Contract Law in Australia

Fourth Edition

Contract Law in Australia

Fourth Edition

J W Carter

BA, LLB (Syd), Ph D (Cantab)

Professor of Commercial Law, University of Sydney
Consultant, Freehills

D J Harland

BA, LLB (Syd), BCL (Oxon)

Emeritus Professor (formerly Challis Professor) of Law,
University of Sydney
Consultant, Clayton Utz

Butterworths
Australia
2002

AUSTRALIA	Butterworths
	Tower 2, 475–495 Victoria Avenue, CHATSWOOD NSW 2067
	On the internet at: www.butterworths.com.au
ARGENTINA	Abeledo Perrot, Jurisprudencia Argentina and Depalma, BUENOS AIRES
AUSTRIA	ARD Betriebsdienst and Verlag Orac, VIENNA
CANADA	Butterworths Canada Ltd, MARKHAM, Ontario
CHILE	Publitecsa and Conosur Ltda, SANTIAGO DE CHILE
CZECH REPUBLIC	Orac sro, PRAGUE
FRANCE	Editions du Juris-Classeur SA, PARIS
HONG KONG	Butterworths Asia (Hong Kong), HONG KONG
HUNGARY	Hvg Orac, BUDAPEST
INDIA	Butterworths India, NEW DELHI
IRELAND	Butterworths (Ireland) Ltd, DUBLIN
ITALY	Giuffré, MILAN
MALAYSIA	Malayan Law Journal Sdn Bhd, KUALA LUMPUR
NEW ZEALAND	Butterworths of New Zealand, WELLINGTON
POLAND	Wydawnictwa Prawnicze PWN, WARSAW
SINGAPORE	Butterworths Asia, SINGAPORE
SOUTH AFRICA	Butterworths Publishers (Pty) Ltd, DURBAN
SWITZERLAND	Stämpfli Verlag AG, BERNE
UNITED KINGDOM	Butterworths Tolley, LONDON, EDINBURGH
USA	LexisNexis, DAYTON, Ohio

National Library of Australia Cataloguing-in-Publication entry

Carter, J. W. (John W.).
Contract law in Australia.
4th ed.
Bibliography.
Includes index.
ISBN 0 409 31876 0 (pbk.).
ISBN 0 409 31875 2.
1. Contracts - Australia. I. Harland, D. J. (David J.),
1940-. II. Title.
346.9402

© 2002 Reed International Books Australia Pty Limited
First edition 1986; Second edition 1991; Third edition 1996

This book is copyright. Except as permitted under the Copyright Act 1968 (Cth), no part of this publication may be reproduced by any process, electronic or otherwise, without the specific written permission of the copyright owner. Neither may information be stored electronically in any form whatsoever without such permission.

Inquiries should be addressed to the publishers.
Edited and typeset in Plantin by Prose Editorial Services.
Printed in Australia by Ligare Pty Ltd.
Visit Butterworths at www.butterworths.com.au

Contents

	Page
Preface	vii
Table of Cases	ix
Table of Statutes	lxv

PART I — INTRODUCTION

1	Introduction	3

PART II — FORMATION OF CONTRACT

2	Agreement	23
3	Consideration	96
4	Intention to Create Legal Relations	163
5	Contracts Requiring Written Evidence	172

PART III — TERMS OF THE CONTRACT

6	Identification of the Terms	199
7	Construction of the Terms	233

PART IV — PARTIES TO THE CONTRACT

8	Capacity	285
9	Privity of Contract and Plurality of Parties	339

PART V — VITIATING FACTORS AND MISLEADING AND DECEPTIVE CONDUCT

10	Misrepresentation	367
11	The Statutory Prohibition of Misleading or Deceptive Conduct	414
12	Mistake	434
13	Duress	486
14	Undue Influence	505
15	Unconscionability	519

PART VI — ILLEGALITY

16	Illegal Contracts	555
17	The Effects of Illegality	604

PART VII — PERFORMANCE AND BREACH

18	Performance and Breach	645

PART VIII — TERMINATION

19	Termination for Breach and Repudiation	687
20	Termination by Frustration	758

PART IX — REMEDIES

21	Damages	815
22	Recovery of Sums Fixed by the Contract	875
23	Restitution	907
24	Specific Performance and Injunction	945

Bibliography 961
Index 969

Preface

The five years which have elapsed since the preparation of the previous edition have been relatively quiet so far as the law of contract is concerned. Nevertheless, we have updated the work to take account of the case law and statutory developments in the period 1996–2001.

It is difficult to single out significant cases worthy of mentioning in a preface. However, the topic of contributory negligence in contract provides an interesting illustration of the interplay between judicial decision and legislative reform. Thus, although in *Astley v Austrust Ltd* (1999) 197 CLR 1; 161 ALR 155 the High Court decided, significantly but unfortunately, that the legislative provisions on contributory negligence do not apply to claims in contract, it was soon followed by legislation reversing that decision in most jurisdictions.

In updating the work we have continued to concentrate on local developments. However, because none of the cases decided since the previous edition have had a major impact on general principles, we have not felt it necessary to restructure the work. We have noted that the concept of good faith is gathering momentum under our law. Some of the influences on contract continue to come from other sources, in particular the decisions (eg *Marks (in a Representative Capacity) v GIO Australia Holdings Ltd* (1998) 196 CLR 494; 158 ALR 333) on s 52 of the *Trade Practices Act 1974* (Cth), and the increasing impact of that Act on contract, through new unconscionable conduct provisions (see [1523]). The continuing role of equity is felt in decisions such as *Garcia v National Australia Bank Ltd* (1998) 194 CLR 395; 155 ALR 614; *Bridgewater v Leahy* (1998) 194 CLR 457; 158 ALR 66; and *Giumelli v Giumelli* (1999) 196 CLR 101; 161 ALR 473. And the High Court has continued to struggle with liability for economic loss in tort (*Perre v Apand Pty Ltd* (1999) 198 CLR 180; 164 ALR 606).

We have endeavoured to state the law on the basis of the reported cases and materials available to us on 1 September 2001. Where possible, we have also taken some of the subsequent material into account.

The work of revising Chapters 2, 8, 9, 11 and 15 has been undertaken by David Harland and our colleague, Elisabeth Peden, to whom we both owe a great debt of gratitude. Elisabeth undertook the principal work involved in revising Chapters 2, 8 and 9, David revised Chapter 11, and they shared the work of revising Chapter 15. Principal responsibility for the balance of the book rests with John Carter.

Jonathan Namey provided conscientious research assistance in updating the statutory provisions for John Carter's chapters.

We should also thank Greg Tolhurst and Elisabeth Peden for their comments and useful information on a number of Chapters. Robert Wilson and the staff of Butterworths have been patient with us and supported this new edition in various ways for which we are very grateful.

From the first edition of the work we have been extremely fortunate in having the benefit of excellent sub-editors. Finally, therefore, we must thank Rosemary Peers for her careful editing of the manuscript, constant attention to detail and her courtesy.

J W Carter
D J Harland
University of Sydney Law School
November 2001

Table of Cases

References are to paragraphs

A v Hayden (1984) ... 1619, 1701, 1702
—v Pelekanakis (1999) ... 1524
Abbott v Lance (1860) ... 250
Abdurahman v Field (1987) ... 1714
Abrahams v Herbert Reiach Ltd [1922] ... 2162
Abram SS Co Ltd v Westville Shipping Co Ltd [1923] ... 1023, 1039, 1045, 1047
Abundant Earth Pty Ltd v R & C Products Pty Ltd (1985) ... 1122
Academy of Health and Fitness Pty Ltd v Power [1973] ... 1050, 1057
Accounting Systems 2000 (Developments) Pty Ltd v CCH Australia Ltd (1993) ... 1109
Acron Pacific Ltd v Offshore Oil NL (1985) ... 2208, 2217
Adam v Newbigging (1888) ... 1065
Adami v Maison de Luxe Ltd (1924) ... 1937
Adams v Lindsell (1818) ... 232, 235
Adamson v New South Wales Rugby League Ltd (1991) ... 1634, 1641
Addis v Gramophone Co Ltd [1909] ... 2103, 2104, 2152
Addison v Brown [1954] ... 1626
Adelaide Petroleum NL v Poseidon Ltd (1988) ... 1108
Adelfamar SA v Silos E Mangimi Martini SpA (The Adelfa) [1988] ... 2066
Adenan v Buise [1984] ... 1404
Adey v Fisher (1914) ... 1028
Adler v Dickson [1955] ... 923, 925
Administration of the Territory of Papua New Guinea v Leahy (1961) ... 409
Administrative and Clerical Officers Association v Commonwealth (1979) ... 2419
Adoption of Children Act (NT), Re (1990) ... 807

Advance Bank of Australia Ltd v Hartshorn (1993) ... 1522
Aerial Advertising Co v Batchelors Peas Ltd (Manchester) [1938] ... 2112, 2117
Afovos Shipping Co SA v Pagnan [1983] ... 727, 1906, 1907, 1909, 1935
A-G v Blake [2001] ... 2103, 2173, 2329
—v Great Southern and Western Ry Co of Ireland [1925] ... 871
—v Manchester Corp [1906] ... 852
A-G (NSW) v Australian Fixed Trusts Ltd [1974] ... 214
—v Mutual Home Loan Fund of Australia Ltd [1971] ... 214
—v Peters (1924) ... 1020, 1022
—v Quin (1990) ... 872
A-G of Duchy of Lancaster v Devonshire (1884) ... 852
A-G of Hong Kong v Humphreys Estate (Queen's Gardens) Ltd [1987] ... 376, 377
AGC (Advances) Ltd v McWhirter (1977) ... 211
—v West (1984) ... 1522
Ahmed v Estate and Trust Agencies (1927) Ltd [1938] ... 2224
Ailsa Craig Fishing Co Ltd v Malvern Fishing Co Ltd [1983] ... 752, 757
Air Great Lakes Pty Ltd v K S Easter (Holdings) Pty Ltd (1985) ... 106, 110, 111, 112, 113, 207, 273, 402, 707, 708
Airways Corporation of New Zealand v Geyserland Airways Ltd [1996] ... 229
Aiton Australia Pty Ltd v Transfield Pty Ltd (1999) ... 271
Ajayi v R T Briscoe (Nigeria) Ltd [1964] ... 372, 378
Akron Securities Ltd v Iliffe (1997) ... 1115, 2336

Alan (WJ) & Co Ltd v El Nasr Export & Import Co [1972] ...372, 380, 1816, 1976
Alati v Kruger (1955) ... 1039, 1050, 1058, 1071, 1945, 2336
Albazero, The [1977] ... 912
Albion Sugar Co Ltd v William Tankers Ltd (The John S Darbyshire) [1977] ... 275
Alcatel Australia Ltd v Scarcella (1998) ... 1983
Alderslade v Hendon Laundry Ltd [1945] ... 763, 764
Aldwell v Bundey (1876) ... 250
Alec Lobb (Garages) Ltd v Total Oil (Great Britain) Ltd [1985] ... 1329, 1509, 1511, 1638, 1643, 1644, 1733, 1736
Alexander v Cambridge Credit Corp (1987) ... 2120, 2121, 2124, 2126,
—v Rayson [1936] ... 1622, 1623, 1715, 1721
Alghussein Establishment v Eton College [1988] ... 1967
Allan v Gotch (1883) ... 1009, 1016, 1021, 1027
Allan (JM) (Merchandising) Ltd v Cloke [1963] ... 1621
Allcard v Skinner (1887) ... 1401, 1404, 1408, 1409, 1411, 1412
—v Walker [1896] ... 1209, 1227, 1228
Allcars Pty Ltd v Tweedle [1937] ... 261, 270
Allen v Allen (1842) ... 808
—v Carbone (1975) ... 273
—v F O'Hearn & Co [1937] ... 906
—v Richardson (1879) ... 1228
Alliance & Leicester Building Society v Edgestop Ltd [1993] ... 1068, 1077
Alliance Acceptance Co Ltd v Hinton (1964) ... 805, 814
Alliance Bank v Broom (1864) ... 355
Allied Marine Transport Ltd v Vale do Rio Doce Navegacao SA (The Leonides D) [1985] ... 111, 112, 229, 354, 379, 1978
Allied Mills Ltd v Gwydir Valley Oilseeds Pty Ltd [1978] ... 2046
Allison v Hewitt (1974) ... 2152, 2165
Alpha Trading Ltd v Dunnshaw-Patten Ltd [1981] ... 628, 1965, 2202

Alucraft Pty Ltd v Grocon Ltd (1994) ... 2107
Aluminium Products (Qld) Pty Ltd v Hill [1981] ... 1036
Amalgamated Collieries of WA Ltd v True (1938) ... 1828
Amalgamated Investment & Property Co Ltd v John Walker & Sons Ltd [1976] ... 2033, 2055
—v Texas Commerce International Bank Ltd [1982] ... 369, 375, 377, 385, 386, 720
Amalgamated Television Services Pty Ltd v Television Corp Ltd [1970] ... 259
Amann Aviation Pty Ltd v Commonwealth (1990) ... 1936, 1970, 1983
Ambassador Refrigeration Pty Ltd v Trocadero Building and Investment Co Pty Ltd [1968] ... 1614
Amev Finance Ltd v Artes Studios Thoroughbreds Pty Ltd (1989) ... 2217
AMEV-UDC Finance Ltd v Austin (1986) ... 2159, 2207, 2211, 2217
Amey v Fifar [1971] ... 865
Amherst v James Walker Goldsmith & Silversmith Ltd [1983] ... 1852
Amoco Australia Pty Ltd v Rocca Bros Motor Engineering Co Pty Ltd (1973) ... 1635, 1636, 1637, 1638, 1639, 1640, 1641,1644, 1646, 1652, 1733
—v—(No 2) [1975] ... 1730, 1733
Amphitrite, The [1921] ... 872
Anaconda Nickel Ltd v Tarmoola Australia Pty Ltd (2000) ... 259, 260, 266, 273
André et Compagnie SA v Marine Transocean Ltd [1981] ... 2058
Andrews v Hopkinson [1957] ... 614, 2138
—v Parker [1973] ... 1632, 1703, 1712
Angel v Jay [1911] ... 1054, 1055
Angelatos v National Australia Bank (1994) ... 1120
Anglia Television Ltd v Reed [1972] ... 2145
Anglo-African Shipping Co of New York Inc v J Mortner Ltd [1962] ... 2224

References are to paragraphs

Table of Cases

Ankar Pty Ltd v National Westminster Finance (Australia) Ltd (1987) ... 113, 119, 733, 740, 1838, 1911, 1917, 1918, 1919, 1952

Annand & Thompson Pty Ltd v Trade Practices Commission (1979) ... 1105

Anon (1455) ... 356

Ansett Transport Industries (Operations) Pty Ltd v Australian Federation of Air Pilots (No 2) [1991] ... 1828

Antaios Compania Naviera SA v Salen Rederierna AB [1983] ... 704, 732, 1984, 1909

Antoniou v Karedis Enterprises Pty Ltd (1995) ... 1112

Antonovic v Volker (1986) ... 1513, 1520, 1522

ANZ Executors & Trustees Ltd v Humes Ltd [1990] ... 2405, 2410

Aotearoa International Ltd v Scancarriers A/S [1985] ... 268

Appleby v Johnson (1874) ... 220

—v Myers (1867) ... 2066, 2074, 2083

Apps (WG) & Sons Pty Ltd & Hurley, Re [1949] ... 267

Aramis, The [1989] ... 925

Archbolds (Freightage) Ltd v S Spanglett Ltd [1961] ... 1611, 1613, 1622, 1701, 1711

Archer v Brown [1985] ... 2153

—v Stone (1898) ... 1242

Arcos Ltd v E A Ronaasen & Son [1933] ... 638, 1813

Arcric Investments Pty Ltd v Ductline Pty Ltd (1992) ... 1105

Ardlethan Options Ltd v Easdown (1915) ... 2136

Argy v Blunts & Lane Cove Real Estate Pty Ltd (1990) ... 1034, 1104, 1112, 1121

Argy Trading Development Co Ltd v Lapid Developments Ltd [1977] ... 372

Aristoc Industries Pty Ltd v R A Wenham (Builders) Pty Ltd [1965] ... 511, 2405

Arkwright v Newbold (1881) ... 1016

Armitage v Nurse [1998] ... 756

Armstrong v Jackson [1917] ... 1054, 1055

Arnison v Smith (1889) ... 1024, 1027

Aroney v Christianus (1915) ... 818, 819

Arrale v Costain Civil Engineering Ltd [1976] ... 315

ASA Constructions Pty Ltd v Iwanov [1975] ... 2165, 2171

Ash Street Properties Pty Ltd v Pollnow (1987) ... 521

Ashbury Railway Carriage Co v Riche (1875) ... 854

Ashby v Tolhurst [1937] ... 762

Ashington Piggeries Ltd v Christopher Hill Ltd [1972] ... 638, 640

Asia Pacific International Pty Ltd v Dalrymple [2000] ... 1513, 1522

Associated Distributors Ltd v Hall [1938] ... 2216

Associated Grocers Co-operative Ltd v Hubbard Properties Pty Ltd (1986) ... 267, 273

Associated Japanese Bank (International) Ltd v Credit du Nord SA [1989] ... 1220, 1224, 1229

Associated Midland Corp Ltd v Bank of NSW (1984) ... 227

Associated Newspapers Ltd v Bancks (1951) ... 1915, 1916, 1937

Astley v Austrust Ltd (1999) ... 107, 118, 635, 1857, 2104, 2124, 2129, 2131

—v Reynolds (1731) ... 1309

Astley Industrial Trust Ltd v Grimley [1963] ... 1927, 1958

Astra Trust Ltd v Adams [1969] ... 275

Athens-MacDonald Travel Service Pty Ltd v Kazis [1970] ... 2153

Atkins v Hill (1775) ... 306

Atlantic Shipping & Trading Ltd v Louis Dreyfus & Co [1922] ... 388

Atlas Express Ltd v Kafco (Importers and Distributors) Ltd [1989] ... 1310, 1312, 1322

Atlas Tiles Ltd v Briers (1978) ... 2167

Atlee v Backhouse (1838) ... 1309

Attica Sea Carriers Corp v Ferrostaal Poseidon Bulk Reederei GmbH [1976] ... 2224

Attwood v Lamont [1920] ... 1649, 1731, 1735

Auckland Harbour Board v The King [1924] ... 871

References are to paragraphs

Aurel Forras Pty Ltd v Graham Karp Developments Pty Ltd [1975] ... 2060, 2067
Austin v Sheldon [1974] ... 2013, 2033
Austotel Pty Ltd v Franklins Selfserve Pty Ltd (1989) ... 377, 378, 2317
Austra Tanks Pty Ltd v Running [1982] ... 1738
Austral Standard Cables Pty Ltd v Walker Nominees Pty Ltd (1992) ... 378, 1945, 1947
Australasian Brokerage Ltd v ANZ Banking Corp Ltd (1934) ... 1066
Australasian Performing Right Association Ltd v Austarama Television Pty Ltd [1972] ... 1259, 1263
Australia and New Zealand Banking Group Ltd v Compagnie d'Assurances Maritimes Aeriennes et Terrestres [1996] ... 730
—v Frost Holdings Pty Ltd [1989] ... 268
—v Westpac Banking Corp (1988) ... 2308
—v Widin (1990) ... 515, 521, 522
Australia Hotel Co Ltd v Moore (1899) ... 1253, 1266
Australian Alliance Assurance Co Ltd v Goodwyn [1916] ... 870
Australian Bank of Commerce Ltd v Perel [1926] ... 1816
Australian Bank Ltd v Stokes (1985) ... 1518
Australian Breeders Co-operative Society Ltd v Jones (1997) ... 1737
Australian Broadcasting Corp v Redmore Pty Ltd (1989) ... 1609, 1613
—v XIVth Commonwealth Games Ltd (1988) ... 273
Australian Capital Territory v Munday (2000) ... 1637
Australian Competition & Consumer Commission v CG Berbatis Holdings Pty Ltd (No 2) (2000) ... 1527
—v Chats House Investments Pty Ltd (1996) ... 1527
—v Leelee Pty Ltd (2000) ... 1524
—v Samton Holdings Pty Ltd (2000) ... 1513, 1528
—v Simply No-Knead (Franchising) Pty Ltd (2000) ... 1527, 1528

Australian Energy Ltd v Lennard Oil NL [1986] ... 712, 718
Australian Gypsum Ltd v Hume Steel Ltd (1930) ... 1259, 1262
Australian Hardwoods Pty Ltd v Commissioner for Railways [1961] ... 2401, 2407
Australian Meat Industry Employees' Union v Frugalis Pty Ltd [1990] ... 627
Australian Mutual Provident Society v 400 St Kilda Road Pty Ltd [1991] ... 1809
—v Chaplin (1978) ... 712
—v Overseas Telecommunications Commission (Australia) [1972] ... 268
Australian National Airlines Commission v Robinson [1977] ... 1811, 1839
Australian Railways Union v Victorian Railway Commissioners (1930) ... 871
Australian Steel & Mining Corp Pty Ltd v Corben [1974] ... 1020, 1024
Australian Woollen Mills Pty Ltd v Commonwealth (1954) ... 207, 239, 311, 318, 409
Australis Media Holdings Pty Ltd v Telstra Corp Ltd (1998) ... 271, 632
Automatic Fire Sprinklers Pty Ltd v Watson (1946) ... 1807, 1930, 1967, 2112, 2221, 2230, 2322
Avery v Bowden (1856) ... 2063
Aviet v Smith & Searle Pty Ltd (1956) ... 238
Avon County Council v Howlett [1983] ... 1209
Avon Finance Co Ltd v Bridger (1979) ... 1273, 1409, 1510
Awwad v Geraghty (a firm) [2000] ... 1630
Axelsen v O'Brien (1949) ... 267
Ayerst v Jenkins (1873) ... 1721
B & B Constructions (Aust) Pty Ltd v Brian A Cheeseman & Associates Pty Ltd (1994) ... 713, 723
B & S Contracts and Design Ltd v Victor Green Publications Ltd [1984] ... 1314, 1322
B(BR) v B(J) [1968] ... 807
Baburin v Baburin [1990] ... 1514
—v—[1991] ... 1513, 1514

References are to paragraphs

Table of Cases

Bacchus Marsh Concentrated Milk Co Ltd v Joseph Nathan & Co Ltd (1919) ... 713, 723, 1261, 1642, 1646
Bacon v Purcell (1916) ... 714, 1823
Bahr v Nicolay (No 2) (1988) ... 273, 710, 711, 713, 922, 1811, 2407
Bain v Fothergill (1874) ... 1230, 2111, 2165
Bainbrigge v Browne (1881) ... 1405, 1408
Baird v BCE Holdings Pty Ltd (1996) ... 1055
Baker v Jones [1954] ... 1626
—v Monk (1864) ... 1506
—v Taylor (1906) ... 251
Bal v Van Standen [1902] ... 232
Balbosa v Ali [1990] ... 741
Baldwyn v Smith [1900] ... 842
Balfour v Balfour [1919] ... 109, 403
—v Hollandia Ravensthorpe NL (1978) ... 1008, 1046
Ballantyne v Phillott (1961) ... 351, 352
—v Raphael (1889) ... 1016, 1020, 1024, 1027
Ballas v Theopilos [1958] ... 248
—v—(No 2) (1957) ... 220, 222, 248, 255
Ballett v Mingay [1943] ... 825
Balmain New Ferry Co Ltd v Robertson (1906) ... 616
Balog v Crestani (1975) ... 1961, 1963
Balt v Onslow (1892) ... 228
Baltic Shipping Co v Dillon (The Mikhail Lermontov) (1991) ... 1522, 1528
—v—(1993) ... 118, 1823, 1832, 1522, 1528, 2067, 2124, 2152, 2153, 2303, 2308, 2314, 2321, 2324, 2336
—v Merchant 'Mikhail Lermontov' (1994) ... 332, 352
Banco de Portugal v Waterlow & Sons Ltd [1932] ... 2136
Banfield v Wells-Eicke (1964) ... 868
Bangladesh Export Import Co Ltd v Sucden Kerry SA [1995] ... 2021
Bank Line Ltd v Arthur Capel & Co [1919] ... 2004, 2026, 2027, 2030, 2040, 2055, 2056, 2058, 2059
Bank of America Australia Ltd v Ceda Jon International Pty Ltd (1988) ... 1656

Bank of Australasia v Adams (1890) ... 1011
—v Palmer [1897] ... 705, 708
Bank of Boston Connecticut v European Grain & Shipping Ltd [1989] ... 1985, 2062, 2067, 2226, 2230
Bank of India v Trans Continental Commodity Merchants Ltd [1982] ... 1603
Bank of New South Wales v Rogers (1941) ... 1048, 1405
Bank of New Zealand v Simpson [1900] ... 717
Bank of Nova Scotia v Hellenic Mutual War Risks Association (Bermuda) Ltd (The Good Luck) [1992] ... 624, 635, 1986
—v Kelly (1973) ... 838, 847
—v MacLellan (1977) ... 339
Banks v Williams (1912) ... 226
Bannerman v White (1861) ... 1061
Banning v Wright [1972] ... 1972
Banque Brussels Lambert SA v Australian National Industries Ltd (1989) ... 610, 724
Barac v Farnell (1994) ... 1631
Barba v Gas & Fuel Corp of Victoria (1976) ... 325, 721
Barber v Fox (1682) ... 319
Barclay v Messenger (1874) ... 1971
Barclays Bank Plc v Boulter [1999] ... 1405
—v Fairclough Building Ltd [1995] ... 2132
—v O'Brien [1994] ... 1405
Barker v Caird (1876) ... 243
—v Clunes MC (1863) ... 858
Barnard v Australian Soccer Federation (1988) ... 1634
Barnes & Co v Toye (1884) ... 810
Barnett v Ira L & A C Berk Pty Ltd (1952) ... 327
Barns v Queensland National Bank Ltd (1906) ... 373
Baroness Wenlock v River Dee Co (1883) ... 852
Barr v Gibson (1838) ... 1216
Barr's Contract, Re [1956] ... 1962
Barrier Wharfs Ltd v W Scott Fell & Co Ltd (1908) ... 273, 712

Barroora Pty Ltd v Provincial Insurance Ltd (1992) ... 918

Barrow Lane & Ballard Ltd v Phillip Phillips & Co Ltd [1929] ... 1219

Barry v Davies [2000] ... 211

Barton v Armstrong [1973] ... 1302, 1305, 1306, 1308, 1318, 1329

Basildon DC v J E Lesser (Properties) Ltd [1985] ... 2132

Bassin v Standen (1945) ... 1609, 1721

Bastard v McCallum [1924] ... 222, 224

Bateman v Slayter (1987) ... 1108, 1121

Batt v Onslow (1892) ... 226, 235

Baume v Commonwealth (1906) ... 2106

Baxton v Kara [1982] ... 2409

Beale v Taylor [1967] ... 2112

Beard v Baulkham Hills Shire Council (1986) ... 1629

—v Wratislaw (1991) ... 1815

Beaton v McDivitt (1987) ... 308, 311, 315, 412, 2038

Beattie v Fine [1925] ... 267

Beaumont v Helvetic Investment Corp Pty Ltd (1982) ... 1518, 1521

Beaven, Re (1912) ... 847

Bedford Insurance Co Ltd v Instituto de Resseguros do Brasil [1985] ... 1614

Beer v Bowden (1976) ... 267

Begbie v State Bank of NSW (1994) ... 1513, 1524, 1528

Behn v Burness (1863) ... 1844, 1967

Behzadi v Shaftesbury Hotels Ltd [1992] ... 119, 1953, 1960

Bell v Lever Bros Ltd [1932] ... 627, 1222, 1223, 1224, 1225, 1229

—v Scott (1922) ... 1942, 1943, 1944

Bell Bros Pty Ltd v Sarich [1971] ... 216

Bellgrove v Eldridge (1954) ... 2155, 2156

Bendigo Central Freezing and Fertiliser Co Ltd v Cunningham [1919] ... 1055

Beneficial Finance Corp Ltd v Karavas (1991) ... 1522

—v Multiplex Constructions Pty Ltd (1995) ... 870

Bennett v Minister for Community Welfare (1992) ... 2120

Bensaude v Thames and Mersey Marine Insurance Co Ltd [1897] ... 2054, 2058

Bentley v Wright [1997] ... 1030

Bentsen v Taylor Sons & Co (No 2) [1893] ... 1917, 1919, 1975

Beresford v Royal Insurance Co [1938] ... 1702

Berg v Sadler [1937] ... 1718

Berger v Boyles [1971] ... 2106

Berger & Co Inc v Gill & Duffus SA [1984] ... 2161, 2306

Bernstein v Pamson Motors (Golders Green) Ltd [1987] ... 1984

Berry v Mahony [1933] ... 2332

Bestoys Pty Ltd v George Wills & Co Ltd (1981) ... 1654

Beswick v Beswick [1968] ... 901, 912, 914, 2406

Bettini v Gye (1876) ... 1848, 1917, 1951

Bettyes v Maynard (1882) ... 1227, 1228

Bevanere Pty Ltd v Lubidineuse (1985) ... 1104, 1106

Beverley's case (1603) ... 839

Bialkower v Acohs Pty Ltd (1998) ... 1113

BICC Plc v Burndy Corp [1985] ... 1979

Bigg v Boyd Gibbins Ltd [1971] ... 207, 209

Biggin v Minton [1977] ... 2170

Bigos v Bousted [1951] ... 1715, 1716

Bill v Darenth Valley Railway Cop (1856) ... 858

Bill Acceptance Corp Ltd v GWA Ltd (1983) ... 1108

Bingham v Bingham (1748) ... 1215, 1228, 1232

Biotechnology Australia Pty Ltd v Pace (1988) ... 108, 112, 261, 270, 338, 2106, 2162

Birkmyr v Darnell (1704) ... 507, 519

Birmingham & District Land Co v London & North Western Railway Co (1888) ... 372

Table of Cases

Birstar Pty Ltd v Proprietors 'Ocean Breeze' Building Units Plan No 3745 (1996) ... 853
Bishop v Taylor (1968) ... 261
Bishop & Baxter Ltd v Anglo-Eastern Trading & Industrial Co Ltd [1944] ... 261
Bishopsgate Insurance Australia Ltd v Commonwealth Engineering (NSW) Pty Ltd [1981] ... 1259, 1262, 1263
Bisset v Wilkinson [1927] ... 1009
Black v Smallwood (1966) ... 862
Black-Clawson International Ltd v Papierwerke Waldhof-Aschaffenburg AG [1981] ... 2059
Blackpool & Fylde Aero Club Ltd v Blackpool Borough Council [1990] ... 212
Blacktown Municipal Council v Doneo [1971] ... 255
Blake v Concannon (1870) ... 820
Blay v Pollard and Morris [1930] ... 1272
Blennerhassett's Institute of Accountancy Pty Ltd v Gairns (1938) ... 811
Bligh v Martin [1968] ... 1219
Bliss v Southeast Thames Regional Health Authority [1987] ... 2152
Bloemen (FJ) Pty Ltd v Gold Coast City Council [1973] ... 1993
Blomley v Ryan (1956) ... 844, 1412, 1507, 1508
Blue Anchor Line Ltd v Alfred C Toepfer International GmbH (The Union Amsterdam) [1982] ... 749
Boardman v McGrath [1925] ... 2165
—v Phipps [1967] ... 2328
Boettcher v Boettcher [1948] ... 355
Bojczuk v Gregorcewicz [1961] ... 811, 813, 829
Bolam v Friern Hospital Management Committee [1957] ... 1857
Bolton v Mahadeva [1972] ... 1831, 1832, 1834, 1835
Bolwell Fibreglass Pty Ltd v Foley [1984] ... 511, 1810, 2323
Bonanza Creek Gold Mining Co v R [1916] ... 852
Boncristiano v Lohmann [1998] ... 2152

Bond v Hongkong Bank of Australia Ltd (1991) ... 1838
Bond Corp Pty Ltd v Thiess Contractors Pty Ltd (1987) ... 1118, 1121
Booker Industries Pty Ltd v Wilson Parking (Qld) Pty Ltd (1982) ... 267, 268, 271, 627, 741
Boomer v Muir (1933) ... 2339
Boone v Eyre (1777) ... 742, 1830
Boothbey v Sowden (1812) ... 360
Borrowman v Free (1878) ... 1815
—v Rossel (1864) ... 1258
Borthwick v Carruthers (1787) ... 801
Bosaid v Andry [1963] ... 272, 1022
Bosnjak v Farrow Services Pty Ltd (in liq) (1993) ... 1518
Bostock & Co Ltd v Nicholson & Sons Ltd [1904] ... 2138
Boston Deep Sea Fishing & Ice Co v Ansell (1888) ... 1986, 2230, 2325
Bot v Ristevski [1981] ... 2237, 2338
Boucaut Bay Co Ltd v Commonwealth (1927) ... 2207, 2209, 2210, 2239
Boulton v Jones (1857) ... 1241
Boustany v Pigott (1993) ... 1512
Bowes v Chaleyer (1923) ... 1813, 1919, 1947, 1952, 1969
—v Shand (1877) ... 702, 1919, 1952
Bowmakers Ltd v Barnet Instruments Ltd [1945] ... 1721, 1723
Bowman v Durham Holdings Pty Ltd (1973) ... 228, 234
Bowring (CT) Reinsurance Ltd v Baxter (The M Vatman and M Ceyhan) [1987] ... 2062
Boyd v Holmes (1878) ... 229
Boyde v Ryan (1947) ... 808
BP Exploration Co (Libya) Ltd v Hunt (No 2) [1979] ... 2059, 2064, 2079, 2081, 2083, 2087, 2335, 2337
BP Refinery (Westernport) Pty Ltd v Shire of Hastings (1977) ... 625, 628
Brabazon v Western Mail Ltd (1985) ... 1113
Brace v Calder [1895] ... 1942, 2044, 2135
Bradbury v Morgan (1862) ... 257
Bradley v H Newsom Sons & Co [1919] ... 1933
Bradley Egg Farm Ltd v Clifford [1943] ... 865, 866

References are to paragraphs

Bradshaw v Gilbert's (Australasian) Agency (Vic) Pty Ltd (1952) ... 1613, 1706
Braham v Walker (1961) ... 248, 1610
Braidotti v Queensland City Properties Ltd (1991) ... 1970
Braithwaite v Foreign Hardwood Co [1905] ... 1943, 1947
Brambles Holdings Ltd v Bathurst City Council [2001] ... 203
Branca v Cobarro [1947] ... 273
Brandt v Liverpool Brazil and River Plate Steam Navigation Co Ltd [1924] ... 925
Breen v Williams (1996) ... 118, 625, 633, 1809, 1857
Bremer Handelsgesellschaft mbH v J H Rayner & Co Ltd [1979] ... 619
—v Vanden Avenne-Izegem PVBA [1978] ... 392, 732, 1919, 1974, 1976, 2042, 2060
Bremer Vulkan Schiffbau und Maschinenfabrik v South India Shipping Corp Ltd [1981] ... 1908, 1936, 1978, 2060
Brenner v First Artists' Management Pty Ltd [1993] ... 2315, 2318, 2335
Bressan v Squires [1974] ... 231, 232, 235
Brew v Whitlock [1967] ... 1629
—v—(No 2) [1967] ... 272, 1730
Brickhill v Cooke [1984] ... 2131
Bridge v Campbell Discount Co Ltd [1962] ... 1502, 2209, 2210, 2216
—v Deacons [1984] ... 1638, 1640, 1641, 1644, 1645, 1651
Bridge Wholesale Acceptance (Aust) Ltd v GVS Associates Pty Ltd (1991) ... 1522
Bridger v Savage (1885) ... 1616
Bridgewater v Leahy (1998) ... 118, 1404, 1416, 1513
Brien v Dwyer (1978) ... 1951, 2237
Bright v Sampson & Duncan Enterprises Pty Ltd (1985) ... 750, 764, 765
Brightman v Lamson Paragon Ltd (1914) ... 1648
Brikom Investments Ltd v Carr [1979] ... 315, 372
Brindley v Scott (1902) ... 1028
Brinkibon Ltd v Stahag Stahl GmbH [1983] ... 204, 231, 234, 235, 238

Brisbane City Council v Group Projects Pty Ltd (1979) ... 2049, 2056
Brisbane Unit Development Corp Ltd v Robertson [1983] ... 1123
Bristol and West Building Society v Mothew [1998] ... 1015
Bristow v Eastman (1794) ... 825
British & Beningtons Ltd v North Western Cachar Tea Co Ltd [1923] ... 525, 1929, 1943
British and American Telegraph Co Ltd v Colson (1871) ... 234
British and Commonwealth Holdings Plc v Quadrex Holdings Inc [1989] ... 1953, 1962
British Bank for Foreign Trade Ltd v Novinex [1949] ... 269
British Car Auctions Ltd v Wright [1972] ... 214
British Columbia etc Saw-Mill Co Ltd v Nettleship (1868) ... 2128
British Electrical & Associated Industries (Cardiff) Ltd v Patley Pressings Ltd [1953] ... 261
British Empire Films Pty Ltd v Oxford Theatres Pty Ltd [1943] ... 338, 340
British Homophone Ltd v Kunz (1935) ... 267
British Movietonews Ltd v London and District Cinemas Ltd [1952] ... 2002, 2019, 2030, 2051, 2056
British South Africa Co v De Beers [1910] ... 852
British Steel Corp v Cleveland Bridge and Engineering Co Ltd (1981) ... 2317
British Sugar Plc v NEI Power Projects Ltd (1997) ... 752
British Traders' Insurance Co Ltd v Monson (1964) ... 2033
British Transport Commission v Gourley [1956] ... 2167
British Waggon Co v Lea & Co (1880) ... 1818
British Westinghouse Electric and Manufacturing Co Ltd v Underground Electric Railways Co of London Ltd [1912] ... 2134
Britt Allcroft (Thomas) LLC v Miller (2000) ... 1122
Brocklehurst deceased; Re; Hall v Roberts [1978] ... 1410

Table of Cases

Brogden v Metropolitan Railway Co (1877) ... 205, 227
Broken Hill Pty Co Ltd v Hapag-Lloyd Aktiengesellschaft [1980] ... 926, 2416
Bromley v Smith [1909] ... 812, 814
Brooks, Re (1903) ... 847
—v Alca (1976) ... 1409
—v Beirnstein [1909] ... 2232
—v Burns Philp Trustee Co Ltd (1969) ... 1627, 1702, 1730, 1731, 1736
—v Wyatt (1992) ... 267
—v—(1994) ... 2169
Brooks Robinson Pty Ltd v Rothfield [1951] ... 511, 1904, 2323, 2339
Broome v Speak [1903] ... 338
Broons, Re [1989] ... 928
Broughton v Knight (1873) ... 840
—v Snook [1938] ... 841
Brown v Brine (1875) ... 342
—v Brown (1905) ... 205
—v Gould [1972] ... 260, 267
—v Jam Factory Pty Ltd (1981) ... 1118, 1121
—v Petranker (1991) ... 764
—v Smitt (1924) ... 1045, 1046, 2336
Brownett v Newton (1941) ... 1726, 1728
Browning v Morris (1778) ... 1720
Brownlie v Campbell (1880) ... 1037, 1228
Brownton Ltd v Edward Moore Inbucon Ltd [1985] ... 1629,
Bruce v Tyley (1916) ... 1818
—v Warwick (1815) ... 817
Brueckner v Carroll (1995) ... 1112
Bruner v Moore [1904] ... 232
Bryan v Maloney (1995) ... 107, 922, 1030
Bryson v Bryant (1992) ... 2326
Buchanan v Byrnes (1906) ... 1936, 2159
Buckenara v Hawthorn Football Club Ltd [1988] ... 1643, 2420
Buckland v Massey [1985] ... 1613
Buckle (A) & Son Pty Ltd v McAllister (1986) ... 1648, 1739
Buckley v Tutty (1971) ... 1634, 1635, 1636, 1642, 1702

Bulk Chartering & Consultants Australia Pty Ltd v T & T Metal Trading Pty Ltd (The Krasnogrosk) (1993) ... 1626
Bunbury Foods Pty Ltd v National Bank of Australasia Ltd (1984) ... 1814
Bunge Corp New York v Tradax Export SA Panama [1981] ... 113, 725, 726, 732, 736, 1852, 1916, 1917, 1918, 1919, 1952, 1968
Bunge SA v Kruse [1980] ... 1922
Burazin v Blacktown City Guardian Pty Ltd (1997) ... 2103
Burg Design Pty Ltd v Wolki (1999) ... 1124
Burge, In The Marriage of (1985) ... 1627
Burgess v Cox [1951] ... 513, 515
Burke v Lfot Pty Ltd (2001) ... 1113
Burke (TM) Estates Pty Ltd v P J Constructions (Vic) Pty Ltd [1991] ... 2336
Burnard v Haggis (1863) ... 825
Burns, Re; Ex parte National Mutual Life Association of Australasia Ltd (1992) ... 360
—v MAN Automotive (Aust) Pty Ltd (1986) ... 2110, 2121, 2123, 2124, 2137
Burns Philp Hardware Ltd v Howard Chia Pty Ltd (1987) ... 718
Burns Philp Trust Co Pty Ltd v Kwikasair Freightlines Ltd (1963) ... 2419
Burrows v Scammell (1881) ... 1252
Burt v Australia and New Zealand Banking Group Ltd (1994) ... 1528
Burton v Palmer [1980] ... 1805
Bush v National Australia Bank Ltd (1992) ... 1261
Busk v Spence (1815) ... 1848
Butler v Craine [1986] ... 521
Butt v M'Donald (1896) ... 1809
Butts v O'Dwyer (1952) ... 627
Byers v Dorotea Pty Ltd (1986) ... 1120, 1123
Byrne v Australian Airlines Ltd (1995) ... 118, 624, 625, 631, 644, 1828, 1967, 2221, 2403
—v Van Tienhoven (1880) ... 235, 244
C & P Haulage v Middleton [1983] ... 2111

References are to paragraphs

Calabar Properties Ltd v Stitcher [1984] ... 2152
Callaghan v O'Sullivan [1925] ... 1628, 1712
Callisher v Bischoffsheim (1870) ... 350, 351
Caltex Oil (Australia) Pty Ltd v Alderton [1964–65] ... 272
—v Best (1990) ... 1617
Camdex International Ltd v Bank of Zambia [1998] ... 1629
Cameron v Hogan (1934) ... 410
—v Qantas Airways Ltd (1994) ... 1528
Cameron (RW) & Co v L Slutzkin Pty Ltd (1923) ... 717, 1234
Cammell Laird & Co Ltd v Manganese Bronze and Brass Co Ltd [1934] ... 639
Campbell v Jones (1796) ... 1806
—v Kitchen & Sons Ltd (1910) ... 718
—v Ridgely (1887) ... 823
Campbell Discount Co Ltd v Gall [1961] ... 1275
Campomar Sociedad Limitada v Nike International Ltd (2000) ... 1105
Canada SS Lines Ltd v The King [1952] ... 748, 764
Canas Property Co Ltd v KL Television Services Ltd [1970] ... 2232
Canberra Advance Bank Ltd v Benny (1992) ... 1983
Candlewood Navigation Corp Ltd v Mitsui OSK Lines Ltd [1986] ... 2104
Cannane v J Cannane Pty Ltd (In Liq) (1998) ... 1618
Canning v Temby (1905) ... 1804, 1852
Caparo Industries Plc v Dickman [1990] ... 1032
Capes v Hutton (1826) ... 806
Capital Finance Co Ltd v Donati (1977) ... 2217
Capital Motors Ltd v Beecham [1975] ... 1036
Car and Universal Finance Co Ltd v Caldwell [1965] ... 1040, 1053, 1246, 1970
Carberry v Gardiner (1936) ... 901
Carello v Jordan [1935] ... 222
Carlill v Carbolic Smoke Ball Co [1893] ... 208, 212, 216, 227, 239, 314, 316, 329, 407, 1616

Carlisle and Cumberland Banking Co v Bragg [1911] ... 1269, 1273
Carlton and United Breweries Ltd v Castlemaine Tooheys Ltd (1986) ... 1654
—v Tooth & Co Ltd (1986) ... 913
Carlton Cricket & Football Social Club v Joseph [1970] ... 864, 865, 866
Carltona Ltd v Commissioners of Works [1943] ... 873
Carmichael v Colonial Sugar Refining Co Ltd (1944) ... 2061
Carney v Herbert [1985] ... 1730, 1737
Carpentaria Investments Pty Ltd v Airs [1972] ... 2407
Carpenter (WR) Finance Corp Ltd v Moloney (1979) ... 1654
Carr v Brisbane City Council [1956] ... 269, 271
—v J A Berriman Pty Ltd (1953) ... 1926, 1927, 1941, 1962
Carrington Slipways Pty Ltd v Patrick Operations Pty Ltd (1991) ... 926
Carson v Rhuddlan Borough Council (1989) ... 267
Carter v Hyde (1923) ... 225, 248, 257, 2409
—v Scargill (1875) ... 1984
—v Silber [1892] ... 819
Cartwright v Hoogstoel (1911) ... 243, 244
Casey's Patents, Re; Stewart v Casey [1892] ... 331
Castlemaine Tooheys Ltd v Carlton & United Breweries Ltd (1987) ... 621, 631
Cathels v CSD (1959) ... 911
Causer v Browne [1952] ... 616, 617
Cavalier Insurance Co Ltd, Re [1989] ... 1614, 1710
Cavalier Marketing (Australia) Pty Ltd v Rasell (1990) ... 640
Cavallari v Premier Refrigeration Co Pty Ltd (1952) ... 222
Cave v MacKenzie (1877) ... 907
CCC Films (London) Ltd v Impact Quadrant Films Ltd [1985] ... 2111, 2112, 2145
Cehave NV v Bremer Handelsgesellschaft mbH (The Hansa Nord) [1976] ... 106, 113, 727, 732, 736, 738, 1913, 1917, 1922, 1926, 1934

Table of Cases

Cellulose Acetate Silk Co Ltd v Widnes Foundry (1925) Ltd [1933] ... 2212
Celthene Pty Ltd v WKJ Hauliers Pty Ltd [1981] ... 926
Central Estates (Belgravia) Ltd v Woolgar (No 2) [1972] ... 1972
Central London Property Trust v High Trees House Ltd [1947] ... 372, 384
Central Queensland Leather Industries Ltd, Re [1969] ... 1728
Chadwick v Manning [1896] ... 382
Chai Sau Yin v Liew Kwee Sam [1962] ... 1705
Challenge Bank Ltd v V L Cooper & Associates Pty Ltd [1996] ... 2135
Champtaloup v Thomas [1976] ... 1971, 1984
Chan v Cresdon Pty Ltd (1989) ... 2404
Chandler v Webster [1904] ... 2067
Channel Tunnel Group Ltd v Balfour Beatty Construction Ltd [1992] ... 1839
Chanter v Hopkins (1838) ... 728, 1845
—v Leese (1838) ... 1967
Chapelton v Barry UDC [1940] ... 616, 617
Chaplin v Hicks [1911] ... 2164
Chapman v Chapman [1954] ... 806
—v Leslie Frewin (Publishers) Ltd [1966] ... 813
—v Wade [1939] ... 1708
Chappel v Hart (1998) ... 2120
Chappell & Co Ltd v Nestlé Co Ltd [1960] ... 327
Chapple v Cooper (1844) ... 810
Charge Card Services Ltd, Re [1989] ... 1816
Charles Rickards Ltd v Oppenhaim [1950] ... 1974
Charter v Sullivan [1957] ... 2140, 2143
Charter Reinsurance Co Ltd v Fagan [1997] ... 704
Charterhouse Credit Co Ltd v Tolly [1963] ... 754
Chatenay v Brazilian Submarine Telegraph Co Ltd [1891] ... 701
Chatterton v Maclean [1951] ... 2232
Chattis Nominees Pty Ltd v Norman Ross Homeworks Pty Ltd (1992) ... 618

Cheall v APEX [1983] ... 1967
Cheers v Pacific Acceptance Corp Ltd (1959) ... 1727
Cheese v Thomas [1994] ... 1402
Chettiar v Chettiar [1962] ... 1718, 1721
Chiarabaglia v Westpac Banking Corp (1989) ... 1108
Chichester v Cobb (1866) ... 346
Child v Commonwealth Development Bank of Australia Ltd (2000) ... 1514
Chillingworth v Esche [1924] ... 273
China National Foreign Trade Transportation Corp v Evlogia Shipping Co SA of Panama (The Mihalios Xilas) [1979] ... 1984, 2232
China Ocean Shipping Co Ltd v P S Chellaram & Co Ltd (1990) ... 379, 761
Christiani & Nielsen Pty Ltd v Goliath Portland Cement Co Ltd (1993) ... 2308
Christie v Robinson (1907) ... 2333
Christopoulos v Angelos (1996) ... 1067
Churchward v R (1865) ... 871
Ciavarella v Balmer (1983) ... 1907, 1949, 1962, 1964, 1973, 1979
CIBC Mortgages Plc v Pitt [1994] ... 1405
Citibank NA v Brown Shipley & Co Ltd [1991] ... 1224
Citicorp Australia Ltd v Hendry (1985) ... 727, 1852, 1950, 2159, 2207, 2211, 2217
City and Westminster Properties (1934) Ltd v Mudd [1959] ... 613
City Bank of Sydney v McLaughlin (1909) ... 843, 846
City Motors (1933) Pty Ltd v Southern Aerial Super Service Pty Ltd (1961) ... 2202, 2221
City of Box Hill v E W Tauschke Pty Ltd [1974] ... 273
City of Gosnells v Roberts (1994) ... 865
Civil Service Co-operative Society of Victoria Ltd v Blyth (1914) ... 1008
Clare v Lamb (1875) ... 1215
Clark v Clark (1882) ... 1023
—v Malpas (1862) ... 1506
—v Urquhart [1930] ... 1068

References are to paragraphs

Clarke v Cobley (1789) ... 823
—v Dickson (1858) ... 1043
—v—(1859) ... 1019, 1026
—v Dunraven [1897] ... 203
—v Tyler (1949) ... 510
Claude Neon Ltd v Hardie [1970] ... 2020, 2040
Clay's Policy of Assurance, Re; Clay v Earnshaw [1937] ... 911
Clea Shipping Corp v Bulk Oil International Ltd (The Alaskan Trader) [1984] ... 2224
Cleary v Australian Co-operative Foods Ltd (Nos 2 & 3) (1999) ... 1103
Cleaver v Mutual Reserve Fund Life Association [1892] ... 911
Clef Aquitaine SARL v Laporte Materials (Barrow) Ltd [2000] ... 1069
Clegg v Wilson (1932) ... 1628, 1712, 1716, 1717, 1718
Clements v London & NW Ry Co [1894] ... 814
Cleveland Petroleum Co Ltd v Dartstone Ltd [1969] ... 1638
Clifford Davis Management Ltd v WEA Records Ltd [1975] ... 1510
Clifton v Coffey (1924) ... 2333
—v Palumbo [1944] ... 207, 209
Clifton Springs Hotel Ltd, Re [1939] ... 226
Clive v Beaumont (1848) ... 222
Clore v Theatrical Properties Ltd [1936] ... 913
Clough v London & North Western Railway Co (1871) ... 1041, 1050
Clydebank Engineering and Shipbuilding Co Ltd v Don Jose Ramos Yzquierdo y Castaneda [1905] ... 2209, 2212, 2215
Clyne v New South Wales Bar Association (1960) ... 1629, 1630
Coal Cliff Collieries Pty Ltd v Sijehama Pty Ltd (1991) ... 268, 271
Coan v Bowles (1691) ... 808
Coast Securities No 9 Pty Ltd v Alabac Pty Ltd [1984] ... 2202
Coastal Estates Pty Ltd v Melevende [1965] ... 1048, 1049, 1050, 1971
Coates v Sarich [1964] ... 2333
Cochrane v Willis (1865) ... 1208, 1219, 2411

Cockshott v Bennett (1799) ... 805, 808
Coddington v Paleologo (1867) ... 1848
Codelfa Construction Pty Ltd v State Rail Authority of New South Wales (1982) ... 119, 621, 625, 629, 703, 712, 713, 714, 718, 719, 2001, 2004, 2008, 2016, 2017, 2036, 2049, 2055, 2056, 2064, 2066
Coghlan v S H Lock (Australia) Ltd (1987) ... 337
Cohen v Cohen (1929) ... 403
—v Kittell (1889) ... 1616
—v Mason [1961] ... 260
—v Roche [1927] ... 516, 2405
Cohen & Co v Ockerby & Co Ltd (1917) ... 1945
Cole v Cunningham (1837) ... 217
Collen v Wright (1857) ... 873
Colley v Overseas Exporters [1921] ... 1809, 2204, 2221
Collier v Morlend Finance Corp (Vic) Pty Ltd (1989) ... 1522
Collin v Holden [1989] ... 514, 519, 521
Collins v Godefroy (1831) ... 342
—v Parker (1984) ... 1518
Collins Marrickville Pty Ltd v Henjo Investments Pty Ltd (1987) ... 1121
Collins Trading Co Pty Ltd v Maher [1969] ... 511
Colman v Eastern Counties Railway Co (1846) ... 853
Colonial Ammunition Co v Reid (1900) ... 223
Colonial Bank of Australasia v Kerr (1889) ... 1408
Comalco Aluminium Ltd v Mogal Freight Services Pty Ltd (1993) ... 1109
Combe v Combe [1951] ... 372
Comco Constructions Pty Ltd v Westminster Properties Pty Ltd (1990) ... 1528
Commerce Consolidated Pty Ltd v Johnstone [1976] ... 1265
Commercial Bank of Australia Ltd v Amadio (1983) ... 118, 1015, 1416, 1503, 1506, 1512, 1513, 1514, 1519, 1522, 1523, 1527, 1528, 1530
—v G H Dean & Co Pty Ltd [1983] ... 273

Table of Cases

Commercial Banking Co of Sydney Ltd v Pollard [1983] ... 1521
Commercial Cable Co v Government of Newfoundland [1916] ... 871
Commission for the New Towns v Cooper (Great Britain) Ltd [1995] ... 1265
Commissioner for Railways (New South Wales) v Quinn (1946) ... 763, 764
Commissioner of Stamp Duties (NSW) v Carlenka Pty Ltd (1995) ... 1261, 1263
Commissioner of State Revenue (Vic) v Royal Insurance Australia Ltd (1994) ... 2326
Commissioner of Taxes (Qld) v Camphin (1937) ... 248
Commonwealth Bank of Australia v Oberdan (2000) ... 1514
—v TLI Management Pty Ltd [1990] ... 724
Commonwealth of Australia v Amann Aviation Pty Ltd (1991) ...118, 1936, 1970, 1983, 2104, 2110, 2111, 2113, 2145, 2161, 2162, 2164, 2323
—v Antonio Giorgio Pty Ltd (1986) ... 256
—v Australian Commonwealth Shipping Board (1926) ... 870
—v Burns [1971] ... 871
—v Colonial Combing Spinning and Weaving Co Ltd (The Wool Tops case) (1922) ... 871
—v Crothall Hospital Services (Aust) Ltd (1981) ... 871
—v Kidman (1923) ... 871
—v Ling (1993) ... 871
—v—(1994) ... 871
—v Mewett (1997) ... 869
—v Verwayen (1990) ... 369, 371, 375, 378, 381, 382, 383, 385, 386, 391, 392, 393, 524, 1513, 1627
Commonwealth Portland Cement Co Ltd v Weber Lohmann & Co Ltd [1905] ... 1843
Commonwealth Trading Bank of Australia v Sydney Wide Stores Pty Ltd (1981) ... 624, 2122
Compagnie Commerciale Sucres et Denrées v C Czarnikow Ltd [1990] ... 1919

Compagnie Francaise des Chemins de Fer Paris Orleans v Leeston Shipping Co Ltd (1919) ... 1054, 1055, 1057
Comptoir Commercial Anversois v Power Son & Co [1920] ... 622, 632, 2040
Comptoir d'Achat et de Vente du Boerenbond Belge SA v Luis de Ridder Limitada (The Julia) [1949] ... 2004, 2030, 2067
Concrete Constructions (NSW) Pty Ltd v Nelson (1990) ... 1104, 1106
Concrete Constructions Pty Ltd v GIO of NSW [1966] ... 901, 914
Concut Pty Ltd v Worrell (2000) ... 347, 1936, 1969
Connolly v United Shire of Beechworth (1874) ... 226, 860
Connor v Spence (1878) ... 2003
—v Stainton (1924) ... 1831
Conroy v Lowndes [1958] ... 2169
Consolidated Neon (Phillips System) Pty Ltd v Tooheys Ltd (1942) ... 2020, 2022
Con-Stan Industries of Australia Pty Ltd v Norwich Winterthur Insurance (Australia) Ltd (1986) ... 382, 629, 644,
Constantinople & Alexandria Hotel Co, Re (Ebbett's case) (1870) ... 805, 817
Construction Engineering (Aust) Pty Ltd v Hexyl Pty Ltd (1985) ... 906, 907
Continental C & G Rubber Co Pty Ltd, Re (1919) ... 2062, 2065, 2067
Cooden Engineering Co Ltd v Stanford [1953] ... 2211
Coogee Esplanade Surf Motel Pty Ltd v Commonwealth (1976) ... 209
—v—(1983) ... 873
Cook v Lister (1863) ... 359, 360
—v Rodgers (1946) ... 2405
—v Wright (1861) ...353
Cook Islands Shipping Co Ltd v Colson Builders Ltd [1975] ... 345
Cooke v Caldwell's Wines Ltd (1925) ... 1069
Cooks v Clayworth (1811) ... 845
Coombs v Bahama Palm Trading Pty Ltd (1991) ... 1518
Cooney v Burns (1922) ... 522, 523
Cooper v Australian Electric Co (1922) Ltd (1922) ... 1811, 2325

References are to paragraphs

—v Phibbs (1867) ... 1011, 1209, 1214, 1227, 1230
Cooper & Sons v Neilson & Maxwell Ltd [1919] ... 2023, 2028
Co-operative Bulk Handling Ltd v Jennings Industries Ltd (1996) ... 918
Co-operative Insurance Society Ltd v Argyll Stores (Holdings) Ltd [1998] ... 2402, 2403
Copperart Pty Ltd, Re (1995) ... 220, 256
Coras v Webb [1942] ... 824
Corio Guarantee Corp v McCallum [1956] ... 1834
Cornelius v Phillips [1918] ... 1614
Cornish & Co v Kanematsu (1913) ... 2016
Corpe v Overton (1833) ... 821
Corser v Commonwealth General Assurance Corp Ltd [1963] ... 261, 268
Corson v Rhuddlan Borough Council (1989) ... 267
Cort v Ambergate Nottingham and Boston and Eastern Junction Railway Co (1851) ... 1933
Corumo Holdings Pty Ltd v C Itoh Ltd (1991) ... 704
Cosgrove v Horsfall (1945) ... 923
Costa Vraca Pty Ltd v Berrigan Weed and Pest Control Pty Ltd (1998) ... 1110
Costello v Loulakas [1938] ... 222
Cottee v Franklins Self-Serve Pty Ltd [1997] ... 213
Couchman v Hill [1947] ... 608, 638, 766
Couglin v Blair (1953) ... 2158
Couldery v Bartrum (1881) ... 360
Coulls v Bagot's Executor and Trustee Co Ltd (1967) ... 302, 319, 322, 360, 901, 903, 911, 912, 930, 2403, 2406
Coulthart v Clementson (1879) ... 257
Courtney & Fairbairn Ltd v Tolaini Bros (Hotels) Ltd [1975] ... 271
Cousins v Freeman (1957) ... 1054, 1230
Coutts & Co v Browne-Lecky [1947] ... 826
Couturier v Hastie (1856) ... 1216, 1217
Cover v McLaughlin (1897) ... 1050

Cowan v O'Connor (1888) ... 231, 236
Cowern v Nield [1912] ... 813, 822
Cox v Phillips Industries Ltd [1976] ... 2152
—v Prentice (1815) ... 1212, 1215
CRA Ltd v NZ Goldfields Investments [1989] ... 2216
Crabb v Arun District Council [1976] ... 377
Craddock Bros v Hunt [1922] ... 1258
Crago v McIntyre [1976] ... 1268
Craig deceased, Re; Meneces v Middleton [1971] ... 1403
Craine v Colonial Mutual Fire Insurance Co Ltd (1920) ... 391, 392, 1972
Crane v Hegeman-Harris Co Inc [1939] ... 1259
Craven-Ellis v Canons Ltd [1936] ... 2313, 2318
Crawford v Mayne Nickless Ltd (1992) ... 643
—v Parish (1991) ... 1077, 1077
Crears v Hunter (1887) ... 355
Credit Lyonnais Bank Nederland NV v Burch [1997] ... 1512
Credit Suisse v Borough Council of Allerdale [1997] ... 852, 853
—v Waltham Forest London Borough Council [1997] ... 853
Crescendo Management Pty Ltd v Westpac Banking Corp (1988) ... 1304, 1305, 1306, 1313, 1321
Cresswell v Potter (1968) ... 1506
Crick v Murray (1882) ... 820
Cricklewood Property and Investment Trust Ltd v Leighton's Investment Trust Ltd [1945] ... 2003, 2004, 2035, 2037, 2044, 2051, 2060, 2061
Criss v Alexander (1928) ... 635, 719
Csomore v Public Service Board of New South Wales (1986) ... 1832, 1939
CSS Investments Pty Ltd v Lopiron Pty Ltd (1987) ... 1810, 1983
CTN Cash and Carry Ltd v Gallaher Ltd [1994] ... 1319
Cudgen Rutile (No 2) Pty Ltd v Chalk [1975] ... 259
Cullen v Bickers (1878) ... 222
—v Thomson (1862) ... 1028
—v Trappell (1980) ... 2167

References are to paragraphs

Cullinane v British 'Rema' Manufacturing Co Ltd [1954] ... 2113
Cumber v Wayne (1721) ... 356, 357
Cumming v Ince (1847) ... 1308, 1325
Cumming & Co Ltd v Hasell (1920) ... 261
Cundy v Lindsay (1878) ... 1241, 1242, 1243, 1254
Currie v Misa (1875) ... 308
Curro v Beyond Productions Pty Ltd (1993) ... 1636, 1637, 1646, 1839, 2415
Curruth v Ern Moro & Amoco Enterprises Pty Ltd (1966) ... 821
Curtis v Chemical Cleaning and Dyeing Co [1951] ... 615, 766
Curwen v Yan Yean Land Co Ltd (1891) ... 1016, 1018, 1027
Custom Credit Corp Ltd v Lupi [1992] ... 1520
Cutter v Powell (1795) ... 1824, 1827, 2015, 2066
Cutts v Buckley (1933) ... 613, 1023
D & C Builders Ltd v Rees [1966] ... 365, 372, 381, 1316
Dagenham (Thames) Dock Co, Re (1873) ... 2240
Dahl v Nelson (1881) ... 2025, 2027, 2056, 2058
Dai v Telstra Corp Ltd (2000) ... 1524
Daily Telegraph Newspaper Co Ltd v McLaughlin [1904] ... 843
Dainford Ltd v Smith (1985) ... 1929, 1941
—v Yulora Pty Ltd [1984] ... 1963, 1979
Dakin (H) & Co Ltd v Lee [1916] ... 1832
Dalgety & Co Ltd v AMP [1908] ... 1017
Dalgety and New Zealand Loan Ltd v C Imeson Pty Ltd [1964] ... 1609, 1614, 1732
Dalgety Australia Ltd v Harris [1977] ... 239, 240
Dalgety Wine Estates Pty Ltd v Rizzon (1979) ... 2416, 2419
Damon Compania Naviera SA v Hapag-Lloyd International SA (The Blankenstein) [1985] ... 1951, 2237
Daniel Doull, In the Estate of (1881) ... 840, 841, 848

Darlington Borough Council v Wiltshier Northern Ltd [1995] ... 912
Darlington Futures Ltd v Delco Australia Pty Ltd (1986) ... 119, 748, 750, 752, 762, 764, 765
Darter Pty Ltd v Malloy [1993] ... 522, 712, 2407
Dataflow Computer Services Pty Ltd v Goodman (1999) ... 1104
Daulia Ltd v Four Millbank Nominees Ltd [1978] ... 250
Davenport v R (1877) ... 1971
David (by her Tutor the Protective Commissioner) v David (1993) ... 838
David Jones Ltd v Lunn (1969) ... 267, 272
David Securities Pty Ltd v Commonwealth Bank of Australia (1992) ... 118, 1010, 2164, 2306, 2318
David T Boyd & Co Ltd v Louca [1973] ... 261
Davidson v Atlas Assurance Co Ltd [1932] ... 1209
Davies, Re [1989] ... 922
—v Beynon-Harris (1931) ... 818
—v Collins [1945] ... 761, 1818
—v Smith (1938) ... 220
Davis v Commissioner for Main Roads (1968) ... 763, 764
—v Jacoby (1934) ... 249
—v Pearce Parking Station Pty Ltd (1954) ... 763, 764
Davis Contractors Ltd v Fareham UDC [1956] ... 2001, 2006, 2017, 2020, 2038, 2043, 2049, 2050, 2056, 2066
Davitt v Titcumb [1989] ... 1702
Day Ford Pty Ltd v Sciacca [1990] ... 1709
De Bernardy v Harding (1853) ... 1991, 2339
De Choisy v Hynes [1937] ... 876
De Francesco v Barnum (1890) ... 808, 814
De Garis v Dalgety & Co Ltd [1915] ... 805, 813, 817, 819
De Garis and Rowe's Lease, Re [1924] ... 2003, 2036, 2060
De La Bere v Pearson [1908] ... 317
De Mattos v Gibson (1858) ... 913

De Soysa v De Pless Pol [1912] ... 2116
Deaves v CML Fire and General Insurance Co Ltd (1979) ... 392, 619, 730
Debenham v Sawbridge [1901] ... 1230
Decro-Wall International SA v Practitioners in Marketing Ltd [1971] ... 1925, 1934, 1967, 2224
Deemcope Pty Ltd v Cantown Pty Ltd [1995] ... 1318
Deepak Fertilisers and Petrochemicals Corp v ICI Chemicals & Polymers Ltd [1999] ... 926
Defina v Kenny (1946) ... 1616
Dehle v Denham (1899) ... 231, 236
Dell v Beasley [1959] ... 1208, 1229, 2411
Demagogue Pty Ltd v Ramensky (1992) ... 2410
—v—(1993) ... 1110
Demetrios v Gikas Dry Cleaning Industries Pty Ltd (1991) ... 1020, 1045
Dencio v Zivanovic (1991) ... 255
Denmark Productions Ltd v Boscobel Productions Ltd [1969] ... 1933, 2045
Dennant v Skinner & Collom [1948] ... 1245
Denny v Hancock (1870) ... 2411
Denny Mott & Dickson Ltd v James B Fraser & Co Ltd [1944] ... 2004, 2006, 2007, 2024, 2027, 2032, 2050, 2051, 2058
Dent v Bennett (1839) ... 1408
Denton v Great Northern Railway Co (1856) ... 208, 317
Derbyshire Building Co Pty Ltd v Becker (1962) ... 642, 1855
Derry v Peek (1889) ... 1025, 1030
Deta Nominees Pty Ltd v Viscount Plastic Products Pty Ltd [1979] ... 517
Deutsche Genossenschaftsbank v Burnhope [1995] ... 703
Deutsche Schachtbau-und Tiefbohrgesellschaft mbH v Shell International Petroleum Co Ltd [1990] ... 402
Devis (W) & Sons Ltd v Atkins [1977] ... 1969
Dewar v Mintoft [1912] ... 2236
Dewhurst v Budget Rent-A-Car System Pty Ltd (1986) ... 1107
Dewhurst (WA) & Co Pty Ltd v Cawrse [1960] ... 205, 238
Di Biase v Rezek [1971] ... 513, 515
Di Dio Nominees Pty Ltd v Brian Mark Real Estate Pty Ltd [1992] ... 704
Diamond v Moore (1931) ... 1936
Dick Bentley Productions Ltd v Harold Smith (Motors) Ltd [1965] ... 610
Dickinson v Dodds (1876) ... 207, 243, 244, 257
Dickson (GC) & Yorston (Builders) Pty Ltd v Hattam [1935] ... 1603
Didymi Corp v Atlantic Lines and Navigation Co Inc (The Didymi) [1988] ... 267
Dies v British and International Mining and Finance Corp Ltd [1939] ... 2324
Dillon v Charter Travel Co Ltd (1989) ... 1520, 2153
Dillwyn v Llewellyn (1862) ... 377
Dimmock v Hallett (1866) ... 1007, 1016, 1023
Dimond v Moore (1931) ... 2034
Dimskal Shipping Co SA v International Transport Workers Federation (The Evia Luck) [1992] ... 1302, 1305, 1310, 1313, 1328, 1329
Dingjan, Re; Ex parte Wagner (1995) ... 1986
Direct Acceptance Finance Ltd v Cumberland Furnishing Pty Ltd [1965] ... 1907, 1925, 1926, 1934, 1936
Ditcham v Worrall (1880) ... 819
DJE Constructions Pty Ltd v Maddocks [1982] ... 1708, 1737
Dobbs v National Bank of Australasia Ltd (1935) ... 1626
Doherty v Allman (1878) ... 2415, 2416, 2417, 2418, 2419, 2420
Doleman & Sons v Ossett Corp [1912] ... 746, 1626
Domb v Isoz [1980] ... 2115
Dominelli Ford (Hurstville) Pty Ltd v Karmot Auto Spares Pty Ltd (1992) ... 1112
Dominion Coal Co Ltd v Dominion Iron & Steel Co Ltd [1909] ...340
Donaldson v Freeson (1934) ... 1715

Table of Cases

Donnell v Bennett (1883) ... 340
Doug Rea Enterprises Pty Ltd v Hymix Australia Pty Ltd [1987] ... 1613
Dougan v Ley (1946) ... 2405, 2408
Douglas, Re; Ex parte Starkey (1987) ... 330
Dowsett v Reid (1912) ... 1209
Doyle v Olby (Ironmongers) Ltd [1969] ... 1068
—v White City Stadium Ltd [1935] ... 813, 816
DPP for Northern Ireland v Lynch [1975] ... 1302, 1304
Drennan v Star Paving Co (1958) ... 387
Dressy Frocks Pty Ltd v Bock (1951) ... 1707
Drexel Burnham Lambert International NV v El Nasr [1986] ... 379
Drinkwater v Arthur (1871) ... 807
Droop v Colonial Bank of Australasia (1880) ... 852
Drozd v Vaskas [1960] ... 1045, 1048
DTR Nominees Pty Ltd v Mona Homes Pty Ltd (1978) ... 713, 1915, 1916, 1941, 1978, 2333
Dublin & Wicklow Ry Co v Black (1852) ... 819
Duggan v Barnes [1923] ... 267
Duncan v Mell (1914) ... 2333
Dunlop v Higgins (1848) ... 222, 235
Dunlop Pneumatic Tyre Co Ltd v New Garage and Motor Co Ltd [1915] ... 2207, 2208, 2209, 2212, 2213, 2214, 2215
—v Selfridge & Co Ltd [1915] ... 309, 319, 901, 904
Dunmore v Alexander (1830) ... 237
Dunn v MacDonald [1897] ... 873
Dunton v Dunton (1892) ... 339, 345
Duralla Pty Ltd v Plant (1984) ... 1023
Dutton v Poole (1678) ... 909
Dyke v McLeish Estates Ltd (1927) ... 1968, 2106
Dyson v Pharmacy Board of NSW (2000) ... 1105
Dyster v Randall & Sons [1926] ... 1242
E E Caledonia Ltd v Orbit Valve Co Europe [1994] ... 763, 764
Eaglesfield v Marquis of Londonderry (1876) ... 1010, 1209

Earhart v William Low Co (1979) ... 2317
Earl of Aylesford v Morris (1873) ... 1504, 1506
Earl of Beauchamp v Winn (1873) ... 1209, 1228, 1230, 1231, 1232
Earl of Chesterfield v Janssen (1751) ... 1504, 1508
Earl v Hector Whaling Ltd [1961] ... 1262
Earle v Peale (1711) ... 815
East v Maurer [1991] ... 1069
Eastern Archipelago Co v R (1853) ... 852
Eastern Counties Railway Co v Hawkes (1855) ... 853
Eastwood v Kenyon (1840) ... 306, 910
Easyfind (NSW) Pty Ltd v Paterson (1987) ... 1209, 1254
Eccles v Bryant [1948] ... 203, 273
Economides v Commercial Assurance Co Plc [1998] ... 1009
Edgington v Fitzmaurice (1885) ... 1009, 1019, 1020, 1025
Edler v Auerbach [1950] ... 1054
Edmunds v Pickering (No 4) (2000) ... 1514
Edwards v Carter [1893] ... 806, 818
—v Skyways Ltd [1964] ... 405
—v Victorian Producers Co-operative Co Ltd (1993) ... 267
—v Worboys (1982) ... 1651
Ee v Kakar (1979) ... 275
Egan v Ross (1928) ... 1275
Eggleston v Marley Engineers Pty Ltd (1979) ... 615, 618
Eighth SRJ Pty Ltd v Merity (1997) ... 1107
Elder Dempster & Co v Paterson Zochonis & Co [1924] ... 923
Elder's Trustee and Executor Co Ltd v Commonwealth Homes and Investment Co Ltd (1941) ... 1048, 1971
Elders Rural Finance Ltd v Smith (1996) ... 1522
Electric Acceptance Pty Ltd v Doug Thorley Caravans (Aust) Pty Ltd [1981] ... 1737
Electrical Enterprises Retail Pty Ltd v Rodgers (1988) ... 1061

References are to paragraphs

Electronic Industries Ltd v David Jones Ltd (1954) ... 527, 1804, 1815
Elias v George Sahely & Co (Barbados) Ltd [1983] ... 273, 514, 515
Elizabeth Bay Developments Pty Ltd v Boral Building Services Pty Ltd (1995) ... 271
Elkington & Co Ltd v Amery [1936] ... 816
Elkoury v Farrow Mortgage Services Pty Ltd (1993) ... 379, 2230
Ellen v Topp (1851) ... 1830, 1942
Ellis v Ellis (1698) ... 815
Ellul v Oakes (1972) ... 515, 606, 610, 2169
Elmslie v FCT (1993) ... 273
Elna Australia Pty Ltd v International Computers (Australia) Pty Ltd (1987) ... 1112
Elpis Maritime Co Ltd v Marti Chartering Co Inc (The Maria D) [1992] ... 513
Embiricos v Sydney Reid & Co [1914] ... 2026, 2027
Empirnall Holdings Pty Ltd v Machon Paull Partners Pty Ltd (1988) ... 205, 229
Empresa Cubana Importada de Alimentos 'Alimport' v Iasmos Shipping Co SA (The Good Friend) [1984] ... 2135
Empresa Exportadora de Azucar v Industria Azucarera Nacional SA (The Playa Larga) [1983] ... 2018, 2040
Engelbach's Estate, Re [1924] ... 911
English v Gibbs (1888) ... 821
English and Australian Copper Co Ltd v Johnson (1911) ... 1929
English and Foreign Co v Arduin (1870) ... 224
English Hop Growers Ltd v Dering [1928] ... 1652
Entores Ltd v Miles Far East Corp [1955] ... 235, 236, 238
Environment Agency (formerly National Rivers Authority) v Empress Car Co (Abertillery) Ltd [1999] ... 2120
Equitable Life Assurance Society v Hyman [2000] ... 631
Equiticorp Finance Ltd v Bank of New Zealand (1993) ... 1304, 1318, 1321
Equity Trustees Executor & Agency Co Ltd and Considine's Contract, Re [1932] ... 2036
Eric Gnapp Ltd v Petroleum Board [1949] ... 1409
Eriksson v Whalley [1971] ... 1909, 1970
Erlanger v New Sombrero Phosphate Co (1878) ... 1043, 1045, 1065
Ernest Beck & Co v K Szymanowski & Co [1924] ... 752, 1977
Errington v Errington [1952] ... 250
Ertel Bieber & Co v Rio Tinto Co Ltd [1918] ... 1625, 2041, 2060, 2062
Esanda Finance Corp Ltd v Peat Marwick Hungerfords (Reg) (1997) ... 1030, 1031, 1032, 1033
—v Plessnig (1989) ... 2159, 2217, 2332
—v Tong (1997) ... 1522
Esanda Ltd v Burgess [1984] ... 112, 613
Eshelby v Federated European Bank Ltd [1932] ... 1832
Esso Australia Resources Ltd v Plowman (1995) ... 631
Esso Petroleum Co Ltd v Commissioners of Customs & Excise [1976] ... 208, 407
—v Harper's Garage (Stourport) Ltd [1968] ... 1634, 1635, 1636, 1637, 1638, 1639, 1640, 1642, 1643, 1644, 1645, 1646, 1647, 1652, 1702, 1733, 1734
—v Mardon [1976] ... 602, 1032, 1033, 1036
Estee Lauder Pty Ltd v Federal Commissioner of Taxation (1989) ... 712
Etablissements Chainbaux SARL v Harbormaster Ltd [1955] ... 1956
Ettridge v Vermin Board of the District of Murat Bay [1928] ... 2157, 2230, 2323
Eudunda Farmers Co-operative Society Ltd v Mattiske (1920) ... 267
Euro-Diam Ltd v Bathurst [1990] ... 730, 1625, 1703, 1715
European Asian of Australia Ltd v Kurland (1985) ... 1508
Evans v Bartlam [1937] ... 1975
—v Benson & Co [1961] ... 1046, 1048, 1064, 1069

Table of Cases

—v Llewellin (1787) ... 1506
—v Ware [1892] ... 812
Evans (J) & Son (Portsmouth) Ltd v Andrea Merzario Ltd [1976] ... 707, 766
Evans Deakin Industries Ltd v Queensland Electricity Generating Board (1984) ... 219
Evans Marshall & Co Ltd v Bertola SA [1973] ... 2418
Eximenco Handels AG v Partrederiet Oro Chief (The Oro Chief) [1983] ... 2405
Export Credits Department v Universal Oil Products Co [1983] ... 2216
Express Airways v Port Augusta Air Services [1980] ... 231, 238
Fablo Pty Ltd v Bloore [1983] ... 520
Faccenda Chicken Ltd v Fowler [1987] ... 633
Facey v Rawsthorne (1925) ... 1973
FAI Traders Insurance Co Ltd v Savoy Plaza Pty Ltd [1993] ... 712
Fairline Shipping Corp v Adamson [1985] ... 229
Falck v Williams [1900] ... 1234
Falconer v Wilson [1973] ... 1961
Falko v James McEwan & Co Pty Ltd [1977] ... 2135, 2152
Familiar Pty Ltd v Samarkos (1994) ... 1513
Fanhaven Pty Ltd v Bain Dawes Northern Pty Ltd [1982] ... 1857
Faram v Kerr (1877) ... 607
Farmer v Honan (1919) ... 273, 710, 712
Farmers' Mercantile Union & Chaff Mills Ltd v Coade (1921) ... 226, 255
Farnworth Finance Facilities Ltd v Attryde [1970] ... 75, 1927
Farr Smith & Co Ltd v Messers Ltd [1928] ... 516, 518
Farrant v Leburn [1970] ... 2237, 2238
Farrow Mortgage Services Pty Ltd v Edgar (1993) ... 1614, 1703, 1720
Fawcett v Smethurst (1914) ... 811
—v Star Car Sales Ltd [1960] ... 1246
FCT v Murry (1998) ... 1642
—v Ranson (1989) ... 111
Fealey, Ex parte (1897) ... 227

Federal Airports Corp v Makucha Developments Pty Ltd (1993) ... 1983
Federal Commerce and Navigation Co Ltd v Molena Alpha Inc [1979] ... 1926, 1932, 1934, 1935, 1937, 1939, 1941
Felthouse v Bindley (1862) ... 224, 229
Felton v Mulligan (1971) ... 1627
Fender v St John-Mildmay [1938] ... 1620, 1632, 1633
Fercometal SARL v Mediterranean Shipping Co SA [1989] ... 1832, 1839, 1943, 1947
Ferguson, Re (1969) ... 1712, 1714, 1720
—v John Dawson & Partners (Contractors) Ltd [1976] ... 719
Fibrosa Société Anonyme v Fairbairn Lawson Combe Barbour Ltd [1942] ... 2067
Fibrosa Spolka Akcyjna v Fairbairn Lawson Combe Barbour Ltd [1943] ... 2023, 2050, 2062, 2065, 2067, 2082, 2301, 2321
Field v Moore (1855) ... 806
Field and the Conveyancing Act, Re [1968] ... 1633, 1736
Filby v Hounsell [1896] ... 273
Financings Ltd v Baldock [1963] ... 2157, 2159, 2217
—v Stimson [1962] ... 244, 256
Finch v Sayers [1976] ... 2015, 2058, 2061
Finchbourne Ltd v Rodrigues [1976] ... 626
Finelvet AG v Vinava Shipping Co Ltd [1983] ... 2028
Fink v Fink (1946) ... 2117, 2163
Finlayson v Carr [1978] ... 410
—v James [1986] ... 1835
Finucane v New South Wales Egg Corp (1988) ... 111, 707, 1105
Fire and All Risks Insurance Co Ltd v Powell [1966] ... 1621, 1623, 1705
Firestone Tyre and Rubber Co Ltd v Vokins & Co Ltd [1951] ... 760
Firth v Halloran (1926) ... 2036
Fisher v Bell [1961] ... 208, 214
Fisher (ET) Pty Ltd v English Scottish & Australian Bank Ltd (1940) ... 360

References are to paragraphs

Fitch v Dewes [1921] ... 1642, 1643, 1648
—v Jones (1855) ... 1616
Fitzgerald v F J Leonhardt Pty Ltd (1997) ... 1602, 1607, 1615, 1620, 1702, 1706, 1710, 1719, 1727, 1728, 1809
—v Masters (1956) ... 272, 1730, 2409
Fitzpatrick v Michel (1928) ... 1009
Fleming v Bank of New Zealand [1900] ... 322
Fleming Bros (Monaro Agencies) Pty Ltd v Smith (1983) ... 1739
Fletcher v Manton (1940) ... 2033
—v Minister for Environment & Heritage (1999) ... 251, 252
Flett v Deniliquin Publishing Co Ltd [1964–65] ... 2335, 2337
Fliegner v MNM Pty Ltd (2000) ... 1110
Flight v Booth (1834) ... 759
Flower v London & NW Ry Co [1894] ... 814
Foakes v Beer (1884) ... 357, 364, 381, 388
Foley v Classique Coaches Ltd [1934] ... 268, 269, 1637
Fong v Cilli (1968) ... 257, 267, 273
Food Corp of India v Antclizo Shipping Corp (The Antclizo) [1987] ... 229
—v Antclizo Shipping Corp [1988] ... 1978
Foran v Wight (1989) ... 119, 382, 1808, 1811, 1815, 1929, 1933, 1935, 1942, 1943, 1945, 1947, 1976, 1978, 2303
Ford v Bartley (1956) ... 1603
Forestry Commission of New South Wales v Stefanetto (1976) ... 2240
Forman & Co Pty Ltd v The Ship 'Liddesdale' [1900] ... 1824, 2325
Forsikringsaktieselskapet Vesta v Butcher [1989] ... 713, 2131
Forslind v Bechely-Crundall 1922 ... 1935
Foster v Driscoll [1929] ... 1625
—v Mackinnon (1869) ... 1273, 1415
Fox v Wood (1981) ... 2121
Fragomeni v Fogliani (1968) ... 2411
Francis v Lyon (1907) ... 702, 2143
Franich v Swannell (1993) ... 1104, 1110

Frank Davies Pty Ltd v Container Haulage Group Pty Ltd (1989) ... 752
Frankcombe v Foster Investments Pty Ltd [1978] ... 2324
Frederick E Rose (London) Ltd v William H Pim Junior & Co Ltd [1953] ... 1061, 1225, 1261, 1263
Freeman v Cooke (1848) ... 382
Freeth v Burr (1874) ... 1938
French (L) & Co Ltd v Leeston Shipping Co Ltd [1922] ... 628
Freshmark Ltd v Mercantile Mutual Insurance (Australia) Ltd [1994] ... 1974
Friedlander v Bank of Australasia (1909) ... 725, 1918
Frobisher (Second Investments) Ltd v Kiloran Trust Co Ltd [1980] ... 621
Frost v Aylesbury Dairy Co Ltd [1905] ... 639
—v Knight (1872) ... 1933, 1937, 1945, 2161
Fry v Lane (1888) ... 1412, 1504, 1506
Fuller's Theatre and Vaudeville Co Ltd v Rofe [1923] ... 1971
Fullers' Theatres Ltd v Musgrove (1923) ... 1041, 1947, 1982, 2407
Furphy v Nixon (1925) ... 1312, 1320
Futuretronics International Pty Ltd v Gadzhis (1990) ... 514, 524, 611, 1108
—v—[1992] ... 1120
Gadd v Thompson [1911] ... 812, 814
Gadsden (J) Pty Ltd v Strider 1 Ltd (The AES Express) (1990) ... 2303
Gall v Mitchell (1924) ... 2411
Gallie v Lee [1969] ... 1270
Galloway v Galloway (1914) ... 1221
Gambrinus Lager Beer Brewery Co Ltd, Re (1886) ... 226
Gamerco SA v ICM/Fair Warning (Agency) Ltd [1995] ... 1610, 2021, 2082
Gandy v Gandy (1885) ... 901
Garcia v National Australia Bank Ltd (1998) ... 118, 879, 1405, 1514
Gardam v George Wills & Co Ltd (1988) ... 1121
Garden Neptune Shipping Ltd v Occidental Worldwide Investment Corp [1990] ... 1077

Table of Cases

Gardiner v Grigg (1938) ... 608, 730
—v Wainfur (1919) ... 815
Gardner v Marsh & Parsons (a firm) [1997] ... 2134
Garnac Grain Co Inc v HMF Faure & Fairclough Ltd [1968] ... 1970, 2149
Garrard v Frankel (1862) ... 1258
Gates v City Mutual Life Assurance Society Ltd (1986) ... 613, 1113
Gator Shipping Corp v Trans-Asiatic Oil Ltd SA (The Odenfeld) [1978] ... 2224
Gaye (No 1) Pty Ltd v Allan Rowlands Holdings Pty Ltd (1993) ... 1610
Geelong Building Society (in liq) v Thomas (1996) ... 1513
Geipel v Smith (1872) ... 1955, 2056
Gelling v Crespin (1917) ... 2014, 2056
Gemmell Power Farming Co Ltd v Nies (1935) ... 635, 720
General Accident Fire and Life Assurance Corp v Tanter (The Zephyr) [1985] ... 364
General Billposting Co Ltd v Atkinson [1909] ... 1994, 1995
General Credits Ltd v Ebsworth [1986] ... 353
General Newspapers Pty Ltd v Telstra Corp (1993) ... 1107, 1110
General Reinsurance Corp v Forsakringsaktiebolaget Fennia Patria [1983] ... 644
Geo Thompson (Aust) Pty Ltd v Vittadello [1978] ... 1936
George v Greater Adelaide Land Development Co Ltd (1929) ... 1610, 1712, 1713, 1714, 1716, 1717, 1718, 1727, 1728
—v Roach (1942) ... 741, 2318
George Barker (Transport) Ltd v Eynon [1974] ... 2224
George Hudson Holdings Ltd v Rudder (1973) ... 228
George Mitchell (Chesterhall) Ltd v Finney Lock Seeds Ltd [1983] ... 752
George Mountreas & Co SA v Navimpex Centrala Navala [1985] ... 2226
George T Collings (Aust) Pty Ltd v HF Stevenson (Aust) Pty Ltd (1991) ... 1514, 1528

George Weston Foods Ltd v Goodman Fielder Ltd (2000) ... 1105
Georgoulis v Mandalinic [1984] ... 221, 233
Geraghty v Minter (1979) ... 1641, 1648, 1650, 1994
Gerraty v McGavin (1914) ... 248, 2060
Giannarelli v Wraith (1988) ... 1036
Gibaud v Great Eastern Railway Co [1921] ... 762
Gibb v Sell [1922] ... 510
Gibbons v Proctor (1891) ... 239
—v Wright (1954) ... 840, 841, 842, 844, 1268
Gibson v Parkes District Hospital (1991) ... 1842
Gidley v Lord Palmerston (1822) ... 873
Gilbert J McCaul (Aust) Pty Ltd v Pitt Club Ltd (1957) ... 1837
—v—(1959) ... 222, 228, 247, 248, 256
Gilbert Stokes & Kerr Pty Ltd v Dalgety & Co Ltd (1948) ... 923
Gilbert-Ash (Northern) Ltd v Modern Engineering (Bristol) Ltd [1974] ... 1825, 1839
Giles v Thompson [1994] ... 1629, 1630
Giliberto v Kenny (1983) ... 619, 722
Gill v Australian Wheat Board [1980] ... 2167
Gillespie Bros & Co Ltd v Cheney Eggar & Co [1896] ... 708, 719
—v Roy Bowles Transport Ltd [1973] ... 763, 764, 765
Gimson v Victorian Workcover Authority [1995] ... 1842
Gino D'Alessandro Constructions Pty Ltd v Powis [1987] ... 520
GIO (NSW) v KS Reed Services Pty Ltd [1988] ... 909
Gipps v Gipps [1978] ... 1022
Giumelli v Giumelli (1999) ... 118, 369, 380, 383
Gjergja v Cooper [1987] ... 217, 239
Glaholm v Hays (1841) ... 1832
Glasbrook Bros Ltd v Glamorgan County Council [1925] ... 343
Glass v Pioneer Rubber Works of Australia Ltd [1906] ... 205
Glazebrook v Woodrow (1799) ... 1830

References are to paragraphs

Glebe Island Terminals Pty Ltd v Continental Seagram Pty Ltd (The Antwerpen) (1993) ... 762, 764
Glegg v Bromley [1912] ... 1629
Glencore Grain Rotterdam BV v Lebanese Organisation for International Commerce [1997] ... 1983
Global Sportsman Pty Ltd v Mirror Newspapers Ltd (1984) ... 1108, 1121
Gloucestershire CC v Richardson [1969] ... 634
Glynn v Margetson & Co [1893] ... 760
Goddard, Ex parte; Re Falvey (1946) ... 865
Godecke v Kirwan (1973) ... 267, 273
Gold Coast Waterways Authority v Salmead Pty Ltd [1997] ... 274
Goldburg v Shell Oil Of Australia Ltd (1990) ... 2111
Goldcorp Exchange Ltd, Re [1995] ... 2302
Goldsbrough Mort & Co Ltd v Carter (1914) ... 703, 2012, 2055, 2060
—v Quinn (1910) ... 248, 1235, 1237, 2169, 2411
Goldsmith v Rodger [1962] ... 1054, 1061
Gollan v Nugent (1988) ... 1619, 1705, 1721, 1723, 1724
Gollin & Co Ltd v Consolidated Fertilizer Sales Pty Ltd [1982] ... 373
—v Karenlee Nominees Pty Ltd (1983) ... 1852
Gompertz v Bartlett (1853) ... 1221
Gonin deceased, Re [1979] ... 404
Good v Cheeseman (1831) ... 360
Goode v Harrison (1821) ... 818
Goodman v Pocock (1850) ... 2233, 2322
Goodwin's of Newtown Pty Ltd v Gurry [1959] ... 214
Gordon v Macgregor (1909) ... 705, 706, 708
Gore v Gibson (1845) ... 842
Gorer v Readon (1869) ... 810
Goring v Goring (1602) ...356
Goss v Chilcott [1996] ... 2306
—v Nugent (1833) ... 705
Gould v Gould [1970] ... 266, 403

—v Vaggelas (1984) ... 1021, 1067, 1068, 1069
Government of Newfoundland v Newfoundland Railway Co (1888) ... 1826, 2233
Government of Swaziland Central Transport Administration v Leila Maritime Co Ltd (The Leila) [1985] ... 385
Gozzard v McKell (1931) ... 1603
GR Securities Pty Ltd v Baulkham Hills Private Hospital Pty Ltd (1996) ... 273
Graham v Baker (1961) ... 1807
—v Freer (1980) ... 1061, 1078
—v Royal National Agricultural and Industrial Association of Queensland [1989] ... 764
—v Voigt (1989) ... 2153
Grainger v Gough [1896] ... 208
Gran Gelato Ltd v Richcliff (Group) Ltd [1992] ... 1077
Grant v Australian Knitting Mills Ltd [1936] ... 638, 639, 640, 1856
—v Dawkins [1973] ... 2171
Graves v Legg (1854) ... 1811, 1830
Gray v Lang (1955) ... 527
—v Motor Accident Commission (formerly State Government Insurance Commission) (1998) ... 2103
—v Pastorelli [1987] ... 1622
Greasley v Cooke [1980] ... 377
Great Amalgamated Gold Mining Co Ltd v Morris (1877) ... 243
Great Northern Railway Co v Witham (1873) ... 223, 249
Greater Pacific Investments Pty Ltd v Australian National Industries Ltd (1996) ... 1045
Greaves & Co (Contractors) Ltd v Baynham Meikle & Partners [1975] ... 632, 1857
Green v Duckett (1883) ... 1309, 1316
—v Green (1989) ... 1619
—v Rose (1900) ... 211
—v Sevin (1879) ... 1960
—v Sommerville (1979) ... 1941
—v Thompson [1899] ... 812
Greenwood v Greenwood (1863) ... 1015
—v Martins Bank Ltd [1933] ... 379

Table of Cases

Greetings Oxford Koala Hotel Pty Ltd v Oxford Square Investments Pty Ltd (1989) ... 2408
Gregory v MAB Pty Ltd (1989) ... 275
—v—[1989] ... 270, 760
Griffith v Brymer (1903) ... 1210
Griffiths v Knight [1960] ... 355
Grineff v Chusov [2000] ... 1514
Groom v Crocker [1939] ... 2131
Grummitt v Natalisio [1968] ... 514, 523
Grundt v Great Boulder Pty Gold Mines Ltd (1937) ... 367, 368, 720, 1975
GSA Group Pty Ltd v Siebe Plc (1993) ... 1809
Guinness Mahon & Co Ltd v Kensington and Chelsea Royal London Borough Council [1999] ... 2318
Gull v Saunders (1913) ... 2128
Gunton v Richmond-upon-Thames London BC [1981] ... 1967
Gurdag v BS Stillwell Ford Pty Ltd (1985) ... 1118
Gurney v Wormersley (1854) ... 1221
Gurr v Forbes (1996) ... 1121
Guy-Pell v Foster [1930] ... 1945
Habib Bank Ltd v Habib Bank AG Zurich [1981] ... 377
Hadley v Baxendale (1854) ... 2108, 2109, 2123, 2124, 2125, 2127, 2128, 2138, 2140, 2142, 2144, 2145, 2151
Haigh v Brooks (1839) ... 350
Hain SS Co Ltd v Tate & Lyle Ltd [1936] ... 755, 761, 1972
Halfpenny v Wilson (1967) ... 1963
Halkett v Earl of Dudley [1907] ... 1984, 2408, 2409
Halkidis v Bugeia [1974] ... 1962
Hall v Busst (1960) ... 268, 269
—v Gilmore [1968] ... 273
—v Wells [1962] ... 822, 824
Halliday v High Performance Personnel Pty Ltd (1993) ... 1629
Halloran v Firth (1926) ... 2036
Halton Pty Ltd v Stewart Bros Drilling Contractors Pty Ltd (1992) ... 1110
Hamer v Sidway 124 NY ... 308
Hamilton v Lethbridge (1912) ... 812, 814, 816, 818, 820

Hammer v Coca-Cola [1962] ... 1938
Hamond v Vam Ltd [1972] ... 260
Hampstead Meats Pty Ltd v Emerson & Yates Pty Ltd [1967] ... 204, 238
Hanave Pty Ltd v Lfot Pty Ltd (1998) ... 1107
—v—(1999) ... 1107, 1110
Hancock v Wilson [1956] ... 261, 267
Haneet Chandru Vaswani v Italian Motors (Sales and Services) Ltd [1996] ... 1941
Hanley v Pease & Partners Ltd [1915] ... 1839
Harbutt's 'Plasticine' Ltd v Wayne Tank and Pump Co Ltd [1970] ... 1926, 1967, 1993, 2155
Hardie (Qld) Employees Credit Union Ltd v Hall Chadwick & Co [1980] ... 1036
Hardie and Lane Ltd v Chilton [1928] ... 1319
Hardman v Booth (1863) ... 1241
Hardwick Game Farm v Suffolk Agricultural Poultry Producers Association [1966] ... 708
Hardy v Motor Insurers' Bureau [1964] ... 1705
Hare v Nicoll [1966] ... 1837
Harling v Eddy [1951] ... 607
Harlingdon and Leinster Enterprises Ltd v Christopher Hull Fine Art Ltd [1991] ... 638, 640
Harnedy v National Greyhound Racing Co Ltd [1944] ... 814
Harnor v Groves (1855) ... 708
Harper v Ashtons Circus Pty Ltd [1972] ... 2130
Harrington v Browne (1917) ... 1919, 1952
Harris v Jenkins [1922] ... 251
—v Nickerson (1873) ... 211, 215
Harrison v National Bank of Australasia Ltd (1928) ... 1507
Harrison & Jones Ltd v Bunten & Lancaster Ltd [1953] ... 1225
Harrison (T & J) v Knowles and Foster [1918] ... 1038
Harry Davies & Co Pty Ltd v East [1925] ... 1808
Harse v Pearl Life Assurance Co [1904] ... 1714, 1716, 1727
Hart v MacDonald (1910) ... 630

—v O'Connor [1985] ... 844, 1502, 1513
—v Swaine (1877) ... 1055
Hartley v Hymans [1920] ... 527
—v Ponsonby (1857) ...345
Hartog v Colin & Shields [1939] ... 1251, 1254
Harvela Investments Ltd v Royal Trust Co of Canada (CI) Ltd [1986] ... 212
Harvey v Edwards Dunlop & Co Ltd (1927) ... 513, 515
—v Facey [1893] ... 209
Hasan v Willson [1977] ...333
Hasell v Bagot Shakes & Lewis Ltd (1911) ... 2142
Hasham v Zenab [1960] ... 2402
Hassard v Smith (1872) ... 841
Hastie v Couturier (1853) ... 1216
Hatcher v White (1953) ... 1713, 1728
Hawker Pacific Pty Ltd v Helicopter Charter Pty Ltd (1991) ... 380, 382, 1310, 1327
Hawkes v Saunders (1782) ... 306
Hawkesbury Development Co Ltd v Landmark Finance Pty Ltd [1962] ... 855
Hawkins v Clayton (1988) ... 625, 635, 1030, 1031, 1067, 1855
Hawthorn Football Club Ltd v Harding [1988] ... 267, 2416, 2420
Hayes v Cable (1962) ... 1613
Haynes v McNeil (1906) ... 205
Hazzell v Hammersmith & Fulham LBC [1990] ... 852
—v—[1992] ... 853, 870
Head v Kelk [1962] ... 260
—v— (1963) ... 519, 1817
Healing Sales Pty Ltd v Inglis Electrix Pty Ltd (1968) ... 105
Hedley Byrne & Co Ltd v Heller & Partners Ltd [1964] ... 107, 1004, 1030, 1032, 1034
Heilbut Symons & Co v Buckleton [1913] ... 611
Heimann v Commonwealth (1938) ... 621, 622, 627, 632
Heine Bros (Aust) Pty Ltd v Forrest [1963] ... 1649, 2420
Heisler v Anglo-Dal Ltd [1954] ... 1969
Helicopter Sales (Australia) Pty Ltd v Rotor-Work Pty Ltd (1974) ... 635
Hempel v Robinson [1924] ... 267, 269

Henderson, Re (1916) ... 822, 824, 825
—v Merrett Syndicates Ltd [1995] ... 635, 1030, 1036
Henjo Investments Pty Ltd v Collins Marrickville Pty Ltd (1988) ... 1112, 1115, 1121, 1123
Henkel v Pape (1870) ... 1234
Henry v Sydney MC (1882) ... 858, 860
Henry Kendall & Sons v William Lillico & Sons Ltd [1969] ... 618, 640, 708
Hensley v Reschke (1914) ... 1929
Henthorn v Fraser [1892] ... 217, 231, 235, 244
Henville v Walker (2001) ... 1112
Heppingstone v Stewart (1910) ... 513, 2403
Herbert Clayton and Jack Waller Ltd v Oliver [1930] ... 2154
Herbert Morris Ltd v Saxelby [1916] ... 1639, 1640, 1649
Hercules Motors Pty Ltd v Schubert (1953) ... 351, 611
Hermann v Charlesworth [1905] ... 1633, 1716, 1717
Herne Bay Steam Boat Co v Hutton [1903] ... 2019
Hewett v Court (1983) ... 511, 1061, 2402, 2410
Heyman v Darwins Ltd [1942] ... 761, 1906, 1930, 1946, 1968, 1970, 1985, 1994
Heywood v Wellers [1976] ... 2152
Hick v Raymond [1893] ... 1804
Hickman v Berens [1895] ... 1253
Hide & Skin Trading Pty Ltd v Oceanic Meat Traders Ltd (1990) ... 704, 712
Higgons v Burton (1857) ... 1242
Hill v C A Parsons & Co Ltd [1972] ... 2420
Hill (DJ) & Co Pty Ltd v Walter H Wright Pty Ltd [1971] ... 615, 618
Hill (t/as R F Hill & Associates) v Van Erp (1997) ... 107, 922, 1030, 1031, 1033, 1034
Hillas & Co Ltd v Arcos Ltd (1932) ... 259, 260, 262, 269, 271, 338
Hills v Manchester & Salford Waterworks Co (1833) ... 858
Hinton v Sparkes (1868) ... 2236
Hirachand Punamchand v Temple [1911] ... 359, 360, 1818

Table of Cases

Hirji Mulji v Cheong Yue SS Co Ltd [1926] ... 2009, 2013, 2050, 2051, 2058, 2062
Hirsch v The Zinc Corp Ltd (1917) ... 2056, 2060, 2062, 2065
Hitchcock v Giddings (1817) ... 1228
Hoad v Scone Motors Pty Ltd [1977] ... 2134
—v Swan (1920) ... 1942, 1970
Hobartville Stud Pty Ltd v Union Insurance Co Ltd (1991) ... 2151
Hobbs v London and South Western Railway Co (1875) ... 2152
—v Petersham Transport Co Pty Ltd (1971) ... 1843, 1857
Hobbs Padgett & Co (Reinsurance) Ltd v JC Kirkland Ltd [1969] ... 261
Hochster v De la Tour (1853) ... 1932, 1937
Hodder v Watters [1946] ... 1041, 2324
Hoenig v Isaacs [1952] ... 1831, 1832, 1834
Hoffman, Re; Ex parte Worrell v Schilling (1989) ... 1048
—v Cali [1985] ... 2158
—v Red Owl Stores Inc (1965) ... 387
Holidaywise Koala Pty Ltd v Queenslodge Pty Ltd [1977] ... 1621
Holland v Eyre (1824) ... 222
—v Wiltshire (1954) ... 1852, 1868, 1970, 1985
Hollier v Rambler Motors (AMC) Ltd [1972] ... 618, 764
Hollywood Premiere Sales Pty Ltd v Faberge Australia (Pty) Ltd (1976) ... 1654
Holman v Johnson (1775) ... 1705, 1709, 1710
Holmes v Burgess [1975] ... 1061
—v Jones (1907) ... 1022, 1069, 1071
Holt v Biroka (1988) ... 1108
Holwell Securities Ltd v Hughes [1974] ... 231, 232, 234
Home Counties Dairies Ltd v Skilton [1970] ... 1649, 1994
Hong Kong Bank of Australia Ltd v Larobi Pty Ltd (1991) ... 1626
Hongkong Fir Shipping Co Ltd v Kawasaki Kisen Kaisha Ltd [1962] ... 731, 732, 734, 736, 738, 754, 1832, 1911, 1917, 1918, 1925, 1926, 1927, 1948, 1957, 1958, 1978, 2002, 2050

Honner v Ashton (1979) ... 1912, 1932, 1934, 1943
Hoobin, Re [1957] ... 2333
Hood v Anchor Line (Henderson Bros) Ltd [1918] ... 208, 617
Hooker (L J) Ltd v W J Adams Estates Pty Ltd (1977) ... 628
Hooker Town Developments Pty Ltd v Director of War Service Homes (1973) ... 1259, 1263
Hooley Hill Rubber and Chemical Co Ltd and Royal Insurance Co Ltd, Re [1920] ... 1009, 1010
Hooper & Grass' Contract, Re [1949] ... 1312, 1316
Hooper Bailie Associated Ltd v Natcon Group Pty Ltd (1992) ... 271
Hope v RCA Photophone of Australia Pty Ltd (1937) ... 707, 708, 718
Hopkinson v Logan (1839) ... 328
Hordern House Pty Ltd v Arnold [1989] ... 211
Horlock v Beal [1916] ... 2003, 2015, 2028, 2054, 2066, 2111
Horne v Barber (1920) ... 1624
Horsfall v Thomas (1862) ... 1018
Hortico (Australia) Pty Ltd v Energy Equipment Co (Australia) Pty Ltd (1985) ... 507
Horton v Jones (1934) ... 520, 718
—v—(1935) ... 266, 404, 412, 519
—v—(No 2) (1939) ... 2307, 2325
—v Westminster Improvement Commissioners (1852) ... 858
Horvath v Commonwealth [1999] ... 815, 824
Hospital Products Ltd v United States Surgical Corp (1984) ... 112, 606, 609, 610, 625, 626, 627, 703, 1809, 2328, 2329
Hospitality Group Pty Ltd v Australian Rugby Union Ltd [2001] ... 2329
Hotham v East India Co (1787) ... 1810, 2202
Houldsworth v City of Glasgow Bank (1880) ... 1116
Hounslow London BC v Twickenham Garden Developments Ltd [1971] ... 1970, 2222, 2224
Household Fire and Carriage Accident Insurance Co (Ltd) v Grant (1879) ... 231, 232, 233, 235
Howard v Currie (1879) ... 846

—v Pickford Tool Co Ltd [1951] ... 1947

—v Shirlstar Container Transport Ltd [1990] ... 1703

Howard F Hudson Pty Ltd v Ronayne (1972) ... 1634, 1637, 1736

Howard Marine and Dredging Co Ltd v A Ogden & Sons (Excavations) Ltd [1978] ... 1036

Howard Smith & Co Ltd v Varawa (1907) ... 209, 273, 513, 712

Howatson v Webb [1908] ... 1272, 1273

Howe v Smith (1884) ... 1852, 1955, 2236

—v Teefy (1927) ... 2164

Howell v Bennett & Fisher Ltd [1966] ... 1017, 1066, 1072

—v Coupland (1876) ... 2014, 2060

Howie v NSW Lawn Tennis Ground Ltd (1956) ... 913

Hoyt's Pty Ltd v Spencer (1919) ... 611, 613, 708

Huddersfield Banking Co Ltd v Henry Lister & Son Ltd [1895] ... 1227, 1228, 1229, 1230, 1232

Hudson v Jope (1914) ... 1050, 1054, 1055, 1227, 1228

Huggins v Wiseman (1690) ... 811

Hughes v Greenwich London Borough Council [1994] ... 627

—v Lord Advocate [1963] ... 2126

—v Metropolitan Railway Co (1877) ... 372, 373, 393, 1974

—v NM Superannuation Pty Ltd (1993) ... 273

—v Western Australian Cricket Association (Inc) (1986) ... 1636

Hughes Aircraft Systems International v Airservices Australia (1997) ... 212, 872

Hughes Bros Pty Ltd v Trustees of the Roman Catholic Church for the Archdiocese of Sydney (1993) ... 1983

Humphries v Proprietors 'Surfers Palms North' Group Titles Plan 1955 (1994) ... 853, 1730

Hungerfords v Walker (1989) ... 118, 2151

Hunt v Silk (1804) ... 2306, 2333

Hunt Contracting Co Pty Ltd v Roebuck Resources NL (1992) ... 1108

Hunter v Walters (1871) ... 1273

Hunter BNZ Finance Ltd v C G Maloney Pty Ltd (1988) ... 1041, 1048

Huppert v Stock Options of Australia Pty Ltd (1965) ... 2102

Hurley v McDonald's Australia Ltd (2000) ... 1527, 1528

Hurst v Bryk [2000] ... 1936

—v Vestcorp Ltd (1988) ... 1237, 1613, 1703, 1728

Huscombe v Standing (1607) ... 1325

Huskisson RSL Sub-Branch Club Ltd v Sullivan (1990) ... 1828

Hussey v Eels [1990] ... 2137

—v Palmer [1972] ... 377

Hutchence v South Sea Bubble Co Ltd (1986) ... 1107, 1122

Hutchinson v McGuren (1910) ... 1028

—v Scott (1905) ... 1621

Hyatt Australia Ltd v LTCB Australia Ltd [1996] ... 915

Hyde v Wrench (1840) ... 251

Hynes v Byrne (1899) ... 1037, 1051

Hyundai Heavy Industries Co Ltd v Papadopoulos [1980] ... 1986, 2157, 2229, 2233, 2324

Hyundai Shipbuilding & Heavy Industries Co Ltd v Pournaras [1978] ... 2229

I & J Securities Pty Ltd v HTW Valuers (BNE) Pty Ltd (2000) ... 1112

IAC (Leasing) Ltd v Humphrey (1972) ... 2217, 2240

Iannotti v Corsaro (1984) ... 1622

ICT Pty Ltd v Sea Containers Ltd (1995) ... 1738, 1739

Iezzi Constructions Pty Ltd v Watkins Pacific (Qld) Pty Ltd [1995] ... 2322

Immer (No 145) Pty Ltd v Uniting Church in Australia Property Trust (NSW) (1993) ... 1971

Imperial Group Pension Trust Ltd v Imperial Tobacco Ltd [1991] ... 1983

Imperial Land Co of Marseilles, Re (Hams' case) (1872) ... 235

—, Re (Harris' case) (1872) ... 235

—, Re (Townsend's case) (1871) ... 235

—, Re (Wall's case) (1872) ... 233, 235

References are to paragraphs

Table of Cases

Imperial Loan Co v Stone [1892] ... 840, 841, 843, 844
Inche Noriah v Shaik Allie Bin Omar [1929] ... 1411
Independent Grocers Co-operative Ltd v Noble Lowndes Superannuation Consultants Ltd (1993) ... 2066, 2315
Inglis v John Buttery & Co (1878) ... 705, 711, 712
Ingram v Little [1961] ... 1245, 1247, 1248, 1254
Inn Leisure Industries Pty Ltd v D F McCloy Pty Ltd (1991) ... 1011, 1012, 1119
Inntrepeneur Pub Co (GL) v East Crown Ltd [2000] ... 708
Insurance Co of Africa v Scor (UK) Reinsurance Co Ltd [1985] ... 1809
Integrated Computer Services Pty Ltd v Digital Equipment Corp (Aust) Pty Ltd (1988) ... 205
Integrated Lighting & Ceilings Pty Ltd v Phillips Electrical Pty Ltd (1969) ... 204, 220
Interfoto Picture Library Ltd v Stiletto Visual Programmes Ltd [1989] ... 617
International Leasing Corp (Vic) Ltd v Aiken [1967] ... 1938, 1970, 1971, 1993, 2207, 2216
International Minerals & Chemical Corp v Helm [1986] ... 2109
International Society of Auctioneers and Valuers (Baillie's case), Re [1898] ... 1241
Investors Compensation Scheme Ltd v West Bromwich Building Society [1998] ... 110, 112, 714
Inwards v Baker [1965] ... 377
IOOF Australia Trustees (NSW) Ltd v Tantipech (1998) ... 1123, 1124
IRAF Pty Ltd v Graham [1982] ... 1739
IRC v Mills [1975] ... 807
Islamic Republic of Iran Shipping Lines v Denby [1987] ... 2328
Ison v Australian Wheat Board (1967) ... 1721, 1725
Issa v Berisha [1981] ... 1256, 1259
Ivanochko v Sych (1967) ... 1229

J & S Holdings Pty Ltd v NRMA Insurance Ltd (1982) ... 1309, 1313, 1316, 1319
J, Re [1909] ... 816
Jackson v Horizon Holidays Ltd [1975] ... 912
—v Union Marine Insurance Co Ltd (1874) ... 749, 1977, 2004, 2015, 2025, 2027, 2042, 2052
Jacob & Youngs Inc v Kent 129 NE ... 1835
Jacobs v Revell [1900] ... 1123
Jacobsen Sons & Co v E Underwood & Son Ltd (1894) ... 254
Jacques v Cut Price Deli Pty Ltd (1993) ... 1107, 1108
JAD International Pty Ltd v International Trucks Australia Ltd (1994) ... 1062
Jaensch v Coffey (1984) ... 1031
Jaggard v Sawyer [1995] ... 2169, 2170, 2329
James v Australian and New Zealand Banking Group Ltd (1986) ... 1412
James (AS) Pty Ltd v Duncan [1970] ... 2132
James Finlay & Co Ltd v NV Kwik Hoo Tong Handel Maatschappij [1929] ... 2135
James Miller & Partners Ltd v Whitworth Street Estates (Manchester) Ltd [1970] ... 712
Janssen Pharmaceutical Pty Ltd v Pfizer Pty Ltd (1986) ... 1107
Jarvis v Pitt Ltd (1935) ... 223
—v Swans Tours Ltd [1973] ... 2153
Je Maintiendrai Pty Ltd v Quaglia (1980) ...373, 380
Jedda Investments Pty Ltd v Krambousanos (1997) ... 1528
Jeffries v Fairs (1876) ... 1212, 1219, 2411
Jenkin v Pharmaceutical Society [1921] ... 852
Jennings v Radio Station KSCS 96.3 Inc 708 SW ... 316
—v Rundall (1799) ... 825
—v Zilahi-Kiss (1972) ... 759, 766
Jericho v Guglielmin [1938] ... 2411
JLW (Vic) Pty Ltd v Tsiloglou (1993) ... 1112, 1113

References are to paragraphs

JNRD and the Protected Estates Act (1992) ... 838
Jobson v Johnson [1989] ... 2211, 2213, 2216, 2240
John G Glass Real Estate Pty Ltd v Karawi Constructions Pty Ltd (1993) ... 1121
John Howard & Co (Northern) Ltd v JP Knight Ltd [1969] ... 206, 275
John McGrath Motors (Canberra) Pty Ltd v Applebee (1964) ... 1026
John Wakim & Sons Pty Ltd v BBA Industries Pty Ltd [2000] ... 273
Johnson v Bones [1970] ... 248
—v Buttress (1936) ... 1404, 1407, 1409, 1410, 1411, 1412, 1414, 1507
—v Clark [1908] ... 807
—v Gore Wood & Co (A firm) [2001] ... 2152
—v Perez (1988) ... 2103, 2104, 2114, 2115, 2131, 2168
Johnson (E) & Co (Barbados) Ltd v NSR Ltd [1997] ... 2033, 2408
Johnson Matthey Ltd v A C Rochester Overseas Corp (1990) ... 716
Johnson Tiles Pty Ltd v Esso Australia Ltd (1999) ... 1110
—v—(2001) ... 1110
Johnsons Tyne Foundary Pty Ltd v Maffra Corporation (1948) ... 860
Johnston v Arnaboldi [1990] ... 1264
—v Commerce Consolidated Pty Ltd [1976] ... 1263
—v Marks (1887) ... 810
Joliffe v Baker (1883) ... 1025
Jon Beauforte (London) Ltd, Re [1953] ... 855
Jones, Re (1881) ... 823
—v Barkley (1781) ... 1808, 1947
—v Bouffier (1911) ... 1712
—v Clifford (1876) ... 1228, 2411
—v Daniel [1894] ... 222
—v Dumbrell [1981] ... 1017
—v Padavatton [1969] ... 109, 266, 403
—v Robinson (1847) ...322
—v Sherwood Computer Services Plc [1992] ... 1626
Jones (AA) & Son Pty Ltd v Weeden (1964) ... 2334
Jorden v Money (1854) ... 382
Joscelyne v Nissen [1970] ... 1263, 1266

Joseph Constantine SS Line Ltd v Imperial Smelting Corp Ltd [1942] ... 2003, 2022, 2044, 2046, 2051, 2055, 2056, 2059, 2062
Junior Books Ltd v Veitchi Co Ltd [1983] ... 2104
Kabwand Pty Ltd v National Australia Bank Ltd (1989) ... 1110
Kaines (UK) Ltd v Osterreichische Warrenhandelsgesellschaft Austrowaren Gesellschaft mbH [1993] ... 2135, 2149
Kalnenas v Kovacevich [1961] ... 514, 522
Kamil Export (Aust) Pty Ltd v NPL (Australia) Pty Ltd (1993) ... 756
Kammins Ballrooms Co Ltd v Zenith Investments (Torquay) Ltd [1971] ... 392, 1048, 1972
Karaguleski v Vasil Bros & Co Pty Ltd [1981] ... 248
Karawi Constructions Pty Ltd v Bonefind Pty Ltd (1993) ... 1112, 1121
Karsales (Harrow) Ltd v Wallis [1956] ... 754
Kathopoulos v Bjelica Investments Pty Ltd (1979) ... 2237
Kaufman v Gerson [1904] ... 1310, 1319
—v McGillicuddy (1914) ... 1994
Kawasaki Steel Corp v Sardoil SpA (The Zuiho Maru) [1977] ... 2051
Keane v Boycott (1795) ... 808
Kearley v Thomson (1890) ... 1707, 1712, 1716, 1718, 1720
Keays v Great Southern Ry Co [1941] ... 814
Keen Mar Corp Pty Ltd v Labrador Park Shopping Centre Pty Ltd (1989) ... 1124
Keighley Maxsted & Co v Durant [1901] ... 901
Kell v Harris (1915) ... 808
Kelly v Caledonian Coal Co (1898) ... 209, 223
Kelner v Baxter (1866) ... 862, 863
Kennard v Bazzan [1962] ... 270
Kennedy v Brown (1863) ...331
—v Panama New Zealand and Australian Royal Mail Co Ltd (1867) ... 1023, 1044, 1061, 1206

Table of Cases

Kenneth Wright Distributors Pty Ltd, Re; W J Vine Pty Ltd v Hall [1973] ... 1629

Kenny & Good Pty Ltd v MGICA (1992) Ltd (1999) ... 1069, 1113, 2120

Kenya Railways v Antares Co Pte Ltd (The Antares) (Nos 1 & 2) [1987] ... 761

Kenyon Son & Craven Ltd v Baxter Hoare & Co Ltd [1971] ... 756

Kern Corp Ltd v Walter Reid Trading Pty Ltd (1987) ... 904

Kerr v Morris [1987] ... 1651

Kerridge v Simmonds (1906) ... 1628

Kershaw v Forster Pastoral Pty Ltd (1985) ... 1815

Kesarmal S/O Letchman Das v NKV Valliappa Chettiar S/O Nagappa Chettiar [1954] ... 1324

Ketsey's case (1631) ... 820

Kettlewell v Refuge Assurance Co [1908] ... 1009, 1028

Khaled v Athanas Bros (Aden) Ltd (1967) ... 251, 252, 255

Khoury v Government Insurance Office of New South Wales (1984) ... 624, 632, 1015, 1971

Kidman v Commonwealth [1926] ... 871

Kilmer v British Columbia Orchard Lands Ltd [1913] ... 2240

King v Ivanhoe Gold Corp Ltd (1908) ... 262

—v Jones (1972) ... 802

—v Poggioli (1923) ... 2169, 2407

—v Smith [1900] ... 1273

King's Motors (Oxford) Ltd v Lax [1970] ... 267

King's Norton Metal Co Ltd v Edridge Merrett & Co Ltd (1897) ... 1243, 1246, 1248

Kingston v Preston (1773) ... 1808

Kirby v Registrar of Titles [1999] ... 864

Kiriri Cotton Co Ltd v Dewani [1960] ... 1720, 1728

Kirkham v Chief Constable of the Greater Manchester Police [1990] ... 1702

Kitchen (J) & Sons Pty Ltd v Stewart's Cash & Carry Stores (1942) ... 223

Kleinwort Benson Ltd v Lincoln City Council [1999] ... 2318

—v Malaysia Mining Corp Berhad [1989] ... 405, 724

Knogo Corp v Halligan (1984) ... 1739

Knowles v Fuller (1947) ... 1603, 1705

Kodros Shipping Corp of Monrovia v Empresa Cubana de Fletes (The Evia (No 2)) [1983] ...734, 2006, 2010, 2028

Konica Business Machines Australia Pty Ltd v Tizine Pty Ltd (1992) ... 1936

Koufos v C Czarnikow Ltd [1969] ... 2104, 2110, 2123, 2124, 2125, 2126, 2128

Krakowski v Eurolynx Properties Ltd (1995) ... 1016, 1026, 1028

Kramer v Duggan (1955) ... 1045, 1054

—v McMahon [1970] ... 1058, 1065

Krell v Henry [1903] ... 1210, 2004, 2008, 2018, 2019, 2035, 2038, 2039, 2052

Kurt Keller Pty Ltd v BMW Australia Ltd [1984] ... 2418

Kwei Tek Chao v British Traders and Shippers Ltd [1954] ... 1972, 1976

L'Estrange v F Graucob Ltd [1934] ... 615, 708

L'Huillier v State of Victoria [1996] ... 872

Lagunas Nitrate Co v Lagunas Syndicate [1899] ... 1023, 1046

Laird v Pim (1841) ... 1986, 2238

Lake v Simmons [1927] ... 1242, 1245, 1246

Lake Macquarie Municipal Council v S & R Bortolus Constructions Pty Ltd [1982] ... 275

Lakshmijit v Sherani [1974] ... 1970

Lam v Ausintel Investments Australia Pty Ltd (1990) ... 1110

Lambert v Lewis [1982] ... 407

Lamont v Heron (1970) ... 220, 273

Lampleigh v Brathwait (1615) ... 306, 330, 331

Land & Homes (WA) Ltd v Roe (1936) ... 826

Landers v Schmidt [1983] ... 2333

Lang v James Morrison & Co Ltd (1911) ... 225

Lansdown v Lansdown (1730) ... 1209
Larkin v Girvan (1940) ...302, 346, 351, 355
Larking v Great Western (Nepean) Gravel Ltd (1940) ... 1972, 2222
Larkins (TJ) & Sons v Chelmer Holdings Pty Ltd and Van Den Broek [1965] ... 1026
Larratt v Bankers and Traders Insurance Co Ltd (1941) ... 392, 393, 1933, 1970, 1971, 1972, 1986, 2157, 2159
Latec Finance Pty Ltd v Knight [1969] ... 227
Laurinda Pty Ltd v Capalaba Park Shopping Centre Pty Ltd (1989) ... 1936, 1938, 1941, 1944, 1961
Lauritzen (J) AS v Wijsmuller BV (The Super Servant Two) [1990] ... 748, 2014, 2043, 2044, 2046, 2051, 2058
Lavarack v Woods of Colchester Ltd [1967] ... 2134
Law v Harrigan (1917) ... 1221
Law Debenture Trust Corp plc v Ural Caspian Oil Corp Ltd [1993] ... 913
Laybutt v Amoco Aust Pty Ltd (1974) ... 248, 257
Lazenby Garages Ltd v Wright [1976] ... 2140, 2143
Le Mans Grand Prix Circuits Pty Ltd v Iliadis [1998] ... 615
Leach Nominees Pty Ltd v Walter Wright Pty Ltd [1986] ... 238
Leaf v International Galleries [1950] ... 610, 1050, 1054, 1061, 1062, 1228, 1229
Leason Pty Ltd v Princes Farm Pty Ltd [1983] ... 1055, 1061
Leda Holdings Pty Ltd v Oraka Pty Ltd (1998) ... 1110, 1124
Lee v Ah Gee [1920] ... 1274
—v Ferno Holdings Pty Ltd (1993) ... 377
—v Sayers (1909) ... 225
—v Showmen's Guild of Great Britain [1952] ... 1626
Leeds & Thirsk Ry v Fearnley (1849) ... 820
Leeds Industrial Co-operative Society Ltd v Slack [1924] ... 2169
Lefkowitz v Great Minneapolis Surplus Store (1957) ... 208

Legione v Hateley (1983) ... 118, 119, 373, 379, 380, 381, 382, 384, 1976, 1979, 1983, 2240, 2332, 2404
Leibler v Air New Zealand Ltd (No 2) [1999] ... 1265
Leighton v Parton [1976] ... 1265
Leighton's Investment Trust Ltd v Cricklewood Property and Investment Trust Ltd [1943] ... 2035
Leipner v McLean (1909) ... 611
Leitch v Natwest Australia Bank Ltd (1995) ... 1524
Leitz Leeholme Stud Pty Ltd v Robinson [1977] ... 1936
Lejo Holdings Pty Ltd v Deutsche Bank (Asia) AG [1988] ... 519
Lemenda Trading Co Ltd v African Middle East Petroleum Co Ltd [1988] ... 1625
Lempriere v Lange (1879) ... 823
Lemura v Coppola [1960] ... 1831, 1832
Leng (Sir WC) & Co Ltd v Andrews [1909] ... 814
Lennon v Scarlett & Co (1921) ... 273, 712
Leonard v Booth (1954) ... 1721
Leonard (JJ) Properties Pty Ltd v Leonard (WA) Pty Ltd (No 2) (1987) ... 1258
Les Affreteurs Reunis SA v Walford Ltd [1919] ... 907
Leslie (R) Ltd v Sheill [1914] ... 823, 825
Leslie Leithead Pty Ltd v Barker (1965) ... 1019
Leslie Shipping Co v Welstead [1921] ... 1936, 2232
Levene v Brougham (1909) ... 825
Lever Bros Ltd v Bell [1931] ... 1255
Levison v Farin [1978] ... 2134
—v Patent Steam Carpet Cleaning Co Ltd [1978] ... 765
Lewandowski v Mead Carney-BCA Pty Ltd [1973] ... 270
Lewes Nominees Pty Ltd v Strang (1983) ... 232, 234, 1837, 2237
Lewis v Alleyne (1888) ... 815
—v Averay [1972] ... 1246, 1247, 1248
—v Bell (1985) ... 630

Table of Cases

Lewis Construction Co Pty Ltd v M Tichauer Societe Anonyme [1966] ... 220, 231, 236

Lexane Pty Ltd v Highfern Pty Ltd [1985] ... 2336

Lexmead (Basingstoke) Ltd v Lewis [1982] ... 2122, 2129

Ley v Dougan (1945) ... 2405

Libyan Arab Foreign Bank v Bankers Trust Co [1989] ... 644, 2061, 2083

Lieberman v Morris (1944) ... 1626, 1627

Life Insurance Co of Australia Ltd v Phillips (1925) ... 701, 708, 710, 1009, 1123, 1234, 1235

Life Savers (A'asia) Ltd v Frigmobile Pty Ltd [1983] ... 760, 765, 926

Lim Teng Huan v Ang Swee Chuan [1992] ... 377

Linden Gardens Trust Ltd v Lenesta Sludge Disposal Ltd [1994] ... 1818

Lindner v Murdock's Garage (1950) ... 1640, 1641, 1648, 1649, 1734

Linnett Bay Shipping Co Ltd v Patraicos Gulf Shipping Co SA (The Al Tawfiq) [1984] ... 2141

Lion White Lead Ltd v Rogers (1918) ... 1926

Lipkin Gorman v Karpnale Ltd [1991] ... 119, 1616, 2308

Lister v Romford Ice and Cold Storage Co Ltd [1957] ... 632, 633, 1855

Little v Trotman (1885) ... 244

Littlewoods Organisation Ltd v Harris [1978] ... 1649

Liverpool Adelphi Loan Association v Fairhurst (1854) ... 825

Liverpool City Council v Irwin [1977] ... 632

Liverpool Marine Credit Co v Hunter (1868) ... 1309

Livingstone v Evans [1925] ... 251

Lloyd v Citicorp Australia Ltd (1986) ... 1855

—v Grace Smith & Co [1912] ... 1028

—v Stanbury [1971] ... 2145

Lloyd's v Harper (1880) ... 907, 912

Lloyds Bank Ltd v Bundy [1975] ... 1410, 1510, 1511, 1512

Loan Investment Corp of Australasia v Bonner [1970] ... 2404

Lobb v Vasey Housing Auxiliary (War Widows Guild) [1963] ... 2015, 2034, 2067, 2081

Lock v Bell [1931] ... 1951

—v Westpac Banking Corp (1991) ... 1809

Lock (SH) (Australia) Ltd v Kennedy (1988) ... 1522, 1656

Lockhart v Barnard (1845) ... 239

—v Osman [1981] ... 1017

Lodder v Slowey [1904] ... 2339

Loftus v Roberts (1902) ... 338

Logwon Pty Ltd v Warringah Shire Council (1993) ... 1254

Lokumal (K) & Sons (London) Ltd v Lotte Shipping Co Pte Ltd (The August Leonhardt) [1985] ... 379

Lolly-Pops (Harbourside) Pty Ltd v Werncog Pty Ltd (1998) ... 234

Lombard North Central Plc v Butterworth [1987] ... 726, 1950, 2158, 2159, 2217

Lombok Pty Ltd v Supetina Pty Ltd (1987) ... 1967, 2333

London and North Western Railway Co v Neilson [1922] ... 761

London and Northern Bank, Re; Ex parte Jones [1900] ... 232, 234

London and South of England Building Society v Stone [1983] ... 2136

London and Westminster Loan and Discount Co Ltd v Bilton (1911) ... 1408

London Chartered Bank of Australia v Lempriere (1873) ... 1028

London Chatham and Dover Railway Co v South Eastern Railway Co [1893] ... 2151

London County Council v Allen [1914] ... 913

London Dock Co v Sinnott (1857) ... 860

London Holeproof Hosiery Co v Padmore (1928) ... 1250

Long v Lloyd [1958] ... 1054, 1061, 1062

Longmate v Ledger (1860) ... 1506, 1508

Longridge v Dorville (1821) ... 306

Lord Elphinstone v Monkland Iron and Coal Co Ltd (1886) ... 2214

References are to paragraphs

Lord Strathcona Steamship Co Ltd v Dominion Coal Co Ltd [1926] ... 913
Loughridge v Lavery [1969] ... 1968
Louth v Diprose (1992) ... 118, 1401, 1404, 1409, 1416, 1512, 1514, 1852, 1955, 1960, 1962, 1964
Lovell & Christmas v Beauchamp [1894] ... 818
Lowe v Hope [1970] ... 2237
Lowe's case (1610) ... 852
Lowe Lippmann Figdor (R) & Franck v AGC (Advances) Ltd [1992] ... 1034
Lu v Lim (1993) ... 1650
Lucas & Tait (Investments) Pty Ltd v Victoria Securities Ltd [1973] ... 2334
Lucy v Commonwealth (1923) ... 2134, 2233, 2420
Lukacs v Wood (1978) ... 1230
Lumley v Ravenscroft [1895] ... 808
—v Wagner (1852) ... 2420
Luna Park (NSW) Ltd v Tramways Advertising Pty Ltd (1938) ... 726, 727, 1813, 1911, 1915, 1916, 1939, 1941, 1972, 2102, 2105, 2106, 2218, 2221
Luxor (Eastbourne) Ltd v Cooper [1941] ... 250, 621, 628, 632, 1809
Lyon v Magnet Nominees Pty Ltd [1978] ... 2237
M & M Civil Engineering Pty Ltd v Sunshine Coast Turf Club [1987] ... 865
M/S Aswan Engineering Establishment Co v Lupdine Ltd [1987] ... 640
M'Cahill v Henty (1878) ... 1707
M'Clure v Ripley (1850) ... 1815
MacAndrew v Chapple (1866) ... 1955
Macaulay v Greater Paramount Theatres Ltd (1921) ... 2408
Macaura v Northern Assurance Co Ltd [1925] ... 904
MacBeath v Haldimand (1786) ... 873
MacCormick v Nowland (1988) ... 1121
MacEwin & Co v Ashwin [1916] ... 876
Mackay v A-G for British Columbia [1922] ... 871
—v Dick (1881) ... 624, 1809, 1810, 2221

Mackenzie v Coulson (1869) ... 1259
—v Rees (1941) ... 1936, 1966
MacKenzie v Royal Bank of Canada [1934] ... 1011, 1023, 1038
Mackman v Stengold Pty Ltd (1991) ... 1121
Macksville & District Hospital v Mayze (1987) ... 1967, 1970
Maclaine v Gatty [1921] ... 1974, 1975
MacLean v Dummett (1869) ... 823
Macleay v Tait [1906] ... 1020, 1024
Macpherson v Kevin J Prunty & Associates [1983] ... 2131
MacRobertson Miller Airline Services v Commissioner of State Taxation (WA) (1975) ... 208, 224, 617, 760
Madden v Kevereski [1983] ... 2169, 2172, 2173
Maddison v Alderson (1883) ... 382, 521, 522
Magee v Pennine Insurance Co Ltd [1969] ... 1229
Magennis v Fallon (1828) ... 1007
Magic Menu Systems Pty Ltd v AFA Facilitation Pty Ltd (1997) ... 1629
Magnacrete Ltd v Douglas-Hill (1988) ... 1305, 1310
Maguire v Makaronis (1997) ... 1015, 1045, 1412, 1414, 2336
—v Simpson (1977) ... 871
Maharaj v Chand [1986] ... 374
Mahkutai, The [1996] ... 925, 926
Mahmoud and Ispahani, Re [1921] ... 1603, 1608, 1611, 1709, 1710
Mahoney v Lindsay (1980) ... 1947
Maiden v Maiden (1909) ... 521
Mailman (GR) & Associates Pty Ltd v Wormald (Aust) Pty Ltd (1991) ... 1852
Mainprice v Westley (1865) ... 211
Majeau Carrying Co Pty Ltd v Coastal Rutile Ltd (1973) ... 644
Majik Markets Pty Ltd v S & M Motor Repairs Pty Ltd (No 1) (1987) ... 1984
Major v Bretherton (1928) ... 708
Makita (Australia) Pty Ltd v Black & Decker (Australasia) Pty Ltd (1990) ... 1107
Malhotra v Choudhury [1980] ... 2165, 2172

References are to paragraphs

Table of Cases

Malik v Bank of Credit and Commerce International SA [1998] ... 2103, 2123

Mallick v Parish (1916) ... 2110

Mallinson v Scottish Australian Investment Co Ltd (1920) ... 722, 1828

Mallozzi Carapelli SpA [1976] ... 271

Malmesbury (Earl) v Malmesbury (Countess) (1862) ... 1256

Malthouse v Adelaide Milk Supply Co-operative Ltd [1922] ... 205, 226

Manchester Diocesan Council v Commercial & General Investments Ltd [1970] ... 228, 255

Mann v Capital Territory Health Commission (1982) ... 2116

Mannai Investments Co Pty Ltd v Eagle Star Life Assurance Co Ltd [1997] ... 1970

Mantovani v Carapelli SpA [1980] ... 1626

Maple Flock Co Ltd v Universal Furniture Products (Wembley) Ltd [1934] ... 1938

Maralinga Pty Ltd v Major Enterprises Pty Ltd (1973) ... 1259, 1260, 1261, 1262, 1263

Marbe v George Edwardes (Daly's Theatre) Ltd [1928] ... 2154

March v E & M H Stramare Pty Ltd (1991) ... 2120, 2121, 2122

Mardorf Peach & Co Ltd v Attica Sea Carriers Corp of Liberia [1977] ... 1911, 1984

Maredelanto Compania Naviera SA v Bergbau-Handel GmbH (The Mihalis Angelos) [1971] ... 1914, 1933, 1969, 2161, 2162

Marek v Australasian Conference Association Pty Ltd [1994] ... 273

Marginson v Ian Potter & Co (1976) ... 502, 507

Marion White Ltd v Francis [1972] ... 1642, 1694

Maritime National Fish Ltd v Ocean Trawlers Ltd [1935] ... 2043

Market Terminal Pty Ltd v Dominion Insurance Co of Australia [1982] ... 1258

Marks v Jolly (1938) ... 1613, 1716, 1718

Marks (in a Representative Capacity) v GIO Australia Holdings Ltd (1998) ... 118, 1068, 1113, 1115, 1116, 2104, 2110

Marriott v Oxford and District Co-operative Society Ltd (No 2) [1970] ... 1967

Marsh v Mackay [1948] ... 2333

Marshall v NM Financial Management Ltd [1997] ... 1634, 1736

Marston Construction Co Ltd v Kigass Ltd (1989) ... 2317

Martin v Gale (1876) ... 815

—v Hogan (1917) ... 1809, 2204, 2221

—v Martin (1959) ... 1715

—v Stout [1925] ... 1930, 1933

Maskell v Horner [1915] ... 1309

Mason v New South Wales (1959) ... 1309, 1312, 1322, 1323

—v Provident Clothing and Supply Co Ltd [1913] ... 1636, 1648, 1735, 1738

Masters v Cameron (1954) ... 273, 2333

Mathew v Bobbins [1980] ... 1409, 1510

Mathieson v Sunshine Wrappings Pty Ltd (1962) ... 1937

Matthes v Carter (1955) ... 520

Matthews v Baxter (1873) ... 842

—v Smallwood [1910] ... 718, 1972

Matthey v Curling [1922] ... 2003, 2036, 2037

Max Garrett (Distributors) Pty Ltd v Tobias (1975) ... 1857

Maxitherm Boilers Pty Ltd v Pacific Dunlop Ltd [1998] ... 617

May v Platt [1900] ... 1266

May & Butcher Ltd v R (1929) ... 267, 268, 635, 2318

Maybury v Atlantic Union Oil Co Ltd (1953) ... 613

Mayers & Co v Johnson & Co [1905] ... 227

Mayfair Trading Co Pty Ltd v Dreyer (1958) ... 1720

Maynard v Goode (1926) ... 712, 1811

Mayson v Clouet [1924] ... 2324

MBP (SA) Pty Ltd v Gogic (1991) ... 2167

McBride v Sandland (1918) ... 521, 522

McCarthy Bros (Milk Vendors) Pty Ltd v Dairy Farmers' Co-operative Milk Co Ltd (1945) ... 1622, 1623
McCauley v Richmond MC (1923) ... 858
McClay v Seeligson (1904) ... 221
McCutcheon v David MacBrayne Ltd [1964] ... 617, 618
McDermott v Black (1940) ... 260, 350, 354
McDonald v Dennys Lascelles Ltd (1933) ... 1808, 1982, 1985, 1986, 1988, 1989, 1991, 2065, 2157, 2228, 2229, 2235, 2237, 2238, 2240, 2324, 2332, 2336
McDonald (AH) & Co Pty Ltd v Wells (1931) ... 1043
McDougall v Aeromarine of Emsworth Ltd [1958] ... 1953, 2306
McEntire v Crossley Bros Ltd [1895] ... 2238
McEvoy v Belfast Banking Co [1935] ... 930
McFarlane v Daniell (1938) ... 1702, 1729, 1730, 1731, 1737
McGregor v McGregor (1888) ... 404
McGruther v Pitcher [1904] ... 913
McHale v Watson (1966) ... 807
McIntyre v Swyny (1893) ... 1010
McKenna v Perecich [1973] ... 1721
—v Richey [1950] ... 2173
McLarnon v McLarnon (1968) ... 1308
McLaughlin v Daily Telegraph Newspaper Co Ltd (No 2) (1904) ... 841, 843
—v Darcy (1918) ... 811, 813
—v Freehill (1908) ... 847
McMahon v Ambrose [1987] ... 521, 522, 524, 2169, 2401, 2403, 2408
—v Gilberd & Co Ltd [1955] ... 216, 239
—v Sydney County Council (1940) ... 2033
McMahon's (Transport) Pty Ltd v Ebbage [1999] ... 229
McNally v Waitzer [1981] ... 1962
McRae v Commonwealth Disposals Commission (1951) ... 753, 1212, 1213, 1217, 1220, 1224, 1801, 1853, 1855, 2111, 2118, 2127, 2163
McTier v Haupt [1992] ... 724

McWilliams' Wines Pty Ltd v LS Booth Wine Transport Pty Ltd (1992) ... 1109
Mears v Safecar Security Ltd [1983] ... 719
Measures Bros Ltd v Measures [1910] ... 2416
Medlin v State Government Insurance Commission (1995) ... 2122
Meehan v Jones (1982) ... 118, 274, 741, 1967
Mehmet v Benson (1965) ... 2407
Melachrino v Nickoll [1920] ... 2148, 2149
Melbourne Banking Corp v Brougham (1879) ... 860
Melbourne Chilled Butter Co Pty Ltd v Downes (1900) ... 227
Melverton v Commonwealth Development Bank of Australia (1989) ... 1522
Mendelson-Zeller Co Inc v T & C Providores Pty Ltd [1981] ... 238
Mendelssohn v Normand Ltd [1970] ... 618, 761, 766
Meng Leong Development Pte Ltd v Jip Hong Trading Co Pte Ltd [1985] ... 1972
Menhaden Pty Ltd v Citibank NA (1984) ... 1104, 1106, 1118
Menzies v Williams (1893) ... 227
Mercantile Credit Co Ltd v Hamblin [1965] ... 1272
Mercantile Credit Ltd v Spinks [1968] ... 815
Mercantile Credits Ltd v Harry [1969] ... 265
Mercantile Union Guarantee Corp Ltd v Ball [1937] ... 813, 814
Meredith v Anthony [1980] ... 267, 273
Meriton Apartments Pty Ltd v McLaurin & Tait (Developments) Pty Ltd (1976) ... 2033
Merritt v Merritt [1970] ... 403
Mersey Steel and Iron Co Ltd v Naylor Benzon & Co (1884) ... 1825, 1937, 1938, 1941, 2230
Messageries Imperiales Co v Baines (1863) ... 913
Metal Fabrications (Vic) Pty Ltd v Kelcey [1986] ... 2133, 2135
Metcalf v Permanent Building Society (1993) ... 1611, 1614

Table of Cases

Metropolitan Electric Supply Co Ltd v Ginder [1901] ... 340
Metropolitan Knitting and Hosiery Co Ltd v Thomas Burnley & Sons Ltd (1924) ... 511, 517
Metropolitan Milk Supply (Greater Brisbane) Ltd v Paulsen [1933] ... 243
Metropolitan Transit Authority v Waverley Transit Pty Ltd [1991] ... 378
Metropolitan Water Board v Dick Kerr & Co Ltd [1917] ... 2002, 2004, 2024, 2029, 2039, 2040, 2064
Meudell v Mayer etc of Bendigo (1900) ... 212
Meynell v Surtees (1855) ... 255, 257
Miba Pty Ltd v Nescor Industries Group Pty Ltd (1996) ... 1108
—v—(1997) ... 1108
Micarone v Perpetual Trustees Australia Ltd (1999) ... 1512, 1528
Michael v Hart & Co [1902] ... 1930
Michael Realty Pty Ltd v Carr [1977] ... 1956
Midland Bank Trust Co Ltd v Hett Stubbs & Kemp [1979] ... 1036
Mikaelion v Commonwealth Scientific and Industrial Research Organisation (1999) ... 1110
Milchas Investments Pty Ltd v Larkin (1989) ... 1120
Miles v New Zealand Alford Estate Co (1886) ... 350, 352, 353
—v Wakefield MDC [1987] ... 1832, 2325
Miliangos v George Frank (Textiles) Ltd [1976] ... 2115
Millars' Karri and Jarrah Co (1902) v Weddel Turner & Co (1908) ... 1938, 1944
Miller v Blankley (1878) ... 823
—v Fiona's Clothes Horse of Centrepoint Pty Ltd (1989) ... 1123
—v Van Heck & Co [1920] ... 2148
Miller Associates (Australia) Pty Ltd v Bennington Pty Ltd (1966) ... 862
Millett v Regent [1975] ... 521, 523
Millichamp v Jones [1982] ... 1968, 2237
Milliner v Milliner (1908) ... 404
Mills v Fox (1887) ... 1228

—v Stokman (1967) ... 511
Milne v A-G (Tas) (1956) ... 207, 409
—v Municipal Council of Sydney (1912) ... 223
Minister for Consumer Affairs v WW Vallack Real Estate Pty Ltd (1986) ... 1517, 1530
Minister for Education v Oxwell [1966] ... 811, 826, 1633
Minister for Lands and Forests v McPherson (1991) ... 1979
Minister of State for the Army v Dalziel (1944) ... 2036
Miramar Maritime Corp v Holborn Oil Trading Ltd [1984] ... 619
Mobil Oil Australia Ltd v Lyndel Nominees Pty Ltd (1998) ... 250
Mohamed v Alaga & Co (a firm) [2000] ... 1630, 1728
Moir v J P Porter & Co Ltd (1979) ... 411
Molton v Camroux (1848) ... 839, 841
—v—(1849) ... 839, 840, 841
Molyneux v Natal Land and Colonization Co Ltd [1905] ... 843, 847
Monarch SS Co Ltd v A/B Karlshamns Oljefabriker [1949] ... 2047, 2120, 2121, 2122, 2124
Mondel v Steel (1841) ... 1832, 2202
Money v Money (No 2) [1966] ... 1633, 1719
—v Ven-Lu-Ree Ltd [1989] ... 267
Moneywood Pty Ltd v Salamon Nominees Pty Ltd (2001) ... 628
Monroe Schneider Associates (Inc) v No 1 Raberem Pty Ltd (1991) ... 1068
Mooney v Williams (1905) ... 222
Moorcock (The) (1889) ... 627
Moorhouse v Angus and Robertson (No 1) Pty Ltd [1981] ... 630
Morgan v Thorne (1841) ... 807
Morgan Crucible Co Plc v Hill Samuel & Co Ltd [1991] ... 1034
Moriarty v Regent's Garage and Engineering Co Ltd [1921] ... 1827
Morlend Finance Corp (Vic) Pty Ltd v Westendorp [1993] ... 1020, 1520, 1522, 1528
Morley v Richardson (1942) ... 1616
Morris, Re (1943) ... 1627

—v Baron & Co [1918] ... 526, 1978
Morrison v Neill (1875) ... 221
—v Robertson 1908 ... 1242
Morton v Lamb (1797) ... 1808
Moschi v Lep Air Services Ltd [1973] ... 113, 507, 1904, 1933, 1947, 1966, 1993, 2116
Moses v Macferlan (1760) ... 2301
—v Northern Assurances Co (1856) ... 1262
Motor Oil Hellas (Corinth) Refineries SA v Shipping Corp of India (The Kanchenjunga) [1990] ... 393, 1815, 1971
Mount Gambier Co-operative Milling Society Ltd v Williams [1921] ... 1019
Mount Tomah Blue Metals Ltd, Re [1963] ... 210
Mountford v Scott [1974] ... 1510
—v— [1975] ... 247, 1510
MS Fashions Ltd v Bank of Credit and Commerce International SA [1993] ... 1814
Mulcahy v Hoyne (1925) ... 393, 1972
Multiplex Constructions Pty Ltd v Abgarus Pty Ltd (1992) ... 2208, 2212
Munchies Management Pty Ltd v Belperio (1988) ... 1064, 1066
Munday & Shreeve v Western Australia [1962] ... 223
Mundy, Re (1963) ... 805, 813, 817
Munro v Morrison [1980] ... 1721
Murphy v Brentwood District Council [1991] ... 119
—v Overton Investments Pty Ltd (2001) ... 1113
—v Timms [1987] ... 355
—v Wright (1992) ... 260
—v Zamonex Pty Ltd (1993) ... 1947, 1978
Musca v Astle Corp Pty Ltd (1988) ... 1113
Muschinski v Dodds (1985) ... 2067
Muskham Finance Ltd v Howard [1963] ... 1272
Mussen v Van Dieman's Land Co [1938] ... 2332
Musumeci v Winadell Pty Ltd (1994) ... 348

Mutual Life & Citizens' Assurance Co Ltd v Evatt (1970) ... 1032
Myam Pty Ltd v Teskera [1971] ... 261
Myers (GH) & Co v Brent Cross Service Co [1934] ... 633
MYT Engineering Pty Ltd v Mulcon Pty Ltd (1999) ... 859
Myton Ltd v Schwab-Morris [1974] ... 2237
Nagle v Feilden [1966] ... 1636
Nagy v Masters Dairy Ltd (1996) ... 1110
Nangus Pty Ltd v Charles Donovan Pty Ltd [1989] ... 2159, 2229
Narich Pty Ltd v Commissioner of Pay-Roll Tax (1983) ... 712
Nash v Inman [1908] ... 810, 816, 829
National Australia Bank Ltd v Hall (1993) ... 1522
—v KDS Construction Services Pty Ltd (1987) ... 741, 1816
—v Nobile (1988) ... 1009
—v Starbronze Pty Ltd [2001] ... 1514
National Carriers Ltd v Panalpina (Northern) Ltd [1981] ... 1936, 2003, 2004, 2005, 2009, 2026, 2034, 2035, 2036, 2037, 2049, 2051, 2052, 2054, 2056
National Mutual Holdings Pty Ltd v Sentry Corp (1989) ... 1616
National Phonograph Co of Australia v Menck (1908) ... 913
National Provincial Bank of England v Jackson (1886) ... 1273
National Savings Bank Association, Re (Hebb's case) (1867) ... 226, 235, 243
National Westminster Bank Plc v Morgan [1985] ... 1404, 1412, 1511, 1512, 1513
Naxakis v Western General Hospital (1999) ... 1857
Nea Agrax SA v Baltic Shipping Co Ltd [1976] ... 260
Neal v Ayers (1940) ... 1068, 1623
Neat Holdings Pty Ltd v Karajan Holdings Pty Ltd (1992) ... 1028
Neeta (Epping) Pty Ltd v Phillips (1974) ... 1955, 1960, 1962, 1964
Neill v Hewens (1953) ... 514
Nelson v Kimberley Homes Pty Ltd (1988) ... 2060

Table of Cases

—v Nelson (1995) ... 1605, 1607, 1615, 1702, 1703, 1710, 1719, 1721
—v Stocker (1859) ... 823
Nemeth v Bayswater Road Pty Ltd [1988] ... 610, 707, 708
Nemtsas v Nemtsas [1957] ... 1274
Netaff Pty Ltd v Bikane Pty Ltd (1990) ... 1113
Nevill v Snelling (1880) ... 1504
Neville v London 'Express' Newspaper Ltd [1919] ... 1629
New South Wales v Bardolph (1934) ... 870, 871, 872, 873
New Zealand Loan and Mercantile Agency Co v Howes (1888) ... 1037, 1054, 1055
New Zealand Shipping Co Ltd v A M Satterthwaite & Co Ltd (The Eurymedon) [1975] ... 208, 349, 364, 925, 926
—v Société des Ateliers et Chantiers de France [1919] ... 1967
Newbigging v Adam (1886) ... 1065
Newbon v City Mutual Life Assurance Society Ltd (1935) ... 1840, 1967, 1975, 1987
Newborne v Sensolid (Great Britain) Ltd [1953] ... 862
Newcastle District Fishermen's Co-Operative Society v Neal (1950) ... 1721, 1723
Newcombe v Newcombe (1934) ... 1805
Newmont Pty Ltd v Laverton Nickel NL (1982) ... 1809
Newry & Enniskillen Ry Co v Coombe (1849) ... 820
News Ltd v Australian Rugby Football League Ltd (1996) ... 1116
Newton v Brownett (1940) ... 1728
—v State Government Insurance Office (Qld) [1986] ... 355
Nicholas v Thompson [1924] ... 1024
Nicholls v Stanton (1915) ... 1706, 1713
—v Taylor [1939] ... 1069
Nichols v Raynbred (1615) ... 1806
Nicholson v Smith (1882) ... 220
Nicholson and Venn v Smith Marriott (1947) ... 1224
Niesmann v Collingridge (1921) ... 273
Nikolaou v Papasavas Phillips & Co (1988) ... 2168
Nina's Bar Bistro Pty Ltd v MBE Corp (Sydney) Pty Ltd [1984] ... 1941, 1947
Nissho Iwai (Australia) Ltd v Oskar [1984] ... 354
Nissho Iwai Australia Ltd v Malaysian International Shipping Corp Berhad (1989) ... 760, 765
Nixon v Furphy (1925) ... 1312, 1320
—v Slater & Gordon (2000) ... 1113
NLS Pty Ltd v Hughes (1966) ... 1936, 2239, 2333
Nobel's Explosives Co v Jenkins & Co [1896] ... 2025
Noble v Maddison (1912) ... 1705, 1708, 1732
Nocton v Lord Ashburton [1914] ... 1032
Nordenfelt v Maxim Nordenfelt Guns and Ammunition Co Ltd [1894] ... 1635, 1636, 1641, 1644, 1647, 1735
Norman Baker Pty Ltd v Baker (1978) ... 805, 817
Norris v Sibberas [1990] ... 1033, 1035
North v Marra Developments Ltd (1981) ... 1705, 1707
North Ocean Shipping Co Ltd v Hyundai Construction Co Ltd (The Atlantic Baron) [1979] ... 345, 1302, 1313, 1322, 1327
North Western Salt Co Ltd v Electrolytic Alkali Co Ltd [1914] ... 1603, 1652
Northern Sandblasting Pty Ltd v Harris (1997) ... 915, 1030
Northland Airlines Ltd v Dennis Ferranti Meters Ltd (1970) ... 222
Norths Ltd v McCaughan Dyson Capel Cure Ltd (1988) ... 410
Norton v Angus (1926) ... 2169, 2170, 2410
Norton Australia Pty Ltd v Streets Ice Cream Pty Ltd (1968) ... 2122
Norwegian American Cruises A/S v Paul Mundy Ltd (The Vistafjord) [1988] ... 369
Norwest Refrigeration Services Pty Ltd v Bain Dawes (WA) Pty Ltd (1984) ... 2151
Norwich City Council v Harvey [1989] ... 923

Norwich Union Fire Insurance Society v William H Price Ltd [1934] ... 1224
Noske v McGinnis (1932) ... 2165
Notcutt v Universal Equipment Co (London) Ltd [1986] ... 2015, 2051, 2058
Nottingham Permanent Benefit Building Society v Thurstan [1903] ... 815, 818
Nowell v Worcester Corp (1854) ... 858
NSW Medical Defence Union Ltd v Transport Industries Insurance Co Ltd (1986) ... 723, 1261, 1263
Nudgee Bakery Pty Ltd's Agreement, Re [1971] ... 265, 644
Nunin Holdings Pty Ltd v Tullamarine Estates Pty Ltd [1994] ... 232
NW Co-operative Freezing & Canning Co Ltd v Easton (1915) ... 216, 255
NW Ry Co v M'Michael (1850) ... 818, 820
Nyulasy v Rowan (1891) ... 243, 254
O'Brien v Australia and New Zealand Bank Ltd (1971) ... 1272
—v Dawson (1941) ... 1961
—v—(1942) ... 273
—v Hooker Homes Pty Ltd (1993) ... 1522
—v McKean (1968) ... 2168
—v O'Brien (1995) ... 804
—v Smolonogov (1983) ... 1104
O'Connor v BDB Kirby & Co [1972] ... 2132
O'Dea v Allstates Leasing System (WA) Pty Ltd (1983) ... 2208, 2214, 2216, 2217, 2238, 2240, 2332
O'Donnell v Thor Industries Pty Ltd (1977) ... 626
O'Halloran Enterprises Pty Ltd v Williamson [1979] ... 216, 248
O'Keefe v Taylor Estates Co Ltd [1916] ... 1064, 1069
O'Loughlin v O'Loughlin [1958] ... 1627, 1730, 1736
O'Reilly v Mackman [1983] ... 1970
O'Rorke v Bolingbroke (1877) ... 1504
O'Rourke v Miller (1985) ... 1970
O'Shanassy v Jachim (1876) ... 807
O'Shea v Sullivan (1994) ... 1118
O'Sullivan v Aarons (1866) ...302

—v Management Agency and Music Ltd [1985] ... 1045, 1401, 1410, 2336
—v National Trustees Executors & Agency Co of A'sia Ltd [1913] ... 266
—v O'Leary [1955] ... 1832, 1834
Oakacre Ltd v Claire Cleaners (Holdings) Ltd [1982] ... 2150, 2171
Oakes v Turquand (1867) ... 1043, 1053
Occidental Worldwide Investment Corp v Skibs A/S Avanti (The Siboen and The Sibotre) [1976] ... 1304, 1310, 1321
Ocean Coal Co Ltd v Powell Duffryn Steam Coal Co Ltd [1932] ... 221
Ocean Tramp Tankers Corp v V/O Sovfracht (The Eugenia) [1964] ... 2017, 2038, 2047, 2050, 2051, 2066
Oceanic Sun Line Special Shipping Co Inc v Fay (1988) ... 616, 617, 760
Ockerby & Co Ltd v Watson (1918) ... 2003
Official Receiver v Feldman (1972) ... 1048
—v Henn (1981) ... 875
Official Trustee in Bankruptcy v Tooheys Ltd (1993) ... 381, 385
Offord v Davies (1862) ... 249
Ogdens Ltd v Nelson [1905] ... 1942
Ogilvie v Ryan [1976] ... 522
Ogle v Comboyuro Investments Pty Ltd (1976) ... 1841, 1933, 1940, 1970, 1972, 2101, 2146
Oldershaw v King (1857) ... 355
Olex Focas Pty Ltd v Skodaexport Co Ltd [1998] ... 1527, 1528
Oliver v Davis [1949] ... 333
Olley v Marlborough Court Ltd [1949] ... 616
Olympia Sauna Shipping Co SA v Shinwa Kaiun Kaisha Ltd (The Ypatia Halcoussi) [1985] ... 1263
On Demand Information Plc v Michael Gerson Finance Plc [2001] ... 1979, 2240
Orion Insurance Co Plc v Sphere Drake Insurance Plc [1992] ... 116, 402
Orr v Ford (1989) ... 393, 2409
Orton v Melman [1981] ... 1738, 1739
Oscar Chess Ltd v Williams [1957] ... 606, 610, 730, 1229

Table of Cases

Oswald Hickson Collier & Co v Carter-Ruck (1982) ... 1651
OTM Ltd v Hydranautics [1981] ... 224
Oudaille v Lawson [1922] ... 1012
Outer Suburban Property Ltd v Clarke [1933] ... 203
Overgrooke Estates Ltd v Glencombe Properties Ltd [1974] ... 1123
Overton v Banister (1844) ... 823
Owendale Pty Ltd v Anthony (1967) ... 1971
Owners of SS 'Mediana' v Owners etc of SS 'Comet' [1900] ... 2106
Owners of SS Istros v F W Dahlstroem & Co [1931] ... 749
Owners of the Dredger Liesbosch v Owners of SS Edison [1933] ... 2121
P v D1 and D2 (The C & J) [1984] ... 2202
P & M Constructions Pty Ltd v Elders Leasing Ltd [1992] ... 217
P's Bill of Costs, Re (1982) ... 1408, 1411
Paal Wilson & Co A/S v Partenreederei Hannah Blumenthal [1983] ...111, 112, 526, 2038, 2045, 2048, 2058, 2064
Pacific Dunlop Ltd v Maxitherm Boilers Pty Ltd (1997) ... 918
Paget v Marshall (1884) ... 1266
Pagnan SpA v Feed Products Ltd [1987] ... 267
—v Tradax Ocean Transportation SA [1987] ... 1856
Palgrave Brown & Son Ltd v Owners of SS Turid [1922] ... 720
Palmdale Insurance Ltd, Re [1982] ... 1942, 2067
Palmer v Bank of NSW [1973] ... 266
—v—(1975) ... 266, 404
—v Carey (1926) ... 2404
—v Hutchinson (1881) ... 873
—v Temple (1839) ... 2333
Pan Atlantic Insurance Co Ltd v Pine Top Insurance Co Ltd [1995] ... 1015, 1023
Pan Foods Co Importers & Distributors Pty Ltd v Australia and New Zealand Banking Group Ltd (2000) ... 704

Pan Ocean Shipping Co Ltd v Creditcorp Ltd (The Trident Beauty) [1994] ... 2232
Panchaud Frères SA v Etablissements General Grain Co [1970] ... 1969, 1975, 1983
Panoutsos v Raymond Hadley Corp of New York [1917] ... 527
Pantalone v Alaouie (1989) ... 2156
Pao On v Lau Yiu Long [1980] ... 330, 349, 362, 363, 716, 721, 1302, 1304, 1313, 1321, 1329
Papastravou v Gavan [1968] ... 1636
Pappas v Poulac Pty Ltd (1983) ... 1107
Paradine v Jane (1647) ... 2003
Parastatidis v Kotaridis [1978] ... 303
Parbury Henty & Co Pty Ltd v General Engineering & Agencies Pty Ltd (1973) ... 222, 516
Park v Allied Mortgage Corp Ltd (1993) ... 1110
Parkdale Custom Built Furniture Pty Ltd v Puxu Pty Ltd (1982) ... 1105
Parker v R-G [1976] ... 1048
—v South Eastern Railway Co (1877) ... 617, 708
Parkin v Thorold (1852) ... 1849
Parramatta City Council v Lutz (1988) ... 1030, 2156
Parsons v BNM Laboratories Ltd [1964] ... 2167
Parsons (H) (Livestock) Ltd v Uttley Ingham & Co Ltd [1978] ... 2123, 2126, 2138
Partridge v Crittenden [1968] ... 208, 214
Pasley v Freeman (1789) ... 1066
Patel v Ali [1984] ... 2410
Patrick Stevedores Operations No 2 Pty Ltd v Maritime Union of Australia (1998) ... 2403
Patterson v Dolman [1908] ... 207, 244, 245
Pattison v Mann (1975) ... 209
Pavey & Matthews Pty Ltd v Paul (1987) ... 105, 118, 119, 520, 2303, 2307, 2308, 2311, 2314, 2325, 2330, 2334, 2337, 2338
Pavia & Co SpA v Thurmann-Nielsen [1952] ... 1952
Payne v Cave (1789) ... 211
—v McDonald (1908) ... 1715

References are to paragraphs

xlvii

—v Wilson (1827) ... 355
Payzu Ltd v Saunders [1919] ... 2149
PC Developments Pty Ltd v Revell (1991) ... 1979, 2207, 2216, 2331
Pearce v Brain [1929] ... 821, 824
—v Brooks (1866) ... 1631
—v Kelly (1919) ... 817
Pearse, Re [1905] ... 360
Pearson (S) & Son Ltd v Dublin Corp [1907] ... 1028, 1123
Peckham v Moore [1975] ... 867
Peek v Derry (1887) ... 1025
—v Gurney (1873) ... 1016, 1019
Peeters v Opie (1677) ... 1806
Pendal Nominees Pty Ltd v Lednez Industies (Australia) Ltd (1996) ... 764
Penfolds Wines Pty Ltd v Elliott (1946) ... 1722, 1723
Pennant Hills Restaurants Pty Ltd v Barrell Insurances Pty Ltd [1977] ... 1036
—v—(1981) ... 2104, 2167, 2168
Pennicott v Pennicott (1936) ... 1936, 1966, 1984
Pennsylvania Shipping Co v Compagnie Nationale de Navigation [1936] ... 1057
Percival v London CC Asylums Committee (1918) ... 223
Perel v Australian Bank of Commerce (1923) ... 1816
Permanent Building Society v Wheeler (1992) ... 1614
Permanent Trustee Australia Ltd v FAI General Insurance Co Ltd (1998) ... 1261
Permanent Trustee Australia Co Ltd v FAI General Insurance Co Ltd (2001) ... 1017
Perpetual Executors and Trustees Association of Australia Ltd v Russell (1931) ... 519, 1715
—v Wright (1917) ... 1715
Perre v Apand Pty Ltd (1999) ... 107, 1030
Perri v Coolangatta Investments Pty Ltd (1982) ... 741, 1804, 1962
Perrin v Reynolds (1886) ... 1230
Perry v Sidney Phillips & Son [1982] ... 2152, 2155, 2168

Petelin v Cullen (1975) ... 1267, 1272, 1274
Peter Turnbull & Co Pty Ltd v Mundus Trading Co (Australasia) Pty Ltd (1954) ... 527, 1929, 1930, 1947, 2202
Petera Pty Ltd v EAJ Pty Ltd (1984) ... 1123
Peters v Fleming (1840) ... 809, 810
—v Tuck (1915) ... 825
—v Schimanski [1975] ... 845
Peters American Delicacy Co Ltd v Champion (1928) ... 626
Peters Ice Cream (Vic) Ltd v Todd [1961] ... 261
Petranker v Brown [1984] ... 1616
Petrofina (Gt Britain) Ltd v Martin [1966] ... 1634
Peyman v Lanjani [1985] ... 1971
Pharmaceutical Society of Great Britain v Boots Cash Chemists (Southern) Ltd [1953] ... 208, 213, 214
—v Dickson [1970] ... 1634, 1637
Phibro Energy AG v Nissho Iwai Corp (The Honam Jade) [1991] ... 1952
Phillips v Brooks Ltd [1919] ... 1246, 1247
—v Ellinson Bros Pty Ltd (1941) ... 520, 527, 1824, 2337
Phoenix General Insurance Co of Greece SA v Halvanon Insurance Co Ltd [1988] ... 1614
Photo Production Ltd v Securicor Transport Ltd [1980] ... 749, 754, 760, 761, 765, 1907, 1926, 1967, 1986, 1988, 1989, 1992, 1993, 2101, 2155, 2158, 2212
Pianta v National Finance & Trustees Ltd (1964) ... 2404
Pickard v Sears (1837) ... 382
Picturesque Atlas Publishing Co Ltd v Phillipson (1890) ... 1037
Pidgeon (FA) & Son Pty Ltd v Danehurst Investments Pty Ltd [1986] ... 2151.
Pigram v Attorney-General (NSW) (1975) ... 2211, 2214
Pillans v Van Mierop (1765) ... 301, 306
Pinnel's Case (1602) ... 356, 357, 358, 364
Pioneer Container, The [1994] ... 926

Table of Cases

Pioneer Shipping Ltd v BTP Tioxide Ltd [1982] ... 702, 2001, 2006, 2010, 2027, 2049
Pirie v Saunders (1961) ... 513, 514
Pitt v Curotta (1931) ... 2332
—v PHH Asset Management Ltd [1994] ... 339
Pitts v Hunt [1991] ... 1705
Placer Development Ltd v Commonwealth (1969) ... 261, 267, 338
Plaimar Ltd v Waters Trading Co Ltd (1945) ... 1809, 2204
Planché v Colburn (1831) ... 2323
Plimmer v Mayor of Wellington (1884) ... 377
Pollock (W & S) & Co v Macrae 1922 ... 757, 1926
Pollway Ltd v Abdullah [1974] ... 2236, 2237
Pondcil Pty Ltd v Tropical Reef Shipyard Pty Ltd (1994) ... 618
Pontypridd Union v Drew [1927] ... 816
Pooraka Holdings Pty Ltd v Participation Nominees Pty Ltd (1991) ... 2151
Poort v Development Underwriting (Victoria) Pty Ltd [1976] ... 2334
—v—(No 2) [1977] ... 1970
Pope & Pearson v The Buenos Ayres New Gas Co (1892) ... 1225
Popiw v Popiw [1957] ... 404
—v—[1959] ... 342, 513, 519
Pordage v Cole (1669) ... 1806, 1811
Port Jackson Stevedoring Pty Ltd v Salmond & Spraggon (Aust) Pty Ltd (The New York Star) (1978) ... 239, 240, 349, 925, 926
—v—(1980) ... 239, 240, 925
—v—[1981] ... 1993
Port Line Ltd v Ben Line Steamers Ltd [1958] ... 913
Port Sudan Cotton Co v Govindaswamy Chettiar & Sons [1977] ... 712
Port Swettenham Authority v T W Wu & Co [1979] ... 624
Porter v Latec Finance (Qld) Pty Ltd (1964) ... 1247
Portman Building Society v Dusangh (2000) ... 1512

Poseidon Ltd v Adelaide Petroleum NL (1992) ... 1110
Postlethwaite v Freeland (1880) ... 1804
Potato Producers Co-operative Ltd v Pavone [1962] ... 1646
Potts v Miller (1940) ... 1069, 1070
Poussard v Spiers (1876) ... 2058
Powell v Jones [1968] ... 267, 273,
—v Lee (1908) ... 217, 226
—v Powell [1900] ... 1405, 1408, 1411
—v Smith (1872) ... 1209, 1266
Power v Kenny [1960] ... 1021
Powys v Brown (1924) ... 2165
Pratten v Thompson (1895) ... 236
Prenn v Simmonds [1971] ... 711, 723
President of India v La Pintada Compania Navigacion SA [1985] ... 2109, 2151
—v Lips Maritime Corp [1988] ... 2151
Preston v Luck (1881) ... 1252
Pretorius Pty Ltd v Muir & Neil Pty Ltd [1976] ... 1613
Price v Easton (1833) ... 901
—v Strange [1978] ... 2169, 2408
Pricom Pty Ltd v Sgarioto (1994) ... 1121
Prince v Haworth (1904) ... 811
Prints for Pleasure Ltd v Oswald-Sealy (Overseas) Ltd [1968] ... 259
Prior v Payne (1949) ... 267
Prioris Pty Ltd v Inscorp Holdings Ltd (1995) ... 1116
Pritchard v Racecage Pty Ltd (1997) ... 1527
Proctor & Gamble Philippine Manufacturing Corp v Kurt A Becher GmbH & Co KG [1988] ... 2161
Production Sheet Metals Pty Ltd, Re [1971] ... 224
Progressive Mailing House Pty Ltd v Tabali Pty Ltd (1985) ... 1930, 1936, 1966, 2036, 2159
Project Blue Moon Pty Ltd v Fairway Trading Pty Ltd [2000] ... 1514
Prometheus, The (1949) ... 873
Provincial and Suburban Bank Ltd, Re (1881) ... 243
Prudential Assurance Co Ltd v C M Breedon Pty Ltd [1994] ... 1229

—v Health Minders Pty Ltd (1987) ... 222
Psaltis v Schultz (1948) ... 1633, 1709, 1937
PT Garuda Indonesia Ltd v Grellman (1992) ... 1628
PT Ltd v Maradona Pty Ltd (1991) ... 842, 1267, 1613
Public Service Employees Credit Union Co-operative Ltd v Campion (1984) ... 1628
Public Trustee v Taylor [1978] ... 1012
Public Works Commissioner v Hills [1906] ... 2208
Pukallus v Cameron (1982) ... 1259, 1262, 1263, 2161
Pullen v Gutteridge Haskins & Davey Pty Ltd [1993] ... 1067, 1857
Purcell v Bacon (1914) ... 1823
Pym v Campbell (1856) ... 707
Qantas Airways Ltd v Cameron (1996) ... 1528
—v Christie (1998) ... 2001
Quadling v Robinson (1976) ... 222
Quadramain Pty Ltd v Sevastapol Investments Pty Ltd (1976) ... 1637, 1638
Queen's Bridge Motors and Engineering Co Pty Ltd v Edwards [1964] ... 2131
Queensland Co-operative Milling Association Ltd v Pamag Pty Ltd (1973) ... 1638, 1642, 1646, 1652
Quenerduaine v Cole (1883) ... 228, 255
Quiggan Bros v Baker [1906] ... 810
Quin v Mutual Acceptance Co Ltd [1968] ... 1713, 1726, 2122, 2131, 2132
R & B Customs Brokers Ltd v United Dominions Trust Ltd [1988] ... 639
R v Brown (1912) ... 2301
—v Clarke (1927) ... 208, 239, 240, 249, 925
—v McDonald (1885) ... 825
—v Paulson [1921] ... 1968
—v Weaver (1931) ... 1009
RACV Investment Co Pty Ltd v Silbury Pty Ltd (1986) ... 1260
Radford v De Froberville [1978] ... 2115, 2156
—v Ferguson (1947) ... 1713

Raffaele v Raffaele [1962] ... 404
Raffles v Wichelhaus (1864) ... 1234
RAIA Insurance Brokers Ltd v FAI Insurance Co Ltd (1993) ... 1108, 1113
Rain v Fullarton (1900) ... 818
Rainbow v Hawkins [1904] ... 211
Raineri v Miles [1981] ... 1852, 1951, 1960
Ramsden v Dyson (1866) ... 377
Ramsgate Victoria Hotel Co Ltd v Montefiore (1866) ... 255
Rance v Kensett (1916) ... 1023
Randazzo v Goulding [1968] ... 267
Rann v Hughes (1778) ... 306
Ratto v Trifid Pty Ltd [1987] ... 522
Rawlins v Wickham (1858) ... 1048
Rawson v Hobbs (1961) ... 1909, 1943, 1969, 1982, 2336
Ray v Davies (1909) ... 624, 2407
—v Druce [1985] ... 2165
Read v Anderson (1882) ... 1616
—v Nerey Nominees Pty Ltd [1979] ... 2131
Real Estate Securities Ltd v Kew Golf Links Estate Pty Ltd [1935] ... 2240
Reardon v Morley Ford Pty Ltd (1980) ... 208, 214, 215
Reardon Smith Line Ltd v Yngvar Hansen-Tangen [1976] ... 106, 638, 703, 713, 714, 715, 736, 1919
Redgrave v Hurd (1881) ... 1022, 1037
Reed v Kilburn Co-operative Society (1875) ... 1817
—v Sheehan (1982) ... 373
Reese Bros Plastics Ltd v Hamon-Sobelco Australia Pty Ltd (1988) ... 238
Reese River Silver Mining Co Ltd v Smith (1869) ... 1037, 1045, 1047
Reg Glass Pty Ltd v Rivers Locking Systems Pty Ltd (1968) ... 633, 1855, 2120
Regalian Properties Plc v London Docklands Development Corp [1995] ... 2317
Regent v Millett (1976) ... 521, 522, 523
Reid v Rush and Tompkins Group Plc [1990] ... 621
Reigate v Union Manufacturing Co (Ramsbottom) Ltd [1918] ... 2161

Table of Cases

Reilly v R [1934] ... 2012
Rejfek v McElroy (1966) ... 1028
Remedios v Kentucky Homes Pty Ltd (1987) ... 1112
Remilton v City Mutual Life Assurance Society Ltd (1908) ... 236
Renard Constructions (ME) Pty Ltd v Minister for Public Works (1992) ... 1809, 1983, 2322, 2339
Reuter v Electric Telegraph Co (1856) ... 852
Reynell v Sprye (1852) ... 1042, 1305, 2235
Reynolds v Atherton (1921) ... 257
—v—(1922) ... 225
—v McGregor [1973] ... 266
Rhodes, Re (1890) ... 847
Rhone v Stephens [1994] ... 908
Rhone Poulenc Agrochimie SA v UIM Chemical Services Pty Ltd (1986) ... 1110
Rian Financial Services Ltd v Alfred Investments Projects Pty Ltd (1988) ... 1954
Rice v Taylor (1969) ... 203, 256
Rich (TP) Investments Pty Ltd v Calderon [1964] ... 1622, 1705
Richards v Bartlet (1584) ... 356
—v Phillips [1968] ... 211
Richardson & Wrench (Holdings) Pty Ltd v Ligon No 174 Pty Ltd (1994) ... 1114
Richardson Spence & Co v Rowntree [1894] ... 617
Riche v Ashbury Railway Carriage Co (1874) ... 852
Riches v Hogben [1985] ... 377, 380, 404, 521
Ricochet Pty Ltd v Equity Trustees Executor & Agency Co Ltd (1993) ... 1112
Riddiford v Warren (1901) ... 1061
Ridge v Baldwin [1964] ... 1970
Riley v Osbourne [1986] ... 521, 523
Rinaldi & Patroni Pty Ltd v Precision Mouldings Pty Ltd [1986] ... 618
Ring (FH) & Co Ltd, Re [1924] ... 226
Ringstad v Gollin & Co Pty Ltd (1924) ... 2024, 2030
Ripka Pty Ltd v Maggiore Bakeries Pty Ltd [1984] ... 1936
Ritchie v Atkinson (1808) ... 1806
Ritter v North Side Enterprises Pty Ltd (1975) ... 1009
River Wear Commissioners v Adamson (1877) ... 703
Riverlate Properties Ltd v Paul [1975] ... 1253, 1265, 1266
Roache v Australian Mercantile Land & Finance Co Ltd (1964) ... 1242
Roadshow Entertainment Pty Ltd v CAN 053 006 269 Pty Ltd Receiver & Manager Appointed (formerly CEL Home Video Pty Ltd) (1997) ... 1978
Robert A Munro & Co Ltd v Meyer [1930] ... 737, 753, 1222, 1228, 1938, 1977,
Roberts, Re (1881) ... 260
—, Re [1905] ... 1209, 1219
—v Gray [1913] ... 816
Roberts (A) & Co Ltd v Leicestershire County Council [1961] ... 1264
Robertson v Wilson (1958) ... 2036, 2037
Robertson & Moffat v Belson [1905] ... 1017
Robertson (JS) (Aust) Pty Ltd v Martin (1956) ... 1981
Robin Pty Ltd v Canberra International Airport Pty Ltd (1999) ... 1104
Robinson v ANZ Banking Group Ltd (1990) ... 1522
—v Balmain New Ferry Co Ltd [1910] ... 616
—v Davison (1871) ... 2015
—v Graves [1935] ... 511
—v Harman (1848) ... 2104
—v McEwan (1865) ... 239
Robinson's Motor Vehicles Ltd v Graham [1956] ... 826
Robophone Facilities Ltd v Blank [1966] ... 2128, 2160, 2207, 2208, 2210
Rock Refrigeration Ltd v Jones [1997] ... 1995
Rogers v Ingham (1876) ... 1209
—v Parish (Scarborough) Ltd [1987] ... 640
—v Whitaker (1992) ... 1857
Rogers (JB) Ltd v Harry Lesnie Ltd (1927) ... 222
Ronald v Lalor (1872) ... 225
Rookes v Barnard [1964] ... 1329

References are to paragraphs

Root v Badley [1960] ... 1055
Roper v Johnson (1873) ... 2133
Roscorla v Thomas (1842) ... 328
Rose v Commissioner of Stamps (SA) (1979) ... 312
Rose & Frank Co v J R Crompton & Bros Ltd [1923] ... 403, 406, 1626
Rosemac Pty Ltd's Caveat, Re (1992) ... 1603
Rosenhain v Commonwealth Bank of Australia (1922) ... 644
Rosenthal & Sons Ltd v Esmail [1965] ... 1981
Ross v Allis-Chalmers Australia Pty Ltd (1980) ... 612
—v Caunters [1980] ... 1036
—v Ratcliff (1988) ... 1611
Ross T Smyth & Co Ltd v T D Bailey Son & Co [1940] ... 1939, 1941
Rossiter v Miller (1878) ... 273
Roufos v Brewster (1971) ... 408
Routledge v Grant (1828) ... 243
Roux v Australian Broadcasting Commission [1992] ... 1629
Rover International Ltd v Cannon Film Sales Ltd [1989] ... 2229, 2238, 2324, 2338
Rowe v Hopwood (1868) ... 819
Rowland v Divall [1923] ... 637, 2306, 2324
Royal Bank of Scotland v Etridge (No 2) [2001] ... 1412
Royal British Bank v Turquand (1856) ... 858
Royal Exchange Assurance v Hall (1952) ... 806
Royal Insurance Australia Ltd v Government Insurance Office of NSW [1994] ... 720
Royscot Trust Ltd v Rogerson [1991] ... 1077
Rudi's Enterprises Pty Ltd v Jay (1987) ... 1967
Rutter v Palmer [1922] ... 763, 764
Ruxley Electronics and Constructions Ltd v Forsyth [1996] ... 1835, 2103, 2156
Ryan v Great Lakes Council (1999) ... 1110
—v Textile Clothing & Footwear Union of Australia [1996] ... 712
Ryder v Taylor (1935) ... 907

—v Wombwell (1868) ... 810
Rymark Australia Development Consultants Pty Ltd v Draper [1977] ... 206
S & E Promotions Pty Ltd v Tobin Bros Pty Ltd (1994) ...376, 378, 382
Sabemo Pty Ltd v North Sydney Municipal Council [1977] ... 2317
Sacher Investments Pty Ltd v Forma Stereo Consultants Pty Ltd [1976] ... 913
Saffron v Société Minière Cafrika (1958) ... 1816
Sagar v H Ridehalgh & Son Ltd [1931] ... 644
Said v Butt [1920] ... 1242
Sainsbury (HR & S) Ltd v Street [1972] ... 2060
Saints Gallery Pty Ltd v Plummer (1988) ... 1121
Salmond & Spraggon (Australia) Pty Ltd v Joint Cargo Services Pty Ltd [1977] ... 240
Sametiet M/T Johs Stove v Istanbul Petrol Rafinerisi A/S (The Johs Stove) [1984] ... 1810
Samuels v Davis [1943] ... 511
San Sebastian Pty Ltd v Minister Administering the Environmental Planning and Assessment Act (1986) ... 1032, 1033
Sander, Re (1934) ... 207
Sanders v Snell (1998) ... 630, 1909
Sanderson Motors (Sales) Pty Ltd v Yorkstar Motors Pty Ltd [1983] ... 2416, 2418
Sanrod Pty Ltd v Dainford Ltd (1984) ... 2151
Santa Martha Baay Scheepvart v Scanbulk A/S (The Rijn) [1981] ... 2162
Sargent v ASL Developments Ltd (1974) ... 1048, 1971, 1974
—v Campbell [1972–73] ... 1025, 1026, 1065
Satellite Estate Pty Ltd v Jaquet (1968) ... 1906, 1941, 1955
Saunders v Anglia Building Society [1971] ... 1269, 1270, 1271, 1272, 1273
—v Edwards [1987] ... 1070, 1703
Savage (JJ) & Sons Pty Ltd v Blakney (1970) ... 610, 612

Table of Cases

Saxon v Saxon [1976] ... 1308
Scally v Southern Health and Social Services Board [1992] ... 631, 635
Scammell (G) & Nephew Ltd v Ouston [1941] ... 258, 260, 261, 267
Scandinavian Trading Tanker Co AB v Flota Petrolera Ecuatoriana [1983] ... 119, 1979, 2211, 2224, 2332
Scanlan's New Neon Ltd v Tooheys Ltd (1943) ... 2003, 2005, 2008, 2009, 2020, 2024, 2029, 2033, 2036, 2045, 2050, 2051, 2052, 2054, 2058
Scarborough v Sturzaker (1905) ... 810
Scarf v Jardine (1882) ... 1040
Scarisbrick v Parkinson (1869) ... 2337, 2338
Scates v King (1870) ... 845
SCF Finance Co Ltd v Masri (No 2) [1987] ... 1612
Schaefer v Schuhmann [1972] ... 404, 1942
Schanka v Employment National (Administration) Pty Ltd (2000) ... 1330
Schebsman, Re [1944] ... 907, 911
Schelde Delta Shipping BV v Astarte Shipping Ltd (The Pamela) [1995] ... 238
Schenker & Co (Aust) Pty Ltd v Maplas Equipment and Services Pty Ltd [1990] ... 764, 767
Schroeder (A) Music Publishing Co Ltd v Macaulay [1974] ... 1510, 1637, 1646, 1653
Schuler (L) AG v Wickman Machine Tool Sales Ltd [1974] ... 704, 712, 718, 727, 730, 1912, 1916, 1918, 1924, 1927, 1970
Schultz v Ocean Accident & Guarantee Corp Ltd (1923) ... 1629
Scotson v Pegg (1861) ... 349
Scott v Avery (1856) ... 1626
—v Bradley [1971] ... 513
—v Brown Doering McNab & Co [1892] ... 1623, 1705
—v Coulson [1903] ... 1221, 1223
—v Davis (2000) ... 2129
Scott Fell (W) & Co v Lloyd (1906) ... 1014
Scottish Australian Investment Co v Walker (1889) ... 818
Scottish Halls Ltd v The Minister (1915) ... 2017

Scottish Petroleum, Re (Maclagan's case) (1882) ... 244
Scottish Special Housing Association v Wimpey Construction UK Ltd [1986] ... 2033
Scriven Bros & Co v Hindley & Co [1913] ... 1234
Scruttons Ltd v Midland Silicones Ltd [1962] ... 319, 901, 905, 924, 925, 926
Seager, Re; Sealey v Briggs (1889) ... 825
Sealand of the Pacific Ltd v Ocean Cement Ltd (1973) ... 1036
Secretary of State for Employment v ASLEF (No 2) [1972] ... 1842
Secretary, Department of Health and Community Services v JWB & SMB (Marion's case) ... 807
Secured Income Real Estate (Australia) Ltd v St Martins Investments Pty Ltd (1979) ... 625, 711, 1809
Seddon v North Eastern Salt Co Ltd [1905] ... 1054, 1255
Seidler v Schallhofer [1982] ... 1619, 1620, 1632
Selectmove Ltd, Re [1995] ... 229
Sellars v Adelaide Petroleum NL (1994) ... 118, 1069, 1113, 2164
Sellin v Scott (1901) ... 813, 820
Selman v Minogue (1937) ... 1069
Senanayake v Cheng [1966] ... 1048, 1054
Seppelt (B) & Sons Ltd v Commissioner for Main Roads (1975) ... 209, 220, 222, 273
Service Station Association Ltd v Berg Bennett & Associates Pty Ltd (1993) ... 1809, 1842, 1983
Seton v Slade (1802) ... 1850
Sevastopoulos v Spanos [1991] ... 520
Seven Seas Properties Ltd v Al-Essa [1988] ... 2165
Shaddock (L) & Associates Pty Ltd v Parramatta City Council (1981) ... 1032, 1034, 1035
Shadwell v Shadwell (1860) ... 349
Sharah v Healey [1982] ... 1651
Sharman v Kunert (1985) ... 1522
Sharneyford Supplies Ltd v Edge [1987] ... 2165
Sharp v Batt (1930) ... 2014, 2046

References are to paragraphs

—v Thomson (1915) ... 1234
Sharpe v Ramage (1995) ... 1112
Shaw v Applegate [1978] ... 2416
—v Ball (1962) ... 2324
—v Groom [1970] ... 1613, 1615, 1620
Sheahan v Workers Rehabilitation and Compensation Corp (1991) ... 343
Shears v Mendeloff (1914) ... 808
Shearson Lehman Hutton Inc v Maclaine Watson & Co Ltd (No 2) [1990] ... 2140
Sheehan, In The Marriage of (1991) ... 1630
—v Zaszlos [1995] ... 273
Sheffield Canal Co v Sheffield and Rotherham Ry Co (1841) ... 251
Shell Oil of Australia Ltd v McIlwraith McEacharn Ltd (1945) ... 913
Shell UK Ltd v Lostock Garage Ltd [1977] ... 624, 629, 1641, 1652, 1702, 2056
Shepherd v Felt and Textiles of Australia Ltd (1931) ... 627, 630, 1809, 1842, 1921, 1969
—v Noyes Bros Pty Ltd (1985) ... 1113
Shepherd (FC) & Co Ltd v Jerrom [1987] ... 2003, 2006, 2046
Shepperd v Ryde Corp (1952) ... 612, 719
Sherwood v Walker ... 1221
Shevill v Builders Licensing Board (1982) ... 1934, 1936, 1938, 1951, 2151, 2159, 2229, 2232
Shiell v Symons [1951] ... 2036, 2037
Shiels v Drysdale (1880) ... 266
Shiloh Spinners Ltd v Harding [1973] ... 1979
Shindler v Northern Raincoat Co Ltd [1960] ... 2135, 2137
Shipley UDC v Bradford Corp [1937] ... 1259
Shipton Anderson & Co v Weil Bros & Co [1912] ... 1812
Shire of Yea v Roberts (1879) ... 269
Shirlaw v Southern Foundries (1926) Ltd [1939] ... 628
Short v Stone (1846) ... 1814
Shuey v United States (1875) ... 246
SIB International SRL v Metallgesellschaft Corp (The Noel Bay) [1989] ... 2148

Sibbles v Highfern Pty Ltd (1987) ... 1947, 1970, 2333
Sibley v Grosvenor (1916) ... 1023, 1028, 1064
Sidney Eastman Pty Ltd v Southern [1963] ... 261
Silovi Pty Ltd v Barbaro (1988) ... 369, 377
Silva v Tarval Pty Ltd (1986) ... 2038
Silverton v SF Carroll Pty Ltd [1983] ... 1123
Sim v Rotherham MBC [1987] ... 1827, 1832
Simmons Ltd v Hay (1964) ... 2004, 2006, 2015, 2039, 2040
Simonius Vischer & Co v Holt [1979] ... 632, 1036, 2121, 2136
Simons v Zartom Investments Pty Ltd [1975] ... 1057, 1123
Simpson v AG [1904] ... 852
—v Hughes (1897) ... 222
—v Surman (1922) ... 1938
Simpson Steel Structures v Spencer [1964] ... 1831, 1834
Sinason-Teicher Inter-American Grain Corp v Oilcakes and Oilseeds Trading Co Ltd [1954] ... 1815
Sinclair v Brougham [1914] ... 2301
—v Preston [1970] ... 1022
—v Schildt (1914) ... 269
Sinclair Scott & Co Ltd v Naughton (1929) ... 273, 513, 718
Sinclair's Life Policy, Re [1938] ... 911
Sindel v Georgiou (1984) ... 1961
Singh v Ali [1960] ... 1722, 1723, 1724
Sita Qld Pty Ltd v Queensland (1999) ... 872
Siu Yin Kwan v Eastern Insurance Co Ltd [1994] ... 906
SJR Investment Co Pty Ltd v Housing Commission of Victoria (1970) ... 2033
Skeate v Beale (1841) ... 1310
Slade v Metrodent Ltd [1953] ... 813
Slade's case (1602) ... 105
Slator v Trimble (1861) ... 820
Slee v Warke (1949) ... 1259, 1262, 2411
Slowey v Lodder (1901) ... 2339
Smeaton Hanscomb & Co Ltd v Sassoon I Setty Son & Co (No 1) [1953] ... 755

Smidt v Tiden (1874) ... 1234
Smith v Bromley (1760) ... 1710
—v Bush [1990] ... 1033, 1034
—v Chadwick (1884) ... 1019, 1021, 1026
—v Hughes (1871) ... 110, 1014, 1250, 1254
—v Jenkins (1970) ... 315, 1705
—v Jones [1954] ... 1258
—v Kay (1859) ... 1021, 1401
—v Land and House Property Corp (1885) ... 1009, 2023
—v Monteith (1844) ... 1309
—v Morgan [1971] ... 268
—v South Wales Switchgear Co Ltd [1978] ... 619, 763, 764
—v Wheatcroft (1878) ... 1248
—v William Charlick Ltd (1924) ... 1301, 1311, 1312, 1318, 1329
—v Yarnold [1969] ... 865
Smith (KA & C) Pty Ltd v Ward (1998) ... 1642, 1738
Smith Bros v Madden Bros [1945] ... 1028
Smith New Court Securities Ltd v Citibank NA [1997] ... 1067, 1068, 2114, 2120
Smyth v Jessep [1956] ... 2239, 2333
Snarski & Snarski v Barbarich [1969] ... 1071, 1123
Snepp v United States 444 US ... 2328
Société Franco Tunisienne D'Armement v Sidermar SpA [1961] ... 2066
Société Italo-Belge pour le Commerce et l'Industrie v Palm and Vegetable Oils (Malaysia) Sdn Bhd (The Post Chaser) [1981] ... 1974, 1976
Solle v Butcher [1950] ... 1012, 1054, 1208, 1209, 1219, 1229, 1230, 1231, 1232, 1254, 1255, 1266
Soper v Arnold (1887) ... 1230
Sotiros Shipping Inc v Sameiet Solholt (The Solholt) [1983] ... 2135, 2137, 2149, 2159
South Australia v Commonwealth (1962) ... 267, 409
—v Johnson (1982) ... 1036, 1068
South Australia Asset Management Corp v York Montague Ltd [1997] ... 1069

South Australian Cold Stores Ltd v Electricity Trust of South Australia (1965) ... 1720
South Australian Commissioner for Railways v Egan (1973) ... 1626
South Australian Railways Commissioner v Egan (1973) ... 1502
South Coast Oils (Qld & NSW) Pty Ltd v Look Enterprises Pty Ltd [1988] ... 272, 273, 513
South Western Mineral Water Co Ltd v Ashmore [1967] ... 1737
Southern Foundries (1926) Ltd v Shirlaw [1940] ... 628, 1902, 1933, 1967
Sowler v Potter [1940] ... 1245
Spectra Pty Ltd v Pindari Pty Ltd [1974] ... 228
Spedley Securities Ltd v Bank of New Zealand (1991) ... 1110
Spence v Crawford [1939] ... 1045, 1046, 2336
Spencer v Harding (1870) ... 207, 208, 212
Spencer's Pictures Ltd v Cosens (1918) ... 220, 254
Spettabile Consorzio Veneziano di Armamento e Navigazione v Northumberland Shipbuilding Co Ltd (1919) ... 1938
Spies v Commonwealth Bank of Australia (1991) ... 351, 1028
Sport Internationaal Bussum BV v Inter-Footwear Ltd [1984] ... 1979
Sportsvision Australia Pty Ltd v Tallglen Pty Ltd (1998) ... 712
Sprague v Booth [1909] ... 1809
Spring v Guardian Assurance Plc [1995] ... 1030, 1032
Spunwill Pty Ltd v BAB Pty Ltd (1994) ... 712
Spurling (J) Ltd v Bradshaw [1956] ... 618, 763
St Clair v Petricevic (1988) ... 1330
St John Shipping Corp v Joseph Rank Ltd [1957] ... 1604, 1607, 1609, 1614, 1623
Stack v Coast Securities (No 9) Pty Ltd (1983) ... 1654
Stanton v Richardson (1872) ... 1955
Stapleton-Bretherton, Re [1941] ... 911
Startup v Macdonald (1843) ... 1815

State Rail Authority of New South Wales v Codelfa Construction Pty Ltd (1982) ... 2064
Steadman v Steadman [1976] ... 521, 522, 524
Steedman v Drinkle [1916] ... 2240, 2332
Steele v Tardiani (1946) ... 1826, 1832, 2314, 2325
Steelwood Carriers Inc of Monrovia Liberia v Evimeria Compania Naviera SA of Panama (The Agios Giorgis) [1976] ... 1839
Steinberg v Scale (Leeds) Ltd [1923] ... 820, 821
Stenhouse Australia Ltd v Phillips [1974] ... 1637, 1702, 1736
Stern v McArthur (1988) ... 1979, 2240, 2336, 2404
Sternbeck v Sternbeck (1968) ... 1302
Stevens v Keogh (1946) ... 1629
Stevenson v Hook (1956) ... 1935, 2322
Stevenson Jaques & Co v McLean (1880) ... 243, 244, 251, 252
Stewart v Kennedy (1890) ... 1266
—v Oriental Fire and Marine Insurance Co Ltd [1985] ... 1614
—v Reavell's Garage [1952] ... 1818
Stickney v Keeble [1915] ... 1852, 1961
Stilk v Myrick (1809) ... 344, 345
Stillwell (BS) & Co Pty Ltd v Budget Rent-A-Car System Pty Ltd [1990] ... 256, 1837
Stillwell Trucks Pty Ltd v Nectar Brook Investments Pty Ltd (1993) ... 410
Stinchcombe v Thomas [1957] ... 231, 266, 2337
Stirling v Maitland (1864) ... 1810
Stirling Properties Ltd v Yerba Pty Ltd (1987) ... 1816
Stockloser v Johnson [1954] ... 2332, 2333
Stocks v Wilson [1913] ... 823, 824
Stocks & Holdings (Constructors) Pty Ltd v Arrowsmith (1964) ... 267
Stocznia Gdanska SA v Latvian Shipping Co [1996] ... 2135, 2224, 2229, 2233
Stone v Wythipol (1583) ... 305
Stoolwinder v Southern Health Care Network (2000) ... 1104

Strada Estates Pty Ltd v Harcla Hotels Pty Ltd (1980) ... 1976
Strang v Owens (1925) ... 1728
Strangborough v Warner (1589) ... 105
Streamline Fashions Pty Ltd, Re [1965] ... 1263
Street v Blay (1831) ... 1061, 1981, 2306
Strickland v Turner (1852) ... 1215
Strikeman v Dawson (1847) ... 823
Ströms Bruks Aktie Bolag v Hutchison [1905] ... 2109
Strongman (1945) Ltd v Sincock [1955] ... 1726
Strover v Harrington [1988] ... 1076
Subdivisions Ltd v Payne [1934] ... 203, 1225, 1732
Suburban Homes Pty Ltd v Topper (1929) ... 1123
Sudbrook Trading Estate Ltd v Eggleton [1983] ... 267, 268, 269
Suisse Atlantique Société d'Armement Maritime SA v NV Rotterdamsche Kolen Centrale [1967] ... 748, 754, 755, 756, 758, 1907, 1937, 2239
Suleman v Shahsavari [1988] ... 2172
Sullivan v Glennon (1986) ... 1970
Sultman v Bond [1956] ... 810, 814, 819
Summergreene v Parker (1950) ... 267, 273
Summers v Commonwealth (1918) ... 644, 1939, 2333
Sumpter v Hedges [1898] ... 1823, 1835, 2325
Sunbird Plaza Pty Ltd v Maloney (1988) ... 507, 1815, 1943, 1969, 1973, 1979, 1983, 2158, 2159, 2229
Sundell (TA) & Sons Pty Ltd v Emm Yannoulatos (Overseas) Pty Ltd (1955) ... 1312, 1316
Surrey County Council v Bredero Homes Ltd [1993] ... 2329
Sutherland Shire Council v Heyman (1985) ... 1034
Sutton v AJ Thompson Pty Ltd (1987) ... 1121
Suttor v Gundowda Pty Ltd (1950) ... 502, 1967
Svanosio v McNamara (1956) ... 1058, 1218, 1219, 1230, 1231, 1255, 2318

Table of Cases

Swain v The Law Society [1982] ... 2131
Swaisland v Dearsley (1861) ... 1237
Sweet & Maxwell Ltd v Universal News Services Ltd [1964] ... 267
Sybron Corp v Rochem Ltd [1984] ... 1018
Sydney City Council v Ilenace Pty Ltd [1984] ... 1730
Sydney Corp v West (1965) ... 750, 754, 762
Sydney MC v M'Beath (1881) ... 858
Sykes v Reserve Bank of Australia (1998) ... 1108
Sykes (F & G) (Wessex) Ltd v Fine Fare Ltd [1967] ... 269
Sykes v Stratton [1972] ... 1714, 1718
Symes v Hughes (1870) ... 1715
Synge v Synge [1894] ... 1942, 1966, 2161
Syros Shipping Co SA v Elaghill Trading Co (The Proodos C) [1981] ... 345, 351, 375, 1304
Sze Hai Tong Bank Ltd v Rambler Cycle Co Ltd [1959] ... 756
Szep v Blanken [1969] ... 1048
Taco Co of Australia Inc v Taco Bell Pty Ltd (1982) ... 1105
Taddy v Sterious [1904] ... 913
Tai Hing Cotton Mill Ltd v Liu Chong Hing Bank Ltd [1986] ... 624, 635, 2148
Talk of the Town Pty Ltd v Hagstrom (1990) ... 1649
Tallerman & Co Pty Ltd v Nathan's Merchandise (Victoria) Pty Ltd (1957) ... 231, 232, 236, 525, 526
Tamplin v James (1880) ... 1251, 2411
Tamplin (FA) SS Co Ltd v Anglo-Mexican Petroleum Products Co Ltd [1916] ... 2008, 2013, 2051, 2052, 2056
Tankexpress A/S v Compagnie Financière Belge des Petroles SA (The Petrofina) [1949] ... 1839
Tasman Express Line Ltd v J I Case (Australia) Pty Ltd (1992) ... 761
Tasmanian Credits Ltd, Re; Ex parte Pitt (1930) ... 255
Tate v Williamson (1866) ... 1403, 1412
Tatem (WJ) Ltd v Gamboa [1939] ... 2039, 2052

Taylor v Allon [1966] ... 239
—v Bowers (1876) ... 1716, 1717, 1724
—v Caldwell (1863) ... 2003, 2012, 2015, 2050, 2053
—v Chester (1869) ... 1707, 1724
—v Johnson (1983) ... 110, 118, 1213, 1224, 1231, 1250, 1251, 1254
—v Oakes Roncoroni & Co (1922) ... 1943
—v Smith [1926] ... 1274
—v Taylor (1890) ... 1624
Taylors Fashions Ltd v Liverpool Victoria Trustees Co Ltd [1982] ... 369, 377
TC Industrial Plant Pty Ltd v Robert's Queensland Pty Ltd (1963) ... 2113, 2133
TCN Channel 9 Pty Ltd v Hayden Enterprises Pty Ltd (1989) ... 704, 2133, 2135, 2137, 2162
Teachers Health Investments Pty Ltd v Wynne [1996] ... 1513
Teheran-Europe Co Ltd v ST Belton (Tractors) Ltd [1968] ... 906
Telstra Corporation Ltd v Optus Communications Pty Ltd (1997) ... 1107
Tenji v Henneberry & Associates Pty Ltd (2000) ... 1115, 1116
Tennants (Lancashire) Ltd v C S Wilson & Co Ltd [1917] ... 2061
Tennent v City of Glasgow Bank (1879) ... 1043
—v Tennents (1870) ... 1015
Terkol Rederierne v Petroleo Brasileiro SA (The Badagry) [1985] ... 629
Tern Minerals NL v Kalbara Mining NL (1990) ... 273
Terrex Resources NL v Magnet Petroleum Pty Ltd [1988] ... 712
Territory Insurance Office v Adlington (1992) ... 380
Texaco Ltd v Mulberry Filling Station Ltd [1972] ... 1645
Thackwell v Barclays Bank Plc [1986] ... 1703, 1710
Thai Trading Co (a firm) v Taylor [1998] ... 1630
Thake v Maurice [1986] ... 603, 2152
Thearle v Keeley (1958) ... 2036
Thomas v Thomas (1842) ...308, 315, 319, 323, 327

References are to paragraphs

Thomas Bates & Son Ltd v Wyndham's Lingerie Ltd [1981] ... 267

Thomas Brown & Sons Ltd v Fazal Deen (1962) ... 1706, 1721, 1723, 1724, 1730, 1737

Thomas National Transport (Melbourne) Pty Ltd v May & Baker (Australia) Pty Ltd (1966) ... 751, 754, 761, 764

Thompson v ASDA-MFI Group Plc [1988] ... 1809, 1967

—v Hudson (1869) ... 2217

—v Palmer (1933) ... 367, 368, 1974

Thompson (WL) Ltd v Robinson (Gunmakers) Ltd [1955] ... 2140

Thomson v McInnes (1911) ... 514, 515

Thorby v Goldberg (1965) ... 270

Thorne v Motor Trade Association [1937] ... 1319

Thorne (L G) & Co Pty Ltd v Thomas Borthwick & Sons (A'Asia) Ltd (1955) ... 707

Thornley v Tilley (1925) ... 712, 720, 2328

Thornton v Shoe Lane Parking Ltd [1971] ... 208, 617

Thoroughgood's case (1584) ... 1269

Thors v Weekes (1989) ... 2040, 2334, 2407

Three Rivers Trading Co Ltd v Gwinear & District Farmers Ltd (1967) ... 262

Thurstan v Nottingham Permanent Benefit Building Society [1902] ... 818

Thwaites v Ryan [1984] ... 521, 522

Tilley v Official Receiver (1960) ... 1816

—v Thomas (1867) ... 1850

Timmerman v Nervina Industries (International) Pty Ltd [1983] ... 264, 268, 1817

Timmins v Moreland Street Property Co Ltd [1958] ... 515

Ting v Blanche (1993) ... 1108

Tinn v Hoffman & Co (1873) ... 228, 239

Tinsley v Milligan [1994] ... 1703, 1721

Tito v Waddell (No 2) [1977] ... 909, 2107

Tobacco Institute of Australia Ltd v Australian Federation of Consumer Organisations Inc (1989) ... 1530

Toby Constructions Products Pty Ltd v Computa Bar (Sales) Pty Ltd [1983] ... 511

Todd v Nichol [1957] ... 404

Todorovic v Waller (1981) ... 2168

Toikan International Insurance Broking Pty Ltd v Plasteel Windows Australia Pty Ltd (1989) ... 110

Tonelli v Komirra Pty Ltd [1972] ... 264

Tonitto v Bassal (1992) ... 513, 515

Toohey v Gunther (1928) ... 913

Tool Metal Manufacturing Co Ltd v Tungsten Electric Co Ltd [1955] ... 372

Tooth v Fleming (1859) ... 235, 236

Tooth & Co Ltd v Barker [1960] ... 913

—v Bryen (No 2) (1922) ... 273

Torkington v Magee [1902] ... 909

Torminster Properties Ltd v Green [1982] ... 2226

Torr v Harpur (1940) ... 759, 2333

Torrance v Bolton (1872) ... 1253

Torvald Klaveness A/S v Arni Maritime Corp [1994] ... 1952

Toscano v Holland Securities Pty Ltd (1985) ... 1517, 1518, 1519

Total Gas Marketing Ltd v Arco British Ltd [1998] ... 730, 741

Total Oil Great Britain Ltd v Thompson Garages (Biggin Hill) Ltd [1972] ... 1936

Toteff v Antonas (1952) ... 1069, 1070, 1071

Toyota Motor Corp Australia Ltd v Ken Morgan Motors Pty Ltd [1994] ... 203, 405, 412

Tozer Kemsley & Millbourn (A'Asia) Pty Ltd v Collier's Interstate Transport Service Ltd (1956) ... 762

Trade Practices Commission v Milreis Pty Ltd (1977) ... 1116

Tramways Advertising Pty Ltd v Luna Park (NSW) Ltd (1938) ... 727, 1911, 1915, 1971, 2218, 2221

Trans Realties Pty Ltd v Grbac [1975] ... 1253

Trans Trust SPRL v Danubian Trading Co Ltd [1952] ... 1919, 2151

References are to paragraphs

Table of Cases

Trans-Pacific Insurance Co (Australia) Ltd v Grand Union Insurance Co Ltd (1989) ... 1809
Transworld Shipping Ltd, Re (1975) ... 873
Trawl Industries of Australia Pty Ltd v Effem Foods Pty Ltd Trading as 'Uncle Bens of Australia' (1992) ... 263, 268, 271, 713
Traywinds Pty Ltd v Cooper [1989] ... 220, 248, 256, 1837
Trazray Pty Ltd v Russell Foundries Pty Ltd (1988) ... 267, 268, 707
Treadwell v Martin (1977) ... 1402
Tremills v Benton (1892) ... 844
Trendtex Trading Corp v Credit Suisse [1982] ... 1629, 1630
Trepca Mines Ltd, Re (No 2) [1962] ... 1630, 1732
Tresize v National Australia Bank Ltd (1994) ... 1405
Tribe v Tribe [1996] ... 1715, 1718
Tricontinental Corp Ltd v HDFI Ltd (1990) ... 735, 740, 1838
Trident General Insurance Co Ltd v McNiece Bros Pty Ltd (1987) ... 917, 926
—v—(1988) ... 118, 902, 903, 905, 907, 911, 912, 917, 918, 919, 920, 921, 922, 926, 2329
Tri-Global (Aust) Pty Ltd v Colonial Mutual Life Assurance Society Ltd (1992) ... 1528
Tropical Traders Ltd v Goonan (1964) ... 1971, 2235, 2332
—v—(No 2) [1965] ... 2332
True v Amalgamated Collieries of WA Ltd [1940] ... 1828
Trueman v Fenton (1777) ...306
Trustees Executors & Agency Co Ltd v Peters (1960) ... 261
Tsakiroglou & Co Ltd v Noblee Thorl GmbH [1962] ... 2005, 2006, 2016
Tsangaris v Gaymark Investments Pty Ltd (1986) ... 2407
Tucker v Godfrey (1862) ... 222
Tufton v Sperni [1952] ... 1404
Tulk v Moxhay (1848) ... 908, 913
Turner v Australasian Coal and Shale Employees Federation (1984) ... 2420
—v Bladin (1951) ... 2406
—v Goldsmith [1891] ... 2012
—v Labafox International Pty Ltd (1974) ... 1974
Turner Kempson & Co Pty Ltd v Camm [1922] ... 222, 224
Turriff Construction Ltd v Regalia Knitting Mills Ltd [1972] ... 2317
Tutt v Doyle (1997) ... 1255
Tweddle v Atkinson (1861) ... 319, 901, 903, 910
Tydhof v Miethke (1982) ... 1258
UBAF Ltd v European American Banking Corp [1984] ... 1036, 1067
UGS Finance Ltd v National Mortgage Bank of Greece and National Bank of Greece SA [1964] ... 754, 758
Ulbrick v Laidlaw [1924] ... 211
Union Bank of Australia Ltd v Puddy [1949] ... 1014
Union Eagle Ltd v Golden Achievement Ltd [1997] ... 1979, 2333
Union Fidelity Trustee Co v Gibson [1971] ... 1410
Union Steamship Co v Ewart (1893) ... 238
Unisys International Services Ltd v Eastern Counties Newspapers Ltd [1991] ... 229
United Australia Ltd v Barclays Bank Ltd [1941] ... 1301, 1971, 1973, 2327
United City Merchants (Investments) Ltd v Royal Bank of Canada [1983] ... 1603
United Dominions Corp (Jamaica) Ltd v Shoucair [1969] ... 526
United Dominions Corp Ltd v Brian Pty Ltd (1985) ... 1014, 2328
United Dominions Trust (Commercial) Ltd v Eagle Aircraft Services Ltd [1968] ... 249, 1836, 1838, 1965
—v Ennis [1968] ... 2216
United Dominions Trust Ltd v Western [1976] ... 1275
United Motels Ltd v Cooper [1964] ... 527
United Scientific Holdings Ltd v Burnley BC [1978] ... 256, 1852, 1949, 1951, 1952, 1962, 1979
United Shoe Machinery Co of Canada v Brunet [1909] ... 1047

References are to paragraphs

United States v Motor Trucks Ltd [1924] ... 1258, 1259
Unity Insurance Brokers Pty Ltd v Rocco Pezzano Pty Ltd (1998) ... 2121
Universal Cargo Carriers Corp v Citati [1957] ... 738, 1814, 1930, 1935, 1942, 1943, 1944, 1955, 1956, 2006, 2014, 2025
Universal Guarantee Pty Ltd v Carlile [1957] ... 222, 224
Universe Tankships Inc of Monrovia v International Transport Workers Federation (The Universe Sentinel) [1983] ... 1313, 1314, 1319, 1322, 1323, 1329,
Unley Democratic Association, Re [1936] ... 2004, 2043
Update Constructions Pty Ltd v Rozelle Child Care Centre Ltd (1990) ... 382, 1991
Upper Hunter County District Council v Australian Chilling & Freezing Co Ltd (1968) ... 260, 263, 264
Upton-on-Severn RDC v Powell [1942] ... 1224
Urquhart v Macpherson (1878) ... 1039, 1051
Vacwell Engineering Co Ltd v BDH Chemicals Ltd [1971] ... 2126
Vadasz v Pioneer Concrete (SA) Pty Ltd (1995) ... 1045, 1402, 1513, 2336
Valentini v Canali (1889) ... 824
Valpy v Manley (1845) ... 1309, 1316
Van den Berg v Giles [1979] ... 2335
Van Der Sterren (H & E) v Cibernetics (Holdings) Pty Ltd (1970) ... 760
Van der Waal v Goodenough [1983] ... 268
Vanbergen v St Edmund's Properties Ltd [1933] ... 389
Vancouver Malt and Sake Brewing Co Ltd v Vancouver Breweries Ltd [1934] ... 1642, 1647
Vandepitte v Preferred Accident Insurance Corp of New York [1933] ... 901
Vantage Navigation Corp v Suhail and Saud Bahwan Building Materials LLC (The Alev) [1989] ... 306, 1320, 1322
Varley v Fotheringham [1905] ... 225

—v Spatt [1955] ... 1603
Varty v British South Africa Co [1964] ... 247
Varverakis v Compagnia de Navegacion Artico SA (The Merak) [1976] ... 275
Vass v Commonwealth (2000) ... 871
Veitch v Sinclair [1975] ... 350, 1219, 1223
Veivers v Cordingley [1989] ... 240, 250
Verna Trading Pty Ltd v New India Assurance Co Ltd [1991] ... 741
Verreault (JE) & Fils Ltee v A-G for Quebec (1976) ... 873
Vickery's Motors Pty Ltd v Tarrant [1924] ... 818, 819
Victoria Laundry (Windsor) Ltd v Newman Industries Ltd [1949] ... 2124, 2127
Viditz v O'Hagan [1900] ... 805
Vigers v Cook [1919] ... 1832
Vimig Pty Ltd v Contract Tooling Pty Ltd (1986) ... 1054
Vine v National Dock Labour Board [1957] ... 1967
Visic v State Government Insurance Commission (1990) ... 922
Vita Food Products Inc v Unus Shipping Co Ltd [1939] ... 1619, 1703
Vitol SA v Norelf Ltd (The Santa Clara) [1996] ... 229, 1970
Vroon BV v Foster's Brewing Group Ltd [1994] ... 203, 268, 625, 1983
W & J Investments Ltd v Bunting [1984] ... 2159, 2160, 2211
WA Pines Pty Ltd v Registrar of Companies [1976] ... 214
WA Woodside Petroeum Development Pty Ltd v H & R E-W Pty Ltd (1997) ... 918
—v—(1999) ... 918
Wadsworth v Lydall [1981] ... 2151
Waghorn v Linden Manufacturing Pty Ltd [1970] ... 1818
Waimond Pty Ltd v Byrne (1989) ... 2131
Wakeling v Ripley (1951) ... 266, 404
Waldron v Tsimiklis (1975) ... 260
Walford v Miles [1992] ... 271
Walk v Matthews (1914) ... 207
Walker v Armstrong (1856) ... 1256

Table of Cases

—v Boyle [1982] ... 766, 1123
Walker Hobson & Hill Ltd v Johnson [1981] ... 1036
Wallace v Brodribb (1985) ... 208, 214, 215
—v Hermans (1974) ... 1971
—v Walplan Pty Ltd (1985) ... 215
Walley v Holt (1876) ... 825
Wallis v Pratt [1910] ... 1911
—v—[1911] ... 638, 751, 1830
Walters v Cooper [1967] ... 1934, 1985
—v Morgan (1861) ... 1013
Waltip Pty Ltd v Capalaba Park Shopping Centre Pty Ltd (1989) ... 1124
Walton Stores Ltd v Sydney City Council [1968] ... 762
Waltons Stores (Interstate) Ltd v Maher (1988) ... 118, 369, 374, 375, 376, 377, 378, 379, 385, 521, 524, 2169, 2317
Warburton v National Westminster Finance Australia Ltd (1988) ... 1275
Ward v Byham [1956] ... 342, 361
—v Ellerton [1927] ... 2333
—v Eltherington [1982] ... 865
—v Griffiths Bros Ltd (1928) ... 2337
Ward (RV) Ltd v Bignall [1967] ... 1815
Wardley Australia Ltd v Western Australia (1992) ... 118, 1067, 1069, 1071, 1112, 1113
Warinco AG v Samor SpA [1979] ... 1938
Waring v S J Brentnall Ltd [1975] ... 1229, 1232
Warlow v Harrison (1858) ... 211
Warner v Elders Rural Finance Ltd (1993) ... 1110
Warner Bros Pictures Inc v Nelson [1937] ... 2420
Warren v Mendy [1989] ... 2420
—v Nut Farms of Australia Pty Ltd [1980] ... 511
Watcham v Attorney-General of the East Africa Protectorate [1919] ... 712, 718
Waters Trading Co Ltd v Dalgety & Co Ltd (1951) ... 923
Waterside Workers' Federation of Australia v Stewart (1919) ... 2215

Wathes (Western) Ltd v Austins (Menswear) Ltd [1976] ... 754
Watson v Campbell (No 2) [1920] ... 819, 825
—v Delaney (1991) ... 521, 522
—v Phibbs (1985) ... 723
—v Prager [1991] ... 1637, 1651
Watson's Bay and South Shore Ferry Co Ltd v Whitfield (1919) ... 872
Watt v Westhoven [1933] ... 1061
Watts v Morrow [1991] ... 2152
Watts Watts & Co Ltd v Mitsui & Co Ltd [1917] ... 2026, 2063
Waugh v Morris (1873) ... 1621, 1622
Way v Latilla [1937] ... 331, 2337
Weatherby v Banham (1832) ... 229
Webb Distributors (Aust) Pty Ltd v State of Victoria (1993) ... 118, 1043, 1116, 1526
Webster, Re (1975) ... 209, 223
Wehr v Thom [1969] ... 1071
Welbourne v Australian Postal Commission (1983) ... 1839
Welby v Drake (1825) ...359
Wells v Birtchnell (1893) ... 207
Wells (Merstham) Ltd v Buckland Sand and Silica Ltd [1965] ... 614
Welston v North Cornwall District Council [1997] ... 1030
Wendt v Bruce (1931) ... 1961, 1971
Wenham v Ella (1972) ... 2104, 2110, 2113, 2114, 2124, 2151, 2173
Wenkheim v Arndt (1873) ... 237
Wenning v Robinson [1964–65] ... 268
Wentworth v Woollahra Municipal Council (1982) ... 2169
Wertheim v Chicoutimi Pulp Co [1911] ... 2141
West v AGC (Advances) Ltd (1986) ... 1517, 1522, 1528
West London Commercial Bank Ltd v Kitson (1884) ... 1010, 1011, 1012
West Midlands Co-operative Society Ltd v Tipton [1986] ... 1969
Westbay Seafoods (Aust) Pty Ltd v Transpacific Standardbred Agency Pty Ltd (1996) ... 1114
Westco Motors Distributors Pty Ltd v Palmer [1979] ... 1654
Western Australian Insurance Co Ltd v Dayton (1924) ... 1974

References are to paragraphs

Western Electric Co (Australia) Ltd v Ward (1933) ... 2208
Westfield Holdings Ltd v ACT Television Pty Ltd (1992) ... 271
Westmelton (Vic) Pty Ltd v Archer and Shulman [1982] ... 1408, 1409, 1411
Westminster Estates Pty Ltd v Calleja (1970) ... 216
—v— [1970] ... 248
Weston v Beaufils (1994) ... 1714
Westpac Banking Corp v Dawson (1990) ... 312
—v Robinson (1993) ... 1015
Westralian Farmers Co-operative Ltd v Southern Meat Packers Ltd [1981] ... 915
Westralian Farmers Ltd v Commonwealth Agricultural Service Engineers Ltd (1936) ... 1821, 1967, 2065, 2067, 2226, 2231
Westwood v Secretary of State for Employment [1985] ... 2134
Wharton v McKenzie (1844) ... 810
Wheeler v Atkinson (1925) ... 1055
—v Sargeant (1893) ... 1408
Wheeler Grace & Pierucci Pty Ltd v Wright (1989) ... 1108, 1121
Whim Well Copper Mines Ltd v Pratt (1910) ... 2015
Whincup v Hughes (1871) ... 2067, 2306
White, Re [1959] ... 806
—v Australian and New Zealand Theatres Ltd (1943) ... 712, 717
—v Bluett (1853) ... 339
—v John Warwick & Co Ltd [1953] ... 764
—v Jones [1995] ... 922, 1030
White and Carter (Councils) Ltd v McGregor [1962] ... 1930, 1940, 1968, 1983, 2137, 2220, 2221, 2223, 2224
White Cliffs Opal Mines Ltd v Miller (1904) ... 231, 254
White Rose Flour Milling Co Pty Ltd v Australian Wheat Board (1944) ... 1316, 1318
White Trucks Pty Ltd v Riley (1948) ... 220, 228, 229, 249, 1940
Whitehead, In the Estate of (1986) ... 360
Whitelaw v Delaney [1914] ... 1228

Whitfeld v De Lauret & Co Ltd (1920) ... 2103
Whitfords Beach Pty Ltd v Gadson [1991] ... 915
Whitlock v Brew (1968) ... 261, 272
Whittet v State Bank of New South Wales (1991) ... 716
Whittingham v Murdy (1889) ... 818
Whundo Copper Syndicate v Ferrari [1962] ... 813
Wickman Machine Tool Sales Ltd v L Schuler AG [1972] ... 730
Wigan v Edwards (1973) ... 341, 350, 353, 1966
—v English & Scottish Law Life Assurance Association [1909] ... 315
Wight v Foran (1987) ... 1933
—v Haberdan Pty Ltd [1984] ... 2406
Wilcher v Steain (1961) ... 1020, 1022, 1037
Wild v Simpson [1912] ... 1707, 1728
Wilde v Gibson (1848) ... 1054
Wilding v Sanderson [1897] ... 1209
Wilkie v London Passenger Transport Board [1947] ... 208
Wilkinson v Clements (1872) ... 2403
—v Coverdale (1793) ... 303
—v Detmold (1890) ... 1022, 1123
—v Osborne (1915) ... 1619, 1620, 1624
Willesden v Webb [1937] ... 267
William Sindall Plc v Cambridgeshire County Council [1994] ... 1077, 1210, 1224, 1229, 1230, 2055, 2169
William Thomas & Sons v Harrowing SS Co [1915] ... 1823, 1832
William Tibbits & Co v Holt (1890) ... 1061
Williams v Bulat [1992] ... 1242
—v Byrnes (1863) ... 216
—v Carwardine (1833) ... 208
—v— (1927) ... 240
—v Johnson [1937] ... 1408
—v Moor (1843) ... 819
—v Moore [1963] ... 1064
—v Roffey Bros & Nicholls (Contractors) Ltd [1991] ... 317, 348, 1314
—v Williams (1853) ... 255
—v— [1957] ... 342
Williamson v Diab [1988] ... 1728

References are to paragraphs

Table of Cases

—v Murdoch (1912) ... 1831
Williamson (J C) Ltd v Lukey (1931) ... 521, 522, 523, 524, 2169, 2401, 2403, 2408, 2413, 2417, 2419
Willmott, Re [1948] ... 806, 818
Wilsher v Essex Area Health Authority [1988] ... 2120
Wilson v Belfast Corp (1921) ... 217, 226
—v Brisbane City Council [1931] ... 1023, 1038
—v Darling Island Stevedoring & Lighterage Co Ltd (1956) ... 901, 905, 907, 919, 923
—v Kingsgate Mining Industries Pty Ltd [1973] ... 390, 393
—v Maynard Shipbuilding Consultants AB [1978] ... 719
—v Union Trustee Co (1923) ... 1038
—v Winton [1969] ... 225
Wilton v Farnworth (1948) ... 1507
Wiluszynski v Tower Hamlets London BC [1989] ... 1832
Wings Ltd v Ellis [1985] ... 2153
Winks v W H Heck & Sons Pty Ltd [1986] ... 712, 1261
Winn v Bull (1877) ... 273
Winterton Constructions Pty Ltd v Hambros Australia Ltd (1991) ... 2326
—v— (1992) ... 1943, 2308
With v O'Flanagan [1936] ... 1017
WMC Resources Ltd v Leighton Contractors Pty Ltd (1999) ... 267
Woden Squash Courts Pty Ltd v Zero Builders Pty Ltd [1976] ... 515
Wollondilly Shire Council v Picton Power Lines Pty Ltd (1994) ... 2216
Wong Lai Ying v Chinachem Investment Co Ltd (1979) ... 2033, 2040
Wood v Little (1921) ... 1624
Wood Factory Pty Ltd v Kiritos Pty Ltd (1985) ... 1936, 1970
Woodar Investment Development Ltd v Wimpey Construction UK Ltd [1980] ... 912, 1933, 1941, 1947
Woodhouse AC Israel Cocoa Ltd SA v Nigerian Produce Marketing Co Ltd [1972] ... 372

Woodside Offshore Petroleum Pty Ltd v Attwood Oceanics Inc [1986] ... 267, 275
Woolf v Associated Finance Pty Ltd [1956] ... 824
—v Collis Removal Service [1948] ... 1993
Woolwich Equitable Building Society v IRC [1993] ... 2308
Woolworths Ltd v Kelly (1991) ... 302, 307, 323, 348, 351
Workers Trust & Merchant Bank Ltd v Dojap Investments Ltd [1993] ... 2333
Workman Clark & Co Ltd v Brazileno [1908] ... 2206
Wright v Carter [1903] ... 1405
—v Dean [1948] ... 1965
—v Gasweld Pty Ltd (1991) ... 1738, 1739
—v Madden [1992] ... 611
—v TNT Management Pty Ltd (1988) ... 1109
—v—(1989) ... 625, 633
Wroth v Tyler [1974] ... 2165, 2172
Wyatt v Ball [1955] ... 308
—v Kreglinger [1933] ... 324, 1634, 1639
Yango Pastoral Co Pty Ltd v First Chicago Australia Ltd (1978) ... 1604, 1607, 1609, 1613, 1614, 1615
Yardley v Saunders [1982] ... 2239, 2333
Yaroomba Beach Development Co Pty Ltd v Coeur de Lion Investments Pty Ltd (1989) ... 721, 1622
Yates Building Co Ltd v F J Pulleyn & Sons (York) Ltd [1976] ... 228
Yeoman Credit Ltd v Apps [1962] ... 757, 759
—v Latter [1961] ... 507
—v Waragowski [1961] ... 2159
Yerkey v Jones (1939) ... 1405, 1408, 1507, 1514
York Air Conditioning & Refrigeration (A'sia) Pty Ltd v Commonwealth (1949) ... 261, 267, 269
York Glass Co Ltd v Jubb (1925) ... 841, 842, 843, 844
Yorke v Lucas (1985) ... 1114, 1121
Yorkshire Insurance Co Ltd v Craine [1922] ... 382, 391, 392, 1972, 1976

References are to paragraphs

Young v Queensland Trustees Ltd (1956) ... 2201
Young & Marten Ltd v McManus Childs Ltd [1969] ... 511, 633
Ypatia Halcoussi (The) [1985] ... 1265
Zamperoni Decorators Pty Ltd v Lo Presti [1983] ... 1831
Zea Star Shipping Co SA v Parley Augustsson (Invest) A/S [1984] ... 2202
Ziel Nominees Pty Ltd v VACC Insurance Co (1975) ... 904
Zimmin v Wentworth Properties Pty Ltd (1959) ... 273
Zoneff v Elcom Credit Union Ltd (1990) ... 1113
Zouch d Abbot & Hallet v Parsons (1765) ... 804, 805, 808
Zsadony v Pizer [1955] ... 2334
Zucker v Straightlace Pty Ltd (1986) ... 1970, 1971
—v—(1987) ... 244

Table of Statutes

References are to paragraphs

UNIFORM COMPANIES LEGISLATION

ACT 1962; NSW 1961; NT 1962;
    QLD 1961; SA 1962; TAS 1962;
    VIC 1961; WA 1961 ... 855
s 19 ... 855

s 20 ... 855
s 20(1) ... 855
s 20(2) ... 855
s 67 ... 1737

COMMONWEALTH

Australian Capital Territory Supreme
    Court Act 1933
s 20 ... 2169
ss 25–34 ... 2169

Australian Securities and Investments
    Commission Act 2001
s 12BA ... 1103
s 12CA ... 1523
s 12CB ... 1523
s 12CC ... 1523
s 12DA ... 1103
Pt 2 ... 1103

Banking Act 1959
s 8 ... 1614

Bankruptcy Act 1966
s 7(1) ... 879
s 58(1) ... 875
s 115 ... 875
s 116 ... 875
s 120 ... 1618
s 121 ... 1618
s 122 ... 875
s 122(1) ... 1618
s 122(2) ... 1618
s 123 ... 875
s 123(1) ... 876
s 125 ... 876
s 126(1) ... 876
s 133 ... 875
s 133(7) ... 875
s 133(8) ... 875
s 187(1) ... 360
s 269(a) ... 876
s 304A ... 876
Pt X ... 360

Bills of Exchange Act 1909
s 8(1) ... 512
s 32(1) ... 333
s 50 ... 1814

Carriage of Goods by Sea Act 1991 ...
    925

Cheques Act 1986
s 35(1)(a) ... 333

Commonwealth Constitution ... 870
s 51(xx) ... 1101
s 83 ... 871

Consumer Credit Code ... 1981
s 21 ... 2241
s 21(1) ... 1617
s 21(2) ... 1617
s 40(1) ... 1617
s 44 ... 1617
s 44(3) ... 1617
s 70 ... 1516
s 71(b) ... 2241
s 169 ... 1617

Corporations Act 2001 (Cth) ... 849,
    850, 855, 1103
s 9 ... 860
s 124 ... 856
s 125(1) ... 856
s 125(2) ... 856
s 126 ... 859, 860, 863
s 127 ... 859, 860
s 128(3) ... 861
s 128(4) ... 861
s 129 ... 861
s 130 ... 861
s 131 ... 863
s 132 ... 863
s 140(1) ... 410
s 140(2) ... 410
s 995 ... 1103, 1104
s 995A ... 1103
s 1324(10) ... 2169

Currency Act 1965
s 16 ... 1815

Defence Act 1903
  s 118 ... 1625
Electronic Transactions Act 1999
  s 5 ... 238
  s 14(1) ... 238
  s 14(2) ... 238
  s 14(3) ... 238
  s 14(4) ... 238
  s 14(7) ... 238
Family Law Act 1975 ... 1633
  s 119 ... 879
Federal Court of Australia Act 1976
  ss 21–33 ... 2169
Financial Services Reform Act 2001 ... 1103
Financial Services Reform (Consequential Provisions) Act 2001 ... 1103, 1523
  Sch 1 ... 1103
Industrial Relations Reform Act 1993 ... 1828
Insurance Contracts Act 1984 ... 904, 1015
  s 37 ... 617
  s 43 ... 1626
  s 48 ... 916, 917
  s 48A ... 916
  s 49 ... 916
  s 51 ... 916
Judiciary Act 1903
  s 31 ... 2169
  s 32 ... 2169
  s 64 ... 871
  Pt IX ... 869
  Pt IXA ... 869
Life Insurance Act 1945
  s 85(1) ... 806
  s 199(2) ... 803
Marine Insurance Act 1909 ... 512
  s 39(1) ... 730
Marriage Act 1961
  s 11 ... 810
  s 111A ... 508, 1633, 1937
Petroleum Retail Marketing Franchise Act 1980
  s 7 ... 1617
Postal Corporation Act 1989
  s 32 ... 235
Reserve Bank Act 1959
  s 36(1) ... 1815
Trade Practices Act 1974 ... 1003, 1530, 1645, 1738
  s 4 ... 642

s 4(1) ... 1524, 1654
s 4B ... 637
s 4D ... 1655
s 4M ... 1655
s 5 ... 1101
s 6 ... 215, 1101, 1654
s 21 ... 1113
s 45 ... 1655
s 45(1) ... 1656
s 45(2) ... 1656
s 45B(1) ... 1656
s 45E(1) ... 1656
s 46 ... 1656
s 47 ... 340, 1656
s 48 ... 913, 1656
s 50 ... 1656
s 51 ... 1655
s 51A ... 1108, 1119
s 51AA ... 1523, 1524, 1526, 1527, 1528
s 51AA(1) ... 1524
s 51AB ... 1523, 1524, 1525, 1526, 1527, 1528
s 51AB(2) ... 1524
s 51AB(3) ... 1524
s 51AB(4) ... 1524
s 51AB(5) ... 1528
s 51AB(6) ... 1524, 1528
s 51AC ... 1523, 1524, 1525, 1526, 1527, 1528
s 51AC(2) ... 1524
s 51AC(3) ... 1524, 1528
s 51AC(3)(k) ... 1503
s 51AC(4) ... 1524, 1528
s 51AC(4)(a)–(e) ... 1524
s 51AC(4)(f)–(k) ... 1524
s 51AC(4)(k) ... 1503
s 51AC(5) ... 1524
s 51AC(6) ... 1524
s 51AC(10) ... 1524
s 51ACAA ... 1525
s 52 ... 766, 1101–1121, 1123, 1124, 1523, 1656, 2164
s 52A ... 1522, 1523, 1524
s 53 ... 1656
s 53(g) ... 1123
s 53A ... 1656
s 53A(2) ... 1330, 1656
s 56 ... 208, 214, 215
s 57 ... 1656
s 60 ... 1330, 1656
ss 63A–65 ... 229
s 65C ... 1656
s 65D ... 1656
s 68 ... 769, 770, 771, 1617
s 68(2) ... 770
s 68A ... 769

Table of Statutes

s 68A(1) ... 771
s 68A(1)(a) ... 771
s 68A(1)(b) ... 771
s 68A(2) ... 771
s 68A(3) ... 771
s 69(1) ... 637
s 70(1) ... 638
s 70(2) ... 638
s 71(1) ... 640
s 71(2) ... 639, 1855
s 72 ... 641
s 74(1) ... 643
s 74(2) ... 643
s 74(3) ... 643
s 75A ... 770, 1617, 1840, 1904, 1970, 1981
s 75A(3)(a) ... 2306
s 75B ... 1114
s 75B(1)(c) ... 1114
s 76 ... 1656
s 78 ... 1656
s 79 ... 1656
s 80 ... 1111, 1330, 1526
s 82 ... 215, 1112, 1113, 1114, 1115, 1118, 1121, 1330, 1526, 1528
s 82(2) ... 1113
s 85 ... 772
s 86(1) ... 1654
s 86(2) ... 1654
s 86A ... 1654
s 87 ... 1113, 1115, 1116, 1120, 1121, 1330, 1526
s 87(1) ... 1656
s 87(1A) ... 1526
s 87(1CA) ... 1526
s 87(1D) ... 1526
s 87(2) ... 1115
s 87(2)(a) ... 1115, 1116, 1656
s 87(2)(b) ... 1115
s 87(2)(c) ... 1115
s 87(2)(d) ... 1115
s 87(2)(e) ... 1115
s 87(2)(f) ... 1115
Pt IV ... 904, 1654, 1655, 1656
Pt IVA ... 1523, 1526
Pt IVB ... 1524
Pt V ... 1101, 1106, 1112, 1654, 1656
Pt V Div 1 ... 1654, 1656
Pt V Div 1A ... 1656
Pt V Div 2 ... 770, 1617
Pt V Div 2A ... 916
Pt VI ... 1654

Trade Practices Amendment Act (No 1) 2001 ... 1113, 1525, 1526, 1528

AUSTRALIAN CAPITAL TERRITORY

Age of Majority Act 1974 ... 803
Apportionment Act 1905
  s 2 ... 1827
  s 4 ... 1827
  s 8 ... 1827
Associations Incorporation Act 1991 ... 864
Commercial Arbitration Act 1986 ...115
  s 46 ...1978
  s 53 ... 1626
  s 55 ... 1626
Consumer Credit Act 1995 ... 1516
Conveyancing and Law of Property Act 1898
  s 30 ... 1505
Credit Act 1985
  s 140 ... 826
Crown Proceedings Act 1992 ... 869
Discrimination Act 1991 ... 882
Domestic Relationships Act 1994
  Pt IV ... 1632
Electronic Transactions Act 2001...238
  s 13(7)(1), (2), (3), (4) ...238
Fair Trading Act 1992 ... 1113
  s 12 ... 1103
  s 13 ... 1525
  s 15(2) ... 1330
  s 21 ... 215
  s 23 ... 1656
  s 26 ... 1330
  ss 28–30 ... 229
Forfeiture of Leases Act 1901
  s 1(1) ... 1970
  s 1(2) ... 1980
Games Wagers and Betting-houses Act 1901
  s 13 ... 1616
Guardianship and Management of Property Act 1991 ... 838
Imperial Acts (Substituted Provisions) Act 1986
  s 3 ... 507, 508, 510, 1505
  s 3(1) ... 505, 506
  Sch 1 ... 505, 506
  Sch 2 Pt 7 cl 5 ... 1505

Sch 2 Pt 7 cl 6 ... 1505
Sch 2 Pt 11 cl 4(1) ... 507, 508, 509, 510
Law of Property (Miscellaneous Provisions) Act 1958
  s 4 ... 1851
Law Reform (Manufacturers Warranties) Act 1977 ... 916
Law Reform (Miscellaneous Provisions) Act 1955
  s 14 ... 2130
  s 15(1) ... 2130
  s 15(3) ... 2130
  s 15(4) ... 2130
  s 54(1) ... 509
  s 54(2) ... 524
Law Reform (Miscellaneous Provisions) Amendment Act 2001 ... 2129
Law Reform (Misrepresentation) Act 1977 ... 1074, 1117
  s 3(a) ... 1059
  s 3(b) ... 1056
  s 3(c) ... 1056
  s 4(1) ... 1076
  s 4(2) ... 1078
  s 5(1) ... 1075
  s 6 ... 1123
Limitation Act 1985
  s 32 ... 334
Married Persons' Property Act 1986
  s 3 ... 879
  s 3(1) ... 879
  s 6 ... 881
Mental Health Act 1962 ... 838
Mental Health (Treatment and Care) Act 1994 ... 838
Mercantile Law Act 1962
  s 15 ... 819
  s 16 ... 1005

Money Lenders Act 1936
  s 13 ... 819
Sale of Goods Act 1896
  s 3(1) ... 511
Sale of Goods Act 1954
  s 5(1) ... 728
  s 7 ... 810, 847
  s 11 ... 1216
  s 12 ... 2012
  s 13(2) ... 2318
  s 15(1) ... 1952
  s 16(1) ... 1981
  s 16(2) ... 727, 1910
  s 16(4) ... 1981
  s 17 ... 637
  s 18 ... 638
  s 19(2) ... 639
  s 19(4) ... 640
  s 20 ... 641
  s 32 ... 1808
  s 33(5) ... 1815
  s 34 ... 624
  s 35(2) ... 1910, 1938
  s 39 ... 1981
  s 41 ... 2139
  s 44 ... 1839
  s 52(1) ... 2204
  s 52(2) ... 1806
  s 53 ... 2140
  s 54 ... 2142
  s 55 ... 2405
  s 56 ... 2138
  s 57 ... 2144
  s 60 ... 211
  s 62(1) ... 736, 1061
  s 62(1A) ... 1061
Sale of Goods Act 1975
  s 3 ... 511
Sale of Goods (Vienna Convention) Act 1987 ... 276

NEW SOUTH WALES

Agricultural Holdings Act 1941 ... 510
Anti-Discrimination Act 1977 ... 882
Associations Incorporation Act 1984 ... 864
Builders Licensing Act 1971
  s 45 ... 520, 2307
Building Operations and Building Materials Control Act 1945 ... 1713
Cattle Slaughtering and Diseased Animals and Meat Act 1902
  s 47 ... 1609, 1614

  s 48 ... 1614
Commercial Arbitration Act 1984 ... 115
  s 46 ... 1978
  s 53 ... 1626
  s 55 ... 1626
Constitution Act 1902
  s 45 ... 871
Consumer Credit Act 1995 ... 1516
Contracts Review Act 1980 ... 769, 772, 1003, 1416, 1526, 1528, 1936, 1981, 1995, 2207

Table of Statutes

s 4(1) ... 1519
s 4(2) ... 1518
s 5 ... 1518
s 6 ... 1518
s 6(1) ... 1518
s 6(2) ... 1518
s 7 ... 1519, 1521, 1522
s 7(1) ... 1519
s 8 ... 1521, 2304
s 9 ... 1520, 1522
s 9(1) ... 1520
s 9(2) ... 1520
s 9(2)(j) ... 1330
s 9(4) ... 1520
s 9(5) ... 1520
s 10 ... 1517, 1530
s 11 ... 1521
s 12 ... 1521
s 16 ... 1521
s 17 ... 1519
s 18 ... 1519
s 21 ... 1518
Sch 1 ... 1521, 2304
Conveyancing Act 1919
  s 13 ... 1851, 1949, 1959
  s 36C ... 914
  s 37C ... 1505
  s 38 ... 312
  s 51A ... 312
  s 54A ... 376
  s 54A(1) ... 509
  s 54A(2) ... 524
  s 54B ... 2166
  s 54B(2) ... 2166
  s 54B(3) ... 2166
  s 55 ... 2409
  s 55(2A) ... 2334
  s 129(1) ... 1970
  s 129(2) ... 1980
  s 133E ... 1837
  s 142 ... 1827
  s 144(1) ... 1827
  s 144(5) ... 1827
  s 149 ... 881
Conveyancing and Law of Property Act 1898
  s 82 ... 806
Credit Act 1984
  s 140 ... 826
Crown Lands Act 1884 ... 1621, 1730
Crown Proceedings Act 1988 ... 869
Electronic Transactions Act 2000
  s 5 ... 238
  s 13(1) ... 238
  s 13(2) ... 238

s 13(3) ... 238
s 13(4) ... 238
s 13(7) ... 238
Fair Trading Act 1987
  s 27 ... 1656
  s 29 ... 1656
  s 41 ... 1108
  s 42 ... 1103
  s 43 ... 1525
  s 45(2) ... 1330
  s 51 ... 215
  s 52 ... 1656
  s 55 ... 1330
  ss 57–59 ... 229
Fisheries and Oyster Farms Act 1935 ... 1723
Frustrated Contracts Act 1978 ... 2304
  s 4 ... 2069
  s 5(1) ... 2073, 2075
  s 5(2)(a) ... 2073
  s 5(3) ... 2073
  s 5(4) ... 2069
  s 6 ... 2070
  s 6(1) ... 2070
  s 6(2) ... 2070
  s 6(3) ... 2070
  s 7 ... 2071
  s 8 ... 2072, 2094
  s 9 ... 2073
  ss 9–13 ... 2077, 2078
  s 10 ... 2073, 2074
  s 11 ... 2074, 2075, 2078
  s 11(1) ... 2074
  s 11(2) ... 2074
  s 12 ... 2075
  s 13 ... 2076
  s 13(1) ... 2076
  s 13(2) ... 2076
  s 14 ... 2077
  s 15 ... 2078
  s 15(1) ... 2078
  s 15(2) ... 2078
  s 15(3) ... 2078
  s 15(4)–(6) ... 2078
  s 15(7) ... 2078
Imperial Acts Application Act 1969
  s 8(1) ... 505, 506, 507, 508, 510
Industrial Relations Act 1996 ... 1828
  s 106 ... 1516
Law Reform (Miscellaneous Provisions) Act 1965
  s 8 ... 2130
  s 9(1) ... 2130
  s 9(2) ... 2130
  s 9(3) ... 2129

References are to paragraphs

Law Reform (Miscellaneous Provisions) Amendment Act 2000 ... 2129
Limitation Act 1969
  s 54 ... 334
Liquor Act 1912 ... 1623
Local Government Act 1919 ... 1035, 1613
  s 311 ... 1603
  s 317A ... 1603
Maintenance, Champerty and Barratry Abolition Act 1993
  s 3 ... 1629
  s 4 ... 1629
  s 6 ... 1629
Married Persons (Equality of Status) Act 1996 ... 879
Married Women's Property Act 1886 ... 879
Mental Health Act 1990 ... 838
Mining on Private Lands Act 1894
  s 33 ... 1621
Minors (Property and Contracts) Act 1970 ... 803, 827
  s 6(1) ... 828
  s 6(3) ... 828
  s 17 ... 828
  s 18 ... 807
  s 19 ... 808, 829
  s 20 ... 834, 835, 836
  s 20(2) ... 834
  s 20(3) ... 834
  s 22 ... 829
  s 23 ... 829
  s 24 ... 829
  s 26 ... 830
  s 27 ... 830
  s 28 ... 835
  s 29 ... 835
  s 30 ... 831
  s 31 ... 832
  s 33 ... 832
  s 34 ... 832
  s 36 ... 832
  s 37 ... 833, 834, 836
  s 38 ... 832
  s 39 ... 831
  s 47 ... 826
  s 48 ... 837
  Sch 1 ... 810, 819
Money-lenders and Infants Loans Act 1941
  s 37 ... 819

Motor Vehicles (Third Party Insurance) Act 1942
  s 10(7) ... 916
Protected Estates Act 1983 ... 838
Property (Relationships) Act 1984
  s 45(1) ... 1632
  s 46 ... 1632
  Pt 4 ... 1632
Real Property Act 1900 ... 1519
Restraints of Trade Act 1976 ... 1636, 1654, 1731
  s 3(1) ... 1738
  s 3(2) ... 1738
  s 3(3) ... 1738
  s 4(1) ... 1738, 1739
  s 4(2) ... 1738
  s 4(3) ... 1738, 1739
  s 4(4) ... 1738
  s 4(5) ... 1738
Sale of Goods Act 1923
  s 4(2) ... 736, 1061
  s 4(2A) ... 1061
  s 4(2A)(a) ... 1059
  s 4(2A)(b) ... 1056
  s 4(5) ... 736
  s 5(1) ... 728
  s 7 ... 810, 847
  s 11 ... 1216
  s 12 ... 2012, 2069
  s 13(2) ... 2318
  s 15(1) ... 1952
  s 16(1) ... 1981
  s 16(2) ... 727, 1910
  s 16(3) ... 1981
  s 18 ... 638, 737
  s 19 ... 737
  s 19(1) ... 639, 640
  s 19(2) ... 640
  s 19(4) ... 737
  s 20 ... 641, 737
  s 31 ... 742, 1808
  s 32(4) ... 1815
  s 33 ... 624
  s 34(2) ... 1910, 1938
  s 38 ... 1981
  s 38(1) ... 1062
  s 38(2) ... 1062
  s 40 ... 2139
  s 43 ... 1839
  s 51(1) ... 2204
  s 51(2) ... 1806, 2204
  s 52 ... 2140
  s 52(2) ... 2140
  s 52(3) ... 2140, 2142
  s 53 ... 2142
  s 53(2) ... 2142, 2148

Table of Statutes

s 53(3) ... 2148
s 54 ... 2138
s 54(1) ... 2138
s 54(2) ... 2138
s 54(3) ... 2138
s 54(4) ... 2138
s 55 ... 2144, 2306
s 56 ... 2405
s 57 ... 737
s 60 ... 211
s 62 ... 737, 772
s 64 ... 772
s 64(1) ... 772
s 64(2) ... 772
s 64(3) ... 640
s 64(4) ... 640
s 66(2) ... 640
Pt III ... 834
Pt VIII ... 640
Sale of Goods (Amendment) Act 1988
   s 3 ... 511
   Sch 1 cl 2 ... 511
Sale of Goods (Vienna Convention) Act 1986 ... 276
Sea-Carriage Documents Act 1997 ... 925
Statute Law (Miscellaneous Provisions) Act 1996

s 4 ... 1005
Sch 5 ... 1005
Supreme Court Act 1970
   s 68 ... 2169
   s 94 ... 2151
Supreme Court Rules
   Pt 15 r 11 ... 1811
Testator's Family Maintenance and Guardianship of Infants Act 1916 ... 1627
Transport Act 1930 ... 2405
Trustee Act 1925 ... 2078
Unlawful Gambling Act 1998
   s 56 ... 1616
Usury Bills of Lading and Written Memoranda Act 1902
   s 9 ... 819
Usury Bills of Lading and Written Memoranda (Repeal) Act 1990
   s 3 ... 1005
Wheat Industry Stabilization Act 1958
   s 11 ... 1725
   s 12 ... 1725
Workers' Compensation Act 1926 ... 2168

NORTHERN TERRITORY

Age of Majority Act 1981 ... 803
Aged and Infirm Persons' Property Act 1979 ... 838
Anti-Discrimination Act 1992 ... 882
Associations Incorporation Act 1963 ... 864
Commercial Arbitration Act 1985 ... 115
   s 46 ... 1978
   s 53 ... 1626
   s 55 ... 1626
Consumer Affairs and Fair Trading Act 1990
   s 26 ... 1656
   s 31 ... 1656
   s 41 ... 1108
   s 42 ... 1103
   s 43 ... 1525
   s 45 ... 1330
   s 52 ... 215
   s 53 ... 1656
   s 55 ... 1330
   ss 57–59 ... 229
   s 62 ... 637

s 63 ... 638
s 64(1) ... 640
s 64(2) ... 639
s 65 ... 641
s 66 ... 643
s 67(1) ... 1904, 1981
s 67(3)(a) ... 2306
s 68 ... 770
s 69 ... 771
Pt V ... 642
Consumer Credit Act 1995 ... 1516
Crown Proceedings Act 1993 ... 869
De Facto Relationships Act 1991
   s 44 ... 1632
Electronic Transactions Act 2000 ... 238
   s 13(7)(1), (2), (3), (4) ... 238
Law of Property Act 2000
   s 5(c) ...524
   s 12 ... 914
   s 56 ... 507, 915, 918, 922
   s 56(7) ... 922
   s 58(2) ...513
   s 62 ... 509

References are to paragraphs

s 65 ...1851
s 70 ... 2166
s 137 ... 1970, 1980
s 210 ... 1505
s 211 ...1827
s 212(1) ...1827
s 213(2) ... 1827
s 221(1) ... 505, 506, 508, 510
Sch 4 ... 505, 506, 508, 510

Law Reform (Miscellaneous Provisions) Act 1956 ... 2130

Law Reform (Miscellaneous Provisions) Amendment Act 2001 ... 2129
s 15 ... 2130
s 16 ... 2130
s 16(2) ... 2130
s 16(2A) ... 2130

Limitation Act 1981
s 41 ... 334

Married Persons (Equality of Status) Act 1989
s 3 ... 879, 881

Mental Health and Related Services Act 1998 ... 838

Racing and Betting Act 1983
s 135 ... 1616

Sale of Goods Act 1972
s 4(2) ... 736, 1061
s 5(1) ... 728
s 7 ... 810, 847
s 10 ... 1216
s 12 ... 2012

s 13(2) ... 2318
s 15(1) ... 1952
s 16(1) ... 1981
s 16(2) ... 727, 1910
s 16(4) ... 1981
s 17 ... 637
s 18 ... 638
s 19(a) ... 639
s 19(b) ... 640
s 20 ... 641
s 31 ... 1808
s 32(5) ... 1815
s 33 ... 624
s 34(2) ... 1910, 1938
s 38 ... 1981
s 40 ... 2139
s 43 ... 1839
s 51(1) ... 2204
s 51(2) ... 1806
s 52 ... 2140
s 53 ... 2142
s 54 ... 2138
s 55 ... 2144
s 56 ... 2405
s 57 ... 737
s 60 ... 211

Sale of Goods Amendment Act 1999
s 2 ... 511

Sale of Goods (Vienna Convention) Act 1987 ... 276

Supreme Court Act 1979
Pt IV ... 2169

QUEENSLAND

Age of Majority Act 1974 ... 803

Anti-Discrimination Act 1991 ... 882

Associations Incorporation Act 1981 ... 864

Commercial Arbitration Act 1990 ... 115
s 46 ... 1978
s 53 ... 1626
s 55 ... 1626

Consumer Credit Act 1994 ... 1516

Credit Act 1987
s 136(1) ... 826

Crown Proceedings Act 1980 ... 869

Electronic Transactions Act 2001 ... 238
s 23(1), (2) ... 238
s 24(1), (2) ... 238

Fair Trading Act 1989 ... 1526
s 37 ... 1108
s 38 ... 1103
s 39 ... 1525
s 40A ... 1330
s 46 ... 215
s 47 ... 1656
s 50 ... 1330
ss 52–55 ... 229
s 107 ... 1123

Guardianship and Administration Act 2000 ... 838

Industrial Relations Act 1999 ... 1828

Land Act 1910–1924 ... 2170

Law Reform Act 1995 ... 2130
s 5 ... 2130
s 10(1) ... 2130
s 10(2) ... 2130
s 10(2A) ... 2130
s 18 ... 879

Table of Statutes

Law Reform (Contributory Negligence) Amendment Act 2001 ... 2129
Limitation of Actions Act 1974
  s 35(3) ... 334
Married Women (Restraint upon Anticipation) Act 1952
  s 2 ... 879
  s 4 ... 881
Married Women's Property Act 1890 ... 879
Mental Health Act 1974 ... 838
Mental Health Act 2000 ... 838
Money-Lenders Act 1916
  s 10 ... 819
Property Law Act 1974 ... 505, 506, 508, 510, 1005
  s 3(2) ... 819
  s 6(d) ... 524
  s 13 ... 914
  s 55 ... 915, 918, 922
  s 55(7) ... 922
  s 56 ... 507
  s 56(2) ... 513
  s 59 ... 509
  s 62 ... 1851
  s 68(1) ... 2165, 2166
  s 69 ... 2409
  s 72 ... 1970
  s 124(1) ... 1970
  s 124(2) ... 1980
  s 128 ... 1837
  s 227 ... 860
  s 230 ... 1505
  s 231 ... 1827
  s 232 ... 1827
  s 233(2) ... 1827
Public Trustee Act 1978 ... 838
Racing and Betting Act 1980
  s 248 ... 1616

Sale of Goods Act 1896
  s 3(1) ... 728
  s 5 ... 810, 847
  s 9 ... 1216
  s 10 ... 2012
  s 11(2) ... 2318
  s 13(1) ... 1952
  s 14(1) ... 1981
  s 14(2) ... 727, 1910
  s 14(3) ... 1981
  s 15 ... 637
  s 16 ... 638
  s 17(1) ... 639
  s 17(2) ... 640
  s 18 ... 641
  s 30 ... 1808
  s 31(4) ... 1815
  s 32 ... 624
  s 33(2) ... 1910, 1938
  s 37 ... 1981
  s 39 ... 2139
  s 42 ... 1839
  s 50(1) ... 2204
  s 50(2) ... 1806
  s 51 ... 2140
  s 52 ... 2142
  s 53 ... 2405
  s 54 ... 2138
  s 55 ... 2144
  s 56 ... 737
  s 59 ... 211
  s 61(2) ... 736, 1061
Sale of Goods (Vienna Convention) Act 1986 ... 276
Statute of Frauds 1972
  s 3 ... 505, 506, 508, 510, 511, 819, 1005
Statute of Frauds and Limitations Act 1867
  s 12 ... 819

SOUTH AUSTRALIA

Age of Majority (Reduction) Act 1971 ... 803
Aged and Infirm Persons' Property Act 1940 ... 838
Apportionment Act 1905
  s 2 ... 1827
  s 3 ... 1827
  s 7 ... 1827
Associations Incorporation Act 1985 ... 864
Commercial Arbitration Act 1986 ... 115
  s 46 ... 1978

s 53 ... 1626
s 55 ... 1626
Consumer Credit Act 1995 ... 1516
Consumer Transactions Act 1972
  s 6(1) ... 637
  s 6(2)–(6) ... 642
  s 6(2) ... 637
  s 6(3) ... 638
  s 6(4) ... 640
  s 6(5) ... 640
  s 6(6) ... 639
  s 7 ... 643
  s 8 ... 770, 771

References are to paragraphs

s 12(1) ... 1984
s 12(3) ... 2306
s 16 ... 770

Crown Proceedings Act 1992 ... 869

De Facto Relationships Act 1996
Pt 2 ... 1632

Electronic Transactions Act 2000
s 5 ... 238
s 13(1) ... 238
s 13(2) ... 238
s 13(3) ... 238
s 13(4) ... 238
s 13(7) ... 238

Fair Trading Act 1987
s 56 ... 1103
s 57 ... 1525
s 59(2) ... 1330
s 65 ... 215
s 66 ... 1656
s 69 ... 1330
ss 71–73 ... 229
s 96 ... 1123

Frustrated Contracts Act 1988
s 3(1) ... 2093, 2095, 2096, 2097
s 3(2) ... 2097
s 3(3) ... 2096
s 3(4) ... 2096
s 4(1)(b) ... 2093
s 4(2) ... 2093
s 4(3) ... 2093, 2097
s 5 ... 2094
s 6 ... 2094
s 6(1) ... 2094
s 6(2) ... 2094
s 7 ... 2097
s 7(1) ... 2092, 2095
s 7(2) ... 2095, 2096
s 7(4) ... 2095
s 7(5) ... 2095
s 7(6) ... 2095
s 7(7) ... 2095
s 8 ... 2098

Guardianship and Administration Act 1993 ... 838

Industrial and Employee Relations Act 1994 ... 1828

Landlord and Tenant Act 1936
s 10 ... 1970
s 11 ... 1980

Law of Property Act 1936
s 16 ... 1851
s 26(1) ... 509
s 26(2) ... 524
s 34(1) ... 914
s 63 ... 1827

s 64 ... 1827
s 68 ... 1827
s 88 ... 1505
ss 92–111 ... 879
s 92(1)(b) ... 879
s 110 ... 881

Law Reform (Miscellaneous Provisions) Act 2001 ... 2129, 2130
s 3 ... 2130
s 7 ... 2130
s 7(3) ... 2130

Limitation of Actions Act 1936
s 42 ... 334

Lottery and Gaming Act 1936
s 50 ... 1616
s 50A ... 1616

Manufacturers Warranties Act 1974 ... 916

Mental Health Act 1993 ... 838

Mercantile Law Amendment Act 1861
s 2 513

Minors' Contracts (Miscellaneous Provisions) Act 1979
s 4 ... 819
s 5 ... 826
s 6 ... 806
s 7 ... 821
s 8 ... 806

Misrepresentation Act 1972 ... 1074, 1117
s 6(1)(a) ... 1059
s 6(1)(b) ... 1056
s 6(1)(c) ... 1056
s 6(2) ... 1052
s 7(1) ... 1076
s 7(2) ... 1078
s 7(3) ... 1075
s 8 ... 1123

Prices Act 1948–1951 ... 1720

Sale of Goods Act 1895
s 2 ... 810, 847
s 6 ... 1216
s 7 ... 2012, 2093
s 8(2) ... 2318
s 10(1) ... 1952
s 11(1) ... 1981
s 11(2) ... 727, 1910
s 11(3) ... 1981
s 12 ... 637
s 13 ... 638
s 14(I) ... 639
s 14(II) ... 640
s 15 ... 641
s 28 ... 1808
s 29(4) ... 1815

Table of Statutes

s 30 ... 624
s 31(2) ... 1910, 1938
s 35 ... 1981
s 37 ... 2139
s 40 ... 1839
s 48(1) ... 2204
s 48(2) ... 1806
s 49 ... 2140
s 50 ... 2142
s 51 ... 2405
s 52 ... 2138
s 53 ... 2144
s 54 ... 737
s 57 ... 211
s 59(2) ... 736, 1061
s 60(1) ... 728

Sale of Goods (Vienna Convention) Act 1986 ... 276
Sex Discrimination Act 1975 ... 882
Statutes Amendment (Enforcement of Contracts) Act 1982
  s 3 ... 505, 506, 507, 508
  s 4 ... 511
Statutes Amendment (Law of Property and Wrongs) Act 1972
  s 11 ... 881
Supreme Court Act 1935
  s 30 ... 2169
Town Planning and Development Act 1920 ... 1727
  s 23 ... 1610
  s 23(c) ... 1610
  s 44 ... 1610

TASMANIA

Age of Majority Act 1973 ... 803
Anti-Discrimination Act 1998 ... 882
Apportionment Act 1871
  s 2 ... 1827
  s 5 ... 1827
  s 7 ... 1827
Associations Incorporation Act 1964 ... 864
Commercial Arbitration Act 1986 ... 115
  s 46 ... 1978
  s 53 ... 1626
  s 55 ... 1626
Consumer Credit Act 1996 ... 1516
Conveyancing and Law of Property Act 1884
  s 15(1) ... 1970
  s 15(2) ... 1980
  s 36(1) ... 509
  s 36(2) ... 524
  s 42 ... 1505
  s 43 ... 881
  s 45 ... 881
  s 61 ... 914
Conveyancing and Law of Property Act 1935
  s 3(XII) ... 881
Crown Proceedings Act 1993 ... 869
Electronic Transactions Act 2000 ... 238
  s 11(1), (2), (3), (4), (7) ... 238
Fair Trading Act 1990 ... 1113
  s 14 ... 1103
  s 15 ... 1525

s 17(2) ... 1330
s 22 ... 215
s 26 ... 1330
s 27 ... 229
s 51 ... 1123
Guardianship and Administration Act 1995 ... 838
Industrial Relations Act 1984 ... 1828
Infants' Relief Act 1875 ... 824
  s 2 ... 819
Limitation Act 1974
  s 29(4) ... 334
Married Women's Property Act 1935
  s 3 ... 879
Mental Health Act 1963
  Pt VI ... 838
Mercantile Law Act 1935
  s 6 ... 506, 507, 508, 510
  s 11 ... 1005
  s 12 ... 513
Minors' Contracts Act 1988 ... 819
  s 4 ... 826
  s 5 ... 824
Powers of Attorney Act 1934
  s 9 ... 914
Racing and Gaming Act 1952
  s 114 ... 1616
Sale of Goods Act 1896
  s 3(1) ... 511, 728
  s 5(2) ... 736, 1061
  s 7 ... 810, 847
  s 9 ... 511
  s 9(3) ... 511
  s 11 ... 1216

s 12 ... 2012
s 13(2) ... 2318
s 15 ... 1952
s 16(1) ... 1981
s 16(2) ... 727, 1910
s 16(3) ... 1981
s 17 ... 637
s 18 ... 638
s 19(a) ... 639
s 19(b) ... 640
s 20 ... 641
s 33 ... 1808
s 34(4) ... 1815
s 35 ... 624
s 36(2) ... 1910, 1938
s 40 ... 1981
s 42 ... 2139
s 45 ... 1839
s 53(1) ... 2204
s 53(2) ... 1806
s 54 ... 2140
s 55 ... 2142
s 56 ... 2405
s 57 ... 2138

s 58 ... 2144
s 59 ... 737
s 62 ... 211
Sale of Goods (Vienna Convention) Act 1987 ... 276
Supreme Court Civil Procedure Act 1932
s 11(7) ... 1851
s 11(13) ... 2169
Tortfeasors and Contributory Negligence Act 1954
s 4(1)(a) ... 2130
s 4(1)(b) ... 2130
Tortfeasors and Contributory Negligence Amendment Act 2000 ... 2129
Unordered Goods and Services Act 1973 ... 229
Wrongs Act 1954
s 2 ... 2130
s 4 ... 2130

VICTORIA

Age of Majority Act 1977 ... 803
Associations Incorporation Act 1981 ... 864
Commercial Arbitration Act 1984 ... 115
s 46 ... 1978
s 53 ... 1626
s 55 ... 1626
Companies (Vic) Code ... 1116
Consumer Credit Act 1995 ... 1516
Credit Act 1984 ... 1522, 1528
s 140 ... 826
Crown Proceedings Act 1958 ... 869
Discharged Soldiers Settlement Act 1917
s 35 ... 1624
Discharged Soldiers Settlement Act 1919
s 35 ... 1624
Electronic Transactions Act 2000
s 5 ... 238
s 13(1) ... 238
s 13(2) ... 238
s 13(3) ... 238
s 13(4) ... 238
s 13(7) ... 238
Equal Opportunity Act 1995 ... 882

Fair Trading Act 1985
s 18 ... 215
s 21 ... 1330
ss 28–30 ... 229
Fair Trading Act 1999
s 4 ... 1108
s 7 ... 1525
s 8 ... 1525
s 9 ... 1102
s 18 ... 1656
Frustrated Contracts Act 1959
s 2 ... 2080
s 3 ... 2087
s 3(1) ... 2079, 2080, 2083
s 3(2) ... 2080, 2081, 2082, 2083, 2084, 2085
s 3(3) ... 2083, 2084, 2085, 2086
s 3(4) ... 2083, 2084, 2085
s 3(5) ... 2083, 2085
s 3(6) ... 2086
s 4(1) ... 2088
s 4(2) ... 2088
s 4(3) ... 2087, 2094
s 4(4) ... 2090
s 4(5) ... 2089
s 5 ... 2091
Goods Act 1958
s 3(1) ... 728
s 4(2) ... 736, 1061
s 7 ... 810, 847

Table of Statutes

s 11 ... 1216
s 12 ... 2012, 2079, 2080
s 13(2) ... 2318
s 15 ... 1952
s 16(1) ... 1981
s 16(2) ... 727, 1910
s 16(3) ... 1981
s 17 ... 637
s 18 ... 638
s 19(a) ... 639
s 19(b) ... 640
s 20 ... 641
s 35 ... 1808
s 36(4) ... 1815
s 37 ... 624
s 38(2) ... 1910, 1938
s 42 ... 1981
s 44 ... 2139
s 47 ... 1839
s 55(1) ... 2204
s 55(2) ... 1806
s 56 ... 2140
s 57 ... 2142
s 58 ... 2405
s 59 ... 2138
s 60 ... 2144
s 61 ... 737
s 64 ... 211
s 86 ... 637
s 87 ... 638
s 88(1) ... 641
s 89(2) ... 640
s 89(3) ... 640
s 90 ... 639
ss 91–93 ... 643
s 94(1) ... 643
s 95 ... 772
s 95(1) ... 770
s 97 ... 771, 772
s 97(1) ... 770
s 99 ... 1981
s 99(1) ... 1981
s 99(2) ... 1981
s 99(3) ... 1981
s 100(1) ... 1061, 1062
s 100(2) ... 1059
s 101(1)(e) ... 2306
s 101(1)(f) ... 2306
s 101(1)(g) ... 2336
s 101(2) ... 1040
ss 103–107 ... 642
s 110 ... 771, 772
s 110(1) ... 770
s 111(2) ... 1059
s 116(1) ... 1612
s 118(1) ... 1981
Pt IV ... 1612, 1981

Guardianship and Administration Act 1986 ... 838
Instruments Act 1958
  s 31(a) ... 860
  s 126 ... 506, 507, 508, 509, 510, 514
  s 128 ... 1005
  s 129 ... 513
Instruments (Corporate Bodies Contracts) Act 1967 ... 860
Land Act 1865 ... 1707
Limitation of Actions Act 1958
  s 24(3) ... 334
Long Service Leave Act 1992 ... 1828
Lotteries, Gaming and Betting Act 1966
  s 15 ... 1616
Marriage Act 1958
  s 156(1)(b) ... 879
  s 157 ... 881
  Pt VIII ... 879
Mental Health Act 1986 ... 838
Prices Regulation Act 1948
  s 25(1) ... 1613
Property Law Act 1958
  s 28B ... 803
  s 41 ... 1851
  s 49(2) ... 2334
  s 55(d) ... 524
  s 56(1) ... 914
  s 146(1) ... 1970
  s 146(2) ... 1980
  s 169 ... 881
  s 175 ... 1505
Sale of Goods (Vienna Convention) Act 1987 ... 276
  s 8 ... 506, 507, 508, 509, 510, 514
  s 9 ... 511
Supreme Court Act 1958
  s 69 ... 824
  s 70 ... 819, 824
  s 71 ... 819
Supreme Court Act 1986
  s 38 ... 2169
  s 49 ... 824
  s 50 ... 819, 824
  s 51 ... 819
  s 53(1) ... 1827
  s 53(4) ... 1827
  s 54 ... 1827
  s 85 ... 1980
Wrongs Act 1958
  s 25 ... 2130
  s 26(1) ... 2130
  s 26(1A) ... 2130
  s 26(1B) ... 2130
Wrongs (Amendment) Act 2000 ... 2129

References are to paragraphs

WESTERN AUSTRALIA

Age of Majority Act 1972 ... 803
Associations Incorporation Act 1987 ... 864
Commercial Arbitration Act 1985 ... 115
   s 46 ... 1978
   s 53 ... 1626
   s 55 ... 1626
Consumer Credit Act 1996 ... 1516
Credit Act 1984
   s 140 ... 826
Crown Suits Act 1947 ... 869
Equal Opportunity Act 1984 ... 882
Fair Trading Act 1987
   s 9 ... 1108
   s 10 ... 1103
   s 11 ... 1525
   s 12(2)(d) ... 1330
   s 19 ... 215
   s 20 ... 1656
   s 23 ... 1330
   ss 28–31 ... 229
   s 34 ... 770
   s 35 ... 771
   s 36 ... 637
   s 37 ... 638
   s 38(1) ... 640
   s 38(2) ... 639
   s 39 ... 641
   s 40 ... 643
   s 41 ... 1904, 1981
   s 41(3)(a) ... 2306
   s 51 ... 1656
   s 52 ... 1656
   s 60 ... 1656
   Pt III ... 642
Gaming and Betting (Contracts and Securities) Act 1985
   s 4 ... 1616
Guardianship and Administration Act 1990 ... 838
Industrial Relations Act 1979 ... 1828
Law Reform (Contributory Negligence and Tortfeasors' Contribution) Act 1947 ... 2130
Law Reform (Property Perpetuities and Succession) Act 1962
   s 25 ... 881
Law Reform (Statute of Frauds) Act 1962
   s 2 ... 505, 506, 508, 510

Limitation Act 1935
   s 44 ... 334
Married Women's Property Act 1892 ... 879
Mental Health Act 1996 ... 838
Mercantile Law Amendment Act 1856 (UK)
   s 3 ... 513
Property Law Act 1969
   s 11 ... 915
   s 11(1) ... 914
   s 21 ... 1851
   s 31 ... 881
   s 34(1) ... 509
   s 36(d) ... 524
   s 81(1) ... 1970
   s 81(2) ... 1980
   s 83C ... 1837
   s 92 ... 1505
   s 130(1) ... 1827
   s 131 ... 1827
   s 134(2) ... 1827
Sale of Goods Act 1895
   s 2 ... 810, 847
   s 4 ... 511
   s 6 ... 1216
   s 7 ... 2012
   s 8(2) ... 2318
   s 10(1) ... 1952
   s 11(1) ... 1981
   s 11(2) ... 727, 1910
   s 11(3) ... 1981
   s 12 ... 637
   s 13 ... 638
   s 14(I) ... 639
   s 14(II) ... 640
   s 15 ... 641
   s 28 ... 1808
   s 29(4) ... 1815
   s 30 ... 624
   s 31(2) ... 1910, 1938
   s 35 ... 1981
   s 37 ... 2139
   s 40 ... 1839
   s 48(1) ... 2204
   s 48(2) ... 1806
   s 49 ... 2140
   s 50 ... 2142
   s 51 ... 2405
   s 52 ... 2138
   s 53 ... 2144
   s 54 ... 737
   s 57 ... 211
   s 59(2) ... 736, 1061

References are to paragraphs

Table of Statutes

s 60(1) ... 511, 728
Sale of Goods (Vienna Convention) Act 1986 ... 276

Statute of Frauds 1677 (UK)
s 4 ... 507, 509
Supreme Court Act 1935
s 25(10) ... 2169

CANADA

Unconscionable Transactions Relief Act RSO, Ontario 1970, c 472 ... 1517

GUANA

Companies Code 1963

s 13 ... 863

INTERNATIONAL

European Community Directive of 1993 on Unfair Terms in Consumer Contracts 1529
Art 4 ... 1528
Hague Rules ... 924
United Nations Convention on Contracts for the International Sale of Goods 1980 (Vienna Convention) ... 119, 511, 1910

Art 14 ... 276
Art 19 ... 224
Art 25 ... 1925, 1927
Art 49 ... 1962
Art 64 ... 1962
Art 71 ... 1839
Art 71(1) ... 1839
Art 71(2) ... 1839
Art 72 ... 1938

NEW ZEALAND

Contracts (Privity) Act 1982 ... 915

Contractual Mistakes Act 1977 ... 1212
s 8 ... 1243

Contractual Remedies Act 1979 ... 1077
s 4(3) ... 1061
s 6 ... 1071
s 7 ... 1938

UGANDA

Rent Restriction Ordinance 1949

s 3(2) ... 1720

UNITED KINGDOM

Age of Majority (Scotland) Act 1969 ... 803
Carriage of Goods by Sea Act 1924 ... 925
Consumer Credit Code ... 512
Contracts (Rights of Third Parties) Act 1999 ... 912, 915
Family Law Reform Act 1969 ... 803
Infants' Relief Act 1874 ... 507, 826
  s 1 ... 824
  s 2 ... 819, 824
Judicature Act 1873
  s 25(6) ... 909
  s 25(7) ... 1851
Law of Property Act 1925
  s 40 ... 509
  s 41 ... 1851
  s 56 ... 914
  s 56(1) ... 914

s 174 ... 1505
Law of Property (Miscellaneous Provisions) Act 1989
  s 2 ... 509, 521
  s 2(1) ... 513
  s 2(3) ... 514
  s 2(5) ... 521
  s 3 ... 2165
Law Reform (Frustrated Contracts) Act 1943 ... 2079
  s 1(2) ... 2091
  s 2(5)(c) ... 2069
Lord Cairns' Act (Chancery Amendment Act 1858) (21 & 22 Vic c 27) ... 524, 2165, 2169, 2171, 2172, 2173
Mercantile Law Amendment Act 1856
  s 3 ... 513

References are to paragraphs

Merchant Shipping (Safety and Load Line Conventions) Act 1932 ... 1615
Minors' Contracts Act 1987
  s 1 ... 824
Misrepresentation Act 1967 ... 1117, 2153
  s 1(a) ... 1059
  s 2(1) ... 1074
Real Property Act 1845
  s 5 ... 914
Rent Restriction Act ... 1229
Road and Rail Traffic Act 1933 ... 1613, 1711
Road Traffic Act 1960
  s 203(3)(a) ... 1705
Sale of Goods Act 1893 ... 615
  s 4 ... 518, 525, 526
  s 11 ... 751
  s 13 ... 751
  s 14 ... 642
  s 61(2) ... 736
Sale of Goods Act 1979 ... 518
  s 14(2) ... 640
  s 14(2A) ... 640
  s 62(2) ... 736
Sale of Reversions Act 1867 ... 1505
Statute of Frauds 1677 (29 Car II c-3) ... 306, 501, 502, 509, 512, 513, 514, 517, 521, 1259, 2307, 2319, 2333
  s 4 ... 403, 503, 504, 505, 507, 519, 524, 1005
  s 17 ... 504, 505, 511, 519
Statute of Frauds (Amendment) Act 1828 (Lord Tenterden's Act) ... 819, 831
  s 6 ... 1005
Statute of Limitations ... 1723, 1724
Supreme Court Act 1981
  s 50 ... 2169

UNITED STATES

Carriage of Goods by Sea Act 1936
  s 1(a) ... 924

Uniform Commercial Code ... 224, 1522
  s 2-201(1) ... 511
  s 2-609(1) ... 1944

Restatement of the Law

Restatement of the Law, Contracts (1932) ... 361
  s 45 ... 387
  s 75(1) ... 309
  s 90 ... 387
  s 346 ... 2156
  s 348 ... 2156
  s 531 ... 249
Restatement of the Law (2d), Contracts (1979) ... 361
  s 1 ... 249
  s 22(2) ... 203
  s 24 ... 207
  s 26 ... 208
  s 32 ... 249
  s 40 ... 253
  s 43 ... 244
  s 45 ... 250
  s 46 ... 246
  s 48 ... 257
  s 51 ... 239
  s 63 ... 237
  s 69 ... 229
  s 71 ... 309
  s 90(1) ... 387
  s 174 ... 1302
  s 175 ... 1302, 1322
  s 205 ... 1809
  s 209(1) ... 708
  s 213 ... 708
  s 243 ... 1966
  s 250 ... 1938
  s 256(1) ... 1945
  s 568 ... 234

PART I
Introduction

Chapter 1

Introduction

General	101
History of Contract	104
Assumptions of Contract Law	108
Theories of Contract	110
The Role of Contract Law	114
Australian Contract Law	117

General

[101] Definition and content. A contract is a legally binding promise or agreement. The person (or persons) who makes a promise is termed the 'promisor'. The person (or persons) to whom the promise is made is termed the 'promisee'.

The law of contract is concerned with four main topics:
(1) the making of the contract;
(2) the content, effect and enforceability of the terms of the contract;
(3) the performance and discharge of the contract; and
(4) rights and remedies in the event of default in the performance of the contract.

More simply, the law of contract is concerned with the formation and enforcement of agreements which are recognised as contractual in nature.

[102] Structure of this book. There may be an appearance of agreement but not the reality of it, or agreeing parties may not intend their agreement to be legally binding, or they may intend this but fail to achieve it for non-satisfaction of the law's criteria of a contract. These matters are the concern of Part II of this book. Ascertaining whether agreement has been reached and if so the agreement's content (its terms) are interrelated processes. Part III deals with identification and construction of the terms of a contract.

Parts IV and V deal respectively with the special positions of particular parties and non-parties and with contracts which may be only contingently binding because, as a result of the circumstances in which contractual assent was given, one party or each party has a right to choose between rescinding and going on with the contract. Part V also deals with the statutory prohibition on misleading and deceptive conduct which has had a major impact on the general law applicable to the rescission of contracts for misrepresentation.

While the entire subject of 'contract' is concerned with the impact of legal rules, there are common law and statutory rules founded in public policy which prohibit the making or implementation of certain agreements or which make certain agreements void or unenforceable. In this book, as in most expositions of contract law, these rules and their effects are discussed under the heading 'Illegality' (Part VI).

Parts VII (Performance and Breach), VIII (Termination) and IX (Remedies) assume the existence of a contract. Part VII discusses the requirements of contractual performance and the circumstances which constitute a breach of contract. Part VIII deals with the existence and exercise by a party of the right to terminate for breach or repudiation, and with the automatic discharge of a contract wrought by an event which has frustrated further performance of the contract.

Remedies available from the courts are treated in the final Part (IX) of the book.

[103] The perfect contract book. The structure described above is fairly traditional. We see it as no more than a logical structure, reflecting an assumed sequence of events. But it is almost certainly not the ideal structure for a contract course, where experience warns against leaving remedies until the end of the teaching program.

If some philanthropist were to gather together a team of authors to write the perfect contract book, the team could be expected to include not only lawyers (both academic and practising) but also business people, philosophers, economists, political scientists, sociologists, anthropologists and psychologists (though never together in the one room!). They would be able to take into account not only the legal decisions and statutes which make up the 'hard' law of contract, but also theories of contract itself and the influence of political, economic and sociological theories and policies, the approaches taken in other legal systems (including customary law), alternative dispute resolution, and the psychology of the contract decision-making process. To do the job properly, the authors ought to have knowledge and experience of the whole range of influences on contract law.

Our aims are more modest. The main goal is to explain the law of contract applied by the courts in the process of resolving contractual disputes. For university students doing contract as part of a law degree that must be a minimum goal. The best way to achieve our goal seems to us to involve a search for principle. At times this may appear doctrinal, or even formalistic,[1] but then that is how contract has been for the past three centuries. On the other hand, it would be wrong to assume that the answers to all the difficult questions are to be found in some pre-conceived general theory. Accordingly, as scholars (and students) of contract law we must

---

1. Cf Brian Coote, 'The Essence of Contract — Part II' (1989) 1 *JCL* 183 at 183–90; and see generally R S Summers, 'Theory, Formality and Practical Legal Criticism' (1990) 106 *LQR* 407.

question whether the principles have been properly applied, formulated or conceived. It is also appropriate to look for guidance in the contract law of other legal systems. But we make no attempt to provide either an exhaustive analysis of the hundreds of thousands of decisions which make up the law of contract or the external, that is non-legal, influences on contract law. An indication of some of the issues raised by external influences is given below.[2]

History of Contract

[104] Relevance. It is a truism to say that the better one's grasp of the historical development of an area of law, the better one's understanding of the modern law. Certainly this is true of the law of contract. Yet no attempt at a full 'historical introduction' is made here.[3]

[105] Forms of action. The story is one of the medieval common law's limiting preoccupation with 'forms of action',[4] those most relevant to the modern notion of contract being debt (to recover a liquidated sum of money) and covenant (an action on an agreement under seal); and above all it is one of the development of the action of assumpsit, and its variants.

The early action of trespass was available in respect of wrongs in which the Crown had a special interest, but trespass 'on the case' became available in respect of purely private wrongs, for example, provision of medical services causing injury to the plaintiff's person. The essence of such an action was misfeasance ('misdoing') but the pleadings (in Latin) would allege that the defendant undertook (assumpsit) the work. Since the focus of modern contract law is legally binding promises, the extension of assumpsit in the early 16th century to embrace non-performance of an undertaking (nonfeasance) marked a most important advance.

Although the importance of the decision for the recognition and enforcement of purely executory promises has probably been overstated,[5] by the time of *Slade's Case*[6] assumpsit was established as an alternative to debt sur contract (debt based on contract) as a remedy for non-payment of a contract price where a contract was fully performed.[7] The availability of the writ of debt, in respect of a claim for goods bargained and sold did not mean that an action on the case was not available. Thus, when John Slade sold goods to Humphrey Morley, but the latter refused to pay for them, Slade could *at his election* maintain either an action in debt or an action on the case in assumpsit. The decision was important in a number of respects, but what needs to be noticed in the present context is that a plaintiff faced with the choice which Slade faced could avoid the wager of law process.

---

2. See [113], [115]–[116].
3. For detailed accounts see, eg Fifoot, *History and Sources of the Common Law*, 1949, pp 217ff; Simpson, *A History of the Common Law of Contract*, 1975.
4. See Maitland, *The Forms of Action at Common Law*, ed Chaytor and Whittaker, 1936.
5. See J H Baker, 'New Light on Slade's Case' [1971] *CLJ* 51, 213; David Ibbetson, 'Sixteenth Century Contract Law: Slade's Case in Context' (1984) 4 *OJLS* 295.
6. (1602) 4 Co Rep 91a; 76 ER 1074.
7. See also [303].

The action was, therefore, procedurally compelling, and the more commonly invoked form of action.

The range of assumpsit was further extended by means of indebitatus assumpsit. It was held that an antecedent debt implied a promise by the debtor to pay that debt. Thus, whereas for an express promise special assumpsit lay, for such an implied promise indebitatus assumpsit was available to the creditor. Some such actions came to be recognised as lying outside contract, in quasi-contract or, as it is now described today, restitution.[8] In *Pavey & Matthews Pty Ltd v Paul*[9] it was held that the promise in such cases is more accurately described as imposed than implied, hence the contrast with a *consensually assumed* contractual liability.[10]

Another important feature of the development of the modern law of contract was the severing of a large part of tort law, namely that concerned with undertakings ('warranties') as to the quality of a contract's subject matter. Originally[11] the action for breach of warranty, being in the nature of the action for deceit, was part of the law of misrepresentation. By the end of the 18th century the action for breach of warranty had lost most of its tortious characteristics and actions on warranties in contracts of sale were declared in assumpsit.

Assume that a plaintiff was always ready, willing and able to perform duly his or her own side of a contract but that the occasion for doing so had not arisen by the time the defendant failed to perform and the contract went off. In the 16th century it was accepted that assumpsit was available to the plaintiff in this 'totally executory' situation as well as where the plaintiff had performed.[12] This development was an element in the establishment of a doctrine of consideration which is considered in detail in Chapter 3. At no time did English law accept that assumpsit should lie in respect of any and every promise. The ill-defined notion in the mid-16th century was that it should lie in respect of promises given for 'good cause'. The subsequent case by case refinement of this notion was anything but scientific and logical but it is clear that the concept of consideration irrevocably characterised the English law of contract as a law of 'bargains'.[13]

[106] Contract or contracts? Awareness of a 'general law of contract' is a phenomenon of the late 19th and early 20th centuries. Previously such legal subjects as, for example, sales and insurance were recognised, but there was not a body of general principles linking them all.[14] Under the synthesising influence of textbooks and law school curricula, the general

---

8. See generally Chapter 23. But see Atiyah, *Essays on Contract*, 1986, p 54.
9. (1987) 162 CLR 221; 69 ALR 577 (see [520], [2308]).
10. See further David Ibbetson, 'Implied Contracts and Restitution: History in the High Court of Australia' (1988) 8 *OJLS* 312.
11. See *Healing Sales Pty Ltd v Inglis Electrix Pty Ltd* (1968) 121 CLR 584. For discussion of the early history see Street, *Foundations of Legal Liability*, 1906, Vol I, pp 374ff; Simpson, *A History of the Common Law of Contract*, 1975, pp 240–7, 535–7.
12. Cf *Strangborough v Warner* (1589) 4 Leon 3; 74 ER 686.
13. See further [309].
14. See *Air Great Lakes Pty Ltd v K S Easter (Holdings) Pty Ltd* (1985) 2 NSWLR 309 at 335.

principles have been derived. It would be easy, though wrong, to assume that such special contracts are the offshoots of the trunk of general principle rather than vice versa.

Therefore, whatever may have been the position at various times in the past, for 100 years the courts have been seeking to find, elucidate and apply general principles. It is simply too late to turn back the clock even if it was ever desirable to do so. Since the usual approach today is to look for guidance in general principles, specific types of contract are regarded as governed by those principles unless there are good reasons for applying special rules. For example, in *The Hansa Nord*,[15] in the sale of goods context, Roskill LJ said[16] that it is 'desirable that the same legal principle should apply to the law of contract as a whole and that different legal principles should not apply to different branches of that law'.

[107] Contract and the law of obligations. Generations of lawyers have been taught that contract and tort cover, generally in a mutually exclusive fashion, the field of common law obligation. Yet it is now clear that there is a substantial degree of concordance of principle and concurrence of causes of action between the two.[17] Thus, the absence of privity of contract, or consideration for an undertaking, are not the obstacles they once were to the recognition of liability. The recognition in *Hedley Byrne & Co Ltd v Heller & Partners Ltd*[18] of the action in tort for negligent advice or statement causing economic loss has protected third parties who relied on such advice or statement to their detriment, to the same extent as the person who paid for the advice or statement.[19] The decision has influenced the courts to extend liability for negligently caused economic loss to a broader category of cases.[20]

That is not to say that tort and contract are mutually exclusive categories. There will often be concurrent remedies in tort and for breach of contract.[21] To this extent, there has been a degree of coalescence of the law of contract and that of tort.[22] But differences continue to manifest themselves,[23] and it is incorrect to say that contract and tort cover the field. Thus, equity continues to be a source of obligation in some cases where there is no contract,[24] and the law also recognises another branch of the law of obligations, based on a concept of unjust enrichment, and known as the law of restitution.[25]

---

15. *Cehave NV v Bremer Handelsgesellschaft mbH* [1976] QB 44 (approved *Reardon Smith Line Ltd v Yngvar Hansen-Tangen* [1976] 1 WLR 989 at 998).
16. [1976] QB 44 at 71.
17. See Keith Mason, 'Contract and Tort: Looking Across the Boundary from the Side of Contract' (1987) 61 *ALJ* 228.
18. [1964] AC 465. See further [1029]–[1036].
19. On the idea that *Hedley Byrne* liability is 'equivalent to contract' see, eg *Hill (t/as R F Hill & Associates) v Van Erp* (1997) 188 CLR 159 at 233.
20. See *Bryan v Maloney* (1995) 182 CLR 609; 128 ALR 163; *Perre v Apand Pty Ltd* (1999) 198 CLR 180; 164 ALR 606.
21. See, eg [1036].
22. Cf Jane Swanton, 'The Convergence of Tort and Contract' (1989) 12 *Syd LR* 40.
23. See *Astley v Austrust Ltd* (1999) 197 CLR 1; 161 ALR 155 (apportionment legislation).
24. See [365]–[387] (promissory estoppel).
25. See further [2302].

These observations raise the question whether the preferable view is that there is a general law of obligations, which manifests itself in particular contracts, particular torts, specific principles of equity and specific responses to unjust enrichment.[26] The authors do not propound this view, which negates the importance of the principles of contract law in establishing the institution which we call contract.

Assumptions of Contract Law

[108] **Paradigm situation.** The modern law of contract assumes freedom of contract, that is, freedom to decide whether to contract and to negotiate contractual terms. It also assumes a paradigm situation of one-to-one negotiation of all the terms of an agreement by parties with equal bargaining strength concerned to maximise their individual positions. It must be recognised that although it is without doubt 'an attribute of a free society ... that it is generally left to parties themselves to make bargains'[27] these assumptions are frequently contradicted or qualified by events in the real world. In many situations adjustments must be made in the conception or application of principle based on these assumptions.

[109] **Qualifications.** Without attempting an exhaustive analysis, four qualifications or contradictions to the paradigm situation, or its implications, may be mentioned.[28]

First, it is apparent that the assumptions are commercially oriented,[29] if not predicated, on both parties entering into the contract for business purposes.[30] Yet, in terms of quantity, and perhaps also in value, far more contracts are entered into by consumers than commercial people. It seems obvious then that a commercial seller may be in a better position, vis-à-vis the protection obtained from the law of contract, than the consumer buyer. This has prompted legislative intervention. Parliament has prohibited the making of some classes of contract, has required that others be in (or evidenced by) writing, has implied non-excludable terms in others, and has provided for a 'cooling-off' period and right of cancellation in some circumstances.[31] Of greatest importance is the recent legislation giving the courts jurisdiction to grant relief from a wide range of 'unjust' contracts.[32]

Second, the proposition that 'will' and 'intention' form the substratum of every contract is heavily attenuated by inequality of bargaining power between the individual and the public corporation or state instrumentality whose power is marked by such bodies' common use of 'standard form contracts'.

---

26. On the relationship between contract, tort and restitution see Mason and Carter, *Restitution Law in Australia*, 1995, paras 310–317.
27. *Biotechnology Australia Pty Ltd v Pace* (1988) 15 NSWLR 130 at 133 per Kirby P.
28. See also [116].
29. And the perspective on commercial behaviour is often that of 19th century methods of contracting. See, eg [203] (limitations on traditional approach to agreement), and further [113].
30. And see [115].
31. Cf [512].
32. See generally [1515]–[1530].

Third, contracts are frequently very informal, with little if any genuine negotiation. The terms implied by law in certain commonly occurring contractual relationships, such as sale of goods, employment and lease, illustrate that it frequently falls to the law of contract itself to complete the parties' bargain.[33]

Fourth, some rules of contract law exhibit a less general bias than the concern with commercial dealings implies. For example, the rules on intention to create legal relations give the appearance of a bias against women and this is sometimes the effect of the decisions.[34]

Theories of Contract

[110] 'Will', 'intent' and the objective theory of contract. Although a subjective intention to contract is in one sense essential in all cases,[35] it is a basic assumption of contract law that whether a contract has been agreed depends more on external manifestation than subjective intention. The modern law applies an 'objective theory of contract'.[36]

The modern concern with 'external manifestation', which implies that parties are to be judged by what they say and do rather than their subjective intentions, means that contract law is not regulated by a 'will theory' under which a subjective meeting of the minds — consensus ad idem — on all the terms of an agreement is essential. Thus, Mason ACJ, Murphy and Deane JJ observed in *Taylor v Johnson*[37] that as between subjective and objective theories of contract 'while the sounds of conflict have not been completely stilled, the clear trend in decided cases and academic writings has been to leave the objective theory in command of the field'.

In fact, however, it is by no means clear what the alleged contrast between subjective and objective theories is meant to convey. The idea that at any time English and Australian law embraced one to the exclusion of the other is not borne out by an examination of the authorities.[38] Thus, the importance of 'external manifestations' was recognised even by those who placed greater emphasis on the need for consensus ad idem than contract lawyers of today. As Blackburn J explained in *Smith v Hughes*:[39]

> If, whatever a man's real intention may be, he so conducts himself that a reasonable man would believe that he was assenting to the terms proposed by the other party, and that other party upon that belief enters into the contract with him, the man thus conducting himself would be equally bound as if he had intended to agree to the other party's terms.

---

33. See generally [631]–[643].
34. See, eg *Balfour v Balfour* [1919] 2 KB 571 (see [403]), although not necessarily in favour of men; see *Jones v Padavatton* [1969] 2 All ER 616 (see [403]).
35. See [111].
36. Recent illustrations include *Toikan International Insurance Broking Pty Ltd v Plasteel Windows Australia Pty Ltd* (1989) 15 NSWLR 641 at 647; *Investors Compensation Scheme Ltd v West Bromwich Building Society* [1998] 1 WLR 896.
37. (1983) 151 CLR 422 at 429; 45 ALR 265.
38. *Air Great Lakes Pty Ltd v K S Easter (Holdings) Pty Ltd* (1985) 2 NSWLR 309 at 335.
39. (1871) LR 6 QB 597 at 607.

The language used by Blackburn J can be explained in terms of estoppel. As Mason ACJ, Murphy and Deane JJ said in *Taylor v Johnson*:[40]

> In practice, as between the contracting parties, there is little difference in the result of the application of the two competing theories since allied with any assertion of the 'subjective theory' is acceptance of one manifestation of the doctrine of estoppel which would ordinarily operate to preclude one who had so conducted himself that a reasonable man would believe that he was assenting to the terms of a proposed contract, from leading evidence as to what his real intentions were.

They went on to explain that the difference between the theories is more evident in 'legal technique', which they illustrated by reference to the consequences of unilateral mistake.[41]

[111] Is a subjective intention to contract essential? That consensus ad idem is still an essential element of contractual formation was treated as self-evident by Lord Diplock in *Paal Wilson & Co A/S v Partenreederei Hannah Blumenthal*,[42] where he described[43] the contrary view as a 'novel heresy'. Similarly, in *Air Great Lakes Pty Ltd v K S Easter (Holdings) Pty Ltd*[44] McHugh JA said that 'an intention to create a legally enforceable contract is a necessary element in the formation of a contract'.

Lord Diplock's statement was made in the context of decisions in which the English courts considered that delay in the prosecution of a submission to arbitration may constitute a contract to abandon the submission.[45] The two controversial elements in these cases are whether the intention to abandon is judged subjectively, and an apparent conflict with the general rule[46] that silence does not constitute acceptance of an offer. Lord Diplock was concerned in particular to reject[47] a submission that where a contract is inferred from conduct — in this context delay — a party may rely on such conduct even though there is no belief that the other party intended to contract.

The relevance of acceptance of an offer by silence[48] to the objective theory is that if a contract may be inferred from conduct, there is no reason why silence, objectively considered, may not constitute a sufficient expression of intention. But, almost invariably, silence will be too equivocal to permit a reasonable person in the position of an offeror to infer that an offer has been accepted by an offeree's silence.[49]

---

40. (1983) 151 CLR 422 at 428.
41. See generally [1238]–[1254].
42. [1983] 1 AC 854.
43. [1983] 1 AC 854 at 917.
44. (1985) 2 NSWLR 309 at 336. But see *Federal Commissioner of Taxation v Ranson* (1989) 90 ALR 533 at 535–6.
45. See also [1978].
46. See [229].
47. [1983] 1 AC 854 at 916–17. Cf at 914, 924. Cf *Air Great Lakes Pty Ltd v K S Easter (Holdings) Pty Ltd* (1985) 2 NSWLR 309 at 330–1; *Finucane v New South Wales Egg Corp* (1988) 80 ALR 486 at 521 (subjective intention a 'factor'). But see *Allied Marine Transport Ltd v Vale do Rio Doce Navegacao SA* [1985] 1 WLR 925 at 936.
48. See further [229].
49. See *Allied Marine Transport Ltd v Vale do Rio Doce Navegacao SA* [1985] 1 WLR 925 at 936–7 (see J Beatson, (1986) 102 *LQR* 19; M J Lawson, [1988] *LMCLQ* 302).

[112] Perspectives of objectivity. The two perspectives for objectivity discussed in the cases[50] are the promisee's perspective or that of a person detached from the parties themselves, that is, the proverbial 'fly on the wall'. Notwithstanding the support which can be found for the latter,[51] the better view is that when the courts speak of an objective theory of contract, they generally mean[52] that words are to be interpreted according to the view which would be taken by a reasonable person *in the position of the person to whom they are addressed*.[53] Thus, in *Paal Wilson & Co A/S v Partenreederei Hannah Blumenthal*[54] Lord Diplock referred[55] to the intention of each party

> ... as it has been communicated to and understood by the other (even though that which has been communicated does not represent the actual state of mind of the communicator) should coincide.

This perspective helps to explain why the approach is never wholly objective.[56]

[113] The changing conceptions of contract. A great deal of attention has been devoted to developing a theory which explains the phenomenon which we describe as 'contract' or 'contract law'.[57] It is difficult to isolate contract theory from substantive principles of contract law. Thus, for example, the 'bargain theory' of consideration[58] has exercised a powerful influence on general contract theory and the conception of what is embraced by 'contract'. Those who suggest[59] that contract is more concerned with 'injurious reliance' than the enforcement of executory promises treat the two as mutually exclusive, whereas it may well be legitimate to conceive of various theories of contract explaining different forms of contract.[60]

The basic principles of contract law were laid down in an economic, social, political and intellectual context different, in important respects,

---

50. Cf Anne De Moor, 'Intention in the Law of Contract: Elusive or Illusory' (1990) 106 *LQR* 632. For a suggestion of a third — promisor objectivity — see William Howarth, 'The Meaning of Objectivity in Contract' (1984) 100 *LQR* 265. This possibility was left open by McHugh JA in *Air Great Lakes Pty Ltd v K S Easter (Holdings) Pty Ltd* (1985) 2 NSWLR 309 at 336.
51. See, eg *Esanda Ltd v Burgess* [1984] 2 NSWLR 139 at 146; *Biotechnology Australia Pty Ltd v Pace* (1988) 15 NSWLR 130 at 153.
52. See, eg *Allied Marine Transport Ltd v Vale do Rio Doce Navegacao SA* [1985] 1 WLR 925 at 936. Cf *Hospital Products Ltd v United States Surgical Corp* (1984) 156 CLR 41 at 62; 55 ALR 417.
53. See J R Spencer, 'Signature, Consent, and the Rule in *L'Estrange v Graucob*' [1973] *CLJ* 104. Cf Esther Stern, 'Objectivity, Legal Doctrine and the Law of Mistaken Identity' (1995) 8 *JCL* 154. For a recent illustration see *Investors Compensation Scheme Ltd v West Bromwich Building Society* [1998] 1 WLR 896 at 912.
54. [1983] 1 AC 854.
55. [1983] 1 AC 854 at 915. The word 'reasonably' should precede the word 'understood' to make the statement more comprehensive (see P S Atiyah, 'The Hannah Blumenthal and Classical Contract Law' (1986) 102 *LQR* 363 at 366).
56. See also [111].
57. For discussion see, eg Brian Coote, 'The Essence of Contract' (1988–89) 1 *JCL* 91 and 183; R A Hillman, 'The Crisis in Modern Contract Theory' (1988) 67 *Texas Law Review* 62. For an analysis from the critical studies perspective see Peter Drahos and Stephen Parker, 'Critical Contract Law in Australia' (1990) 3 *JCL* 31.
58. See [309].
59. Cf P S Atiyah, 'Contracts, Promises and the Law of Obligations' (1978) 94 *LQR* 193.

from today's. They were developed under the influence of the forces of individualism, competitiveness, laissez-faire, an intellectual climate characterised by a high regard for general principle (both moral and legal), and economic dominance of a free market economy. Atiyah has observed, 'although freedom of contract is by no means dead in the law courts, even among lawyers the decline has been evident'.[61]

In a small and beguiling American work,[62] which the author describes as a 'study in what might be called the process of doctrinal disintegration',[63] Professor Gilmore argued that the general theory of the law of contract was an artificial construct derived by 19th century law teachers and judges rather than something truly to be found in the reasons for decision in the major contract cases from which they drew support. In a passage characteristic of his style, Gilmore observed:[64]

> The instinctive hope of the great system-builders was, no doubt, that the future development of the law could be, if not controlled, at least channelled in an orderly and rational fashion. That hope has proved, in our century of war and revolution, delusive. The systems have come unstuck and we see, presently, no way of glueing them back together again. But it is possible to learn as much from a failed experiment as from a successful one. Our observations of how the general theory of contract was put together and how it fell apart may stand us in good stead when next we feel ourselves in a mood to build something.

Gilmore concludes by speculating that the death of classical contract theory which he accepts has occurred, may herald a new theory. Atiyah also concludes his study by suggesting that 'the time is plainly right for a new theoretical structure for contract, which will place it more firmly in association with the rest of the law of obligations'.[65]

It would be a mistake to see the modern institution of contract as based exclusively, or even perhaps mainly, on a laissez-faire philosophy derived from the 19th century.[66] There is undoubtedly a tension between classical contract theory and the reality of contract bargaining. Take, for example, the legal principle that a promise freely made should be performed.[67] This is no more than an expression of a basic moral presumption that if you

---

60. Cf Ian R Macniel, 'Efficient Breach of Contract: Circles in the Sky' (1982) 68 *Virginia Law Review* 947; Samuel Stoljar, 'Enforcing Benevolent Promises' (1989) 12 *Syd LR* 17 especially at 31, 35; Brian Coote, 'The Essence of Contract — Part II' (1989) 1 *JCL* 183 at 190–1, 201–3.
61. *The Rise and Fall of Freedom of Contract*, 1979, p 716.
62. *The Death of Contract*, 1974. For analysis see R E Speidel, 'An Essay on the Reported Death and Continued Vitality of Contract' (1975) 27 *Stanford LR* 1161; D B King, 'Reshaping Contract Theory and Law: Death of Contracts II' (1994) 7 *JCL* 245 and 8 *JCL* 16. The enduring interest in Gilmore's book is shown by the publication of a symposium in (1995) 90 *Northwestern ULR* 1.
63. *The Death of Contract*, 1974, p 101.
64. *The Death of Contract*, 1974, p 102.
65. *The Rise and Fall of Freedom of Contract*, 1979, p 778.
66. Cf *Air Great Lakes Pty Ltd v K S Easter (Holdings) Pty Ltd* (1985) 2 NSWLR 309 at 338.
67. See, eg *Moschi v Lep Air Services Ltd* [1973] AC 331 at 346; *The Hansa Nord* [1976] QB 44 at 71; *Bunge Corp New York v Tradax Export SA Panama* [1981] 1 WLR 711 at 715; *Ankar Pty Ltd v National Westminster Finance (Australia) Ltd* (1987) 162 CLR 549 at 556–7; 70 ALR 641.

make a promise you should keep it.[68] The legal tension which arises when the enforcement of the promise will cause hardship is no more than a manifestation of the moral dilemma which arises when the promise is found to be improvident. It is trite to say that the courts are not insensitive to the need to make the law produce just solutions.

We have seen that many traditional assumptions of contract law are, in the modern world, subject to qualifications. Not only does the law give content to the word 'freely',[69] but there are also qualifications to the proposition that a promise freely made should be performed.[70] Indeed, although Australian law has been slow in developing the concept, a concept of good faith in contract is now beginning to emerge.[71] The fact that the law is now more generous (or flexible) in defining qualifications than under 'classical' theory is no more than a reflection of the changes in society's perception of the strength of the moral presumption.[72] Courts, being generally on the conservative side, have simply been slower in responding than most members of the community would have liked and this has led to legislative intervention.[73]

It is more difficult today than in the past to see contract law as a coherent whole for four reasons. First, the courts have become more pragmatic in their decisions. Second, legislation usually operates by qualifying, rather than redefining, existing legal principles. Third, contract law today is more complex than in the 19th century. And, fourth, principles cannot be formulated solely from a commercial perspective: the law of contract is more general than that.

---

68. See Rawls, *A Theory of Justice*, 1973, p 342. Cf Atiyah, *The Rise and Fall of Freedom of Contract*, 1979, p 431; Andrew Phang, 'Security of Contract and the Pursuit of Fairness' (2000) 16 *JCL* 120. For a more general approach see Fried, *Contract as Promise*, 1981. Cf F H Easterbrook, 'The Inevitability of Law and Economics' (1989) 1 *Legal Educ Rev* 1.
69. See, eg [1063] (fraud), [1206] (mistake), Chapter 13 (duress), Chapter 14 (undue influence) and [1512] (unconscionability).
70. See, eg [751] (interpretation of exclusion clauses), [1606] (public policy) and [2207] (penalty clauses).
71. See H O Hunter, 'The Duty of Good Faith and Security of Performance' (1993) 6 *JCL* 19; Roger Brownsword, 'Two Concepts of Good Faith' (1994) 7 *JCL* 197; J W Carter and M P Furmston, 'Good Faith and Fairness in the Negotiation of Contracts' (1994-95) 8 *JCL* 1 and 93; John Adams, 'The Economics of Good Faith in Contract' (1995) 8 *JCL* 126; E Allan Farnsworth, 'Good Faith in Contract Performance', in Beatson and Friedmann, eds, *Good Faith and Fault in Contract Law*, 1995, p 153; S M Waddams, 'Good Faith, Unconscionability and Reasonable Expectations' (1995) 9 *JCL* 55; A F Mason, 'Contract, Good Faith and Equitable Standards in Fair Dealing' (2000) 116 *LQR* 66; Elisabeth Peden, 'Incorporating Terms of Good Faith in Contract Law in Australia' (2001) 23 *Syd LR* 222. Cf Mr Justice Steyn, 'The Role of Good Faith and Fair Dealing in Contract Law: A Hair-Shirt Philosophy?' [1991] *Denning LJ* 131. See further [271], [1809], [1842], [1993].
72. Cf Andrew Phang, 'Security of Contract and the Pursuit of Fairness' (2000) 16 *JCL* 120.
73. See [109].

The Role of Contract Law

[114] Consistency and certainty.[74] Consistency and certainty in the law are not merely an indulgence for the benefit of lawyers and law students: they are essential to confident planning for the future by all. But what must be acknowledged is something which the lawyer, steeped in doctrine, has not always been prepared to recognise, namely, that doctrine is formed not in a vacuum but in response to particular problems in time and space.

Similarly, the future viability of legal doctrine depends on considerations extrinsic to the system of doctrine itself, in general its capacity to provide just and efficient solutions to contemporary disputes.

[115] Dispute resolution. The study of contract law is principally a study of legal decisions. Yet, the role of contract law in determining the resolution of contractual disputes can be overestimated. The cost and delay involved in litigation are considerable, notwithstanding persistent attempts to reduce both. Arbitration, as an alternative, has often proved to be even more expensive and time consuming.[75] Both also involve considerable indirect and non-financial costs; for example, expenditure of the parties' own time and energy in preparing for trial, and the worry and mental strain imposed on the litigants and their witnesses.

These problems would not disappear if our adversarial system of litigation were to be abandoned in favour of an inquisitional model. But the law now encourages (by institutional means) the conciliation process as part of 'alternative' dispute resolution processes. These conspire or should conspire to make resort to the courts and to arbitration a last resort. Yet it is the ordinary courts (and, to a lesser extent, arbitration) that give life, power and practical significance to the general principles of contract law in society.

As well as reducing the role played by the general principles of contract law by its incursions into the substantive law,[76] parliament has established various tribunals, commissions, boards and committees with jurisdiction to hear and determine particular classes of contractual or contract-related disputes. Examples are industrial tribunals in relation to employment disputes, and consumer tribunals in relation to disputes arising out of the supply of goods or services (particularly credit) by traders to consumers. A number of reasons for this development can be cited. They include: that a just solution is more likely to emanate from persons having *specialist expertise* and experience than from those expert in abstract legal principles; that the *amount at stake* does not warrant the exhaustive factual and legal exploration to which adversaries before the ordinary courts are entitled; and that there is a *public interest* in the ascertainment of the truth and the resolution of certain classes of contractual or contract-related disputes

---

74. Cf Treitel, *Doctrine and Discretion in the Law of Contract*, 1981.
75. But improvements have been made; see **ACT:** *Commercial Arbitration Act* 1984; **NSW:** *Commercial Arbitration Act* 1984; **NT:** *Commercial Arbitration Act* 1985; **Qld:** *Commercial Arbitration Act* 1990; **SA:** *Commercial Arbitration Act* 1986; **Tas:** *Commercial Arbitration Act* 1986; **Vic:** *Commercial Arbitration Act* 1984; **WA:** *Commercial Arbitration Act* 1985.
76. See [109].

which is inhibited by the ordinary courts' application of the technical rules of evidence and procedure.

It should be noted that many of the recent attempts to devise procedures to avoid the need to resort to litigation themselves involve contracts. Thus, where parties to a contractual dispute agree to use a mediator to assist the resolution, the procedure is itself a contractual one.

[116] The commercial decision-making process. There is little empirical research into the extent to which contract law plays a role in the commercial decision-making process. What evidence there is suggests that business people are prone to make contracts and to solve contractual disputes without reference or with minimal reference to the applicable legal principles.[77]

There are various reasons for this phenomenon, including: ignorance; sheer pressure of day-to-day business makes formality and explicitness in contracting an unwelcome burden; insistence on such formality and explicitness offends by suggesting distrust; the possible need of business people in dispute to have commercial dealings and relations with each other in the future; distrust of lawyers or a perception that they charge too much; the fact that when negotiating a settlement disputants are in control of both the direct result and its foreseeable consequences whereas litigation is nothing if not uncertain; the possibility of disclosure, either to the other party in the course of the interlocutory steps of discovery of documents and answering of interrogatories, or to the public in the course of the final hearing, of facts which a disputant would prefer to have remain private; that litigating itself, irrespective of the result, may damage one's commercial reputation by suggesting that the litigant is not 'realistic' or 'commercial'; and a perception by the disputant and by others that inability to settle is a mark of failure and defeat.

Nevertheless, in the day-to-day activities of any business the law is there, giving to every action a legal consequence. The presumption is that an agreement which satisfies the law's requirements is legally binding as a contract.[78] Business people who are informed on the law of contract may in fact be in a much better position to make decisions, or to understand the consequences of their own decisions than those with whom they contract. The fact that it is rare[79] for parties to reach agreements binding only 'in

---

77. See, eg L M Friedman and S Macaulay, 'Contract Law and Contract Teaching: Past, Present, and Future' [1967] *Wisconsin Law Rev* 805; S Macaulay, 'Non-Contractual Relations in Business' (1963) 28 *Am Soc Rev* 55; H Beale and T Dugdale, 'Contracts between Businessmen; Planning and the Use of Contractual Remedies' (1975) 2 *Brit J Law & Soc* 18; Stewart Macaulay, 'Elegant Models, Empirical Pictures and the Complexities of Contract' (1977) 11 *Law and Society Rev* 507; Yates, *Exclusion Clauses in Contracts*, 2nd ed, 1982, Chapter 1; MacNeil, *The New Social Contract; an Inquiry into Modern Contractual Relations*, 1980; R B Ferguson, 'The Adjudication of Commercial Disputes and the Legal System in Modern England' (1980) 7 *Brit J Law & Soc* 141; R Lewis, 'Contracts Between Businessmen; Reform of the Law of Firm Offers and an Empirical Study of Tendering Practices in the Building Industry' (1982) 9 *Brit J Law & Soc* 153.
78. See [405].
79. See, eg *Orion Insurance Co Plc v Sphere Drake Insurance Plc* [1992] 1 Lloyd's Rep 239.

honour' is itself an indication that commercial people respect the legal sanctions provided by contract law.

Although no-one would suggest that we should abandon contract theory because business people do not make it their business to determine how they are affected, a strong argument can be made for making it simpler and more accessible. That is one function of this and other books, particularly those[80] which are pitched at an audience which is more concerned with the basic applications of the law than detailed analysis of legal principle. It is also a justification for the creation of alternative dispute resolution procedures.

Practising and academic lawyers of today must see contract law for what it is: *one* means of resolving questions and disputes arising from broken agreements.[81] Its content is not inevitable and immutable, and its future depends on its economic and social environment as well as on factors intrinsic to the legal system and its personnel.[82] As Professor Coote[83] states:

> Contract remains alive at common law and its retention can be justified so long as the balance of advantage to society remains with providing a facility by which parties are able to take legal contractual obligations upon themselves.

Australian Contract Law

[117] **The 'flavour' of Australian contract law.** Australian contract law is derived from English law. However, English decisions (unless already adopted) are no longer binding on Australian courts. It is now possible, in the case of the High Court,to refer to nearly a century of case law. It would be surprising if this did not produce an Australian slant to our contract law. The fact that Australian social and legal culture differs from those of other countries itself implies that our contract jurisprudence will have distinctive features. It is therefore appropriate to speak of an 'Australian law of contract'.[84]

---

80. See, eg Carter, *Outline of Contract Law in Australia*, 2nd ed, 1994.
81. For an analysis of the role of contract theory in the provision of advice by practising lawyers see John Swan, 'Party Autonomy and Judicial Intervention: The Impact of Fairness in Commercial Contracts' (1994) 7 *JCL* 1. Cf John Gava and Peter Kincaid, 'Contract and Conventionalism: Professional Attitudes to Changes in the Law of Contract in Australia' (1996) 10 *JCL* 141.
82. See Adams and Brownsword, *Understanding Contract Law*, 1987.
83. Brian Coote, 'The Essence of Contract — Part II' (1989) 1 *JCL* 183 at 201. See also J W Carter, 'Contract, Restitution and Promissory Estoppel' (1989) 12 *UNSWLJ* 30 at 31, 58; Sir Gerard Brennan, 'Opening Address [to the First *Journal of Contract Law* Conference]' (1990) 3 *JCL* 85.
84. For a more radical approach see M P Ellinghaus, 'An Australian Contract Law?' (1989) 2 *JCL* 13. Contrast John Gava, 'An Australian Contract Law? — A Reply' (1998) 12 *JCL* 242.

The first step in identifying the 'flavour' of Australian contract law involves an appreciation of the nature of the cases in which those principles have been applied.[85] Given the traditional rural basis of the economy, and the importance attached by Australian people to home ownership, it is to be expected that by far the most common type of contract to have come before the Australian courts is the sale of land contract. Until quite recently,[86] nearly all the leading High Court cases in contract were decisions on that type of contract. In this respect there is a contrast with English law, which is based mainly on commercial contracts of arbitration, insurance, charterparty and sale of goods. This is a reflection of the role of London as a centre for contract dispute resolution in Europe, even where the contract does not involve residents of the United Kingdom.[87] The discussion in this book of recent decisions concentrates on Australian cases, and the main relevance of English cases lies in giving an account of commercial contracts.

The second step is an acknowledgment of the role which statute now plays in Australian contract law. Although there is no statute codifying contract law,[88] the legislation is extensive. Much of this, such as statutes which regulate bills of exchange, marine insurance, partnership and commercial sale of goods contracts, is derived from English statutes. On the other hand, consumer protection, trade practices and fair trading legislation is more extensive in Australia than in other countries.[89] In particular, the statutory prohibition on conduct that is misleading or deceptive or is likely to mislead or deceive[90] has created a norm of conduct having considerable impact on contract law. Although the legislation includes remedial provisions which operate in conjunction with contract principles, the impact is in many cases to displace those principles.[91]

---

85. See further J W Carter and Andrew Stewart, 'Commerce and Conscience: The High Court's Developing View of Contract' (1993) 23 *UWALR* 49.
86. See [118].
87. See Lord Goff, 'Opening Address [to the Second *Journal of Contract Law* Conference]' (1992) 5 *JCL* 1.
88. For discussion see F M B Reynolds, 'Contract: Codification, Legislation and Judicial Development' (1995) 9 *JCL* 11; S M Waddams, 'Codification, Law Reform and Judicial Development' (1996) 9 *JCL* 192; Dame Mary Arden, 'Time for an English Commercial Code?' [1997] *CLJ* 516. In New Zealand several important areas of contract law are regulated by statutes, enacted not as an 'enduring code, so much as a liberating device' (Richard Sutton, 'Commentary on "Codification, Law Reform and Judicial Development"' (1996) 9 *JCL* 200 at 201).
89. For a general review see L J Priestley, 'Contract — The Burgeoning Maelstrom' (1988) 1 *JCL* 15.
90. See Chapter 11.
91. See generally David Harland, 'The Statutory Prohibition on Misleading or Deceptive Conduct in Australia and its Impact on the Law of Contract' (1995) 111 *LQR* 100. Cf Nicholas Seddon, 'Australian Contract Law: Maelstrom or Measured Mutation?' (1994) 7 *JCL* 93.

[118] Innovation by the High Court. The third step involves an appreciation of a feature to which Sir Anthony Mason drew attention when writing in the first issue of the *Journal of Contract Law*. Referring to the break with the English legal system,[92] and the innovative approach of many recent High Court decisions, he said that the law of contract has recently awoken from a 'long slumber'.[93] Arguably, only in the last decade or so have the High Court's judgments in contract been truly 'innovative'. Thus, in the first edition of this book we referred to several cases of the early 1980s in which the court showed itself to be willing to mould old doctrine to suit the needs of current social and legal conditions.[94] It was noted that these cases all involved sale of land transactions, and the point was made that the innovation was for the most part couched in terms of equitable principle rather than common law.[95] In drawing attention in the second edition to subsequent innovations[96] we noted that the decisions were more concerned with ordinary commercial contracts than land transactions, and not driven exclusively by a desire to promote equitable principles.

Since publication of the second edition there have been relatively few High Court decisions significantly affecting the core of contract law, and it is not possible to discern an overriding concern. The period has been one of consolidation rather than innovation, particularly in the contexts of contract damages[97] and implied terms.[98] The equitable principles have been further refined.[99] In addition, however, there have been decisions which, although not strictly contractual in nature, have a significant impact on contract law, particularly in contexts of restitution[100] and the trade practices legislation.[101]

---

92. See Sir Anthony Mason, 'Australian Contract Law' (1988) 1 *JCL* 1.
93. See Sir Anthony Mason, Book Review (1989) 1 *JCL* 265.
94. These were: *Meehan v Jones* (1982) 149 CLR 571; 42 ALR 463 (see [274]); *Taylor v Johnson* (1983) 151 CLR 422; 45 ALR 265 (see [1254]); *Commercial Bank of Australia Ltd v Amadio* (1983) 151 CLR 447; 46 ALR 402 (see [1512]); *Legione v Hateley* (1983) 152 CLR 406; 46 ALR 1 (see [373], [1979]).
95. See Anthony Mason, 'The Place of Equity and Equitable Remedies in the Contemporary Common Law World' (1994) 110 *LQR* 238.
96. Reference was made to: *Pavey & Matthews Pty Ltd v Paul* (1987) 162 CLR 221 (see [520], [2308]); *Waltons Stores (Interstate) Ltd v Maher* (1988) 164 CLR 387; 76 ALR 513 (see [376]); *Trident General Insurance Co Ltd v McNiece Bros Pty Ltd* (1988) 165 CLR 107; 80 ALR 574 (see [917]); *Hungerfords v Walker* (1989) 171 CLR 125; 84 ALR 119 (see [2151]).
97. See *Commonwealth of Australia v Amann Aviation Pty Ltd* (1991) 174 CLR 64; 104 ALR 1 (see [2111]); *Baltic Shipping Co v Dillon (The Mikhail Lermontov)* (1993) 176 CLR 344; 111 ALR 289 (see [2153]); *Astley v Austrust Ltd* (1999) 197 CLR 1 (see [2129]).
98. See *Byrne v Australian Airlines Ltd* (1995) 185 CLR 410; 131 ALR 422; *Breen v Williams* (1996) 186 CLR 71; 138 ALR 259.
99. See *Louth v Diprose* (1992) 175 CLR 621; 110 ALR 1 (undue influence and unconscionable conduct in relation to gift); *Garcia v National Australia Bank Ltd* (1998) 194 CLR 395; 155 ALR 614 (undue influence); *Bridgewater v Leahy* (1998) 194 CLR 457; 158 ALR 66 (unconscionable conduct); *Giumelli v Giumelli* (1999) 196 CLR 101; 161 ALR 473 (promissory estoppel).
100. See, eg *David Securities Pty Ltd v Commonwealth Bank of Australia* (1992) 175 CLR 353 (restitution of money paid under mistake of law); *Baltic Shipping Co v Dillon (The Mikhail Lermontov)* (1993) 176 CLR 344 (total failure of consideration).

[119] Modernising and internationalising contract law. There are many decisions, in which the High Court, while not exactly being innovative, has modernised contract law.[102] This process is also (perhaps more so) apparent in the decisions of the State Supreme Courts and the Federal Court. Although space does not permit us to highlight particular cases here, they are discussed throughout the book. We do not intend by referring exclusively to the High Court's decisions to undervalue or trivialise those contributions.

It is frequently difficult to discern whether Australian law is diverging from English law in the formulation of principle rather than (as the traditional contrast between sale of land and commercial contracts would suggest) in the application of common principles.[103] It is also true that judges of the High Court have enjoyed high regard as expositors of the law of contract, and their contract judgments have often been cited in the courts of England and other Commonwealth countries. Australian cases therefore sometimes form the basis for changes in the law of other jurisdictions. An extremely important example[104] of this has arisen in the law of restitution, where the High Court's decision in *Pavey & Matthews Pty Ltd v Paul*[105] to adopt unjust enrichment was followed in England.[106]

While it might be objected that *Pavey & Matthews* was not a decision applying contract principles, the adoption was symptomatic of what is arguably the most significant development in the past decade. This development might be termed the 'internationalisation' of the common law, including contract law.[107] It has, moreover, been reinforced (or hastened) by the adoption[108] of the *United Nations Convention on Contracts for the International Sale of Goods* 1980.[109] Far from being dead, contract law

---

101. See, eg *Wardley Australia Ltd v State of Western Australia* (1992) 175 CLR 514; 109 ALR 247 (limitation of actions); *Webb Distributors (Aust) Pty Ltd v State of Victoria* (1993) 179 CLR 15; 117 ALR 321 (approach to discretionary jurisdiction — see [1116]); *Sellars v Adelaide Petroleum NL* (1994) 179 CLR 332; 120 ALR 16 (assessment of damages); *Marks (in a Representative Capacity) v GIO Australia Holdings Ltd* (1998) 196 CLR 494; 158 ALR 333 (assessment of damages — see [1113]).
102. See, eg *Codelfa Construction Pty Ltd v State Rail Authority of New South Wales* (1982) 149 CLR 337; 41 ALR 367 (see [629], [713], [2017]); *Ankar Pty Ltd v National Westminster Finance (Australia) Ltd* (1987) 162 CLR 549 (see [1918]); *Foran v Wight* (1989) 168 CLR 385; 88 ALR 413 (see [1942]).
103. Thus, with *Legione v Hateley* (1983) 152 CLR 406 may be contrasted *Scandinavian Trading Tanker Co AB v Flota Petrolera Ecuatoriana* [1983] 2 AC 694 (see [1979]) in which there was no relief from the 'forfeiture' produced by exercise of a contractual right to terminate. But see *Darlington Futures Ltd v Delco Australia Pty Ltd* (1986) 161 CLR 500; 68 ALR 85 where the High Court had occasion to disagree with the English approach to limitation clauses in contracts; see [752].
104. For another illustration see *Behzadi v Shaftesbury Hotels Ltd* [1992] Ch 1.
105. (1987) 162 CLR 221 (see [520], [2308]).
106. See *Lipkin Gorman v Karpnale Ltd* [1991] 2 AC 548. Compare, in tort, the reliance on Australian law in *Murphy v Brentwood District Council* [1991] 1 AC 398 (see J G Fleming, (1990) 106 *LQR* 525).
107. See Sir Anthony Mason, 'Changing the Law in a Changing Society' (1993) 67 *ALJ* 568, especially at 570–3; Lord Oliver of Aylmerton, 'Requiem for the Common Law?' (1993) 67 *ALJ* 675, especially at 686–7; H O Hunter and J W Carter, 'Is Commercial Law Becoming a World Law?' (1996) 2 *NZBLQ* 161. See also Arthur Rosett, 'UNIDROIT Principles and Harmonization of International Commercial Law: Focus on Chapter 7' [1997] *Uniform Law Review* 441.
108. See [276].

appears to be entering a stage where there is a high degree of common principle between common law jurisdictions such as Australia,[110] and also to some extent between these jurisdictions and those which otherwise operate under civil law principles. The development also militates against the view that we were inclined to express in previous editions, namely, that a general Australian contract law was being formulated.

---

109. See also the *UNIDROIT Principles For International Commercial Contracts* (1994) which, although not having the force of law, provide a facility for the adoption of common principles to govern contracts between parties who operate under different systems of law. See M P Furmston, 'Unidroit Principles For International Commercial Contracts' (1996) 10 *JCL* 11; Roy Goode, 'International Restatements of Contract and English Law' [1997] *Uniform Law Review* 231.
110. It is perhaps unfortunate that the United Kingdom has not yet adopted the *United Nations Convention on Contracts for the International Sale of Goods* 1980. See Johan Steyn, 'The Vienna Convention: A Kind of Esperanto', in Birks, ed, *The Frontiers of Liability*, 1994, Vol 2, p 12.

PART II
Formation of Contract

Chapter 2

Agreement

Introduction 201
Offer 207
   Offer and Invitation to Treat 208
   Offers to Unascertained Persons 216
   Necessity for Communication of Offer 217
Acceptance 218
   What Amounts to Acceptance 218
   Who May Accept? 225
   Communication of Acceptance 226
   The Postal Acceptance Rule 230
   The Requirement of Knowledge 239
Duration of Offers 242
   Revocation 243
   Rejection 251
   Lapse of Time 254
   Offers Subject to Condition 256
   Death of Offeror or Offeree 257
Uncertainty and Incompleteness 258
Impact of Vienna Convention 276

Introduction

[201] Importance of agreement. The law of contract is concerned with the rights and obligations which arise from the making of a promise which the law will enforce. Except in the case of contracts under seal,[1] such consequences arise only when two or more parties have reached agreement, and the starting point of our study must therefore be the rules employed by the law in identifying those circumstances in which parties who are alleged to have become contractually bound will be regarded as having reached agreement. The foundation of the legal relations which we call contract is

---

1. See Chapter 3.

thus the agreement of the parties, and this remains so even though the law increasingly imposes rights and obligations upon contracting parties without reference to the question of what their real intentions may have been.[2] In the absence of agreement (or, perhaps more accurately, in the absence of circumstances which the law treats as giving rise to agreement),[3] there can be no contract. Of course, although the existence of agreement is essential, it is not of itself sufficient, for an agreement may fail to take effect as an enforceable contract because of the absence of another essential element, such as consideration[4] or contractual intention[5] or some required formality.[6]

[202] **The traditional approach.** The traditional approach to the question whether parties contemplating a contract have concluded negotiations and reached agreement is to inquire whether there has been both offer and acceptance; that is, a clear indication ('offer') by one party (the 'offeror') of a willingness to be bound on certain terms, accompanied by an unqualified assent to that offer communicated by the other party (the 'offeree') to the offeror ('acceptance'). So accustomed have lawyers become to the analysis of problems of formation of contract in terms of offer and acceptance that it is often overlooked that this method of analysis is of comparatively recent origin and appears indeed to have developed in the 19th century as a result of the need to provide a framework for the increasing number of cases where parties dealt with each other at a distance by communicating by letter or telegram (or, more recently, by telephone, telex or facsimile).[7]

[203] **Limitations on traditional approach.** So embedded in the thinking of lawyers has offer and acceptance become that some writers insist that the correspondence of offer and acceptance is an inevitable requirement of contractual agreement.[8] And yet in some important situations such an analysis can be maintained only at the cost of much artificiality. Where a contract is formed by both parties signing a written document, it may sometimes be possible to regard the party who signs first as being the offeror,[9] and yet it will usually be a matter of chance which party happens to put pen to paper first. Moreover, contracts for the sale of land are very commonly formed by the parties (or their representatives) exchanging duplicate copies of the agreement, so that each party possesses a copy signed by the other. In such a case it seems pointless (as well as

---

2. For examples of situations in which certain of the legal consequences of a contract are established by law irrespective of what the parties (or, more likely, one of them) may have intended, see the discussion in Chapter 7 of legislation affecting exclusion clauses in consumer transactions.
3. See [206].
4. See Chapter 3.
5. See Chapter 4.
6. See Chapter 4.
7. S J Stoljar, 'Offer, Promise and Agreement' (1955) 50 *Northwestern ULR* 445 at 453–6; H K Lücke, 'Striking a Bargain' (1962) 3 *Adel LR* 293. See also A W B Simpson, 'Innovation in Nineteenth Century Contract Law' (1975) 91 *LQR* 247.
8. Salmond and Williams, *Principles of the Law of Contracts*, 1945, p 70.
9. See, eg *Outer Suburban Property Ltd v Clarke* [1933] SASR 221 (intending purchaser signing document which was later signed on behalf of vendor).

artificial) to attempt to analyse the formation of agreement in terms of a succession of offer and acceptance.[10]

The classic illustration of a case which seems to defy analysis in terms of offer and acceptance is *Clarke v Dunraven*[11] where the owners of yachts entered in a race run by a yachting club agreed with the club to be bound by the club rules. When the defendant's yacht, in breach of the rules, collided with that of the plaintiff, it was held that each owner had impliedly contracted with every other owner to be bound by the rules. The House of Lords had little difficulty in holding that such a series of contracts had arisen (the main point of discussion being the correct interpretation of the rules), and yet it seems impossible to provide a satisfactory analysis explaining this result in terms of offer and acceptance.[12] It is suggested that the true situation is that concurrence of offer and acceptance is not an inevitable prerequisite of a binding agreement.[13] In the cases just discussed, indeed, such a concurrence need not be sought for, as there is little doubt on the facts that agreement has in fact been reached. It is in cases where one party denies the other party's claim that agreement had been finalised that an analysis of the facts in terms of offer and acceptance will prove useful. Offer and acceptance is thus seen as an analytical tool which, in at least the great majority of disputed cases, will illuminate the one ultimate question with which the law is here concerned, namely whether the parties had completed negotiations envisaging an agreement and had in fact reached agreement.

The student reading textbook accounts of the law of offer and acceptance (and judicial opinions on problems of formation of contract) should always bear in mind that the analytical problem involved in approaching any given factual situation is one of stating the facts in a form which has usually not been done by the parties themselves. Business people do not always (or even normally) conduct negotiations in terms of such concepts as offer, acceptance, revocation and counter-offer with which the student will be familiar by the time this chapter has been read.[14] It will be shown later, for example, that a statement described by its author as an 'acceptance' may

---

10. Such an analysis is perhaps more realistic where the exchange takes place by mail: see, eg *Eccles v Bryant* [1948] 1 Ch 93; *Rice v Taylor* (1969) 89 WN (Pt 1) (NSW) 596.
11. [1897] AC 59.
12. Although attempts have been made to establish the contrary, the view expressed in the text has been convincingly established by Treitel, *The Law of Contract*, 10th ed, 1999, pp 45–6. 'I think it takes some ingenuity, at times, to reconcile the practice of the common law with the theory of offer and acceptance as elements of contract': *Subdivisions Ltd v Payne* [1934] SASR 214 at 220 per Napier J, discussed by H K Lücke (1962) 3 *Adel LR* 293. See also *Vroon BV v Foster's Brewing Group Ltd* [1994] 2 VR 32 and more recently *Brambles Holdings Ltd v Bathurst City Council* [2001] NSWCA 61 at paras 71–81 per Heydon JA, but compare *Toyota Motor Corp Australia Ltd v Ken Morgan Motors Pty Ltd* [1994] 2 VR 106 at 177–8 per Tagdell J.
13. Thus it has been said in the United States that 'a manifestation of mutual assent may be made even though neither offer nor acceptance can be identified and even though the moment of formation cannot be determined' (*Restatement (2d) Contracts*, §22(2)).
14. 'It would be ludicrous to suppose that business men couch their communications in the form of a catechism or reduce their negotiations to such a species of interrogatory as was formulated in the Roman *Stipulatio*': Cheshire and Fifoot, *Law of Contract*, 3rd ed, 1952, p 28.

very well be, in legal effect, a 'counter-offer'. Our task is rather to look to the intentions of the parties as disclosed by their words and conduct and to attempt, by applying such concepts to the facts, to see whether agreement was ever reached.

[204] **Lengthy negotiations.** Where agreement has been reached after lengthy negotiations, the analysis of those negotiations in terms of offer and acceptance may at times seem rather unrealistic. In particular, where a series of offers are put and rejected and replaced by counter-proposals, it will be a matter of pure chance as to which of the parties is ultimately seen as offeror and which as offeree ('acceptor').[15] It is suggested that this should not disturb us, for in such cases the analysis will usually indicate whether or not the party is correct who insists that at some point in time negotiations ceased and final agreement was reached. So long as the analytical tools employed enable us to answer this ultimate question, it matters not which party made the final offer which was converted into a contract on acceptance by the other party.[16] It is true that the arbitrary characterisation of one of the parties as acceptor rather than offeror may have crucial consequences when the question arises as to the place where a contract was formed,[17] but this is a result not so much of the inadequacies of the rules governing formation of contract but of the use of those rules to solve an entirely different problem for which they may not be well suited.

[205] **Agreement inferred from conduct.** The formation of agreement will in many cases be inferred from the conduct of the parties. Sometimes there may be no identifiable offer and acceptance because the parties have not expressly discussed the formation of contract but have indicated by their conduct that they did in fact intend to contract.[18] In many cases a more realistic explanation is that by the time a dispute arises, perhaps many years after the alleged contract was entered into, no direct evidence is available of what was said by the parties and yet their conduct is consistent only with the hypothesis that an agreement was in fact made by them.[19] In other cases an express offer has been made which was never expressly accepted or rejected, but the subsequent conduct of the offeree in performing the acts contemplated in the offer indicate an intention to accept.

Thus, in *Brown v Brown*[20] the defendant instructed her architect to prepare a contract and call for tenders for the erection of a house. The architect, acting under the defendant's instructions, accepted the plaintiff's tender. The defendant never signed the contract, nor was she aware of its

---

15. For examples, see *Hampstead Meats Pty Ltd v Emerson & Yates Pty Ltd* [1967] SASR 109; *Integrated Lighting & Ceilings Pty Ltd v Phillips Electrical Pty Ltd* (1969) 90 WN (Pt l) (NSW) 693. See also *Brinkibon Ltd v Stahag Stahl GmbH* [1983] 2 AC 34 at 40.
16. The problems which arise where each party attempts to contract on the basis of his own set of printed terms arise not so much from an arbitrary labelling of one party as 'offeror' and the other as 'offeree' but from the insistence that offer and acceptance must exactly correspond: see [222].
17. See [236].
18. See, eg *Haynes v McNeil* (1906) 8 WALR 186; *Glass v Pioneer Rubber Works of Australia Ltd* [1906] VLR 754.
19. See *W A Dewhurst & Co Pty Ltd v Cawrse* [1960] VR 278 at 282.

terms, but the house was built and certain interim payments were made by the defendant, and in correspondence she referred to 'the contract'. In these circumstances it was held that she was bound by the written contract. It will be noted that in cases such as this the defendant's consent is inferred from conduct, even though it may be impossible to establish a precise point in time when the offer of the other party was accepted. (This type of situation must be clearly distinguished from that of an offer of a unilateral contract,[21] calling for acceptance by performance of the act stipulated in the offer; we are here concerned with contracts where the commencement of performance by the offeree is seen as implying a promise to complete that performance, that is an acceptance, giving rise to a bilateral contract, is inferred from the actions of the offeree.)

[206] **Objective approach.** It must be remembered that, as is indicated more fully elsewhere, the law is in general concerned with the interpretation which would be placed upon the words and actions of the parties by a reasonable person, rather than upon their subjective intentions.[22] This approach is based partly upon practical problems of proof, and partly upon the notion that a person is entitled to act on the basis that what another appears to intend will be binding upon him or her. Thus an offer must normally be interpreted in the sense in which it would reasonably be understood by an ordinary person, even though the offeror's actual meaning was otherwise. Likewise, even if a party is convinced that a contract was formed on the sending of a letter by that party, no contract will result if 'the meaning that would be conveyed to an ordinary sensible person by that letter' was that there was no binding contract and that the matter was still open to negotiation.[23]

Conversely, acts otherwise amounting to acceptance are not prevented from being effective because of a reservation not communicated to the other party.[24] Further, the law will sometimes hold that an acceptance by mail is effective even though, unknown to the offeree, a letter withdrawing the offer had previously been posted to him.[25] Nonetheless, the frequency with which such cases occur should not be exaggerated, for in the great majority of cases a person's apparent intention will in fact reflect their real intention. The extent to which our law has committed itself to the objective approach in respect of questions of intention is a matter of dispute, but it is in general true to say that the common law is in principle committed to an objective approach, even though occasionally this approach is not applied

---

20. (1905) 5 SR (NSW) 146. For further examples see *Brogden v Metropolitan Railway Co* (1877) 2 App Cas 666; *Malthouse v Adelaide Milk Supply Co-operative Ltd* [1922] SASR 572; *Empirnall Holdings Pty Ltd v Machon Paull Partners Pty Ltd* (1988) 14 NSWLR 523. See also *Integrated Computer Services Pty Ltd v Digital Equipment Corp (Aust) Pty Ltd* (1988) 5 BPR 97,326.
21. Discussed [249]–[250].
22. See [110], [606], [703], [1024], [1213].
23. *John Howard & Co (Northern) Ltd v J P Knight Ltd* [1969] 1 Lloyd's Rep 364.
24. *Rymark Australia Development Consultants Pty Ltd v Draper* [1977] Qd R 336.
25. See [244].

with complete consistency.[26] Much of the difficulty of the law of mistake (discussed in Chapter 12) arises from confusion over this point.

Offer

[207] **Definition.** An offer may be described as the indication by one person to another of his or her willingness to enter into a contract with that person on certain terms.[27] The statement alleged to be an offer must indicate a willingness by the offeror to be bound without further negotiation as to the terms of the proposed contract. Although the making of an offer cannot, of course, in itself give rise to a contract, an offer does have legal significance in that it creates in the offeree a power subsequently to create a contract by the offeree's unilateral action, that is, by accepting the offer (provided that the offer has not previously been withdrawn or otherwise terminated).[28]

Whether a statement is an offer depends on whether the person to whom it is addressed would reasonably interpret it as such, and this question depends on the interpretation of what has been said by the parties. Where it is alleged, for example, that a letter or series of letters should be read as containing an offer, the correspondence as a whole must be looked at, and it is not permissible to regard a particular phrase or sentence as amounting to an offer to contract if the correspondence as a whole indicates a contrary intention. A good example is to be found in *Australian Woollen Mills Pty Ltd v The Commonwealth*,[29] where letters were held to contain merely a statement of government policy as to a proposed subsidy scheme for manufacturers rather than an offer capable of acceptance by the plaintiff manufacturer.

It is not legitimate to interpret as an offer a statement of intention as to a future course of action, not put forward as an offer and not inviting acceptance or rejection.[30] As it is the intention of the alleged offeror which is decisive, a statement containing the word 'offer' may nonetheless indicate that the word is being used in its frequent colloquial sense of indicating merely a willingness to commence negotiations.[31] This is especially true where a document is drawn up by lay people without professional assistance, though it would seem that in doubtful cases there will be some tendency to interpret the word in the narrower sense in which it is used in this chapter.[32] In a number of cases a statement which its maker described

---

26. See the discussion in *Air Great Lakes Pty Ltd v K S Easter (Holdings) Pty Ltd* (1985) 2 NSWLR 309. For a useful comparison of common law and civil law approaches see F Kessler and E Fine, 'Culpa in Contrahendo' (1964) 77 *Harv LR* 401.
27. The American *Restatement (2d) Contracts*, §24 puts it thus: 'An offer is the manifestation of willingness to enter into a bargain, so made as to justify another person in understanding that his assent to that bargain is invited and will conclude it'.
28. *Corbin on Contracts*, Vol 1, 1963, p 24.
29. (1954) 93 CLR 546.
30. *Milne v A-G (Tas)* (1956) 95 CLR 460. See also *Re Sander* (1934) 7 ABC 129 (statement by father that he hoped to be able to repay his son's debt not a promise to pay); *Walk v Matthews* (1914) 18 CLR 440 (promise by father to leave child a share of his estate a representation of intention, not a contractual promise).
31. *Spencer v Harding* (1870) LR 5 CP 561; *Clifton v Palumbo* [1944] 2 All ER 497.
32. *Patterson v Dolman* [1908] VLR 354; *Bigg v Boyd Gibbins Ltd* [1971] 2 All ER 183.

as an 'agreement' was held to be merely an offer as it was clear that there was no concluded agreement,[33] and a statement which is expressed as an acceptance may yet be in the circumstances clearly merely an offer.[34]

Offer and Invitation to Treat

[208] Invitation to treat distinguished from offer. The question often arises as to whether a seller who has indicated a desire to sell certain goods has made an offer which, on acceptance, is capable of binding the seller. Very often the seller will be regarded as having merely issued what is usually called an 'invitation to treat' — a request to others to make offers or to engage in negotiations with a sale in mind. If the seller has only issued an invitation to treat, a reply to the invitation will at most be an offer (even if phrased in terms of acceptance) which the seller has the option to accept or reject. (Of course, the reply itself will not necessarily amount to an offer — it may itself be merely an indication of willingness to negotiate.) The question of whether a statement is properly to be regarded as an offer depends on the interpretation reasonably to be placed upon it by one in the position of the person to whom it was addressed. In all cases the question to be asked is whether the statement can be taken as indicating an intention by the alleged offeror to be bound, without further discussion or negotiation, on acceptance of the terms set out by the offeror.

Rules have been developed by the courts as to some commonly recurring situations, but these rules simply indicate the normal inference to be drawn in such situations as to intention. Care must be taken not to apply them mechanically, for it is always possible that the language used, or the surrounding circumstances (including previous discussion between the parties), will indicate that the normal inference would be inappropriate in a particular factual situation. It may also be noted that there remain commonly recurring situations where the appropriate prima facie analysis of the facts in terms of offer and acceptance may still cause difficulties. Stephen J remarked that '[the] doctrine, of the formation of contracts by offer and acceptance, encounters difficulties when sought to be applied, outside the realms of commerce and conveyancing, to the everyday contractual situations which are a feature of life in modern urban communities'.[35]

It has often been held that the circulation by a merchant of price lists or of other promotional material giving particulars of merchandise which he or she has for sale does not amount to the making of an offer. This is so

---

33. *Dickinson v Dodds* (1876) 2 Ch D 463.
34. *Wells v Birtchnell* (1893) 19 VLR 473 (document stating 'I agree to purchase' merely an offer as no previous offer made). A purported but ineffective acceptance will very often have effect as a counter-offer: see [219].
35. *MacRobertson Miller Airline Services v Commissioner of State Taxation (WA)* (1975) 133 CLR 125 at 136; 8 ALR 131 (a case in which it was said that the issue of an airline ticket to an intending passenger amounts to an offer which is accepted by the passenger orally or (more usually) by conduct in retaining the ticket without objecting to any of the conditions contained on it). See also *Hood v Anchor Line (Henderson Bros) Ltd* [1918] AC 837 at 846; *Wilkie v London Passenger Transport Board* [1947] 1 All ER 258 at 259; *New Zealand Shipping Co Ltd v A M Satterthwaite & Co Ltd* [1975] AC 154 at 167.

even though the material may refer to the seller 'offering for sale' the goods concerned, for in that case the word 'offer' will normally be read in its colloquial sense of indicating a willingness to consider a sale while still retaining the freedom to reject any particular proposal which may be made in response to the 'offer'. Thus, in *Spencer v Harding*[36] it was held that a circular stating 'we are instructed to offer to the trade for sale' certain described goods was merely an invitation to treat and not an offer capable of acceptance. The same result follows where goods are advertised for sale[37] or are displayed for sale in a retail shop.[38] The result reached in such cases is often put on the basis that were the seller to be regarded as making an offer, the number of orders (that is, binding acceptances) received would be potentially limitless and might well exceed the seller's total stock.[39] In that event the seller could not, if further stock could not be procured, actually perform each contract, but would be liable in damages to each customer whose order was not filled. But the difficulty that the seller cannot know in advance how many orders will be received could be met, if an offer were in fact intended, by an express provision limiting the seller's liability to the amount of stock in hand or, in the case of a poster displayed at the point of sale, by removal of the poster when stocks were exhausted.[40]

There is certainly no rule that an advertisement is never capable of taking effect as an offer.[41] Thus, in *Carlill v Carbolic Smoke Ball Co*[42] the defendant advertised its medical preparation in a number of newspapers and stated that '£100 reward will be paid by the Carbolic Smoke Ball Company to any person who contracts the increasing epidemic influenza ... after having used the ball ... according to the printed directions supplied with each ball'. The plaintiff, who caught influenza despite having, on reading the advertisement, used the smoke ball as directed, claimed payment of £100 and was held to be entitled to succeed. A number of issues, to which reference will be made later, were involved in this case, but the point relevant here is that the judges were unanimous in regarding the advertisement as an offer, which was accepted by those members of the public who used the balls on the faith of the advertisement and yet caught influenza. The advertisement was one for a unilateral contract (a promise in return for an act)[43] and acceptance occurred by the plaintiff's conduct

---

36. (1870) LR 5 CP 561. See also *Grainger v Gough* [1896] AC 325 at 333–4.
37. *Partridge v Crittenden* [1968] 2 All ER 421.
38. *Pharmaceutical Society of Great Britain v Boots Cash Chemists (Southern) Ltd* [1953] 1 QB 401; *Fisher v Bell* [1961] 1 QB 394. Cf *Reardon v Morley Ford Pty Ltd* (1980) 33 ALR 417 (a decision on s 56 of the *Trade Practices Act* 1974 (Cth)), not followed in *Wallace v Brodribb* (1985) 58 ALR 737.
39. See, eg *Grainger v Gough* [1896] AC 325 at 333–4; *Esso Petroleum Ltd v Commissioners of Customs & Excise* [1976] 1 All ER 117 at 126.
40. As to the latter point see *Esso Petroleum Ltd v Commissioners of Customs & Excise* [1976] 1 All ER 117 at 124, 126 (per Lord Russell). In that case at least two of the Law Lords (Lords Simon and Wilberforce) regarded the display by petrol station proprietors of posters promising a 'gift' for every four gallons of petrol purchased as an offer.
41. For American examples see *Restatement (2d) Contracts*, §26; *Lefkowitz v Great Minneapolis Surplus Store* 86 NW 2d 689 (1957).
42. [1893] 1 QB 256. For a very interesting discussion of the background to this famous case see A W B Simpson, 'Quackery and Contract Law: The Case of the Carbolic Smoke Ball' (1985) 14 *J Leg Studies* 345.
43. See [249].

without any direct contact with the defendant prior to her lodging her claim for the sum of £100. The fact that the nature of the proposed transaction involves no negotiation between the parties no doubt explains why cases of advertisements offering rewards for the return of lost or stolen property, or for the supply of information leading to the arrest or conviction of criminals, are almost always treated by the courts as amounting to offers.[44]

The argument that the advertisement in *Carlill's* case was a mere vague puff, not capable of giving rise to a contract, was met by pointing to the precision with which the promise to pay the reward was made (despite the extravagance of the claims made in regard to the efficacy of the preparation). The conclusive point was perhaps that the advertisement went on to state that '£1,000 is deposited with the Alliance Bank, shewing our sincerity in the matter', though it should not be assumed that the result would necessarily have been different in the absence of this statement. The advertisement had to be read in its plain meaning, as the public would understand it, and so regarded, it was held that it would be understood by the public as an offer which was to be acted upon. Similarly, although the display of goods for sale will not normally be regarded as constituting an offer for sale, the display of an automatic vending machine apparently constitutes an offer which is accepted by those customers who insert their money into the machine.[45]

[209] Statement of price. The question often arises as to whether a statement by a seller, made in answer to an inquiry, of the price at which he or she is prepared to sell goods amounts to an offer. The circumstances may indicate that the seller is prepared to be bound without further negotiations, and that such questions as to the time when the goods are to be delivered will be settled by reference to terms which are implied by law in the absence of express agreement. However, the more valuable the subject matter of the transaction is and the more complex the contemplated transaction, the less likely it is that an agreement on price without more will be held to bind the parties. For example, in *Howard Smith & Co Ltd v Varawa*[46] it was alleged that an agreement for the sale of a steamship at a price of £28,000 was to be found in a series of international telegrams exchanged between the parties. Griffith CJ commented:[47]

> No doubt a contract for the purchase of a named ship for a lump sum without more may be a good and complete contract. But it is highly improbable that it would be made unless both parties were familiar with the subject matter, and were ad idem as to what was intended to be included by

---

44. Treitel, *The Law of Contract*, 10th ed, 1999, p 13. See, eg *Williams v Carwardine* (1833) 5 Car & P 566; 172 ER 1101; *R v Clarke* (1927) 40 CLR 227. Query the application of the reward cases in *Denton v Great Northern Railway Co* (1856) J E & B 860; 119 ER 701 where a majority held that the publication of a railway timetable amounted to an offer accepted by any intending passenger who tendered the price of a ticket.
45. See *Thornton v Shoe Lane Parking Ltd* [1971] 2 QB 163 at 169 per Lord Denning MR.
46. (1907) 5 CLR 68.
47. (1907) 5 CLR 68 at 76. See also *Kelly v Caledonian Coal Co* (1898) 19 LR (NSW) 1 (statement of price at which coal would be supplied over 18-month period held not to amount to a promise to supply in the absence of any reference to quantity to be delivered); *Re Webster* (1975) 132 CLR 270.

the name of the ship, and it seems to me still more improbable when one of the parties had no acquaintance with the subject matter which was at a distance of several thousand miles. Was it intended to include the apparel and furniture of the ship, which was a passenger ship, or not? Was the delivery to be immediate or deferred, and to whom and where was it to be made? ... Upon the sale of a ship certain matters must be provided for, either expressly or by implication. In this case there is no express provision, and the circumstances do not afford grounds for any definite implication.

A number of cases have involved contracts for the sale of land. Quite apart from the question of price, a large number of important questions arise in such cases: for example, whether vacant possession is to be given (a matter of particular importance if the property is tenanted); whether encumbrances such as existing mortgages are to be discharged prior to conveyance of title; (in the case of land not under Torrens system title) the nature of the title which the purchaser must accept; and the time within which the transaction is to be completed by transfer of title and payment of purchase price. These matters are normally governed by quite lengthy and detailed written contracts drawn up by the parties' legal advisers (or, in some States, land agents). Such a formal contract is not, however, essential, and provided that the parties have identified the subject matter and agreed on a price, the most informal agreement (usually called an 'open contract') may be effective as a binding contract, and the types of questions referred to above will be governed by terms implied, in the absence of express agreement, by the common law or by statute.[48] The mere fact, however, that parties to such transactions do not normally intend to be bound until a contract governing such matters has been entered into and that the terms implied by law into open contracts are frequently considered as giving insufficient protection to the parties (especially vendors) means that the courts will look particularly carefully at the correspondence[49] for some clear indication that, despite the absence of agreement on details, a concluded contract was really intended by the parties.

> It is true that there can be a concluded agreement for the sale of land which merely fixes the parties, the subject matter and the price ... But very often the absence of any reference to matters which one would normally expect to be the subject of negotiation has been taken as a strong indication that no definite concluded agreement has been reached.[50]

Thus in *Harvey v Facey*[51] a telegram stating 'Lowest cash price for Bumper Hall Pen £900' sent in reply to a telegram asking 'Will you sell us Bumper Hall Pen [a farm]? Telegraph lowest cash price', was held not to be

---

48. As to implied terms see generally Chapter 6. For a discussion of open contracts for the sale of land see Stonham, *Law of Vendor and Purchaser*, 1964, pp 105 ff.
49. Contracts for the sale of land must generally be evidenced in writing to be enforceable: see Chapter 5.
50. *Pattison v Mann* (1975) 13 SASR 34 at 37 per Bray CJ.
51. [1893] AC 552. See also *Clifton v Palumbo* [1944] 2 All ER 497; *B Seppelt & Sons Ltd v Commissioner for Main Roads* (1975) 1 BPR 9147; *Coogee Esplanade Surf Motel Pty Ltd v The Commonwealth* (1976) 50 ALR 363. Compare *Bigg v Boyd Gibbins Ltd* [1971] 2 All ER 183, where *Harvey v Facey* and *Clifton v Palumbo* were distinguished on the facts of the case. The more detailed and definite a proposal is, the more likely it is to be construed as an offer: see Schlesinger, ed, *Formation of Contracts*, 1968, Vol 1, pp 323–9, 346.

an offer. The mere statement of the lowest price the vendor would accept contained no implied promise to sell at that price.

[210] Application for shares or debentures. A person applying, in response to a prospectus, for the issue to him or her of shares or debentures in a company is regarded as making an offer, which must be accepted by the company before any contract arises. The reason the prospectus is regarded as an invitation to treat is that the directors of the company are taken to reserve the right (indeed such a right is usually expressly stated) to reject applications in the event of an over-subscription. But in appropriate circumstances this may not be the correct inference. Thus in *Re Mount Tomah Blue Metals Ltd*[52] a company in financial difficulties sent a circular to existing shareholders appealing for funds (in respect of which debentures were to be issued to secure the amounts advanced) to enable the company to make an arrangement with creditors in an attempt to avoid liquidation proceedings. It was held in these circumstances that the sending of the circular was an offer, which had been accepted by those shareholders who had responded by sending money to the company.

[211] Auction sales. It is well established that an auctioneer who puts property up for sale is not offering to sell but is issuing a request for bids. Each bid made at the auction is an offer, and no contract is formed until the auctioneer accepts the highest bid by 'knocking down' the goods and declaring them sold. It follows that until acceptance any bid may be withdrawn under the principle that an offer can be withdrawn at any time prior to acceptance.[53] This rule is now codified in the sale of goods legislation.[54]

It also follows, as was held in *Harris v Nickerson*[55] that an advertisement of an auction sale is simply a declaration of intention to hold the sale, not an offer binding the auctioneer to any prospective purchaser who claims compensation for expenses wasted in travelling to the sale only to find that the sale is cancelled. Some doubt exists, however, where an auction sale is stated to be 'without reserve', that is, where the property is to be sold to the highest bidder and no right is reserved by the seller to withdraw the property if the bidding does not reach the minimum reserve price (set in advance but not normally communicated to the bidders).[56] Prima facie the above rules would indicate that the highest bidder has no recourse if the property is not knocked down to him or her, despite the fact that the failure

---

52. [1963] ALR 346.
53. *Payne v Cave* (1789) 3 TR 148; 100 ER 502.
54. **ACT**: *Sale of Goods Act* 1954, s 60; **NSW**: *Sale of Goods Act* 1923, s 60; **NT**: *Sale of Goods Act* 1972, s 60; **Qld**: *Sale of Goods Act* 1896, s 59; **SA**: *Sale of Goods Act* 1895, s 57; **Tas**: *Sale of Goods Act* 1896, s 62; **Vic**: *Goods Act* 1958, s 64; **WA**: *Sale of Goods Act* 1895, s 57. On sales by auction generally see Sutton, *Sales and Consumer Law in Australia and New Zealand*, 4th ed, 1995, paras 23.1–23.14.
55. (1873) LR 8 QB 286.
56. Where the seller does not expressly reserve a right to bid on his or her own behalf, it is unlawful for the seller or anyone on his or her behalf to bid, and any sale contravening this rule may be treated as fraudulent by the buyer: see the provisions of the sale of goods legislation cited in fn 54. Such a right to bid serves a similar function to that of setting a reserve price in that the seller is protected against the risk of the property being sold at what he or she regards as an unacceptably low price.

to do so would amount to a disregard by the auctioneer of the condition as to the sale being without reserve.

However, the recent case of *Barry v Davies*[57] has held that the highest bidder at an auction for goods advertised for sale on a 'without reserve' basis, has a contractual claim against the auctioneer. Basically, Mr Barry went to an auction to bid for some 'engine analysers', which had an approximate value of £14,000 each. The auctioneer stated the auction would be without reserve. Mr Barry was the only bidder and bid £200 per machine. The auctioneer refused to accept such a low bid and later the machines were sold for £750 each. Mr Barry successfully sued the auctioneer for breach of contract and recovered £27,600 in damages. Prior to *Barry v Davies*, *Warlow v Harrison*[58] was the leading case. There, the plaintiff bid at an auction sale which was advertised to be without reserve. A higher bid was made but the plaintiff, on being advised that the bidder was in fact the owner, refused to bid further, whereupon the lot was knocked down to the owner. The plaintiff sued the auctioneer claiming damages, arguing that the auctioneer was in breach of a duty owed by him to the plaintiff. This argument depended on a contract for the sale of the horse having arisen, but it was held that as the horse had never been knocked down to the plaintiff, under the rule in *Payne v Cave*, no contract of sale had ever arisen. However, the majority of the Court of Exchequer Chamber considered that the plaintiff would have succeeded if he had alleged a separate contract whereby the auctioneer promised that the sale should be without reserve. On this reasoning a contract is formed between the auctioneer and the highest bona fide bidder.[59] The majority of the Court of Appeal in *Barry v Davies* agreed with this approach.

A number of difficulties arise out of the reasoning in *Warlow v Harrison*. It has been doubted whether the highest bidder in such a situation supplies any consideration for the promise of the auctioneer. Moreover, the court in *Warlow v Harrison* appeared to consider that the auctioneer is under no liability unless the auction is actually commenced and the conditions of sale breached, and this point was relied upon in *Harris v Nickerson* when it was held that a complete failure to hold an advertised auction gives no contractual claim to a disappointed bidder. It is difficult to see any ground of policy why a distinction should be made between the two cases. However, although *Warlow v Harrison* has been criticised,[60] it has never been overruled and its reasoning was in fact applied by the Victorian Supreme Court in *Ulbrick v Laidlaw*.[61] In that case the plaintiff and another bidder each made the same bid but the auctioneer did not see the plaintiff's

57. [2000] 1 WLR 1962, noted, Carter (2001) 17 *JCL* 69.
58. (1858) 1 El & El 299, 309; 120 ER 920, 925.
59. Possibly the contract would be with the seller himself or herself rather than the auctioneer in cases where the identity of the seller is disclosed: see *Mainprice v Westley* (1865) 34 LJQB 229; *Rainbow v Hawkins* [1904] 2 KB 322. See also *Hordern House Pty Ltd v Arnold* [1989] VR 402.
60. See the exchange of views in (1952) 68 *LQR* 238, 457; (1953) 69 *LQR* 21.
61. [1924] VLR 274. But cf *AGC (Advances) Ltd v McWhirter* (1977) 1 BPR 9454. In *Ulbrick v Laidlaw* the court also rejected the argument that the question of bona fides was to be finally decided by the auctioneer. It is unclear how far the auctioneer has a discretion in this regard: see *Green v Rose* (1900) 21 NSWLR (Eq) 226; *Richards v Phillips* [1968] 2 All ER 859.

bid and knocked the property down to the other bidder. Despite a term in the conditions of sale governing the auction that in the event of a dispute between purchasers the property would be put up again, the auctioneer refused to re-open the matter. It was held that the auctioneer was under a contractual obligation to any bona fide disputant to put the property up again.

The other interesting point arising from *Barry v Davies* is the question of damages. The court assessed the bidder's damages in the same way they would have approached an action by a buyer against a seller for failure to deliver goods. The better view may be that there is a contract between the auctioneer and all the bidders at an auction, and the general measure of damages should be the loss of chance[62] of being the highest bidder.

[212] **Tenders**. Companies desiring to purchase bulk supplies of goods (often to be delivered in instalments) over a lengthy period of time will often advertise requesting tenders from potential suppliers. Contracts for the carrying out of building or engineering works are also very frequently entered into in this way, as are many contracts with government bodies. Tendering may also be selected as the means by which a vendor is to sell goods. The person calling for tenders will usually give instructions (called the specifications) as to the form which the tender is to take and as to the matters to be covered by the tender. The specifications can be very lengthy documents and, especially in the practice of many government authorities, may contain detailed standard terms of contract to be agreed to by the tenderer. Persons wishing to tender are normally required to submit sealed tenders, which are not opened until after the time for lodging of tenders has passed. It is well established that, even though the form of the tender and its detailed conditions may have been drawn up by the person calling for tenders, that person does not in so doing normally make any offer to prospective tenderers. Each tenderer has made an offer, which the offeree may then accept or reject, and the offeree is under no obligation to accept any tender.

Thus, in *Meudell v Mayor etc of Bendigo*[63] a municipal council called for tenders for the loan to the council of money, to be secured by the issue of debentures, and stated that tenders of the highest premium would have preference and debentures might be allotted proportionately to tenderers of even rates. It was held that the plaintiff had no cause of action when his tender was not accepted, even though the amount tendered for by others at rates higher than or equal to that offered by the plaintiff did not equal the total amount for which tenders were invited. In *Meudell's* case there was language in the prospectus for the loan which pointed to the council reserving a right to refuse to accept any tender. This right is usually expressly reserved when tenders are invited. It would seem, however, that it is not strictly necessary for this right to be reserved. Thus, in *Spencer v Harding*[64] tenders were invited for the purchase of goods and it was held that, although nothing had been said on the point in the document calling for tenders, the seller was not bound to sell to the person submitting the

62. As to loss of chance damages see [2163]–[2164].
63. (1900) 26 VLR 158.
64. (1870) LR 5 CP 561.

highest tender. It was suggested in *Spencer v Harding* that in the event of the person advertising for tenders promising to accept the most favourable tender, the advertisement could be regarded as an offer which had been accepted by the highest (in the case of a sale) or lowest (in the case of the supply of goods or performing of services) tenderer.[65]

Until very recently the point appeared not to have arisen for decision, no doubt because of the almost invariable practice of expressly reserving the right not to accept any tender, but a similar result could perhaps be reached by analogy with the cases on auctions without reserve discussed in the previous paragraph. In fact the process of entering into a contract by way of competitive tender is very similar to making a sale by way of auction, and it would be difficult to distinguish the two cases in principle. On the somewhat unusual facts of *Harvela Investments Ltd v Royal Trust Company of Canada (CI) Ltd*,[66] where two parties were invited to make sealed competitive bids for shares on certain terms and it was stated that the sellers bound themselves to accept the highest bid, it was recently held that the seller was bound to the highest bidder. Equally, in particular circumstances the facts may indicate a contractual commitment as to how the evaluation of tenders will be carried out.[67]

[213] **Self-service stores**. It has for long been assumed, following the principles discussed above, that the display of goods in a shop does not amount to an offer by the shopkeeper to sell, but merely to an invitation to treat. It was not, however, until the decision in *Pharmaceutical Society of Great Britain v Boots Cash Chemists (Southern) Ltd*[68] that it was decided that the rule was the same where goods were displayed in such a manner as to require customers to select for themselves the items which they wished to purchase. The defendants were charged with a breach of legislation requiring the sale of certain proprietary medicines to be effected by or under the supervision of a registered pharmacist. Supervision was provided at the cashier's desk to which customers were required to take items which they wished to purchase. It was held that the display of goods in this manner amounted only to an invitation to customers to make an offer to buy, and that as such an offer was accepted at the cashier's desk no infringement had occurred.

The reasoning applied by the court in the *Boots* case has, however, been criticised.[69] The major reason the court was not prepared to hold that an offer was made to customers was that it assumed that in that event the offer would be accepted when the customer selected an item from the shelves and that the customer would technically be in breach of contract if he or she later decided to buy a substitute item or not to buy at all.[70] However, if

---

65. This view appears to have had the support of Bowen LJ in *Carlill v Carbolic Smoke Ball Co* [1893] 1 QB 256 at 269.
66. [1986] 1 AC 207.
67. *Hughes Aircraft Systems International v Airservices Australia* (1997) 146 ALR 1. See also *Blackpool & Fylde Aero Club Ltd v Blackpool Borough Council* [1990] 1 WLR 1195, criticised by A Phang, 'Tenders and Uncertainty' (1991) 4 *JCL* 46.
68. [1953] 1 QB 401.
69. See Unger (1953) 16 *MLR* 369; Williams (1953) 10 *NILQ* 117; Treitel, *The Law of Contract*, 10th ed, 1999, pp 12–13; cf Montrose (1954) 10 *NILQ* 178; (1955) 4 *Amer Jnl Comp L* 235.

the shopkeeper was in fact to be regarded as making an offer, the most natural inference would surely be that the customer had not finally indicated an intention to buy (and thus to accept the offer) until the item was presented at the cashier's desk (or, possibly, until it was actually paid for).[71] Despite such criticisms, the rule that it is the customer who makes an offer in a self-service store appears now to be well established, and may perhaps be justified on the basis that in the absence of a very clear indication of contrary intention the shopkeeper should not be assumed to have relinquished the right to refuse to sell to customers whom he or she considers undesirable, or to limit the number of items in short supply which he or she is prepared to sell to each customer. The above analysis does, however, serve to illustrate the difficulties which may arise in commonplace situations in determining who should be regarded as offeror and who as offeree.

[214] **Meaning of 'offer' in statutory offences.** *Pharmaceutical Society of Great Britain v Boots Cash Chemists (Southern) Ltd*[72] shows that the contractual principles of offer and acceptance may be thought to have practical significance in situations involving no action for breach of contract. A number of English cases have been concerned with the meaning to be given to the word 'offer' in the context of statutory offences prohibiting a person from offering goods for sale in certain circumstances, and in those cases it has been held that parliament must be assumed to have used the word in its technical contractual meaning, rather than in its broader colloquial sense. Consequently it has been held that such statutes were not infringed where goods were displayed for sale in a shop window,[73] or advertised in a newspaper,[74] or offered for sale by an auctioneer.[75] Such cases are valuable in affording guidance on the contractual principles relevant in certain typical situations (the more so as many issues are rarely the subject of judicial decision because of the unlikelihood of contractual claims which usually involve quite small amounts of money being litigated or, if litigated, reported). Nonetheless, it is very doubtful whether as a matter of policy such technicality is desirable, for the result would seem to be to thwart the legislative intention and to result in legislation becoming unnecessarily complicated as amendments are made to overcome the effect of such decisions.[76]

---

70. This reasoning was perhaps not strictly necessary for the decision, for each of the members of the Court of Appeal agreed with the reasons of Lord Goddard CJ at first instance who stated ([1952] 2 QB 795 at 802) that even if a contract was formed when the customer selected goods from the shelves, the sale would still, on the facts, have been made under the supervision of the pharmacist.
71. For a discussion of some American cases suggesting this analysis see Schlesinger, ed, *Formation of Contracts*, 1968, Vol 1, pp 336–8. For a discussion as to whether, on a prospective purchaser entering a store, there may arise a limited contract (to the effect that any shopping trolley supplied will be reasonably fit for its purpose) see *Cottee v Franklins Self-Serve Pty Ltd* [1997] 1 Qd R 469.
72. [1953] 1 QB 401.
73. *Fisher v Bell* [1961] 1 QB 394.
74. *Partridge v Crittenden* [1968] 2 All ER 421.
75. *British Car Auctions Ltd v Wright* [1972] 1 WLR 1519.
76. See Note (1961) 1 *Adel LR* 221; J C Smith, 'Civil Law Concepts in the Criminal Law' (1972) 31 *CLJ* 197.

The courts in Australia seem prepared to read such phrases as 'offer for sale' in their ordinary sense, unless a technical meaning is clearly required, and it is unlikely, therefore, that the English cases referred to would be followed in Australia. Thus, in *Goodwin's of Newtown Pty Ltd v Gurry*[77] it was held that in the context of legislation designed to regulate retail shopping hours the word 'offer' must be read in the manner in which it is used in everyday use, and in *Attorney-General (NSW) v Mutual Home Loan Fund of Australia Ltd*[78] it was held that the word, when appearing in legislation regulating advertisements offering to sell shares in a company, must be read in a non-contractual sense as including invitations to treat.

[215] **Invitations to treat and bait advertising**. The fact that the offering of goods for sale is interpreted as being merely an invitation to treat means that consumers will normally have no contractual protection where a retailer has engaged in the practice which has become known as 'bait advertising'. This expression refers to the practice of advertising goods at attractive bargain prices, being goods which the advertiser does not in fact intend to sell in more than minimal quantities, if at all. Often the essential purpose of the advertiser is to persuade customers to purchase other more expensive (and, to the seller, more profitable) items. In some cases the customer will be told that the advertised item is not available at all, whereas in other cases that item may be made available to the persistent but only after considerable effort, usually involving strong disparagement of the 'bait', has been expended in an attempt to 'switch' the customer to a more expensive item.

The *Trade Practices Act* 1974 (Cth), following widespread criticism of this selling technique, now provides in s 56 that a corporation[79] shall not, in trade or commerce, advertise for supply at a specified price goods or services if there are reasonable grounds, of which the corporation is aware, or ought reasonably to be aware, for believing that the corporation will not be able to offer for supply those goods or services at that price for a period that is, and in quantities that are, reasonable having regard to the nature of the market in which the corporation carries on business and the nature of the advertisement. Even if this cannot be shown, an offence is committed by the advertisers if they do not in fact supply, unless they offer to supply (and, if the offer is accepted, do in fact supply) the advertised goods or services, or equivalent alternatives, within a reasonable time. Thus a retailer advertising 'specials' for sale may well be in breach of s 56 if only limited quantities are available and the position has not been made clear in the advertisement. An infringement of s 56 is a criminal offence and a

---

77. [1959] SASR 295.
78. [1971] 2 NSWLR 162, followed in *Attorney-General (NSW) v Australian Fixed Trusts Ltd* [1974] 1 NSWLR 110. See also *WA Pines Pty Ltd v Registrar of Companies* [1976] WAR 149. Cf *Reardon v Morley Ford Pty Ltd* (1980) 33 ALR 417 (a decision on s 56 of the *Trade Practices Act* 1974 (Cth)), not followed in *Wallace v Brodribb* (1985) 58 ALR 737.
79. Although the section is expressed to apply only to action by a corporation, the effect of s 6 of the *Trade Practices Act* is that non-corporate traders may in fact be caught in other situations where the Commonwealth has legislative power to control their activities (eg where the activity occurs in the course of interstate trade or in trade within the ACT or NT).

heavy maximum penalty may be imposed. Section 56 does not of itself alter the contractual principles discussed above, but a person suffering loss as a result of a contravention of s 56 now has a statutory right to damages under s 82 of the *Trade Practices Act*.[80] Thus, a person incurring expense in travelling to an advertised sale might now be able to recover damages under s 82, even though there would be no contractual claim to recover such damages.[81] All States have also enacted legislation dealing with bait advertising.[82]

Offers to Unascertained Persons

[216] Offer to public at large. An offer is normally addressed to a specific identified person or persons. However, an offer may be made to the public at large. It was at one time thought that to regard documents such as advertisements offering rewards as being contractual offers was somehow legally impossible as amounting to regarding the advertisement as a 'contract with the whole world'. The thought seems to have been that as no specific offerees were identified, the advertisement could not take effect as an offer but could at most amount to an invitation to treat, that is, an invitation to the public to come forward and make offers to the advertiser. The fallacy of this view was well stated by Bowen LJ in *Carlill v Carbolic Smoke Ball Co*:[83]

> It was also said that the contract is made with all the world — that is, with everybody; and that you cannot contract with everybody. It is not a contract made with all the world ... It is an offer made to all the world; and why should not an offer be made to all the world which is to ripen into a contract with anybody who comes forward and performs the condition? It is an offer to become liable to any one who, before it is retracted, performs the condition, and, although the offer is made to the world, the contract is made with that limited portion of the public who come forward and perform the condition on the faith of the advertisement.

Although it is convenient to refer to an offer made to a large group of unascertained persons as an 'offer to the world', the exact scope of the offer depends, of course, on the language used. Thus an offer may be restricted to certain classes of person, or it may be expressed in general terms but subject to the exclusion of a specific category of persons.[84] In *Westminster Estates Pty Ltd v Calleja*[85] it was argued that the principle that an offer may be made to unascertained persons was restricted to the 'advertisement' cases. Helsham J held, however, that the principle is of general operation, so that an offer to 'A or his nominee' is effective and may be accepted by

---

80. For decisions on s 56 see *Reardon v Morley Ford Pty Ltd* (1980) 33 ALR 417; *Wallace v Brodribb* (1985) 58 ALR 737; *Wallace v Walplan Pty Ltd* (1985) 8 FCR 14 (affirmed (1985) 8 FCR 27).
81. *Harris v Nickerson* (1873) LR 8 QB 286 (see [211]).
82. **ACT**: *Fair Trading Act* 1992, s 21; **NSW**: *Fair Trading Act* 1987, s 51; **NT**: *Consumer Affairs and Fair Trading Act* 1990, s 52; **Qld**: *Fair Trading Act* 1989, s 46; **SA**: *Fair Trading Act* 1987, s 65; **Tas**: *Fair Trading Act* 1990, s 22; **Vic**: *Fair Trading Act* 1985, s 18; **WA**: *Fair Trading Act* 1987, s 19.
83. [1893] 1 QB 256 at 268. The facts of this case were set out at [208].
84. *McMahon v Gilberd & Co Ltd* [1955] NZLR 1206 (advertisement offering refund of 'deposit' on return of empty bottles directed to consumers to the exclusion of bottle dealers).

the nominee once appointed, even though the nominee's identity was not ascertainable at the time the offer was made.

Necessity for Communication of Offer

[217] Offer ineffective until communicated. It is frequently stated that an offer is ineffective until it is communicated to the offeree. Thus, for example, Kay LJ stated in *Henthorn v Fraser*[86] that 'an offer to sell is nothing until it is actually received'. It might be asked whether such a rule has any practical significance, unless it refers to the rule[87] that the performance of an act in ignorance of an offer cannot amount to acceptance even though the act performed happens to fulfil precisely the conditions laid down in the offer. In such a case it can hardly be said that the parties have come to any agreement. However, the rule does have further significance, for a person may hear from a third source that another intends to make an offer to him or her. It would seem that even though A may express an intention to make an offer to B, no power of acceptance is created in B until such time, if ever, as A's offer is communicated to B by A or by someone acting with A's authority.[88] The natural inference in such a situation would be that until such time as such communication has occurred, A has not finally decided to be exposed to the potential liability which would arise once the offer becomes effective. Thus in *Banks v Williams*[89] it was held that a decision of the Minister for Public Instruction approving the purchase of certain goods was not an offer capable of acceptance when it was communicated without authority by the Under Secretary of the Minister's Department.

---

85. (1970) 91 WN (NSW) 222, followed in *O'Halloran Enterprises Pty Ltd v Williamson* [1979] VR 33. See also *Williams v Byrnes* (1863) 3 SCR (NSW) (App) 14 at 16–17; *NW Co-operative Freezing & Canning Co Ltd v Easton* (1915) 11 Tas LR 65 (application for shares directed to provisional directors of company about to be formed held to be an offer to the company when formed); *Bell Bros Pty Ltd v Sarich* [1971] WAR 157.
86. [1892] 2 Ch 27 at 37. But see *P & M Constructions Pty Ltd v Elders Leasing Ltd* [1992] 1 Qd R 264 at 280–1.
87. See [239].
88. *Cole v Cottingham* (1837) 8 Car & P 75; 173 ER 406 (expression to third party of intention to marry C, not uttered in hearing of C nor communicated to C with authority of speaker, held not to be an offer).
89. (1912) 12 SR (NSW) 382. See also *Powell v Lee* (1908) 99 LT 284 (where the unauthorised communication was, for reasons which are not clear, treated as an acceptance rather than an offer; the reasoning is, however, equally applicable to an unauthorised communication of an offer); *Wilson v Belfast Corp* (1921) 55 ILT 205 (resolution of city council held not to be an offer, partly on ground that publication not authorised); *Gjergja v Cooper* [1987] VR 167 at 196–7, 206, 208–9 per Ormiston J.

Acceptance

What Amounts to Acceptance

[218] Necessity for acceptance. Where an offer has been made, a contract binding the parties will result when, and only when, the offeree has clearly accepted the offer. Normally acceptance is not effective until it has been communicated to the offeror, and this requirement will be considered later. Our concern here is with the kind of declaration of consent to the contract proposed by the offeror which must be made in order to constitute an effective acceptance. In the majority of cases the consent will be expressed but, as we have seen,[90] that consent will sometimes be implied from the conduct rather than the express words of the acceptor. There must be a clear indication of consent to the terms proposed.

[219] Acceptance must correspond with offer. The offer and acceptance must precisely correspond; that which has been proposed by the offeror must be accepted in toto, no more and no less. Any departure from the offer will result in the purported acceptance being ineffective. Such a purported acceptance is not without significance as it will normally, even though worded as an acceptance, amount to a new offer (described as a 'counter-offer') which, if accepted by the original offeror (now the offeree in respect of the counter-offer), will result in a contract.[91] Of course, if the counter-offer itself is not accepted, neither party is bound.

[220] Acceptance must be unequivocal. Acceptance must be unequivocal in that nothing further is left to be negotiated between the parties and the language used must be such as would clearly convey a definite decision by the offeree to be bound by the terms of the offer.[92] Whether this has been in fact done involves interpreting the language used by the offeree. Even if the offeree does not say in so many words 'I accept your offer', it is sufficient if he or she clearly indicates that he or she is treating the offer as accepted, for example, by informing the offeror that he or she has taken steps to perform by ordering goods or materials which he or she must acquire in order to perform his or her part of the bargain.[93] Where one states that one 'desires' or 'intends' to accept an offer, the context may be such as to indicate that one has definitely bound oneself rather than merely stating an intention to do so at some future time.[94] On the other hand, where a telegram which prima facie indicates an intention to accept states that a letter will be sent containing details of the offeree's

---

90. See [205].
91. See, eg *Evans Deakin Industries Ltd v Queensland Electricity Generating Board* (1984) 1 BCL 334.
92. *Appleby v Johnson* (1874) LR 9 CP 158; *Ballas v Theophilos (No 2)* (1957) 98 CLR 193. See also *Spencer's Pictures Ltd v Cosens* (1918) 18 SR (NSW) 102.
93. *White Trucks Pty Ltd v Riley* (1948) 66 WN (NSW) 101; *Integrated Lighting & Ceilings Pty Ltd v Phillips Electrical Pty Ltd* (1969) 90 WN (Pt 1) (NSW) 693.
94. *Nicholson v Smith* (1882) 22 Ch D 640; *Ballas v Theophilos (No 2)* (1957) 98 CLR 193 at 205; *B Seppelt & Sons Ltd v Commissioner for Main Roads* (1975) 1 BPR 9147 at 9149; *Traywinds Pty Ltd v Cooper* [1989] 1 Qd R 222. See also *Re Copperart Pty Ltd* (1995) 16 ACSR 351.

position, the inference is likely to be drawn that the telegram is not intended to be a binding acceptance.[95]

[221] Offers presenting alternatives. Although acceptance must correspond exactly with the offer, it is important to remember that an offer may in fact present several alternatives to the offeree. Thus, where an offer is made for the sale of a specified number of shares in a company, a purported acceptance in respect of part only will be ineffective, though such an acceptance would be valid if the offer were to sell those shares or such lesser number as the purchaser might wish.[96] Similarly, if the owner of land writes to a person offering in the alternative to sell or lease the land on certain terms, a reply agreeing to purchase is clearly a valid acceptance.[97]

[222] Additional or different terms. Perhaps the commonest situation where a purported acceptance is ineffective and operates merely as a counter-offer is where it proposes one or more terms which are in addition to, or at any rate different in some respects from, those contained in the offer to which it refers. A purported acceptance which agrees to the offer in general terms but which seeks to qualify the scope of some of the detailed provisions contained in it is at most a counter-offer.[98] Thus an offer for the purchase of land is not rendered binding by an 'acceptance' which contains terms not contained in the offer; and this will be so even if the terms (for example, a requirement that the purchaser pay a deposit) are normally agreed to in that type of transaction.[99] On the other hand, an acceptance would no doubt be effective if it did not depart from the terms of the offer but simply set out expressly what would be implied by law in the absence of express agreement.

Difficulty frequently arises where an offeree who is alleged to have accepted chose to describe in his or her own words the effect of the offer, for in such cases it will often be arguable that the words used by the offeree would in fact produce a different effect in substance from those used in the offer. The problem was well described by Gibbs J in remarks which, although made in the context of a purported exercise of an option, are of general application:[100]

> [It] is not always easy to determine whether the purported exercise of an option should be understood as attempting to vary the terms of the option or as intending to accept its terms without modification, notwithstanding that

---

95. *Davies v Smith* (1938) 12 ALJ 258; *Lewis Construction Co Pty Ltd v M Tichauer Société Anonyme* [1966] VR 341. Cf *Lamont v Heron* (1970) 45 ALJR 102.
96. *McClay v Seeligson* (1904) 7 WALR 87; *Ocean Coal Co Ltd v Powell Duffryn Steam Coal Co Ltd* [1932] 1 Ch 654.
97. *Morrison v Neill* (1875) 1 VLR (L) 287. See also *Georgoulis v Mandalinic* [1984] 1 NSWLR 612.
98. See, eg *Holland v Eyre* (1825) 2 Sim & St 194; 57 ER 319; *Tucker v Godfrey* (1862) 1 SCR (NSW) 292; *Mooney v Williams* (1905) 3 CLR 1; *Bastard v McCallum* [1924] VLR 9; *Carello v Jordan* [1935] QSR 294.
99. *Cullen v Bickers* (1878) 12 SALR 5; *Jones v Daniel* [1894] 2 Ch 332.
100. *Quadling v Robinson* (1976) 137 CLR 192 at 201; 10 ALR 319. See also *Cavallari v Premier Refrigeration Co Pty Ltd* (1952) 85 CLR 20; *Ballas v Theophilos (No 2)* (1957) 98 CLR 193 at 204–6, 209–11; *Gilbert J McCaul (Aust) Pty Ltd v Pitt Club Ltd* (1959) 59 SR (NSW) 122; *Prudential Assurance Co Ltd v Health Minders Pty Ltd* (1987) 9 NSWLR 673.

they may have been misdescribed, or notwithstanding that the grantee of the option may have indicated that he intends to perform the contract in a manner for which the terms of the option do not provide. It must of course depend upon the proper construction of the document by which the grantee purports to exercise an option whether it amounts to an absolute and unqualified acceptance of the rights and liabilities conditionally created by the option.

The question is always whether or not the statement alleged to have been an acceptance is properly to be interpreted as an unqualified acceptance of the offer. It is possible that a reference to an additional term should be read as a proposal for the modification of the agreement, but that the maker of the statement intends to be immediately bound whether or not the modification is agreed to by the other party. Thus, for example, in *J B Rogers Ltd v Harry Lesnie Ltd*[101] directors of the plaintiff and defendant companies agreed upon a contract of a year's duration and at the same time agreed that a proposal for an option for the renewal of the contract be submitted to the plaintiff, the director conducting the negotiations on behalf of the plaintiff having no authority to agree to that aspect of the defendant company's proposals. It was held that in the circumstances the parties intended to be immediately bound by the initial contract, irrespective of whether the option proposal were accepted.[102] In other cases an acceptance will be effective even though accompanied by a request for some indulgence as to the manner in which the obligations under the contract are to be performed. Thus, for example, a request by a buyer that delivery should be made on a certain date will not, even though the offer does not refer to such date, prevent the acceptance being effective if it is clear that the acceptance is not made conditional upon the seller agreeing to that date.[103]

The above discussion must not, however, be allowed to obscure the fact that an acceptance conditional upon the offeror's agreement to any variation from the terms of the offer will be ineffective. In *Northland Airlines Ltd v Dennis Ferranti Meters Ltd*[104] a telegram purporting to accept an offer for the sale of an aeroplane required delivery to be made within 30 days. As the offer said nothing concerning the date of delivery, the seller would have been obliged to deliver within a reasonable time.[105] Thirty days was not in the circumstances of this case synonymous with a reasonable time, and the buyer's requirement of delivery within that period prevented his telegram taking effect as an acceptance, even though the parties did not consider the date of delivery to be important. In other words, any variation in the effect of the offer (and not, as seems sometimes to be assumed, only a material or important variation) prevents a contract being formed. It is otherwise

---

101. (1927) 27 SR (NSW) 427.
102. See also *Turner Kempson & Co Pty Ltd v Camm* [1922] VLR 498; *Universal Guarantee Pty Ltd v Carlile* [1957] VR 68; *Parbury Henty & Co Pty Ltd v General Engineering & Agencies Pty Ltd* (1973) 47 ALJR 336.
103. *Dunlop v Higgins* (1848) 1 HLC 381; 9 ER 805. See also *Clive v Beaumont* (1848) 1 De G & Sm 397; 63 ER 1121; *Costello v Loulakas* [1938] St R Qd 267; *Simpson v Hughes* (1897) 66 LJ Ch 334; *B Seppelt & Sons Ltd v Commissioner for Main Roads* (1975) 1 BPR 9147.
104. (1970) 114 Sol J 845.
105. See [1804].

where the variation is solely in favour of the offeror. In *Ex parte Fealey*[106] the defendant placed an order for insertion of a half-inch advertisement in the plaintiff's newspaper. The plaintiff accepted by inserting a one-inch advertisement. As the rate for one inch was the same as for half an inch it was held that the defendant was liable for the cost of the advertisement.[107]

[223] **Acceptance of tenders**. We have already referred to the practice of companies desiring to purchase bulk supplies of goods over a lengthy period of time, or to have building or engineering work carried out, to contract by way of calling for tenders. We have seen[108] that persons submitting tenders will be regarded as making an offer, which the person requesting tenders is then free to accept or reject. Many difficulties occur in practice as to the precise effect of an 'acceptance' of a tender. If, on interpretation of the specifications and tender it appears that the acceptor is definitely agreeing to purchase, for example, specified quantities of goods, there is no problem and both parties are bound. However, what at first sight appears to be a definite agreement may on closer examination turn out to be merely what is generally called a 'standing offer'. For example, in *Colonial Ammunition Co v Reid*[109] the plaintiff promised to supply the government with ammunition on certain terms for a period of seven years. When the government subsequently purchased ammunition from another supplier, the plaintiff sued alleging a breach of contract. There was no express promise in the agreement which had been signed that the government would purchase from the plaintiff all the ammunition it required. The court refused in the circumstances of the case to imply such a promise, with the result that despite the 'acceptance' of the plaintiff's promise there was no binding contract. The plaintiff's promise amounted to a standing offer, such that a contract was formed each time a specific order was placed in accordance with its terms. There was, however, no obligation on the government to place any order and, moreover, although bound by any orders previously placed, the plaintiff could have withdrawn his offer at any time, despite his promise to keep it open for seven years. In this respect a standing offer is as freely revocable as any other offer.[110]

Often, however, the language used and the circumstances of the case will indicate that the person accepting the tender, while not bound to take any stated quantity of what is being offered, does agree to take all of his or her requirements, whatever they may turn out to be, of the goods or services offered. In that case the acceptor is bound to take his or her actual requirements from the successful tenderer and will be liable in breach of

---

106. (1897) 18 LR (NSW) 282.
107. However, although a plaintiff in a suit for the specific performance of a contract unenforceable unless evidenced in writing (see [519]) may in some cases be able to waive a term agreed on solely for the plaintiff's benefit but not included in the writing, this principle does not apply where the question is whether there was ever an agreement reached between the parties: *Bastard v McCallum* [1924] VLR 9.
108. See [212].
109. (1900) 21 LR (NSW) 338.
110. *Great Northern Railway Co v Witham* (1873) LR 9 CP 16; *Kelly v Caledonian Coal Co* (1898) LR (NSW) 1; *Percival v London CC Asylums Committee* (1918) 87 LJKB 677; *Munday & Shreeve v Western Australia* [1962] WAR 65; *Re Webster* (1975) 132 CLR 270; 6 ALR 65.

contract upon dealing elsewhere. As a corollary, the tenderer is likewise bound to supply in accordance with the other's requirements.[111] Thus, for example, in *Milne v Municipal Council of Sydney*[112] the plaintiff agreed to do all the mechanical repairs required to the defendant's electrical plant for a period of 12 months at specified rates of payment. Although it was impossible to say at the date of contract precisely what work would in the event require to be performed, the obligations of the parties were sufficiently clearly defined and there were indications in the written agreement that both parties regarded themselves as bound for the period of 12 months. In these circumstances the High Court of Australia held that there should be implied a promise by the defendant to employ the plaintiff to the exclusion of other persons to do those repairs. The defendant therefore was bound to employ the plaintiff, the plaintiff's promise being more than simply a standing offer.

A supplier of goods may well, as a matter of commercial convenience and efficiency, supply to a regular customer a price list indicating the prices at which the supplier is prepared, for a stated period of time, to supply commonly ordered goods. Unless there is an agreement by the customer to order either a minimum quantity or the actual requirements for the customer's own business, the arrangement amounts only to a standing offer. The distinction between a standing offer and a contract binding both parties is clear enough in principle, but in practice can give rise to very difficult problems of interpretation in ascertaining the true intention of the parties.

[224] **The battle of the forms.** The increasing use of standard forms in business dealings gives rise to a problem which is well described by American commentators as 'the battle of the forms'.[113] Where, for example, the purchase of goods is contemplated, the buyer and seller may each use in the process of negotiation their own printed forms setting out the terms on which they propose to deal. As each party's form will be drafted in a manner designed to protect its own interests, the forms will almost inevitably be in conflict on some points, and this fact may produce quite unexpected results. Thus in *Butler Machine Tool Co Ltd v Ex-cell-O Corp (England) Ltd*[114] a seller quoted a price for certain machinery subject to the seller's own conditions (which included a clause enabling the seller to vary the price of the machinery in certain circumstances). The buyer subsequently requested the supply of the machinery, using its own order form containing its own terms. The seller acknowledged this order on a form of acknowledgment of order supplied by the buyer. When the seller later claimed to be entitled to an increased payment in reliance on its price variation clause, it was held that as the buyer's order form contained no such clause, that order was not an acceptance but a counter-offer, which

---

111. *Milne v Municipal Council of Sydney* (1912) 14 CLR 54; *Jarvis v Pitt Ltd* (1935) 54 CLR 506. See also *J Kitchen & Sons Pty Ltd v Stewart's Cash & Carry Stores* (1942) 66 CLR 116. As to the consideration for such a requirements contract, see [340]. See generally M Howard, 'The Requirements and the Output Contracts' (1967) 2 *Univ of Tas LR* 446.
112. (1912) 14 CLR 54.
113. See, eg Fuller and Eisenberg, *Basic Contract Law*, 5th ed, 1990, pp 596–627.
114. [1979] 1 WLR 401. See also *OTM Ltd v Hydranautics* [1981] 2 Lloyd's Rep 211.

had been accepted by the seller. The seller was therefore bound by the buyer's terms. Where in such cases the seller does not acknowledge the buyer's counter-offer, it may well be held to have been accepted by conduct if the goods in question are later in fact supplied.[115]

In other cases where a dispute arises before the seller supplies the goods it may be held that, contrary to what will usually be the clear assumption of the parties, no contract at all exists.[116] This result can in some situations be particularly harsh, especially when the parties have agreed on all essentials and the variations between the competing sets of conditions are relatively minor. Consequently in some overseas jurisdictions a purported acceptance which contains terms which are different from those in the offer is effective as an acceptance if those new terms do not materially alter the terms of the offer; the new terms are treated as proposals for additions to the contract which the offeror will be deemed to have agreed to if they are not expressly objected to.[117] It seems clear that such an approach is inconsistent with the principles of formation of contract applied by the Australian courts,[118] though its adoption would prevent a party being able to escape from a contract on the basis of a minor variation between the forms employed by the parties.[119] It would in practice, however, often be extremely difficult to distinguish between new terms which were only 'minor' and those which 'materially altered' the terms of the original offer.

Who May Accept?

[225] **Offer may be accepted only by offeree**. An offer may be accepted only by the person or persons to whom it is addressed.[120] Thus if an offer is made by A to B, and B purports to accept on behalf of herself and C, no contract results and B's action is in fact not an acceptance but a counter-offer.[121] In most cases it will be clear enough who is entitled to accept, but where doubt arises the offer must be carefully construed to ascertain who is

---

115. See *Re Production Sheet Metals Pty Ltd* [1971] QWN 16.
116. *Bastard v McCallum* [1924] VLR 9; *Turner Kempson & Co Pty Ltd v Camm* [1922] VLR 498. Compare *Universal Guarantee Pty Ltd v Carlile* [1957] VR 68.
117. See, eg *Uniform Commercial Code* (US), §2-207. See also *United Nations Convention on Contracts for the International Sale of Goods* (1980), Art 19; as to the application of this Convention in Australia see [276]. See also E H Hondius and Ch Mahé, 'The Battle of the Forms: Towards a Uniform Solution' (1998) 12 *JCL* 268.
118. See *Bastard v McCallum* [1924] VLR 9, applying *Felthouse v Bindley* (1862) 11 CBNS 869; 142 ER 1037 (see [229]). But see *English and Foreign Co v Arduin* (1870) LR 5 HL 64. For the view that an exception may exist where a customer is handed a ticket containing contractual exemption clauses see *MacRobertson Miller Airline Services v Commissioner of State Taxation (WA)* (1975) 133 CLR 125 at 137–9 per Stephen J (but contrast Jacobs J at 142–4); 8 ALR 131; see further M Powell, 'Acceptance by Silence in the Law of Contract' (1977) 5 *ABLR* 260.
119. In such cases 'there is often a suspicion, if not a moral certainty, that the provision which one or both parties now contends should control is one of which neither party was particularly cognizant, and one which, if contested during negotiations, would have been deleted by the party in whose favour it ran': Murray, *Cases and Materials on Contracts*, 1969, p 146.
120. *Reynolds v Atherton* (1922) 127 LT 189.
121. *Ronald v Lalor* (1872) 3 VR (E) 98; *Lee v Sayers* (1909) 28 NZLR 804; *Lang v James Morrison & Co Ltd* (1911) 13 CLR 1. Cf *Wilson v Winton* [1969] Qd R 536 (acceptance effective where offeree acting as agent for undisclosed principals and thus was personally bound).

entitled to accept.[122] Thus where two directors of a company offered, in a circular addressed to shareholders, to sell their shares in the company, it was necessary to construe the terms of the offer to ascertain whether the offer could be accepted only by the shareholders acting as a group, or whether it was open to acceptance by any individual shareholder.[123]

Communication of Acceptance

[226] Acceptance effective on communication. An acceptance is generally effective to conclude a contract only when the fact of acceptance is communicated to the offeror. Until such time the offeror is free to withdraw the offer. It is normally only when the offeror knows that the proposal has been accepted that we can say that the parties have reached agreement. Thus it is, for example, well established that a person who makes an offer to a company to purchase shares in that company may withdraw that offer before being notified of the company's acceptance, and this is so even though the company may in fact already have allotted shares to the offeror in the company's share register.[124] On the other hand, it is not necessary that a formal notice of allotment be given, and knowledge of the allotment may be inferred from the conduct of the parties, for example, by the company sending to the applicant notice of a call in respect of money due for the shares or by the applicant participating in a meeting of shareholders.[125] An offeror may have authorised an agent to receive notification of acceptance on the offeror's behalf, and in such a case notice to the agent is treated as the equivalent of notice to the offeror personally; the offeror is not, however, bound if the agent has authority merely to transmit the notification rather than to receive it on the offeror's behalf.[126]

Moreover, unless there are special circumstances indicating that actual communication is not necessary, the very fact that an offeree, though having decided to accept, has not yet informed the other party of that decision will usually imply that the offeree has not yet finally made a commitment. Accordingly, the offeree will not be bound even though the decision to accept has been conveyed to the offeror by someone acting without authority to do so.[127]

[227] Offeror may dispense with need for communication. The requirement that acceptance is ineffective until notified to the offeror is one insisted on primarily in the interests of the offeror, and accordingly the

---

122. *Carter v Hyde* (1923) 33 CLR 115.
123. *Varley v Fotheringham* [1905] SALR 19.
124. *Re National Savings Bank Association (Hebb's Case)* (1867) LR 4 Eq 9; *Re F H Ring & Co Ltd* [1924] SASR 138.
125. *Re Gambrinus Lager Beer Brewery Co Ltd* (1886) 12 VLR 446; *Malthouse v Adelaide Milk Supply Co-operative Ltd* [1922] SASR 572; *Re F H Ring & Co Ltd* [1924] SASR 138; *Re Clifton Springs Hotel Ltd* [1939] VLR 27. But see *Farmers' Mercantile Union & Chaff Mills Ltd v Coade* (1921) 30 CLR 113.
126. *Batt v Onslow* (1892) 13 LR (NSW) Eq 79.
127. *Connolly v United Shire of Beechworth* (1874) 5 AJR 50 (resolution of corporation not an acceptance without communication); *Powell v Lee* (1908) 99 LT (NS) 284 (unauthorised communication of decision of governing body of school not an acceptance). See also *Banks v Williams* (1912) 12 SR (NSW) 382; *Wilson v Belfast Corp* (1921) 55 ILT 205.

need for notification may be dispensed with by the offeror. Thus the offeror may, expressly or by implication, specify that acceptance is to be communicated in a particular manner, in which case an acceptance communicated in that manner will be effective whether or not the communication is actually received by the offeror.[128] This reasoning is one of the bases for the rule whereby a posted acceptance will often be effective on posting rather than on delivery.[129]

In many cases an offer will be interpreted as contemplating that acceptance may take the form of performance of an act rather than of the making of a counter-promise, and in such a case the offeror will be held to have dispensed with the necessity of communication of acceptance. It was on this basis that it was held in *Carlill v Carbolic Smoke Ball Co*[130] that a contract was made as soon as the plaintiff had performed the condition set out in the offer contained in the company's advertisement of its preparation.[131] Likewise, if a person wishing to buy goods from a distant seller writes ordering the goods and indicates that the seller, if wishing to accept the offer, should promptly ship the goods without first replying, the contract is made as soon as the goods are shipped.[132] Where it is not obvious from the facts that communication of acceptance is not required, the offer must clearly indicate an intention to this effect if the normal rule is to be displaced.[133]

[228] **Method of acceptance prescribed by offeror.** The offeror may prescribe the manner in which acceptance is to be made, and if the offeror has insisted upon this as the prescribed method of acceptance, a purported acceptance in any other manner is not an effective acceptance. 'The offeror creates the power of acceptance; and he has full control over the character and extent of the power that he creates.'[134] Thus, for example, it has been held that the fact that the offeror has made the offer by telegram is an implied indication that a prompt reply is expected and that consequently an acceptance sent by ordinary mail will be ineffective.[135]

However, in most cases an offeror in indicating that acceptance may be made in a particular manner will not be taken to have insisted that that is the exclusive method of acceptance. In such cases any alternative method of acceptance which is as prompt as, and no less advantageous to the offeror than, the prescribed method will suffice.[136] Therefore an offer requesting a reply 'by return of post' will normally be regarded as indicating

---

128. *Latec Finance Pty Ltd v Knight* [1969] 2 NSWR 79 at 81; *Associated Midland Corp Ltd v Bank of NSW* (1984) 51 ALR 641.
129. See [230]–[238].
130. [1893] 1 QB 256. See [208].
131. Consequently communication of acceptance is usually not required by an offer of a unilateral contract. It should, however, be remembered that the performance of an act as acceptance does not necessarily indicate that the contract is unilateral: see [249].
132. *Brogden v Metropolitan Railway Co* (1877) 2 App Cas 666 at 691; *Menzies v Williams* (1893) 10 WN (NSW) 13; *Melbourne Chilled Butter Co Pty Ltd v Downes* (1900) 25 VLR 559; *Mayers & Co v Johnson & Co* [1905] QWN 39. See also *Ex parte Fealey* (1897) 18 LR (NSW) 282.
133. *Latec Finance Pty Ltd v Knight* [1969] 2 NSWR 79.
134. *Corbin on Contracts*, Vol 1, 1963, p 88.
135. *Quenerduaine v Cole* (1883) 32 WR 185.

merely a requirement of a prompt reply rather than as stipulating that acceptance must be by letter and no other means. Consequently a reply by telegram or by some other means, received no later than a letter by post would normally reach its destination, would comply with the terms of the offer.[137] If an offeror wishes the prescribed method of acceptance to be the only method permissible, this intention must be made quite clear. But if this is done, the direction is effective and any purported acceptance which does not comply is at best a counter-offer, which the original offeror is then free either to accept or reject.[138]

[229] **Silence as acceptance**. Although there is curiously little authority on the point, it is accepted that an offeror cannot compel an offeree to take positive steps to reject an offer by the device of stating that unless it is heard to the contrary the offer will be assumed to have been accepted. If in such a case the offeree decides not to accept, and therefore simply ignores the offer, there will be no acceptance and hence no contract. Thus, in *Felthouse v Bindley*[139] an uncle wrote to his nephew proposing to buy the latter's horse and said 'if I hear no more about him, I consider the horse mine at £30/15/0'. The nephew did not reply, and it was held that 'it is ... clear that the uncle had no right to impose upon the nephew a sale of his horse for £30/15/0 unless he chose to comply with the condition of writing to repudiate the offer'.[140] It is by no means clear, however, just how far this principle may be taken. There would seem to be no reason in principle why parties should not be bound where they have previously dealt with each other and established an arrangement whereby an offer is taken to have been agreed to if not promptly rejected.

Such an arrangement had been made in the Victorian case of *Boyd v Holmes*[141] where the plaintiff, a merchant in China, had for some time been consigning shipments of tea to the defendant, a Melbourne merchant, who subsequently sold the tea in Melbourne on behalf of them both. The plaintiff had, before shipping the consignment in dispute, cabled the

---

136. *Tinn v Hoffman & Co* (1873) 29 LT 271; *Balt v Onslow* (1892) 13 LR (NSW) Eq 79; *White Trucks Pty Ltd v Riley* (1948) 66 WN (NSW) 101; *Manchester Diocesan Council v Commercial & General Investments Ltd* [1970] 1 WLR 241; *George Hudson Holdings Ltd v Rudder* (1973) 128 CLR 387; *Yates Building Co Ltd v R J Pulleyn & Sons (York) Ltd* [1976] EG 123; *Spectra Pty Ltd v Pindari Pty Ltd* [1974] 2 NSWLR 617.
137. *Tinn v Hoffman & Co* (1873) 29 LT 271. It would be otherwise if the offeror's stipulation should be read as partly motivated by a desire to receive clear written evidence of the acceptance so as to avoid the risk of mistakes occurring in the transmission of a message by, eg, telegram or telephone: see Treitel, *The Law of Contract*, 10th ed, 1999, pp 29–30.
138. *Gilbert J McCaul (Aust) Pty Ltd v Pitt Club Ltd* (1959) 59 SR (NSW) 122; *Bowman v Durham Holdings Pty Ltd* (1973) 131 CLR 8; 2 ALR 193. But contrast *Manchester Diocesan Council v Commercial & General Investments Ltd* [1970] 1 WLR 241 at 246.
139. (1862) 11 CBNS 869; 142 ER 1037. See also *Empirnall Holdings Pty Ltd v Machon Paull Partners Pty Ltd* (1988) 14 NSWLR 523; *McMahon's (Transport) Pty Ltd v Ebbage* [1999] 1 Qd R 185. See generally C J Miller, 'Felthouse v Bindley Re-Visited' (1972) 35 *MLR* 489; M Powell, 'Acceptance by Silence in the Law of Contract' (1977) 5 *ABLR* 260. See also [111].
140. (1862) 11 CBNS 869 at 875; 142 ER 1037 at 1040.
141. (1878) 4 VLR (E) 161. See also *Empirnall Holdings Pty Ltd v Machon Paull Partners Pty Ltd* (1988) 14 NSWLR 523; *Re Selectmove Ltd* [1995] 1 WLR 474.

defendant details of the cost of the tea and, relying on a previous arrangement between them, took the defendant's failure to reply as an acceptance of his proposal. The Full Court of the Victorian Supreme Court held that the arrangement relied upon by the plaintiff had in fact not been complied with as it had previously been altered so as to apply only when further particulars (such as the quantity obtainable and freight costs) were supplied by the plaintiff. The court seems, however, clearly to have assumed (as had been held by the trial judge) that had the then existing arrangement been complied with the defendant would have been bound.

While it is clear that, at any rate in the absence of any previous arrangement between the parties, silence as such will not bind an offeree, it would seem that the performance by the offeree of some act clearly indicating an intention to accept would suffice to bind him or her. It is generally assumed that, apart from the effect of recent statutory provisions which are discussed below, where a seller without previous request sends goods to a person accompanied by a statement that the recipient will be assumed to have agreed to buy if he or she does not return them, the recipient will be bound if the goods are used, or dealt with, in such a way as to indicate an intention to buy (as, for example, by making a gift of the goods to a friend).[142] Normally at least, mere silence and inactivity are equivocal[143] but here the recipient has done more than simply remain silent (which does not in itself indicate a decision one way or the other) and has done something from which an intention to accept may reasonably be inferred.[144] It is true that an acceptance has not been communicated to the offeror, but the offeror has clearly indicated that such notification is not expected and we have already seen that in many cases an offeror will be taken to have dispensed with the necessity of communicating acceptance.

It is difficult to reconcile such an approach with *Felthouse v Bindley*,[145] discussed above, where it was held that no contract had been made, even though the nephew had stated to an auctioneer, whom he had employed to sell a number of horses, that the horse in question was not to be auctioned as it had already been sold to his uncle. In *Felthouse v Bindley* the offeree was the seller and the action of the seller in thus dealing with his own property may have been regarded as equivocal,[146] but otherwise the decision seems difficult to support.[147] Further, if an offeree remains silent because intending to accept, it would seem harsh if the offeree were unable

---

142. Some support for this view may be obtained from *Weatherby v Banham* (1832) 5 C & P 228; 172 ER 950. See also *Restatement (2d) Contracts*, §69; Schlesinger, ed, *Formation of Contracts*, 1968, Vol II, pp 1096–1108.
143. See *Allied Marine Transport Ltd v Vale do Rio Doce Navegacao SA* [1985] 2 All ER 796; *Unisys International Services Ltd v Eastern Counties Newspapers Ltd* [1991] 1 Lloyd's Rep 538; but see *Vitol SA v Norelf Ltd (The Santa Clara)* [1996] 3 All ER 193.
144. See *Empirnall Holdings Pty Ltd v Machon Paull Partners Pty Ltd* (1988) 14 NSWLR 523; *Airways Corporation of New Zealand v Geyserland Airways Ltd* [1996] 1 NZLR 116.
145. The action was brought by the uncle against the auctioneer, the uncle arguing that a contract had been formed by virtue of which property in the horse had passed to him and that the auctioneer's oversight in selling the horse to a third party constituted the tort of conversion. Keating J, while agreeing with the decision, considered that the result might have been different if the question had arisen as between the uncle and the nephew.

to enforce the contract even though having done precisely what was requested by the offeror. In such a situation the American law would probably permit the offeree to enforce the contract,[148] and it is suggested that there is no reason the same rule should not be followed by Australian courts.[149] So long as the offeree is not prejudiced by becoming bound when remaining silent with no intention of accepting, the offeree is adequately protected and there is no need for a rigid insistence that silence in the face of an offer must always be without contractual effect.

The practice (known as 'inertia selling') of sending unsolicited goods to a person, accompanied by a statement that if the goods are not returned within a stated period the recipient will be taken to have agreed to buy them, has at times been very common (especially in regard to relatively small items, such as books and records, which may easily be sent by post). The practice is objectionable on a number of counts. People might often be confused as to their legal position and may pay for the goods in the mistaken belief that they are bound to do so. Moreover, although it is clear that the recipient is under no legal obligation to go to the trouble and expense of returning the goods, doing so may often be the only effective way of ensuring that annoying demands for payment are not made. Consequently the legislature has stepped in to provide that in many circumstances the making of a demand for payment for unsolicited goods is an offence.[150] It is also provided that where the sender does not collect the goods within a certain period of time, the goods become the property of the recipient, in effect as a gift. The details of this legislation are beyond the scope of this work, but the possible relevance of the inertia selling legislation should always be borne in mind when the problems discussed in this paragraph are being considered.

The Postal Acceptance Rule

[230] Acceptance effective on posting. Perhaps the main exception (an exception of considerable importance in commercial dealings) to the

---

146. *Cheshire, Fifoot and Furmston's Law of Contract*, 13th ed, 1996, pp 48–50. On the need for a 'definite overt act' where communication of acceptance has been dispensed with see *White Trucks Pty Ltd v Riley* (1948) 66 WN (NSW) 101. Cf the suggestion that *Felthouse v Bindley* indicates that there need be no communication of acceptance only where the offeror stipulates the overt act which will suffice for acceptance: Salmond and Williams, *Principles of the Law of Contracts*, 1945, pp 82–3.
147. See, eg *Anson's Law of Contract*, 27th ed, 1998, p 49; *Chitty on Contracts*, 26th ed, 1989, Vol 1, p 62.
148. See *Restatement (2d) Contracts*, §69 and Schlesinger, ed, *Formation of Contracts*, 1968, Vol II, pp 1096–8.
149. But see *Fairline Shipping Corp v Adamson* [1985] QB 180 at 188–9 where Kerr J considered that the suggested rule cannot fit into the accepted law of offer and acceptance. See also *Food Corp of India v Antclizo Shipping Corp (The Antclizo)* [1987] 2 Lloyd's Rep 130 at 146 per Nicholls LJ.
150. **Cth**: *Trade Practices Act* 1974, ss 63a–5; **ACT**: *Fair Trading Act*, 1992, ss 28–30; **NSW**: *Fair Trading Act* 1987, ss 57–9; **NT**: *Consumer Affairs and Fair Trading Act* 1990, ss 57–9; **Qld**: *Fair Trading Act* 1989, ss 52–5; **SA**: *Fair Trading Act* 1987, ss 71–3; **Tas**: *Unordered Goods and Services Act* 1973; *Fair Trading Act* 1990, s 27; **Vic**: *Fair Trading Act* 1985, ss 28–30; **WA**: *Fair Trading Act* 1987, ss 28–31. The legislation also deals with unordered services and directory entries.

principle that acceptance is not effective until communicated to the offeror occurs in cases where the postal acceptance rule applies. In such cases the acceptance is effective immediately a properly pre-paid and addressed letter is posted. Thus a contract is formed on posting even though the offeror is then ignorant of that fact, and even though the letter is delayed in transmission, or may be lost in the post and therefore never ultimately delivered. It is essential to realise, however, that it is by no means in all cases where acceptance is made by post that acceptance will be effective on posting.

[231] **When rule applies**. In the leading case which finally established the rule in England it was emphasised that its application was limited 'to cases in which by reason of general usage, or of the relations between the parties to any particular transactions, or of the terms in which the offer is made, the acceptance of such offer by a letter through the post is expressly or impliedly authorised'.[151] A few years later the notion of the rule depending on some form of 'authorisation' of the use of the post was criticised in *Henthorn v Fraser*,[152] where the principle was reformulated by Lord Herschell as follows:

> It strikes me as somewhat artificial to speak of the person to whom the offer is made as having the implied authority of the other party to send his acceptance by post. He needs no authority to transmit the acceptance through any particular channel; he may select what means he pleases, the post office no less than any other. The only effect of the supposed authority is to make the acceptance complete so soon as it is posted, and authority will obviously be implied only when the tribunal considers that it is a case in which this result ought to be reached. I should prefer to state the rule thus: Where the circumstances are such that it must have been within the contemplation of the parties that, according to the ordinary usages of mankind, the post might be used as a means of communicating the acceptance of an offer, the acceptance is complete as soon as it is posted.

Henthorn v Fraser shows that, although the postal acceptance rule will normally arise where the offer was itself made by post, this is by no means essential. In that case the plaintiff called at the office of a firm (the defendant) with which he had been negotiating for the purchase of some houses. A written offer was then handed to him which he took away to consider. The next day he posted from the town in which he lived (which was some distance from the town in which the defendant's office was located) a letter accepting the offer. In the meantime a letter withdrawing the offer had been posted by the defendant but was not received by the plaintiff until after he had posted his acceptance. For reasons which will be explained later, the letter of revocation could be effective only on receipt by the plaintiff (the postal acceptance rule having no application to revocation of offers)[153] but nonetheless the revocation was received by the plaintiff

---

151. *Household Fire and Carriage Accident Insurance Co (Ltd) v Grant* (1879) LR 4 Ex D 216 at 228 per Baggallay LJ.
152. [1892] 2 Ch 27 at 33, see also at 36 per Kay LJ; *White Cliffs Opal Mines Ltd v Miller* (1904) 4 SR (NSW) 150; *Tallerman & Co Pty Ltd v Nathan's Merchandise (Vic) Pty Ltd* (1957) 98 CLR 93 at 111–12; *Holwell Securities Ltd v Hughes* [1974] 1 All ER 161; *Bressan v Squires* [1974] 2 NSWLR 460.
153. See [244].

before his acceptance letter had been delivered. There would thus be a contract only if his acceptance had been effective when posted, and the court held that this was indeed the case. The offer by its terms was to remain open for 14 days,[154] so an immediate reply was clearly not contemplated, and as the defendant knew that the plaintiff lived in a different town the proper inference was that both parties contemplated that if the plaintiff accepted he might very well do so by post. The postal acceptance rule applies to communications by telegram as well as those by letter.[155]

In many (if not most) cases the parties will in fact be quite unaware of the postal acceptance rule, and it seems clear that the relevant question is whether it can reasonably be inferred that the parties contemplated the likelihood of acceptance by post rather than whether they contemplated what the legal effect of such a method of acceptance would be.[156]

[232] When postal rule displaced. The postal acceptance rule is, however, always liable to be displaced by appropriate circumstances. We have already seen that an offeror has full control over the character and extent of the power of acceptance that the offer creates,[157] and consequently it is always open to the offeror to indicate that acceptance will not be binding until it is communicated. This will be so if the offer stipulates that it may be accepted by 'notice' to the offeror within a stated period of time.[158] In such cases everything depends on the correct interpretation in the circumstances of the language used, and slight differences in terminology can be of crucial significance (for example, if in the case just referred to the offer called for 'notice posted' or 'acceptance in writing' within the time limit).[159]

The postal acceptance rule became established against the background of assumptions that the postal service was both speedy and reliable. In light of

---

154. However, as there was in this case no consideration for an option, the offer could nonetheless be withdrawn at any earlier time provided that this was done before it had been effectively accepted: see [247].
155. *Cowan v O'Connor* (1888) 20 QBD 640; *Dehle v Denham* (1899) 1 N & S 128; *Lewis Construction Co Pty Ltd v M Tichauer Société Anonyme* [1966] VR 341. See also *Brinkibon Ltd v Stahag Stahl GmbH* [1983] 2 AC 34. As to a telegram sent through the post office to a telex receiver see *Express Airways v Port Augusta Air Services* [1980] Qd R 543.
156. *Bressan v Squires* [1974] 2 NSWLR 460 at 461–2. But cf *Holwell Securities Ltd v Hughes* [1974] 1 All ER 161 at 166–7 per Lawton LJ.
157. See [228].
158. *Holwell Securities Ltd v Hughes* [1974] 1 All ER 161; *Bressan v Squires* [1974] 2 NSWLR 460. Both cases involved the exercise of an option; in such a case the offeror is bound during the period of the option while the offeree is not (see [247]), and this fact may have made the courts more disposed than might otherwise have been the case to hold that the language used was sufficient to oust the postal acceptance rule. See also *Nunin Holdings Pty Ltd v Tullamarine Estates Pty Ltd* [1994] 1 VR 74.
159. A desire to avoid the necessity for such fine distinctions was one reason for the vigorous dissent by Bramwell LJ in *Household Fire and Carriage Accident Insurance Co (Ltd) v Grant* (1879) LR 4 Ex D 216, but his prediction that the effect of the rule established by the majority would be that it would be obviated by offerors using words indicating the necessity for actual communication has not been borne out in practice: see his remarks at 236, 238–9.

public debate in recent years questioning both of these assumptions, the practice of phrasing offers so as to exclude the operation of the rule may become more popular in practice. It often happens that an offer will be stated to be open for a certain period of time, there being no indication one way or the other as to whether actual notice is envisaged. It can be argued that as the purpose of the offeror in setting such a time limit is probably to ensure that the offeror can, once the period has expired, safely act on the footing that the offer has been rejected, the offeror should be regarded as impliedly indicating that acceptance will be effective only on receipt. The cases, so far as they touch this point, seem to point to the contrary conclusion,[160] perhaps on the basis that it is a simple matter for the offeror's intention to be indicated clearly and that, once it appears that the postal acceptance rule is prima facie applicable, at least some indication of contrary intention other than the mere fixing of a time limit on the validity of the offer should be shown.[161]

It may be that in some cases the very nature of the subject matter may indicate that the postal acceptance rule is not to apply, on the grounds that in such cases its application would produce an absurd or inconvenient result.[162] In *Tallerman & Co Pty Ltd v Nathan's Merchandise (Vic) Pty Ltd*[163] two members of the High Court were prepared to assume that actual communication would be essential where firms of solicitors were conducting a highly contentious correspondence relating to possible settlement of a dispute over the terms of a contract previously entered into between their clients.[164] It is true that 'courts in more recent times and in the light of modern means of communication have shown no disposition to extend the [postal acceptance rule]',[165] and this point is illustrated later when the cases dealing with situations where communication is virtually instantaneous are discussed.[166] However, the application of the rule may well yet vary with changing commercial practices. It has in recent years become increasingly common for business communications to be conveyed by means of courier services and it may be that, where communication in this manner is shown to have been contemplated by the parties (either from the manner of transmission of the offer or from practice in previous dealings between them), a letter of acceptance would be held to be effective once handed to the courier.[167]

---

160. *Bruner v Moore* [1904] 1 Ch 305; *Jacobsen Sons & Co v E Underwood & Son Ltd* 1894 1 SLT 578. See also *Lewes Nominees Pty Ltd v Strang* (1983) 57 ALJR 823.
161. It has been suggested that in such cases the correct inference to be drawn is that the acceptance must be posted within such a time that it would normally be received before the expiry of the time limit: D M Evans, 'The Anglo-American Mailing Rule' (1966) 15 *ICLQ* 553 at 569, 574. The offeror may, of course, expressly stipulate this result (see [234]) but it is suggested that it is rather artificial to read such an inference into the mere fixing of a time limit without further elaboration.
162. *Holwell Securities Ltd v Hughes* [1974] 1 All ER 161 at 166–7 per Lawton LJ.
163. (1957) 98 CLR 93 at 111–12 per Dixon CJ and Fullagar J.
164. In *Holwell Securities Ltd v Hughes* [1974] 1 All ER 161 at 167 Lawton LJ considered that the special nature of an option contract was such as to render the rule inapplicable. The other members of the court did not approach the question on this basis, and the point was referred to but left open by Bowen CJ in Eq in *Bressan v Squires* [1974] 2 NSWLR 460.
165. *Bressan v Squires* [1974] 2 NSWLR 460 at 462 per Bowen CJ in Eq.
166. See [238].

The postal acceptance rule depends on the letter of acceptance having been properly pre-paid and deposited with the post office, and so where a letter was handed to a postal delivery officer in a street, and it was established that the post office regulations forbade postal delivery officers to accept letters in this way, it was held that the letter had not been posted for the purposes of the postal acceptance rule.[168] If the offeree wrongly addresses the letter of acceptance so that it is delayed in delivery, the acceptance will not be effective until it is actually delivered. Presumably the acceptance would be effective on posting if the letter was, despite the incorrect address, in fact delivered in the normal time. The point would be important if the offeror purported to revoke while the letter was in the course of transmission. Where the delay is caused by the offeror giving a wrong or incomplete address it would seem that, at least where the error is not one which should have been obvious to the offeree, the acceptance will be effective on posting even though delivery is delayed because of the use of an incorrect address.[169]

The cases holding an acceptance to have been effective on posting assume that at the time the post office remained in existence as a medium of communication between the parties' addresses, and hence it was held in a South African case to be inapplicable when postal communication had been suspended because of war.[170] The same reasoning would apply where at the time of posting it was general knowledge that postal communication was disrupted because of industrial action and a letter of acceptance was as a result delivered late. Perhaps the result would be otherwise if disruption such as a 'go-slow' strike had occurred before the posting of the offer and was continuing at the time of posting of the acceptance.

[233] Acceptance lost in post. The postal acceptance rule protects the acceptor not just against the risk of delay in the acceptance being transmitted but also against the risk of it being lost and never reaching the offeror. Thus in *Household Fire and Carriage Accident Insurance Co (Ltd) v Grant*[171] the defendant applied in writing for shares in the plaintiff company. A letter advising of the allotment of shares to him was posted to the defendant but was never received by him. When the company later sued to recover money owing in respect of the purchase of the shares, the defendant argued that, as he was liable only if there was a contract binding

---

167. An argument against this view would be that at least where the courier is employed by the offeree he retains the right to withdraw the letter until it is actually delivered. Loss of control is one argument cited to support the postal acceptance rule, but it is semble not a determining basis of the rule: see [235].
168. *Re London and Northern Bank: Ex parte Jones* [1900] 1 Ch 220. The question was whether the offer had been accepted prior to the communication of a revocation of the offer; the offeree was unable to prove that the acceptance had been properly posted by the postman before this time.
169. Cf *Re London and Northern Bank: Ex parte Jones* [1900] 1 Ch 220. See also *Adams v Lindsell* (1818) 1 B & Ald 681; 106 ER 250 (delay caused by misdirection of an offer ignored in determining whether acceptance posted in time; sed quaere whether this should be so where offeree should have realised that offer had been delayed). See further Treitel, *The Law of Contract*, 10th ed, 1999, pp 26–7.
170. *Bal v Van Standen* [1902] TS 128.
171. (1879) LR 4 Ex D 216. See also *Re Imperial Land Co of Marseilles, Wall's Case* (1872) LR 15 Eq 18; *Georgoulis v Mandalinic* [1984] 1 NSWLR 612.

him to take the shares, the fact that he had never received notice of the acceptance of his offer was fatal. It was held that the contract had been formed on the posting of the letter of allotment.

[234] **Intermediate situations.** In situations where the parties contemplate that acceptance may well be made by post but for some reason the acceptance is held not to have been effective on posting, it does not necessarily follow that the acceptance will take effect only when actually read by the offeror. If it is contemplated that acceptance will be by post, it may well be that an acceptance, though not effective on posting, will nonetheless take effect on delivery to the offeror's address even if not actually read until some later time.[172] Moreover, it is not uncommon for a formal offer to make an express provision as to when acceptance will be effective. In *Bowman v Durham Holdings Pty Ltd*,[173] for example, an option provided that any exercise of the option by mail would be deemed to have been given at the time when the letter would in the ordinary course of post be delivered. The letter was in fact not delivered until after the expiry date of the option but, it being proved that it would in the ordinary course have been delivered on that day, it was held that the exercise of the option had been made in due time.

[235] **Justifications of the rule.** The postal acceptance rule has had a somewhat controversial history. Although it can be traced back to *Adams v Lindsell*[174] in 1818, that case was not conclusive and there was a series of conflicting decisions[175] until the matter was settled in 1879 by *Household Fire and Carriage Accident Insurance Co (Ltd) v Grant*.[176] Most of the reasons given in the cases for the existence of the rule have been criticised as unsound.[177] Perhaps the argument most commonly advanced initially was that the post office was the agent of the offeror (or, alternatively, the

---

172. See *Holwell Securities Ltd v Hughes* [1974] 1 All ER 161 at 164. See also *Re London and Northern Bank: Ex parte Jones* [1900] 1 Ch 220 at 224; *Brinkibon Ltd v Stahag Stahl GmbH* [1983] 2 AC 34 at 43 per Lord Fraser. However, in *Lolly-Pops (Harbourside) Pty Ltd v Werncog Pty Ltd* (1998) NSW Conv R 55-861, Young J considered that in such circumstances acceptance by letter is communicated when the letter is opened in the ordinary course of business, or would have been opened, had ordinary business practice been followed. *Restatement (2d) Contracts*, §568 goes further and holds that any written acceptance will be effective when it comes into the possession of the person addressed or when it has been deposited in some place which has been authorised by that person as the place for communications to be deposited.
173. (1973) 131 CLR 8. See also *Lewes Nominees Pty Ltd v Strang* (1983) 57 ALJR 823.
174. (1818) 1 B & Ald 681; 106 ER 250.
175. For cases supporting the view that communication was essential see, eg *British and American Telegraph Co Ltd v Colson* (1871) LR 6 Exch 108; *Re Imperial Land Co of Marseilles; Townsend's Case* (1871) LR 13 Eq 148. For cases supporting the rule as finally established see, eg *Dunlop v Higgins* (1848) 1 HLC 381; 9 ER 805; *Re Imperial Land Co of Marseilles; Hams' Case* (1872) 7 Ch App 587. An early Australian authority supporting the rule that acceptance was complete upon posting is *Tooth v Fleming* (1859) Legge 1152.
176. (1879) LR 4 Ex D 216.
177. See generally P H Winfield, 'Some Aspects of Offer and Acceptance' (1939) 55 *LQR* 499; D M Evans, 'The Anglo-American Mailing Rule' (1966) 15 *ICLQ* 553; R A Samek, 'A Reassessment of the Present Rule Relating to Postal Acceptance' (1961) 35 *ALJ* 38; S Gardner, 'Trashing with Trollope: a Deconstruction of the Postal Rules in Contract' (1992) 12 *Oxford J Legal Studies* 170.

common agent of both parties) to receive the communication and that therefore the acceptance should be treated as having been communicated to the offeror upon posting.[178] This reasoning was answered, in a frequently cited passage, by Kay LJ in *Henthorn v Fraser*:[179]

> That reason is not satisfactory. The post office are only carriers between them. They are agents to convey the communication, not to receive it. The communication is not made to the post office, but by their agency as carriers. The difference is between saying 'Tell my agent A, if you accept', and 'Send your answer to me by A'. In the former case A is to be the intelligent recipient of the acceptance, in the latter he is only to convey the communication to the person making the offer which he may do by a letter, knowing nothing of its contents. The post office are only agents in the latter sense.

Another argument is that the acceptance is effective on posting because the offeree has then done all that can be done to communicate acceptance and should not be responsible for what might happen after losing control over the letter.[180] The difficulty with this argument is that in other situations the argument affords no comfort to an offeree if circumstances beyond his or her control result in the offeror being unaware of his or her acceptance, for example where, unknown to the offeree, a telephone line goes dead or a telex machine fails to transmit a message.[181] The difficulty arises because where negotiations are carried out at a distance by use of the postal service, some time must elapse when one of the parties is ignorant of a vital fact. If acceptance is effective on posting, the offeror will be bound without knowing it until the acceptance is received. The only other solution which was ever seriously considered in English law (namely, that acceptance would be effective only on receipt) would result in the acceptor being bound for a certain period of time without knowing it (that is, until becoming aware that the acceptance had been received by the offeror). The fact is that the postal acceptance rule has been settled as a matter of convenience and the present authors would agree with the conclusion of an eminent American writer:[182]

---

178. See, eg *Re National Savings Bank Association (Hebb's Case)* (1867) LR 4 Eq 9; *Household Fire and Carriage Accident Insurance Co (Ltd) v Grant* (1879) LR 4 Ex D 216 at 221; *Byrne v Van Tienhoven* (1880) 5 CPD 344.
179. [1892] 2 Ch 27 at 35–6. For a further discussion of this distinction see *Batt v Onslow* (1892) 13 LR (NSW) Eq 79.
180. See, eg *Dunlop v Higgins* (1848) 1 HLC 381; 9 ER 805; *Re Imperial Land Co of Marseilles; Wall's Case* (1872) LR 15 Eq 18; *Household Fire and Carriage Accident Insurance Co (Ltd) v Grant* (1879) LR 4 Ex D 216 at 223.
181. *Entores Ltd v Miles Far East Corp* [1955] 2 QB 327. Some American courts, relying on a regulation of the US Post Office entitling a person depositing a letter in the mail to reclaim it, have held that as the sender of a letter no longer loses the right of control the postal acceptance rule is no longer applicable in that country. For a convincing argument that the rule does not in fact rest on the test of control see C L Pannam, 'Postal Regulation 289 and Acceptance of an Offer by Post' (1960) 2 *MULR* 388 (where the US cases are discussed). The Australian Postal Corporation General Postal Services Terms and Conditions (made under the Australian *Postal Corporation Act* 1989 (Cth), s 32) provide for the return of articles before delivery: cl 48. However, there is no absolute right in the sender to the return of articles because certain conditions must be fulfilled, eg an authorised person must determine that there are special reasons for the withdrawal or return of the article or that the addressee has consented to its return.

[235]

One of the parties must carry the risk of loss and inconvenience. We need a definite and uniform rule as to this. We can choose either rule; but we must choose one. We can put the risk on either party; but we must not leave it in doubt. The party not carrying the risk can then act promptly and with confidence in reliance on the contract; the party carrying the risk can insure against it if he so desires. The business community could no doubt adjust itself to either rule; but the rule throwing the risk on the offeror has the merit of closing the deal more quickly and enabling performance more promptly.

Mention must be made of one further aspect of the operation of the postal acceptance rule, a factor which helps to explain its survival despite the criticisms which have been made of it.[183] In many legal systems an offer made in a business context will be assumed, in the absence of express provision to the contrary, to be a firm offer which may not be revoked before the offeree has had a reasonable opportunity to consider whether or not to accept.[184] By contrast, at common law an offer, even though expressly stated to be open for a certain period of time, may always be revoked at any time prior to acceptance, the only exception being where separate consideration has been provided for an option contract.[185] One effect of the postal acceptance rule is to limit the offeror's power of revocation, especially as it is established that the rule only applies to acceptances and that a revocation by letter is effective only when communicated.[186] In a number of cases the result has been that a revocation communicated after the posting of a letter of acceptance has been held to be ineffective, and the courts have emphasised the need, where the parties are not in instantaneous communication with each other, for the acceptor to be able to act immediately on the basis that the contract is binding once the letter of acceptance is posted.[187] Were the law otherwise it would always be possible that the offer might be revoked before the acceptance was delivered, and the offeree could not safely incur liabilities under the contract (as where, for example, a seller needs to purchase goods to fulfil a contract).

[236] **Postal rule and the place and time of formation of contract.** We have already seen that where it applies the postal acceptance rule operates to protect the offeree against the risk of delay or loss in the course

---

182. *Corbin on Contracts*, Vol 1, 1963, p 337. See also *Bressan v Squires* [1974] 2 NSWLR 460 at 461 (where Bowen CJ In Eq stated that the rule 'it seems, is really based upon notions of expediency and convenience, as these are envisaged by the courts from time to time'): *Brinkibon v Stahag Stahl GmbH* [1983] AC 34.
183. See A Nussbaum, 'Comparative Aspects of the Anglo-American Offer-And-Acceptance Doctrine' (1936) 36 *Col LR* 920. For a further useful comparative discussion of the postal acceptance rule see P H Winfield, 'Some Aspects of Offer and Acceptance' (1939) 55 *LQR* 499.
184. See Schlesinger, ed, *Formation of Contracts*, 1968, especially Vol 1, pp 162-3, for the conclusion, based upon a comparative study, that in general in legal systems which make acceptance effective on posting, offers are normally revocable, whereas in those systems where posted acceptance is effective only on receipt, the offer will normally be irrevocable for a period of time.
185. See [247], [254].
186. See [244].
187. *Re Imperial Land Co of Marseilles; Harris' Case* (1872) 7 Ch App 587 at 594-5; *Byrne v Van Tienhoven* (1880) 5 CPD 344 at 348. See also *Henthorn v Fraser* [1892] 2 Ch 27 at 36-7; *Brinkibon Ltd v Stahag Stahl GmbH* [1983] 2 AC 34 at 41.

of transmission of the letter, and also to protect against revocation of the offer after the acceptance has been posted. The rule also has a number of other important implications. The question of the place of formation of a contract is often important in relation to the jurisdiction of a court to entertain an action on the contract, and also in relation to the application of the conflict of laws rules concerning the law to be applied to contracts where the parties are in different jurisdictions.[188] A contract is formed at the place where the final act regarded as completing the contract occurred. Thus, where the postal acceptance rule applies, Australian courts will regard the contract as having been made in the place where the acceptance was posted, whereas in other cases the contract is made at the place where acceptance is communicated to the offeror.[189] In other cases it will be important to fix with precision the time when a contract was made, for the calculation of the price to be paid for property sold (for example, where shares are sold by reference to the market price) or the calculation of just what is included in a sale (for example, the sale of a business at a stated price plus the value of stock in hand) may by the terms of the contract require to be made by reference to the date of the making of the contract.[190] Indeed, the functions served by the rule are so many and diverse that it has been forcefully argued that it is unsatisfactory to have just one general rule which must then automatically be applied in all situations, but this argument has not in fact been adopted by the courts.[191]

[237] **Withdrawal of acceptance by post.** Mention must finally be made of one much disputed point, namely whether an offeree who posts a letter of acceptance may effectively retract the acceptance by speedier means of communication (for example, a telegram or telephone call) reaching the offeror before the letter of acceptance.[192] There is curiously little authority on the point. A Scottish case is often cited as suggesting that withdrawal of the acceptance would be effective[193] whereas a New Zealand case tends to the contrary conclusion.[194] A logical application of the postal acceptance rule would prevent the withdrawal having effect, and would also prevent the offeree being able to speculate at the offeror's expense (for example, where the contract is for the purchase of property such as company shares which may fluctuate rapidly in value). On the other hand, there would seem to be little harm in allowing retraction, especially as, being unaware of the

---

188. See Nygh, *Conflict of Laws in Australia*, 6th ed, 1995, pp 51–3, 303–4, 308.
189. *Cowan v O'Connor* (1888) 20 QBD 640; *Pratten v Thompson* (1895) 11 WN (NSW) 162; *Dehle v Denham* (1899) 1 N & S 128; *Remilton v City Mutual Life Assurance Society Ltd* (1908) 10 WALR 19; *Entores Ltd v Miles Far East Corp* [1955] 2 QB 327; *Tallerman & Co Pty Ltd v Nathan's Merchandise (Vic) Pty Ltd* (1957) 98 CLR 93; *Lewis Construction Co Pty Ltd v M Tichauer Société Anonyme* [1966] VR 341.
190. *Tooth v Fleming* (1859) Legge 1152.
191. See D M Evans, 'The Anglo-American Mailing Rule' (1966) 15 *ICLQ* 553; Schlesinger, ed, *Formation of Contracts*, 1968, Vol 11, pp 1393ff. See also *Brinkibon Ltd v Stahag Stahl GmbH* [1983] 2 AC 34 at 40 per Lord Wilberforce.
192. A useful discussion, which reviews the conflicting opinions of the text writers, is A H Hudson, 'Retractation of Letters of Acceptance' (1966) 82 *LQR* 169.
193. *Dunmore v Alexander* (1830) 9 Sh (Ct of Sess) 190. It is not clear that the case involved the postal acceptance rule at all.
194. *Wenkheim v Arndt* (1873) 1 JR 73. The case is very briefly reported and at least a contributory factor to the decision was a strong doubt as to whether the retraction was sent by a person authorised to act on the acceptor's behalf.

acceptance, the offeror will not have acted on it and will in fact know just what the position is at an earlier point of time.[195] Even if the withdrawal of an acceptance is held in principle to be ineffective, it would obviously be unjust to hold the offeror bound if, relying on the revocation at its face value, it assumed there was no contract and altered its position (for example, by selling the goods the subject of the offer to a third party) on the assumption that the offer had been rejected. In such a case the purported withdrawal of acceptance would no doubt be treated as either an offer to rescind the contract or a repudiation of it justifying the offeror in terminating the contract, or as giving rise to an estoppel preventing the offeree from enforcing the contract.[196]

[238] **Instantaneous communication**. The postal acceptance rule, while firmly established, will not be readily extended by the courts. It can be argued that wherever the parties are communicating at a distance the offeree should be held to have effectively accepted if all has been done to communicate an acceptance by approved methods. This argument was, however, rejected in *Entores Ltd v Miles Far East Corp*[197] where, when an offer was made by telex machine from the plaintiff in London to the defendant in Holland and was accepted by the defendant by telex message, the question arose as to whether the contract was concluded in Holland or in London. The court considered that there was no justification for extending the postal acceptance rule and held that where the parties were in instantaneous communication the general rule that acceptance is ineffective before communicated prevailed. As a result, the contract was held to have been made in London. In the case of communication by mechanical means such as telephone, telex or fax[198] communication is for all practical purposes simultaneous and hence is to be assimilated to cases where parties are negotiating in each other's presence.[199]

The *Entores* case was subsequently applied by the House of Lords on very similar facts, but it was pointed out that the circumstances may sometimes dictate a different result:[200]

> Since 1955 the use of telex communication has been greatly expanded, and there are many variants on it. The senders and recipients may not be the principals to the contemplated contract. They may be servants or agents with limited authority. The message may not reach, or be intended to reach, the designated recipient immediately; messages may be sent out of office

---

195. C L Pannam, 'Postal Regulation 289 and Acceptance of an Offer by Post' (1960) 2 *MULR* 388 at 396.
196. *Restatement (2d) Contracts*, §63, comment c; Treitel, *The Law of Contract*, 10th ed, 1999, pp 27–8.
197. [1955] 2 QB 327, followed in *Aviet v Smith and Searls Pty Ltd* (1956) 73 WN (NSW) 274; *W A Dewhurst & Co Pty Ltd v Cawrse* [1960] VR 278; *Hampstead Meats Pty Ltd v Emerson Yates Pty Ltd* [1967] SASR 190; *Mendelson-Zeller Co Inc v T & C Providores Pty Ltd* [1981] 1 NSWLR 366; *Express Airways v Port Augusta Air Services* [1980] Qd R 543; *Reese Bros Plastics Ltd v Hamon-Sobelco Australia Pty Ltd* (1988) 5 BPR 11,106. For an interesting discussion of further problems arising in this context see B Coote, 'The Instantaneous Transmission of Acceptances' (1971) 4 *NZULR* 331.
198. Eg *Reese Bros Plastics Ltd v Hamon-Sobelco Australia Pty Ltd* (1988) 5 BPR 11,106.
199. For an early New Zealand case applying this rule to acceptance by telephone see *Union Steamship Co v Ewart* (1893) 13 NZLR 9.

hours, or at night, with the intention, or upon the assumption, that they will be read at a later time. There may be some error or default at the recipient's end which prevents receipt at the time contemplated and believed in by the sender. The message may have been sent and/or received through machines operated by third persons. And many other variations may occur. No universal rule can cover all such cases: they must be resolved by reference to the intentions of the parties, by sound business practice and in some cases by a judgment where the risks should lie.

It would follow from the above that if a person accepted an offer by telephone and because of some failure in the telephone system the acceptance was not heard by the offeror, there would be no contract at that time.[201]

The case of email communications is still unclear.[202] Some suggest the postal acceptance rule would apply,[203] whereas others disagree. There may also be a distinction between cases of contracting by email (where perhaps the postal acceptance rule should apply) and contracting over the internet through a merchant's e-commerce website (where perhaps the receipt rule should apply). In the case of email there may be a further distinction between email over the internet and email where there is a direct link between the parties' computers.

Most States have recently enacted legislation concerning Electronic Transactions.[204] However, this legislation does not seem to change the existing law, as similar issues arise as to the method and place of an effective acceptance (including the issue of effective receipt). The legislation covers the time and place of dispatch and receipt of electronic communications, unless regulations exempt particular electronic communications.[205] It supplies default rules that apply if the parties have not agreed otherwise. The relevant section in the legislation provides that electronic communications[206] will be taken to have been dispatched when they enter a

---

200. *Brinkibon Ltd v Stahag Stahl GmbH* [1983] 2 AC 34 at 42 per Lord Wilberforce. For a possible example of such a situation see *Leach Nominees Pty Ltd v Walter Wright Pty Ltd* [1986] WAR 244 (offeror contemplating acceptance by use of the public telex facility). It would follow that where a telex or fax is sent and received outside of normal office hours it may not be regarded as received until the following normal opening hours: see *Schelde Delta Shipping BV v Astarte Shipping Ltd (The Pamela)* [1995] 2 Lloyd's Rep 249.
201. Normally the offeree will realise that the message has not been received. But if the offeree reasonably believes that the message has been received and the offeror ought to have realised that this was the case, the offeror may be estopped from saying that the message of acceptance was not received: see *Entores Ltd v Miles Far Fast Corp* [1955] 2 QB 327 at 333 per Denning LJ.
202. See K O'Shea and K Skeahan, 'Acceptance of Offers by Email — How far should the Postal Acceptance Rule Extend?' (1997) 13 *QUTLJ* 247.
203. See, eg Chissick and Kelman, *Electronic Commerce Law and Practice*, 1999, pp 73ff.
204. *Electronic Transactions Act* 2000 (NSW); *Electronic Transactions (Victoria) Act* 2000 (Vic); *Electronic Transactions Act* 2000 (SA); *Electronic Transactions Act* 2000 (Tas); *Electronic Transactions Act* 2000 (NT); *Electronic Transactions Act* 2001 (ACT); *Electronic Transactions Act* 2001 (Qld), which differs slightly from the other pieces of legislation. See also *Electronic Transactions Act* 1999 (Cth). Western Australia is considering a similar Bill. It is possible other States will enact similar legislation. For a discussion to the background of the legislation see C Tay, 'Contracts, Technology and Electronic Commerce: the evolution continues' (1998) 9 *JLIS* 177; A Upcroft, 'E-commerce: Global or local? An Australian Case Study' (1999) 10 *JLIS* 112.

single information system out of the control of the originator.[207] Furthermore, if the addressee has designated an information system for receiving electronic communications, then the time of receipt will be when that communication enters that information system.[208] However, if there is no designated system, then receipt will be the time when the communication comes to the attention of the addressee.[209] The legislation provides no guidance as to when an information system will be 'designated' and presumably it is a question of construction.

The Requirement of Knowledge

[239] Necessity of knowledge of offer. It is clear in principle that acceptance cannot occur if the offeree is in fact ignorant of the offer. Consequently, where an offer is made for a reward to be paid in return for the performing of some act (for example, the supplying of information relating to the commission of a crime), the mere fact that a person by chance happens to perform that act while ignorant of the offer will not result in any contract being formed. Unless the person performing the act called for is 'acting on or in pursuance of or in reliance upon or in return for'[210] the consideration contained in the offer, the parties cannot be said in even the most extended sense to have reached an agreement capable of having contractual effect. It is true that one case involving such a reward offer can be read as holding that the offer could be accepted by a person who did not know of it,[211] but it is not clear from the report if this was in fact the reasoning of the court and, in any event, subsequent cases have made it clear that the decision, if it did so decide, must be regarded as wrong.[212]

---

205. *Electronic Transactions Act* 2000 (NSW), s 13(7); *Electronic Transactions (Victoria) Act* 2000 (Vic), s 13(7); *Electronic Transactions Act* 2000 (SA), s 13(7); *Electronic Transactions Act* 2000 (Tas), s 11(7); *Electronic Transactions Act* 2000 (NT), s 13(7); *Electronic Transactions Act* 2001 (ACT), s 13(7); contrast *Electronic Transactions Act* 2001 (Qld), which does not provide this exclusion. See also *Electronic Transactions Act* 1999 (Cth), s 14(7)
206. These are defined in the Acts to mean '(a) a communication of information in the form of data, text or images by means of guided or unguided electromagnetic energy, or both or (b) a communication of information in the form of sound by means of guided or unguided electromagnetic energy, or both, where the sound is processed at its destination by an automated voice recognition system'. There are minor differences in the Queensland definition.
207. *Electronic Transactions Act* 2000 (NSW), s 13(1) and (2); *Electronic Transactions (Victoria) Act* 2000 (Vic), s 13(1) and (2); *Electronic Transactions Act* 2000 (SA), s 13(1) and (2); *Electronic Transactions Act* 2000 (Tas), s 11(1) and (2); *Electronic Transactions Act* 2000 (NT), s 13(1) and (2); *Electronic Transactions Act* 2001 (ACT), s 13(1) and (2); *Electronic Transactions Act* 2001 (Qld), s 23(1) and (2). See also *Electronic Transactions Act* 1999 (Cth), s 14(1) and (2).
208. *Electronic Transactions Act* 2000 (NSW), s 13(3); *Electronic Transactions (Victoria) Act* 2000 (Vic), s 13(3); *Electronic Transactions Act* 2000 (SA), s 13(3); *Electronic Transactions Act* 2000 (Tas), s 11(3); *Electronic Transactions Act* 2000 (NT), s 13(3); *Electronic Transactions Act* 2001 (ACT), s 13(3); *Electronic Transactions Act* 2001 (Qld), s 24(1). See also *Electronic Transactions Act* 1999 (Cth), s 14(3).
209. *Electronic Transactions Act* 2000 (NSW), s 13(4); *Electronic Transactions (Victoria) Act* 2000 (Vic), s 13(4); *Electronic Transactions Act* 2000 (SA), s 13(4); *Electronic Transactions Act* 2000 (Tas), s 11(4); *Electronic Transactions Act* 2000 (NT), s 13(4); *Electronic Transactions Act* 2001 (ACT), s 13(4); *Electronic Transactions Act* 2001 (Qld), s 24(2). See also *Electronic Transactions Act* 1999 (Cth), s 14(4).

It seems that, consistently with the above reasoning, no contract would result if two offers in identical terms should happen to cross in the post, each party being unaware of the offer of the other.[213]

Where an offer calls for acceptance by the performance of an act, it may be that a person commences performance in ignorance of the offer but becomes aware of it before completing performance. It is reasonable to assume in such a case, in the absence of any clear evidence to the contrary, that such continued performance was at least partly motivated by the offer. In such a case there would in principle, at least in the absence of any contrary intention indicated by the offeror, appear to be a binding contract once the performance is complete.[214]

[240] **Is knowledge sufficient?** A more difficult question is whether, once it is shown that a person was aware of an offer and subsequently performed the act requested by the offeror, it necessarily follows that agreement has been reached. In *R v Clarke*[215] a reward was offered by the Western Australian government 'for such information as shall lead to the arrest and conviction of the person or persons' who committed the murders of two police officers. Clarke, who knew of the offer, gave information that led to the arrest of one person and the conviction of that person and another for the murder of one of the officers. There is considerable doubt as to whether Clarke had in any event brought himself within the terms of the offer,[216] but the case was not decided on this point. The trial judge had found that, on Clarke's own evidence, he had given the information only after his own arrest in order to save himself from an unfounded charge of one of the murders. The High Court of Australia held that there was no justification for interfering with this finding and that as Clarke had not performed the conditions of the offer acting on the faith of or in reliance on the offer, no contract resulted and he was not entitled to the reward. In reaching this conclusion the court had to distinguish *Williams v*

---

210. *R v Clarke* (1927) 40 CLR 227 at 231 per Isaacs ACJ. See also *Lockhart v Barnard* (1845) 14 M & W 674; 153 ER 646 (information called for in reward offer must be given not in mere conversation but with a view to its being acted on); *Gjergja v Cooper* [1987] VR 167 at 206, 208–11 per Ormiston J (acceptance must be 'truly responsive' to the offer).
211. *Gibbons v Proctor* (1891) 64 LT 594.
212. See, eg *Carlill v Carbolic Smoke Ball Co* [1892] 2 QB 484 at 489; *R v Clarke* (1927) 40 CLR 227; *McMahon v Gilberd & Co Ltd* [1955] NZLR 1206; *Taylor v Allon* [1966] 1 QB 304; *Dalgety Australia Ltd v Harris* [1977] 1 NSWLR 324; *Port Jackson Stevedoring Pty Ltd v Salmond & Spraggon (Aust) Pty Ltd* (1978) 139 CLR 231; 18 ALR 333. (The point was not expressly discussed when the case was appealed to the Privy Council: (1980) 144 CLR 300; 30 ALR 588.) See also *Australian Woollen Mills Pty Ltd v The Commonwealth* (1954) 92 CLR 424.
213. See *Tinn v Hoffman & Co* (1873) 29 LT 271; cf Seddon and Ellinghaus, *Cheshire and Fifoot's Law of Contract*, 7th Aust ed, 1997, p 114.
214. See *Restatement (2d) Contracts*, §51. *Robinson v McEwan* (1865) 2 WW & A'B(L) 65 possibly supports this view, though the facts are somewhat unclear.
215. (1927) 40 CLR 227.
216. The reward was offered for information leading to the arrest and conviction of the person or persons who committed the murders. Clarke's evidence did not lead to the arrest of one of the convicted murderers (who was arrested before the information was given) and it led only to the conviction of the persons who committed one of the two murders in question. In cases of this kind, as in any other, offer and acceptance must precisely correspond: see [219]–[224].

Carwardine,[217] another case involving the offer of a reward for information leading to the discovery of the persons who committed a particular murder. The jury found that the plaintiff gave the necessary information not for the sake of the reward but to ease her guilty conscience. It seems clear that the plaintiff was aware of the offer,[218] and the significance of the decision therefore lies in the fact that she was held entitled to recover although her motive in giving the information was not to obtain the reward.

The principle to be applied in such cases was well stated by Starke J in *R v Clarke*:[219]

> In my opinion the true principle applicable to this type of case is that unless a person performs the conditions of the offer, acting upon its faith or in reliance on it, he does not accept the offer and the offeror is not bound to him. As a matter of proof any person knowing of the offer who performs its conditions establishes prima facie an acceptance of that offer ... It is an inference of fact and may be excluded by evidence ... The statements or conduct of the party himself uncommunicated to the other party, or the circumstances of the case, may supply that evidence. Ordinarily, it is true, the law judges of the intention of a person in making a contract by outward expression only by words or acts communicated between them ... But when the offeror, as in the anomalous case under consideration, has dispensed with any previous communication to himself of the acceptance of the offer the law is deprived of one of the means by which it judges of the intention of the parties, and the performance of the conditions of the offer is not in all cases conclusive for they may have been performed by one who never hears of the offer or who never intended to accept it.

The court in *R v Clarke* considered that Clarke's own evidence was sufficient to rebut the prima facie inference which arose upon proof of knowledge of the offer followed by the performance by him of the conditions of the offer. Higgins J so decided on the basis that Clarke had admitted that although he had seen the offer, he had forgotten it at the time when he gave the information. 'Ignorance of the offer is the same thing whether it is due to never hearing of it or to forgetting it after hearing.'[220] The case is sometimes regarded as having turned on this point,[221] but Isaacs ACJ and Starke J do not appear to have regarded the evidence as going as far. Although they considered that Clarke must be treated as having been aware of the offer at the relevant time, they nonetheless concluded that his admission as to his motives in giving the information totally displaced any intention on his part to claim the reward.[222] The distinction between *R v Clarke* and *Williams v Carwardine* then comes down to a difference in the weight of the evidence in the two cases. In *R v Clarke* Isaacs ACJ[223] regarded *Williams v Carwardine* as being a doubtful case on its facts but one where a majority at least of the court considered that the

---

217. (1833) 5 Car & P 566; 172 ER 1101.
218. See in particular Denman CJ and Littledale J at (1833) 5 Car & P 566 at 574; 172 ER 1101 at 1104.
219. (1927) 40 CLR 227 at 244.
220. (1927) 40 CLR 227 at 241.
221. Seddon and Ellinghaus, *Cheshire and Fifoot's Law of Contract*, 7th Aust ed, 1997, pp 111–112.
222. Starke J entertained doubts as to whether the evidence did in fact go so far, but felt unable to disturb the factual finding made by the trial judge.
223. (1927) 40 CLR 227 at 232.

motive of the informant in giving the information was not totally inconsistent with an intention also to claim the reward.

All of the members of the court in *R v Clarke* appear to have assented to the proposition that any person knowing of an offer who subsequently performs its conditions prima facie establishes an acceptance of the offer.[224] In subsequent Australian cases this point has, however, given rise to some controversy. In *Dalgety Australia Ltd v Harris*[225] Glass JA held that there can be no such general proposition and that each case requires an individual examination of the facts to see whether the conduct relied upon both as acceptance and performance was actuated by the offer at least in part. He instanced the case where the conduct might be explicable by reference to a contract with a third party. This view was repeated by Glass JA, and was adopted by Hutley JA, in *Salmond & Spraggon (Australia) Pty Ltd v Joint Cargo Services Pty Ltd*.[226] On appeal to the High Court Mason and Jacobs JJ (and apparently Barwick CJ) considered this approach to be incorrect,[227] and it is suggested that, at any rate for Australian courts, the matter must now be regarded as settled.

[241] **Should acceptance be required in reward cases?** It should be pointed out that not all legal systems approach the question of reward offers to the public at large as raising questions of contract law. In German law, for example, such an offer is regarded as a unilateral juristic act immediately binding on the offeror and not requiring acceptance.[228] A person giving the requested information is therefore entitled to the reward even though being at the time totally ignorant of the offer. A strong argument has been made that a similar approach should be adopted by the common law, on the ground that the offeror has in such cases got what was asked for and that there seems no reason in justice that it should not be paid for.[229]

Duration of Offers

[242] **Offer ceasing to be effective**. A purported acceptance which appears at first sight to be effective may fail to create a contract because the offer has ceased to be effective. This may have occurred because of lapse of time, positive withdrawal by the offeror or a number of other factors which we shall consider below. Another way of putting the matter is to say that acceptance must take place within the period of duration of the power of

---

224. This proposition was applied in *Veivers v Cordingley* [1989] 2 Qd R 278.
225. [1977] 1 NSWLR 324 at 328. Mahoney JA (at 331) was inclined to the contrary view. As Samuels JA concurred in both judgments it is not clear what view he took on this point.
226. [1977] 1 Lloyd's Rep 445.
227. *Port Jackson Stevedoring Pty Ltd v Salmond & Spraggon (Aust) Pty Ltd* (1978) 139 CLR 231. The point was not expressly discussed when the case was appealed to the Privy Council: (1980) 144 CLR 300.
228. Bürgerliches Gesetzbuch art 657; Cohn, *Manual of German Law*, 2nd ed, 1968, Vol 1, p 146. See also *Restatement (2d) Contracts*, §523, comment c.
229. Atiyah, *An Introduction to the Law of Contract*, 5th ed, 1995, pp 64–5; A H Hudson, 'Gibbons v Proctor Revisited' (1968) 84 *LQR* 503.

acceptance created by the offeror in making the offer. A purported acceptance occurring outside of this period can at best be a counter-offer.

Revocation

[243] Offer may be revoked prior to acceptance. Except for the case where the parties have entered into an option contract,[230] an offer may be withdrawn or revoked by the offeror at any time before it has been accepted. Thus, for example, there are many cases where a person has applied to purchase shares in a company and has been held to have been entitled to withdraw the offer provided that this was done before the company had accepted by giving a notice of allotment of the shares.[231] The offeror may revoke even though the offer expressly states that it is to remain open for a specified period of time which has not, at the time of revocation, expired.[232]

[244] Communication of revocation. Revocation is made effective by the offeree being informed that the offeror no longer wishes to proceed with the proposed transaction and any form of language which clearly indicates this intention will suffice. Thus in *Financings Ltd v Stimson*[233] the defendant had made an offer to enter into a hire-purchase agreement with a finance company. The defendant subsequently decided not to go ahead but he did not in terms revoke his offer because he believed incorrectly that his offer had already been accepted. He did, however, make it clear that he did not wish to proceed with the transaction and it was held that he had revoked his offer even though the actual language used by him was more appropriate to a case of rescission of a previously concluded contract.

Revocation is not effective until communicated to the offeree (or someone who is authorised by the offeree to receive such communications).[234] It is of great importance in this context to appreciate that the postal acceptance rule applies only to acceptances and never operates to render a revocation effective on posting. Consequently, where the postal acceptance rule applies an acceptance will be effective on posting even though prior to that time the offeror has sent a letter revoking the offer.[235] It is, of course, otherwise if the offeree has received the letter of

---

230. See [247].
231. *Re National Savings Bank Association (Hebb's Case)* (1867) LR 4 Eq 9; *Barker v Caird* (1876) 14 SCR (NSW) 358; *Great Amalgamated Gold Mining Co Ltd v Morris* (1877) 11 SALR 9; *Re Provincial and Suburban Bank Ltd* (1881) 7 VLR(E) 63; *Metropolitan Milk Supply (Greater Brisbane) Ltd v Paulsen* [1933] St R Qd 53.
232. *Routledge v Grant* (1828) 4 Bing 653; 130 ER 920; *Dickinson v Dodds* (1876) 2 Ch D 463; *Nyulasy v Rowan* (1891) 17 VLR 663; *Stevenson Jaques & Co v McLean* (1880) 4 QBD 346; *Cartwright v Hoogstoel* (1911) 105 LT 628.
233. [1962] 3 All ER 386.
234. *Financings Ltd v Stimson* [1962] 3 All ER 386.
235. *Byrne v Van Tienhoven* (1880) 5 CPD 344; *Stevenson Jaques & Co v McLean* (1880) 5 QBD 346; *Re Scottish Petroleum (Maclagan's Case)* (1882) 51 LJ Ch 841; *Henthorn v Fraser* [1892] 2 Ch 27. It would seem reasonable to hold, at least where negotiations have been conducted by post, that a letter of revocation should be effective when delivered to the offeree, even if not in fact read by the offeree until some later time: see *Zucker v Straightlace Pty Ltd* (1987) 11 NSWLR 87. This raises considerations similar to those referred to at [234].

revocation before posting an acceptance. This rule has been justified on the following basis:[236]

> If the defendants' contention were to prevail no person who had received an offer by post and had accepted it would know his position until he had waited such a time as to be quite sure that a letter withdrawing the offer had not been posted before his acceptance of it. It appears to me that both legal principles, and practical convenience require that a person who has accepted an offer not known to him to have been revoked, shall be in a position safely to act upon the footing that the offer and acceptance constitute a contract binding on both parties.

Although a revocation of an offer is ineffective unless communicated to the offeree, it is not essential that the communication be made by the offeror (or even by someone acting with the authority of the offeror). In *Dickinson v Dodds*[237] the defendant offered on Wednesday to sell a property to the plaintiff, the offer to be left open until 9 am on the following Friday. The plaintiff was subsequently told by a third party that the defendant 'had been offering or agreeing to sell' the property to someone else, whereupon the plaintiff purported to accept the offer. It was held that the plaintiff must have been aware that the defendant was no longer minded to sell to him and that his acceptance was ineffective as it occurred after the offer had been revoked. The decision itself is unsatisfactory in a number of respects. There is some language in the judgments suggesting that the mere fact of sale, unknown to the offeree, of property the subject of an offer might be sufficient to revoke the offer. While consistent with a subjective theory of contractual agreement, the subsequent cases apply an objective approach[238] and make it plain that knowledge of revocation by the offeree is essential,[239] and the judgments in *Dickinson v Dodds* do in fact emphasise that the plaintiff was aware of the offeror's change of heart.

Another unsatisfactory feature of the decision is that there was apparently no evidence as to how the third party had come to know of the defendant's actions. Moreover, his information that the defendant was 'offering or agreeing to sell' would seem to be at least consistent with the making of an offer not at that stage accepted which was not necessarily inconsistent with the continuance of the offer previously made to the plaintiff. Nonetheless, the court considered that on the facts (which are perhaps imperfectly summarised in the report) the plaintiff must have been as clearly aware of the withdrawal of the offer as if he had been told so directly by the defendant. The issue in such cases must ultimately be as to the correct inference to be drawn from the facts. The essential question should be as to the effect which the information conveyed to him should reasonably have had upon the mind of the offeree, and the following comment from the American Restatement summarises well the relevant considerations:[240]

> [M]ere negotiations with a third person, or even a definite offer to a second offeree, may be consistent with an intention on the part of the offeror to

---

236. *Byrne v Van Tienhoven* (1880) 5 CPD 344 at 348–9 per Lindley J.
237. (1876) LR 2 Ch D 463.
238. See [206].
239. *Little v Trotman* (1885) 6 ALT 252; *Patterson v Dolman* [1908] VLR 354; *Cartwright v Hoogstoel* (1911) 105 LT 628.
240. *Restatement (2d) Contracts*, §43, comment d.

honor an acceptance by the original offeree. Even a binding contract with a third person may be expressly subject to any rights arising under the outstanding offer. Moreover, a mere rumor does not terminate the power of acceptance, if the offeree disbelieves it and is reasonable in doing so, even though the rumor is later verified. The basic standard to which the offeree is held is that of a reasonable person acting in good faith.

[245] **Revocation of multiple offers.** The fact that revocation is ineffective unless communicated means that an offeror who concurrently offers property for sale to a number of different persons may be in difficulty if more than one of those persons accept. In *Patterson v Dolman*[241] A posted to B an offer to sell certain goods and also offered to sell the same goods to C. Both B and C posted acceptances. A carried out his contract with C (whose acceptance had been posted first), and B sued A for damages. The trial judge held that as the subject matter had been sold to C, there was no contract with B. On appeal the Full Court of the Supreme Court of Victoria held that this conclusion was clearly incorrect as B had no knowledge of this sale when he accepted. The result is that in such a case the seller can only carry out the contract with one acceptor, but will be liable in damages to the others. The offeror in such a situation would therefore be wise to make it clear that the offer is being made to more than one person and that it is open to acceptance only by the first person to notify acceptance.

[246] **Revocation of offers to public.** We have seen that an offer may be made to the public at large or to an indeterminate number of persons.[242] In such a case the offeror does not know the identity of the persons who have become aware of the offer and who may be contemplating accepting. The question of how such an offer may be revoked does not appear to have arisen before an Australian or English court, but was considered by the Supreme Court of the United States in the frequently cited case of *Shuey v United States*.[243] It was there held that where an offer of a reward was made by publication of a public notice, that offer could be withdrawn by a similar notice given the same notoriety as had been given to the offer. As this had been done well before the plaintiff purported to accept, he was not entitled to the reward even though he was in fact ignorant of the revocation. It is likely that this approach would be followed by Australian courts in cases where no feasible substitute approach was available, as insistence on actual communication of revocation would in practice make revocation of such offers impossible. Publication of such a notice of revocation may not be effective immediately, as there must presumably be 'publicity equivalent to that given the offer, including in appropriate cases a reasonable time for equivalent indirect circulation'.[244] Such an offer would, irrespective of attempts made to revoke it, in any event ultimately lapse by expiry of time.[245]

---

241. [1908] VLR 354.
242. See [216].
243. 92 US 73 (1875).
244. *Restatement (2d) Contracts*, §46, comment b.
245. See [255].

[247] Revocation and option contracts. An exception to the rule that an offer may be withdrawn at any time prior to acceptance occurs in the case of an option contract. Option contracts usually relate to a contemplated sale of property and under such a contract the person to have the benefit of the option (the 'optionee') gives consideration for the promise of the other party (the 'optionor') to sell provided that, within the period of validity of the option, the right of the optionee under the option is exercised. Upon exercise of the option both parties are bound by a contract of sale, but until that time only the optionor is bound; the optionee is free to decide whether or not to proceed with the proposed transaction. The consideration provided by the optionee for the option is the price paid for the optionor forgoing during the period of the option the right to sell elsewhere (or to decide not to sell at all).

The option contract may provide that if the option is exercised the amount paid as consideration for the option will be credited towards the purchase price of the property sold, but this depends on the terms of the contract. Particularly where the period during which the option may be exercised is a lengthy one the consideration paid for the option may be a considerable sum, but it is also quite common for option contracts to provide for a purely nominal consideration (typically $1). As is shown later,[246] a purely nominal consideration is nonetheless sufficient consideration to support a contract and this principle applies to options as to any other kind of contract.[247] It appears that an option granted by deed has the same effect even though no consideration is given for the grant of the option.[248]

Options are frequently used in many commercial situations. A common example is where a company is about to embark on a project such as a new shopping centre development. The company may need, if the project is to be viable, to purchase from different owners several adjoining blocks of land and may be unwilling to bind itself to purchase any block until it is sure that it will in fact be able to purchase all the land necessary for the project. The company may therefore negotiate the purchase of options in respect of the various blocks of land. Similarly, the completion of such a project will necessitate the obtaining of planning and other permissions from various government authorities. For a major undertaking the obtaining of all necessary approvals may be a very lengthy and expensive process, and the obtaining of a series of options over the land enables the company to proceed in the knowledge that it will, if the project goes ahead, be able to acquire the land while nonetheless not having bound itself to do so, thus avoiding the risk of being bound to purchase land for which it would have no use if it ultimately appeared for some reason that the project was not possible.

Recent important developments in the law of promissory estoppel mean that in certain circumstances an offeror who has promised to keep an offer

---

246. See [327].
247. *Mountford v Scott* [1975] 1 Ch 258.
248. See, eg *Gilbert J McCaul (Aust) Pty Ltd v Pitt Club Ltd* (1959) 59 SR (NSW) 122 at 123; *Mountford v Scott* [1975] 1 Ch 258 at 265; *Varty v British South Africa Co* [1964] 2 All ER 975 at 981–2.

open may well not be able to revoke with impunity even though there is no consideration for an option contract.[249]

[248] Juristic nature of options. It is necessary to note a 'standing controversy'[250] as to the juristic nature of an option contract. The view which commands majority support in the Australian cases is that an option is an irrevocable offer; that is, an offer coupled with a contract that the offer will not be revoked during the period of time, if any, specified in the option.[251] There is also, however, considerable support for the view that an option is a conditional contract; that is, a contract to sell upon condition that the optionee within the stipulated time shall bind him or herself by complying with the conditions laid down for the exercise of the option.[252] On this view, on exercise of the option what was originally a conditional contract becomes fully binding on both parties, whereas on the irrevocable offer approach the exercise of the option is an acceptance giving rise to a new contract. It would seem that in any event where an option is not simply expressed as such but is worded in such a way as to suggest that it is either an irrevocable offer or a conditional contract, the form of words used in the contract is controlling.[253] It has been said also that in most cases it makes no difference which view is correct as to the nature of an option,[254] though difficulties may arise in some situations; for example, where an option is expressed to be exercisable by the optionee or a nominee of the optionee and where it is argued that the benefit of an option has been assigned. The nature of these difficulties and other questions relating to the exercise of options are beyond the scope of this work.[255]

It should finally be noted that where the contract of purchase which will bind both parties on the exercise of an option is of a kind (usually one for the acquisition of an interest in land) which will be specifically enforceable, then the option contract is itself specifically enforceable. One result of this is that the optionee acquires a proprietary interest in the property which is the subject matter of the transaction and can prevent the optionor dealing with the property inconsistently with the option.[256] The nature and

---

249. See generally on promissory estoppel [365]–[387].
250. *Braham v Walker* (1961) 104 CLR 366 at 376 per Dixon CJ.
251. See, eg *Ballas v Theophilos (No 2)* (1957) 98 CLR 193 at 207–8; *Commissioner of Taxes (Qld) v Camphin* (1937) 57 CLR 127; *Gerraty v McGavin* (1914) 18 CLR 152 at 163; *Gilbert J McCaul (Aust) Pty Ltd v Pitt Club Ltd* (1959) 59 SR (NSW) 122; *Goldsbrough Mort & Co Ltd v Quinn* (1910) 10 CLR 674 at 690–2; *Karaguleski v Vasil Bros & Co Pty Ltd* [1981] 1 NSWLR 267.
252. See, eg *Ballas v Theophilos* [1958] VR 576; *Goldsbrough Mort & Co Ltd v Quinn* (1910) 10 CLR 674 at 678–9; *Laybutt v Amoco Aust Pty Ltd* (1974) 132 CLR 57 at 75–6; 4 ALR 482; *Traywinds Pty Ltd v Cooper* [1989] 1 Qd R 222.
253. See *Carter v Hyde* (1923) 33 CLR 115 at 123; *Johnson v Bones* [1970] 1 NSWR 28; *O'Halloran Enterprises Pty Ltd v Williamson* [1979] VR 33; *Westminster Estates Pty Ltd v Calleja* [1970] 1 NSWR 526.
254. *Ballas v Theophilos (No 2)* (1957) 98 CLR 193 at 207. See also *Carter v Hyde* (1923) 33 CLR 115 at 123; *Laybutt v Amoco Aust Pty Ltd* (1974) 132 CLR 57 at 73.
255. See H K Lücke, 'Options' (1968) 3 *Adel LR* 197; C J Rossiter, 'Options to Acquire Interests in Land — Freehold and Leasehold' (1982) 56 *ALJ* 576, 624; Farrands, *The Law of Options*, 1992.
256. See, eg *Commissioner of Taxes (Qld) v Camphin* (1937) 57 CLR 127.

consequences of the remedy of specific performance are discussed in Chapter 24.

[249] Unilateral contracts. We have previously come across situations where an offer takes the form of a promise given in return for the performing of an act rather than in return for a counter-promise.[257] A typical example of such a case is the offer of a reward for the giving of certain information relating to the commission of a crime or the offer of a reward for the return of lost property. In such cases, the performing of the act called for is the acceptance of the offer, the offeror being taken to have impliedly dispensed with the necessity for notice of acceptance. In such a case the person accepting is never bound by any executory obligation as no performance has been promised to the offeror. Such contracts are usually referred to as 'unilateral' contracts, in contrast to 'bilateral' contracts where a promise is given in return for a promise.[258]

Where an offer is made which contemplates a unilateral contract, the performance of the act called for will constitute both the acceptance and the furnishing of consideration by the offeree. In some cases the act contemplated is such that it will involve a performance spread over a period of time. Judicial examples of such acts include 'if you walk to York, I will give you £100'[259] and an offer of £100 to any person who should swim 100 yards in the harbour on the first day of the year.[260] In such a case the terms of the offer indicate that the offeror does not contemplate that a person wishing to claim the reward will promise to perform the act in question. A person who commences to perform indicates a hope to qualify for the reward, but is not promising to complete performance and, if the effort is abandoned halfway through, would not be in breach of contract in so doing. Of course, there would be no entitlement to the reward because the conditions on which the reward is payable have not been complied with; nor could payment of part of the reward be claimed, because nothing was promised to the part-performer.

It is important to bear in mind that the fact that an intention to accept is indicated by commencement of performance does not necessarily mean that a unilateral contract is involved. The correct interpretation of the offer may well be that no express acceptance is required, but that on commencement of performance the offeree should be taken impliedly to have promised to complete the performance; that is, a bilateral contract has been made, the acceptance taking the form of a counter-promise implied from conduct.[261] If, for example, I say that I shall pay a house painter $1000 to paint my house while I am away on holidays, a bilateral contract is clearly formed if the painter promises to do so. But if the painter says that

---

257. See [208], [227], [239]–[240].
258. For a discussion of the distinction see *United Dominions Trust (Commercial) Ltd v Eagle Aircraft Services Ltd* [1968] 1 WLR 74 at 83–4, where it is pointed out that 'bilateral' is strictly inappropriate, for such contracts may well have more than two parties. Likewise, the phrase 'unilateral' obscures the fact that we are speaking of a contract involving at least two parties, even though only one is bound by any outstanding obligation.
259. *Great Northern Railway Co v Witham* (1873) LR 9 CP 16 at 19 per Brett J.
260. *R v Clarke* (1927) 40 CLR 227 at 233 per Isaacs ACJ.
261. As to acceptance implied from conduct generally see [205].

he or she is not certain whether jobs currently in hand will be finished in time to permit this, I may well reply that, although I realise there is no promise to do the work, I shall pay the painter $1000 if the house is in fact painted. If the painter did in fact commence the work, it would be likely to be held that, although there was no promise in advance to do so, once it was commenced the painter had impliedly promised to complete the work.[262] In that event the painter would not be free to withdraw leaving me with a partially painted house, simply because it is most unlikely that this was ever contemplated by us. In all cases the correct inference must be determined by an examination of what was said by the parties, and it appears that in cases of doubt the courts are likely to lean towards inferring that a bilateral rather than a unilateral contract was contemplated.[263]

[250] **Revocation and unilateral contracts.** A difficulty arises as to whether an offer of a unilateral contract may be revoked after an offeree has commenced performance but before it has been completed. This question has given rise to much debate[264] but is the subject of curiously little authority, no doubt because the point will only relatively rarely cause difficulty in practice. It is difficult to see how a unilateral contract may be said to have been performed prior to complete performance by the offeree, because while it has only been partially performed the offeree is at all times free to withdraw. If, therefore, we are to say that the offeree has not accepted until the performance is complete, may not the offeror revoke the offer on the principle that an offer may be revoked at any time prior to acceptance? Often the offeree will have expended considerable time and energy, and perhaps expense, in a partial performance and it is usually thought that it would be unjust if the offeree were to be deprived of the opportunity to complete performance and to become entitled to claim the benefit promised by the offeror.

An American writer has suggested that an offer of a unilateral contract should be read as containing an implied subsidiary promise that the offer will not be revoked once performance has commenced.[265] Some support for such an approach may be gained from the early New South Wales case

---

262. See Treitel, *The Law of Contract*, 10th ed, 1999, pp 37–8.
263. *White Trucks Pty Ltd v Riley* (1948) 66 WN (NSW) 101 is apparently an example. See also the often cited but ambiguous remarks of Erle CJ in *Offord v Davies* (1862) 12 CBNS 748 at 757; 142 ER 1336 at 1340. There is considerable authority for this proposition in American law, a good example being *Davis v Jacoby* 34 P 2d 1026 (1934). *Restatement (2d) Contracts*, §32 states that in cases of doubt the offeree has the choice of accepting either by promising to perform or rendering performance. The original *Restatement* (in §531) stated the rule suggested in the text. The change in approach is a consequence of the abandonment in the *Restatement (2d)* of the distinction between bilateral and unilateral contracts: see §1, Reporter's Note.
264. See, eg H W Ballantine, 'Acceptance of Offers for Unilateral Contracts by Partial Performance of Service Requested' in Association of American Law Schools, *Selected Readings on the Law of Contracts*, 1931, p 312; D O McGovney, 'Irrevocable Offers' in *Selected Readings on the Law of Contracts*, 1931, p 300; M Wormser, 'The True Conception of Unilateral Contracts' in *Selected Readings on the Law of Contracts*, 1931, p 307; S J Stoljar, 'The False Distinction between Bilateral and Unilateral Contracts' (1955) 64 *Yale LJ* 515.
265. D O McGovney, 'Irrevocable Offers' in *Selected Readings on the Law of Contracts*, 1931, p 300.

of *Abbott v Lance*[266] although both the agreement and the reasoning of the court are not altogether clear. That case was applied by the Full Court of the Supreme Court of Queensland in *Veivers v Cordingley*.[267] The relevant facts of *Abbott v Lance* are that Lance had offered to sell certain stations to Abbott on certain terms, but Abbott was not willing to accept until he had inspected the stations, which were situated about 500 miles away. It was therefore agreed that Abbott would have two months for the purpose of inspection and that if within that time Abbott offered to purchase on Lance's terms, Lance would sell on those terms. There was a promise that Lance was in the meantime free to sell to anyone else, but that if Abbott made within the two months a bona fide offer to buy on Lance's terms Lance would, if he had already sold, pay the sum of £100 to Abbott. Abbott therefore commenced to ride to inspect the stations, but when about halfway was overtaken by a letter from Lance advising that the stations had been sold. The question was whether Abbott was entitled to recover £100 from Lance. The objection was made that no contract had been formed as Lance could withdraw his offer at any time and Abbott was not bound to purchase. (He was presumably not bound either to inspect the property.) The court appears to have regarded the arrangement as involving a unilateral offer to keep the offer of sale open (or alternatively to pay £100) if Abbott should inspect the properties and make a bona fide offer to buy. The court considered that the principle that an offer may be retracted before acceptance was not applicable, the part performance of the journey by Abbott constituting sufficient consideration to prevent revocation of the unilateral offer.

The promise not to revoke the unilateral offer in *Abbott v Lance* was an express offer, but there would seem little difficulty in implying such an offer in an appropriate case. Part performance of the act called for could then be regarded as sufficient consideration for the promise not to revoke.[268] If this analysis is accepted by the courts, it would, of course, not be possible to imply a promise not to revoke if the offeror expressly reserved the power to revoke at any time, or if the facts gave rise to an inference that the offeree took the risk of revocation even after he or she had commenced performance.[269] Moreover, revocation would apparently still be effective if the offeree had not commenced to perform but had merely made preparations to perform.[270]

---

266. (1860) Legge 1283.
267. [1989] 2 Qd R 278.
268. In *Errington v Errington* [1952] 1 KB 290 at 295 Denning LJ considered that a unilateral offer could not be revoked once the offerees had entered on performance, but he did not discuss any theory upon which this result could be reached. Similarly in *Daulia Ltd v Four Millbank Nominees Ltd* [1978] 1 Ch 231 Goff LJ, with whom Buckley and Orr LJJ agreed, considered that there must be an implied obligation on the part of the offeror not to prevent the condition imposed in his offer becoming satisfied, that obligation arising as soon as the offeree starts to perform. Consequently, once the offeree has embarked upon performance it will be too late for the offeror to revoke. The point was regarded as doubtful in *Aldwell v Bundey* (1876) 10 SALR 118.
269. See *Luxor (Eastbourne) Ltd v Cooper* [1941] AC 109, especially per Lord Russell at 124. See further [628].
270. See *Restatement (2d) Contracts*, §45, comment f.

Cases may have to be considered on their facts, following the recent Full Federal Court decision of *Mobil Oil Australia Ltd v Lyndel Nominees Pty Ltd*.[271] There, some service station franchisees claimed that Mobil had promised them some years of free tenure if they could achieve certain sales records for a number of years. The franchisees argued that as they had commenced performance, Mobil could not implement its purported revocation of those alleged offers. The Full Federal Court disagreed. The court considered all the authorities and arguments concerning whether unilateral offers should be able to be revoked once the act of acceptance has commenced. Their Honours did not think that it would be universally unjust for an offeror to revoke an offer, even if acceptance had commenced.[272] Furthermore, to the extent that earlier authorities made such a suggestion, the court disagreed.[273] However, they stated that: 'In the circumstances of a particular case, it may be appropriate to find that the offeror has entered into an implied ancillary contract not to revoke, or that the offeror is estopped from falsifying an assumption, engendered by it, that the offeree will not be deprived of the chance of completing the act of acceptance'.[274] On the facts before them, their Honours did not think it was unjust of Mobil to revoke the offer. The franchisees would benefit if they in fact performed the act of acceptance, since their businesses would be successful. Furthermore, the court did not think, even if there was a contract not to revoke, that the revocation would have been ineffective. Their Honours thought that in the absence of any specific relief, such as an injunction, the revocation would be effective though the offeror would be liable in damages.

Rejection

[251] Offer terminated by rejection. An offer is terminated once rejected by the offeree.[275] The offeror is in such circumstances entitled to assume that the offer is no longer open to acceptance and that there is therefore no necessity to revoke it if no longer wishing to contract on the terms of the offer. A counter-offer is treated as impliedly rejecting an offer.[276] It follows that any subsequent attempt by the offeree to accept can at most be a counter-offer which the offeror is free to accept or reject. Of course, an offeree will often reject an offer by making a counter-offer on terms more favourable to the offeree in the hope that the original offeror will accept them. The original offeror may well reject the counter-offer, but in terms which indicate that the original offer is still open. In such a case the offeror has renewed that original offer and the offeree may accept, but only because following the rejection the offeror chose to repeat the offer.[277]

---

271. (1998) 153 ALR 198.
272. (1998) 153 ALR 198 at 224.
273. (1998) 153 ALR 198 at 228.
274. (1998) 153 ALR 198 at 228.
275. *Stevenson Jaques & Co v McLean* (1880) 5 QBD 346; *Khaled v Athanas Bros (Aden) Ltd* (1967) 1 BPR 9310 (PC); *Fletcher v Minister for Environment & Heritage* (1999) 73 SASR 474.
276. *Hyde v Wrench* (1840) 3 Beav 334; 49 ER 132; *Baker v Taylor* (1906) 6 SR (NSW) 500; *Harris v Jenkins* [1922] SASR 59.

[252] **What amounts to rejection.** It will sometimes be difficult to tell whether or not an offeree has in fact rejected an offer. In *Stevenson Jaques & Co v McLean*[278] an offer was made for the sale of goods at a cash price. The buyer telegraphed asking whether the seller would consider credit terms. The seller treated this as a rejection and sold the goods elsewhere, but before the buyer had received the seller's telegram advising of this fact he (the buyer) had sent a telegram accepting the offer. It was held that there was a contract. The buyer's original telegram could not be read as a counter-offer or rejection of the offer, but rather as the making of an inquiry for information which the buyer desired to have before he finally decided whether or not to accept the offer. Similarly, where an offeree did not expressly reject an offer but advised the offeror that he wished to take time to consult with his partners before coming to a decision, it was held that the offer had not been rejected and was still open for acceptance.[279]

As the implied intention of the person making the counter-offer is the basis of the rule that a counter-offer operates as a rejection of an offer, it would seem that the rule would have no application if a person made a counter-offer while at the same time making it clear that the original offer had not been definitely rejected. Thus if an offeree should reply to the offeror that the offer was still being considered but he or she would be willing to buy the property offered immediately if the other would reduce the price by $500, the offeree should, it is submitted, subsequently be able to accept the original offer.[280]

[253] **Time when rejection effective.** A rejection would in principle operate to terminate an offer only when received by the offeror. There appears to be no authority as to the situation where an offer is rejected by letter and then a letter purportedly accepting is subsequently posted. If the letter of acceptance arrived before the letter of rejection, there would presumably be a contract. But if the letter of rejection arrived first, the offeror should be entitled to rely upon that, with the result that the acceptance should then operate at most as a counter-offer, even though the postal acceptance rule might in the circumstances otherwise apply and even though the acceptance was posted prior to the offeror's receipt of the rejection.[281]

Lapse of Time

[254] **Offer open for stated period.** An offer will in some circumstances lapse by virtue of the passage of time without the necessity for revocation

---

277. *Sheffield Canal Co v Sheffield and Rotherham Ry Co* (1841) Ry & Can Cas 121; *Livingstone v Evans* [1925] 4 DLR 769; *Khaled v Athanas Bros (Aden) Ltd* (1967) 1 BPR 9310 (PC).
278. (1880) 5 QBD 346.
279. *Khaled v Athanas Bros (Aden) Ltd* (1967) 1 BPR 9310 (PC). See also *Fletcher v Minister for Environment & Heritage* (1999) 73 SASR 474, where it was held that commencing proceedings amounted to revocation by conduct.
280. See *Corbin on Contracts*, Vol 1, 1963, p 92.
281. See *Restatement (2d) Contracts*, §40. Cf C D Ashley, 'Must the Rejection of an Offer be Communicated to the Offeror' in Association of American Law Schools, *Selected Readings on the Law of Contracts*, 1931, p 246.

by the offeror. We have seen that an offer, even though stated to be open for a certain period of time, may be revoked if it has not been accepted. But the stipulation of the time period, while not preventing earlier revocation by the offeror, does have the effect that the offer automatically lapses on the expiry of that period, with the result that a subsequent acceptance is ineffective.[282] An interesting application of this rule appeared in *White Cliffs Opal Mines Ltd v Miller*[283] where negotiations were carried out between a representative of the New South Wales government and the Australian representative of a London company. An offer was made to the company and was stated to be open until 30 June. On 30 June, London time, the company sent a cable of acceptance, but it was by then 1 July in New South Wales. It was held that the meaning of the words '30th June' was in the circumstances to be governed by New South Wales law and that the acceptance was too late.

[255] **Offer of indefinite duration.** Where no time for acceptance is prescribed in the offer, the offer must be accepted within a reasonable time.[284] What is a reasonable time will, of course, depend upon the circumstances. Where an offer is made after protracted negotiations a longer time may be allowed than would otherwise have been the case.[285] An enforceable option will normally specify the period during which it may be exercised. However, if none is stated, an option to purchase property the value of which is affected by the changing conditions which time and the vicissitudes of business bring must be exercised promptly,[286] and indeed the fact that under an option only one party is bound would seem to indicate that a shorter period may there be reasonable than if there were no option.[287] Where an offer is made by telegram or telex it will normally be inferred that a prompt reply is expected, so that an acceptance by letter would be too late.[288]

The theoretical basis of the rule that where no time for acceptance is stated acceptance must occur within a reasonable time is still not settled. The rule is perhaps generally assumed to be based upon an implied term in the offer,[289] but it has more recently been held that a better explanation is that if the offeree does not accept within a reasonable time he or she must be treated as having rejected it.[290] This approach would enable the court to have regard not just to the facts as they existed at the time when the offer

---

282. *Jacobsen Sons & Co v E Underwood & Son Ltd* (1894) 1 SLT 578; *Spencer's Pictures Ltd v Cosens* (1918) 18 SR (NSW) 102. See also *Nyulasy v Rowan* (1891) 17 VLR 663.
283. (1904) 4 SR (NSW) 150.
284. *Ramsgate Victoria Hotel Co Ltd v Montefiore* (1866) LR 1 Ex 109; *NW Co-operative Freezing & Canning Co Ltd v Easton* (1915) 11 Tas LR 65; *Re Tasmanian Credits Ltd; Ex parte Pitt* (1930) 25 Tas LR 111; *Ballas v Theophilos (No 2)* (1957) 98 CLR 193; *Manchester Diocesan Council v Commercial & General Investments Ltd* [1970] 1 WLR 241. But see *Farmers' Mercantile Union & Chaff Mills Ltd v Coade* (1921) 30 CLR 113; *Blacktown Municipal Council v Doneo* [1971] 1 NSWLR 157.
285. *Khaled v Athanas Bros (Aden) Ltd* (1967) 1 BPR 9310 (PC).
286. *Ballas v Theophilos (No 2)* (1957) 98 CLR 193 at 197.
287. *Ballas v Theophilos (No 2)* (1957) 98 CLR 193. As to option contracts see [247]–[248].
288. *Quenerduaine v Cole* (1883) 32 WR 185.
289. *Meynell v Surtees* (1855) 25 LJ Ch 257; *Dencio v Zivanovic* (1991) 105 FLR 117.
290. *Manchester Diocesan Council v Commercial & General Investments Ltd* [1970] 1 WLR 241. See also *Williams v Williams* (1853) 17 Beav 213; 151 ER 1015.

was made, but also to facts subsequently occurring. In the case in question the judge therefore felt able to take into account a letter by the offeree which, while not clearly then accepting the offer, clearly indicated an intention to do so, thus excluding the possibility of imputing to him a rejection of the offer. In another case where it was held that acceptance had been made within a reasonable time the court had regard to the fact that the offeror had received and acquiesced in notice of acceptance without making any suggestion that it was out of time.[291] Perhaps this must be regarded as a case where the offeror's actions could be regarded as affording relevant evidence as to what the parties considered a reasonable time to be in the circumstances. Where an acceptance is made too late, it will usually be possible to regard the purported acceptance as a counter-offer which the original offeror may choose to accept (and which may well be accepted by conduct rather than expressly, especially if the offeror does not raise any objection to the acceptance being late).

Offers Subject to Condition

[256] Conditional offers. An offer may be made subject to an express or implied condition that the offer is to be open only for so long as a certain state of affairs continues to exist. If that state of affairs ceases to exist, the offer automatically lapses. Thus, where a person makes an offer for the purchase of goods, it will often be proper to infer that the offer was made conditionally on the goods remaining in substantially the same condition until the time of acceptance. If in such a case the goods are, subsequently to the making of the offer, extensively damaged, a purported acceptance will not bind the offeror.[292]

Death of Offeror or Offeree

[257] The effect of death on an offer. There is curiously little authority on the effect on an offer of the death of the offeror. Although it is sometimes stated without qualification than an offer may not be accepted after the death of the offeror,[293] it seems that acceptance will be effective if the offeree accepts before receiving notice of the death of the offeror.[294] The latter solution would certainly be the more equitable of the two.[295]

---

291. *Khaled v Athanas Bros (Aden) Ltd* (1967) 1 BPR 9310 (PC).
292. *Financings Ltd v Stimson* [1962] 3 All ER 386. See also *Rice v Taylor* (1969) 89 WN (Pt 1) (NSW) 596 at 602 per Jacobs JA. As to the application of a similar rule where a clause in a lease granting an option to renew makes exercise of the option conditional on performance by the lessee of all of his or her obligations under the lease see *Gilbert J McCaul (Aust) Pty Ltd v Pitt Club Ltd* (1959) 59 SR (NSW) 122 (applied *Commonwealth of Australia v Antonio Giorgio Pty Ltd* (1986) 67 ALR 244; *Re Copperart Pty Ltd* (1995) 16 ACSR 351); *B S Stilkwell & Co Pty Ltd v Budget Rent-A-Car System Pty Ltd* [1990] VR 589 (but cf *Traywinds Pty Ltd v Cooper* [1989] 1 Qd R 222)). See also *United Scientific Holdings Ltd v Burnley BC* [1978] AC 904 at 928–9, 945–6, 951, 961–2. See further [1837].
293. See *Meynell v Surtees* (1855) 25 LJ Ch 257 at 260; *Dickinson v Dodds* (1876) 2 Ch D 463 at 475; *Reynolds v Atherton* (1921) 125 LT 690 at 695–6.
294. *Fong v Cilli* (1968) 11 FLR 495. See also *Bradbury v Morgan* (1862) 1 H & C 249; 158 ER 877; *Coulthart v Clementson* (1879) 5 QBD 42. Contrast *Restatement (2d) Contracts*, §48 (power of acceptance terminated by death of offeror whether or not offeree has notice of the death).

It likewise appears that an offer is generally not capable of acceptance by the executor or personal representatives of a deceased offeree, on the basis that the offer is intended to be made to a living person.[296] However, where an option has been granted for consideration (for example, an option to purchase land or a business) we are no longer concerned with a mere offer. Where the subject matter of the proposed principal contract is such that that contract could be specifically enforced,[297] the granting of the option creates a right of a proprietary nature which can normally be bought and sold like other proprietary rights. If in such a case the beneficiary of the option should die, the option can be exercised by the beneficiary's personal representatives unless the circumstances show that the option was intended to be purely personal.[298] Indeed, where there is no option, if the language of an offer is such as to show that it was contemplated that the offer was to stand on foot for some period of time and that it might be accepted by the personal representatives if the offeree should die before acceptance, there would seem to be no reason the personal representatives could not accept as we should then be simply concerned with one form of an offer made to persons who were unascertained at the date when the offer was made.[299]

Uncertainty and Incompleteness

[258] **General principles.**[300] Even though there might at first sight appear to be in a particular situation a correspondence of offer and acceptance resulting in a binding contract, it will on occasion be held that there is in truth no concluded agreement capable of being enforced. Contract results from the agreement of the parties and it has frequently been said that the courts will not draft a contract for the parties where they have failed to reach agreement. In such cases the parties themselves may have considered they had reached finality, but the courts will regard them as not having passed beyond the stage of negotiation. Two related, but conceptually distinct, principles are here involved. In the first place, the language used by the parties may be such that the court is unable to attribute to it a sufficiently precise and clear meaning in order to identify the scope of the rights and obligations agreed to. In such a case there is in fact no concluded agreement and the alleged contract will be held to be void for uncertainty. Second, even though the language used is perfectly clear in its meaning, if some important part of the transaction is yet to be agreed upon there is, despite appearances, in truth no completed agreement and the alleged contract will fail for incompleteness. In any

---

295. Semble an option may be exercised after the death of the grantor provided that the option was not intended to last only during the life of the grantor and provided that the proposed contract was not personal to the grantor: *Laybutt v Amoco Aust Pty Ltd* (1974) 132 CLR 57 at 75-6.
296. *Reynolds v Atherton* (1921) 125 LT 690.
297. See, eg [2404].
298. *Carter v Hyde* (1923) 33 CLR 115; see also *Laybutt v Amoco Aust Pty Ltd* (1974) 132 CLR 57 at 75-6.
299. See [216].
300. H K Lücke, 'Illusory, Vague and Uncertain Contractual Terms' (1977) 6 *Adel LR* 1.

given case there may in fact be elements both of uncertainty and incompleteness.[301]

[259] Contracts upheld where possible. This area of the law is of considerable importance in practice. Many important business agreements are concluded informally and will often contain language which may seem perfectly adequate to commercial parties no matter how it might appear to the critical mind of the lawyer. Moreover, very often an agreement is intended to govern a complex business relationship over an extended period of time and it will in practice be impossible or undesirable to provide for all likely eventualities with the precision which more traditional theory might demand. The general principles applicable have been laid down in fairly clear terms, but a variety of approaches is used to uphold an agreement wherever possible and it is frequently very difficult to apply the general principles with confidence to concrete factual situations. The courts are here faced with a conflict between the desire, on the one hand, to avoid making such efforts to enforce an uncertain or incomplete agreement so that what is enforced is something that the parties did not in fact agree to and, on the other hand, to uphold reasonable expectations of parties who believed they had a contract and to avoid 'the reproach of being the destroyer of bargains'.[302]

There has in recent years been a tendency for the courts to be more astute than previously in finding ways in which to uphold agreements, especially commercial arrangements. The prevailing judicial attitude was summarised as follows by Macfarlan J in *Prints for Pleasure Ltd v Oswald-Sealy (Overseas) Ltd*:[303]

> It is obvious, in my opinion, that in dealings between business people there cannot always be certainty or predictability about the future course of events arising out of or in the performance of a business relationship which they desire to, and may lawfully, create. The course of business often means that this must be so and it would, as Lord Tomlin said,[304] be a reproach upon the law if parties who intended to agree, and believed they had agreed in this way, should be told that their agreement for legal reasons had never come into existence. In the present case the agreement was concerned with establishing throughout a period of time in the future marketing and business relations between the applicant and the respondent but the performance of that agreement according to its provisions plainly envisaged that future acts would be done and decisions made while this relationship continued to exist ... In a business relationship of this kind, which was intended to exist throughout some time in the future, it is in my opinion inevitable that the shifts and changes of events, over many of which the parties could not have any control, would produce unpredictable influences upon such a business relationship.

---

301. A good example is *G Scammell & Nephew Ltd v Ouston* [1941] AC 251 (see [261]).
302. *Hillas & Co Ltd v Arcos Ltd* (1932) 147 LT 503 at 512 per Lord Tomlin.
303. [1968] 3 NSWR 761 at 765-6. See also *Amalgamated Television Services Pty Ltd v Television Corp Ltd* [1970] 3 NSWR 85; *Cudgen Rutile (No 2) Pty Ltd v Chalk* [1975] AC 520; (1974) 49 ALJR 22; *Anaconda Nickel Ltd v Tramoola Australia Pty Ltd* (2000) 22 WAR 101.
304. *Hillas & Co Ltd v Arcos Ltd* (1932) 147 LT 503 at 512.

[260] **Difficulty of interpretation distinguished from absence of meaning.** It has frequently been said that the courts will interpret the language used broadly and fairly (especially when approaching a document drafted by laypersons)[305] and that it is their duty to place a reasonable meaning on that language unless this is 'utterly impossible'.[306] While it may be questioned whether the courts do in fact always avoid the temptation 'to repose on the easy pillow of saying that the whole is void for uncertainty'[307] (alternatively described by Goff LJ as 'a counsel of despair'),[308] the prevailing approach is one of upholding agreements wherever possible. Difficulty of interpretation must be distinguished from absence of meaning:[309]

> But a contract of which there can be more than one possible meaning or which when construed can produce in its application more than one result is not therefore void for uncertainty. As long as it is capable of a meaning, it will ultimately bear that meaning which the courts, or in an appropriate case, an arbitrator, decides is its proper construction: and the court or arbitrator will decide its application. The question becomes one of construction, of ascertaining the intention of the parties, and of applying it ... So long as the language employed by the parties, to use Lord Wright's words in *G Scammell & Nephew Ltd v Ouston*[310] is not 'so obscure and so incapable of any definite or precise meaning that the court is unable to attribute to the parties any particular contractual intention', the contract cannot be held to be void or uncertain or meaningless. In the search for that intention, no narrow or pedantic approach is warranted, particularly in the case of commercial arrangements. Thus will uncertainty of meaning, as distinct from absence of meaning or of intention, be resolved.

[261] **External standard.** Provisions which are apparently vague or uncertain can frequently be given substance if there is some external yardstick or standard by appeal to which the content of the agreement can be more precisely defined.[311] Thus, an agreement to hire a motor car on the terms of the 'usual hiring agreement' of the plaintiff or of any other company nominated by the plaintiff was valid.[312] The agreement gave a very wide discretion to the plaintiff, but once the plaintiff nominated a company which did in fact have a 'usual' hiring agreement used by it the obligations of the parties were sufficiently defined. It is also not uncommon

---

305. See *Hillas & Co Ltd v Arcos Ltd* (1932) 147 LT 503 at 514; *Cohen v Mason* [1961] Qd R 518.
306. *Brown v Gould* [1972] Ch 53 at 57; *Hammond v Vam Ltd* [1972] 2 NSWLR 16 at 18. See also *Murphy v Wright* (1992) NSW Conv R 55-652 at 59-733.
307. *Re Roberts* (1881) 19 Ch D 520 at 529, discussed in *Brown v Gould* [1972] Ch 53 at 57.
308. *Nea Agrax SA v Baltic Shipping Co Ltd* [1976] 1 QB 933 at 948.
309. *Upper Hunter County District Council v Australian Chilling & Freezing Co Ltd* (1968) 118 CLR 429 at 436-7 per Barwick CJ. See also *Head v Elk* [1962] NSWR 1363 at 1370-1; *McDermott v Black* (1940) 63 CLR 161; *Waldrom v Tsimiklis* (1975) 12 SASR 481; *Anaconda Nickel Ltd v Tarmoola Australia Pty Ltd* (2000) 22 WAR 101.
310. [1941] AC 251 at 268.
311. See generally *York Air Conditioning & Refrigeration (A'sia) Pty Ltd v The Commonwealth* (1949) 80 CLR 11; *Peters Ice Cream (Vic) Pty Ltd v Todd* [1961] VR 485; *Placer Development Ltd v The Commonwealth* (1969) 121 CLR 353; *Biotechnology Australia Pty Ltd v Pace* (1988) 15 NSWLR 130.
312. *Allcars Pty Ltd v Tweedle* [1937] VLR 35. The total rental and the terms of payment were set out in the agreement.

for the parties to agree expressly on some aspects of their bargain and then to provide that, except as inconsistent with the express agreement, the parties shall be bound by the terms of a nominated standard form contract. Once that standard form is identified, the content of the parties' agreement is clear.[313] On the other hand, an agreement to take a motor vehicle on 'hire-purchase terms' was void when it appeared that there were a great variety of hire-purchase terms in use.[314] Had there been evidence that there were, as a matter of fact and commercial practice, any 'usual' hire-purchase terms in general use the court would have had a yardstick by which to establish the scope of the obligation.

In *Whitlock v Brew*[315] an agreement for the sale of land provided that the purchaser would grant a lease of a defined portion of the land to a named oil company. The land was to be used for the purposes of a petrol station (already established there) and the lease was to be 'upon such reasonable terms as commonly govern such a lease'. It was held that the provision was void as it neither specified nor provided a means for determining the period for which the lease should be granted nor the rent which should be payable. There was no evidence that there was in fact any set of reasonable terms in common use for leases of this kind, but even if there had been such evidence it may well not have assisted on the vital points of the length of the lease and the rent.

[262] Reasonableness standard. On other occasions the standard of reasonableness will be called in aid. In *Hillas & Co Ltd v Arcos Ltd*[316] buyers agreed to buy from Russian sellers '22,000 standards of Russian softwood goods of fair specification over the season 1930'. The agreement also contained an option for the buyers to take a further '100,000 standards for delivery during 1931'. The option clause did not specify what kinds, sizes or qualities of timber were to be supplied nor did it define the dates and ports of shipment and discharge. The House of Lords held that the option must be read as requiring the standards to be 'of fair specification' and that in the case of the parties disagreeing the court could ascertain what quality, times of delivery etc would be reasonable in the circumstances. The court was influenced, as in many other cases, by the fact that the parties themselves thought they had a concluded agreement. The fact that the parties themselves had, by their actions in carrying out the sale and purchase of 22,000 standards under the initial part of the contract, attributed meaning to the agreement was also important and in fact, as we

---

313. See, eg *Trustees Executors & Agency Co Ltd v Peters* (1960) 102 CLR 537; *Sidney Eastman Pty Ltd v Southern* [1963] NSWR 815.
314. *G Scammell & Nephew Ltd v Ouston* [1941] AC 251.
315. (1968) 118 CLR 445. Cf *Hancock v Wilson* [1956] St R Qd 266 (agreement to grant an easement valid); *Hobbs Padgett & Co (Reinsurance) Ltd v J C Kirkland Ltd* [1969] 2 Lloyd's Rep 547 (suitable arbitration clause). See also *Bishop & Baxter Ltd v Anglo-Eastern Trading & Industrial Co Ltd* [1944] 1 KB 12; *British Electrical & Associated Industries (Cardiff) Ltd v Patley Pressings Ltd* [1953] 1 WLR 280; *Cumming & Co Ltd v Hasell* (1920) 28 CLR 508 (cf *David T Boyd & Co Ltd v Louca* [1973] 1 Lloyd's Rep 209); *Corser v Commonwealth General Assurance Corp Ltd* [1963] NSWR 225; *Bishop v Taylor* (1968) 118 CLR 518; *Myam Pty Ltd v Teskera* [1971] VR 725.
316. (1932) 147 LT 503. See also *King v Ivanhoe Gold Corp Ltd* (1908) 7 CLR 617.

shall see later, where an agreement has been partly performed the courts are particularly reluctant to hold it void for uncertainty.

Similar to the appeal to the standard of reasonableness is that to the understanding or practice of business people. Thus, in *Three Rivers Trading Co Ltd v Gwinear & District Farmers Ltd*[317] it was held that a contract for the sale of '400 tons approximately' of barley was valid. The word 'approximately' could be given a quite sufficient meaning by commercial people and the contract would be satisfied by a delivery of such quantity as was practicable, delivery of a ton or so short of (or in excess of) 400 tons being a good delivery under the contract.

[263] **Effect of provision not immediately ascertainable.** In many cases the exact implications of a phrase will be uncertain only in the sense that its exact implications in a given situation may be seen only when certain facts not yet ascertained (and perhaps not ascertainable until some future point of time) have in fact been ascertained. If, for example, a farmer agrees to sell the whole of a currently growing crop of wheat at a certain figure per bushel, the total price will not be known until the crop has been harvested and the quantity produced measured, but when this has been done the price can be easily ascertained. As the contract itself provides the necessary standard and nothing depends on future agreement between the parties, the contract is enforceable. Likewise, Barwick CJ remarked that a contract to build a bridge 'at cost' would be enforceable: 'to my mind, generally speaking, the concept of a cost of doing something is certain in the sense that it provides a criterion by reference to which the rights of the parties may ultimately and logically be worked out, if not by the parties then by the courts'.[318]

[264] **'Rise and fall' clauses.** The principle referred to in the previous paragraph is frequently relied upon in the context of contracts (such as building and engineering contracts) whose performance is likely to extend over a period of time. Where a contractor agrees to complete a project for a specified sum, the contract price is fixed even though subsequent increases in the costs of labour and materials may render the contract quite unprofitable. To overcome this problem, the parties will often agree on a 'rise and fall' clause under which the price may be adjusted in the event of defined variations in costs. (In times of relatively high inflation the price is in general much more likely to rise than to fall, but in the case of some materials there can be quite marked fluctuations up or down in market prices.) A rise and fall clause will seek to define those cost alterations which may be taken into account and to provide some formula according to which the adjusted price is to be objectively calculated. Some such clauses are extremely complex and frequently refer to indexes of the costs of materials and labour produced by the Australian Bureau of Statistics or other bodies.[319]

---

317. (1967) 111 Sol Jo 831.
318. *Upper Hunter County District Council v Australian Chilling & Freezing Co Ltd* (1968) 118 CLR 429 at 437. But see *Trawl Industries of Australia Pty Ltd v Effem Foods Pty Ltd* (1992) 27 NSWLR 326.

[265] **Area of operation uncertain.** One final form of uncertainty should be mentioned. It may well be that the words used by the parties are clear in their meaning, but that the operation of the agreement is not clear either because there is no set of facts upon which it can operate or because there is more than one set of facts which are within those words and the agreement does not indicate the set on which it is to operate. In such a case the agreement fails because the area of its operation is not stated with certainty. Thus in *Mercantile Credits Ltd v Harry*[320] the defendant guaranteed the performance by two named persons of their obligations under a lease with the plaintiff. There were in fact two leases between these persons and the plaintiff which answered the description in the guarantee, but as the terms of the guarantee made it clear that it related to one lease only and the guarantee did not define to which of the leases it referred, the plaintiff's action on the guarantee failed.

[266] **Uncertainty and intention to contract.** A number of cases have involved an arrangement under which the plaintiff agreed to look after an elderly and infirm person for the rest of his or her life in return for a rather vague promise of future reward. The issue usually arises when the elderly person dies without having made provision (or having made what is alleged to be an inadequate provision) for the other. The facts of the cases, of course, vary in the degree of uncertainty involved, but in a number of cases it has been held that the arrangement was too uncertain to be contractual (though in some cases it was held that compensation could be recovered on a quantum meruit basis).[321] In other cases, however, an arrangement of this type will be upheld.[322] A similar case is *Wakeling v Ripley*,[323] where a husband and wife were persuaded by the wife's brother to come to Australia and live with him there, in return for his promise to leave them all his property on his death and in the meantime to provide them with a home and 'living'. Had the validity of this contract been disputed while the agreement was still largely executory, the contract might well have been held to be unenforceable. However, the dispute did not arise until some time after the husband and wife had taken up residence in Australia, which involved serious steps for them as they had sold their home in England and the husband had resigned his university lectureship.[324] It was held that they were entitled to damages for breach of contract. It should be noted that

---

319. For some examples of such clauses see Dorter and Sharkey, *Building and Construction Contracts in Australia*, 2nd ed, 1990, paras 10.120–10.260. For examples of cases where a rise and fall clause was argued to be uncertain see *Upper Hunter County District Council v Australian Chilling & Freezing Co Ltd* (1968) 118 CLR 429; *Tonelli v Komirra Pty Ltd* [1972] VR 737; *Timmerman v Nervina Industries (International) Pty Ltd* [1983] 1 Qd R 1.
320. [1969] 2 NSWR 248. See also *Re Nudgee Bakery Pty Ltd's Agreement* [1971] Qd R 24.
321. See *Shiels v Drysdale* (1880) 6 VLR (E) 126; *Horton v Jones* (1935) 53 CLR 475; *Stinchcombe v Thomas* [1957] VR 509; *Reynolds v McGregor* [1973] QL 314. As to recovery on quantum meruit where there is no actionable agreement in existence, see [2317], [2318].
322. See *O'Sullivan v National Trustees Executors & Agency Co of A'sia Ltd* [1913] VLR 173; *Palmer v Bank of NSW* [1973] 2 NSWLR 244 (affirmed on other grounds (1975) 133 CLR 150).
323. (1951) 51 SR (NSW) 183.
324. As to the significance of a contract having been largely performed see [269].

[266]   Contract Law in Australia

Wakeling v Ripley turned mainly on the question of whether the parties intended that their agreement should be legally enforceable. As is shown later,[325] there is a presumption (which may be, as was the case here, rebutted) that domestic arrangements are not intended to be legally enforceable. Uncertainty in the terms of such an agreement is, even though it might not be so extreme of itself as to render the agreement void on that ground, nonetheless often relevant as a factor indicating that the agreement is to be regarded as one not intended to be legally enforceable.[326]

[267] **Agreement incomplete.** It has often been said that a contract will fail for incompleteness where, even though the language used may be quite clear in its meaning, some essential or important part of the bargain is yet to be agreed.[327] In a contract of sale price is obviously a vital element and therefore there will be no contract if the parties provide that the price is to be agreed by them at a future date. This principle has been applied where a lease contains an option for the lessee to enter into a renewal of the lease at a rental to be agreed and it has been held that in such cases the option will be void.[328] It is otherwise, however, if a contract of sale or lease provides that in default of agreement between the parties the rental or price is to be determined according to some formula or machinery not depending on further agreement between the parties.[329] Thus this may be determined by a named third party or pursuant to a clause providing for arbitration, provided that the arbitration clause is drawn so as to cover this matter.[330]

[268] **Implication of terms.** A seemingly incomplete agreement will often be enforced because the courts will imply in the contract terms relating to essential matters which the parties themselves have not expressly

---

325. Chapter 4.
326. See, eg *Jones v Padavatton* [1969] 1 WLR 328; *Gould v Gould* [1970] 1 QB 275. As to the relationship between uncertainty and intention to contract see also *Anaconda Nickel Ltd v Tarmoola Australia Pty Ltd* (2000) 22 WAR 101.
327. See, eg *Hempel v Robinson* [1924] SASR 288; *May & Butcher Ltd v R* (1929) [1934] 2 KB 17n; *Willesden v Webb* [1937] QWN 8; *G Scammell & Nephew Ltd v Ouston* [1941] AC 251; *Summergreene v Parker* (1950) 80 CLR 304; *South Australia v The Commonwealth* (1962) 108 CLR 131 at 145; *Stocks & Holdings (Constructors) Pty Ltd v Arrowsmith* (1964) 112 CLR 647; *David Jones Ltd v Lunn* (1969) 91 WN (NSW) 468; *Woodside Offshore Petroleum Pty Ltd v Attwood Oceanics Inc* [1986] WAR 253. As to the ambiguity of 'essential' in this context see *Pagnan SpA v Feed Products Ltd* [1987] 2 Lloyd's Rep 601.
328. *Eudunda Farmers Co-operative Society Ltd v Mattiske* (1920) SALR 309; *King's Motors (Oxford) Ltd v Lax* [1970] 1 WLR 426 (doubted by the English Court of Appeal in *Carson v Rhuddlan Borough Council* (1989) 59 P & CR 185); *Randazzo v Goulding* [1968] Qd R 433. See also *Duggan v Barnes* [1923] VLR 27; *Fong v Cilli* (1968) 11 FLR 495; *British Homophone Ltd v Kunz* (1935) 152 LT 589; *Re W G Apps & Sons Pty Ltd & Hurley* [1949] VLR 7. Cf *Thomas Bates & Son Ltd v Wyndham's Lingerie Ltd* [1981] 1 WLR 505; *Beer v Bowden* (1976) [1981] 1 WLR 522 (in both of which cases there was no option but the rental in the latter years of a lengthy lease was to be as agreed between the landlord and the tenant); *Hancock v Wilson* [1956] St R Qd 266; *Trazray Pty Ltd v Russell Foundries Pty Ltd* (1988) NSW Conv R 55–393.
329. *Brown v Gould* [1972] Ch 53; *Booker Industries Pty Ltd v Wilson Parking (Qld) Pty Ltd* (1982) 149 CLR 600; 43 ALR 68; *Prior v Payne* (1949) 23 ALJ 298; *Sudbrook Trading Estate Ltd v Eggleton* [1983] 1 AC 444. See also *Hawthorn Football Club Ltd v Harding* [1988] VR 49; *Corson v Rhuddlan Borough Council* (1989) 59 P & CR 185.

dealt with. These terms may be implied under a rule of law relating to the type of transaction in question or may be implied from the particular facts.[331]

On the other hand, it has recently been said that 'the law does not permit a court to imply a term into a bargain between parties for the purposes of making their bargain an enforceable contract'.[332] What this statement indicates is that the greater the number of important matters not expressly dealt with the more likely it is that the court will conclude that the parties were in truth not finally agreed on a bargain. Much may also depend on whether the contract in question is 'one of the kind with which courts have a lawyerly familiarity' as a result of which 'they may feel confident enough in their ability to fill in the gaps which the parties have left' or whether it involves a novel or complex commercial undertaking dependent on factors 'incapable of being readily valued according to pre-existing or reasonable ascertainable external standards'.[333] However, where the court concludes that the parties had really reached a bargain, much can then be the subject of implication. For example, reference was made earlier to an 'open' contract for the sale of land[334] where, provided that the parties have identified the parties to the sale, the property and the price, terms will be implied as to the many other matters which may arise in the course of performance (and which are usually agreed upon expressly in a formal contract). Similarly, where an agreement for the supply of services or the sale of goods is silent as to the price, there is an implied obligation to pay a

---

330. It is unclear whether a contract is valid which leaves terms to be settled by one of the parties to the contract (as opposed to a third party), or whether such a provision, at least when it relates to an essential matter, brings into play the doctrine of illusory consideration (discussed [336]–[340]): see, eg *Beattie v Fine* [1925] VLR 363; *York Air Conditioning & Refrigeration (A'sia) Pty Ltd v The Commonwealth* (1949) 80 CLR 11 at 29; *Powell v Jones* [1968] SASR 394; *Placer Development Ltd v The Commonwealth* (1969) 121 CLR 353; *Godecke v Kirwan* (1973) 129 CLR 629; 1 ALR 457; *Edwards v Victorian Producers Co-Operative Co Ltd* (1993) 62 SASR 415. Where essential terms have been agreed by the parties and other matters are left to be determined by the solicitors for one of the parties, the contract is valid, at least where it is expressly or impliedly provided that the solicitors must act reasonably: *Axelsen v O'Brien* (1949) 80 CLR 219; *Sweet & Maxwell Ltd v Universal News Services Ltd* [1964] 2 QB 699; *Godecke v Kirwan*, above; *Meredith v Anthony* [1980] 2 NSWLR 784. See also *Associated Grocers Co-operative Ltd v Hubbard Properties Pty Ltd* (1986) 42 SASR 321. See M Howard, 'Terms to be Supplied by a Contracting Party' (1982) 56 *ALJ* 77. A question arises as to whether the court itself can intervene in appropriate cases where the machinery established in the contract to determine an essential matter breaks down (eg where one party refuses to appoint a valuer). In *Sudbrook Trading Estate Ltd v Eggleton* [1983] 1 AC 444 the House of Lords (overruling a number of earlier authorities) held that it could, but the position in Australia is as yet not clear: see *Booker Industries Pty Ltd v Wilson Parking (Qld) Pty Ltd* (1982) 149 CLR 600 (but compare *Brooks v Wyatt* (1992) 112 FLR 12 where Kearney J regarded the majority in *Booker Industries* as having approved the reasoning of Lord Diplock in *Sudbrook Estates*). See also *Didymi Corp v Atlantic Lines and Navigation Co Inc (The Didymi)* [1988] 2 Lloyd's Rep 108 (provision for hire of ship to be equitably decreased in certain circumstances by an amount to be agreed by the parties held to relate to a subsidiary matter, referring to an objective standard, and to be a matter of machinery and an enforceable obligation); *Money v Ven-Lu-Ree Ltd* [1989] 3 NZLR 129 (PC); *WMC Resources Ltd v Leighton Contractors Pty Ltd* (1999) 20 WAR 489 (where a contract provides a value to be determined by an agreed valuer without specifying criteria, the value would only be open to challenge if the valuer had not acted honestly and in good faith).

reasonable sum. This is so at least where the services have been performed or the goods delivered. Where a purely executory contract provides for the payment of a reasonable price (or uses a similar formula, such as 'stock at valuation') the better view is that the contract is enforceable, and indeed this is probably also true even if nothing at all is said as to price, provided of course that it is clear that the parties were not still negotiating.[335]

In *May & Butcher Ltd v R*[336] an agreement for the sale of tentage at prices to be agreed upon was held unenforceable because a vital term had still to be agreed between the parties. The court refused to imply a term that in the absence of agreement a reasonable price would be paid, on the basis that to do so would be to impose a provision inconsistent with the express provisions of the contract. On the other hand, in *Foley v Classique Coaches Ltd*[337] the plaintiff sold land to the proprietors of a motor coach business subject to the purchasers entering a separate agreement to purchase from the plaintiff, who owned a petrol station on adjoining land still owned by him, all the petrol required for their business 'at a price to be agreed by the parties ... from time to time'. The land was conveyed and some three years later the purchasers claimed they were not bound to purchase petrol from the plaintiffs. It was held that a term must be implied that the petrol sold was to be of reasonable quality and at a reasonable price and that if there were any dispute between the parties on the latter point this should be determined by arbitration under the arbitration clause contained in the contract. The two cases are not easy to reconcile though there were a number of distinctions drawn between this contract and that in *May & Butcher*. It appears that an important factor was that here the parties had acted under the contract for three years and an important consideration in the plaintiff's mind in selling the land at the price agreed upon was

331. As to this distinction see [632].
332. *Australia and New Zealand Banking Group Ltd v Frost Holdings Pty Ltd* [1989] VR 695 at 702, relying on *Aotearoa International Ltd v Scancarriers A/S* [1985] 1 NZLR 513 at 556 (PC).
333. *Trawl Industries of Australia Pty Ltd v Effem Foods Pty Ltd* (1992) 27 NSWLR 326 at 332–3, 334 per Kirby P. See also *Coal Cliff Collieries Pty Ltd v Sijehama Pty Ltd* (1991) 24 NSWLR 1 at 38 per Handley JA; *Vroon BV v Foster's Brewing Group Ltd* [1994] 2 VR 32.
334. [209].
335. *Wenning v Robinson* [1964–65] NSWR 614; *Timmerman v Nervina Industries (International) Pty Ltd* [1983] 1 Qd R 1. See also *Australia and New Zealand Banking Group Ltd v Frost Holdings Pty Ltd* [1989] VR 695. As to sale of goods see [2318]. In Australia, it appears that *Hall v Busst* (1960) 104 CLR 206, despite differences in the reasoning of the majority, lays down that a contract for the sale of land will be void even when it expressly provides that the price shall be a reasonable price (though relief may sometimes be possible where possession has been taken of the land): *Australian Mutual Provident Society v Overseas Telecommunications Commission (Australia)* [1972] 2 NSWLR 806; *Van der Waal v Goodenough* [1983] 1 NSWLR 81; see also *Corser v Commonwealth General Assurance Corp Ltd* [1963] NSWR 225; *Timmerman v Nervina Industries (International) Pty Ltd* [1983] 1 Qd R 11; *Trazray Pty Ltd v Russell Foundries Pty Ltd* (1988) NSW Conv R 55–393. The position is different in England: *Sudbrook Trading Estate Ltd v Eggleton* [1983] 1 AC 444. In *Booker Industries Pty Ltd v Wilson Parking (Qld) Pty Ltd* (1982) 149 CLR 600 Brennan J suggested that *Hall v Busst* may require reconsideration in light of this decision.
336. (1929) [1934] 2 KB 17n. Cf *Smith v Morgan* [1971] 1 WLR 803.
337. [1934] 2 KB 1.

obviously his expectation of continued benefit from sales of petrol to the defendant.

[269] Executed contracts. Where a contract which is prima facie incomplete has been largely performed by one or both parties, the courts are much more likely to imply terms in order to avoid the injustice which would arise if a party who had performed was unable to enforce the contract against the other party. 'In a commercial agreement the further the parties have gone on with their contract, the more ready are the courts to imply any reasonable term so as to give effect to their intentions.'[338] A similar approach is adopted where a contract is uncertain. 'When the parties have shown by their conduct that they understand and can apply the terms of a contract without difficulty, a court should be very reluctant indeed to pay no attention to such conduct by holding that the terms of the contract are unintelligible by reason of uncertainty.'[339] In such situations the courts tend to uphold the contract on the basis that by their actions in performance the parties have supplied the elements which previously were absent. (This was an important factor in the decision of the House of Lords in *Hillas & Co Ltd v Arcos Ltd*.)[340] The same end result is sometimes reached on the basis, which is probably the more accurate in terms of principle,[341] that an implied contract, incorporating as many as possible of the terms of the original agreement, has come into existence.[342]

[270] Party having wide discretion as to performance. We have already seen that no contract results where an essential part of an agreement is left to the future agreement of the parties. Similarly, no contract results where there is reserved to one party a discretion as to whether or not to perform, in this case because the apparent consideration provided by that party is in fact illusory. The doctrine of illusory consideration is discussed later.[343] It is, however, essential to bear in mind that the fact that a party is given a wide latitude of choice as to how to perform does not render the agreement void, so long as nothing is left for future agreement between the parties and so long as the area within which that latitude is to be had is clearly laid down. The distinction was discussed by Menzies J in *Thorby v Goldberg*:[344]

> It is an objection to a contract if one party is left to choose whether he will perform it but it is an entirely different matter if there is an obligation to do a specified thing of a general description but it is left to the party who is to

---

338. *F & G Sykes (Wessex) Ltd v Fine Fare Ltd* [1967] 1 Lloyd's Rep 53 at 57 per Denning MR; see also *Foley v Classique Coaches Ltd* [1934] 2 KB 1; *Hempel v Robinson* [1924] SASR 288; *Sudbrook Trading Estate Ltd v Eggleton* [1983] 1 AC 144. Cf *Carr v Brisbane City Council* [1956] St R Qd 402. It is perhaps on this ground that *Shire of Yea v Roberts* (1879) 5 VLR (E) 222 is to be explained; the case is difficult to reconcile with *Hall v Busst* (1960) 104 CLR 206 (discussed in fn 318) which was itself a case where the contract was largely executed on both sides.
339. *York Air Conditioning and Refrigeration (A'sia) Pty Ltd v The Commonwealth* (1949) 80 CLR 11 at 53 per Latham CJ. See also *Hempel v Robinson* [1924] SASR 288; *Sinclair v Schildt* (1914) 16 WALR 100.
340. (1932) 147 LT 503 (see [262]).
341. Contrast H K Lücke, 'Illusory, Vague and Uncertain Contractual Terms' (1977) 6 *Adel LR* 1 at 9–11.
342. *British Bank for Foreign Trade Ltd v Novinex* [1949] 1 KB 623.
343. See [336]–[340].

perform it to choose the particular thing that he will do in performance of it. An arrangement with an artist that he should for a specified fee paint a portrait of a particular person if the artist, upon seeing the proposed sitter, should decide to do so would be no contract to paint a portrait whereas an arrangement that the artist would for a specified fee paint a portrait of such person as he, the artist, should choose would be a contract.

[271] **Good faith and agreement to negotiate.**[345] Despite a dictum of Lord Wright[346] to the contrary, the prevailing view in the cases has, at least until recently, been that an agreement whereby the parties agree to negotiate in the future on some fundamental matter will not be enforced, either on the basis that the agreement is uncertain or that the consideration is illusory.[347] The approach favoured by Lord Wright was to say that in such a case there was, if there were good consideration, in strict theory a binding contract to negotiate, even though damages might often be nominal because of the uncertain value of the opportunity to negotiate. As a result of the decision of the House of Lords in 1992 in *Walford v Miles*[348] English law has clearly opted for the conclusion that an agreement to negotiate in good faith is unenforceable. In that case Lord Ackner, with whom all their Lordships agreed, said[349] that 'the concept of a duty to carry on negotiations in good faith is inherently repugnant to the adversarial position of the parties when involved in negotiations' and that such a duty 'is as unworkable in practice as it is inherently inconsistent with the position of a negotiating party'. With this should be contrasted *Coal Cliff Collieries Pty Ltd v Sijehama Pty Ltd*,[350] decided by the NSW Court of Appeal shortly before *Walford v Miles*. Kirby P, with whom Waddell A-JA agreed 'generally', rejected the notion that a contract to negotiate in good faith is unknown to the law and agreed with Lord Wright that such a promise would in some cases, depending on its terms and construction, be enforceable. Handley JA, on the other hand, considered that a promise to negotiate in good faith is illusory and cannot be binding, there being 'no identifiable criteria by which the content of the obligation to negotiate in good faith can be determined'.[351] It is suggested that the view of the majority in the *Coal Cliff* case is correct in principle, though in many cases a successful plaintiff will have difficulty in recovering more than nominal

---

344. (1965) 112 CLR 597 at 613 (see also at 605). See also *Allcars Pty Ltd v Tweedle* [1937] VLR 35; *Kennard v Bazzan* [1962] NSWR 1383; *Lewandowski v Mead Carney-BCA Pty Ltd* [1973] 2 NSWLR 640; *Biotechnology Australia Pty Ltd v Pace* (1988) 15 NSWLR 130; *Gregory v MAB Pty Ltd* [1989] 1 WAR 1.
345. See J W Carter and M P Furmston, 'Good Faith and Fairness in the Negotiation of Contracts' (1994) 8 *JCL* 1 and 93.
346. *Hillas & Co Ltd v Arcos Ltd* (1932) 147 LT 503 at 515.
347. *Carr v Brisbane City Council* [1956] St R Qd 402; *Courtney & Fairbairn Ltd v Tolaini Bros (Hotels) Ltd* [1975] 1 WLR 297; *Mallozzi Carapelli SpA* [1976] 1 Lloyd's Rep 407.
348. [1992] 2 AC 128. See I Brown, 'The Contract to Negotiate: a Thing Writ in Water?' [1992] *JBL* 353.
349. [1992] 2 AC 128 at 138.
350. (1991) 24 NSWLR 1. As to the enforceability of an agreement to submit a dispute to conciliation or mediation see *Hooper Bailie Associated Ltd v Natcon Group Pty Ltd* (1992) 28 NSWLR 194. See also *Elizabeth Bay Developments Pty Ltd v Boral Building Services Pty Ltd* (1995) 36 NSWLR 709; *Aiton Australia Pty Ltd v Transfield Pty Ltd* (1999) 153 FLR 236.

damages. It is significant that the majority in the *Coal Cliff* case, despite their view on the point of principle, held that on the facts of that case the promise was unenforceable and that, even were that not so, there were too many imponderable factors 'to venture what might have been achieved in good faith negotiations had they continued'[352] and that as a result the plaintiff would in any event have been unable to recover more than nominal damages.[353]

[272] **Severance**. Another aspect of the desire of the courts to uphold wherever possible an agreement which the parties thought resulted in a binding contract is to be seen in their attempts to 'sever' that portion of a contract which is void as being either too vague or incomplete. Where severance is possible the void clause is ignored and the rest of the contract enforced, whereas if severance is not possible the whole contract must fail. Thus, for example, in *Whitlock v Brew*,[354] which was discussed earlier,[355] the clause providing for a lease of a portion of the land agreed to be sold was held to be void for uncertainty. As this provision was a material part of the agreement it was inseverable with the result that the whole contract was void. Most of the cases dealing with the question of whether a void clause can be severed have arisen in the context of provisions which are illegal or void on the grounds of public policy, and detailed discussion of the relevant principles is most conveniently made in that context.[356] The Australian cases show, however, that the question can equally arise in the context of vague or incomplete contracts. Where a provision relating to some inessential or incidental matter is meaningless there will usually be little difficulty in deciding that the provision may be severed.[357] It seems that the test to be applied is whether the parties must be taken to have intended that the offending provision should be severable. Another way of putting this is to ask whether the parties intended that, if the clause in question could not for any reason take effect, the whole contract must fail.[358] If the answer to this question of construction is negative, then even a clause relating to a quite important matter will be severable.[359]

---

351. (1991) 24 NSWLR 1 at 33. In *Trawl Industries of Australia Pty Ltd v Effem Foods Pty Ltd* (1992) 27 NSWLR 326 Samuels JA at 343 considered the conclusion of the majority in the *Coal Cliff* case to be not wholly consistent with what was said by a majority of the High Court in *Booker Industries Pty Ltd v Wilson Parking (Qld) Pty Ltd* (1982) 149 CLR 600 at 604. *Coal Cliff* has been applied since: see, eg *Australis Media Holdings Pty Ltd v Telstra Corporation Ltd* (1998) 43 NSWLR 104. However, the Court of Appeal did not find it necessary to choose between the different approaches of Kirby P and Handley JA. See also *Aiton v Transfield* (2000) 16 BCL 60; (1999) 153 FLR 236.
352. (1991) 24 NSWLR 1 at 32. See also *Westfield Holdings Ltd v ACT Television Pty Ltd* (1992) 5 BPR 11,615.
353. See also Jeannie Marie Paterson, 'The Contract to Negotiate in Good Faith: Recognition and Enforcement' (1996) 10 *JCL* 120.
354. (1968) 118 CLR 445.
355. See [261].
356. See [1729]–[1739].
357. See, eg *Bosaid v Andry* [1963] VR 465; *Caltex Oil (Aust) Pty Ltd v Alderton* [1964–65] NSWR 456.
358. See, eg *Fitzgerald v Masters* (1956) 95 CLR 420; *Brew v Whitlock (No 2)* [1967] VR 803; *Whitlock v Brew* (1968) 118 CLR 445; *David Jones Ltd v Lunn* (1969) 91 WN (NSW) 468.

[273] **'Subject to contract'**. Very frequently a document has been signed which prima facie is capable of constituting a binding contract, but it appears from the document that the parties contemplate that a further formal contract will subsequently be drawn up and executed. The difficulty in such cases is to know whether, pending the execution of the formal contract, there is a binding agreement or whether neither party is bound until such time, if ever, as the formal contract comes into force. The leading Australian case is *Masters v Cameron* in which it was said:[360]

> Where parties who have been in negotiation reach agreement upon terms of a contractual nature and also agree that the matter of their negotiation shall be dealt with by a formal contract, the case may belong to any of three classes. It may be one in which the parties have reached finality in arranging all the terms of their bargain and intend to be immediately bound to the performance of those terms, but at the same time propose to have the terms restated in a form which will be fuller or more precise but not different in effect. Or, secondly, it may be a case in which the parties have completely agreed upon all the terms of their bargain and intend no departure from or addition to that which their agreed terms express or imply, but nevertheless have made performance of one or more of the terms conditional upon the execution of a formal document. Or, thirdly, the case may be one in which the intention of the parties is not to make a concluded bargain at all, unless and until they execute a formal contract.

In cases falling within the first two classes referred to in *Masters v Cameron* the parties are immediately bound. They have reached finality in negotiating the terms of their bargain and intend to be bound but yet intend to have those terms stated later in a form which is fuller or more precise. An example of a case falling within the first class is *Branca v Cobarro*[361] where a written agreement for the sale of a mushroom farm was stated to be a 'provisional agreement until a fully legalised agreement' was drawn up and signed. It was held that the provisional agreement was fully effective until such time (if ever) that the further agreement was drawn up and signed. Consequently neither party could withdraw. In cases of this type lay people have often drawn up the initial agreement themselves but desire that it ultimately be 'put into a more formal and professional shape'[362] by a solicitor who will, however, not be able to vary the agreement. Strictly speaking the latter agreement could not, as a purely grammatical matter, have precisely the same effect as the original agreement[363] and it would therefore appear that the more formal agreement, once entered into, discharges and replaces the earlier agreement.[364] Certainly there are cases where the parties intend to be

---

359. See, eg *David Jones Ltd v Lunn* (1969) 91 WN (NSW) 468; *South Coast Oils (Qld & NSW) Pty Ltd v Look Enterprises Pty Ltd* [1988] 1 Qd R 680.
360. *Masters v Cameron* (1954) 91 CLR 353 at 360.
361. [1947] 1 KB 854. See also *Rossiter v Miller* (1878) 3 App Cas 1124; *Lennon v Scarlett & Co* (1921) 29 CLR 499; *Tooth & Co Ltd v Bryen (No 2)* (1922) 22 SR (NSW) 541; *City of Box Hill v E W Tauschke Pty Ltd* [1974] VR 39; *Powell v Jones* [1968] SASR 394; *Lamont v Heron* (1970) 45 ALJR 102; *Commercial Bank of Australia Ltd v G H Dean & Co Pty Ltd* [1983] 2 Qd R 204; *South Coast Oils (Qld & NSW) Pty Ltd v Look Enterprises Pty Ltd* [1988] 1 Qd R 680; *Associated Grocers Cooperative Ltd v Hubbard Properties Pty Ltd* (1986) 42 SASR 321.
362. *Rossiter v Miller* (1878) 3 App Cas 1124 at 1143 per Lord Hatherley.
363. H K Lücke, 'Arrangements Preliminary to Formal Contracts' (1967) 3 *Adel LR* 46.

bound immediately while expecting to make a later more formal document containing by agreement additional terms. Whether or not (as is suggested in some recent decisions) such cases really amount to a fourth class of case, the initial agreement will in such a situation be enforceable unless superseded by a later agreement.[365]

Cases falling into the second category are relatively uncommon. In such instances there is also an immediately binding contract. In *Niesmann v Collingridge*[366] an option provided that the defendant granted the plaintiff 'the firm offer' of certain land at a stated price, part to be payable 'on the signing of the contract', part three months afterwards and the balance three years after the signing of the contract. It was held that there was an immediately binding contract. The execution of the formal contract was not a condition of the existence of a binding contract, but the obligation to pay the price by instalments was conditional on that execution. The agreement was not expressed to be 'subject to' the execution of a formal contract, the reason for the reference to that contract being to fix the date of payment of the first and subsequent instalments of purchase money. Consequently, the first step in carrying out specific performance was the ordering of the settlement and execution of a formal contract.

The third, and most common, type of case referred to in *Masters v Cameron* is where the parties intend that there shall be no binding contract unless and until the formal contract comes into force.[367] The parties may well not intend any further negotiation as to the terms of their bargain but wish to remain free to withdraw until that later stage. Very commonly this is done where intending purchasers of a house have entered an informal agreement but wish to consult their solicitor before finally binding themselves. The phrases 'subject to contract' and 'subject to the preparation of a formal contract' prima facie create a strong presumption that the agreement is not binding.[368] The presumption is particularly strong where 'subject to contract' is used. Where the parties merely contemplate the subsequent execution of a formal contract, but do not express their agreement to be subject to or conditional upon the execution of a formal

---

364. See *Branca v Cobarro* [1947] 1 KB 854 at 858, 859; *Lamont v Heron* (1970) 45 ALJR 102 at 104; *Sinclair Scott & Co Ltd v Naughton* (1929) 43 CLR 310 at 317.
365. See, eg *GR Securities Pty Ltd v Baulkham Hills Private Hospital Pty Ltd* (1996) 40 NSWLR 631; *Tern Minerals NL v Kalbara Mining NL* (1990) 3 WAR 486; *Anaconda Nickel Ltd v Tarmoola Australia Pty Ltd* (2000) 22 WAR 101. There is some apparently contradictory authority on this point in Queensland: see, eg *Sheehan v Zaszlos* [1995] 2 Qd R 210 and *Marek v Australasian Conference Association Pty Ltd* [1994] 2 Qd R 521.
366. (1921) 29 CLR 177. See also *Godecke v Kirwan* (1973) 129 CLR 629; *Meredith v Anthony* [1980] 2 NSWLR 784; *Bahr v Nicolay (No 2)* (1988) 164 CLR 604; 78 ALR 1.
367. For examples see *Allen v Carbone* (1975) 132 CLR 528; *Barrier Wharfs Ltd v W Scott Fell Co Ltd* (1908) 5 CLR 647; *Chillingworth v Esche* [1924] 1 Ch 97; *Eccles v Bryant* [1948] 1 Ch 93; *Farmer v Honan* (1919) 26 CLR 183; *Sinclair Scott & Co Ltd v Naughton* (1929) 43 CLR 310; *Summergreene v Parker* (1950) 80 CLR 304; *Winn v Bull* (1877) 7 Ch D 29; *Zimmin v Wentworth Properties Pty Ltd* (1959) SR (NSW) 101.
368. *Chillingworth v Esche* [1924] 1 Ch 97; *Masters v Cameron* (1954) 91 CLR 353. For exceptional cases see *Filby v Hounsell* [1896] 2 Ch 737; *Hall v Gilmore* [1968] Qd R 406.

contract it is a question whether the parties intended to be immediately bound.[369] Although subsequent conduct of the parties may generally not be referred to in construing the terms of a previously concluded contract,[370] such conduct may be considered when the question is whether prior dealings between the parties gave rise to a binding contract.[371] Moreover, most cases holding an agreement to be one not binding until the execution of the formal contract have dealt with agreements relating to land. In fact, in New South Wales where there is a practice that real estate is sold by exchange of contracts, it has been said there is a rebuttable presumption that there is no contract until exchange, even where there is written evidence of a putative contract.[372] It has been suggested that an immediately binding contract may more readily be found with at least some other types of agreement.[373] Further, vagueness in an important clause in the agreement is another factor which may influence the court to hold that the parties are not bound until the formal contract is executed.[374] Where there is held to be no binding contract and a deposit has been paid, it is normally inferred that the payment was an anticipatory one, pending the execution of the formal contract, and that until this occurs it may be recovered by the intending purchaser.[375]

[274] **'Subject to finance'**. An agreement for the sale of land will sometimes state that it is made subject to finance being obtained. The object of such a provision is to enable the purchaser to avoid being liable if unable to obtain the loan needed to complete the transaction, while protecting the vendor in preventing the purchaser from declining to proceed for some reason unrelated to the availability of finance. House purchasers who must rely on obtaining a loan from a bank or other financial institution will wish to ensure that they are not bound to the vendor until such time as they are assured that the loan will be forthcoming. Usually financial institutions will not commit themselves to granting a loan until they have inspected the property involved and the process of granting final approval of the loan can take some time. If the purchasers do bind themselves and the loan is subsequently refused, the purchasers will usually be forced to breach the contract and will be liable to

---

369. *Commercial Bank of Australia Ltd v G H Dean & Co Pty Ltd* [1983] 2 Qd R 204; *Elias v George Sahely & Co (Barbados) Ltd* [1983] 1 AC 646; *Fong v Cilli* (1968) 11 FLR 495; *Niesmann v Collingridge* (1921) 29 CLR 177; *Powell v Jones* [1968] SASR 394; *Winn v Bull* (1877) 7 Ch D 29 at 32; *Marek v Australasian Conference Association Pty Ltd* [1994] 2 Qd R 521. For a good example where the court was divided in such a case see *O'Brien v Dawson* (1942) 66 CLR 18. As to what evidence is admissible to prove such an intention see *Air Great Lakes Pty Ltd v K S Easter (Holdings) Pty Ltd* (1985) 2 NSWLR 309.
370. See [712].
371. See, eg *Howard Smith & Co Ltd v Varawa* (1907) 5 CLR 68; *B Seppelt & Sons Ltd v Commissioner for Main Roads* (1975) 1 BPR 9147; *Australian Broadcasting Corp v XIVth Commonwealth Games Ltd* (1988) 18 NSWLR 540; *Hughes v NM Superannuation Pty Ltd* (1993) 29 NSWLR 653; *Elmslie v Federal Commissioner of Taxation* (1993) 118 ALR 357. See further [712].
372. *John Wakim & Sons Pty Ltd v BBA Industries Pty Ltd* [2000] NSW Conv R 55-946.
373. *City of Box Hill v E W Tauschke Pty Ltd* [1974] VR 39; *Commercial Bank of Australia Ltd v G H Dean & Co Pty Ltd* [1983] 2 Qd R 204.
374. *Farmer v Honan* (1919) 26 CLR 183.
375. *Chillingworth v Esche* [1924] 1 Ch 97; *Masters v Cameron* (1954) 91 CLR 353.

forfeit to the vendor any deposit (usually a substantial amount in contracts for the sale of land) they have paid on entering into the contract.[376] The purchaser in such a case might usually prefer to obtain an option for such period as is likely to be needed to arrange finance, but this approach will often be unattractive to the vendor because during the period of validity of the option the vendor cannot sell to anyone else, while the purchaser has a complete discretion as to whether or not to proceed with the purchase.[377] A 'subject to finance' clause represents an attempt to balance the interests of both parties.

There had been a considerable diversity of view in the Australian cases as to the effect of such a provision, some cases holding that a 'subject to finance' clause was void for uncertainty and that the whole contract consequently was void.[378] On this view a finance clause had a similar effect to a 'subject to contract' clause. These cases will not be discussed, because the decision of the High Court in *Meehan v Jones*[379] has now largely settled the Australian law so far as this point is concerned. In *Meehan v Jones* a contract for the sale of land contained a clause stating that the contract was executed subject to 'the purchaser or his nominee receiving approval for finance on satisfactory terms and conditions in an amount sufficient to complete the purchase'. In an action by the purchaser for specific performance it was held that the contract was valid, the finance clause being neither void for uncertainty nor one which rendered the consideration supplied by the purchaser illusory.

The finance clause was to be read as leaving it to the purchaser to decide whether the terms on which finance was available were satisfactory, though it was not necessary to decide whether the test as to his satisfaction was subjective (finance which he honestly considered satisfactory) or objective (finance which ought reasonably to satisfy him).[380] It appears that, whichever interpretation is correct, such a clause will not now be held to be void for uncertainty. Gibbs CJ said:[381]

> If the words of the condition are understood to import a subjective test ... it is impossible in my opinion to regard the condition as uncertain. The question whether the purchaser does think the finance satisfactory is a simple question of fact ... On the other hand, if the test is an objective one, and the question is whether the finance ought reasonably to be regarded as satisfactory, I should not have thought that the clause is too indefinite for the courts to be able to attribute any particular contractual intention to the parties.

---

376. As to forfeiture of deposits see [2333].
377. As to the effect of an option see [247]–[248].
378. See J P Swanton, '"Subject to Finance" Clauses in Contracts for the Sale of Land' (1984) 58 *ALJ* 633 and 690 (where the New Zealand and English cases and the considerable literature on the subject are also referred to).
379. (1982) 149 CLR 571.
380. Gibbs CJ considered that the purchaser must only act honestly. Mason and Wilson JJ discussed but did not decide the point. Murphy J held that there was no justification for implying that the purchaser must act reasonably and remarked (at 597) that 'implication of the word "honest" as qualifying the satisfaction adds nothing'. See also *Gold Coast Waterways Authority v Salmead Pty Ltd* [1997] 1 Qd R 246 at 358–8 per McPherson JA.
381. (1982) 149 CLR 571 at 579.

The court also held that the finance clause did not render the contract void as one based on an illusory consideration. The reasoning expressed in support of this conclusion differs, perhaps the most satisfactory being that of Mason J, namely that the purchaser's obligation to act at least honestly (and perhaps honestly and reasonably) in considering whether the finance available was satisfactory meant it was not a case where one party had a discretion as to whether or not to perform.[382]

Although many difficult questions will still arise as to the precise obligations of the parties,[383] it now appears that normally where a contract for the sale of land contains a clause stating that the contract is 'subject to finance' or some similar phrase, the contract will be valid. Previously, because of the unsettled state of the law, finance clauses frequently dealt in some detail with such matters as the amount of finance to be raised, the rate of interest and length of the loan. This was done in an attempt to lessen the risk of the clause being held to be void for uncertainty. As a result of *Meehan v Jones* it would appear that it will now normally not be necessary to go into such detail for that reason, but defining such matters may well avoid subsequent disputes and also lessen the extent of the purchaser's ability to avoid the contract.

[275] Other conditional contracts. The normal effect of a provision that a contract is made 'subject to finance' appears now to be settled in Australia, but many other cases may occur of a contract being expressed to be subject to some specified event or condition. In each case the question arises whether the parties are not bound (and either may therefore unilaterally withdraw) unless and until that event occurs or condition is fulfilled. The intention of the parties must be ascertained from their agreement and this will often be no easy task, as shown by the differing opinions which have been expressed in a number of cases as to the position where a sale has been stated to be 'subject to' survey, running trials or the like.[384] The ambiguity of the word 'condition'[385] is another source of difficulty.

---

382. (1982) 149 CLR 571 at 590. As to illusory consideration see [336]–[340].
383. J P Swanton, '"Subject to Finance" Clauses in Contracts for the Sale of Land' (1984) 58 *ALJ* 633 and 690.
384. See, eg *Astra Trust Ltd v Adams* [1969] 1 Lloyd's Rep 81; *John Howard & Co (Northern) Ltd v J P Knight Ltd* [1969] 1 Lloyd's Rep 364; *Varverakis v Compagnia de Navegacion Artico SA (The Merak)* [1976] 2 Lloyd's Rep 250; *Albion Sugar Co Ltd v William Tankers Ltd (The John S Darbyshire)* [1977] 2 Lloyd's Rep 457; *Ee v Kakar* (1979) 40 P & CR 223; *Lake Macquarie Municipal Council v S & R Bortolus Constructions Pty Ltd* [1982] LGRA 292; *Woodside Offshore Petroleum Pty Ltd v Atwood Oceanics Inc* [1986] WAR 253; *Gregory v MAB Pty Ltd* (1989) 1 WAR 1.
385. See [730].

Impact of Vienna Convention

[276] International sales of goods. Certain contracts are now subject to special rules laid down by the *United Nations Convention on Contracts for the International Sale of Goods* 1980 (often referred to as the Vienna Convention). This Convention entered into force in Australia on 1 April 1989.[386]

It is beyond the scope of this work to discuss the circumstances in which the Convention will apply to a contract and the content of the rules laid down in such cases. It should be borne in mind, however, that some of the rules of the Convention on formation of contract differ in important respects from those discussed in this chapter. For example, under Article 14 an offer cannot be revoked if it indicates, whether by stating a fixed time for acceptance or otherwise, that it is irrevocable. This contrasts with the refusal of our law of contract otherwise to recognise the concept of a 'firm offer'.[387]

---

386. **ACT**: *Sale of Goods (Vienna Convention) Act* 1987; **NSW**: *Sale of Goods (Vienna Convention) Act* 1986; **NT**: *Sale of Goods (Vienna Convention) Act* 1987; **Qld**: *Sale of Goods (Vienna Convention) Act* 1986; **SA**: *Sale of Goods (Vienna Convention) Act* 1986; **Tas**: *Sale of Goods (Vienna Convention) Act* 1987; **Vic**: *Sale of Goods (Vienna Convention) Act* 1987; **WA**: *Sale of Goods (Vienna Convention) Act* 1986. For a discussion of the Convention see Honnold, *Uniform Law for International Sales under the 1980 United Nations Convention*, 2nd ed, 1991.
387. See [235], [243], [247].

Chapter 3

Consideration

General .... .301
    Introduction *301*
    Historical Development *305*
    Definition *307*
    Consideration Not Required for Deeds *312*
    Executory and Executed Consideration *313*
    Referability of Consideration *315*

Consideration Must Move from the Promisee .... .319

The Sufficiency Rule .... .323
    General *323*
    Adequacy *325*

Past Consideration .... .328
    The General Rule *328*
    Executed Consideration *329*
    Exceptions *333*

Illusory Consideration .... .336

Existing Legal Duties .... .341
    Introduction *341*
    Public Duties *342*
    Contractual Duties *344*
    Compromise and Forbearance to Sue *350*
    Part Payment of Debt *356*
    Criticism *361*

Promissory Estoppel .... .365
    Estoppel Generally *365*
    Estoppel in the Context of a Pre-existing Legal Relationship *371*
    Estoppel Where no Pre-existing Legal Relation .. *374*
    Elements of Promissory Estoppel *378*
    Operation of the Doctrine — Remedies *383*

Discharge, Variation and Related Concepts .... .388
    Discharge and Variation *388*
    Estoppel, Election and Waiver *390*

General[1]

Introduction

[301] Why we have a requirement of consideration. At the heart of the law of contract is a thesis that certain promises may be enforced in a court of law. The concept of consideration owes its existence to attempts to define those promises which are 'contractual' and legally enforceable from that specific perspective. The concept does not determine whether a promise has been made: it determines whether the promise should be recognised as creating an obligation capable of being described as 'contractual'. Therefore, while some promises are merely gratuitous, for example, a promise to make a gift of money, a contractual promise is given in return for something of value, for example, a promise to pay money in return for a promise to deliver goods. That something of value is called consideration.

At times the concept is spoken of almost as a living thing, so (metaphorically) contractual promises are 'supported' by consideration, and consideration must 'move' from the promisee. The consideration put forward may itself be 'good' (recognised in law) or 'bad' (not recognised). Again, the courts are accustomed to say that consideration must be 'sufficient' to justify the enforcement of a promise. Again, some promises are clothed with consideration, whereas others are 'naked', that is, not supported by consideration.[2]

[302] Why consideration? No legal system can countenance the proposition that any and every promise imposes a legal obligation. All systems insist on some indicia that a promise is to give rise to legal, as distinct from purely moral or commercial, enforceability. Some legal systems distinguish between promises which are legally binding and those which are not by reference only to the seriousness of intent which characterises a promise, a test which can be satisfied by a gratuitous promise.[3] While the common law insists upon an intention to be bound by a promise,[4] it holds that an agreement is not a contract unless consideration is present.

It follows from the conception of contract as an institution accepted by society as a means of giving *legal* effect to promises that some criterion for enforceability must be developed within the law of contract itself. 'Consideration' was the criterion adopted in English law and accepted in Australia. In *Coulls v Bagot's Executor and Trustee Co Ltd*[5] Windeyer J

---

1. See, eg K O Shatwell, 'The Doctrine of Consideration in the Modern Law' (1955) 1 *Syd LR* 289; Sutton, *Consideration Reconsidered*, 1974; M P Ellinghaus, 'Consideration Reconsidered Considered' (1975) 10 *MULR* 267; K C T Sutton, 'Promises and Consideration' in Finn, ed, *Essays on Contract*, 1987, p 35.
2. Hence the description of some promises as 'nudum pactum' (ex nudo pacto non oritur actio). See, eg *Pillans v Van Mierop* (1765) 3 Burr 1663 at 1670, 1671; 97 ER 1035 at 1038, 1039.
3. See the discussion by the English Law Revision Committee, *Sixth Interim Report*, Cmd 5449, 1937, para 26.
4. Cf Chapter 4.
5. (1967) 119 CLR 460.

observed:[6] 'Whether we like them or not, the rules relating to consideration seem to me a stubborn part of our law. They cannot be displaced by courts by head-on collision'.

More than one rationale has been offered for consideration. The promisee under a gratuitous promise has a less compelling claim on the law to enforce the promise than a promisee who 'bought' a promise by furnishing consideration for it. Enforcement of gratuitous promises could prejudice those, such as creditors, who have given value to the promisor. The doctrine also protects, deservedly or not, the person who, having made a gratuitous promise rashly, subsequently has regrets.

To the modern reader, the rules which we discuss in this chapter, and the difficulties encountered in applying those rules, not to mention defining the concept itself, raise serious doubts as to the utility of the concept in the modern world. Perhaps this disquiet arises from four misconceptions. First, it is probably misleading to conceive of consideration as a single concept which may be defined succinctly. In fact, the concept seems better understood as a description of a not wholly precise or internally consistent set of rules with a common objective.

Second, even though consideration is *a* criterion of enforceability, it is wrong to regard consideration as the *sole* criterion. The reality is that promises which are not supported by consideration are frequently enforced, although important questions arise as to whether these promises are enforced as contracts (or under contract law).

Third, in the majority of cases consideration does not pose any real difficulties. Many contracts, particularly those of consumers, involve the exchange of goods or services for money and the question of consideration is usually not controversial in these contracts.

Fourth, consideration reflects a feature which is common to both consumer and commercial contracts, namely, that promises are not made 'in the air'. Rather, they are made *in return for* something. Moreover, the requirement of consideration does not mean that promises are only binding if the promisee has actually given over some benefit. An important feature of consideration is therefore that a promise may be binding on the promisor before the promisor has received any part of the promisee's performance.

[303] **Form and content of promise.** Whether the promise is to do something, for example, to take out an insurance policy in the plaintiff's name;[7] or to forbear from doing something, for example, to refrain from enforcing a judgment for debt or other legal right;[8] and whether the promise is expressed in absolute terms or subject to one or more qualifications, the promise is enforceable only if consideration was given for it.

Consideration is concerned with the enforceability of promises *as promises*. A promise without consideration may, when coupled with

6. (1967) 119 CLR 460 at 499. See also *Woolworths Ltd v Kelly* (1991) 22 NSWLR 189 at 221 (consideration 'deeply embedded in Australian law'). Cf *O'Sullivan v Aarons* (1866) 5 SCR (NSW) L 353; *Larkin v Girvan* (1940) 40 SR (NSW) 365.
7. As in *Wilkinson v Coverdale* (1793) 1 Esp 75; 170 ER 284.
8. See, eg *Parastatidis v Kotaridis* [1978] VR 449.

subsequent events, give rise to rights and duties other than contractual rights and duties. First, the promisor (such as a person who has agreed to provide services) may have embarked upon a performance of the promise and may have performed negligently, causing injury or loss to the promisee. In that case the promisor stands to be liable to the promisee for negligence in tort, though not, in the absence of consideration, in contract.[9]

Second, one of the alleged weaknesses of consideration under Australian law is that it gives insufficient recognition to the phenomenon of reliance, and denies the contractual significance of a promise which, though not supported by consideration, has been the subject of injurious reliance. However, under the doctrines of estoppel,[10] a promisor may be precluded from acting inconsistently with a promise, that is, precluded from enforcing his or her legal rights, even though there was no consideration for the promise.

[304] Consideration required for legally binding promise. The proposition that consideration is an essential element of a contract is most easily understood if conceived of as being concerned with the essential elements of a legally binding *promise* or undertaking. A person is bound to perform a promise only if consideration was given for it.[11] A few simple illustrations may be given.

(1) Assume an agreement to buy and to sell, what constitutes consideration? The seller provides consideration for the buyer's promise to pay the price by promising to transfer ownership. Similarly, the buyer's promise to pay the price constitutes consideration for the seller's promise to transfer ownership.

(2) Assume a partnership agreement between solicitors, what constitutes consideration? The promises of a partner under the agreement are the consideration for the promises by the other partners.

(3) Assume that A pays an architect who promises to design a house, what is the consideration for the promise? It is no more and no less than the payment to the architect.

Historical Development

[305] Origins.[12] In the 16th century the scope of the action of assumpsit was allowed to expand at the expense of the older forms of action, particularly the action of debt sur contract. Moreover, it offered a remedy in situations in which the older forms of writ had not. As assumpsit became at the end of the 16th century and in the first half of the 17th century a general remedy for all breaches of parol promises or undertakings, the doctrine of consideration developed as a requirement of promissory liability. In its earliest usage in the present context the word 'consideration' bore the very general connotation of 'reason for enforceability'. So,

---

9. *Wilkinson v Coverdale* (1793) 1 Esp 75; 170 ER 284.
10. See [365]–[387].
11. Indeed, as explained later (see [319]–[322]) a promisor is bound to perform a promise only if consideration was given for it by the promisee.
12. See Simpson, *A History of the Common Law of Contract*, 1975.

[305] assumpsit would lie in respect of a parol promise only if the promise had been supported by a good reason for enforceability.

Naturally, there were attempts at more concrete definition. In 1583 in *Stone v Wythipol*[13] Coke argued that 'every consideration that doth charge the defendant in an assumpsit, must be to the benefit of the defendant or charge of the plaintiff, and no case can be put out of this rule'. This early suggestion that a legally sufficient consideration necessarily involved benefit to the defendant-promisor or detriment to the plaintiff-promisee has had an enduring influence.[14]

[306] **Lord Mansfield's attempts to modify the rule.** Although the doctrine that English law enforced only promises supported by 'consideration' was accepted in the 17th century and the first half of the 18th century, Lord Mansfield, who became Chief Justice of the King's Bench in 1756, did not acquiesce.

In *Pillans v Van Mierop*[15] he suggested that consideration was no more than one form of evidence of an intention that a promise was to be legally binding. On this view consideration was essential only where it afforded the only evidence of an intention to contract. Accordingly, and in particular, if a promise was in writing or was evidenced by writing, the writing might serve as an evidentiary substitute for consideration. But in *Rann v Hughes*[16] it was said:[17]

> All contracts are ... distinguished into agreements by specialty, and agreements by parol; nor is there any such third class as some of the counsel have endeavoured to maintain, as contracts in writing. If they be merely written and not specialties, they are parol, and a consideration must be proved.

Similarly, it was also decided that compliance with the *Statute of Frauds* 1677 (Imp) did not take away the necessity for consideration.[18]

Lord Mansfield's second assault on the doctrine which, if it had succeeded, would have effectively emptied the requirement of consideration of any force, was his suggestion that a pre-existing moral obligation was a good consideration for a later promise to discharge that obligation. Thus, in *Hawkes v Saunders*[19] he said:

> Where a man is under a moral obligation, which no Court of Law or Equity can inforce, and promises, the honesty and rectitude of the thing is a consideration ... [T]he ties of conscience upon an upright mind are a sufficient consideration.

---

13. (1583) Cro Eliz 126 at 126; 78 ER 383 at 384.
14. See [308].
15. (1765) 3 Burr 1663; 97 ER 1035.
16. (1778) 7 TR 350n; 101 ER 1014.
17. (1778) 7 TR 350n at 350n; 101 ER 1014 at 1014.
18. For a suggested return to the views of Lord Mansfield see English Law Revision Committee, *Sixth Interim Report*, Cmd 5449, 1937, paras 29–30. And cf *Vantage Navigation Corp v Suhail and Saud Bahwan Building Materials LLC (The Alev)* [1989] 1 Lloyd's Rep 138 at 145 ('[u]ltimately the question of consideration is a formality'); R S Summers, 'The Formal Theory of Law — Criteria of Validity for Contracts' (1995) 9 *JCL* 29 at 30–1.
19. (1782) 1 Cowp 289 at 290; 98 ER 1091. Cf *Atkins v Hill* (1775) 1 Cowp 184; 98 ER 1088; *Trueman v Fenton* (1777) 2 Cowp 544; 98 ER 1232.

In the 19th century the courts began to define the concept in a more doctrinal way. Thus, it was said[20] that any 'act of the plaintiff, however, from which the defendant derives a benefit or advantage, or any labour, detriment, or inconvenience sustained by the plaintiff, is a sufficient consideration to support a promise'. Lord Mansfield's view, though criticised in the meanwhile, was only authoritatively rejected in 1840 in *Eastwood v Kenyon*.[21] The plaintiff (Eastwood) was the executor of the will of one John Sutcliffe. At the time of his death, Sutcliffe had owned some cottages. The person entitled to the cottages after Sutcliffe's death was his daughter Sarah, who was under 21 years of age and therefore lacked contractual capacity.[22] The plaintiff was her guardian. He benefited her in three ways: he paid for her maintenance and education; he paid for improvement of the cottages; and he paid the interest falling due under the mortgage securing money which he had borrowed to improve the cottages. The plaintiff had also borrowed £140 from one Blackburn and gave him a promissory note for that sum. After Sarah turned 21 she promised the plaintiff to pay the £140 and in fact did pay one year's interest on that amount to Blackburn. Afterwards Sarah married the defendant who, knowing the above facts, also promised the plaintiff to pay the amount of the promissory note.

In giving the judgment of the Queen's Bench, Lord Denman CJ said that if Lord Mansfield had indeed considered the rule against enforcement of gratuitous promises too narrow and maintained that all promises deliberately made ought to be held binding, this 'would annihilate the necessity for any consideration at all, in as much as the mere fact of giving a promise creates a moral obligation to perform it'.[23] Lord Denman observed:[24]

> The enforcement of such promises by law, however plausibly reconciled by the desire to effect all conscientious engagements, might be attended with mischievous consequences to society; one of which would be the frequent preference of voluntary undertakings to claims for just debts. Suits would thereby be multiplied, and voluntary undertakings would also be multiplied, to the prejudice of real creditors. The temptations of executors would be much increased by the prevalence of such a doctrine, and the faithful discharge of their duty be rendered more difficult.

Describing the consideration propounded in the instant case as 'past' consideration and not requested by either the defendant or by his wife before their marriage, the court distinguished the case from those in which the promisor had previously requested the expenditure in question and subsequently promised to pay the amount expended.[25]

---

20. *Longridge v Dorville* (1821) 5 B & Ald 117 at 122; 106 ER 1136 at 1138.
21. (1840) 11 Ad & El 438; 113 ER 482.
22. See [802], [804]–[826].
23. (1840) 11 Ad & El 438 at 450; 113 ER 482 at 486.
24. (1840) 11 Ad & El 438 at 450–1; 113 ER 482 at 487.
25. Cf *Lampleigh v Brathwait* (1615) Hob 105; 80 ER 255 and see further [313]–[314], [330].

Definition

[307] Introduction. When the existence or validity of a propounded consideration is in question, what was in fact the agreement of the parties must first be determined. It is only necessary to determine its effectiveness as consideration if what the plaintiff propounds as consideration did indeed form part of the parties' bargain.[26] Conversely, a promise is not rendered binding by the fact that there was at hand some 'price' which would have served as a good consideration, if in fact this was not the agreed price as indicated by the parties' agreement. Having identified the agreement between the parties, we need a definition of consideration, to be applied to determine whether, as a matter of law, consideration is present.

All definitions of the concept import the notion of a consideration *for one party's promise*, or bundle of promises. Consideration may be and often is itself a promise (or a bundle of promises), but it is always *for* the other party's undertaking (or undertakings) and it is not strictly accurate to speak of consideration *for a contract*. The basic contrast in the definitions discussed below is between a focus on an element of bargain and analysis in terms of benefit and detriment. We suggest that today consideration may be defined *as some act or forbearance involving legal detriment to the promisee, or the promise of such an act or forbearance, furnished by the promisee as the agreed price of the promise*. This definition directs attention to two aspects of consideration: first, that it must have been agreed upon as the price of a promise; and, second, that some prices agreed upon will not serve as valid consideration.

[308] Definition in terms of benefit and detriment. In *Currie v Misa*[27] it was suggested:

> A valuable consideration, in the sense of the law, may consist either in some right, interest, profit, or benefit accruing to the one party, or some forbearance, detriment, loss or responsibility given, suffered or undertaken by the other ...

This definition has the appeal of simplicity, but it suffers from the defect that it does not require consideration to be causally connected with the promise which it is propounded to support. A person may suffer a detriment, or confer a benefit, without being asked to do so. Such a person does not make a bargain, although there may be a hope, or expectation, that something will be received from the person on whom the benefit was conferred, or that someone will reverse the detriment. So there is at least a need to imply, or infer, an element of cause and effect between the promise and the consideration.[28]

It is clear that benefit to the promisor is not essential: the promisor may have stipulated for the promisee's benefiting a third party. For example, in the case of a guarantee, the consideration for the promise of the guarantor (promisor) is the advancing of money or credit by the creditor (promisee)

---

26. See *Woolworths Ltd v Kelly* (1991) 22 NSWLR 189 and further [315]–[318]. But cf [348] (whether factual benefit sufficient).
27. (1875) LR 10 Ex 153 at 162. Cf *Thomas v Thomas* (1842) 2 QB 851 at 859; 114 ER 330 at 333–4.
28. Cf *Beaton v McDivitt* (1987) 13 NSWLR 162 at 181. See further [348].

to the principal debtor (third party). It follows that detriment incurred by a promisee is a valid consideration whether or not it involves benefit to the promisor. The fact that it usually does benefit the promisor may be seen as merely explaining why the promisor wanted the promisee to incur the particular detriment in question.

Can consideration be adequately defined simply in terms of detriment to the promisee? It is certainly not required that the promisee should have been 'actually worse off' as a result of furnishing consideration. If A promises to pay B money in consideration of B's refraining from drinking, using tobacco, swearing and playing cards or billiards for money until B becomes 21 years of age, B's refraining may be good consideration although it may in fact have benefited B (and not A).[29] On the other hand, Professor Williston, in reference to unilateral contracts[30] described[31] 'as accurate as a brief general statement can be' the statement that the:

> ... requirement ordinarily stated for the sufficiency for consideration (sometimes stated as the 'reality' of consideration) to support a promise is, in substance, a detriment incurred by the promisee or a benefit received by the promisor at the request of the promisor.

The introduction of an element of request is an improvement on the *Currie v Misa* definition, but Williston recognised that his 'definition' required some modification in its application to bilateral contracts. The reason for this is that, as was illustrated earlier,[32] a promise still to be performed ('executory promise') is a recognised form of consideration even though it is extremely difficult to see how the mere making of a promise is detrimental or the conferral of a benefit.

[309] Definition in terms of bargain. Sir Frederick Pollock put forward[33] the following definition: 'An act or forbearance of the one party, or the promise thereof is the price for which the promise is bought.' Its elegance, and approval by the House of Lords in *Dunlop Pneumatic Tyre Co Ltd v Selfridge & Co Ltd*,[34] assured this definition of a very prominent place in the modern law of contract.

American law embraced the bargain theory of consideration with complete enthusiasm. Thus, the *Restatement of the Law of Contracts* (1932), §75(1) defined consideration as follows:

> Consideration for a promise is
>
> (a) an act other than a promise, or
>
> (b) a forbearance, or
>
> (c) the creation, modification or destruction of a legal relation, or
>
> (d) a return promise
>
> bargained for and given in exchange for the promise.

---

29. *Hamer v Sidway* 124 NY 538; 27 NE 256 (1891).
30. See on the unilateral contract concept [249].
31. *Williston on Contracts*, 3rd ed, Vol 1, §102, pp 375-6. Cf *Wyatt v Ball* [1955] St R Qd 515 at 524.
32. See [304].
33. *Pollock's Principles of Contract*, 8th ed, 1911, p 175. Cf Salmond and Williams, *Principles of the Law of Contracts*, 2nd ed, 1945, p 101.
34. [1915] AC 847 at 855.

On the other hand, Professor Corbin refrained from attempting a dogmatic definition of consideration, preferring to beg the question by saying[35] that consideration is 'one of those factors that have been held, more or less generally, to be sufficient to make a promise enforceable'.

The definition in the *Restatement (2d) Contracts* (1979), §71 is more elaborate than its predecessor, but to the same effect in emphasising a necessary element of bargain. It states:

> (1) To constitute consideration, a performance or a return promise must be bargained for.
>
> (2) A performance or return promise is bargained for if it is sought by the promisor in exchange for his promise and is given by the promisee in exchange for that promise.
>
> (3) The performance may consist of
>
> (a) an act other than a promise, or
>
> (b) a forbearance, or
>
> (c) the creation, modification, or destruction of a legal relation.
>
> (4) The performance or return promise may be given to the promisor or to some other person ...[36]

[310] Consideration as the 'reason' for enforcement. Criticisms of a definition of consideration as the 'price' of a promise apply à fortiori to a 'definition' of consideration suggested by Professor Atiyah[37] as 'a reason for enforcement' of a promise. The vagueness of this concept scarcely needs to be pointed out. Professor Treitel observes[38] in his critique of Atiyah's analysis: 'to say that consideration is a reason for enforcing a promise, and that courts will enforce promises when the justice of the case requires it points to a difficulty, but it does not solve any problems'.

To describe consideration as a reason for enforcement acknowledges the purpose of and difficulties with the doctrine of consideration but offers nothing in its place.

[311] Conclusion. Australian courts have embraced the bargain theory of consideration,[39] although not as strongly as the American courts.[40] A definition of consideration as a price furnished for a promise is unobjectionable, but how far does it go in explaining the modern doctrine?

The generality of the definition safeguards it from the kinds of criticism which can be made of the more explicit benefit-detriment approach. The latter attempts, albeit unsuccessfully, to specify those characteristics which an act or forbearance must possess if it is to be a good consideration. 'Price' correctly insists that the parties' agreement on the particular act or forbearance as the consideration for the promise is essential, but says

---

35. *Corbin on Contracts*, Vol 1, 1963, §110, p 492.
36. The section also states that it may 'be given by the promisee or by some other person', but this does not represent Australian law; see [319].
37. Atiyah, *Consideration in Contracts: A Fundamental Restatement*, 1971, p 60.
38. G H Treitel, 'Consideration: a Critical Analysis of Professor Atiyah's Fundamental Restatement' (1976) 50 *ALJ* 439 at 449.
39. *Australian Woollen Mills Pty Ltd v The Commonwealth* (1954) 92 CLR 424.
40. *Beaton v McDivitt* (1987) 13 NSWLR 162 at 181.

nothing as to the qualities which a particular act or forbearance must possess in order to be accepted by the courts as a valid consideration.

There is still the problem of how promises exchanged under an executory contract can be consideration for one another. It is the presence or absence of consideration as at the time of the making of the agreement that is in issue. An executory contract therefore raises the question, how does a promise made by A support a reciprocal promise by B, where A has done nothing at that time beyond furnishing a promise in return for B's promise? It cannot be answered that it is because B's promise is legally binding on B, since whether this is so will depend on whether A's promise is good consideration for B's. The only alternative to this circle is to recognise that certain promises have an institutional backing — the law of contract — and are binding because of each promisor's assumption of contractual (as distinct from, for example, moral) responsibility to the other for the promise.[41]

Consideration Not Required for Deeds

[312] Simple contracts and specialties. According to the common law, consideration is an essential element of a 'simple', 'parol' or 'informal' contract. This chapter is concerned with simple contracts, not with formal ones, and references in this chapter to 'contracts' must be understood as limited in this way.

Consideration is not required for formal promises under seal. These are a form of 'specialty' or 'deed' and are enforceable as such. Promises under seal are called 'covenants' and are enforceable although consideration was not given for them. The deed may be a bilateral (or multilateral) instrument between two (or more) parties. Alternatively, it may be a unilateral covenant ('deed poll') made by one or more persons to other persons who, although identified in the instrument, do not join in its execution. The solemnity of 'form' may be seen as a justification for enforcement of a promise which the law accepts as an alternative to consideration.

Formal contracts may be conceived of as documents which are sealed and delivered and intended to take effect as deeds. Legislation impinges on the general law requirements.[42] For example, s 38 of the *Conveyancing Act 1919* (NSW) requires that every deed be signed as well as sealed and be attested by at least one witness not a party to the deed; provides for what is a 'sufficient' signing; and provides that 'every instrument expressed to be an indenture or deed, or to be sealed which is signed and attested in accordance with this section, shall be deemed to be sealed'. That section does not affect the execution of deeds by corporations but s 51A of the same Act contains special provisions in that respect.[43]

---

41. See the analysis by Brian Coote, 'The Essence of Contract — Part II' (1989) 1 *JCL* 183 especially at 191ff.
42. On deeds generally see *Norton on Deeds*, 2nd ed, 1928. See also notes in (1978) 52 *ALJ* 391 and 454; (1980) 54 *ALJ* 46 and 424; and Mr Justice Needham, 'Deeds-Formalities' (1985) 1 *Aust Bar Rev* 3.
43. See *Westpac Banking Corp v Dawson* (1990) 19 NSWLR 614.

[312]   Contract Law in Australia

Notwithstanding that there may be no consideration for a promise made by deed, the promise is enforceable in the same way as a contractual promise, in the sense that contract damages may be obtained for breach of the promise. However, if there is no consideration for the promise, it remains a 'gratuitous' promise and because equity does not assist a volunteer may not be amenable to relief by way of specific performance.[44] On the other hand, a document may be executed and take effect as a deed and yet also satisfy the legal requirements for a binding contract. In particular, the promises made in the deed may be supported by consideration so that all remedies are (potentially) available.

A document may be executed under seal yet operate only as an informal agreement (and as such have to satisfy the requirement of consideration) because it was not intended to take effect as a deed.[45] This possibility is more likely to suggest itself where the party in question is a body corporate than in other cases.

Executory and Executed Consideration

[313] **Promise as consideration.** Many contracts involve a bundle of promises (rather than a single promise) on the part of *each* party to be performed at different times. The promises, or some of them, furnished by the contracting parties may fall due for performance concurrently. On the other hand, there may be no concurrence of performance between the promises or between any two of the promises of the respective parties. Some promises may be due for performance almost immediately after the making of the contract and others much later. But importantly, each party's *promises* represent the consideration for those of the other.

In these situations the promise of a party becomes binding at the time it was made,[46] rather than when the other party performs the promises. The fact that the promise has not fallen due for performance signifies that the consideration is *executory* in nature, and the contracts are described as *bilateral* because the agreement is formed by an exchange of mutual or reciprocal promises. Common examples are contracts of employment, contracts for the sale of land and contracts for the sale of goods in the commercial context, where payment and delivery are commonly postponed.

[314] **Act or forbearance as consideration.** Where the proper view is that a person has bargained for an act or forbearance itself as the consideration for a promise, the promisor signifies consent to be bound by the promise upon the doing of the act or the giving of the forbearance, and not before.[47] Assume that the owner of a lost dog promises a reward for its return. No one is contractually bound to search for the animal, but if a finder returns the dog in acceptance of the offer, the owner may be contractually bound to pay the reward.[48] At its inception, the contract so

44. See generally Chapter 24.
45. *Rose v Commissioner of Stamps (SA)* (1979) 22 SASR 84.
46. The promise may be breached before it was due to be performed; see [1928].
47. See also [318].
48. *Carlill v Carbolic Smoke Ball Co* [1893] 1 QB 256 (see [216]).

made is executory on one side (the owner's) only, the consideration on the other side (the finder's) being executed at that time. From this perspective the contract is 'unilateral', there being only one executory promise.

The word 'executed' is somewhat ambiguous. In the present context it means that all that is required to entitle a promisee to call for performance by the promisor is the doing of the act. Rather than making a promise, the promisee provides consideration for the promise by action or forbearance, as requested.[49]

Referability of Consideration

[315] Motive and consideration. It is usually said that motive and consideration are not the same thing.[50] But such statements must be treated with caution. After all, consideration for a promise is the very thing that will motivate the making of a promise and the provision of consideration.[51] But it is nevertheless true that a good motive for making a promise does not amount to consideration for the promise. Generally, each party to a contract enters into it in the hope and expectation of deriving some benefit from it. So, A, when entering into a contract, may hope and expect that a benefit will be derived by reason of B's participation. Yet the obtaining of that benefit, while it may be A's motive, is not the consideration for A's promise. Analysis of the circumstances may reveal that the agreed upon consideration was something else, the benefit being only what one or both parties expected A would derive from performance of the contract.

The discussion of motive is one way of introducing an element of considerable significance in the law of consideration, namely, the referability of consideration to the promise which is sought to be enforced. It is no consideration 'to refrain from a course of conduct which it was never intended to pursue'.[52] There must be some connection between a promise which is sought to be enforced and the consideration which is alleged to support the promise. Although it is not necessary that a propounded consideration should have been the *only* inducement for a promise, it is necessary that it was *an* inducement.[53] The converse is true also: once it appears that a requested act or forbearance follows a request, inducement may be presumed. Therefore, the onus of establishing the contrary is on the promisor.[54]

The issue of referability is most frequently raised in the context of unilateral contracts, and attempts to distinguish contractual promises from conditional gift promises.

---

49. See further [315]–[318], [353].
50. See, eg *Thomas v Thomas* (1842) 2 QB 851 at 859–60; 114 ER 330 at 333–4. But cf the civil law concept of 'causa': *Smith v Jenkins* (1970) 119 CLR 397 at 411.
51. Cf *Beaton v McDivitt* (1987) 13 NSWLR 162 at 181. And see Samuel Stoljar, 'Bargain and Non-bargain Promises' (1988) 18 *UWALR* 119.
52. *Arrale v Costain Civil Engineering Ltd* [1976] 1 Lloyd's Rep 98 at 106. And cf *Wigan v English & Scottish Law Life Assurance Association* [1909] 1 Ch 291.
53. *Brikom Investments Ltd v Carr* [1979] QB 467 at 490.
54. See [240].

[316] **Conditional gift promises and contracts.** A promise in the form 'I will do act A if and when event B occurs' appears to be a gratuitous promise, the performance of which is contingent on the occurrence of the event. A clear example is a promise by X to pay Y $100 if X has this amount in his or her pocket on returning from a shopping trip.

A promise in the form 'I will do act A if and when event B occurs' is not converted into a contract merely by reason of the fact that the person to whom the promise is made has the capacity to bring about event B. Thus, if Y accompanies X on the shopping trip, the mere fact that Y is in a position to pay for X's purchases does not give X's statement contractual force. Although it is necessarily assumed that Y did not provide consideration by promising that event B would occur, the absence of such a promise is not of itself a reason for denying that the promise is enforceable as a contract by the promisee.

Cases such as *Carlill v Carbolic Smoke Ball Co*[55] illustrate quite clearly that a promisee may provide consideration by doing an act which was not promised. The act must be requested by the promisor. So, for example, 'I will pay $20 to any person who returns my lost dog to me', is a promise which may be found to be supported by consideration if it is properly interpreted as a request to look for the dog. Equally, however, the presence of a request is not conclusive. For example, common sense tells us that if X promises Y that Y may have X's television set if Y turns it on this is not a contract. Intuitively, we know that the act of turning on the television set is not consideration for the promisor's promise, even though requested by the promisor. The promise is still no more than a promise to make a gift. The difficulty lies in explaining this intuition by reference to consideration itself.

The form of the promise cannot be conclusive. A promise in the form 'I will give $20 to the first member of the class who raises his or her hand' will be construed as a conditional promise of a gift, whereas one in the form, 'I will pay $20 to the first person who removes a load of rubbish from my house' is more likely to be interpreted as a promise made in consideration of an act. Given the definitions discussed above,[56] the answer must in all cases be found in the element of bargain. The question in each case is whether the event was stipulated for as the 'price' of the promise or merely as a condition precedent on fulfilment of which the promise, still gratuitous, was to operate.

[317] **Absence of obvious benefit or detriment.** The rule that although consideration must be sufficient it need not be adequate[57] means that equivalence of benefit and detriment in the act and performance of the promise is not required. The fact that a promisor has made a bad bargain is not a ground for saying that consideration was absent from the promisor's promise. Nevertheless, in the nature of things, the question 'contract or gift promise' will arise where the event is not of obvious benefit to the promisor or detriment to the promisee.

---

55. [1893] 1 QB 256 (see [216]). Cf *Jennings v Radio Station KSCS 96.3 Inc* 708 SW 2d 60 (1986).
56. See [307]–[311].
57. See generally [323]–[327].

De La Bere v Pearson[58] was an action against a newspaper proprietor for damages for breach of a contract to use due care in the giving of financial advice. The newspaper invited readers to address requests for financial advice to its city editor. The requests and replies were, if the defendant so chose, to be published in the newspaper and such publication might have a tendency to increase sales. The plaintiff sought advice on investment and asked for the name of a 'good' stockbroker. The city editor handed the plaintiff's letter to an outside broker and the plaintiff sent him money for investment. The broker sent the plaintiff contract notes but did not purchase the securities. He was not a member of the Stock Exchange and was, in fact, an undischarged bankrupt. The city editor could, if he had made inquiries, have discovered these facts. The English Court of Appeal held that there was consideration for an implied undertaking to take reasonable care, in the fact that by sending his letter inquiring on the basis that it might be published if the defendant so chose, the plaintiff had conferred a benefit on the defendant. Implicit in this holding is the view that the permission to publish was the bargained-for consideration for the defendant's implied promise of due care, not merely a part of a condition to be fulfilled by the plaintiff in order to get gratuitous advice.[59]

[318] The *Woollen Mills* case. In *Australian Woollen Mills Pty Ltd v The Commonwealth*[60] the plaintiff, a manufacturer of worsted cloth, purchased large quantities of raw wool between 1939 and the end of 1948. It claimed from the Commonwealth a sum of £108,871, said to be due under a series of alleged contracts by virtue of which the Commonwealth had promised to pay a subsidy.

The history surrounding the case begins during the Second World War when the British government purchased the Australian wool clip with the exception of wool required for local manufacture. A local manufacturer, such as the plaintiff, which required wool was forced to purchase from the Australian government rather than from growers. Growers received a subsidy and local manufacturers benefited from lower prices. A return to normal wool sale practices — auction sales to local and overseas manufacturers — was to take place in 1947. Market forces would almost certainly push prices up to the disadvantage of local manufacturers such as the plaintiff. So the Commonwealth devised a subsidy plan the aim of which was to maintain the price of wool purchased by Australian manufacturers for domestic use. In June and August 1946 the Prices Commissioner announced that the amount of the subsidy was to be calculated by reference to the difference between the current basic price of wool for domestic production and the average market price for each auction series. The amount was to be determined by the Australian Wool Realisation Commission. Subsequently, the subsidy scheme was discontinued.

---

58. [1908] 1 KB 280. Cf *Denton v Great Northern Railway Co* (1856) 5 El & Bl 860; 119 ER 701.
59. But see the interpretation of the case in *Williams v Roffey Bros & Nicholls (Contractors) Ltd* [1991] 1 QB 1 at 22.
60. (1954) 92 CLR 424.

[318]

The plaintiff alleged a promise by the Commonwealth that, in consideration that the plaintiff would purchase wool for domestic consumption, the Commonwealth would pay a subsidy. It was alleged that the plaintiff made purchases of wool 'in pursuance of the said agreement'. The High Court said:[61]

> In cases of this class it is necessary, in order that a contract may be established, that it should be made to appear that the statement or announcement which is relied on as a promise was really offered as consideration for the doing of the act, and that the act was really done in consideration of a potential promise inherent in the statement or announcement. Between the statement or announcement, which is put forward as an offer capable of acceptance by the doing of an act, and the act which is put forward as the executed consideration for the alleged promise, there must subsist, so to speak, the relation of a quid pro quo. One simple example will suffice to illustrate this. A, in Sydney, says to B in Melbourne: 'I will pay you £1000 on your arrival in Sydney'. The next day B goes to Sydney. If these facts alone are proved, it is perfectly clear that no contract binding A to pay £1000 to B is established. For all that appears there may be no relation whatever between A's statement and B's act. It is quite consistent with the facts proved that B intended to go to Sydney anyhow, and that A is merely announcing that, if and when B arrives in Sydney, he will make a gift to him. The necessary relation is not shown to exist between the announcement and the act. Proof of further facts, however, might suffice to establish a contract. For example, it might be proved that A, on the day before the £1000 was mentioned, had told B that it was a matter of vital importance to him (A) that B should come to Sydney forthwith, and that B objected that to go to Sydney at the moment might involve him in financial loss. These further facts throw a different light on the statement on which B relies as an offer accepted by his going to Sydney. They are not necessarily conclusive but it is now possible to infer (a) that the statement that £1000 would be paid to B on arrival in Sydney was intended as an offer of a promise, (b) that the promise was offered as the consideration for the doing of an act by B, and (c) that the doing of the act was at once the acceptance of an offer and the providing of an executed consideration for a promise. The necessary connection or relation between the announcement and the act is provided if the inference is drawn that A has requested B to go to Sydney.

Turning to the facts before the court it was said[62] to be 'impossible to find anywhere anything in the nature of a request or invitation to purchase wool'. Nor was there anything to suggest 'that the payment of subsidy was put forward in order to induce any manufacturer to purchase wool'. And there was no evidence 'that the payment of subsidy and the purchase of wool were regarded as related in such a way that the one was a consideration for the other'. Applying the statement quoted above, the High Court held:[63]

> If we ask (what we think is the real and ultimate question) whether there is a promise offered in consideration of the doing of an act, as a price which is to be paid for the doing of an act, we cannot find such a promise. No relation of quid pro quo between a promise and an act can be inferred.

An appeal to the Privy Council was dismissed.[64]

---

61. (1954) 92 CLR 424 at 456–7.
62. (1954) 92 CLR 424 at 461.
63. (1954) 92 CLR 424 at 461.

Consideration Must Move from the Promisee

[319] The rule. By the mid-19th century,[65] if not earlier,[66] it was established that consideration must move from the promisee.[67] Accordingly, it is not enough that a promise was made to the person seeking to enforce it; it is also required that that person (and not some third party) should have given consideration for the promise.

[320] Relation with privity of contract rule. It might be thought that the requirements that a person seeking to enforce an agreement should have been a party to the 'promise' (the privity rule) and a party to the 'bargain' (the consideration rule) are in truth one and the same. However, the cases[68] support the view that privity and the requirement that consideration move from the promisee are two related but distinct rules. Thus, a person to whom a promise has been made may not have furnished consideration, and since a person may have furnished consideration for a promise yet not be the person to whom that promise was made, the two requirements are doctrinally distinct.

[321] Consideration need not move to the promisor. As has already been illustrated,[69] there is no rule that the promisor must receive the benefit of the consideration provided by a promisee.

Of course, in most cases the promisee will have provided consideration for the promisor's benefit. But when the rule of consideration requires that a party seeking to enforce a promise provide consideration it does not also require that the promisor be the person who received the consideration. So, A might make a promise to deliver goods to B in return for a promise by B to pay the price to C. That promise is made to B who, as promisee must, in order to obtain a legally enforceable promise, provide consideration. The consideration is the promise, made by B, to pay C.

[322] Joint promisees. In *Coulls v Bagot's Executor and Trustee Co Ltd*[70] C granted to the O company, in consideration of £5, a right to quarry and remove stone from his land and a right of way. The O company also promised to pay royalties. The agreement contained a paragraph reading:

> I authorise the above company to pay all money connected with this agreement to my wife, Doris Sophia Coulls and myself, Arthur Leopold Coulls as joint tenants (or tenants-in-common?) (the one which goes to living partner).

---

64. See (1955) 93 CLR 546.
65. See, eg *Thomas v Thomas* (1842) 2 QB 851 at 859; 114 ER 330 at 333–4; *Tweddle v Atkinson* (1861) 1 B & S 393 at 398, 399; 121 ER 762 at 763–4.
66. Cf *Barber v Fox* (1682) 2 Wms Saund 134 at 137; 85 ER 859 at 866.
67. For more recent authorities see, eg *Dunlop Pneumatic Tyre Co Ltd v Selfridge & Co Ltd* [1915] AC 847; *Scruttons Ltd v Midland Silicones Ltd* [1962] AC 446; *Coulls v Bagot's Executor and Trustee Co Ltd* (1967) 119 CLR 460.
68. See [903].
69. See [308].
70. (1967) 119 CLR 460.

The agreement was signed by C and his wife and by a representative of the O company. C was survived by his wife. A majority of the High Court construed the quoted paragraph as a revocable mandate from C which was revoked by his death. For the majority, the contract was one between C (alone) and the O company, and no promise was made to C's wife. Therefore, Mrs C, not being privy to the promise, could not enforce it.

Barwick CJ and Windeyer J dissented. They construed the contract as a *promise* to pay C and Mrs C, which was not revoked on C's death. Moreover, in the view of Barwick CJ and Windeyer J, Mrs C was a party to the contract, so that the contract was between O on the one hand and C and Mrs C on the other. A term of that contract was a promise by O to pay C and Mrs C jointly. On this approach, because C and Mrs C were joint promisees, the doctrine of privity of contract presented no obstacle to enforcement by Mrs C. But did it matter that she had not herself furnished consideration? Barwick CJ and Windeyer J thought not.[71] Taylor and Owen JJ agreed in rejecting the contention that if one only of two joint promisees provides the consideration for the promise the other cannot enforce the promise.[72] Windeyer J summarised the position in these terms:[73]

> Still, it was said, no consideration moved from her. But that, I consider, mistakes the nature of a contract made with two or more persons jointly. The promise is made to them collectively. It must, of course, be supported by consideration, but that does not mean by consideration furnished by them separately. It means a consideration given on behalf of them all, and therefore moving from all of them. In such a case the promise of the promisor is not gratuitous; and, as between him and the joint promisees, it matters not how they were able to provide the price of his promise to them.

Thus, the requirement that consideration must move from the promisee is satisfied if consideration moves from one or some of two or more joint promisees. A fortiori it is satisfied where the plaintiff furnishes part of the consideration, the rest being furnished by the co-joint promisees.[74]

The Sufficiency Rule

General

[323] **The rule.** The rule that consideration must be sufficient requires that what is put forward as consideration reach a threshold of legal recognition. But once this threshold is reached no inquiry is required into how valuable the consideration is. Thus, the rule is frequently expressed in the form 'consideration must be sufficient but need not be adequate'.[75] Sufficient consideration is often described as 'good' or 'valuable' consideration. The sufficiency rule therefore prompts the question: what

---

71. (1967) 119 CLR 460 at 478–9, 492–3.
72. (1967) 119 CLR 460 at 486. McTiernan J expressed no opinion.
73. (1967) 119 CLR 460 at 493.
74. *Jones v Robinson* (1847) 1 Ex 454; 154 ER 193; *Fleming v Bank of New Zealand* [1900] AC 577.
75. For the reasons supporting the approach see *Woolworths Ltd v Kelly* (1991) 22 NSWLR 189 at 193–4.

does the law recognise as valuable? The simple answer is that anything which is not unlawful may count as consideration 'in the eye of the law'.[76] Where a promise is put forward as consideration it must be one which a court, if called upon to do so, would enforce.

The rule requiring sufficiency of consideration applies both to consideration in the form of an executory promise and executed consideration in the form of an act. Indeed, when determining whether a promise is consideration, the promisee will not be permitted to say that the promise was consideration if the performance of the promise would not be 'valuable' as understood in this context.

Many of the 'rules' of consideration involve the application of a rule that consideration must be sufficient. These are treated under separate headings.

[324] **Consideration must be legal.** Since the law cannot contemplate as valuable something which is illegal, there is a general requirement that the consideration put forward to support a promise must, at least, be lawful. A promise the performance of which would necessarily be illegal is no consideration. For example, a contract killer could hardly put forward the promise to kill as a legally valid consideration.

The same result obtains, although for less compelling reasons, where the promise is merely unenforceable on public policy grounds. *Wyatt v Kreglinger*[77] illustrates this. The employers, by letter, promised a wool broker employed by them that on his retirement they would pay him a 'pension' or 'remuneration' of £200 per year provided he did not enter the wool trade and did 'nothing at any time to [their] detriment (fair business competition excepted)'. Two interpretations of the letter were possible: first, that it was a promise of payment subject to fulfilment of certain contingencies; and, second, that it was a promise of payment in consideration of promises by the employee not to enter the wool trade and not to injure the employers in their business. On the basis that the latter view was correct, the court considered the employers' promise not enforceable because the employee's promises were unenforceable as in unreasonable restraint of trade.[78]

If illegality enters the picture only by reason of the *manner* of performance which the plaintiff has chosen, the contract (being capable of being performed legally) is valid, but public policy may prevent the plaintiff from enforcing it.[79]

Adequacy

[325] **Consideration need not be 'adequate'.** It is well established that the 'inadequacy' of consideration is no ground of objection.[80] 'Adequacy'

---

76. *Thomas v Thomas* (1842) 2 QB 851 at 859; 114 ER 330 at 333–4.
77. [1933] 1 KB 793.
78. See [1634].
79. See [1622]. However, where the performance of a promise is illegal, the contract may have to be treated as illegal from its very inception. See [1610]. For the impact of subsequent illegality see [2040]–[2042]. On the severance of invalid from valid promises see [1729], [1730], [1731].

[325]

denotes 'adequacy in value', by comparison with the (objective) value of the promise which it supports. On the other hand, 'sufficiency' of consideration describes 'legally sufficient' consideration, that is, as a synonym for its 'validity' or 'effectiveness'.

Thus, a propounded consideration which satisfies all those tests which it must satisfy in order to make a promise legally binding is 'sufficient' and it does not matter that its value is not 'adequate' in comparison with the value of the promise. For example, if Janice decides to sell her motor car to Fred for $1000, her promise to sell is sufficient consideration for Fred's promise to purchase even though the vehicle has a market value of $500. The consideration provided by Janice is sufficient even though, objectively, it looks inadequate.

[326] **Situations where adequacy is relevant.** Although the law governing the formation of contracts is not concerned with the adequacy of consideration, and inadequacy as such does not negate the validity of consideration, it may be relevant to issues of economic duress,[81] undue influence[82] and unconscionability,[83] as well as the availability of the remedy of specific performance.[84]

[327] **Nominal consideration.** It clearly follows from the lack of concern with adequacy that a purely nominal consideration will suffice to make a promise binding. Payment of ten dollars (or a promise to pay that amount) is often used in commercial contracts to support quite onerous promises. The parties to such agreements are simply invoking a device which the law allows in order to render binding a promise which may be gratuitous. They could equally use another device which the law allows to achieve that purpose, namely, the formality of a deed or specialty.

In *Thomas v Thomas*[85] John Thomas said (the evening before he died) that he wanted his widow to have his house and its contents or £100 instead. A few days later the executors of John's will agreed in writing with the widow that in consideration of their desire to carry out John's wishes and also the widow's undertaking to pay £1 per year towards the ground rent and to keep the house in repair, they would transfer the house to her for life upon her request. It was held that the widow's agreement to pay £1 per annum and to keep the premises in repair was a good consideration for the promise to convey. An argument that on the proper construction of the agreement the widow's promise was a mere proviso or condition attached to a promise of a gift by the executors was rejected.

80. See, eg *Alexander v Rayson* [1936] 1 KB 169 at 182; *Barba v Gas & Fuel Corp of Victoria* (1976) 136 CLR 120; 12 ALR 649.
81. See, eg [1312].
82. See, eg [1407].
83. See, eg [1508].
84. See Meagher, Gummow and Lehane, *Equity: Doctrines and Remedies*, 3rd ed, 1992, para 2005.
85. (1842) 2 QB 851; 114 ER 330. Compare the holding in *Barnett v Ira L & A C Berk Pty Ltd* (1952) 52 SR (NSW) 268 that the heavily qualified and thus minimal obligations undertaken by the seller of a motor car in that case were sufficient to support a promise to buy.

Whether the promisor actually places a value on what represents a nominal consideration is also irrelevant. Thus, in *Chappell & Co Ltd v Nestlé Co Ltd*[86] Chappell owned the copyright in a popular tune, 'Rockin Shoes', and Nestlé manufactured chocolates. Nestlé offered the public 'records' of the tune (actually thin films of cellulose acetate mounted on cardboard) in return for payment of 1s 6d and production of the wrappers from three bars of their chocolate. Under copyright legislation it was permissible for Nestlé to use the copyright provided the copyright owner was paid a certain percentage of the 'ordinary retail selling price' of the record. Chappell argued that this contemplated a selling price consisting of money alone, with the result that the section did not permit Nestlé to do what it had done. Nestlé argued that the selling price in the instant case did consist of money alone, namely 1s 6d, the supply of the three wrappers being merely a qualifying condition to be satisfied by persons wishing to buy the records. The House of Lords, by a three to two majority, rejected this contention, holding that since Nestlé's purpose was to increase sales of its chocolate, the supply of the three wrappers, constituting evidence of such sales, formed part of the consideration.

Past Consideration

The General Rule

[328] Past consideration no consideration. In *Roscorla v Thomas*[87] the plaintiff's pleadings alleged that 'in consideration that the plaintiff, at the request of the defendant, had bought of the defendant a certain horse, at and for a certain price, the defendant promised the plaintiff that the said horse was sound and free from vice'. They went on to complain that the horse was not sound and free from vice. What consideration had the plaintiff, on this pleading, furnished for the promise ('warranty')? Certainly not the buying of the horse since that transaction preceded the giving of the warranty: that was held to be a 'past' consideration, or more accurately, no consideration. It was also held that a warranty as to soundness and freedom from vice was not an implied term of the contract of sale itself, the consideration for which would have been the plaintiff's promise to accept the goods and pay their price.[88] There being no consideration for the warranty, the plaintiff failed.

Assume that A, being already indebted to B, promises to pay on a future date. The only consideration for A's promise, the antecedent debt, is a 'past consideration' which is no consideration.[89] Instead of or in addition to the promise to pay, there may be a giving of security, for which likewise the past consideration (the debt) is no consideration. However, in some such cases it may be legitimate to infer that there was a promise to forbear from

---

86. [1960] AC 87.
87. (1842) 3 QB 234; 114 ER 496.
88. In this respect the case might well be decided differently today under the sale of goods legislation. For the terms implied thereby see [637]–[641].
89. *Hopkinson v Logan* (1839) 5 M & W 241; 151 ER 103. For a statutory exception see [333].

enforcing the original legal liability. If this is so, and was the agreed consideration for the promise or security, the promise is binding.[90]

Executed Consideration

[329] **The concept.** Executed consideration and past consideration are distinct. In the case of executed consideration the act or forbearance supplied is a part of the same transaction as the promise sought to be enforced. In the case of past consideration, the promise is made after an independently constituted and concluded transaction. That transaction may explain the promisor's motive of gratitude or sense of moral obligation in giving the subsequent promise, but this is legally irrelevant.

For example, if A finds and returns B's goods and B then promises A a reward, the return of the goods is a past consideration for B's promise. But if B had advertised a reward for the return of the goods and A had returned the goods relying on the advertisement, A would have furnished an executed consideration. The classic example of an executed consideration is *Carlill v Carbolic Smoke Ball Co.*[91]

[330] **Request for performance.** In *Lampleigh v Brathwait*[92] Brathwait, having committed murder, asked Lampleigh to use his best efforts to procure a pardon from the King. Lampleigh was active and incurred expense to this end, and later Brathwait promised to pay him £100. He did not pay. In Lampleigh's action in assumpsit, Brathwait argued that his promise to pay had been gratuitous, the only consideration to be found being past. But the court rejected this argument. The reasoning of the court[93] suggests that what is crucial is the fact that the promisee did not spontaneously provide the services but did so in response to the promisor's request. The court seems to have treated request, response and promise of payment as all part of the same transaction, rather than treating the first two as a closed transaction followed by the promise of payment.

A *promise* given at the request of the defendant prior to the rendering of services, and on the understanding that the promisor is to be 'paid', will support a subsequent promise by the requesting party to pay for the services rendered.[94]

[331] **Implied promise to pay for services rendered.** *Lampleigh v Brathwait*[95] was decided in 1615, some two centuries before the clear rejection of moral obligation as a good consideration.[96] Two rationalisations have emerged in modern times of a promisor's liability on a promise to pay an amount for services which were earlier requested.[97] One is that the request followed by the meeting of it creates an implied contract to pay a

---

90. See [351].
91. [1893] 1 QB 256 (see [216]).
92. (1615) Hob 105; 80 ER 255.
93. (1615) Hob 105 at 106; 80 ER 255 at 255.
94. *Pao On v Lau Yiu Long* [1980] AC 614 (see [349]). See also *Re Douglas; Ex parte Starkey* (1987) 75 ALR 97.
95. (1615) Hob 105; 80 ER 255 (see [330]).
96. See [306].
97. See S J Stoljar, 'The Consideration of Request' (1966) 5 *MULR* 314.

reasonable amount. Any subsequent promise to pay a stipulated amount then serves as *evidence* against the promisor of what is a reasonable amount.[98] According to this explanation, the consideration for the promise is the actual supply of the services. The other rationalisation is that the original request and response import an agreement to pay an amount yet to be agreed by the parties and that the actual agreeing on an amount simply fixes that amount. Under this approach there is a (later) contract the consideration for which is found in the settlement of the quantum of liability.

In *Re Casey's Patents; Stewart v Casey*[99] owners of patent rights agreed to give their manager a one-third share in the patents in consideration of his services in working the patents. It was argued that, on its true construction, the agreement was one to reward for past services only. Both of the analyses summarised above are present in the following passage from the judgment of Bowen LJ:[100]

> Now, the fact of a past service raises an implication that at the time it was rendered it was to be paid for, and, if it was a service which was to be paid for, when you get in the subsequent document a promise to pay, that promise may be treated either as an admission which evidences or as a positive bargain which fixes the amount of that reasonable remuneration on the faith of which the service was originally rendered. So that here for past services there is ample justification for the promise to give the third share.

Where it is impossible to apply either analysis, but it is clear that the services have not been rendered gratuitously, the recipient of the benefit of the services may come under an obligation to make restitution.[101]

[332] Accord and satisfaction. Another analysis of fact situations where a promise is made in consideration of the performance of a contract, is that the promise forms part of an accord and satisfaction, the parties agreeing on the amount specified in substitution for their rights and duties under the already existing contract.[102] On this view, the consideration for the promise is the promisee's releasing or agreeing to release rights under a prior contract.[103]

Exceptions

[333] Bills of exchange. In order that a holder of a bill of exchange should enjoy the special rights and protection available to a 'holder for value,' it is necessary that the holder should have given valuable consideration for it. Section 32(1) of the *Bills of Exchange Act* 1909 (Cth)[104] provides that 'valuable consideration for a bill may be constituted by

---

98. See *Kennedy v Brown* (1863) 13 CBNS 677; 143 ER 268.
99. [1892] 1 Ch 104.
100. [1892] 1 Ch 104 at 115–16.
101. Cf *Way v Latilla* [1937] 3 All ER 759 and see further Chapter 23. See also Fung, *Pre-contractual Liability Rights and Remedies: Restitution and Promissory Estoppel*, 1999, Chs 5 and 6.
102. See further [354].
103. A transaction which fails to take effect as a release cannot take effect as an accord and satisfaction. See *Baltic Shipping Co v Merchant 'Mikhail Lermontov'* (1994) 36 NSWLR 361 at 370.
104. See also *Cheques Act* 1986 (Cth), s 35(1)(a).

(a) any consideration sufficient to support a simple contract; or (b) an antecedent debt or liability'. Paragraph (b) signifies a 'past consideration' which is for this purpose as effective as sufficient consideration.

The antecedent debt or liability must, in general, be that of the promisor or drawer of the bill rather than that of a third party.[105] At least where the antecedent debt or liability is that of a third party, there must be some relationship between the receipt of the bill and the third party's antecedent debt or liability. For example, the promisor or drawer may have obtained the recipient's forbearance or promise to forbear from suing the third party. Even where an antecedent debt or liability exists, a 'consideration sufficient to support a simple contract' would exist if the bill was truly given in return for a promise to forbear from enforcing that debt or liability.

Where there has been a contract for the supply of goods or services for a price and the price has not been paid but a cheque has been given for the amount of the price and not honoured on presentation, the supplier is usually entitled to sue either on the original contract or on the cheque.[106] The supplier will usually sue on the cheque because defences relating to the goods or services are only available to an action on the dishonoured cheque if they establish a total failure of the consideration[107] for which the cheque was given. The defences are available to an action for the contract price even if there was no total failure of consideration.[108]

[334] Acknowledgment of debt. In the case of a debt, recovery of which would otherwise be barred by the relevant statute of limitations, an acknowledgment of the debt (including an acknowledgment by part payment) by the debtor 'revived' the cause of action so that the limitation period commenced to run as from the time of the acknowledgment. This rule, developed by the courts, was said to be sustained by the view that the acknowledgment imported a promise to pay the debt. Such an implied promise, being given without consideration, could not itself be sued upon as a contract. It is, of course, difficult to see what justification could be offered for having a limitation period, in respect of a cause of action which had accrued perhaps years previously, run from the time of that later promise. However, any need to resolve this difficulty is now obviated by legislative provisions which dispense with the requirement of consideration or provide that the cause of action is deemed to have accrued on and not before the date of the acknowledgment or last payment.[109]

[335] Ratification by minor. At common law, voidable contracts of a minor could be rendered binding by being ratified by the minor once the minor attained majority.[110] Thus, by virtue of a gratuitous unilateral act, a person may become liable on a promise on which he or she had not been

---

105. Cf *Oliver v Davis* [1949] 2 KB 727; *Hasan v Willson* [1977] 1 Lloyd's Rep 43.
106. See [1816].
107. See generally [2306].
108. See, eg [2138].
109. See generally **ACT**: *Limitation Act* 1985, s 32; **NSW**: *Limitation Act* 1969, s 54; **NT**: *Limitation Act* 1981, s 41; **Qld**: *Limitation of Actions Act* 1974, s 35(3); **SA**: *Limitation of Actions Act* 1936, s 42; **Tas**: *Limitation Act* 1974, s 29(4); **Vic**: *Limitation of Actions Act* 1958, s 24(3); **WA**: *Limitation Act* 1935, s 44.
110. See [819].

liable previously, either during infancy or after majority and before ratification.[111]

Illusory Consideration

[336] The concept. Sometimes it is said that a propounded consideration is no consideration because it is 'illusory'. The characterisation of a consideration as 'illusory' obscures rather than clarifies, and the word has been used to refer to conceptually different things. Thus, a promise which is no more than a promise to perform a contractual duty already owed to the other party[112] and a promise to do something which the law declares to be illegal[113] could be called illusory considerations. Other illustrations might be promises agreed to be binding in honour only and not at law,[114] or promises accompanied by an exclusion of all liability for any breach.[115]

If the expression, 'illusory consideration' has any utility it is in describing a promise, performance of which would be at the sole discretion of the promisor. Because of the reservation of discretion, the promise cannot be regarded as a sufficient consideration.[116] It is also, perhaps, useful in describing promises which are unenforceable on the basis of uncertainty.[117]

[337] Relevance mainly to executory consideration. It is executory rather than executed considerations which are usually described as 'illusory'. The promise will have been formulated in language by the parties and will need to be so formulated by the plaintiff in his or her pleadings. Analysis of the parties' language or the attempt to plead the consideration may reveal a 'vague' promise. Just as the defendant's promise must be sufficiently certain in meaning to be enforceable[118] so must the plaintiff's own promise which is put forward as consideration.[119]

[338] Discretionary promises. In *Placer Development Ltd v The Commonwealth*[120] there was a written agreement between the Commonwealth and the plaintiff company (Placer) which contemplated that Placer would form a company (the Timber Company) to produce plywood and other timber products in what was then the Territory of Papua and New Guinea. It contained the following clause:

> If customs duty is paid upon the importation into Australia of the plywood, veneers, logs and other products of the Timber Company, and is not remitted, the Commonwealth will pay to the Timber Company a subsidy

---

111. For legislative reform, see [824], [827]–[837].
112. See generally [344]–[349].
113. See [324].
114. See [406].
115. Cf [760].
116. See [338].
117. See [337], [339].
118. See [258]–[275].
119. Cf *Coghlan v S H Lock (Australia) Ltd* (1987) 8 NSWLR 88 at 94 (PC) (promise to entertain a request not consideration).
120. (1969) 121 CLR 353. See also *British Empire Films Pty Ltd v Oxford Theatres Pty Ltd* [1943] VLR 163; *Biotechnology Australia Pty Ltd v Pace* (1988) 15 NSWLR 130 at 151.

upon the exportation of these products from the Territory for entry into Australia of an amount or at a rate determined by the Commonwealth from time to time, but the amount of subsidy paid shall not exceed the amount of customs duty paid and not remitted ...

The High Court held by a three to two majority that the agreement did not oblige the Commonwealth to determine an amount or rate of subsidy, to pay a subsidy of an amount or rate sufficient to recoup the customs duty paid and not remitted, or, indeed, to pay any subsidy at all. Kitto J, who delivered one of the majority judgments, said:[121]

> [T]he general principle is established which Vaughan Williams LJ in *Loftus v Roberts*,[122] expressed in words that were subsequently adopted by Lord Wrenbury, as Buckley J, in *Broome v Speak*.[123] It is that wherever words which by themselves constitute a promise are accompanied by words showing that the promisor is to have a discretion or option as to whether he will carry out that which purports to be the promise, the result is that there is no contract on which an action can be brought at all. The succinct statement of the principle in *Leake on Contracts*, 3rd ed, p 3: 'Promissory expressions reserving an option as to the performance do not create a contract' was approved by the Lord Justice, as it was later by Lord Wright in *Hillas & Co Ltd v Arcos Ltd*.[124]

On the other hand, Menzies J (one of the dissentients) said:[125]

> It appears to me that two interpretations of the clause are open. First that it creates no legal obligation at all because what it provides is an illusory promise on the part of the Commonwealth. The second is that it does create an obligation when the conditions stated are fulfilled (1) to determine a subsidy within the limit and (2) to pay the subsidy determined.
>
> According to the former interpretation, if the Commonwealth were to determine a subsidy upon imported products it would still be under no obligation to pay the subsidy so determined; according to the latter the Commonwealth's obligation is both to determine what the subsidy is to be and then to pay it.

Menzies J's preference was for the latter interpretation. And the case was clearly one in which much could be said in favour of both views. However, it does little credit to a government to make a promise in a commercial context and then be permitted to say that the promise was merely illusory and not real. We are inclined to think that the promise should have been treated as enforceable.

[339] Vague and uncertain promises. As noted earlier,[126] motive is distinct from consideration. But assume that the consideration propounded by a promisee is a promise to show love and affection or a promise not to complain. Are such promises of no value in the eye of the law because they are of no economic value? A pertinent question is whether such a promise could be enforceable in the sense that damages could be awarded for its breach. No authority is known to deny such a remedy.

---

121. (1969) 121 CLR 353 at 356. Cf at 359–61.
122. (1902) 18 TLR 532 at 534.
123. [1903] 1 Ch 586 at 599.
124. (1932) 147 LT 503 at 517.
125. (1969) 121 CLR 353 at 363. Cf at 370–1.
126. See [315].

In principle, if even nominal damages would be awarded, the promise should serve as good consideration just as a promise to pay a nominal sum does.[127] In *Dunton v Dunton*,[128] a majority of the Full Court of the Supreme Court of Victoria held to be a valid consideration a woman's promise to her former husband not at any time to commit 'any act whereby she or [her former husband] shall or may become subjected to personal hate, contempt, or ridicule', and to 'conduct herself with sobriety, and in a respectable, orderly and virtuous manner, and with all respect' to her former husband. Hood J, dissenting, would have held the wife's promise too indefinite to be enforceable and therefore no consideration.

White v Bluett[129] is sometimes cited as an illustration of illusory consideration. The defendant was sued by his late father's executor on a promissory note which he had given to his father in respect of a loan. The defence was that he had had just grounds to complain of the distribution which his father had made of his property among his children and that his father had admitted the justice of his complaint; that 'it was agreed by and between the said J Bluett [the father] and the defendant, that the defendant should forever cease to make such complaints'; and that in consideration of that agreement, the father agreed to discharge him from liability on the note and the cause of action in respect of it. The court considered the pleaded consideration to be no consideration. Pollock CB observed[130] that since the son had no legal right to challenge the father's distribution, 'the son's abstaining from doing what he had no right to do can be no consideration'. Pollock CB and Alderson B noted in effect that since anyone could complain about anything, a contrary holding would mean that a consideration would always be ready to be fabricated and called into service to support any promise.

Precisely why (except for policy reasons) a promise to desist from complaining should have been held to be no consideration is not entirely clear. This might have been clear if the court had discussed whether there was a compromise of a claim made by the son.[131] There was no suggestion that the complaints had not been made or that they were not bona fide, and in particular there was no suggestion that the plaintiff had manufactured or contrived a consideration. However, neither difficulty in determining whether the promise to desist was or was not performed, nor the lack of a convenient basis for measurement of any loss or damage caused to the father by a breach (that is by the son's renewal of his complaints), can scarcely be reasons for the invalidity of consideration.

[340] Requirements contracts.[132] A 'requirements contract' is a contract by which a party, who needs supplies of a particular product for a business, undertakes to buy all the requirements of the business for a fixed period from a particular supplier in return for the latter's promise to

---

127. Cf *Bank of Nova Scotia v MacLellan* (1977) 78 DLR (3d) 1.
128. (1892) 18 VLR 114.
129. (1853) 23 LJ (NS) Ex 36.
130. (1853) 23 LJ (NS) Ex 36 at 37. But see *Pitt v PHH Asset Management Ltd* [1994] 1 WLR 327 at 332.
131. See generally [350]–[355].
132. See J M Adams, 'Consideration for Requirements Contracts' (1978) 94 *LQR* 73.

supply.[133] The price and other terms on which supply is to be made and accepted are stipulated. The agreement will not oblige the buyer to call for any supply at all, the undertaking being in substance no more than not to buy from any other sources.[134]

The counterpart of a requirements contract, namely, an undertaking to sell to the other party on stated terms any product of a certain description which the supplier may have during a stipulated period, though uncommon, is also conceivable.[135]

In both classes of case consideration is regarded as being present even though the value of the undertaking is substantially contingent on the will of the party giving it.[136]

Existing Legal Duties[137]

Introduction

[341] Promise to perform existing legal duty not consideration. Since contract law recognises as valid only those promises which are supported by consideration, that requirement applies to promises by parties to existing contracts in the same way as it applies to promises by persons who are not already contractually bound. A variation to a contract will of necessity involve one party making a fresh promise or changing the content of an existing promise.[138] Either way there is a new promise ('variation promise') which is binding only if supported by consideration.

As a matter of strict logic, it is difficult to see how an agreement to do what the promisee is already bound to do can constitute consideration for a variation promise. This is, in fact, one aspect of a particular (and troublesome) manifestation of the sufficiency rule. Thus, the traditional view is that the promise to perform (or the performance of) a pre-existing duty is not sufficient consideration for a variation promise. For example, if S has agreed to sell goods to B for $1000, but S and B agree that the price will be increased to $2000, there is no consideration moving from the promisee (S), if S has done no more than repeat its promise to deliver.

The general principle was stated by Mason J in *Wigan v Edwards*[139] in these terms:[140]

> The general rule is that a promise to perform an existing duty is no consideration, at least when the promise is made by a party to a pre-existing contract, when it is made to the promisee under that contract, and it is to do

---

133. See, eg *Dominion Coal Co Ltd v Dominion Iron & Steel Co Ltd* [1909] AC 293.
134. *Metropolitan Electric Supply Co Ltd v Ginder* [1901] 2 Ch 799. Such a contract may be invalid under the *Trade Practices Act* 1974 (Cth), s 47.
135. *Donnell v Bennett* (1883) 22 Ch D 835.
136. See *British Empire Films Pty Ltd v Oxford Theatres Pty Ltd* [1943] VLR 163.
137. See A G Davis, 'Promise to Perform an Existing Duty' (1938) 6 *Camb LJ* 202; J W Carter, 'The Renegotiation of Contracts' (1998) 13 *JCL* 185 (and commentary thereon by S M Waddams, (1998) 13 *JCL* 199; M P Furmston, (1998) 13 *JCL* 210).
138. See generally on variation [388], [389].
139. (1973) 47 ALJR 586; 1 ALR 487.
140. (1973) 47 ALJR 586 at 594. Walsh J agreed.

no more than the promisor is bound to do under that contract. The rule expresses the concept that the new promise, indistinguishable from the old, is an illusory consideration. And it gives no comfort to a party who by merely threatening a breach of contract seeks to secure an additional contractual benefit from the other party on the footing that the first party's new promise of performance will provide sufficient consideration for that benefit.

The statement implicitly recognises two exceptions to the rule: it does not apply when the promise is made to a third party: and consideration is present where the plaintiff's existing legal duty is exceeded. These and other exceptions are considered later.[141] More generally, the words 'at least' indicate that Mason J was confident of the rule's operation only within a narrow sphere. In fact, the rule has been questioned and come under so much criticism that its scope and validity are now matters of considerable doubt. It is convenient to consider the decided cases in categories of pre-existing duties.

Public Duties

[342] **Is a promise to perform public duty consideration?** In general the courts have treated the promise to perform a public duty as not being sufficient consideration. Thus, in *Collins v Godefroy*[142] the plaintiff sued to recover compensation for his loss of time in attending court under subpoena as a witness for the defendant. It was held that since the law imposed a duty on a person subpoenaed to attend at the court from time to time to give evidence, a promise to remunerate him for doing so was without consideration. Assuming its validity, the principle applies equally to promises not to do that which the general law prohibits as to promises to do that which it compels.[143]

However, in several cases the rule has been avoided, and its validity questioned. A leading case is *Ward v Byham*.[144] The unmarried parents of a child separated and the mother became housekeeper to a man who, with the mother, was ready to let the child live with them. The mother wrote to the father asking that she have the child and that he pay her the £1 per week he was already paying a neighbour to maintain the child. The father wrote agreeing 'providing you can prove that she will be well looked after and happy and also that she is allowed to decide for herself whether or not she wishes to come and live with you'. The child went to live with the mother to whom the father paid £1 a week until, some seven months later, the mother married, whereupon the father ceased paying. In the father's appeal against a judgment based on failure to perform the agreement, Morris and Parker LJJ, in brief judgments, held that by the terms of the letter the mother's obligation was to prove something to the father and because this went beyond her statutory duty to maintain the child the father's promise was therefore supported by consideration.[145]

However, Lord Denning MR said:[146]

---

141. See [343], [345]–[355], [358]–[360].
142. (1831) 1 B & Ad 950; 109 ER 1040.
143. *Brown v Brine* (1875) LR 1 Ex 5. Cf [339].
144. [1956] 2 All ER 318.

I approach the case ... on the footing that, in looking after the child, the mother is only doing what she is legally bound to do. Even so, I think that there was sufficient consideration to support the promise. I have always thought that a promise to perform an existing duty, or the performance of it, should be regarded as good consideration, because it is a benefit to the person to whom it is given. Take this very case. It is as much a benefit for the father to have the child looked after by the mother as by a neighbour. If he gets the benefit for which he stipulated, he ought to honour his promise, and he ought not to avoid it by saying that the mother was herself under a duty to maintain the child.

Similarly, in *Williams v Williams*,[147] although a majority of the English Court of Appeal was able to find (or perhaps invent) consideration, in the duty being exceeded, Lord Denning MR reiterated his view that a promise to perform an existing duty is sufficient consideration to support a promise, 'so long as there is nothing in the transaction which is contrary to the public interest'.[148] In *Popiw v Popiw*[149] Hudson J accepted what Lord Denning had said in these cases as a correct statement of the law, but he was also able to find (or invent) consideration.

[343] Promise to exceed duty good consideration. The leading case *Glasbrook Bros Ltd v Glamorgan County Council*,[150] while acknowledging the rule, illustrates that there will be good consideration if the person subject to the public duty promises to do more than what that duty calls for.

There was a strike at the plaintiff company's mine and the manager requested that the defendant council provide a resident garrison of police in order to ensure the protection of the 'safety men'. The police thought this unnecessary and that adequate protection could be provided in other ways. But, at the manager's insistence, the council agreed and the manager promised to pay the cost of rationing the garrison and for its services at specified rates. The council's action to recover £2200 succeeded, since the supply of the garrison went beyond the protection which the police were bound by law to provide.

Contractual Duties

General rules

[344] Promise to perform contractual duty not consideration. In *Stilk v Myrick*[151] two sailors deserted their ship in the course of a voyage and the captain, being unable to find replacements, promised the remaining eight members of the crew (including the plaintiff) that he would

---

145. It might have been possible to find consideration in an implied promise by the mother not to bring affiliation proceedings against the father but for the fact that her evidence was that she had not at any time intended to bring such proceedings and that it was too late for her to bring them once she ceased to be a single woman.
146. [1956] 2 All ER 318 at 319.
147. [1957] 1 WLR 148.
148. [1957] 1 WLR 148 at 151.
149. [1959] VR 197.
150. [1925] AC 270. See also *Sheahan v Workers Rehabilitation and Compensation Corp* (1991) 101 ALR 431 at 440–1.
151. (1809) 2 Camp 317; 170 ER 1168.

divide the wages which the two deserters would have earned among them upon their working the vessel home. The plaintiff completed the voyage and sued for his share. By his original employment contract the plaintiff was to be paid £5 per month and was bound to do all he could under the 'emergencies of the voyage'. Lord Ellenborough held that there was no consideration for the promise since the position resulting from the desertion of the two sailors was as much 'an emergency of the voyage' as their deaths would have been. Since the plaintiff was already bound by his contract to do all that he could to work the ship home, his promise to do this was no consideration for the promise of extra payment.

Although the decision may actually have been based on considerations of public policy, viz, that to allow the action might reward extortion, the case has been taken as authority for the proposition that neither performance of, nor a promise to perform, a contractual duty already owed to the promisor, is good consideration for the promise by the latter.

[345] **Promise or performance beyond existing duty as consideration.** Decisions such as *Stilk v Myrick*[152] will be distinguishable if the plaintiff has made a promise which in some way goes beyond the pre-existing contractual duty. Similarly, the existing duty rule will not apply if the duty has been exceeded. Thus, in *Hartley v Ponsonby*[153] a shortage of crew made it *perilous* to continue the voyage with the result that the remaining crew were not bound to continue to serve and a contract for additional payment if they did so was held binding.

Exceptions

[346] **Promises with different contents.** In *Larkin v Girvan*[154] Jordan CJ observed that there is a special class of case in which it is necessary to see if consideration was furnished by the promisor as well as by the promisee, namely '[w]here the promise sought to be enforced is found to be a promise to do something which the promisor is already bound to do by a prior enforceable contract with the promisee'. In that case a landowner (the plaintiff) contracted for a builder (the defendant) to build a house for her. There were disputes over alleged defects and the plaintiff threatened to refer the dispute to arbitration under the building contract. The builder promised to remedy any defects within six months if she would not resort to arbitration. She agreed and later sued for breach of the builder's undertaking. Jordan CJ apparently had no difficulty in regarding the *content* of the promise to forbear from arbitrating as having legal value, but observed that if the builder's promise had not gone beyond the duty which he already owed to the owner, mutuality would have been lacking with the result that the promise to remedy defects within six months would not have been binding, and, presumably, the owner's only remedy would have been

---

152. (1809) 2 Camp 317; 170 ER 1168 (see [344]).
153. (1857) 7 E & B 872; 119 ER 1471. See also *Dunton v Dunton* (1892) 18 VLR 114; *Cook Islands Shipping Co Ltd v Colson Builders Ltd* [1975] 1 NZLR 422; *North Ocean Shipping Co Ltd v Hyundai Construction Co Ltd (The Atlantic Baron)* [1979] QB 705; *Syros Shipping Co SA v Elaghill Trading Co (The Proodos C)* [1981] 3 All ER 189.
154. (1940) 40 SR (NSW) 365 at 368.

to sue on the original contract. However, he said that the builder had furnished consideration by admitting the owner's claim which he had previously disputed, thereby saving her the trouble and expense of arbitration.

[347] Termination of the contract. The principle that a promise to perform a contractual obligation already owed to the other party is no consideration for a return promise by the latter has no application where the earlier obligation is, as part of the agreement, terminated or discharged.[155] In other words, if the existing duty is discharged by a contract which includes a promise with the same content as the original promise, the promise will be regarded as binding because consideration is present in the parties' agreement that the original duty is to be discharged.

Nor, generally, will the principle apply if the first agreement can be lawfully terminated. For example, assume that an employee demands higher wages for work which is being done under a contract of employment terminable by one week's notice by either party. Assume also that, although agreeing to do so, the employer does not pay the increase. Clearly, if the employee had terminated the original contract by one week's notice, a fresh contract importing the new wage rate for the future would be binding. Unless the circumstances are such that it is impossible to interpret the second contract as a termination of the first, a court will discern an implied agreement to terminate the original contract and consideration will be present.[156]

[348] Factual benefit to promisor.[157] In *Williams v Roffey Bros & Nicholls (Contractors) Ltd*[158] the English Court of Appeal held that the existing duty rule will not apply if the promisor receives factual benefits from the performance of the duty, or the promisor avoids a 'disbenefit' which might have resulted from the other party's failure to perform.

The plaintiff contracted to do carpentry work on 27 flats in a block which the defendants had contracted to refurbish. The agreed price was £20,000. Of this £16,200 had been paid when the financial difficulties of the plaintiff prompted the defendants to promise to pay an extra sum of £10,300, payable at the rate of £575 for each flat in respect of which the carpentry work was completed. It seems that there was a promise to complete the work. Between the making of this agreement and the plaintiff's abandonment of the work some eight more flats were completed. Subject to a deduction for certain defects in the work, the court held that the plaintiff was entitled to recover £4600. The obvious objection to this decision is that the plaintiff did less than his contractual duty in performing the work.

---

155. See further [350]–[355], [388].
156. But cf *Concut Pty Ltd v Worrell* (2000) 176 ALR 693.
157. See J W Carter, Andrew Phang and Jill Poole, 'Reactions to Williams v Roffey' (1995) 8 *JCL* 248; Andrew Phang, 'Acceptance by Silence and Consideration Reined In' [1994] *LMCLQ* 336; Mindy Chen-Wishart, 'Consideration: Practical Benefit and the Emperor's New Clothes' in Beatson and Friedmann, eds, *Good Faith and Fault in Contract Law*, 1995, p 123.
158. [1991] 1 QB 1. See Brian Coote, 'Consideration and Benefit in Fact and in Law' (1990) 3 *JCL* 23; John Adams and Roger Brownsword (1990) 53 *MLR* 536; Andrew Phang (1991) 107 *LQR* 21.

The work which was done could nevertheless have been regarded as sufficient consideration had the second agreement been in the form of a termination of the old and substitution of the new,[159] but the trial judge said this was not the intention of the parties. How then did the court find consideration to be present?

Glidewell LJ expressed the law in this way:[160]

(i) if A has entered into a contract with B to do work for, or to supply goods or services to, B in return for the payment by B; and

(ii) at some stage before A has completely performed his obligation under the contract B has reason to doubt whether A will, or will be able to, complete his side of the bargain; and

(iii) B thereupon promises A an additional payment in return for A's promise to perform his contractual obligations on time; and

(iv) as a result of giving his promise, B obtains a practical benefit, or obviates a disbenefit; and

(v) B's promise is not given as a result of economic duress or fraud on the part of A; then

(vi) the benefit to B is capable of being consideration for B's promise, so that the promise will be legally binding.

The benefits which the defendants were said to have obtained (and 'disbenefits' which they may have avoided) were a measure of protection against the risk that as a result of the main contract to refurbish they would be liable to pay liquidated damages, and the avoidance of the trouble and expense of finding a replacement for the plaintiff. This pragmatic approach to consideration was also applied by Russell and Purchas LJJ. The former was prepared to adopt[161] such an approach where the promisor gains an advantage arising out of the continuing relationship with the promisee, and the latter emphasised[162] the 'commercial advantage to both sides' in the agreement.

With respect, it is difficult to reconcile this approach with the prior case law. Moreover, if factual benefit is capable of being regarded as consideration the reality is that the existing duty rule no longer applies, for these types of benefits will be present in every case.[163] Although it can certainly be argued that the existing duty rule should be abolished,[164] this was not the intention of the court. In any event, the more fundamental criticism which can be advanced against the case is simply that the consideration requirement was applied in a way which is contrary to that adopted by the High Court.[165] The statement of Glidewell LJ expresses the consideration provided by the plaintiff in element (iv), whereas the consideration in fact offered by the defendants is in element (iii). In other words, the consideration which was said to support the promise was not in

---

159. See [347]. Similarly, estoppel was not discussed because the point had not been raised at the trial.
160. [1991] 1 QB 1 at 15–16.
161. [1991] 1 QB 1 at 19.
162. [1991] 1 QB 1 at 22.
163. See Brian Coote, 'Consideration and Benefit in Fact and in Law' (1990) 3 *JCL* 23, and note his analysis (at 27–8) of the case from the unilateral contract perspective.
164. See further [364].
165. See [311], [318], [341]. Cf *Woolworths Ltd v Kelly* (1991) 22 NSWLR 189 at 204.

fact referable to the promise. Nevertheless, the case has not so far been doubted and was in fact applied in the Supreme Court of New South Wales by Santow J in *Musumeci v Winadell Pty Ltd*.[166]

[349] Promise to perform a duty to third party consideration. If A already owes a contractual duty to X, and B promises to pay A a specified sum in consideration for A's promise to perform (or actual performance of) the duty owed to X, B is bound by the promise since A is regarded as having provided consideration in the promise to perform (or the performance of) the duty owed to X.

In *Shadwell v Shadwell*,[167] the plaintiff, a practising barrister, when he was already engaged to marry Ellen Nicholl, received a letter from his uncle, the defendant, which contained a statement that as he was 'glad to hear' of the intended marriage and, as he 'promised to assist' the plaintiff 'at starting', was 'happy' to say that he would pay '£150 yearly during my life and until your annual income derived from your profession of a Chancery barrister shall amount to 600 guineas'. The marriage occurred but there was no suggestion that the plaintiff had promised his uncle that he would proceed with the marriage. The plaintiff's annual income as a barrister at no time reached 600 guineas. The yearly instalments of £150 were not all paid during the uncle's life and, after his death, his legal personal representatives were sued by the nephew for the arrears. A majority of the court held that the nephew had provided consideration by marrying. It was said[168] that this involved both a detriment to the nephew and a benefit to the uncle. The detriment was that the nephew 'may have made a most material change in his position, and induced the object of his affection to do the same, and may have incurred pecuniary liabilities resulting in embarrassments, which would be in every sense a loss if the income which had been promised should be withheld'. The benefit to the uncle was that the marriage was 'an object of interest to a near relative'.

Unfortunately, the majority judgment does not advert to the fact that the marriage was nothing more than a performance of an existing contractual obligation. Thus, it does not consider such possibilities as that consideration might exist in the nephew's actually marrying as distinct from breaching the contract to marry and paying damages for that breach, or in the nephew's forgoing the right to negotiate with Ellen Nicholl for a discharge of the contract to marry. So far as the suggested benefit to the uncle is concerned, the majority judgment itself described it as a merely 'sentimental' one. Thus, although *Shadwell v Shadwell* may exemplify the proposition that performance of an existing contractual duty owed to a third party can be good consideration, the actual reasoning of the majority judgment lends little support to it.[169]

However, the view that either a promise to perform or the actual performance of an existing contractual duty is capable of being sufficient consideration was confirmed by the Privy Council in *The Eurymedon*.[170] A

---

166. (1994) 34 NSWLR 723.
167. (1860) 9 CBNS 159; 142 ER 62.
168. (1860) 9 CBNS 159 at 174; 142 ER 62 at 68.
169. See also *Scotson v Pegg* (1861) 6 H & N 295; 158 ER 121; *Chichester v Cobb* (1866) 14 LT 433.

firm of stevedores negligently unloaded goods from a ship with consequent damage to the goods. The consignee sued the stevedores for damages. The stevedores, who were bound by a contract with the shipowner to unload the goods, pleaded a clause which specified the time limit within which such an action could be brought. This clause was in fact contained in a contract to which it was not otherwise a party, and the issue was whether the stevedores had provided consideration. It was held that, vis-à-vis the consignee, the stevedores' unloading was consideration notwithstanding that they were already contractually bound to the shipowner. The majority said:[171]

> An agreement to do an act which the promisor is under an existing obligation to a third party to do, may quite well amount to valid consideration and does so in the present case: the promisee obtains the benefit of a direct obligation which he can enforce.

Similarly, in *Pao On v Lau Yiu Long*[172] the plaintiffs promised the defendants, who were the majority shareholders of a public company, to perform contractual obligations which the plaintiffs already owed to the public company in consideration of a promise of indemnity given by the defendants. It was held that the plaintiffs' promise could be sufficient consideration for the defendant's promise of indemnity. The Privy Council did not doubt[173] 'that a promise to perform, or the performance of, a pre-existing contractual obligation to a third party can be valid consideration'.

It might be argued that, where the propounded consideration is *executory*, that is, a promise to perform the duty owed to the third party, detriment is involved in that the person giving that promise is exposed to a second possible action for breach of the same contractual promise, whereas if the propounded consideration is *executed*, that is, the actual performance of the duty already owed to the third party, no detriment is involved. However, the cases clearly support the view that to distinguish between the giving of a promise to perform obligations under a contract with a third party and actual performance of them is commercially unacceptable. Either may count as good and sufficient consideration.

Compromise and Forbearance to Sue[174]

[350] Consideration in compromise. If it stood alone the existing duty rule would be a serious obstacle to the orderly settlement of contractual disputes. Assume that A and B are subject to a contract which, when properly interpreted, obliges A to do X. Assume further that A is under the honest misapprehension that the contract requires A to do Y, an act which is less beneficial to B than X. Now, B could go to court and ask for a ruling on what the contract requires A to do. But the prospect of litigation is never

---

170. *New Zealand Shipping Co Ltd v A M Satterthwaite & Co Ltd* [1975] AC 154. See further on the case [925].
171. [1975] AC 154 at 168. See also *Port Jackson Stevedoring Pty Ltd v Salmond & Spraggon (Aust) Pty Ltd (The New York Star)* (1978) 139 CLR 231 at 243–4; 18 ALR 333 (adopted (1980) 144 CLR 300; 30 ALR 588 (PC)).
172. [1980] AC 614.
173. [1980] AC 614 at 632.
174. Cf S J Stoljar, 'The Consideration of Forbearance' (1965) 5 *MULR* 34.

inviting and the law should encourage A and B to settle their dispute. Assume then that A and B enter into an agreement whereby B agrees to accept act Z, the benefit of which to B lies somewhere between that of A doing X and A doing Y, in return for A's promise to abandon the claim that A is entitled to perform by doing Y. Assume finally that B discovers the true construction of the original contract and refuses to honour the agreement to accept Z as performance. In order to enforce the agreement by B, A must show that consideration was provided by promising to do Z. Application of the existing duty rule would necessarily lead to the conclusion that no consideration was provided. After all, A has promised to do *less* than what the contract requires. However, by interpreting the second agreement as a bona fide compromise of the dispute the law regards B's promise as supported by consideration.

The guiding principle, as stated by Mason J in *Wigan v Edwards*,[175] is that:[176]

> a promise to do precisely what the promisor is already bound to do is a sufficient consideration, when it is given by way of a bona fide compromise of a disputed claim, the promisor having asserted that he is not bound to perform the obligation under the pre-existing contract or that he has a cause of action under that contract.

The leading modern cases[177] show that the giving up of a seriously asserted claim may result in an enforceable compromise if the assertion was made bona fide.[178]

[351] Claim may be bad in law. What is the position if it transpires that the claim by one (or both) of the parties under the original contract was unfounded? Consistently with what is said above,[179] the compromise contract is still valid. The fact that the claim is bad in law does not prevent its compromise being valuable consideration.[180] It does not matter that the promisee knew the promisor's claim to be bad. Nor is it necessary for the promisee to have issued proceedings to enforce the claim. Again, a promise to abandon a suit in whole or part *already commenced* is a valuable consideration where there was a bona fide claim.[181] Similar principles apply where there is a promise to forbear (or actual forbearance) to enforce a claim, rather than its abandonment.[182]

---

175. (1973) 47 ALJR 586.
176. (1973) 47 ALJR 586 at 594–5.
177. See, eg *Callisher v Bischoffsheim* (1870) LR 5 QB 449; *Miles v New Zealand Alford Estate Co* (1886) 32 Ch D 266; *McDermott v Black* (1940) 63 CLR 161; *Wigan v Edwards* (1973) 1 ALR 497; 47 ALJR 586.
178. In some cases it will be found that the plaintiff furnished valuable consideration, if not by surrendering a claim of right, then by delivering up into the possession of the defendant a document which creates or supports the existence of that right and which it was in the defendant's interests to have. See *Haigh v Brooks* (1839) 10 A & E 309; 113 ER 119; *Veitch v Sinclair* [1975] 1 NZLR 264.
179. See [350].
180. See, eg *Callisher v Bischoffsheim* (1870) LR 5 QB 449; *Spies v Commonwealth Bank of Australia* (1991) 24 NSWLR 691 at 698.
181. See *Butler v Fairclough* (1917) 23 CLR 78 at 96 and further [352].
182. See, eg *Larkin v Girvan* (1940) 40 SR (NSW) 365; *Hercules Motors Pty Ltd v Schubert* (1953) 53 SR (NSW) 301; *Ballantyne v Phillott* (1961) 105 CLR 379; *The Proodos C* [1981] 3 All ER 189 at 192; *Woolworths Ltd v Kelly* (1991) 22 NSWLR 189.

It must be acknowledged that acceptance of compromise of a bona fide claim as consideration derives more from practical necessity than from logic. It would be intolerable that it should be open to a party to undo a compromise by showing that after all the other party's claim could not have succeeded. On the other hand, where it transpires that the claim was not even an arguable one, it is difficult to find anything of legal value which the claimant has surrendered.

[352] **Claim must be honestly made.** A promise not to sue at all, that is, an abandonment of a substantive claim, is a valuable consideration, if there be either liability or a bona fide belief of liability.[183] If it were not for the requirement that the claim be 'a serious claim honestly made'[184] it would be possible by issuing or threatening the issue of proceedings, or by withholding performance of an existing contract, to extract an unfair advantage. In *Ballantyne v Phillott*[185] Dixon CJ, when inquiring into what 'value or import' was to be found in the alleged surrender of rights in that case, observed that the other party could have expected trouble if he had not settled. Since this can probably be said in relation to all serious claims which are asserted bona fide, it indicates a 'benefit' to the other party which will be inherent in every giving up of such a claim. Moreover, true to its lack of concern with adequacy of consideration, so long as the claim is honestly made it does not matter that one party benefits more from the compromise than the other.[186]

[353] **Vexatious and frivolous claims.** Is 'good faith' the only test which the asserted claim must satisfy? In *Miles v New Zealand Alford Estate Co*[187] Bowen LJ considered[188] that it must also appear that the claim was not vexatious or frivolous. In *Wigan v Edwards*[189] the High Court did not decide whether the more stringent formulation of Bowen LJ was correct. All members of the court held that a vendor's undertaking was binding, as having been given as part of a compromise of the purchasers' claim — that they were not bound to perform — in which they honestly believed. Mason J also considered that the claim was not frivolous or vexatious. Clearly, it would be unlikely for a court to find that a claim which a contracting party honestly believed to be well founded was in fact vexatious or frivolous.[190]

[354] **Accord and satisfaction.** Analysis of a compromise agreement may yield more than one possible legal construct. The bargained-for consideration may be the release of a cause of action, or a promise of

---

183. *Butler v Fairclough* (1917) 23 CLR 78 at 96.
184. *Miles v New Zealand Alford Estate Co* (1886) 32 Ch D 266 at 283 per Cotton LJ.
185. (1961) 105 CLR 379 at 390.
186. Cf *Baltic Shipping Co v Merchant 'Mikhail Lermontov'* (1994) 36 NSWLR 361 at 371.
187. (1886) 32 Ch D 266.
188. (1886) 32 Ch D 266 at 291–2. The views of Cotton LJ and Fry LJ on this question (see at 283–4, 297–8) were less clear though not contradictory of that of Bowen LJ.
189. (1973) 47 ALJR 586.
190. In *Cook v Wright* (1861) 1 B & S 559 at 569; 121 ER 822 at 826 the asserted claim was referred to as 'a reasonable claim on one side which it was bona fide intended to pursue'. See also *General Credits Ltd v Ebsworth* [1986] 2 Qd R 162.

release.[191] In each case it is said that an 'accord', that is, agreement, has been reached, but only in the former is the cause of action extinguished immediately. In the former there is an 'accord and satisfaction', effective at law, by virtue of the acceptance of the new promise in satisfaction of the cause of action. The latter — a mere promise to release — is called an 'accord executory'. Although effective in equity as a contract itself, the cause of action is extinguished only when the promise is performed.

Identification of the bargained-for consideration has presented particular difficulty in this context. In *McDermott v Black*[192] Dixon J explained:[193]

> The essence of accord and satisfaction is the acceptance by the plaintiff of something in place of his cause of action. What he takes is a matter depending on his own consent or agreement. It may be a promise or contract or it may be the act or thing promised. But, whatever it is, until it is provided and accepted the cause of action remains alive and unimpaired. The accord is the agreement or consent to accept the satisfaction. Until the satisfaction is given the accord remains executory and cannot bar the claim. The distinction between an accord executory and an accord and satisfaction remains as valid and as important as ever. An accord executory neither extinguishes the old cause of action nor affords a new one ... An executory promise or series of promises given in consideration of the abandonment of the claim may be accepted in substitution or satisfaction of the existing liability. Or, on the other hand, promises may be given by the party liable that he will satisfy the claim by doing an act, making over a thing or paying an ascertained sum of money and the other party may agree to accept, not the promise, but the act, thing or money in satisfaction of his claim. If the agreement is to accept the promise in satisfaction, the discharge of the liability is immediate; if the performance, then there is no discharge unless and until the promise is performed.

Although usually the subject of an express agreement, there is no objection to an implied abandonment of a claim. For example, in *Allied Marine Transport Ltd v Vale do Rio Doce Navegacao SA (The Leonides D)*[194] the English Court of Appeal pointed out that a reference to arbitration might be discharged by the parties conducting themselves in a way which shows that each has abandoned its claim to receive an award.

[355] **Forbearance to sue.** A promise not to sue for a limited period, definite or indefinite, is a valuable consideration where the substantive claim is one for which the other party is liable.[195] Thus, if A owes B $10,000 due on 1 March, on that day A may ask B not to sue for the debt. An agreement might be reached, providing that in consideration of B not suing until, say, 1 June, A agrees to grant B a mortgage of A's house. The promise by B may be enforced by A. The same is true if, *at A's request*, B forbears to sue until 1 June on the understanding that A will provide a mortgage as security. In such a case the issue will usually be whether B has provided consideration for A's promise. Where the promise to forbear is not for a fixed time, a reasonable time is implied,[196] but where the agreed

---

191. Cf *Nissho Iwai (Australia) Ltd v Oskar* [1984] WAR 53.
192. (1940) 63 CLR 161.
193. (1940) 63 CLR 161 at 183–5.
194. [1985] 1 WLR 925 at 933. Whether the claimant's cause of action remains intact is a separate question.
195. *Butler v Fairclough* (1917) 23 CLR 78 at 96.

consideration is simply actual forbearance the notion of forbearance for a reasonable period is apparently not implied, 'some degree of' or a 'certain amount of' forbearance being sufficient.[197]

A forbearance to sue, whether in a court of law or some other forum for dispute resolution, is distinguishable from the giving up of a claim.[198] The giving up of a claim raises the single issue of the legal value of the abandonment of an invalid claim. A forbearance may or may not raise this issue, but any forbearance which is less than permanent will raise the different question whether a forbearance must be of certain minimum duration in order to be valid consideration. Since forbearance from acting in a specified way is generally a valid consideration, it is in principle difficult to see why a forbearance from issuing proceedings, or from further prosecuting particular proceedings already on foot, for even a very short time, should not be a good consideration since the adequacy of consideration is not a concern of the courts. This approach has in fact been taken in the cases.[199] Thus, a creditor's forbearance (or the promise thereof) will support a promise by the debtor to pay interest on the debt or to furnish security for it, or to procure a guarantee or other species of promise by a third party. However, mere temporary forbearance to sue where there is no liability is no consideration, even if the claim is disputed.[200]

It is no part of the law that contracts involving these forms of consideration must be express, or that these forms of consideration must have been identified by the parties expressly. Thus, a request to forbear, while essential, need not be express.[201] However, a forbearance (like a release) not requested expressly or by implication, or requested but given without being induced by that request, is no consideration.[202] The cases suggest that a request will be easily inferred, at least where a debtor promises the creditor to secure payment of the debt.[203] Careful construction of documents and analysis of all the circumstances may warrant a finding that there was an implied promise to surrender a cause of action or to forbear from suing and that the parties had agreed that this, or the actual surrender or forbearance itself, was the consideration bargained for by the promisee as the price of a promise which itself may have been implied rather than express. The difficult question is: on the facts, was a release or forbearance, or a promise of one or the other, requested?

---

196. *Payne v Wilson* (1827) 7 B & C 423; 108 ER 781; *Oldershaw v King* (1857) 2 H & N 517; 157 ER 213.
197. *Alliance Bank v Broom* (1864) 2 Dr & Sm 289 at 292; 62 ER 631 at 632–3.
198. See *Larkin v Girvan* (1940) 40 SR (NSW) 365 (arbitration).
199. See *Alliance Bank v Broom* (1864) 2 Dr & Sm 289; 62 ER 631; *Boettcher v Boettcher* [1948] Qd St R 73; *Griffiths v Knight* [1960] SR (NSW) 353.
200. *Butler v Fairclough* (1917) 23 CLR 78 at 96.
201. *Crears v Hunter* (1887) 19 QBD 341; *Newton v State Government Insurance Office (Qld)* [1986] 1 Qd R 431 at 444.
202. See *Murphy v Timms* [1987] 2 Qd R 550.
203. See, eg *Alliance Bank v Broom* (1864) 2 Dr & Sm 289; 62 ER 631.

Part Payment of Debt

The rule: not consideration

[356] Origin of the rule. Before the doctrine of consideration developed as a constraint on the action of assumpsit, the proposition that part payment of a debt could not satisfy the debt was judicially accepted, at least as early as 1455.[204] The rule was stated by the Court of Common Pleas in 1602 in *Pinnel's Case*:[205]

> It was resolved by the whole court, that payment of a lesser sum on the day in satisfaction of a greater, cannot be any satisfaction for the whole, because it appears to the Judges that by no possibility, a lesser sum can be a satisfaction to the plaintiff for a greater sum: but the gift of a horse, hawk, or robe, etc., in satisfaction is good. For it shall be intended that a horse, hawk, or robe, etc., might be more beneficial to the plaintiff than the money, in respect of some circumstance, or otherwise the plaintiff would not have accepted of it in satisfaction. But when the whole sum is due, by no intendment the acceptance of parcel can be a satisfaction to the plaintiff ...

The judgment goes on to make it clear that, payment of a lesser sum having been made earlier than the date for payment, the defendant might have succeeded if he had pleaded an accord and satisfaction rather than that he had made part payment which the plaintiff had accepted in full satisfaction.

Pinnel's Case was an action on a bond. A century later in *Cumber v Wayne*[206] the King's Bench held that where a debt of £15 was owed, payment of a smaller amount could not be relied on as a satisfaction unless there was consideration for the relinquishment of the balance, and similarly that the creditor's agreement to accept a promissory note for £5 was not a good plea to an action for the £15.

[357] Acceptance of the rule under the modern law. Although the origin of the rules relating to surrender of the whole or part of a debt antedates the origin of the contractual doctrine, and notwithstanding that, conceptually, the extinguishment of a chose in action such as a debt differs from the giving of a promise, by the time *Pinnel's Case*[207] was decided, it was probably accepted that consideration was necessary for the creation of promissory obligation. The modern cases refer to *Pinnel's Case* and *Cumber v Wayne*[208] as illustrating the contractual doctrine of consideration. This explanation received the imprimatur of the House of Lords in *Foakes v Beer*.[209]

Mrs Beer was the judgment creditor of Dr Foakes for £2090.19.0. They entered into a written agreement reciting his request for time to pay and the parties' agreement that 'in consideration' of his paying to her £500

---

204. *Anon* (1455) YB 33 Henry IV f 48 pl 32; *Anon* (1495) YB 10 Henry VII f 4 pl 4.
205. (1602) 5 Co Rep 117a; 77 ER 237. See also *Richards v Bartlet* (1584) 1 Leon 19; 74 ER 17; *Goring v Goring* (1602) Yelv 11; 80 ER 8.
206. (1721) 1 Stra 426; 93 ER 613.
207. (1602) 5 Co Rep 117a; 77 ER 237.
208. (1721) 1 Stra 426; 93 ER 613.
209. (1884) 9 App Cas 605. See Janet O'Sullivan, 'In Defence of Foakes v Beer' [1996] *CLJ* 219.

forthwith in part-satisfaction 'and on condition of his paying' £150 on 1 July and 1 January or within one calendar month after each of those days in each year until the full sum of £2090.19.0 should have been fully paid and satisfied, she agreed not to enforce the judgment. Foakes ultimately paid off the judgment debt but Beer sued him for £360, the interest on the judgment. He pleaded the agreement, and she replied that the agreement was not binding for lack of consideration. The plea was held bad. Even if there was a promise by Beer to forgive the whole debt (including interest), which was not considered to be the proper construction of the agreement, there was no consideration to support the promise.

Exceptions

[358] Deeds and nominal consideration. The easiest way to make binding a promise to accept part of a debt as a discharge of the whole is to put the agreement in a deed. Consideration is not then required.[210]

Apart from the deed (and of course compromise of the claim),[211] a familiar way of finding consideration is in the presence of nominal consideration. This device was recognised in *Pinnel's Case*[212] itself, in references to 'the gift of a horse, hawk, or robe, etc [which] might be more beneficial to the plaintiff than the money'. Similarly, payment at a date before the debt is due, payment at a place selected for the convenience of the creditor (not being the place originally agreed), or the acceptance of a bill of exchange (other than a personal cheque) all count as nominal consideration.

The presence of consideration is enough to take the agreement outside the general rule even though it will usually be purely nominal. The impact is that a promise to accept $999 in discharge of a debt of $1000 presently due is not supported by consideration whereas a promise to accept $1 and an old sandshoe in complete discharge of the $1000 debt is enforceable. The absurdity of this is patent.

[359] Part payment of a debt by a third party. Acceptance by a creditor of part payment by a third party in full settlement is a good defence to the creditor's action against the debtor for the balance.[213] The explanation usually given is that it would be a fraud on the third party or a breach of contract (which the court will not facilitate) if the creditor were allowed to recover.

[360] Compositions with creditors under the *Bankruptcy Act* 1966 (Cth). Section 187(1) of the *Bankruptcy Act* 1966 (Cth) defines 'composition' for the purposes of Pt X of that Act as an arrangement by which the creditors of a debtor:

---

210. See generally [312].
211. See [350]–[355].
212. (1602) 5 Co Rep 117a; 77 ER 237 (see [356]).
213. *Welby v Drake* (1825) 1 C & P 557; 171 ER 1315; *Cook v Lister* (1863) 13 CB (NS) 543 at 595; 143 ER 215 at 235–6; *Hirachand Punamchand v Temple* [1911] 2 KB 330.

(a) agree to accept payment of the debts due to them by instalments; or

(b) agree to accept, in full satisfaction of the debts due to them, less than the full amount of those debts, whether in the form of money or other property and whether by instalments or otherwise.

Each creditor agrees to forgo in part his or her legal rights in consideration of a similar undertaking by each other creditor party to the composition,[214] and so it is clear that the composition is enforceable as between the creditor parties to it. Assuming that the debtor is a party to the composition so that no difficulty of privity of contract exists,[215] the composition will be binding if the debtor has procured the participation of the creditors in the composition.[216] Where, however, is the consideration moving from the debtor which enables the debtor to defend an action by a creditor for recovery of the full amount of the debt?

First, the principle of *Coulls v Bagot's Executor and Trustee Co Ltd*[217] may be available: each creditor's promise may have been made to the debtor and the other creditors jointly and so be enforceable by the debtor so long as consideration has been furnished by the debtor's co-joint promisees.

Second, there are suggestions that it would be fraud on the other creditors (and on the debtor) for a creditor to recover in breach of the composition agreement since, by the making of the agreement, the other creditors have been induced to refrain from seeking recovery of their debts and the debtor from paying them, with the result that the plaintiff creditor would get an unintended preference.[218]

Finally, it has been suggested[219] that 'compositions with creditors may be valid despite the absence of consideration or despite the inability to perceive consideration moving from the debtor'.

Criticism

[361] Introduction. The most fundamental question about consideration today is whether the requirement should be retained. In 1937 the English Law Revision Committee said[220] 'inconvenience and possible injustice resulting from the doctrine of consideration raise the question whether it presents countervailing advantages which justify its retention'. Developments since 1937, not only in the pragmatic approach to consideration which pervades the commercial contract cases,[221] but also in the law of estoppel,[222] indicate that a requirement of consideration is more

---

214. *Boothbey v Sowden* (1812) 3 Camp 175; 170 ER 1346; *Good v Cheeseman* (1831) 2 B & Ad 328; 109 ER 1165.
215. See generally Chapter 9.
216. See, eg *Re Burns; Ex parte National Mutual Life Association of Australasia Ltd* (1992) 117 ALR 174.
217. (1967) 119 CLR 460 (see [322]).
218. See *Cook v Lister* (1863) 13 CBNS 543 at 595; 143 ER 215 at 235. Cf *Couldery v Bartrum* (1881) 19 Ch D 394; *Hirachand Punamchand v Temple* [1911] 2 KB 330; *Re Pearse* [1905] VLR 446; *E T Fisher Pty Ltd v English Scottish & Australian Bank Ltd* (1940) 64 CLR 84.
219. See *Estate of Whitehead (dec'd)* (1986) 44 SASR 402 at 406.
220. *Sixth Interim Report*, Cmd 5449, 1937, para 26.
221. See further [364].
222. See [365]–[387].

likely to cause inconvenience than injustice. There is in fact little likelihood of the requirement being abolished, even if that were thought desirable.[223]

Another, also fairly fundamental question, is whether contract law should not develop the enforcement of promises without a requirement of consideration being satisfied. This point was alluded to earlier in the discussion of contract theory.[224] It may also be pointed out that American law, under the guidance of the *Restatements*,[225] has got on quite well with a body of law dealing with the enforcement of promises not supported by consideration.[226]

There is an air of unreality to many of the rules discussed above, and their operation has been criticised. For example, in *Ward v Byham*,[227] Lord Denning MR accepted as a general proposition that performance of or a promise to perform an existing legal duty of any class should be regarded as good consideration because[228] 'it is a benefit to the person to whom it is given', and if a person 'gets the benefit for which he stipulated he ought to honour his promise'.

We concentrate on the existing duty rules as those most in need of reform. There is, however, a more general approach to the law which should be mentioned, namely, the adoption of a subjective notion of consideration.[229]

[362] Public policy. The distinction between a promise to perform an existing duty owed to a party to a contract and one owed to a third party seems illogical, particularly where (as in *Pao On v Lau Yiu Long*)[230] the defendant has a financial interest in the performance of the contract with the third party. The promise is still to do precisely what is required under an existing obligation. There is no public policy objection to regarding the promise as a sufficient consideration, particularly when regard is had to the concept of economic duress.[231]

Similarly, the distinction between a promise to perform a public duty and a promise to perform a private (contractual) duty is artificial. Consideration is an inappropriate mechanism for controlling the promises of those subject to a duty owed to the public at large. While it would, for example, be against the public interest to permit a public officer to recover a promised reward for carrying out official duties, no comparable considerations apply in the case of a promise to perform contractual obligations owed to a party to a contract. Thus, we agree with the view that a promise to perform a public duty should be regarded as a sufficient

---

223. Cf Samuel Stoljar, 'Bargain and Non-bargain Promises' (1988) 18 *UWALR* 119.
224. See [113].
225. See further [387] (promissory estoppel).
226. But cf Samuel Stoljar, 'Estoppel and Contract Theory' (1990) 3 *JCL* 1.
227. [1956] 2 All ER 318 (see [342]).
228. [1956] 2 All ER 318 at 319.
229. See [364].
230. [1980] AC 614 (see [349]).
231. See further [363].

consideration.[232] But the enforcement of the promise which it supports should be denied if public policy so requires.[233]

[363] Economic duress. Given that a promisor (A) has regarded a promise by B to perform an existing duty as consideration for a promise on A's part, the law serves no useful purpose in denying the enforceability of A's promise on the basis that it was not given for value. What is of concern to the law is that A's promise should not have been obtained by extortion. Thus, A's promise to pay B extra money if B will do that which B is already contractually bound to A to do may raise the spectre of economic duress. Why would A make or promise an additional payment unless B was refusing to perform without it? If the circumstances satisfy the tests for operative economic duress,[234] the contract will be voidable by A even if consideration is present.

It is suggested that public policy has no real relevance to the contractual duty cases[235] and that promises to perform such duties should be regarded as valid. The relevance of economic duress is that if a party entered into the agreement as a result of duress there is a right to avoid the contract. The same is true of promises induced by factors such as misrepresentation. Although such factors do not deny the validity of the promise, they nevertheless provide an important safety valve.

[364] Business practice and subjectivity in consideration. Consideration is neither entirely logical nor internally consistent. In many respects the concept is very subjective. In other words, in deciding whether there is something of value, the law generally takes the view that (absent policy issues) what a promisor regards as valuable will amount to consideration. We can see this, for example, in the rule that consideration must be sufficient but need not be adequate. This illustrates that the courts are alive to the need to protect properly negotiated agreements by which each party considers that a valuable benefit has been obtained under a contract.

On the other hand, we have seen that objectivity is sometimes insisted on in the context of the existing duty rule. In other words, because the promise to perform a duty already owed is objectively equal to that duty, and because the duty already exists, there is no consideration. It is by no means clear that this approach reflects what goes on in contract practice. Indeed, as far back as *Foakes v Beer*[236] Lord Blackburn said:[237]

> What principally weighs with me in thinking that Lord Coke [in *Pinnel's Case*][238] made a mistake of fact is my conviction that all men of business, whether merchants or tradesmen, do every day recognise and act on the ground that prompt payment of a part of their demand may be more beneficial to them than it would be to insist on their rights and enforce

---

232. Arguably this would be a return to what may have been the original approach, see [345].
233. See generally on public policy [1619]–[1653].
234. See generally Chapter 13.
235. See *Pao On v Lau Yiu Long* [1980] AC 614 at 634–5.
236. (1884) 9 App Cas 605.
237. (1884) 9 App Cas 605 at 622.
238. (1602) 5 Co Rep 117a; 77 ER 237.

payment of the whole. Even where the debtor is perfectly solvent, and sure to pay at last, this often is so. Where the credit of the debtor is doubtful it must be more so.

Although he did not dissent from the opinion that a promise to pay part of a debt cannot be consideration, other judges have not been so timid. For example, the majority decision in *The Eurymedon*[239] is clearly based on the need to ensure that legal recognition is given to commercial understandings as to responsibility in arrangements for the carriage of goods.

The question may therefore be raised, in relation to the existing duty rule: why not regard the promise to perform such a duty as valid consideration whenever the other party treated it as valuable? Adoption of this view does not involve the abolition of the requirement of consideration. In fact, it merely requires an extension of the view that the bargain element — a central feature of consideration — may be satisfied even though, objectively, the bargain had no value.

Promissory Estoppel[240]

Estoppel Generally

[365] Impact of estoppel. Criticism of the consideration requirement must be made with an appreciation of what has been happening, particularly in recent years, under the guise of estoppel. To say that a person is 'estopped' is to say that a person is 'precluded'. Estoppel therefore refers to situations where a person is precluded from saying something. That 'something' varies, but it relevantly refers to the denial of the consequences achieved by conduct following a representation or promise.

Many of the possible injustices of consideration have been averted by use of estoppel. For example, in *D & C Builders Ltd v Rees*[241] Lord Denning MR expressed the view[242] that the principle of promissory estoppel

> has been applied to cases where a creditor agrees to accept a lesser sum in discharge of a greater. So much so that we can now say that, when a creditor and a debtor enter upon a course of negotiation, which leads the debtor to suppose that, on payment of the lesser sum, the creditor will not enforce payment of the balance, and on the faith thereof the debtor pays the lesser sum and the creditor accepts it as satisfaction: then the creditor will not be

---

239. [1975] AC 154 (see [349]). See also *General Accident Fire and Life Assurance Corp v Tanter (The Zephyr)* [1985] 2 Lloyd's Rep 529 at 538.
240. See, eg Paul Finn, 'Equitable Estoppel' in Finn, ed, *Essays in Equity*, 1985, p 59; J W Carter, 'Contract, Restitution and Promissory Estoppel' (1989) 12 *UNSWLJ* 30; K E Lindgren, 'Estoppel in Contract' (1989) 12 *UNSWLJ* 153; Patrick Parkinson, 'Equitable Estoppel: Developments after Waltons Stores (Interstate) Ltd v Maher' (1990) 3 *JCL* 50; Justice D N Angel, 'Some Reflections on Privity, Consideration, Estoppel and Good Faith' (1992) 66 *ALJ* 484; Michael Spence, 'Australian Estoppel and the Protection of Reliance' (1997) 11 *JCL* 203. See also Rory Derham, 'Estoppel by Convention' (1997) 71 *ALJ* 860 and 956; Andrew Robertson, 'The Failure of Economic Analysis of Promissory Estoppel' (1999) 15 *JCL* 69.
241. [1966] 2 QB 617.
242. [1966] 2 QB 617 at 624.

allowed to enforce payment of the balance when it would be inequitable to do so ...

Whether this statement is a perfectly accurate assessment of the law may be debated, but it is nevertheless clear that all the rules on consideration must be taken with a very large grain of estoppel flavoured salt.

[366] Forms of estoppel. If the terminology is taken seriously there is a veritable smorgasbord of concepts to choose from under the heading of estoppel. References may be found to common law estoppel, estoppel in pais, estoppel by representation, estoppel by convention, equitable estoppel, promissory estoppel, *High Trees* estoppel, proprietary estoppel, estoppel by acquiescence, estoppel of record and issue estoppel. Some of these — the list is not exhaustive — such as 'issue estoppel' have nothing to do with consideration.

If ever these expressions were intended to describe distinct types of estoppel, they do not do so today. Clearly, some are merely alternative descriptions of the same thing, and many may be grouped together by reference to a unifying concept of unconscionability.[243] The broad traditional division is between common law estoppels, based on representations of fact, and equitable versions relying on promises or assurances. However, even this division must now be regarded as of doubtful validity.

[367] Object of estoppel. In *Thompson v Palmer*[244] Dixon J explained that the object of estoppel 'is to prevent an unjust departure by one person from an assumption adopted by another as the basis of some act or omission which, unless the assumption be adhered to, would operate to that other's detriment'. In *Grundt v Great Boulder Pty Gold Mines Ltd*[245] he explained the meaning of this in these terms:[246]

> This means that the real detriment or harm from which the law seeks to give protection is that which would flow from the change of position if the assumption were deserted that led to it. So long as the assumption is adhered to, the party who altered his situation upon the faith of it cannot complain. His complaint is that when afterwards the other party makes a different state of affairs the basis of an assertion of right against him then, if it is allowed, his own original change of position will operate as a detriment. His action or inaction must be such that, if the assumption upon which he proceeded were shown to be wrong and an inconsistent state of affairs were accepted as the foundation of the rights and duties of himself and the opposite party, the consequence would be to make his original act or failure to act as a source of prejudice.

[368] Protection of reliance. A significant feature of estoppel is that, to a greater extent than is allowed for under the bargain theory of consideration,[247] it protects a person from the injurious consequences of reliance. In *Thompson v Palmer*[248] Dixon J said:[249]

---

243. See [369].
244. (1933) 49 CLR 507 at 547.
245. (1937) 59 CLR 641.
246. (1937) 59 CLR 641 at 674–5.
247. See [309].
248. (1933) 49 CLR 507.

Whether a departure by a party from the assumption should be considered unjust and inadmissible depends on the part taken by him in occasioning its adoption by the other party. He may be required to abide by the assumption because it formed the conventional basis upon which the parties entered into contractual or other mutual relations, such as bailment; or because he has exercised against the other party rights which would exist only if the assumption were correct ... ; or because knowing the mistake the other laboured under, he refrained from correcting him when it was his duty to do so; or because his imprudence, where care was required of him, was a proximate cause of the other party's adopting and acting upon the faith of the assumption; or because he directly made representations upon which the other party founded the assumption. But, in each case, he is not bound to adhere to the assumption unless, as a result of adopting it as the basis of action or inaction, the other party will have placed himself in a position of material disadvantage if departure from the assumption be permitted.

And in *Grundt v Great Boulder Pty Gold Mines Ltd*[250] Dixon J said:[251]

> One condition appears always to be indispensable. [The party who has adopted the assumption] must have so acted or abstained from acting upon the footing of the state of affairs assumed that he would suffer a detriment if the opposite party were afterwards allowed to set up rights against him inconsistent with the assumption. In stating this essential condition, particularly where the estoppel flows from representation, it is often said simply that the party asserting the estoppel must have been induced to act to his detriment. Although substantially such a statement is correct and leads to no misunderstanding, it does not bring out clearly the basal purpose of the doctrine.

[369] **Unconscionability.** The recent authorities have tended to unify the various types of estoppel and to insist that the doctrine should not be seen as a 'series of independent rules'.[252] It is clear that, in this unification or rationalisation, a key component is 'unconscionability'. That is to say, a person will be estopped only (assuming other criteria to be satisfied) if it would be unconscionable to depart from the assumption relied upon by the other party.[253] Indeed, the clear trend of the authorities is to treat unconscionability as the touchstone for all relevant forms of estoppel.[254]

[370] **Relevance.** Our main concern is with gratuitous promises, and the extent to which estoppel is a means of enforcing such promises. Because of this, we concentrate on promissory estoppel. We need to consider the

---

249. (1933) 49 CLR 507 at 547.
250. (1937) 59 CLR 641.
251. (1937) 59 CLR 641 at 674–5.
252. *Commonwealth of Australia v Verwayen* (1990) 170 CLR 394 at 411; 95 ALR 321. See also A F Mason, 'Contract, Good Faith and Equitable Standards in Fair Dealing' (2000) 116 *LQR* 66 at 91. The point was left open in *Giumelli v Giumelli* (1999) 196 CLR 101 at 112; 161 ALR 473.
253. See further [381], and generally on unconscionability Chapter 15.
254. See, eg *Amalgamated Investment & Property Co Ltd v Texas Commerce International Bank Ltd* [1982] QB 84 at 106; *Taylors Fashions Ltd v Liverpool Victoria Trustees Co Ltd* [1982] QB 133n at 151; *Waltons Stores (Interstate) Ltd v Maher* (1988) 164 CLR 387 at 404, 419; 76 ALR 513; *Silovi Pty Ltd v Barbaro* (1988) 13 NSWLR 466 at 472; *Norwegian American Cruises A/S v Paul Mundy Ltd (The Vistafjord)* [1988] 2 Lloyd's Rep 343; *Commonwealth of Australia v Verwayen* (1990) 170 CLR 394 especially at 409ff, 431ff, 453–4, 500.

circumstances which give rise to an estoppel and the relation between estoppel and promises supported by consideration. Recalling the idea that estoppel refers to an ability to deny, we are concerned with the inability to deny that a promise is binding even though the promise is not actually supported by consideration.

Of course, merely saying that a person may be precluded from denying that a promise was made does not take us very far. We also need to know how far the estoppel extends, that is, its impact on rights and remedies. Here a word of caution is necessary. It is misleading, and generally wrong, to say that a promise binding by virtue of estoppel has the same effect as a promise binding because it is supported by consideration. Further guidance can be gained from two contrasting perspectives.

First, a promise may be made in the context of a pre-existing legal relationship, such as a contractual relationship. The issue may then arise whether the person who made the promise is estopped (precluded) from setting up a right arising from that relationship. Generally, estoppel is given a sufficient operation merely by regarding the promise as a valid defence to the assertion of the right which arose from the relationship.

Second, a promise may be made in a situation where there is no pre-existing legal relationship. A holding of estoppel is likely to be much more controversial, since the effect may be to preclude the promisor from asserting that no rights arose from the promise. By definition there is no consideration, and so the *direct* enforcement of the promise results in the promisee acquiring legal (or equitable) rights which would not otherwise exist. To allow the promisee to treat the promise as fully binding tends to contradict the consideration requirement. Yet this is, on occasion, the practical result.

It follows from this that another way of expressing the two perspectives is to say that estoppel may be 'defensive' or 'offensive'. In its former guise estoppel is sometimes described as a rule of evidence. That is to say, the operation of estoppel is not to create or change legal rights or obligations, so much as to preclude a party from setting up the legal rights or obligations which govern the parties' relationship. From the second perspective estoppel may be used more aggressively, to assist in the creation of rights where none existed before.

Estoppel in the Context of a Pre-existing Legal Relationship

[371] **Introduction.** The least controversial context for estoppel is where there is a pre-existing legal relationship between the person who made a representation, promise or assurance and the person to whom it was made. Notwithstanding our contractual focus, it is clear that the legal relation need not be contractual in character.[255]

---

255. See, eg *Commonwealth of Australia v Verwayen* (1990) 170 CLR 394 (pre-existing relation of plaintiff and defendant).

[372] The principle in *Hughes*' case. Until 1983 there was some doubt as to whether a principle of promissory estoppel was applicable in Australia. In England there was support for a doctrine of promissory estoppel having the effect of precluding a promisor from resiling from a promise, at least without first giving reasonable notice to the other party that the operation of the contract is to be reinstated. A statement in *Hughes v Metropolitan Railway Co*[256] was the origin of this. In a much cited passage, Lord Cairns LC said:[257]

> ... it is the first principle upon which all Courts of Equity proceed, that if parties who have entered into definite and distinct terms involving certain legal results — certain penalties or legal forfeiture — afterwards by their own act or with their own consent enter upon a course of negotiation which has the effect of leading one of the parties to suppose that the strict rights arising under the contract will not be enforced, or will be kept in suspense, or held in abeyance, the person who otherwise might have enforced those rights will not be allowed to enforce them where it would be inequitable having regard to the dealings which have thus taken place between the parties.

The case was treated by Denning J in *Central London Property Trust v High Trees House Ltd*[258] as authority for the existence of a general principle of estoppel, certainly in equity and perhaps also at common law, which would seem wide enough to embrace, in appropriate circumstances, a promise not to enforce (or a promise to suspend) legal contractual rights. In *High Trees* the plaintiff leased a block of flats to the defendant under a 99-year lease. The war made the flats difficult for High Trees to let out and it was clear that it could not pay the rent out of the profits from lettings. In 1940 the plaintiff agreed to reduce the rent and the reduced rent was paid. In 1945 (by which time the flats were again fully let) the plaintiff asserted that it was entitled to the full rent and brought proceedings to recover the amount of the additional rent for the last two quarters of 1945. Denning J considered that the parties' intention was that the reduction should continue only as long as the low occupancy rate due to the war continued, with the result that by its own terms the arrangement had ended in early 1945. The defendant was therefore liable to pay the amount of the original rent thereafter.

More importantly for present purposes, Denning J considered that if the plaintiff had sued for the rent forgone from 1940 to 1945, it would not have been able to go back on its promise. He said:[259]

> The courts have not gone so far as to give a cause of action in damages for the breach of such a promise, but they have refused to allow the party making it to act inconsistently with it. It is in that sense, and that sense only, that such a promise gives rise to an estoppel.

That an estoppel could arise out of a promised suspension of contractual rights was accepted by the House of Lords in *Tool Metal Manufacturing Co Ltd v Tungsten Electric Co Ltd*[260] and the Privy Council in *Ajayi v R T Briscoe (Nigeria) Ltd*.[261]

---

256. (1877) 2 App Cas 439. See also *Birmingham & District Land Co v London & North Western Railway Co* (1888) 40 Ch D 268 at 285–6.
257. (1877) 2 App Cas 439 at 448.
258. [1947] KB 130.
259. [1947] KB 130 at 134.

[373] **Recognition in Australia.** Although it was not until 1983, when the High Court decided *Legione v Hateley*,[262] that promissory estoppel was authoritatively recognised in Australia, it would be wrong to say that there was no support for the limited form of promissory estoppel recognised in England.[263] The importance of *Legione v Hateley* was the confirmation of the principle at the highest level.

In *Legione v Hateley* a contract for the sale of land provided for completion on 1 July 1979. Time for completion was of the essence of the contract. The contract also provided that, in the event of breach, a party was not entitled to enforce rights and remedies without first giving to the other a written notice specifying the default and stating the intention to enforce his rights and remedies unless the default was made good within 14 days. If such a notice was given and not complied with, the contract provided that it was to 'become rescinded upon the expiry of the period'. The purchasers failed to complete on 1 July 1979 and the vendors duly gave a notice expiring at midnight on 10 August 1979. On 9 August, a member of the firm of solicitors representing the purchasers telephoned the solicitors for the vendors and spoke to a Ms Williams. His evidence was that he told Ms Williams that the purchasers had arranged bridging finance and would be ready to settle on the following Friday, that is, 17 August, and that she replied 'I think that'll be all right but I'll have to get instructions'. On 14 August 1979 the vendors' solicitors advised the purchasers' solicitors by letter that the vendors declined to sign the transfer of land as the contract 'had been rescinded'. They demanded immediate possession of the land. The purchasers contested the validity of the purported rescission and on 15 August tendered payment of the balance purchase price but the tender was rejected.

The purchasers sought specific performance in the Supreme Court of Victoria and the vendors counter-claimed for a declaration that they had validly rescinded the contract. The trial judge found for the vendors. On appeal, the Full Court by majority held that the vendors were estopped from asserting that the contract had been rescinded prior to the tender on 15 August 1979. The vendors appealed to the High Court. In a joint judgment, Gibbs CJ and Murphy J noted that it was not suggested by counsel for the vendors that the Full Court had erred in holding that promissory estoppel was part of the law of Victoria, and proceeded to review the broad basis of the doctrine in the speech of Lord Cairns in *Hughes v Metropolitan Railway Co.*[264] In another joint judgment, Mason and Deane JJ thought[265] that there was strong English authority for a limited

260. [1955] 2 All ER 657. See also *Combe v Combe* [1951] 2 KB 215; *D & C Builders Ltd v Rees* [1966] 2 QB 617; *W J Alan & Co Ltd v El Nasr Export & Import Co* [1972] 2 QB 189; *Woodhouse AC Israel Cocoa Ltd SA v Nigerian Produce Marketing Co Ltd* [1972] AC 741; *Argy Trading Development Co Ltd v Lapid Developments Ltd* [1977] 1 WLR 444 at 456–7; *Brikom Investments Ltd v Carr* [1979] QB 467.
261. [1964] 1 WLR 1326.
262. (1983) 152 CLR 406; 46 ALR 1.
263. See, eg *Je Maintiendrai Pty Ltd v Quaglia* (1980) 26 SASR 101; *Gollin & Co Ltd v Consolidated Fertilizer Sales Pty Ltd* [1982] Qd R 435; *Reed v Sheehan* (1982) 56 FLR 206. But cf *Barns v Queensland National Bank Ltd* (1906) 3 CLR 925.
264. (1877) 2 App Cas 439 at 448 (see [372]).

doctrine of promissory estoppel, albeit 'restricted to precluding departure from a representation by a person in a pre-existing contractual relationship that he will not enforce his strict contractual rights'. They said:[266]

> The clear trend of recent authorities, the rationale of the general principle underlying estoppel in pais, established equitable principle and the legitimate search for justice and consistency under the law combine to persuade us to conclude that promissory estoppel should be accepted in Australia as applicable between parties in such a relationship.

Gibbs CJ and Murphy J were satisfied as to the existence of those elements necessary to give rise to a promissory estoppel in the context of the case at hand, whereas Mason and Deane JJ (and also Brennan J) thought it impossible to read into Ms Williams's statement any promise or representation to the effect that unless they were advised otherwise, the purchasers could disregard the lapsing of time fixed by the vendor's notice. Accordingly, on this issue[267] the purchasers failed.[268]

Estoppel Where no Pre-existing Legal Relation

[374] Introduction. In 1986 the Privy Council suggested in *Maharaj v Chand*[269] that the 'frontiers' of promissory estoppel are still being worked out. Although that may well still be true, in the High Court's landmark decision in *Waltons Stores (Interstate) Ltd v Maher*,[270] promissory estoppel was applied where there was no pre-existing contractual relation, and an offensive stance for the doctrine was effectively recognised in the decision to award damages. The current uncertainty relates to the impact of that decision on estoppel in general and the relationship between promissory estoppel and the doctrine of consideration in particular.[271]

[375] Estoppel and consideration. Estoppel may operate if, at the time when the promisor seeks to go back on a promise, the circumstances are such that it would be *unjust, unconscionable or inequitable* to allow the promisor to go back on the promise. This operation of estoppel does not depend on the presence of consideration. Such detriment as the promisee may have suffered by reliance on the promise is not a consideration for that promise because, although foreseeable by the promisor, it had not been bargained for. The absence of consideration precludes an ordinary contractual action for damages to enforce the promise. This has often been expressed by saying that estoppel does not create a cause of action where none existed before. Metaphorically, promissory estoppel operates 'as a shield and not as a sword'.[272]

---

265. (1983) 152 CLR 406 at 432.
266. (1983) 152 CLR 406 at 434–5.
267. See also [1979] (relief against forfeiture).
268. See also [1976].
269. [1986] AC 898 at 908.
270. (1988) 164 CLR 387 (see [376]).
271. See further [375], [377], [385]–[386].
272. See, eg *The Proodos C* [1981] 3 All ER 189 at 191; *Amalgamated Investment & Property Co Ltd v Texas Commerce International Bank Ltd* [1982] QB 84 at 105; *Commonwealth of Australia v Verwayen* (1990) 170 CLR 394 at 434ff.

[375]

Opinions are divided on whether this remains an accurate way of expressing the position. In *Waltons Stores (Interstate) Ltd v Maher*[273] the High Court gave effect to an estoppel by awarding damages. On one view this is the direct enforcement of estoppel as a cause of action. However, the result may be viewed differently, by asserting that once an estoppel has arisen, and the defendant is entitled to some relief, the precise form of relief depends on the way in which the estoppel arises, and the discretion of the court.[274]

[376] **Promise to complete transaction on agreed terms.** In *Waltons Stores (Interstate) Ltd v Maher*[275] Mr and Mrs Maher (the Mahers) negotiated with Waltons Stores (Interstate) Ltd (Waltons) for the lease by the latter of a commercial property which the Mahers owned in Nowra. After demolishing an old building on the land, the Mahers were to erect a new building by 5 February 1984. On 21 October 1983 a draft agreement for lease was sent to the Mahers' solicitors. Amendments were discussed and Waltons' solicitors were informed that the Mahers had begun to demolish the old building. On 7 November Waltons' solicitors were told that it would be impossible for the new building to be completed on time unless the agreement was completed in the next day or two. As they were also told, the Mahers did not want to demolish a new part of the old building until it was clear that there were no problems. This conversation proved to be crucial. That same day Waltons' solicitors sent to the Mahers' solicitors fresh documents incorporating the amendments agreed on by the solicitors and stating 'we have not yet obtained our client's specific instructions to each amendment requested, but we believe that approval will be forthcoming. We shall let you know tomorrow if any amendments are not agreed to'.

On 11 November, the documents executed by the Mahers were forwarded to Waltons' solicitors 'by way of exchange', and the Mahers began to demolish the new portion of the old building. Unfortunately, Waltons, who knew what the Mahers were doing, altered its retailing policy. Having received advice that because contracts had not been exchanged it was not bound to proceed, Waltons instructed its solicitors to 'go slow'. The Mahers commenced construction of the new building which was 40 per cent complete by 19 January 1984 when Waltons informed the Mahers of its intention not to sign the proposed lease. At no time prior to this letter was there any indication that the amendments were unacceptable or that Waltons would not exchange contracts.

Notwithstanding the substantial negotiations which had taken place, there was no pre-existing legal relationship between Waltons and the Mahers which would, under earlier views of promissory estoppel, have justified a finding that Waltons was estopped from denying a promise to grant a lease to the Mahers. However, Kearney J awarded the Mahers damages, holding that Waltons was estopped from denying that a

---

273. (1988) 164 CLR 387 (see [376]).
274. See further [383]–[387].
275. (1988) 164 CLR 387. See K C T Sutton, 'Contract by Estoppel' (1988) 1 *JCL* 205; C N H Bagot, 'Equitable Estoppel and Contractual Obligations in the Light of *Waltons v Maher*' (1988) 62 *ALJ* 926.

concluded contract by way of exchange existed. An appeal to the New South Wales Court of Appeal was dismissed.

A further appeal to the High Court was also dismissed.[276] A majority of the court[277] applied promissory estoppel. In their view there was an implied promise to complete the transaction which Waltons was estopped from denying.[278] Mason CJ and Wilson J said:[279]

> [T]he doctrine extends to the enforcement of voluntary promises on the footing that a departure from the basic assumptions underlying the transaction between the parties must be unconscionable. As failure to fulfil a promise does not of itself amount to unconscionable conduct, mere reliance on an executory promise to do something, resulting in the promisee changing his position or suffering detriment, does not bring promissory estoppel into play. Something more would be required. *A-G of Hong Kong v Humphreys Estate (Queen's Gardens) Ltd*[280] suggests that this may be found, if at all, in the creation or encouragement by the party estopped in the other party of an assumption that a contract will come into existence or a promise will be performed and that the other party relied on that assumption to his detriment to the knowledge of the first party.

Deane J and Gaudron J (like the Court of Appeal) based their decisions on common law estoppel. Thus, Deane J thought that Waltons was bound to adhere to an assumption that a binding contract existed, and Gaudron J held that Waltons was bound by an assumption of fact that contracts had been exchanged.

On either view the Mahers were entitled to substantial damages. For the majority the basis was that the Mahers' reliance on the promise had generated an equity in their favour. That is to say, they had a right to the fulfilment of the promise by Waltons to complete the transaction. Normally this would have been enforced by an order for specific performance. But because specific performance was no longer appropriate,[281] they were entitled to damages in lieu of specific performance.[282] This was the means by which the assumption of the Mahers was protected and by which Waltons was prevented from engaging in unconscionable conduct.[283] For Deane J and Gaudron J, relying on common law estoppel, the basis for the action in damages was breach of the contract which Waltons was estopped from denying.[284]

[377] Promise to grant proprietary interest where terms still to be agreed. Prior to *Waltons Stores (Interstate) Ltd v Maher*,[285] promises to

---

276. It was also held that s 54A of the *Conveyancing Act* 1919 (NSW) did not preclude the Mahers from obtaining relief; see [521].
277. Mason CJ, Wilson and Brennan JJ.
278. Contrast *A-G of Hong Kong v Humphreys Estate (Queen's Gardens) Ltd* [1987] AC 114.
279. (1988) 164 CLR 387 at 406.
280. [1987] AC 114.
281. Contrast *S & E Promotions Pty Ltd v Tobin Bros Pty Ltd* (1994) 122 ALR 637 where relief analogous to specific performance was granted.
282. See *S & E Promotions Pty Ltd v Tobin Bros Pty Ltd* (1994) 122 ALR 637 at 640. See generally on damages in lieu of specific performance [2169]–[2173].
283. See further [385].
284. Cf [386].
285. (1988) 164 CLR 387 (see [376]).

grant proprietary interests in land were sometimes enforced, notwithstanding that terms were still to be agreed. Indeed, unlike *Waltons v Maher*, where a contractual relation was clearly contemplated, it was not crucial for there to be an intention to enter any contractual relation. This form of estoppel was usually referred to as 'proprietary estoppel' or 'estoppel by acquiescence'.

Where it applies to such a promise, since the doctrine estops the landowner from denying that the rights or interest exist, an order to transfer or grant as promised may be made. A required circumstance is 'detrimental reliance' by the promisee, and in most cases this has taken the form of effecting improvements on the promisor's land. Thus, a landowner's promise that another has or shall have the land or an interest in it, although not supported by consideration and therefore not enforceable contractually, may, with other circumstances, activate the equitable doctrine of estoppel.[286]

In *Austotel Pty Ltd v Franklins Selfserve Pty Ltd*[287] a letter of intent was given by Franklins to enter into a lease for the purpose of opening a supermarket in Mosman (Sydney). For two reasons this did not constitute a contract. First, Franklins said on a number of occasions that entry into a formal contract would have to wait until other projects were completed. Franklins did, however, say that it would honour the letter of intent save in 'extenuating circumstances'. Second, there was an increase in the floor area for the supermarket so that the rent for the lease was never agreed. Franklins sought an order for the grant of a lease of part of commercial premises in the course of construction. Although no formal lease was signed, Franklins did incur substantial costs and had communicated commercially significant information to Austotel about the setting up of a supermarket. Austotel was under pressure from its financiers to provide evidence of commitment on the part of Franklins. This was given in the form of letters from Franklins to the financiers. One actually said that Franklins had entered into a lease. Ultimately, however, Austotel discontinued negotiations with Franklins and leased the supermarket to another party.

The main argument put forward by Franklins, based on promissory estoppel, was rejected by a majority of the court. Kirby P emphasised the relative equality in bargaining positions of the parties and said[288] that the court should be slow to allow promissory estoppel to operate in clear contradiction to the intention of the parties. Franklins consciously refrained from entering into the lease for good commercial reasons, but it misjudged

---

286. See, eg *Dillwyn v Llewellyn* (1862) 4 De GF & J 517; 45 ER 1285; *Ramsden v Dyson* (1866) LR 1 HL 129; *Plimmer v Mayor of Wellington* (1884) 9 App Cas 699; *Inwards v Baker* [1965] 2 QB 29; *Hussey v Palmer* [1972] 1 WLR 1286; *Crabb v Arun District Council* [1976] Ch 179; *Greasley v Cooke* [1980] 1 WLR 1306; *Riches v Hogben* [1986] 1 Qd R 315; *Lim Teng Huan v Ang Swee Chuan* [1992] 1 WLR 113. For discussion see J D Davies, 'Informal Arrangements Affecting Land' (1979) 8 *Syd LR* 578; Meagher, Gummow and Lehane, *Equity: Doctrines and Remedies*, 3rd ed, 1992, paras 1715–1727. See also *Lee v Ferno Holdings Pty Ltd* (1993) 33 NSWLR 404 (specific performance on basis of estoppel by convention).
287. (1989) 16 NSWLR 582.
288. (1989) 16 NSWLR 582 at 585.

the hold which it had over Austotel. Similarly, Rogers AJA said that for Franklins to succeed it was necessary that an 'equity' in its favour had arisen from the combination of encouragement that a lease would be entered into, and Austotel standing by while expenditure was incurred. But, in his view, it was clear that Franklins had intentionally refrained from entering into the lease and from discussing the price element which proved to be crucial. It was simply impossible, in his view, to identify an assumption on the basis of which Franklins was encouraged to proceed. He said[289] Franklins had made a 'deliberate gamble' that the contract would not materialise.

Priestley JA would have held in favour of Franklins. He pointed to a difference between the estoppel found in *Waltons v Maher*, where there is no dispute about the terms of the agreement, but the terms of the agreement are not enforceable, and the present case, where the plaintiff sought relief of a proprietary kind even though there was no agreement on terms. As is explained above, typical of the latter type of estoppel is the encouragement by the defendant that the plaintiff spend money on the defendant's property in the belief that an interest in that property will be obtained by contract. Priestley JA said that analysis in a series of recent English cases,[290] approved by the Privy Council in *A-G of Hong Kong v Humphreys Estate (Queen's Gardens) Ltd*,[291] if applicable in Australia, would justify the expansion of the scope of promissory estoppel as stated in *Waltons v Maher*. He expressed the principle as follows:[292]

> For equitable estoppel to operate there must be the creation or encouragement by the defendant in the plaintiff of an assumption that a contract will come into existence or a promise be performed or an interest granted to the plaintiff by the defendant, and reliance on that by the plaintiff, in circumstances where departure from the assumption by the defendant would be unconscionable.

The granting of a proprietary remedy — an interest in the defendant's land — is then seen merely as the most appropriate way of giving effect to the equity raised by promissory estoppel. Kirby P agreed with this analysis. But Priestley JA dissented in its application to the facts by concluding that although Franklins was not 'finally committed in a legal sense', it was as a matter of practicality bound to proceed. Austotel had represented that it was unconditionally bound to grant a lease and Franklins relied to its disadvantage to an extent where it was unconscionable for Austotel to be permitted to deny the promise to grant the lease.

While this analysis still awaits express approval by the High Court, it is consistent with that court's attempts to consolidate the various forms of estoppel by means of the unconscionability concept.[293]

---

289. (1989) 16 NSWLR 582 at 620.
290. Such as *Crabb v Arun District Council* [1976] Ch 179; *Taylors Fashions Ltd v Liverpool Victoria Trustees Co Ltd* [1982] QB 133n esp at 145–155; *Habib Bank Ltd v Habib Bank AG Zurich* [1981] 1 WLR 1265 esp at 1285; *Amalgamated Investment & Property Co Ltd v Texas Commerce International Bank Ltd* [1982] QB 84 esp at 104.
291. [1987] AC 114.
292. (1989) 16 NSWLR 582 at 610 (qualifying what he had said in *Silovi Pty Ltd v Barbaro* (1988) 13 NSWLR 466 at 472).
293. See [369].

Elements of Promissory Estoppel

[378] **Introduction.** Although, given the flexibility and indeed the wide-ranging nature of the concept, it is difficult to isolate particular elements as essential to promissory estoppel, it is important to make some attempt at this process. In *Ajayi v R T Briscoe (Nigeria) Ltd*[294] the Privy Council explained[295] the principle that if one party to a contract agrees without fresh consideration 'not to enforce his rights an equity will be raised in favour of the other party'. It continued:[296]

> This equity is, however, subject to the qualifications (1) that the other party has altered his position, (2) that the promisor can resile from his promise on giving reasonable notice which need not be a formal notice, giving the promisee a reasonable opportunity of resuming his position, (3) the promise only becomes final and irrevocable if the promisee cannot resume his position.

In *Waltons Stores (Interstate) Ltd v Maher*[297] Brennan J said:[298]

> In my opinion, to establish an equitable estoppel, it is necessary for a plaintiff to prove that (1) the plaintiff assumed that a particular legal relationship then existed between the plaintiff and the defendant or expected that a particular legal relationship would exist between them and, in the latter case, that the defendant would not be free to withdraw from the expected legal relationship; (2) the defendant has induced the plaintiff to adopt that assumption or expectation; (3) the plaintiff acts or abstains from acting in reliance on the assumption or expectation; (4) the defendant knew or intended him to do so; (5) the plaintiff's action or inaction will occasion detriment if the assumption or expectation is not fulfilled; and (6) the defendant has failed to act to avoid that detriment whether by fulfilling the assumption or expectation or otherwise.

Brennan J's formulation has been referred to in several subsequent cases, without disapproval.[299] However, it has not been approved by the High Court, and it may be that element (1) places undue emphasis on the need for an assumption or expectation that a particular *legal* relationship existed or would exist.[300]

[379] **Promise may be express or implied.** It is clear from *Legione v Hateley*,[301] and many other cases,[302] that the promise relied upon must be unequivocal, or clear and unambiguous. However, as was pointed out in

---

294. [1964] 1 WLR 1326.
295. [1964] 1 WLR 1326 at 1330.
296. [1964] 1 WLR 1326 at 1330.
297. (1988) 164 CLR 387.
298. (1988) 164 CLR 387 at 428–9.
299. See, eg *Metropolitan Transit Authority v Waverley Transit Pty Ltd* [1991] 1 VR 181 at 208; *Austotel Pty Ltd v Franklins Selfserve Pty Ltd* (1989) 16 NSWLR 582 at 610; *Commonwealth of Australia v Verwayen* (1990) 170 CLR 394 at 502.
300. On the interpretation and application of elements (4) and (5) see *Austral Standard Cables Pty Ltd v Walker Nominees Pty Ltd* (1992) 26 NSWLR 524 at 540; *S & E Promotions Pty Ltd v Tobin Bros Pty Ltd* (1994) 122 ALR 637 at 653–4.
301. (1983) 152 CLR 406 (see [373]).
302. See, eg *Allied Marine Transport Ltd v Vale do Rio Doce Navegacao SA (The Leonides D)* [1985] 1 WLR 925 at 937; *China Ocean Shipping Co Ltd v P S Chellaram & Co Ltd* (1990) 28 NSWLR 354 at 367, 379 (affirmed (1992) 176 CLR 695); *Elkoury v Farrow Mortgage Services Pty Ltd* (1993) 114 ALR 541 at 548.

that case, the promise may be implied: it need not be expressly made. Nevertheless, words which are unclear or equivocal will not usually be a sufficient basis from which to imply a promise giving rise to a case of promissory estoppel.[303]

Traditionally, the courts have been reluctant to treat silence as a promise.[304] But in appropriate cases silence may amount to a promise.[305] This was in fact the position in *Waltons Stores (Interstate) Ltd v Maher*,[306] where silence on the part of Waltons was regarded as implying a promise to complete the transaction.

[380] Reliance and detriment. One form of consideration is the incurring of a detriment. But in the typical context in which promissory estoppel is relied upon there will be only acquiescence by the promisee, and any change of position will have occurred collaterally. It will not have been *bargained for* by the promisor. Such a change of position will therefore not suffice as the consideration necessary as an element of contract. Nevertheless, once reliance is established, particularly definite and substantial reliance, the need to protect the promisee from retraction of the promise will become apparent. In *Giumelli v Giumelli*[307] Gleeson CJ, McHugh, Gummow and Callinan JJ adopted the reasoning of McPherson J in *Riches v Hogben*,[308] including the statement that 'it is not the existence of an unperformed promise that invites the intervention of equity but the conduct of the plaintiff in acting upon the expectation to which it gives rise'.

Je Maintiendrai Pty Ltd v Quaglia[309] illustrates the difficulty inherent in the concept or concepts indicated by such expressions as 'detriment', 'material disadvantage' and 'action in reliance'. A lessor agreed at the lessee's request, but without consideration, to accept a reduced rent for an indefinite period. About 18 months later the lessor claimed and sued for the arrears of the full rent. King CJ thought it clear that there could be no estoppel unless the promisee had altered his or her position on the faith of the promise and saw no valid distinction in this respect between estoppel by representation of fact and promissory estoppel. Thus, he did not accept the view, which Lord Denning MR expressed in *W J Alan & Co Ltd v El Nasr Export & Import Co*,[310] that it sufficed that the promisee had 'acted upon the promise', detriment being unnecessary. King CJ saw as necessary that resiling from the promise would 'result in some detriment and therefore some injustice' to the other party.[311] He was not prepared to disturb the finding of the trial judge that there was detriment to the lessee by virtue of

---

303. *Drexel Burnham Lambert International NV v El Nasr* [1986] 1 Lloyd's Rep 356 at 365. Contrast *Flinn v Flinn* [1999] 3 VR 712 at 738 (proprietary estoppel).
304. For a recent reminder see *Allied Marine Transport Ltd v Vale do Rio Doce Navegacao SA (The Leonides D)* [1985] 1 WLR 925 at 937.
305. Cf *Greenwood v Martins Bank Ltd* [1933] AC 51.
306. (1988) 164 CLR 387 (see [376]). Contrast *K Lokumal & Sons (London) Ltd v Lotte Shipping Co Pte Ltd (The August Leonhardt)* [1985] 2 Lloyd's Rep 28.
307. (1999) 196 CLR 101 at 121.
308. [1985] 2 Qd R 292 at 300–1.
309. (1980) 26 SASR 101.
310. [1972] 2 QB 189 at 213.
311. (1980) 26 SASR 101 at 106.

the accumulation of arrears of rent of the magnitude concerned. White J, also accepting that detriment was an essential element of promissory estoppel, found it in the lessee's continuing to pay rent, albeit a reduced rent, and electing to continue to be liable as lessee. Cox J dissented precisely on the ground that he could not find on the evidence that detriment had been established.

In *Legione v Hateley*[312] Mason and Deane JJ held[313] it to be an essential element that the promisee must have adopted the promise 'as the basis of action or inaction', and thus be placed 'in a position of material disadvantage' if the promisor were allowed to withdraw the promised indulgence without notice.

[381] Unconscionability. Consistently with the doctrine's origins in equity, relief on the basis of promissory estoppel is in the nature of discretionary equitable relief against the operation of the common law. Relief will be granted in favour of a promisee only if it would be unconscionable for the promisor to go back on the promise. Unconscionability is therefore the 'driving force' behind promissory estoppel.[314] In *Legione v Hateley*[315] the purchasers had sufficient funds to complete when the extension of time expired, and so missed the chance of completing by that time. That provided an element of detriment which would have made it unconscionable for the vendor to depart from the promise, had it been unequivocally made. Whether it would have been present if the purchasers had not had sufficient funds by that time, and the vendor (while the period of the extension was running) had purported to terminate, is open to considerable doubt.

Relief will not be granted if the promisee is not acting in good conscience. This is illustrated by the judgment of Lord Denning MR in *D & C Builders Ltd v Rees*.[316] A debtor's wife, as agent of the debtor, knowing that the creditor was in financial trouble, offered payment of a proportion of the debt in full satisfaction, insisting that if this was not accepted, nothing would be paid. The creditor agreed, and was paid accordingly. Subsequently, it sued for the residue. While Wynn LJ held for the creditor on the ground of lack of consideration, Lord Denning MR and Danckwerts LJ held in its favour on the ground that the wife's undue pressure on the creditor prevented that true accord which would be necessary before equity would interfere with the creditor's exercise of its legal rights. Lord Denning MR's view was that a creditor would normally be estopped in equity by a promise to accept payment from the debtor of a lesser sum in satisfaction of a larger debt where both creditor and debtor had acted on it, but that this was so only where it would be 'inequitable' for

---

312. (1983) 152 CLR 406 (see [373]).
313. (1983) 152 CLR 406 at 437. See also *Hawker Pacific Pty Ltd v Helicopter Charter Pty Ltd* (1991) 22 NSWLR 298 at 308; *Territory Insurance Office v Adlington* (1992) 84 NTR 7 at 10–11, 15.
314. *Commonwealth of Australia v Verwayen* (1990) 170 CLR 394 at 407. See also Anthony Mason, 'The Place of Equity and Equitable Remedies in the Contemporary Common Law World' (1994) 110 *LQR* 238 at 254, 256.
315. (1983) 152 CLR 406 (see [373]).
316. [1966] 2 QB 617. See also *Official Trustee in Bankruptcy v Tooheys Ltd* (1993) 29 NSWLR 641 (misrepresentation).

the creditor to insist on his or her legal rights, that is, in accordance with *Foakes v Beer*.[317] In the instant case there was inequitable conduct by or on behalf of the debtor in the form of pressure applied to the creditor in exploitation of the creditor's desperate financial position at the time.

[382] **Representations of fact.** Prior to the decision of the House of Lords in *Jorden v Money*[318] there was ample authority for the existence of a principle, operative at common law as well as in equity, of estoppel arising from a representation of existing fact, which representation it was reasonable to expect would be acted upon by the representee. The object of relief was to make good the representation by holding the representor to the assumption.[319] But in *Jorden v Money* the holding of Lord Cranworth LC and Lord Brougham was that the established doctrine of estoppel by representation was confined in its operation to representations *of fact* and did not extend to representations *of intention as to the future or to promises*. And in *Maddison v Alderson*[320] the House confirmed[321] that *Jorden v Money* had decided 'that the doctrine of estoppel by representation is applicable only to representations as to some state of facts alleged to be at the time actually in existence, and not to promises de futuro, which, if binding at all, must be binding as contracts'.

The High Court was content in *Legione v Hateley*[322] to confine this line of authority to representations of fact. It could not be treated as denying the possibility of promissory estoppel operating to preclude reliance on contractual rights. At the same time, the court was sceptical not only of the distinction, but also of the need for a pre-existing legal relationship. Following hints in *Foran v Wight*[323] that *Jorden v Money* might not be followed in Australia, it is arguable that the High Court held in *Commonwealth of Australia v Verwayen*[324] that an 'estoppel, whether common law or equitable, may be founded on a future as well as a present fact'.[325] It is also clear that a promise which is not supported by

---

317. (1884) 9 App Cas 605.
318. (1854) 5 HLC 180; 10 ER 868.
319. See, eg *Pickard v Sears* (1837) 6 Ad & El 469; 112 ER 179; *Freeman v Cooke* (1848) 2 Ex 654; 154 ER 652.
320. (1883) 8 App Cas 467. See also *Yorkshire Insurance Co Ltd v Craine* [1922] 2 AC 541.
321. (1883) 8 App Cas 467 at 473 per the Earl of Selborne LC. See also *Chadwick v Manning* [1896] AC 231 at 238, where the Privy Council approved the headnote to *Jorden v Money* including the passage that to 'raise an equity in such a case (to restrain a person possessing a legal right from enforcing it), there must be a misrepresentation of existing facts, and not of mere intention'. And see Samuel Stoljar, 'Enforcing Benevolent Promises' (1989) 12 *Syd LR* 17 at 24–8.
322. (1983) 152 CLR 406 (see [373]).
323. (1989) 168 CLR 385 at 411–12, 435–6; 88 ALR 413. But cf *Con-Stan Industries of Australia Pty Ltd v Norwich Winterthur Insurance (Australia) Ltd* (1986) 160 CLR 226 at 244–5; 64 ALR 481. And see the judgment of Priestley JA in *Update Constructions Pty Ltd v Rozelle Child Care Centre Ltd* (1990) 20 NSWLR 251 (see Peta Spender, (1991) 4 *JCL* 158).
324. (1990) 170 CLR 394 (see Michael Spence, (1991) 107 *LQR* 221).
325. Sir Anthony Mason, 'Changing the Law in a Changing Society' (1993) 67 *ALJ* 568 at 572. See also A F Mason, 'Contract, Good Faith and Equitable Standards in Fair Dealing' (2000) 116 *LQR* 66 at 90. Cf *Hawker Pacific Pty Ltd v Helicopter Charter Pty Ltd* (1991) 22 NSWLR 298 at 307.

consideration may, in limited cases, be given effect and enforced in the same way as a representation of fact is enforced in cases of estoppel.[326] The safeguards for the doctrine of consideration are two-fold. First, the moulding of the remedy to suit the circumstances;[327] and, second, the insistence on unconscionable conduct.

Operation of the Doctrine — Remedies

[383] Generally. The remedy granted in the context of estoppel will be proportionate to the detriment suffered by the promisee in reliance on the representation, promise or assurance. However, the detriment may be interpreted in more than one way.[328] In broad terms, a choice is to be made between two perspectives on relief.

First, it may be appropriate to permit the promisor to resile from the representation or promise. In such a case the operation of estoppel means that the promisee is granted a remedy (usually the award of a money sum) proportionate to the actual detriment suffered by reason of its reliance.

Second, it may be appropriate to hold the promisor to the assumption generated by the promise. In such a case the operation of estoppel means that the promisee is granted relief equivalent to enforcement of the promise.

Once the basis for relief has been decided it is necessary to consider the form of relief. The overriding concern is again to ensure that the relief is appropriate relief. In *Giumelli v Giumelli*[329] an estoppel was based on a promise to confer an interest in land on which the plaintiff built. The question of relief then arose. Was the plaintiff entitled to receive a transfer of an interest in the land, or did equity merely require an order for money payment? The plaintiff had given up a particular career path in order to improve the property. In the view of Gleeson CJ, McHugh, Gummow and Callinan JJ[330] an order for payment of a money sum was more appropriate than one for the acquisition of title. Nevertheless, the sum was to be assessed by reference to the value of the property in question rather than the loss of income which the plaintiff suffered by relying on the promise, and secured by an equitable charge.

[384] Suspension and termination of the promisor's rights. One operation of the doctrine of promissory estoppel is to *suspend* the promisor's rights. This is illustrated by cases such as *Central London Property Trust v High Trees House Ltd*[331] and was the point at issue in *Legione v Hateley*.[332]

---

326. See Anthony Mason, 'The Place of Equity and Equitable Remedies in the Contemporary Common Law World' (1994) 110 *LQR* 238 at 254. Cf *S & E Promotions Pty Ltd v Tobin Bros Pty Ltd* (1994) 122 ALR 637 at 653.
327. See further [385].
328. See *Commonwealth of Australia v Verwayen* (1990) 170 CLR 394 at 413, 415, 453–4, 487.
329. (1999) 196 CLR 101. See David Wright [1999] *CLJ* 476; James Edelman, 'Remedial Certainty or Remedial Discretion in Estoppel after Giumelli?' (1999) 15 *JCL* 179. Contrast *Flinn v Flinn* [1999] 3 VR 712 at 750.
330. (1999) 196 CLR 101 at 125.
331. [1947] KB 130 (see [372]).
332. (1983) 152 CLR 406 (see [373]).

Promissory estoppel may achieve a *termination* of rights. However, estoppel is permanent only where (1) a permanent abrogation has been promised; and (2) such detriment has been suffered as to make it impossible for the promisee to resume his or her position.

[385] Enforcement of an equity. One approach to remedies in the context of promissory estoppel is to say that the court should enforce the equity which arises from reliance by the promisee on the promise. There are many cases which extol the virtues of equitable relief and its flexibility in moulding the remedy to suit the needs of the case.[333] Under this approach, the court will determine the *minimum equity* and such relief as is necessary to protect the promisee.[334] Thus, one explanation of *Waltons Stores (Interstate) Ltd v Maher*[335] is the enforcement of an 'equity' generated by the promisee's reliance on the implied promise. An order for damages may be made, but only if that is necessary for giving effect to the equity.[336]

Taken to its ultimate conclusion, the approach suggests that a promise founding a promissory estoppel is *never* directly enforced. Rather, it is the promisee's equity which is enforced.[337] Although this assists in keeping the operation of promissory estoppel distinct from the enforcement of contractual promises supported by consideration, it does make the law more complex, and is arguably fictional, since the reality is that a promise which is not supported by consideration forms the basis for the promisee's claim in damages. In *Commonwealth of Australia v Verwayen*[338] Mason CJ said that promissory estoppel has 'undermined the idea that voluntary promises cannot be enforced in the absence of consideration'. It is nevertheless clear, not only that the courts have not resumed the approach[339] taken in the 18th century of 'making representations good',[340] but also that where promises are in effect enforced, the remedy is not necessarily equivalent to that available for breach of a contractual promise.

It will be explained later[341] that the usual method of calculating damages for breach of contract is to place the promisee in the position which it would have occupied had the promise been performed. However, this is not

---

333. See, eg *Amalgamated Investment & Property Co Ltd v Texas Commerce International Bank Ltd* [1982] QB 84 at 103, 122; *Waltons Stores (Interstate) Ltd v Maher* (1988) 164 CLR 387 at 419; *Commonwealth of Australia v Verwayen* (1990) 170 CLR 394 at 412, 442; *Official Trustee in Bankruptcy v Tooheys Ltd* (1993) 29 NSWLR 641 at 650.
334. See, eg *Waltons Stores (Interstate) Ltd v Maher* (1988) 164 CLR 387 at 419; *Commonwealth of Australia v Verwayen* (1990) 170 CLR 394 at 411, 429, 501. See also Anthony Mason, 'The Place of Equity and Equitable Remedies in the Contemporary Common Law World' (1994) 110 *LQR* 238 at 254.
335. (1988) 164 CLR 387 (see [376]). Cf *Government of Swaziland Central Transport Administration v Leila Maritime Co Ltd (The Leila)* [1985] 2 Lloyd's Rep 172 at 179.
336. See, eg *Waltons Stores (Interstate) Ltd v Maher* (1988) 164 CLR 387 at 405; *Commonwealth of Australia v Verwayen* (1990) 170 CLR 394 at 411–12, 475–6, 487, 501.
337. See *Commonwealth of Australia v Verwayen* (1990) 170 CLR 394 at 434ff.
338. (1990) 170 CLR 394 at 410. Cf *Amalgamated Investment & Property Co Ltd v Texas Commerce International Bank Ltd* [1982] QB 84 at 131 ('matter of semantics').
339. See [382].
340. See Anthony Mason, 'The Place of Equity and Equitable Remedies in the Contemporary Common Law World' (1994) 110 *LQR* 238 at 254.
341. See [2110].

necessarily the proper approach to promises not supported by consideration but given effect to under promissory estoppel. In this regard *Waltons v Maher* must be regarded as exceptional, since an expectation method of calculation was there adopted. Often, in responding to reliance, the appropriate way of enforcing the promise is by a restorative award for reliance loss. Thus, if A makes a promise to B, and B relies on the promise by expending money, it may only be appropriate to award B the money spent.[342] Similarly, if B relies on the promise by providing services, the reasonable value of the services rendered should be awarded. Awarding B expectation damages for A's nonperformance of the promise, while in some cases necessary, cannot be supported as a general rule because that would be inconsistent with the general acceptance consideration as a requirement for the direct enforcement of promises.

[386] Giving effect to the assumption. In *Commonwealth of Australia v Verwayen*[343] Deane J developed the view that there is one doctrine of estoppel based on the prevention of departures from assumptions generated by promises or representations. In his view, whether arising from a promise or a representation of fact, the object of estoppel is to give effect to the assumption. Therefore, if A represents, or promises, that a contractual relation exists, or will exist, between A and B (the person to whom the promise or representation was made) and the requirements of estoppel are satisfied, the court must give effect to the assumption and treat A as contractually bound to B or bound to enter into the contract with B. Dawson J adopted a similar approach.[344]

[387] The American doctrine. American law has, for a considerable period of time, countenanced a cause of action based on promissory estoppel.[345] In the Californian case, *Drennan v Star Paving Co*,[346] the plaintiff general contractor relied on the defendant paving subcontractor's bid (the lowest received by the plaintiff) in calculating the amount of his own bid, which was accompanied by a nomination of the defendant for the paving work. The plaintiff's bid was the lowest and he was awarded the contract. The defendant refused to do the paving work, asserting that it had made a mistake in its bid and that it could not do the work for the amount of its bid. The plaintiff had to engage another contractor to do the paving work at a price exceeding the amount of the defendant's bid. He succeeded in an action for damages in the amount of the excess.

At that time §90 of the *Restatement of Contracts* (1932) stated:

> A promise which the promisor should reasonably expect to induce action or forbearance of a definite and substantial character on the part of the promisee and which does induce such action or forbearance is binding if injustice can be avoided only by enforcement of the promise.

---

342. Cf *Commonwealth of Australia v Verwayen* (1990) 170 CLR 394.
343. (1990) 170 CLR 394 at 434ff.
344. See (1990) 170 CLR 394 at 453ff. Cf *Amalgamated Investment & Property Co Ltd v Texas Commerce International Bank Ltd* [1982] QB 84 at 105–7.
345. See, eg S D Henderson, 'Promissory Estoppel and Traditional Contract Doctrine' (1969) 78 *Yale LJ* 343.
346. 51 Cal 2d 409; 333 P 2d 757 (1958).

The court thought the case analogous to that of a unilateral contract, that is, an offer of a promise to be accepted by action, noting that according to §45 of the *Restatement*, if part of the consideration requested by the offeror is given or tendered by the offeree in response, the offeror ceases to be free to revoke. Traynor J (for the majority) said:[347]

> Whether implied in fact or law, the subsidiary promise serves to preclude the injustice that would result if the offer could be revoked after the offeree had acted in detrimental reliance thereon. Reasonable reliance resulting in a foreseeable prejudicial change in position affords a compelling basis also for implying a subsidiary promise not to revoke an offer for a bilateral contract ...

Holding that there was an implied promise not to revoke, the court further held that §90 made it unnecessary to find any consideration for that implied promise and allowed reasonable reliance to make that promise binding. Traynor J said[348] that the 'very purpose of §90 is to make a promise binding even though there was no consideration "in the sense of something that is bargained for and given in exchange".[349] Reasonable reliance serves to hold the offeror in lieu of the consideration ordinarily required to make the offer binding'.

Section 90(1) of the *Restatement (2d) Contracts* (1979) now provides:

> A promise which the promisor should reasonably expect to induce action or forbearance on the part of the promisee or a third person and which does induce such action or forbearance is binding if injustice can be avoided only by enforcement of the promise. The remedy granted for breach may be limited as justice requires.

Under the first *Restatement* the action or forbearance had to be of 'a definite and substantial character'. Thus, the provision is now wider than previously. Moreover, the last sentence of §90(1) has been added to allow a court to mould the remedy as justice requires. This reflects the tendency of American courts[350] to adopt a broad and flexible approach to the concept. Under the current §90(1) there must be action or forbearance, but it need not be by the promisee. Thus, a third person who relies on the promisor's promise may be afforded a remedy. Not only does §90 dispense with the requirement of consideration, it is also opposed to the rule of privity of contract.

Discharge, Variation and Related Concepts

Discharge and Variation

[388] Discharge. Once a contract has been discharged by performance[351] there remains no executory undertaking to be discharged. On the other hand, where either or both parties have obligations to perform, the discharge or extinguishment of those obligations (often termed 'rescission')

---

347. 51 Cal 2d 409; 333 P 2d 757 at 760 (1958).
348. 51 Cal 2d 409; 333 P 2d 757 at 760 (1958).
349. *Corbin on Contracts*, Vol 1, 1963, §§634ff.
350. Cf *Hoffman v Red Owl Stores Inc* 133 NW 2d 267 (1965).
351. See Chapter 18.

by an agreement between the parties necessarily requires consideration. The contract, although arising in the context of a pre-existing contract, is subject to the ordinary requirements of contract law.

If executory on *both* sides, the requirement of consideration to support the agreement for discharge will ordinarily present no difficulties. Consideration is necessarily present if there are mutual releases of the outstanding obligations. For each party's release, the reciprocal release of the other is consideration.[352]

However, if a contract remains executory on one side only, even if only to a minor extent, the question whether an agreed discharge or promise of discharge of the executory obligation is supported by consideration presents more difficulty. Clearly, the doctrine of consideration requires that, unless made by deed, such a discharge must be supported by a fresh consideration.[353] This is so whether or not the time has arrived for performance. If that time has not yet arrived, the release is of an outstanding primary obligation fixed by the contract, for example, a promise to paint a portrait where payment has been made in advance. If that time has arrived, the release is of the defaulting party's obligations consequential upon performance or breach, for example, of an indebtedness for the price of goods or services supplied or an obligation to pay damages for breach of contract.

In most cases, if consideration is present it will be in the form of a compromise. In other words, the contract to discharge the unperformed part of a contract will arise out of a bona fide dispute in relation to the contract. This area of the law has already been discussed.[354]

[389] **Variation.** Variation of a subsisting contract is theoretically distinct from an agreement for complete discharge. On any conventional description of the concept of a variation, it does not include an agreement to discharge the contract altogether.[355] The same is true where the parties, as well as agreeing to discharge the pre-existing contract, substitute a fresh contract. The second contract cannot be regarded as a mere variation of the first, since the intention is to replace the first, or the outstanding obligations of the parties, with a second contract.[356]

On the other hand, the agreement may be to do no more than vary the pre-existing contract, by changing one or more terms (or the obligations created) without actually discharging the contract. For example, the parties to a contract for the sale of goods under which the buyer is required to pay a price of $1000 might agree to increase the price to $1500. Clearly, there must be some consideration for the buyer's promise to pay the higher price, as the buyer was contractually entitled to receive the goods for the lesser sum. We have already seen this principle in operation in the context of

---

352. Unless the reciprocal obligations outstanding are comparable obligations to pay or release liquidated sums. See [356]–[361].
353. See *Atlantic Shipping & Trading Ltd v Louis Dreyfus & Co* [1922] 2 AC 250 at 262–3 (release of an accrued cause of action); *Foakes v Beer* (1884) 9 App Cas 605 (release of part of a debt — see [357]).
354. See [350]–[355].
355. See [526].
356. See [526].

promises to perform pre-existing duties.[357] The orthodox view is that the seller's promise to deliver the goods cannot itself be consideration for the buyer's promise to pay the higher price.

A variation may incipiently involve a potential benefit and a potential detriment to each party. In any such case, consideration is clearly present for each party's agreement to the variation. An example is a variation in the currency in which money is to be paid under the contract. It is immaterial that, as events transpire, the change to a different currency appears to benefit one party only. So, if in our example above, the buyer had originally agreed to pay $1000 in Australian currency, but later agreed to pay $1000 in United States currency, the later promise is supported by consideration, in the form of the seller's promise to accept a different currency.

However, consideration will not be present where a variation is exclusively for the benefit of one party. Where the nature of a variation may be equivocal, extrinsic evidence may show that it was made for the benefit of one party only. Thus, the suggested consideration for a seller's granting of an extension of time for payment and the seller's promise not to serve a bankruptcy notice, might be a change in the place where payment is to be made, but once it is shown that this change was also made for the buyer's convenience alone, it is disqualified as a consideration.[358]

Estoppel, Election and Waiver

[390] Doctrines available. Discharge and variation depend on a bilateral consensus. But a contracting party may, in effect unilaterally, lose rights available under a contract. This is usually explained by reference to the related concepts of 'estoppel', 'election' and 'waiver'. Although the precise interrelationship of these doctrines is uncertain,[359] it is clear that they operate in a way which is distinct from discharge and variation. Generally, whereas consideration is required for discharge or variation, it is not necessary for the operation of concepts such as estoppel, election and waiver.[360] Unfortunately, however, the law is complex, and not characterised by a high degree of coherence or consistency. For present purposes it is sufficient to explain how these concepts operate without the need for consideration.[361]

In order to highlight these issues, and to avoid detailed anticipation of future discussions, it is proposed to take 'waiver' as the focus, although this is the most troublesome concept of all. The looseness with which the term is used is notorious, and this is not the place to examine the doctrine exhaustively.[362]

[391] Waiver meaning election. One sense of the word 'waiver' is to describe an election between rights.[363] Assume that one party to a contract (the promisee) is entitled to terminate the contract for the promisor's

---

357. See [341]–[349].
358. See *Vanbergen v St Edmund's Properties Ltd* [1933] 2 KB 223, a case of creditor and debtor.
359. Cf *Wilson v Kingsgate Mining Industries Pty Ltd* [1973] 2 NSWLR 713 at 730.
360. See [392].
361. Cf [525]–[527] (formal requirements).

breach of contract.³⁶⁴ The law does not require that the promisee terminate; the promisee may prefer to 'affirm' the obligation to perform the contract, and actually perform or call on the promisor to perform. But termination and affirmation are mutually inconsistent rights and the exercise of one is necessarily a rejection of the other.³⁶⁵

Apart from such cases of conscious election between rights, the promisee may engage in conduct which would be justifiable only if an election had been made one way or the other. If so, the alternative right ceases to be available: it is regarded as having been lost in just the same way as if the promisee had consciously (expressly) elected in favour of one right and against the other.³⁶⁶

[392] **Waiver meaning estoppel.** The concept of 'waiver' of a right is broad enough to embrace not only the giving up of one right in favour of another but also conduct which makes it unfair, inequitable or unconscionable for the promisee to insist on the right.³⁶⁷ The broad distinction between waiver in the sense of election, and waiver in the sense of estoppel is that while the former focuses on the words and conduct of the promisee, the second focuses more on the reliance by the promisor on what the promisee has said or done.³⁶⁸

Assume that one party to a contract (the promisee) possesses the right to terminate for the breach and also the right to claim damages for the breach. For example, a buyer would be in this position where a seller of goods has not met a delivery date and time of delivery is of the essence.³⁶⁹ The buyer is not obliged to exercise the right of termination, the buyer may request the seller to deliver on a later (named) date, and the seller might rely on this by making arrangements for the delivery of the goods on that day. If the seller tenders (offers) the goods to the buyer, the buyer is not permitted to reject them on the ground of late delivery. The buyer is regarded as having 'waived' the right of termination in the sense that the buyer is precluded (estopped) from relying on the right of termination³⁷⁰ because:

---

362. See, eg Ewart, *Waiver Distributed*, 1917; S J Stoljar, 'The Modification of Contracts' (1957) 35 *Can Bar Rev* 485; Tony Dugdale and David Yates, 'Variation, Waiver and Estoppel — A Re-Appraisal' (1976) 39 *MLR* 681; H K Lücke, 'Non-contractual Arrangements for the Modification of Performance: Forbearance, Waiver and Equitable Estoppel' (1991) 21 *UWALR* 149; J W Carter, 'Waiver (of Contractual Rights) Distributed' (1991) 4 *JCL* 59. See also [1972].
363. See, eg *Craine v Colonial Mutual Fire Insurance Co Ltd* (1920) 28 CLR 305 at 326 (affirmed sub nom *Yorkshire Insurance Co Ltd v Craine* [1922] 2 AC 541); *Commonwealth of Australia v Verwayen* (1990) 170 CLR 394 at 406.
364. See generally on termination for breach Chapter 19.
365. See *Commonwealth of Australia v Verwayen* (1990) 170 CLR 394 at 421–2 and [1971], [1972].
366. For detailed discussion of the requirements of election see [1047]–[1048], [1970]–[1972].
367. Cf *Larratt v Bankers and Traders Insurance Co Ltd* (1941) 41 SR (NSW) 215 at 227; *Kammins Ballrooms Co Ltd v Zenith Investments (Torquay) Ltd* [1971] AC 850 at 883.
368. *Craine v Colonial Mutual Fire Insurance Co Ltd* (1920) 28 CLR 305 at 326 (affirmed sub nom *Yorkshire Insurance Co Ltd v Craine* [1922] 2 AC 541).
369. For the meaning of this expression see [1848].
370. See also [1975], [1976].

(1) it has expressly or impliedly represented that the goods will not be rejected;
(2) the seller has relied to its detriment on that representation by attempting to deliver the goods; and
(3) it would be unjust or unconscionable to permit the buyer to exercise the legal right of termination.

Whereas it is an essential ingredient of waiver in the sense of estoppel that the seller should have changed its position in reliance on what the buyer has said,[371] this is not an essential element of waiver in the sense of election.[372] Similarly, although there is no requirement of unconscionability in the context of election,[373] no estoppel will arise in the absence of unconscionability.[374] Again, although waiver in the sense of election requires 'knowledge' of the circumstances,[375] waiver in the sense of estoppel does not require knowledge.[376]

[393] **Effect of waiver.** What both these forms of waiver have in common is that there is no requirement of consideration. We have seen that estoppel is independent of consideration.[377] Waiver in the sense of election does not signify that the promisee has purported to contract out of the right, the position is simply that the promisee has engaged in conduct (which may in some cases be no more than silence) showing that one of the rights available to the promisee has been rejected in favour of another. Thus, although no longer able to choose one of the rights available in respect of the promisor's breach, the promisee still has the right to sue for breach of contract.

To conclude that a right has been 'waived' might be thought to suggest that the right has been lost. But that is not necessarily the case. In order to determine what precisely is the effect of waiver it is necessary to examine the basis for the conclusion. A 'waiver' which is an election between inconsistent rights is final in the sense that the inconsistent right is permanently lost. On the other hand, a waiver which is an estoppel may involve no more than a temporary suspension of contractual rights.[378] Unless it would be inequitable so to allow, the right may be reasserted upon the giving of reasonable notice.[379]

---

371. See *Wilson v Kingsgate Mining Industries Pty Ltd* [1973] 2 NSWLR 713 at 731; *Commonwealth of Australia v Verwayen* (1990) 170 CLR 394 at 407, 450.
372. See *Commonwealth of Australia v Verwayen* (1990) 170 CLR 394 at 422, and further [1974].
373. But, as Lord Wilberforce said in *Johnson v Agnew* [1980] AC 367 at 398: 'Election, though the subject of much learning and refinement, is in the end a doctrine based on simple considerations of common sense and equity'.
374. See [369], [381].
375. Cf *Craine v Colonial Mutual Fire Insurance Co Ltd* (1920) 28 CLR 305 at 326 (affirmed sub nom *Yorkshire Insurance Co Ltd v Craine* [1922] 2 AC 541); *Deaves v CML Fire and General Insurance Co Ltd* (1979) 143 CLR 24 at 42; 23 ALR 539. See further on the requirement [1971].
376. Cf *Bremer Handelsgesellschaft mbH v Vanden Avenne-Izegem PVBA* [1978] 2 Lloyd's Rep 109 at 127.
377. See, eg [380].
378. See, eg *Motor Oil Hellas (Corinth) Refineries SA v Shipping Corp of India (The Kanchenjunga)* [1990] 1 Lloyd's Rep 391 at 399.

There is an important contrast between the right of termination which the buyer enjoyed in the examples given and the right to damages which accrued to the buyer when the breach of contract occurred. The right to damages is regarded as a more significant matter. Standing alone, an election in respect of a right of termination does not extend to the promisee's right to compensation. In order for that right to be lost the general rule is that there must be consideration.[380] However, in some cases waiver will have a greater effect than a mere election. So, 'waiver' has sometimes been used to describe loss of a right to claim damages following breach. There are two categories of case.

First, the requirement of consideration may be satisfied. For example, a party to a contract might agree to accept payment of $1000 in return for a promise to 'waive' the right to claim damages. An appropriate construction of the word in that context would be to describe an agreement to compromise the claim.[381]

Second, there may be an estoppel in relation to the right to claim damages. However, in order for that to occur, it would need to be shown the promise or representation on which the party has relied extended further than the right of termination to include the right to sue for damages.

It is suggested, however, that there is nothing to be gained in employing 'waiver' to describe any of the above situations. Indeed, there is much to be lost in utilising such an ambiguous word, which serves more to confuse than to clarify.[382]

---

379. Cf *Hughes v Metropolitan Railway Co* (1877) 2 App Cas 439 at 452; *Commonwealth of Australia v Verwayen* (1990) 170 CLR 394 at 474–5.
380. See *Motor Oil Hellas (Corinth) Refineries SA v Shipping Corp of India (The Kanchenjunga)* [1990] 1 Lloyd's Rep 391.
381. See *Mulcahy v Hoyne* (1925) 36 CLR 41 at 58. Cf *Orr v Ford* (1989) 167 CLR 316 at 337–8; 84 ALR 146 (acquiescence).
382. Cf *Larratt v Bankers and Traders Insurance Co Ltd* (1941) 41 SR (NSW) 215 at 226.

Chapter 4

Intention to Create Legal Relations

General 401
Family, Social and Domestic Agreements 403
Commercial Agreements 405
Particular Situations 409
Conclusion 412

General

[401] Intention to create legal relations an essential element. Does the furnishing of consideration, as Williston argued,[1] import an intention that the promise so 'bought' be legally binding and so render superfluous any separate inquiry on whether the promise is intended to be legally binding? Conversely, is consideration merely one form of evidence of intention to create legal relations not warranting the status of an independent element of a contract? We have already seen that the answer to the latter question is 'no'.[2] The former question is answered 'no' in this chapter.

Consideration and intention to create legal relations are clearly interrelated. The presence of the former suggests the presence of the latter. However, the law requires that, in addition to agreement and consideration, a third element is necessary to a contract, namely, an intention to create legal relations.[3] Equally, since a contract is a 'legally binding *agreement*', it would be paradoxical if an agreement could be held a contract in the face of the parties' intention that it should not give rise to legal rights and obligations. Therefore, a common positive intention not to contract will be respected.

The requirement that there be an intention to create legal relations does not mean that a party seeking to enforce a contract must show that the

---
1. *Williston on Contracts*, 3rd ed, Vol 1, §21.
2. See [306].
3. See H K Lücke, 'The Intention to Create Legal Relations' (1970) 3 *Adel LR* 419.

parties consciously adverted to the legal implications of what they were doing. Moreover, because the test of intention is objective,[4] it is not usually open to one party to prove that subjectively a *unilateral* intention was that legal relations should not arise.[5] Therefore, in practice, the issue of intention to create legal relations does not often arise. Accordingly, apart from the uncommon cases where the parties agree that their agreement is not to attract legal consequences,[6] the issue is determined as an inference of fact in the drawing of which two rebuttable presumptions of fact,[7] based on common experience, play a part.

[402] **Intention may be express or implied.** The presence or absence of the intention to be legally bound depends on the facts of each case.[8] The relevant intention may be express or implied.[9] However, in the case of parties at arm's length, and in particular, in the case of commercial agreements, an intention that the agreement was not intended to be legally binding will not lightly be inferred. On the other hand, in the case of consensual relations between close friends or members of a family, it will be more easily inferred that agreement and consideration were not accompanied by contractual intent.

Although the requirement of intention is of general application, it is convenient to consider the cases in classes.

Family, Social and Domestic Agreements

[403] **Presumption that such agreements held not binding.** Experience of life shows that close relatives do not usually intend the various arrangements which they make to create legal relations and that they prefer to rely on 'family ties of mutual trust and affection'.[10] The law therefore recognises a rebuttable presumption of fact that relatives, such as husband and wife and parent and child, do not intend their agreements to be contracts.

The justification for the presumption does not exist — and so the presumption does not arise or is rebutted — where husband and wife have ceased living in amity and have separated or are about to separate at the time of the making of the agreement.[11] In the leading case, *Balfour v Balfour*,[12] a wife could not, for medical reasons, accompany her husband from England back to Ceylon (his place of employment) and he orally promised to pay her an allowance of £30 per month until she could rejoin

4. See [110]–[112].
5. Cf [707].
6. See [406].
7. See [403], [405].
8. See *Air Great Lakes Pty Ltd v K S Easter (Holdings) Pty Ltd* (1985) 2 NSWLR 309 at 336; *Orion Insurance Co Plc v Sphere Drake Insurance Plc* [1992] 1 Lloyd's Rep 239 at 263, 301.
9. See, eg *Deutsche Schachtbau-und Tiefbohrgesellschaft mbH v Shell International Petroleum Co Ltd* [1990] AC 295 at 315 (reversed on another point at 329).
10. *Jones v Padavatton* [1969] 2 All ER 616 at 621 per Salmon LJ.
11. *Merritt v Merritt* [1970] 2 All ER 760.
12. [1919] 2 KB 571.

him. This promise was held not binding for lack of an intention that the understanding should be legally enforceable. Atkin LJ said:[13]

> ... there are agreements between parties which do not result in contracts within the meaning of that term in our law. The ordinary example is where two parties agree to take a walk together, or where there is an offer and an acceptance of hospitality. Nobody would suggest in ordinary circumstances that those agreements result in what we know as a contract, and one of the most usual forms of agreement which does not constitute a contract appears to me to be the arrangements which are made between husband and wife. It is quite common, and it is the natural and inevitable result of the relationship of husband and wife, that the two spouses should make arrangements between themselves ... those agreements, or many of them, do not result in contracts at all, and they do not result in contracts even though there may be what as between other parties would constitute consideration for the agreement ... It constantly happens, I think, that such arrangements made between husband and wife are arrangements in which there are mutual promises, or in which there is consideration in form within the definition that I have mentioned. Nevertheless they are not contracts, and they are not contracts because the parties did not intend that they should be attended by legal consequences.

In *Cohen v Cohen*,[14] Dixon J, by similar reasoning, held an arrangement between an intending husband and wife as to a dress allowance to the latter not a contract. After referring to questions of consideration, and s 4 of the *Statute of Frauds* 1677 (Imp), he said:[15]

> But these matters only arise if the arrangement which the plaintiff made with the defendant was intended to affect or give rise to legal relations or to be attended with legal consequences (*Balfour v Balfour*;[16] *Rose & Frank Co v J R Crompton & Bros Ltd*[17]). I think it was not so intended. The parties did no more, in my view, than discuss and concur in a proposal for the regular allowance to the wife of a sum which they considered appropriate to their circumstances at the time of marriage.

Although it is right for the courts to exercise a degree of vigilance in ensuring that the courts are not used as a forum for purely vindictive litigation in relation to agreements which no reasonable person would regard as having the force of law, it is by no means clear that the decisions reached in the above cases would be reached today. Normal court procedures exist to deal with vexatious litigants, and the courts must be careful to see that agreements which are intended to be taken seriously are observed. To leave the wife in *Balfour v Balfour* without a means of supporting herself seems entirely unjustified and smacks of bias against married women. Moreover, as has been pointed out,[18] Atkin LJ failed to distinguish a purely social promise — the agreement for a walk — which is not intended to be enforceable, from a 'benevolent' promise contemplating reliance of a serious or injurious kind.

---

13. [1919] 2 KB 571 at 578-9.
14. (1929) 42 CLR 91.
15. (1929) 42 CLR 91 at 96.
16. [1919] 2 KB 571.
17. [1923] 2 KB 261 at 288; [1925] AC 445.
18. Samuel Stoljar, 'Enforcing Benevolent Promises' (1989) 12 *Syd LR* 17 at 19–20.

[403]

In *Jones v Padavatton*[19] an arrangement was reached between a mother and her 34-year-old daughter that the mother would maintain her at a specified rate if she would go to England and read for the Bar with a view to practising later in Trinidad. This arrangement necessitated the daughter's abandoning a comfortable flat and a secure remunerative job in Washington and her seven-year-old son's education there. After her arrival in England there was a variation to the arrangements under which the mother purchased a house in which the defendant could live. Rooms were let to tenants, but none of the rental payments were remitted to the mother, who was paying off a substantial mortgage. Even though the daughter did not live with her mother, was well above the age of majority and had a family of her own, the English Court of Appeal held that there was no intention to be legally bound. Although the court was also influenced by elements of uncertainty in the arrangements with respect to the house,[20] it may be asked whether it would today be appropriate to treat such an arrangement as attracting a presumption that there was no intention to create legal relations.

[404] **Rebuttal of the presumption.** In many cases agreements between husband and wife have been upheld as contracts, for example, a written partnership;[21] an agreement to pay and accept a stipulated weekly amount for maintenance and to indemnify as part of a compromise of litigation comprising cross-summonses for assault;[22] an agreement by the wife to return to live with her husband in consideration of the husband's promise to transfer title to the matrimonial home into both names.[23]

Other cases have involved promises, usually by an elderly or disabled person, to devise or otherwise make over title to property (often a residence) to a friend or relative in consideration of the promisee's taking up residence with the promisor and/or rendering or promising to render household and/or personal services to the promisor.[24] It is not difficult to infer the requisite intention to create legal relations, at least where implementation of the arrangement requires the promisee to give up or dispose of existing advantages, for example, an advantageous existing place of residence, perhaps some distance away.[25]

Commercial Agreements

[405] **Presumption that parties intend to be legally bound.** It follows from what was said above[26] that in commercial agreements it is rare for the conclusion to be drawn that the parties did not intend their agreement to

19. [1969] 2 All ER 616.
20. Cf *Gould v Gould* [1970] 1 QB 275.
21. *Milliner v Milliner* (1908) 8 SR (NSW) 471.
22. *McGregor v McGregor* (1888) 21 QBD 424.
23. *Popiw v Popiw* [1957] VR 197.
24. Cf *Horton v Jones* (1935) 53 CLR 475; *Wakeling v Ripley* (1951) 51 SR (NSW) 183; *Todd v Nichol* [1957] SASR 721; *Raffaele v Raffaele* [1962] WAR 29; *Schaefer v Schuhmann* [1972] AC 572; *Palmer v Bank of NSW* (1975) 133 CLR 150; 7 ALR 671; *Riches v Hogben* [1985] 2 Qd R 292 (affirmed [1986] 1 Qd R 315).
25. But see *Re Gonin deceased* [1979] Ch 16.
26. See especially [401].

be attended by legal consequences. Only rarely will the presumption be rebutted, and the onus of establishing that a commercial agreement was not to create legal relations rests on the party so contending.[27]

Where an express exclusion of that intention is alleged, the words used must be clear and unambiguous. In *Edwards v Skyways Ltd*[28] the use of the words 'ex gratia' to describe a promise of payment was held by Megaw J as insufficient to negative contractual intention. The words were construed to signify only that the promisor did not admit a liability to make the payment. And in *Kleinwort Benson Ltd v Malaysia Mining Corp Berhad*[29] the English Court of Appeal said that if it is alleged that a commercial agreement was not intended to have legal force this must be justified by proof of a separate agreement to that effect.

[406] Honour clauses. So called 'honour clauses' declare that an agreement is not to be legally binding, with the result that the agreement is 'binding in honour only'. Such clauses are not often encountered. They might be used where the parties are prepared to rely on non-legal sanctions, for example, their ongoing commercial dealings with each other, as an inducement to performance.

In the leading case *Rose & Frank Co v J R Crompton & Bros Ltd*[30] an agreement between an English manufacturer and a New York dealer giving the latter certain selling rights in respect of the former's products contained the following 'Honourable Pledge clause':

> This arrangement is not entered into, nor is this memorandum written, as a formal or legal agreement, and shall not be subject to legal jurisdiction in the law courts either in the United States or England, but is only a definite expression and record of the purpose and intention of the parties concerned, to which they each honourably pledge themselves ...

The clause was held effective according to its terms. In the English Court of Appeal, Scrutton LJ observed that in social and family relations an intention not to create legal relations is readily implied, whereas in business matters the reverse is ordinarily the case, but that even in business matters there is no reason why the parties could not 'exclude all idea of settling disputes by any outside intervention, with the accompanying necessity of expressing themselves so precisely that outsiders may have no difficulty in understanding what they mean'.[31] The House of Lords agreed with this conclusion.

[407] Promotional puff. As is noted elsewhere,[32] the extravagant, non-specific language of the advertiser may fail to satisfy the criteria of a representation of fact. Such language may also fail as the basis itself of *contractual* obligation for the reason that this was not intended. So, in *Lambert v Lewis*[33] a manufacturer's advertising literature accompanying its

---

27. Cf *Toyota Motor Corp Australia Ltd v Ken Morgan Motors Pty Ltd* [1994] 2 VR 106 at 150, 177.
28. 1964] 1 All ER 494.
29. [1989] 1 WLR 379.
30. [1923] 2 KB 261; [1925] AC 445. See also [1626].
31. [1923] 2 KB 261 at 288.
32. See [603], [1007].
33. [1982] AC 225.

[407]

dual purpose towing hitches stated that they were 'foolproof' and 'required no maintenance'. The English Court of Appeal agreed with the trial judge's conclusion that the advertiser's claims 'were not intended to be, nor were they acted upon as being express warranties'.[34] On the other hand, an argument of 'mere puff' failed in *Carlill v Carbolic Smoke Ball Co*[35] if for no other reason, because the defendant declared that it had deposited £1000 with a bank to show its 'sincerity in the matter' of a promised £100 reward to any person who contracted influenza after using the defendant's smoke ball in accordance with the directions.

In *Esso Petroleum Ltd v Commissioners of Customs and Excise*[36] the issue before the House of Lords was whether certain goods — 'World Cup coins' — were 'produced ... for sale' and therefore chargeable to purchase tax under tax legislation. These coins were of no intrinsic value, but bore the likenesses of the English soccer team. As part of a promotional scheme by Esso, they were provided to motorists. One coin was given for every four gallons of Esso petrol which motorists purchased. The members of the House of Lords who expressed an opinion on the question of whether Esso or the service station proprietors on the one hand, and motorists on the other, intended that there should be a legally binding obligation to supply the coins were evenly divided. One view emphasised the commercial advantage which Esso and the proprietors expected from the sales promotion, and held legal relations to be intended. The other emphasised the language used in the promotional material (for example, 'free', 'gifts'), the unlikelihood of legal proceedings if coins were not supplied, the coins' lack of intrinsic value and the fact that it is, after all, legally possible to make gifts within a commercial setting.

[408] Unsatisfactoriness of distinction between 'family, social and domestic agreements' and 'commercial agreements'. The supposed simple distinction between 'family, social and domestic agreements' and 'commercial agreements' can be misleading. This is illustrated by *Roufos v Brewster*.[37] Mr and Mrs Brewster conducted a motel business at Coober Pedy and their son-in-law, Mr Roufos, ran a store there. Roufos took the Brewsters' truck on his semi-trailer to Adelaide for repairs and an arrangement was made between Mrs Brewster and her daughter (Mrs Roufos) that Mr Roufos should engage a driver to drive the truck back to Coober Pedy on the footing that he might, if he wished, send back a load of his own goods on the truck. This arrangement was implemented, but the truck was damaged en route. The Brewsters sued Roufos for damages for breach of contract to recover the cost of repairs. Bray CJ observed:[38]

> It is true that the appellant is the son-in-law of the respondents, but they were conducting separate businesses at Coober Pedy, there was, according to the evidence of Mrs Roufos, intermittent hostility between Mr Roufos and his parents-in-law, and the appellant had an important commercial interest in the transport of his liquor to Coober Pedy for the purpose of his new

---

34. [1982] AC 225 at 263 (on appeal the House of Lords did not discuss the issue).
35. [1893] 1 QB 256 (see [208]).
36. [1976] 1 All ER 117.
37. (1971) 2 SASR 218.
38. (1971) 2 SASR 218 at 222.

restaurant ... just as the respondents had a commercial interest in regaining the use of their truck as soon as possible. The whole setting of the arrangement is commercial rather than social or domestic.

Particular Situations

[409] Schemes propounded by governments and intergovernmental agreements. A government or governmental agency may administer a scheme, plan or policy involving the prospect of governmental subsidies or other assistance to persons who satisfy stated criteria. Typically these persons will be required to 'co-operate', at the very least by applying for the benefit and furnishing information, and perhaps by doing other acts. A person aggrieved by refusal of benefits may seek to enforce the scheme, plan or policy as a contract. On the basis of the issues discussed in earlier chapters, the scheme, plan or policy may fail as a contract because:

(1) on a proper construction, the words used did not amount to an offer or acceptance (as the case may be);[39] or

(2) what is propounded by the claimant as consideration was in truth a condition precedent,[40] or was not furnished with reference to the offer.[41]

An alternative rationalisation is that there was no intention to create legal obligations. The circular or other document announcing or explaining the scheme, plan or policy may be regarded by the court as 'administrative' as distinct from 'contractual', and as distinct from an offer of a contract. In *The Administration of the Territory of Papua New Guinea v Leahy*[42] McTiernan J expressed the relevant principle as it applied to the facts of that case as follows:[43]

> The arrangement consisted of agreed promises but that is not enough to make a contract, unless it was the common intention of the parties to enter into legal obligations, mutually communicated, expressly or impliedly. It was not an express or implied term of the arrangement that the respondent should make any payment for the treatment of the cattle. I cannot agree that the Administration through its officers intended to enter into legal relations when, at the request of the respondent, it undertook the organisation of the tick eradication campaign with respect to his cattle. The conduct of the parties constituted an administrative arrangement by which the Administration in pursuance of its agricultural policy, gave assistance to an owner of stock to prevent that stock contracting a disease which was prevalent in the Territory. The work done by the Administration was analogous to a social service which generally does not have as its basis a legal relationship of a contractual nature and from which no right of action would arise in favour of the citizen who is receiving the services if the Government acts inefficiently in performing them.

---

39. Cf *Australian Woollen Mills Pty Ltd v The Commonwealth* (1954) 92 CLR 424 at 460–5.
40. See [316].
41. See [315], [318].
42. (1961) 105 CLR 6. See also *Milne v A-G for the State of Tasmania* (1956) 95 CLR 460 at 472–3. And cf *South Australia v The Commonwealth* (1962) 108 CLR 130.
43. (1961) 105 CLR 6 at 11.

In such cases the proper view to be taken is that it was intended to attract political and administrative rather than contractual sanctions.[44]

[410] The constitutions of voluntary associations. The constitutive rules of an association may be sought to be enforced as a contract. It may, however, be argued that particular sets of rules were not intended to create legal relations with the result that breach of them was not actionable. The leading case is *Cameron v Hogan*[45] in which the plaintiff alleged that he had been wrongfully expelled from the Australian Labor Party of the State of Victoria. In denying him declaratory and injunctive relief, Rich, Dixon, Evatt and McTiernan JJ said that the test was whether a member enjoyed under the rules 'some civil right of a proprietary nature proper to be protected',[46] and remarked that membership of the Party carried with it 'no tangible or practical proprietary right'.[47] In *Finlayson v Carr*,[48] the test of 'tangible or practical proprietary right' led to a conclusion that the rules and regulations of the Australian Jockey Club did create a contractual relationship between its members.

In the case of companies registered under the *Corporations Act* 2001 (Cth), s 140(1) provides that a company's constitution (if any) and any replaceable rules that apply to the company have effect as a contract:[49]

(a) between the company and each member;

(b) between the company and each director and company secretary; and

(c) between a member and each other member;

under which each person agrees to observe and perform the constitution and rules so far as they apply to that person.

This binds each to observe and perform the provisions of the constitution and rules so far as applicable to the person in question,[50] and so appears to obviate the necessity of any inquiry as to whether the general law requirement of contractual intent is satisfied. Whether this apparent effect could be negated by an 'honour clause'[51] in the constitution is doubtful, because the legislation reveals an intention that part of the price for the benefits of registration shall be enforceability at the instance of individual members.

[411] Other cases. It must not be assumed that there is an exhaustive list of classes of case in which there is no intention to create legal relations, or that any one system of classification is 'correct'. In particular agreements, the allowance to one party of a wide discretion as to performance, for example 'at the pleasure of the Board of Directors of the [defendant]

---

44. See H K Lücke, 'The Intention to Create Legal Relations' (1970) 3 *Adel LR* 419 at 425–8; Dennis Rose, 'The Government and Contract', in Finn, ed, *Essays on Contract*, 1987, pp 238–42.
45. (1934) 51 CLR 358.
46. (1934) 51 CLR 358 at 377.
47. (1934) 51 CLR 358 at 378.
48. [1978] 1 NSWLR 657.
49. As to whether members are bound by modifications of the constitution see *Corporations Act* 2001 (Cth), s 140(2).
50. Cf *Norths Ltd v McCaughan Dyson Capel Cure Ltd* (1988) 12 ACLR 739; *Stillwell Trucks Pty Ltd v Nectar Brook Investments Pty Ltd* (1993) 115 ALR 294 at 300.
51. See [406].

company and subject to its sole discretion',[52] the vagueness of the language of a promise and the importance or otherwise of the agreement to the parties may all influence the decision on whether there was an intention to create legal relations.

Conclusion

[412] Overlap between intention, agreement and consideration. Frequently there is overlap between the issue of intention to create legal relations and the issues of agreement and consideration. This is perhaps more obvious, if, instead of speaking of 'intention to create legal relations', we speak of 'intention to be immediately committed to a contract'. The more firm the intention to create legal rights and obligations immediately, the more probable it is that the terms of agreement will be certain and particular. Conversely, vagueness and generality of terms may point to an absence of contractual intent.[53] The other overlap, that between consideration and intention to create legal relations, is well established.[54]

Horton v Jones[55] illustrates the interrelationship of all three elements. In that case there were issues as to: (1) whether a woman's promise to a person since deceased to enter into his service and to act as his secretary, housekeeper and nurse for the rest of his life was too vague and uncertain to constitute consideration for the deceased's promise to leave her his 'fortune'; and (2) whether the parties' language was that of legal obligation. Evatt and McTiernan JJ observed[56] in relation to the plaintiff, it is 'not suggested that her past was not honourable, *but it cannot be measured by any legal standards*'.

---

52. *Moir v J P Porter & Co Ltd* (1979) 103 DLR (3d) 22.
53. See *Toyota Motor Corp Australia Ltd v Ken Morgan Motors Pty Ltd* [1994] 2 VR 106 at 130, 202.
54. See [306], [336], [401].
55. (1935) 53 CLR 475. See also *Beaton v McDivitt* (1987) 13 NSWLR 162.
56. (1935) 53 CLR 475 at 492 (emphasis supplied).

Chapter 5

Contracts Requiring Written Evidence

Introduction 501
The *Statute of Frauds* 502
   Relevant Provisions 503
   Operation of the Statute and Derivative Legislation in Australia ... 505
Compliance with the Requirements 513
   Note or Memorandum 513
   Sale of Goods 516
Effect of Noncompliance 519
   Position at Common Law 519
   Position in Equity 521
Rescission, Variation and Related Concepts 525

Introduction

[501] Writing not generally required. A fact which often surprises the layperson is that there is no general rule requiring contracts to be in writing. Usually, a contract is valid and enforceable even though it is wholly oral or partly oral and partly written. Similarly, a contract may be inferred from conduct. Where writing is required this is because of the operation of statute.[1] In such cases, statute may require the contract itself to be in writing or merely require written evidence of the contract. In this chapter we deal mainly with requirements which are derived from the *Statute of Frauds* 1677 (Imp). It is, as we shall see,[2] sufficient for there to be written evidence of a promise within the statute.

    An imposed requirement of writing need not be exclusive, there may be *alternative* ways of satisfying the statute. For example, in the case of a sale of goods within the statutory requirements discussed in this chapter,[3] the

---

1. Or the intention of the parties. See [273] ('subject to contract').
2. See [513]–[516].
3. See [511].

contract will be binding on a purchaser who has paid part of the price. And in what is a quite remarkable gloss on the *Statute of Frauds*, courts of equity have worked out a 'doctrine of part performance' which effectively permits enforcement of the contract even if there is no written evidence at all.[4]

The *Statute of Frauds*

[502] Purpose of the statute. Requirements of writing have three main functions. First, an *evidentiary* function, a way of preventing perjury and ensuring that reliable evidence is received. Second, a *cautionary* function of forcing parties to think carefully about the transaction before signing the document. Third, there is a *channelling* function: parties may be forced to use a particular form, and similar agreements are given a similar form.

The preamble to the *Statute of Frauds* 1677 (Imp) stated its purpose as the prevention of 'many fraudulent practices, which are commonly endeavoured to be upheld by perjury and subornation of perjury'. Thus, a requirement of writing was imposed as a formal ingredient of certain specified types of promises. The preamble looks to the first of the three functions. Arguably, however, only the cautionary function has real importance in the context of the modern law of contract. The whittling away at the scope of the *Statute of Frauds* reflects a feeling that oral evidence is today more reliable. The fact that the main examples of contracts where writing remains essential are those involving land, where enormous sums of money may be involved, shows the relevance of the cautionary function. In the main area where new (and more onerous) requirements have been imposed, consumer credit transactions, the cautionary function is patent.

The evidentiary function of the *Statute of Frauds* is reflected in the procedural requirement that the statute be specifically pleaded when relied upon to defeat a claim.[5] The defendant must allege and prove the existence of facts which bring the contract within the statute.[6] It is sufficient for the defendant to prove the existence of a promise within the statute, and that the formal requirements have not been complied with. Moreover, the defendant will succeed even if the contract contains another or alternative promise, which need not be evidenced in writing and which the plaintiff might perform at his or her option.[7]

Relevant Provisions

[503] Section 4. The central provision of the statute, s 4, provided as follows:

> And be it further enacted that from and after the said 24th day of June no action shall be brought whereby to charge any executor or administrator upon any special promise, to answer damages out of his own estate; or whereby to charge the defendant upon any special promise to answer for the debt, default or miscarriages of another person; or to charge any person upon any agreement made upon consideration of marriage; or upon any

---

4. See [521]–[524].
5. See, eg *Suttor v Gundowda Pty Ltd* (1950) 81 CLR 418 at 440.
6. *Marginson v Ian Potter & Co* (1976) 136 CLR 161 at 168; 11 ALR 64.
7. *Marginson v Ian Potter & Co* (1976) 136 CLR 161 at 168–9.

[503]

contract or sale of lands, tenements or hereditaments, or any interest in or concerning them; or upon any agreement that is not to be performed within the space of one year from the making thereof, unless the agreement upon which such action shall be brought, or some memorandum or note thereof shall be in writing, and signed by the party to be charged therewith, or some other person thereunto by him lawfully authorized.

The choice of promises (contracts) seems particularly arbitrary, but Professor Simpson[8] has suggested a unifying feature, namely, that they became actionable at common law through the new action of assumpsit on an oral agreement even though, previously, the contracts would not have been actionable in the absence of a sealed instrument. The statute is from that perspective a conservative measure designed to 'put the clock back, substituting ... the signature for the seal'. In respect of these informal contracts there was also the requirement of consideration. Although Lord Mansfield suggested that writing dispensed with that requirement, this was rejected towards the end of the 18th century.[9]

[504] **Section 17.** The second main provision was s 17 which provided:

And be it further enacted by the authority aforesaid, that from and after the said 24th day of June no contract for the sale of any goods, wares, or merchandises, for the price of ten pounds sterling or upwards, shall be allowed to be good, except the buyer shall accept part of the goods so sold, and actually receive the same, or give something in earnest to bind the bargain, or in part of payment, or that some note or memorandum in writing of the said bargain be made and signed by the parties to be charged by such contract, or their agents thereunto lawfully authorized.

Although this section applied the requirement of writing to contracts for the sale of goods in the same way as s 4 applied it to the classes of contract there listed, there were two distinctions. First, s 17 applied only to contracts for the sale of goods if the price exceeded £10 and would not have applied to the vast majority of sale transactions. Second, alternatives to the requirement of writing were stated so that, for example, a buyer's acceptance of goods would take the contract of sale outside the operation of the statute even though it specified a price in excess of £10.

A contrast may also be found in the language used to describe the effect of s 17 ('no contract ... shall be allowed to be good') and that stated in s 4 ('no action shall be brought'). However, this must now be taken to have had no significance.[10]

Operation of the Statute and Derivative Legislation in Australia

[505] **Statute part of received law.** The *Statute of Frauds* 1677 (Imp) formed part of the received law of the Australian Colonies on their settlement in the 18th century. However, in most jurisdictions some

8. Simpson, *A History of the Common Law of Contract*, 1975, p 610.
9. See [306] and Simpson, *A History of the Common Law of Contract*, 1975, pp 617–19.
10. See [519].

amendment has been made in the operation of s 4, and s 17 no longer applies in any jurisdiction.[11]

In the Australian Capital Territory, New South Wales, Queensland, the Northern Territory and South Australia s 4 of the *Statute of Frauds* has been declared no longer to be in force.[12] Even in Tasmania, Victoria and Western Australia, where s 4 is to some extent still in force, the important aspects of the section have been replaced by local enactments. Section 2 of the *Law Reform (Statute of Frauds) Act* 1962 (WA) deserves mention in this connection as it continues the operation of s 4 in that State but requires it to be read as if certain words were omitted.

Before analysing the content and impact of the requirement of writing, it is necessary to consider each of the classes of contract enumerated in ss 4 and 17, and to indicate the current position in Australia.

[506] Special promises by an executor or administrator to answer damages out of his or her own estate. In Tasmania this class of contract is required to be evidenced by writing.[13]

In all other jurisdictions[14] no requirement of writing is applicable. This type of contract has, in any event, no practical significance to the modern law of contract. An executor (or administrator) is normally liable only to the extent of the assets of the deceased and, for reasons which are not relevant to this work, it is rare for such a person to enter into contracts which impose a personal liability.

[507] Contracts of guarantee. The words of s 4 of the *Statute of Frauds* 1677 (Imp), requiring a contract whereby the defendant is charged on any 'special promise to answer for the debt, default or miscarriages of another person' to be evidenced by writing, have their main application in respect of what are more economically described as contracts of guarantee.[15]

For example, a person (A) may wish to borrow money from another person (B), but B may be in some doubt as to A's ability to repay the loan, or merely wish to have some protection (other than to resort to litigation against A) in the event of A defaulting under the contract. B might therefore require a third person (C) to guarantee A's performance of the contract. Thus, contemporaneously with the loan between A and B, C may promise to guarantee A's performance in consideration of B making the loan. The relation of the parties under such an arrangement is that C is the

11. For derivative legislation see [511].
12. **ACT**: *Imperial Acts (Substituted Provisions) Act* 1986, s 3(1) and Sch 1; **NSW**: *Imperial Acts Application Act* 1969, s 8(1); **NT**: *Law of Property Act* 2000, s 221(1) and Sch 4; **Qld**: *Statute of Frauds* 1972, s 3 (itself repealed by the *Property Law Act* 1974); **SA**: *Statutes Amendment (Enforcement of Contracts) Act* 1982, s 3.
13. See *Mercantile Law Act* 1935 (Tas), s 6.
14. **ACT**: *Imperial Acts (Substituted Provisions) Act* 1986, s 3(1) and Sch 1; **NSW**: *Imperial Acts Application Act* 1969, s 8(1); **NT**: *Law of Property Act* 2000, s 221(1) and Sch 4; **Qld**: *Statute of Frauds* 1972, s 3 (itself repealed by the *Property Law Act* 1974); **SA**: *Statutes Amendment (Enforcement of Contracts) Act* 1982, s 3; **Vic**: *Instruments Act* 1958, s 126 (as substituted by the *Sale of Goods (Vienna Convention) Act* 1987 (Vic), s 8); **WA**: *Law Reform (Statute of Frauds) Act* 1962, s 2.
15. For a wider interpretation see *Moschi v Lep Air Services Ltd* [1973] AC 331 at 347–8.

guarantor (or surety), B the creditor and A the principal debtor. The promise by C was required by s 4 to be evidenced by writing.

In the Northern Territory, Queensland, Tasmania, Victoria and Western Australia contracts of guarantee are required by local enactment to be in writing or evidenced by writing.[16] On the other hand, in the Australian Capital Territory, New South Wales and South Australia there is no such requirement.[17]

In view of the fact that writing is required in a majority of Australian jurisdictions it is appropriate to mention the distinction between a guarantee and an indemnity. In *Moschi v Lep Air Services Ltd*[18] Lord Diplock explained:[19]

> It follows from the legal nature of the obligation of the guarantor to which a contract of guarantee gives rise that it is not an obligation himself to pay a sum of money to the creditor, but an obligation to see to it that another person, the debtor, does something; and that the creditor's remedy for the guarantor's failure to perform it lies in damages for breach of contract only.

As he went on to point out, this is true even if the debtor's own obligation, the subject of the guarantee, is to pay a sum of money. The creditor's ability to proceed against the guarantor depends on default by the principal debtor. In the example given above, A must default in the repayment of the loan before B can call upon C to pay.

On the other hand, where a contract of indemnity is present, liability is independent of default by the debtor. In *Birkmyr v Darnell*[20] the following illustration was given. If two persons go into a shop, one of whom intends to purchase goods and the other, in order to obtain credit for the first person, promises to pay the seller if the first person does not, the contract is one of guarantee. But if the second person says 'let him have the goods, I will be your paymaster', that is a personal undertaking to purchase the goods which provides an indemnity for the shopkeeper. In this case the shopkeeper can sue the second person, who has given the indemnity, without seeking payment from the first person and without proving default by that person.

The importance of the distinction between guarantee and indemnity is that whereas the requirement of writing applies to the former, it does not apply to the latter, the words of the statute not being descriptive of a contract of indemnity. Whether a contract is one of indemnity or guarantee depends on the construction of the contract. For example, in *Yeoman Credit Ltd v Latter*[21] the plaintiffs, a finance company, let a motor car on hire-

---

16. See **NT**: *Law of Property Act* 2000, s 56; **Qld**: *Property Law Act* 1974, s 56; **Tas**: *Mercantile Law Act* 1935, s 6; **Vic**: *Instruments Act* 1958, s 126 (as substituted by the *Sale of Goods (Vienna Convention) Act* 1987 (Vic), s 8); **WA**: *Statute of Frauds* 1677 (Imp), s 4. The wording of the Northern Territory and Queensland provisions are in a simplified form, employing the word 'guarantee'.
17. See **ACT**: *Imperial Acts (Substituted Provisions) Act* 1986, s 3 and Sch 2, Pt 11, cl 4(1); **NSW**: *Imperial Acts Application Act* 1969, s 8(1); **SA**: *Statutes Amendment (Enforcement of Contracts) Act* 1982, s 3. But see [512] (credit legislation).
18. [1973] AC 331.
19. [1973] AC 331 at 348. Cf at 344–5.
20. (1704) 1 Salk 27; 91 ER 27.
21. [1961] 1 WLR 828.

purchase terms to the first defendant. At the same time the second defendant signed a document headed 'Hire-purchase indemnity and undertaking', which provided that the second defendant would 'indemnify' the plaintiffs 'against any loss resulting from or arising out of' the hire-purchase contract. The court held that the contract was one of indemnity, not merely a guarantee. The plaintiffs were therefore able to succeed in their action against the second defendant even though their contract with the first defendant was void by reason of the *Infants' Relief Act* 1874 (UK). However, the words chosen by the parties are not conclusive. A contract described as 'guarantee' may actually provide for an indemnity, or an obligation of some other nature. It is, moreover, a mistake to regard all guarantees as conforming to the analysis made by Lord Diplock in *Moschi*.[22]

If A promises to discharge a liability to which A or A's property is already subject, the contract is not within the statute.[23] But the interest in property must not be merely 'commercial': A must possess a legal or equitable right in the property.

[508] Contracts made in consideration of marriage. In Tasmania a contract made in consideration of marriage is required to be in writing or evidenced by writing.[24] In the other jurisdictions the requirement of writing is no longer applicable.[25]

This provision does not refer to a promise to marry. Thus, if A promises to marry B, the contract need not be evidenced by writing.[26] However, if A makes a promise to B, for example, to pay $100 per week to C (A's daughter) during A's lifetime in consideration of B's marriage to C, the contract must be evidenced by writing.

[509] Contracts for the sale of land or an interest in land. In all Australian jurisdictions, contracts for the sale of land, or an interest in land, must be written or evidenced by writing.[27] Section 54A(1) of the *Conveyancing Act* 1919 (NSW) is representative of these provisions. It provides as follows:[28]

> No action or proceedings may be brought upon any contract for the sale or other disposition of land or any interest in land, unless the agreement upon which such action or proceedings is brought, or some memorandum or note

---

22. See, eg *Hortico (Australia) Pty Ltd v Energy Equipment Co (Australia) Pty Ltd* (1985) 1 NSWLR 545 at 550; *Sunbird Plaza Pty Ltd v Maloney* (1988) 166 CLR 245; 77 ALR 205.
23. *Marginson v Ian Potter & Co* (1976) 136 CLR 161.
24. See *Mercantile Law Act* 1935 (Tas), s 6.
25. **ACT**: *Imperial Acts (Substituted Provisions) Act* 1986, s 3 and Sch 2, Pt 11, cl 4(1); **NSW**: *Imperial Acts Application Act* 1969, s 8(1); **NT**: *Law of Property Act* 2000, s 221(1) and Sch 4; **Qld**: *Statute of Frauds* 1972, s 3 (itself repealed by the *Property Law Act* 1974); **SA**: *Statutes Amendment (Enforcement of Contracts) Act* 1982, s 3; **Vic**: *Instruments Act* 1958, s 126 (as substituted by the *Sale of Goods (Vienna Convention) Act* 1987 (Vic), s 8); **WA**: *Law Reform (Statute of Frauds) Act* 1962, s 2.
26. In any event, by virtue of s 111a of the *Marriage Act* 1961 (Cth) breach of such a promise does not give rise to a liability to pay damages.
27. On whether a land contract must be in writing see *Marist Bros v Community of Harvey* (1994) 14 WAR 69. See also Nicholas Seddon, 'Contracts for the Sale of Land: Is a Note or Memorandum Sufficient?' (1987) 61 *ALJ* 406.

thereof, is in writing, and signed by the party to be charged or by some other person thereunto lawfully authorised by the party to be charged.

This is by far the most important of the contracts enumerated in the *Statute of Frauds* 1677, as is indicated by the fact that a requirement of writing exists in all Australian jurisdictions.[29] The equitable doctrine of part performance[30] also has its main application in respect of such contracts.

[510] **Contracts not to be performed within a year.** In Tasmania a contract which is not to be performed within the space of one year from its making is required to be evidenced by writing.[31] Writing is not required in the other jurisdictions.[32]

In *Clarke v Tyler*[33] Dixon J said that for a contract 'to answer the description of an agreement that is not be to performed within the space of one year ... it is necessary that it should be of such a character that performance within a year by either side is impossible from the beginning'. In that case a share-farming agreement, which contained no express provision as to duration, was held to be within the rule because the *Agricultural Holdings Act* 1941 (NSW) applied and prohibited termination before the expiry of 12 months. The position would have been different if termination within the 12-month period had been permitted by the statute.

[511] **Sale of goods.** In Tasmania and Western Australia a contract for the sale of goods of value at or above a specified amount must comply with one of the requirements set out in legislation derived from s 17. Thus, the *Sale of Goods Act* 1896 (Tas) provides, in s 9:[34]

> (1) A contract for the sale of any goods of the value of $20 or upwards shall not be enforceable by action unless the buyer shall accept part of the goods so sold and actually receive the same, or give something in earnest to bind the contract, or in part payment, or unless some note or memorandum in writing of the contract be made and signed by the party to be charged or his agent in that behalf.

---

28. See also **ACT**: *Law Reform (Miscellaneous Provisions) Act* 1955, s 54(1); **NT**: *Law of Property Act* 2000, s 62; **Qld**: *Property Law Act* 1974, s 59; **SA**: *Law of Property Act* 1936, s 26(1); **Tas**: *Conveyancing and Law of Property Act* 1884, s 36(1); **Vic**: *Instruments Act* 1958, s 126 (as substituted by the *Sale of Goods (Vienna Convention) Act* 1987 (Vic), s 8); **WA**: *Statute of Frauds* 1677 (Imp), s 4.
29. In England, *Law of Property (Miscellaneous Provisions) Act* 1989 (UK), s 2 (repealing s 40 of the *Law of Property Act* 1925 (UK)) provides that the contract must be in writing.
30. See [521]–[524].
31. See *Mercantile Law Act* 1935 (Tas), s 6.
32. See **ACT**: *Imperial Acts (Substituted Provisions) Act* 1986, s 3 and Sch 2, Pt 11, cl 4(1); **NSW**: *Imperial Acts Application Act* 1969, s 8(1); **NT**: *Law of Property Act* 2000, s 221(1) and Sch 4; **Qld**: *Statute of Frauds* 1972, s 3 (itself repealed by the *Property Law Act* 1974); **SA**: *Statutes Amendment (Enforcement of Contracts) Act* 1982, s 3; **Vic**: *Instruments Act* 1958, s 126 (as substituted by the *Sale of Goods (Vienna Convention) Act* 1987 (Vic), s 8); **WA**: *Law Reform (Statute of Frauds) Act* 1962, s 2.
33. (1949) 78 CLR 646 at 653. And see *Gibb v Sell* [1922] VLR 561.
34. See also **WA**: *Sale of Goods Act* 1895, s 4. Repeal of the Western Australian provision has been recommended by the Law Reform Commission of Western Australia, *Report on the Sale of Goods Act* 1895, Project No 89, 1998. See J W Carter, 'Sale of Goods Reform in Western Australia' (1999) 15 *JCL* 58.

(2) The provisions of this section apply to every such contract, notwithstanding that the goods may be intended to be delivered at some future time, or may not at the time of such contract be actually made procured or provided or fit or ready for delivery or some act may be requisite for the making or completing thereof or rendering the same fit for delivery.

(3) There is an acceptance of goods within the meaning of this section when the buyer does any act in relation to the goods which recognizes a pre-existing contract of sale, whether there be an acceptance in performance of the contract or not.

In all other jurisdictions the relevant provision of the sale of goods legislation has been repealed.[35]

It will be noticed that the amount, $20, is the decimal equivalent of the £10 stated over 300 years ago in the *Statute of Frauds* 1677 (Imp). Needless to say, $20 seems totally unrealistic today.[36] Four further features of s 9 deserve mention. First, it is sufficient for the party to be charged to sign the note or memorandum.

Second, s 9 applies notwithstanding that the goods are to be delivered at a future time, or are presently not fit for delivery.

Third, there is a definition of 'acceptance'.[37]

Fourth, in order for s 9 to apply the subject matter must be 'goods', as defined. Section 3(1) of the *Sale of Goods Act* 1896 (Tas) states:[38]

'Goods' include all chattels personal other than things in action and money. The term includes emblements, industrial growing crops, and things attached to or forming part of the land which are agreed to be severed before sale or under the contract of sale.

This definition does not embrace a contract the subject matter of which is work and materials.[39] Although there is an element of product supply in such contracts, as where a builder supplies the materials (such as timber) required in the construction of a set of cupboards, the courts have distinguished a work and materials contract from one of pure sale on the basis of the element of labour, that is, the supply of services.

The test to be applied was stated by Greer LJ, in *Robinson v Graves*,[40] in terms of the 'substance' of the contract. He said that if you find the

35. See **ACT**: *Sale of Goods Act* 1975, s 3; **NSW**: *Sale of Goods (Amendment) Act* 1988, s 3 and Sch 1, cl 2; **NT**: *Sale of Goods Amendment Act* 1999, s 2; **Qld**: *Statute of Frauds* 1972, s 3 (itself repealed by the *Property Law Act* 1974); **SA**: *Statutes Amendment (Enforcement of Contracts)* 1982, s 4; **Vic**: *Sale of Goods (Vienna Convention) Act* 1987, s 9. No requirement of writing applies to contracts of sale governed by the *United Nations Convention on Contracts for the International Sale of Goods* 1980.
36. Under the *Uniform Commercial Code* (US), §2-201(1) the threshold is $500.
37. This definition distinguishes acceptance in performance (see [1981]). Under s 17 of the *Statute of Frauds* 1677 (Imp) both parties had to sign and there was no definition of acceptance. The effect of s 9(3) is to codify the previous law on acceptance. See *Metropolitan Knitting and Hosiery Co Ltd v Thomas Burnley & Sons* Ltd (1924) 35 CLR 232 at 240. See further [517].
38. See also *Sale of Goods Act* 1895 (WA), s 60(1).
39. On the distinction between sale of an interest in land and a sale of goods see, eg *Mills v Stokman* (1967) 116 CLR 61; *Warren v Nut Farms of Australia Pty Ltd* [1980] WAR 136.
40. [1935] 1 KB 579 at 587.

[511] substance of the contract to be the skill and labour involved in the production of the article the subject of the contract, so that the transfer of materials in addition to the skill involved is only 'ancillary', the contract is a work and materials contract rather than a sale of goods. The fact that property in the materials is intended to pass on delivery to the buyer is a factor, but no more, in favour of the contract being one for the sale of goods rather than a work and materials contract.[41]

The following may be taken as illustrations of the distinction. A contract to paint a portrait has been held to be a contract for work and materials,[42] whereas a dentist's contract to supply a set of false teeth has been described as one for the sale of goods.[43] A contract to construct and install a cocktail cabinet has been interpreted as one for work and materials,[44] as has one for the supply and installation of lecture theatre seats.[45] Similarly, a contract to construct a house on the builder's premises and to deliver it to a site selected by the other party is not a contract for the sale of goods but is, instead, a contract for work and materials.[46]

The expression 'work and materials contract' has been described as imprecise,[47] and the distinction between such a contract and one for the sale of goods criticised as being imprecise and artificial.[48] By and large the distinction has been drawn for the purpose of avoiding the requirement of writing. The illustrations given above certainly indicate that the distinction is frequently a fine one. They also indicate the difficulty of predicting when a contract which contains an element of work and labour will be treated as one for the sale of goods.

[512] **Other legislation.** Apart from the provisions derived from the *Statute of Frauds* 1677 (Imp), examples of formal requirements may be found in legislation governing other types of contracts. The most important example is the *Consumer Credit Code*, under which a credit provider must comply with detailed provisions relating to the form and content of contracts which involve the supply of credit. The provisions apply to contracts of sale or loan as well as certain contracts of guarantee with a credit provider. Examples in Commonwealth legislation include contracts for marine insurance, which are inadmissible in evidence in an action for recovery of a loss unless the contract is embodied in a marine policy in accordance with the provisions of the *Marine Insurance Act* 1909; and bills of exchange which are required by s 8(1) of the *Bills of Exchange Act* 1909 to be in writing.

The consequences of a failure to comply with a requirement of writing imposed by provisions derived from the *Statute of Frauds* 1677 (Imp) are dealt with later in this chapter.[49] However, it should not be assumed that

---

41. See *Collins Trading Co Pty Ltd v Maher* [1969] VR 20; *Bolwell Fibreglass Pty Ltd v Foley* [1984] VR 97 at 108–9.
42. *Robinson v Graves* [1935] 1 KB 579.
43. *Samuels v Davis* [1943] 1 KB 526 at 529. See also *Toby Constructions Products Pty Ltd v Computa Bar (Sales) Pty Ltd* [1983] 2 NSWLR 48 (computer system).
44. *Brooks Robinson Pty Ltd v Rothfield* [1951] VLR 405.
45. *Aristoc Industries Pty Ltd v R A Wenham (Builders) Pty Ltd* [1965] NSWR 581.
46. *Hewett v Court* (1983) 149 CLR 639.
47. *Young & Marten Ltd v McManus Childs Ltd* [1969] 1 AC 454 at 476.
48. *Hewett v Court* (1983) 149 CLR 639 at 646, 655; 46 ALR 87.

the same consequences apply in relation to other types of contracts subjected to a requirement of writing. For example, a contract which is not evidenced by writing as required by the *Statute of Frauds* (or derivative legislation) is merely rendered unenforceable, it is not void; whereas the failure to comply with the requirements imposed by other statutes may in fact render the contract void. The failure to follow a statutory requirement may have other consequences as well. For example, the failure to comply with the requirements of the *Consumer Credit Code* may subject the credit provider to a pecuniary penalty, but no such consequence follows merely from a failure to comply with the requirements derived from the *Statute of Frauds*.

Compliance with the Requirements

Note or Memorandum

[513] Contents of the document. The *Statute of Frauds* 1677 (Imp) required either the contract to be in writing or the existence of a written 'memorandum or note' of the contract. Needless to say, the concept of a memorandum or note of the contract immediately raises the issue of the information which must be contained in the document.

The note or memorandum must, generally speaking, contain all the terms of the contract,[50] or at least all the 'essential' terms.[51] Accordingly, the parties to the contract must be identified. The 'naming of a party is sufficient if he is joined or nominated in the instrument by a sufficiently identifiable description'.[52]

Second, the note or memorandum must state the consideration for the promise sought to be enforced. For example, in *Burgess v Cox*[53] a contract for the sale of a holiday camp was agreed, but the note relied on made no reference to the inclusion in the sale of the deposits which had been received by the vendor from prospective guests. The contract was therefore unenforceable. However, in jurisdictions where contracts of guarantee are still subjected to the requirement, statutory provisions specifically allow for the sufficiency of writing which makes no reference to the consideration for the promise sued on.[54]

Third, the note or memorandum must sufficiently describe the subject matter of the contract. For example, in *Pirie v Saunders*[55] a reference in a

---

49. See [519]–[524].
50. *Sinclair Scott & Co Ltd v Naughton* (1929) 43 CLR 310 at 318. This is the position under *Law of Property (Miscellaneous Provisions) Act* 1989 (UK), s 2(1).
51. *Harvey v Edwards Dunlop & Co Ltd* (1927) 39 CLR 302 at 307.
52. *Di Biase v Rezek* [1971] 1 NSWLR 735 at 741–2.
53. [1951] Ch 383. It would seem that Harman J's refusal in this case to grant relief claimed in favour of a party willing to submit to the omitted term was wrong: *Scott v Bradley* [1971] Ch 850.
54. See **NT**: *Law of Property Act* 2000, s 58(2); **Qld**: *Property Law Act* 1974, s 56(2); **Tas**: *Mercantile Law Act* 1935, s 12; **Vic**: *Instruments Act* 1958, s 129; **WA**: *Mercantile Law Amendment Act* 1856 (UK), s 3 (adopted by 31 Vic No 8).
55. (1961) 104 CLR 149.

document to the sale of 'part of Lot B, Princes Highway, Sylvania Heights' was said not to be sufficient.

Although the note or memorandum will usually come into existence after the contract has been agreed, this is not always the case. For example, a written offer may be orally accepted[56] and the offer, 'by its subsequent acceptance',[57] becomes the note or memorandum. Although the document must recognise the existence of the contract sued on, there is no requirement that it be made for that purpose. For example, in *Popiw v Popiw*[58] an affidavit sworn by the respondent in proceedings which sought a determination of the question whether the applicant was entitled to an interest in the matrimonial home was held to be, in form, a sufficient memorandum of a contract to dispose of an interest in land. The case also illustrates the principle that the document must have been in existence at the time of the proceedings. Since the affidavit was sworn after commencement, fresh proceedings by the applicant were required.[59]

[514] Signature. The concept of 'signature' under the *Statute of Frauds* 1677 (Imp) is a fairly loose one. The requirement is signature by the party to be charged under the contract or by that person's agent, 'lawfully' authorised.[60] However, the courts have striven to widen the requirement so as not to allow the statute to be the engine of injustice. In *Thomson v McInnes*[61] Griffith CJ said that the statute contemplated 'three different modes of signature, first, by a person with his own hand, secondly, by an amanuensis signing the name of another person in that other person's presence by his direction, and, thirdly, by an agent'. Signature by an agent, for example one party's solicitor,[62] will bind that party if the agent has authority to sign. Except in Victoria, the authority of the agent need not be in writing.[63]

Where the name of the party to be charged appears on the alleged note or memorandum, for example, because it was typed in by the other party, the so-called 'authenticated signature fiction' may apply. Thus, if the party to be charged expressly or impliedly acknowledges the writing as an authenticated expression of the contract the typed words will be deemed to be his or her signature. But this principle has no application to a document 'which is not in some way or other recognisable as a note or memorandum of a concluded agreement'.[64]

---

56. *Heppingstone v Stewart* (1910) 12 CLR 126. But see *Howard Smith & Co Ltd v Varawa* (1907) 5 CLR 68 at 79.
57. *Pirie v Saunders* (1961) 104 CLR 149 at 154.
58. [1959] VR 197. See also *Elpis Maritime Co Ltd v Marti Chartering Co Inc (The Maria D)* [1992] 1 AC 21; *Tonitto v Bassal* (1992) 28 NSWLR 564.
59. See also *South Coast Oils (Qld & NSW) Pty Ltd v Look Enterprises Pty Ltd* [1988] 1 Qd R 680 at 690-1.
60. Contrast *Law of Property (Miscellaneous Provisions) Act* 1989 (UK), s 2(3) (signature by both parties).
61. (1911) 12 CLR 562 at 573.
62. See, eg *Kalnenas v Kovacevich* [1961] WAR 188; *Elias v George Sahely & Co (Barbados) Ltd* [1983] 1 AC 646.
63. See s 126 of the *Instruments Act* 1958 (Vic) (as substituted by the *Sale of Goods (Vienna Convention) Act* 1987 (Vic), s 8). See *Grummitt v Natalisio* [1968] VR 156; *Collin v Holden* [1989] VR 510; *Futuretronics International Pty Ltd v Gadzhis* (1990) [1992] 2 VR 217.

[515] **Joinder of documents.** The writing may be found in one or more documents: there is no requirement that a single document contain all the evidence.[65] In *Thomson v McInnes*[66] Griffith CJ said:[67]

> It is well known that the note or memorandum which the statute requires need not be contained in one piece of paper. It is sufficient if the note signed by the party to be charged refers to some other document in such a way to incorporate it with the document signed, so that they can be read together. That has been settled for a long time. But the whole contract must be shown by the writing. The reference, therefore, in the document signed must be to some other document as such, and not merely to some transaction or event in the course of which another document may or may not have been written.

The document so referred to may be identified by verbal evidence, but the bargain must be completed. For example, in *Thomson v McInnes* itself, the document referred to contemplated the payment of a deposit under a contract for the sale of land but failed to fix the amount. There was, therefore, no sufficient note or memorandum.[68]

Subsequent decisions have taken the matter further than the views expressed in *Thomson v McInnes* would justify. Thus, in *Harvey v Edwards Dunlop & Co Ltd*[69] the High Court proceeded on the basis that a reference to some other 'transaction' is sufficient if the transaction contains all the terms in writing. Direct reference in one document to another is therefore not essential. For example, the later document may refer to an agreement the effect of which can be explained by oral evidence. Similarly, in *Elias v George Sahely & Co (Barbados) Ltd*[70] the Privy Council approved a statement in *Timmins v Moreland Street Property Co Ltd*[71] to the effect that once the required memorandum contains some reference, express or implied, to some other document or transaction, evidence may be given to identify the other document, or explain the other transaction, and to identify any document relating to it. If the oral evidence leads to another document which, when placed side by side with the later document, indicates a connection between them, that is sufficient.[72]

Sale of Goods

[516] **Note or memorandum.** The issues likely to be raised in relation to the note or memorandum required under the sale of goods legislation will appear from the above discussion. The important point with regard to the

---

64. *Pirie v Saunders* (1961) 104 CLR 149 at 154. See also *Neill v Hewens* (1953) 89 CLR 1.
65. *Tonitto v Bassal* (1992) 28 NSWLR 564.
66. (1911) 12 CLR 562.
67. (1911) 12 CLR 562 at 569.
68. See also *Australia and New Zealand Banking Group Ltd v Widin* (1990) 102 ALR 289 at 300 (document did not refer to transaction).
69. (1927) 39 CLR 302 at 307. See also *Ellul v Oakes* (1972) 3 SASR 377 at 383; *Woden Squash Courts Pty Ltd v Zero Builders Pty Ltd* [1976] 2 NSWLR 212. Cf *Tonitto v Bassal* (1992) 28 NSWLR 564. Contrast *Di Biase v Rezek* [1971] 1 NSWLR 735.
70. [1983] 1 AC 646 at 655.
71. [1958] 1 Ch 110 at 130.
72. *Burgess v Cox* [1951] Ch 383 at 388.

[517] sale of goods contract is that writing is only one of a number of possible ways in which the statute may be satisfied. Of course, if the sale of goods contract happens to come within the classes of contract discussed above, for example, because it is not to be performed within the space of one year, there must be writing because the alternative methods of satisfying the requirement specified in the sale of goods legislation will not be available.[73]

[517] **Acceptance of goods.** Under the definition of acceptance in the sale of goods legislation[74] the crucial question is whether the buyer has done any *act in relation to the goods* which *recognises a pre-existing contract* of sale. This is a question of fact.[75]

If a buyer actually receives goods the subject of an oral contract of sale, and treats the goods as his or her own property, they will be regarded as 'accepted' as required by legislation.[76] Words or conduct of a more equivocal nature may, on the facts of a particular case, constitute acceptance. But what if the goods which have been 'accepted' were not delivered pursuant to the contract sued on? The matter arose in *Metropolitan Knitting and Hosiery Co Ltd v Thomas Burnley & Sons Ltd*[77] where an action was brought on two contracts of sale one of which was denied by the defendants who raised the defence that s 17 of the *Statute of Frauds* 1677 (Imp), which was then in force, had not been complied with. In their pleadings the plaintiffs alleged 'acceptance' of part of the goods and the trial judge directed the jury that in order to satisfy the statute the plaintiffs had to show that the goods were accepted *under the contract sought to be enforced*, and not under the contract which had been denied by the defendants. A majority of the High Court considered that this direction was proper, and agreed that an honest belief by the defendants that they were receiving goods under some contract other than that sued on was material. On the other hand, Isaacs J considered[78] that the word 'act' in the legislative description of acceptance excluded 'secret qualification and undisclosed error' and emphasised the objectivity of the provision. Moreover, in his view[79] the only 'recognition' of a contract required by acceptance was the recognition under 'some contract of sale' between the parties.

[518] **Earnest and part payment.** Enforcement of an oral contract for the sale of goods will be possible if the buyer gives something 'in earnest to bind the contract, or in part payment'. Although not restricted to monetary payments, a clear example of the former is the payment of a monetary

---

73. For illustrative purposes reference can be made to the following cases which deal with the requirement of writing in relation to sale of goods: *Cohen v Roche* [1927] 1 KB 169 (signature); *Farr Smith & Co Ltd v Messers Ltd* [1928] 1 KB 397 (signature by agent); *Parbury Henty & Co Pty Ltd v General Engineering & Agencies Pty Ltd* (1973) 47 ALJR 336 (contract acknowledged by letter).
74. See [511].
75. *Metropolitan Knitting and Hosiery Co Ltd v Thomas Burnley & Sons Ltd* (1924) 35 CLR 232 at 243.
76. For an illustration see *Deta Nominees Pty Ltd v Viscount Plastic Products Pty Ltd* [1979] VR 167.
77. (1924) 35 CLR 232.
78. (1924) 35 CLR 232 at 240.
79. (1924) 35 CLR 232 at 242.

deposit, that is, a payment made at the time of formation in order to show the genuineness of the buyer. It is a sum of money which is liable to be forfeited to the seller if the contract goes off without default on the seller's part.[80] Although a deposit is almost invariably credited towards the payment of the price of the goods, it is distinguishable from a pure part payment by reason of the fact that it is normally subject to forfeiture in the event of the payer's default.[81] A part payment may be made in advance, but is more frequently made in exchange for the goods.

The relation between deposits and part payments was considered by Wright J in *Farr Smith & Co Ltd v Messers Ltd*.[82] A contract for the sale of a quantity of wood was repudiated by the sellers before delivery. The buyers had promised to make payments by way of cash and bills of exchange and they relied on this as something given in earnest, to bind the contract. Alternatively, they relied on the payment later received by the sellers by virtue of the bills of exchange. Wright J considered that nothing had been given in 'earnest'. He said[83] that an earnest must be a 'tangible thing' given 'at the moment when the contract is concluded', as a 'guarantee' that the buyer will fulfil the contract. Clearly, the plaintiffs had given nothing in earnest on the facts of this case; but, equally clearly, their payment constituted a payment under the contract. The defence based on s 4 of the *Sale of Goods Act* 1893 (UK)[84] therefore failed. The case indicates that a buyer's *promise* to pay the price of the goods the subject of the contract does not amount either to an earnest or a part payment.

Effect of Noncompliance

Position at Common Law

[519] Contract unenforceable but not void. Until the middle of the 19th century the prevailing view was that noncompliance with the requirements of the *Statute of Frauds* 1677 (Imp) rendered the contract void.[85] However, it is now accepted that the contract is unenforceable but not void. This is true in respect of both s 4 and s 17 and their modern equivalents. Thus, their effect is said to be 'procedural',[86] preventing any action on the contract but not denying its existence. Clearly, an action for damages for breach of contract is not possible because such an action is brought directly on the contract. In the language of s 4, the plaintiff is seeking to 'charge' the defendant on the contract. But it is also true that if money has been paid under a contract which does not comply with the requirement of writing and is therefore unenforceable, the 'payee may rely upon such contract to protect his position against a plaintiff seeking to establish some countervailing claim'.[87]

---

80. See also [2236].
81. See [2333].
82. [1928] 1 KB 397.
83. [1928] 1 KB 397 at 408.
84. There is no such requirement under the *Sale of Goods Act* 1979 (UK).
85. See, eg *Birkmyr v Darnell* (1704) 1 Salk 27; 91 ER 27; and see Simpson, *A History of the Common Law of Contract*, 1975, pp 609, 612–13.
86. See, eg *Popiw v Popiw* [1959] VR 197 at 200.

[519]

Where a contract contains several promises, some but not all of which are required to be evidenced by writing, the absence of a written note or memorandum renders the whole contract unenforceable unless the promises are severable. In this context[88] 'severable' means that the promises are 'not only themselves severable but may be referred to and supported by independent or divisible considerations or divisible parts of a consideration capable of distribution'.[89] In other words, the plaintiff must show that the promise being enforced is not one required to be evidenced by writing, and that the form of the contract is such that the consideration for this promise is separate from the consideration supporting the unenforceable promises.

[520] Claims dehors the contract. A plaintiff who is unable to sue on a contract because of noncompliance with the formal requirements applicable is not necessarily precluded from obtaining relief on a claim which is independent of the contract.

In *Horton v Jones*[90] Jordan CJ said[91] that if 'a person does acts for the benefit of another in the performance of a contract which is unenforceable' by reason of the statute, and the other 'accepts the benefit of those acts', an action in restitution to 'obtain reasonable remuneration' will be available. This approach was approved by the High Court in *Pavey & Matthews Pty Ltd v Paul*.[92] In that case Pavey & Matthews (the builder) sued Ms Paul to recover a reasonable sum for work done and materials supplied at her request. The defence was that s 45 of the *Builders Licensing Act* 1971 (NSW) made the building contract, under which the work was done, unenforceable. It required any building contract under which the builder, as holder of a licence under the Act, undertook to carry out any building work (or to vary any building work or the manner of carrying out any building work) to be *in writing* and signed by each of the parties. It declared unenforceable *against the other party* to the contract any contract which did not comply with s 45. The defence was tried by Clarke J as a separate preliminary issue on certain agreed facts including that the contract was unenforceable by reason of noncompliance with s 45. He decided the issue in favour of the builder, but an appeal to the New South Wales Court of Appeal was allowed.[93] A further appeal to the High Court was (by majority) allowed.

It is important to notice that the claim was not brought on the contract. Such a claim was clearly prohibited. Rather, the action was a restitutionary claim for 'reasonable remuneration' (described as a 'quantum meruit')

---

87. *Head v Kelk* (1963) 63 SR (NSW) 340 at 348. See also *Lejo Holdings Pty Ltd v Deutsche Bank (Asia) AG* [1988] 2 Qd R 30 at 43. Cf *Perpetual Executors and Trustees Association of Australia Ltd v Russell* (1931) 45 CLR 146. See Mason and Carter, *Restitution Law in Australia*, 1995, para 1019.
88. See also [272], [1729]–[1739].
89. *Horton v Jones* (1935) 53 CLR 475 at 485. See also *Collin v Holden* [1989] VR 510 at 512–13.
90. (1934) 34 SR (NSW) 359.
91. (1934) 34 SR (NSW) 359 at 367 (affirmed on other grounds (1935) 53 CLR 475).
92. (1987) 162 CLR 221 at 250; 69 ALR 577. See also *Phillips v Ellinson Bros Pty Ltd* (1941) 65 CLR 221 at 246.
93. See (1985) 3 NSWLR 114.

based, so the High Court held, on unjust enrichment.[94] The obligation to pay a reasonable sum was not contractual in nature, it was an obligation imposed by law, and s 45 was held not to apply to such a claim. Thus, although no action on the contract was available, an action to recover the reasonable value of the services rendered was available. The High Court did not see this decision as frustrating the purpose of the section, that is, to provide protection for a building owner.[95] As Deane J said:[96]

> The building owner remains entitled to enforce the contract. He cannot, however, be forced either to comply with its terms or to permit the builder to carry it to completion. All that he can be required to do is to pay reasonable compensation for work done of which he has received the benefit and for which in justice he is obligated to make such a payment by way of restitution. In relation to such work, he can rely on the contract, if it has not been rescinded, as to the amount of remuneration and the terms of payment. If the agreed remuneration exceeds what is reasonable in the circumstances, he can rely on the unenforceability of the contract with the result that he is liable to pay no more than what is fair and reasonable.

Pavey & Matthews Pty Ltd v Paul shows that a plaintiff is entitled to recover in respect of a fully performed but unenforceable contract. The action is for restitution and the price specified in the contract is evidence of the plaintiff's entitlement.[97] However, if performance is only partial, recovery will not usually be possible. Recovery of the reasonable value of work done as restitution is, however, open where the defendant has accepted the benefit of the work, and the contract has been rescinded or discharged. The usual situation is where the plaintiff has validly terminated the contract, for example, because of a serious breach or repudiation by the defendant.[98]

It is essential that the policy behind the statutory requirement of writing be considered. In *Pavey & Matthews Pty Ltd v Paul* the conclusion was that this did not extend to a claim in restitution. However, there may be situations in which the policy of the statute requires a different conclusion.[99]

Position in Equity[100]

[521] Doctrine of part performance. Rigid adherence to the common law position, even allowing for restitutionary claims discussed above,[101] and for the fairly generous interpretation of concepts such as signature,[102]

---

94. See further [2308].
95. Brennan J (dissenting) considered that the protective function of s 45 would have been frustrated by a decision in the builder's favour.
96. (1987) 162 CLR 221 at 263. See also *Gino D'Alessandro Constructions Pty Ltd v Powis* [1987] 2 Qd R 40. Cf *Fablo Pty Ltd v Bloore* [1983] 1 Qd R 107.
97. See *Horton v Jones* (1934) 34 SR (NSW) 359 at 367–8 (affirmed on other grounds (1935) 53 CLR 475); and further [2337], [2338].
98. See *Matthes v Carter* (1955) 55 SR (NSW) 357 and generally Mason and Carter, *Restitution Law in Australia*, 1995, paras 1031–1032.
99. See, eg *Sevastopoulos v Spanos* [1991] 2 VR 194.
100. See Spry, *Equitable Remedies*, 5th ed, 1997, pp 248–88.
101. See [520].
102. See *Australia and New Zealand Banking Group Ltd v Widin* (1990) 102 ALR 289 at 301.

[521]

would cause injustice and allow the *Statute of Frauds* 1677 (Imp) itself to be the protector of fraudulent persons. It was not long[103] before equity developed what is known as the 'doctrine of part performance'.[104]

Where the plaintiff establishes sufficient acts of part performance to justify equitable intervention notwithstanding that the contract is oral, the defendant is, as Lord Selborne LC explained in *Maddison v Alderson*,[105] '"charged" upon the equities resulting from the acts done in execution of the Contract, and not (within the meaning of the statute) upon the contract itself'. In such a case the 'equity' which arises is to have the 'entire contract carried into execution by both sides'.[106]

The reason for equitable intervention, in the face of the statute, is that the acts of part performance make it unconscientious for the defendant to plead the statute as a bar to the plaintiff's claim.[107] We are concerned, therefore, with conduct which renders it inequitable or unconscionable for the defendant to rely on the statute. Of course, if the court is to intervene, by ordering specific performance of the oral contract, the contract must be amenable to relief by specific performance.[108] For example, if personal services are involved, specific performance may not be ordered even if part performance is established.[109]

Although the doctrine of part performance has fairly recently been considered by both the House of Lords[110] and the High Court,[111] there is still uncertainty as to the requirements of the doctrine. For example, there seems to be a conflict of opinion in Australia on the order in which matters are considered. Glass JA said in *Millett v Regent*[112] that the 'accepted practice is to deal with the unwritten contract first and then to consider the acts of part performance, disregarding the oral agreement'. Support for Glass JA's opinion can be found in *Steadman v Steadman*,[113] but it is contrary to *Thwaites v Ryan*.[114]

---

103. The origins are far from clear. See Simpson, *A History of the Common Law of Contract*, 1975, pp 613–16.
104. The doctrine no longer applies in England because the *Law of Property (Miscellaneous Provisions) Act* 1989 (UK), s 2 states that a contract for the sale or other disposition of an interest in land can only be made in writing. But cf s 2(5) (saving of constructive trusts) and see *Butler v Craine* [1986] VR 274.
105. (1883) 8 App Cas 467 at 475. See also *McBride v Sandland* (1918) 25 CLR 69 at 77; *Ash Street Properties Pty Ltd v Pollnow* (1987) 9 NSWLR 80 at 84, 101; *McMahon v Ambrose* [1987] VR 817 at 851.
106. *JC Williamson Ltd v Lukey* (1931) 45 CLR 282 at 300.
107. See Meagher, Gummow and Lehane, *Equity: Doctrines and Remedies*, 3rd ed, 1992, para 2045.
108. See generally [2403].
109. See, eg *Maiden v Maiden* (1909) 7 CLR 727 at 737.
110. *Steadman v Steadman* [1976] AC 536 (see [522]).
111. *Regent v Millett* (1976) 133 CLR 679; 10 ALR 496 (see [522]).
112. [1975] 1 NSWLR 62 at 73 (affirmed without reference to the point sub nom *Regent v Millett* (1976) 133 CLR 679).
113. [1976] AC 536 at 556. See also *Watson v Delaney* (1991) 22 NSWLR 358 at 363 ('tentative preference' for the view).
114. [1984] VR 65 at 77, followed in *Riley v Osbourne* [1986] VR 193 at 198–9 (reluctantly); *Butler v Craine* [1986] VR 274 at 282. Cf *McMahon v Ambrose* [1987] VR 817 at 846–7.

Three principal issues arise and are dealt with below.[115] However, part performance should not be seen as the only qualification to the operation of the *Statute of Frauds* 1677 (Imp). It is now clear that estoppel may have the same effect as part performance, namely, the availability of specific performance where there is no legally enforceable contract.[116]

[522] Referability. The first issue is referability. To what extent must the acts relied upon as part performance be referable to the contract sued on?

In *Maddison v Alderson*[117] Lord Selborne LC said that the 'acts relied upon as part performance must be unequivocally and in their own nature, referable to some such contract as that alleged'. There are two aspects to this classic statement. There is a requirement that the acts be 'unequivocal'; and a requirement of referability to 'some such contract', not simply 'a contract'. Although the 'unequivocal' act requirement has generally been insisted on,[118] it is doubtful whether the word has been literally interpreted. And the requirement of 'some such contract', although insisted on in many High Court decisions,[119] was rejected by a majority of the House of Lords in *Steadman v Steadman*,[120] a decision which indicates that it is impossible to keep the two aspects of referability distinct from one another.

In *Steadman v Steadman* an agreement was reached under which the plaintiff agreed to surrender her interest in a house, which was owned jointly by herself and the defendant, to the defendant. It was also agreed:

- that a maintenance order in favour of the plaintiff should be discharged;
- that a maintenance order for a child of the marriage should continue; and
- that arrears of maintenance should be remitted save for a sum of £100 which was subsequently paid by the defendant.

When the plaintiff refused to sign a transfer of the house the defendant relied on the following facts as part performance justifying an order for specific performance: (1) payment of the £100; (2) intimation of the agreement to the magistrate's court and the abandonment of attempts to have all arrears of maintenance remitted; and (3) the dispatch to the plaintiff's solicitor of the transfer which the plaintiff refused to sign and the cost of its preparation. A majority held that sufficient part performance was established and specific performance was therefore ordered. This would seem to have been on the basis that referability requires that the acts of part performance, when considered in the light of the circumstances of the case, point to some contract between the parties on the balance of probabilities, and indicate the nature of the oral agreement alleged or consistent with

---

115. See [522]–[524].
116. See *Riches v Hogben* [1985] 2 Qd R 292 (affirmed [1986] 1 Qd R 315); *Waltons Stores (Interstate) Ltd v Maher* (1988) 164 CLR 387; 76 ALR 513 (see [376]); *Collin v Holden* [1989] VR 510; and the discussion by K G Nicholson, 'Riches v Hogben: Part Performance and the Doctrines of Equitable and Proprietary Estoppel' (1986) 60 *ALJ* 345.
117. (1883) 8 App Cas 467 at 479. See also *Cooney v Burns* (1922) 30 CLR 216 at 243.
118. See, eg *McBride v Sandland* (1918) 25 CLR 69 at 78.
119. See, eg *McBride v Sandland* (1918) 25 CLR 69; *J C Williamson Ltd v Lukey* (1931) 45 CLR 282.
120. [1976] AC 536.

it.[121] This is wider than the requirement, traditionally applied in Australia, that the acts be referable to some such contract as that alleged, that is (broadly) a contract relating to land. Accordingly, in the absence of High Court approval of *Steadman*, Australian courts have continued to insist on the traditional requirement.[122] Moreover, the House of Lords treated the payment of money as an act of part performance notwithstanding that payment, even of the full purchase price of land, has in the past been regarded as an equivocal act.[123]

Whatever formulation of the requirement of referability is preferred, it must not be forgotten that each case will depend on its own facts and that different conclusions may result notwithstanding a similarity of the acts relied upon. For example, in *McBride v Sandland*[124] the taking of possession of land was held not to be sufficient part performance. On the other hand, in *Regent v Millett*[125] purchasers of land relied on the following acts as part performance under an oral contract for the sale of land:

- the taking of possession;
- the fact that they had effected repairs to improvements on the land;
- renovations and additions to the improvements; and
- the making of mortgage payments.

The High Court held that the giving and taking of possession was itself sufficient part performance. *McBride v Sandland* was distinguished on the ground that in that case the taking of possession was 'referable to some authority other than the contract alleged'.[126] In that case, the possession taken by the defendant (and her husband) was referable to a lease between the plaintiff and the defendant's husband, and not referable to an option to purchase the land in respect of which part performance was alleged.

A lessee's continuation in possession of land may be evidence of part performance of an agreement for a lease, but not if the lessee continues to pay the same rent because that renders the act equivocal.[127] Where the same rent is paid the position may be simply that the lessor has made a decision not to recover possession; but an increase in rent is some evidence of fresh agreement.

[523] Performance of the contract. The second issue is this: to what extent must the acts relied on be performance of the contract? In *J C Williamson Ltd v Lukey*[128] Dixon J said that the acts must have been done in 'actual performance' of the contract which in fact existed between the parties. Clearly, this excludes acts which have been done but were not

---

121. *Ogilvie v Ryan* [1976] 2 NSWLR 504 at 520.
122. See, eg *Ogilvie v Ryan* [1976] 2 NSWLR 504; *Thwaites v Ryan* [1984] VR 65; *Ratto v Trifid Pty Ltd* [1987] WAR 237 at 258; *McMahon v Ambrose* [1987] VR 817 at 847; *Australia and New Zealand Banking Group Ltd v Widin* (1990) 102 ALR 289 at 305.
123. See Spry, *Equitable Remedies*, 5th ed, 1997, p 274.
124. (1918) 25 CLR 69.
125. (1976) 133 CLR 679. See also *Watson v Delaney* (1991) 22 NSWLR 358.
126. (1976) 133 CLR 679 at 683.
127. *Kalnenas v Kovacevich* [1961] WAR 188 at 193; *Darter Pty Ltd v Malloy* [1993] 2 Qd R 615 at 623.
128. (1931) 45 CLR 282 at 300.

part of the contract. Thus, preparatory acts, such as the preparation of the assignment of a lease, have been held not to be sufficient.[129] It would also exclude acts which might otherwise be unequivocal such as a taking of possession of land where the contract does not require this. But in *Regent v Millett*[130] the High Court considered that the taking of possession was a sufficient act even though the contract did not require it. The court said[131] that the 'utility of the equitable doctrine would be reduced to vanishing point' if it were necessary for the acts to be 'in compliance with a requirement of the contract'. Thus, it may be that it is sufficient for the act to be done pursuant to the contract even though the act is not 'required'. The High Court left open the position with regard to an act which is neither required nor permitted by the contract. In the New South Wales Court of Appeal there had been a difference of opinion. Hutley JA had expressed the view[132] that if acts are done which unequivocally point to a contract the doctrine of part performance should be applicable, 'if other conditions are fulfilled', even though the acts are 'neither required by the contract nor ... expressly authorised', provided they are done in consequence of the agreement. On the other hand, Glass JA said[133] that acts done in consequence of the oral agreement, 'but not in execution of it, are excluded from consideration', because they are neither required nor authorised by the agreement. The third member of the court, Mahoney JA, expressed no view on the matter.

[524] Scope of the doctrine. Most of the cases on the doctrine of part performance involve contracts which relate to land. Clearly, its main application is to such contracts and the modern statutory provisions derived from s 4 of the *Statute of Frauds* 1677 (Imp) expressly preserve the doctrine in that context.[134]

The reason the doctrine has been discussed mainly in the context of contracts involving land is that the remedy of specific performance, so important in the context of the doctrine, has its main application to such contracts. But a third issue in relation to part performance is whether it applies beyond land contracts. The doctrine has been discussed, if not actually applied, in the context of other types of contracts[135] and there is no reason, in principle, for not applying the doctrine outside the context of land if specific performance is available.[136] Of course, the diminished

---

129. *Cooney v Burns* (1922) 30 CLR 216. See also *Grummitt v Natalisio* [1968] VR 156 (expenditure on surveying and related matters not part performance of contract for sale of land).
130. (1976) 133 CLR 679 (see [522]).
131. (1976) 133 CLR 679 at 683. See also *Riley v Osbourne* [1986] VR 193.
132. Sub nom *Millett v Regent* [1975] 1 NSWLR 62 at 66.
133. [1975] 1 NSWLR 62 at 71.
134. See **ACT**: *Law Reform (Miscellaneous Provisions) Act* 1955, s 54(2); **NSW**: *Conveyancing Act* 1919, s 54a(2); **NT**: *Law of Property Act* 2000, s 5(c); **Qld**: *Property Law Act* 1974, s 6(d); **SA**: *Law of Property Act* 1936, s 26(2); **Tas**: *Conveyancing and Law of Property Act* 1884, s 36(2); **Vic**: *Property Law Act* 1958, s 55(d); **WA**: *Property Law Act* 1969, s 36(d).
135. See, eg *J C Williamson Ltd v Lukey* (1931) 45 CLR 282; *Steadman v Steadman* [1976] AC 536 at 570.
136. See Meagher, Gummow and Lehane, *Equity: Doctrines and Remedies*, 3rd ed, 1992, para 2043.

importance of formal requirements outside the context of land means that the issue is not particularly important in practice.

The doctrine of part performance has one important limitation, namely, it cannot be used to found an action for common law damages for breach of contract.[137]

Rescission, Variation and Related Concepts

[525] When variation must be written. Where a contract is *not* required to be evidenced by writing any variation of the terms of the contract may be made by a purely oral agreement. However, where there is such a requirement the variation must also be so evidenced because the writing must contain all the terms. If the variation is purely oral it cannot, subject perhaps to the doctrine of part performance, be enforced and the 'original contract in writing stands unaffected'.[138]

In *British & Beningtons Ltd v North Western Cachar Tea Co Ltd*[139] several contracts for the sale of tea required delivery to be made in London. Because of congestion in the Port of London the vessels carrying the tea were diverted to various other ports and the ensuing delay was the subject of disputes between the parties to the contracts. An oral agreement was alleged to have then been made under which the buyers agreed to take delivery, at the ports where the tea had been discharged, in return for a reduction in price. This was an oral variation of the written contracts which existed and was unenforceable by reason of s 4 of the *Sale of Goods Act* 1893 (UK) which was in force at the time. Accordingly, the contracts had to be enforced in their original, unaltered, form.

[526] Variation distinguished from rescission. Although a variation of a contract required to be evidenced by writing must be similarly evidenced, the contract may be validly rescinded by an oral agreement. An agreement to rescind discharges the parties from the duty to perform their contractual obligations. It may replace the obligations with a set of new obligations, in which case that contract will probably be evidenced by writing. If there is no such fresh agreement, or it is unenforceable, the parties are still discharged and the consequences which flow from rescission, or 'abandonment' as it is sometimes termed, are implied by law.[140] Rescission may take place by reason of express or implied agreement, or even by the conduct of the parties in abandoning the performance of the contract.[141]

---

137. See, eg *McMahon v Ambrose* [1987] VR 817 at 828. However, damages based on *Lord Cairns' Act (Chancery Amendment Act* 1858 (UK) (21 & 22 Vic c 27) see generally [2169]–[2173]) may be available; see *Waltons Stores (Interstate) Ltd v Maher* (1988) 164 CLR 387 (see [376]); but cf *Commonwealth of Australia v Verwayen* (1990) 170 CLR 394 at 439; 95 ALR 321. For discussion of whether a claim for damages may be based on breach of the statutory prohibition (see [1102]) on misleading and deceptive conduct see *Futuretronics International Pty Ltd v Gadzhis* (1990) [1992] 2 VR 217.
138. *Tallerman & Co Pty Ltd v Nathan's Merchandise (Victoria) Pty Ltd* (1957) 98 CLR 93 at 113.
139. [1923] AC 48.
140. See *Paal Wilson & Co A/S v Partenreederei Hannah Blumenthal* [1983] 1 AC 854 at 915.

In *Morris v Baron & Co*[142] an action was brought to recover the price of goods sold and delivered by the plaintiff to the defendants. The defendants conceded the claim but made a counter-claim, alleging non-delivery of other goods. This was based alternatively on the original contract and an agreement reached in settlement of a previous action between the parties. The settlement contract did not comply with s 4 of the *Sale of Goods Act 1893* (UK) and, on the assumption that it should have complied with that provision, was held to be unenforceable. So far as the distinction between rescission and variation is concerned, Viscount Haldane said[143] it is 'essential', if the agreement is to amount to a complete rescission, 'that there should have been made manifest the intention in any event of a complete extinction of the first and formal contract, and not merely the desire of an alteration, however sweeping, in terms which still leave it subsisting'. In this case the parties had agreed to discharge the original contract and to replace it with a fresh set of obligations with the result that neither the original agreement nor the substituted agreement could be the source of an action by the defendants.

Unless the parties have expressly stated that their prior agreement is to be 'terminated', 'rescinded', 'abrogated', 'abandoned', 'discharged', or have used some similar expression, it may be difficult to decide whether the subsequent agreement is a mere variation or a rescission. In *Morris v Baron & Co* various tests were suggested, such as inquiring whether the two agreements deal with the same subject matter in such a way that it is impossible for both to be performed, or whether the subsequent contract is inconsistent to an extent which goes to the 'root' of the prior contract.

In *Tallerman & Co Pty Ltd v Nathan's Merchandise (Victoria) Pty Ltd*[144] Dixon CJ and Fullagar J expressed the view that the distinction between variation and rescission is not a satisfactory one. Similarly, in *United Dominions Corp (Jamaica) Ltd v Shoucair*[145] Lord Devlin, when delivering the advice of the Privy Council in that case, admitted that logic might dictate the interpretation of even a minor contractual variation as the rescission of the prior contract and the substitution of a new contract. He recognised that this view had been rejected in *Morris v Baron & Co* for the very sensible reason that it would not accord with the intention of the parties, assuming the variation to be purely oral, for there to be no enforceable agreement between them. This leads to the proposition that in considering the effect of a subsequent oral agreement it is always material to examine the intention of the parties and, in particular, to ask whether they intend the prior contract to be rescinded if the subsequent contract is unenforceable. In other words, if the parties' agreement for rescission is contingent on the substitution of a new and enforceable contract, the rescission will not take effect if the subsequent agreement is unenforceable by reason of a statutory requirement of writing.[146] It was on this basis that a

141. See [111], [1978].
142. [1918] AC 1.
143. [1918] AC 1 at 19.
144. (1957) 98 CLR 93 at 113.
145. [1969] 1 AC 340 at 348, 349.
146. See *Tallerman & Co Pty Ltd v Nathan's Merchandise (Victoria) Pty Ltd* (1957) 98 CLR 93 at 123.

variation of the rate of interest payable on a loan was held not to extinguish the prior debt and mortgage in the *United Dominions* case.

[527] Variation distinguished from forbearance and related concepts. The fact that an oral variation of a contract required to be evidenced by writing is unenforceable has given rise to some artificial distinctions designed to prevent the statutory requirement causing obvious injustice. A decision which indicates the kinds of distinctions which have been drawn is *Hartley v Hymans*.[147] A contract for the sale of goods required delivery to be made, at a specified rate per week, starting in the month of September and being completed by 15 November. In fact, deliveries commenced on 29 November, but the buyer, while complaining of delay, urged the seller to deliver, and accepted two deliveries in December and one in the following February. However, in March the buyer purported to cancel the contract on the ground of late delivery and the seller sued to recover damages for the buyer's refusal to accept the balance of the goods. McCardie J held that time had originally been of the essence of the contract,[148] which meant that the buyer could have terminated the performance of the contract when delivery did not commence by the required date.[149] It was held, however, that the buyer had in fact 'waived' the right to insist that the contract period terminated on 15 November, that is, elected[150] not to terminate, and that as this was evidenced by writing the seller was able to succeed in his action.

Alternatively, McCardie J held: (1) that the buyer was estopped[151] from saying that the period for delivery had expired; and (2) that a new agreement could be implied, from the letters which passed between the parties, extending the period for delivery. But in the course of reaching those conclusions it was also said that a party's election in favour of a right will be effective even if oral, as it does not involve a variation of the contract. The position will be different where the conduct goes further. For example, if its effect is to substitute a different term in the contract writing will be required.[152] It is also established that estoppel may be purely oral for the reason that it does not vary the contract but, instead, disentitles parties, such as the buyer in *Hartley v Hymans*, from relying on their strict legal rights.[153]

A distinction is drawn between a variation of the terms of the contract and an arrangement in relation to the mode or manner of performance. It is well established that no writing is required for the latter.[154] For example, a forbearance by one party in the performance of a contract, such as a seller's forbearance to deliver at the request of the buyer, is effective, even if purely oral, to prevent insistence on the original delivery date, provided there is

---

147. [1920] 3 KB 475.
148. For the meaning of this expression see [1848], [1949].
149. For the meaning of termination see [1985].
150. See further [1971].
151. See generally [365]–[387], [1974]–[1976].
152. See *Phillips v Ellinson Bros Pty Ltd* (1941) 65 CLR 221 at 244.
153. See, eg *Panoutsos v Raymond Hadley Corp of New York* [1917] 2 KB 473. Cf *Peter Turnbull & Co Pty Ltd v Mundus Trading Co (Australasia) Pty Ltd* (1954) 90 CLR 235 (see [1947]).
154. See, eg *Phillips v Ellinson Bros Pty Ltd* (1941) 65 CLR 221 at 233, 244.

sufficient evidence.[155] Therefore, in the example just given, even though there is no variation of the terms of the contract, the buyer is not entitled to sue the seller for not delivering at the appointed time, and cannot refuse to take delivery on the ground that the goods have not been delivered at the time stipulated in the contract.

---

155. See *Electronic Industries Ltd v David Jones Ltd* (1954) 91 CLR 288; *Gray v Lang* (1955) 56 SR (NSW) 7 at 11, 12; *United Motels Ltd v Cooper* [1964] NSWR 1252 at 1254.

PART III
Terms of the Contract

Chapter 6

Identification of the Terms

Introduction 601
Express Terms 602
   Pre-contractual Statements 602
   Incorporation of Terms 615
Implied Terms 620
   General 620
   Terms Implied in Fact 625
   Terms Implied in Law 631
   Terms Implied by Statute 636
   Terms Implied by Custom or Usage. 644

Introduction

[601] **Term may be express or implied.** Subject to certain statutory restrictions[1] a contract may be wholly oral, or partly oral and partly written. When used in its most general sense the word 'term' describes any clause or provision in a contract, whether written or oral.

Apart from the terms *expressly stated* in the contract, *implied* terms may govern the parties' relationship. Therefore, in order to identify the terms of a contract it is not always sufficient merely to look at the contract itself, assuming that it is in writing, or to ask what the parties actually said, if the contract is merely oral.

We include in the category of express terms those incorporated into the contract, for example, by means of a notice displayed at the time the contract is entered into. However, some such terms are actually implied terms.[2] In some cases statements made before the contract was entered into may be intended to take effect as terms. However, not all such statements operate as terms.[3]

---

1. See generally Chapter 5.
2. See [618].
3. See generally [602]–[619].

Express Terms

Pre-contractual Statements[4]

Classification

[602] Purpose of classification. The purpose of classifying statements made prior to entry into the contract is straightforward: a statement which is not a term has no contractual force. The basic classification is between terms and representations. In this context the word 'term' has a narrower meaning than stated above, and describes a contractual statement which amounts to an undertaking or guarantee ('warranty'), by the maker of the statement, of its truth or that the maker had reasonable grounds for making it. In most cases the promisor is strictly liable on the undertaking to guarantee the truth of the statement, liability in damages does not depend on whether reasonable care was exercised.[5]

Statements which take effect as collateral contracts are dealt with later.[6]

[603] Puffs. At the lowest end of the scale are laudatory statements not intended to be taken seriously. 'Sales' talk or 'puffery' on behalf of a seller of goods, for example, that a motor vehicle is the 'best on the market', does not have contractual force.[7]

[604] Representations. Between puffs and terms is the category of representations. Those are factual statements which induce the representee to enter into the contract but which are not guaranteed by their maker. Frequently such a statement is described as a 'mere' representation, reflecting the absence of contractual intent.[8]

Because a representation has no contractual force, its falsity does not give rise to a claim for damages for breach of contract. If the representor has been guilty of fraud the representee is able to pursue a remedy in tort, and in certain circumstances negligence on the part of a representor may also provide the representee with a claim for common law damages. However, if the representation is innocently made there is no liability in damages at common law and the representee's only remedy is rescission.[9] Under statute a misrepresentation, whatever its character, may give rise to a claim for damages.[10]

[605] Terms. Assuming that a pre-contractual statement is a term of the contract, it takes effect as an express term. Most of the cases concern

---

4. See D E Allan, 'The Scope of the Contract' (1967) 41 *ALJ* 274.
5. Contrast *Esso Petroleum Co Ltd v Mardon* [1976] QB 801 (see [1133]).
6. See [611]–[614].
7. Reference should be made to cases on what constitutes an offer for examples of puffs. See [208]. See also [407], [1007]. Cf *Thake v Maurice* [1986] QB 644 at 685 (surgeon's 'therapeutic reassurance').
8. Although in practice rare, a representation may be reproduced in a memorandum of a contract, and yet retain its character as a representation. See further [609], [724], [1057]–[1059].
9. See generally Chapter 10.
10. See further [1073]–[1078] (misrepresentation legislation), Chapter 11 (misleading and deceptive conduct).

statements of fact, and when such a statement is a term it is usually referred to as a 'warranty'. However, this is merely a conventional expression and when classified under the tripartite classification[11] may be more accurately described as a 'condition' or an 'intermediate' term.[12] The fact that the statement is a term means that its breach gives rise to a claim for damages. It is therefore necessary to consider whether it is a condition, warranty or an intermediate term only if the promisee claims to be entitled to terminate the performance of the contract.[13]

What distinguishes a term from a mere representation is the intention of the maker of the statement to guarantee its truth.[14]

Relevant factors

[606] Intention of parties. Although the basis upon which pre-contractual statements are classified is the intention of the parties, the court must be objective and ask what conclusion a reasonable person in the position of the person to whom the statement was made would have reached.[15] If such a person would have concluded that the maker of the statement intended to guarantee its truth, it is a term whether or not there was an actual intention to accept contractual responsibility.[16]

The criterion of intention is easy to state but difficult to apply. In order to decide the issue the courts have regard to various factors and these are considered in the paragraphs which follow.

[607] Time of statement. The proximity between the statement made and entry into the contract may be considered relevant to the intention of the parties, because the shorter the period of time the more likely it is that the statement induced entry into the contract. For example, in *Harling v Eddy*[17] the defendant put a heifer up for auction and, when there was no bid, stated that there was nothing wrong with the animal and that he would absolutely guarantee her in every respect. He also said that he would take the heifer back if she was no good. The plaintiff thereupon bid for the heifer which was sold to him. Within four months the animal died from tuberculosis and she must have been suffering from this disease when sold to the plaintiff. The court held that the defendant's statement was a term of the contract and that he was liable in damages. The close proximity between the statement and entry into the contract was one factor which justified this conclusion.

This factor can hardly be conclusive, because the proximity of the statement and entry into the contract may only establish that the

---

11. See [725]–[738].
12. See [734].
13. For the meaning of termination see [1985], and generally on termination for breach of a term [1911]–[1927].
14. See [606].
15. See, eg *Hospital Products Ltd v United States Surgical Corp* (1984) 156 CLR 41 at 61; 55 ALR 417. Cf *Oscar Chess Ltd v Williams* [1957] 1 WLR 370 at 375 (a statement is a term if an 'intelligent bystander would reasonably infer' that its truth was being guaranteed). See further [610].
16. See, eg *Ellul v Oakes* (1972) 3 SASR 377 at 381.
17. [1951] 2 KB 739. Cf *Faram v Kerr* (1877) 3 VLR (L) 146.

representee relied on the statement when entering into the contract, and is entitled to rescind the contract for misrepresentation. Conversely, the fact that there is delay does not necessarily indicate that a statement was not to have contractual force.

[608] **Content of the statement.** The more important the content of a statement the more likely it is that the parties intended it to be a term of the contract. Importance must, of course, depend on the circumstances of the case. For example, in *Couchman v Hill*[18] Couchman purchased a heifer from Hill at a price of £29. The contract was entered into at an auction and before making his bid Couchman asked whether the heifer had been served. Both the seller and the auctioneer replied that the heifer was unserved. This was clearly important because the heifer was young, but the statement turned out to be false and Couchman suffered loss when the heifer died from the early pregnancy. His action for damages for breach of contract was successful because the statement was found to be an offer which became a term of the contract when Couchman bid and the animal was knocked down to him.[19]

[609] **Existence of written memorandum.** If the parties execute a memorandum of the terms of the contract which does not include a pre-contractual statement later relied on as a term, the representee will find it difficult to establish that the statement was a term. As a matter of common sense, the failure to include the statement is some indication that it was not intended to be a term.[20]

On the other hand, the failure of the parties to execute a written memorandum is no evidence at all of whether the statement relied on is a term of the contract.

If a statement is made, and then later recorded in writing, that is 'good evidence' that the statement was intended to be a term in the sense that its truth was guaranteed.[21]

[610] **Knowledge and expertise of the parties.** Perhaps the most important factor is the relative positions of the parties, and their respective knowledge of the facts. In *Ellul v Oakes*[22] the plaintiffs claimed damages for breach of contract, based on a statement that a property which they purchased from the defendant was sewered. This statement had been made in certain advertising material and the court found that the defendant had guaranteed the truth of the statement. It was obviously within the knowledge of the defendant whether his property was sewered and the plaintiffs, who were ignorant of the fact that the property was served by a septic tank, were justified in regarding the statement as more than a mere representation.

---

18. [1947] 1 KB 554. See also *Gardiner v Grigg* (1938) 38 SR (NSW) 524.
19. See further [766].
20. See *Hospital Products Ltd v United States Surgical Corp* (1984) 156 CLR 41 at 62 and further [708].
21. *Oscar Chess Ltd v Williams* [1957] 1 WLR 370 at 376.
22. (1972) 3 SASR 377.

On the other hand, in *Oscar Chess Ltd v Williams*,[23] Williams sold his mother's car to Oscar Chess in the belief that it was a 1948 model Morris, a fact which he conveyed to Oscar Chess and seemed to be confirmed by the registration book which he produced during negotiations. In fact the car was a 1939 model and Oscar Chess claimed damages for breach of contract. There was no doubt that the statement had some importance, the difference in value between the respective models being about £115. However, the court held that the statement was not a term because there was nothing to indicate that Williams was guaranteeing the year of manufacture. All that he had done was to repeat information conveyed by the registration book: he had no expertise in the matter. In fact, the party who might be expected to have expertise was Oscar Chess who were car dealers.

Oscar Chess was distinguished in *Dick Bentley Productions Ltd v Harold Smith (Motors) Ltd*.[24] Harold Smith, the sellers of a motor car, said that the vehicle had been fitted with a replacement engine and gearbox and had travelled only 20,000 miles since these were fitted. Dick Bentley purchased the vehicle in reliance on the statement but later discovered that it was false. In an action for breach of contract the trial judge found that the vehicle had in fact travelled nearly 100,000 miles. In holding that the statement was a term of the contract the English Court of Appeal emphasised the fact that Harold Smith were motor dealers, and in a better position to ascertain the history of the vehicle than a private seller. *Oscar Chess* was distinguishable because the seller there honestly believed on reasonable grounds that the statement made was true. Moreover, he was in no better position to ascertain the facts than the purchaser. In the *Dick Bentley* case the sellers were in a superior position.

A statement by Lord Denning MR in the *Dick Bentley* case gives rise to some difficulty. He said[25] that if a statement 'is made in the course of dealings for a contract for the very purpose of inducing the other party to act upon it, and actually induces him to act upon it, by entering into the contract, that is prima facie ground for inferring that it was intended' as a term of the contract. This implies that inducement and reliance give rise to a presumption that a statement is a term, and would justify a court in holding that statement effective as a term even though there is no further proof of an intention to guarantee the truth of the statement. However, that would be contrary to *J J Savage & Sons Pty Ltd v Blakney*,[26] where the High Court rejected an argument similar to that of Lord Denning. Although the case was decided in the collateral contract context, the better view is that the position is no different where the alleged term is part of a single contract.[27]

---

23. [1957] 1 WLR 370.
24. [1965] 1 WLR 623.
25. [1965] 1 WLR 623 at 627.
26. (1970) 119 CLR 435 at 442. See also *Hospital Products Ltd v United States Surgical Corp* (1984) 156 CLR 41 at 61, 116.
27. See *Nemeth v Bayswater Road Pty Ltd* [1988] 2 Qd R 406 at 416–17; *Banque Brussels Lambert SA v Australian National Industries Ltd* (1989) 21 NSWLR 502 at 524. But cf *Ellul v Oakes* (1972) 3 SASR 377 at 387.

In the *Dick Bentley* case Lord Denning went on to say[28] that the maker of the statement can rebut the presumption by showing 'that he was in fact innocent of fault in making it, and that it would not be reasonable in the circumstances for him to be bound by it'. However, the traditional view is that whether the maker of the statement was in some way at fault does not come into the matter.[29] The focus of the inquiry is what a reasonable person in the other person's position would conclude, and this leaves little room for discussion of 'fault' by the maker of the statement.

The expertise of a party may be important in another respect, namely, to distinguish a mere statement of opinion from a statement of fact guaranteed by its maker. For example, where the owner of a gallery stated that a painting was a 'Constable', the court said that the statement was in all probability a term of the contract.[30] Without the element of expertise the statement would have been regarded as a statement of opinion.

Collateral contracts[31]

[611] Form and nature. There are two forms of collateral contracts. The first arises where A enters into a contract with B after a statement by B has effect as a promise in a contract between A and B which is collateral to the main contract between the same parties. The second form operates where A enters into a contract with C after a statement by B which has effect as a contract between A and B which is collateral to the main contract between A and C.

The nature of collateral contracts appears from a statement made by Lord Moulton in *Heilbut Symons & Co v Buckleton*:[32]

> It is evident, both on principle and on authority, that there may be a contract the consideration for which is the making of some other contract. 'If you will make such and such a contract I will give you one hundred pounds,' is in every sense of the word a complete legal contract. It is collateral to the main contract, but each has an independent existence, and they do not differ in respect of their possessing to the full the character and status of a contract.

It can be seen that the consideration provided for the collateral contract is entry into the main contract, that is an executed consideration.[33] It is not possible to infer a collateral contract the consideration for which is the entry into the main contract if the main contract was agreed prior to the making of the statement subsequently relied upon as a collateral contract.[34] The consideration in such a case would be past consideration.[35]

The three practical virtues of collateral contracts are:

(1) where the main contract is illegal, the collateral contract may be the subject of a claim even though the main contract is not enforceable;[36]

---

28. [1965] 1 WLR 623 at 627-8.
29. See, eg *Ellul v Oakes* (1972) 3 SASR 377 at 388-9.
30. *Leaf v International Galleries* [1950] 2 KB 86.
31. K W Wedderburn, 'Collateral Contracts' [1959] *CLJ* 58.
32. [1913] AC 30 at 47. See also *Hoyt's Pty Ltd v Spencer* (1919) 27 CLR 133 at 139.
33. See generally [313]–[314].
34. *Hercules Motors Pty Ltd v Schubert* (1953) 53 SR (NSW) 301.
35. See [328].

(2) where a contract is required to be evidenced by writing the collateral contract may not need to be so evidenced;[37] and

(3) assuming a collateral contract of the second type, the privity of contract rule is avoided.[38]

[612] **Elements.** In *J J Savage & Sons Pty Ltd v Blakney*[39] the High Court held that in order to establish a collateral contract in respect of a statement of fact three elements must be established:

(1) that the statement was intended to be relied on;

(2) reliance by the party alleging the existence of the contract; and

(3) an intention, on the part of the maker of the statement, to guarantee its truth.

The facts illustrate the importance of the third element. The plaintiff purchased a cabin cruiser from the defendant. During negotiations the defendant recommended that the vessel be fitted with a particular type of engine, and said that it would have an estimated maximum speed of 15 miles per hour. An itemised specification and quotation was later provided which made no reference to the speed of the vessel. The plaintiff purchased the vessel with the recommended engine installed, but found it to be incapable of travelling at 15 miles per hour. He therefore claimed damages for breach of an alleged speed warranty. The plaintiff said that he would not have purchased the vessel had the statement not been made, and the Full Court of the Supreme Court of Victoria held that it could be relied on as a collateral contract. On appeal, the High Court said that the plaintiff had established a misrepresentation but not a collateral contract. What the lower court had neglected, and the plaintiff was unable to prove, was the element of guarantee, that is, an intention on the part of the defendant to guarantee ('warrant') the truth of the statement.

Savage v Blakney also illustrates the difficulty of establishing a collateral contract based on a statement which is, in essence, an expression of opinion.[40] This difficulty did not arise in *Shepperd v Ryde Corp*,[41] where the plaintiff entered into a contract for the sale of land after the Ryde Corp had said that it would maintain an area of land (which it owned) located near the land purchased as a park. The High Court was satisfied that the plaintiff would not have entered into the contract but for the statement made, and also that Ryde Corp was in fact promising to maintain the land in question as a park. The consideration for this promise was the plaintiff's entry into the contract of sale and a collateral contract was therefore established. The plaintiff had at least made out a prima facie case for relief.

---

36. See [1726].
37. *Leipner v McLean* (1909) 8 CLR 306. A collateral contract to sign the memorandum of a contract required to be evidenced by writing must be similarly evidenced: *Futuretronics International Pty Ltd v Gadzhis* (1990) [1992] 2 VR 217; *Wright v Madden* [1992] 1 Qd R 343.
38. See further [614].
39. (1970) 119 CLR 435.
40. See also *Ross v Allis-Chalmers Australia Pty Ltd* (1980) 32 ALR 561.
41. (1952) 85 CLR 1.

He was able therefore to obtain an injunction[42] restraining the Ryde Corp from using or permitting the park to be used for any other purpose.

[613] Requirement of consistency. According to the decision of the High Court in *Hoyt's Pty Ltd v Spencer*[43] a statement will not take effect as a collateral contract if it is inconsistent with the main contract. A lease contained a term providing for termination by the lessor on his giving at least four weeks' notice in writing of his intention to terminate. The lessees alleged the existence of a promise by the lessor not to exercise his contractual right unless requested or required by his head lessors to do so. When the lessor exercised his contractual right to terminate despite the absence of any such request or requirement, the lessees sought to use the promise as the basis for a claim for damages. The High Court held that the action could not be maintained because the promise was not consistent with the terms of the main contract. Isaacs J said[44] that a 'principle' which 'must govern the bargain of a contractual promise made in consideration of entering into the main contract is that the parties shall have and be subject to *all* (not some only) of the respective benefits and burdens of the main contract'. It was because the promise was at variance with the main contract (the lease) that the lessees' action failed. To hold otherwise would have been, in Isaacs J's words,[45] to make the collateral contract the 'dominant' contract.

Although *Hoyt's v Spencer* has been the subject of criticism,[46] the High Court has shown no inclination to overrule it.[47] But there are decisions which indicate that the requirement of consistency is not applied in England,[48] and it is arguable that the doctrine of promissory estoppel will now allow a plaintiff such as the lessees to recover damages.[49] Moreover, if the lessees had refused to vacate the premises, the promise by the lessor would have been a defence to an action for possession. The main objection which could have been raised, absence of an existing contractual relation at the time of the statement, would not now be a bar to promissory estoppel.[50]

[614] Contract with third party. The elements of a collateral contract with a third party do not differ greatly from those applicable where the contract is between the parties to the main contract. As in that context, of crucial importance is the intention of the maker of a statement of fact to guarantee its truth, or the presence of a promissory undertaking. For example, in *Andrews v Hopkinson*[51] the plaintiff acquired a second-hand

---

42. See generally [2415]–[2420].
43. (1919) 27 CLR 133.
44. (1919) 27 CLR 133 at 146.
45. (1919) 27 CLR 133 at 148. See also *Cutts v Buckley* (1933) 49 CLR 189 at 201; *Maybury v Atlantic Union Oil Co Ltd* (1953) 89 CLR 507.
46. See, eg Nicholas Seddon, 'A Plea for the Reform of the Rule in *Hoyt's Pty Ltd v Spencer*' (1978) 52 *ALJ* 372.
47. See *Gates v City Mutual Life Assurance Society Ltd* (1986) 160 CLR 1; 63 ALR 600. And see *Esanda Ltd v Burgess* [1984] 2 NSWLR 139.
48. *City and Westminster Properties (1934) Ltd v Mudd* [1959] Ch 129.
49. See J C Phillips and J W Carter, 'The Demise of Hoyt's Pty Ltd v Spencer' (1989) 2 *JCL* 181. Cf *State Rail Authority of New South Wales v Heath Outdoor Pty Ltd* (1986) 7 NSWLR 170 at 193.
50. See [374].

motor car from a finance company on hire-purchase terms. Prior to the contract being entered into the defendant, a motor dealer, had said: 'It's a good little bus. I would stake my life on it. You will have no trouble with it'. Unfortunately, the vehicle had a defect which rendered it unroadworthy and the plaintiff was injured when a collision occurred owing to the defect. McNair J held[52] that the statement made by the defendant 'amounted at least to a warranty that the car was in good condition and reasonably fit for use on a public highway'. The consideration for this undertaking was the plaintiff's entry into the hire-purchase contract with the finance company. The breach of the undertaking was therefore a breach of a contract collateral to the hire-purchase contract. It might, however, be argued that McNair J was wrong to accept the defendant's statement as a contractual undertaking, rather than a puff or a mere representation.[53]

The requirement of consistency, applicable where the collateral contract is between the same parties, does not apply where the contract is with a third person. In other words, because they are between different persons, it is not necessary to consider whether the collateral contract is consistent with the main contract.

In so far as collateral contracts with third parties have been used as a device for avoiding the privity of contract rule, recent statutory provisions make them less important than was formerly the case.[54]

Incorporation of Terms[55]

[615] Incorporation by signature. The most obvious way by which terms are incorporated into a contract is by the parties signing ('executing') a document. If execution occurs, knowledge of the terms need not be established. In other words, a party may be bound even though not knowing the terms of the contract.[56] This was established in *L'Estrange v F Graucob Ltd*[57] where Ms L'Estrange, the proprietor of a cafe business, entered into a contract for the purchase of an automatic vending machine. She signed a document headed 'sales agreement' which stated that it contained 'all the terms and conditions' under which she had purchased the machine. The document also provided that 'any express or implied condition, statement, or warranty, statutory or otherwise' which was not stated in the document was excluded. Ms L'Estrange found the machine to be unsatisfactory and brought an action claiming the return of the money she had paid and damages for breach of a term, which she alleged was implied by the *Sale of Goods Act* 1893 (UK), requiring the machine to be fit for the purpose for which she purchased it.[58] However, the Divisional

---

51. [1957] 1 QB 229.
52. [1957] 1 QB 229 at 235.
53. *Wells (Merstham) Ltd v Buckland Sand and Silica Ltd* [1965] 2 QB 170 illustrates a stronger fact situation.
54. See [915], [916].
55. Yates, *Exclusion Clauses in Contracts*, 2nd ed, 1982, pp 45–64; Malcolm Clarke, 'Notice of Contractual Terms' [1976] *CLJ* 51.
56. But see [1267]–[1275].
57. [1934] 2 KB 394. For critical analysis see J R Spencer, 'Signature, Consent, and the Rule in *L'Estrange v Graucob*' [1973] *CLJ* 104.
58. See [639].

Court held that no such term could be implied as it was excluded by the document which she had signed.[59] The document contained the terms of the contract even though it had not been read.

The position in *L'Estrange v Graucob* might have been different had the defendant misrepresented the effect of the document. Thus, in *Curtis v Chemical Cleaning and Dyeing Co*[60] Ms Curtis took a dress to the defendants' shop for dry cleaning and was asked to sign a document headed 'Receipt'. On inquiring into the reason for this, the shop assistant said that the defendants would not accept liability for certain specified risks, namely, damage to the beads and sequins with which the dress was trimmed. In fact, the receipt contained a much wider exclusion which was relied on in the present action for damages based on negligence. The court held that the document could not be treated as incorporating the wide exclusion clause, because of the misrepresentation which had been made. Somervell LJ (with whom Singleton LJ agreed) said[61] that 'owing' to the misrepresentation the exclusion clause 'never became part of the contract'. However, Denning LJ said that the conduct of the defendants merely disentitled them from relying on the exclusion except in relation to beads and sequins. He also said[62] that a failure to draw attention to the existence or extent of the exclusion clauses might in some cases preclude reliance. However, because of the absence of any general duty of disclosure in contract[63] this could only be true in the case of an unusually wide exclusion of liability.

A difficult area concerns documents which, although signed, are not obviously contractual in character. For example, if, in *Curtis*, the shop assistant had said nothing, the plaintiff could have argued that a document headed 'Receipt' did not express contractual terms.[64] In *Le Mans Grand Prix Circuits Pty Ltd v Iliadis*[65] the Victorian Court of Appeal would seem to have taken a broader view. In that case a printed document which was signed by the respondent included clauses set out in the format of contractual terms. These clauses were introduced by the words 'In consideration of'. Nevertheless, the Court of Appeal (Batt JA dissenting) held that the respondent was entitled to regard the document as a registration form which he was asked to sign because he was about to drive one of the respondent's cars on a go-kart track. An employer had booked the track for use by its employees, and the respondent was not a party to that contract. Reference was made by Tadgell JA (with whom Winneke P agreed)[66] to the fact that there was 'no obvious commercial relationship' between the appellant and the respondent, and the absence of any payment by the respondent to the appellant. However, the respondent was at least an invitee and, given its form, the document might reasonably have been

---

59. But see now [770].
60. [1951] 1 KB 805.
61. [1951] 1 KB 805 at 808.
62. [1951] 1 KB 805 at 809.
63. See generally [1014].
64. See [1951] 1 KB 805 at 809. See also [617].
65. [1998] 4 VR 661.
66. See [1998] 4 VR 661 at 667. See also at 663, 668 per Tadgell JA ('marketing ... or registration' or 'application' form).

regarded as contractual in character. It is therefore difficult to reconcile the approach of the court with the rationale for the rule in *L'Estrange v F Graucob* which does not depend on proof that the document has been read, or that the party who relies on a signed document as a contract brought the character of the document to the other party's attention.

The problem also arises where the document is signed after the terms of the contract have been orally agreed. Usually it is appropriate to regard the document as replacing the oral terms, but what if the document is signed after the contract has been performed? The matter arose in *D J Hill & Co Pty Ltd v Walter H Wright Pty Ltd*.[67] The defendants agreed to carry machinery for the plaintiffs, and after the machinery was delivered two documents were signed which made reference to the 'terms and conditions' on the back of the documents. It transpired that the machinery had been damaged in transit and the defendants sought to defend the plaintiffs' action for damages by relying on an exclusion clause on the back of the documents. The Full Court of the Supreme Court of Victoria held that the documents signed were not contractual in character because signature occurred after the contract had been performed. Accordingly, the exclusion clause was no defence to the action. The decision was followed, with reluctance, by Hogarth J in *Eggleston v Marley Engineers Pty Ltd*.[68] He said that documents of the type considered in *Hill v Wright* should be classified as contractual. We would agree with this view, at least in the context of a commercial contract where the parties know that a document with express terms will be presented at some stage in the transaction, and a previous course of dealing is followed.

The conclusion whether a document should be regarded as contractual will to some extent depend on the knowledge, or assumed knowledge, of how people do business. Clearly, this may vary over time.

[616] Incorporation by notice. Where no document is signed by the parties, the usual way by which terms are incorporated is by one of the parties giving the other notice of the terms of the contract. It is difficult to state the legal requirements here beyond saying that the notice must be 'reasonable'. That is, the party relying on the terms must show that, in the circumstances, reasonable steps were taken to bring the terms to the attention of the other party.[69]

Most of the cases concern exclusionary terms which a party seeks to rely on in order to exclude, restrict, or qualify liability under the contract. For example, in *Chapelton v Barry UDC*[70] the plaintiff claimed damages for negligence when he was injured by falling through one of the defendant's deck chairs. The chairs had been in a pile next to a notice stating the rate of hire and 'respectfully' requesting the public to obtain tickets from chair attendants. The plaintiff had taken his ticket without looking at it, and therefore did not see a statement on the ticket excluding liability for 'any accident or damage arising from hire of chair'. The court held that, in the

---

67. [1971] VR 749. See further [618].
68. (1979) 21 SASR 51.
69. *Balmain New Ferry Co Ltd v Robertson* (1906) 4 CLR 379 at 386 (affirmed sub nom *Robinson v Balmain New Ferry Co Ltd* [1910] AC 295).
70. [1940] 1 KB 532.

[616]   Contract Law in Australia

absence of any warning, the ticket could not be relied upon as sufficient notice of the exclusion clause which it purported to incorporate.[71]

Unless a course of dealing is proved between the parties,[72] the notice must be given prior to or contemporaneously with entry into the contract. For example, in *Olley v Marlborough Court Ltd*[73] the plaintiff left jewellery in her room when staying at the defendant's hotel. By reason of the defendant's negligence the jewellery was stolen and it sought to rely on a notice placed in the plaintiff's bedroom which excluded liability for valuables which were not handed to the defendant's manageress for safe custody. The English Court of Appeal held that the contract was formed when the plaintiff paid for her room in advance at the reception desk. The notice in the bedroom did not state a term of the contract because it was not brought to the plaintiff's attention before the contract was formed.[74]

[617]   **The ticket cases.** The principle of the 'ticket cases' is that where one party makes an offer to contract on terms stated on or referred to in a document (usually no more than a ticket) given to the other party, that party's decision to keep the document indicates assent to a contract on the terms stated or referred to.[75] For example, in *Parker v South Eastern Railway Co*[76] the plaintiffs claimed compensation for the loss of luggage. The luggage had been deposited with the defendants at their cloakroom. A ticket which was received by each plaintiff when the articles were deposited restricted the defendants' liability. The court said that assent to the terms of the ticket did not depend on actual knowledge of its contents.[77] Evidence of assent to the terms was found in the plaintiffs' failure to hand the ticket back to the clerk.

Parker's case[78] suggests that in considering the application of the ticket cases there are, potentially, three questions to be asked:[79]

(1)   Did the person who received the ticket know that there was writing on the ticket?

(2)   Did that person know that the ticket referred to terms?

(3)   Did the party relying on the terms do what was reasonable to bring notice of the existence of the terms sought to be incorporated to the other party's attention?

Despite its constant repetition in the cases, the first question is hardly ever crucial. If it is established that the person who received the ticket did not know that there was writing on it, the writing cannot be relied on as

---

71. See also *Causer v Browne* [1952] VLR 1, and further [617].
72. See [618].
73. [1949] 1 KB 532.
74. See also *Oceanic Sun Line Special Shipping Co Inc v Fay* (1988) 165 CLR 197; 79 ALR 9.
75. See *McCutcheon v David MacBrayne Ltd* [1964] 1 WLR 125 at 131.
76. (1877) 2 CPD 416.
77. A misdirection by the judge at the trial meant that a new trial had to be ordered.
78. (1877) 2 CPD 416 at 423.
79. This analysis was approved by the House of Lords in *Hood v Anchor Line (Henderson Bros) Ltd* [1918] AC 837, a case adopted by the High Court in *MacRobertson Miller Airline Services v Commissioner of State Taxation* (1975) 133 CLR 125; 8 ALR 131.

incorporating contractual terms. But the point seems to be that in cases where actual knowledge is lacking, knowledge of writing is a step towards proving constructive knowledge of the terms. The ticket cases will not apply if the person who received the ticket did not know that the ticket referred to terms *and* insufficient notice was given by the other party.[80] However, even if the person did not know or believe that the writing contained (or referred to) contractual terms, the terms will be incorporated (and be contractually binding) if the ticket was delivered in circumstances indicating that sufficient notice was given that the writing contained contractual terms. Provided sufficient notice of the nature of the document is given, it does not matter that the recipient did not in fact read the terms or was incapable of doing so.[81]

For the ticket cases to apply, the party relying on the ticket must also lead a reasonable person to believe that the ticket is a contractual document. Thus, in *Chapelton v Barry UDC*[82] the ticket cases did not apply because the ticket was no more than a receipt: there was no basis for saying that the contract was written rather than oral or inferred from conduct. As Slesser LJ pointed out,[83] the defendant had made a general offer to the public and there was 'no reason' anybody taking one of the chairs 'should necessarily obtain a receipt at the moment he took the chair — and, indeed, the notice is inconsistent with that, because it "respectfully requests" the public to obtain receipts for their money'. Similarly, in *Causer v Browne*,[84] where a docket was given when a dress was left for cleaning, the ticket cases did not apply because the defendants had not proved that the document would reasonably be understood as stating the terms of the contract.

The ticket cases are based on an analysis which treats the failure to reject the ticket as the acceptance, by conduct, of the offer of a *written* contract.[85] Since in most cases tickets are proffered on a 'take it or leave it' basis, this is largely fictional. Nevertheless, the absence of an ability to reject the ticket and negotiate the terms of the contract will prevent this line of cases applying. Thus, in *Thornton v Shoe Lane Parking Ltd*[86] the document relied on as a ticket incorporating contractual terms was issued by an automatic machine inside the entrance to a car park. Lord Denning MR explained[87] that the ticket cases did not apply because any person who received the ticket could not negotiate: 'He may protest to the machine, even swear at it; but it will remain unmoved'. However, on the assumption that the ticket cases applied, the defendant could not rely on the ticket as incorporating terms, because the plaintiff had no knowledge that the ticket contained terms and the defendant had not done all that was reasonable to bring the terms to the plaintiff's notice. The term in issue sought to exclude liability for any personal injury suffered by the plaintiff while he was on the

---

80. See *Richardson Spence & Co v Rowntree* [1894] AC 217; *Oceanic Sun Line Special Shipping Co Inc v Fay* (1988) 165 CLR 197.
81. See, eg *Hood v Anchor Line (Henderson Bros) Ltd* [1918] AC 837.
82. [1940] 1 KB 532 (see [616]).
83. [1940] 1 KB 532 at 537.
84. [1952] VLR 1.
85. But cf *Maxitherm Boilers Pty Ltd v Pacific Dunlop Ltd* [1998] 4 VR 559 at 568.
86. [1971] 2 QB 163.
87. [1971] 2 QB 163 at 169–70.

defendant's premises. Emphasis was placed by Lord Denning MR on the fact that the ticket contained an exclusionary term which was unusually wide for the type of contract in issue. Megaw LJ emphasised[88] that the restriction was not usual in the class of contract before the court, and Sir Gordon Willmer considered[89] that more notice was required in the case of such a 'stringent' term.

As was pointed out in *Interfoto Picture Library Ltd v Stiletto Visual Programmes Ltd*,[90] *Thornton* illustrates a refinement of the approach in *Parker's* case, from an analysis of the terms as a whole to consideration of particular terms. In *Interfoto* some photographs were sent to the defendant, at its request, for possible inclusion in a client presentation. Enclosed in the sealed envelope containing the photographs was a delivery note which stated that a 'holding fee' of £5 was payable for photographs retained for longer than 14 days following delivery. The defendant, who did not know that the term was present, contended that it did not govern the contract. In fact the plaintiffs received 47 photographs and retained them for two weeks, for which the fee claimed was £3783.50. Dillon LJ described[91] this fee as 'exorbitant', and the court (applying *Thornton*) held that, having regard to the onerous nature of the clause, insufficient notice had been given. In the result £3.50 per transparency per week was allowed as a reasonable fee.[92]

[618] Incorporation by course of dealing.[93] A course of dealing occurs when the contract at issue between the parties is preceded by a series of transactions over time. Such a course of dealing may have the effect of incorporating terms into a contract. For example, an oral contract may contain *implied terms* incorporated by the course of dealing. It is now established that in order to rely on a course of dealing one party need not show that the other party had actual knowledge of the terms. Thus, in *Henry Kendall & Sons v William Lillico & Sons Ltd*[94] a long and consistent course of dealing, and the failure to object to the terms, was held to imply assent to the incorporation of the terms contained in 'sold notes' as terms of the contract, even though these were received after an oral contract had been agreed between the parties.[95]

In order to decide whether the terms are incorporated by the course of dealing regard must be had to the extent of dealing between the parties and the steps taken. The course of dealing must be consistent and sufficiently long. For example, in *J Spurling Ltd v Bradshaw*[96] a course of dealing was

88. [1971] 2 QB 163 at 172. See also *Oceanic Sun Line Special Shipping Co Inc v Fay* (1988) 165 CLR 197 at 229; *Maxitherm Boilers Pty Ltd v Pacific Dunlop Ltd* [1998] 4 VR 559 at 569.
89. [1971] 2 QB 163 at 174.
90. [1989] QB 433. Cf *Insurance Contracts Act* 1984 (Cth), s 37.
91. [1989] QB 433 at 436. The court left open the possibility that the clause might have been an unenforceable penalty. See generally [2207]–[2217].
92. As on a quantum meruit (see [2307]).
93. See Jane Swanton, 'Incorporation of Contractual Terms by a Course of Dealing' (1989) 1 *JCL* 223.
94. [1969] 2 AC 31.
95. The contrary view of Lord Devlin in *McCutcheon v David MacBrayne Ltd* [1964] 1 WLR 125 at 134, that actual knowledge of the terms is required, was disapproved. See [1969] 2 AC 31 at 90, 104–5, 130.

established by reason of the fact that the parties had contracted on 'many' occasions prior to the contract which gave rise to the dispute. And in *Henry Kendall & Sons v William Lillico & Sons Ltd* the course of dealing extended over three or four years and involved three or four transactions each month. By way of contrast, no course of dealing was established in *D J Hill & Co Pty Ltd v Walter H Wright Pty Ltd*,[97] even though the parties had contracted on a number of occasions. A clearer case is *Hollier v Rambler Motors (AMC) Ltd*,[98] where there were only three or four transactions spread over a period of five years. Moreover, if there is inconsistency in the dealings between the parties the court may conclude that there is no course of dealing.[99]

To what extent is it necessary that the terms sought to be incorporated be received prior to the formation of the contract? *Spurling v Bradshaw* proceeds on the basis that the time at which the document is received is not crucial if a course of dealing is established. In other words, although in a single transaction a document might come too late,[100] the existence of a course of dealing implies that even a document received after formation may be incorporated. No doubt the time at which the document comes into existence is relevant to the sufficiency of notice, but in *Hill v Wright*, where no course of dealing was established, the court appears to have considered that a document received after the contract has been performed cannot be contractual in nature and that it is only in respect of contractual documents that the course of dealing basis for incorporation can apply. It is difficult to accept this as an accurate statement of the law, because the contract is oral rather than written.[101] If the court meant to say that the receipt of a document after the contract has been performed attracts a requirement of actual knowledge,[102] this is inconsistent with the law stated in *Henry Kendall & Sons v William Lillico & Sons Ltd*. The degree of knowledge possessed by a party denying that terms have been incorporated by a course of dealing is merely a factor to be considered.[103]

[619] Incorporation by reference. In commercial contracts it is quite common for the parties to record the bare essentials of the contract in a document and for the document to refer to, and incorporate, a set of terms, such as the standard form of a trade association,[104] the standard terms of one of the parties[105] or the terms of another contract related to the transaction.[106]

---

96. [1956] 1 WLR 461.
97. [1971] VR 749 (see [615]).
98. [1972] 2 QB 71.
99. See, eg *McCutcheon v David MacBrayne Ltd* [1964] 1 WLR 125.
100. See [616].
101. See *Chattis Nominees Pty Ltd v Norman Ross Homeworks Pty Ltd* (1992) 28 NSWLR 338 at 343. Cf *Mendelssohn v Normand Ltd* [1970] 1 QB 177 at 182. Contrast *Rinaldi & Patroni Pty Ltd v Precision Mouldings Pty Ltd* [1986] WAR 131. See also *Pondcil Pty Ltd v Tropical Reef Shipyard Pty Ltd* (1994) ATPR Digest ¶46-134 (see S Kapnoullas, (1996) 10 *JCL* 173).
102. See [1971] VR 749 at 752, 753–4. But cf *Eggleston v Marley Engineers Pty Ltd* (1979) 21 SASR 51 at 62–5.
103. *Hollier v Rambler Motors (AMC) Ltd* [1972] 2 QB 71 at 77–8.
104. See, eg *Bremer Handelsgesellschaft mbH v J H Rayner & Co Ltd* [1979] 2 Lloyd's Rep 216.
105. See, eg *Smith v South Wales Switchgear Co Ltd* [1978] 1 WLR 165.

This method of incorporation is not limited to commercial contracts. For example, the parties to a contract for the sale of land might incorporate the terms stated in a standard contract approved or issued by a body such as a law society or real estate institute.[107] It is also employed in the context of insurance contracts.[108]

Implied Terms

General

[620] **Reasons for implication.** There are three main reasons for implying terms into a contract. The first reason, which gives rise to a category known as 'terms implied in fact' is the need to give business efficacy to a contract. Second, terms may be implied from the nature of the contract itself or the obligations it creates. Third, terms may be implied by statute. The second and third reasons, taken together, give rise to a category of 'terms implied by law'.

There are other, and less important, reasons for implication. Thus, reference was made above[109] to implication by course of dealing, and we later deal, briefly, with custom or usage as a reason for implying terms.[110]

The line of demarcation between the various bases for implication cannot always be sharply drawn. They tend to 'merge imperceptibly'[111] into one another.

[621] **Onus of proof.** In the case of terms implied in fact, the presumption is that the contract is effective without the term. Accordingly, the onus of proving that a term should be implied into the contract rests on the party so alleging.[112] The onus is most difficult to discharge in detailed commercial contracts simply because the contract will look to state all the terms of the bargain.[113] If the onus is discharged the term is deemed to have been implied from the time of contractual formation.[114] The same approach is taken to terms implied by custom or usage.[115]

Where the term in question is of the implied in law variety the onus of proof is different. Once the contract (or the obligations it creates) has been shown to be of a nature which justifies an implication, whether under the common law or statute, the term is presumed to be part of the contract. It

---

106. See, eg *Miramar Maritime Corp v Holborn Oil Trading Ltd* [1984] AC 676 (bill of lading incorporating terms of charterparty).
107. See, eg *Giliberto v Kenny* (1983) 48 ALR 620.
108. But see *Deaves v CML Fire and General Insurance Co Ltd* (1979) 143 CLR 24; 23 ALR 539.
109. See [618].
110. See [644].
111. Glanville Williams, 'Language and the Law — IV' (1945) 61 *LQR* 384 at 401.
112. *Heimann v The Commonwealth* (1938) 38 SR (NSW) 691 at 695; *Luxor (Eastbourne) Ltd v Cooper* [1941] AC 108 at 137.
113. See *Codelfa Construction Pty Ltd v State Rail Authority of New South Wales* (1982) 149 CLR 337; 41 ALR 367. Cf *Reid v Rush and Tompkins Group Plc* [1990] 1 WLR 212 (employment contract).
114. *Frobisher (Second Investments) Ltd v Kiloran Trust Co Ltd* [1980] 1 WLR 425 at 432.
115. See [644].

is therefore up to the party who alleges that the term should not be implied to prove this.[116] However, where a term is implied by virtue of statute, exclusion of the term by agreement may be prohibited.[117]

[622] Issue of law. Whether a term should be implied into a contract is an issue of law to be decided by the court on the basis of the other terms of the contract and the evidence admissible on the issue.[118]

[623] Admissible evidence. Where it is alleged that a term should be implied by law it appears that the court is not limited to a consideration of the contract itself. Thus, extrinsic evidence is admissible to support or rebut the implication, even if the parol evidence rule otherwise applies.[119]

The law is not so clear with respect to terms implied in fact. The main consideration with respect to such terms is the construction of the contract. However, even if the contract is in writing, regard may also be had to the circumstances surrounding the contract in order to establish the 'factual matrix' against which the parties contracted.[120] On the other hand, evidence of the parties' negotiations is not admissible for the purpose of implying a term.[121]

[624] Implied legal duties. Where a term is implied into a contract it will usually embody a contractual promise and therefore create a legal duty. For example, where a sale of goods contract attracts the term requiring the goods to be fit for the buyer's purpose,[122] the effect of the term is to impose a legal duty on the seller. If the duty is created by a contractual term, a failure to discharge the duty will amount to a breach of contract.

A party to a contract may, however, be subject to an implied legal duty independently of a contractual term. Thus, a duty may be implied by law from the nature of the parties' relationship. For example, a customer owes a duty to exercise reasonable care in drawing cheques on an account with its banker.[123] Alternatively, the duty may be implied by statute. For example, the sale of goods legislation imposes on a seller of goods a legal duty to deliver the quantity of goods stated in the contract.[124] Some duties, such as the duty to co-operate or exercise good faith in the performance of a contract,[125] are sometimes based on an implied term, but on other

---

116. *Heimann v The Commonwealth* (1938) 38 SR (NSW) 691 at 695–6. See also *Castlemaine Tooheys Ltd v Carlton & United Breweries Ltd* (1987) 10 NSWLR 468.
117. See [769]–[772].
118. *Re Comptoir Commercial Anversois v Power Son & Co* [1920] 1 KB 868; *Heimann v The Commonwealth* (1938) 38 SR (NSW) 691 at 695.
119. See [719].
120. See [713].
121. See [719].
122. See [639].
123. *Commonwealth Trading Bank of Australia v Sydney Wide Stores Pty Ltd* (1981) 148 CLR 304; 35 ALR 513 (see J W Carter, (1982) 98 *LQR* 19). But there is no duty to examine accounts: *Tai Hing Cotton Mill Ltd v Liu Chong Hing Bank Ltd* [1986] AC 80.
124. See **ACT**: *Sale of Goods Act* 1954, s 34; **NSW**: *Sale of Goods Act* 1923, s 33; **NT**: *Sale of Goods Act* 1972, s 33; **Qld**: *Sale of Goods Act* 1896, s 32; **SA**: *Sale of Goods Act* 1895, s 30; **Tas**: *Sale of Goods Act* 1896, s 35; **Vic**: *Goods Act* 1958, s 37; **WA**: *Sale of Goods Act* 1895, s 30.
125. See [1809].

occasions the duty has been inferred by the court solely by the construction of the contract and without the need for implying a term.[126] Generally, however, the courts have preferred to employ an implied term analysis in the creation of legal duties, rather than to imply the duty simpliciter.[127]

An implied legal duty need not be contractual in character and need not give rise to a right to claim damages in the event that it is not discharged. An example is the common law duty of an insured to disclose material facts to an insurer.[128] And a legal duty, such as that of a bailee to take reasonable care of the bailor's goods, may arise even though there is no contractual relation, for example, because the bailment is not supported by consideration.[129] However, this work is concerned with legal duties present in contracts, and generally these arise by virtue of contractual terms.

Terms Implied in Fact[130]

[625] Requirements for implication. The requirements for implication in respect of terms implied in fact depend in the first instance on a classification of the contract. If the contract is a formal contract which is complete on its face, the requirements are those stated by Lord Simon, delivering the advice of the majority of the Privy Council, in *BP Refinery (Westernport) Pty Ltd v Shire of Hastings*:[131]

> Their Lordships do not think it necessary to review exhaustively the authorities on the implication of a term in a contract which the parties have not thought fit to express. In their view, for a term to be implied, the following conditions (which may overlap) must be satisfied: (1) it must be reasonable and equitable; (2) it must be necessary to give business efficacy to the contract so that no term will be implied if the contract is effective without it; (3) it must be so obvious that 'it goes without saying'; (4) it must be capable of clear expression; (5) it must not contradict any express term of the contract.

However, these requirements are particularly 'strict'[132] or 'stringent',[133] perhaps overly so. Thus, in relation to informal contracts which are not complete on their face, the High Court in *Byrne v Australian Airlines Ltd*[134] approved the following statement by Deane J in *Hawkins v Clayton*:[135]

---

126. See, eg *Mackay v Dick* (1881) 6 App Cas 251 at 263.
127. See, eg *Ray v Davies* (1909) 9 CLR 160 at 170; *Byrne v Australian Airlines Ltd* (1995) 185 CLR 410 at 449; 131 ALR 422. But see *Shell UK Ltd v Lostock Garage Ltd* [1977] 1 All ER 481 at 487.
128. See *Khoury v Government Insurance Office of NSW* (1984) 165 CLR 622; 54 ALR 639; *Bank of Nova Scotia v Hellenic Mutual War Risks Association (Bermuda) Ltd (The Good Luck)* [1992] 1 AC 233.
129. See *Port Swettenham Authority v T W Wu & Co* [1979] AC 580.
130. H K Lücke, 'Ad Hoc Implications in Written Contracts' (1973) 5 *Adel LR* 32.
131. (1977) 180 CLR 266 at 282–3; 16 ALR 363 (approved *Secured Income Real Estate (Australia) Ltd v St Martins Investments Pty Ltd* (1979) 144 CLR 596 at 605–6; 26 ALR 567; *Codelfa Construction Pty Ltd v State Rail Authority of New South Wales* (1982) 149 CLR 337 at 347).
132. *Wright v TNT Management Pty Ltd* (1989) 85 ALR 442 at 459.
133. *Vroon BV v Foster's Brewing Group Ltd* [1994] 2 VR 32 at 68.
134. (1995) 185 CLR 410 at 422, 442 (see Gregory Tolhurst and J W Carter, 'The New Law on Implied Terms' (1996) 11 *JCL* 76). See also *Breen v Williams* (1996) 186 CLR 71; 138 ALR 259 (see J W Carter and G J Tolhurst, (1997) 12 *JCL* 152; Jane Swanton and Barbara McDonald, (1997) 71 *ALJ* 332 and 413).

where it is apparent that the parties have not attempted to spell out the full terms of their contract, a court should imply a term by reference to the imputed intention of the parties if, but only if, it can be seen that the implication of the particular term is necessary for the reasonable or effective operation of a contract of that nature in the circumstances of the case. The general statement of principle is subject to the qualification that a term may be implied in a contract by established mercantile usage or professional practice or by a past course of dealing between the parties.

It would appear that, in applying Deane J's statement it is both legitimate and necessary to consider the matters referred to in the *BP Refinery* case. The difference is that these are more in the nature of factors to be considered than essential requirements. Nevertheless, a term cannot be implied into an informal contract if it is unnecessary to do so, and the term must also be consistent with express terms.

[626] Reasonable and equitable. Although it is not sufficient to justify an implication that it be reasonable to imply a term,[136] any term which is sought to be implied must operate reasonably and equitably between the parties. For example, in *Peters American Delicacy Co Ltd v Champion*[137] a contract between manufacturers and a retailer of ice cream provided: 'Prices are subject to alteration on giving customer seven days' notice in writing'. It was argued that the clause was governed by an implied term entitling the manufacturers to fix 'reasonable' prices. But a majority of the court said that such a term would be both unfair and unreasonable from the manufacturers' standpoint, since they might be required, by litigation 'to enter into a full examination of ... manufacturing costs and expenses'[138] in order to prove that any price was reasonable. It would also have been unfair to the retailer to oblige him to pay any price considered reasonable by the manufacturers.[139]

[627] Necessary to give business efficacy. At the heart of factual implication is the idea that a term should only be implied if it is necessary[140] to make the contract effective in a business sense. If the contract is commercially effective without the term, the court will not imply it.[141] But a term will be implied if without it the contract would be unworkable.[142]

The leading authority on business efficacy is *The Moorcock*,[143] where the plaintiff's vessel suffered damage when lying at the defendants' jetty. The

---

135. (1988) 164 CLR 539 at 573; 78 ALR 69. See also *Hospital Products Ltd v United States Surgical Corp* (1984) 156 CLR 41 at 121.
136. See, eg *Hospital Products Ltd v United States Surgical Corp* (1984) 156 CLR 41 at 139.
137. (1928) 41 CLR 316.
138. (1928) 41 CLR 316 at 324. Contrast *Finchbourne Ltd v Rodrigues* [1976] 3 All ER 581.
139. See also *O'Donnell v Thor Industries Pty Ltd* (1977) 136 CLR 296; 14 ALR 61; *Hospital Products Ltd v United States Surgical Corp* (1984) 156 CLR 41 at 95.
140. *Hospital Products Ltd v United States Surgical Corp* (1984) 156 CLR 41; *Hughes v Greenwich London Borough Council* [1994] 1 AC 170.
141. See, eg *Bell v Lever Bros Ltd* [1932] AC 161 at 226; *Heimann v The Commonwealth* (1938) 38 SR (NSW) 691 at 695; *Australian Meat Industry Employees' Union v Frugalis Pty Ltd* [1990] 2 Qd R 201.
142. *Hospital Products Ltd v United States Surgical Corp* (1984) 156 CLR 41 at 66.
143. (1889) 14 PD 64.

defendants had agreed to allow the plaintiff to discharge and load his vessel at their wharf and for that purpose to be moored alongside the jetty. During low tide the vessel, as the parties contemplated, rested on the mud at the bottom of the River Thames. Damage to the vessel was found to have been occasioned by a ridge of hard ground beneath the mud and the plaintiff claimed compensation. The English Court of Appeal said that a term had to be implied into the contract imposing an obligation on the defendants to see that the bottom of the river was reasonably fit, or to exercise reasonable care in finding out its condition, and to advise the plaintiff of its condition. Bowen LJ said:[144]

> In business transactions such as this, what the law desires to effect by the implication is to give such business efficacy to the transaction as must have been intended at all events by both parties who are business men; not to impose on one side all the perils of the transaction, or to emancipate one side from all the chances of failure, but to make each party promise in law as much, at all events, as it must have been in the contemplation of both parties that he should be responsible for in respect of those perils or chances.

Since the parties knew that the vessel would rest on the bottom at low tide, it was obvious that the contract could not be performed unless the ground was safe. Moreover, the plaintiff was entitled to take up the position that the defendants, who could be assumed to know the state of the river, had accepted responsibility. Accordingly, the plaintiff was able to recover damages for breach of contract.[145]

It is common for a contract to involve co-operation between the parties and it requires little imagination to imply a term creating the duty to co-operate or at least not to do anything which will frustrate the operation of the contract.[146] In fact, the need for business efficacy may give rise to an implication which imposes an obligation on both parties. For example, in *Booker Industries Pty Ltd v Wilson Parking (Qld) Pty Ltd*[147] a lease conferred an option of a further term on the lessee, and provided for the payment of 'such rental as may be mutually agreed ... and failing agreement then such rental as may be fixed by an arbitrator' nominated in accordance with the lease. The High Court held that a term should be implied requiring both parties to do all that was reasonably necessary to procure the nomination of an arbitrator. Therefore, once the lessee had exercised the option for renewal, and only the rental was left to be determined, the parties were required to follow the procedure for nomination provided for by the lease and an order for specific performance was made.[148]

[628] Obviousness. In *Shirlaw v Southern Foundries (1926) Ltd*[149] Mackinnon LJ said:[150]

> Prima facie that which in any contract is left to be implied and need not be expressed is something so obvious that it goes without saying; so that, if,

---

144. (1889) 14 PD 64 at 68.
145. See also *Shepherd v Felt and Textiles of Australia Ltd* (1931) 45 CLR 359.
146. See [1809]–[1810].
147. (1982) 149 CLR 600; 43 ALR 68.
148. See also *Butts v O'Dwyer* (1952) 87 CLR 267.
149. [1939] 2 KB 206 (affirmed sub nom *Southern Foundries (1926) Ltd v Shirlaw* [1940] AC 701).
150. [1939] 2 KB 206 at 227.

while the parties were making their bargain, an officious bystander were to suggest some express provision for it in their agreement, they would testily suppress him with a common 'Oh, of course!'

The operation of the requirement can be seen by contrasting two cases on commission agency contracts. In *Luxor (Eastbourne) Ltd v Cooper*[151] the plaintiff sought to recover the payment alleged to be due under a contract with the defendants which provided for the payment of commission on 'completion' of the sale of two leasehold cinemas with a purchaser introduced by the plaintiff. A prospective purchaser, able and willing to buy the properties, was found by the plaintiff, but no draft contract was ever submitted to the defendants who ultimately sold the properties to another person. The plaintiff alleged that a term should be implied to the effect that the defendants would do nothing to prevent completion of a sale and deprive the plaintiff of commission, at least without 'reasonable cause'. The House of Lords held that no such term could be implied as it would have prevented the defendants dealing with their own property. It was by no means obvious that the defendants were giving up their freedom of disposal, particularly in view of the fact that the agent did not promise to find a purchaser, or even to use due diligence.

On the other hand, in *Alpha Trading Ltd v Dunnshaw-Patten Ltd*[152] the defendants agreed to pay the plaintiffs commission out of the proceeds of a contract for the sale of goods if a purchaser was introduced by the plaintiffs. The plaintiffs introduced a company which entered into a contract with the defendants. However, owing to the default of the defendants under the contract of sale, this contract was not completed and no proceeds were received. The English Court of Appeal, distinguishing *Luxor v Cooper* where no contract of sale had been entered into, implied a term to the effect that the defendants would not do anything which would prevent the plaintiffs receiving commission. Because in *Alpha Trading* a contract of sale had been agreed with a purchaser introduced by the plaintiffs, it was obvious that the defendants could not have complete freedom in the matter, and could not deprive the plaintiffs of the benefit of their labours.[153] Accordingly, the plaintiffs recovered the agreed commission by way of damages for breach of the term implied into the agency contract.

Even the requirement of obviousness may lead to debate. For example, in the *Southern Foundries* case the House of Lords was split three to two on the implication of the term when affirming the decision of the English Court of Appeal where there had also been a difference of opinion.[154]

[629] Clarity of expression. For a term to be implied it must be capable of clear expression and reasonably certain in its operation.[155] There is a link with the requirement of obviousness since a term which is unclear is not

---

151. [1941] AC 108. Cf *L J Hooker Ltd v W J Adams Estates Pty Ltd* (1977) 138 CLR 52; 13 ALR 161.
152. [1981] QB 290 (see J W Carter, (1982) 45 *MLR* 220). See also *Moneywood Pty Ltd v Salamon Nominees Pty Ltd* (2001) 177 ALR 390 at 395–6, 407 (terms implied *in law* in estate agency contracts). See further [2202].
153. But cf *L French & Co Ltd v Leeston Shipping Co Ltd* [1922] 1 AC 451.
154. See also *BP Refinery (Westernport) Pty Ltd v Shire of Hastings* (1977) 180 CLR 266.
155. See, eg *Terkol Rederierne v Petroleo Brasileiro SA (The Badagry)* [1985] 1 Lloyd's Rep 395 at 401.

likely to be obvious to both parties. For example, in *Codelfa Construction Pty Ltd v State Rail Authority of New South Wales*[156] the High Court refused to imply a term into a construction contract because it was impossible to say, with any degree of certainty, what the term would have said. The parties had contracted under the misapprehension that construction work could proceed on a three shifts per day basis. Although an injunction obtained by local residents made this impossible, it was by no means clear what term the parties would have included to deal with the eventuality.

It is probably true to say that if the court can see, for example from the arguments of counsel, that various terms *could* be implied, it will be reluctant to reach the conclusion that one particular formulation was a necessary implication.

[630] Consistency. The term sought to be implied must be consistent with the other terms of the contract,[157] and not deal with a matter already sufficiently dealt with by the contract. For example, in *Shepherd v Felt and Textiles of Australia Ltd*[158] a term was implied into an agency contract requiring the agent to render faithful and loyal service to his principal. This was implied, even though there was an express term requiring the agent to use his 'best endeavours' to obtain orders for the principal, because there was no inconsistency between the terms.[159] Nor could it be said that the express term had dealt exhaustively with the obligations of the agent.

In *Hart v MacDonald*[160] a written contract for the erection of a dairy plant and butter factory provided: 'It is to be understood that there is no agreement or understanding between [the parties] not embodied' in the document. The High Court held that this did not preclude the implication of a promise by the defendant to commence the business of dairying upon the erection of plant, and to carry on that business so that he would be able to pay for the plant. This term was necessary because the contract provided for payment out of the proceeds of butter manufactured within the butter factory. The term stating that there was no agreement other than that embodied in the contract did not preclude this implication. Griffith CJ said[161] that the implication was 'necessary', and arose 'upon a proper construction of the express words'; O'Connor J said[162] that the implication was 'embodied in the contract just as effectively as if it were written therein'; and Isaacs J explained[163] that the express term only excluded what was 'extraneous' to the written contract, and did not exclude an implication arising on a 'fair construction of the agreement itself'.

---

156. (1982) 149 CLR 337 (see J W Carter, [1983] *CLJ* 199). See also *Con-Stan Industries of Australia Pty Ltd v Norwich Winterthur Insurance (Australia) Ltd* (1986) 160 CLR 226 at 24; 64 ALR 4811. Cf *Shell UK Ltd v Lostock Garage Ltd* [1977] 1 All ER 481.
157. See, eg *Sanders v Snell* (1998) 196 CLR 329; 157 ALR 491.
158. (1931) 45 CLR 359. Contrast *Moorhouse v Angus and Robertson (No 1) Pty Ltd* [1981] 1 NSWLR 700.
159. The term may have been of the implied in law variety, but the position is the same with regard to consistency; see [635].
160. (1910) 10 CLR 417.
161. (1910) 10 CLR 417 at 421.
162. (1910) 10 CLR 417 at 427.
163. (1910) 10 CLR 417 at 430. Cf *Lewis v Bell* (1985) 1 NSWLR 731 at 736.

Terms Implied in Law

[631] Requirements for implication. Where a term is implied as a matter of law, rather than because of the factual circumstances of the case, it is usually implied because of the nature of the contract itself: because the same term has been implied in contracts of this nature in the past. Usually the contract is a very informal type, often with no written terms at all. However, because the terms are in the nature of default rules,[164] applicable on the basis of the parties' presumed intention, existence of writing does not of itself preclude an implication by the court.

The list of contracts which attract terms implied in law is not closed,[165] and a term may be implied in law in a new situation. However, it must be *necessary* to make the new implication.[166]

[632] Distinguishing legal from factual implication.[167] Although the implication of any term is a question of law for the court,[168] there are two quite significant distinctions between factual and legal implication.

First, there is a difference in the onus of proof.[169] Where a term is implied in fact the onus is on the party alleging the implication; the onus is on the other party when the term is implied in law, assuming that, in the past, a particular term has been implied into the type of contract before the court.

Second, there are important differences in the factors relevant to implication. In particular, 'reasonableness' is more important to legal implication and a term may be implied by law, on the ground that it is reasonable to do so, even though the 'business efficacy' and 'obviousness' criteria of terms implied in fact are not satisfied.[170] It is also the case that a term may be implied in law even though it lacks the necessary precision of a term implied in fact.[171]

It is sometimes said that there is a third distinction, namely that the *presumed* intention of the parties is the rationale for terms implied in law, whereas *actual* intention is the rationale of terms implied in fact.[172] Even if this distinction is helpful, which may be doubted, it is impossible to find any consistent approach in the cases.[173]

---

164. See *Equitable Life Assurance Society v Hyman* [2000] 3 WLR 529 at 539.
165. *Castlemaine Tooheys Ltd v Carlton & United Breweries Ltd* (1987) 10 NSWLR 468 at 487.
166. See *Scally v Southern Health and Social Services Board* [1992] 1 AC 294 (see Peter Brereton, (1992) 5 *JCL* 264); *Byrne v Australian Airlines Ltd* (1995) 185 CLR 410 at 450; *Esso Australia Resources Ltd v Plowman* (1995) 183 CLR 10; 128 ALR 391. See Elisabeth Peden, 'Policy Concerns in Terms Implied in Law' (2001) 117 *LQR* 459.
167. See J F Burrows, 'Implied Terms and Presumptions' (1968) 3 *NZULR* 121.
168. *Re Comptoir Commercial Anversois v Power Son & Co* [1920] 1 KB 868; *Heimann v The Commonwealth* (1938) 38 SR (NSW) 691 at 695.
169. See [621].
170. See, eg *Liverpool City Council v Irwin* [1977] AC 239.
171. *Lister v Romford Ice and Cold Storage Co Ltd* [1957] AC 555 at 576.
172. *Greaves & Co (Contractors) Ltd v Baynham Meikle & Partners* [1975] 1 WLR 1095 at 1099.

Nevertheless, once a term has been implied, it is often difficult to tell whether the court's decision is based on factual or legal implication. Thus, some terms which have been based on the requirement of business efficacy look, in the final analysis, to be terms implied in law, because they involve the 'imposition of legal duties in cases where the law thinks that policy requires it'.[174] Moreover, where an informal contract is in issue it may now be very difficult to draw the line between factual and legal implication.

[633] **Illustrations.** To decide whether a term is implied it is necessary to classify the contract. By way of illustration, reference can be made to terms usually implied in employment contracts, bailment contracts and contracts for work and materials.[175]

Where an employment contract exists the court will, in the absence of express exclusion (or the imposition of a more onerous duty), imply a term requiring the employee to exercise 'proper or reasonable care' in the discharge of duties under the contract.[176] Where the contract is for the provision of services by a professional person, such as a solicitor, insurance broker or engineer, the term will require the exercise of the degree of care expected of a person in the profession, trade or industry possessing the particular special skill.[177]

A bailment contract imposes on the bailee an obligation not to convert the bailor's goods and to exercise reasonable care.[178]

Where a contract involves the execution of work and the supply of materials, such as in the building of a house, the law implies terms requiring the contractor to use reasonable care in doing the work and to supply materials which are of 'good quality' and 'fit for the purpose' for which they are supplied.[179]

[634] **Unjust or unreasonable terms not implied.** A term will not be the subject of legal implication if, in the circumstances of the case, it is unjust or unreasonable to imply it. For example, in *Gloucestershire CC v Richardson*,[180] a builder was employed by the council to build extensions to a technical college and in doing so used concrete supplied by a supplier nominated, as required in the contract, by the County architect. The cement was defective and delays occurred in the building of the extensions.

---

173. See, eg *Luxor (Eastbourne) Ltd v Cooper* [1941] AC 108 at 137; *Khoury v Government Insurance Office of NSW* (1984) 165 CLR 622 at 635–6; *Australis Media Holdings Pty Ltd v Telstra Corp Ltd* (1998) 43 NSWLR 104 at 123. For discussion see Jane Swanton, 'Implied Contractual Terms: Further Implications of Hawkins v Clayton' (1992) 5 *JCL* 127.
174. *Simonius Vischer & Co v Holt* [1979] 2 NSWLR 322 at 348.
175. For the impact of statute see [642]–[643].
176. *Lister v Romford Ice and Cold Storage Co Ltd* [1957] AC 555. See also *Faccenda Chicken Ltd v Fowler* [1987] Ch 117 (implied duty of good faith or fidelity). There may also be an obligation to provide a safe system of work: *Wright v TNT Management Pty Ltd* (1989) 85 ALR 442 at 459.
177. See, eg *Breen v Williams* (1996) 186 CLR 71 (doctor). See further [1857].
178. See, eg the discussion in Palmer, *Bailment*, 2nd ed, 1991, pp 44–61.
179. *G H Myers & Co v Brent Cross Service Co* [1934] 1 KB 46 at 55 (approved *Young & Marten Ltd v McManus Childs Ltd* [1969] 1 AC 454; adopted *Reg Glass Pty Ltd v Rivers Locking Systems Pty Ltd* (1968) 120 CLR 516).
180. [1969] 1 AC 480.

As the council would not provide compensation for the builder in respect of the defects he abandoned the work. One issue before the House of Lords was whether the implied term of quality, normally present in a work and materials contract,[181] was implied in the contract between the builder and the council. It was held that the term was not present because it would have been unjust to imply it. The supplier had been nominated by the council, the builder had no right to veto the nomination and was bound by terms which, as between the builder and the supplier, severely restricted the builder's rights in respect of defective supply. The restriction would effectively have prevented the builder obtaining compensation from the supplier and it would therefore have been unjust to hold the builder liable to the council on an implied term.

[635] **Consistency and concurrent duties.** The requirement of consistency between express and implied terms also applies where the term is the subject of legal implication. Thus, in *Gemmell Power Farming Co Ltd v Nies*[182] the defendant alleged the breach of a contract of hire on the basis of an implied term covering the fitness of a tractor for the hirer's purpose. It was held that the existence of an express warranty (cl 7) and an exclusion of liability (cl 8) combined to exclude the alleged implied term by virtue of their inconsistency with the term sought to be implied.[183]

Where there is a duty under the law of tort, for example, to exercise reasonable care, the courts have in recent years been reluctant to imply a contractual term which would have the effect of increasing one party's obligations under a contract which is not obviously incomplete.[184] However, these cases do not deny the ability to imply a term to *define* the standard of care.[185]

The cases also indicate that a tortious duty of care — which would frequently operate in a similar way to a term implied in law — will not be imposed where the contract is intended to be a complete statement of the parties' obligations.[186] The converse is not, however, correct. Thus, it is now clear that a term may be implied to create a contractual duty which mirrors the tortious duty.[187] Since the contract provides the setting for the tortious duty, it would be peculiar for the tortious duty to displace the term which would otherwise be implied as a matter of law. Thus, generally, a

---

181. See [633].
182. (1935) 35 SR (NSW) 469. See also *Helicopter Sales (Australia) Pty Ltd v Rotor-Work Pty Ltd* (1974) 132 CLR 1. Contrast *Criss v Alexander* (1928) 28 SR (NSW) 297.
183. Cf *May and Butcher Ltd v R* (1929) [1934] 2 KB 17n.
184. See, eg *Tai Hing Cotton Mill Ltd v Liu Chong Hing Bank Ltd* [1986] AC 80; *Hawkins v Clayton* (1988) 164 CLR 539; *Scally v Southern Health and Social Services Board* [1992] 1 AC 294.
185. See [1855].
186. See also *Bank of Nova Scotia v Hellenic Mutual War Risks Association (Bermuda) Ltd (The Good Luck)* [1992] 1 AC 233.
187. See *Astley v Austrust Ltd* (1999) 197 CLR 1 at 21–3; 161 ALR 155 (approving *Henderson v Merrett Syndicates Ltd* [1995] 2 AC 145 at 193–4 and disapproving *Hawkins v Clayton* (1988) 164 CLR 539 at 585). See Barbara McDonald, 'Solicitors' Liability: Tort, Contract or Both?' (1991) 4 *JCL* 121.

professional person will be subject to concurrent duties in contract and tort.[188]

Terms Implied by Statute

[636] Extent of legislative intervention. The category of terms implied by statute is a large one, and it is beyond the scope of this work to give any more than an outline of the relevant provisions. The treatment will not extend beyond contracts for the supply of goods and services, and emphasis will be given to supply by way of sale. It should perhaps be pointed out that many of the terms now implied by statute were at one time implied at common law.

Sale of goods

[637] Implied terms relating to title. In a contract of sale, unless the circumstances of the contract are such as to show a different intention, s 17 of the *Sale of Goods Act* 1923 (NSW)[189] provides that there is:

(1) an implied condition on the part of the seller that in the case of a sale the seller has a right to sell the goods, and that in the case of an agreement to sell the seller will have a right to sell the goods at the time when the property is to pass;

(2) an implied warranty that the buyer will have and enjoy quiet possession of the goods; and

(3) an implied warranty that the goods are free from any charge or encumbrance in favour of any third party not declared or known to the buyer before or at the time when the contract is made.

Because the first implied term is a condition, a right to terminate for breach of an implied condition is established by proof that the seller had no right to sell.[190] On the other hand, because the applicable implied terms are warranties where the buyer's quiet possession of the goods is interfered with, or there is a charge or encumbrance on the goods, the buyer must be satisfied with a claim for damages.[191]

Similar terms are implied by s 69(1) of the *Trade Practices Act* 1974 (Cth) into contracts for the 'supply' (which includes sale) of goods to a consumer[192] by a corporation.[193]

[638] Correspondence with description.[194] Under s 18 of the *Sale of Goods Act* 1923 (NSW)[195] a condition is implied into a contract for the sale

188. See further [1857].
189. See also **ACT**: *Sale of Goods Act* 1954, s 17; **NT**: *Sale of Goods Act* 1972, s 17; **Qld**: *Sale of Goods Act* 1896, s 15; **SA**: *Sale of Goods Act* 1895, s 12; **Tas**: *Sale of Goods Act* 1896, s 17; **Vic**: *Goods Act* 1958, s 17; **WA**: *Sale of Goods Act* 1895, s 12.
190. See, eg *Rowland v Divall* [1923] 2 KB 500 (see [2306]).
191. For the distinction between conditions and warranties see [726]–[730].
192. For the definition of 'consumer' see s 4B.
193. See also *Consumer Affairs and Fair Trading Act* 1990 (NT), s 62; *Fair Trading Act* 1987 (WA), s 36; cf *Consumer Transactions Act* 1972 (SA), s 6(1), (2); *Goods Act* 1958 (Vic), s 86, none of which require the supplier to be a corporation.
194. See Brian Coote, 'Correspondence with Description in the Law of Sale of Goods' (1976) 50 *ALJ* 17.

of goods by description, requiring the goods to correspond with that description. A similar implied term is provided for, in contracts for the 'supply' of goods (including sale otherwise than by auction) to a consumer, by s 70(1) of the *Trade Practices Act* 1974 (Cth).[196] For the term to be implied the buyer must rely on the description when entering into the contract.[197]

Two main issues may arise in the application of s 18: whether the sale is *by description*, and whether the goods delivered (or tendered) correspond with that description. In *Wallis v Pratt*[198] sellers agreed to sell goods described in the contract as 'common English sainfoin'. The sale was by description because the description was the means by which the subject matter of the contract had been identified.[199] Where the goods are selected by a consumer from a retailer's stock, as in the normal retail sale, the transaction need not be a sale by description. However, if, for example, the consumer asks to buy 'a hot water bottle', the sale will be by description because the goods are being chosen on the basis of a particular description.[200] Section 70(2) of the *Trade Practices Act* 1974 (Cth) perhaps takes the matter a little further by expressly providing that a supply of goods is not prevented from being a supply by description 'by reason only that, being exposed for sale ... they are selected by the consumer'.

Correspondence with description is more complex. The court must first identify the words which actually describe the goods. Words directed solely to quality are not part of the goods' description,[201] whereas the elements used to identify the goods usually are. Thus, in *Wallis v Pratt* the descriptive words were 'common English sainfoin'. The sellers were in breach of contract because they delivered goods of another description, namely, 'giant sainfoin'. There is a tendency to distinguish commercial contracts, for example, for the sale of commodities such as wheat, from other types of contracts.[202] In the former, every detail of the description may be essential and the slightest deviation a breach of condition.[203] But in other contracts the non-correspondence must relate to a substantial ingredient of the 'identity' of the goods sold before there is a breach of the implied condition.[204]

---

195. See also **ACT**: *Sale of Goods Act* 1954, s 18; **NT**: *Sale of Goods Act* 1972, s 18; **Qld**: *Sale of Goods Act* 1896, s 16; **SA**: *Sale of Goods Act* 1895, s 13; **Tas**: *Sale of Goods Act* 1896, s 18; **Vic**: *Goods Act* 1958, s 18; **WA**: *Sale of Goods Act* 1895, s 13.
196. See also *Consumer Affairs and Fair Trading Act* 1990 (NT), s 63; *Fair Trading Act* 1987 (WA), s 37; cf *Consumer Transactions Act* 1972 (SA), s 6(3); *Goods Act* 1958 (Vic), s 87. Unlike the *Trade Practices Act* 1974 (Cth) provision, these do not require the supplier to be a corporation.
197. See *Harlingdon and Leinster Enterprises Ltd v Christopher Hull Fine Art Ltd* [1991] 1 QB 564 (see Ian Brown, (1990) 106 *LQR* 561).
198. [1911] AC 394.
199. It was, in addition, a sale by sample.
200. See *Grant v Australian Knitting Mills Ltd* [1936] AC 85 at 100.
201. See *Ashington Piggeries Ltd v Christopher Hill Ltd* [1972] AC 441.
202. See *Reardon Smith Line Ltd v Yngvar Hansen-Tangen* [1976] 1 WLR 989 at 998.
203. See, eg *Arcos Ltd v E A Ronaasen & Son* [1933] AC 470.
204. *Couchman v Hill* [1947] KB 554 at 559, as interpreted in *Reardon Smith Line Ltd v Yngvar Hansen-Tangen* [1976] 1 WLR 989.

[639] **Fitness for purpose.** Under s 19(1) of the *Sale of Goods Act* 1923 (NSW),[205] a condition requiring the goods to be fit for the buyer's purpose will be implied if:[206]

- the buyer made a particular purpose known to the seller;
- the purpose was made known in such a way as to show reliance on the seller's skill or judgment; and
- the goods were of a description which it was in the course of the seller's business to supply (as manufacturer or otherwise).

An example is provided by *Frost v Aylesbury Dairy Co Ltd*[207] where milk was supplied by the defendants who were dealers in milk. A breach of the implied condition of fitness for purpose was established by proof that the milk contained typhoid fever germs. The sellers said that they had taken special precautions to ensure that only pure milk would be supplied. The milk was obtained for the purpose of human consumption and in the circumstances it was clear that the buyer had relied on the sellers' skill or judgment. There was no doubt that it was in the course of the sellers' business to supply goods described as 'milk'. The case also illustrates that the liability of sellers is strict in relation to purpose (and quality) since the defect in the goods was latent.[208]

In order for the condition to be implied the buyer need not rely exclusively on the seller's skill or judgment.[209]

A corresponding term, in relation to 'supply' (including sale otherwise than by auction) to a consumer, is implied by s 71(2) of the *Trade Practices Act* 1974 (Cth). The requirements for implication are more readily satisfied.[210] In particular, the condition will be implied unless the circumstances show that the buyer did not rely, or that it was unreasonable for the buyer to rely, on the seller's skill or judgment.[211]

[640] **Merchantable quality.** Section 19(2) of the *Sale of Goods Act* 1923 (NSW)[212] states that where goods are bought by description from a seller

---

205. See also **ACT**: *Sale of Goods Act* 1954, s 19(2); **NT**: *Sale of Goods Act* 1972, s 19(a); **Qld**: *Sale of Goods Act* 1896, s 17(1); **SA**: *Sale of Goods Act* 1895, s 14(I); **Tas**: *Sale of Goods Act* 1896, s 19(a); **Vic**: *Goods Act* 1958, s 19(a); **WA**: *Sale of Goods Act* 1895, s 14(I).
206. This is, however, subject to a proviso 'that in the case of a contract for the sale of a specified article under its patent or other trade name there is no implied condition as to its fitness for any particular purpose'. The proviso has been narrowly interpreted. See, eg *Grant v Australian Knitting Mills Ltd* [1936] AC 85 at 99.
207. [1905] 1 KB 608.
208. See generally on standard of duty [1853]–[1857].
209. *Cammell Laird & Co Ltd v Manganese Bronze and Brass Co Ltd* [1934] AC 402.
210. However, the supplier must be a corporation. See also *Consumer Affairs and Fair Trading Act* 1990 (NT), s 64(2); *Fair Trading Act* 1987 (WA), s 38(2); cf *Consumer Transactions Act* 1972 (SA), s 6(6); *Goods Act* 1958 (Vic), s 90, where there is no such requirement.
211. See *R & B Customs Brokers Ltd v United Dominions Trust Ltd* [1988] 1 WLR 321 (see Sally Jones and David Harland, (1990) 2 *JCL* 266).
212. See also **ACT**: *Sale of Goods Act* 1954, s 19(4); **NT**: *Sale of Goods Act* 1972, s 19(b); **Qld**: *Sale of Goods Act* 1896, s 17(2); **SA**: *Sale of Goods Act* 1895 s 14(II); **Tas**: *Sale of Goods Act* 1896, s 19(b); **Vic**: *Goods Act* 1958, s 19(b); **WA**: *Sale of Goods Act* 1895, s 14(II). Cf *Sale of Goods Act* 1979 (UK), s 14(2), under which an implied term of 'satisfactory quality' replaces the merchantable quality term.

who deals in goods of that description there is an implied condition that the goods purchased are of 'merchantable quality'. The provision is subject to a proviso that if the buyer has examined the goods there is no implied condition as regards defects which such an examination 'ought to have revealed'.

The requirement that the goods be 'bought' by description means that there must have been a sale by description;[213] and the requirement is the same as in s 19(1). Thus, the seller's business must include a willingness to accept orders for goods of that description.[214] The proviso indicates that a buyer who has not examined the goods will be in a better position than one who has. However, the proviso will not prevent the condition being implied, and a breach established, in relation to latent defects in the goods, that is, those not discoverable by an examination of the goods.

For example, in *Grant v Australian Knitting Mills Ltd*[215] the plaintiff purchased woollen underwear from a retailer and contracted dermatitis because of the presence of a chemical irritant in the garments. The implied condition was established, and a breach proved, even though the defect in the goods could not have been discovered by any examination by either the buyer or the retailer. Moreover, liability was established without any proof by the buyer that the retailer had failed to exercise reasonable care. The Privy Council said:[216]

> [W]hatever else merchantable may mean, it does mean that the article sold, if only meant for one particular use in ordinary course, is fit for that use; merchantable does not mean that the thing is saleable in the market simply because it looks all right; it is not merchantable in that event if it has defects unfitting it for its only proper use but not apparent on ordinary examination ...

The statement indicates that 'merchantable' means 'saleable', but also indicates that the purpose to which the goods are put is relevant in determining whether the goods are merchantable. It can also be inferred that in cases where goods can be put to more than one use it may be difficult to decide whether the goods are merchantable. Where a range of purposes is possible it would seem that, at common law, regard must be had to the description of the goods, the price at which they are sold and the range of purposes.[217] Generally, goods are merchantable if fit for at least one of the range of purposes to which the goods are usually put.

The fact that purpose is relevant to both fitness for purpose and merchantable quality indicates that there is an overlap between ss 19(1) and 19(2). For example, in *Grant v Australian Knitting Mills Ltd* a breach of both implied conditions was established. It is also fair to say that the decisions have tended to widen the fitness for purpose provision at the expense of the merchantable quality provision.[218]

---

213. See [638].
214. See *Ashington Piggeries Ltd v Christopher Hill Ltd* [1972] AC 441.
215. [1936] AC 85.
216. [1936] AC 85 at 99–100.
217. See, eg *Henry Kendall & Sons v William Lillico & Sons Ltd* [1969] 2 AC 31.
218. See, eg *Ashington Piggeries Ltd v Christopher Hill Ltd* [1972] AC 441.

In respect of 'consumer' sales covered by Pt VIII of the *Sale of Goods Act* 1923 (NSW) there is no implied condition of merchantable quality as regards 'defects brought to the buyer's notice before the contract was entered into'.[219] There is also, in s 64(3), a definition of 'merchantable quality' in the following terms:[220]

> Without limiting the meaning of the expression 'merchantable quality', goods of any kind which are the subject of a contract for a consumer sale are not of merchantable quality if they are not as fit for the purpose or purposes for which goods of that kind are commonly bought as is reasonable to expect having regard to their price, to any description applied to them by the seller and to all other circumstances.

A condition of merchantable quality is also implied by s 71(1) of the *Trade Practices Act* 1974 (Cth), where a corporation supplies (including sale otherwise than by auction) goods to a consumer, in the course of a business, except as regards defects specifically brought to the consumer's attention before the contract was made. If the consumer examined the goods prior to the contract being made there is no implied condition as regards defects which the examination ought to have revealed.[221] Section 66(2) provides a definition of 'merchantable quality', similar to that quoted above.

An important question of interpretation arises in respect of these statutory definitions of merchantable quality.[222] At common law goods commonly used for more than one purpose would clearly be unmerchantable only if of no use for any of the range of purposes.[223] Suitability for one such purpose may therefore be sufficient. Although, in theory, the effect of the definitions may be to narrow the common law, by emphasising purpose for use rather than saleable quality, s 64(3) of the *Sale of Goods Act* (NSW) is at least as wide as the common law because it is introduced by words which preserve any wider meaning. One view is that these definitions merely reproduce the common law.[224] There is, however, authority to suggest that the law has been changed, and that the effect of the definitions is to require goods, commonly used for a number of purposes, to be suitable for all of those purposes.[225]

---

219. Section 64(4). Cf *Consumer Transactions Act* 1972 (SA), s 6(4); *Goods Act* 1958 (Vic), s 89(3).
220. See also *Goods Act* 1958 (Vic), s 89(2). Cf *Consumer Transactions Act* 1972 (SA), s 6(5).
221. See also *Consumer Affairs and Fair Trading Act* 1990 (NT), s 64(1); *Fair Trading Act* 1987 (WA), s 38(1); cf *Goods Act* 1958 (Vic), s 89(3), all provisions which do not require the supplier to be a corporation.
222. For discussion see Taperell, Vermeesch and Harland, *Trade Practices and Consumer Protection*, 3rd ed, 1983, paras 1725–1727. In England, the implied term of 'satisfactory quality' (which replaces the merchantable quality term) is described in s 14(2A) of the *Sale of Goods Act* 1979 (UK). See *Benjamin's Sale of Goods*, 5th ed, 1997, paras 11-026–11-043.
223. See *Henry Kendall & Sons v William Lillico & Sons Ltd* [1969] 2 AC 31.
224. See *M/S Aswan Engineering Establishment Co v Lupdine Ltd* [1987] 1 WLR 1 at 14. See also *Harlingdon and Leinster Enterprises Ltd v Christopher Hull Fine Art Ltd* [1991] 1 QB 564.
225. See *Rogers v Parish (Scarborough) Ltd* [1987] QB 933; *Cavalier Marketing (Australia) Pty Ltd v Rasell* (1990) 96 ALR 375 (see Kenneth Sutton, (1991) 4 *JCL* 235).

[641] Sale by sample. Section 20 of the *Sale of Goods Act* 1923 (NSW)[226] provides that, in the case of a sale by sample, there are three implied conditions, requiring:

(1) that the bulk correspond with the sample in quality;

(2) that the buyer have a reasonable opportunity of comparing the bulk with the sample; and

(3) that the goods be free from any defect rendering them unmerchantable which would not be apparent on reasonable examination of the sample.

A contract is one for sale by sample if there is an express or implied term to that effect.[227]

Section 72 of the *Trade Practices Act* 1974 (Cth) is similar, and applicable to the 'supply' (which includes sale otherwise than by auction), of goods by a corporation to a consumer.[228]

Further illustrations

[642] Supply of goods other than by sale. Because the provisions of the *Trade Practices Act* 1974 (Cth) in relation to title, description, quality, fitness and sample apply to the *supply* of goods they also apply to an exchange, lease, hire or hire-purchase of goods.[229] In addition, there is provision in the legislation of some States and the Northern Territory for the implication of terms, for example, in the case of a lease of goods to a consumer, similar to those implied where the transaction is by way of sale.[230]

Where no legislative provisions deal with the implication of terms in contracts for the supply of goods, the common law must be relied on for the implication of terms. In *Derbyshire Building Co Pty Ltd v Becker*[231] Kitto J said:[232]

> The authorities concerning the nature of an implied term in a contract of bailment ... are not uniform. But the weight of judicial opinion is, I think, in favour of applying to all contracts for the supply of chattels, including contracts of bailment, the principles laid down with respect to sales in s 14 of the *Sale of Goods Act* 1893 (UK).

For example, where goods are hired there is, at common law, an implied term that the goods are fit for the hirer's purpose provided, of course, that

---

226. See also **ACT**: *Sale of Goods Act* 1954, s 20; **NT**: *Sale of Goods Act* 1972, s 20; **Qld**: *Sale of Goods Act* 1896, s 18; **SA**: *Sale of Goods Act* 1895, s 15; **Tas**: *Sale of Goods Act* 1896, s 20; **Vic**: *Goods Act* 1958, s 20; **WA**: *Sale of Goods Act* 1895, s 15.
227. But note the definition in s 88(1) of the *Goods Act* 1958 (Vic) which gives the concept a wider application in consumer sales.
228. See also *Consumer Affairs and Fair Trading Act* 1990 (NT), s 65; *Fair Trading Act* 1987 (WA), s 39 which do not require the supplier to be a corporation.
229. See s 4 and discussion in Taperell, Vermeesch and Harland, *Trade Practices and Consumer Protection*, 3rd ed, 1983, para 423.
230. See generally **NT**: *Consumer Affairs and Fair Trading Act* 1990, Pt V; **SA**: *Consumer Transactions Act* 1972, s 6(2)–(6); **Vic**: *Goods Act* 1958, ss 103–107; **WA**: *Fair Trading Act* 1987, Pt III.
231. (1962) 107 CLR 633.
232. (1962) 107 CLR 633 at 649.

the hirer has communicated the specific purpose in such a way as to indicate reliance on the supplier's skill or judgment.[233]

[643] **Supply of services.** It will already have been noticed that the tendency of recent legislation is to extend the categories of contracts in which terms are implied by statute. A notable further extension is in respect of contracts for the provision of 'services'.

Under s 74(1) of the *Trade Practices Act* 1974 (Cth), where a corporation supplies services to a consumer in the course of a business there is an implied 'warranty' that the services will be rendered 'with due care and skill'. There is also an implied 'warranty' that any materials supplied in connection with the services will be 'reasonably fit for the purpose' for which they are supplied. Under s 74(2), if the consumer has made known, either expressly or impliedly, any 'particular' purpose for which the services are required, 'or the result that he or she desires the services to achieve', there is an implied 'warranty' that the services and the materials supplied will be reasonably fit for that purpose or of such a nature and quality 'that they might reasonably be expected to achieve that result'.[234] However, there is no such implied warranty where the circumstances indicate that the consumer did not rely, or that it would have been 'unreasonable' for the consumer to rely, on the corporation's skill or judgment.[235]

It is arguable that, in one respect, the terms relating to quality and fitness implied by legislation in contracts for services are narrower than those implied at common law. The legislation describes them as 'warranties' whereas at common law they are probably 'conditions'.[236] In another respect, however, the terms have a wider application because the requirements for implication are easier to satisfy than the common law requirements.

In cases where the *Trade Practices Act* 1974 (Cth) does not apply, and there is no State or Territory legislation governing the contract,[237] the common law position obtains. There is, therefore, an implied term that the services will be rendered with due care and skill,[238] and also implied terms regulating the quality and fitness of any goods supplied.[239]

Terms Implied by Custom or Usage

[644] **Requirements for implication.** A term may sometimes be implied into a contract by reason of a custom or usage in the market. The phrase 'custom or usage' includes established mercantile usage or professional practice.[240] The parties are regarded as having contracted on

---

233. See further Carter, *Breach of Contract*, 2nd ed, 1991, paras 229, 263–65.
234. See *Crawford v Mayne Nickless Ltd* (1992) 59 SASR 490.
235. Services of a professional nature provided by a qualified architect or engineer are excluded from the operation of the section. Note also the more general qualifications in s 74(3).
236. See [734]. But note *Goods Act* 1958 (Vic), s 94(1) (sale of goods and services).
237. But see *Consumer Affairs and Fair Trading Act* 1990 (NT), s 66; *Consumer Transactions Act* 1972 (SA), s 7; *Goods Act* 1958 (Vic), ss 91–3; *Fair Trading Act* 1987 (WA), s 40.
238. See [633].
239. See [642].

the basis of any custom or usage applicable and the term is implied in accordance with the custom or usage.

For a term to be implied the custom or usage must be proved to be 'notorious, certain, legal and reasonable'.[241] For example, in *Sagar v H Ridehalgh & Son Ltd*[242] the defendants, who employed the plaintiff as a weaver, made deductions from the plaintiff's wages in respect of cloth which had not been properly woven. A usage in the Lancashire region, where the plaintiff worked, was established which justified the deduction. The fact that some mill-owners in the region did not make deductions did not prevent the usage being applied because there was evidence that over 85 per cent of the mills in the county made such deductions.

Evidence of actual market practices is nevertheless crucial. Thus, in *Con-Stan Industries of Australia Pty Ltd v Norwich Winterthur Insurance (Australia) Ltd*[243] the appellants before the High Court failed to establish a term alleged to be implied into contracts between themselves and their insurers on the basis of commercial custom or usage. The implied term would have precluded the insurer making any claim against the appellants if the broker to whom they paid a premium did not pass it on, or would have required the insurers to look to the broker for payment whether or not the premium had been paid to the broker. There was no proof that insurers in the market invariably, or even regularly, abstained from making claims against insureds in cases where the broker defaulted and in the absence of such proof there was no basis for implication on the ground of custom or usage. However, the court made it clear that universal acceptance of a custom is not essential.

A term which is inconsistent with the express terms of the contract will not be implied even if the custom or usage is established. Thus, in *Summers v The Commonwealth*[244] a contract was entered into for the supply of 671 cubic feet of marble for Australia House, London. The contract required the size of each block to be full enough 'to admit of its being worked and polished in London without blemish on every side if need be, to the size set out in the schedule' to the contract. The supplier alleged the existence of a trade usage under which it was sufficient for him to supply blocks of marble from which a number of the schedule sized blocks could be cut. The court was not satisfied that the usage was established; but said that, even if this was the case, no term could have been implied because the usage was inconsistent with the express term.[245] Similarly, a term cannot be implied if the trade usage establishes a matter dealt with sufficiently by the express terms.[246]

---

240. See *Byrne v Australian Airlines Ltd* (1995) 185 CLR 410 at 440.
241. *Halsbury's Laws of England*, 4th ed, 1974, Vol 9, para 353. See also *Majeau Carrying Co Pty Ltd v Coastal Rutile Ltd* (1973) 129 CLR 48 at 61; 1 ALR 1.
242. [1931] 1 Ch 310.
243. (1986) 160 CLR 226. See also *Byrne v Australian Airlines Ltd* (1995) 185 CLR 410 at 423.
244. (1918) 25 CLR 144 (affirmed (1919) 26 CLR 180).
245. See also *Rosenhain v Commonwealth Bank of Australia* (1922) 31 CLR 46 at 53; *Con-Stan Industries of Australia Pty Ltd v Norwich Winterthur Insurance (Australia) Ltd* (1986) 160 CLR 226 at 236–7.
246. *Re Nudgee Bakery Pty Ltd's Agreement* [1971] Qd R 24.

Establishing a course of conduct in a given market does not indicate that a term giving contractual effect to that course of conduct can be implied. It is necessary for the course of conduct to have a binding effect in the market, that is to say, the merchants who operate in the market must regard themselves as bound by the usage unless it has been expressly *excluded*.[247]

---

247. See *General Reinsurance Corp v Forsakringsaktiebolaget Fennia Patria* [1983] QB 856. See also *Libyan Arab Foreign Bank v Bankers Trust Co* [1989] QB 728.

Chapter 7

Construction of the Terms

General..701
The Parol Evidence Rule...................................705
   Formulations of the Rule.................................. 705
   Application of the Parol Evidence Rule..................... 707
   The Evidence Excluded..................................... 709
Evidence of Factual Matrix.................................713
Exceptions to the Parol Evidence Rule......................716
Classification of Terms....................................724
   General... 724
   The Tripartite Classification............................. 725
   Promises and Contingencies................................ 739
   Other Types of Terms...................................... 743
Exclusion Clauses..748
   General... 748
   Operation at Common Law................................... 750
   Operation under Statute................................... 769

General

[701] Meaning of 'construction'. We explored in the previous chapter the processes by which courts *identify* the terms agreed upon by the parties. Having arrived at the position where the terms of the contract are known, it is now necessary to consider the impact which those terms have. This is achieved by interpreting the words used; a process known as *construction* of the contract.

'Construction' describes two things:[1] determining the *meaning* of words used to express the terms of the contract; and the means by which particular *legal effects* are ascribed to the terms which make up a contract.

In most cases the determination of meaning requires no more than a reading of the contract in its context. Because meaning is essentially the linguistic significance of words, prior decisions on the meaning of terms in other contracts are not likely to be particularly helpful. But when we move from meaning to legal effect the process of construction becomes more dynamic. Construction here is much more concerned with rights and remedies created by the contract. Experience shows that legal effect is seldom discovered by a mere reading of a document; an understanding of case law is frequently necessary.

[702] **Issue of law.** At least where the contract is expressed or evidenced (wholly or partly) in a document, 'construction' raises an issue of law not fact.[2] The basis for this rule is historical rather than logical. Lord Diplock once described it as a 'legacy of the system of trials by juries who might not all be literate'.[3]

[703] **Construction and intention.** The primary 'object'[4] of construction is to determine the intention of the parties. Thus, when a court construes a contract it does so in order to determine and give effect to the intention of the parties. Intention may be actual, expressed or implied:

- 'Actual' intention is the intention subjectively (actually) held by the parties.
- 'Expressed' intention is the intention disclosed in the words of the contract.
- 'Implied' (or inferred or imputed) intention is the intention which is attributed to the parties in relation to matters on which no intention has been expressed.

When it is said that construction depends on the 'intention' of the parties it is clear that the word is being used objectively.[5] References to intention are not to the parties' actual intentions, still less to their desires, aspirations or expectations.[6] 'Intention' therefore refers to expressed intention, to be ascertained from the words used.[7] Where no intention is expressed, intention must be determined by implication. It will be implied, inferred or imputed on the basis of the words used, read in context and in the light of

1. Cf *Chatenay v Brazilian Submarine Telegraph Co Ltd* [1891] 1 QB 79 at 85 (adopted *Life Insurance Co of Australia Ltd v Phillips* (1925) 36 CLR 60 at 78).
2. *Bowes v Shand* (1877) 2 App Cas 455 at 462; *Francis v Lyon* (1907) 4 CLR 1023 at 1040.
3. *Pioneer Shipping Ltd v BTP Tioxide Ltd* [1982] AC 724 at 736.
4. *River Wear Commissioners v Adamson* (1877) 2 App Cas 743 at 763.
5. *Reardon Smith Line Ltd v Yngvar Hansen-Tangen* [1976] 1 WLR 989 at 996. See also *Hospital Products Ltd v United States Surgical Corp* (1984) 156 CLR 41 at 62; 55 ALR 417; [110], [206].
6. See *Codelfa Construction Pty Ltd v State Rail Authority of New South Wales* (1982) 149 CLR 337; 41 ALR 367 at 352–3.
7. *Goldsbrough Mort & Co Ltd v Carter* (1914) 19 CLR 429 at 447; *Deutsche Genossenschaftsbank v Burnhope* [1995] 1 WLR 1580 at 1589. Cf Sir Johan Steyn, 'Written Contracts: To What Extent May Evidence Control Language?' [1988] *CLP* 23.

principles of contract law. This is an objective inquiry, which, at least at the level of meaning, refers to what a reasonable person in the position of the party to whom the words were addressed would regard as the other party's intention.[8]

It may seem peculiar, even absurd, that in determining what parties intended by their contract their actual intention should not be considered relevant. This approach is readily explained at the time of its development, since the parties to an action were not originally permitted to give evidence in court.[9] But the fact that the parties may now give evidence has not changed the law, although it has resulted in a greater reliance on the context of the contract. Perhaps the main virtue of the rule is that it protects the integrity of the bargain. Contracts very frequently affect third parties. It would be wrong to allow the rights of such persons to be denied by permitting the parties to contradict the intention expressed in their document. The approach also serves to control evidence in court, where a great deal of time might be wasted in hearing what the parties thought their contract meant. The purpose of the doctrine of rectification, considered later,[10] is to allow parties to have documents which do not accurately record their bargain corrected. But this does not allow a party to deny an accurate expression merely on the basis that the contract does not reflect that party's subjective understanding of the words chosen. In any event, 'construction' is directed to legal effect as well as linguistic meaning, and evidence of what lay people understood as the legal significance of words in a contract cannot control the effect of their bargain. Typically, where legal effect is at issue, 'implied' intention refers to the intention 'imputed' to the parties on the basis of what the contract says, its context and legal decisions.

[704] Approach to construction: issues for analysis. It is essential, given the objective approach to contract construction, that the courts adopt a sensible approach. Their function is to give effect to the bargain, not to deny its efficacy by a restrictive technical analysis. This finds its expression in a number of ways. For example, as a general rule, where a contract is construed the court will apply a presumption that the parties did not intend its terms to operate unreasonably.[11] Therefore, where a particular construction would achieve an unreasonable result the court will be reluctant to accept that this was meant by the parties.[12] Nevertheless, the court has no jurisdiction to reject an interpretation, clearly intended by the parties, merely because it is in its view unreasonable or because it produces unreasonable results.[13]

Second, a commonsense approach must be taken, particularly in commercial contracts which are expressed in an imperfectly constructed document. Thus, Lord Diplock has said[14] that 'if detailed semantic and

---

8. See [112]. On that basis, the approach applies to documents associated with contracts, such as termination notices. See [1970].
9. See Law Commission, *The Parol Evidence Rule*, Law Com No 154, 1986, para 2.4.
10. See [1256]–[1266]. See also [723].
11. See, eg *L Schuler AG v Wickman Machine Tool Sales Ltd* [1974] AC 235.
12. See, eg *TCN Channel 9 Pty Ltd v Hayden Enterprises Pty Ltd* (1989) 16 NSWLR 130 at 146.
13. See *Charter Reinsurance Co Ltd v Fagan* [1997] AC 313; [1996] 2 WLR 726 at 759 (interpretation must conform to the intention of the parties). See further [765].

syntactical analysis of words in a commercial contract is going to lead to a conclusion that flouts business commonsense, it must be made to yield to business commonsense'.

Third, there must be rules governing the forensic material which can be received to assist in the construction process. The role of context in determining meaning must be fully acknowledged. Linguists have, of course, emphasised this point as crucial; lawyers have recognised it only recently.[15]

The issues referred to above are general ones, relevant to both meaning and legal effect. The general approach today is to apply the same construction rules no matter what the form or nature of the clause or contract. In other words, the relevant principles do not depend on whether the contract is for the sale of goods or the provision of services and so on. However, the nature of the contract must be taken into account when considering the parties' intention, and some types of contracts and clauses still give rise to particular difficulties.[16]

Since construction issues arise in relation to all contracts, it is not possible to discuss all issues which may be framed in terms of construction in one chapter. Our concern is with three areas:

- the raw material which may be used to construe a contract;[17]
- the classification of contractual terms;[18] and
- the construction of exclusion clauses.[19]

The Parol Evidence Rule[20]

Formulations of the Rule

[705] Introduction. One of the least satisfactory chapters in the law of contract concerns what is referred to as the parol evidence rule. It is usually spoken of as a well-understood, even clearly defined concept, yet in fact it is possible to find various formulations of the rule. The formulation of Lord Blackburn in *Inglis v John Buttery & Co*,[21] was adopted by Isaacs J in *Gordon v Macgregor*.[22] Lord Blackburn said:[23]

---

14. *Antaios Compania Naviera SA v Salen Rederierna AB* [1985] AC 191 at 201. See also *Hide & Skin Trading Pty Ltd v Oceanic Meat Traders Ltd* (1990) 20 **NSWLR** 310 at 313–14; *Di Dio Nominees Pty Ltd v Brian Mark Real Estate Pty Ltd* [1992] 2 VR 732 at 740.
15. The relevant context is now usually termed the 'factual matrix'. See [713]–[715].
16. For example, the approach to the construction of contracts of guarantee is usually said to be 'stricter' than the approach to contracts generally. See *Corumo Holdings Pty Ltd v C Itoh Ltd* (1991) 24 NSWLR 370 at 377. But cf *Pan Foods Co Importers & Distributors Pty Ltd v Australia and New Zealand Banking Group Ltd* (2000) 202 CLR 351 at 360, 374 per Kirby J (ordinary rules of commercial construction apply, at least in context of surety for reward).
17. See [705]–[723] (the 'parol evidence rule' and its exceptions).
18. See [724]–[747].
19. See [748]–[772].
20. Cf H K Lücke, 'Contracts in Writing' (1966) 40 *ALJ* 265.
21. (1878) 3 App Cas 552.
22. (1909) 8 CLR 316 at 323.

Now, I think it is quite fixed — and no more wholesome or salutary rule relative to written contracts can be devised — that where parties agree to embody, and do actually embody, their contract in a formal written deed, then in determining what the contract really was and really meant, a court must look to the formal deed and to that deed alone. That is only carrying out the will of the parties.

In its working paper on the parol evidence rule, the Law Commission identified[24] three rules which, either separately or together, have been referred to as the parol evidence rule. The first rule says that where a document exists, other evidence of the terms of the document is not admissible. The second rule prohibits evidence of other terms not included 'expressly or by reference' in the document. The third rule excludes evidence of 'its writer's intended meaning'. The conclusion of the Law Commission, in its final report,[25] was that the second rule, if it ever existed, no longer exists as a rule of contract law.

In so far as the rules do in fact operate (which seems to be the Australian position), it is important to appreciate that the first is a rule of evidence rather than one of contract law. It is concerned with the *exclusiveness* of the writing. On the other hand, the second rule, if valid, expresses the *conclusiveness* of the document as to the terms agreed between the parties. It is a rule of contract law and not a rule of evidence. The third rule is also a substantive one. Even so, the courts have not drawn a sharp distinction between the second and third rules. For example, the formulation in *Inglis v John Buttery & Co* is, in effect, an amalgam of the two.

[706] A suggested formulation. We would express the parol evidence rule as excluding extrinsic evidence in determining the meaning or legal effect of words used in a document which the parties have adopted as contractual or as evidencing their contract in whole or in part.

To return to the rules identified above,[26] an examination of how the third rule is applied is in our view sufficient to show why, in practice, the second rule does not operate.[27] Although we therefore agree with the Law Commission's conclusions, we would give the third rule a slightly broader interpretation.[28] This means that the formulation approved by Isaacs J in *Gordon v Macgregor*[29] is not today to be applied to determine 'what the contract really was': it is restricted to what was 'really meant'. This includes the legal effect of the document and the terms stated.

---

23. (1878) 3 App Cas 552 at 577. Cf *Goss v Nugent* (1833) 5 B & Ad 58 at 64–5; 110 ER 713 at 716; *Bank of Australasia v Palmer* [1897] AC 540 at 545.
24. *Working Paper No 70*, 1976, para 4.
25. *The Parol Evidence Rule*, Law Com No 154, 1986. See Geoffrey Marston, [1986] *CLJ* 192; J W Carter, 'The Parol Evidence Rule: The Law Commission's Conclusions' (1988) 1 *JCL* 33.
26. See [705].
27. See [707]–[708].
28. See [710]–[712].
29. (1909) 8 CLR 316 at 323 (see [705]).

Application of the Parol Evidence Rule[30]

[707] Establishing the terms of the bargain. Logically, the initial step in any case is to identify the terms of the contract. Although this may sound obvious, there are cases in which the parol evidence rule has been applied to restrict evidence of the terms of the contract. In *L G Thorne & Co Pty Ltd v Thomas Borthwick & Sons (A'Asia) Ltd*[31] buyers under a contract for the sale of certain drums of neatsfoot oil claimed damages because the oil supplied was not equal to a sample given by the sellers prior to the contract being entered into. The buyers had to prove that the contract was a sale by sample.[32] However, the memorandum of the contract made no reference to the sale being by sample and a majority of the court held that evidence which might show that this was a *term of the contract* was excluded by the parol evidence rule. A different majority of the court held that the rule did not operate to prevent the reception of extrinsic evidence establishing that the buyers entered into a *collateral contract* containing a promise that the oil delivered would be equal to the sample supplied. A new trial, limited to this issue, was justified as it had not been considered by the trial judge.

It need hardly be said that this conclusion lacked logic, and had no effect other than to cause increased expense for the parties. We consider that this approach no longer represents the law and that the dissenting judgment of Herron J should be applied. He said:[33]

> The writing must in a proper case be compared with the negotiations, which must be provisionally received in evidence, before it can safely be said what was covered by the suggested final writing. Thus, the *applicability of the [parol evidence] rule and the effect of the rule are distinct things.*

Alternatively, as McHugh JA expressed it in *State Rail Authority of New South Wales v Heath Outdoor Pty Ltd*,[34] the parol evidence rule has 'no operation until it is first determined' that the terms of the contract are in writing. On this approach it is proper for the court to receive evidence of the prior negotiations to decide what terms expressed the contract before applying the parol evidence rule.

In England, the Court of Appeal in *J Evans & Son (Portsmouth) Ltd v Andrea Merzario Ltd*[35] applied the same approach as Herron J. The plaintiffs imported a moulding machine in a container which was lost during the voyage from Rotterdam to Tilbury. They had employed the defendants as forwarding agents to make the necessary transport arrangements. In the past transport had been arranged in crates stored below deck, and when the defendants proposed a change to container transport they assured the plaintiffs that containers containing the

---

30. See Andrew Stewart, 'Oral Promises, Ad Hoc Implication and the Sanctity of Written Agreements' (1987) 61 *ALJ* 119.
31. (1955) 56 SR (NSW) 81.
32. See [641].
33. (1955) 56 SR (NSW) 81 at 94 (italics added).
34. (1986) 7 NSWLR 170 at 191. See also *Nemeth v Bayswater Road Pty Ltd* [1988] 2 Qd R 406 at 413; *Trazray Pty Ltd v Russell Foundries Pty Ltd* (1988) NSW Conv R ¶55-393.
35. [1976] 2 All ER 930. See also *Finucane v New South Wales Egg Corp* (1988) 80 ALR 486.

plaintiffs' goods would not be carried on deck. However, the machine in question had been placed in a container which was carried on deck and that was the reason for the plaintiffs' loss. Roskill LJ said:[36] 'The court is entitled to look at and should look at all the evidence from start to finish in order to see what the bargain was that was struck between the parties.' In those circumstances the court held that the assurance by the defendants had contractual effect.

In *Hope v RCA Photophone of Australia Pty Ltd*,[37] Latham CJ said that 'there are exceptional cases where the parties to a contract have not expressed all the terms of their contract in writing, and, accordingly, parol evidence is admitted to complete the written contract'. However, we see no reason for describing this process as exceptional. In truth, it is merely part of the process of discovering the terms of the bargain. In fact, many of the cases which have hitherto been treated as exceptions to the parol evidence rule should now be treated as part of the process of term identification. The classic example is *Pym v Campbell*[38] where evidence of an oral condition precedent[39] to formation was treated as receivable under an exception to the parol evidence rule. The better view is that whether a document is binding as a contract is not an issue determined by application of the rule, and may (where necessary) be determined objectively by extrinsic evidence.[40]

[708] The concept of integration. A contractual document may be executed with the intention of superseding entirely all prior negotiations in relation to the subject matter dealt with by the document.[41] The effect of such a document is to *integrate* the bargain in written form.[42] Such a document discharges any prior oral agreement, evidence of which becomes inadmissible because of the parol evidence rule. A second form of integration is where a document embodies, in whole or in part, the parties' agreement without discharging a prior oral agreement. The document is conclusive evidence of the contract or that part recorded in writing.[43]

Two illustrations may be given to show the difference between the two types of integration. First, assume that A rings an airline and books a seat on a plane from Sydney to London. The next day A pays the fare and receives a ticket which A and the airline expressly agree upon as stating all the terms of the contract. The ticket is the written contract and the contract made over the telephone is completely discharged.[44]

36. [1976] 2 All ER 930 at 935.
37. (1937) 59 CLR 348 at 357.
38. (1856) 6 E & B 370; 119 ER 903.
39. For the condition precedent concept see [741].
40. *Air Great Lakes Pty Ltd v K S Easter (Holdings) Pty Ltd* (1985) 2 NSWLR 309 at 331, 333, 337.
41. *Harnor v Groves* (1855) 15 CB 667 at 674; 139 ER 587 at 590 (adopted *Gordon v Macgregor* (1909) 8 CLR 316 at 319–20, 322–3).
42. *Air Great Lakes Pty Ltd v K S Easter (Holdings) Pty Ltd* (1985) 2 NSWLR 309 at 336; *Nemeth v Bayswater Road Pty Ltd* [1988] 2 Qd R 406 at 413. Cf *Restatement (2d) Contracts* (1979), §213.
43. *Bank of Australasia v Palmer* [1897] AC 540 at 545; *Hoyt's Pty Ltd v Spencer* (1919) 27 CLR 133 at 144. Cf *Restatement (2d) Contracts* (1979), §209(1) ('a writing or writings constituting a final expression of one or more terms of an agreement').
44. Cf *Parker v South Eastern Railway Co* (1877) 2 CPD 416 at 421.

Second, assume that B and C have dealt with each other for many years in transactions for the sale of fish food. Always, when the goods are delivered, B receives C's invoice which has a number of terms. If B orders goods from C over the telephone, and these are subsequently delivered, the fact that the terms of the contract are embodied in the invoice does not imply that the contract is in writing. Rather, the contract is oral, but B is bound by the terms of the invoice by reason of the course of dealing.[45]

Confusion arises in the application of the parol evidence rule because of statements that where there is a document that looks to be contractual it should be presumed to be the contract. The parol evidence rule is then applied to exclude evidence to the contrary. Even if this approach is accepted, the presumption is variable in force and may be rebutted.[46] In *Gillespie Bros & Co v Cheney Eggar & Co*[47] Lord Russell CJ said that

> ... although when the parties arrive at a definite written contract the implication or presumption is very strong that such contract is intended to contain all the terms of their bargain, it is a presumption only, and it is open to either of the parties to allege that there was, in addition to what appears in the written agreement, an antecedent express stipulation not intended by the parties to be excluded, but intended to continue in force with the express written agreement.

The parol evidence rule will not apply where the document in question is clearly not the memorandum of the agreement between the parties,[48] and the rule should not be used to exclude evidence that the document is not intended to integrate the contract.

A contract may contain an express integration clause. These take various forms, including the 'entire agreement' provision commonly found in commercial contracts.[49] For example, in *Hope v RCA Photophone of Australia Pty Ltd*,[50] the document said that it was the 'entire understanding' of the parties with reference to the subject matter of the contract, and that the contract contained no terms other than those expressed. The High Court held that the clause was conclusive that the terms of the contract were as stated in the document.[51]

The Evidence Excluded

[709] Extrinsic evidence need not be oral. Where the parol evidence rule applies it excludes three types of extrinsic evidence:

---

45. See *Hardwick Game Farm v Suffolk Agricultural Poultry Producers Association* [1966] 1 WLR 287 at 340 (affirmed sub nom *Henry Kendall & Sons v William Lillico & Sons Ltd* [1969] 2 AC 31). Cf [618].
46. *Gordon v Macgregor* (1909) 8 CLR 316 at 320, 323–4; *Major v Bretherton* (1928) 41 CLR 62 at 67–8.
47. [1896] 2 QB 59 at 62. See also *Life Insurance Co of Australia Ltd v Phillips* (1925) 36 CLR 60 at 71, 76. Cf *Nemeth v Bayswater Road Pty Ltd* [1988] 2 Qd R 406 at 414.
48. *Bank of Australasia v Palmer* [1897] AC 540.
49. See *Inntrepeneur Pub Co (GL) v East Crown Ltd* [2000] 2 Lloyd's Rep 611.
50. (1937) 59 CLR 348 (see [718]). See also *L'Estrange v F Graucob Ltd* [1934] 2 KB 394 (see [615]).
51. However, an integration clause may be ineffective, as a prohibited exclusion clause or unjust term. See generally [769]–[772], [1118], [1124], [1515]–[1530].

(1) evidence of the actual (subjective) intentions of the parties;
(2) evidence of the parties' prior negotiations; and
(3) evidence of the parties' subsequent conduct.

The rule is not limited to oral extrinsic evidence, it applies also to documentary evidence. For example, evidence of the parties' negotiations is considered to be extrinsic if contained in a letter, facsimile, or electronic mail.

[710] **Intention.** Where a written document is put forward as the contract, or a part of the contract integrated by the document, direct evidence of the intention of the parties is not admissible (it is also not relevant), and the expression of intention in the document must govern.[52]

[711] **Prior negotiations.** The negotiations of the parties prior to entry into the contract are excluded by the parol evidence rule and cannot be called in aid when interpreting the document.[53] In *Prenn v Simmonds*[54] Lord Wilberforce explained that the reason for excluding prior negotiations is 'not a technical one or even mainly one of convenience ... it is simply that such evidence is unhelpful'.

Prior negotiations might be thought by lay people to provide evidence of what the parties intended, but to the lawyer they are unhelpful because of the difficulty of extracting a clear meaning from the divergent views expressed, and which are presumed to have been superseded by the execution of a final memorandum. It is also true that consideration of prior negotiations would prolong litigation and add to its expense.

[712] **Subsequent conduct.**[55] There is considerable authority for the proposition that, as a general rule, the subsequent conduct of the parties cannot be used for the purpose of construing the terms of a written contract ex post facto.[56]

Against this line of authority there is *Watcham v Attorney-General of the East Africa Protectorate*,[57] where subsequent conduct was used to decide the scope of an ambiguous title to land. The decision has been relied on in Australia on a number of occasions. For example, in *Farmer v Honan*[58] Isaacs and Rich JJ cited the case as authority for the proposition that the conduct of the parties may be used to 'elucidate the contract, where its terms are doubtful'. In *Howard Smith & Co Ltd v Varawa*[59] Griffith CJ said that on the question whether the parties had in fact concluded an

---

52. *Farmer v Honan* (1919) 26 CLR 183 at 195; *Life Insurance Co of Australia Ltd v Phillips* (1925) 36 CLR 60 at 71; *Bahr v Nicolay (No 2)* (1988) 164 CLR 604 at 616–17, 651; 78 ALR 1.
53. See, eg *Inglis v John Buttery & Co* (1878) 3 App Cas 552 at 577; *Secured Income Real Estate (Australia) Ltd v St Martin's Investments Pty Ltd* (1979) 144 CLR 596 at 606; 26 ALR 567; *Bahr v Nicolay (No 2)* (1988) 164 CLR 604 at 617.
54. [1971] 1 WLR 1381 at 1384.
55. See Stephen Charles, 'Interpretation of Ambiguous Contracts by Reference to Subsequent Conduct' (1991) 4 *JCL* 16.
56. See, eg *Inglis v John Buttery & Co* (1878) 3 App Cas 552 at 572; *Maynard v Goode* (1926) 37 CLR 529 at 538.
57. [1919] AC 533. See further [718].
58. (1919) 26 CLR 183 at 197. Cf *Thornley v Tilley* (1925) 36 CLR 1 at 11.

agreement evidenced by written documents, 'any statements or conduct' on their part, after the date of alleged formation 'inconsistent with the existence of a concluded contract' were relevant.

However, in England the law is clear that subsequent conduct cannot be used to interpret a contract. Thus, in *L Schuler AG v Wickman Machine Tool Sales Ltd*[60] Lord Wilberforce described *Watcham* as a 'precedent which ... had long been recognised to be nothing but the refuge of the desperate', and *Watcham* was confined to its own special facts. In so deciding the House of Lords confirmed the general proposition, expressed in *James Miller & Partners Ltd v Whitworth Street Estates (Manchester) Ltd*,[61] that evidence of subsequent conduct is excluded. The exclusion was there based on the view that the contract might be given one meaning on the day when the document comes into existence but another, and different, meaning during the course of performance because of what the parties have done. Indeed, its meaning might change more than once. From this perspective, the exclusion of subsequent conduct is simply an affirmation that the meaning and effect of a contract must (in the absence of an agreed variation)[62] be determined once and for all at the time of agreement.

These English decisions were treated by the Privy Council as expressing Australian law in *Australian Mutual Provident Society v Chaplin*,[63] and were subsequently referred to without disapproval by the High Court in *Codelfa Construction Pty Ltd v State Rail Authority of New South Wales*.[64] How then do we reconcile the fact that Australian courts have sometimes allowed evidence of subsequent conduct to be used as an aid to interpretation? In *Port Sudan Cotton Co v Govindaswamy Chettiar & Sons*,[65] Lord Denning MR said that subsequent conduct may be used to establish the existence of a concluded contract. The justification which he gave was that the subsequent conduct is admissible if it amounts to an admission that there is a contract. This may suggest a general rationale of estoppel, and explain the statement by Griffith CJ in *Howard Smith & Co Ltd v Varawa*. However, we would not describe estoppel as an exception to the parol evidence rule,[66] because the evidence is not directed to the construction of the document.[67]

In *FAI Traders Insurance Co Ltd v Savoy Plaza Pty Ltd*[68] the Appeal Division of the Supreme Court of Victoria had no doubt that, at present,

59. (1907) 5 CLR 68 at 78. See also *Barrier Wharfs Ltd v W Scott Fell & Co Ltd* (1908) 5 CLR 647; *Lennon v Scarlett & Co* (1921) 29 CLR 499; *Terrex Resources NL v Magnet Petroleum Pty Ltd* [1988] 1 WAR 144 at 160; *Darter Pty Ltd v Malloy* [1993] 2 Qd R 615 at 619 and [273].
60. [1974] AC 235 at 261. See also [718].
61. [1970] AC 583.
62. See further [718], [719].
63. (1978) 18 ALR 385 at 392. See also *Narich Pty Ltd v Commissioner of Pay-Roll Tax* (1983) 50 ALR 417 at 420–1.
64. (1982) 149 CLR 337.
65. [1977] 2 Lloyd's Rep 5 at 11. See also *Winks v W H Heck & Sons Pty Ltd* [1986] 1 Qd R 226 at 233; *Australian Energy Ltd v Lennard Oil NL* [1986] 2 Qd R 216 at 237. Cf *Estee Lauder Pty Ltd v Federal Commissioner of Taxation* (1989) 86 ALR 415 at 419–20.
66. Cf *James Miller & Partners Ltd v Whitworth Street Estates (Manchester) Ltd* [1970] AC 583 at 611, 615; and see generally [365]–[387], [1974]–[1976].
67. See also [716].

Australian law does not permit reliance on subsequent conduct as either a general aid to construction or under an exception to the parol evidence rule applicable in cases of ambiguity.[69] However, in *Spunwill Pty Ltd v BAB Pty Ltd*[70] Santow J expressed a contrary view, and it must be conceded that the extent to which subsequent conduct may be relied upon in construing a contract remains uncertain.[71]

Evidence of Factual Matrix

[713] Factual matrix concept. In *Reardon Smith Line Ltd v Yngvar Hansen-Tangen*[72] Lord Wilberforce explained that, when construing a contract, the court must 'place itself in thought in the same factual matrix as that in which the parties were' when the contract was made. Therefore, notwithstanding the parol evidence rule, the court is able to receive evidence of the circumstances surrounding the contract, and the aim, object or commercial purpose of the contract on the basis that it forms part of the factual matrix against which the parties contracted.

The High Court adopted Lord Wilberforce's approach in *Codelfa Construction Pty Ltd v State Rail Authority of New South Wales*.[73] Mason J said[74] that the word or expression at issue must be 'susceptible of more than one meaning' in order to justify the use of surrounding circumstances. Isaacs J had expressed the same view in *Bacchus Marsh Concentrated Milk Co Ltd v Joseph Nathan & Co Ltd*[75] when he said that it is legitimate to adduce evidence of surrounding circumstances in order to prove that 'words susceptible of more than one meaning are applicable to one only of those meanings'. However, the practice of courts in constantly taking the factual matrix into account without first establishing that words in issue are 'susceptible of more than one meaning' suggests that these statements cannot be taken at face value. Alternatively, we could say that since virtually every English word or expression is capable of more than one meaning, evidence of context must always be admitted when determining the meaning or legal effect of the word or expression.[76]

---

68. [1993] 2 VR 343. See also *Ryan v Textile Clothing & Footwear Union of Australia* [1996] 2 VR 235 at 238.
69. See further [718].
70. (1994) 36 NSWLR 290. Contrast *Sportsvision Australia Pty Ltd v Tallglen Pty Ltd* (1998) 44 NSWLR 103 at 116.
71. See *Hide & Skin Trading Pty Ltd v Oceanic Meat Traders Ltd* (1990) 20 NSWLR 310 at 327–8 where Priestley JA suggested that a broad interpretation of *White v Australian and New Zealand Theatres Ltd* (1943) 67 CLR 266 (see [717]) might legitimise the reception of such evidence; but cf the view of Kirby P (at 315–16).
72. [1976] 1 WLR 989 at 997.
73. (1982) 149 CLR 337. See further [719]. See also *DTR Nominees Pty Ltd v Mona Homes Pty Ltd* (1978) 138 CLR 423 at 429; 19 ALR 223; *Bahr v Nicolay (No 2)* (1988) 164 CLR 604 at 616, 651; *Forsikringsaktieselskapet Vesta v Butcher* [1989] AC 852 at 909.
74. (1982) 149 CLR 337 at 350. Stephen and Wilson JJ agreed.
75. (1919) 26 CLR 410 at 427.
76. See *Trawl Industries of Australia Pty Ltd v Effem Foods Pty Ltd Trading as 'Uncle Bens of Australia'* (1992) 27 NSWLR 326 at 358–9. Cf *B & B Constructions (Aust) Pty Ltd v Brian A Cheeseman & Associates Pty Ltd* (1994) 35 NSWLR 227.

[714] **Surrounding circumstances.** The factual matrix is established by a consideration of the setting of the contract. Thus, in *Reardon Smith Line Ltd v Yngvar Hansen-Tangen*[77] Lord Wilberforce said that no contracts are 'made in a vacuum: there is always a setting in which they have to be placed'. The 'surrounding circumstances' represent this setting.[78] However, the phrase is an 'imprecise' one, which Lord Wilberforce said can be 'illustrated but hardly defined'.

For example, in *Bacon v Purcell*[79] a contract for the sale of cattle provided for delivery on or before 26 April. The Privy Council held, in the light of the circumstances surrounding the contract, that this meant that the seller had to be ready to begin delivery on 26 April and to complete it with all reasonable dispatch. Having regard to the quantity of cattle involved, and the place and conditions under which delivery was to take place, the parties could not have intended that all the cattle would be handed over on one day.

More recently, and somewhat controversially, in *Codelfa Construction Pty Ltd v State Rail Authority of New South Wales*[80] the High Court held that evidence of discussions between the parties to a construction contract, prior to the contract being executed, was admissible for the purpose of establishing the common understanding of the parties in relation to a matter of fact, namely, that work would be carried out on the basis of three eight-hour shifts per day.

[715] **Aim or object of contract.** All contracting parties have some aim or object in mind when agreeing to contract, and entry into the contract is no doubt motivated by the view that their particular aim will be attained. Although direct evidence of aim or object cannot be received by the court, the circumstances surrounding the contract will frequently provide evidence, which is admissible, of what reasonable persons would have had in mind.

For example, in *Reardon Smith Line Ltd v Yngvar Hansen-Tangen*[81] a series of charterparties were entered into so as to make available to the charterers a medium sized tanker suitable for use as such. The terms of the charterparties to some extent confirmed this. It was contended that phrases which had been inserted in the charterparties, for example 'to be built by Osaka Shipbuilding Co Ltd', took effect as contractual terms of description. However, when regard was had to the object and purpose of the charterparties it was clear that no particular significance was to be attached to the insertions, which were made for the purpose of identification: to enable the charterers of the vessel to locate it and, if they

77. [1976] 1 WLR 989 at 995.
78. Query whether it includes all material (reasonably available to the parties) which would have 'affected the way in which the language of the document would have been understood by a reasonable' person as suggested by Lord Hoffmann in *Investors Compensation Scheme Ltd v West Bromwich Building Society* [1998] 1 WLR 896 at 912–13. See Sir Christopher Staughton, 'How Do Courts Interpret Commercial Contracts?' [1999] *CLJ* 303 at 307.
79. (1916) 22 CLR 307.
80. (1982) 149 CLR 337. See further [719].
81. [1976] 1 WLR 989.

wished, to sub-dispose of it. The factual matrix included the fact that the vessel had not been constructed when the charterparties were entered into, and that the vessel could only be described by reference to such matters as its builder and place of construction. Accordingly, the insertions were not a necessary part of the contractual descriptions of the vessels. In any event, although it could also be said that it was built by another company, the vessel was built by Osaka since it planned, organised and directed the building of the vessel.

Exceptions to the Parol Evidence Rule

[716] **Introduction.** Traditionally, expositions of the parol evidence rule have focused on a large number of exceptions to the rule. However, if the views expressed above are correct, the list of exceptions is in truth a small one.

Thus, if we put to one side the cases[82] which have treated the parol evidence rule as relevant to the determination of the terms of the bargain, on the basis that the rule is only concerned with the interpretation of the concluded bargain, exceptions must relate to evidence directed to the meaning or legal effect of words. Therefore, evidence of a collateral contract is not received under an exception to the rule. More generally, evidence relating to the validity or enforceability of the contract is unaffected by the parol evidence rule: since the evidence does not relate to the meaning or legal effect of the words used, the parol evidence rule has no operation. Accordingly, evidence of matters such as incapacity, misrepresentation, mistake and illegality,[83] or evidence as to the availability of remedies such as specific performance and injunction is not directed to construction, even if there is a document expressing the terms of the contract. Such evidence is outside the scope of the parol evidence rule, because the evidence is concerned with the ability of a party to enforce the document, or rights arising from the document. Similarly, evidence of matters subsequent to contract is also unaffected, unless it relates to the interpretation of the contract. Accordingly, evidence of breach of contract, a variation of the terms, or of conduct on the basis of which an estoppel is raised, all fall outside the rule.[84]

This suggests, as a basic criterion for concluding that an exception to the rule operates, a case in which a party is entitled to adduce extrinsic evidence of the meaning or scope of words or their legal effect. The chief examples of exceptions are therefore situations in which one party is permitted to give evidence of actual intention, prior negotiations or

---

82. See [707].
83. Cf *Pao On v Lau Yiu Long* [1980] AC 614 at 631.
84. Although in *Johnson Matthey Ltd v A C Rochester Overseas Corp* (1990) 23 NSWLR 190 at 195–6 McLelland J held that evidence of an estoppel by convention is not admissible, at least where there is an entire agreement clause, the decision was not followed by Rolfe J in *Whittet v State Bank of New South Wales* (1991) 24 NSWLR 146 at 153. For discussion see Rory Derham, 'Estoppel by Convention — Part I' (1997) 71 *ALJ* 860 at 868–9.

subsequent conduct for the purpose of construing the words in the document.

[717] **Identification of the subject matter of the contract.** Where the description of the subject matter of a contract is uncertain or ambiguous, the subject matter may be identified by extrinsic evidence.[85] For example, in *White v Australian and New Zealand Theatres Ltd*[86] a written contract between two theatrical artists and a theatre company stated that the 'sole professional services' of the artists had been engaged on certain terms. But the contract did not define what 'sole professional services' meant, and the High Court held that extrinsic evidence was properly admitted to establish that it included work in producing a revue to be staged by the theatre company.

[718] **Ambiguity in contract.** Ambiguity may be 'patent', that is, apparent on the face of the document. Alternatively, it may be 'latent' because a word or description, superficially referring to one person or thing, is found to be equally applicable to more than one person or thing. In either case extrinsic evidence can be used to resolve the ambiguity. The rationale is that if the evidence were not admitted the contract (or at least the ambiguous part) would be void for uncertainty.

Matthews v Smallwood[87] illustrates patent ambiguity. A lease conferred a right of re-entry on the lessor in the event of any breach by the lessee 'of the covenant hereinbefore contained and on his part to be performed'. Since there were numerous covenants contained in the prior part of the deed, Parker J found a case of patent ambiguity. In order to resolve the ambiguity regard was had to the counterpart of the lease, which employed the plural 'covenants' and justified the conclusion that there was a clerical error in the lease. Accordingly, the right of re-entry came into operation on the breach by the lessee of any of the prior covenants.

Latent ambiguity was alleged in *Hope v RCA Photophone of Australia Pty Ltd*,[88] where a lease of 'electrical-sound reproduction equipment' described in the schedule to the contract made no mention of whether the equipment was to be new or used. The contention of the defendant was that the plaintiffs were in breach by supplying equipment which was not new. Since the agreement did not describe the equipment as 'new' the defendant had to establish, by extrinsic evidence, that the plaintiffs had promised to supply new equipment. But the court held that the general description of the subject matter did not create any ambiguity, and the extrinsic evidence could not be received.

If a case of ambiguity is established, is the court entitled to receive evidence of the subsequent conduct of the parties in order to resolve the ambiguity? In *Sinclair Scott & Co Ltd v Naughton*,[89] Isaacs J said that if there is any ambiguity in the document which lets in extrinsic evidence, conduct by which both parties concur in placing the same construction on

---

85. *Bank of New Zealand v Simpson* [1900] AC 182; *R W Cameron & Co v L Slutzkin Pty Ltd* (1923) 32 CLR 81.
86. (1943) 67 CLR 266.
87. [1910] 1 Ch 777.
88. (1937) 59 CLR 348.

words that 'are in themselves of doubtful construction, sometimes, but very rarely, may be accepted'. In *Watcham v Attorney-General of the East Africa Protectorate*[90] the Privy Council went even further, saying that in the interpretation of a modern instrument in which there is ambiguity, either latent or patent, 'evidence may be given of user under it to show the sense in which the parties to it used the language they have employed, and their intention in executing the instrument as revealed by their language interpreted in this sense'.

The matter was considered in *L Schuler AG v Wickman Machine Tool Sales Ltd*.[91] In that case a distributorship agreement made visits by Wickman to Schuler's clients a 'condition' of the contract. Schuler contended that this meant that any failure by Wickman to visit Schuler's clients would constitute a breach of an essential term of the contract. Wickman contended that the word 'condition' was ambiguous, and that the subsequent conduct of the parties could be used to interpret it. The choice of the word certainly gave rise to a difficulty of construction, because the word is used in so many senses.[92] But it was unanimously held that subsequent conduct could not be used as an aid to interpretation. Even on the assumption that there was ambiguity, Lord Simon said[93] that there were sound reasons for rejecting such evidence. First, it might be 'misleading' to allow evidence of subsequent conduct without also considering direct evidence of the parties' intentions, and the exclusion of prior negotiations implied that subsequent conduct had also to be excluded. Second, it could only be relevant to consider evidence of what the words in the document actually meant by what they said, but subsequent conduct might merely be referable to what the parties meant to say. Third, the 'practical difficulties involved in admitting subsequent conduct as an aid to interpretation' were said to be only 'marginally, if at all, less than are involved in admitting evidence of prior negotiations' which are excluded from consideration.

It is not easy to reconcile these two lines of approach,[94] but the answer may lie either in differing conceptions of what constitutes ambiguity or in the difference between construction to determine meaning and construction to determine legal effect. In *Schuler* the ambiguity was not such as to prevent a meaning being given to the word; rather it was in the nature of uncertainty as to the *legal effect* of the word used. There is in such a context no scope for an exception to the parol evidence rule since legal effect must be attributed on the basis of the words used unless the subsequent conduct of the parties creates an estoppel (precluding a party from relying on a particular legal effect),[95] or a variation of the contract. On the other hand, where there is a genuine case of ambiguity as to *meaning*, the court must resolve the matter in some way, and it cannot as in *Schuler*,

---

89. (1929) 43 CLR 310 at 327. See also *Campbell v Kitchen & Sons Ltd* (1910) 12 CLR 515 at 527. Cf *Horton v Jones* (1934) 34 SR (NSW) 359 at 364 (affirmed (1935) 53 CLR 475).
90. [1919] AC 533 at 540.
91. [1974] AC 235 (see J H Baker, [1973] *CLJ* 196).
92. See [726], [730].
93. See [1974] AC 235 at 268–9.
94. The need for reconciliation arises from the approval of *Schuler* in *Codelfa Construction Pty Ltd v State Rail Authority of New South Wales* (1982) 149 CLR 337.
95. *Australian Energy Ltd v Lennard Oil NL* [1986] 2 Qd R 216 at 237.

rely on prior decisions as to the effect of the words used in order to impute an intention. Unless the ambiguity is resolved the clause in question will be void for uncertainty. Since it is therefore necessary to give some meaning to the words, there seems no objection to the use of subsequent conduct, provided the conduct is mutual rather than unilateral.[96]

[719] **Implied terms.** Evidence of the factual matrix[97] may be used in determining whether a term should be implied. However, it is not entirely clear how far extrinsic evidence may be received under an exception to the parol evidence rule.

In considering whether a term should be implied in law[98] the court may have regard to extrinsic evidence for the purpose of supporting or rebutting a presumption that the term should be implied. For example, in *Gillespie Bros & Co v Cheney Eggar & Co*[99] evidence of a pre-contractual conversation between the parties was admitted for the purpose of showing that buyers of goods had expressly made known to the sellers the purpose for which the goods were required in such a way as to indicate reliance on the sellers' skill or judgment. This was because the buyers alleged the breach of a term requiring the goods to be fit for the buyers' purpose which would only be implied if the buyers had made their purpose known in such a way as to indicate reliance on the sellers' skill or judgment.[100] Conversely, in *Mears v Safecar Security Ltd*,[101] subsequent conduct was used to rebut the implication of a term providing for payment of wages to an employee during a period when he was absent from work through illness. It was not the policy of his employers to pay sick pay and the employee did not request payment during his illness.

The position with regard to terms implied in fact was discussed by the High Court in *Codelfa Construction Pty Ltd v State Rail Authority of New South Wales*.[102] It was held that evidence of discussions between the parties prior to entry into the contract had been properly admitted for the purpose of deciding whether a term was to be implied into the contract. Having regard to the existence of a formal document in that case it might be argued that the court applied an exception to the parol evidence rule. Moreover, Mason J said[103] that prior negotiations of the parties were not admissible evidence. On the other hand, he was concerned to emphasise[104] three points: first, that the implication of a term is, in essence, a process of construction; second, that the prior discussions were not negotiations about the terms of the contract; and, third, that the common understanding between the parties on the way in which performance would take place, evidenced by the prior discussions, was part of the factual

---

96. If the conduct is by one party only, the evidence cannot be regarded as admissible except as evidence of an estoppel. Cf *Burns Philp Hardware Ltd v Howard Chia Pty Ltd* (1987) 8 NSWLR 642 at 645–6, 657.
97. See [713].
98. See [631]–[635].
99. [1896] 2 QB 59. See also *Criss v Alexander* (1928) 28 SR (NSW) 297.
100. See [639].
101. [1983] QB 54.
102. (1982) 149 CLR 337 (see [629], [713]).
103. (1982) 149 CLR 337 at 354.
104. (1982) 149 CLR 337 at 353–4. See also [629].

background to the contract. Stephen J and Wilson J agreed with the analysis by Mason J and the other members of the court certainly did not take a wider view. This suggests that the court was restricting the admissible evidence to that justified by the factual matrix concept.

It is not easy to see how regard can be had, in cases like *Codelfa*, to the prior discussions of the parties while at the same time saying that implication is essentially a matter of construction. No doubt construction plays a part in implication, particularly with respect to the requirement of consistency with express terms, but consideration of the requirement of obviousness may require the court to have regard to the negotiations of the parties, because the officious bystander is deemed to be present during negotiations. This is, it is suggested, better explained by saying that the parol evidence rule does not apply: the issue can be treated as part of the process of term identification, not within the parol evidence rule.[105]

Even if the parol evidence rule otherwise applies, there is no objection to the use of extrinsic evidence for the purpose of implying a term where the evidence is necessary to identify or explain the subject matter of the contract. Thus, in *Shepperd v Ryde Corp*[106] a contract for the sale of land described it as being 'part of the vendor's Housing Project No 4'. The High Court held that reference to the project let in extrinsic evidence in order to ascertain the project and its features. When this evidence was considered it led to the implication of a term which operated in favour of the purchaser. The plan comprising the Housing Project referred to parkland (including that adjacent to the land purchased) reserved as an amenity for the common advantage of purchasers and justified the implication of a term obliging the Corporation to maintain the areas referred to as parkland.

[720] **Custom, usage and course of dealing.** The requirements for implication of a term on the basis of custom or usage were explained earlier.[107] The custom must be notorious, certain, legal and reasonable. If there is a document which does not express the custom or usage, and if the ordinary meaning of the words stated is relied on, no evidence of custom or usage may be adduced.[108] The fact that evidence of the custom or usage is admissible in situations where some other meaning is relied on indicates that it does form an exception to the parol evidence rule. And if the document refers to a custom, but does not explain it, extrinsic evidence may be received to explain the custom. However, the custom must be consistent with the express terms of the contract.[109]

Where parties have previously dealt with each other on a regular basis, so that there is a course of dealing, evidence of this may be used to incorporate terms into the contract,[110] or to negative the implication of a term which

---

105. See [707]. For English decisions which may support the reception of evidence of the subsequent conduct for the purpose of implication on this basis see *Ferguson v John Dawson & Partners (Contractors) Ltd* [1976] 3 All ER 817; *Wilson v Maynard Shipbuilding Consultants AB* [1978] QB 665. Cf *Mears v Safecar Security Ltd* [1983] QB 54.
106. (1952) 85 CLR 1 (see also [612]).
107. See [644].
108. *Thornley v Tilley* (1925) 36 CLR 1; *Royal Insurance Australia Ltd v Government Insurance Office of NSW* [1994] 1 VR 123 at 133.
109. See, eg *Palgrave Brown & Son Ltd v Owners of SS Turid* [1922] 1 AC 397.

would otherwise be implied.[111] In addition, if the course of dealing has the effect of placing a particular meaning on the terms of a document, the parties may be bound by that course of dealing, even if it involves the admission of subsequent conduct as evidence. The basis may be a variation of the contract — if the contract would not otherwise possess the meaning attributed to it — or the existence of estoppel precluding the parties from denying that the contract is to be interpreted in accordance with their course of dealing.[112]

[721] **Consideration.** In *Pao On v Lau Yiu Long*,[113] Lord Scarman, when delivering the advice of the Privy Council, expressed the law as follows:[114]

> There is no doubt ... that extrinsic evidence is admissible to prove the real consideration where (a) no consideration, or a nominal consideration, is expressed in the instrument, or (b) the expressed consideration is in general terms or ambiguously stated, or (c) a substantial consideration is stated, but an additional consideration exists. The additional consideration must not, however, be inconsistent with the terms of the written instrument. Extrinsic evidence is also admissible to prove the illegality of the consideration.

[722] **Identity of parties or their relationship.** Extrinsic evidence may be admissible to prove the parties to a contract where the document does not make this matter clear. Frequently, the circumstances surrounding the contract will identify the parties with sufficient precision. But extrinsic evidence may also be admitted if there is ambiguity. For example, in *Giliberto v Kenny*[115] an action for specific performance was brought on an alleged contract for the sale of land evidenced by a document which in one part described the purchaser as 'Mrs Kenny' and in another as 'Mr Kenny'. The document was signed by Mrs Kenny and the High Court held that extrinsic evidence was admissible for the purpose of showing that Mrs Kenny was acting as agent for her husband and herself. There was clearly a case of patent ambiguity and the trial judge was justified in relying on facts known to the parties to the contract.

Extrinsic evidence may also be used to identify the relationship of a party or the capacity in which he or she contracted.[116] For example, extrinsic evidence might be used to explain that a person who appears to be a party to the contract is in fact the agent of a principal on whose behalf the contract was made.

[723] **Rectification.** A well-established exception to the parol evidence rule arises where rectification of a written document is sought. Extrinsic evidence of the parties' intention is admissible to rectify the document so

---

110. See [618].
111. See *Gemmell Power Farming Co Ltd v Nies* (1935) 35 SR (NSW) 469 at 476.
112. *Amalgamated Investment & Property Co Ltd v Texas Commerce International Bank Ltd* [1982] QB 84 at 121. Cf *Grundt v Great Boulder Pty Gold Mines Ltd* (1937) 59 CLR 641 at 657, 674.
113. [1980] AC 614.
114. [1980] AC 614 at 631. See also *Barba v Gas & Fuel Corp of Victoria* (1976) 136 CLR 120 at 131–2; 12 ALR 649; *Yarooma Beach Development Co Pty Ltd v Coeur de Lion Investments Pty Ltd* (1989) 18 NSWLR 398 at 407.
115. (1983) 48 ALR 620.
116. See *Mallinson v Scottish Australian Investment Co Ltd* (1920) 28 CLR 66 at 75.

that it expresses that intention.[117] The purpose of rectification is, as Isaacs J explained in *Bacchus Marsh Concentrated Milk Co Ltd v Joseph Nathan & Co Ltd*,[118] not to import additional or different terms into contracts, but, instead, 're-form instruments so as to make them accord with what the parties actually agreed to, or with what one party intended and the other party knew the first intended'.

One feature of this exception is unsatisfactory. If a party claims that the document should be rectified the result may be to let in evidence which turns out to be irrelevant because the claim is rejected by the court.[119] There is obviously a prolongation of proceedings and an increase in the cost of the litigation. As a practical matter, it may be difficult for the court to disregard the evidence entirely when construing the contract.[120]

Classification of Terms[121]

General

[724] Purpose of classification. One purpose of classifying contractual terms, which has already been referred to, is to distinguish express terms from implied terms.[122] Terms may also be classified from the point of view of whether they survive termination, and a distinction drawn between substantive terms and procedural terms.

Another purpose of classification is to see whether the term is capable of being breached, and a distinction then drawn between promises and contractual undertakings on the one hand, and non-promissory terms, such as definitional terms, factual statements and terms providing for contingencies, on the other.[123] For example, in *Kleinwort Benson Ltd v Malaysia Mining Corp Berhad*[124] a 'comfort letter' stated that it was the 'policy' of Malaysia Mining to ensure that its subsidiary, to whom money had been lent by Kleinwort, 'is at all times in a position to meet its liabilities' to Kleinwort. When the subsidiary defaulted Kleinwort sought payment from Malaysia Mining. Kleinwort relied on the comfort letter, contending that the statement of policy was a promissory obligation to ensure that the subsidiary would repay its loan. The English Court of Appeal held that the statement was not promissory in character. Accordingly, Malaysia Mining was not liable when it changed its policy and refused to meet the subsidiary's liabilities.

---

117. See, eg *NSW Medical Defence Union Ltd v Transport Industries Insurance Co Ltd* (1986) 6 NSWLR 740.
118. (1919) 26 CLR 410 at 427. See generally on rectification [1256]–[1266].
119. See *Prenn v Simmonds* [1971] 1 WLR 1381 at 1383; *B & B Constructions (Aust) Pty Ltd v Brian A Cheeseman & Associates Pty Ltd* (1994) 35 NSWLR 227 at 232–3.
120. But see *Watson v Phipps* (1985) 63 ALR 321 at 323.
121. See Carter, *Breach of Contract*, 2nd ed, 1991, Chapter 4.
122. See [601].
123. See, eg *McTier v Haupt* [1992] 1 VR 653.
124. [1989] 1 WLR 379. See also *Commonwealth Bank of Australia v TLI Management Pty Ltd* [1990] VR 510. Contrast *Banque Brussels Lambert SA v Australian National Industries Ltd* (1989) 21 NSWLR 502 (see Alan Tyree, (1990) 2 JCL 279).

In deciding whether the promisee is entitled to terminate the performance of the contract,[125] or can merely claim damages, a 'tripartite classification' of terms has been adopted.[126]

The Tripartite Classification

[725] Basis of classification. Under the tripartite classification the issue is whether a term is a condition, a warranty or an intermediate term. In theory this classification is always based on the intention of the parties, as expressed in the contract. It is therefore an issue of construction.[127] However, sometimes the construction issue is predetermined by statute.[128]

Conditions and warranties

[726] Conditions as important terms. A promisee who establishes that the promisor has breached a condition is both entitled to terminate the performance of the contract and to claim damages for its breach.[129] Because a breach of a condition gives rise to a right to terminate the performance of the contract, a condition is a particularly important contractual term.[130]

[727] Definition of condition in sale of goods. Although the distinction between conditions and warranties figures prominently in the sale of goods legislation, there is no express definition of the word 'condition'. Nevertheless, the term is inferentially defined by s 16(2) of the *Sale of Goods Act* 1923 (NSW)[131] as a term *any* breach of which[132] 'may give rise to a claim for damages' and to a 'right to reject the goods and treat the contract as repudiated'. This reference to treating the contract as repudiated is a reference to termination by the buyer for the seller's breach of condition. By the same reasoning, a seller may terminate for breach of condition by the buyer.

The definition of condition stated in the sale of goods legislation is of general application.[133] However, in *Tramways Advertising Pty Ltd v Luna Park (NSW) Ltd*[134] Jordan CJ distinguished two types of conditions, namely, those requiring 'strict' compliance and those requiring 'substantial'

---

125. For the meaning of 'termination' see [1840], [1985].
126. See [725]–[748].
127. *Friedlander v Bank of Australasia* (1909) 8 CLR 85 at 99; *Bunge Corp New York v Tradax Export SA Panama* [1981] 1 WLR 711.
128. See further [737].
129. See, eg *Lombard North Central Plc v Butterworth* [1987] 1 QB 527 at 535. See further [2102].
130. *Luna Park (NSW) Ltd v Tramways Advertising Pty Ltd* (1938) 61 CLR 286; *Bunge Corp New York v Tradax Export SA Panama* [1981] 1 WLR 711.
131. See also **ACT**: *Sale of Goods Act* 1954, s 16(2); **NT**: *Sale of Goods Act* 1972, s 16(2); **Qld**: *Sale of Goods Act* 1896, s 14(2); **SA**: *Sale of Goods Act* 1895, s 11(2); **Tas**: *Sale of Goods Act* 1896, s 16(2); **Vic**: *Goods Act* 1958, s 16(2); **WA**: *Sale of Goods Act* 1895, s 11(2).
132. Subject to the de minimis rule: *Cehave NV v Bremer Handelsgesellschaft mbH (The Hansa Nord)* [1976] QB 44 at 69.
133. *L Schuler AG v Wickman Machine Tool Sales Ltd* [1974] AC 235.
134. (1938) 38 SR (NSW) 632 at 641–2 (reversed on other grounds sub nom *Luna Park (NSW) Ltd v Tramways Advertising Pty Ltd* (1938) 61 CLR 286).

compliance. The first type of condition corresponds to that defined by the sale of goods legislation. The second differs from the first because only a 'substantial' breach will give rise to a right to terminate. In view of the subsequent emergence of the intermediate term concept[135] this refinement in classification is probably now unnecessary.[136]

The fact that any breach of a term classified as a condition gives rise to a right to terminate implies that the right may accrue even though the promisor's breach does not cause any loss or damage to the promisee.[137] Although this legitimises the classification of a term which provides a contractual right to terminate for any breach as a 'condition',[138] it is misleading to treat the existence of a contractual right to terminate for breach as on a par with breach of condition for purposes other than the existence of a right to terminate.[139]

[728] Definition of warranty in sale of goods. Section 5(1) of the *Sale of Goods Act* 1923 (NSW) states:[140]

> 'Warranty' means an agreement with reference to goods which are the subject of a contract of sale, but collateral to the main purpose of such contract, the breach of which gives rise to a claim for damages, but not to a right to reject the goods and treat the contract as repudiated.

Under this definition there is no right to terminate for breach of warranty, and the contrast between condition and warranty is therefore established. Although the Act's concept of a warranty,[141] as a term the breach of which gives rise to a right to claim damages but not to a right to terminate, has been applied generally (and not restricted to sale of goods contracts),[142] in modern commercial contracts the word 'warranty' is frequently used as a general description of the parties' express undertakings.[143]

[729] Weaknesses of the distinction. The definitions stated above might give the impression that the words 'condition' and 'warranty' now have settled meanings and that the distinction between them is clear. However, this is not the case, and one weakness of the distinction is that the words are used in other senses as well.[144]

The major weakness of the distinction is its simplistic nature, that is, the idea that all terms are so straightforward that they can be classified as either

---

135. See [731]–[738].
136. See [1911]; but cf *Citicorp Australia Ltd v Hendry* (1985) 4 NSWLR 1 at 27.
137. See [1911].
138. See, eg *Afovos Shipping Co SA v Pagnan* [1983] 1 WLR 195 at 203.
139. See [1935], [2159], [2229].
140. See also **ACT**: *Sale of Goods Act* 1954, s 5(1); **NT**: *Sale of Goods Act* 1972, s 5(1); **Qld**: *Sale of Goods Act* 1896, s 3(1); **SA**: *Sale of Goods Act* 1895, s 60(1); **Tas**: *Sale of Goods Act* 1896, s 3(1); **Vic**: *Goods Act* 1958, s 3(1); **WA**: *Sale of Goods Act* 1895, s 60(1).
141. The idea that breach of warranty does not give rise to a right to terminate is historically inaccurate and based on a misinterpretation of Lord Abinger CB's famous statement in *Chanter v Hopkins* (1838) 4 M & W 399 at 404; 150 ER 1484 at 1486–7. See Carter, *Breach of Contract*, 2nd ed, 1991, paras 412–13.
142. See *Associated Newspapers Ltd v Bancks* (1951) 83 CLR 322 at 339.
143. See further [730], [734].
144. See further [730].

important (conditions) or unimportant (warranties). This neglects the obvious fact that some terms are ambivalent in that they may be important in some situations but unimportant in others.[145] The distinction is simplistic for another reason as well, namely, the conception of a contractual term as creating a single obligation. In fact, contractual terms are often composite, creating a number of obligations.[146] In practice, therefore, the distinction must be applied to each obligation contained in a contractual term rather than to the term as a whole.[147]

A final weakness of the distinction is its inflexibility. Because a term must be classified at the moment of formation, on the basis of construction, no regard can be had to any actual breach; at best the court can consider *possible* breaches.[148] The distinction therefore places a court in a rather restricted position and encourages the treatment of terms as conditions. For example, assume that a court is construing a term in a standard form contract for the sale of goods. If it can foresee that some breaches of the term might have serious consequences, the court is virtually obliged, in any choice between condition and warranty, to choose the former, irrespective of how minor the breach before the court actually is, because of the possibility of prejudice to a party to a subsequent contract on the same form. Until recently this encouraged the avoidance of contracts on the ground of a technical breach for the purpose of taking advantage of a change in market price for the subject matter of the contract.

[730] **Other meanings.** 'Condition' and 'warranty' have a number of meanings and are frequently used in senses different from those described above.[149] First, the word 'condition' is sometimes used as a synonym for 'term'.[150] It then describes any term of the contract, whatever its nature.[151] This is the case, for example, in the expression 'conditions of sale'.

Second, the word 'condition' may also describe a contingency, that is, an event which is not certain to occur but which must occur before performance under a contract becomes due. For example, if A's obligation to perform under a contract with B is dependent on the issue of a licence to export goods by a certain date, the issue of the licence is the 'condition' (contingency) which must be satisfied if A is to come under an obligation to perform.[152] Of course, the fulfilment of the contingency may also be promised.[153]

Three other meanings of the word 'warranty' may be noted:

---

145. See further [731], [732].
146. See, eg *Associated Newspapers Ltd v Bancks* (1951) 83 CLR 322.
147. Cf [1949].
148. See [1913].
149. See *Total Gas Marketing Ltd v Arco British Ltd* [1998] 2 Lloyd's Rep 209 at 218 (source of recurring confusion).
150. For a more detailed treatment see S J Stoljar, 'The Contractual Concept of Condition' (1953) 69 *LQR* 485.
151. Cf *Wickman Machine Tool Sales Ltd v L Schuler AG* [1972] 1 WLR 840 at 850 (affirmed sub nom *L Schuler AG v Wickman Machine Tool Sales Ltd* [1974] AC 235) where the usage of 'condition' adopted by the sale of goods legislation is described as the lawyer's 'term of art' and contrasted with the common meaning of the word.
152. See further [739], [1805]–[1810]; [1836]–[1838].
153. See [740].

- to describe any contractually binding promise, whatever its nature,[154] as where a contract states that each party gives certain (enumerated) 'warranties' to the other;
- to describe the executory undertaking or promise in a collateral contract;[155] or
- to describe an essential contractual promise,[156] although it is now rare for the word to be used in this sense outside the context of insurance.[157]

Intermediate terms

[731] The *Hongkong Fir* case. In *Hongkong Fir Shipping Co Ltd v Kawasaki Kisen Kaisha Ltd*[158] the English Court of Appeal interpreted a seaworthiness term in a time charterparty. This stated that the vessel was 'in every way fitted for ordinary cargo service'. Upjohn LJ said[159] that the term was not a condition and that the remedies open to the charterers, on breach by the shipowners, depended 'entirely on the nature of the breach and its foreseeable consequences'.

Diplock LJ explained the position in the following way:[160]

> No doubt there are many simple contractual undertakings, sometimes express but more often because of their very simplicity ... to be implied, of which it can be predicated that every breach of such an undertaking must give rise to an event which will deprive the party not in default of substantially the whole benefit which it was intended that he should obtain from the contract. And such a stipulation, unless the parties have agreed that breach of it shall not entitle the non-defaulting party to treat the contract as repudiated, is a 'condition'. So too there may be other simple contractual obligations of which it can be predicated that *no* breach can give rise to an event which will deprive the party not in default of substantially the whole benefit which it was intended that he should obtain from the contract; and such a stipulation, unless the parties have agreed that breach of it shall entitle the non-defaulting party to treat the contract as repudiated, is a 'warranty'.
>
> There are, however, many contractual undertakings of a more complex character which cannot be categorised as being 'conditions' or 'warranties' ... Of such undertakings all that can be predicated is that some breaches will and others will not give rise to an event which will deprive the party not in default of substantially the whole benefit which it was intended that he should obtain from the contract; *and the legal consequences of a breach of such an undertaking, unless provided for expressly in the contract, depend upon the nature of the event to which the breach gives rise and do not follow automatically from a prior classification of the undertaking as a 'condition' or a 'warranty'*.

---

154. See *Oscar Chess Ltd v Williams* [1957] 1 WLR 370 at 374.
155. See, eg *Gardiner v Grigg* (1938) 38 SR (NSW) 524 at 531.
156. *Marine Insurance Act* 1909 (Cth), s 39(1). See also *Australia and New Zealand Banking Group Ltd v Compagnie d'Assurances Maritimes Aeriennes et Terrestres* [1996] 1 VR 561 at 567–8.
157. See *Deaves v CML Fire and General Insurance Co Ltd* (1979) 143 CLR 24 at 63; 23 ALR 539; *Euro-Diam Ltd v Bathurst* [1990] 1 QB 1 at 40.
158. [1962] 2 QB 26.
159. [1962] 2 QB 26 at 64.
160. [1962] 2 QB 26 at 69–70 (italics supplied).

Thus, the seaworthiness undertaking was too complex in nature to be classified as either a condition or a warranty. All that could be said was that some breaches would be serious (for example, a breach causing the vessel to sink) and others only minor (for example, one making repair work of a single day's duration necessary).[161]

There is a difference between the approach of Upjohn LJ and that of Diplock LJ. The latter treated the case as one in which the à priori classification of condition or warranty simply failed to come up with an answer. Upjohn LJ, on the other hand, appears to have been of the view that the term was a warranty, and he implicitly rejected the proposition that there can be no termination for breach of warranty.[162]

[732] **Definition.** Although there is no express reference to a category of 'intermediate' terms in *Hongkong Fir Shipping Co Ltd v Kawasaki Kisen Kaisha Ltd*,[163] subsequent decisions have treated it as having given birth to such a category.[164] As a matter of definition, an intermediate term is one the importance of which lies somewhere between a condition and a warranty. A term can only be so classified after it has been found, on the basis of construction, to be neither a condition nor a warranty.[165] The breach of such a term gives rise to a right to claim damages, but only if the consequences are sufficiently serious does a right to terminate arise.

Intermediate terms have also been described as 'innominate' terms.[166] The rationale for this terminology is that the character of the term in question cannot be judged by construction, so that it takes on the 'character'[167] of a condition or a warranty in accordance with the seriousness of the actual breach established.

By and large the two expressions have been treated as interchangeable.[168] However, since most of the terms in this third category are so construed because they are capable of being breached in various ways[169] it seems better to acknowledge their intermediate status than to imply that they cannot be classified at all.

Scope of the classification

[733] **General application.** The tripartite classification is of general application, in the sense that it is not restricted to particular kinds of contracts or terms.[170] The classification is applicable to both express and

---

161. For the position in the *Hongkong Fir* case see [1958].
162. See further [738].
163. [1962] 2 QB 26. The catchwords to the headnote refer to 'intermediate stipulation'.
164. See, eg *The Hansa Nord* [1976] QB 44 at 60.
165. *Bunge Corp v Tradax Export SA* [1980] 1 Lloyd's Rep 294 at 309 (affirmed sub nom *Bunge Corp New York v Tradax Export SA Panama* [1981] 1 WLR 711).
166. See, eg *Antaios Compania Naviera SA v Salen Rederierna AB* [1985] AC 191 at 200.
167. *Bunge Corp New York v Tradax Export SA Panama* [1981] 1 WLR 711 at 719.
168. See *Bremer Handelsgesellschaft mbH v Vanden Avenne-Izegem PVBA* [1978] 2 Lloyd's Rep 109 at 113.
169. See [1917], [1922].
170. See *Ankar Pty Ltd v National Westminster Finance (Australia) Ltd* (1987) 162 CLR 549; 70 ALR 641 (see J W Carter and J C Phillips, 'Construction of Contracts of Guarantee and the Hongkong Fir Case' (1988) 1 *JCL* 70). But see [736].

implied terms. All that is necessary for the term to be the subject of the classification is the capability of breach.[171] Thus, it applies equally to undertakings as to the truth of a present (or past) fact and to promises that things will happen in the future.

Generally, however, the courts have not applied it to 'time stipulations', that is, terms which state the time for performance.[172] Of course, it is always open to the parties to a contract to classify a term by express provision, but this is use of the classification, not its avoidance.

[734] Conventional descriptions of terms. Primarily because of the variety of meanings attributed to the word 'warranty', the conventional description of a term as a warranty may not be an accurate expression of its place in the tripartite classification. For example, the 'warranty of seaworthiness' found, expressly or impliedly, in charterparties is not strictly a warranty, it is an intermediate term unless the parties have expressly provided to the contrary.[173] By way of contrast, one (at least) of the 'warranties' implied by the common law into contracts for work and materials[174] — that requiring the contractor to supply materials fit for the other party's purpose — must, as a matter of construction, usually be a condition.[175]

[735] Terms providing for contingencies. An important type of contractual term which does not fall within the tripartite classification is that which merely provides for a contingency.[176] For example, if A agrees to pay B $1000 if fire destroys B's motor car before 1 March, that part of the term which qualifies A's promise to pay is not governed by the tripartite classification and it is not appropriate to ask whether destruction by fire before 1 March is important to the parties. The position is simply that A cannot be called upon to perform unless a fire takes place and destroys B's motor car before 1 March.[177]

[736] Sale of goods law.[178] In *The Hansa Nord*[179] the English Court of Appeal applied the analysis made in *Hongkong Fir Shipping Co Ltd v Kawasaki Kisen Kaisha Ltd*[180] to a contract for the sale of goods. Although the judgments in the case exhibit differences of approach to the issue, the

---

171. For illustrations of non-promissory terms which are not subject to the distinction see [744], [745], [747].
172. See further [1952].
173. *Hongkong Fir Shipping Co Ltd v Kawasaki Kisen Kaisha Ltd* [1962] 2 QB 26. See also *Kodros Shipping Corp of Monrovia v Empresa Cubana de Fletes (The Evia (No 2))* [1983] 1 AC 736 at 765 ('safe port warranty').
174. See [633].
175. However, the terms implied under statute into consumer transaction are 'warranties'. See [643]. But because there is no statutory definition of the 'warranty', it is arguable that termination is available under the general law; see Taperell, Vermeesch and Harland, *Trade Practices and Consumer Protection*, 3rd ed, 1983, para 1760.
176. See further [739], [1837].
177. See, eg *Tricontinental Corp Ltd v HDFI Ltd* (1990) 21 NSWLR 689 (entitlement to make demand under underpinning agreement).
178. See J W Carter and C Hodgekiss, 'Conditions and Warranties: Forebears and Descendants' (1977) 8 *Syd LR* 31.
179. [1976] QB 44 (see F M B Reynolds, (1976) 92 *LQR* 17).
180. [1962] 2 QB 26.

[736] Contract Law in Australia

unifying feature was that s 61(2) of the *Sale of Goods Act* 1893 (UK),[181] which preserved the 'rules of the common law' permitted recourse to decisions prior to the passing of the Act. It was important for the court to find some such provision because the sale of goods legislation codified the prior law on the subject.[182]

There is no Australian case in which *The Hansa Nord* has been applied, and the application of that case in Australia is, to some extent at least, uncertain. However, the utility of the *Hongkong Fir* case must outweigh the technical arguments which can be made against its application to a sale of goods contract. Alternatively, the sale of goods legislation should be amended, as has occurred in New South Wales.[183]

[737] **Effect of statute.** We have already seen that where a term is implied by statute the legislation will generally provide a classification, in terms of either a condition or a warranty. This is the case, for example, with the sale of goods legislation.[184] In theory this is a prima facie classification only since the legislation permits the parties to reach agreement for some other classification. Thus, s 57 of the *Sale of Goods Act* 1923 (NSW)[185] provides that where 'any right, duty, or liability would arise under a contract of sale by implication of law, it may be negatived or varied by express agreement, or by the course of dealing between the parties, or by usage, if the usage be such as to bind both parties to the contract'. For example, the implied condition requiring goods the subject of the sale to be of merchantable quality may be reduced to the status of a warranty by a term which makes it clear that the buyer is to have no right to reject the goods for a breach in relation to quality.[186]

In practice, the ability to alter the nature of terms implied by statute is frequently restricted to contracts between commercial enterprises. For example, in respect of 'consumer' sales, as defined by s 62 of the *Sale of Goods Act* 1923 (NSW), a provision which purports to 'exclude or restrict the operation' of ss 18, 19 or 20 (except s 19(4)) 'or any liability of the seller for a breach of a condition or warranty implied by any provision of those sections is void'.[187]

[738] **Criticism.** Although the analysis in *Hongkong Fir Shipping Co Ltd v Kawasaki Kisen Kaisha Ltd*,[188] from which the tripartite classification is

---

181. See now *Sale of Goods Act* 1979 (UK), s 62(2). For equivalent provisions see **ACT**: *Sale of Goods Act* 1954, s 62(1); **NSW**: *Sale of Goods Act* 1923, s 4(2); **NT**: *Sale of Goods Act* 1972, s 4(2); **Qld**: *Sale of Goods Act* 1896, s 61(2); **SA**: *Sale of Goods Act* 1895, s 59(2); **Tas**: *Sale of Goods Act* 1896, s 5(2); **Vic**: *Goods Act* 1958, s 4(2); **WA**: *Sale of Goods Act* 1895, s 59(2).
182. The decision was approved by the House of Lords in *Reardon Smith Line Ltd v Yngvar Hansen-Tangen* [1976] 1 WLR 989 (see [715]). See also *Bunge Corp New York v Tradax Export SA Panama* [1981] 1 WLR 711 (see [1952]).
183. *Sale of Goods Act* 1923 (NSW), s 4(5). See further [738].
184. See, eg [637].
185. See also **NT**: *Sale of Goods Act* 1972, s 57; **Qld**: *Sale of Goods Act* 1896, s 56; **SA**: *Sale of Goods Act* 1895, s 54; **Tas**: *Sale of Goods Act* 1896, s 59; **Vic**: *Goods Act* 1958, s 61; **WA**: *Sale of Goods Act* 1895, s 54.
186. Cf *Robert A Munro & Co Ltd v Meyer* [1930] 2 KB 312 (see [1977]).
187. Section 64(1). See further [769]–[772].
188. [1962] 2 QB 26.

derived, should be accepted as an accurate analysis of the law, and a useful reminder that the existence of a right to terminate the performance of a contract does not always depend on the breach of a term classified as a condition, the preference for a tripartite, rather than bipartite, classification can be criticised.

It is doubtful whether the decision in the *Hongkong Fir* case necessitated the creation of a third category of intermediate terms. Upjohn LJ seems to have considered that a serious breach of warranty would give rise to a right to terminate.[189] Although it might be argued that the definition of 'warranty' in the sale of goods legislation[190] precludes this, Ormrod LJ in *The Hansa Nord*[191] thought that, even in the sale of goods context, termination for breach of warranty could be based on a de facto failure of consideration, rather than the existence of a third type of term. Moreover, the concept of the intermediate term has had the effect of making it virtually impossible to conclude that a term was intended by the parties to be a mere warranty and this class of express terms is, for practical purposes, virtually closed. Some, at least, of the terms which have in the past been construed as warranties[192] must be regarded as ripe for reclassification as intermediate terms.

Promises and Contingencies

[739] Distinguishing promises from contingencies. A term which expresses a promise that an event will occur (or will not occur) or an undertaking as to the truth of a present (or past) fact is treated as embodying a contractual obligation, the breach of which gives rise to a claim for damages.[193] Such a term is distinguishable from one which qualifies the obligation of a party by providing for a contingency.[194] For example, if a contract for the sale of goods provides that the obligation of the parties to perform is subject to the issue of an export licence, but neither party undertakes to obtain the licence, the issue of a licence is merely a contingency on which the obligation of the parties to perform depends.[195]

The obvious distinction between a term stating an undertaking and a term which merely provides for a contingency is that the latter does not provide a basis for a damages claim if the contingency is not fulfilled.

[740] Promises which state contingencies. A term may embody both a promise and a contingency. For example, if a sale of goods contract between A and B not only makes A's obligation to perform dependent on the issue of the licence, but also contains a promise by B to obtain the export licence by a specific date, the condition (contingency) is of a promissory kind because B has promised to see that it is fulfilled.

---

189. See [731]. See also *Universal Cargo Carriers Corp v Citati* [1957] 2 QB 401 at 431.
190. See [728].
191. [1976] QB 44 at 84.
192. See, eg *Universal Cargo Carriers Corp v Citati* [1957] 2 QB 401 (term in charterparty requiring vessel to be loaded prior to expiry of lay days).
193. For the assessment of damages see Chapter 21.
194. See also [735].
195. See also [730] and further [740], [1807].

Therefore, if B fails to obtain the licence by the specified date, not only is B unable to enforce A's obligations, but B is also liable in damages for breach of contract. The former consequence arises from the contingent nature of A's obligation, the latter consequence from the fact that B has promised to fulfil the contingency. The tripartite classification then becomes applicable and the question may arise whether the obligation to obtain the licence by the specified date is a condition in the strict sense. If it is, A is entitled to terminate the performance of the contract.[196]

[741] **Conditions precedent and subsequent.** Where the occurrence of an event is a *condition precedent*, the existence of the contract, or the obligation of one party (or both parties) to perform is subject to the prior occurrence of a specified event. Whether the failure of the event to occur means that there is no contract, or simply no obligation to perform, depends on the intention of the parties.[197] For example, in *George v Roach*[198] an agreement for the sale of a business provided that a newspaper agency should be purchased at the value placed on it by a named valuer. The person named refused to value the agency and a majority of the High Court held that valuation by the person named was a 'condition precedent' to the existence of a contract between the parties and that the refusal to value meant that there was no contract.

In the same way the parties to a contract may express an intention that a particular event is to terminate the obligation of the parties to perform, or a relation created by the contract, or to give either (or both) of the parties the right to terminate the further performance of the contract. The occurrence of the event referred to is then a *condition subsequent*.[199] For example, the parties to a sale of goods contract might provide that neither is obliged to perform if an export licence is not obtained by a specified date. The occurrence of the event — failure to obtain the licence by the specified date — terminates the obligation of the parties to perform.[200]

Because the distinction affected the onus of proof, the distinction between conditions precedent and conditions subsequent was more significant in times when precise pleading was important. The onus of proving the fulfilment of a condition precedent rests on the plaintiff in the action whereas the defendant bears the onus of proving that a condition subsequent has occurred.[201] Now that the fulfilment of conditions precedent is the subject of an implied averment[202] the distinction is not particularly important. In any event, the utility of the distinction is

---

196. Hence the expression 'promissory condition': see, eg *Tricontinental Corp Ltd v HDFI Ltd* (1990) 21 NSWLR 689 at 702–3. Cf *Ankar Pty Ltd v National Westminster Finance (Australia) Ltd* (1987) 162 CLR 549 at 555–6. See further [742].
197. See [273]–[275].
198. (1942) 67 CLR 253. Contrast *Booker Industries Pty Ltd v Wilson Parking (Qld) Pty Ltd* (1982) 149 CLR 600; 43 ALR 68.
199. See, eg *National Australia Bank Ltd v KDS Construction Services Pty Ltd* (1987) 163 CLR 668; 76 ALR 27.
200. However, where such an event may occur as the result of a breach of contract the courts are reluctant to treat its occurrence as of itself terminating the obligation of the parties to perform, as this might allow a party to profit by his or her own wrong. See [1967].
201. See, eg *Verna Trading Pty Ltd v New India Assurance Co Ltd* [1991] 1 VR 129.
202. See [1811].

doubtful, because the terms 'precedent' and 'subsequent' merely express contrasting time relations. In fact, the difference between conditions precedent and conditions subsequent is largely semantic[203] for the simple reason that whether the 'condition' is 'precedent' or 'subsequent' depends on the perspective of the individual. Thus, a provision which is termed a 'condition precedent' may operate as a condition subsequent.[204]

In *Perri v Coolangatta Investments Pty Ltd*[205] Gibbs CJ explained that the crucial issue is always the *effect* of the 'condition' because, 'provided the effect of a condition is clearly understood its classification may be merely a matter of words'. Thus, it is important to distinguish events which must occur for the formation of a binding contract from events which merely condition a party's obligation to perform. Where there is no contract until the event in question occurs either party may resile prior to the occurrence of the event without being held liable in damages for breach of contract. And the courts generally say that it is not open to one party to overlook ('waive') the non-occurrence of the event and to claim a right to enforce the 'contract'. The 'condition' must be for that party's benefit alone and that is more likely to be the position where the event conditions the obligation of one party to perform.[206] By contrast, where the event merely makes a party's obligation to perform contingent, neither party is entitled to withdraw from the contract until it is clear that the event will not occur, in the case of a condition precedent, or the event has actually occurred, in the case of a condition subsequent.

[742] Confusion between promise and contingency.[207] It is usual to refer to conditions precedent and subsequent as terms of the contract,[208] and this, unfortunately, leads to some confusion between promises and contingencies. Although it is reasonable to refer to a term classified as a condition as a 'condition precedent', it is not necessary for a condition precedent to be stated in a contractual term. For example, the phrase 'subject to approval by X' may operate to indicate the existence of a condition precedent to the formation of a contract.[209] It is difficult to say that this type of condition precedent is a term when there is no contract until the event occurs. More accurately the expression describes the *event* (the approval by X) which must occur before a contract is formed.

Confusion between promises and contingencies is present in the sale of goods legislation. For example, s 31 of the *Sale of Goods Act* 1923 (NSW) provides[210] that, unless the parties have agreed to the contrary, 'delivery of

---

203. *Meehan v Jones* (1982) 149 CLR 571 at 582; 42 ALR 463. But see D W McMorland, 'A New Approach to Precedent and Subsequent Conditions' (1980) 4 *Otago LR* 469.
204. See *Total Gas Marketing Ltd v Arco British Ltd* [1998] 2 Lloyd's Rep 209 (see B J Davenport, (1999) 115 *LQR* 11).
205. (1982) 149 CLR 537 at 541; 41 ALR 441. Cf Holmes, *The Common Law*, ed by M De W Howe, 1963, p 247.
206. Contrast *Balbosa v Ali* [1990] 1 WLR 914 at 919.
207. See G H Treitel, '"Conditions" and "Conditions Precedent"' (1990) 106 *LQR* 185; J W Carter, 'Conditions and Conditions Precedent' (1991) 4 *JCL* 90.
208. The usage goes back at least as far as *Boone v Eyre* (1777) 1 H Bl 273n; 126 ER 160.
209. See generally [275].
210. For the corresponding provisions see [1808].

[742]   Contract Law in Australia

the goods and payment of the price are concurrent conditions, that is to say, the seller must be ready and willing to give possession of the goods to the buyer in exchange for the price, and the buyer must be ready and willing to pay the price in exchange for possession of the goods'. Having regard to the definition of 'condition' referred to earlier,[211] it might be thought that the failure of the buyer to be ready and willing to pay the price is a breach which gives rise to a right to terminate. However, that is not usually the case. The purpose of s 31 is to state that the seller's obligation to deliver is *contingent* on the buyer's readiness and willingness to pay the price. It expresses a presumption of concurrent performance, and makes the readiness and willingness of the buyer a condition precedent to the obligation of the seller to deliver.[212] The fact that the buyer impliedly promises to be ready and willing means that an absence of readiness or willingness on the buyer's part at the time appointed for acceptance (and payment) constitutes a breach of contract. But the seriousness of the breach depends, in the first instance, on a classification of the term rather than the operation of s 31.[213]

Other Types of Terms

[743] Essential and fundamental terms. So far as the right to terminate is concerned, a term cannot be more essential or fundamental than a condition. It is more common to refer to time stipulations which are conditions as 'essential' terms[214] but this is merely an illustration of preferred terminology.

However, it is sometimes suggested that conditions must be distinguished from essential or fundamental terms in the construction of contractual right to terminate,[215] and the application of exclusion clauses.[216]

[744] Definitional terms. Some contractual terms do no more than define the meaning of words appearing in the contract. For example, a term might provide that 'month' means 'calendar month'. Obviously, these terms do not embody promises.

[745] Exclusion clauses. An important category of contractual terms, referred to collectively in this work as 'exclusion clauses', operate to exclude, restrict or qualify the rights of the parties. They are also referred to as 'exemption' clauses or 'exception' clauses. These do not usually embody contractual undertakings.

The rules governing the construction of exclusion clauses are discussed later in this chapter.[217]

[746] Procedural terms. Some contractual terms lay down procedures to be followed in defined situations. For example, a contract may contain

---

211. See [727].
212. For the concept of readiness and willingness to perform see [1929].
213. See [1919], [1951].
214. See generally [1950]–[1953].
215. See [727] and further [2159]. See also [1935] (anticipatory breach).
216. See [755].
217. See [750]–[768].

an arbitration clause which applies in the event of a dispute between the parties. Such a clause specifies the procedure for the resolution of disputes.

Only where a procedural term embodies a contractual undertaking is it meaningful to speak of the term being breached. For example, an arbitration clause is capable of being breached.[218]

[747] **Agreed damages clauses.** Agreed damages clauses, which purport to quantify the damages which are to be payable in the event of breach, are distinguishable from those so far considered because they deal with the secondary obligation of a party after breach, rather than a primary obligation.[219]

Agreed damages terms are governed by a distinction between liquidated damages clauses and penalties.[220] The term is not enforceable if it is a penalty.

Exclusion Clauses[221]

General

[748] **Types of exclusion clauses.** Exclusion clauses are of three main types. These may be illustrated and distinguished by consideration of the effect of an exclusion clause on a party's right to terminate the performance of a contract for breach of contract.[222]

The first type operates to *exclude* the rights which a party would otherwise possess under a contract by reason of the other terms of the contract, or a rule or presumption of law. For example, a clause may exclude the right to terminate for breach, thus obliging the promisee to perform notwithstanding the breach.

The second type *restricts* the rights of one party without necessarily excluding the liability of the other party. For example, the clause might provide that only a particular type of breach is to give rise to the right of termination.

The third type *qualifies* rights by subjecting them to specified procedures. For example, a promisee's right to terminate may be subject to a requirement of exercise within a specified period of time.

The principles stated in the paragraphs which follow are applicable to each type of clause. Thus, in *Darlington Futures Ltd v Delco Australia Pty Ltd*[223] the High Court decided that a clause which restricts or partially excludes the liability of a party by limiting it to a specific sum is governed by the same rules as a total exclusion. The principles have also sometimes been applied to other types of terms, on the basis that they are analogous to

---

218. *Doleman & Sons v Ossett Corp* [1912] 3 KB 257. On when a right to terminate may be based on breach of a procedural term see [1919].
219. For the distinction between primary and secondary obligations see [1989], [2101], [2158].
220. See [2207]–[2217].
221. See Yates, *Exclusion Clauses in Contracts*, 2nd ed, 1982, Chapters 4–6.
222. See further [1977].
223. (1986) 161 CLR 500; 68 ALR 385. See further [752].

exclusion clauses.[224] Nevertheless, for a clause to be exclusionary it must operate for the benefit of one party only. For example, in *Suisse Atlantique Société d'Armement Maritime SA v NV Rotterdamsche Kolen Centrale*[225] a liquidated damages clause[226] fixing the liability of charterers for detention of the vessel was said not to be exclusionary because it operated, potentially, for the benefit of both parties. It provided for the payment of $1000 per day even if the shipowners suffered a lesser loss by reason of the charterers' breach of contract.

[749] **Function of exclusion clauses.**[227] Traditionally, exclusion clauses have been treated as having the function of providing *defences* to possible actions for breach of contract.[228] Two consequences of this approach may be noticed at this stage:

- it implies that exclusion clauses are applied after liability under the contract (or in tort) has been established; and
- it means that even if the clause excludes all liability there is still, in theory at least, a breach of contract on the part of the promisor.[229]

The second function of exclusion clauses is to define contractual duties and obligations. Exclusion clauses have been applied in this way in shipping cases.[230] However, most exclusion clauses can be treated as definitions. In *Photo Production Ltd v Securicor Transport Ltd*[231] Securicor agreed to provide a night patrol service at Photo Production's factory under a standard form contract, cl 1 of which provided that under 'no circumstances' would Securicor be 'responsible for any injurious act or default by any employee ... unless such act or default could have been foreseen and avoided by the exercise of due diligence' on its part. The same term went on to provide that Securicor would not 'in any event' be 'responsible for' any loss suffered by Photo Production through 'fire or any other cause, except in so far as such loss is solely attributable to the negligence' of an employee of Securicor 'acting within the course' of his or her employment. Photo Production claimed damages from Securicor for the loss suffered when an employee of Securicor, who had satisfactory references and had been employed for over three months, set fire to the premises. Apparently, the fire had been started deliberately, but not necessarily with the intention of causing serious damage. But the fire got out of control and substantial damage occurred.

Lord Wilberforce adopted the traditional approach. He found a breach by Securicor in its failure to comply with an implied term requiring it to provide the service with due and proper regard to the safety and security of

---

224. See, eg *Canada SS Lines Ltd v The King* [1952] AC 192 (indemnity provision); *J Lauritzen AS v Wijsmuller BV (The Super Servant Two)* [1990] 1 Lloyd's Rep 1 at 12 (cancellation clause). But see [764].
225. [1967] 1 AC 361.
226. See generally on agreed damages clauses [2207]–[2217].
227. See Coote, *Exception Clauses*, 1964, Chapter 1.
228. See, eg *Owners of SS Istros v F W Dahlstroem & Co* [1931] 1 KB 247.
229. *Blue Anchor Line Ltd v Alfred C Toepfer International GmbH (The Union Amsterdam)* [1982] 2 Lloyd's Rep 432 at 436.
230. See *Jackson v Union Marine Insurance Co Ltd* (1874) LR 10 CP 125.
231. [1980] AC 827 (see Brian Coote, 'The Second Rise and Fall of Fundamental Breach' (1981) 55 *ALJ* 788).

Photo Production's premises. However, as a matter of construction Securicor's liability for this breach had been excluded by cl 1 of the contract. Lords Salmon, Keith and Scarman agreed with this approach.

On the other hand, Lord Diplock saw cl 1 as defining Securicor's obligations. In the absence of the exclusion clause, he said the primary obligations of Securicor would have included an implied 'absolute obligation to procure that the visits by the night patrol to the factory were conducted by natural persons who would exercise reasonable skill and care for the safety of the factory'. However, Lord Diplock explained:[232]

> That primary obligation is modified by the exclusion clause. Securicor's obligation to do this is not to be absolute, but is limited to exercising due diligence in its capacity as employer of the natural persons by whom the visits are conducted, to procure that those persons shall exercise reasonable skill and care for the safety of the factory.

On this analysis, the effect of the exclusion clause was to prevent the events which had occurred constituting a breach of contract on the defendants' part. Accordingly the plaintiffs' action failed.

The precise function of any exclusion clause must depend on the construction of the contract. However, the influence of the traditional approach is such that the courts generally prefer to treat them as possible defences.

Operation at Common Law

[750] **Question of construction.** The application of exclusion clauses at common law depends on the intention of the parties. It is therefore a question of construction.[233] This may be described as the 'primary' rule. There are, however, particular ('secondary') rules which assist in the application of the primary rule in cases where the clause does not expressly deal with the circumstances which have occurred. Often these rules are no more than particular applications, or adaptations, of general approaches to construction, employed for the purpose of inferring the parties' intention.

Although traditionally the courts' approach to exclusion clauses has been hostile, the recent cases illustrate a more balanced approach.[234] This has become possible because of the statutory protection of contracting parties in weak bargaining positions.[235] Indeed, in the context of commercial contracts the better view is that exclusion clauses are to be treated in the same way as other types of contractual provision. Thus, in *Darlington Futures Ltd v Delco Australia Pty Ltd*[236] the High Court said:[237]

---

232. [1980] AC 827 at 851. Earlier (at 847) he said that the defendants had committed a 'fundamental breach'. Presumably this was directed to the defendants' position apart from the exclusion clause.
233. *Sydney Corp v West* (1965) 114 CLR 481; *Darlington Futures Ltd v Delco Australia Pty Ltd* (1986) 161 CLR 500.
234. See, eg *Bright v Sampson & Duncan Enterprises Pty Ltd* (1985) 1 NSWLR 346 at 365.
235. See [769]–[772].
236. (1986) 161 CLR 500.
237. (1986) 161 CLR 500 at 510. But cf *Bright v Sampson & Duncan Enterprises Pty Ltd* (1985) 1 NSWLR 346 at 359.

[T]he interpretation of an exclusion clause is to be determined by construing the clause according to its natural and ordinary meaning, read in the light of the contract as a whole, thereby giving due weight to the context in which the clause appears including the nature and object of the contract, and, where appropriate, construing the clause *contra proferentem* in case of ambiguity.

Accordingly, the secondary rules considered below are, generally, no more than rules of thumb. Indeed, it may be that some of the rules are no longer useful, even as rules of thumb.

[751] Construction contra proferentem. An exclusion clause is 'ordinarily construed strictly against the proferens',[238] that is, against the party relying on the clause. For example, in *Wallis v Pratt*[239] a term in a contract for the sale of goods provided: 'Sellers give no warranty expressed or implied as to growth, description or any other matters.' The contract required the delivery of seed described as 'common English sainfoin' but the sellers delivered, and the buyers accepted, different goods, namely, 'giant sainfoin'. The seed delivered was inferior to that provided for by the contract and the buyers claimed damages for breach of the condition implied by s 13 of the *Sale of Goods Act* 1893 (UK),[240] which required the goods to correspond with their contractual description. The buyers relied on the quoted clause. The House of Lords held that the clause only covered a breach of warranty and did not apply to the breach of condition which had occurred. The fact that the effect of s 11 of the *Sale of Goods Act* 1893 (UK)[241] was to reduce the buyer's rights to those applicable for breach of warranty — because the goods had been accepted — did not affect the matter. The term breached retained its character as a condition: only the rights of the buyers had been changed.

[752] Application of the contra proferentem rule. The contra proferentem rule is a general rule of construction and therefore applies to any *ambiguous* clause, exclusionary or otherwise. Nevertheless, two points need to be noted.

First, although the rule is only relevant in cases of ambiguity in construction, the courts have tended to create ambiguity artificially, by a process of strict construction. For example, in *Ernest Beck & Co v K Szymanowski & Co*[242] a contract to sell a quantity of '200 yards reels' of cotton thread provided 'the goods delivered shall be deemed to be in all respects in accordance with the contract' unless within 14 days notice was received by the seller 'of any matter or thing by reason whereof ... the goods are not in accordance with the contract'. The buyer discovered that the reels had less than 200 yards of cotton, but failed to complain within the 14-day period. The House of Lords held that the clause did not apply because it was restricted to goods delivered, whereas the buyer's complaint was in relation to goods not delivered. The decision was possible only

---

238. *Thomas National Transport (Melbourne) Pty Ltd v May & Baker (Australia) Pty Ltd* (1966) 115 CLR 353 at 376.
239. [1911] AC 394.
240. See [638].
241. See [1981].
242. [1924] AC 43.

because of the very strict interpretation of the clause. It is by no means clear that the result in *Beck v Szymanowski* would be the same today. The clause was not ambiguous on its face, and there seems no compelling reason to create an ambiguity by strict construction. The proper approach, as expressed by the High Court in *Darlington Futures Ltd v Delco Australia Pty Ltd*[243] is to construe the clause in accordance with ordinary construction principles, and only if ambiguity is then found should the contra proferentem rule be applied.

Second, as *Darlington* also makes clear,[244] suggestions in *Ailsa Craig Fishing Co Ltd v Malvern Fishing Co Ltd*[245] that rules such as the contra proferentem rule should not be vigorously applied to clauses which merely limit liability, are not relevant in Australia where the various types of exclusion are all subject to the same rules.[246]

[753] Seriousness of breach. Common sense tells us that the more serious the breach of contract the less likely it is for the parties to the contract to have intended an exclusion clause to apply. Although the cases support such a statement,[247] much confusion has arisen from attempts to describe in advance the type of breach which will not be covered by an exclusion clause. For example, use has been made of concepts of 'fundamental' and 'total' breach.[248] However, it is the 'degree of seriousness'[249] which counts, not whether a particular epithet is applicable to the breach.

Although it is necessary to consider the more particular descriptions, the cases should now be seen as illustrating the straightforward proposition that the more serious the breach sought to be covered, the less likely that the parties intended liability to be excluded.

[754] Fundamental breach.[250] In *Suisse Atlantique Société d'Armement Maritime SA v NV Rotterdamsche Kolen Centrale*[251] the House of Lords approved 'a rule of construction' stated by Pearson LJ in *UGS Finance Ltd v National Mortgage Bank of Greece and National Bank of Greece SA*[252] that 'normally an exception or exclusion clause or similar provision in a contract should be construed as not applying to a situation created by a fundamental breach of contract'. But, as Pearson LJ pointed out: 'This is not an

---

243. (1986) 161 CLR 500 at 510 (see [750]).
244. See Sir Anthony Mason, 'Australian Contract Law' (1988) 1 *JCL* 1 at 5.
245. [1983] 1 WLR 964 at 970. See also *George Mitchell (Chesterhall) Ltd v Finney Lock Seeds Ltd* [1983] 2 AC 803 at 813–14.
246. For the interpretation of a clause excluding liability for 'consequential loss' see *British Sugar Plc v NEI Power Projects Ltd* (1997) 87 BLR 45; *Frank Davies Pty Ltd v Container Haulage Group Pty Ltd* (1989) 98 FLR 289 at 313.
247. See, eg *Robert A Munro & Co Ltd v Meyer* [1930] 2 KB 312 (see [1977]); *McRae v Commonwealth Disposals Commission* (1951) 84 CLR 377 at 398.
248. See [754], [757].
249. Brian Coote, 'The Second Rise and Fall of Fundamental Breach' (1981) 55 *ALJ* 788 at 801.
250. See, eg Brian Coote, 'The Rise and Fall of Fundamental Breach' (1966) 40 *ALJ* 336. Cf E J Hayek, 'Exemption Clauses — The Canadian Approach' (1991) 4 *JCL* 51.
251. [1967] 1 AC 361 (see G H Treitel, (1966) 29 *MLR* 546).
252. [1964] 1 Lloyd's Rep 446 at 453. See also *Thomas National Transport (Melbourne) Pty Ltd v May & Baker (Australia) Pty Ltd* (1966) 115 CLR 353 at 377.

independent rule of law imposed by the court on the parties willy-nilly in disregard of their contractual intention.'

When approving this principle, the judges in *Suisse Atlantique* were concerned to disapprove statements in earlier cases[253] that, *as a matter of law,* exclusion clauses never apply to fundamental breach. Similar disapproval had already been expressed by the High Court in *Sydney Corp v West*.[254] Subsequently, the English courts developed a second version of the fundamental breach rule, originally based on termination for fundamental breach,[255] but ultimately indistinguishable from the first version. However, in *Photo Production Ltd v Securicor Transport Ltd*[256] the House of Lords rejected this formulation of the rule.[257]

It remains to consider what the courts mean by 'fundamental' breach. At the lowest it describes any breach which provides (or would apart from the exclusion clause provide) the promisee with a right to terminate the performance of the contract.[258] At the highest it describes a total nonperformance of the contract.[259] Somewhere between these conceptions is the idea that a breach is fundamental if it satisfies the requirements applied under the doctrine based on *Hongkong Fir Shipping Co Ltd v Kawasaki Kisen Kaisha Ltd*.[260] However, for the reasons stated above,[261] and the confusion which the fundamental breach concept has created, it is doubtful whether the concept has any real utility. In fact, the rule of construction approved in *Suisse Atlantique* is hardly ever referred to now.

[755] **Breach of fundamental term.**[262] In *Smeaton Hanscomb & Co Ltd v Sassoon I Setty Son & Co (No 1)*[263] Devlin J stated that it is a 'principle of construction' that exclusion clauses do not apply 'if the beneficiary has committed a breach of a fundamental term of the contract'. Thus, in cases such as *Hain SS Co Ltd v Tate & Lyle Ltd*,[264] where deviation by a vessel carrying goods from the agreed route is treated as the breach of a fundamental term, exclusion clauses have been held not to apply.

What, then, is a fundamental term? Devlin J said in *Smeaton Hanscomb* that a fundamental term is something 'narrower than a condition', and gave as an example of the breach of such a term the supply of pine logs under a contract for the sale of goods requiring the delivery of mahogany logs. If it is helpful to consider whether the term breached is fundamental, such a

---

253. See, eg *Karsales (Harrow) Ltd v Wallis* [1956] 1 WLR 936 at 940.
254. (1965) 114 CLR 481.
255. See [1993].
256. [1980] AC 827 (see [749]).
257. The decisions in *Charterhouse Credit Co Ltd v Tolly* [1963] 2 QB 683 and *Wathes (Western) Ltd v Austins (Menswear) Ltd* [1976] 1 Lloyd's Rep 14 were overruled.
258. *Suisse Atlantique Société d'Armement Maritime SA v NV Rotterdamsche Kolen Centrale* [1967] 1 AC 361 at 397.
259. *Suisse Atlantique Société d'Armement Maritime SA v NV Rotterdamsche Kolen Centrale* [1967] 1 AC 361 at 431.
260. [1962] 2 QB 26 (see [1958]).
261. See [753].
262. See, eg Lord Devlin, 'The Treatment of Breach of Contract' [1966] *CLJ* 192. Contrast C D Drake, 'Fundamentalism in Contract' (1967) 30 *MLR* 531.
263. [1953] 1 WLR 1468 at 1470.
264. [1936] 2 All ER 597. See further [761].

term may be implied, it need not be expressly stated in the contract. In fact, most fundamental terms are implied terms.

In *Suisse Atlantique Société d'Armement Maritime SA v NV Rotterdamsche Kolen Centrale*[265] the House of Lords made it clear that there is no rule of law preventing the application of exclusion clauses to the breach of a fundamental term.[266] Moreover, if, as Devlin J suggested in *Smeaton Hanscomb*, a fundamental term is more important than a condition, breach of the former brings into play the rule of construction applicable on fundamental breach,[267] since the breach of a fundamental term is clearly a 'fundamental' breach.[268]

[756] **Wilful breach.** If an exclusion clause does not expressly exclude liability for wilful breach it will usually be construed so as not to apply to such a breach, on the basis that this may legitimately be presumed to have been the intention of the parties. Conversely, an exclusion clause may restrict the defendant's responsibility to cases of 'wilful' default or breach.[269]

In *Sze Hai Tong Bank Ltd v Rambler Cycle Co Ltd*,[270] English sellers agreed to sell a quantity of bicycle parts to buyers in Singapore. The goods were sent by sea and a bill of lading was issued acknowledging that the goods were to be delivered in Singapore. It contained an exclusion clause stating that the 'responsibility of the carrier, whether as carrier or as custodian or bailee of the goods shall be deemed ... to cease absolutely after they are discharged' from the ship. On arrival of the goods in Singapore the buyers, who wished to obtain the goods without paying for them, obtained a letter of indemnity from the Sze Hai Tong Bank Ltd in favour of the shippers. This was presented to the shipping company's agents. A delivery order was then issued and the goods delivered to the buyers even though they did not present the bill of lading as they should have done. In an action by the sellers against the bank, it was conceded that the bank's liability depended on whether the shipping company was liable for delivering the goods without any bill of lading being presented. Although the shipping company sought to rely on the exclusion clause, the Privy Council held that it did not apply. Lord Denning, delivering the advice of the Board, said[271] that the clause had to be 'modified so as not to permit the shipping company deliberately to disregard its obligations as to delivery'.

The decision in *Sze Hai Tong* must be seen as based on the construction of the clause, rather than a rule of law. Thus, in *Kamil Export (Aust) Pty Ltd v NPL (Australia) Pty Ltd*[272] the appellate division of the Supreme Court of

---

265. [1967] AC 361. But see Yates, *Exclusion Clauses in Contracts*, 2nd ed, 1982, pp 196-214.
266. It was, perhaps, prepared to except cases where the 'main purpose' rule applies. But this now seems very doubtful. See [760].
267. See [754].
268. *Suisse Atlantique Société d'Armement Maritime SA v NV Rotterdamsche Kolen Centrale* [1967] 1 AC 361 at 422.
269. See, eg *Kenyon Son & Craven Ltd v Baxter Hoare & Co Ltd* [1971] 1 WLR 519. As to the exclusion of trustees' liability for wilful default and 'gross negligence' see *Armitage v Nurse* [1998] Ch 241 (see Nicholas McBride, [1998] *CLJ* 33).
270. [1959] AC 576.
271. [1959] AC 576 at 587.

Victoria read down an exclusion, on the basis of the presumed intention of the parties, so as not to apply to a loss resulting from a deliberate conversion of goods. The conversion occurred when there was a release of the goods to their consignee without the shipper's consent, and as in *Sze Hai Tong Bank Ltd v Rambler Cycle Co Ltd*, the bill of lading was not produced.

[757] **Total breach.** The concept of 'total' breach was applied by the House of Lords in *W & S Pollock & Co v Macrae*[273] where a contract for the building and installation of a set of motor engines provided that all goods were supplied on the basis that the builders were not liable for 'direct or consequential damages arising from defective material or workmanship'. In an action by the builders for the balance due under the contract the buyers claimed the return of money paid, and compensation for the engines not being in accordance with the contract. Lord Dunedin said[274] that the exclusion clause had no application to 'damage arising when there has been a total breach of contract by failing to supply the article truly contracted for'. On the facts he said that there was 'such a congeries of defects as to destroy the workable character of the machine'[275] and that this amounted to a total breach. The other members of the House of Lords concurred.

The total breach concept is difficult to distinguish from fundamental breach. Indeed, they have sometimes been treated as the same thing,[276] and there is some evidence of the English courts applying the total breach concept as a rule of law, without proper regard to the construction of the contract.[277] However, like fundamental breach, it is clear that it is a rule of construction only.[278]

[758] **Supply of a different article.** The cases provide many illustrations, mostly fictional, of situations where a supplier of goods is unable to hide behind an exclusion clause because of supply of an article different from that contracted for. Thus, if the contract requires the supply of cheese the supplier cannot rely on an exclusion clause as protection from the consequences of a supply of chalk.[279]

In *Suisse Atlantique Société d'Armement Maritime SA v NV Rotterdamsche Kolen Centrale*[280] Lord Wilberforce said that since contracting parties can 'hardly be supposed to contemplate such a mis-performance, or to have provided against it without destroying the whole contractual substratum, there is no difficulty' in holding exclusion clauses to be inapplicable to such cases. However, as he was at pains to point out,[281] a breach which is serious

---

272. (1993) [1996] 1 VR 538 at 547, 553 (see Brian Coote, (1997) 12 *JCL* 169). See also *Suisse Atlantique Société d'Armement Maritime SA v NV Rotterdamsche Kolen Centrale* [1967] 1 AC 361.
273. 1922 SC (HL) 192.
274. 1922 SC (HL) 192 at 199.
275. 1922 SC (HL) 192 at 200.
276. See, eg *Farnworth Finance Facilities Ltd v Attryde* [1970] 1 WLR 1053.
277. See *Yeoman Credit Ltd v Apps* [1962] 2 QB 508 at 520.
278. See *Ailsa Craig Fishing Co Ltd v Malvern Fishing Co Ltd* [1983] 1 WLR 964.
279. *UGS Finance Ltd v National Mortgage Bank of Greece and National Bank of Greece SA* [1964] 1 Lloyd's Rep 446 at 453.
280. [1967] 1 AC 361 at 433.
281. [1967] 1 AC 361 at 431.

enough to entitle the promisee to refuse to perform the contract, in this context to refuse to accept the different article, 'may be reduced in effect, or made not a breach at all, by the terms of the [exclusion] clause'.

It will also have been noticed that supply of a different article has been used to illustrate other rules, such as the total breach rule,[282] which is itself a guide to the dangers involved in treating the supply of a different article as any more than an indication that the exclusion is not, as a matter of construction, likely to apply. It may be, however, that the presumption is stronger in the case of the supply of a different article, particularly if the breach is wilful.

[759] The rule in *Flight v Booth*.[283] Where a contract for the sale of land is entered into it may contain an 'errors or misdescriptions clause' to which the rule in *Flight v Booth*[284] applies. In that case the clause provided that if by mistake the land was improperly described, this was not to vitiate the sale. Rather, compensation was to be paid. There was found to be a misdescription in the property sold, and the court stated the following principle:[285]

> [W]here the misdescription, although not proceeding from fraud, is in a material and substantial point, so far affecting the subject-matter of the contract that it may reasonably be supposed that, but for such misdescription, the purchaser might never have entered into the contract at all, in such case ... the purchaser is not bound to resort to the clause of compensation. Under such a state of facts, the purchaser may be considered as not having purchased the thing which was really the subject of the sale ...

On the facts there was such a discrepancy as to entitle the purchaser to terminate the performance of the contract: the exclusionary clause did not apply to restrict the purchaser to the recovery of 'compensation' under the clause.

This rule is, in essence, a form of the fundamental breach rule. Theoretically, like all the others considered, it is a rule of construction. However, it is in practice applied unless the parties have in the clearest words excluded its operation.[286] Attempts are sometimes made to give the rule an application, beyond sale of land contracts to contracts generally, or to other types of exclusion clauses.[287] This should be discouraged because of the accepted practice peculiar to real estate.

[760] The main purpose rule. What is usually described as the 'main purpose' rule has two aspects. One aspect was expressed thus by Lord Halsbury LC in *Glynn v Margetson & Co*:[288] 'Looking at the whole of the instrument, and seeing what one must regard ... as its main purpose, one must reject words, indeed whole provisions, if they are inconsistent with

---

282. See [757].
283. See Charles Harpum, 'Exclusion Clauses and Contracts for the Sale of Land' [1992] *CLJ* 263 at 270ff.
284. (1834) 1 Bing NC 370; 131 ER 1160.
285. (1834) 1 Bing NC 370 at 377; 131 ER 1160 at 1162–3.
286. See, eg *Torr v Harpur* (1940) 40 SR (NSW) 585; *Jennings v Zilahi-Kiss* (1972) 2 SASR 493.
287. See, eg *Yeoman Credit Ltd v Apps* [1962] 2 QB 508 at 523.
288. [1893] AC 351 at 357.

what one assumes to be the main purpose of the contract'. He explained the main purpose of the contract before the court as being the delivery of perishable goods pursuant to a contract for carriage by sea. Although there was a clause in the contract permitting the carrier to 'proceed to and stay' at a series of ports 'for the purpose of delivering coals, cargo, or passengers or for any other purpose whatsoever', this had to be construed in the light of the main purpose of the contract. The carriage provided for was between Malaga and Liverpool and the cargo was found to be damaged owing to the delay involved in the vessel travelling 350 miles from Malaga to Burriana on the east coast of Spain before retracing her course. Had the vessel not deviated the cargo would have arrived in good condition, and so the contract was construed as if there was no liberty to deviate except to call at a port (or ports) in the course of the agreed voyage. In the result, the carrier could not invoke the clause.

The second form of the main purpose rule is indistinguishable from the fundamental breach rule. If the breach by the promisor is so serious that application of the exclusion clause to the breach would defeat the main purpose of the contract, the court will presume that the parties did not intend the exclusion clause to apply.

The continued existence of the main purpose rule as a rule of construction has been acknowledged,[289] and courts have not usually interpreted literally an exclusion which would destroy contractual intent. Thus, it might be considered illusory to say 'I promise to do X', if the agreement totally excludes any liability for a failure to do X.[290] However, it is doubtful whether there is a rule of law even in this context.[291] Moreover, it is now clear that even as a rule of construction it is not as wide as originally conceived. For example, in *Photo Production Ltd v Securicor Transport Ltd*[292] Lord Diplock restricted the main purpose rule to clauses which would deprive the parties' agreement of the 'legal characteristics of a contract'. More recently, in *Nissho Iwai Australia Ltd v Malaysian International Shipping Corp Berhad*[293] the High Court held that an exclusion clause may apply to an event defeating the main object of the contract. It was also said that if the happening of the event covered by the clause will *always* defeat the main object of the contract, the clause will apply.

[761] **The deviation cases.**[294] A carrier of goods by sea who deviates from the agreed voyage thereby loses the benefit of exclusion clauses in the contract which would otherwise apply.[295] The rule is also applicable to

---

289. See, eg *H & E Van Der Sterren v Cibernetics (Holdings) Pty Ltd* (1970) 44 ALJR 157.
290. See *Firestone Tyre and Rubber Co Ltd v Vokins & Co Ltd* [1951] 1 Lloyd's Rep 32 at 39. But see [270], [336], [411].
291. But cf *MacRobertson Miller Airline Services v Commissioner of State Taxation (WA)* (1975) 133 CLR 125; 8 ALR 131; *Gregory v MAB Pty Ltd* [1989] 1 WAR 1 at 14.
292. [1980] AC 827 at 850. See also *Life Savers (A'asia) Ltd v Frigmobile Pty Ltd* [1983] 1 NSWLR 431 at 435–6 (cf S W Cavanagh, 'The Ultimate Exclusion Clause' (1985) 59 *ALJ* 67 at 75–6); *Oceanic Sun Line Special Shipping Co Inc v Fay* (1988) 165 CLR 197; 79 ALR 9.
293. (1989) 167 CLR 219; 86 ALR 375.
294. See John Livermore, 'Deviation, Deck Cargo and Fundamental Breach' (1990) 2 *JCL* 241; Brian Coote, 'Deviation and the Ordinary Law' in Rose, ed, *Lex Mercatoria: Essays on International Commercial Law in Honour of Francis Reynolds*, 2000, p 13.

other contracts of carriage[296] by land or rail. It may, indeed, apply to all bailment contracts.[297]

The basis for the rule is a matter of debate. In *Photo Production Ltd v Securicor Transport Ltd*[298] Lord Wilberforce, referring to the cases on carriage by sea, suggested two possibilities: either the deviation rule is one of construction or the cases on which it is based 'should be considered as a body of authority sui generis with special rules derived from historical and commercial reasons'.[299] The preferable view is that the deviation rule is based on the construction of the contract. Therefore, whether an exclusion clause applies after deviation must depend on its scope: there is no rule of law prohibiting its application.[300] Moreover, since deviation usually arises on the breach of a fundamental term, the construction basis brings the cases into line with other rules.

This is supported, at least in contexts other than carriage by sea, by the decision of the High Court in *Thomas National Transport (Melbourne) Pty Ltd v May & Baker (Australia) Pty Ltd*.[301] The plaintiff claimed damages as compensation for the damage to their goods while in the possession of Thomas National Transport (the carrier), which had agreed to carry the goods and to deliver them to consignees located interstate. The driver of the vehicle carrying the goods back to the carrier's central depot stored them overnight in his garage where they were damaged by fire. This was a deviation from the usual arrangements, made necessary because the carrier's depot was closed for the night, but nevertheless held to be a breach of contract. The terms of the contract provided that the 'consignors', that is the plaintiff, had to accept 'responsibility for any damage or loss of any goods' while in the carrier's custody; and that 'no responsibility' was accepted by the carrier 'for any loss of, or damage to' the goods 'either in transit or in storage for any reason whatsoever'. Nevertheless, a majority of the High Court held that the provision did not exclude liability for the damage which had occurred after the breach by deviation.

[762] The four corners rule. What is frequently referred to as the 'four corners' rule has been stated in various ways but probably that most often

---

295. See, eg *Hain SS Co Ltd v Tate & Lyle Ltd* [1936] 2 All ER 597.
296. See *London and North Western Railway Co v Neilson* [1922] 2 AC 263; *Thomas National Transport (Melbourne) Pty Ltd v May & Baker (Australia) Pty Ltd* (1966) 115 CLR 353.
297. See, eg *Davies v Collins* [1945] 1 All ER 247. Cf *Mendelssohn v Normand Ltd* [1970] 1 QB 177 at 184.
298. [1980] AC 827 at 845.
299. In *Hain SS Co Ltd v Tate & Lyle Ltd* [1936] 2 All ER 597 the House of Lords seems to have proceeded on the basis that it is 'termination of the contract' for breach which prevents the application of exclusion clauses in the deviation cases. Lord Wilberforce's statement in *Photo Production* was based on the rationale that the deviation cases cannot be regarded as laying down 'different rules as to contracts generally' from those stated in *Heyman v Darwins Ltd* [1942] AC 356, which excludes the possibility of the deviation cases depending on the fact of termination.
300. Cf *China Ocean Shipping Co Ltd v P S Chellaram & Co Ltd* (1990) 28 NSWLR 354; *Tasman Express Line Ltd v J I Case (Australia) Pty Ltd* (1992) 111 FLR 108 at 111.
301. (1966) 115 CLR 353. See also *Kenya Railways v Antares Co Pte Ltd (The Antares) (Nos 1 & 2)* [1987] 1 Lloyd's Rep 424 (loading of cargo).

quoted is Scrutton LJ's formulation in *Gibaud v Great Eastern Railway Co*:[302]

> The principle is well known ... that if you undertake to do a thing in a certain way, or to keep a thing in a certain place, with certain conditions protecting it, and have broken the contract by not doing the thing contracted for in the way contracted for, or not keeping the article in the place in which you have contracted to keep it, you cannot rely on the conditions which were only intended to protect you if you carried out the contract in the way in which you had contracted to do it.

Therefore, a contractor who breaches the contract by stepping outside the 'four corners' of the contract will generally lose the protection of the exclusion clause. This has its main, indeed almost exclusive application, in the context of bailment contracts. In *Sydney Corp v West*[303] the High Court held that the rule is one of construction. The plaintiff parked his car in the defendant's car park, and received a ticket which stated that the ticket had to be presented before the vehicle was taken from the car park. In addition, there were terms excluding the liability of the defendants, for, among other things, the 'loss or damage to any vehicle ... however such loss [or damage] may arise or be caused'. The evidence indicated that the defendant delivered the vehicle to a third party without any authorisation by the plaintiff, and notwithstanding the third party's inability to produce a parking ticket. In fact, a 'duplicate' was issued to the third party. A majority of the High Court held that the defendant was unable to rely on the clause excluding liability. Barwick CJ and Taylor J said that the clause had no application where the defendant, as bailee, had been negligent *and* dealt with the plaintiff's goods in a way which was neither authorised nor permitted by the contract. Windeyer J said that the contract was breached because the defendant did not do what it had contracted to do in the way in which it had contracted to do it. It had obtained possession of the vehicle and undertook to release it only on presentation of the ticket, but had in fact released the vehicle without the ticket being produced.

The four corners rule is straightforward and simple, perhaps deceptively so as it may be difficult to decide whether an act is authorised by the contract without first bringing the exclusion clause into account to determine what is, in fact, authorised.[304] Nevertheless, as a rule of construction, it is undoubtedly valid.[305]

[763] **Negligence.** Whether an exclusion clause applies to protect a party from liability for negligence is, of course, a question of construction. However, because negligence frequently results in personal injury or property damage rather than mere economic loss, it is usually said that the intention to exclude liability for negligence must be clearly expressed.[306] An

---

302. [1921] 2 KB 426 at 435.
303. (1965) 114 CLR 481. See also *Tozer Kemsley & Millbourn (A'Asia) Pty Ltd v Collier's Interstate Transport Service Ltd* (1956) 94 CLR 384; *Walton Stores Ltd v Sydney City Council* [1968] 2 NSWR 109.
304. Cf *Ashby v Tolhurst* [1937] 2 KB 242.
305. This was approved by the High Court in *Darlington Futures Ltd v Delco Australia Pty Ltd* (1986) 161 CLR 500. See *Glebe Island Terminals Pty Ltd v Continental Seagram Pty Ltd (The Antwerpen)* (1993) 40 NSWLR 206. Cf [761].
306. See [764].

express reference to negligence is sufficient.[307] However, a clause does not expressly exclude negligence unless it actually uses that word or a synonym.[308]

In cases where there is no express reference to negligence the issue is whether an intention to exclude liability should be imputed to the parties on the basis of the words used. An important consideration is whether the defendant can be held liable in the absence of negligence. If negligence is the only basis for liability that will usually be a sufficient reason for saying that the clause must apply to cases of negligence. For example, in *Alderslade v Hendon Laundry Ltd*[309] the plaintiff left ten handkerchiefs with the defendants for laundering. These were not returned and an action for damages was brought based on the defendants' negligence. A clause in the contract limited the liability of the defendants to a 'maximum amount allowed for lost or damaged articles' equal to '20 times the charge made for laundering'. That amount was less than the value of the ten handkerchiefs. The court said that the defendants could not be held liable in the matter of returning the goods except through negligence on their part, and that the clause must therefore have been intended to cover loss of the handkerchiefs through lack of care on their part.

A similar approach was taken by the High Court in *Davis v Pearce Parking Station Pty Ltd*.[310] The plaintiff parked her car at the defendant's parking station, paid a fee and received a receipt, described as a 'parking check'. This contained a term stating that the vehicle was garaged 'at the owner's risk', and excluding the defendant's responsibility 'for loss or damage of any description'. Due to negligence on the defendant's part the vehicle was stolen from the station. Eventually it was recovered, but badly damaged. The plaintiff therefore claimed damages for negligence. It was held that the exclusion clause protected the defendant. The court said that although the contract created a bailment relationship, the defendant could exclude its liability for negligence if the words in the contract were clear enough to apply to the circumstances which had occurred. In deciding that the words were sufficiently clear, the court was influenced by the fact that the defendant made a very small charge for the custody of valuable goods. Even though the damage was a result of the defendant's negligence, a reasonable person in the plaintiff's position would have treated the clause as indicating that it was necessary to insure the vehicle in order to be protected.

However, as Scrutton LJ explained in *Rutter v Palmer*,[311] the rule is not invariable:[312] the position is simply that the exclusion clause will 'more readily' exclude liability for negligence where that is the only basis of the defendant's liability. Moreover, it is always appropriate to consider the type of clause in issue. For example, in *Commissioner for Railways (New South*

---

307. See, eg *J Spurling Ltd v Bradshaw* [1956] 1 WLR 461.
308. See *Smith v South Wales Switchgear Co Ltd* [1978] 1 All ER 18 at 22, 26 (disapproving *Gillespie Bros & Co Ltd v Roy Bowles Transport Ltd* [1973] QB 400 at 420, 421). See also *E E Caledonia Ltd v Orbit Valve Co Europe* [1994] 1 WLR 1515 at 1520 and further [764].
309. [1945] 1 KB 189.
310. (1954) 91 CLR 642. Cf *Davis v Commissioner for Main Roads* (1968) 117 CLR 529.
311. [1922] 2 KB 87 at 92.
312. See further [764].

Wales) v Quinn[313] a (time limitation) provision dealt with the time within which a claim for loss or damage to goods tendered for conveyance by rail had to be lodged with the Commissioner. Rich J said[314] that the term did not have as its object the 'demarcation of liability'; rather its object was to 'impose a time bar and a requirement of notice'.

[764] The *Canada SS* rules.[315] In *Canada SS Lines Ltd v The King*[316] the Privy Council restated the approach to exclusion of liability for negligence in three rules. These are construction rules and should not be treated as if they had statutory force.[317] Under the first rule an express exclusion of liability for negligence must be given effect and is sufficient to exclude liability.[318]

Under the second rule, where there is no express reference to negligence, the court must consider whether the words used are wide enough, with any doubt (ambiguity) being resolved contra proferentem.[319] Clauses purporting to exclude 'all liability' or 'any loss' have generally been treated as *insufficient* to exclude liability for negligence; but the addition of the words 'whatever its cause' or 'howsoever caused' has been treated as a sufficient indication of an intention to exclude liability for negligence.[320] Nevertheless, the use of these (or similar) words is not conclusive,[321] and it is arguable that they are not today necessary to achieve protection from liability for negligence. Moreover, as we have seen,[322] if the defendant's duty is such that it cannot be liable in the absence of negligence this is a proper basis for saying that the clause must apply. Thus, in *Davis v Pearce Parking Station Pty Ltd*[323] it was pointed out that, as a bailee, the defendant could not be held liable 'for loss or damage occurring without negligence', and the clause was therefore taken to cover such liability.

There are nevertheless cases in which an exclusion clause will be held not to apply even though negligence is the only basis for liability. Thus, in *Hollier v Rambler Motors (AMC) Ltd*[324] the plaintiff left his car at the defendant's premises for repair. When a fire caused damage to his car he claimed damages, relying on the defendant's negligence. Since the only basis for liability for loss by fire was negligence, the defendant's argument that a clause stating that the defendant was 'not responsible for damage caused by fire' applied looked to be a sound one.[325] However, the court said that ample content would be given to the clause by treating it as a warning

---

313. (1946) 72 CLR 345.
314. (1946) 72 CLR 345 at 356. See also at 365, 372, 385.
315. See J W Carter, '"Commercial" Construction and the Canada SS Rules' (1995) 8 *JCL* 69.
316. [1952] AC 192 at 208.
317. See, eg *Smith v South Wales Switchgear Co Ltd* [1978] 1 All ER 18 at 22.
318. See [763].
319. Cf *Darlington Futures Ltd v Delco Australia Pty Ltd* (1986) 161 CLR 500 at 510 (see [750]).
320. See *Rutter v Palmer* [1922] 2 KB 87 at 94; *Commissioner for Railways (New South Wales) v Quinn* (1946) 72 CLR 345 at 372; *Gillespie Bros & Co Ltd v Roy Bowles Transport Ltd* [1973] QB 400.
321. See, eg *Smith v South Wales Switchgear Co Ltd* [1978] 1 All ER 18.
322. See [763].
323. (1954) 91 CLR 642 at 651 (see [763]).
324. [1972] 2 QB 71 (see Brian Coote, [1973] *CLJ* 14).

to the plaintiff that the defendant would not be liable in the absence of negligence. The basis for this decision was that an ordinary person in the position of the plaintiff would not have drawn the conclusion that liability was being excluded. *Alderslade v Hendon Laundry Ltd*[326] was distinguished on the basis that in that case an ordinary person would have known that negligence was being excluded. *Hollier* illustrates the relevance to the construction of the clause of the class of person to whom the clause is addressed: had the contract been a commercial one the result would probably have been different.

The third rule stated in the *Canada SS* case draws on a statement in *Alderslade*.[327] If the words used are wide enough to cover liability for negligence it must be considered whether 'the head of damage may be based on some ground other than that of negligence'. Therefore, if, as a matter of construction the words used are wide enough to cover negligence, a court must consider the possible bases for the defendant's liability before reaching a conclusion on whether in fact liability for negligence has been excluded. However, the other head of damage must 'not be so fanciful or remote that the proferens cannot be supposed to have desired protection against it'.[328] This rule has given rise to considerable controversy. Four points may be made.

First, the rule should be taken not too literally. Thus, it is now clear that the Privy Council overstated the position when it said that the existence of a possible head of damage other than negligence is 'fatal' to the application of the clause to negligence.[329]

Second, although the usual case where the third rule applies is where the defendant is subject to a contractual and a tortious duty, the mere fact that a defendant is subject to liability in both tort and contract is not a sufficient basis for concluding that the clause can be avoided simply by suing in tort.[330] What is required is for the duties to be of a different nature. For example, in *White v John Warwick & Co Ltd*[331] the plaintiff hired a tradesman's cycle from the defendant under a contract which obliged the latter to maintain it in working order. When the machine was in need of repair the defendant supplied a replacement. Owing to a defect in the nut which held the saddle in place, the plaintiff suffered injury when the saddle shifted forward and he was thrown to the ground. The plaintiff sued in contract and in tort but the defendant relied on an exclusion of liability 'for personal injury to the riders of the machines' as a defence to both claims. The English Court of Appeal held that there were two bases of liability. The contract head of liability was strict in nature, while that in tort depended on proof of negligence. The plaintiff conceded that the clause prevented

---

325. In fact, the court did not consider that the clause had been incorporated into the contract: see [618].
326. [1945] 1 KB 189 (see [763]).
327. [1945] 1 KB 189 at 192.
328. See *Canada SS Lines Ltd v The King* [1952] AC 192 at 208.
329. See *Hollier v Rambler Motors (AMC) Ltd* [1972] 2 QB 71 at 80.
330. See, eg *Bright v Sampson & Duncan Enterprises Pty Ltd* (1985) 1 NSWLR 346 at 356–7.
331. [1953] 1 WLR 1285. For illustrations of contracts imposing a strict liability see [1856].

success on the contract claim. The clause did not expressly refer to negligence and it was held not to govern that liability on the basis that sufficient scope was given to the clause by treating it as applicable to the claim in contract. It followed that the clause did not prevent a claim in negligence based on the breach of a duty of care.[332]

Third, in Australia there is authority for the proposition that the *Canada SS* rules do not apply to indemnity clauses.[333]

Fourth, there is dicta in recent Australian cases that the *Canada SS* rules are no longer valid. In *Schenker & Co (Aust) Pty Ltd v Maplas Equipment and Services Pty Ltd*[334] the Appeal Division of the Supreme Court of Victoria said that they were in effect rejected by the High Court in *Darlington Futures Ltd v Delco Australia Pty Ltd*.[335] It is, however, doubtful whether this is true. Negligence was not at issue in *Delco*. There is, moreover, abundant Australian authority for the proposition that an intention to exclude liability for negligence must be clearly expressed.[336] Since this is all that the *Canada SS* rules actually require,[337] the matter must await a decision by the High Court.

[765] **Reasonableness.** Under statute the reasonableness of an exclusion clause may be crucial.[338] At common law it is merely a factor to be considered when inferring the intention of the parties as to the scope of the clause. If an exclusion clause operates unreasonably in relation to particular breaches, that is some indication that the parties did not intend the clause to apply to such breaches.[339]

It has occasionally been suggested that reasonableness has a greater significance at common law. For example, in *Gillespie Bros & Co Ltd v Roy Bowles Transport Ltd*[340] Lord Denning MR said that a refusal to enforce 'unreasonable' clauses was the basis for the reluctance of courts to permit

332. Because there was no finding of negligence by the trial judge a new trial was ordered.
333. *Schenker & Co (Aust) Pty Ltd v Maplas Equipment and Services Pty Ltd* [1990] VR 834. See also *Pendal Nominees Pty Ltd v Lednez Industries (Australia) Ltd* (1996) 40 NSWLR 283 at 289. Contrast *E E Caledonia Ltd v Orbit Valve Co Europe* [1994] 1 WLR 1515.
334. [1990] VR 834 at 846 (see Peter Brereton, (1991) 4 JCL 261). See also *Glebe Island Terminals Pty Ltd v Continental Seagram Pty Ltd (The Antwerpen)* (1993) 40 NSWLR 206 at 242–4. Cf *Brown v Petranker* (1991) 22 NSWLR 717 at 722. But cf *Graham v The Royal National Agricultural and Industrial Association of Queensland* [1989] 1 Qd R 624 at 630.
335. (1986) 161 CLR 500.
336. See, eg *Commissioner for Railways (New South Wales) v Quinn* (1946) 72 CLR 345 at 371; *Davis v Pearce Parking Station Pty Ltd* (1954) 91 CLR 642 at 649; *Davis v Commissioner for Main Roads* (1968) 117 CLR 529 at 537; *Bright v Sampson & Duncan Enterprises Pty Ltd* (1985) 1 NSWLR 346 at 359.
337. Cf *Thomas National Transport (Melbourne) Pty Ltd v May & Baker (Australia) Pty Ltd* (1966) 115 CLR 353 at 376–7, where Windeyer J (whose judgment was approved in *Delco*) cited the *Canada SS* case by way of authority for general principles governing the exclusion of liability for negligence. Cf *Davis v Pearce Parking Station Pty Ltd* (1954) 91 CLR 642 at 651.
338. See [769], [771].
339. Cf [704].
340. [1973] QB 400 at 415–17. See also *Levison v Patent Steam Carpet Cleaning Co Ltd* [1978] QB 69 at 79–80.

the exclusion of liability for negligence. He suggested that a clause is unreasonable if it would be unconscionable to allow the defendant to rely on it. However, in the same case, Buckley LJ expressed the orthodox position as follows:[341]

> It is not ... the function of a court ... to fashion a contract in such a way as to produce a result which the court considers that it would have been fair or reasonable for the parties to have intended. The court must attempt to discover what they did in fact intend. In choosing between two or more equally available interpretations of the language used it is of course right that the court should consider which will be likely to produce the more reasonable result, for the parties are more likely to have intended this than a less reasonable result.

More recently, the courts have rejected Lord Denning's approach.[342] For example, although *Photo Production Ltd v Securicor Transport Ltd*[343] indicates that it is relevant to consider the reasonableness of the clause, the case illustrates that in contracts between commercial enterprises a clause is not likely to be regarded as unreasonable in operation. In fact the court was impressed by how reasonable the clause in issue was.

[766] Oral representations and promises. Most cases on the interpretation of exclusion clauses concern attempts to escape liability for breach of contract or negligence. Although such a clause may also apply to pre-contractual statements, a party cannot rely on an exclusion clause to escape liability for a fraudulent misrepresentation.[344] There are two further points.

First, an oral promise or representation may preclude reliance on an exclusion clause in a way which would be inconsistent with the representation. For example, in *Mendelssohn v Normand Ltd*[345] the plaintiff drove into the defendant's garage and received a ticket from the attendant which purported to exclude liability for loss of the contents of the plaintiff's vehicle. The plaintiff had valuable jewellery in a suitcase on the back seat of the car and he naturally wished to lock the vehicle. However, the attendant told him that that was not permitted, and said that he would see to it that the vehicle was locked. The suitcase was stolen because the vehicle was not locked and the court held that the defendant could not rely on the exclusion clause because the attendant's statement had the effect of overriding the exclusion.[346]

Second, a representation or assurance may not only override an exclusion, but also form the basis for a claim in contract or tort. For

---

341. [1973] QB 400 at 421. See also *Bright v Sampson & Duncan Enterprises Pty Ltd* (1985) 1 NSWLR 346 at 366. Cf *Life Savers (A'asia) Ltd v Frigmobile Pty Ltd* [1983] 1 NSWLR 431 at 439.
342. But see M H Ogilvie, 'Fundamental Breach Excluded but not Extinguished: Hunter Engineering v Syncrude Canada' (1990) 17 *CBLJ* 74.
343. [1980] AC 827 (see [749]). See also *Darlington Futures Ltd v Delco Australia Pty Ltd* (1986) 161 CLR 500 at 507–8; *Nissho Iwai Australia Ltd v Malaysian International Shipping Corp Berhad* (1989) 167 CLR 219.
344. See, eg *Jennings v Zilahi-Kiss* (1972) 2 SASR 493 at 410. See also [1123] (misleading and deceptive conduct).
345. [1970] 1 QB 177.
346. This is also an alternative analysis of *Curtis v Chemical Cleaning and Dyeing Co* [1951] 1 KB 805 (see [615]).

example, the assurance in *J Evans & Son (Portsmouth) Ltd v Andrea Merzario Ltd*,[347] as well as overriding the exclusionary provisions of the contract, which would have precluded the plaintiffs claiming damages, provided the basis for the claim. Although there are statements in the English cases[348] which suggest that it is immaterial whether the statement relied on as overriding the exclusion clause is a representation, a promise or part of a collateral contract, it may be important to consider the nature and effect of the statement. If the plaintiff is merely concerned to show that the exclusion clause does not apply, it probably does not matter whether it is in fact a promise or merely a representation: where the plaintiff has relied on the oral statement this will preclude the defendant from invoking the exclusion. However, in cases where the statement forms the basis for the plaintiffs' action in damages, it may be crucial to analyse the nature of the statement.[349] Although a claim for damages in tort or under statute may be made if the statement is a fraudulent (or negligent) misrepresentation,[350] or amounts to conduct prohibited by statute,[351] no claim for contract damages is available unless the statement is in fact a promise[352] supported by consideration.[353] This was the position in *Evans v Merzario*, but will not be so in all cases.

[767] **Third parties.** By virtue of the privity of contract rule,[354] exclusion clauses only protect the parties to the contract. This means that where a party to a contract sues a third party whose negligence has caused loss or damage, the third party will not be permitted to invoke the clause even though it purports to protect the third party. However, in some cases the third party has been able to prove the existence of a promise under which the protection of the exclusion clause is extended beyond the contract in which it is contained.[355] Thus, stevedores have been found to have the benefit of exclusion clauses contained in the bill of lading, evidencing a contract between the carrier and the consignee for the carriage of goods, to which the stevedores are not parties.[356]

[768] **Termination.** The general rule is that termination of the performance of a contract, whether for breach or by frustration, does not of itself prevent reliance on such a clause. The question remains one of intention.[357]

---

347. [1976] 2 All ER 930 (see [707]). Cf *Couchman v Hill* [1947] KB 554 (see [608]).
348. See, eg *Mendelssohn v Normand Ltd* [1970] 1 QB 177 at 186.
349. It is, perhaps, easier to justify rescission; see *Walker v Boyle* [1982] 1 WLR 495.
350. See generally [1025]–[1036]. And see [1076] (statutory right to damages for innocent misrepresentation).
351. For example, under s 52 of the *Trade Practices Act* 1974 (Cth). See [1081], and generally Chapter 11.
352. See generally [605]–[610]. If the statement takes effect as a collateral contract there is the problem of consistency explained in [613].
353. The statement must also be sufficiently definite. See generally Chapters 2 and 3.
354. See generally Chapter 9.
355. See also *Schenker & Co (Aust) Pty Ltd v Maplas Equipment and Services Pty Ltd* [1990] VR 834, which illustrates that the same effect may be achieved through indemnity provisions.
356. See [923]–[926].
357. See [1993].

Operation Under Statute

[769] Forms of statutory control. One feature of contract law in recent years has been the amount of legislative intervention against exclusion clauses. Some provisions, such as ss 68 and 68A of the *Trade Practices Act* 1974 (Cth) are aimed directly at exclusion clauses.[358] Others, such as the *Contracts Review Act* 1980 (NSW) are more general, being aimed at 'unjust', 'unconscionable' or 'unfair' contractual terms.[359] An exclusion clause will come under this form of control if it is found to be deserving of the description used by the statute.

The paragraphs which follow deal in general terms with the impact of such provisions.[360]

[770] Prohibited exclusion clauses. Some statutory provisions prohibit the use of exclusion clauses and make no allowance for 'reasonable' operation. For example, s 68 of the *Trade Practices Act* 1974 (Cth)[361] prohibits the use of clauses which 'exclude, restrict or modify' (or have the effect of excluding, restricting or modifying) the application of the provisions of Div 2 of Pt V of the Act, the exercise of a right conferred, or any 'liability' for breach of a condition or warranty implied by such a provision, or the application of s 75A of the Act.

Although it will be necessary to construe the contract to see whether the clause in issue excludes, restricts or modifies,[362] once this is established it is unnecessary to consider whether or not the parties intended the clause to apply. Assume, for example, that a corporation attempts to limit its liability for breach of the condition that goods sold by it are of merchantable quality.[363] A consumer who has purchased a washing machine, and who suffers loss as a consequence of the breach of that implied term, will not be limited in a claim for damages by the exclusion clause because s 68 renders it void.

[771] Permitted use of exclusion clauses. Statutory provisions which prohibit the use of 'unreasonable' exclusion clauses impliedly permit the use of exclusion clauses which are not unreasonable. For example, s 68A(1) of the *Trade Practices Act* 1974 (Cth)[364] provides that a term in a contract for the supply of goods or services to a consumer is not void under s 68 by reason only of the fact that it limits the liability of the corporation, in any of the ways specified in s 68A(1)(a) or (b). This provision applies to goods or services which are not of a kind ordinarily acquired for personal, domestic

---

358. See [770].
359. See generally [1515]–[1530].
360. Detailed treatment will be found in more specialised works. See, eg Taperell, Vermeesch and Harland, *Trade Practices and Consumer Protection*, 3rd ed, 1983, paras 1742–54; 1771–76.
361. See also *Consumer Affairs and Fair Trading Act* 1990 (NT), s 68; *Fair Trading Act* 1987 (WA), s 34. Cf *Consumer Transactions Act* 1972 (SA), ss 8, 16; *Goods Act* 1958 (Vic), ss 95(1), 97(1), 110(1).
362. And note in that regard s 68(2).
363. See [640].
364. See also *Consumer Affairs and Fair Trading Act* 1990 (NT), s 69; *Fair Trading Act* 1987 (WA), s 35. Cf *Goods Act* 1958 (Vic), ss 97, 110; *Consumer Transactions Act* 1972 (SA), s 8.

or household use or consumption. But even if the goods or services are not of that kind, s 68A(1) will not apply if the consumer establishes that it is not 'fair or reasonable' for the corporation to rely on the term.[365]

[772] Scope of the legislative provisions. The legislative provisions do not apply to all contracts. For example, the *Trade Practices Act* 1974 (Cth) provisions, referred to above,[366] are restricted to contracts for the supply of goods or services to a 'consumer' (as defined).[367]

A second type of limitation is that, generally, prohibitions in relation to the use of exclusion clauses apply only to terms implied by the Acts in which the prohibitions are contained. For example, s 64(1) of the *Sale of Goods Act* 1923 (NSW)[368] renders provisions in a consumer sale void, but only so far as they purport to exclude or restrict the terms implied by the Act, or any liability of the seller for a breach of such a term.[369] However, there is nothing to prevent a seller limiting the operation of an *express* term of the contract, although in some circumstances relief may be given against the operation of the clause, for example, if it is found to be an unjust provision under the *Contracts Review Act* 1980 (NSW).[370]

---

365. Section 68A(2). The matters to be considered are set out in s 68A(3).
366. See [771].
367. See also *Sale of Goods Act* 1923 (NSW), s 64 (consumer sales, as defined by s 62); *Goods Act* 1958 (Vic), ss 95, 97, 110 (sale, or agreement to sell, goods and services as defined by s 85).
368. The same is true of similar provisions in other legislation, including the *Trade Practices Act* 1974 (Cth).
369. The existence of the express condition or warranty does not negative a condition as to merchantable quality implied by the Act: s 64(2).
370. But see Law Reform Commission of NSW, *Issues Paper on Sale of Goods*, IP 5, 1988, para 3.21.

PART IV
Parties to the Contract

Chapter 8

Capacity

Minors	.802
The Age of Majority	802
Contractual Capacity of Minors	804
Contracts for Necessaries	809
Contracts Not for Necessaries	817
Minors' Contracts in New South Wales	827
Mental Disability (Including Intoxication)	.838
Corporations	.849
Vires	851
Expression and Formation of Contractual Assent	857
Pre-incorporation Contracts	862
Unincorporated Associations	.864
The Crown and its Instrumentalities	.869
Bankrupts	.874
Married Women	.877

[801] **Introduction.** There is a presumption at common law that a person who enters into a contract has full capacity to do so. In certain limited cases a person who is under some disability will be exempted fully or partially from the normal rule. Such cases of incapacity are few, and persons alleging that they are protected from the normal consequences of their actions must bear the burden of proving incapacity.[1] This chapter is concerned with those limited cases where a contracting party has less than full contractual capacity.

Minors

The Age of Majority

[802] **Introduction.** By about the 17th century the common law had established 21 as the age at which a person attained adult status for most

---
1. *Borthwick v Carruthers* (1787) 1 TR 648; 99 ER 1300.

purposes. This remained substantially unchanged until quite recently. It was at 21 that a person became entitled to exercise civic responsibilities and to accept civic offices. It was at this age that he or she became fully bound by contracts and transfers of property. Certain limited exceptions to the general rule have been established in modern times by legislation, but for most purposes an individual was not regarded by the law as a fully responsible citizen, relieved of legal disabilities fixed by reference to age, until he or she attained the age of 21.[2] It is not surprising that those jurisdictions which adopted the common law generally adopted also the notion that the age of majority should be 21. Thus the age of majority was until quite recently 21 throughout Australia. A similar position prevailed in Canada, and in most of the American States.

Certain factors, many of relatively recent development, have contributed towards a climate of opinion that the traditional age of 21 is not necessarily the most desirable.[3] An important factor has been an increased awareness of the fact that historically the age of 21 was arrived at because of factors which bear little relevance to modern society. In England, prior to the Norman Conquest, there was no fixed rule as to the age of majority and there appears to have been a tendency to settle upon different ages for different classes of society. Gradually, however, the age at which a military tenant became of age became the age for all. And this age, it seems, was arrived at primarily because it was felt that it was only then that a young knight would have the physical strength, necessitated by the very heavy and bulky armour then in vogue, required to enable him to discharge his military duties.[4]

> Historically the concept is one of property rights in and power over children, as much as of a duty to protect them ... [T]he time has now come when it is in the interest of society generally as well as the individual young people concerned to eradicate from our legal system any residual traces there may be of a legal age of majority imposed for the sole purpose of furthering the interest or serving the convenience of any person or bodies of persons other than the child himself.[5]

Another factor which has undoubtedly influenced views on the age of majority has been medical evidence relating to the maturation process. There is a considerable body of evidence stating that for about the last 100 years there has been a significant trend towards earlier physical maturity in both boys and girls. Of perhaps greater influence has been the belief that the improvement of educational standards has resulted in young people being much better informed as to the world around them than was previously the case. Moreover, the majority of young people will be earning their own living for a considerable period before they turn 21.

2. See generally *King v Jones* (1972) 129 CLR 221.
3. See generally *Report of the Committee on the Age of Majority* ('The Latey Committee Report') 1967, Cmnd 3342; NSW Law Reform Commission, *Report on Infancy in Relation to Contracts and Property*, LRC 6, 1969.
4. Pollock and Maitland, *History of English Law Before the Time of Edward I*, 2nd ed, re-issued 1968, Vol 2, pp 438–9; T E James, 'The Age of Majority' (1960) 4 *Amer Jnl of Legal History* 22.
5. Latey Committee Report, p 23.

While these considerations may point towards the desirability of reducing the age of majority, they do not of themselves compel the selection of one age rather than another. The selection of any age must necessarily be to some extent an arbitrary process. It would indeed be possible to provide that capacity should depend on the maturity and discretion of each individual, but it is suggested that the requirements of certainty and predictability render the establishment of some general rule a practical necessity. It remains true, however, that no matter what age is selected, some people will be fully mature in all senses prior to the attainment of that age, whereas others will not be so until considerably later (and perhaps never).

[803] **Lowering the age of majority.** Such factors resulted, in the space of only a very few years, in the approach generally taken towards the question of the most desirable age of majority being altered drastically. There has indeed been a quite remarkable reversal of an attitude which had been accepted without serious questioning for several centuries. In England and Scotland, following the comprehensive report of the Committee on the Age of Majority, the age of majority was, for most purposes, lowered to 18 years in 1969.[6] This action was followed by a spate of similar developments in other jurisdictions, the general tendency being to lower the age at which full legal capacity is attained to 18. In 1969 the New South Wales Law Reform Commission, in its *Report on Infancy in Relation to Contracts and Property*, recommended that full capacity to contract and deal with property be granted at the age of 18 years. This recommendation was implemented by the passing of the *Minors (Property and Contracts) Act* 1970. As a result of subsequent legislation, the age of majority is now 18 years in all Australian States.[7] One incidental result of this reform has been that the word 'minor' is now generally used to refer to persons under the age of majority, rather than the term 'infant'. At common law 'infant' was used somewhat inappropriately to refer to anyone under the age of 21 years.

The effect of this legislation is, of course, that a contracting party aged 18 years or over will, in the absence of special factors such as mental illness or drunkenness, be unable to rely upon lack of contractual capacity as a defence to an action for breach of contract. Although a person does not attain adult status until the age of 18, there are some limited instances where legislation has provided that in respect of particular types of contract a person under that age shall be treated as though of full age.[8]

---

6. *Family Law Reform Act* 1969 (UK); *Age of Majority (Scotland) Act* 1969 (UK).
7. **ACT**: *Age of Majority Act* 1974; **NT**: *Age of Majority Act* 1981; **Qld**: *Age of Majority Act* 1974; **SA**: *Age of Majority (Reduction) Act* 1971; **Tas**: *Age of Majority Act* 1973; **Vic**: *Age of Majority Act* 1977; **WA**: *Age of Majority Act* 1972.
8. See, eg **Cth**: *Life Insurance Act* 1995, s 199(2) (person who has attained age of 16 has same capacity in relation to life policy as person who has attained the age of 18); **Vic**: *Property Law Act* 1958, s 28B (contracts by minors with registered building societies etc for repayment of loans valid).

Contractual Capacity of Minors[9]

[804] Incapacity not absolute. One of the most important instances of contractual incapacity is that arising from minority. The incapacity of minors is regarded as a protection for minors against the consequences of their own actions and presumed lack of discretion and judgment. It was always recognised, however, that the satisfactory protection of minors required that in certain instances their actions should be binding on them. The point was forcibly made by Lord Mansfield in the leading case of *Zouch d Abbot & Hallet v Parsons*:[10]

> Miserable must the condition of minors be; excluded from the society and commerce of the world; deprived of necessaries, education, employment, and many advantages; if they could do no binding acts. Great inconvenience must arise to others, if they were bound by no act. The law, therefore, at the same time that it protects their imbecility and indiscretion from injury, through their own imprudence, enables them to do binding acts, for their own benefit.

Similar considerations also dictated that even those acts of minors which were not binding on them should not normally be completely devoid of legal effect, for if this were so the result would be that whereas minors were not bound by their contracts, neither could they acquire any enforceable rights under them. Moreover, minors do not enjoy any general immunity from the operation of statutes of limitation.[11] A minor who had purchased defective merchandise would no doubt find somewhat puzzling a concept of 'protection' which prevented the minor from enforcing the seller's contractual guarantee as to the quality of the goods sold. It was therefore established that the contracts of minors were normally only voidable in the sense that although they were not themselves bound, they could if they chose enforce any resulting rights against an adult party. Further, they could generally render such contracts completely binding by confirming them on attaining majority.

[805] Classification of minors' contracts. Under the common law the contracts of minors may be classified into two broad categories. In certain limited cases a minor is bound because the contract falls into the category of contracts for necessaries. In the great majority of cases a contracting minor is not bound. The minor may avoid the contract at his or her election, although an adult contracting with the minor will be bound at the suit of the minor and cannot plead the minor's lack of capacity as a defence.[12] Although most contracts are not binding on minors in the sense that they may repudiate them and thereby avoid liability, the exact nature of such contracts is a matter of some difficulty. Some contracts are binding on minors unless repudiated either during minority or within a reasonable time of attaining majority. What is a reasonable time depends on the

---

9. See generally Harland, *Law of Minors in Relation to Contracts and Property*, 1974, esp Chapter 2; D R Percy, 'The Present Law of Infants' Contracts' (1975) 53 *Can Bar Rev* 1.
10. (1765) 3 Burr 1794 at 1801; 97 ER 1103 at 1106–7.
11. See *O'Brien v O'Brien* (1995) 35 NSWLR 664.
12. See, eg *Zouch d Abbot & Hallet v Parsons* (1765) 3 Burr 1794, 97 ER 1103; *Cockshott v Bennett* (1788) 2 TR 763; 100 ER 411.

circumstances of each case, but once such a reasonable time has elapsed, or if the contract is effectively confirmed after majority, the former minor is bound.[13] Inaction is, in such a case, fatal. Other contracts are not binding on the minor unless ratified on attaining majority. In such cases some positive act whereby the minor adopts or confirms the contract is necessary in order that he or she should become bound by it.

Two qualifications must be made to the classification of minors' contracts outlined above. In Victoria it is provided by statute that most contracts, other than for necessaries, made by minors are 'void'. If this word were to be interpreted literally it would follow that such contracts, while clearly not binding the minor, could also not be enforced by the minor. It will be shown later[14] that the legislation has been applied in such a way as to make it doubtful whether the position is in fact different from that in States where the common law rules are in force. Moreover, there is authority that even under the common law some contracts entered into by minors are completely void. Thus, it has sometimes been said that a trading contract entered into by a minor is void, and yet it is recognised that such contracts may be enforced by the minor, a result impossible to justify if the contract were in truth devoid of any legal effect.[15] It has frequently been asserted that a contract necessarily prejudicial to a minor is void.[16] These statements have, however, usually been made in the context of an attempt to enforce a contract by an adult who had contracted with a minor and it is clearly immaterial in such actions whether the contract is void or voidable. It would seem in principle that, in the interests of minors themselves, such contracts should not be held to be absolutely void. Changing circumstances may make it desirable for a minor to enforce a contract which, when made, may have seemed prejudicial. Moreover, to hold a transaction void would mean that it could not, as is normally the case at common law, be ratified and made fully binding by the minor on attaining majority. In a few cases a purported ratification was in fact held to be ineffective on this ground.[17] The interests of minors would be best protected if they were given an opportunity to decide for themselves, when of full age, whether or not they should be bound. 'It is better for infants, that they shall have an election.'[18]

This account of the law relating to minors' contracts is for the most part concerned with the rules of the common law as to the contracts of minors, for those rules are still, subject to some statutory modification, in force in all States other than New South Wales. In New South Wales those rules have been superseded by a new statutory code embodying radically

13. *Re Constantinople & Alexandria Hotel Co (Ebbett's Case)* (1870) LR 5 Ch App 302; *Re Mundy* (1963) 19 ABC 165 at 171; *Norman Baker Pty Ltd v Baker* (1978) 3 ACLR 856. Possibly the position was different if the contract remained purely executory: *De Garis v Dalgety & Co Ltd* [1915] SALR 102 at 143.
14. See [824].
15. See Salmond and Winfield, *Principles of the Law of Contracts*, 1927, pp 448–50; Pollock's *Principles of Contract*, 13th ed, 1950, pp 47–9.
16. See, eg *Viditz v O'Hagan* [1900] 2 Ch 87 at 97; *De Garis v Dalgety & Co Ltd* [1915] SALR 102.
17. See, eg *De Garis v Dalgety & Co Ltd* [1915] SALR 102; *Alliance Acceptance Co Ltd v Hinton* (1964) 1 DCR (NSW) 5.
18. *Zouch d Abbot & Hallet v Parsons* (1765) 3 Burr 1 794 at 806; 97 ER 1103 at 1109–10. But see [807] as to very young children.

different principles, and the position in that State must therefore be discussed separately.[19]

[806] The duration of incapacity. The incapacity of infancy remained at common law until the infant attained the age of 21, and could not be removed at any earlier stage. In many legal systems a minor may be freed, either partially or wholly, from incapacity by emancipation from parental control,[20] but this was never so at common law. In many systems also the consent of a parent or other guardian may give validity to a particular transaction entered into by a minor.[21] Despite some early dicta to the contrary, this is not the case at common law.[22] Similarly, it became established that the courts had no general power to approve and thus render binding a contract or disposition of property into which a minor proposed to enter. The Court of Chancery had an inherent jurisdiction to approve of certain dealings in respect of a minor's property, but this jurisdiction was very narrow in scope. There is no principle that the court has power to consent to a transaction simply because it is beneficial to the minor, though in some cases legislation provides for such a procedure in respect of particular types of transaction.[23] A number of other provisions have been enacted to mitigate, by providing that minors shall be treated in certain specific situations as though they were of full age, what was felt to be the undue severity of the common law.[24] More general provisions have now been enacted in two States. The provisions in New South Wales allowing minors to be granted contractual capacity by court order in certain circumstances are discussed later.[25] In South Australia a court may approve a minor's contract and thus render it as binding as it would have been if the minor had been of full age; a court may also appoint a person to transact any specified business, or business of a specified class, on behalf of a minor, and any liabilities incurred by that person are enforceable against the minor.[26]

[807] Whether degrees of minority recognised. It has been said that the law recognises no degrees of minority, so that a person who has almost reached the age of majority is just as much a minor as a child of tender years.[27] While this is generally true, some qualification is necessary. In the first place, it seems that the acts of a minor who is so young as to be incapable of understanding the nature of his or her actions are totally void rather than, as is generally true of the acts of a minor, merely voidable.[28]

---

19. See [827]–[837].
20. See *Amos & Walton's Introduction to French Law*, 3rd ed, 1967, p 46; Cohn, *Manual of German Law*, 2nd ed, 1968, Vol 1, p 76.
21. See Cohn, *Manual of German Law*, 2nd ed, 1968, Vol 1, p 76.
22. *Field v Moore* (1855) 7 De G M & G 691 at 706–7; 44 ER 269 at 275; *Capes v Hutton* (1826) 2 Russ 357; 38 ER 370. For a statutory exception see *Life Insurance Act* 1945 (Cth), s 85(1).
23. See, eg *Edwards v Carter* [1893] AC 360; *Royal Exchange Assurance v Hall* (1952) 53 SR (NSW) 107; *Chapman v Chapman* [1954] AC 429. See also *Re Willmott* [1948] St R Qd 256; *Re White* [1959] VR 661. For an example of such legislation see *Conveyancing and Law of Property Act* 1898 (NSW), s 82.
24. See [803].
25. See [830].
26. *Minors' Contracts (Miscellaneous Provisions) Act* 1979 (SA), ss 6, 8.
27. *Morgan v Thorne* (1841) 7 M & W 400 at 408; 151 ER 821 at 825.

Whether a particular minor is capable of such understanding appears to be a question of fact in each case depending upon the stage of development of the individual child, and also upon the nature and complexity of the transaction involved. Likewise, the age of an individual minor was (and remains to be) of considerable importance in many tort situations.[29] Moreover, it will be shown later that the age of a minor is one factor to be considered in deciding whether a particular contract is binding upon the minor as a contract for necessaries.[30]

[808] **Minority as a personal privilege.** Many statements may be found to the effect that minority is a personal privilege which may be availed of only by the minor.[31] This statement is not entirely accurate, for there are some instances when minority may be relied on as a defence by one who has dealt with a minor. Thus, it is established that specific performance will not be decreed in favour of a minor, and a defendant who relies on this rule is obviously taking advantage of the minority of the plaintiff.[32] Likewise at common law a person who contracted to purchase land could object to a title which was defective because of a conveyance by a minor at an earlier point in the chain of title.[33] Similarly, a defendant in a tort action for inducing breach of contract can establish as a defence that the person allegedly induced was a minor and therefore was not bound by the contract.[34]

The true meaning of the rule that minority is a personal privilege is that it is only the minor and not any other party to the transaction who may elect to repudiate a transaction which is voidable on the ground of minority.[35] Thus an adult who contracts with a minor is in most cases liable in an

---

28. *Johnson v Clark* [1908] 1 Ch 303 at 311–12; *Drinkwater v Arthur* (1871) 10 SCR (NSW) 193 at 205–7, 228–9; *O'Shanassy v Jachim* (1876) 1 App Cas 82 at 89; *B(BR) v B(J)* [1968] P 466 at 473. See also *IRC v Mills* [1975] AC 38 at 53. The common law on this point is preserved in NSW by the *Minors (Property and Contracts) Act* 1970, s 18.
29. See, eg *McHale v Watson* (1966) 115 CLR 199 (liability of child in negligence). See also *Re Adoption of Children Act* (1990) 71 NTR 26 (consent of minor to adoption of her child); *Secretary, Department of Health and Community Services v JWB and SMB* (*Marion's* case) (1992) 175 CLR 218; 106 ALR 385 (consent of intellectually disabled person to medical treatment).
30. See [810].
31. See, eg *Coan v Bowles* (1691) 1 Show 165 at 171; 89 ER 514 at 518; *Keane v Boycott* (1795) 2 Hy Bl 511 at 515; 126 ER 676 at 678.
32. *Lumley v Ravenscroft* [1895] 1 QB 683; *Boyd v Ryan* (1947) 48 SR (NSW) 163. It is apparently otherwise where the contract has been ratified upon majority: *Kell v Harris* (1915) 15 SR (NSW) 473. The rule is based upon the fact that such a contract cannot normally be enforced against the minor and hence the mutuality necessary as a condition for the grant of the remedy of specific performance (see [2408]) is lacking. Where the contract can be enforced against the minor (eg under the *Minors (Property and Contracts) Act* 1970 (NSW), s 19) the remedy would no doubt be granted in a suitable case.
33. *Allen v Allen* (1842) 2 Dr & War (Ir) 307 at 339. This is the position at common law. As to the position with Torrens title land see Francis, *Law and Practice Relating to Torrens Title in Australasia*, 1973, Vol 2, pp 3–7.
34. *De Francesco v Barnum* (1890) 45 Ch D 430; *Shears v Mendeloff* (1914) 30 TLR 342. It is not clear whether the contracts in these cases were regarded as void or voidable. If they were merely voidable a different result might have been reached.
35. See, eg *Zouch d Abbot & Hallet v Parsons* (1765) 3 Burr 1794; 97 ER 1103; *Cockshott v Bennett* (1788) 2 TR 763; 100 ER 411.

action brought by the minor to enforce the contract, even though he or she could not have enforced the contract as against the minor.

Contracts for Necessaries

[809] Concept of 'necessaries'. The only exception to the common law rule that minors are not bound by contracts is that they are liable on their contracts for necessaries, and this remains the law in all States except New South Wales. Coke laid down, in a passage which has been frequently cited in later cases, that 'an infant may bind himself to pay for his necessary meat, drinks, apparell, necessary physicke, and such other necessaries, and likewise for his good teaching or instruction, whereby he may profite himself afterwards'.[36] The word 'necessaries' is rather misleading in that it implies that only the bare essentials of life are included. Further, it obscures the fact that the concept is a relative one, as what could amount to necessaries may vary considerably according to the circumstances of the particular individual. Thus, it was said in *Peters v Fleming*:[37]

> It is perfectly clear, that from the earliest time down to the present, the word necessaries was not confined, in its strict sense, to such articles as were necessary to the support of life, but extended to articles fit to maintain the particular person in the state, station, and degree in life in which he is; and therefore we must not take the word 'necessaries' in its unqualified sense, but with the qualification above pointed out.

[810] Relevant factors. The question is whether what was supplied was in fact necessary for the individual minor concerned. In jurisdictions other than New South Wales,[38] the sale of goods legislation, codifying the common law, provides that 'where necessaries are sold and delivered to an infant ... he must pay a reasonable price therefor. "Necessaries" in this section mean goods suitable to the condition in life of such infant, ... and to his actual requirements at the time of the sale and delivery'.[39] It is necessary to examine the social position and means (both present and prospective) of the minor, as well as his or her age and occupation. Regard must be paid to the type of goods which someone in the minor's situation might reasonably have been expected to possess.[40] A married minor is on these principles liable not only for necessary goods purchased for his or her personal use, but also for those purchased by him or her for his or her spouse and children.[41]

---

36. Co Lit, §172a.
37. (1840) 6 M & W 42 at 46–7; 151 ER 314 at 315–16.
38. Section 7 of the *Sale of Goods Act* 1923 (NSW) no longer applies to contracts by minors: *Minors (Property and Contracts) Act* 1970, First Sch. See further [829].
39. **ACT**: *Sale of Goods Act* 1954, s 7; **NT**: *Sale of Goods Act* 1972, s 7; **Qld**: *Sale of Goods Act* 1896, s 5; **SA**: *Sale of Goods Act* 1895, s 2; **Tas**: *Sale of Goods Act* 1896, s 7; **Vic**: *Goods Act* 1958, s 7; **WA**: *Sale of Goods Act* 1895, s 2.
40. *Wharton v McKenzie* (1844) 5 QB 606; 114 ER 1378; *Ryder v Wombwell* (1868) LR 4 Ex 32; *Nash v Inman* [1908] 2 KB 1; *Scarborough v Sturzaker* (1905) 1 Tas LR 117.
41. *Chapple v Cooper* (1844) 13 M & W 252; 153 ER 105. Query the position of a minor engaged to be married: *Quiggan Bros v Baker* [1906] VLR 259; *Sultman v Bond* [1956] St R Qd 180. Following the provisions of the *Marriage Act* 1961 (Cth), s 11 on marriageable age there will in any event be few cases of married minors.

It is not sufficient to show that the goods in question were capable of being necessaries for the particular minor. It is essential to show in addition that they were in fact necessary for the minor in that he or she was not already adequately supplied with similar goods. Whether or not the supplier was aware of this fact is irrelevant.[42] Thus, in *Nash v Inman*[43] an undergraduate had purchased, but not paid for, a number of fancy waistcoats. When it was proved on the evidence of the defendant's father that he was, at the time of the purchase, already adequately supplied with clothes provided by the father, it was held that the question of whether the waistcoats were capable of being necessaries did not arise. This rule puts the trader who has supplied goods to a minor in a difficult position, as the onus of proving that the minor was not adequately supplied lies on the trader, but the rule has been justified on the basis that otherwise the protection afforded to minors would be seriously diminished.

The courts have attempted to draw a distinction between articles of utility (which might be necessaries) and purely luxurious articles (which cannot be necessaries).[44] It cannot be said that the attempt has been particularly successful. The truth is that what might be considered to be essential items by some, would appear to others to be mere extravagances. Articles of ornament, so long as they were not too extravagant for the particular minor and were such as one in the minor's social position might be expected to possess, may in fact be held to be necessaries.[45]

[811] **Services as necessaries.** Although most of the cases deal with necessary goods, the concept is by no means so limited. A minor is no less bound to pay for necessary services rendered. Thus, a minor may be liable for the supply of medical services,[46] for the supply of transportation,[47] and for legal services.[48] Contracts for the education of the minor may also be binding.[49]

[812] **Employment contracts.** A minor may also be bound by contracts of employment and of apprenticeship. In the case of an apprentice the contract is to some extent a contract for education, but this is not essential and a minor is bound by contracts of employment whereby he or she is enabled to earn a living, even though no element of instruction is involved.[50] The question has arisen in a number of cases where the issue was whether a covenant in restraint of trade[51] contained in a contract made during minority was binding on the employee.

---

42. *Barnes & Co v Toye* (1884) 13 QBD 410; *Johnstone v Marks* (1887) 19 QBD 509.
43. [1908] 2 KB 1.
44. *Peters v Fleming* (1840) 6 M & W 42; 151 ER 314; *Ryder v Wombwell* (1868) LR 4 Ex 32.
45. See, eg *Gorer v Readon* (1869) 20 LT 40.
46. *Huggins v Wiseman* (1690) Carth 110; 90 ER 669.
47. *Fawcett v Smethurst* (1914) 84 LJKB 473 at 475. But see *Bojczuk v Gregorcewicz* [1961] SASR 128 (see [813]).
48. *Prince v Haworth* (1904) 20 TLR 313; *McLaughlin v Darcy* (1918) 18 SR (NSW) 585 at 595.
49. *Blennerhassett's Institute of Accountancy Pty Ltd v Gairns* (1938) 55 WN (NSW) 89; *Minister for Education v Oxwell* [1966] WAR 39.

[813] Benefit alone insufficient. There has been a tendency in more recent years to extend the scope of the concept of contracts for necessaries. In a number of cases, minors have been held liable on contracts which, while not strictly contracts of employment or instruction, were regarded as being sufficiently analogous or incidental thereto as to justify their enforcement. In *McLaughlin v Darcy*,[52] for example, a professional boxer, who was about to embark on a tour of the United States in order to obtain boxing engagements, was held liable to a solicitor whom he had employed to assist him in obtaining a passport (a matter of some difficulty owing to wartime controls).[53] It might be thought that these cases were tending to establish a rule that any contract which is for the minor's benefit is binding on the minor. There are many statements in the older cases to this effect, and the proposition has been repeated in some more modern decisions.[54] Confusion has been caused by the fact that some such statements were referring to a quite distinct proposition[55] to the effect that even a contract which is prima facie one for necessaries is not binding on the minor if it contains terms which are so onerous as to render the contract one that is not on the whole for his or her benefit.

It is clearly established, however, that benefit alone is never sufficient to render a contract binding upon a minor. The contract must, in addition, be capable of being brought within the confines of the rather technical concept of a contract for necessaries. If the rule were otherwise, the frequent insistence by the judges that some articles could not be necessary for any minor, no matter how wealthy, would have been quite unnecessary. Moreover, it is established that a minor is never bound by a trading contract, no matter how beneficial the contract may have been. Thus, in *Cowern v Nield*[56] a minor who had established himself in business was not bound by a contract whereby he agreed to sell goods in the course of his business, and such a minor was likewise held in *Mercantile Union Guarantee Corp Ltd v Ball*[57] to be not liable under a contract for goods acquired by him for use in the business. This distinction gives rise to some difficulties in application, but the distinction itself is well established.

50. *Green v Thompson* [1899] 2 QB 1; *Gadd v Thompson* [1911] 1 KB 304; *Evans v Ware* [1892] 3 Ch 502; *Bromley v Smith* [1909] 2 KB 235. Compare *Hamilton v Lethbridge* (1912) 14 CLR 236 (a case involving articles of clerkship) where it was assumed that any contract could be avoided on majority in respect of obligations which were still unperformed, even though the contract might bind the minor during minority; the case ultimately was decided on the ground that the contract had in any event been ratified after majority. For an anomalous common law rule concerning the enforceability of a minor's apprenticeship contract see *Chitty on Contracts*, 26th ed, 1989, Vol 1, p 379. Regard must now be had to legislation concerning apprenticeships.
51. See generally [1634]ff.
52. (1918) 18 SR (NSW) 585.
53. See also *Doyle v White City Stadium Ltd* [1935] 1 KB 110; *Chaplin v Leslie Frewin (Publishers) Ltd* [1966] Ch 71.
54. For example, *De Garis v Dalgety & Co Ltd* [1915] SALR 102 at 156; *Slade v Metrodent Ltd* [1953] 2 QB 112.
55. See [814].
56. [1912] 2 KB 419.
57. [1937] 2 KB 498. See also *Sellin v Scott* (1901) 1 SR (NSW) Eq 64; *Whundo Copper Syndicate v Ferrari* [1962] WAR 24; *Re Mundy* (1963) 19 ABC 165.

A final illustration of the limited scope of the concept of necessaries may be seen in the case of *Bojczuk v Gregorcewicz*.[58] A minor who desired to emigrate from Poland to Australia requested her uncle, already living in Australia, to purchase for her a ticket for her passage and agreed to repay the amount involved after her arrival in Australia. When she refused to do so the uncle sued her, and the question of her liability turned upon whether, had she purchased the ticket herself, that contract would have been one for necessaries. The court found as a matter of fact that the contract was clearly for her benefit, but nonetheless dismissed the uncle's claim. She did not come to Australia for the purpose of furthering her education or to obtain employment, and the contract could not be regarded as one for necessaries or analogous thereto.

[814] Overall benefit to minor. It was shown above that the mere fact that a contract may be said to be for the benefit of a minor does not render the contract binding on the minor. A separate, though closely related point, is that even those contracts which may be prima facie binding as contracts for necessaries will not bind a minor if they contain provisions which are so unfair as to render the contract as a whole one that is, in the circumstances, not for his or her benefit. The issue has normally arisen in the cases in the context of contracts of employment or instruction, but there seems no doubt that the same principles apply generally to contracts for necessaries.[59]

A striking illustration is afforded by *De Francesco v Barnum*,[60] which concerned an agreement whereby a minor was to be bound apprentice for a period of seven years to be taught stage dancing. The minor agreed not to accept any professional engagement during that period without the consent of the master, but the master was under no obligation to provide employment or to maintain her while unemployed. The master also reserved a unilateral right to terminate the apprenticeship if, after a fair trial, he considered her unfit for stage dancing. When the master sued the defendant for the tort of inducing the minor away from her employment, it was held that the contract was not binding on her and hence no action lay for enticement. There was no doubt that the master was a very competent instructor and that his training school was well conducted. Nonetheless, the contract was extremely one-sided and gave to the master an inordinate power without any correlative obligation on his part.

In *De Francesco v Barnum* it was emphasised that the occurrence in a contract of a clause clearly disadvantageous to a minor does not necessarily mean that the contract must fail:[61]

> [I]t is obvious that the contract of apprenticeship or the contract of labour must, like any other contract, contain some stipulations for the benefit of the one contracting party, and some for the benefit of the other ... The Court

---

58. [1961] SASR 128.
59. *Mercantile Union Guarantee Corp Ltd v Ball* [1937] 2 KB 498; *Sultman v Bond* [1956] St R Qd 180; *Alliance Acceptance Co Ltd v Hinton* (1964) 1 DCR (NSW) 5.
60. (1890) 45 Ch D 430.
61. (1890) 45 Ch D 430 at 439. See also *Clements v London & NW Ry Co* [1894] 2 QB 482.

must look at the whole contract, having regard to the circumstances of the case, and determine ... whether the contract is or is not beneficial.

It is on this basis that a minor has been held bound in a number of cases by a clause in restraint of trade contained in an employment or apprenticeship contract.[62] Among the relevant factors in determining whether a particular provision has the effect of rendering a contract as a whole unfair is whether the provision is of a type that is common in contracts of the kind in question, but it is ultimately for the court to decide whether, despite the provision objected to, the contract as a whole can be said to be beneficial to the minor. Where, for example, a minor enters into a contract (such as one for the purchase of goods or services on credit, or for personal transportation), the presence in the contract of a wide exclusion clause may well produce the result that the contract is not binding on the minor, even if the clause is of a type commonly found to be used in such transactions.[63] In *Mercantile Union Guarantee Corp Ltd v Ball*[64] a minor was sued for arrears of instalments under a hire-purchase agreement in respect of a motor lorry which the defendant used in a haulage contracting business which he operated. It was held that the contract was not in any event capable of being one for necessaries but that, even if it were a contract for necessaries, such contracts must be on the whole beneficial to the minor. The acquisition of a large and expensive lorry on onerous hire-purchase terms could not be for the defendant's benefit, even though it was recognised that the terms of the hire-purchase agreement were those common in such contracts.

[815] Loans for the purchase of necessaries. Minors are only liable on contracts for necessaries as such: they are not liable to repay a loan given for necessaries, the rationale being that they might dissipate the money.[65] (Such contracts are made 'void' by statute in Victoria.)[66] However, at common law a person purchasing necessaries for a minor at the minor's request may recover the reasonable cost thereof from the minor,[67] and in equity one who lends money to a minor for the purchase of necessaries is subrogated to the seller's rights against the minor in respect of so much of the money as was actually spent on necessaries.[68] The lender has a similar right where the money is used to discharge liabilities under a contract which is binding on the minor until avoided and which has not been avoided by the minor.[69]

---

62. See, eg *Bromley v Smith* [1909] 2 KB 235; *Gadd v Thompson* [1911] 1 KB 304. Cf *Sir W C Leng & Co Ltd v Andrews* [1909] 1 Ch 763. *Hamilton v Lethbridge* (1912) 14 CLR 236 is sometimes assumed to be an example of such a case (see particularly the statement by Barton J at 253) but the case was in fact decided on a different ground — see fn 49 above. As to covenants in restraint of trade see [1634]ff.
63. *Flower v London & NW Ry Co* [1894] 2 QB 65; *Keays v Great Southern Ry Co* [1941] Ir R 534; *Harnedy v National Greyhound Racing Co Ltd* [1944] Ir R 160.
64. [1937] 2 KB 498.
65. *Lewis v Alleyne* (1888) 4 TLR 560.
66. See [824].
67. *Earle v Peale* (1711) 1 Salk 386; 91 ER 336; *Ellis v Ellis* (1698) 5 Mod 368; 87 ER 711.
68. *Martin v Gale* (1876) 4 Ch D 428; *Gardiner v Wainfur* (1919) 89 LJ Ch 98. See also *Mercantile Credit Ltd v Spinks* [1968] QWN 32.

[816] **Executory contracts for necessaries.** The extent to which a minor is liable on an executory contract for necessaries is a matter of considerable controversy. One view is that a minor's liability for necessaries is never contractual, the liability being one imposed by law in respect of benefits actually received.[70] The other view is that in respect of necessaries a minor does have, by way of exception to the general rule, contractual capacity and is, therefore, bound by an executory contract.[71]

Most commentators hold that a minor is not bound by an executory contract for the sale of goods.[72] On this view the minor is bound only by a restitutionary obligation to pay a reasonable price for necessary goods actually supplied to the minor. This view is based in part on the wording of the sale of goods legislation[73] which provides that 'where necessaries are sold and delivered to an infant ... he must pay a reasonable price therefor. "Necessaries" in this section mean goods suitable to the condition in life of such infant, ... and to his actual requirements at the time of the sale and delivery'. As this provision is thought to have been intended merely to codify the common law, it would follow that the same rule ought to apply to contracts for the supply of necessary services. Most commentators, however, recognise, though often with reluctance,[74] that contracts of employment and analogous contracts are binding even though still executory. That this is so was established by *Roberts v Gray*[75] which involved a professional billiards player who had agreed to participate in a world tour with an established player, the contract being regarded as analogous to a contract of apprenticeship. He was held liable in damages when he refused to commence the tour.

There seems to be no reason in principle why a minor should not be liable for breach of an executory contract for necessary goods or services, although if performance is to take place at too distant a time in the future the question of whether it was in fact beneficial for the minor to be bound so far in advance would arise as a separate issue. It must be admitted that the point is certainly not settled and that the relatively few relevant dicta are conflicting.

Contracts Not for Necessaries

[817] **Voidable contracts.** Those contracts which are not contracts for necessaries are said to be voidable in the sense that they can be avoided by

---

69. *Nottingham Permanent Benefit Building Soc v Thurstan* [1903] AC 6. In that case the minor had attained his majority and had not repudiated the contract. Query if the result would have been the same had he been sued while still a minor. See also *Horvath v Commonwealth of Australia* [1999] 1 VR 643 at 652 per Tadgell JA, 654 per Ormiston JA, 664–5 per Phillips JA.
70. *Nash v Inman* [1908] 2 KB 1 at 8–9; *Re J* [1909] 1 Ch 574 at 577; *Hamilton v Lethbridge* (1912) 14 CLR 236 at 261; *Pontypridd Union v Drew* [1927] 1 KB 214 at 220; *Elkington & Co Ltd v Amery* [1936] 2 All ER 86 at 88.
71. *Nash v Inman* [1908] 2 KB 1 at 11–13; *Roberts v Gray* [1913] 1 KB 520.
72. See in particular P H Winfield, 'Necessaries under the *Sale of Goods Act* 1893' (1942) 58 *LQR* 83.
73. See [810].
74. See in particular the note by P A Landon, (1935) 51 *LQR* 270.
75. [1913] 1 KB 520. See also *Doyle v White City Stadium Ltd* [1935] 1 KB 110.

an election by the minor, although the other contracting party is bound and may not plead the lack of capacity of the minor. (This common law rule has been affected in Victoria by legislation rendering many contracts other than those for necessaries 'void'; the position under this legislation is discussed later.)[76] The contract can be enforced by the minor either during minority or after attaining majority.[77] The position of an adult against whom a minor enforces a contract is unclear. If there remain obligations to be performed by the minor in the future it might well be that at a later date the minor might undergo a change of heart and refuse to perform the obligations. It has been suggested that the granting of a judgment in favour of the minor would render the contract binding,[78] but, as the courts generally have no power to approve a contract on behalf of a minor and thus render it binding, this must be regarded as very doubtful.

Although most contracts are not binding on minors in the sense that they may repudiate them and thereby avoid liability, the exact nature of such contracts is a matter of some difficulty. Some contracts are binding unless repudiated either during minority or within a reasonable time of attaining majority. What is a reasonable time depends on the circumstances of each case, but once such reasonable time has elapsed, or if the contract is effectively confirmed after majority, the former minor is bound.[79] Inaction is, in such a case, fatal. Other contracts are not binding on the minor unless ratified by the minor on attaining majority. In such cases some positive act whereby the minor adopts or confirms the contract is necessary in order that he or she should become bound by it.

[818] **Contracts binding unless repudiated.** The scope of the category of contracts which are binding unless repudiated is most unclear. It certainly includes contracts whereby a minor acquires property of a permanent nature to which continuing obligations are attached.[80] A clear example is a contract under which a minor acquires a leasehold interest in land.[81] The same rule applies where a minor acquires an estate in land,[82] although in most cases it is difficult to see what continuing obligations the minor is subject to under the contract following completion.[83] Presumably the rule was developed by analogy to the rules relating to conveyances. It is settled that the conveyance of an interest in land by or to a minor will vest title in the grantee, although the title will revest in the grantor if the minor subsequently repudiates the conveyance before the lapse of a reasonable time after attaining majority.[84] A contract whereby a minor purchases

76. See [824].
77. *Bruce v Warwick* (1815) 6 Taunt 118; 128 ER 978; *Pearce v Kelly* (1919) 20 SR (NSW) 88 at 92–3.
78. H J Hartwig, 'Infants' Contracts in English Law' (1966) 15 *ICLQ* 780 at 808.
79. See *Re Constantinople & Alexandria Hotel Co (Ebbett's Case)* (1870) LR 5 Ch App 302; *Re Mundy* (1963) 19 ABC 165 at 171; *Norman Baker Pty Ltd v Baker* (1978) 3 ACLR 856. Possibly the position was different if the contract remained purely executory: *De Garis v Dalgety & Co Ltd* [1915] SALR 102 at 143.
80. *NW Ry Co v M'Michael* (1850) 5 Ex 114 at 124; 155 ER 49 at 54; *Whittingham v Murdy* (1889) 60 LT 956.
81. *Davies v Beynon-Harris* (1931) 47 TLR 424.
82. *Whittingham v Murdy* (1889) 60 LT 956; *Scottish Australian Investment Co v Walker* (1889) 10 LR (NSW) 32 at 39.
83. Treitel, *The Law of Contract*, 10th ed, 1999, p 491.

shares from a company, at any rate if the shares are not fully paid up, is in the same category.[85] So too are contracts for marriage settlements[86] and contracts for the purchase of the goodwill of a business.[87] A similar rule applies to a minor who joins a partnership.[88] There is some support for a wider view that to be included also within this category are all contracts involving continuing rights and duties under which a minor has taken a benefit.[89] No satisfactory reason for the existence of this separate category has been advanced.[90]

[819] Contracts not binding unless ratified. It is now generally accepted that, despite a few statements to the contrary, most contracts are not binding on a minor unless ratified by him or her on attaining majority. In this case a minor who takes no positive step to confirm the contract is not bound by it. The minor is bound only if he or she affirms it on attaining majority. The distinction was made clear by the appropriate forms of common law pleading. In the ordinary case a person sued in respect of a contract entered into during minority could simply plead that he or she was a minor at the time of contract. If established, this was a complete defence unless the plaintiff in turn established a ratification of the contract.[91] On the other hand, where the contract was of the type which was binding unless repudiated, a simple plea of minority was bad. The plea must further have alleged that the contract had been repudiated during minority or within a reasonable time of attaining majority.[92] A ratification is an intentional recognition of a previous contract, a confirmation of it with the intention of rendering it binding.[93] This rule was felt to be undesirable in that it could leave a minor open to undesirable pressure from creditors to ratify, on turning 21, contracts previously entered into as a result of youthful indiscretion. Consequently, the effect of ratification was restricted in England in 1828 by the *Statute of Frauds (Amendment) Act (Lord Tenterden's Act)*. It was thereby provided that:

---

84. See, eg *Rain v Fullarton* (1900) 21 LR (NSW) Eq 311; *Thurstan v Nottingham Permanent Benefit Building Soc* [1902] 1 Ch 1 (affirmed [1903] AC 6); *Re Willmott* [1948] St R Qd 256. The rule stated in the text relates to the position at common law. As to the position with Torrens title land see Francis, *Law and Practice Relating to Torrens Title in Australasia*, 1973, Vol 2, pp 3–7.
85. *NW Ry Co v M'Michael* (1850) 5 Ex 114; 155 ER 49. See also *Vickery's Motors Pty Ltd v Tarrant* [1924] VLR 195.
86. *Edwards v Carter* [1893] AC 360.
87. *Aroney v Christianus* (1915) 15 SR (NSW) 118.
88. *Goode v Harrison* (1821) 5 B & Ald 147; 106 ER 1147; *Lovell & Christmas v Beauchamp* [1894] AC 607 at 611.
89. *Hamilton v Lethbridge* (1912) 14 CLR 236 at 256; *Anson's Law of Contract*, 27th ed, 1998, p 215.
90. See generally Treitel, *The Law of Contract*, 10th ed, 1999, p 508.
91. *Williams v Moor* (1843) 11 M & W 256; 152 ER 798; *Aroney v Christianus* (1915) 15 SR (NSW) 118.
92. *Dublin & Wicklow Ry Co v Black* (1852) 8 Ex 181; 155 ER 1310; *Carter v Silber* [1892] 2 Ch 278 at 284. This is certainly so where the defendant has reached majority when sued. The position is possibly otherwise if he or she is still a minor when sued — see [820].
93. *Rowe v Hopwood* (1868) LR 4 QB 1; *Ditcham v Worrall* (1880) 5 CPD 410; *Sultman v Bond* [1956] St R Qd 180.

[N]o action shall be maintained whereby to charge any person upon any promise made after full age to pay any debt contracted during infancy, or upon any ratification made after full age of any promise or simple contract made during infancy, unless such promise or ratification shall be made by some writing signed by the party to be charged therewith.

Similar legislation was enacted in Queensland, New South Wales and the Australian Capital Territory (but has since been repealed in New South Wales and Queensland).[94] In Western Australia and the Northern Territory the United Kingdom legislation is apparently still in force, being Imperial legislation which originally applied to the colonies and has never been replaced. The United Kingdom legislation was originally in force in South Australia for the same reason.[95] However, in South Australia it has been provided by the *Minors' Contracts (Miscellaneous Provisions) Act* 1979, s 4, that where a person has entered into a contract that is, by reason of his or her minority at the time of entering into the contract, unenforceable against him or her, the contract shall remain unenforceable against him or her unless it is ratified by him or her, in writing, on or after the day on which he or she attains his or her majority. It has been assumed that this provision supplements the provision of *Lord Tenterden's Act* discussed above.[96] However, it may be that the effect of s 4 is to impliedly repeal that provision of *Lord Tenterden's Act* in South Australia for by virtue of s 4 any contract (presumably including one resulting in the creation of a debt) coming within the section is unenforceable unless ratified in writing. (If this view is correct, query the position in regard to a debt incurred otherwise than by way of contract, for example, a gratuitous loan.) It appears that s 4 was intended to abolish the distinction between contracts binding unless repudiated and those not binding unless ratified,[97] but it is arguable that contracts of the former type are not 'unenforceable' by reason of minority and are therefore not affected by s 4.[98]

In interpreting *Lord Tenterden's Act* the courts drew a fine distinction between a mere ratification and a fresh promise. The result was that a fresh promise to perform a promise or simple contract (other than a debt) made during minority was actionable though not in writing.[99]

In Victoria it is further provided that any agreement, whether in writing or not, made after majority to repay a loan contracted during minority is void.[100]

---

94. **ACT**: *Mercantile Law Act* 1962, s 15; **NSW**: *Usury Bills of Lading and Written Memoranda Act* 1902, s 9, repealed by *Minors (Property and Contracts) Act* 1970, First Sch; **Qld**: *Statute of Frauds and Limitations Act* 1867, s 12, repealed by *Statute of Frauds* 1972, s 3 (in turn repealed by *Property Law Act* 1974, s 3(2)).
95. See *De Garis v Dalgety & Co Ltd* [1915] SALR 102.
96. See Sutton, *Sales and Consumer Law in Australia and New Zealand*, 4th ed, 1995, p 109.
97. *Forty-first Report of the Law Reform Committee of South Australia Relating to the Contractual Capacity of Infants*, 1977, p 7.
98. Seddon and Ellinghaus, *Cheshire & Fifoot's Law of Contract*, 7th Aust ed, 1997, p 662.
99. *Ditcham v Worrall* (1880) 5 CPD 410; *Watson v Campbell (No 2)* [1920] VLR 347; *Vickery's Motors Pty Ltd v Tarrant* [1924] VLR 195. (Although these cases were decided on s 2 of the *Infants' Relief Act* 1874 (UK) or its Victorian equivalent, the wording of that legislation was, for the purposes of the present distinction, identical with *Lord Tenterden's Act*.)

In Victoria the legislation concerning ratification goes even further. The effect of the provision is that no action shall be brought on any promise made after majority to pay any debt contracted during minority, or on a ratification made after majority of any promise or contract made during minority, whether or not there was any new consideration for the promise or ratification.[101] The distinction noted above between ratification and a fresh promise is relevant here, with the result that in that State a fresh promise to perform a promise or contract other than a debt will be enforceable though a mere ratification is not.[102]

[820] **Repudiation.** A contract which is not binding on a minor may be repudiated by the minor during minority.[103] No formalities are required for the repudiation of a contract by a minor, the repudiation often in practice taking the form of an assertion of a defence based on lack of capacity when steps are taken to enforce the contract. There is some inconclusive authority that any repudiation during minority is not in itself binding and may later be withdrawn, at any rate on attaining majority.[104] While most of these statements were made in the context of contracts which concerned land or shares and which were binding until repudiated, it has been held that the principle is of general application.[105] Such a principle is at least logical, for just as a minor could not be bound by way of contract because of inexperience and immaturity, it might seem inconsistent if the minor were allowed finally to determine a contract which might in fact turn out to be beneficial and which he or she could, in the absence of an effective repudiation, affirm on attaining majority. On the other hand, if such a repudiation were capable of being subsequently withdrawn, those with whom the minor had dealt would have been placed in a position of great uncertainty and hardship.

---

100. *Supreme Court Act* 1986 (Vic), s 51. An exception is made in Victoria in favour of a person who in good faith, for value and without notice, is the holder or an assignee of an instrument relating to the agreement; that person may recover from the minor the amount secured by the instrument and if that person does so recover then the minor may recover that amount from the person to whom the minor gave the instrument. Section 51 replaces *Supreme Court Act* 1958 (Vic), s 71. Earlier ACT (*Money-lenders Act* 1936, s 13), NSW (*Money-lenders and Infants Loans Act* 1941, s 37) and Qld (*Money-Lenders Act* 1916, s 10) provisions have been repealed.
101. *Supreme Court Act* 1986 (Vic), s 50, replacing *Supreme Court Act* 1958 (Vic), s 70. Tasmania had legislation to the same effect as s 70 (*Infants' Relief Act* 1875, s 2), but this was repealed by the *Minors' Contracts Act* 1988 (Tas). As this provision (and also *Lord Tenterden's Act*) contemplates the promise or ratification being unenforceable by action rather than void, it seems that they may have effect for certain purposes: see Salmond and Williams, *Principles of the Law of Contracts*, 2nd ed, 1945, p 312; see also [519]–[520].
102. Query the effect of a fresh promise, at least in the absence of new consideration, to perform a contract which is rendered 'void' by the legislation. As to these contracts see [824].
103. *Newry & Enniskillen Ry Co v Coombe* (1849) 3 Ex 565; 154 ER 970; *Steinberg v Scala (Leeds) Ltd* [1923] 2 Ch 452.
104. *NW Ry Co v M'Michael* (1850) 5 Ex 114 at 127; 155 ER 49 at 55; *Slator v Trimble* (1861) 14 Ir CLR 342 at 351–2. There is also some authority for the view that a contract which is beneficial to a minor cannot be repudiated by the minor during minority, even though he or she could repudiate it on majority: *Hamilton v Lethbridge* (1912) 14 CLR 236 at 261–2.
105. *Sellin v Scott* (1901) 1 SR (NSW) Eq 64.

Another difficulty arises in regard to the effect of repudiation. A contract which is not binding unless ratified does not require repudiation and thus the minor is not bound by any obligations arising under the contract, whether or not those obligations have already accrued. In the case of contracts which are binding until repudiated, the minor is not liable in respect of any obligations which would not have accrued until after the repudiation. As regards those obligations which have already become due prior to the repudiation the position is less clear, although there is some authority that the minor is bound.[106] On this view a minor who leases a flat and repudiates on being sued for arrears of rent is free from any future liability for rent, but remains liable for arrears of rent already accrued due at the time of the repudiation.

[821] **Effect of repudiation on obligations of minor.** A minor is clearly not liable in respect of any future obligations under a repudiated contract. Apart from the possible exception discussed in the preceding paragraph, this is true also in respect of obligations which have accrued due, but remain unperformed, at the time of repudiation. Thus a minor who purchases non-necessary goods is not obliged to pay the purchase price, even though he or she may in fact have received and used those goods.

To the extent, however, that a minor has performed his or her obligations, the effect of repudiation is much less drastic. One might expect that a minor who has paid money under a contract could, following upon repudiation, recover that money, at least where the minor is able to make substantial restitution of any consideration received. It appears, however, that the minor may recover only if there has been a total failure of consideration.[107] In other words, the minor may recover the money only in the relatively rare event that he or she has received no benefit at all under the contract. As to this issue, the question of whether the minor could effect justice by returning what had been received in substantially its original condition is irrelevant. The result of these decisions is rather curious in that whereas the law is perhaps too eager to protect a minor in respect of a purely executory contract, it is very reluctant to intervene to give relief in respect of acts which have been performed under the contract. The rule can obviously operate very arbitrarily. A minor who made a small advance payment in respect of services to be performed in the future (for example, a course of instruction to be given over an extended period of time) may recover the payment if repudiation precedes commencement of performance. On the other hand, if the minor has made a substantial or total payment in advance, once some portion, no matter how small, of the services contracted for has been rendered he or she may recover no part of the money paid.

---

106. *Ketsey's Case* (1631) Cro Jac 320; 79 ER 274; *Leeds & Thirsk Ry v Fearnley* (1849) 4 Ex 26; 154 ER 1110; *Blake v Concannon* (1870) 1 R 4 CL 323. Contra *Newry & Enniskillen Ry Co v Coombe* (1849) 3 Ex 565; 154 ER 970; *NW Ry Co v M'Michael* (1850) 5 Ex 114; 155 ER 49; *Crick v Murray* (1882) 3 LR (NSW) 20. See further A H Hudson, (1957) 35 Can Bar Rev 1213.
107. See, eg *Corpe v Overton* (1833) 10 Bing 252; 131 ER 901; *English v Gibbs* (1888) 9 LR (NSW) 455; *Steinberg v Scala (Leeds) Ltd* [1923] 2 Ch 452; *Curruth v Ern Moro & Amoco Enterprises Pty Ltd* (1966) 60 QJP 106. As to the cases dealing with contracts rendered 'void' by statute see [824].

Following the rule relating to the recovery of money, it has been held that a minor who has transferred goods under a contract may upon repudiation recover those goods only if he or she has received no part of the consideration promised for them.[108] Thus, if a minor agrees to sell a motor cycle, but later regrets the decision and repudiates, the minor is not bound by any outstanding obligations under the contract. If the cycle has already been delivered to the purchaser, the minor may not insist on its return if any part, even though it may be only a small deposit, of the purchase price has been received. It is doubtful whether the extension of the rule to a claim for the recovery of property is justified in principle. The cases involving a claim by a minor for the payment of a sum of money are but a special application of the general rule that an action for restitution will lie where money has been paid for a consideration which has wholly failed.[109] Such actions are actions alleging the existence of a debt (a claim of entitlement to payment of a specified sum of money) and are not appropriate where it is claimed that where a voidable title to a specific chattel has passed, the person transferring the title may, on avoiding the transaction, claim that the title has revested in him or her and that he or she is therefore entitled to recover what is now once again his or her own property.

It is well established that a minor who has transferred land or to whom land has been transferred may repudiate the transfer and thereby revest the title in the original owner.[110] The same rule has been applied to some transfers of personal property, but the position where goods have been transferred has been little discussed and is the subject of conflicting authority.[111] The view that a minor who has transferred title to goods may not later revest title in himself or herself by repudiating the transaction may perhaps be justified on the practical grounds that severe uncertainty and hardship could thereby be caused to others, especially subsequent purchasers, but in that case the rule against recovery should apply whether or not the minor had actually received any portion of the consideration promised.

In South Australia it is now provided that where a person has avoided a contract on the grounds of his or her minority and, before the avoidance of the contract, property passed under it to another party to the contract, a court may order restitution of that property.[112] Such an order may be made on such terms and conditions as the court considers just and may be made notwithstanding that the minor has received some benefit under the contract or that any other party has partly performed his or her obligations under the contract. Thus, a minor who has transferred property to an adult party may obtain an order for the recovery of that property even though he or she has received some consideration for it. (The court would no doubt normally make such an order conditional on restoration of the consideration received, at any rate if the minor still retained it.) It is not clear whether this provision would apply where a minor has paid money to

---

108. *Pearce v Brain* [1929] 2 KB 310.
109. See generally [2306], [2318], [2321].
110. See cases cited in [818].
111. The cases are discussed in Harland, *Law of Minors in Relation to Contracts and Property*, 1974, pp 13–15, 23–4.
112. *Minors' Contracts (Miscellaneous Provisions) Act* 1979, s 7.

the other contracting party; it is arguable that in such a case 'property' has 'passed' under the contract.[113] It is clear that the provision has no application where property has passed to a minor who is seeking to divest himself or herself of it or the adult party is seeking to recover it.

[822] **Effect of repudiation on obligations of adult.** An adult contracting with a minor is in no better position than the minor. If the adult has delivered non-necessary goods to a minor who refuses to pay for them, it is generally assumed that the adult cannot recover that property. Certainly, if this remedy were available, one would have expected that it would have been referred to in the many cases where a supplier sued a minor for the price of goods which were held not to be necessaries. There is some authority that an adult seller who terminates a contract for breach upon the minor purchaser's refusal to pay the price for goods purchased on credit thereby revests in the seller ownership of the goods, which could then be recovered in an action based on the right of ownership.[114] Further, it has been submitted above that in principle repudiation of a contract by a minor should revest title in any goods transferred to the minor under the contract. The existence of either of these supposed remedies is, however, doubtful.

It was held in the much criticised case of *Cowern v Nield*[115] that an adult who had paid for goods which the minor seller later refused to deliver could not recover his money. It has been suggested that in situations where a minor could have recovered upon a total failure of consideration, a similar remedy should be available to an adult,[116] and this suggestion seems clearly correct in principle.

[823] **Effect of fraud by minor.** An adult who contracts with a minor as a result of a fraudulent representation by the minor that he or she is of full age is in a stronger position.[117] It is clearly established that in such a case the minor is not estopped by fraud from relying on lack of capacity as a defence if the minor is sued on the contract. Nor may the minor be sued in an action in tort for deceit, because although a minor is generally liable for his or her torts, the minor is not liable in tort where the awarding of damages would amount to the indirect enforcement of an unenforceable contract.[118] Nonetheless, the minor's fraud does make certain relief available to the other party in equity, though the extent of this relief is a matter of debate. Certainly the minor is liable in equity to restore property which remains in his or her possession and which had been obtained as a result of the minor's fraud. The minor may be required to release the other party from obligations or acts induced by the fraud.[119]

---

113. Contrast Seddon and Ellinghaus, *Cheshire & Fifoot's Law of Contract*, 7th Aust ed, 1997, p 662.
114. *Re Henderson* (1916) 12 Tas LR 40 but contrast *Hall v Wells* [1962] Tas SR 122 at 129. See R W Clarke, 'Contracts for Sale of Non-necessary Goods, Vendor's Remedies Against an Infant Purchaser' (1981) 7 *Univ Tas LR* 85.
115. [1912] 2 KB 419.
116. See Sutton, *Sales and Consumer Law in Australia and New Zealand*, 4th ed, 1995, pp 118–9.
117. See generally Sutton, *Sales and Consumer Law in Australia and New Zealand*, 4th ed, 1995, pp 113–8.
118. See further [825].
119. *R Leslie Ltd v Sheill* [1914] 3 KB 607.

Thus in *Lemprière v Lange*[120] a lease was ordered to be delivered up and cancelled, and in *Clarke v Cobley*[121] a minor was ordered to return to the plaintiff promissory notes obtained by him. It also seems that if the fraudulent minor were actively seeking as plaintiff the assistance of the court, such assistance would be given only on terms that the minor made good the fraudulent representation (or at least restored any benefits obtained).[122] Although this relief would in many cases go a long way towards restoring to the adult what he or she had lost as a result of the minor's fraud, equity stops short of enforcing the contract. No award of damages against the minor will be made. A minor who has obtained a loan by fraud and has spent the proceeds may not be forced to repay the sum borrowed. Where the minor has obtained property and disposed of it, the minor may not be ordered to pay the value of that property. 'Restitution stopped where repayment began.'[123]

There is one possible exception to the principle that a minor who has disposed of the property obtained as a result of perpetrating a fraud cannot be liable. Under the equitable doctrine of tracing, property which belongs in equity to one person may in certain circumstances be followed into the hands of another who holds property or a fund which may be said to represent the original property. In *R Leslie Ltd v Sheill*[124] Lord Sumner suggested that these principles might be applied to a fraudulent minor. It would follow on this view that where a minor borrows money and spends that money on the purchase of a motor car, the lender would be able to recover the value of the car. The remedy of tracing is, however, strictly a proprietary one, so that if the car has depreciated in value this loss will fall on the lender. Similarly, if the minor has subsequently sold the car and dissipated the proceeds so that there are no tangible assets which could be said to represent the money borrowed, no recovery would be possible.[125] The practical difficulties involved in applying the principles of tracing would no doubt frequently make such a right of recovery more theoretical than real, but the remedy, if available, could clearly serve in many situations to prevent substantial injustice.

The scope of the equitable remedy of restitution is, however, severely limited. It applies only in cases of fraud, and it seems that an express representation by the minor that he or she was of full age is required.[126] The hardship which could be caused by the common law rules would

---

120. (1879) 12 Ch D 675.
121. (1789) 2 Cox 173; 30 ER 80.
122. *Overton v Banister* (1844) 3 Hare 503 at 506; 67 ER 479 at 481; *R Leslie Ltd v Sheill* [1914] 3 KB 607 at 626.
123. *R Leslie Ltd v Sheill* [1914] 3 KB 607 at 618.
124. [1914] 3 KB 607.
125. *Stocks v Wilson* [1913] 2 KB 235, which was criticised in *R Leslie Ltd v Sheill* [1914] 3 KB 607, must be regarded as of doubtful authority in so far as a minor was ordered to pay the amount received by him for property of which he had disposed without any inquiry being made as to whether he still retained that money or its proceeds. The same may be said of *Campbell v Ridgely* (1887) 13 VLR 701.
126. *Stikeman v Dawson* (1847) 1 De G & Sm 90; 63 ER 984. See also *Nelson v Stocker* (1859) 4 De G & J 458; 45 ER 178; *MacLean v Dummett* (1869) 22 LT 710; *Miller v Blankley* (1878) 38 LT 527; *Re Jones* (1881) 18 Ch D 109. The contrary view is argued by P S Atiyah, 'The Liability of Infants in Fraud and Restitution' (1959) 22 MLR 273.

undoubtedly be mitigated to a substantial extent were the courts to apply generally a principle analogous to that of tracing, and if this approach were adopted there is no reason the remedy should not be made available to a minor seeking to recover money or property from an adult. It has indeed been argued that the general equitable principle of tracing is applicable in all cases irrespective of fraud[127] but it is doubtful whether this is in fact the case.

[824] **Statutory modification of the common law.** The rules described above were modified in England by the passing of the *Infants' Relief Act* 1874 (UK). This legislation was substantially adopted in Tasmania by the *Infants' Relief Act* 1875 (Tas) and, with one alteration, by Victoria in ss 69 and 70 of the *Supreme Court Act* 1958. The *Infants' Relief Act* was generally regarded as being most unsatisfactory and has recently been repealed in England[128] and in Tasmania.[129] In Victoria ss 69 and 70 of the *Supreme Court Act* 1958 (Vic) have been replaced by ss 49 and 50 of the *Supreme Court Act* 1986 (Vic). (These sections have been somewhat simplified but are to substantially the same effect as their predecessors.)[130] Section 49 (which corresponds to s 1 of the English Act of 1874) provides that:

> The following contracts entered into by a minor are void:
>
> (a) Contracts for the repayment of money lent or to be lent;
>
> (b) Contracts for payment for goods supplied or to be supplied, other than necessaries;
>
> (c) Accounts stated.

The English Act (and previously s 69 of the Victorian Act) rendered the enumerated contracts 'absolutely void'. The omission of the epithet 'absolutely' in the new Victorian provision presumably has no substantive effect. Section 50 of the Victorian Act (corresponding to s 2 of the English Act) relates to the ratification of a contract entered into during minority and has already been discussed.[131]

It will be noticed that s 49 does not apply to all contracts, other than those for necessaries, into which a minor may enter, but only to the three types of contract enumerated. It does not, for example, apply to contracts for the supply of services to a minor or to contracts of employment. Nor does it apply to those contracts[132] which are binding on a minor unless and until repudiated by him or her.

The question of the effect of the *Infants' Relief Act* and similar provisions upon the previous law has given rise to much controversy. One might have

---

127. P S Atiyah, 'The Liability of Infants in Fraud and Restitution' (1959) 22 MLR 273.
128. *Minors' Contracts Act* 1987 (UK), s 1.
129. *Minors' Contracts Act* 1988 (Tas), s 5.
130. For the history see *Horvarth v Commonwealth of Australia* [1999] 1 VR 643 at 662–8 per Phillips JA.
131. See [819]. Section 49 (and previously s 69) refers to contracts 'for payment for goods' rather than, as did the English Act, to contracts 'for goods'.
132. Discussed [818]. Section 49 may perhaps apply if a contract of the type described therein can be regarded as coming within the category of contracts binding unless repudiated; eg a contract for the supply of goods under a credit sale contract or a contract of lease would arguably be such a contract.

expected that a contract which was rendered 'absolutely void' by s 1 was one which, unlike a contract unenforceable against a minor at common law, could not be enforced by the minor. If this were the result it would follow that a minor who had purchased defective goods would fail if he or she sought to recover damages in an action based on breach of a term, express or implied, relating to the quality of goods, and it has generally been assumed that, despite the wording of the legislation, the minor's right to enforce a contract was not affected.[133] The contrary view had, however, strong supporters[134] and the point was never definitively determined. It should be noted that the insertion of the words 'for payment' in the Victorian Act may render contracts for the supply of goods void in so far as a minor's promise to pay the purchase price was concerned, leaving such contracts otherwise unaffected and enabling the minor to enforce the contract against the adult. It is, however, arguable that it is the contract for supply as a whole that is void, but that the words 'for payment' render the legislation applicable only to contracts for the supply of goods on credit, leaving cash sales unaffected.[135]

If the word 'void' were to be literally interpreted it might be thought that it would follow that a minor who had paid money pursuant to a contract within the legislation would be able to recover the amount paid. A similar argument could be made in respect of goods transferred by the minor, although there would still be some force in the argument that delivery with an intention to pass property would be effective to pass title even though the contract pursuant to which the delivery was made was void. The cases, however, appear to establish that the same rule applies as with a contract governed by the common law, that is that money or property is irrecoverable unless the minor has suffered a total failure of consideration in the sense that he or she has in fact received no part of the benefits promised.[136]

The generally accepted view as to the effect of a delivery of goods to a minor who purchases under a 'void' contract is that the delivery, provided it was made with the intention to pass property, will be effective to do so.[137]

[825] Liability in tort. At common law a minor, at any rate when old enough to appreciate the seriousness and consequences of his or her action, is liable in tort.[138] This is, however, subject to the important qualification that a minor is not liable in tort where to hold the minor liable would amount to the indirect enforcement of an otherwise unenforceable

---

133. See, eg Seddon and Ellinghaus, *Cheshire & Fifoot's Law of Contract*, 7th Aust ed, 1997, pp 653–5.
134. See in particular Treitel, *The Law of Contract*, 6th ed, 1983, pp 422–3.
135. See Seddon and Ellinghaus, *Cheshire & Fifoot's Law of Contract*, 7th Aust ed, 1997, p 652; Sutton, *Sales and Consumer Law in Australia and New Zealand*, 4th ed, 1995, p 107.
136. *Valentini v Canali* (1889) 24 QBD 166 appeared to suggest that money could be recovered where the minor could make substantial restitution of any consideration received by him (see also *Coras v Webb* [1942] St R Qd 66 at 73); subsequent cases have, however, interpreted *Valentini v Canali* as establishing the rule stated in the text: *Pearce v Brain* [1929] 2 KB 310; *Woolf v Associated Finance Pty Ltd* [1956] VLR 51. See also Mason and Carter, *Restitution Law in Australia*, 1995, para 1017.
137. *Stocks v Wilson* [1913] 2 KB 235 at 246–7; *Re Henderson* (1916) 12 Tas LR 40 at 41; *Hall v Wells* [1962] Tas SR 122 at 123–8.

contract. Thus, a minor who hires goods and damages them by negligent use may not be sued in tort, for to allow such an action would, it is said, in substance amount to holding the minor liable for the misperformance of the contract.[139] On the other hand, the minor is not totally immune in that he or she will be liable if the wrongful act, 'though concerned with the subject matter of a contract, and such that, but for the contract, there would have been no opportunity of committing it, is nevertheless independent of the contract in the sense of not being an act of the kind contemplated by it'.[140] Thus, where a minor hired a horse and was expressly told that it was not fit for jumping, he was held liable in tort when the horse was injured in attempting to jump it over a fence. The act of jumping the horse was in the circumstances 'not within the object and purpose of the hiring'.[141] Likewise a minor who hired a chattel was held liable in detinue when he failed, because he had wrongfully disposed of it to a third party, to return it on the expiration of the hiring.[142] The same reasoning was applied where it was sought to make a minor who had misappropriated money liable in quasi-contract.[143]

Perhaps the most important application of the above rule is in cases where a minor has induced another by fraud to enter into a contract. The fraud is usually, though not necessarily, a misrepresentation by the minor that he or she is of full age. We have seen that that fraud does not, whether by the operation of an estoppel or otherwise, render a minor liable on the contract.[144] Further, the minor cannot be held liable for the tort of deceit, for to do so, it is said, would be to enforce indirectly the unenforceable contract.[145] Thus, for example, the rule prevents a person, who was induced by the fraud of a minor to lend money to the minor, from recovering damages in deceit, even though it might well be said that the result of such an action would not be to enforce the contract of loan but to effect restitution to the defrauded party and to prevent the minor from obtaining an undeserved windfall at the expense of the party who had been deceived. (The severity of the application of this rule may be mitigated in some cases where the equitable principle of restitution is applicable.)[146] On similar reasoning it has generally been assumed that a minor who has purchased goods under a contract which is not binding on the minor cannot be sued in tort if he or she keeps the goods but refuses to pay for them.[147]

---

138. See, eg *Jennings v Rundall* (1799) 8 TR 335 at 337; 101 ER 1419 at 1421; *Bristow v Eastman* (1794) 1 Esp 172; 170 ER 317; *R v McDonald* (1885) 15 QBD 323 at 328; *Re Henderson* (1916) 12 Tas LR 40.
139. *Jennings v Rundall* (1799) 8 TR 335; 101 ER 1419.
140. *Pollock's Principles of Contract*, 13th ed, 1950, p 63.
141. *Burnard v Haggis* (1863) 14 CB (NS) 45; 143 ER 360.
142. *Ballett v Mingay* [1943] 1 KB 281. See also *Walley v Holt* (1876) 35 LT 631.
143. *Bristow v Eastman* (1794) 1 Esp 172; 170 ER 317; *Re Seager; Sealey v Briggs* (1889) 60 LT 665; *Peters v Tuck* (1915) 11 Tas LR 30. But see *R Leslie Ltd v Sheill* [1914] 3 KB 607 at 621.
144. See, eg *Levene v Brougham* (1909) 25 TLR 265; *R Leslie Ltd v Sheill* [1914] 3 KB 607; *Watson v Campbell (No 2)* [1920] VLR 347.
145. See, eg *Liverpool Adelphi Loan Association v Fairhurst* (1854) 9 Ex 422; 156 ER 180; *R Leslie Ltd v Sheill* [1914] 3 KB 607.
146. See [823].

Capacity [827]

[826] **Guarantees of contractual obligations of a minor.** A minor who wishes to purchase goods or services on credit will, because of the danger that he or she will not be contractually liable, usually find that the prospective supplier is not prepared, on becoming aware of the minor's age, to proceed with the proposed transaction. The supplier will sometimes, however, be prepared to contract with the minor if the latter's obligations are guaranteed by some responsible adult, such as the minor's parent. It was held in *Coutts & Co v Browne-Lecky*,[148] that an adult was not liable on his or her guarantee of a minor's contract where that contract was rendered 'absolutely void' by the Infants' Relief Act 1874 (UK). There being no principal obligation, there could be no accessory obligation under which the guarantor could be liable. This decision is not directly applicable in those jurisdictions where a minor's contract is, unless for necessaries, merely voidable at the minor's option and not void. However, it seems that as the obligation of a guarantor is an accessory obligation, the guarantor will not be liable, at any rate where, as will usually be the case when a guarantor is called upon to pay, the minor has repudiated the principal contract.[149] An adult will in any event be liable if the contract is construed as one of indemnity rather than of guarantee, because in that case the adult is liable as a principal irrespective of whether the minor is also liable.[150] These difficulties are avoided in New South Wales, South Australia and Tasmania where it is provided that a guarantor of a minor's contract is bound to the extent to which the guarantor would have been bound if the minor had been of full age.[151]

Minors' Contracts in New South Wales

[827] **Background.** There has for some time been considerable dissatisfaction with the law concerning minors' contracts as being an area of the law which, perhaps more than most other areas, has retained with relatively little modification basic approaches developed several centuries ago but which, despite the antiquity of its general principles, remains subject to quite unnecessary complexity and uncertainty. Thus it has been remarked that 'the complexities of the law are not related to the needs of

---

147. See *Chitty on Contracts*, 28th ed, 1999, Vol I, para 6-133. But see *Re Henderson* (1916) 12 Tas LR 40 (see [822]).
148. [1947] KB 104, followed in *Robinson's Motor Vehicles Ltd v Graham* [1956] NZLR 545.
149. *Land & Homes (WA) Ltd v Roe* (1936) 39 WALR 27 (where the opinion was expressed that possibly the guarantor would be liable if the minor failed, following upon repudiation, to return property which he or she had received under the contract). See also *Minister for Education v Oxwell* [1966] WAR 39 at 40.
150. As to the distinction between guarantee and indemnity see [1507].
151. **NSW**: *Minors (Property and Contracts) Act* 1970, s 47; **SA**: *Minors' Contracts (Miscellaneous provisions) Act* 1979, s 5; **Tas**: *Minors' Contracts Act* 1988, s 4. Note also that under the consumer credit legislation similar provision is made in respect of the liability of certain persons under a guarantee (which is defined to include indemnity) in respect of a regulated contract where the debtor is a minor; this provision does not, however, apply unless a prominent warning is given in the prescribed manner that the guarantor may not have the right to recover from the minor amounts that the guarantor is liable to pay: **ACT**: *Credit Act* 1985, s 140; **NSW**: *Credit Act* 1984, s 140; **Qld**: *Credit Act* 1987, s 136(1); **Vic**: *Credit Act* 1984, s 140; **WA**: *Credit Act* 1984, s 140.

the persons affected by it. It is said that it is unfair to those who deal with infants and disadvantageous to infants themselves in that others are deterred from dealing with them'.[152] As a result of such dissatisfaction, the New South Wales Law Reform Commission recommended in 1969 the adoption of a new statutory code[153] and this recommendation was implemented by the passing of the *Minors (Property and Contracts) Act* 1970.[154] A number of other law reform bodies have examined the matter and it has correctly been remarked that 'it is perhaps indicative of the difficulties in this area of law that these reports do not disclose a common approach, still less, a common set of recommendations'.[155]

The New South Wales legislation is a bold attempt to recast almost completely the law of minors' contracts, and the attempt made to deal with some of the difficulties referred to earlier in this chapter is therefore of interest to lawyers in other jurisdictions.

[828] **'Civil acts' which are 'presumptively binding'.** The *Minors (Property and Contracts) Act* is intended to be a code replacing the common law rules (s 17), although we shall see that those rules may on occasion supply some guidance in interpreting the Act. The central concept in the legislation is that of a 'civil act', which is defined to mean 'any act relating to contractual or proprietary rights or obligations or to any chose in action, whether having effect at law or in equity' (s 6(1)). This broad concept has been adopted from the civil law notion of an 'act in the law' or 'juristic act', which has been defined as 'an expression of will, the intention and normal effect of which is to produce a lawful change in the legal position of its author'.[156] The scheme of the Act is to deal with the effect of a civil act in which a minor has participated, and the Act therefore has important implications far beyond the law of contract.

The following discussion will be confined to the impact of the legislation upon the law of contract, but it is important to notice that in practice one of the most important types of civil act will be a contract and, as incidental thereto, an election to rescind or determine a contract for fraud, mistake, breach or any other cause. A disposition of property (also defined in broad terms in s 6(1)) is also a civil act. Many civil acts in which a minor participates are rendered 'presumptively binding' on the minor. This phrase may at first sight be somewhat misleading in that it may be thought to imply that there is only a prima facie presumption, which might in appropriate circumstances be rebutted, that such civil acts will bind the

---

152. *Report of the Committee on the Age of Majority* ('Latey Committee Report'), 1967, Cmnd 3342, pp 74–5.
153. *Report on Infancy in Relation to Contracts and Property*, LRC 6, 1969.
154. See generally Harland, *Law of Minors in Relation to Contracts and Property*, 1974; D J Harland, 'The Contractual Capacity of Minors — A New Approach' (1973) 7 *Syd LR* 41.
155. *Forty-first Report of the Law Reform Committee of South Australia Relating to the Contractual Capacity of Infants*, 1977, p 4. See also Law Commission, *Law of Contract — Minors' Contracts*, Law Com No 131, 1984; Victorian Chief Justice's Law Reform Committee, *Infancy* (No 3), 1970; Law Reform Commission of Tasmania, *Report on Contracts and the Disposition of Property by Minors*, Report No 48, 1987; Law Reform Commission of Western Australia, *Report on Minors' Contracts* (Project No 25, Pt 11) 1988.
156. *Amos and Walton's Introduction to French Law*, 3rd ed, 1967, p 21.

minor. However, under s 6(3) a presumptively binding civil act is one which is as binding on a minor as if he or she were not under the disability of infancy at the time of his or her participation in the civil act. In other words, the validity of the civil act may not be attacked on the basis that one of the parties to it is a minor, but defences based on other vitiating factors (such as fraud, mistake or illegality) remain available.

[829] **Beneficial contracts.** Section 19 provides that where a minor participates in a civil act and such participation is for the minor's benefit, at the time of participation, that civil act is presumptively binding on the minor.[157] An important effect of s 19 is that where a minor has entered into a contract, the sole question arising when it is sought to determine whether the minor may escape liability on the ground of minority is whether entering into the contract was for his or her benefit. It is no longer necessary to ask whether the contract is capable of falling within the technical and narrow category of contracts for necessaries. In circumstances such as those arising in *Bojczuk v Gregorcewicz*[158] the minor would be presumptively bound. It is presumably necessary that the contract be on the whole beneficial in that it contains no unduly harsh or onerous provisions, and the principles developed at common law and discussed previously[159] will no doubt be of assistance. Moreover, a contract to buy goods which were beyond a minor's financial means or were of a kind with which the minor was already adequately supplied could hardly be said to be for the minor's benefit even though the contract was perfectly fair in its terms, and in such cases the types of consideration discussed in *Nash v Inman*[160] will continue, it is submitted, to be relevant. Nonetheless, a minor may be bound under s 19 in a much wider range of circumstances than is the case at common law, and in particular there is in New South Wales no longer any absolute rule that a minor will never be bound by a trading contract or a contract of loan. It is also clear that where s 19 applies the minor is presumptively bound even though the contract is executory.[161]

[830] **Grant of capacity.** We have seen[162] that at common law there is no means whereby a minor may, prior to attaining the age of majority, be freed from the disabilities of minority, whether by parental emancipation or judicial decree. Section 26 now empowers the Supreme Court to make an order granting a minor capacity to enter into all civil acts (amounting to a general grant of adult capacity for the purposes of civil acts). The court may also grant capacity to enter into any description of civil acts or a specific civil act. Courts of petty sessions may also grant capacity in certain circumstances in respect of a particular proposed contract (s 27). No such order may be made unless the court is satisfied that the making of the order

---

157. See also s 22 (civil act entered into by a minor pursuant to a contractual or other duty binding on him or her is itself presumptively binding on the minor), s 23 (investment made by a minor in certain government securities is presumptively binding), and s 24 (civil act presumptively binding in favour of third parties in certain circumstances).
158. [1961] SASR 128, discussed [813].
159. See [814].
160. [1908] 2 KB 1.
161. Compare the position at common law re necessaries — see [816].
162. See [806].

will be for the benefit of the minor, and any contract or other civil act entered into pursuant to such an order is presumptively binding on the minor. While this procedure will no doubt not be frequently used, it nonetheless provides a useful measure of flexibility which was previously lacking.

[831] **Affirmation.** In many cases a contract which is not initially presumptively binding on a minor will subsequently be rendered so. Once a minor attains the age of 18, he or she may affirm, and thus render presumptively binding on the minor, any civil act in which he or she participated during minority (s 30). An incentive towards affirmation is provided by the fact that the minor may not enforce against any other party a contract which is not presumptively binding on the minor (s 39). Unlike the position in those Australian jurisdictions which retain *Lord Tenterden's Act* (1828) (Imp),[163] it is not necessary that the affirmation be in writing and, indeed, it is expressly provided that the affirmation may be by conduct. Although a minor may not affirm a contract while a minor, it may be affirmed on the minor's behalf by a court if the court considers that affirmation will be for his or her benefit: s 30.

[832] **Repudiation.** A minor who has entered into a contract which is not presumptively binding on him or her may repudiate that contract at any time prior to the minor's 19th birthday, provided that the contract is not, at the time of repudiation, for the minor's benefit (s 31). The repudiation is, however, ineffective unless certain formalities, requiring the service of written notice, are complied with (s 33). Alternatively, a court may repudiate on behalf of the minor at any time prior to his or her 18th birthday, provided that the contract does not appear to the court to be for the benefit of the minor (s 34). A minor is not, of course, bound by a contract which is not presumptively binding on him or her, but it will nonetheless often be important for the minor to ensure that an effective repudiation is made. In the first place, any contract which is not presumptively binding on the minor will automatically become so if not effectively repudiated prior to his or her 19th birthday (s 38). Moreover, the important powers of the courts, discussed below, to adjust the rights of the parties to a contract which is not presumptively binding arise only once the contract has been repudiated.

Under the previous law an adult who contracted with a minor might be placed in a position of considerable hardship. In most cases the adult could not enforce the contract against the minor. But nor could the adult safely assume that the contract would not be enforced against him or her at some future time, for although the minor could elect to repudiate the contract the adult had no such privilege. Section 36 attempts to overcome this problem by providing that any person interested in a contract into which a minor has entered may require a court to elect to affirm or to repudiate on behalf of the minor.

[833] **Adjustment upon repudiation.** Upon repudiation of a contract the courts acquire jurisdiction under s 37 to adjust the rights of the parties

---

163. See [819].

to the contract. Section 37 is a key provision in the Act and gives the courts a wide discretion in attempting to produce a result that is fair to all parties. The court may, if it thinks fit, confirm (and enforce) the contract in whole or in part, but except in so far as it adopts this course its basic aim is to be to attempt so far as is practicable to restore the parties to their positions prior to the time that the contract was made. This aim is, however, qualified where one of the parties has derived 'property, services or other things' under the contract. In that case an adult party will be ordered to make just compensation for what he or she has received, and a party who is (or was, at the time of contracting) a minor will be ordered to make just compensation to the extent that what the minor received is for his or her benefit. Presumably such compensation will be ordered only where the benefit received is not capable of being restored to the other party. Except in so far as compensation must be ordered in respect of benefits which have been received and cannot be returned (for example, the benefit of services rendered under the contract) the court's discretion is not limited. The courts will no doubt aim to strike a fair balance between the conflicting interests of the parties. On the one hand, there is the interest of the minor that his or her economic position should not be severely affected as a result of his or her lack of discretion and experience. On the other hand, it is often harsh to inflict the whole of such a loss on an adult party, especially if there was no unfair dealing by the adult and he or she reasonably assumed that the minor was aged 18 or over.

[834] Adjustment where disposition of property presumptively binding. No repudiation, and no adjustment of rights under s 37, may be made of a civil act which is presumptively binding on a minor. This point assumes added importance by reason of the fact that although a contract may not be presumptively binding on a minor, a disposition of property made pursuant to that contract may be presumptively binding. Section 20 provides that where a disposition of property is made by a minor pursuant to a contract and he or she receives at least part of the consideration therefor, the disposition of property is presumptively binding on the minor provided that the consideration of the other party is not, at the time of the disposition, manifestly inadequate. Similarly, where a disposition of property is made to a minor pursuant to a contract, he or she is presumptively bound by the disposition if the consideration promised by the minor is not, at the time of the disposition, manifestly excessive.

Section 20 does not render the contract as such presumptively binding on the minor, who will not be liable under the contract in respect of any outstanding obligations on his or her part, but he or she will be unable to insist on the property transferred being revested in the party who made the disposition.[164] Consequently, if a minor agrees to purchase a motor car and title has passed to the minor by delivery, he or she may not, if the price to be paid is not manifestly excessive, unilaterally insist upon the seller taking

164. Section 20(3) provides that 'save to the extent to which, under Pt III of the *Sale of Goods Act* 1923 (NSW), or otherwise, a promise may operate as a disposition of property, subsection (2) of this section does not make presumptively binding on a minor a promise by him which is the whole or part of the consideration for a disposition of property to him'.

[834]

back the vehicle and returning any money paid by the minor. On the other hand, as the contract of sale is not presumptively binding on the minor, the seller may not, unless the contract has been affirmed, sue the minor for any balance outstanding of the purchase price. Alternatively, once the contract has been repudiated (and the seller may if necessary require a court to elect on behalf of the minor whether the contract is to be affirmed or repudiated), the court must, if requested by the seller, make an order under s 37, but in that case the court is not bound, in assessing the compensation to be paid by the minor, by the contractually agreed price. Similarly, where a minor agrees to sell to an adult property for a price which is not manifestly inadequate and receives part of the purchase price (it may be only a small deposit on the total price), the minor cannot, once having transferred title in the property sold, insist upon that property being returned, even though the contract of sale is not presumptively binding on the minor. If the contract is affirmed the minor may sue the buyer for the balance outstanding. If the contract is repudiated, the purchaser will, unless the court in exercising its powers under s 37 decides to confirm the contract, be ordered to pay just compensation, which may be found by the court to be in excess of the purchase price.

[835] **Certificates under ss 28 and 29.** Sections 28 and 29 provide a procedure whereby the presumptively binding nature of a disposition of property for consideration made by or to a minor may be established at the time when the disposition is made. Once a disposition becomes presumptively binding in this manner, the same consequences flow as where a disposition has become presumptively binding under s 20. The disposition must be made pursuant to a certificate, issued not more than seven days before the making of the disposition, given by the Public Trustee or an independently instructed and employed solicitor. The certificate must state a number of matters referred to in ss 28 and 29, including that the person giving it is satisfied that the consideration is not manifestly excessive or inadequate as the case may be.

[836] **Difficulties in making adjustment upon repudiation.** The common law rules as to the position of the parties to a contract which has been repudiated on the grounds of incapacity of one of the parties are uncertain and can operate very harshly. This complex problem can probably only be handled satisfactorily by granting a fairly wide discretion to the courts. On this ground the power granted to the New South Wales courts under s 37 is to be welcomed, although the extent to which the courts must order the payment of compensation for benefits actually received is somewhat obscure and may lead to difficulties in the future. The provisions concerning presumptively binding dispositions of property are perhaps more controversial, for it may seem harsh that a minor should be necessarily bound under s 20 by a disposition of property where the minor has agreed to purchase some extravagant luxury, albeit at a fair price. The view of the New South Wales Law Reform Commission, on whose draft Bill the Act is based, was that as a general rule a completed transfer of property should not be able to be later unsettled on the ground of lack of capacity.[165] And it should be remembered that these provisions will not

apply where the consideration agreed to is manifestly inadequate or excessive.

[837] **Liability in tort.** One further matter arising under the New South Wales Act must be briefly noted. The rule protecting a minor from liability in tort where the cause of action in tort is in substance a cause of action in contract[166] is abolished by s 48. Thus a minor who, by a fraudulent representation as to his or her age, induces another to contract with him or her, will be liable for the tort of deceit, although the contract is not thereby rendered binding on the minor. The practical result is that tort damages for loss actually suffered, though not contract damages for any loss of expected profit,[167] may be recovered.

Mental Disability (Including Intoxication)

[838] **Introduction.** 'The law relating to the contracts of mentally incompetent persons is not now, and so far as I can tell, never was in a satisfactory state.'[168] The reason for this kind of observation is that the courts have tried to accommodate two inconsistent propositions. One is that where a contracting party's mental capacity does not reach the relevant legal standard, assent should be treated as a nullity, and the contract as absolutely void. The other is that a contracting party who has some, albeit inadequate, understanding, should not be allowed to disown assent, thereby depriving the other party of a contract.

Five matters should be noted. First, it is not vital for present purposes to choose between such expressions as 'insanity', 'lunacy', 'mental illness', 'mental disability' or 'mental incapacity'. The legal threshold for contractual assent has been laid down in other terms which will shortly be noted. Second, we are not primarily concerned here with persons in respect of whom there has been a finding under the relevant legislation that they are incapable of managing their property and affairs, control and management of which have been vested in a committee or official. The general scheme of the legislation[169] is that so long as the management and control continues, the committee or official has defined powers in relation to the property and affairs of the person, but the effect as against other parties of contracts entered into by that person varies depending on the applicable legislation.[170] Third, there will be a composite treatment of

---
165. *Report on Infancy in Relation to Contracts and Property*, LRC 6, 1969, p 86.
166. See [825].
167. As to this distinction see [1069].
168. *Bank of Nova Scotia v Kelly* (1973) 41 DLR (3d) 273 at 288–9.
169. **ACT**: *Mental Health Act* 1962; *Mental Health (Treatment and Care) Act* 1994; *Guardianship and Management of Property Act* 1991; **NSW**: *Mental Health Act* 1990; *Protected Estates Act* 1983; **NT**: *Mental Health and Related Services Act* 1998; *Aged and Infirm Persons' Property Act* 1979; **Qld**: *Guardianship and Administration Act* 2000; *Mental Health Act* 1974; *Mental Health Act* 2000; *Public Trustee Act* 1978; **SA**: *Aged and Infirm Persons' Property Act* 1940; *Guardianship and Administration Act* 1993; *Mental Health Act* 1993; **Tas**: *Mental Health Act* 1963 Pt VI; *Guardianship and Administration Act* 1995; **Vic**: *Mental Health Act* 1986; *Guardianship and Administration Act* 1986; **WA**: *Mental Health Act* 1996; *Guardianship and Administration Act* 1990.

mental disability and intoxication by alcohol or other drugs because both are governed by the same principles. Accordingly, cases involving mental disability and drunkenness will be cited without distinction.

Fourth, we are not concerned here with cases in which the plea of non est factum would be available in accordance with the ordinary principles governing that plea.[171] Fifth, although a contract may be found not binding in accordance with the principles discussed below, there remains the possibility of a liability in restitution for necessaries supplied.[172]

[839] General principle. Despite earlier authority to the contrary, the general principle of the common law developed that a person (not being a person 'found' or 'certified' as insane) was not allowed to 'stultify' or 'disable' himself or herself, that is, to escape responsibility for acts by setting up his or her own mental incapacity or drunkenness.[173] But by 1848, Pollock CB, for the Court of Exchequer, in *Molton v Camroux*[174] could state the 'modern' law in terms which have not been departed from since, as follows:[175] ' ... unsoundness of mind (as also intoxication) would now be a good defence to an action upon a contract, if it could be shewn that the defendant was not of capacity to contract, and the plaintiff knew it'.

The two elements of contractual incapacity on the ground of mental disability (which expression is used as extending to disability arising from intoxication by alcohol or other drugs) are thus: (1) the necessary degree of influence on the mind; and (2) knowledge thereof in the other party.

[840] Extent of influence. Mental disability will not necessarily signify contractual incapacity: questions of degree are involved. The test of the nature and extent of influence has been variously described, for example, 'so lunatic, or drunk, as not to know what he was about when he made a promise or sealed an instrument',[176] not 'capable of understanding the nature of the contract',[177] not 'capable of understanding what he was about'.[178] The extent of capacity which must be possessed is not fixed but is relative to the particular contract, instrument or transaction in question.[179] In *Gibbons v Wright*[180] the High Court said that each party must have 'such soundness of mind as to be capable of understanding the general nature of what he is doing by his participation'[181] and 'the capacity to understand [the] transaction when it is explained'.[182] The court thought that ordinarily

---

170. See eg *JNRD and the Protected Estates Act* (1992) 28 NSWLR 728; *David by her Tutor the Protective Commissioner v David* (1993) 30 NSWLR 417.
171. See[1267]–[1275].
172. See [847]. And see [809]–[816].
173. *Beverley's Case* (1603) 4 Co Rep 123b; 76 ER 1118.
174. (1848) 2 Ex 487; 154 ER 584 (affirmed (1849) 4 Ex 17; 154 ER 1107).
175. (1848) 2 Ex 487 at 501; 154 ER 584 at 589.
176. *Molton v Camroux* (1849) 4 Ex 17 at 19; 154 ER 1107 at 1108 per Patteson J for the Exchequer Chamber.
177. *Boughton v Knight* (1873) LR 3 P & D 64 at 72.
178. *Imperial Loan Co v Stone* [1892] 1 QB 599 at 601 per Lord Esher MR.
179. *In the estate of Daniel Doull* (1881) 7 VLR (IP & M) 70; *Gibbons v Wright* (1954) 91 CLR 423 at 437–9; *Scott v Wise* [1986] 2 NZLR 484.
180. (1954) 91 CLR 423.
181. (1954) 91 CLR 423 at 437.

what was to be understood was the 'broad operation' or 'general purport' of an instrument but that in some cases it might be the effect of a wider transaction which the instrument was a means of carrying out.

[841] **Awareness of other party.** The courts came to allow an exception to the principle that 'no man of full age shall be received in any plea by the law to stultify and disable his own person'[183] if it could be shown that the other contracting party had 'imposed upon' or 'taken advantage of' the mental incompetent, and this test has always been satisfied by (indeed it seems to have become equated with) proof that he or she knew or ought to have known of the incapacity.[184] Lopes LJ in *Imperial Loan Co v Stone*[185] (in a passage later apparently approved by the High Court)[186] summarised the principle to be deduced from the cases in these terms:[187] 'A defendant who seeks to avoid a contract on the ground of his insanity, must plead and prove, not merely his incapacity, but also the plaintiff's knowledge of that fact, and unless he proves these two things he cannot succeed'.

[842] **Void or voidable?** Notwithstanding dicta in some early cases favouring voidness,[188] it is now established that the resultant contract is not void but is voidable and therefore (assuming lucidity of mind at the time of ratification) ratifiable by the disabled party.[189] In other words, the distinction is between lack of intention to sign (somnambulists writing their name in their sleep[190] or lunatics writing their name in a frenzy, unaware of the motions their hands are performing)[191] and persons who intend to sign but lack understanding: the former makes the 'contract' void ab initio and affords the defence 'non est factum' ('it is not the party's deed') whereas the latter makes it voidable only. The elements of the plea non est factum are considered elsewhere[192] and they are applicable to the case of a contract signed by a mentally defective person. There will, in such a case, be an issue as to the nature and extent of the mental incompetent's lack of understanding of the document[193] but it may be that he or she will have

---

182. (1954) 91 CLR 423 at 438.
183. *Littleton's Tenures*, S 405.
184. *Molton v Camroux* (1848) 2 Ex 487; 154 ER 584 (affirmed (1849) 4 Ex 17; 154 ER 1107); *Hassard v Smith* (1872) Ir R 6 Eq 429 at 433; *In the Estate of Daniel Doull* (1881) 7 VLR (IP & M) 70; *Imperial Loan Co v Stone* [1892] 1 QB 599; *McLaughlin v Daily Telegraph Newspaper Co Ltd (No 2)* (1904) 1 CLR 243 at 272; *York Glass Co Ltd v Jubb* (1925) 134 LT 36; *Broughton v Snook* [1938] 1 All ER 481; *Gibbons v Wright* (1954) 91 CLR 423 at 441.
185. [1892] 1 QB 599 at 602–3.
186. *Gibbons v Wright* (1954) 91 CLR 423 at 441.
187. [1892] 1 QB 599 at 603; and cf to the same effect Lord Esher MR at 601.
188. For example, *Gore v Gibson* (1845) 13 M & W 523; 153 ER 260.
189. *Matthews v Baxter* (1873) LR 8 Ex 132 (explaining *Gore v Gibson* (1843) 13 M & W 623; 153 ER 260); *Baldwyn v Smith* [1900] 1 Ch 588; *York Glass Co Ltd v Jubb* (1925) 134 LT 36; *Gibbons v Wright* (1954) 91 CLR 423 at 441–3, 449.
190. The illustration comes from *Gore v Gibson* (1845) 13 M & W 623 at 627; 153 ER 260 at 262.
191. The illustration comes from *Gibbons v Wright* (1954) 91 CLR 423 at 443.
192. See [1267]–[1275].
193. See *PT Ltd v Maradona Pty Ltd* (1991) 25 NSWLR 643 (mental incapacity preventing any understanding at all of a transaction held to mean that there was no intention to sign and that pleas of non est factum therefore succeeded).

little difficulty in satisfying the court that the signing occurred without negligence on his or her part.

[843] Executed and executory contracts. The requirement that the other party must have known of the disability developed in cases in which contracts had been executed and it was impossible for the status quo to be restored. In such cases the other party's change of position gave rise to some 'equity' or claim of right which competed with sympathy for the mentally disabled person. But where the contract remains entirely executory, it can reasonably be argued that it should be, if not void ab initio, at least voidable without proof of knowledge in the other party. Yet the English courts have declined to distinguish between executed and executory contracts in this respect.[194] The suggested distinction would have scope to operate as between a mentally incapable principal and agent appointed without consideration flowing from the latter for the appointment. In *McLaughlin v Daily Telegraph Newspaper Co Ltd (No 2)*[195] the High Court held that a power of attorney executed by an insane person (who had lucid intervals) whose insanity was known to the person who procured its execution was 'void' (so that shares of the insane person which had been transferred by the attorney had to be re-registered in his name notwithstanding that the companies and the purchasers had no notice of the insanity). Special leave to appeal was refused by the Privy Council which saw no reason to doubt the correctness of the High Court's judgment.[196] It was suggested in the High Court that even if the attorney had not known of the insanity the result might have been the same.[197]

It seems that there are still two open questions in Australia in relation to executory contracts of a mentally incapable person: whether the other party's awareness of the disability is essential, and whether such contracts are void or voidable. It is thought that in principle awareness should be an essential element and that the contract should be treated as voidable rather than void.

[844] Unfairness without knowledge of mental disability. It has been suggested that even though a contracting party's mental condition is not known to the other party, the contract will not stand at law if it is 'unfair',[198] for example, where the consideration moving to the incompetent is disproportionately small. This question had been unresolved by authority,[199] but recently the Privy Council held in *Hart v*

---

194. *Imperial Loan Co v Stone* [1892] 1 QB 599 at 601; *York Glass Co Ltd v Jubb* (1925) 134 LT 36 per Sir Ernest Pollock MR.
195. (1904) 1 CLR 243.
196. Sub nom *Daily Telegraph Newspaper Co Ltd v McLaughlin* [1904] AC 776 at 780. And see *Molyneux v Natal Land and Colonization Co Ltd* [1905] AC 555 at 563–4.
197. (1904) 1 CLR 243 at 274–6. It is interesting that notwithstanding the holding of 'voidness', the court was able, a few years later, to hold the former lunatic liable for monies obtained by the attorney (his wife) from his bank on the ground that the self-styled agent had applied them for his benefit and that he, upon regaining his sanity, had not repudiated the transaction: *City Bank of Sydney v McLaughlin* (1909) 9 CLR 615.
198. Cf 'In order to avoid a fair contract of the ground of insanity, the mental incapacity of the one must be known to the other of the contracting parties': *Imperial Loan Co v Stone* [1892] 1 QB 599 at 603 per Lopes LJ.

O'Connor[200] that where the unsoundness of a contracting party's mind is not known to the other contracting party, the validity of the contract is to be determined by the same standards as the validity of a contract by a person of sound mind, so that mere 'unfairness' of the contract does not vitiate it. The better view appears to be that where it has been introduced, the notion of unfairness has referred to the competent party's taking advantage of the other's condition, an over-reaching which gross inadequacy of consideration may tend to show.[201] It is questionable whether, since the modern development of the principles relating to unconscionable bargains,[202] the kind of unfair contract referred to should be treated otherwise than as one example of a contract governed by those principles rather than as one to be treated under the rubric of mental incapacity.

[845] **A more flexible position in equity?** Although a contract may be valid at law in accordance with the foregoing principles, equity may refuse specific performance and even order rescission upon proof of a less substantial overbearing. In such a case equity acts upon the ground of constructive fraud; see the discussion of unconscionable exploitation of inequality of bargaining power in Chapter 15. But often, while having enough misgivings to refuse specific performance, the court has also refused rescission, leaving the other party to the common law remedy of damages.[203]

[846] **Ratification.** Once a contracting party has recovered mental capacity, words or conduct consistent only with the contract's continuance will render it binding. If rescission does not take place promptly, his or her silence, while others alter their positions on the footing of the contract's subsistence, may be deemed an affirmation.[204]

[847] **Necessaries.** Under the general law, in respect of necessaries supplied to him or her, the mentally disabled person was bound by a contract implied at law to pay a reasonable price, though only out of and to the extent of his or her own property and only if the circumstances did not displace the notion of obligation, for example, by indicating a supply by way of gift.[205] The sale of goods legislation now provides that 'where

---

199. *York Glass Co Ltd v Jubb* (1925) 134 LT 36 per Sargant LJ; *Gibbons v Wright* (1954) 91 CLR 423 at 444.
200. [1985] AC 1000.
201. *Tremills v Benton* (1892) 18 VLR 607; and cf the facts of *Blomley v Ryan* (1956) 99 CLR 362.
202. See Chapter 15.
203. As in *Cooks v Clayworth* (1811) 18 Ves Jun 12; 34 ER 222; *Scates v King* (1870) 1 VLR (Eq) 100; *Peters v Schimanski* [1975] 2 NZLR 328.
204. *Howard v Currie* (1879) 5 VLR (E) 87; *City Bank of Sydney v McLaughlin* (1909) 9 CLR 615.
205. *Re Rhodes* (1890) 44 Ch D 94; *Re Brooks* (1903) 21 WN (NSW) 4; *McLaughlin v Freehill* (1908) 5 CLR 858; *Re Beaven* (1912) 105 LT 784; *Bank of Nova Scotia v Kelly* (1973) 41 DLR (3d) 273. The obligation to pay for necessaries is imposed even in systems based on the Roman Law which adopt the subjective rule that mental disability precludes the possibility of consensual obligation: *Molyneux v Natal Land and Colonization Co Ltd* [1905] AC 555. See also [809]–[816]; Mason and Carter, *Restitution Law in Australia*, 1995, paras 831, 832.

necessaries are sold and delivered to a person who, by reason of mental incapacity or drunkenness, is incompetent to contract, he must pay a reasonable price therefor'.[206] Clearly, the 'reasonable price' referred to will not necessarily be the contract price.

[848] **Burden of proof.** The onus of proof of mental disability rests on the person setting it up, but where such disability of a permanent nature is established, the onus of proving that the contract was made during a lucid interval is on the other party.[207]

Corporations

[849] **Meaning of 'corporation'.** A corporation is an individual or group of individuals invested with legal personality (the capacity to have legal rights and duties) other than that legal personality which is allowed to each individual upon birth in our legal system. Since our legal system recognises all individuals as having legal personality from birth, it is sometimes said that corporations (or 'bodies corporate') are entities having 'artificial' or 'fictional' legal personality as contrasted with the 'natural' legal personality of the individual. But strictly speaking, all legal personality is a construct of the legal system and is to this extent artificial.

Corporations may be corporations sole or corporations aggregate. The former consists of one individual who is an office-holder. The latter comprises two or more individuals. Illustrations are universities, local government councils and companies which are incorporated upon registration under the *Corporations Act* 2001 (Cth).

[850] **Three aspects of contracts by corporations.** There are three aspects of the contracts by corporations which call for discussion: (a) vires, that is, the power or capacity of the body corporate to become legally bound; (b) the making of the decision to contract (corresponding to the natural person's mental act of assenting to contract); and (c) the mode of expression of contractual assent (this has always posed special difficulties for bodies corporate since they lack the normal contracting 'equipment' of the natural person, namely a mouth with which to speak and a hand with which to write). Another area of difficulty which we shall have to consider is that of pre-incorporation contracts.[208]

Our main concern here is with companies governed by the corporations legislation.[209]

---

206. **ACT**: *Sale of Goods Act* 1954, s 7; **NSW**: *Sale of Goods Act* 1923, s 7; **NT**: *Sale of Goods Act* 1972, s 7; **Qld**: *Sale of Goods Act* 1896, s 5; **SA**: *Sale of Goods Act* 1895, s 2; **Tas**: *Sale of Goods Act* 1896, s 7; **Vic**: *Goods Act* 1958, s 7; **WA**: *Sale of Goods Act* 1895, s 2.
207. *In the Estate of Daniel Doull* (1881) 7 VLR (IP & M) 70.
208. See generally Ford, Austin and Ramsay, *Ford's Principles of Corporations Law*, 10th ed, 2001, Chs 12–15.
209. See the *Corporations Act* 2001 (Cth).

Vires

[851] The doctrine of ultra vires. The doctrine of 'ultra vires' is a doctrine that where an entity's legal capacity is limited, a purported contractual assent lying outside that capacity (ultra vires) is a nullity.[210]

[852] Chartered companies. A chartered company is a company which has been granted corporate personality by the issue of a charter from the Crown. Chartered companies are not common in Australia but a well-known example is the Bank of New South Wales, now named Westpac Banking Corporation. It has been said that a chartered company has the full legal capacity of an individual on the ground that the King's charter could not alter the common law, which did not recognise legal persons with differing legal capacities.[211]

On this view, the doctrine of ultra vires did not invalidate such a company's transactions with outsiders,[212] though acts in excess of the company's objects as stated in the charter would be a ground for proceedings for repeal of the charter.[213] But Street's conclusion was that where it could be shown that a grant of a charter was for a particular purpose the doctrine probably applied, whereas where the charter could not be traced, the common law attached to the corporation 'all the capacity of citizens'.[214]

[853] Statutory companies. A statutory company is a company established by a special Act of parliament passed for that purpose. The intention of parliament was always regarded as paramount in any attempt to define the legal capacity of statutory companies.[215] The development of the concept of ultra vires with respect to statutory companies in many railway company cases decided about the middle of the 19th century,

---

210. On the doctrine as it applied to the registered company, see Davies, *Gower's Principles of Modern Company Law*, 6th ed, 1997, Chapter 8; Ford, Austin and Ramsay, *Ford's Principles of Corporations Law*, 10th ed, 2001, pp 629–32.
211. *Lowe's Case* (1610) 9 Co Rep 122; 77 ER 909; *Hazzell v Hammersmith and Fulham LBC* [1990] 2 WLR 1038. A charter must, if possible, be interpreted so as not to conflict with the common law (*Simpson v AG* [1904] AC 476 at 511) but if there is a clear conflict it is wholly void (*AG of Duchy of Lancaster v Devonshire* (1884) 14 QBD 195 at 208).
212. See *Reuter v The Electric Telegraph Co* (1856) 6 El & Bl 341; 119 ER 892; *Riche v Ashbury Carriage Co* (1874) LR 9 Ex 224 at 263–4; *Droop v Colonial Bank of Australasia* (1880) 6 VLR (E) 228 at 234; *Baroness Wenlock v River Dee Co* (1883) 36 Ch D 675 at 685; *AG v Manchester Corp* [1906] 1 Ch 643 at 651; *British South Africa Co v De Beers* [1910] 1 Ch 354 at 374; *Bonanza Creek Gold Mining Co v R* [1916] AC 566 at 582; and *Jenkin v Pharmaceutical Society* [1921] 1 Ch 392 at 398; *Credit Suisse v Borough Council of Allerdale* [1997] QB 306; [1996] 3 WLR 894 at 918–19 per Neill LJ, 931 per Hobhouse LJ.
213. As in *Eastern Archipelago Co v R* (1853) 2 E & B 856; 118 ER 988.
214. Street, *Ultra Vires*, 1930, p 17, and see generally pp 18–22.
215. See, eg *Hazzell v Hammersmith and Fulham LBC* [1992] 2 AC 1; [1991] 2 WLR 372; *Credit Suisse v Borough Council of Allerdale* [1997] QB 306; [1996] 3 WLR 894; *Humphries v Proprietors 'Surfers Palms North' Group Titles Plan 1955* (1994) 179 CLR 597; 121 ALR 1; *Credit Suisse v Waltham Forest London Borough Council* [1997] QB 362; [1996] 3 WLR 943, CA. See also *Birstar Pty Ltd v The Proprietors 'Ocean Breeze' Building Units Plan No 3745* (1996) Unreported, SC (Qld) (CA) 30 April 233/1995.

originating in *Colman v Eastern Counties Railway Co*[216] and culminating in *Eastern Counties Railway Co v Hawkes*,[217] is thus to be viewed as the product of statutory interpretation and was always subject to the unlikely event that a contrary intention existed in the special Act governing a particular company. Today too, where a corporation derives its corporate personality from its own special Act, the legislative intention as discerned in that Act is the primary source of the law governing its contractual capacity.

[854] **Doctrine of ultra vires applied to registered companies.** The modern company mostly takes the form of a company incorporated under the general companies legislation upon public registration. In this context the doctrine of ultra vires was that such a company's legal capacity was limited by reference to its objects as stated in its registered memorandum, and that a purported contractual assent lying outside that capacity (ultra vires) was a nullity.[218] (Even the assent or ratification of all shareholders could not prevail against this doctrine.) The doctrine distinguished the registered company from the chartered company and identified it with the statutory company formed for particular purposes.[219]

The fate of contracts could depend on a fine process of construction of a company's memorandum of association (a document which typically had not been present to the minds of the contracting parties), and led to attempts by the drafters of object clauses in memoranda of association to evade the rigour of the doctrine and to protect company directors by giving them the widest powers and discretions imaginable, and to efforts by the courts to apply the doctrine notwithstanding these attempts, yet to circumvent it in order to prevent injustice in particular cases.

[855] **Australian uniform companies legislation of 1961 and 1962.** Section 19 of the Australian 'uniform' companies legislation of 1961 and 1962[220] gave capacity to registered companies by providing that they should have most 'common form powers', unless expressly excluded or modified by the memorandum or articles. More importantly, s 20 attacked the ultra vires doctrine head on. It was thought unjust to outsiders that a company's ultra vires contractual undertaking should be void[221] and there had been several recommendations that the doctrine should be abrogated or substantially modified.[222] Section 20(1) provided that:

> No act of a company (including entering into an agreement by the company) and no conveyance or transfer of property, whether real or personal, to or by a company shall be invalid by reason only of the fact that the company was without capacity or power to do such an act or to execute or take such conveyance or transfer.

---

216. (1846) 10 Beav 1; 50 ER 481.
217. (1855) 5 HLC 331; 10 ER 928.
218. See *Ashbury Railway Carriage Co v Riche* (1875) LR 7 HL 653 at 678, 686.
219. (1875) LR 7 HL 653 at 693.
220. **ACT**: *Companies Ordinance* 1962; **NSW**: *Companies Act* 1961; **NT**: *Companies Ordinance* 1962; **Qld**: *Companies Act* 1961; **SA**: *Companies Act* 1962; **Tas**: *Companies Act* 1962; **Vic**: *Companies Act* 1961; **WA**: *Companies Act* 1961.
221. *Re Jon Beauforte (London) Ltd* [1953] Ch 131 was often cited in support.
222. Cohen Committee, 1945, Cmnd 6659, para 12; Jenkins Committee, 1962, Cmnd 1749, paras 35–42.

But s 20(2) provided that any such lack of capacity or power might be asserted or relied upon in certain classes of proceedings.

The cases decided under ss 19 and 20[223] did not explore some of the more difficult questions raised by s 20 for the purposes of contract law and they were ultimately replaced by provisions now contained in the *Corporations Act* 2001 (Cth).

[856] *Corporations Act* 2001 (Cth). Section 124 of the *Corporations Act* now provides that a company has the legal capacity of a natural person as well as certain specified powers peculiarly appropriate to companies. Under s 125(1) of the *Corporations Act*, if a company has a constitution, it may contain an express restriction on, or a prohibition of, the company's exercise of any of its powers. However, s 125(1) states that 'exercise of a power by the company is not invalid merely because it is contrary to an express restriction or prohibition in the company's constitution'. Again, under s 125(2) of the *Corporations Act* 2001 (Cth), if a company has a constitution, it may set out the company's objects. However, s 125(2) also states that an 'act of the company is not invalid merely because it is contrary to or beyond any objects in the company's constitution'.

Expression and Formation of Contractual Assent

[857] Agency principles. All contracts by bodies corporate must be made through the instrumentality of human beings. It is necessary to consider briefly the general principles governing the making of contracts through agents. A natural person may become bound contractually if a contract is made by that person or an agent. The most straightforward case is the one where the contract falls within the actual authority delegated by the principal to an agent. Thus, where A authorises B to buy a horse from C up to a price of $5000 and B buys it from C for $4500, B has contracted within the authority given and A is bound. Actual authority may be express (as in the illustration) or implied (as, for example, from a position or office to which A has appointed B). If B's authority is exceeded, A is prima facie not bound but may be bound in two situations. First, A may have previously represented to C that B does have authority from A to make the particular contract or to make contracts of a class which includes the particular one. Although B does not have that authority when contracting with C (A may have revoked B's authority and forgotten to inform C of this) A will be bound contractually to C because, so far as C was concerned, B had 'apparent' or 'ostensible' authority from A to make that contract. Second, although B had neither actual nor apparent authority, A will become bound by a contract which B makes on A's behalf if A 'ratifies' ('adopts' or 'affirms') the contract. Thus, the legal acts which will cause a natural person to become contractually bound are the act of contracting itself, of delegation of authority, a representation or holding out, and finally an act of ratification.

---

223. The case in which the sections were most closely examined was *Hawkesbury Development Co Ltd v Landmark Finance Pty Ltd* [1962] 2 NSWLR 782 esp at 794–8.

[858] **Special role of common seal.** The common seal of a body corporate is the physical object (nowadays generally a stamp) designed to impress on documents the 'signature' of the corporation. The common law had two rules which provided the framework for the decision of virtually all corporate contractual cases apart from those where a statutory provision governed the making of contracts. The two rules are the positive corporate seal rule[224] and the negative corporate seal rule.[225] These may be expressed as aspects of the one rule, namely, that the common seal was the one and only legally cognisable expression of an act of a body corporate. The positive corporate seal rule was that wherever the common seal appeared, the corporate mind had expressed itself and questions of irregularity internal to the corporation antecedent to the affixing of the common seal were not to be entered into.[226] The negative corporate seal rule was that without the appearance of the common seal, the corporation's assent could not be proved and so the corporation was not bound.[227] There were very few exceptions to the negative corporate seal rule. So long as the negative corporate seal rule applied, there was no scope for development of agency principles in the context of company contracts, but legislation has now substantially modified the strictness of the common law.

[859] **Contracts by companies and company agents under the Corporations Act.** Sections 126 and 127 of the *Corporations Act* deal with the position of an agent exercising a company's power to make contracts, and the execution of documents. Section 126 provides:

(1) A company's power to make, vary, ratify or discharge a contract may be exercised by an individual acting with the company's express or implied authority and on behalf of the company. The power may be exercised without using a common seal.

(2) This section does not affect the operation of a law that requires a particular procedure to be complied with in relation to the contract.

These provisions apply to all corporations incorporated or taken to be incorporated under the legislation. However, they do not prevent a company from making, varying or discharging a contract under its common seal.[228]

[860] **Contracts by agents of other corporations.** Sections 126 and 127 apply to all companies incorporated or deemed to be incorporated under the legislation.[229] Victoria and Queensland have legislated generally

---

224. See K E Lindgren, 'The Positive Corporate Seal Rule and Exceptions Thereto and the Rule in *Turquand's* case' (1973) 9 *MULR* 192.
225. See K E Lindgren, 'The Negative Corporate Seal Rule and Exceptions Thereto' (1974) 9 *MULR* 411.
226. *Hills v Manchester & Salford Waterworks Co* (1833) 5 B & Ad 315; 110 ER 1011; *Horton v Westminster Improvement Commissioners* (1852) 7 Ex 780; 155 ER 1165; *Nowell v Worcester Corp* (1854) 9 Ex 457; 156 ER 195; *Bill v Darenth Valley Railway Co* (1856) 1 H & N 305; 156 ER 1219; *Royal British Bank v Turquand* (1856) 6 El & Bl 327; 119 ER 886.
227. *Barker v Clunes MC* (1863) 2 W & W (L) 315; *Sydney MC v M'Beath* (1881) 2 NSWR 142; *Henry v Sydney MC* (1882) 3 NSWR 264; *McCauley v Richmond MC* (1923) 23 SR (NSW) 279.
228. See s 127. See also *MYT Engineering Pty Ltd v Mulcon Pty Ltd* (1999) 162 ALR 441.

in respect of the making, otherwise than under seal, of contracts by other bodies corporate. The *Instruments (Corporate Bodies Contracts) Act* 1967 (Vic) (inserting s 31(a) in the *Instruments Act* 1958 (Vic)) and s 227 of the *Property Law Act* 1974 (Qld) enable them to make, vary or discharge contracts in the same modes as individuals. The sections do not prevent such bodies corporate from making, varying or discharging a contract under their common seals.

In the other jurisdictions where the common law applies, in the absence of any special provision in the incorporating statute, a contract is not binding unless under seal except where inconvenience amounting almost to necessity or essentiality to the achievement of the purpose of incorporation demands otherwise. Thus the contract will be binding where the corporation is a trading company and the contract is in the course of trading, and where a contract is of little importance and of a frequently occurring kind so that it would be obstructive of the corporation's interests to require sealing. A company may also be liable in some cases where the other party has performed a contract and the company has taken the benefit of that performance.[230]

[861] Reliable appearance of assent. The *Corporations Act* 2001 (Cth) contains provisions which facilitate proof by the outsider of a reliable appearance of corporate assent in relation to company dealings and virtually abolish the doctrine of constructive notice in relation to the contracts of corporations.[231] Certain assumptions may be made by a person having dealings with a company, or a person having dealings with a person, who has acquired or purports to have acquired title to property from a company (whether directly or indirectly). The company is not entitled to repudiate these assumptions in relation to those dealings. The assumptions are set out in s 129 and include, for example, that the constitution of the company has been complied with and that a person held out by the company to be an officer or agent of the company has been duly appointed and has authority to exercise the powers and perform the duties customarily exercised or performed by an officer of the kind concerned. A person is not entitled to make such assumptions if he or she knew or suspected that the assumption was incorrect (s 128(4)).

The presence of fraud or forgery by those representing the company will not disentitle the outsider to make the assumptions referred to above unless the person has actual knowledge of the fraud or forgery (s 128(3)).

Section 130 of the *Corporations Act* abolishes the doctrine of constructive notice except where a document has been lodged by a company in respect of a registrable charge created by it. Thus an expression of contractual assent which appears by reference to other criteria to bind a company will not be defeated merely because the outsider, if he or she had read the

---

229. See definition of 'company' in s 9 of the *Corporations Act*.
230. See *London Dock Co v Sinnott* (1857) 8 El & Bl 347; 120 ER 129; *Henry v Sydney MC* (1882) 3 NSWLR 264 at 269, 270; *Connolly v Beechworth Shire* (1876) 2 VLR (E) 1; *Melbourne Banking Corp v Brougham* (1879) 4 App Cas 156. See also *Johnsons Tyne Foundary Pty Ltd v Maffra Corporation* (1948) 77 CLR 544.
231. For a discussion of problems in applying these provisions see Ford, Austin and Ramsay, *Ford's Principles of Corporations Law*, 10th ed, 2001, Ch 13.

publicly available documents, would have known or suspected that the person with whom he or she was dealing was not entitled to commit the company.

Pre-incorporation Contracts

[862] Pre-incorporation contracts under the general law. It is common for those (called 'promoters') who are forming and registering a company to wish to conclude a contract on its behalf before time has permitted its incorporation. Indeed, often it is the opportunity of making the contract that prompts the decision to form a company to take advantage of it. Under the general law a contract made on behalf of a non-existent company did not bind the company once it was incorporated; nor could the company ratify it, although it might bind the signatories personally.[232]

Thus it has been said that where, because a company has not been incorporated, no-one would otherwise be bound by the contract, the signatories will be bound. However, ultimately it became clear that expressed in this way the principle was too wide. Where it is clear that the parties intend to contract with the company and that signatures are added merely to authenticate the signature of the company, and it transpires that the company was not in existence, there is no contract with anyone.[233]

[863] Pre-incorporation contracts under the *Corporations Act* 2001 (Cth). It has been thought inconvenient and possibly unjust (1) that a company should not, upon incorporation, be able to ratify a pre-incorporation contract made for it so as to become bound and benefited by it; (2) concomitantly, that there should be no right for the signatories to be relieved of liability; and (3) that no-one should be liable in 'the authentication cases'.[234]

Section 131 of the *Corporations Act* empowers a company within a reasonable time after incorporation to ratify its pre-incorporation contracts entered into a reasonable time before incorporation. Ratification may be effected in the same manner as that allowed for the making of a contract in s 126. Upon ratification the company is bound and benefited by the contract as if it had been incorporated prior to the contract and had been a party to it. Where ratification does not occur, the person or persons who purported to execute the contract on behalf of the non-existent company (the 'promoters') are liable in damages equal to the amount for which the company would have been liable if it had been formed and ratified, but had failed to perform any of its obligations under the contract and the contract had been discharged by reason thereof. The section treats identically promoters who execute a contract in the name of a non-existent company

---

232. *Kelner v Baxter* (1866) LR 2 CP 174.
233. See *Newborne v Sensolid (Great Britain) Ltd* [1953] 1 All ER 708; *Black v Smallwood* (1966) 117 CLR 52 and *Miller Associates (Australia) Pty Ltd v Bennington Pty Ltd* (1975) 7 ALR 144.
234. See *Jenkins Committee Report*, 1962, Cmnd 1749, para 44; *Ghana Report*, p 32 and s 13 of the *Ghanaian Companies Code* 1963; *Final Report of the Special Committee to Review the Companies Act*, New Zealand, 1973, paras 105–7.

and those who contract as agents or trustees for a proposed company. Thus the distinction between the cases where the promoters would be personally bound[235] and the authentication cases is no longer important. In such proceedings against the promoters, the court may, where the company has been formed but has not ratified the contract, order the company to transfer or pay to a contracting party named in the order, property or an amount not exceeding the benefit received by the company as a result of the contract, and/or to pay the whole or a specified portion of the damages for which the promoters are found liable. Even where ratification occurs, the promoters remain contingently liable, since it is provided that if the company fails to perform all or any of its contractual obligations, by reason of which the contract is discharged, the court may, in proceedings brought against the company for damages for breach of contract, order the promoters to pay to the plaintiff the whole or a specified portion of the damages for which the company is found liable. The promoters may, by the written consent of the other contracting party, be released from liability in relation to the contract (s 132). Similarly, where the pre-incorporation contract is discharged and replaced by a fresh post-incorporation contract, the liability of the promoters is discharged.

Unincorporated Associations

[864] **General.** Unlike the corporation, an unincorporated association has no legal personality distinct from that of its members.[236] It is therefore true to say both that it has no contractual capacity and that its contractual capacity is co-extensive with that of its members. An association is like a crowd: one can say that 'the crowd is still there' when in fact the individuals constituting it are changing continually and only the object of their interest is constant.[237]

[865] **Identification of contracting party.** If there is an intention to contract with the 'entity' or the members as they exist from time to time, the contract is a nullity.[238] But in order to sustain the expectation of the parties that they are creating legal rights and obligations, a court will attempt to find an intention to contract with natural persons, be they the members of the association at the time of the contract or, as is more commonly found, all or some of the members of its managing committee or council.

---

235. See, eg *Kelner v Baxter* (1866) LR 2 CP 174 (see [874]).
236. See *Kirby v Registrar of Titles* [1999] 1 VR 861 at 869 per Mandie J. These associations may be incorporated by registration as companies limited by guarantee under the *Companies Code*. Alternatively, a simpler and less expensive means of incorporation is available under the following: **ACT**: *Associations Incorporation Act* 1991; **NSW**: *Associations Incorporation Act* 1984; **NT**: *Associations Incorporation Act* 1963; **Qld**: *Associations Incorporation Act* 1981; **SA**: *Associations Incorporation Act* 1985; **Tas**: *Associations Incorporation Act* 1964; **Vic**: *Associations Incorporation Act* 1981; **WA**: *Associations Incorporation Act* 1987.
237. Cf *Carlton Cricket & Football Social Club v Joseph* [1970] VR 487 at 488.
238. *Ex parte Goddard; Re Falvey* (1946) 46 SR (NSW) 289 at 296; *Carlton Cricket & Football Social Club v Joseph* [1970] VR 487; *Amey v Fifar* [1971] 1 NSWLR 685.

In *Bradley Egg Farm Ltd v Clifford*,[239] for example, where a poultry farmer had had certain of his fowls tested by the unincorporated Lancashire Union Poultry Society to ascertain if they had certain diseases and the fowls had to be destroyed as a result of tests conducted by an employee of the Society's council, the farmer succeeded not only against the employee but against the members of the council. Scott LJ said:[240]

> That the plaintiff intended to make a real contract with somebody is beyond doubt but it is equally beyond doubt that they had never formed any intention in their own minds beyond the vague one of making a contract with the person or persons the law would hold responsible on the contract. They did not, of course, think about it at all; they merely assumed, with the confidence natural to a nation which normally carries out its contracts, that somebody would be responsible. They expected performance and not breach; but the rest was assumption which they never even began to think out.
>
> In these circumstances, what is the function of the law? Surely it is to imply an intention on the plaintiffs' part to make their contract with the person or persons whom alone in the circumstances of the case the law regards as the persons responsible. That cannot be the society, for it does not exist. The law, therefore, has to choose from the various persons associated together under the umbrella of the society's name, those most concerned in the function of making contracts, those of the associated persons who were most directly concerned, and to discard those who were, for any reason, least directly concerned.

The members who had no liability beyond their annual membership subscription were discarded and the members of the executive council were chosen to bear legal liability. In New South Wales and Queensland the same approach has been taken with the same adverse result for office-holders and committee members.[241]

[866] Long-term contracts. The approach enunciated by Scott LJ in *Bradley Egg Farm Ltd v Clifford*[242] is not so readily available in relation to contracts whose performance extends beyond the period of incumbency of the committee members, councillors or office-holders. Constitutions frequently provide for an annual election of officers and so there is a good chance that some, or even all, of those in office when a long-term contract is made, will not be in office at the time of breach or litigation. A court will not so readily infer that the persons in office originally were parties to such

---

239. [1943] 2 All ER 378.
240. [1943] 2 All ER 378 at 386. And cf *Ex parte Goddard; Re Falvey* (1946) 46 SR (NSW) 289 at 295-7 per Jordan CJ for the Full Court.
241. Cf *Ex parte Goddard; Re Falvey* (1946) 46 SR (NSW) 289; *Smith v Yarnold* [1969] 2 NSWR 410; *M & M Civil Engineering Pty Ltd v Sunshine Coast Turf Club* [1987] 2 Qd R 401. See also *City of Gosnells v Roberts* (1994) 12 WAR 437. It is suggested in the judgment of Herron CJ in the second case that in order to be liable, committee members must have acted personally in connection with the making of the contract. In *Ward v Eltherington* [1982] Qd R 561, McPherson J preferred the view that committee members were liable, by reason not of their participation, but of their status as committee members. The former view had been advocated by R M Stonham in 'Clubs — Contractual Liability of Members and Committeemen' (1943) 17 *ALJ* 7 and the latter by K L Fletcher in 'Unincorporated Associations and Contract' (1979) 11 *UQLJ* 53 at 63-4.
242. [1943] 2 All ER 378 at 386 (see [865]).

a contract. So in *Carlton Cricket & Football Social Club v Joseph*[243] Gowans J held that the two signatories (the club's president and secretary), on behalf of the Fitzroy Football Club, the committee members at the time of the contract and the club members at that time were not bound by a 21-year licence agreement, with the result that no-one was bound by it. The following passage from his Honour's judgment is instructive of the approach likely to be taken to long-term contracts:[244]

> It may be taken on the evidence that the committee authorised the making of the Carlton agreement. But there is nothing to show that they authorised it to be made in such terms as to make themselves liable, and the actual document does not purport to make them liable. Whatever might be the position in the case of a simple transaction of a final and complete character such as the purchase of goods, or the doing of a single act of the kind dealt with in *Bradley Egg Farm Ltd v Clifford*,[245] when the committee might be regarded as pledging the personal credit of the committee members, the members of the committee could not be regarded in the circumstances of this case as authorising the undertaking of obligations of the kind dealt with in the document in such a way as to make themselves personally liable for the performance of those obligations over the years. The further alternative that is presented is that the two signatories made themselves personally liable. Here no question of authority arises. It is a simple case of whether the signatories were themselves the contracting parties. Again in some cases this might be the proper inference, for example where an official of a club gives an order for goods. He may then pledge his own credit in order to get the goods. But, in my opinion, it is fantastic to suggest that that is the case here, having regard to the nature of the transaction with which the document was concerned, and in the face of the language in which the document was couched.

[867] **Employment.** The unincorporated association as employer generates peculiar analytical difficulties, if only because the fact that its staff work and are paid over many years suggests that at each moment they have a contract of employment with someone. In *Peckham v Moore*,[246] which concerned a long-term contract between a professional footballer and the unincorporated Canterbury Bankstown District Rugby League Football Club, the solution proffered was that the employee contracted with the members of the original committee but promised them that he would continue to provide his services to their successors and that they promised that their successors would employ him. It was held that when he was injured in the course of his employment some years after his initial engagement, his employers were the members of the committee at that time rather than the original committee. Samuels JA said[247] that if a successor committee had refused to make use of the plaintiff's services, he would have had an action for breach of contract against the members of the original committee.

---

243. [1970] VR 487.
244. [1970] VR 487 at 499.
245. [1943] 2 All ER 378.
246. [1975] 1 NSWLR 353 (noted (1975) 49 *ALJ* 543).
247. [1975] 1 NSWLR 353 at 371.

[868] Other difficulties and reform. The inability of the law to accommodate contracts with unincorporated associations has prompted judicial observations on the need for reform.[248]

Moreover, the foregoing treatment has been concerned only with the difficulty of identifying the contracting parties and thus the persons liable in a contractual action. Further difficulties arise as to the rights, if any, of the parties held contractually liable to reimburse themselves out of the funds of the association or to recover from the members by way of indemnity, and as to an association's capacity to be the recipient of gifts (particularly bequests and devises) and to be owner and occupier of property.[249] All these difficulties are substantially overcome if an association is incorporated.[250]

The Crown and its Instrumentalities[251]

[869] Procedure: the Crown as litigant. The common law rule that the Crown, being the fountain of justice, could not be forced as defendant into the courts of the land, and so could not be made liable in respect of contractual undertakings, has been overcome by legislation. In Australia that legislation is to be found in the *Judiciary Act* 1903 (Cth) and an Act in each State.[252] Even when the rule applied it was necessary to distinguish from 'the Crown', public officers and bodies which might be created as bodies corporate, that is, bodies invested with a legal personality of their own delineated in the charter or Act of parliament setting them up, such as the Australian Broadcasting Corporation, the Australian Wheat Board, the New South Wales Egg Corporation. If their charter or special Act did not say otherwise, their possession of legal personality meant that there was no procedural impediment to their being sued and found liable on contracts made by them.

[870] Ultra vires. The doctrine of ultra vires[253] is an important limitation on the contractual capacity of the 'commissions', 'boards', 'councils', and 'authorities' that are a familiar feature of modern regulatory and welfare legislation.[254] Further, subject to statutory provision, their contracts must

---

248. See, eg *Banfield v Wells-Eicke* (1964) [1970] VR 81 at 485–6 per Gowans J.
249. See generally, Robert Baxt, 'The Dilemma of the Unincorporated Association' (1973) 47 *ALJ* 305.
250. See [864].
251. Cf Hogg, *Liability of the Crown in Australia, New Zealand and the United Kingdom*, 2nd ed, 1989; Dennis Rose, 'The Government and Contract', in Finn, *Essays on Contract*, 1987, Ch 9; Seddon, *Government Contracts: Federal, State and Local*, 2nd ed, 1999.
252. **Cth**: *Judiciary Act* 1903, Pts IX and IXA; **ACT**: *Crown Proceedings Act* 1992; **NSW**: *Crown Proceedings Act* 1988; **NT**: *Crown Proceedings Act* 1993; **Qld**: *Crown Proceedings Act* 1980; **SA**: *Crown Proceedings Act* 1992; **Tas**: *Crown Proceedings Act* 1993; **Vic**: *Crown Proceedings Act* 1958; **WA**: *Crown Suits Act* 1947; and see eg *Commonwealth of Australia v Mewett* (1997) 191 CLR 471; 146 ALR 299 at 304–7 per Dawson J (with whom McHugh J agreed), 317–18 per Toohey J, 341–9 per Gummow and Kirby JJ; see also P W Hogg, 'Suits against the Commonwealth and the States in the Federal Jurisdiction' (1970) 44 *ALJ* 425.
253. See the earlier discussion ([851]–[856]) in the context of corporations.

be made under common seal unless they fall within one of the exceptions to the negative corporate seal rule.[255]

Does the doctrine of ultra vires apply to the executive government itself? There is no vires limit on the contractual capacity of the Crown in a unitary system. The question in Australia eventually is whether the vesting of legislative power with respect to particular matters in the Commonwealth parliament somehow operates to render a Commonwealth contract with respect to other matters invalid, and perhaps whether a State contract is similarly ultra vires if made with respect to a subject matter on which the Constitution gives the Commonwealth parliament the exclusive power to make laws. Little light is shed on this question by the express provisions of the Commonwealth Constitution. There is some authority for the view that statutory authority is necessary for any Commonwealth contract which is not 'in the ordinary course of administering a recognised part of the government of the State'.[256] Tying the Commonwealth's contractual capacity to a law of the Commonwealth has the effect of limiting that capacity to an extent commensurate with the Commonwealth's legislative capacity. The alternative (and it is thought the preferable) view is that contractual rights and duties are created by voluntary act rather than by statute with the result that the Commonwealth's contracting power is not limited in the same way as its legislative power.[257]

[871] **Parliamentary control over public monies.** It has been, at least since the Revolution Settlement of 1688, an undoubted rule of law that money cannot be paid out of consolidated revenue without parliamentary authority[258] and money so paid is paid illegally and can be recovered, at least if it can be traced.[259] The rule was so notorious that the content of the Crown's contractual obligation could be impliedly qualified by reference to parliament's appropriating the funds.[260]

In the earlier cases this limitation was sometimes spoken of as going to the capacity of the executive government to become contractually bound

---

254. See, eg *Commonwealth v Australian Commonwealth Shipping Board* (1926) 39 CLR 1; *Hazzell v Hammersmith and Fulham London Borough Council* [1992] AC 1; *Beneficial Finance Corp Ltd v Multiplex Constructions Pty Ltd* (1995) 36 NSWLR 510 at 539 per Young J
255. See [858].
256. *New South Wales v Bardolph* (1934) 52 CLR 455 at 508 per Dixon J and at 496, 502–3, 508, 514; cf *Commonwealth v Australian Commonwealth Shipping Board* (1926) 39 CLR 1; and *Australian Alliance Assurance Co Ltd v Goodwyn* [1916] QSR 135.
257. See Enid Campbell, 'Commonwealth Contracts' (1970) 44 *ALJ* 14, 'Federal Contract Law' (1970) 44 *ALJ* 580, and 'Agreements about the Exercise of Statutory Powers' (1971) 45 *ALJ* 338.
258. This principle is now embodied in s 83 of the Commonwealth Constitution and in analogous provisions of the State Constitutions, eg the *Constitution Act* 1902 (NSW), s 45.
259. *Auckland Harbour Board v The King* [1924] AC 318; *Commonwealth v Burns* [1971] VR 825. Cf *Commonwealth v Crothall Hospital Services (Aust) Ltd* (1981) 36 ALR 567. It has been questioned whether s 64 of the *Judiciary Act* 1903 (Cth) has destroyed the Commonwealth's cause of action for recovery of monies so paid: *Commonwealth v Crothall Hospital Services (Aust) Ltd* (1981) 36 ALR 567 at 580 citing *Maguire v Simpson* (1977) 139 CLR 362 at 387–8.
260. See, eg *Churchward v The Queen* (1865) LR 1 QB 173.

[871] and there were references to the invalidity or non-existence of a contract made without parliamentary authority or appropriation.[261] In *AG v Great Southern and Western Ry Co of Ireland*[262] Viscount Haldane described a contractual undertaking of the Crown as a 'liability in rem', that is, a liability to pay out of the funds which parliament chooses to supply but not a liability extending beyond this. An approach which attacked the contract at its formation was thought to be the only one consistent with a government that was 'responsible'. But in *Kidman v The Commonwealth*[263] Viscount Haldane expressed the view that the absence of an appropriation 'did not make the contract null and ultra vires; it made it not enforceable because there was no res against which to enforce it'.[264] It is now accepted that absence of parliamentary appropriation does not go to validity but is an answer to a claim to enforce recovery of a money judgment arising out of the contract.[265]

[872] **Fettering of the executive government's and parliament's discretion.** Two propositions conflict. First, the Executive cannot by contract disable itself from exercising statutory discretion to be exercised in public interest.[266] In particular, they should not be bound by the contracts made by yesterday's government to act or not to act, or to legislate or not to legislate, in a certain way. Second, it is in the Crown's interest that it be, and be known as, a contracting party which is bound to perform rather than as one which is free to disown its contracts. Every contract (save one which the Crown performs at the moment of making it) involves a restriction on the Crown's freedom of action in the future.

Contractual obligations, particularly long-term ones, have been seen to conflict with the former ideal. The desirability of an unfettered discretion can influence the construction of the extent of obligation being assumed by the Crown in a particular contract.[267] Yet it is not possible to 'read down' the Crown's obligations in all cases. It has been argued that where the Crown breaks a contract in what it conceives to be the public interest, the

---

261. See, eg *Commercial Cable Co v Government of Newfoundland* [1916] 2 AC 610 at 617; *Mackay v A-G for British Columbia* [1922] AC 457 at 461; *Commonwealth v Colonial Combing Spinning and Weaving Co Ltd* (*The Wool Tops* case) (1922) 31 CLR 421.
262. [1925] AC 754 at 771–4.
263. [1926] ALR 1 at 2 (in argument).
264. The Supreme Court (sub nom *Commonwealth v Kidman* (1923) 23 SR (NSW) 590 at 599) had described the contracts as being 'of no force and effect *so far as they purported to bind the Commonwealth to the expenditure of public money*' (italics supplied).
265. *Australian Railways Union v Victorian Railway Commissioners* (1930) 44 CLR 319 at 353; *New South Wales v Bardolph* (1934) 52 CLR 455. See also *Commonwealth v Ling* (1993) 118 ALR 309 (affirmed on other grounds (1994) 51 FCR 88); *Vass v Commonwealth of Australia* (2000) 169 ALR 486.
266. See *Attorney-General (NSW) v Quin* (1990) 170 CLR 1; 93 ALR 1 at 11 per Mason CJ. See also *Sita Qld Pty Ltd v Queensland* (1999) 164 ALR 18 at 23 per Dowsett J; *L'Huillier v State of Victoria* [1996] 2 VR 466 at 479, 480, 482–3 per Callaway JA, with whom Charles JA agreed, CA (exercise of public law discretion).
267. Cf *The Amphitrite* [1921] 3 KB 500; *Watson's Bay and South Shore Ferry Co Ltd v Whitfield* (1919) 27 CLR 268; *Hughes Aircraft Systems International v Airservices Australia* (1997) 146 ALR 1 at 49–50 per Finn J. And see P W Hogg, 'The Doctrine of Executive Necessity in the Law of Contract' (1970) 44 *ALJ* 154.

general principles of contract law requiring payment of damages adequately govern the respective positions of the contracting parties.[268] Yet there is authority for the view that the Crown is not even liable in damages in the case of contracts 'which concern the welfare of the State' as distinct from 'commercial contracts'.[269] In the case of commercial contracts such as a contract to pay for advertising, the Crown is clearly liable and must perform subject to the provision by parliament of sufficient monies.[270]

[873] **Agency principles.** It is necessary, if government is to be workable and contractual responsibility of the Crown is to mean anything at all, that powers vested in Ministers be capable of being exercised by their officers. 'The whole system of departmental organisation and administration is based on the view that ministers, being responsible to Parliament, will see that important duties are committed to experienced officials. If they do not do that, Parliament is the place where complaint must be made against them.'[271] So, principles of actual and ostensible authority of agents are applicable to contracts made by government officers.[272] A court will more easily find that an officer has ostensible authority in the case of contracts providing for the carrying on of the ordinary, well recognised activities or functions of government than in the case of extra-ordinary contracts.[273]

A civil servant who makes contracts for the government in the course of employment will not be personally liable unless there is the clearest evidence of an intention to contract personally.[274] The courts have been influenced by this principle and by considerations of public policy to hold that a civil servant, unlike an agent of a private principal,[275] does not impliedly warrant to persons with whom he or she deals that there was authority to bind the Crown and so is not liable to them in an action for 'breach of warranty of authority', that is, for not having authority to commit the Crown contractually to them.[276]

Bankrupts

[874] **General.** Bankruptcy does not affect contractual capacity, that is, the capacity of a person to become contractually bound, but affects the

268. See P W Hogg, 'The Doctrine of Executive Necessity in the Law of Contract' (1970) 44 *ALJ* 154 at 159.
269. *The Amphitrite* [1921] 3 KB 500 at 503.
270. *New South Wales v Bardolph* (1934) 52 CLR 455.
271. *Carltona Ltd v Commissioners of Works* [1943] 2 All ER 560 at 563 per Lord Greene MR.
272. *J E Verreault & Fils Ltee v A-G for Quebec* (1976) 57 DLR (3d) 403; *Coogee Esplanade Surf Motel Pty Ltd v Commonwealth* (1983) 50 ALR 363; *R v Transworld Shipping Ltd* (1975) 61 DLR (3d) 304. And cf *New South Wales v Bardolph* (1934) 52 CLR 455 at 495.
273. *New South Wales v Bardolph* (1934) 52 CLR 455 at 496, 503, 507.
274. *MacBeath v Haldimand* (1786) 1 TR 172; 99 ER 1036; *Gidley v Lord Palmerston* (1822) 3 B & B 275; 129 ER 1290; *Palmer v Hutchinson* (1881) 6 App Cas 619.
275. As to which the leading case is *Collen v Wright* (1857) 8 E & B 647; 120 ER 241.
276. *Dunn v MacDonald* [1897] 1 QB 555 at 558; *The Prometheus* (1949) 82 Ll L Rep 859.

operation of contracts made by a person who is at the time, or subsequently becomes, bankrupt.[277]

[875] Effect of bankruptcy upon pre-bankruptcy contracts. Upon bankruptcy, contracts previously entered into do not come to an end: the bankrupt's contractual rights vest under s 58(1) of the *Bankruptcy Act 1966* (Cth) in the trustee in bankruptcy for the benefit of the bankrupt's creditors.[278] The trustee must perform or procure performance of the contract if the other party is to remain liable to perform it. However, s 133 of the Act empowers the trustee to disclaim by signed writing, amongst other things, any 'unprofitable contract' that forms part of the property of the bankrupt and any other such contract with the leave of the court. Thus, the trustee has an election as to whether or not to continue to perform a contract or cause or permit its performance, so as to entitle the trustee to a continued performance of it by the other party. Under the section, where the other party applies to the trustee requiring election, and, for 28 days thereafter or such extended period as is allowed by the court, the trustee has declined or neglected to disclaim, the trustee loses the right to disclaim and is deemed to have adopted the contract.

Further, 'The Court may, on the application of a person who is, as against the trustee, entitled to the benefit or subject to the burden of a contract made with the bankrupt, make an order rescinding the contract on such terms as to payment by or to either party of damages for the non-performance of the contract, or otherwise, as the Court considers just and equitable' and 'Damages so payable may be proved as a debt in the bankruptcy'.[279] It can be assumed that a disclaimer by the trustee of a contract which is 'unprofitable' from the trustee's viewpoint will often signify the loss of a contract which would have been 'profitable' to the other contracting party. The section contemplates that damages may be awarded to the other party for the loss of the contract and that he or she may qualify as a creditor in the bankruptcy in respect of those damages.

Rights accrued prior to bankruptcy against the bankrupt out of a contract (for example, a right to sue for a debt or for damages for breach of contract) are converted into a right to prove as a creditor in the bankruptcy. Indeed, as noted above, loss caused to the other contracting party by a disclaimer entitles that person to prove in the bankruptcy for that loss as for damages. Property which has passed to the other party under the contract may, depending upon the circumstances, have to be disgorged for the benefit of creditors generally. Examples are the doctrine of relation back (expressed in the *Bankruptcy Act* 1966 (Cth), ss 58(1), 115, 116, 123) and the undue preference provisions (s 122). These expressions refer to aspects of bankruptcy law which are based on the premise that insolvency does not occur at the moment of time when the court order is made by which a person becomes bankrupt but is a state of affairs which exists over a period down to that time. The doctrine of relation back and the undue preference

---

277. As to the effect of a company's winding up and voluntary administration see Ford, Austin and Ramsay, *Ford's Principles of Corporations Law*, 10th ed, 2001, paras 26.092, 27.123.
278. For an illustration, see *Official Receiver v Henn* (1981) 40 ALR 569.
279. *Bankruptcy Act* 1966 (Cth), s 133(7), (8).

provisions are designed to ensure an evenhanded treatment of the bankrupt's creditors and in particular to recapture for the benefit of all creditors property which passed from the bankrupt while insolvent and payments, made while the bankrupt was insolvent, by which particular creditors were preferred over others.

Where continued performance by the other party would involve giving credit or further credit to the bankrupt, it appears that in view of the fact that there is no assurance that the creditor will be paid in full, he or she is entitled to refuse to perform other than for payment in cash.

[876] Effect of bankruptcy upon post-bankruptcy contracts. A bankrupt can continue to incur contractual obligations subject to the trustee's right to intervene and disclaim. In the absence of such intervention, a post-bankruptcy contract binds the bankrupt. Just as the *Bankruptcy Act* 1966 (Cth), s 123(1) protects pre-bankruptcy dispositions, s 126(1) provides:[280]

> A transaction by a bankrupt with a person dealing with him in good faith and for valuable consideration in respect of property acquired by the bankrupt on or after the day on which he became a bankrupt is, if completed before any intervention by the trustee, valid against the trustee, and any estate or interest in that property which, by virtue of this Act, is vested in the trustee shall determine and pass in such manner and to such extent as is necessary for giving effect to the transaction.

In order to have access to the property vested in the trustee, the other contracting party would need to implicate the trustee by getting approval of the contract, that is, an election by the trustee not to disclaim.

In view of the limited means available to a bankrupt to satisfy judgments, the Act prohibits the bankrupt under penalty from entering into certain types of transaction without disclosing that he or she is an undischarged bankrupt. For example, s 269(a) prohibits the obtaining of credit to the extent of a prescribed amount or more[281] without disclosing his or her status as an undischarged bankrupt. Where a bankrupt contracts in breach of this prohibition the contract is unenforceable by the bankrupt and the other party is entitled to rescind the contract.[282]

Married Women

[877] Position at common law. To the modern reader the common law on married women's contracts must be regarded as a most unhappy chapter of the law. The general rule at common law was that a married woman lacked contractual capacity and that her contracts were void because she had no legal personality separate from that of her husband. Moreover, by virtue of the marriage her property was vested in her husband. It is lack of property which has been the source of the contractual disadvantage

---

280. See also *Bankruptcy Act* 1966 (Cth) s 125.
281. Section 269(a) nominates the amount of $3000, but by virtue of a complicated procedure set out in s 304a this amount is altered quarterly following the Consumer Price Index.
282. *De Choisy v Hynes* [1937] 4 All ER 54; *MacEwin & Co v Ashwin* [1916] NZLR 1028.

experienced by married women until recent times. Lack of the capacity to own property signifies not only that a person is precluded from making those contracts by which property is disposed of or acquired, but perhaps more importantly, that there is no fund out of which the person's contractual liabilities can be satisfied, for which reason others will not deal with the person on credit terms.

[878] **Position in equity.** The position at law was mitigated by equity's development of the doctrine of the married woman's separate estate. If property were conveyed to her husband or to trustees by words which indicated that it was for her sole and separate use, equity required her husband or trustee to hold his legal interest as trustee for her and to facilitate dispositions by her. This, and powers granted to her which related to the enjoyment and disposition of the separate estate, made it possible for a married woman's contractual liability to be satisfied to the extent of her separate estate which she had at the time of contracting. Clearly, this liability was not personal but proprietary, that is to say, the married woman was subject, not to an absolute and unlimited contractual liability, but to a liability qualified and limited by reference to particular property which she had owned at a particular moment of time.

[879] **Statutory modification.** Legislation towards the end of the 19th century[283] enlarged the proprietary contractual capacity of married women by building upon equity's doctrine of the separate estate. It enacted, in effect, that in the case of women marrying after a date specified, all their property, no matter when acquired, should be their separate estate; and that in the case of women married prior to that date, property acquired after it should be their separate estate whereas that which they had acquired before it should remain subject to the existing common law and equitable principles. The legislation provided that to the extent of her separate estate as so enlarged, a married woman should be capable of binding herself by any contract, not merely those incidental to the enjoyment and disposition of her separate estate, and of suing and being sued in contract.

The other development occurred when it was enacted[284] that every contract made by a married woman (otherwise than as agent) should bind her separate estate whether she possessed any at the time of contracting or not (except property the subject of a restraint upon anticipation).[285] By limiting her liability to the extent of her property, the legislation still recognised that the married woman's contractual liability was proprietary rather than personal, though the liability was enlarged to the extent of her separate estate as it might exist at any time and from time to time. Some States legislated to remove this anomaly by providing that a married woman should be capable of being liable in all respects as if she were a single

283. See, eg *Married Women's Property Act* 1886 (NSW).
284. The current legislation is: **ACT**: *Married Persons' Property Act* 1986, s 3(1); **NSW**: *Married Persons (Equality of Status) Act* 1996; **NT**: *Married Persons (Equality of Status) Act* 1989; **SA**: *Law of Property Act* 1936, ss 92–111; **Tas**: *Married Women's Property Act* 1935; **Vic**: *Marriage Act* 1958, Pt VIII; **WA**: *Married Women's Property Act* 1892. Legislation to the same effect in Queensland (*Married Women's Property Act* 1890) was repealed by the *Law Reform Act* 1995 (Qld).
285. See [880].

woman[286] but in other jurisdictions, the married woman's contractual liability was left as proprietary. However, s 7(1) of the *Bankruptcy Act* 1966 (Cth) provides that the Act 'extends to debtors being married women' and since an inability to be made bankrupt seems to have been the only consequence of the fact that a married woman's liability was proprietary rather than personal, the section has, in effect, made her liability personal.[287]

The practical effect of the legislation is that a married woman now has full contractual capacity,[288] subject only to the continued operation in some jurisdictions of restraints upon anticipation. There is now express provision to this effect in Queensland.[289]

[880] **Restraints upon anticipation.** Another source of distinction between the contractual capacity of married women and other persons is the doctrine of the restraint upon anticipation. It was possible for persons minded to vest property in a married woman to ensure that it would be preserved for her benefit and would not be disposed of by her under the influence of her present husband or any future husband.

The technique used was to provide in the dispositive documents that the disponee was not to possess the power of anticipation or alienation. Such a provision invalidated any transaction which would have the effect of disposing of the corpus of the property. The woman was entitled to the use, enjoyment and benefit of the property and of any income from it but she was not entitled to dispose of the property or subject it to a liability. The restraint took effect upon marriage and was co-extensive with her status as a 'married woman'. A restraint upon anticipation deprived a married woman of contractual capacity to the extent that it rendered the property subject to it immune from liability to satisfy her contractual obligations. Property subject to the restraint when the contract was made and the income arising thereafter from that property were immune, but pre-contract income, being at her free disposal, was available to satisfy her contractual liability.

[881] **Legislative modification of the restraint upon anticipation.** In New South Wales alone it is still possible to create restraints upon anticipation. The courts are, however, empowered to release a married woman's property from a restraint upon anticipation where this is for her benefit and with her consent.[290] There is a similar power in Tasmania, Victoria and Western Australia.[291] However, this will be relevant only where

---

286. **SA**: *Law of Property Act* 1936, s 92(1)(b); **Tas**: *Married Women's Property Act* 1935, s 3; **Vic**: *Marriage Act* 1958, s 156(1)(b). See also **ACT**: *Married Persons' Property Act* 1986, s 3; **NT**: *Married Persons (Equality of Status) Act* 1989, s 3. Similar legislation in Queensland (*Married Women (Restraint upon Anticipation) Act* 1952, s 2) was repealed by the *Law Reform Act* 1995 (Qld).
287. See also *Family Law Act* 1975 (Cth), s 119 (either party to a marriage may bring proceedings in contract or in tort against the other).
288. See *Garcia v National Australia Bank Ltd* (1998) 194 CLR 395 at 422; 155 ALR 614 at 634 per Kirby J
289. See *Law Reform Act* 1995 (Qld), s 18 (married person has independent legal personality and same capacity as that person would have if unmarried).
290. **NSW**: *Conveyancing Act* 1919, s 149.

the restraint was created before 1936, 1956 and 1963 respectively. While the Australian Capital Territory, Tasmania, Victoria and Western Australia[292] and probably the Northern Territory[293] have legislated to prevent further imposition of restraints, they have left existing restraints intact. Queensland and South Australia have invalidated existing restraints as well.[294] It is surmised that there can be very few restraints upon anticipation in effect in Australia today.

[882] **Anti-discrimination legislation.** What has been said above is directed to 'capacity' and says nothing as to decisions not to contract with married women or to contract with them only on special terms which might be the subject of 'anti-discrimination' legislation.[295]

---

291. **Tas**: *Conveyancing and Law of Property Act* 1884, s 43; **Vic**: *Property Law Act* 1958, s 169; **WA**: *Property Law Act* 1969, s 31.
292. **ACT**: *Married Persons' Property Act* 1986, s 6; **Tas**: *Conveyancing and Law of Property Act* 1884, s 45 (inserted by *Conveyancing and Law of Property Act* 1935, s 3(XII)); **Vic**: *Marriage Act* 1958, s 157; **WA**: *Property Law Act* 1969, s 31 (replacing *Law Reform (Property Perpetuities and Succession) Act* 1962, s 25).
293. In NT *Married Persons (Equality of Status) Act* 1989, s 3, has semble the same effect.
294. **Qld**: *Married Women (Restraint upon Anticipation) Act* 1952, s 4; **SA**: *Statutes Amendment (Law of Property and Wrongs) Act* 1972, s 11, substituting a new s 110 of the *Law of Property Act* 1936.
295. See, eg *Sex Discrimination Act* 1975 (SA); *Anti-Discrimination Act* 1977 (NSW); *Anti-Discrimination Act* 1991 (Qld); *Discrimination Act* 1991 (ACT); *Equal Opportunity Act* 1995 (Vic); *Equal Opportunity Act* 1984 (WA); *Anti-Discrimination Act* 1992 (NT); *Anti-Discrimination Act* 1998 (Tas).

Chapter 9

Privity of Contract and Plurality of Parties

The Privity Doctrine...................................901
    General.. 901
    'Exceptions' to the Privity Doctrine 905
    The Legal Effects of Contracts for the Benefit of a Third Party 910
    Attempts to Impose Contractual Burdens on Third Parties 913
    Legislation and Suggestions for Reform..................... 914
    The Future of the Privity Doctrine in Australia 917
    The Special Case of Third Parties and the Benefit of Exclusion
        Clauses 923
Plurality of Parties 927

The Privity Doctrine

General

[901] The basic rule. The privity of contract doctrine states that only the parties to a contract are legally bound by and entitled to enforce it.[1] Viscount Haldane LC expressed the basic rule in *Dunlop Pneumatic Tyre Co Ltd v Selfridge & Co Ltd*:[2]

> My Lords, in the law of England, certain principles are fundamental. One is that only a person who is a party to a contract can sue on it. Our law knows nothing of a jus quaesitum tertio arising by way of contract. Such a right may be conferred by way of property, as, for example, under a trust, but it

---

1. Leading authorities include *Price v Easton* (1833) 4 B & Ad 433; 110 ER 518; *Tweddle v Atkinson* (1861) 1 B & S 393; 121 ER 762; *Gandy v Gandy* (1885) 30 Ch D 57 at 69; *Keighley Maxsted and Co v Durant* [1901] AC 240 at 246; *Dunlop Pneumatic Tyre Co Ltd v Selfridge & Co Ltd* [1915] AC 847; *Vandepitte v Preferred Accident Insurance Corp of New York* [1933] AC 70 at 79, 82; *Carberry v Gardiner* (1936) 36 SR (NSW) 559 at 573, 574; *Wilson v Darling Island Stevedoring & Lighterage Co Ltd* (1956) 95 CLR 43 at 66, 67, 80; *Scruttons Ltd v Midland Silicones Ltd* [1962] AC 446 at 467, 472, 494; *Concrete Constructions Pty Ltd v GIO of NSW* [1966] 2 NSWR 609 at 615–18; *Beswick v Beswick* [1968] AC 58 at 72, 83, 92–3, 95.
2. [1915] AC 847 at 853.

[901] cannot be conferred on a stranger to a contract as a right to enforce the contract in personam.

And in *Coulls v Bagot's Executor and Trustee Co Ltd*[3] Barwick CJ said:[4]

> It must be accepted that, according to our law, a person not a party to a contract may not himself sue upon it so as directly to enforce its obligations. For my part, I find no difficulty or embarrassment in this conclusion. Indeed, I would find it odd that a person to whom no promise was made could himself in his own right enforce a promise made to another.

A third party may be benefited or burdened in fact by performance of the contract, but according to the privity doctrine only the contracting parties are benefited and burdened in law by the making of the contract.

[902] **The impact of the *Trident* decision.** In *Trident General Insurance Co Ltd v McNiece Bros Pty Ltd*[5] a majority of the High Court of Australia recently decided that a company which was intended to be benefited by an insurance policy could, even though it was not a party to the contract of insurance and provided no consideration for it, recover from the insurance company the indemnity promised in the policy. Three members of the court held that the company could sue directly on the contract. This approach, were it to become established, would be a direct modification of the doctrine of privity and, indeed, could hardly in principle be limited to contracts of insurance. However, both the other two members of the majority (who proceeded on different doctrinal bases) and the two dissenting judges disagreed with this approach. In the result the status of the privity doctrine in Australia must be said to be in a state of flux. Since the likely impact of the *Trident* decision cannot be understood without an appreciation of the traditional privity doctrine, analysis of the case is deferred until later.[6]

[903] **Historical development of the doctrine.** The rule that consideration must move from the promisee[7] is often regarded as being conceptually distinct from the requirement of the privity doctrine that a promise is enforceable only at the instance of the promisee, although commonly a third party beneficiary of a promise will be disentitled to enforce it on both grounds. In *Coulls v Bagot's Executor and Trustee Co Ltd*[8] Windeyer J posed the issue in these terms:[9]

> By the common law of England only those who are parties to a contract can sue upon it. For us that statement is incontrovertible. But what exactly is meant by it? Is there a useful distinction between denying a right of action to a person because no promise was made to him, and denying a right of action to a person to whom a promise was made because no consideration for it moved from him?

His Honour noted that a third party beneficiary was said to fail in some cases because he was not the promisee and in others because he had not

3. (1967) 119 CLR 460.
4. (1967) 119 CLR 460 at 478.
5. (1988) 165 CLR 107.
6. See [917]–[922].
7. See [319]–[322].
8. (1967) 119 CLR 460.
9. (1967) 119 CLR 460 at 494.

furnished consideration, and that in the reports of the 16th and 17th centuries were cases in which persons who were neither 'privy to the promise' nor 'privy to the consideration' had succeeded in assumpsit. In particular, his Honour noted cases in which it was said that either the promisee or the third party beneficiary might sue.

As Windeyer J observed,[10] the early cases conflict because during the 16th, 17th and 18th centuries the doctrine of consideration was in process of formation, and because, before *Tweddle v Atkinson*,[11] the question whether, and in what circumstances, third parties should be allowed to bring assumpsit was not settled. But the doctrine was, after that case, taken as settled that they could not.[12]

Although it has been strongly argued that the requirements of consideration and privity are but different ways of stating the one rule, the weight of authority supports the existence of two separate though interrelated principles.[13]

The formula 'consideration must move from the promisee' assumes satisfaction of the privity requirement; it is only to the promisee that the requirement of consideration need be applied.

[904] Illustrations. The privity doctrine has an impact in commonly occurring situations. First, a manufacturer (A) may, by the contract by which it sells goods to a wholesaler, importer or distributor (B), seek to restrict any retailer (C) to whom B sells as to the terms on which the retailer (C) may sell.[14] C is not bound by the contract between A and B and the contract between B and C is not enforceable by A. Assume that by the contract with A, B promises A to include in any contracts between B and retailers to whom B sells, undertakings by them. If B does so, but a retailer (C) breaches its undertaking, A cannot sue C because A is not a party to the contract between B and C.[15] If B fails to include the undertaking, B has breached the contract with A and is liable to A in damages but the assessment of these will proceed on the footing that if B had included the undertaking, it would not have been enforceable by A.

Second, a building contract is enforceable only as between the parties to it, for example, proprietor and builder, and any subcontracts are enforceable only as between the parties to them, for example, builder and subcontractor.

Third, and by way of elaboration on the first illustration, a succession of contracts will characterise the chain of supply of consumer products. There may be contracts by which the manufacturer acquires the materials and services involved in the manufacturing process. If the manufacturer is

---

10. (1967) 119 CLR 460 at 498.
11. (1861) 1 B & S 393; 121 ER 762.
12. In *Tweddle v Atkinson* (1861) 1 B & S 393; 121 ER 762 the plaintiff was a stranger to both the promise and the consideration and the judgments referred to the latter alone. Yet the case has been treated as authority for the proposition not only that consideration must move from the promisee but also that only the promisee can enforce the contract.
13. *Trident General Insurance Co Ltd v McNiece Bros Pty Ltd* (1988) 165 CLR 107 at 115–16 per Mason CJ and Wilson J and at 164 per Toohey J.
14. Arrangements of the kind described in this paragraph are now prohibited by Pt IV of the *Trade Practices Act* 1974 (Cth).
15. *Dunlop Pneumatic Tyre Co Ltd v Selfridge & Co Ltd* [1915] AC 847.

[904]

foreign, there will be a contract between it and an importer. There will be contracts between the manufacturer (or importer) and wholesalers/distributors. There will be contracts by which retailers purchase their stock. Finally, there will be contracts between retailers and consumers.

Fourth, under the general law, insurance and life assurance policies were, in the absence of statutory modification,[16] enforceable only as between the parties to them, that is to say, the insurer and the proposer. So, where a sole trader or partners take out a fire insurance policy and the insured property is subsequently sold to a company (including a company in which they may be the principal shareholders) the company cannot enforce the policy against the insurer because of the privity doctrine and any fire will have caused the sole trader or partners, as distinct from the company, no loss.[17] Similarly, where a landowner contracts to sell, the privity doctrine prevents the purchaser from enforcing the vendor's fire insurance policy, and, assuming the contract of sale to be one of which specific performance would be ordered, the vendor is entitled to be paid the sale price notwithstanding damage to or destruction of the property and so will suffer no loss in that event.[18]

'Exceptions' to the Privity Doctrine

[905] **Are there true exceptions?** In various situations a third party intended to be benefited by a contract to which he or she is not party may nonetheless have a remedy against the party who promised to confer the benefit. This is sometimes said to be because the case comes within an exception to the privity doctrine. However, the better analysis is that stated by Deane J in *Trident General Insurance Co Ltd v McNiece Bros Pty Ltd*:[19]

> If a third party is to be entitled to rights and subject to obligations in relation to a contract to which he is a stranger, those rights and obligations must have some basis, either in statutory provision or in common law principle, beyond the mere contract ... On the other hand, if they arise by reason of the operation of some other principle or some statutory provision, the rule of privity will have nothing to say to them. It is in that context that it would seem accurate to say, as Fullagar J[20] and Lord Reid[21] have suggested, that there are no true exceptions at common law to the rule of privity.

[906] **Agency.** That a contract burdens and benefits a party who enters into it by an agent does not suggest a qualification of the general rule since the agent contracts 'on behalf of' the principal. What is clearly exceptional, however, is the agency doctrine of the undisclosed principal. An undisclosed principal is a person for whom another acts as agent but whose existence and identity is not disclosed to the person with whom the agent is

---

16. The Australian Law Reform Commission recommended reform of the privity doctrine in the context of the insurance problem discussed here. See now the *Insurance Contracts Act* 1984 (Cth): see [916].
17. Cf *Macaura v Northern Assurance Co Ltd* [1925] AC 619.
18. *Ziel Nominees Pty Ltd v VACC Insurance Co* (1975) 180 CLR 173; 7 ALR 667; *Kern Corp Ltd v Walter Reid Trading Pty Ltd* (1987) 163 CLR 164; 71 ALR 417.
19. (1988) 165 CLR 107 at 143; see also at 134–5 per Brennan J.
20. *Wilson v Darling Island Stevedoring & Lighterage Co Ltd* (1956) 95 CLR 43 at 67.
21. *Scruttons Ltd v Midland Silicones Ltd* [1962] AC 446 at 473.

dealing. In *Teheran-Europe Co Ltd v S T Belton (Tractors) Ltd*,[22] Lord Denning MR described the doctrine of the undisclosed principal as an 'anomaly' which was 'justified by business convenience' and stated it thus:[23]

> It is a well-established rule of English law that an undisclosed principal can sue and be sued upon a contract, even though his name and even his existence is undisclosed, save in those cases where the terms of the contract expressly or impliedly confine it to the parties to it.

Lord Diplock expressed the position only a little differently:[24]

> Where an agent has ... actual authority and enters into a contract with another party intending to do so on behalf of his principal, it matters not whether he discloses to the other party the identity of his principal, or even that he is contracting on behalf of a principal at all, if the other party is willing or leads the agent to believe that he is willing to treat as a party to the contract anyone on whose behalf the agent may have been authorised to contract. In the case of an ordinary commercial contract such willingness of the other party may be assumed by the agent unless either the other party manifests his unwillingness or there are other circumstances which should lead the agent to realise that the other party was not so willing.

The agent or the undisclosed principal, but not both, can sue and be sued on the contract. If the agent sues, the damages are for the loss suffered by the agent, on the footing that the agent was principal.[25] While a person with appropriate authority from an undisclosed principal can make the latter party to a contract, he or she is not thereby constituted trustee of the contract for the undisclosed principal. The High Court has accepted the possibility, however, that such an agent might contract not 'as agent' at all but 'as trustee', in which case the undisclosed party will not be liable on the contract.[26]

[907] **Trusteeship.**[27] A trustee holds property upon trust for beneficiaries (or 'cestuis que trust'). The implication of the trust concept for property consisting of contractual rights must now be considered:[28]

> One distinction between agency and trusteeship is that 'the trustee does not bring his cestuis que trust into any contractual relationship with third parties, while it is the normal function of an agent to do so'.[29]

A trustee contracts as principal for the benefit of a cestui que trust. An agent contracts for a principal or principals of which he or she may himself or herself be one.

It is well established that a contracting party may be trustee for a third party of that chose in action which is constituted by the benefit of a

---

22. [1968] 2 QB 545. See also *Siu Yin Kwan v Eastern Insurance Co Ltd* [1994] 1 All ER 213.
23. [1968] 2 QB 545 at 552. Sachs LJ seems to have agreed with Lord Denning's formulation: at 561. On the doctrine of the undisclosed principal generally, see Reynolds and Davenport, *Bowstead and Reynolds on Agency*, 16th ed, 1996, pp 408–26.
24. [1968] 2 QB 545 at 555.
25. *Allen v F O'Hearn & Co* [1937] AC 213 at 218.
26. *Construction Engineering (Aust) Pty Ltd v Hexyl Pty Ltd* (1985) 155 CLR 541; 58 ALR 411.
27. On trusteeship of the benefit of contractual rights generally, see Meagher and Gummow, *Jacobs' Law of Trusts in Australia*, 6th ed, 1997, pp 17–29.
28. *Construction Engineering (Aust) Pty Ltd v Hexyl Pty Ltd* (1985) 155 CLR 541 at 546.
29. Pettit, *Equity and the Law of Trusts*, 5th ed, 1984, p 24; *Cave v MacKenzie* (1877) 46 LJ Ch 564 at 567.

contract.[30] In such a case, the third party beneficiary, not being a party to the contract, cannot directly exercise the remedies or obtain the relief available to a party, but may, by proceedings in equity against the trustee, compel the trustee to enforce the contract. Enforcement will be for the benefit of the beneficiary. In particular, damages will be assessed by reference to the beneficiary's loss and will be held on trust for him or her.

Whether a contracting party has constituted himself or herself trustee is a question of intention. It is difficult to reconcile the decided cases on the issue 'trust or no trust'. In *Ryder v Taylor*,[31] Nicholas J thought it necessary to show an intention 'to confer on him some right in relation to some property, and to confer this right in such a way that it can not be destroyed or varied by the actions of the parties to the contract alone: ...'. While a term of the contract that it shall not be varied or rescinded without the third party's consent may well suggest a trust, there is no reason in principle why there should not be a trust of a promise which is susceptible to variation or even termination.[32] In *Re Schebsman*,[33] du Parcq LJ observed:[34]

> It is true that, by the use possibly of unguarded language, a person may create a trust, as Monsieur Jourdain talked prose, without knowing it, but unless an intention to create a trust is clearly to be collected from the language used and the circumstances of the case, I think that the court ought not to be astute to discover indications of such an intention.

There has been much uncertainty as to when the courts will recognise a trust of a contract for the benefit of a third party and this has limited the extent to which the trust device could mitigate the hardship which could otherwise be caused by the privity doctrine. In *Wilson v Darling Island Stevedoring & Lighterage Co Ltd*[35] Fullagar J said that it was 'difficult to understand the reluctance which courts have sometimes shown to infer a trust in such cases' and more recently this difficulty was shared by at least four members of the High Court in *Trident General Insurance Co Ltd v McNiece Bros Pty Ltd*.[36] As is shown later,[37] one effect of the *Trident* case is likely to be that Australian judges will in future be more willing than has been the case in the past to infer a trust in favour of a third party beneficiary.

[908] **Privity of estate.** Property law allows for third parties to be benefited and burdened by contractually created obligations. The benefit and burden of the obligation are sometimes said to be 'annexed to the land' and the genesis of this exception to the privity doctrine does indeed lie in the law of real property rather than in that of contract.

30. See, eg *Les Affréteurs Réunis SA v Walford Ltd* [1919] AC 801; *Wilson v Darling Island Stevedoring & Lighterage Co Ltd* (1956) 95 CLR 43.
31. (1935) 36 SR (NSW) 31 at 48. See also *Lloyd's v Harper* (1880) 16 Ch D 290.
32. Cf Fullagar J in *Wilson v Darling Island Stevedoring & Lighterage Co Ltd* (1956) 95 CLR 43 at 67–8: 'I cannot see why it should be necessary that such a trust should be irrevocable; a revocable trust is always enforceable in equity while it subsists'.
33. [1944] 1 Ch 83.
34. [1944] 1 Ch 83 at 104.
35. (1956) 95 CLR 43 at 67.
36. (1988) 165 CLR 107 at 120 (per Mason CJ and Wilson J), 146–7 (per Deane J) and 166 (per Toohey J).
37. See [919], [922].

The assignee of land subject to a lease is benefited by certain covenants which the original lessee gave to the original lessor and the assignee of the lease itself is bound by those covenants. Easements and covenants restrictive of the use of land, if appropriately created, benefit and burden not only the immediate parties to their creation but also their successors in title.[38] In the leading case on restrictive covenants, *Tulk v Moxhay*,[39] the plaintiff, owner of vacant ground in Leicester Square and of several of the houses forming the Square, sold the ground to one Elms, who, by the deed of conveyance, for himself, his heirs and assigns covenanted with the plaintiff, his heirs, executors and assigns, that Elms, his heirs and assigns would keep and maintain the ground as a square garden and pleasure ground for the use as such by the plaintiff's tenants. After several intervening conveyances, the land came into the hands of the defendant, who had taken his title with knowledge of the covenant.

Lord Cottenham LC observed (twice) that the question was not whether the covenant ran with the land but whether 'an equity is attached to the property by the owner' and whether the purchaser took with notice. The Lord Chancellor observed that if a purchaser with notice were not bound, a vendor could never be sure that the benefited land retained by him or her would not be rendered worthless.

Briefly, in order for the *Tulk v Moxhay* doctrine to operate, a restriction must touch or concern the land of the covenantor purportedly burdened and accommodate the land of the covenantee purportedly benefited, and the respective lands burdened and benefited must be at the time of creation of the restriction, and subsequently remain, in separate ownership. The doctrine applies only to negative covenants; it does not allow enforcement of a positive covenant (such as an obligation to spend money on improving the land or repairing structures on it).[40] The *Tulk v Moxhay* doctrine has been subjected to severe limitations and has been modified by statute.[41]

[909] Assignment of contractual rights. In many cases a contracting party can effectively assign the benefit of the other party's outstanding obligation. Assignability of contractual rights, which is usually considered in the context of assignability of 'choses in action', embraces 'rights of a proprietorial or quasi-proprietorial nature which are claimable or enforceable by action, such as a right to sue for a debt, or for damages for breach of contract'.[42] '"Chose in action" is a known legal expression used to describe all personal rights of property which can only be claimed or enforced by action, and not by taking physical possession'.[43] Choses in action could generally not be assigned at common law, that is to say, ownership of the chose and the consequential right to sue the debtor could not be transferred to the assignee. However, choses in action were assignable in equity. Section 25(6) of the *Judicature Act* 1873 (UK) provided a statutory procedure for assignment of a debt or other legal chose

---

38. On the subject generally, see Bradbrook and Neave, *Easements and Restrictive Covenants in Australia*, 1981.
39. (1848) 2 Ph 774; 41 ER 1143.
40. *Rhone v Stephens* [1994] 2 All ER 65.
41. See Bradbrook and Neave, *Easements and Restrictive Covenants in Australia*, 1981.
42. Starke, *Assignments of Choses in Action in Australia*, 1972, p 1.
43. *Torkington v Magee* [1902] 2 KB 427 at 430 per Channell J.

in action, and every Australian jurisdiction has enacted a very similar provision. An account of the requirements for an effective statutory or equitable assignment of a chose in action, and of those types of contractual rights which are not assignable, is beyond the scope of this work.[44] The point to be made here is that where an assignee can enforce a chose in action created by a contract to which the assignee is not a party, the cause of action is one to enforce what the law regards as a form of property right and is therefore not inconsistent with the privity of contract doctrine.

It should be noted that generally speaking the assignment of contractual obligations is not possible,[45] though all parties involved may (by what is called 'novation') agree to substitute one contract for another (for example, to substitute one purchaser of property for the original purchaser). Moreover, in the case of death or bankruptcy of a contracting party, the contractual liability of the deceased or bankrupt passes to the deceased's legal personal representative or the bankrupt's trustee in bankruptcy, but only to the extent of available assets in their hands, and subject, in the case of the trustee in bankruptcy, to the trustee's power to disclaim certain contracts.

The Legal Effects of Contracts for the Benefit of a Third Party

[910] Generally. A, being indebted to another (TP), may make an agreement with B that for good consideration moving from A to B, B promises A that B will pay A's debt to TP. TP is not party to the promise (and is not party to the consideration either). If we remove the indebtedness of A to TP, it is conceivable that A may wish to benefit TP out of charity, friendship, moral obligation or family relationship.

In the unsatisfactorily reported case in 1678, *Dutton v Poole*,[46] a father, at the request of his son and heir, refrained from selling a wood in order to raise portions for his younger children, in consideration of which the son and heir promised to pay his sister £1000. The son and heir was held to be liable to his sister: 'there was such apparent consideration of affection from the father to his children, for whom nature obliges him to provide, that the consideration and promise to the father may well extend to the children'.[47]

Dutton v Poole does not represent the modern law. When it was decided, moral obligation was accounted consideration. That notion was rejected in 1840 in *Eastwood v Kenyon*[48] and in 1861 in *Tweddle v Atkinson*[49] in which Blackburn J said that *Dutton v Poole* could no longer be supported since natural love and affection were not a sufficient consideration to support an

---

44. See Meagher, Gummow and Lehane, *Equity: Doctrines and Remedies*, 3rd ed, 1992, Chapter 6; Starke, *Assignments of Choses in Action in Australia*, 1972.
45. There is some authority that in certain cases a person taking the benefit of a grant must accept certain associated burdens. The scope and, indeed, validity of such a principle is unclear: compare eg *Tito v Waddell (No 2)* [1977] Ch 106 with *Government Insurance Office (NSW) v K A Reed Services Pty Ltd* [1988] VR 829, discussed in E Aughterson, 'In Defence of the Benefit and Burden Principle' (1991) 65 *ALJ* 319.
46. (1678) 2 Lev 210; 83 ER 523.
47. (1678) 2 Lev 210 at 211–12; 83 ER 523 at 524 per Scroggs CJ.
48. (1840) 11 Ad & E 438; 113 ER 482.
49. (1861) 1 B & S 393; 121 ER 762.

action of assumpsit. In that case two fathers, in consideration of an intended marriage between their children, contracted between themselves that they would each pay a sum of money to the intended husband. The latter failed in an action against his wife's father's executors, notwithstanding the family relationships involved.

[911] Performance and variation of contracts which provide for benefits to third parties. Assume that upon the proper construction of a contract A and B are the parties to it; that B promises A that B will pay TP; and that A does not hold that promise upon trust for TP.[50] It is a consequence of the privity doctrine that A and B can, by agreement between themselves and without reference to TP, vary their contract by reducing the amount of the payment to TP or eliminating the provision for that payment entirely.[51]

But A is not entitled unilaterally to vary the contract by substituting himself or someone else as payee in lieu of TP, and B is entitled to insist on paying TP in accordance with the original contract.[52] (Payments which B has made or will make to TP under the contract, although gratuitous as between B and TP, vest in TP.)[53] The position would be different if the contract obliged B to pay TP or as A might direct, in that a particular direction given is but a revocable mandate which could be revoked by A, at least before payment was made.[54]

[912] Enforcement and remedies — exclusion of the 'third party beneficiary'. The privity doctrine insists that a contracting party alone is entitled to exercise any remedies provided by the contract itself, to terminate for breach or repudiation, to sue for damages or specific performance, to choose between rights or remedies and to choose not to enforce the contract at all. If the promisee obtains an order for specific performance, this will give the third party beneficiary the benefit which he or she contemplated getting from the contract. For example, in *Beswick v Beswick*[55] a man sold his business as a coal merchant to his nephew in consideration of, inter alia, the nephew's promise to pay, after his uncle's death, a weekly amount to his aunt (that is, the uncle's widow) for her life. The aunt was not a party to the agreement. After her husband's death she brought an action against the nephew. She did so in two capacities: as legal personal representative (in this case, administratrix) of the deceased, and in her own right.

Although it was held that she was not entitled to enforce the contract as third party beneficiary, she was, in her capacity as administratrix, entitled

---

50. And that, despite some of the judgments in *Trident General Insurance Co Ltd v McNiece Bros Pty Ltd* (1988) 165 CLR 107, TP has no action against B on the contract: see [917]–[922].
51. See, eg *Cleaver v Mutual Reserve Fund Life Association* [1892] 1 QB 147; *Re Engelbach's Estate* [1924] 2 Ch 348; *Re Clay's Policy of Assurance; Clay v Earnshaw* [1937] 2 All ER 548; *Re Sinclair's Life Policy* [1938] Ch 799. These cases all involved insurance policies, as to which special statutory provisions now apply: see [916].
52. *Re Schebsman* [1944] Ch 83; *Cathels v CSD* (1959) 79 WN (NSW) 271; *Re Stapleton-Bretherton* [1941] Ch 482.
53. *Re Schebsman* [1944] Ch 83; *Cathels v CSD* (1959) 79 WN (NSW) 271.
54. *Re Stapleton-Bretherton* [1941] Ch 482; *Coulls v Bagot's Executor and Trustee Co Ltd* (1967) 119 CLR 460.
55. [1968] AC 58 (see [914]).

to an order for specific performance of the nephew's undertaking and since this had been to pay money to her in her own right, she benefited in fact in her capacity as third party beneficiary.

The remedy of damages raises special difficulties and the law is still uncertain. For whose loss or damage is the award made? Does the contracting party hold the award for himself or herself? Assume that by a contract between A and B, B promises A to pay $500 to TP. One view has been that A can recover only for A's own loss or damage and that this will always signify an award of nominal damages only. At the other extreme is the view espoused by the Court of Appeal in *Jackson v Horizon Holidays Ltd*.[56] The court upheld an award of damages for breach of contract to a husband and father against a travel agency, assessed by reference to the loss suffered by all members of his family. Lord Denning MR, drawing on a passage from the judgment of Lush LJ in *Lloyd's v Harper*,[57] concluded that one who contracts for the benefit of members of a group is entitled to recover damages for their monetary loss and, where appropriate, for their discomfort, vexation and upset, and will be liable to account to them in due course. This view was disapproved by all members of the House of Lords in *Woodar Investment Development Ltd v Wimpey Construction UK Ltd*,[58] though Lord Scarman (with some support from Lord Salmon and Lord Russell of Killowen) expressed a willingness to reconsider the denial by English law of a jus quaesitum tertio if there should be further delay in the implementation of the recommendations of the Law Revision Committee's *Sixth Interim Report*.[59] Lord Wilberforce thought it 'a question of great doubt and difficulty'[60] whether in the absence of evidence of trusteeship, agency or sustaining of loss by a contracting party, the latter could recover any but nominal damages and on what principle, and Lord Scarman thought that this question required further consideration by the House.

The two questions concerning damages posed earlier were discussed by Windeyer J in *Coulls v Bagot's Executor and Trustee Co Ltd*.[61] His Honour thought that while A might not be able to recover $500 which B had promised A to pay to TP, the ordinary rules for the assessment of damages would, in some cases, give A substantial unliquidated damages which could be more or less than the $500 promised to be paid.[62] Windeyer J's approach towards damages in third party beneficiary contracts was described by Mason CJ and Wilson J as being plainly correct in *Trident General Insurance Co Ltd v McNiece Bros Pty Ltd*.[63]

---

56. [1975] 3 All ER 92.
57. (1880) 16 Ch D 290 at 321.
58. [1980] 1 All ER 571.
59. Cmd 5449, 1937. There has been more recent reform following Law Commission Report, *Privity of Contract: Contracts for the Benefit of 3rd Parties*, Law Com No 242, 1996, which led to the enactment of *Contracts (Rights of Third Parties) Act* 1999. See [915].
60. [1980] 1 All ER 571 at 577. Lord Salmon agreed with him (at 583). For special cases concerning certain contracts relating to property, where substantial damages may be recovered, see eg *The Albazero* [1977] AC 74; *Darlington Borough Council v Wiltshier Northern Ltd* [1995] 1 WLR 68.
61. (1967) 119 CLR 460 at 501–2.
62. And see Lord Upjohn in *Beswick v Beswick* [1968] AC 58 at 101 to the same effect.
63. (1988) 165 CLR 107 at 119. See also at 158 per Dawson J.

His Honour instanced situations in which A was relying on the payment to discharge or reduce an indebtedness to TP, or in which TP was to use the $500 in a joint venture with A. The damages awarded would be by reference to A's own loss. This accords with the privity doctrine and requires that the second question posed earlier be answered to the effect that A's damages recovered are held by A for A alone. Ex hypothesi, A did not hold the contractual rights as agent or trustee for TP; why should A hold damages awarded for breach of them as trustee for TP?

The inadequacy of damages as a remedy for breach of a contract to pay money to a third party suggests that specific performance is an appropriate remedy for such a breach.[64]

Attempts to Impose Contractual Burdens on Third Parties

[913] **Attempts to extend the principle derived from *Tulk v Moxhay* to goods.** Does 'privity of estate'[65] also qualify the operation of the general doctrine of privity of contract in relation to personal property?[66] The question arose in several cases in relation to disputes between the buyer of a ship and its charterer under a subsisting charterparty (a contract by which a ship or a part thereof is let by the shipowner to another for a specified time or purpose) whose existence and terms were known to the buyer at the time of the purchase.[67] The Privy Council in *Lord Strathcona Steamship Co Ltd v Dominion Coal Co Ltd*[68] upheld an injunction obtained by the charterer against such a 'buyer with notice' restraining him from using the ship inconsistently with the charterparty. Notwithstanding the attempt of the Privy Council to show otherwise, it is submitted that the land law's requirements previously noted are not satisfied in such a case. For one thing, there is no property of the charterer benefited standing against the ship burdened.

The *Strathcona* case has been considered by Australian courts.[69] As a Privy Council decision it has in the past been accepted as binding. In *Shell Oil Co of Australia Ltd v McIlwraith McEacharn Ltd*,[70] Jordan CJ explained it as depending upon the 'peculiar value' of a ship to a charterer, and would have limited recognition of 'the *Strathcona* principle' by reference to the remedy of injunction. *Strathcona* has been similarly confined in England[71]

---

64. Cf *Beswick v Beswick* [1968] AC 58 at 89, 101–2; *Coulls v Bagot's Executor & Trustee Co Ltd* (1967) 119 CLR 460 at 503; *Trident General Insurance Co Ltd v McNiece Bros Pty Ltd* (1988) 165 CLR 107 at 119–20. And see [2406].
65. See [908].
66. This question is discussed at some length in *Cheshire and Fifoot's Law of Contract*, 7th Aust ed, 1997, pp 252–6.
67. Cf *DeMattos v Gibson* (1858) 4 De G & J 276; 45 ER 108; *Messageries Imperiales Co v Baines* (1863) 7 LT 763; *London County Council v Allen* [1914] 3 KB 642; *Lord Strathcona Steamship Co Ltd v Dominion Coal Co Ltd* [1926] AC 108.
68. [1926] AC 108.
69. See *Shell Oil Co of Australia Ltd v McIlwraith McEacharn Ltd* (1945) 45 SR (NSW) 144 at 150 per Jordan CJ; *Toohey v Gunther* (1928) 41 CLR 181 at 208 per Higgins J; *Howie v NSW Lawn Tennis Ground Ltd* (1956) 95 CLR 132 at 156 per Dixon CJ, McTiernan and Fullagar JJ; *Tooth & Co Ltd v Barker* [1960] NSWR 51 at 64 per McLelland CJ in Eq. See also *Carlton and United Breweries Ltd v Tooth & Co Ltd* (1986) 7 IPR 581.
70. (1945) 45 SR (NSW) 144.

and was not followed in *Port Line Ltd v Ben Line Steamers Ltd*[72] by Diplock J, who held that it was wrongly decided.

Against the measure of success enjoyed by the attempts to extend the land law's restrictive covenant to personalty, is to be seen the courts' consistent rejection of attempts to cause contracts to maintain selling prices to run with the subject goods so as to oblige subsequent buyers in favour of the original seller.[73]

Legislation and Suggestions for Reform

[914] Non-party to instrument taking interest in property. At common law there was a technical rule that a person could not take an immediate interest in property or the benefit of any covenant under an indenture which purported to be inter partes unless named as a party in the indenture. Section 5 of the *Real Property Act* 1845 (UK) eliminated this requirement, though the legislation was limited to immediate estates or interests in, and conditions or covenants respecting, real property. In England the section was replaced by s 56(1) of the *Law of Property Act* 1925 (UK) which referred to 'land or other property' and to a 'conveyance or other instrument'. Moreover, 'property' was defined in that Act to include any chose in action. There are counterpart provisions operating in the Australian States and the Northern Territory[74] of which s 36C of the *Conveyancing Act* 1919 (NSW) is typical:

> (1) A person may take an immediate or other interest in land or other property, or the benefit of any condition, right of entry, covenant, or agreement over or respecting land or other property, although he may not be named as a party to the assurance or other instrument.
>
> (2) Such person may sue, and shall be entitled to all rights and remedies in respect thereof as if he had been named as a party to the assurance or other instrument.

In *Beswick v Beswick*[75] the question of the impact of s 56 of the *Law of Property Act* 1925 (UK) on the doctrine of privity of contract was considered by the House of Lords. It will be recalled[76] that in that case a coal merchant (A) agreed with his nephew (B) to transfer to the latter the goodwill and trade utensils of his business in consideration of B's employing him as a consultant at £6.10.0 per week for the rest of his life and after A's death paying to his widow (TP) an annuity charged on the business at the rate of £5 week for her life. TP was not a party to the agreement. After A's death, B paid one sum of £5 to TP but declined to

---

71. *Clore v Theatrical Properties Ltd* [1936] 3 All ER 483; *Law Debenture Trust Corp plc v Ural Caspian Oil Corp Ltd* [1993] 2 All ER 355.
72. [1958] 2 QB 146.
73. *Taddy v Sterious* [1904] 1 Ch 354; *McGruther v Pitcher* [1904] 2 Ch 306; *National Phonograph Co of Australia v Menck* (1908) 7 CLR 481 at 516–17 per Griffith CJ (and on appeal (1911) 12 CLR 15 at 22). The practice of resale price maintenance is now prohibited by the *Trade Practices Act* 1974 (Cth), s 48.
74. **NSW**: *Conveyancing Act* 1919, s 36C; **Qld**: *Property Law Act* 1974, s 13 (but note this omits 'or other property'); **SA**: *Law of Property Act* 1936, s 34(1); **Tas**: *Conveyancing and Law of Property Act* 1884, s 61 and *Powers of Attorney Act* 1934, s 9; **Vic**: *Property Law Act* 1958, s 56(1); **WA**: *Property Law Act* 1969, s 11(1); **NT**: *Law of Property Act* 2000, s 12 (omits or 'other property'). There is semble no such legislation in the ACT.
75. [1968] AC 58.
76. See [912].

pay more. TP, having taken out letters of administration in respect of A's estate, took proceedings both in her capacity as administratrix and also in her personal capacity against B seeking specific performance of the agreement. She was held to be entitled, as administratrix, to an order for specific performance.

However, the Court of Appeal had also held[77] that s 56 of the *Law of Property Act* 1925 entitled her to enforce the contract in her own right as a contract made for her benefit. The House of Lords rejected this proposition, holding that s 56(1) was part of a consolidating Act and was intended merely to reproduce the effect of s 5 of the *Real Property Act* 1845.

The precise effect of s 56(1) and the significance for it of *Beswick v Beswick* are not free from difficulty. It is clear that it does not suffice to activate the section that an instrument is for the benefit of a third party. The better view seems to be that what is necessary and sufficient to activate the provision is that the instrument purports to contain a grant to or covenant with a third party.

The argument that the section appears in a consolidating statute may not be available in respect of its Australian counterparts. However, the provision has been narrowly construed in Australia also.[78]

[915] Recommendations for reform. The desirability of the privity doctrine in so far as it prevents the imposing of a contractual burden on a non-party is not under challenge. But where a contract purports to benefit a third party it has been thought unsatisfactory that that person should have no rights in respect of variation, termination or enforcement of the contract or in respect of any damages recovered for breach. There have been several official inquiries into the privity doctrine.[79] In Australia, the parliaments of Western Australia, Queensland and the Northern Territory have modified the privity rule. The provisions are to be found in s 11 of the *Property Law Act* 1969 (WA); s 55 of the *Property Law Act* 1974 (Qld)[80] and s 56 of the *Law of Property Act* 2000 (NT). Although by no means identical, the provisions entitle the third party beneficiary to enforce the contract; allow the immediate parties to vary or discharge the contract prior to its

---

77. [1966] Ch 538.
78. See *Concrete Constructions Pty Ltd v GIO of NSW* [1966] 2 NSWR 609; *Sacher Investments Pty Ltd v Forma Stereo Consultants Pty Ltd* [1976] 1 NSWLR 5 at 12.
79. See the *Sixth Interim Report* of the English Law Revision Committee, Cmd 5449, 1937, paras 41–9; Law Commission Report, *Privity of Contract: Contracts for the Benefit of 3rd Parties*, Law Com No 242, 1996, which led to the enactment of *Contracts (Rights of Third Parties) Act* 1999. For a discussion of the legislation see generally Merkin, ed, *Privity of Contract*, 2000. See also Report of the New Zealand Contracts and Commercial Law Reform Committee (whose draft bill was enacted in practically identical form in the *Contracts (Privity) Act* 1982 (NZ)).
80. And see New Zealand's *Contracts (Privity) Act* 1982. On the WA section see *Westralian Farmers Co-operative Ltd v Southern Meat Packers Ltd* [1981] WAR 241; *Whitfords Beach Pty Ltd v Gadson* [1991] 6 WAR 537. On the Qld section see *Northern Sand Blasting Pty Ltd v Harris* (1997) 188 CLR 313; *Hyatt Australia Ltd v LTCB Australia Ltd* [1996] 1 Qd R 260; Des Butler, 'Enforcement of Third Party Rights in Queensland Pursuant to Property Law Act 1974 (Qld), s 55' (1998) 14 *QUTLJ* 73, and on all three pieces of legislation, see Andrew Rogers, 'Contract and Third Parties' in Finn, ed, *Essays on Contract*, 1987, p 81; Louise Wilson, 'Contract and Benefits for Third Parties' (1987) 11 *Syd LR* 230.

being 'adopted' (Western Australia) or 'accepted' (Queensland and Northern Territory) by the third party beneficiary but not thereafter; protect the defendant in proceedings brought by the third party beneficiary as regards defences which would have been available if the third party beneficiary had been named as a party to the contract; and subject the third party beneficiary to obligations which the contract purports to impose on him or her.

[916] **Other legislation.** Other statutes may be seen to modify the operation of the privity doctrine in particular contexts. Examples are legislation which imposes liability on manufacturers in favour of consumers,[81] legislation providing that compulsory third party motor vehicle insurance shall indemnify non-party drivers[82] and, most importantly, recent legislation providing for enforcement of insurance policies by persons other than the proponent and the insurer.[83]

The Future of the Privity Doctrine in Australia

[917] **The *Trident* decision.** In *Trident General Insurance Co Ltd v McNiece Bros Pty Ltd*[84] Blue Circle Southern Cement Ltd entered into a contract of insurance with Trident. Subsequently to the issuing of the policy McNiece became the principal contractor for construction work being carried out at the plant of Blue Circle. The policy covered, among other things, liability to the public for accidents occurring during this construction work and the policy defined 'the assured' as including, in addition to Blue Circle, all its contractors and subcontractors. A worker was seriously injured at the construction site and recovered judgment against McNiece. McNiece claimed indemnity under the policy for the amount of the judgment but Trident denied liability. The New South Wales Court of Appeal held[85] that McNiece could recover on the ground that at common law a beneficiary under a contract of liability insurance can sue on the policy even though it is not a party to the contract and provides no consideration for it. On appeal to the High Court it was held by a five to two majority that McNiece could recover, but the approaches of the majority differed to such an extent that there is no majority support for any one approach. The case is important because of its implications generally for the privity doctrine in Australia; were the facts of the case to occur now, McNiece would be able to recover from Trident by virtue of s 48 of the *Insurance Contracts Act* 1984 (Cth).[86]

[918] **An action on the contract?** Mason CJ and Wilson J, in their joint judgment in *Trident General Insurance Co Ltd v McNiece Bros Pty Ltd*,[87] considered that there was much substance in criticisms which have been

---

81. For example, **Cth**: *Trade Practices Act* 1974, Pt V, Div 2A; **ACT**: *Law Reform (Manufacturers Warranties) Act* 1977; **SA**: *Manufacturers Warranties Act* 1974.
82. For example, *Motor Vehicles (Third Party Insurance) Act* 1942 (NSW), s 10(7).
83. *Insurance Contracts Act* 1984 (Cth), ss 48, 48A, 49, 51.
84. (1988) 165 CLR 107 (see Peter Kincaid, 'The Trident Insurance Case: Death of Contract?' (1989) 2 *JCL* 160).
85. (1987) 8 NSWLR 270.
86. See [916].
87. (1988) 165 CLR 107.

made of the common law privity doctrine. They concluded that 'it is the responsibility of this court to reconsider in appropriate cases common law rules which operate unsatisfactorily and unjustly'[88] and that 'the principled development of the law' required that McNiece be entitled to succeed.[89] While their Honours had in this case only to decide whether the old rules continue to apply to a policy of insurance, it seems unlikely that, faced with a third party beneficiary contract of a different kind, they would apply a different rule. (They did, however, refer to the likelihood in such cases of insurance as the presence of some degree of reliance, often probably not adequately protected by the doctrine of estoppel, by the third party as a factor which should influence the development of the law.) It would appear that Mason CJ and Wilson J would allow an action by a third party whenever there is a contractual intention to benefit the third party,[90] subject to the preservation of the right of the contracting parties to vary or rescind the contract (unless the third party had relied on the contract to his or her detriment) and subject also to the availability in an action by the third party of defences against a contracting party. Toohey J also held that McNiece could recover on the policy. While he stated the principle upon which his decision was based in narrow terms confined to certain insurance situations,[91] Toohey J recognised that a decision in favour of McNiece would inevitably have implications for privity of contract in other situations[92] and it would seem that his approach would be similar to that of Mason CJ and Wilson J.[93]

[919] Revival of the trust device? Deane J in *Trident General Insurance Co Ltd v McNiece Bros Pty Ltd*[94] felt unable to take the step of holding that in a situation such as this the third party has a direct right of action on the contract. He considered that criticism of the privity doctrine has often been flawed by an incomplete perception of the extent to which its practical effect is confined and qualified by the application of other principles.[95] In some cases injustice could be avoided by the application of the principles of estoppel or unjust enrichment (but these had not been relied upon in this case). Deane J, agreeing with an earlier comment of Fullagar J,[96] found it difficult to understand the reluctance which courts have often shown to infer a trust in third party beneficiary cases and considered that this had

---

88. (1988) 165 CLR 107 at 123.
89. (1988) 165 CLR 107 at 124.
90. They semble would not go further and require, as does the *Property Law Act* 1974 (Qld) s 55 and *Law of Property Act* 2000 (NT), s 56 (see [915]), an indication of intention that the third party should be able to sue on the contract: see at 123. For a comparison of the Queensland Act with the general law following the *Trident* case see C A C MacDonald, 'The High Court, Contract and Remedies' (1989) 5 *QUTLJ* 35.
91. (1988) 165 CLR 107 at 172.
92. (1988) 165 CLR 107 at 163.
93. See also *Barroora Pty Ltd v Provincial Insurance Ltd* (1992) 26 NSWLR 170. In *Co-operative Bulk Handling Ltd v Jennings Industries Ltd* (1996) WAR 257 the Full Supreme Court of Western Australia held that *Trident* was not limited to 'liability' insurance. Nor was there an inference that only those persons who were intended to be insured under the contract and who acted on such assumption and suffered detriment were entitled to the benefit of the exception. See also *Pacific Dunlop Ltd v Maxitherm Boilers Proprietary Ltd* (1997) 9 ANZ Insurance Cases 61-357; *WA Woodside Petroleum Development Pty Ltd v H & R E-W Pty Ltd* (1997) 18 WAR 539; and on appeal (1999) 20 WAR 380.
94. (1988) 165 CLR 107.
95. (1988) 165 CLR 107 at 144.
96. In *Wilson v Darling Island Stevedoring & Lighterage Co Ltd* (1956) 95 CLR 43 at 67.

often been caused by a failure to appreciate the innate flexibility of the law of trusts.[97] He considered that the requisite intention to create a trust should be inferred if it clearly appears that it was the intention of the promisee that the third party should be entitled to insist upon performance of the promise and receipt of the benefit and if trust is, in the circumstances, the appropriate legal mechanism for giving effect to that intention.[98] In Deane J's view the prima facie effect of the policy here was to create a trust for McNiece and it was difficult to conceive of circumstances which would negative or modify that conclusion. However, as the case had not been argued on the basis of a trust, McNiece should be given leave to join Blue Circle in the proceedings and Trident should be allowed, if it could, to place before the court material showing that there were circumstances precluding or modifying the trust which the policy would otherwise have created.

[920] **Unjust enrichment?** The final member of the court in *Trident General Insurance Co Ltd v McNiece Bros Pty Ltd*[99] who would allow McNiece to recover was Gaudron J, who did so on a principle of unjust enrichment.[100] Her Honour held that a promisor who has accepted an agreed consideration for a promise to benefit a third party is unjustly enriched to the extent that the promise is unfulfilled and the non-fulfilment does not attract proportional legal consequences. The right of the third party to sue is not a right to sue on the contract, but rather a right independent of, but ordinarily corresponding in content and duration with, the obligation owed under the contract by the promisor to the promisee.[101]

[921] **The dissenting judgments in *Trident*.** Brennan and Dawson JJ considered in *Trident General Insurance Co Ltd v McNiece Bros Pty Ltd*[102] that this was not an appropriate situation for the High Court to overturn well-established doctrine. The Court of Appeal had held that an exception to the privity doctrine existed in respect of liability insurance contracts, but neither Brennan nor Dawson JJ could see any conceptual basis on which such contracts should be treated differently from other types of contract. Both thought that the path of future development to avoid any injustice caused by the doctrine lay in the further development of other principles such as those relating to the law of trusts, estoppel and damages.

[922] **Conclusion.** The path of future development of the privity doctrine in Australia following the decision of the High Court in *Trident General Insurance Co Ltd v McNiece Bros Pty Ltd*[103] is unclear. It may be that when

---

97. (1988) 165 CLR 107 at 146–7.
98. (1988) 165 CLR 107 at 147. Mason CJ and Wilson J (at 121) seemed to think it was the intention of both parties that was relevant.
99. (1988) 165 CLR 107.
100. As to unjust enrichment generally see Chapter 23. For a discussion in the context of the privity doctrine see Mason and Carter, *Restitution Law in Australia*, 1995, paras 1841–2.
101. Deane J, (1988) 165 CLR 107 at 145–6, considered that in some circumstances an action founded on unjust enrichment might perhaps be available to the third party, but he did not find it necessary to pursue this question. For criticisms of Gaudron J's approach towards unjust enrichment see K B Soh, 'Privity of Contract and Restitution' (1989) 105 *LQR* 4; D A Butler, 'Privity of Contract in Queensland' (1990) 10 *QL* 147.
102. (1988) 165 CLR 107.
103. (1988) 165 CLR 107.

the issue again comes before the High Court a majority will be prepared, where a contract shows a clear intention to benefit a third party, to hold that at common law the third party may sue on the contract. If this step is taken, it is difficult to see the right to sue being restricted to situations involving insurance policies. At the very least it seems that courts will be much more willing than in the past to find an intention to create a trust in favour of the third party. (As we saw earlier,[104] Deane J's judgment centred on this point, but it was also made by Mason CJ and Wilson J and by Toohey J.)[105] It is also likely that there will be further development of the law relating to the measure of damages, to estoppel, and perhaps also to unjust enrichment, to minimise any risk of injustice. It may also be that the courts may in some situations feel less pressure than would otherwise be the case to grant a tort remedy in negligence to a person suffering economic loss as a result of a breach of a contract to which that person was not a party.[106] It should be noted that the general law will apparently still be relevant even in jurisdictions such as Queensland, Northern Territory and Western Australia which have legislated so as to grant a right of action to the third party beneficiary. This is because where the statute is not applicable, due to, for example, the beneficiary not accepting within a reasonable time as required by the *Property Law Act* 1974 (Qld), s 55,[107] (and *Law of Property Act* 2000 (NT), s 56) it may well be that the beneficiary will nonetheless be held entitled, for example, under a trust arising under the general law.[108]

It should finally be noted that where a third party beneficiary may in principle be entitled to sue, it will in some cases be difficult to decide whether a particular person was intended to benefit directly under the contract or was merely one who in some incidental way would benefit if it is performed. The latter 'incidental beneficiary' will in any event not be able to enforce the contract, and this would seem to be the case whether the action is brought under an expanded common law rule or under legislation such as that enacted in Queensland, Northern Territory and Western Australia. Thus where an injured employee sued an insurance company with whom his employer held a policy, it was held, distinguishing *Trident*, that the words of the policy promised indemnity only to the employer and not to the employee, and that as a consequence the action must fail.[109]

---

104. See [919].
105. (1988) 165 CLR 107 at 120–1, 166. See also *Bahr v Nicolay (No 2)* (1988) 164 CLR 604 at 618–19 per Mason CJ and Dawson J.
106. See, eg *White v Jones* [1995] 2 WLR 187; *Bryan v Maloney* (1995) 182 CLR 609; *Hill v Van Erp* (1997) 188 CLR 159 and the discussion in D Beyleveld and R Brownsword, 'Privity, Transitivity and Rationality' (1991) 54 *MLR* 48.
107. See *Re Davies* [1989] 1 Qd R 48.
108. See D A Butler, 'Privity of Contract in Queensland' (1990) 10 *QL* 147. The *Property Law Act* 1974 (Qld), s 55(7) (and *Law of Property Act* 2000 (NT), s 56(7)) expressly preserves rights or remedies arising apart from that provision.
109. *Visic v State Government Insurance Commission* (1990) 3 WAR 122.

The Special Case of Third Parties and the Benefit of Exclusion Clauses[110]

[923] **The *Elder Dempster* case and its sequelae.** Bills of lading attempt to exclude or limit liability in respect of the cargo, not only of the immediate issuer of the bill (shipowner or carrier), but of other persons involved in their carriage as well. Is such a non-issuer entitled to the protection of such an exclusion clause? It will be noted that literally he or she seeks not to enforce a promise but to take the benefit of a defence. In *Elder Dempster & Co v Paterson Zochonis & Co*[111] a bill issued by a carrier which purported to protect 'the shipowners' as well as the charterer was held by all members of the House of Lords to be effective for that purpose. Viscount Cave said, 'It may be that the owners were not directly parties to the contract; but they took possession of the goods ... on behalf of and as the agents of the charterers, and so can claim the same protection as their principals'.[112]

This may be called a principle of 'vicarious immunity'.[113] In two New South Wales cases, *Gilbert Stokes & Kerr Pty Ltd v Dalgety & Co Ltd*[114] and *Waters Trading Co Ltd v Dalgety & Co Ltd*,[115] non-issuers succeeded similarly.

Lines of reasoning other than a theory of vicarious immunity leading to the same result were available and referred to in these cases, such as that the carrier who had issued the bill had contracted as agent of the defendant, or that a collateral bailment agreement came into existence between the plaintiff and the defendant incorporating the exclusion clause in the bill of lading.

In *Cosgrove v Horsfall*[116] and *Adler v Dickson*[117] injured passengers suing employees of the carrier were met with defences based on exclusion clauses in the agreement between plaintiff and carrier. In *Cosgrove v Horsfall* a free bus pass issued to Cosgrove by a transport authority stipulated that neither it nor its servants should be liable to him for, inter alia, injury. The Court of Appeal held that the defendant Horsfall, a bus driver, could not rely on the agreement because he was not a party to it. In *Adler v Dickson*, Mrs Adler, while a passenger on the P & O Steamship, *Himalaya*, was injured, allegedly as a result of the negligence of the master and boatswain whom she sued. Conditions on her ticket exempted the company from liability including liability in respect of injury occasioned by negligence of the company's servants. All three members of the Court of Appeal agreed that the conditions did not, expressly or by implication, deprive the plaintiff of the right to sue the servants.

---

110. The expression 'exclusion clause' is used to comprehend exclusion, exemption, exception and limitation (both time limitation and monetary limitation) clauses.
111. [1924] AC 522.
112. [1924] AC 522 at 534.
113. Cf Coote, *Exception Clauses*, 1964, pp 119ff.
114. (1948) 48 SR (NSW) 435 per Owen J.
115. (1951) 52 SR (NSW) 4.
116. (1945) 62 TLR 140.
117. [1955] 1 QB 158.

Denning LJ thought that *Elder Dempster* allowed protection to stevedores and others because 'although they were not parties to the contract nevertheless they participated in the performance of it, and the exception clause was [by necessary implication] made for their benefit whilst they were so performing it'.[118] Jenkins and Morris LJJ, while noting that the ticket did not purport to protect the company's servants, thought that even if it had done so, the privity doctrine would have prevented them from relying on it.

In *Wilson v Darling Island Stevedoring & Lighterage Co Ltd*,[119] the High Court by a three to two majority overruled *Gilbert Stokes* and *Waters Trading* and held that an exclusion clause in a bill of lading which purported to protect 'the Carrier or his Agents or servants' did not protect a stevedore which was the agent of the issuer (in this case the carrier which issued the bill was the shipowner) because the stevedore could not sue or be sued on a contract to which it was not a party.[120]

[924] **Midland Silicones.** The privity rule was applied by the House of Lords in *Scruttons Ltd v Midland Silicones Ltd*[121] to deny the protection of an exclusion clause in a bill of lading to a stevedore. The bill was signed on behalf of the shipowner and provided for a monetary ceiling on the liability of the 'carrier' which was defined in standard form to include 'the owner or the charterer who enters into a contract of carriage with a shipper'.[122]

Lord Morris observed[123] that there is no difference in principle between A's promises to B (in each case for good consideration) that A will make a gift to C and that A will not claim from C that which C ought to pay to A. The House held that the term 'carrier' did not include the stevedores, that the bill did not, expressly or by implication, purport to extend the benefit of the limitation on liability provision to stevedores, and that the carrier did not contract as agent for the stevedores. But Lord Reid held out some hope for the agency argument in a different factual context:[124]

> I can see a possibility of success of the agency argument if (first) the bill of lading makes it clear that the stevedore is intended to be protected by the provisions in it which limit liability, (secondly) the bill of lading makes it clear that the carrier, in addition to contracting for these provisions on his own behalf, is also contracting as agent for the stevedore that these provisions should apply to the stevedore, (thirdly) the carrier has authority from the stevedore to do that, or perhaps later ratification by the stevedore would suffice, (fourthly) that any difficulties about consideration moving from the stevedore were overcome.

---

118. [1955] 1 QB 158 at 182–3.
119. (1956) 95 CLR 43.
120. Various possible grounds for distinguishing *Elder Dempster* were suggested, particularly by Fullagar J. But compare the recent decision by the Court of Appeal in *Norwich City Council v Harvey* [1989] 1 All ER 1180, criticised by Palmer, *Bailment*, 2nd ed, 1991, pp 1625–31, 1645–53.
121. [1962] AC 446.
122. The bill was expressly made subject to the *Carriage of Goods by Sea Act* 1936 (US) whereby the US adopted the Hague Rules with certain variations and the definition of 'carrier' was contained in s 1(a) of the Act.
123. [1962] AC 446 at 494.
124. [1962] AC 446 at 474.

[925] ***The Eurymedon*** **and** ***The New York Star.*** The question before the Privy Council in *New Zealand Shipping Co Ltd v A M Satterthwaite & Co Ltd (The Eurymedon)*[125] was whether the bill of lading there in question (which was in a form in use prior to *Scruttons Ltd v Midland Silicones Ltd*[126] and had not been drawn in the light of that case) satisfied Lord Reid's requirements.[127]

The bill of lading issued by the carrier to the consignor-manufacturer of an expensive drilling machine was for its shipment from Liverpool to Wellington in New Zealand. The machine was damaged, allegedly as a result of the negligence of the stevedore ('New Zealand Shipping') at a time by which the consignee (Satterthwaite) had become the holder of the bill and bound by its terms and owner of the goods.[128] Importantly, for several years, the stevedore had carried out all the stevedoring work in Wellington in respect of the carrier's ships; the carrier was a wholly owned subsidiary of the stevedore; and the stevedore generally acted as the carrier's agent in New Zealand. The bill provided as follows:

> It is hereby expressly agreed that no servant or agent of the carrier (including every independent contractor from time to time employed by the carrier) shall in any circumstances whatsoever be under any liability whatsoever to the shipper, consignee or owner of the goods or to any holder of this bill of lading for any loss or damage or delay of whatsoever kind arising or resulting directly or indirectly from any act, neglect or default on his part while acting in the course of or in connection with his employment and, without prejudice to the generality of the foregoing provisions in this clause, every exemption, limitation, condition and liberty herein contained and every right, exemption from liability, defence and immunity of whatsoever nature applicable to the carrier or to which the carrier is entitled hereunder shall also be available and shall extend to protect every such servant or agent of the carrier acting as aforesaid and for the purpose of all the foregoing provisions of this clause the carrier is or shall be deemed to be acting as agent or trustee on behalf of and for the benefit of all persons who are or might be his servants or agents from time to time (including independent contractors as aforesaid) and all such persons shall to this extent be or be deemed to be parties to the contract in or evidenced by this bill of lading.

The bill incorporated the Hague Rules scheduled to the *Carriage of Goods by Sea Act* 1924 (UK), with the result that the carrier and the ship were discharged from all liability in respect of cargo damage unless suit was brought against them within one year after delivery. Was the stevedore also entitled to the benefit of this time bar clause?

The bill clearly purported to protect the stevedore but was the stevedore a contracting party? Lord Wilberforce, speaking for the majority, analysed the transaction as follows:[129]

---

125. [1975] AC 154.
126. [1962] AC 446.
127. [1975] AC 154 at 166 per Lord Wilberforce for the majority.
128. In some cases at least, by accepting a bill of lading and asking for delivery of the goods, a consignee becomes entitled to the benefit of, and bound by, the bill's terms vis-à-vis the carrier: *Brandt v Liverpool Brazil and River Plate Steam Navigation Co Ltd* [1924] 1 KB 575; *The Aramis* [1989] 1 Lloyd's Rep 213. There is legislation dealing with this in most Australian jurisdictions: see *Carriage of Goods By Sea Act* 1991 (Cth), *Sea-Carriage Documents Act* 1997 (NSW); and for a discussion see Frances Hannah, 'Sea Carriage Documents', Chapter 8, in White, ed, *Australian Maritime Law*, 2nd ed, 2000.

[T]he bill of lading brought into existence a bargain initially unilateral but capable of becoming mutual, between the shipper and the appellant [stevedore], made through the carrier as agent. This became a full contract when the appellant performed services by discharging the goods. The performance of these services for the benefit of the shipper was the consideration for the agreement by the shipper that the appellant should have the benefit of the exemptions and limitations contained in the bill of lading.

The dissentients, Viscount Dilhorne and Lord Simon of Glaisdale, accepted that a third party could be protected by a clause appropriately framed.

In view of the close association between the stevedore and the carrier in *The Eurymedon*, it could hardly be suggested that the stevedore, when commencing to provide services, did not know of the bill of lading or of its terms. Analysis in terms either of acceptance by its act of the shipper's offer to exempt, or of the exchange of that act for a promise by the shipper,[130] sits comfortably with this fact. The question of whether the stevedore had supplied consideration was discussed earlier.[131]

The High Court and the Privy Council, following *The Eurymedon*, held a stevedore entitled to the benefit of a time bar clause in the bill of lading issued by the charterer in *Port Jackson Stevedoring Pty Ltd v Salmond & Spraggon (Aust) Pty Ltd (The New York Star)*.[132]

Thirty-seven cartons of razor blades had been shipped on the *New York Star* from Canada to Sydney, where the stevedore unloaded them and stored them in its wharfside shed, from which 33 cartons were stolen. The shipment was covered by a bill of lading issued by the charterer to, and accepted by, the consignor, and transmitted to and accepted by the plaintiff consignee by the time of the loss. Clause 2 of the bill was identical to the clause in *The Eurymedon* quoted above (which has come to be called the '*Himalaya* clause' after the name of the ship in *Adler v Dickson*)[133] and as in that case there was a one year time bar provision. Further, as in that case, the stevedore had for years acted as stevedore in the discharge of the carrier's ships in the port of discharge. It knew the contents (including the *Himalaya* clause) of the carrier's form of bill of lading for shipments to Australia.

There were two principal issues: was the stevedore entitled to such protection as the time bar clause offered? And, if so, did that clause, properly construed, cover the facts? Only the former need be discussed here. The High Court by a three to two majority answered it 'yes'. The *Himalaya* clause clearly satisfied the first and second of Lord Reid's requirements, and according to their Honours forming the majority on the first issue, Barwick CJ, Mason and Jacobs JJ, the facts supported an inference of fact that the carrier had contracted with the stevedore's authority.

---

129. [1975] AC 154 at 167–8.
130. Cf [1975] AC 154 at 168 per Lord Wilberforce.
131. See [349].
132. (1978) 139 CLR 231 (HC); (1980) 144 CLR 300 (PC).
133. [1955] 1 QB 158 (see [923]).

In relation to Lord Reid's fourth condition, Mason and Jacobs JJ thought that the relevant provisions of the bill constituted an offer capable of acceptance and that when the stevedore, knowing of it and of its conditions, performed its conditions by unloading, it accepted that offer and provided the consideration for it.[134] By contrast, Barwick CJ thought that the provisions constituted at the outset an agreement with the stevedore as distinct from an offer to it, for which the stevedore gave consideration by unloading. His Honour said,[135] 'I can see no validity in a suggestion that the bill of lading could not at the one time contain a contract of carriage between the consignor and carrier and an arrangement between consignor and stevedore, made through the agency of the carrier, to regulate the relationship of consignor and stevedore, when the stevedoring work was undertaken' and described[136] the arrangement as 'a compact with agreed conditions to attend the performance of certain acts, which are not promised to be done' whose essential characteristic is 'to provide an agreed consequence to future action should that action take place: to attach conditions to a relationship arising from conduct'. On this approach 'the performance of the contemplated act both supplies the occasion for those conditions to operate and the consideration which makes the arrangement contractual'.[137]

The Privy Council found Barwick CJ's analysis to be 'in substantial agreement with and indeed to constitute a powerful reinforcement of one of the two possible bases put forward in the Board's judgment'[138] in *The Eurymedon* for holding the stevedore entitled to the benefit of the exemption clause. Since the stevedore is, on either the reasoning of Barwick CJ or that of Mason and Jacobs JJ, a principal contracting party, questions as to how far a third party beneficiary under a contract can enforce that contract do not arise.

In *The Mahkutai*,[139] the Privy Council approved the bilateral contract approach taken in *The Eurymedon* and *The New York Star* and indicated that it might even take the approach further.[140] As the case dealt with a jurisdiction clause rather than an exemption clause the Privy Council did not think it appropriate to do so in that case.

Sequelae of *The Eurymedon* and *The New York Star*. Subsequent Australian cases have held that the principles enunciated in *The Eurymedon*[141] and *The New York Star*[142] apply to carriage of goods by road as well as by sea and to other exemption clauses as well as to time bar clauses; and that ratification, one of the two alternative limbs of Lord Reid's

---

134. Citing *R v Clarke* (1927) 40 CLR 227 at 244 per Starke J.
135. (1968) 139 CLR 231 at 243 (emphasis supplied).
136. (1968) 139 CLR 231 at 244.
137. (1968) 139 CLR 231 at 244.
138. (1980) 144 CLR 300 at 305.
139. [1996] AC 650; noted [1997] *LMCLQ* 1.
140. '[T]he time may well come when, in an appropriate case, it will fall to be considered whether the courts should take what may legitimately be perceived to be the final, and inevitable, step in this development, and recognise in these cases, a fully fledged exception to the doctrine of privity of contract, thus escaping from all the technicalities which the courts are now faced in English law': [1996] AC 650 at 664 per Lord Goff.
141. [1975] AC 154.
142. (1978) 139 CLR 231 (HC); (1980) 144 CLR 300 (PC).

third condition in *Midland Silicones*, may take the form of the third party's pleading the exemption clause.[143]

In *Celthene Pty Ltd v WKJ Hauliers Pty Ltd*,[144] Yeldham J in the Supreme Court of New South Wales held that consideration had been supplied by a driver of a subcontractor (the subcontractor and its driver were both sued) notwithstanding that at the time of performance he had not known of the existence of the clause.[145] In *Life Savers (Australasia) Ltd v Frigmobile Pty Ltd*[146] there was no antecedent established business connection between the carrier and its subcontractor as there had been in *The Eurymedon* and *The New York Star*, but the subcontractor had accepted delivery of the consignment (of chocolate) from the plaintiff/consignor on an invoice of the carrier's signed by the subcontractor's driver and by the consignor. The case was treated by the New South Wales Court of Appeal as one of an offer by the consignor of the immunity to the subcontractor direct if he would carry the goods and of acceptance of the offer by the acceptance of the goods on that basis.

These two New South Wales cases suggest that many third party beneficiaries of exclusion clauses will have little difficulty in meeting Lord Reid's third and fourth conditions.[147] Hutley JA's observation in the *Life Savers* case seems most apposite: 'The form of contract here used, patterned on provisions in favour of stevedores and other subcontractors in bills of lading, strains doctrines of privity of contract and consideration but these difficulties have been overcome'.[148]

One final speculation may be permitted. If in future Australian law is to permit a third party intended to be benefited by a contract a direct right of action on the contract[149] there would seem no obvious reason why this approach should not also apply to the benefit of exclusion clauses.[150] If so, the niceties of analysis raised by *The Eurymedon* and *The New York Star* could be sidestepped.

---

143. *Celthene Pty Ltd v WKJ Hauliers Pty Ltd* [1981] 1 NSWLR 606; *Life Savers (Australasia) Ltd v Frigmobile Pty Ltd* [1983] 1 NSWLR 431. But compare the comments of Kirby P and Handley JA in *Carrington Slipways Pty Ltd v Patrick Operations Pty Ltd* (1991) 24 NSWLR 745 and see D Malcolm, 'The Negligent Pilot and the *Himalaya* Clause: a Saga of Disagreement' (1993) 67 *ALJ* 14.
144. [1981] 1 NSWLR 606.
145. With respect, it is difficult to support the holding that consideration could be furnished in ignorance of, and without reference to, the offer: see [315]–[318]. As to ratification in such a context see also *Trident General Insurance Co Ltd v McNiece Bros Pty Ltd* (1987) 8 NSWLR 270 at 282 per McHugh JA; Palmer, *Bailment*, 2nd ed, 1991, pp 1617–20.
146. [1983] 1 NSWLR 431.
147. For a discussion of the two New South Wales cases, see S W Cavanagh, 'The Ultimate Exclusion Clause' (1985) 59 *ALJ* 67. As to the possibility of the carrier obtaining a stay of proceedings where the consignor or consignee sues the third party in contravention of an express promise in the bill of lading not to do so see *Broken Hill Pty Co Ltd v Hapag-Lloyd Aktiengesellschaft* [1980] 2 NSWLR 572. See also *Deepak Fertilisers and Petrochemicals Corporation v ICI Chemicals & Polymers Ltd* [1999] 1 Lloyd's Rep 387.
148. [1999] 1 Lloyd's Rep 387 at 438. For a discussion of these difficulties see Palmer, *Bailment*, 2nd ed, 1991, pp 1605b ff. As to a special rule which apparently arises under the law of bailment see *The Pioneer Container* [1994] 2 All ER 250 and Palmer, *Bailment*, 2nd ed, 1991, pp 1631–45.
149. See the discussion in [918]–[922] of *Trident General Insurance Co Ltd v McNiece Bros Pty Ltd* (1988) 165 CLR 107.
150. See also *The Mahkutai* [1996] AC 650 at 664–5 per Lord Goff.

Plurality of Parties

[927] Introduction. Of present concern is the promise which is given by or to two or more persons, such as a promise by A and B (co-promisors) to C, or by A alone to B and C (co-promisees). Difficult questions of construction may arise as to the nature of a promise made by co-promisors and of one made to co-promisees. There is also a series of rules as to various other matters, for example the effect of the death of a co-promisor or co-promisee, the effect of a release in favour of one co-promisor or a release by one co-promisee. Considerations of space prevent a discussion of these rules here, but such may be found elsewhere.[151] All that is attempted here is to describe in general terms the types of promises which may be encountered.

[928] Co-promisors. A distinction is made between 'joint', 'joint and several' and 'several' promisors. A joint promise is of the form 'A and B together promise C to pay C $1000'. A joint and several promise is of the form 'A and B together promise C, and A separately promises C, and B separately promises C, to pay C $1000', the promise by A and B together being the joint promise and the two separate promises, one by A and the other by B, being the several promises.

Joint promises and joint and several promises are alike in that only one performance is promised ('to pay C $1000') and once the promisee (C) receives payment C no longer has a cause of action. By contrast, purely several promises are cumulative and in terms of the illustration would have had A and B each promising $1000, that is, $2000 in all.

A joint promise by two or more persons creates a single obligation incumbent upon both or all. The theory of a joint and several obligation is that it creates both a joint obligation incumbent upon all and a number of several obligations respectively incumbent upon each one; but the several obligations are non-cumulative, so that (as with purely joint liability) performance by any one will discharge all.[152] The common law presumption is that a promise by two or more is made jointly but the question is one of intention and in some cases is affected by legislation.

[929] Co-promisees. A promise to co-promisees jointly is of the form 'A promises B and C together to pay X $1000' and a promise to them jointly and severally[153] is of the form 'A promises B and C together and A promises B separately and A promises C separately to pay X $1000'.

As noted above,[154] purely several promises are cumulative and just as this was illustrated there by promises by A and B each to pay C $1000, so it can be illustrated here by A's promise to B to pay B $1000 and A's promise to C to pay C $1000, two promises which oblige A to pay $2000 in all ($1000 to B and $1000 to C). It can also be illustrated by A's promise to B to pay X $1000 and A's separate promise to C to pay X $1000, two separate

---

151. See *Halsbury's Laws of Australia*, 'Contract', pp 197, 531-7; Williams, *Joint Obligations*, 1949.
152. Williams, *Joint Obligations*, 1949, p 24. See also *Re Broons* [1989] 2 Qd R 315.
153. The early law did not recognise this possibility.
154. See [928].

promises which also oblige A to pay $2000 in all (the whole $2000 to X). The present concern is not with such purely separate and cumulative promises. The position of co-promisees is more complex than that of co-promisors. Co-promisee questions, like co-promisor questions, are logically distinct from questions as to the content of the promise. But the existence and extent of the interests of the co-promisees in the subject matter of the contract and in performance of the promise can influence a decision as to whether the promise is to the co-promisees jointly, jointly and severally, or severally. The law seeks to give effect to the parties' intention as expressed. Where co-promisees have no beneficial interest in the contract's subject matter or performance, a promise is seen to be made to them jointly.

[930] Co-promisees: consideration moving from one. It seems to have been accepted in *Coulls v Bagot's Executor and Trustee Co Ltd*[155] that where consideration is furnished by one joint promisee, the promise is enforceable by all the joint promisees: vis-à-vis the promisor, the consideration has been furnished by all. By contrast, consideration must move from each several promisee.[156]

---

155. (1967) 119 CLR 460 (see [322]).
156. For the position of joint and several promisees, see *McEvoy v Belfast Banking Co* [1935] AC 24, discussed by LSJB, (1935) 51 *LQR* 419; and Treitel, *The Law of Contract*, 10th ed, 1999, pp 536–7.

PART V
Vitiating Factors and Misleading and Deceptive Conduct

Chapter 10

Misrepresentation

General	1001
Elements of Misrepresentation	1006
False Factual Statement	*1006*
Reliance	*1019*
Materiality	*1023*
Fraudulent Misrepresentation	1025
Negligent Misrepresentation	1029
Innocent Misrepresentation	1037
Rescission for Misrepresentation	1039
Exercise of the Right of Rescission	*1039*
Restrictions on Rescission	*1042*
Damages for Misrepresentation	1063
Introduction	*1063*
Damages at Common Law	*1066*
Damages Under Statute	*1073*

General

[1001] Introduction. It was explained earlier[1] that where a statement is made by one person which induces another to enter into a contract, the statement may take effect as a *term* of that contract or a collateral contract. It was, however, also said that a false statement may still give rise to rights and remedies even though it is not effective as a term of the contract. This distinction is often expressed as a contrast between a 'warranty', in the broad sense of a legally binding promise, and a 'mere representation'. In this chapter we consider the legal characteristics[2] which such statements must possess in order to be a source of rights and remedies under the law of misrepresentation, the various types of misrepresentation[3] and the content of the rights and remedies themselves.[4]

---

1. See [602]–[614].
2. See [1006]–[1024].
3. See [1025]–[1038].

[1001]   Although statutory provisions specifically designed to reform the law of misrepresentation are discussed in the present chapter,[5] more recent statutory developments in the area of misleading or deceptive conduct, which are more broadly based (but impinge considerably on the law of misrepresentation), are discussed in the next chapter.[6]

[1002]   Definition and effect. A misrepresentation is a false statement of a material fact made by one person (the representor) to another (the representee) in order to induce the representee to enter into the contract and which has this effect. The misrepresentation does not prevent the contract coming into being: the contract is not void.[7] Instead, the basic response of the law of misrepresentation to this 'misinformation' is to say that because the representee's decision to contract was based on a false understanding, the representee is entitled to treat the contract as if it never existed. This entitlement, or right of avoidance, is termed the right of 'rescission'.

Rescission is the principal remedy for misrepresentation.[8] Damages for breach of contract are necessarily excluded if the contract is rescinded. However, if the contract is not rescinded, and the false statement of fact is also a term of the contract, damages for breach of contract may be claimed.[9] Whether or not the contract is rescinded, damages may be recoverable in tort (if the misrepresentation was fraudulent or made in breach of a duty of care) or under statute (for example, because it amounts to misleading or deceptive conduct).

[1003]   Common law, equity and statute. Prior to the fusion of law and equity, jurisdiction over misrepresentation was exercised both at common law and in equity. The right of rescission for misrepresentation was available on a much more liberal basis in equity than at common law. On the other hand, the common law courts exercised a jurisdiction to award damages in cases of fraud not generally possessed by the equity courts. The fusion of law and equity has, except perhaps in one area,[10] made the distinction largely of historical interest, although it is still helpful to recall the origins of the current principles.

In recent years the legal and equitable principles have been affected by statute. For present purposes it is sufficient to make three points. First, as might be expected, certain aspects of the law of misrepresentation have been reformed and rationalised.[11]

Second, the introduction of statutory prohibitions on certain kinds of conduct, by the *Trade Practices Act* 1974 (Cth) and fair trading legislation, has made the law of misrepresentation much less significant than it was formerly. False factual statements are relevant examples of such conduct.[12]

---

4.   See [1039]–[1072].
5.   See [1056], [1059], [1073]–[1078].
6.   Chapter 11. See also [1003].
7.   But see [1206], [1240], [1244] (mistake).
8.   Cf [2412] (refusal of specific performance).
9.   See [1036], [1058].
10. See [1060]–[1062].
11. See [1056], [1059], [1073]–[1078].
12. See Chapter 11.

Third, a pre-contract misrepresentation may be a factor relevant to a grant of relief under statutes such as the *Contracts Review Act* 1980 (NSW),[13] under which relief is available in respect of a contract which is 'unjust in the circumstances'.

[1004] Types of misrepresentation. Misrepresentations are classified as either *fraudulent* or *innocent*. The category of innocent misrepresentation is essentially residual, containing all non-fraudulent misrepresentations. Following the recognition of a remedy in damages for negligent misstatement in *Hedley Byrne & Co Ltd v Heller & Partners Ltd*,[14] it has become usual, at least for the purpose of analysis, to refer to a category of *negligent* misrepresentation, that is, one made in breach of a duty of care.

[1005] When writing required. The part of s 4 of the *Statute of Frauds* 1677 (Imp)[15] requiring promises to guarantee the performance of an obligation to be evidenced by writing[16] was supplemented by s 6 of *Lord Tenterden's Act* (the *Statute of Frauds Amendment Act* 1828 (Imp)). This provided that no action could be brought based upon a representation or assurance as to the credit or ability of a person unless it was in writing and signed by the defendant. The provision, which seems still to be in force in the Northern Territory, South Australia and Western Australia, was enacted because of the circumvention of s 4 by pleadings alleging a fraudulent misrepresentation of creditworthiness. Local enactments to the same effect can be found in the Australian Capital Territory, Tasmania and Victoria.[17] But in New South Wales and Queensland the legislation has been repealed.[18]

The discussion in the Report of the New South Wales Law Reform Commission[19] provides strong grounds for repeal of the provision, which has the anomalous effect that absence of written evidence is a defence to a claim for damages for fraudulent misrepresentation but not negligent misrepresentation.[20] Moreover, the requirements of writing in relation to contracts of guarantee have been repealed in some Australian jurisdictions, and a different provision has been enacted to deal with the guarantee of credit contracts.[21]

---

13. See [1520]. See also [1524] (trade practices legislation).
14. [1964] AC 465.
15. See generally [502]–[512].
16. See [507].
17. See **ACT**: *Mercantile Law Act* 1962, s 16; **Tas**: *Mercantile Law Act* 1935, s 11; **Vic**: *Instruments Act* 1958, s 128.
18. See **NSW**: *Usury, Bills of Lading and Written Memoranda (Repeal) Act* 1990, s 3 (itself repealed by the (NSW) *Statute Law (Miscellaneous Provisions) Act* 1996, s 4, Sch 5); **Qld**: *Statute of Frauds* 1972, s 3 (itself repealed by the *Property Law Act* 1974).
19. *Representations as to Credit*, LRC 57, 1988.
20. The legislative prohibitions on misleading or deceptive conduct discussed in Chapter 11 only serve to emphasise the anomaly.
21. See [507], [512].

Elements of Misrepresentation

False Factual Statement

General

[1006] False factual statement a misrepresentation. A misrepresentation is a representation which does not accord with the true facts (past or present). Therefore, promises or assurances for the future, statements of intention, expressions of opinion, advertising 'puffs', and representations of law have all, on occasions, been distinguished from the representation of fact essential to an operative misrepresentation.

However, a representation need not be express, since the words and circumstances may *imply* a representation as to a matter of fact, especially as to the state of mind of the maker of the statement.[22]

[1007] Advertising 'puffs'. The reason given for the exclusion of advertising 'puffs' (for example, 'a desirable residence for a family of distinction')[23] is that such statements are not reasonably understood to be statements of fact.

Promises and statements of intention or opinion

[1008] Promises and assurances. A promise or assurance for the future cannot be presently true or false, and does not of itself constitute a misrepresentation.[24] For example, in *Civil Service Co-operative Society of Victoria Ltd v Blyth*[25] a rule of a co-operative society empowered the directors to suspend withdrawals by members. The plaintiffs were promised that the rule would not be enforced against them. Griffith CJ and Barton J pointed out that this was not a representation of an existing fact which could give rise to a right to rescind a contract to take shares in the society.

Whether words are promissory or representational is a question of substance or effect, and not merely one of grammar. A promissory statement implies that the maker intends and believes that the promise or assurance will be fulfilled. In *Balfour v Hollandia Ravensthorpe NL*[26] an agent for a vendor of land told prospective purchasers that in two years' time they would be able to borrow from a particular building society an amount equal to 90 per cent of the value of the land on the security of a first mortgage over it. It was held that a representation of fact had been made, namely, a representation (1) as to the existing policy of the building society; and (2) as to the agent's state of knowledge of that policy.

---

22. See further [1009]. On whether silence may be a misrepresentation see [1013]–[1018].
23. *Magennis v Fallon* (1828) 2 Mol 561 at 588; LR 2 Ir 167. In *Dimmock v Hallett* (1866) LR 2 Ch App 21 similar indulgence was shown to 'a mere flourishing description by an auctioneer'.
24. But see [1109] (impact of legislation on misleading or deceptive conduct).
25. (1914) 17 CLR 601.
26. (1978) 18 SASR 240.

[1009] Statements of intention and opinion. A statement of present intention may not be fulfilled because of a change of mind or of other circumstances, but cannot be presently true or false unless the intention is not entertained at all.[27] A similar comment can be made of expressions of opinion. Neither constitutes a representation of fact. Again, a statement of belief is not a misrepresentation if it was honestly held.[28]

In *Bisset v Wilkinson*[29] the vendor of a farm said that its carrying capacity in winter was 2000 sheep. The primary question was whether in all the circumstances this was a statement of fact or one of opinion. The Privy Council said[30] it was proper to take into account 'the material facts of the transaction, the knowledge of the parties respectively, and their relative positions, the words of representation used, and the actual condition of the subject matter spoken of'. Emphasising that, as both parties knew, the vendor never carried on sheep-farming on the unit in question, the trial judge's view that the purchasers were not justified in regarding the vendor's words as anything more than an expression of his opinion was upheld. On the separate question whether the vendor honestly held that opinion, there was also a finding in his favour.[31]

Statements of intention or opinion at least imply that the state of the maker's mind is consistent with them, that is, that the person holds the intention or opinion professed. If this is not so, there will be a fraudulent misrepresentation. *Edgington v Fitzmaurice*[32] involved a statement in a prospectus of the objects for which the money raised by the issue of debentures would be used. A subscriber sought a refund, alleging fraudulent misrepresentation. In a famous passage Bowen LJ said:[33]

> A mere suggestion of possible purposes to which a portion of the money might be applied would not have formed a basis for an action of deceit. There must be a misstatement of an existing fact: but the state of a man's mind is as much a fact as the state of his digestion. It is true that it is very difficult to prove what the state of a man's mind at a particular time is, but if it can be ascertained, it is as much a fact as anything else. A misrepresentation as to the state of a man's mind is, therefore, a misstatement of fact.

For example, in *Ritter v North Side Enterprises Pty Ltd*[34] a purchaser of land alleged a fraudulent misrepresentation by the vendor's agent, namely, that although the agent had assured him that the property would be

---

27. See *Allan v Gotch* (1883) 9 VLR (L) 371 per Higinbotham J.
28. See *Economides v Commercial Assurance Co Plc* [1998] QB 587 (see Malcolm Clarke, [1998] *CLJ* 24).
29. [1927] AC 177.
30. [1927] AC 177 at 183. See also *National Australia Bank Ltd v Nobile* (1988) 100 ALR 227 at 235.
31. If an agent of an insurer makes a representation as to the existing practice and course of business of the insurer in dealing with insureds, it will be treated as one of fact (see *Kettlewell v Refuge Assurance Co* [1908] 1 KB 541) but if it is a statement as to legal rights under the policy it will be treated as an expression of the agent's opinion. Cf *Re Hooley Hill Rubber and Chemical Co Ltd and Royal Insurance Co Ltd* [1920] 1 KB 257; *Life Insurance Co of Australia Ltd v Phillips* (1925) 36 CLR 60 per Isaacs J.
32. (1885) 29 Ch D 459.
33. (1885) 29 Ch D 459 at 483.
34. (1975) 132 CLR 301; 6 ALR 125.

sewered within four months, the agent knew that it would not be, or made the representation recklessly, not caring whether it would be sewered within that time or not. The High Court held that the representation alleged involved an assertion by the agent that he believed that the area would be sewered within four months, that is, that there was a representation as to the agent's statement of mind, and that a fraudulent misrepresentation of fact had therefore been sufficiently alleged.

A statement of opinion usually implies that facts are known which could justify the opinion. In *Smith v Land and House Property Corp*,[35] in which a vendor described the tenant of the property for sale as 'a most desirable tenant', Bowen LJ said:[36]

> [I]t is often fallaciously assumed that a statement of opinion cannot involve the statement of a fact. In a case where the facts are equally well known to both parties, what one of them says to the other is frequently nothing but an expression of opinion. The statement of such opinion is in a sense a statement of a fact, about the condition of the man's own mind, but only of an irrelevant fact, for it is of no consequence what the opinion is. But if the facts are not equally known to both sides, then a statement of opinion by the one who knows the facts best involves very often a statement of a material fact, for he impliedly states that he knows facts which justify his opinion.

Similarly, to 'say that a flat will let for six guineas a week cannot be a statement to that effect as an existing fact, but it does involve certainly a representation that the person making it entertains that opinion, and possibly a representation that facts are known to him that justify that opinion'.[37]

Representations of law

[1010] General rule. It is usually said that a statement of law is not a representation of fact. In fact, composite statements of fact and law are more common than pure representations of law. In this connection in *Eaglesfield v Marquis of Londonderry*[38] Jessel MR said:[39]

> A misrepresentation of law is this: when you state the facts, and state a conclusion of law, so as to distinguish between facts and law. The man who knows the facts is taken to know the law; but when you state that as a fact which no doubt involves, as most facts do, a conclusion of law, that is still a statement of fact and not a statement of law.

Jessel MR instanced as statements of fact which nevertheless involve conclusions of law, statements such as that a woman is 'a single woman of a large fortune', and that a man is 'the eldest son of a marriage', and said:[40] 'There is not a single fact connected with personal *status* that does not, more or less, involve a question of law.'

The basis for the approach to statements of law is that one can only ever express an *opinion* as to the law on an issue until a court adjudicates on it.

---

35. (1885) 28 Ch D 7.
36. (1885) 28 Ch D 7 at 15.
37. *Fitzpatrick v Michel* (1928) 28 SR (NSW) 285 at 289. See also *R v Weaver* (1931) 45 CLR 321 at 353.
38. (1876) 4 Ch D 693.
39. (1876) 4 Ch D 693 at 702.
40. (1876) 4 Ch D 693 at 703.

Indeed, given that the High Court has rejected the distinction between mistake of fact and mistake of law, in the context of the recovery of payments made under mistake,[41] it is suggested that this is the only possible rationale for the continued application of the distinction in the present context.[42] Accordingly, a person who states the law on a subject is to be understood as representing only an opinion as to what it is,[43] and whether the statement involves a misrepresentation is to be determined in the same way as a statement of opinion.[44]

[1011] **Private rights and status.** It appears that only pure statements as to the law will be treated as representations of law, since only these can be regarded as statements of opinion.

A representation as to a person's private rights,[45] the effect of a private instrument,[46] and even the effect of *private* Acts of parliament,[47] have been held to involve representations of fact for the purpose of the distinction. In *Cooper v Phibbs*[48] Lord Westbury said that the distinction was one between private rights which were treated as matters of fact and 'the general law — the ordinary law of the country'.

[1012] **Fraud.** A person who knowingly misrepresents the law makes a fraudulent misrepresentation.[49] This is because, even as an expression of opinion, it can be implied that the person holds the opinion. Thus, in *Public Trustee v Taylor*,[50] a representation that land was owned in a specified way was held to be a representation of law, but, being fraudulent, was actionable nonetheless. In *Oudaille v Lawson*[51] a weekly tenant of an apartment house agreed to sell furniture and his interest in the business and during the negotiations represented that the rental could not be increased because it was up to the level allowable under war regulations. In fact he knew that they could not apply. The New Zealand Court of Appeal held that although the misrepresentation was as to a question of law, when persons state an opinion on such a matter which in truth is not their real opinion, there is a misrepresentation of fact to which the ordinary rules apply.

---

41. See *David Securities Pty Ltd v Commonwealth Bank of Australia* (1992) 175 CLR 353; 109 ALR 57. See also [1209], [2301].
42. Cf Bibi Sangha, 'The Law/Fact Distinction in Contract: A Lawyer's Plaything?' (1994) 7 JCL 113.
43. Cf *West London Commercial Bank Ltd v Kitson* (1884) 13 QBD 360; *McIntyre v Swyny* (1893) 14 LR (NSW) L 436; *Re Hooley Hill Rubber and Chemical Co Ltd and Royal Insurance Co Ltd* [1920] 1 KB 257.
44. See [1009], [1112].
45. *Cooper v Phibbs* (1867) LR 2 HL 149; *MacKenzie v Royal Bank of Canada* [1934] AC 468 at 476; *Inn Leisure Industries Pty Ltd v D F McCloy Pty Ltd* (1991) 100 ALR 447 at 462–3.
46. *Bank of Australasia v Adams* (1890) 8 NZLR 119.
47. *West London Commercial Bank Ltd v Kitson* (1884) 13 QBD 360. Contrast *Inn Leisure Industries Pty Ltd v D F McCloy Pty Ltd* (1991) 100 ALR 447 at 461 (representation of result obtained by applying public Act one of law).
48. (1867) LR 2 HL 149.
49. *West London Commercial Bank Ltd v Kitson* (1884) 13 QBD 360 per Bowen LJ; *Inn Leisure Industries Pty Ltd v D F McCloy Pty Ltd* (1991) 100 ALR 447 at 460–1.
50. [1978] VR 289.
51. [1922] NZLR 259. Cf *Solle v Butcher* [1950] 1 KB 671 (see [1229]).

Conduct and silence

[1013] Question of fact. Whether words or conduct constitute a representation in the circumstances of a particular case is a question of fact for the court and 'a single word, or ... a nod or a wink, or a shake of the head, or a smile intended to induce' may amount to representation.[52]

[1014] Positive statement or conduct generally required. The general principle is that, in the absence of a special relationship between them, parties negotiating a contract are not obliged to look after each other's interests. They are therefore entitled to be silent and to disclose nothing. Non-disclosure of facts, albeit material and important facts, is not a misrepresentation.[53] Thus, generally, a representation must be found in some positive statement or conduct.

However, the legislation on misleading or deceptive conduct has a much broader impact, and silence may amount to misleading or deceptive conduct even though it does not count as a misrepresentation under the general law.[54]

[1015] Duties to disclose.[55] There are exceptional classes of contract in which, because only one of the two parties will know the material facts, the law imposes a duty to disclose them to the other party. Thus, there is a duty of disclosure where a fiduciary duty arises in the negotiation of a contract, or the contract or the relationship created by the contract is fiduciary in character.[56]

The most important of these 'contracts of utmost good faith' (contracts uberrimae fidei) is that of insurance. The general law imposes on a person proposing insurance, or life assurance (the proponent), a duty to disclose to the insurer, whether asked or not, all facts which a prudent insurer would reasonably consider material to the decision whether to undertake the insurance at all and, if so, on what terms and at what premium. Non-disclosure renders the insurance contract voidable at the instance of the insurer.[57]

On the other hand, a contract of guarantee falls outside the class of contracts uberrimae fidei, and the law does not impose on the creditor a

---

52. *Walters v Morgan* (1861) 3 De GF & J 718 at 724; 45 ER 1056 at 1059.
53. See, eg *Smith v Hughes* (1871) LR 6 QB 597; *W Scott Fell & Co v Lloyd* (1906) 4 CLR 572; *Union Bank of Australia Ltd v Puddy* [1949] VLR 242 at 247; *United Dominions Corp Ltd v Brian Pty Ltd* (1985) 157 CLR 1 at 5–6; 60 ALR 741.
54. See [1110].
55. See S M Waddams, 'Pre-contractual Duties of Disclosure' in Cane and Stapleton, eds, *Essays for Patrick Atiyah*, 1991, p 237. Cf Charles Harpum, 'Selling Without Title: A Vendor's Duty of Disclosure?' (1992) 108 *LQR* 281.
56. See *Maguire v Makaronis* (1997) 188 CLR 449 at 495; 144 ALR 729; *Bristol and West Building Society v Mothew* [1998] Ch 1 at 18. In particular circumstances, property agreements between members of a family may be contracts uberrimae fidei. See *Greenwood v Greenwood* (1863) 2 De GJ & Sm 28; 46 ER 285; *Tennent v Tennents* (1870) LR 2 Sc & Div 6.
57. *Khoury v Government Insurance Office of New South Wales* (1984) 165 CLR 622; 54 ALR 639. On the requirement of inducement see *Pan Atlantic Insurance Co Ltd v Pine Top Insurance Co Ltd* [1995] 1 AC 501. In most cases the general law on the duty of disclosure is now regulated by the *Insurance Contracts Act* 1984 (Cth).

duty of utmost good faith in favour of the surety or guarantor. There is, however, a duty on the creditor to disclose to the intending surety anything which is not naturally to be expected in the relation between the debtor and creditor.[58]

[1016] **Statements partially true.** Non-disclosure, if combined with additional features, may amount to a misrepresentation. Thus, a statement which is partially true may amount to a misrepresentation. Accordingly, a statement which is literally true may be a misrepresentation because it gives a false impression by not telling the whole truth. For example, in *Dimmock v Hallett*[59] a vendor of an estate represented that the farms on it were fully let, but omitted to say that the tenants had given notice to quit, and his representation was held to be false. More recently, in *Krakowski v Eurolynx Properties Ltd*[60] it was held that where negotiations for the sale of property had taken place on a particular footing, a representation that the terms of the lease instrument were unaffected by any other contractual arrangement was implied from the failure to bring a separate agreement with the lessee to the purchaser's attention.

However, in *Arkwright v Newbold*,[61] James LJ cautioned against a finding of fraudulent misrepresentation based on mere omission, insisting[62] on some 'active misstatement of fact, or, at all events, such a partial and fragmentary statement of fact as that the withholding of that which is not stated makes that which is stated absolutely false'.

[1017] **Change in circumstances.** The time at which a representation must be evaluated is when the representee enters into the contract. If the facts change between the time when a representation is made and the time when the representation is acted upon, the statement becomes a false statement of fact. For example, in *With v O'Flanagan*[63] the defendant, a medico who wished to sell his practice, represented in January that it had brought in £2000 per annum for the preceding three years, and that he had a panel of 1480 patients. Although this statement was then true, it had ceased to be so by the time the contract was signed in May. Because of illness, the defendant was absent from the practice from time to time with the result that the takings of the practice dwindled to virtually nothing, and the number of panel patients fell to 1260. The purchaser rescinded the contract when it discovered these facts immediately after completing the purchase. The English Court of Appeal held that the rescission was valid. A duty to disclose a change in facts was not limited to cases of uberrimae fidei, or cases where the representation in question was that the representor had a certain intention.

---

58. See *Commercial Bank of Australia Ltd v Amadio* (1983) 151 CLR 447 at 454–8, 485; 46 ALR 402. On the proper rationalisation of the principle see *Westpac Banking Corp v Robinson* (1993) 30 NSWLR 668 at 687ff (see Duncan Murdoch, (1995) 8 *JCL* 286).
59. (1866) LR 2 Ch App 21. Cf *Peek v Gurney* (1873) LR 6 HL 377; *Curwen v Yan Yean Land Co Ltd* (1891) 17 VLR 745; *Allan v Gotch* (1883) 9 VLR (L) 371; *Ballantyne v Raphael* (1889) 15 VLR 538.
60. (1995) 183 CLR 563; 130 ALR 1.
61. (1881) 17 Ch D 301.
62. (1881) 17 Ch D 301 at 317–18.
63. [1936] Ch 575.

The principle is of broader application. If a person who has made a representation which is not immediately acted upon finds that the facts change, that person must disclose the change to the representee before the representation is acted upon. Two situations must be distinguished. First, the representor may have become aware of the true facts *which existed at the time of the representation*.[64] Second, as in *With v O'Flanagan*, the circumstances which falsify the representation may arise to the representor's knowledge *after the representation was made* and before contract.[65] In each case, continuance of negotiations and agreement to contract give rise to a presumption that the representation continues down to contract. Knowledge by that time of the true facts makes the representation fraudulent. Where such subsequent falsifying circumstances arise unbeknown to the representor, a misrepresentation is still taken to have been made at the time of contracting, but it is an innocent misrepresentation.

[1018] **Fraudulent concealment.** Finally, a person may make a misrepresentation by deliberately concealing something, such as a defect in property, so as to cause a contracting party to gain a false impression.[66] Of course, such a misrepresentation is always a fraudulent one.

Reliance

[1019] **Intention of the representor.** The representor must have intended the representation to reach, and induce to contract, the representee who claims to have been induced to contract. In *Peek v Gurney*[67] the plaintiff bought shares from existing shareholders in reliance on the prospectus which the promoters had issued upon formation of the company and which contained false statements. The House of Lords held that the prospectus had been addressed to the public, inviting them to take shares *originally as allottees*. There was no communication between the promoters and the plaintiff, who, by contrast with the original allottees, had no rights against them in respect of the misrepresentation. Once the allotment was completed, the prospectus had done its work and was a spent force.

Similarly, it appears that even where there is a misrepresentation directly by A to B in one context and later B acts in reliance on it in a different context not involving A, the misrepresentation is no longer operative.[68] On the other hand, there is a misrepresentation by A to B where A communicates the misrepresentation to X with the intention and effect of having it reach and be acted on by B.[69] It suffices that A intends a

---

64. *Robertson & Moffat v Belson* [1905] VLR 555; *Dalgety & Co Ltd v AMP* [1908] VLR 481; *Howell v Bennett & Fisher Ltd* [1966] SASR 188; *Lockhart v Osman* [1981] VR 57.
65. *Dalgety & Co Ltd v AMP* [1908] VLR 481; *Jones v Dumbrell* [1981] VR 199; *Permanent Trustee Australia Co Ltd v FAI General Insurance Co Ltd* (2001) 50 NSWLR 679.
66. *Horsfall v Thomas* (1862) 1 H & C 90; 158 ER 813; *Curwen v Yan Yean Land Co Ltd* (1891) 17 VLR 745. Cf *Sybron Corp v Rochem Ltd* [1984] 1 Ch 112.
67. (1873) LR 6 HL 377.
68. See *Peek v Gurney* (1873) LR 6 HL 377 at 411.

representation to reach and be acted on by either a class of which B is a member, or even, as *Peek v Gurney* acknowledges, by the public at large.[70]

The representor's ultimate motive or purpose in making the representation is irrelevant as a matter of law, but the intention to induce is essential.[71]

[1020] Reliance a question of fact. Whether a person has been induced by the representation to enter into the contract, or to persist in an intention to contract,[72] is an issue of fact. The representation must be shown to have reached and misled the mind of the person taking the decision to contract.[73]

Typically, there will be multiple inducements leading to the formation of a contract. The representation, to be operative, need not have been the sole, or nowadays, particularly in cases of fraud, even the decisive inducement: it suffices that it was a 'real' inducement, that is, it materially affected the representee's decision to contract.[74] Where an action for damages is brought, the acting in reliance on the misrepresentation is also the loss or damage which is an essential ingredient in that cause of action.[75]

[1021] Burden of proof. The onus of proof rests on the person setting up the misrepresentation. However, if the statement is one which by its nature was calculated to induce the representee to contract, it will be inferred that the representation did in fact induce entry into the contract if, after becoming aware of it, the representee entered into the contract. Thus, the representor must prove that there was in fact no reliance by the representee.[76]

The presumption of inducement is strongest in cases of fraud. In *Smith v Kay*[77] Lord Chelmsford LC said:[78]

> But can it be permitted to a party who has practised a deception, with a view to a particular end, which has been attained by it to speculate upon what might have been the result if there had been a full communication of the truth?

---

69. The courts have also been prepared to hold a company a representee where its formation was in contemplation and the representation was made to its promoters. See *Mount Gambier Co-operative Milling Society Ltd v Williams* [1921] SASR 185; *Leslie Leithead Pty Ltd v Barker* (1965) 65 SR (NSW) 172.
70. Cf *Clarke v Dickson* (1859) 6 CBNS 453; 141 ER 533; *Edgington v Fitzmaurice* (1885) 29 Ch D 459.
71. *Smith v Chadwick* (1884) 9 App Cas 187.
72. *Australian Steel & Mining Corp Pty Ltd v Corben* [1974] 2 NSWLR 202.
73. See *Macleay v Tait* [1906] AC 24; *A-G of New South Wales v Peters* (1924) 34 CLR 146.
74. *Edgington v Fitzmaurice* (1885) 29 Ch D 459; *Ballantyne v Raphael* (1889) 15 VLR 538; *Wilcher v Steain* (1961) 79 WN (NSW) 141; *Demetrios v Gikas Dry Cleaning Industries Pty Ltd* (1991) 22 NSWLR 561 at 569; *Morlend Finance Corp (Vic) Pty Ltd v Westendorp* [1993] 2 VR 284 at 304.
75. *Macleay v Tait* [1906] AC 24.
76. *Smith v Chadwick* (1884) 9 App Cas 187 at 196; *Allan v Gotch* (1883) 9 VLR (L) 371; *Power v Kenny* [1960] WAR 57.
77. (1859) 7 HLC 750; 11 ER 299.
78. (1859) 7 HLC 750 at 759; 11 ER 299 at 303.

The factual inference of inducement ordinarily arises from the making of fraudulent representations, and this imposes on the representor an onus to lead evidence to displace that inference, even though the ultimate onus of proving inducement always rests on the plaintiff.[79]

[1022] Discovery of true position. Even if the representee subsequently, but before contract, discovers that it is not wholly true, it need not follow that inducement is absent.[80] Yet there are cases where these circumstances existed but the representor was able to disprove inducement. In *Holmes v Jones*,[81] for example, owners of a pastoral property, in offering it for sale, made false statements as to the numbers of stock upon it. The purchaser refused the offer, and later, having become aware of the inaccuracy of the statements, negotiated to buy on a totally different basis as regards stock, inspected the property and stock, and as a result of the inspection contracted on the new basis. The High Court held that he was not induced by the misrepresentations made by the vendors in the first instance.[82]

Of course, where it is shown that the representee did in fact rely exclusively upon his or her own inquiries or inspection, inducement will have been disproved.[83] But it does not follow from the mere fact that the representee has had an *opportunity* of verifying the truth of the representation, but has not done so, that inducement can be deemed not to have occurred. As Jessel MR said in *Redgrave v Hurd*:[84] 'Where you have neither evidence that he knew facts to show that the statement was untrue, or that he said or did anything to show that he did not actually rely upon the statement, the inference remains that he did so rely ...'. For example, if a vendor makes a representation concerning a property, and the purchaser has the opportunity of inspecting it but does not do so, the representation may still be held to have induced the purchase. Other illustrations are cases where the representation could have been falsified by an inspection of documents which were available to the representee.[85]

A representee may know that a representation is false in a material particular, but not know the extent of the falsity. In *Gipps v Gipps*[86] the New South Wales Court of Appeal held that such a representee was not thereby defeated in her action for fraud. The case arose out of the sale of the plaintiff's shares in a family company to her husband. The representations related to the cost value of the stock in hand of the company, and to the average net yearly profit after tax for certain financial years. The plaintiff knew only that the figures supplied were *to some extent* wrong. The court said[87] that even complete knowledge of the falsity will not necessarily negate the operation of a representation and that only if

---

79. *Gould v Vaggelas* (1984) 157 CLR 215; 56 ALR 31.
80. *Sinclair v Preston* [1970] WAR 186.
81. (1907) 4 CLR 1692.
82. Cf *A-G of New South Wales v Peters* (1924) 34 CLR 146; *Bosaid v Andry* [1963] VR 465.
83. *Wilcher v Steain* (1961) 79 WN (NSW) 141 at 144.
84. (1881) 20 Ch D 1 at 22.
85. See *Wilkinson v Detmold* (1890) 16 VLR 439.
86. [1978] 1 NSWLR 454.
87. [1978] 1 NSWLR 454 at 460 (following *Sinclair v Preston* [1970] WAR 186 at 191).

'knowledge is of the falsity of representations, and that knowledge is accepted as true so that the false belief is wholly dissipated does knowledge defeat the representation'. These principles may assume particular importance where an agreement for the sale of a business was preceded by numerous representations as to aspects of asset backing and profitability.

Materiality

[1023] Representation must be of a material fact. In the case of a fraudulent misrepresentation it has always been sufficient to show misrepresentation as to any part of that which induced the party to enter into the contract. A stricter view was formerly taken with respect to a purely innocent misrepresentation. In *Kennedy v Panama New Zealand and Australian Royal Mail Co Ltd*[88] Blackburn J said:[89]

> [W]here there has been an innocent misrepresentation or misapprehension, it does not authorise a rescission, unless it is such as to shew that there is a complete difference in substance between what was supposed to be and what was taken, so as to constitute a failure of consideration.

This common law requirement no longer governs the right to rescind for misrepresentation:[90] it is now sufficient to find a 'material' representation. Unfortunately, the word 'material' has been used in various ways, including as a general description of the kind of misrepresentation which will be recognised, and in factual descriptions of the misrepresentation involved in the particular case.[91] The usage has been loose and confused. At times it has been used in association with 'inducement', or in the connotation of 'inducing',[92] and at others, with a more general reference, apparently to 'representation'.[93] And in *Smith v Land and House Property Corp*[94] Baggallay LJ applied 'material' or its derivatives to both 'misrepresentation' and 'influence'.

[1024] Relevance of materiality. A 'material representation' might signify either a 'relevant' one or a 'substantial' one. In relation to inducement, 'material' might signify:

- influencing the mind in fact either:

    (1) at all; or

    (2) to a sufficient extent to be recognised at law; or

---

88. (1867) LR 2 QB 580.
89. (1867) LR 2 QB 580 at 587.
90. See further [1038]. But see [1061] (sale of goods).
91. See, eg *Clark v Clark* (1882) 8 VLR (L) 303; *Smith v Land and House Property Corp* (1885) 28 Ch D 7; *Cutts v Buckley* (1933) 49 CLR 189.
92. See, eg *Rance v Kensett* (1916) 16 SR (NSW) 285; *Duralla Pty Ltd v Plant* (1984) 2 FLR 342 at 346–7. See also *Dimmock v Hallett* (1866) LR 2 Ch App 21 ('calculated materially to mislead').
93. See, eg *Sibley v Grosvenor* (1916) 21 CLR 469; *Abram SS Co Ltd v Westville Shipping Co Ltd* [1923] AC 773 at 778; *Wilson v Brisbane City Council* [1931] QSR 360; *MacKenzie v Royal Bank of Canada* [1934] AC 468 at 475. Cf *Pan Atlantic Insurance Co Ltd v Pine Top Insurance Co Ltd* [1995] 1 AC 501. See also *Lagunas Nitrate Co v Lagunas Syndicate* [1899] 2 Ch 392 ('innocent misrepresentations of material facts').
94. (1885) 28 Ch D 7.

- of a kind which, in an objective sense, is calculated to influence the mind either:
  (1) of the particular plaintiff; or
  (2) of a reasonable person.

In the cases there are illustrations of both a subjective approach[95] and an objective approach.[96]

In cases of fraud, materiality is in itself irrelevant, whether applied to 'misrepresentation' or to 'inducement', and is not an issue to be pursued. The relevance is as to the response in fact to the misrepresentation, that is, 'Was the representation a real inducement or not'?[97] It seems, however, that 'materiality' in an objective sense may still have some part to play even in such cases. First, if a statement is of a kind calculated to induce persons or the particular person to contract, it may be difficult for the representor to contend successfully that it was understood and believed that others would understand it in a different sense. In this way materiality in the objective sense of 'calculated to induce' is relevant to whether the representor had the necessary intention to induce.[98]

Second, where a statement is of that kind, the courts are prepared to infer that it did in fact induce the representee to contract.[99]

In these ways materiality assists in proving both the purpose and the fact of inducement. Moreover, this exposition is applicable to innocent misrepresentations as well as to fraudulent ones, since an intention and effect of inducing are essential to both.

Fraudulent Misrepresentation

[1025] Concept of fraud. Actual dishonesty, that is, knowledge that the representation was untrue, is the hallmark of fraud. Such dishonesty is a necessary element, additional to those already considered,[100] which must be present before a misrepresentation will be characterised as 'fraudulent'.

The modern law has its origin in *Derry v Peek*.[101] Sir Henry Peek sued the directors of a tramway company for damages for fraudulent misrepresentation by statements in a prospectus that the company had the right to use steam or other mechanical power, on the faith of which statements he applied for and was allotted shares in the company. The truth was that an Act of parliament gave the company only a contingent possibility of obtaining the right referred to, dependent on the consents of the Board of Trade and of the corporations of Plymouth and Devonport. These consents were refused as to a material portion of the tram-line. Later, the company was compulsorily wound up. Stirling J dismissed the

---

95. *Ballantyne v Raphael* (1889) 15 VLR 538.
96. *Arnison v Smith* (1889) 41 Ch D 348.
97. *Nicholas v Thompson* [1924] VLR 554 at 565–6; *Australian Steel & Mining Corp Pty Ltd v Corben* [1974] 2 NSWLR 202.
98. See *Nicholas v Thompson* [1924] VLR 554.
99. See *Macleay v Tait* [1906] AC 24.
100. See [1006]–[1024].
101. (1889) 14 App Cas 337.

action but the English Court of Appeal[102] reversed that decision, holding that the defendants were liable to the plaintiff for the loss sustained by him by reason of his having taken the shares. The basis on which the directors were liable was that they had *no reasonable ground* for the belief they sincerely entertained.

The defendants appealed to the House of Lords which held that lack of reasonable grounds for believing that their statement was true was not fraud on the directors' part, and that in an action for deceit nothing less than actual fraud must be proved. So long as the directors honestly believed that their prospectus was true, fraud was ruled out. At best, lack of reasonable grounds for a belief is merely an aid in determining whether the belief is genuinely held, and in this case it was quite credible that the directors' minds dwelt only upon the statutory power to use steam and overlooked the condition to which that power was subject. Their carelessness was not to be equated with deceitfulness.[103]

Under *Derry v Peek*, 'fraud' embraces situations in which the representor:

- *lacked belief* in the truth of the representation; or
- made it recklessly, *not caring* whether it was true or false.

On analysis, actual dishonesty and recklessness may merge into lack of belief in the truth of a statement so that nowadays the test is usually stated as a unitary one: did the maker honestly believe that the representation was true? It is to this extent that moral culpability is vital in fraud.

[1026] State of representor's mind. When fraud is alleged, the inquiry must always be as to the subjective state of the representor's mind. For example, where a statement is ambiguous, the decisive criterion is whether the representor believed it to be true according to its meaning as understood by the representor. The question concerning the maker's state of mind is whether the statement, *as its maker believed it would be understood*, conveys a true or false impression.[104] For example, in *John McGrath Motors (Canberra) Pty Ltd v Applebee*[105] the High Court held that a satisfactory finding about fraud by the sellers of a business could not be made without ascertaining how *they had understood* the advertisement for which they were responsible.

[1027] Intention and motive. A person who makes a statement without belief in its truth will usually do so intending to cause loss, that is, to defraud someone. But this is not an essential element: it is sufficient (and essential) that the test for all operative misrepresentations be satisfied, that is, that the representor intended that the statement should reach the plaintiff and that the plaintiff should act upon it.[106] Accordingly, the

---

102. Sub nom *Peek v Derry* (1887) 37 Ch D 541.
103. See also *Joliffe v Baker* (1883) 11 QBD 255; *Edgington v Fitzmaurice* (1885) 29 Ch D 459; *Sargent v Campbell* [1972–73] ALR 708.
104. See, eg *Clarke v Dickson* (1859) 6 CBNS 453; 141 ER 533; *Smith v Chadwick* (1884) 9 App Cas 187; *T J Larkins & Sons v Chelmer Holdings Pty Ltd and Van Den Broek* [1965] Qd R 68; *Krakowski v Eurolynx Properties Ltd* (1995) 183 CLR 563 at 577.
105. (1964) 110 CLR 656. See also *Sargent v Campbell* [1972–73] ALR 708.

distinction is between the ultimate purpose or motive of the defendant (which is irrelevant) and immediate intention (which is relevant).

[1028] Pleading and proving fraud. Fraud must be distinctly alleged and proved.[107] It is notoriously difficult to prove. Although only the civil onus of proof applies, that is to say proof on a preponderance of probabilities,[108] the gravity of the imputation is taken into account.[109] The difficulty in convincing the court (even after allowing for the drawing of inferences of fact) of the presence of the necessary moral turpitude has left many plaintiffs unsuccessful.[110] Where fraud alone is pleaded and is not proved, relief will not be given on the footing that the evidence establishes innocent misrepresentation, but rescission is allowable if innocent misrepresentation is pleaded in the alternative.[111]

An action for damages for fraud lies against the deceiver, whoever that is. For example, in *Cullen v Thomson*[112] the manager and assistant manager of a company who knowingly joined with the directors in the preparation of false and fraudulent reports were held liable in damages for fraud although the plaintiff, when he bought shares in the company in reliance on the reports, did not know of their involvement or give credit to it, but knew of and gave credit only to the involvement of the directors. Lord Westbury LC said that '[a]ll persons directly concerned in the commission of a fraud are to be treated as principals'[113] and are liable notwithstanding that their participation was not known at the time.

Rescission is, by its nature, available only against the other party to the contract.[114] However, where fraud is committed by an agent within the scope of the agent's authority, a principal will be liable to pay damages for deceit and the person deceived may also rescind the contract with the principal.[115]

---

106. See *Arnison v Smith* (1889) 41 Ch D 348 at 370; *Ballantyne v Raphael* (1889) 15 VLR 538; *Curwen v Yan Yean Land Co Ltd* (1891) 17 VLR 745; *Allan v Gotch* (1883) 9 VLR (L) 371.
107. See *Krakowski v Eurolynx Properties Ltd* (1995) 183 CLR 563 at 573, 579.
108. *Neat Holdings Pty Ltd v Karajan Holdings Pty Ltd* (1992) 110 ALR 449 at 449–50, HC.
109. *Smith Bros v Madden Bros* [1945] QWN 33; *Rejfek v McElroy* (1966) 112 CLR 517; *Spies v Commonwealth Bank of Australia* (1991) 24 NSWLR 691 at 693.
110. This serves to underline the importance of statutory developments in the area of misleading or deceptive conduct, where, although the civil remedies approximate those available in cases of fraud, there is no imputation of deceit. See Chapter 11. Cf [1074]–[1078] (misrepresentation legislation).
111. *London Chartered Bank of Australia v Lempriere* (1873) LR 4 PC 572; *Brindley v Scott* (1902) 2 SR (NSW) Eq 49; *Hutchinson v McGuren* (1910) 10 SR (NSW) 449; *Adey v Fisher* (1914) 14 SR (NSW) 407.
112. (1862) 6 LT 870.
113. (1862) 6 LT 870 at 874; and cf *Sibley v Grosvenor* (1916) 21 CLR 469 esp at 474–5, 484–5.
114. For the position of third parties whose rights derive from the contract see [1052]–[1053].
115. *Kettlewell v Refuge Assurance Co* [1908] 1 KB 545; *Lloyd v Grace Smith & Co* [1912] AC 716. See also *S Pearson & Son Ltd v Dublin Corp* [1907] AC 351 at 354. But cf *Sibley v Grosvenor* (1916) 21 CLR 469 at 474.

Negligent Misrepresentation

[1029] Elements. Negligence, as a tort, comprises three elements:
(1) a duty of care;
(2) breach of that duty by the defendant; and
(3) loss or damage (suffered by the plaintiff) caused by the breach.

Whereas a contractual duty is consensual, a duty in tort is imposed. A duty of care is therefore imposed by law. Unlike a claim in respect of a breach of contract, a plaintiff's cause of action in tort for negligence is not complete without proof of loss or damage.[116] Whether a duty of care exists depends on the circumstances.[117] Since the duty in relation to misrepresentation is informed to a large extent by general considerations of tort law rather than contract, consideration of the circumstances in which the law implies a duty of care is beyond the scope of this work. The main object of the discussion below is to indicate relevant considerations in a particular context. That context is the making of a negligent misrepresentation or misstatement, or the giving of careless information or advice, in breach of a duty of care. The three elements of negligence then become:

(1) a duty owed by the representor to the representee to take due care to ensure that the representation is true and reliable;
(2) failure by the representor to take such due care; and
(3) loss or damage caused by the falsity of the representation.

[1030] *Hedley Byrne* **principle.** Nearly 80 years after *Derry v Peek*,[118] in *Hedley Byrne & Co Ltd v Heller & Partners Ltd*[119] the House of Lords took the step which had been left open in that case, namely, the recognition of a tortious liability for a statement carelessly made, and not constituting fraud.

Giving negligent advice does not cause an immediate loss. The loss suffered depends on how the advice is used, a matter over which the representor may have no control. The 'field of liability for mere economic loss is a comparatively new and developing area of the law of negligence';[120] and courts have been reluctant to find a legal duty to take care not to cause economic loss in the making of statements, breach of which would give rise, potentially, to indeterminate liability. Thus, in *Hawkins v Clayton*[121] Deane J said that claims for economic loss are 'special' in the sense that

---

116. See further [1067], [2106].
117. See [1031]–[1035].
118. (1889) 14 App Cas 337 (see [1025]).
119. [1964] AC 465.
120. *Bryan v Maloney* (1995) 182 CLR 609 at 618; 128 ALR 163.
121. (1988) 164 CLR 539 at 576; 78 ALR 69. See also *Bryan v Maloney* (1995) 182 CLR 609 at 618; *Hill (t/as R F Hill & Associates) v Van Erp* (1997) 188 CLR 159 at 192, 197, 229–30; 142 ALR 687; *Esanda Finance Corp Ltd v Peat Marwick Hungerfords (Reg)* (1997) 188 CLR 241 at 254, 272, cf at 263–4; 142 ALR 750; *Perre v Apand Pty Ltd* (1999) 198 CLR 180 at 192–3, 209; 164 ALR 606. For the policy considerations see *Bryan v Maloney* (1995) 182 CLR 609 at 618–19; and generally Jane Stapleton 'Duty of Care and Economic Loss: A Wider Agenda' (1991) 107 LQR 249.

[1030]

they usually involve reliance or the assumption of responsibility or both. These elements may be present in a case of negligent misrepresentation, under the *Hedley Byrne* principle.[122] Nevertheless, in the general law of negligence it is now clear that claims for economic loss are no longer particularly 'special'.[123]

To return to the specific category of negligent misrepresentation, an action will be available where an assumption of responsibility by a defendant is causally related through inducement and reliance to the plaintiff's economic loss.[124] Since the plaintiff's concern is to establish a duty of care, there is no requirement that the statement be a factual representation, at least in the narrow senses described above.[125] Thus, a statement of opinion, or an undertaking, may constitute a statement within the *Hedley Byrne* principle.[126] Nevertheless, the usual requirements of misrepresentation will often be satisfied. For example, if an opinion is expressed in terms of advice it can usually be said that a false statement of fact is present, because the maker of the statement has impliedly represented that care was taken in expressing the opinion.

[1031] Foreseeability not enough. The most difficult issue in cases of alleged negligent misrepresentation is whether the defendant owed a duty of care to the plaintiff. Because, in nearly all cases, the damage is 'mere economic loss' rather than physical injury or damage to property, or economic loss consequent on physical injury, the fact that the defendant could reasonably have foreseen that the plaintiff would suffer loss or damage if reasonable care was not exercised is not a sufficient basis for proof of a duty of care in relation to information or advice under the *Hedley Byrne* principle.[127]

Something more must be shown. Defining that additional element has proved difficult.[128] Initially, the law concentrated on whether a special

---

122. *Spring v Guardian Assurance Plc* [1995] 2 AC 296.
123. The key cases are: *Bryan v Maloney* (1995) 182 CLR 609 (see Barbara McDonald and Jane Swanton, (1995) 69 *ALJ* 687; J G Fleming, (1995) 111 *LQR* 362); *Hill (t/as R F Hill & Associates) v Van Erp* (1997) 188 CLR 159 (see Jane Swanton and Barbara McDonald, (1997) 71 *ALJ* 822); *Northern Sandblasting Pty Ltd v Harris* (1997) 188 CLR 313; 146 ALR 572; *Perre v Apand Pty Ltd* (1999) 198 CLR 180 (see Jane Swanton and Barbara McDonald, (2000) 74 *ALJ* 17; Joseph Tesvic, (2000) 22 *Syd LR* 297). See also *White v Jones* [1995] 2 AC 207 (see Barbara McDonald and Jane Swanton, (1995) 69 *ALJ* 577; Alec Hayon, [1995] *CLJ* 239; Tony Weir, (1995) 111 *LQR* 357; John Murphy, [1996] *CLJ* 43).
124. See *Hill (t/as R F Hill & Associates) v Van Erp* (1997) 188 CLR 159 at 170, 197; *Esanda Finance Corp Ltd v Peat Marwick Hungerfords (Reg)* (1997) 188 CLR 241 at 257. See also *Spring v Guardian Assurance Plc* [1995] 2 AC 296 at 316; *Henderson v Merrett Syndicates Ltd* [1995] 2 AC 145 at 179.
125. See [1006]-[1012]. As to whether silence may amount to breach of a duty of care in this context see *Bentley v Wright* [1997] 2 VR 175 at 180-3.
126. See *Parramatta City Council v Lutz* (1988) 12 NSWLR 293 at 317. See also *Welston v North Cornwall District Council* [1997] 1 WLR 570 at 587 (negligent recommendation; see Richard Mullender, (1999) 62 *MLR* 425).
127. See, eg *Jaensch v Coffey* (1984) 155 CLR 549 at 575; 54 ALR 417; *Hawkins v Clayton* (1988) 164 CLR 539 at 553; *Hill (t/as R F Hill & Associates) v Van Erp* (1997) 188 CLR 159 at 174; *Esanda Finance Corp Ltd v Peat Marwick Hungerfords (Reg)* (1997) 188 CLR 241 at 249, 252, 266, 271-2.
128. See [1032].

relationship existed between the plaintiff and defendant. However, it is now clear that the *Hedley Byrne* principle is broader. It will apply in cases where the defendant professes to have special care or skill. More generally, even if the defendant does not profess to have special care or skill, a realisation on the part of the representor that the representee will rely on the statement is an important consideration.[129] The existence of a request for the information or advice is therefore important, particularly in demonstrating reliance. However, it is not essential[130] and the *Hedley Byrne* principle may therefore apply where information or advice is communicated to a third party.[131]

[1032] Existence of special relationship not essential. A duty of care will arise if there existed a special relationship between the representor and representee. Thus, in *Nocton v Lord Ashburton*[132] it was held that the fiduciary relationship[133] which existed between a solicitor and his client gave rise to a duty of care. One important feature of *Hedley Byrne & Co Ltd v Heller & Partners Ltd*[134] was the House of Lords' rejection of the argument that a fiduciary relationship is an essential ingredient of the duty of care.

At its narrowest, therefore, the *Hedley Byrne* principle posits either that the maker of the statement occupied a position involving the profession of special care or skill, or represented that the special skill or care was possessed. The majority Privy Council decision in *Mutual Life & Citizens' Assurance Co Ltd v Evatt*[135] sought to confine the principle to such cases. In the English cases, such as *Esso Petroleum Co Ltd v Mardon*,[136] a duty has been imposed where the only person qualified (or at least the person best qualified) to make a reliable statement was the representor. Ormrod LJ said[137] that the effect of the Privy Council's stricture in *Evatt* would be that the *Hedley Byrne* principle would be 'so radically curtailed as to be virtually eliminated'.

When *Evatt* was before the High Court, Barwick CJ said that the duty of care arises:[138]

> whenever a person gives information or advice to another ... upon a serious matter, [in] circumstances [where] the speaker realises ... or ought to realise that he is being trusted ... to give the best of his information or advice as a basis for action on the part of the other party and it is reasonable in the circumstances for the other party ... to act upon that information [or] advice.

---

129. See [1034], [1035]. For cases of pre-contract misrepresentation see [1033].
130. See [1033].
131. See, eg *Esanda Finance Corp Ltd v Peat Marwick Hungerfords (Reg)* (1997) 188 CLR 241 at 252.
132. [1914] AC 932.
133. For the incidents of such a relationship see [2329].
134. [1964] AC 465.
135. (1970) 122 CLR 628.
136. [1976] QB 801 (see [1033]). See also *Spring v Guardian Assurance Plc* [1995] 2 AC 296 (see Tom Allen, (1995) 58 *MLR* 553).
137. [1976] QB 801 at 827.
138. (1968) 122 CLR 556 at 572–3. Cf *Caparo Industries Plc v Dickman* [1990] 2 AC 605 at 635–6, 637–8.

The adoption of Barwick CJ's statement in subsequent High Court decisions[139] amounts to a rejection of the majority view in *Evatt*. Therefore, the principle of liability for negligent misstatement is not limited to persons who have or profess to have skill and competence commensurate with those who carry on a business or profession.[140]

[1033] Pre-contract misrepresentation. Although the precise scope of the *Hedley Byrne* principle remains unclear, no court has yet held that the relationship between parties negotiating a contract is itself enough to give rise to a duty of care. Nevertheless, the cases illustrate situations in which a duty of care has arisen in that context. For example, in *Esso Petroleum Co Ltd v Mardon*[141] an oil company was held liable in damages for a negligent forecast or estimate of the gallonage consumption or throughput of a petrol service station, made to a person who was induced thereby to become tenant of the station. Lord Denning MR said:[142]

> [I]f a man, who has or professes to have special knowledge or skill, makes a representation by virtue thereof to another — be it advice, information or opinion — with the intention of inducing him to enter into a contract with him, he is under a duty to use reasonable care to see that the representation is correct, and that the advice, information or opinion is reliable. If he negligently gives unsound advice or misleading information or expresses an erroneous opinion, and thereby induces the other side into a contract with him, he is liable in damages.

Esso Petroleum v Mardon is typical, in that usually representations by a contracting party will be made because of the representor's greater familiarity with (or access to) information concerning the subject matter of the contract. There is nothing to suggest that the principle formulated by Lord Denning MR should not be applied in Australia.[143] In cases where the plaintiff requests the information or advice, and the information or advice is given in the form of a representation made with the intention of inducing entry into a contract, the duty of care will be readily found and treated as breached if entry into a disadvantageous contract was induced (at least partially) by the representation.[144] However, a request is not essential.[145]

[1034] Realisation that statement will be relied upon. An important element in determining the existence of a duty of care is the realisation on the part of the representor that the representee will rely on the statement.[146] For example, in *L Shaddock & Associates Pty Ltd v Parramatta City*

---

139. See *L Shaddock & Associates Pty Ltd v Parramatta City Council* (1981) 150 CLR 225 at 250; 36 ALR 385; *San Sebastian Pty Ltd v Minister Administering the Environmental Planning and Assessment Act* (1986) 162 CLR 340 at 356–7, 371; 68 ALR 161; *Esanda Finance Corp Ltd v Peat Marwick Hungerfords (Reg)* (1997) 188 CLR 241 at 255, 261.
140. See also *Esanda Finance Corp Ltd v Peat Marwick Hungerfords (Reg)* (1997) 188 CLR 241 at 265.
141. [1976] QB 801.
142. [1976] QB 801 at 820.
143. See *Norris v Sibberas* [1990] VR 161 at 171.
144. Cf *San Sebastian Pty Ltd v Minister Administering the Environmental Planning and Assessment Act* (1986) 162 CLR 340 at 358, 366.
145. See *Hill (t/as R F Hill & Associates) v Van Erp* (1997) 188 CLR 159 at 184; *Esanda Finance Corp Ltd v Peat Marwick Hungerfords (Reg)* (1997) 188 CLR 241 at 252, 256, 262, 310. Cf *Smith v Bush* [1990] 1 AC 831 at 871.

Council[147] a local government council was held liable to pay damages for the negligent supply of information to a prospective purchaser of land as to whether the land was affected by any road widening proposal.

It is, however, open to the representor to disclaim any duty of care which would otherwise arise. Thus, in *Hedley Byrne & Co Ltd v Heller & Partners Ltd*[148] itself, the maker of the statement disclaimed liability and this was sufficient to prevent the finding of a duty of care.[149] Similarly, if a contract is agreed, the defendant may rely on an exclusion clause in the contract.[150]

[1035] Seriousness of the occasion. A distinction can be drawn between informal situations in which information or advice is sought, where the existence of a duty of care is unlikely to be found, and more formal occasions in which it is appropriate to find a duty of care.[151]

In *L Shaddock & Associates Pty Ltd v Parramatta City Council*,[152] the council had, through an unidentified officer, orally represented (in a telephone conversation) to the plaintiffs' solicitor, a Mr Carroll, that certain land which the plaintiffs were contemplating purchasing for redevelopment was not affected by any road widening proposal of the council. On the following day Carroll lodged with the council an application in a standard form seeking a certificate under the *Local Government Act* 1919 (NSW). In addition it asked whether the property was 'affected or proposed to be affected by any of the following ... Road widening or re-aligning proposals'. A fee for the certificate was enclosed, but no fee was tendered for the additional information, and none was customarily sent or required. In response to his application Carroll received a certificate from the council. The local road widening proposals were not so included and there was no statutory obligation to include the information in the certificate. Although road widening proposals had not been formally adopted by the council, there was little doubt in May 1973 (when Carroll made his oral and written inquiries) that they would be implemented and would seriously affect such a property. In fact, the proposals were embodied in a plan in the council's records and the council had referred to them in certificates in relation to other land in the vicinity. Carroll, relying on previous experience, believed that the absence of any notation as to a local road widening proposal indicated that there was no such proposal. The trial judge found that it was the practice of the council to answer inquiries as to the existence of road widening proposals on the law stationer's form by making an appropriate endorsement on the

---

146. See *Sutherland Shire Council v Heyman* (1985) 157 CLR 424 at 486; 60 ALR 1; *R Lowe Lippmann Figdor & Franck v AGC (Advances) Ltd* [1992] 2 VR 671. Cf *Smith v Bush* [1990] 1 AC 831 at 862, 871–2; *Morgan Crucible Co Plc v Hill Samuel & Co Ltd* [1991] Ch 295.
147. (1981) 150 CLR 225 (see [1035]). Contrast *Argy v Blunts & Lane Cove Real Estate Pty Ltd* (1990) 94 ALR 719.
148. [1964] AC 465.
149. But see [1122].
150. The privity rule will normally prevent reliance on an exclusion where the duty of care is owed to a person who is not a party to a contract. Cf *Hill (t/as R F Hill & Associates) v Van Erp* (1997) 188 CLR 159 at 181–2.
151. See, eg *Norris v Sibberas* [1990] VR 161 at 172.
152. (1981) 150 CLR 225.

certificate; and that in the light of this practice Carroll was led to believe, by the absence of any such notification on the certificate received by him, that there were no relevant road widening proposals. The plaintiffs contracted to purchase the property.

The High Court was unanimously of the view that the *Hedley Byrne* principle is not limited to persons who carry on a business or profession or persons who profess to have skill and competence commensurate with those who carried on such a business or profession, and that it is not limited to the giving of advice as distinct from factual information. Accordingly, the council was held liable.

[1036] Cause of action in both tort and contract. With the growth of the tort of negligence, concurrent causes of action in contract and tort arise in a number of situations.[153] For example, if a professional adviser gives negligent advice in the performance of a contract, the negligent advice may constitute the breach of an express or implied term requiring competent advice to be given.[154] Therefore, the giving of negligent advice may constitute a tort which is also a breach of contract, thus providing the client with a choice between suing for damages in tort or in contract.[155]

More relevant to the present context is the situation where negligence advice precedes entry into the contract. The crucial issue is whether the rights and obligations created by the resultant contract supersede and replace the tortious duty of care. *Esso Petroleum Co Ltd v Mardon*[156] decides that it does not. The same approach has been taken in Canada[157] and New Zealand.[158] It is submitted that this is correct. However, it is possible to find expressions of a contrary view.[159]

Innocent Misrepresentation

[1037] Introduction. As has been explained,[160] under the common law rescission was not permitted for innocent misrepresentation except where

---

153. See, eg F M B Reynolds, 'Tort Actions in Contractual Situations' (1985) 11 *NZULR* 215; Sir Robin Cooke, 'Tort and Contract' in Finn, ed, *Essays on Contract*, 1987, p 222; Jane Swanton, 'Concurrent Liability in Tort and Contract: the Problem of Defining the Limits' (1996) 10 *JCL* 21.
154. See further [635], [1857], [2104].
155. See, eg *Midland Bank Trust Co Ltd v Hett Stubbs & Kemp* [1979] Ch 384; *Ross v Caunters* [1980] Ch 297; *Hardie (Qld) Employees Credit Union Ltd v Hall Chadwick & Co* [1980] Qd R 362; *Aluminium Products (Qld) Pty Ltd v Hill* [1981] Qd R 33; *Henderson v Merrett Syndicates Ltd* [1995] 2 AC 145 (see J D Heydon, (1995) 111 *LQR* 1; Steve Hedley, [1995] *CLJ* 27). Cf *Giannarelli v Wraith* (1988) 165 CLR 543; 81 ALR 417.
156. [1976] QB 801 (see [1033]). See also *Howard Marine and Dredging Co Ltd v A Ogden & Sons (Excavations) Ltd* [1978] 1 QB 574; *UBAF Ltd v European American Banking Corp* [1984] QB 713.
157. *Sealand of the Pacific Ltd v Ocean Cement Ltd* (1973) 33 DLR (3d) 625.
158. *Capital Motors Ltd v Beecham* [1975] 1 NZLR 576; *Walker Hobson & Hill Ltd v Johnson* [1981] 2 NZLR 532 at 540.
159. See *Pennant Hills Restaurants Pty Ltd v Barrell Insurances Pty Ltd* [1977] 2 NSWLR 827 at 844–5; cf *Simonius Vischer & Co v Holt* [1979] 2 NSWLR 322 at 349–54. The point was conceded in *South Australia v Johnson* (1982) 42 ALR 161.
160. See [1023].

the misrepresentation was so fundamental that the party misled could establish a complete difference in substance between what was supposed to be and what was in fact supplied.[161] However, in equity the representor, notwithstanding the absence of moral delinquency, is not permitted to enforce a contract against the representee by specific performance.[162] Moreover, the representee, as the party misled, is permitted to rescind the contract ab initio, provided the parties can be restored, substantially, to their pre-contractual positions.[163]

[1038] **The current approach.** Subject to the discussion below[164] of sale of goods transactions, the fusion of the administration of law and equity has established that the equitable rule applies to all cases of misrepresentation. Nevertheless, the position remains that damages are not available for a misrepresentation which is purely innocent, that is, neither fraudulent nor negligent, unless there is a cause of action under statute.[165]

The requirement of a representation in relation to a *material* fact, which is the usual formulation of the type of misrepresentation which gives rise to a right of rescission,[166] is broader than the common law requirement of a complete difference of substance described above.[167] Therefore, although a 'substantial' difference will be sufficient, it is no longer necessary, and a misrepresentation need be no more than 'material' in an *objective* sense.[168] Moreover, it would seem that even 'materiality' has now been rejected as an independent test in cases of misrepresentation, fraudulent or otherwise.[169]

Rescission for Misrepresentation[170]

Exercise of the Right of Rescission

[1039] **General.** For all classes of operative misrepresentation, the innocent party has a right to rescind the contract ab initio, that is to say, as from the beginning. Although the representee's consent to contract is real, it has been given under a misapprehension caused by the other contracting party, and the representee is entitled to choose either to withdraw assent

---

161. 'Error in substantialibus sufficient to annul the whole contract': *Brownlie v Campbell* (1880) 5 App Cas 925 at 937 per Lord Selborne LC. And cf *New Zealand Loan and Mercantile Agency Co v Howes* (1888) 4 QLJ 73; *Picturesque Atlas Publishing Co Ltd v Phillipson* (1890) 16 VLR 675 at 680; *Hynes v Byrne* (1899) 9 QLJ 154; *Wilcher v Steain* (1961) 79 WN (NSW) 141.
162. *Reese River Silver Mining Co v Smith* (1869) LR 4 HL 64 per Lord Cairns; *Redgrave v Hurd* (1881) 20 Ch D 1.
163. See further [1043]–[1046].
164. See [1060]–[1062].
165. See [1076], Chapter 11 (impact of legislation on misleading or deceptive conduct).
166. See [1023]–[1024].
167. See [1023], [1037].
168. *T & J Harrison v Knowles and Foster* [1918] 1 KB 608. Cf *Wilson v Brisbane City Council* [1931] QSR 360 at 374 et seq; *Wilson v Union Trustee Co* (1923) 44 ALT 165; *MacKenzie v Royal Bank of Canada* [1934] AC 468.
169. See [1024].
170. For an historical perspective see Janet O'Sullivan, 'Rescission as a Self-help Remedy: A Critical Analysis' [2000] *CLJ* 509.

and be relieved of the contract, or to affirm it and continue bound and benefited by it.[171]

Since the contract is valid until rescinded, it may create rights and duties in the parties, or cause property to pass from one to the other. The right of the misled party should be seen primarily as a right to be relieved of the contract.[172] This is evident when the court *declares* that a purported rescission was effective, but even where it *orders* that a contract be set aside, it does so by virtue of the right to rescind vested in the party misled and that person's expression of an election to rescind.

[1040] Unequivocal conduct required. Rescission must be overt, that is to say, by words or conduct. It is also said that it must be clear and unequivocal, so that the other contracting party knows that the contract is not to proceed. Similarly, it is usually required that the election to rescind be communicated to the other party.[173] However, in exceptional cases this may not be necessary. Thus, in *Car and Universal Finance Co Ltd v Caldwell*[174] a fraudulent buyer passed a worthless cheque and absconded so that it was impossible for the seller to communicate his election to rescind. However, on discovering the fraud, the seller informed the police and took other steps which, although not amounting to communication or repossession, were held to be sufficient.

[1041] Position after rescission. Since an effective rescission for misrepresentation inducing a contract annuls the contract, it causes any property which has passed or vested by reason of the contract to re-vest in the pre-contract owner.[175] The misled party's act of rescission causes title to property to divest and to re-vest in the party originally entitled.

A party who received payment will be liable after rescission to make pecuniary restitution,[176] and one who has taken delivery or possession of property will be liable to return it. This last obligation involves a duty to use reasonable care to preserve the property to enable restoration of what was received, so far as this is reasonably practicable, and a duty not to abandon the property without adequate notice to the other party.[177]

Restrictions on Rescission

Introduction

[1042] Types of restrictions. A variety of circumstances may restrict the exercise of the right of rescission.[178] However, in the case of fraudulent

---

171. See, eg *Urquhart v Macpherson* (1878) 3 App Cas 831; *Abram SS Co Ltd v Westville Shipping Co Ltd* [1923] AC 773; *Alati v Kruger* (1955) 94 CLR 216.
172. See *Alati v Kruger* (1955) 94 CLR 216.
173. *Scarf v Jardine* (1882) 7 App Cas 345 at 360, 361. See also [1971].
174. [1965] 1 QB 525. For a statutory recognition of the case see *Goods Act* 1958 (Vic), s 101(2).
175. Cf *Clough v London & North Western Railway Co* (1871) LR 7 Ex 26 at 34; *Hunter BNZ Finance Ltd v C G Maloney Pty Ltd* (1988) 18 NSWLR 420 at 420–1.
176. See further [1044].
177. Cf *Fullers' Theatres Ltd v Musgrove* (1923) 31 CLR 524; *Hodder v Watters* [1946] VLR 222.
178. Cf [1967]–[1984] (restrictions on termination).

misrepresentation (except where the rights of innocent third parties intervene) there is no moral right in the representor to resist the innocent party's claim to be relieved of the contract: 'Once make out that there is anything like deception and no contract resting in any degree on that foundation can stand.'[179]

The following restrictions on rescission are not mutually exclusive: the same facts may establish more than one.[180]

Impossibility of restitutio in integrum

[1043] The process of rescission. Rescission is both a right and a process. The elements of exercise of the *right* were explained above.[181] References there to matters such as the re-vesting of property illustrate that rescission has important consequential effects. In this regard rescission is also a *process* of restoration. In order for a valid rescission for a pre-contract misrepresentation, both parties must make restitution. The requirement of restitutio in integrum is usually expressed in terms of a requirement that the parties be restored to their pre-contract positions.[182] The essence of restitutio as a restriction on rescission is the proposition that the right is not available if the process cannot be satisfactorily completed. It applies to all cases of rescission for misrepresentation, whether fraudulent or innocent.

It follows that although it is sufficient for the representor's rescission to achieve restitutio, this is not necessary provided that the court may do so by appropriate orders. For example, if a contract for the sale of land is rescinded by the purchaser, the requirement is that the purchaser must be able to restore to the vendor the subject property in the state in which the vendor had owned it before the contract. If that can only be effectively done by means of court orders, these will be made in favour of *both* parties if restitutio is possible.

Undoubtedly, however, there will be cases in which restitutio is not possible, and in which the rescission will be invalid notwithstanding the representee's right of rescission. For example, in *Clarke v Dickson*[183] the plaintiff had subscribed for shares in a mining company to be worked on the cost book principle. The mine was worked in 1854, 1855 and 1856 and the plaintiff was paid dividends in the form of bonus shares. In 1857 the company was converted into a limited liability company. The company was wound up. Then the plaintiff discovered that fraudulent representations had been made prior to entry into the contract. The plaintiff's shareholding

---

179. *Reynell v Sprye* (1852) 1 De GM & G 660 at 708; 42 ER 710 at 728 per Lord Cranworth LJ.
180. Discretionary factors influence the requirement of restitutio in integrum. See [1045].
181. See [1039]–[1041].
182. See, eg *Erlanger v New Sombrero Phosphate Co* (1878) 3 App Cas 1218 at 1278, 1279; *A H McDonald & Co Pty Ltd v Wells* (1931) 45 CLR 506 at 513–14. But see [2336].
183. (1858) EB & E 148; 120 ER 463. Compare cases holding that rescission of a contract to purchase shares is not available once winding up of the company has commenced: *Oakes v Turquand* (1867) LR 2 HL 325; *Tennent v City of Glasgow Bank* (1879) 4 App Cas 615; *Webb Distributors (Aust) Pty Ltd v State of Victoria* (1993) 179 CLR 15; 119 ALR 577.

in a company incorporated with limited liability was not even substantially what he had received initially: restitutio in integrum was impossible, quite apart from the intervention of the rights of third parties which the winding up itself involved.

What must be considered, therefore, is the extent to which restitutio must be possible before a rescission will be held valid.

[1044] **Common law and equity.** In relation to rescission, the common law courts did not exercise a jurisdiction to adjust the rights of parties so as to make allowances for changes in position since contract. Therefore, a misled party's rescission of the contract was either itself and without the necessity or possibility of a court order, totally effective to annul the contract (where perfect restitution was possible) or totally ineffective (where perfect restitution was not possible). Although in the former case an action for restitution, in the form of a claim to recover money paid (on the basis of a total failure of consideration)[184] would succeed, it followed that, in the latter case, a plaintiff's action to recover a sum as money paid would be defeated by reason of the defendant's part performance.[185]

This strict rule of precise restitutio was the necessary conclusion from the rule of a complete difference in substance applied by the common law courts to innocent misrepresentation.[186] The requirement of restitutio in equity was substantial restoration of the parties to their pre-contractual positions, or more simply, *substantial restitution*.[187] It was equity's more flexible approach to remedies which made rescission more liberally available. Where it was not possible for the representee to achieve restitutio in integrum, equity by its orders would often be able to achieve it. And the more lenient requirement of a 'material'[188] misrepresentation ensured that the representee would be far better placed in any claim for rescission. Nevertheless, even in such cases it must be possible to 'do what is practically just between the parties'.[189]

[1045] **Equitable rule prevails.** Subject to the discussion below of sale of goods contracts,[190] the position today, following the fusion in administration of law and equity, is that the equitable rule prevails and governs the requirement of restitutio in integrum.

The leading case is *Alati v Kruger*.[191] The buyer of a fruit business sought rescission on the ground of fraudulent misrepresentation. The misrepresentation was proved, and the buyer had certainly purported to rescind the contract. However, the property to be handed back had deteriorated since contract. Moreover, the lease had been assigned by the vendors, the buyer had actually carried on the business and made a loss,

---

184. For the meaning of this expression see [2306].
185. *Kennedy v Panama New Zealand and Australian Royal Mail Co Ltd* (1867) LR 2 QB 580 at 587. See Mason and Carter, *Restitution Law in Australia*, 1995, paras 1320, 1433.
186. See [1037].
187. See Mason and Carter, *Restitution Law in Australia*, 1995, paras 1305, 1318.
188. See [1024].
189. See [1045].
190. See [1060]–[1062].
191. (1955) 94 CLR 216.

and the business had ultimately closed down. Dixon CJ, Webb, Kitto and Taylor JJ noted that the impossibility of precise restitutio would have precluded rescission at common law then added:[192]

> But it is necessary here to apply the doctrines of equity, and equity has always regarded as valid the disaffirmance of a contract induced by fraud even though precise restitutio in integrum is not possible, if the situation is such that, by the exercise of its powers, including the power to take accounts of profits and to direct inquiries as to allowances proper to be made for deterioration, it can do what is practically just between the parties, and by so doing restore them substantially to the status quo: *Erlanger v New Sombrero Phosphate Co*;[193] *Brown v Smitt*;[194] *Spence v Crawford*.[195] It is not that equity asserts a power by its decree to avoid a contract which the defrauded party himself has no right to disaffirm, and to revest property the title to which the party cannot affect. Rescission for misrepresentation is always the act of the party himself: *Reese River Silver Mining Co Ltd v Smith*.[196] The function of a court in which proceedings for rescission are taken is to adjudicate upon the validity of a purported disaffirmance as an act avoiding the transaction ab initio, and, if it is valid, to give effect to it and make appropriate consequential orders: see *Abram SS Co Ltd v Westville Shipping Co Ltd*.[197] The difference between the legal and the equitable rules on the subject simply was that equity, having means which the common law lacked to ascertain and provide for the adjustments necessary to be made between the parties in cases where a simple handing back of property or repayment of money would not put them in as good a position as before they entered into their transaction, was able to see the possibility of restitutio in integrum, and therefore to concede the right of a defrauded party to rescind, in a much wider variety of cases than those which the common law could recognise as admitting of rescission. Of course, a rescission which the common law courts would not accept as valid cannot of its own force revest the legal title to property which had passed, but if a court of equity would treat it as effectual the equitable title to such property revests upon the rescission.

Thus, the rescission was held valid, although the position might have been different if the buyer had abandoned the business so that it ceased to exist.[198]

Although, usually, the contract must be rescinded as a whole, in some cases where substantial restitutio in integrum is impossible, a court may make a declaration for partial rescission. In *Vadasz v Pioneer Concrete (SA) Pty Ltd*[199] a creditor represented that a guarantee would apply only to debts incurred by a company after its signing, that is, its future debts. However, the guarantee in fact related to both past and future debts. Although the

---

192. (1955) 94 CLR 216 at 223–4. See also *Kramer v Duggan* (1955) 55 SR (NSW) 385; *O'Sullivan v Management Agency and Music Ltd* [1985] QB 428 at 457; *Demetrios v Gikas Dry Cleaning Industries Pty Ltd* (1991) 22 NSWLR 561 at 573–4.
193. (1878) 3 App Cas 1218 at 1278, 1279.
194. (1924) 34 CLR 160 at 165, 169.
195. [1939] 3 All ER 271 at 279, 280.
196. (1869) LR 4 HL 64 at 73.
197. [1923] AC 773.
198. See *Drozd v Vaskas* [1960] SASR 88.
199. (1995) 184 CLR 102; 130 ALR 570 (see J W Carter and Gregory Tolhurst, (1996) 10 *JCL* 167; Dominic O'Sullivan, (1997) 113 *LQR* 16). See also David Wright, 'Fiduciaries, Rescission and the Recent Change to the High Court's Equity Jurisprudence' (1998) 13 *JCL* 166.

guarantor sought an order rescinding the guarantee in toto, the creditor had conferred benefits on the company after the guarantee was given. The High Court held[200] that if 'such complete and unconditional relief is to be granted, it must be on some basis other than mere entitlement to a practical restoration of the status quo upon rescission or "disaffirmance" of a contract induced by fraud'. In the result, partial rescission was granted, so as to leave the guarantee standing for so much of the debts as the guarantor had been willing to guarantee.[201]

[1046] **Illustrations.** In *Balfour v Hollandia Ravensthorpe NL*[202] it was held that the deterioration of a house since it was occupied by the purchasers was not a ground for denying effect to the purchasers' rescission of the contract of sale for fraudulent misrepresentation by the vendor's employee, but that to the extent that the deterioration was caused by the purchasers' act (as distinct from diminution in value due to changes in the economy) they would be required to make compensation for it.

In *Brown v Smitt*,[203] a purchaser of land who had entered into possession and improved the land was allowed to rescind and to recover as restitution: (a) the value which he had added to the land by those permanent improvements which were not mere matters of taste and enjoyment; and (b) the cost of necessary repairs, but not his 'collateral' losses arising from the contract, such as losses incurred in carrying on a business on the land.

A court will be the more ready to assist the misled party in cases where the representor was fraudulent, or stood in a fiduciary relation to the representee. That is to say, provided always the substantial identity of the subject matter remains, the court will be the more ready to use its powers to make orders for compensation or indemnity in such cases.[204]

Affirmation

[1047] **Affirmation as a restriction on rescission.** Following a representor's misrepresentation, the decision to rescind rests with the representee. The decision to rescind is a species of election, and the representee is perfectly entitled to elect to *affirm* the contract. The rule is that once such an election has taken place, rescission ceases to be available: affirmation is a bar to rescission. The basis of the rule is that 'rescission' and 'affirmation' are mutually exclusive rights: it is a condition of the enjoyment of either one that the other be abandoned. Affirmation may be express or implied. The former occurs when there is a conscious choice by the representee to affirm the contract. The latter occurs when the choice is inferred on the basis of what the representee has said and done. In essence, the basis for inferring (or imputing) affirmation is a finding that the

---

200. (1995) 184 CLR 102 at 112 per Deane, Dawson, Toohey, Gaudron and McHugh JJ.
201. Contrast *Greater Pacific Investments Pty Ltd v Australian National Industries Ltd* (1996) 39 NSWLR 143 at 151; *Maguire v Makaronis* (1997) 188 CLR 449.
202. (1978) 18 SASR 240.
203. (1924) 34 CLR 160.
204. See *Lagunas Nitrate Co v Lagunas Syndicate* [1899] 2 Ch 392 per Rigby LJ; *Spence v Crawford* [1939] 3 All ER 271; *Evans v Benson & Co* [1961] WAR 12.

representee has behaved in a way which is consistent only with an election in favour of affirmation having been made.

Analysis of the restriction requires a consideration of the elements of affirmation. As in the case of rescission,[205] an election must be made in clear and unequivocal terms, and so an election to rescind or to affirm will not be found unless there are clear and unequivocal words or conduct.[206] The representee must also have sufficient knowledge to make the election.[207]

Although there is a substantial body of law in the context of misrepresentation, it is not peculiar to that context. In fact, affirmation is no more than a specific application of the general requirement of election between inconsistent rights.[208]

[1048] Knowledge of the representee. The question of election does not arise until the party misled acquires knowledge that the representation was false. The representee is entitled to believe the representation, at least until there is some cause for suspicion, and usually beyond that stage.[209] Accordingly, mere partial information giving some cause for suspicion will not suffice,[210] and a right to rescind may exist notwithstanding the lapse of a considerable time since the making of the contract.[211]

Is it sufficient to an affirmation merely that the representee has become aware of *the facts* which falsified the representation, or is it also necessary that the representee should know of the *right* to rescind?[212] In *Coastal Estates Pty Ltd v Melevende*,[213] Melevende purchased eight allotments upon a seaside subdivision on Westernport Bay, Victoria from Coastal Estates. Melevende alleged that he had been induced to purchase by the fraudulent misrepresentation and sued to recover the money paid under the contract on the basis that it had been rescinded. The trial judge found that the purchase had been induced by fraud. But the defence of affirmation was put forward, raising the question whether Melevende had, by his conduct, elected to affirm the contract so that it was not open to him to rescind it when he issued his summons. The contract was entered into in September 1960. Melevende first knew in April or May 1961 that the representations were untrue, and he endeavoured by telephone to get agents to sell the land. In January 1962 he was completely satisfied that the representations

---

205. See [1040].
206. Cf *Reese River Silver Mining Co v Smith* (1869) LR 4 HL 64 at 74; *United Shoe Machinery Co of Canada v Brunet* [1909] AC 330; *Abram SS Co Ltd v Westville Shipping Co Ltd* [1923] AC 773 at 779. For the impact of delay see [1050].
207. See [1048].
208. See [1971]. See also [391] ('waiver').
209. *Rawlins v Wickham* (1858) 3 De G & J 304; 44 ER 1285.
210. See *Drozd v Vaskas* [1960] SASR 88 at 95–6; *Hunter BNZ Finance Ltd v C G Maloney Pty Ltd* (1988) 18 NSWLR 420 at 435; *Re Hoffman; Ex parte Worrell v Schilling* (1989) 85 ALR 145 at 150. Cf *Senanayake v Cheng* [1966] AC 63 at 78–9.
211. For the impact of delay see [1050].
212. This question arises in respect of all cases of election, and there is no reason for thinking that the answer given in the context of rescission for misrepresentation should be any different from the answer given in other contexts such as termination for breach or repudiation. See [1971]. For the distinction between election between rights and election between remedies see [1973].
213. [1965] VR 433.

were lies. He went on paying instalments of interest under the contract up to and including March 1962, and instalments of principal monthly up to and including June 1962. He also paid rates on the land in October 1961 and 1962. Although he decided to rescind the contract in April or May 1962, it was not until September 1962, just before the summons was issued, that he saw a solicitor and was informed of his legal rights. He said that he had paid rates because he 'didn't know what to do about it'. The Victorian Full Court decided in favour of Melevende.

The judgments support the proposition that, leaving aside questions of estoppel, where a misrepresentation is fraudulent it is necessary to a binding election to affirm that the defrauded party should have known of the right to rescind as well as of the falsifying facts.[214] The analysis relies on a distinction between two sources for a right to elect, namely, the general law (of misrepresentation) and the express terms of the contract. In relation to the latter the view was expressed that knowledge sufficient to justify a finding of affirmation is knowledge of the facts which activate the term in the contract. However, in the former, knowledge of the right to rescind was said to be essential. It was because none of the acts after the visit to the solicitor were inconsistent with the exercise of the right of rescission that Melevende was held not to have elected to affirm the contract. Had the right been conferred by the terms of the contract, a greater number of acts would have been in issue, and payment of the instalments of the price would probably have constituted affirmation.

More generally, the case seems to assert that knowledge of the right to rescind is a *general* requirement in cases other than those in which the right is expressly conferred by the contract. We have great difficulty in seeing the basis or logic for this. Modern authority in the context of an election to affirm following breach or repudiation[215] suggests that awareness of the right, as distinct from knowledge of the facts giving rise to that right, is not in general necessary. There is no reason this should not also apply to affirmation following misrepresentation inducing the making of the contract.[216] Moreover, if a representee discovers that a representation was false, but only later discovers that it was fraudulently so, the representee does not, upon making the latter discovery, acquire a fresh right to rescind. Any prior election to affirm will preclude rescission.[217]

The impact of the view in *Melevende* is that a representee who is legally represented may be treated differently to one who is not, due to the legal adviser's knowledge of the law. It is difficult to believe that in all the cases where a representee has been held to have affirmed a contract following misrepresentation there was knowledge of the right to rescind. As is explained later,[218] the High Court has left open the correctness of the analysis in *Melevende*. What seems to us the appropriate rationale for saying that the distinction between implied rights and those expressly conferred is

---

214. See also *Parker v R-G* [1976] 1 NSWLR 342 at 359; *Hunter BNZ Finance Ltd v C G Maloney Pty Ltd* (1988) 18 NSWLR 420 at 436.
215. See [1971].
216. See *Kammins Ballrooms Co Ltd v Zenith Investments (Torquay) Ltd* [1971] AC 850 at 878, 883, but cf at 873.
217. See *Evans v Benson & Co* [1961] WAR 12.
218. See [1971].

erroneous is that the principles of election are concerned with consistency of conduct. They rely on the inferences legitimately drawn from the conduct of people with knowledge of the circumstances giving rise to rights, and suggest that it is quite legitimate to draw an inference of affirmation where a person does an act inconsistent with the exercise of the right to rescind. Similar considerations led Pincus J in *Re Hoffman; Ex parte Worrell v Schilling*[219] to reject the distinction and to treat knowledge of the facts as enough for a binding election to affirm even in cases of fraud.

It may, however, be conceded that in the absence of knowledge of the right to rescind, conduct, particularly in cases of fraud, may need to be 'more convincing', such as by positively showing an intention to affirm,[220] or by showing the exercise of proprietary rights or contractual rights adverse to the other party or to his or her detriment.[221] However, these are matters of proof not principle.

[1049] Conduct of the representor. One other feature of conduct should be noticed. Because principles of election concentrate on the conduct of the party required to elect, it is not usually necessary to consider the conduct of the other party, in this context the representor. However, a representee may find that the right of rescission is not available following reliance by the representor on the words or conduct of the representee. This is the application of principles of estoppel.[222] For example, in *Coastal Estates Pty Ltd v Melevende*,[223] Sholl J said:[224]

> If the defrauded party does not know that he has a legal right to rescind, he is ... bound by acts which on the face of them are referable only to an intention to affirm the contract, [where] those acts are 'adverse to' the opposite party, ie, [where] they involve something to the other party's prejudice or detriment, as eg, if the defrauded party goes into possession of property sold to him by the contract, or accepts some other benefit thereunder.

It is significant that the representee may be bound by such acts where there is no knowledge of the right to rescind. This shows that, even if there is no election to affirm, clear and unequivocal conduct *relied upon by the representor* may preclude the representee from asserting a valid exercise of the right of rescission, at least where it would be unconscionable for the representee to insist on the right of rescission.

[1050] Delay. It is sometimes said that rescission must be 'prompt'. However, as a general principle this cannot be accepted as correct. Thus, when this word is used in the cases it will usually be used either to emphasise that the representee has elected in time,[225] or to emphasise a

---

219. (1989) 85 ALR 145 at 151–2.
220. Cf *Szep v Blanken* [1969] SASR 65 at 74–5; *Official Receiver v Feldman* (1972) 4 SASR 246 at 254, 270.
221. *Elder's Trustee and Executor Co Ltd v Commonwealth Homes and Investment Co Ltd* (1941) 65 CLR 603 at 618; *Sargent v ASL Developments Ltd* (1974) 131 CLR 634 at 657–8; 4 ALR 257.
222. See also [392], [1974].
223. [1965] VR 433.
224. [1965] VR 433 at 443.
225. See, eg *Alati v Kruger* (1955) 94 CLR 216 at 223.

peculiar feature of the contract which the representee seeks to rescind. For example, in *Coastal Estates Pty Ltd v Melevende*,[226] Sholl J and Adam J considered the word appropriate to cases where the representee seeks to rescind a contract for the purchase of shares, because of their fluctuating value and the possibility of third parties being prejudiced.

The general principle applicable to delay would seem to be that the representee must elect within a reasonable period of time,[227] and that the particular period of time is governed by whether the delay is sufficient to constitute unequivocal conduct amounting to affirmation. Normally, silence is equivocal conduct and inaction alone, even until the other party takes proceedings to enforce the contract, will not defeat rescission. Generally, therefore, it is permissible for the party misled to postpone making an election so long as nothing is done to affirm the contract.[228] It is therefore important to distinguish purely executory contracts from those which have been fully[229] or partially performed. Where the contract is executory a longer period is likely to be allowed.[230]

Substantial delay will often be accompanied by conduct and circumstances which will be held to show that the party misled has evinced an intention that the contract is to proceed. Illustrations of affirmative conduct might be found, for example, where a representee, rather than rescinding, has been negotiating for payment of compensation in respect of deficiencies in a property bought,[231] or has treated and dealt with the subject matter of the contract in ways consistent only with ownership of it.[232] Affirmative conduct of this kind may also make it impossible for the party misled to make restitutio in integrum[233] to the representor, that is to say, the same conduct may give rise to both bars to rescission.[234]

[1051] Scope of affirmation. The representee cannot affirm in part and rescind in part[235] unless the contract is 'divisible'. But, of course, if there are two quite unconnected representations, affirmation of the contract after the discovery of the falsity of one would not preclude rescission upon the later discovery of the falsity of the other.

Third parties' rights

[1052] Intervention of rights of third parties prevents rescission. Since a contract induced by misrepresentation is valid until rescinded, its performance may cause property to pass to a third party, who thereby acquires rights contingent on its validity at the time of acquisition. The rule

---

226. [1965] VR 433 at 443, 452.
227. See [1984]. Cf *Leaf v International Galleries* [1950] 2 KB 86.
228. *Clough v London & North Western Railway Co* (1871) LR 7 Ex 26 at 34.
229. Cf [1054].
230. See, eg *Academy of Health and Fitness Pty Ltd v Power* [1973] VR 254.
231. Cf *Cover v McLaughlin* (1897) 18 LR (NSW) Eq 107.
232. As in *Hudson v Jope* (1914) 14 SR (NSW) 351.
233. See generally [1043]–[1046].
234. Alternatively, where equitable adjustments are necessary, the representee may be barred by the defence of laches. See Mason and Carter, *Restitution Law in Australia*, 1995, para 2713.
235. *Urquhart v Macpherson* (1878) 3 App Cas 831 at 837–8; *Hynes v Byrne* (1899) 9 QLJ 154 at 157–8.

is that once a third party has, for valuable consideration and without notice of the misrepresentation, acquired rights under a voidable contract, the contracting party's right of rescission is barred. In this way the interposition of the third party's rights constitutes a restriction on the right of rescission.[236]

[1053] **Illustration.** As an illustration, consider a case where a buyer of goods (B), by a fraudulent misrepresentation, induces the owner (A) to sell to B and that after the sale B purports to sell the goods to an unsuspecting third party (C). B's fraudulent misrepresentation might be B's identity, the misrepresentation being that B is a person of some status. The misrepresentation might induce A (a shopkeeper) to sell goods to B on credit, after which sale B sells or otherwise disposes of them to C who takes them without notice of the fraud and for valuable consideration before A has rescinded the contract of sale. A loses the right to rescind and so cannot recover the goods from C.[237]

If in the above illustration A were still allowed to rescind, C would have to return the goods to A and would be relegated to an action for damages against B, which may well prove fruitless.[238] However if, as in *Car and Universal Finance Co Ltd v Caldwell*,[239] the seller (A) is able to rescind the contract before the innocent third party acquires rights in the goods, then A's rescission will have been effective and C must return the goods.

Execution of the contract

[1054] **Rule in *Seddon's* case.** In the present context,[240] to say that a contract has been 'executed' means that it has been discharged by complete performance in all respects. Some cases suggest that execution of the contract is a bar to rescission for innocent misrepresentation.

The executed contract restriction is usually described as the 'rule in *Seddon's* case', a reference to *Seddon v North Eastern Salt Co Ltd*.[241] A narrower source is *Wilde v Gibson*,[242] where a purchaser of land sought to rescind after the contract had been completed by the conveyance of title. The ground alleged was that the vendor had fraudulently concealed the existence of a deed poll in her title, but the purchaser failed because the evidence did not establish fraud as pleaded. Lord Campbell said that although the court will not compel a party to complete a contract induced by a non-fraudulent misrepresentation, once the matter has passed from contract to conveyance the court will not intervene in the absence of actual fraud. He observed that there would be no certainty if transactions could be set aside upon discovery at distant times that a pre-contractual representation had been false.

---

236. Section 6(2) of the *Misrepresentation Act* 1972 (SA) expressly preserves the restriction imposed by the interposition of a third party's rights.
237. But see [1245] (contract may be void for mistake).
238. Cf *Oakes v Turquand* (1867) LR 2 HL 325 (subscription for shares in a company by a fraudulent prospectus).
239. [1965] 1 QB 525 (see [1040]).
240. See also [1255] (mistake).
241. [1905] 1 Ch 326.
242. (1848) 1 HLC 605; 9 ER 897.

[1054]

There is some justification for applying the restriction to land transactions where contract and completion are distinct legal steps, the purchaser having the opportunity after contract to investigate the vendor's title and to make objections and raise requisitions in accordance with the contract's terms before being compellable to complete.[243] In Australia, the executed contracts exception has been considered applicable to land transactions[244] and contracts for the sale of a business.[245] But in *Seddon's* case, Joyce J said the rule applied to an action for rescission by a purchaser of shares,[246] suggesting a broader application than land contracts. On the other hand, even allowing for exceptions,[247] *Seddon's* case has been distinguished and criticised.[248] The idea that the equitable doctrine of rescission for innocent misrepresentation should be excluded by execution of the contract has been described as 'curious',[249] because the representee may only know of the misrepresentation after title and possession have been obtained. Lord Denning repeatedly said[250] both that the supposed rule had been too widely stated by Joyce J, and that it was to be limited to misrepresentations as to title in the case of contracts for the sale of land.

Significantly, an alternative ground for Joyce J's decision was that the purchaser had affirmed the contract. It is often the case that once ownership has passed, acts of affirmation will occur which will bar the exercise of the buyer's right of rescission.[251] Further, Joyce J doubted that there was a misrepresentation at all. It is thought that the dangers sought to be avoided by the rule are adequately provided for by other rules, such as the restriction implied by the requirement of substantial restitution,[252] the impact of affirmation of the contract,[253] and the interposition of rights of innocent third parties.[254] The observation of the Privy Council in *Senanayake v Cheng*[255] seems to be of general application: 'Of greater importance than seeking in a case such as the present to attach the label of one or other of these words ['executed' or 'executory'] are the questions whether restitutio in integrum is substantially possible and whether rescission is timely and just and fair.'

---

243. Thus, the rule applies to leases: *Angel v Jay* [1911] 1 KB 666.
244. *Kramer v Duggan* (1955) 55 SR (NSW) 385; and cf *Cousins v Freeman* (1957) 58 WALR 79.
245. *Vimig Pty Ltd v Contract Tooling Pty Ltd* (1986) 9 NSWLR 731.
246. See also *Compagnie Francaise des Chemins de Fer Paris Orleans v Leeston Shipping Co Ltd* (1919) 1 Ll L Rep 235; *Edler v Auerbach* [1950] 1 KB 359.
247. See [1055].
248. See, eg H A Hammelman, 'Seddon v North Eastern Salt Co' (1939) 55 *LQR* 90.
249. *Armstrong v Jackson* [1917] 2 KB 822 at 825.
250. See *Solle v Butcher* [1950] 1 KB 671 at 695; *Leaf v International Galleries* [1950] 2 KB 86 at 90; *Goldsmith v Rodger* [1962] 2 Lloyd's Rep 249.
251. See, eg *Leaf v International Galleries* [1950] 2 KB 86; *Long v Lloyd* [1958] 2 All ER 402.
252. See [1043]–[1046].
253. See [1047]–[1051].
254. See [1052]–[1053]. Cf *New Zealand Loan and Mercantile Co Agency v Howes* (1888) 4 QLJ 73.
255. [1966] AC 63 at 83. And see *Hudson v Jope* (1914) 14 SR (NSW) 351 (conveyance of wrong parcel — but for her affirmation, purchaser would have been entitled to rescind).

[1055] Scope of the rule. Even if valid outside the land context, the rule in *Seddon's* case does not apply where there has been mere partial execution.[256] A particular difficulty in applying the rule arises where property is not unitary but is composite and heterogeneous (as in a contract for the sale of a business) and passes to the purchaser at different times. In the New Zealand case *Root v Badley*[257] the question asked in this situation was whether the contract was still *substantially* executory.

Execution of the contract is not a restriction in cases of fraudulent misrepresentation, the presence of fraudulent intent being a much more weighty factor than the dividing line between contract and conveyance.[258] Nor is it applicable where there has been fundamental mistake involving a complete failure of consideration so that even at common law relief would have been available,[259] or where the party against whom rescission is sought had made the contract in breach of a fiduciary duty owed to the other party.[260]

There is authority deciding that the rule in *Seddon's* case is not a bar to rescission for innocent misrepresentation inducing contracts for the sale of goods or shares.[261]

[1056] Statutory amendment. The rule has been abolished in the Australian Capital Territory and South Australia.[262] It is not a bar to rescission that a conveyance, transfer or other document has been registered at a public registry office in pursuance of the contract.[263]

The rule has also been abolished, in the context of sale of goods, in New South Wales.[264]

Pre-contract representation also a term of the contract

[1057] The alleged restriction. A pre-contract representation may also be a term of the contract. This may be because there is a contractual document containing a term to the same effect as the representation, or because the intention of the parties was that the statement was to take effect as a term of the contract under the principles discussed earlier.[265]

---

256. *Compagnie Francaise des Chemins de Fer Paris Orleans v Leeston Shipping Co Ltd* (1919) 1 Ll L Rep 235.
257. [1960] NZLR 760.
258. See, eg *Hart v Swaine* (1877) 7 Ch D 42; *Wheeler v Atkinson* (1925) 28 WALR 12; *Angel v Jay* [1911] 1 KB 666.
259. *New Zealand Loan and Mercantile Agency Co v Howes* (1888) 4 QLJ 73; *Hudson v Jope* (1914) 14 SR (NSW) 351.
260. See, eg *Armstrong v Jackson* [1917] 2 KB 822; *Bendigo Central Freezing and Fertiliser Co Ltd v Cunningham* [1919] VLR 387.
261. *Leason Pty Ltd v Princes Farm Pty Ltd* [1983] 2 NSWLR 381 (goods); *Baird v BCE Holdings Pty Ltd* (1996) 40 NSWLR 374 at 379 (shares). See also [1056].
262. See **ACT**: *Law Reform (Misrepresentation) Act* 1977, s 3(b); **SA**: *Misrepresentation Act* 1972, s 6(1)(b).
263. See **ACT**: *Law Reform (Misrepresentation) Act* 1977, s 3(c); **SA**: *Misrepresentation Act* 1972, s 6(1)(c).
264. See *Sale of Goods Act* 1923 (NSW), s 4(2a)(b).
265. See [602]–[610].

Rescission is not a remedy for breach of contract,[266] so the question may arise whether the representor can rely on the representation as a ground for rescission. In some cases it has been suggested that the incorporation of the representation as a term prevents rescission.[267] However, there is also authority to the effect that rescission as for a pre-contract misrepresentation remains available.[268] In our view, these decisions should be accepted as correct in the absence of evidence of an intention that the parties' rights and remedies are to be found exclusively in the contract itself.

Usually, the fact that it is a term means that the falsity of the representation is also a breach of contract sounding in damages.[269] Even if the rule has validity in the context of innocent misrepresentation, there may still be a right of *termination* for breach of the term, for example, because it is a condition.[270] However, exercise of the right of termination does not have the same effect as rescission, since the contract is discharged as to the future only.

[1058] Nature of the misrepresentation. Where the misrepresentation is fraudulent, rescission is available even if the representation has been incorporated as a contractual term.[271] Therefore, the incorporation restriction, if valid at all, applies only to cases where the representation is innocent.[272] The rationale would be that the remedy of rescission ceases to be available because the statement has lost its character as a representation.

[1059] Statutory amendment. Following legislative reform in England,[273] it is now provided in the Australian Capital Territory and South Australia that incorporation of a misrepresentation as a term of the contract does not bar rescission.[274]

Sections 100(2) and 111(2) of the *Goods Act* 1958 (Vic) state that incorporation is not a bar in respect of consumer sales and leases. And, in the context of sale of goods, s 4(2A)(a) of the *Sale of Goods Act* 1923 (NSW) provides that incorporation of a representation as a term of the contract does not deprive the representee of the remedies for misrepresentation.

Sale of goods

[1060] Relevant issues. Two features of contracts for the sale of goods call for comment:[275]

---

266. See [1904].
267. See, eg *Pennsylvania Shipping Co v Compagnie Nationale de Navigation* [1936] 2 All ER 1167 at 1171.
268. *Compagnie Francaise des Chemins de Fer Paris Orleans v Leeston Shipping Co Ltd* (1919) 1 Ll L Rep 235 at 237–8; *Academy of Health and Fitness Pty Ltd v Power* [1973] VR 254; *Simons v Zartom Investments Pty Ltd* [1975] 2 NSWLR 30 at 36.
269. Although it would be unusual for it to do so, the term may still have the character of a mere representation. See [604].
270. See generally [1911]–[1921].
271. *Alati v Kruger* (1955) 94 CLR 216 at 222; *Kramer v McMahon* [1970] 1 NSWR 194 at 204.
272. Cf *Svanosio v McNamara* (1956) 96 CLR 186 at 205.
273. See *Misrepresentation Act* 1967 (UK), s 1(a).
274. See **ACT**: *Law Reform (Misrepresentation) Act* 1977, s 3(a); **SA**: *Misrepresentation Act* 1972, s 6(1)(a).

(1) whether the rules of equity affording relief of rescission for innocent misrepresentation apply; and

(2) the impact on a buyer's right of rescission of 'acceptance' of goods by the buyer.

[1061] Applicability of equitable rules. Under the common law applicable prior to the enactment of the sale of goods legislation, once the property in a specific chattel had passed to the buyer, the buyer had no right to return a chattel, re-vest the property in the seller and recover the price (if paid) even though there was a breach of contract or misrepresentation by the seller.[276] There were, however, exceptions. Thus, a term of the contract might provide for a contrary result.[277] Rescission was also available in cases of fraud, or where, in the case of an innocent misrepresentation, there was a complete difference in substance between what was received and what was represented.[278]

Since the rules of equity providing for rescission for innocent misrepresentation had not been applied to contracts for the sale of goods when the administration of the systems of common law and equity were fused in the Judicature reforms, it could not be argued with any confidence that there was a case of a conflict or variance between common law and equity resulting in the supremacy of the equitable rule. Accordingly, when the sale of goods legislation provided[279] that 'the rules of the common law', including those relating to the effect of fraud and misrepresentation, should continue to apply to contracts for the sale of goods so far as not inconsistent with the express provisions of the legislation,[280] this was interpreted in some cases[281] as referring to the rules of common law as distinct from those of equity, rather than the common law in the general sense of unenacted law. Nonetheless, the contrary view has been expressed,[282] and in the majority of cases[283] the courts have simply assumed that the remedy of rescission for innocent misrepresentation is available under equitable principles.

---

275. See M G Bridge, 'Misrepresentation and Merger: Sale of Land Principles and Sale of Goods Contracts' (1985) 20 *UBC LR* 53 at 89ff; NSW Law Reform Commission, *Report on Sale of Goods Law*, LRC 51, 1987, Chapter 2.
276. See, eg *Street v Blay* (1831) 2 B & Ad 456; 109 ER 1212; *William Tibbits & Co v Holt* (1890) 16 VLR 714.
277. Cf *Bannerman v White* (1861) 10 CBNS 844; 142 ER 685.
278. *Kennedy v Panama New Zealand and Australian Royal Mail Co Ltd* (1867) LR 2 QB 580 at 587 (see [1037]). See J C Smith, 'The Right to Rescind for Breach of Condition in a Sale of Specific Goods under the *Sale of Goods Act*, 1893' (1951) 14 *MLR* 173.
279. See **ACT**: *Sale of Goods Act* 1954, s 62(1); **NSW**: *Sale of Goods Act* 1923, s 4(2); **NT**: *Sale of Goods Act* 1972, s 4(2); **Qld**: *Sale of Goods Act* 1896, s 61(2); **SA**: *Sale of Goods Act* 1895, s 59(2); **Tas**: *Sale of Goods Act* 1896, s 5(2); **Vic**: *Goods Act* 1958, s 4(2); **WA**: *Sale of Goods Act* 1895, s 59(2).
280. The wording of the provisions varies, but the substance is the same. The problem is one aspect of a wider issue of the applicability of equitable principles to sale of goods transactions. See NSW Law Reform Commission, *Issues Paper on Sale of Goods*, IP 5, 1988, pp 12–13; *Hewett v Court* (1983) 149 CLR 639; 46 ALR 87.
281. See, eg *Riddiford v Warren* (1901) 20 NZLR 572; *Watt v Westhoven* [1933] VLR 458; *Holmes v Burgess* [1975] 2 NZLR 311.
282. See *Graham v Freer* (1980) 35 SASR 424. Cf *Electrical Enterprises Retail Pty Ltd v Rodgers* (1988) 15 NSWLR 473.

The fact that equitable jurisdiction was not invoked in the sale of goods context prior to the Judicature reforms and enactment of sale of goods legislation is not a good reason for continuing to exclude the remedy today, and the better view is that, in legislation intending to codify the law, 'common law' means 'non-statutory' law.[284]

In the Australian Capital Territory and New South Wales[285] the issue has been settled by provisions stating that equitable rules apply to misrepresentation.

[1062] Effect of buyer's acceptance of goods. Once the buyer has 'accepted' goods under a contract for the sale of goods, the contract cannot be terminated for breach of condition.[286] In *Leaf v International Galleries*[287] Denning LJ suggested that a misrepresentation which induces the contract is less potent than a condition, so that acceptance must also preclude rescission for misrepresentation. However, the better view is that since termination and rescission are distinct rights, the loss of one does not necessarily imply the loss of the other.[288]

In many cases where acceptance has occurred, affirmation will also have occurred. Yet there will be some situations in which acceptance will occur before the representee knew or could reasonably have known of the misrepresentation, and so, before the representee was in a position either to affirm or rescind. Moreover, in New South Wales, s 38(2) of the *Sale of Goods Act* 1923 (NSW)[289] expressly provides that rescission for misrepresentation is governed by the general law and not the provision governing acceptance (s 38(1)). And s 100(1) of the *Goods Act* 1958 (Vic) allows rescission of a consumer sale before, or within a reasonable period after, acceptance of the goods.

Damages for Misrepresentation

Introduction

[1063] Remedies for deceit. The most elemental system of justice will afford a remedy to the person who is induced to rely, detrimentally, on another's fraud. The limited remedies which eventually came to be allowed

---

283. See *Leaf v International Galleries* [1950] 2 KB 86; *Long v Lloyd* [1958] 2 All ER 402; *Goldsmith v Rodger* [1962] 2 Lloyd's Rep 249; *Leason Pty Ltd v Princes Farm Pty Ltd* [1983] 2 NSWLR 381. Cf *Frederick E Rose (London) Ltd v William H Pim Junior & Co Ltd* [1953] 2 QB 450 (rectification).
284. See G L Williams, 'Language and the Law — III' (1945) 61 *LQR* 293 at 302.
285. See **ACT**: *Sale of Goods Act* 1954, s 62(1a); **NSW**: *Sale of Goods Act* 1923, s 4(2a). Cf *Goods Act* 1958 (Vic), s 100(1) (consumer sale). And see *Contractual Remedies Act* 1979 (NZ), s 4(3).
286. See [1981].
287. [1950] 2 KB 86 at 90–1. Cf *Long v Lloyd* [1958] 2 All ER 402.
288. See *JAD International Pty Ltd v International Trucks Australia Ltd* (1994) 50 FCR 378 at 385 and Mason and Carter, *Restitution Law in Australia*, 1995, para 2323.
289. A similar reform is recommended by the Law Reform Commission of Western Australia, *Report on the Sale of Goods Act 1895*, Project No 89, 1998. See J W Carter, 'Sale of Goods Reform in Western Australia' (1999) 15 *JCL* 58.

for innocent misrepresentation stood in contrast to the more comprehensive redress which was available for fraud.

The common law gave two remedies to the person induced to make a disadvantageous contract by the other contracting party's fraudulent misrepresentation: damages and, as has already been explained,[290] the right to rescind the contract. The law relating to damages for fraudulent misrepresentations inducing a person to contract flows from the redress which the law provides for 'deceit'.

[1064] **Rescission and damages.** As with any operative misrepresentation, the party misled has the choice of rescinding or affirming the contract. However, damages and rescission are not mutually exclusive. The right of action in deceit is distinct from, independent of and cumulative upon the right to be relieved of the contract.[291] Accordingly, it lies against a representor who is not a contracting party.[292] Moreover, although damages may be recovered whether or not the innocent party has rescinded the contract,[293] the measure of damages may vary.[294]

On the other hand, even if the contract has also been breached, a party who rescinds for misrepresentation cannot sue for damages for breach of contract because the rescission is ab initio and the contract is gone.

[1065] **No damages in equity.** Generally, damages are not available for innocent misrepresentation. Such a statement relies on the fact that courts of equity did not have a general power to award compensation. However, in working out rescission, orders for the payment of money may be made as incidents of rescission. Such orders are in the nature of restitution, and ultimately based on the prevention or reversal of unjust enrichment.[295] However, although perhaps with the same rationale, there is a power to grant an 'indemnity' in certain cases, that is, a power to award to a representee money payable to a third party in consequence of the representor's misrepresentation.[296]

The rule that damages cannot be recovered for an innocent misrepresentation is qualified in two main ways. First, the comments above in relation to deceit apply also to innocent misrepresentations which are within the concept of negligent misstatement.[297] Second, and more significantly, damages may be available under statute.[298]

---

290. See [1039]–[1041].
291. *Sibley v Grosvenor* (1916) 21 CLR 469 per Griffith CJ; *Munchies Management Pty Ltd v Belperio* (1988) 84 ALR 700 at 710.
292. See [1028].
293. See, eg *O'Keefe v Taylor Estates Co Ltd* [1916] St R Qd 301; *Evans v Benson & Co* [1961] WAR 12; *Williams v Moore* [1963] SR (NSW) 765.
294. See [1071]–[1072].
295. Cf Daniel Friedmann, 'Valid, Voidable, Qualified, and Non-existing Obligations: An Alternative Perspective on the Law of Restitution' in Burrows, ed, *Essays on the Law of Restitution*, 1991, p 262. See generally Chapter 23.
296. See, eg *Erlanger v New Sombrero Phosphate Co* (1878) 3 App Cas 1218 per Lord Blackburn; *Newbigging v Adam* (1886) 34 Ch D 582 (affirmed sub nom *Adam v Newbigging* (1888) 13 App Cas 308); *Kramer v McMahon* [1970] 1 NSWLR 194 at 206; *Sargent v Campbell* [1972–73] ALR 708.
297. See generally [1029]–[1036].
298. See [1073] and generally Chapter 11.

Damages at Common Law

[1066] Proof of damage essential. A plaintiff suing in tort for deceit or negligence will fail if no loss or damage is proved to have been suffered by having acted upon the misrepresentation.[299] The classic statement is to be found in Buller J's judgment in *Pasley v Freeman*:[300]

> The foundation of this action is fraud and deceit in the defendant, and damage to the plaintiffs. And the question is, whether an action thus founded can be sustained in a court of law. Fraud without damage, or damage without fraud, gives no cause of action; but where these two concur an action lies ...

No cognisable loss or damage occurs where a person is induced by fraud to perform an existing legal obligation, for example, to perform a binding contract.[301] Nor is the requirement of loss or damage satisfied merely by proof that the plaintiff did not make the profit which would have been made if the representation had been true.[302]

[1067] Accrual of the cause of action. Since loss or damage is an essential element of the cause of action for deceit or negligence, the cause of action generally accrues only when that loss or damage exists. The relevant period under the statute of limitations for commencement of proceedings begins to run from that time.[303] By contrast, the limitation period in an action for breach of contract commences to run when the contract is breached.

In the present context loss or damage usually occurs when the resultant contract proves to be disadvantageous. However, the High Court's decision in *Wardley Australia Ltd v State of Western Australia*[304] indicates that the general rule is less rigorously applied than in the past. For example, in *Christopoulos v Angelos*[305] it was held that where damage depended on action being taken by the dominant owner to enforce a right of way, a cause of action based on negligent misrepresentation by solicitors did not arise when the purchasers completed the purchase.

Similarly, although the general rule is that damages are assessed at the time when the transaction was entered into, this is not invariably the case.[306] Moreover, the approach does not preclude an award for consequential loss or damage.

---

299. See, eg *Munchies Management Pty Ltd v Belperio* (1988) 84 ALR 700 at 707.
300. (1789) 3 TR 51 at 56; 100 ER 450 at 453.
301. *Australasian Brokerage Ltd v ANZ Banking Corp Ltd* (1934) 52 CLR 430.
302. *Howell v Bennett & Fisher Ltd* [1966] SASR 188.
303. See, eg *Hawkins v Clayton* (1988) 164 CLR 539. Cf *UBAF Ltd v European American Banking Corp* [1984] QB 713.
304. (1992) 175 CLR 514; 109 ALR 247. Although decided by reference to a cause of action for misleading or deceptive conduct prohibited by statute (see Chapter 11), the same rules apply to cases of fraud.
305. (1996) 41 NSWLR 700 at 705, 711. See also *Pullen v Gutteridge Haskins & Davey Pty Ltd* [1993] 1 VR 27 at 66–71.
306. See *Gould v Vaggelas* (1984) 157 CLR 215 at 220; *Smith New Court Securities Ltd v Citibank NA* [1997] AC 254.

[1068] **Causation and remoteness.** In order for a plaintiff to recover substantial damages for a wrong committed by the defendant, two elements must be present:
(1) the loss or damage in respect of which the plaintiff claims compensation must have been *caused* by the wrong; and
(2) the loss or damage must *not be too remote*.

These two requirements therefore apply to an action for damages in tort for misrepresentation, that is, for fraud or negligence.[307] The test of causation is the same in both deceit or negligence.[308]

However, the remoteness criterion is more generous in deceit than negligence.[309] In cases of deceit the plaintiff is, subject to principles governing mitigation of loss,[310] entitled to recover any loss which is a direct and natural consequence of acting on the misrepresentation.[311] On the other hand, the (general) criterion that the loss or damage must have been reasonably foreseeable applies to a claim for damages for negligent misrepresentation.

[1069] **Measure of damages.** The measure of damages in tort for fraud or negligence emphasises the prejudice or disadvantage suffered by reason of the representee's alteration of position.[312] This is the 'out of pocket test', that is, how much the plaintiff is worse off by reason of having acted upon the misrepresentation. Broadly expressed, this measure is the difference between the financial position in which the representee would have been if the false representation had not been made, and the representee's actual position. A more comprehensive way of stating the position was stated by Dixon J in *Potts v Miller*:[313]

> [T]he measure of damages in an action of deceit consists in the loss or expenditure incurred by the plaintiff in consequence of the inducement upon which he relied, diminished by any corresponding advantage in money or money's worth obtained by him on the other side ...

So, in *O'Keefe v Taylor Estates Co Ltd*[314] the plaintiff sued for £200 being the contract price for the defendant to agist his cattle on the plaintiff's land. The defendant pleaded fraudulent misrepresentation. It was held that he could recover the expense which he had incurred in removing his cattle to

---

307. The statutory provisions apportioning responsibility on the basis of contributory negligence (see [2129]) will usually not apply to cases of fraud: *Alliance & Leicester Building Society v Edgestop Ltd* [1993] 1 WLR 1462.
308. The criterion for remoteness may be more generous in tort than contract. See [2126].
309. See *South Australia v Johnson* (1982) 42 ALR 161 at 169–170.
310. See, eg *Neal v Ayers* (1940) 63 CLR 524; *Monroe Schneider Associates (Inc) v No 1 Raberem Pty Ltd* (1991) 104 ALR 397 at 412.
311. *Clark v Urquhart* [1930] AC 28 at 68; *Doyle v Olby (Ironmongers) Ltd* [1969] 2 QB 158; *Smith New Court Securities Ltd v Citibank NA* [1997] AC 254 (see Jennifer Payne, [1997] *CLJ* 17); Roger Halson, [1997] *LMCLQ* 423. Cf *Gould v Vaggelas* (1984) 157 CLR 215 at 221; *Marks (in a Representative Capacity) v GIO Australia Holdings Ltd* (1998) 196 CLR 494 at 512; 158 ALR 333.
312. See also *Toteff v Antonas* (1952) 87 CLR 647 at 650; *Wardley Australia Ltd v State of Western Australia* (1992) 175 CLR 514 at 530.
313. (1940) 64 CLR 282 at 297. See also *Toteff v Antonas* (1952) 87 CLR 647 at 650–1; *Gould v Vaggelas* (1984) 157 CLR 215 at 220–1, 242–3, 254–5.
314. [1916] St R Qd 301.

the land. If he had paid the £200 in advance, rescission alone would have given him a right only to be reimbursed that sum, but the presence of fraud would have given him *damages* for the expense thrown away as well. The expenditure must be causally connected with the fraud and it must have been truly lost to the plaintiff, rather than adequately reflected in the value of property retained, or spent to make the plaintiff the owner of such property.[315]

In *Holmes v Jones*[316] the High Court contrasted the measure of damages for fraud inducing the making of a contract with that for breach of contract[317] (or 'warranty' in the broad sense of contractual undertaking). O'Connor J said:[318]

> Damages for a breach of warranty are given on the principle that, where a person contracts to do something, and fails to do it, he must put the other party in the same position as if the thing had been done, so far as money can do it. But where the complaint is that the contract has been induced by a fraudulent misrepresentation, the remedy for that wrong is to put the party, who has been induced to make the contract, as far as possible in the position he would have been in if he had not entered into the contract. To put him into that position he must be recompensed for the damage he has sustained by entering into the contract. In order to ascertain the extent of that damage the whole contract must be looked at. If it should turn out that though in one respect the contract is less beneficial to the other party than it would have been if the representation had been true, yet in other respects, it is so profitable that on the whole he loses nothing, no damage has resulted from his entering into the contract and he cannot recover.

The contrast is therefore between:

- *fraud*: compensating the plaintiff for loss or damage suffered by reason of entering into the contract; and
- *breach of contract*: putting the plaintiff in the position which would have been occupied had the contract been performed.

This contrast means that a benefit which would have been accrued had the representation been true is not recoverable as damages for fraud. It is nevertheless true that loss of a business opportunity may be recoverable, for example, where entry into the contract deprived the representee of the opportunity.[319]

In principle,[320] there is no reason why the measure of damages in tort for fraud should differ from the measure in tort for negligence. Thus, the distinction drawn by O'Connor J in *Holmes v Jones* is as applicable to a claim based on negligent misrepresentation as it is to a claim based on fraud. However, in the context of negligence the position is complicated by

---

315. Cf *Cooke v Caldwell's Wines Ltd* (1925) 25 SR (NSW) 161; *Selman v Minogue* (1937) 37 SR (NSW) 280; *Nicholls v Taylor* [1939] VLR 119; *Evans v Benson & Co* [1961] WAR 12.
316. (1907) 4 CLR 1692.
317. See Chapter 21.
318. (1907) 4 CLR 1692 at 1709.
319. See *Sellars v Adelaide Petroleum NL* (1994) 179 CLR 332; 120 ALR 16, especially at 335 where the standard of proof is explained. Cf *East v Maurer* [1991] 1 WLR 461 (see Jonathan Marks, (1992) 108 *LQR* 386; Simon Evans, (1993) 6 *JCL* 73); *Clef Aquitaine SARL v Laporte Materials (Barrow) Ltd* [2000] 3 WLR 1760.
320. And subject to the points in [1068] concerning causation and remoteness.

the fact that the plaintiff may also have a cause of action in contract which is based on the defendant's negligence. For example, assume that a valuer negligently values a property at $8 million when its real value — that is, the valuation which would be placed on the property by a valuer exercising due care — is $5 million. If the plaintiff lends $7 million on the security of the property, it has lent $2 million more than its true value. Of course, if the borrower defaults, so that the property has to be sold, the amount realised on the sale will depend on movements in the property market. Thus, the value of the property may have fallen with the result that it is sold for only $3 million. What is the measure of the plaintiff's damages? Does the measure differ between contract and tort if the negligence is the breach of a contractual duty of care?[321]

As will be explained later,[322] when applying the concepts of causation and remoteness the courts have been reluctant to countenance different awards, depending on whether the plaintiff sues in tort or contract. Although the question of measure of damages is logically a distinct issue on which there is in principle a genuine difference between contract and tort, in *South Australia Asset Management Corp v York Montague Ltd*[323] the House of Lords suggested that the liability of a negligent valuer of property should be the same in contract and tort. Thus, in the example given above, the House of Lords said that the maximum which the plaintiff may recover — whether it sues in tort or contract — is $3 million. That measure is the difference between the actual valuation ($8 million) and the valuation which would be placed on the property by a valuer exercising due care ($5 million). The result is that $1 million of the $4 million loss realised on sale of the property is not recoverable. This was said to be attributable to the fall in market prices for which the defendant could not be held responsible.

The *South Australia Asset Management Corp* decision was subsequently considered by the High Court in *Kenny & Good Pty Ltd v MGICA (1992) Ltd*.[324] Although it would appear that a majority of the court rejected the approach of the House of Lords, it is far from clear what principles should be applied. Some judges spoke in terms of whether the loss attributable to the fall in market prices was caused by the defendant's negligence. Others spoke in terms of remoteness, and McHugh J considered that the result depended on whether the circumstances showed that the defendant had agreed that the valuation would remain valid for a particular period. In the result, however, the decisions of the lower courts (which refused to follow the approach in *South Australia Asset Management Corp*) were affirmed. This suggests that, in the example above, the plaintiff would recover $4 million as damages.

---

321. See generally D W McLauchlan, 'A Damages Dilemma' (1997) 12 *JCL* 114; Brian Coote, 'Is there Hope, Still, for Negligent Valuers' (1997) 12 *JCL* 145. See also [1071], [1072], [2104].
322. See [2104], [2126].
323. [1997] AC 191 (see D W McLauchlan, (1997) 113 *LQR* 421; Janet O'Sullivan, [1997] *CLJ* 19; Jane Stapleton, (1997) 113 *LQR* 1; John Wightman, (1998) 61 *MLR* 68).
324. (1999) 199 CLR 413; 163 ALR 611 (see D W McLauchlan and C E F Rickett, (2000) 116 *LQR* 1).

[1070] **Relevance of market value.** In applying the measure of damages explained above, the first question to ask is what the plaintiff parted with in reliance on the fraudulent misrepresentation. It is the 'real' or 'fair' value which is to be regarded and not the 'market' value, which may, after all, be inflated by the very fraudulent misrepresentation in question.[325] Where the plaintiff is a buyer this is the total contract price which was paid. In *Toteff v Antonas*[326] the vendor of a business fraudulently misrepresented the takings. The contract apportioned the total price of £2200 between goodwill (£200), plant (£1750) and stock (£250). The fair value of the business as a going concern was £900. The trial judge awarded damages of £200, on the basis that the misrepresentation related to the goodwill alone, but the High Court held that the misrepresentation had induced the purchaser to part with £2200 for the business as a whole and that damages equal to £1300 (£2200–£900) should have been awarded.

If what the plaintiff received in return was valueless, the total price paid is the measure of compensation. But if property is received and retained by the plaintiff, damages must be reduced by the value of the property at the time of receipt. Any subsequent decrease (or increase) in value will be disregarded as too remotely connected with the inducement.[327]

[1071] **Position where contract affirmed.** Assume that a seller (S) makes a fraudulent misrepresentation concerning the quality of a property. Assume also that if the representation had been true the property's value would have been $150,000, whereas in fact its fair value is $100,000. If we further assume that the buyer (B) was induced by the fraudulent representation to buy it for $120,000, but that B chose to affirm the transaction and to retain the property, the measure of B's loss is the difference between the price paid and the value of the property.[328] Thus, the out of pocket test entitles B to $20,000 ($120,000–$100,000). B cannot recover $30,000 ($150,000–$120,000), since that is the breach of contract measure.[329]

If the fair value of the land had in fact been, say, $125,000, instead of $100,000, no damages would be payable at all for misrepresentation (since the tortious measure is $120,000–$125,000), even though, had the truth of the statement been warranted as a term of the contract, B could have recovered $25,000 ($150,000–$125,000) for breach of contract.[330]

[1072] **Position where contract rescinded.** Rescission of the contract in the first example given above[331] would entitle B to a refund of the purchase price ($120,000). The value of the property is irrelevant. If the land had been worth $150,000, instead of $100,000, B is still limited, in a claim in

---

325. *Potts v Miller* (1940) 64 CLR 282. For the relevant date see *Saunders v Edwards* [1987] 1 WLR 1116.
326. (1952) 87 CLR 647.
327. *Potts v Miller* (1940) 64 CLR 282. But cf [1069] (position of negligent valuer).
328. *Toteff v Antonas* (1952) 87 CLR 647 at 650; *Alati v Kruger* (1955) 94 CLR 216 at 222; *Wardley Australia Ltd v State of Western Australia* (1992) 175 CLR 514 at 530.
329. But cf *Wehr v Thom* [1969] WAR 39; *Snarski & Snarski v Barbarich* [1969] WAR 46. And contrast *Contractual Remedies Act* 1979 (NZ), s 6.
330. See *Holmes v Jones* (1907) 4 CLR 1692.
331. See [1071].

restitution or in tort, to recovery of the purchase price. There is a clear contrast with the 'loss of bargain' measure, which would apply on termination of the contract for breach by S.[332] This would produce an additional sum of $30,000 as compensation, that is, the difference between the contract price and the market price ($150,000–$120,000).

Now assume this change in the figures. If the land had in fact been worth, say, $115,000, and S had made a representation which, had it been true, would have made the land worth $115,000 no damages would be payable at all for breach of contract, had the truth of the statement been warranted. The measure for 'loss of bargain' would be nominal,[333] since B has made a bad bargain. B is entitled, by rescinding the contract, to recover the total amount paid. But B would fail in an action for additional damages (other than for costs incurred) because B has suffered no loss.

Damages Under Statute

Introduction

[1073] **General.** Legislation affects the law relating to damages for misrepresentation inducing contracts in two ways. First, there are statutes the object of which is to reform directly the common law of misrepresentation.[334] Second, there are statutes which, in conferring rights of damages, for example, in respect of misleading or deceptive conduct, impact on the law of misrepresentation by making analysis of the common law incomplete.[335]

Misrepresentation legislation

[1074] **Application of the legislation.** The origin of legislation dealing specifically with misrepresentation is the *Misrepresentation Act* 1967 (UK).[336] Similar legislation has been enacted in the *Misrepresentation Act* 1972 (SA) and the *Law Reform (Misrepresentation) Act* 1977 (ACT).[337]

The *Misrepresentation Act* 1972 (SA) applies to misrepresentations made 'in the course of a trade or business' for the purpose of inducing a person to make a contract or to pay money or dispose of property. It makes such conduct an offence by the person by whom the trade or business is conducted and the actual representor, who are both liable to be fined. The *Law Reform (Misrepresentation) Act* 1977 (ACT) has the same effect with respect to misrepresentations made 'in the course of trade or commerce'.

Of more concern, however, is the expansion of the civil remedies for misrepresentation.

---

332. See [2157]–[2161].
333. See *Howell v Bennett & Fisher Ltd* [1966] SASR 189. On the concept of 'nominal' damages see [2106].
334. See [1074]–[1078].
335. See Chapter 11.
336. Prompted by the *Tenth Report* of the Law Reform Committee, Cmd 1782, 1962. See Ian Brown and Adrian Chandler, 'Deceit, Damages and the *Misrepresentation Act* 1967, s 2(1)' [1992] *LMCLQ* 40
337. See also WA Law Reform Commission, *Report on Innocent Misrepresentation*, Project No 22, 1973.

[1075] Damages in lieu of rescission. The court is conferred with a *discretionary power*, notwithstanding rescission or a right to rescind, to declare the contract to be subsisting and to award such damages as it considers fair and reasonable.[338]

[1076] Right to damages. The most significant impact of the legislation is to confer a right to damages in respect of innocent misrepresentations which would not give rise to such a right at common law.[339] The right given to recover damages is *limited* by three considerations.

First, the misrepresentation must have been made by a representor (defendant) who is a person who might be loosely described as one who is interested in the transaction. That person may be:

- another party to the contract;
- a person acting for or on behalf of the defendant; or
- a person who receives a direct or indirect consideration or material advantage as a result of the formation of the contract.

Second, the circumstances must be such that the defendant (whether or not the actual representor) would, *if the representation had been fraudulent*, have been liable in damages to the contracting party misled.[340] Thus, the plaintiff must show detrimental reliance on a misrepresentation which would at least constitute an innocent misrepresentation.[341]

Third, the operation of the provisions is subject to statutory defences.[342]

[1077] Nature and measure of damages. The damages recoverable as a result of the legislation are in the nature of damages for the tort of deceit. This, it would seem, follows from the way in which the legislation operates. Rather than deeming the representation to be a term of the contract,[343] the legislation, while not changing the character of the representation, confers a right to damages where the misrepresentation, though innocent, would have given rise to a liability in damages had it been fraudulent.[344]

It also follows that the relevant measure of damages is not the expectation basis as on a breach of contract.[345] Rather, the court must assess how much worse off the plaintiff is by reason of having made the contract.[346] The

---

338. See **ACT**: *Law Reform (Misrepresentation) Act* 1977, s 5(1); **SA**: *Misrepresentation Act* 1972, s 7(3).
339. See **ACT**: *Law Reform (Misrepresentation) Act* 1977, s 4(1); **SA**: *Misrepresentation Act* 1972, s 7(1).
340. See [1077].
341. Cf *Strover v Harrington* [1988] Ch 390 (knowledge of agent fatal).
342. See [1078].
343. As under the *Contractual Remedies Act* 1979 (NZ), which assimilates the remedies for breach of contract and pre-contract misrepresentation.
344. But the plaintiff does not plead fraud as the basis for the claim: *Garden Neptune Shipping Ltd v Occidental Worldwide Investment Corp* [1990] 1 Lloyd's Rep 330 (see Richard Hooley, (1991) 107 *LQR* 31).
345. But cf *William Sindall Plc v Cambridgeshire County Council* [1994] 1 WLR 1016 at 1037, 1045 (see Hugh Beale, (1995) 111 *LQR* 60; A J Oakley, [1995] *CLJ* 17). On the relevance of contributory negligence see *Crawford v Parish* (1991) 105 FLR 361 at 367; *Gran Gelato Ltd v Richcliff (Group) Ltd* [1992] Ch 560 (see Peter Cane, (1992) 108 *LQR* 539; Adrian Chandler and Stephen Higgins, [1994] *LMCLQ* 326); *Alliance & Leicester Building Society v Edgestop Ltd* [1993] 1 WLR 1462.

tortious test therefore governs remoteness, and it has been held that the effect of the characterisation of the award is to incorporate the general rule in relation to fraud[347] that the representor is liable for any loss which is a direct and natural consequence of acting on the misrepresentation.[348] However, given that it is no defence for the representor to prove an honest belief in the truth of the representation[349] this seems a peculiar result.

[1078] Statutory defences. Absence of belief in the truth of the representation or knowledge of its falsity is the basic criterion for deceit.[350] Absence of reasonable grounds did not constitute deceit, though gross negligence may have suggested that degree of reckless indifference for the truth which had come to be treated as absence of belief in the truth of the representation.[351] A consequence of the *Hedley Byrne* principle is that absence of reasonable grounds may amount to carelessness and give rise to a liability under that principle.[352] Honesty alone would be sufficient to defeat a common law action for deceit, and exercise of reasonable care would preclude a claim under the *Hedley Byrne* principle. It is, however, a statutory defence to the action for damages under the misrepresentation legislation that the defendant acted *both* honestly and reasonably.[353] This means that the representor must not only have *believed* that the representation was true, but also have had *reasonable grounds* for that belief.

What if the defendant was not the actual representor? Section 4(2) of the *Law Reform (Misrepresentation) Act* 1977 (ACT) provides that it is a defence if *both* the defendant and the actual representor believed on reasonable grounds that the representation was true. By contrast, s 7(2) of the *Misrepresentation Act* 1972 (SA) provides a defence if the defendant did not know and could not reasonably be expected to have known that the representation had been made or that it was untrue.

---

346. The discussion in [1066]–[1072] applies.
347. See [1068].
348. See *Royscot Trust Ltd v Rogerson* [1991] 2 QB 297; *William Sindall Plc v Cambridgeshire County Council* [1994] 1 WLR 1016. Cf *Crawford v Parish* (1991) 105 FLR 361 at 366. For commentary see A J Oakley, [1992] *CLJ* 9; John Wadsley, (1992) 55 *MLR* 698.
349. See [1078].
350. See generally [1025]–[1027].
351. See [1025].
352. See generally [1029]–[1036].
353. See **ACT**: *Law Reform (Misrepresentation) Act* 1977, s 4(2); **SA**: *Misrepresentation Act* 1972, s 7(2). The defence is not applicable to a claim for rescission and consequential relief: *Graham v Freer* (1980) 35 SASR 424.

Chapter 11

The Statutory Prohibition of Misleading or Deceptive Conduct and the Law of Contract[1]

Misleading or Deceptive Conduct 1101
The Statutory Remedies 1111
Actions Based on the Statutory Prohibition
   Compared with Actions under the General Law of Contract . 1117
Disclaimers, Exclusion and Acknowledgment
   and Merger Clauses 1122

Misleading or Deceptive Conduct

[1101] Introduction. Section 52 of the *Trade Practices Act* 1974 (Cth) prohibits misleading or deceptive conduct when occurring in trade or commerce. It thereby establishes a general norm of conduct to govern commercial behaviour. Unlike the position under similar legislation in many other countries, enforcement is not entrusted solely or even principally to a public enforcement agency (in this case the Australian Competition and Consumer Commission, previously the Trade Practices Commission), but very wide rights of action to seek damages and other orders are given to private individuals (and corporations). This has resulted in the legislation having a quite dramatic impact on the general law of contract, such that the possibility of remedies based on s 52 must be considered in practically any commercial litigation based on contractual disputes. The impact has been particularly great in many situations where

---

1. This chapter is based on the more extensive discussion appearing in David Harland, 'The Statutory Prohibition of Misleading or Deceptive Conduct in Australia and its Impact on the Law of Contract' (1995) 111 *LQR* 100.

previously a remedy, if any at all was available, would have had to be sought under the law as to misrepresentation.

Section 52 of the *Trade Practices Act* 1974 (Cth) provides that 'a corporation shall not, in trade or commerce, engage in conduct that is misleading or deceptive or is likely to mislead or deceive'.[2]

The *Trade Practices Act* contains very important provisions dealing with competition law and prohibits a variety of practices which restrict competition. The Act also contains the principal federal provisions dealing with consumer protection. Section 52 appears among these provisions (contained in Pt V of the Act), which represented the first major federal legislation specifically aimed at consumer protection and, because of their wide substantive scope and the important enforcement mechanisms provided, the *Trade Practices Act* quickly became the single most important consumer protection enactment in Australia.

In common with most of the provisions of the Act defining prohibited conduct, s 52 speaks of conduct by 'a corporation'. This is because the Act relies for its constitutional validity principally on the power of the Commonwealth Parliament to make laws with respect to 'foreign corporations, and trading or financial corporations formed within the limits of the Commonwealth'.[3] However, ss 5 and 6 of the Act give these provisions an extended operation in some instances where other heads of federal legislative power can be relied upon. Thus, for example, any trader, whether incorporated or not, may be caught by the Act in respect of conduct occurring in interstate trade or commerce. It should be remembered that where the business activity of an unincorporated sole trader or partnership is not subject to the *Trade Practices Act* it will be subject to the fair trading legislation of the appropriate State or Territory.

[1102] The fair trading legislation of the States. The consumer protection legislation of the States operates concurrently with the federal legislation, the former complementing the latter in respect of, inter alia, matters outside of the legislative competence of the Commonwealth parliament. The need for federal/State co-operation in the field of consumer protection was recognised almost immediately after the enactment in 1974 of the *Trade Practices Act*. Ultimately, in order to overcome problems caused by limitations on federal legislative power, each State and the two Territories enacted 'fair trading' legislation which, with relatively minor exceptions, copies those of the consumer protection provisions of the *Trade Practices Act* which prohibit unfair marketing practices but applies the prohibitions to persons generally, whether incorporated or not. Subject to this point, what is said in the remainder of this chapter about s 52 of the *Trade Practices Act* and the remedies available under it is, in general, applicable also to the corresponding provisions of the fair trading legislation.[4]

---

2. For a useful overview of s 52 see R French, 'A Lawyer's Guide to Misleading or Deceptive Conduct' (1989) 63 *ALJ* 250. For more extensive discussions see Healey and Terry, *Misleading and Deceptive Conduct*, 1991; Lockhart, *The Law of Misleading or Deceptive Conduct*, 1998.
3. *Constitution*, s 51(xx).

[1103] Misleading or deceptive conduct and financial services.
Section 52 of the *Trade Practices Act* originally applied to all types of transactions (or proposed transactions). However, under the *Australian Securities and Investments Commission Act* 2001 (Cth) (the *ASIC Act*)[5] the consumer protection provisions of the *Trade Practices Act* no longer apply to conduct in relation to financial services,[6] which is now regulated by equivalent provisions inserted in the *ASIC Act* and enforced by the Australian Securities and Investments Commission. The *ASIC Act* equivalent of s 52 of the *Trade Practices Act* is s 12DA.[7] As the *ASIC Act* provisions regulating misleading or deceptive conduct are, within their sphere of operation, almost identical to those of the *Trade Practices Act* which are the concern of this chapter they will not be discussed further here. It should, however, be noted that as a result of amendments expected to commence on 11 March 2002, s 12DA will in future apply to 'persons', in this respect following the approach of the fair trading legislation of the States and Territories rather than that of s 52.[8]

[1104] 'In trade or commerce'. One limiting factor on s 52 (and on the corresponding provisions of the fair trading legislation)[9] is that it applies only to conduct which occurs 'in trade or commerce'. This phrase was intended to make it clear that the new standards of behaviour laid down by the Act were to be imposed only on those who could be said in some sense to be acting in a business capacity rather than in a purely private capacity. It is largely for this reason that s 52 does not have the effect of totally supplanting the general law as to misrepresentation.

Difficult questions can arise as to when conduct can be said to occur 'in' trade or commerce,[10] but this will not be pursued here because the borderline cases are for the most part likely to arise in other than contractual contexts. It should, however, be noted that s 52 is not limited to

---

4. **ACT**: *Fair Trading Act*, 1992, s 12; **NSW**: *Fair Trading Act*, 1987, s 42; **NT**: *Consumer Affairs and Fair Trading Act* 1990, s 42; **Qld**: *Fair Trading Act* 1989, s 38; **SA**: *Fair Trading Act* 1987, s 56; **Tas**: *Fair Trading Act* 1990, s 14; **Vic**: *Fair Trading Act* 1999, s 9; **WA**: *Fair Trading Act* 1987, s 10. Unlike the other jurisdictions, the Queensland provisions on damages (see [1112]) and other orders (see [1115]) are limited to consumers.
5. See Pt 2 (Australian Securities and Investments Commission and consumer protection in relation to financial services), replacing corresponding provisions inserted in 1998 in the former *Australian Securities and Investments Commission Act* 1989.
6. 'Financial service' is defined in *ASIC Act*, s 12BA, which is to be replaced by a new definition contained in s 12BAB: *Financial Services Reform Act* 2001 (this provision is expected to commence on 11 March 2002). See also the new s 12DA(1A), which will exclude from the scope of the provision conduct contravening certain sections of the *Corporations Act* 2001. As to the meaning of 'in relation to financial services' see *Cleary v Australian Co-operative Foods Ltd (Nos 2 & 3)* (1999) 32 ACSR 701.
7. Note that s 12DA does not apply to dealings in securities, as to which see *Corporations Act* 2001, s 995 (see also s 995A providing that s 995 operates to the exclusion of the fair trading legislation (discussed in [1102])). Following provisions, expected to commence on 11 March 2002, of the *Financial Services Reform Act* 2001, s 995 will be replaced by s 1041H; see also s 1041K (to exclude the operation of the fair trading legislation in certain cases).
8. See *Financial Services Reform (Consequential Provisions) Act* 2001, Schedule 1, Item 29.
9. Note, however, that there is no such limitation in *Corporations Act* 2001 (Cth), s 995 (as to which see [1103]).

conduct occurring in the normal or regular course of a trader's business. It has been held that the sale by a corporation of its only capital asset may be conduct in trade or commerce, and consequently a company selling its beauty salon business was held to be acting in trade or commerce, even though it was not in the business of buying and selling such assets.[11] By way of contrast, the sale by an individual of a non-business asset (for example, the family home) is not in trade or commerce.[12] Where a financial institution such as a bank gives information, that conduct may be in trade or commerce even though the information was given gratuitously to someone not a customer of the bank.[13]

[1105] Misleading or deceptive conduct. 'To mislead' means 'to lead into error' (and 'deceive' does not seem to add anything to this). It is not necessary to show any intention to mislead or deceive. Section 52 prohibits conduct having (or capable of having) the stated result, irrespective of fault or moral blameworthiness on the part of the actor. It is not essential that any person has been misled or deceived, so long as the conduct has a real capacity or tendency (though not merely a remote possibility) to do so. Evidence of deception may be persuasive, but this is not essential or conclusive, the question of whether particular conduct is misleading or deceptive being ultimately one for the court itself to determine in an objective manner.[14]

Despite some support for the proposition that, in judging the capacity of conduct to mislead or deceive, one should look to the likely effect of the conduct on the 'reasonable man',[15] the weight of authority was until very recently in favour of a less stringent test, that having the most favour being to assess the effect of the conduct 'on a person, not particularly intelligent or well informed, but perhaps of somewhat less than average intelligence and background knowledge, although the test is not the effect on a person who is, for example, quite unusually stupid'.[16] There was, however, much

10. *Concrete Constructions (NSW) Pty Ltd v Nelson* (1990) 169 CLR 594. See D Harland, 'Misleading or Deceptive Conduct: The Breadth and Limitations of the Prohibition' (1991) 4 *JCL* 107.
11. *Bevanere Pty Ltd v Lubidineuse* (1985) 59 ALR 334. This is semble not affected by the narrowing of the concept brought about by *Concrete Constructions (NSW) Pty Ltd v Nelson* (1990) 169 CLR 594. For a discussion of a difference of opinion as to whether representations concerning conditions of employment made by an employer to existing or prospective employees is conduct 'in' trade or commerce see, eg *Stoolwinder v Southern Health Care Network* (2000) 177 ALR 501. On the disputed point of whether one not otherwise acting in trade or commerce may become liable by virtue of acting 'in' the trade or commerce of another see, eg *Robin Pty Ltd v Canberra International Airport Pty Ltd* (1999) 179 ALR 449; *Dataflow Computer Services Pty Ltd v Goodman* (1999) 168 ALR 169.
12. *O'Brien v Smolonogov* (1983) 53 ALR 107; *Argy v Blunts of Lane Cove Real Estate Pty Ltd* (1990) 94 ALR 719; *Franich v Swannell* (1993) 10 WAR 459.
13. *Menhaden v Citibank NA* (1984) 55 ALR 709.
14. See in particular *Parkdale Custom Built Furniture Pty Ltd v Puxu Pty Ltd* (1982) 149 CLR 191; 42 ALR 1; *Taco Co of Australia Inc v Taco Bell Pty Ltd* (1982) 42 ALR 177; *Arcric Investments Pty Ltd v Ductline Pty Ltd* (1992) ATPR 41-180.
15. See in particular *Parkdale Custom Built Furniture Pty Ltd v Puxu Pty Ltd* (1982) 149 CLR 191 at 199 per Gibbs CJ.
16. *Annand & Thompson Pty Ltd v Trade Practices Commission* (1979) 25 ALR 91 at 102 per Franki J.

support for an even wider approach which would look to all who come within the relevant section of the public, 'including the astute and the gullible, the intelligent and the not so intelligent, the well educated as well as the poorly educated'.[17]

However, in *Campomar Sociedad Limitada v Nike International Ltd*[18] the High Court recently said, without discussing the previous cases favouring a more lenient approach, that in cases of representations made to the public one has regard to 'ordinary' or 'reasonable' members of the class of prospective purchasers addressed. Whether this signals a different approach in the future is not altogether clear,[19] though the difference in practice between the various verbal formulations might well be less than might at first sight appear.

The question of the correct approach is particularly important in cases involving mass media advertising or other conduct directed at the public at large. It probably has little direct impact in the context of one-to-one negotiations (as opposed to statements contained in promotional material), except that the discussion of this issue does emphasise that in every case one must look at the audience to which conduct is directed. It would seem to follow that just as in advertising cases a vulnerable group may apparently be misled where a more sophisticated or expert group might not, so also the characteristics and vulnerabilities (at least where known to the other party) of an individual engaged in contract negotiations must be taken into account when determining whether or not a representation made during those negotiations was misleading.[20]

[1106] Misleading or deceptive conduct and consumers. Section 52 appears in Pt V of the Act, which is headed 'Consumer Protection'. However, s 52 is not expressly limited to conduct directed to consumers. It is essential to realise that although it has been suggested from time to time that s 52 should be read down so as to be contravened only by conduct which is in some sense directed to consumers, it is now well established that s 52 is not so restricted in scope. However, although the very strong weight of authority in the Federal Court was in favour of this position,[21] in what is now the leading decision on the point the High Court reached this result only by a bare majority.[22] In the result the courts have rejected what would be one way of limiting what some would regard as an unacceptable impact on the general law as it applies to many purely commercial transactions. The approach adopted reflects the view that although the Division of the

---

17. See in particular *Taco Co of Australia Inc v Taco Bell Pty Ltd* (1982) 42 ALR 177 at 202 per Deane and Fitzgerald JJ.
18. (2000) 169 ALR 677.
19. Compare eg *George Weston Foods Ltd v Goodman Fielder Ltd* (2000) 49 IPR 553 with *Dyson v Pharmacy Board of New South Wales* (2000) 50 NSWLR 523.
20. Lockhart J appeared to take this approach in *Finucane v NSW Egg Corp* (1988) 80 ALR 486. Quaere whether the maker of the representation must be aware of the idiosyncrasies of the other.
21. See in particular *Menhaden v Citibank NA* (1984) 55 ALR 709; *Bevanere Pty Ltd v Lubidineuse* (1985) 59 ALR 334.
22. *Concrete Constructions (NSW) Pty Ltd v Nelson* (1990) 169 CLR 594; 92 ALR 193. See further D Harland, 'Misleading or Deceptive Conduct: The Breadth and Limitations of the Prohibition' (1991) 4 *JCL* 107 at 115–17.

Act in which s 52 appears was designed to further the protection of consumers against unfair trading practices, the legislature has taken the view that this policy will best be effectuated through a general ban on misleading conduct in the marketplace, irrespective of whether the interests of any individual consumer are directly affected in any particular case. There have been literally hundreds of reported cases under s 52, but relatively few of these involve either the Australian Competition and Consumer Commission (or its predecessor the Trade Practices Commission) or private consumers, most having been brought by trade rivals of the defendant (attacking, for example, allegedly misleading advertising of a competitor) or by a disgruntled party to a commercial contract complaining of misleading representations allegedly made by the other party to the contract.

[1107] Literal truth, the overall impression and puffery. A statement may be misleading or deceptive although literally true. 'Half-truths' and ambiguities may result in deception.[23] One must look to the overall impression created by the conduct. This is particularly true where contractual negotiations extend over a period of time.[24]

We have seen that in some cases conduct which might at first sight appear to be a misrepresentation has been held to be mere puffery, not attracting legal consequences.[25] Similarly, 'puffery' may be a defence to a claim that s 52 has been contravened.[26] But the more specific and precise (and thus capable of being proved to be true or false) a statement is, the more likely it is that the defence of puffery will fail.[27] The commentators generally agree that the defence that a seller's claim is only puffery, not be taken seriously and not attracting liability, is less likely to succeed under the statutory prohibition than under the general law. This is no doubt generally true, especially in cases of advertising and other promotional activity, and, given the public policy goals underlying the statute, any other result would be surprising. Nonetheless, there have been indications of some judicial disquiet that s 52 liability may at times too readily attach in commercial transactions, that some measure of judicial restraint may be called for, and that 'in the ordinary course of commercial dealings, a certain amount of "puffing" or exaggeration is to be expected'.[28]

---

23. See in particular *Janssen Pharmaceutical Pty Ltd v Pfizer Pty Ltd* (1986) ATPR 40–654; *Hutchence v South Sea Bubble Co Ltd* (1986) 64 ALR 330; *Makita (Australia) Pty Ltd v Black & Decker (Australasia) Pty Ltd* (1990) ATPR 41–030; *Telstra Corporation Ltd v Optus Communications Pty Ltd* (1997) ATPR 41-541.
24. See in particular *Pappas v Soulac Pty Ltd* (1983) 50 ALR 231; *Jacques v Cut Price Deli Pty Ltd* (1993) ATPR (Digest) 46–102.
25. See [1007.]
26. See generally Healey and Terry, *Misleading and Deceptive Conduct*, 1991, pp 220–1, 298–300; Lockhart, *The Law of Misleading or Deceptive Conduct*, 1998, pp 77–80.
27. See *Dewhurst v Budget Rent-A-Car System Pty Ltd* (1986) ATPR 40–648 (claim to be leader in rental car market for luxury cars misleading as rival company in fact had larger share of that market).
28. *General Newspapers Pty Ltd v Telstra Corp* (1993) ATPR 41–274 at 41,690 per Davies and Einfeld JJ. See also *Jacques v Cut Price Deli Pty Ltd* (1993) ATPR (Digest) 46–102. For recent examples of such an approach in the context of real estate advertising see *Eighth SRJ Pty Ltd v Merity* (1997) 7 BPR 97635; *Havave Pty Ltd v Lfot Pty Ltd* (1998) ATPR 41-658 (reversed on other grounds (1999) ATPR 41-687).

[1108] **Promises, predictions and opinions.** There is much authority for the proposition that for conduct to be misleading or deceptive it must involve, at least by implication, a representation as to some past or present fact.[29] While this conclusion arguably imposes an unnecessary gloss on the statutory language,[30] one well-established consequence is that the mere fact that a promise is not fulfilled or that a prediction or promise proves to be incorrect does not involve the speaker in a contravention of s 52.[31]

However, this distinction is in any event by no means as limiting as might at first appear because, influenced by the approach taken under the common law on a similar point arising as to misrepresentation,[32] the courts have often held that a person making a representation as to the future or expressing an opinion will be taken also to have impliedly made a representation as to present fact, and if that implied representation is misleading then s 52 will be taken to have been contravened. To quote from one of the leading cases on this point:[33]

> A statement which involves the state of mind of the maker ordinarily conveys the meaning (expressly or by implication) that the maker of the statement had a particular state of mind when the statement was made and, commonly at least, that there was basis for that state of mind.

Applicants relying on a representation as to the future now have their evidentiary burden considerably eased by s 51A, inserted in the *Trade Practices Act* in 1986. Section 51A provides that where a corporation makes a representation with respect to any future matter and it does not have reasonable grounds for making the representation, the representation shall be taken to be misleading. Most importantly, s 51A also provides that in such cases the corporation shall, unless it adduces evidence to the contrary, be deemed not to have had reasonable grounds for making the representation.[34] This easing of the onus of proof will often be a significant advantage to an applicant, especially if the relevant events occurred some time prior to the trial.

There are a number of difficulties in the interpretation of s 51A and its full implications have yet to be developed by the courts. It may well be that one effect of s 51A is that a contracting party who is unable to establish that at the time of contracting he or she then had the intention and perhaps also the ability to perform the contract will be in contravention of s 52.[35] A

---

29. See in particular *Global Sportsman Pty Ltd v Mirror Newspapers Ltd* (1984) 55 ALR 25.
30. See, eg *Adelaide Petroleum NL v Poseidon Ltd* (1988) ATPR 40-901; *Holt v Biroka* (1988) 13 NSWLR 629; *Hunt Contracting Co Pty Ltd v Roebuck Resources NL* (1992) ATPR 41-193.
31. See, eg *Bill Acceptance Corp Ltd v GWA Ltd* (1983) 50 ALR 242.
32. See [1008]-[1009].
33. *Global Sportsman Pty Ltd v Mirror Newspapers Ltd* (1984) 55 ALR 25 at 31 per Bowen CJ, Lockhart and Fitzgerald JJ.
34. In the majority of jurisdictions the fair trading legislation goes further and provides that the representor has the onus of establishing reasonable grounds: **NSW**: *Fair Trading Act* 1987, s 41; **NT**: *Consumer Affairs and Fair Trading Act* 1990, s 41; **Qld**: *Fair Trading Act* 1989, s 37; **Vic**: *Fair Trading Act* 1999, s 4; **WA**: *Fair Trading Act* 1987, s 9.
35. See in particular *Futuretronics International Pty Ltd v Gadzhis* [1992] 2 VR 217 and references there discussed.

statement (express or implied) of a person's present belief or expectation about some future state of affairs will often, perhaps usually, also amount to a representation as to the future for the purposes of the operation of s 51A.[36] Moreover, it seems that in some (not clearly defined) cases a positive unqualified prediction may be misleading in contravention of s 52, even if the speaker had reasonable grounds for believing the prediction would be fulfilled, if in the circumstances some qualification is required as a matter of fair trading.[37]

Many cases involve the expression of an opinion as to an existing state of affairs and in such a case s 51A has no application. The onus of establishing the falsity of any implied representations therefore rests on the applicant. Nonetheless, claims based on expression of opinions may well succeed, either because it is established that the speaker did not in fact hold the opinion or, in many cases, because there was no reasonable basis for it.[38]

[1109] Breach of contract as a contravention of s 52? It is convenient to note here a recent approach which, if established and extended to its logical conclusion, could expand enormously the ability of a contracting party to rely on the statutory remedies in addition to those available at common law. A majority of the Full Court of the Federal Court held in *Accounting Systems 2000 (Developments) Pty Ltd v CCH Australia Ltd*[39] that the mere giving of a contractual warranty as to a presently existing state of affairs may, if false, amount to conduct in contravention of s 52. On the other hand, it has been held in the Supreme Court of New South Wales that the mere performance of a contract does not carry with it a representation that the contract was being properly performed.[40] However, a false representation that a party had the proper competence and skill to carry out a contract will contravene s 52.[41]

[1110] Silence and s 52. We have seen that under the general law, subject to limited exceptions, mere silence does not amount to a representation.[42] It is now well established that a failure to speak may amount to misleading or deceptive conduct even though there would in the same circumstances be no actionable misrepresentation at common law.[43]

---

36. See, eg *Ting v Blanche* (1993) 118 ALR 543; *Sykes v Reserve Bank of Australia* (1998) 88 FCR 511 but compare *Jacques v Cut Price Deli Pty Ltd* (1993) ATPR (Digest) 46-102; *Miba Pty Ltd v Nescor Industries Group Pty Ltd* (1996) 141 ALR 525 (on appeal (1997) 150 ALR 633).
37. See in particular *Wheeler Grace & Pierucci Pty Ltd v Wright* (1989) ATPR 40-940 per Lee J; *Bowler v Hilda Pty Ltd* (1998) 80 FCR 191.
38. See, eg *Bateman v Slayter* (1987) 71 ALR 553; *Chiarabaglia v Westpac Banking Corp* (1989) ATPR 40-971; *RAIA Insurance Brokers Ltd v FAI Insurance Co Ltd* (1993) ATPR 41-225.
39. (1993) 114 ALR 355. See also *Wright v TNT Management Pty Ltd* (1988) 15 NSWLR 679 per McHugh JA (dissenting).
40. *McWilliams' Wines Pty Ltd v L S Booth Wine Transport Pty Ltd* (1992) 25 NSWLR 723.
41. *Comalco Aluminium Ltd v Mogal Freight Services Pty Ltd* (1993) ATPR (Digest) 46-106.
42. See [1013]-[1018].
43. See in particular *Rhône Poulenc Agrochimie SA v UIM Chemical Services Pty Ltd* (1986) 68 ALR 77; *Kabwand Pty Ltd v National Australia Bank Ltd* (1989) ATPR 40-950; *Franich v Swannell* (1993) 10 WAR 459.

It seems that the existence of a duty of disclosure under the general law is still highly relevant in determining whether non-disclosure contravenes s 52. In other circumstances, at least generally, if not necessarily always, a failure to reveal facts will not be misleading unless the circumstances are such as to give rise to a reasonable expectation that if some relevant fact exists it would be disclosed.[44] In those circumstances a failure to disclose can thus be seen to be misleading. One question on which there has been a difference of judicial opinion is whether a failure to disclose can be misleading only where the person whose conduct is complained of actually knew of the relevant fact and intentionally refrained from disclosing it.[45]

Although the approach just outlined gives an important conceptual focus to the problem of when silence can be misleading, it is still difficult to predict just when the courts will infer a reasonable expectation that if certain facts existed they would be disclosed. While the circumstances of a case will at times be held to give rise to a reasonable expectation of disclosure,[46] courts have on the whole been wary of holding that a failure to disclose a fact which would not have been a misrepresentation under the general law constituted a contravention of s 52.[47] Moreover, in the context of contractual negotiations (somewhat different considerations may apply in the case of advertising and promotional activity) a number of judges have been concerned that s 52 not be applied so as to impose what they would see to be unduly restrictive inhibitions on commercial negotiations. Thus, a warning has been given about the danger of imposing between parties negotiating commercial contracts at arm's length obligations which may be quite contrary to ordinary commercial expectations.[48] Likewise, it has been commented that it has not been suggested that s 52 strikes at the traditional secretiveness of the bargaining process and that 'no-one expects all the cards to be on the table'.[49]

---

44. See, eg *Demagogue Pty Ltd v Ramensky* (1993) ATPR 41-203; *Warner v Elders Rural Finance Ltd* (1993) ATPR 41-238; *General Newspapers Pty Ltd v Telstra Corp* (1993) ATPR 41-274. For some recent applications of this approach see *Nagy v Masters Dairy Ltd* (1996) 150 ALR 273; *Leda Holdings Pty Ltd v Oraka Pty Ltd* (1998) ATPR 41-601.
45. Compare eg *Spedley Securities Ltd v Bank of New Zealand* (1991) ATPR 41-143 and *Fliegner v MNM Pty Ltd* (2000) NSW Conv R 55-937 with *Nagy v Masters Dairy Ltd* (1996) 150 ALR 273 and *Johnson Tiles Pty Ltd v Esso Australia Ltd* (2001) ATPR 41-794. Quaere how far cases of 'mere' silence raising this issue will in any event occur: see, eg *Demagogue Pty Ltd v Ramensky* (1993) ATPR 41-203 per Black CJ and *Johnson Tiles Pty Ltd v Esso Australia Ltd* (1999) ATPR 41-696 and (2000) ATPR 41-743 per Merkel J.
46. For recent examples see, eg *Hanave Pty Ltd v Lfot Pty Ltd* (1999) ATPR 41-687; *Costa Vraca Pty Ltd v Berrigan Weed and Pest Control Pty Ltd* (1998) 155 ALR 714; *Mikaelion v Commonwealth Scientific and Industrial Research Organisation* (1999) 163 ALR 172.
47. See, eg *Ryan v Great Lakes Council* (1999) 102 LGERA 123 (no implied representation from sale of oysters that they were uncontaminated).
48. *Lam v Ausintel Investments Australia Pty Ltd* (1990) 97 FLR 458; *Halton Pty Ltd v Stewart Bros Drilling Contractors Pty Ltd* (1992) ATPR 41-158.
49. *Poseidon Ltd v Adelaide Petroleum NL* (1992) ATPR 41-164 at 49,227 per Burchett J. See also *General Newspapers Ltd v Telstra Corporation* (1993) ATPR 41-274 at 41,690 per Davies and Einfeld JJ; *Park v Allied Mortgage Corp Ltd* (1993) 45 FCR 164.

The Statutory Remedies

[1111] Introduction. Although the substantive scope of s 52 is obviously an essential aspect of the impact it has had, of at least equal importance are the very liberal provisions of the Act as to the remedies available in the event of contravention.

Many of the cases in which s 52 has been invoked have been applications for an injunction under s 80 made by a competitor of the person who has allegedly engaged in misleading conduct. This aspect of s 52's operation has had a profound impact on the law of tort, especially in the context of the common law tort of passing off.[50] It is not proposed to discuss this remedy further as it will have little impact as an alternative to actions based on contract. Section 80 could, however, be useful in certain circumstances, such as if conduct in breach of a franchise or distribution agreement also was misleading or deceptive.[51]

[1112] Damages. Perhaps the most important provision in the context of our present concern is s 82, which provides that 'a person who suffers loss or damage by conduct of another person that was done in contravention of a provision of ... Part V [which is where s 52 appears] may recover the amount of the loss or damage by action against that other person or against any person involved in the contravention'.[52]

The test of applicability of s 82 is one of causation. The suffering of loss or damage is an essential element of the cause of action[53] (and hence purely nominal damages cannot be awarded in a s 82 action).[54] It is not sufficient for an applicant merely to prove a contravention of s 52. It has not infrequently happened that, although misleading or deceptive conduct has been established, an action claiming damages under s 82 has nonetheless failed because the applicant was unable to prove that he or she suffered any loss or damage as a result of that conduct.[55] This will be the case where, for example, it appears that the misleading conduct did not in fact induce the applicant to enter into the contract being complained of because the applicant knew the representation to be false or for some reason was not influenced by it in deciding to enter into the contract.

The misleading conduct need not be the sole factor inducing the contract.[56] Direct evidence of inducement is not essential and, indeed, as is the case at common law in actions of deceit, if it is established that

---

50. See, eg R French, 'The Law of Torts and Pt V of the Trade Practices Act' in Finn, ed, *Essays on Torts*, 1989, pp 183–202.
51. See also the suggestion that continuing conduct in breach of a promise, the making of which was a contravention of s 52, may perhaps be enjoined: C E K Hampson, 'Blocked Contractual Arteries? Try a Section 52 By-pass' (1993) 1 *TPLJ* 22 at 34–6.
52. See generally Healey and Terry, *Misleading and Deceptive Conduct*, 1991, pp 362–73; Lockhart, *Law of Misleading or Deceptive Conduct*, 1998, Chapter 11.
53. See, eg *Remedios v Kentucky Homes Pty Ltd* (1987) ATPR 40–799; *Elna Australia Pty Ltd v International Computers (Australia) Pty Ltd* (1987) 75 ALR 271; *Wardley Australia Ltd v Western Australia* (1992) 175 CLR 514; 109 ALR 247.
54. *JLW (Vic) Pty Ltd v Tsiloglou* (1993) ATPR 41–257.
55. For an example see *Ricochet Pty Ltd v Equity Trustees Executor and Agency Co Ltd* (1993) ATPR 41–236.

misleading representations likely to induce entry into a contract were made and that the applicant subsequently entered the contract and suffered loss, an inference of reliance is likely to be drawn unless the defendant shows that other relevant circumstances existed.[57] Failure by an applicant to take reasonable action in his or her own interests to check the veracity of a representation does not prevent recovery, though it seems that in some circumstances such failure may be so extreme as to break the causal link between contravention and loss.[58] The Act makes no express provision for apportionment of damages for contributory negligence and the High Court has recently held that no such doctrine should be read into s 82.[59]

[1113] **Measure of damages.** Section 82 makes no provision as to how damages are to be assessed. The High Court of Australia had held that the tort measure of damages would be appropriate in most, if not all, cases involving misleading or deceptive conduct.[60] Under this approach one asks how much 'worse off' the applicant was as a result of the contravention, rather than whether 'the non-attainment of a benefit or the non-realisation of a profit'[61] has resulted in a loss of bargain ('expectation loss').[62] There was considerable judicial restiveness[63] at what was perceived by some to be the injustice of this approach, as well as criticism of it in the literature.[64]

The High Court revisited this issue in *Marks v GIO Australia Holdings Ltd*.[65] All members of the court agreed that the approach towards relief under s 82 was not to be confined by analogy with the law of contract or tort. However, in a joint judgment McHugh, Hayne and Callinan JJ held that in s 52 cases the remedy under s 82 should be available only to those who are worse off as a result of the contravention of s 52 and stated that 'we

56. See, eg *Elna Australia Pty Ltd v International Computers (Australia) Pty Ltd* (1987) 75 ALR 271; *Henjo Investments Pty Ltd v Collins Marrickville Pty Ltd* (1988) 79 ALR 83; *Sharpe v Ramage* (1995) ATPR 41-398; *Henville v Walker* (2001) 182 ALR 37 (HC).
57. See *Dominelli Ford (Hurstville) Pty Ltd v Karmot Auto Spares Pty Ltd* (1992) ATPR 41-198; *Ricochet Pty Ltd v Equity Trustees Executor and Agency Co Ltd* (1993) ATPR 41-236.
58. See, eg *Argy v Blunts and Lane Cove Real Estate Pty Ltd* (1990) 94 ALR 719 at 742-4 per Hill J; *Karawi Constructions Pty Ltd v Bonefind Pty Ltd* (1993) ATPR 41-265; *Brueckner v Carroll* (1995) ATPR 41-379; *Henville v Walker* (2001) 182 ALR 37 (HC) at 41 (per Gleeson CJ), 70-1 (per McHugh J, with whom Gummow J agreed).
59. *Henville v Walker* (2001) 182 ALR 37. The decision confirms the prior general assumption that damages may not be reduced because of the plaintiff's own contributory negligence — see eg *Antoniou v Karedis Enterprises Pty Ltd* (1995) ATPR 41-400. For another approach relying on s 87 of the Act see *I & L Securities Pty Ltd v HTW Valuers (BNE) Pty Ltd* (2000) 179 ALR 89. See also J C Campbell, 'Contribution, Contributory Negligence and s 52 of the Trade Practices Act' (1993) 67 *ALJ* 87 and 177; N Seddon, 'Misleading Conduct: The Case for proportionality' (1999) 71 *ALJ* 146.
60. *Gates v CML Life Assurance Society Ltd* (1986) 160 CLR 1; 63 ALR 600. See also *Wardley Australia Ltd v Western Australia* (1992) 175 CLR 514.
61. *Shepherd v Noyes Bros Pty Ltd* (1985) ATPR 40-588 at 46,750 per Spender J.
62. On this distinction see further [1069]-[1072].
63. Described by Kirby J in *Marks v GIO Australia Holdings Ltd* (1998) 196 CLR 494 at 543-4.
64. See eg D Price, 'Opening Gates: The Measure of Damages under the Trade Practices Act' (1994) 1 *CCCL* 257, but compare C Colvin, 'Tales of the unexpected: Damages for lost expectations' (1997) 5 *TPLJ* 17.

do not accept that a person suffers injury simply because a hoped for advantage does not materialise'.[66] Gaudron and Gummow JJ agreed that on the facts of the case the plaintiffs could not recover but reached this conclusion on the basis of causation. It is not clear whether they would have approached the question of assessment of damages as narrowly as did the other members of the majority. Kirby J dissented and, while not finding it necessary ultimately to decide the effect of s 82,[67] considered that the Act's provisions should be interpreted broadly.[68] In the result little practical guidance is given as to the assessment of damages under s 82.[69] It seems likely that in s 52 cases damages will still normally be assessed on the 'worse off' approach reminiscent of the law of deceit and that this will not include damages for the loss of expectation of profits following the misleading representation of contractual terms.[70] On the other hand, one should not make too much of this distinction, because in many cases little end difference will result, no matter what measure of damages is adopted. Moreover, if an applicant can prove that, in reliance on misleading conduct, he or she refrained from making a different profitable contract, that lost profit can be recovered.[71] In these circumstances the 'reliance loss' approach of the law of tort resembles in practice the 'expectation loss' aspect of damages in the law of contract.

Many of the cases involve consequential losses, and much depends on the estimation of the judge.[72] At least where the loss or damage is of a kind which cannot be precisely estimated, the court must do the best it can, even if a certain amount of speculation or guesswork is involved.[73]

Damages under s 82 are not limited to purely economic loss, but may include damages for injury to reputation or for disappointment or mental distress,[74] though, as s 82 is based on compensation, exemplary damages

65. (1998) 196 CLR 494. See S Lo, 'Expectation Damages under the Trade Practices Act s 82' (2001) 9 *C&CLJ* 174.
66. (1998) 196 CLR 494 at 515.
67. Kirby J decided the case on the basis of s 87, discussed at [1115].
68. See, however, *Kenny & Good Pty Ltd v MGICA (1992) Ltd* (1999) 199 CLR 413 at 461; 163 ALR 611, where in a joint judgment with Callinan J, Kirby J said that very often in s 52 cases the amount of damages would coincide with that in a common law action in deceit.
69. For an illustration see the discussions in *Murphy v Overton Investments Pty Ltd* (2001) ATPR 46-819.
70. As to the distinction between 'reliance' and 'expectation' damages see [1069], [1071], [2210], [2211]. See also *Henville v Walker* (2001) 182 ALR 37 at 72 per McHugh J (with whom Gummow J agreed) arguing that normally in a s 52 case the claimant's loss will be greater on a reliance than on an expectation basis.
71. *Sellars v Adelaide Petroleum NL* (1994) 179 CLR 332; 120 ALR 16 establishes that although the ordinary civil standard of the balance of probabilities applies to the issue of whether the applicant suffered some loss of a commercial opportunity having some (not negligible) value, the value of that chance is to be ascertained by reference to the degree of probabilities or possibilities (ie some damages can be recovered even though there was a less than 50 per cent chance of that opportunity in fact proving to be profitable).
72. For a discussion of some of the difficulties see *Netaff Pty Ltd v Bikane Pty Ltd* (1990) 26 FCR 305.
73. See, eg *Sellars v Adelaide Petroleum NL* (1994) 179 CLR 332; *RAIA Insurance Brokers Ltd v FAI General Insurance Co Ltd* (1993) ATPR 41-225; *JLW (Vic) Pty Ltd v Tsiloglou* (1993) ATPR 41-257.

cannot be recovered.[75] The Act makes no express provision as to the recovery of contribution or indemnity when two or more persons are liable, though it is possible that a right to contribution will arise on general principles, or, in some cases, under State law.[76]

Until recently one practical disadvantage of reliance on s 82 was that subs (2) imposed a relatively short limitation period of three years. However, as from 26 July 2001 the period became six years.[77] Moreover, time runs from the date on which the cause of action accrued, and the High Court has held that in the case of misleading conduct inducing a contract this is not necessarily the date the contract is made but may be considerably later.[78] The task of ascertaining precisely when loss is suffered for this purpose gives rise to many difficulties which seem certain to be the subject of continuing litigation

[1114] **Damages against 'any person involved'.** One final aspect of s 82 which should be noted is that it allows recovery not just against the person who actually contravened s 52, but also against 'any person involved in the contravention'. Section 75B defines this phrase so as to include those involved in a variety of accessory ways, that most commonly relied on being that the person sued was 'directly or indirectly, knowingly concerned in, or party to, the contravention' (s 75B(1)(c)). As we shall see,[79] this provision is of great significance as it very considerably extends the circle of people who can be made personally liable for a contravention of s 52. It is important to note that whereas liability under s 52 is strict, a person can be held liable as a 'person involved' in a contravention only if he or she can be shown to have had knowledge of the essential elements constituting the contravention.[80] This added evidentiary burden has frequently, however, not prevented applicants recovering damages against such a person.

[1115] **Other orders under s 87.** In addition to the remedies already discussed, s 87 of the *Trade Practices Act* allows the court to make a wide variety of orders against a person who was engaged in conduct in contravention of, inter alia, s 52, or against a person who was involved in such a contravention. These orders may be made in favour of a person who has suffered or is likely to suffer loss or damage as a result of the contravention and are to be made if the court considers such orders to be

---

74. See *Brabazon v Western Mail Ltd* (1985) ATPR 40-549; *Zoneff v Elcom Credit Union Ltd* (1990) ATPR 41-058; *Nixon v Slater & Gordon* (2000) 175 ALR 15.
75. See, eg *Musca v Astle Corp Pty Ltd* (1988) 80 ALR 251.
76. For recent discussions see, eg *Bialkower v Acohs Pty Ltd* (1998) 83 FCR 1; *Burke v Lfot Pty Ltd* (2001) 178 ALR 161 (leave to appeal to the High Court granted). See also the articles cited at n 59.
77. See *Trade Practices Amendment Act (No 1)* 2001, noting s 21 (new period applies to prior conduct if previous limitation period had not expired at commencement date).
78. *Wardley Australia Ltd v Western Australia* (1992) 175 CLR 514. The ACT and Tas *Fair Trading Acts* do not contain a limitation period. The others have a three-year period except for Victoria, which has six years.
79. See [1121].
80. See, eg *Yorke v Lucas* (1985) 158 CLR 661; 61 ALR 307; *Richardson & Wrench (Holdings) Pty Ltd v Ligon No 174 Pty Ltd* (1994) 123 ALR 681; *Westbay Seafoods (Aust) Pty Ltd v Transpacific Standardbred Agency Pty Ltd* (1996) ATPR (Digest) 46-162.

appropriate to compensate the affected person in whole or in part for the loss or damage or to prevent or reduce the loss or damage. The orders which may be made include the orders mentioned in subs 87(2). These are quite wide-ranging in scope and include an order declaring the whole or any part of a contract to be void (para (a)), an order varying a contract (para (b)), an order directing the refund of money or return of property (para (c)), an order for the payment of the amount of loss or damage suffered by a person (para (d)), an order directing the repair of goods (para (e)) or the supply of specified services (para (f)).

Although earlier cases often took a rather restrictive view, it is now clear that s 87 gives the courts a very wide discretion.[81] Where orders for money compensation are made a similar approach to that taken in assessing s 82 damages is to be taken, except that s 87 extends to situations where loss has not yet occurred but is 'likely' to be suffered and the orders may be designed to 'prevent or reduce' loss.[82]

By far the most common application of s 87 has been, where a contract has been shown to have been induced by conduct in contravention of s 52, the making of orders declaring the contract void and, where appropriate, ordering the return of money or property. Such orders have the effect of orders rescinding the contract and have very frequently been sought by applicants and granted by the courts. It has become accepted that the court has a discretion under s 87. One consequence of this has been that in deciding whether or not to set aside the contract the court is not bound by (though it would have regard to) the limitations arising under the general law on the right to rescind for misrepresentation.[83] This is no doubt an important reason for the frequency with which such orders have been sought.

[1116] Possible limitation on the scope of s 87 orders. The availability of s 87 as a basis for rescission orders was placed in some question by the decision of the High Court in *Webb Distributors (Aust) Pty Ltd v Victoria*.[84] The case concerned the question of whether shareholders in some building societies were prevented by the winding up of those societies from rescinding their contracts for the purchase of shares, or recovering damages, on the basis of alleged fraudulent representation. It was held that on the basis of the rule in *Houldsworth v City of Glasgow Bank*,[85] given statutory recognition in the *Companies (Victoria) Code*, such relief was not available once a company was wound up. It was further held, in response to an argument based on an alleged contravention of s 52, that the *Trade Practices Act* was not to be seen as eliminating 'by a side-wind' the detailed provisions established for more than 100 years to govern the winding up of a company. The majority further commented that in *Trade Practices Commission v Milreis Pty Ltd*[86] Brennan and Deane JJ (then members of the

---

81. See in particular *Akron Securities Ltd v Iliffe* (1997) 41 NSWLR 353 per Mason P; *Marks v GIO Australia Holdings Ltd* (1998) 196 CLR 494.
82. *Marks v GIO Australia Holdings Ltd* (1998) 196 CLR 494.
83. See in particular *Henjo Investments Pty Ltd v Collins Marrickville Pty Ltd* (1988) 79 ALR 83; *Tenji v Henneberry & Associates Pty Ltd* (2000) 98 FCR 324.
84. (1993) 179 CLR 15.
85. (1880) 5 App Cas 317.

Federal Court) 'made it clear that s 87(2)(a) is not to be understood as conferring a power to declare void a contract which was valid at its inception, other than through the operation of some other provision of the *Trade Practices Act* or by reason of some alteration in circumstances'.

It is not possible here to analyse fully the implications of the *Milreis* and *Webb Distributors* decisions. It is perhaps surprising that the majority of the High Court should, in a very brief reference to s 87, have thrown doubt on the settled practice of the Federal Court in setting aside contracts (those orders seeming to rely essentially on para (2)(a)) though without referring to this consequence of what is at least arguably an unnecessarily restrictive reading of the legislation. The courts appear for the most part to have continued to make orders of the kind previously made.[87] Moreover, it was recently held[88] by a Full Court of the Federal Court that these observations in *Webb Distributors* were apparently obiter dicta and must be regarded as having been overtaken by the width of operation attributed to s 87 in *Marks v GIO Australia Holdings Ltd*.[89]

Actions Based on the Statutory Prohibition Compared with Actions under the General Law of Contract

[1117] The impact of s 52. The combination of the breadth of s 52 and the liberal remedies available under the Act has had a profound impact on the law of contract. For the most part this is because reliance on these provisions will often allow relief where this would be difficult, or the remedies available to the plaintiff less attractive, if resort had to be made to the general law. Many obstacles placed in the plaintiff's way, particularly under the rules as to contractual terms and misrepresentation, can be to a significant extent sidestepped by reliance on the statutory remedies. This area of law is very complex, difficult to apply and arguably much in need of reform.[90] We have seen that although South Australia and the Australian Capital Territory adopted misrepresentation legislation based on the *Misrepresentation Act* 1967 (UK), the other Australian jurisdictions did not follow suit.[91]

[1118] Damages for misrepresentation. The common law insisted on maintaining a distinction between those representations which become incorporated as terms of a contract and those which are regarded as amounting merely to representations. Contractual damages are available only where a term of a contract has been broken. No damages (whether

---

86. (1977) 29 FLR 144.
87. See, however, cases such as *Prioris Pty Ltd v Inscorp Holdings Ltd* (1995) 124 FLR 409; *News Ltd v Australian Rugby Football League Ltd* (1996) ATPR 41-521.
88. *Tenji v Henneberry & Associates Pty Ltd* (2000) 98 FCR 324.
89. (1988) 196 CLR 494.
90. For a useful discussion see D E Allan, 'The Scope of the Contract' (1967) 41 *ALJ* 274.
91. **SA**: *Misrepresentation Act* 1972; **ACT**: *Law Reform (Misrepresentation) Act* 1977. See [1056], [1059], [1074]–[1078].

contractual or otherwise) are recoverable under the general law in respect of a mere innocent misrepresentation.[92] It is perhaps in creating what amounts to a statutory right to damages for innocent misrepresentation that s 52, in conjunction with s 82, has had its greatest impact on the law of contract.

Many difficulties arising in this area and facing a plaintiff can be largely overcome by a resort to the statutory remedies.[93] The issue of contractual intention[94] is irrelevant in a s 52 action. The parol evidence rule and merger or integration clauses[95] do not oust s 52 (though the latter may, as we shall see, have some evidentiary effect).[96] The rather strict approach adopted by the Australian courts towards collateral contracts[97] is not a limitation in an action based on s 52. It is not necessary under s 52 to establish the dishonest intention which is an essential element of the tort of deceit.[98] Nor is it necessary to establish any degree of fault, so that if carelessly given advice or information can be said to involve misleading conduct, damages can be recovered without resort to the difficulties[99] facing one relying on the common law tort of negligent misrepresentation.[100]

[1119] Conduct not amounting to misrepresentation. Not only does the statutory action allow damages to be recovered for misrepresentation, but this may at times be possible in respect of conduct which would not be regarded under the general law as amounting to misrepresentation. Thus we have seen that silence may amount to conduct in contravention of s 52 in circumstances where there would be no misrepresentation at common law.[101] The evidentiary provision in s 51A places an onus on the defendant which will often be of very significant benefit to a plaintiff[102] and is in some cases likely to produce a different result from that which would be reached under the general law, even though similar basic principles are applied both under the law as to misrepresentation and s 52 in relation to promises and other representations as to future matters. It seems likely that at least some representations which would be dismissed as puffing under the general law will amount to conduct in contravention of s 52.[103] Traditionally misrepresentations of law have not been actionable under the common law as to misrepresentation.[104] Although the question of the effect under the

---

92. See [1038], [1063], [1065].
93. For examples see *Brown v The Jam Factory Pty Ltd* (1981) 35 ALR 79; *Gurdag v BS Stillwell Ford Pty Ltd* (1985) 61 ALR 689.
94. See [604]–[610].
95. See [705]–[723].
96. See [1124].
97. See [611]–[614].
98. See [1025]–[1028].
99. See [1029]–[1036].
100. For illustrations of such situations see, eg *Menhaden Pty Ltd v Citibank NA* (1984) 55 ALR 709; *Bond Corp Pty Ltd v Thiess Contractors Pty Ltd* (1987) 71 ALR 615. However, it has been held that not every careless mistake amounts to misleading or deceptive conduct: see *O'Shea v Sullivan* (1994) ATPR (Digest) 46-124.
101. See [1110].
102. See [1108].
103. See [1107].
104. See [1010]–[1012].

Act of misrepresentations of law has not been fully ventilated, it seems that in at least some cases misrepresentations of law can contravene s 52.[105]

[1120] **Rescission.** Where a contract has been induced by an innocent misrepresentation which is not a term of the contract, the only remedy available under the general law is rescission of the contract. While this is often a useful remedy for the victim of misrepresentation, we have seen that it can also be a fragile one in that the right to rescind can be lost in a variety of ways.[106] As an example of the operation of s 52 in this context, in *Byers v Dorotea Pty Ltd*[107] contracts to buy home units were induced by misleading representations. A purported rescission by the buyers for innocent misrepresentation was held to be ineffective because occurring after affirmation of the contract, but the court nonetheless gave relief having the same practical effect as rescission by making an order under s 87 for the return of deposits. To the extent that the courts have the power to make orders having the effect of rescission (a matter discussed earlier),[108] the discretion available to the courts under s 87 of the *Trade Practices Act* affords much more flexibility than do the rules of the general law. Although the courts have been reluctant to make orders under s 87 which would amount to forms of specific performance,[109] great flexibility is granted which can prove very useful in an appropriate case.

[1121] **Liability of 'persons involved'.** One of the great attractions for plaintiffs of actions based on the *Trade Practices Act* is the prospect of obtaining orders for damages or compensation not only against the other contracting party but also against others who were in some way involved in the negotiations. This follows partly from the fact that orders under ss 82 and 87 can be obtained not only against those who directly contravened the Act, but against all those 'involved in' the contravention.[110] Thus, for example, where a company leases commercial premises or sells a franchise or a business or other property, directors and executives of the company may well be personally liable.[111] Not only does this obviously increase the likelihood of any order being actually satisfied if the company itself is of doubtful solvency, but one suspects that the prospect of their personal assets being at risk may often make those controlling companies more willing to negotiate settlement than might otherwise be the case. This type of ancillary liability does involve proof of some element of fault, but in many cases those involved in the negotiations may well themselves be liable as a principal contravener, in which case no element of intentional wrongdoing or fault need be established. On this basis orders have

---

105. See in particular *Inn Leisure Industries Pty Ltd v D F McCloy Pty Ltd* (1991) 28 FCR 151.
106. See [1042]–[1062].
107. (1986) 69 ALR 715.
108. See [1116].
109. See, eg *Milchas Investments Pty Ltd v Larkin* (1989) 96 FLR 464; *Futuretronics International Pty Ltd v Gadzhis* [1992] 2 VR 217; but see *Angelatos v National Australia Bank* (1994) ATPR 41-333.
110. See [1114].
111. See, eg *Collins Marrickville Pty Ltd v Henjo Investments Pty Ltd* (1987) 72 ALR 601 (affirmed (1988) 79 ALR 83); *Bateman v Slayter* (1987) 71 ALR 553; *Wheeler Grace & Pierucci Pty Ltd v Wright* (1989) ATPR 40-940.

frequently been obtained against real estate agents who have made representations in the course of negotiating leases in shopping centres or other transactions.[112] Of course, where an agent is itself in contravention of the Act, directors and salespersons of the agent may also incur personal liability as persons involved in that contravention. It should also be noted that where a private vendor is, because not acting in trade or commerce, not liable under the Act, a real estate agent employed by that vendor is acting in trade or commerce and thus may be liable.[113] In such a case the vendor may well be liable as one 'involved in' the contravention by the real estate agent. Professional advisers involved in negotiations on behalf of a client may also incur liability,[114] perhaps usually as persons 'involved in' a contravention by their client but in some cases also as a principal contravener. (In some cases persons such as agents will be regarded as merely passing on information obtained from others and, because not personally making any misleading representation, not contravening s 52;[115] just how far this notion of a 'mere conduit' or 'implied disclaimer' may be taken as a defence to a claim based on s 52 raises considerable difficulties,[116] but in some cases the court has had little difficulty in holding liable real estate agents using information supplied by clients.)[117]

Disclaimers, Exclusion and Acknowledgment and Merger Clauses

[1122] Disclaimers. Where a representation is made which, taken by itself, would be misleading or deceptive, a contemporaneous and prominent disclaimer or qualification may in principle remove the likelihood of the representation misleading those to whom it is directed. However, the courts have shown considerable reluctance to hold that disclaimers contained in point of sale signs or product labels are sufficiently prominent and compelling to produce this result.[118] In any event, this line of reasoning will rarely be applicable in the case of a contractual disclaimer, as the contract containing the disclaimer will usually be entered into some

---

112. See, eg *Brown v The Jam Factory Pty Ltd* (1981) 35 ALR 79; *MacCormick v Nowland* (1988) ATPR 40-852.
113. See, eg *Argy v Blunts & Lane Cove Real Estate Pty Ltd* (1990) 94 ALR 719; *Pricom Pty Ltd v Sgarioto* (1994) ATPR (Digest) 46-135.
114. See *Sutton v A J Thompson Pty Ltd* (1987) 73 ALR 233. See also *Bond Corp Pty Ltd v Thiess Contractors Pty Ltd* (1987) 71 ALR 615; *Mackman v Stengold Pty Ltd* (1991) ATPR 41-105.
115. See *Yorke v Lucas* (1985) 158 CLR 661 at 666. See also *Global Sportsman Pty Ltd v Mirror Newspapers Ltd* (1984) 55 ALR 25; *Saints Gallery Pty Ltd v Plummer* (1988) 80 ALR 525; *Gurr v Forbes* (1996) ATPR 41-491.
116. See *Gardam v George Wills & Co Ltd* (1988) 82 ALR 415.
117. See, eg *John G Glass Real Estate Pty Ltd v Karawi Constructions Pty Ltd* (1993) ATPR 41-249; *Karawi Constructions Pty Ltd v Bonefind Pty Ltd* (1993) ATPR 41-265.
118. See, eg *Abundant Earth Pty Ltd v R & C Products Pty Ltd* (1985) 59 ALR 211; *Hutchence v South Sea Bubble Co Pty Ltd* (1986) 64 ALR 330; *Britt Allcroft (Thomas) LLC v Miller* (2000) ATPR 41-776 (affirmed on appeal; (2000) ATPR 41-792).

time subsequently to the making of the representation complained of, thus failing to satisfy the requirement of contemporaneity.

[1123] Exclusion clauses. Clauses attempting to exclude or limit liability for innocent misrepresentation will, it seems, be effective according to their terms in relation to innocent misrepresentation.[119] Such clauses are, however, usually regarded as a matter of construction as not applying to fraud. If intended to apply to fraud they would appear in any event to be ineffective, for a clause purporting to exempt from liability for fraud would presumably be contrary to public policy and thus void.[120]

It is well established that exclusion clauses (or clauses purporting to acknowledge that no misrepresentation occurred) are not effective to exclude liability for a contravention of s 52, nor may they limit the scope of liability (for example, by placing a monetary limit on liability for damages).[121] As an example, in *Byers v Dorotea Pty Ltd*[122] purchasers of home units purported to rescind the contracts of purchase on the grounds of innocent misrepresentation. It was held that this claim failed, partly because of an exclusion clause in the contract, but the purchasers nonetheless obtained relief based on a contravention of s 52.

A variety of reasons have been given for this result, but perhaps the most convincing is that on public policy grounds the courts will not allow the norm of conduct established in the public interest by s 52 to be evaded. It should be borne in mind that not only will a clause which purports to exclude liability be void, but that the mere use of such a clause would appear to contravene s 53(g) of the Act, which prohibits false or misleading representations 'concerning the existence, exclusion or effect of any condition, warranty, guarantee, right or remedy'. Persons contravening s 53(g) are exposed to criminal as well as civil sanctions.[123]

---

119. *Life Insurance Co of Australia Ltd v Phillips* (1925) 36 CLR 60 at 82, 87; *Silverton v S F Carroll Pty Ltd* [1983] 1 Qd R 72 at 80–1; *Brisbane Unit Development Corp Ltd v Robertson* [1983] 2 Qd R 105 at 108. But see *Byers v Dorotea Pty Ltd* (1986) 69 ALR 714 at 724–5, and cf *Overbrooke Estates Ltd v Glencombe Properties Ltd* [1974] 1 WLR 1335; *Walker v Boyle* [1982] 1 All ER 634.
120. *S Pearson & Son Ltd v Dublin Corp* [1907] AC 353; *Suburban Homes Pty Ltd v Topper* (1929) 35 ALR 294; *Snarski & Snarski v Barbarich* [1969] WAR 46. See also [766]. 'Exclusion' or 'compensation' clauses will not necessarily be effective in the face of all forms of mistake or misdescription either: see [759] and cf *Wilkinson v Detmold* (1890) 16 VLR 439; *Jacobs v Revell* [1900] 2 Ch 858; *Simons v Zartom Investments Pty Ltd* [1975] 2 NSWLR 30. Under the misrepresentation legislation a contractual term purporting to exclude any liability or remedy by reason of a pre-contract misrepresentation is 'of no effect' except to the extent that the court may allow such reliance as is fair and reasonable in the circumstances of the case: **ACT**: *Law Reform (Misrepresentation) Act* 1977, s 6; **SA**: *Misrepresentation Act* 1972, s 8.
121. See *Petera Pty Ltd v EAJ Pty Ltd* (1984) 7 FCR 375; *Byers v Dorotea Pty Ltd* (1986) 69 ALR 715; *Henjo Investments Pty Ltd v Collins Marrickville Pty Ltd* (1988) 79 ALR 83; *IOOF Australia Trustees (NSW) Ltd v Tantipech* (1998) 156 ALR 470. See generally Healey and Terry, *Misleading and Deceptive Conduct*, 1991, pp 202–9, 312–30; Andrew Terry, 'Disclaimers and Deceptive Conduct' (1986) 14 *ABLR* 478. In some jurisdictions it is expressly provided that attempts to contract out of the fair trading legislation (see [1102]) are ineffective: see Qld s 107; SA s 96; Tas s 51.
122. (1986) 69 ALR 715.
123. See *Miller v Fiona's Clothes Horse of Centrepoint Pty Ltd* (1989) ATPR 40-963.

[1124] Acknowledgment and merger clauses. Many clauses seek not so much directly to exclude liability but seek to avoid the operation of s 52 by providing evidence of some factual matter. Thus, for example, a purchaser of goods may acknowledge that they are in accordance with the contract and that no representations not recorded in the written contract were made; a lessee of a shop in a shopping centre may acknowledge that no representations not recorded in the lease or acknowledgment were made or that, if made, they were not relied upon by the lessee. A suitably drafted clause may be of some evidentiary value in helping to establish that no representation such as that alleged was made or that the particular applicant did not in fact act in reliance on, and therefore did not suffer loss as a result of, any contravention of s 52 that may be established. Such a clause is not, of course, conclusive. It seems likely that an acknowledgment clause contained in a standard form contract and not specifically drawn to the attention of the party sought to be affected will have little, if any, effect. The practice appears to have grown up in some cases of requiring lessees in shopping centres to sign a 'deed of acknowledgment' as a document quite separate from the lease agreement. Such documents are more likely to have some evidentiary effect, but even they will be subjected to close scrutiny by the courts.[124]

---

124. See, eg *Keen Mar Corp Pty Ltd v Labrador Park Shopping Centre Pty Ltd* (1989) ATPR (Digest) 46–048; *Waltip Pty Ltd v Capalaba Park Shopping Centre Pty Ltd* (1989) ATPR 40–975; *Leda Holdings Pty Ltd v Oraka Pty Ltd* (1998) ATPR 41-601; *IOOF Australia Trustees (NSW) Ltd v Tantipech* (1998) 156 ALR 470; *Burg Design Pty Ltd v Wolki* (1999) 162 ALR 639.

Chapter 12

Mistake

General 1201
   Types of Mistake 1202
   Approaches to Mistake 1205
   Mistake and Other Doctrines 1210

Common Mistake 1214
   Common Mistake Rendering Contract Void 1215
   Rescission for Common Mistake 1226

Mutual Mistake 1233
   Mutual Mistake Rendering Contract Void 1233
   Rescission for Mutual Mistake 1236

Unilateral Mistake 1238
   General 1238
   Unilateral Mistake Rendering Contract Void 1240
   Rescission for Unilateral Mistake 1252

Restrictions on Rescission for Mistake 1255

Rectification 1256
   General 1256
   Nature of Agreement Relied Upon and Relevant Intention 1259
   Proof of Intention 1262
   Rectification for Unilateral Mistake 1264

Non Est Factum 1267

General

[1201] Introduction. 'Mistake' is a difficult part of contract law. Contracting parties' decisions and actions are often influenced by 'mistake' ('error' or 'misapprehension'). Indeed, perhaps in most contracts one party at least is mistaken to some degree as to the extent of benefit it will provide. Obviously, such unilateral mistakes of motive cannot be relieved against. The two essential questions with which 'mistake' is concerned are:

- when will mistake be 'operative'? and
- what effect does the mistake have?

The second question may be rephrased as:

- what do we mean by 'operative'? or
- what remedies are available for mistake?

Of course, it is always assumed that one party, whether sharing the mistake or not, resists the claim for relief, that is to say, asserts that the contract is binding according to its terms. However, it is only a small proportion of mistakes that will, on any reckoning, be cognisable in contract law, that is, constitute 'operative mistake'. Thus, the mere presence of 'mistake' does not signify legal consequences. Moreover, most situations in which one or both parties are mistaken are resolved by the application of legal doctrines other than those peculiar to contract law.

Before considering further the legal doctrine of mistake in contract, it is appropriate to make some attempt at classifying factual situations which might be analysed under the rubric of mistake.

Types of Mistake

[1202] Common mistake. The words 'common' and 'mutual' are used to describe mistake situations where both parties are mistaken. In this work, a mistake is described as 'common' where it is *shared by both parties*, that is, where they make the same mistake. For example, a seller and buyer of goods may contract under the mistaken belief that the goods existed when the contract was made, whereas in truth they have been destroyed.

Although, in the case of operative common mistake, the bargain fails for want of subject matter, it should not be thought that a contract is always, or even usually, ineffective merely because both parties are mistaken. Were the law otherwise, all contracts induced by innocent misrepresentation would fail.

One further distinction may be drawn. Whereas mistake proceeding from misrepresentation is induced, in many cases a mistake will be spontaneous, in the sense that it was not induced by the words or conduct of the other. Common sense tells us that the law is more likely to provide relief in respect of induced mistakes than spontaneous mistakes.

[1203] Mutual mistake. Although the word 'mutual' has often been used to refer to shared mistakes, as illustrated above,[1] we draw a distinction between common and mutual mistake. The word 'mutual' describes situations where, although parties may both be mistaken, their mistakes may differ. In such cases, the objective facts are equivocal and the subjective states of mind of the parties are at odds.

Such parties are at cross-purposes in contract formation: consensus ad idem is only apparent since, in truth, the *parties mean different things*. For example, parties may contract for the sale and purchase of a horse of a certain name, or of a house in a street of a certain name, whereas in truth

---

1. See [1202].

there exist two horses with that name, or two streets of that name, the seller intending to refer to one and the buyer to the other.

[1204] Unilateral mistake. In the case of common mistake both parties are in error. In the case of mutual mistake, it is not clear that either party can be described as being 'in error'. On the other hand, a unilateral mistake is *a mistake by one party only, the other not being mistaken at all*. For example, one party may be mistaken as to the true identity of the other contracting party. Where such a mistake has legal consequences, it will be found that the non-mistaken party knows of the other party's mistake.

There is scope for a great variety of situations according to whether the non-mistaken party knows or suspects that the other party is mistaken or has even caused or contributed to the mistake. However, most cases of unilateral mistake occur when the parties disagree as to the meaning of the contract. Once it is acknowledged or held that the understanding of one party is 'correct', the case becomes one of unilateral mistake. In these cases, at the time of contracting, one party apprehends the position correctly and the other does not.

Approaches to Mistake

[1205] Generally. There are five possibilities to be considered in any analysis of the consequences of mistake in contract. First, and by far the most common situation, the mistake may have no effect at all, because it is neither operative nor the result of a representation by one of the parties.

Second, the presence of mistake may be relevant to equitable relief, to set aside the contract, to refuse specific performance or to order rectification.[2]

Third, the mistake may be associated with a right to rescind a contract ab initio ('from the beginning'). Since all cases of misrepresentation inducing a contract exemplify mistake, a right of rescission will arise in all such cases. However, these cases are analysed under the rubric of misrepresentation, not mistake.[3]

Fourth, the mistake may be operative in the sense that it renders the contract void ab initio, that is, the contract never came into existence.[4]

Fifth, mistake may be a basis for recovering money paid. This is governed by principles regulating restitution for unjust enrichment. Unless the payer has simply paid more than was due, a payment made under a valid contract is not recoverable merely on the basis of mistake. The plaintiff must therefore establish that the contract was void or has been validly rescinded.[5]

[1206] Common law. At common law, that is, prior to the fusion of law and equity, mistake was a very narrow doctrine. Thus, putting rescission for fraud to one side, a mistake operative at common law may negative

2. See [1207], [1208], [1237], [1256]–[1266], [2411].
3. See generally Chapter 10 and further [1208]. Similarly, the mistake may be caused by the breach of a statutory prohibition, for example, the prohibition on misleading and deceptive conduct, and statutory relief may then be available. See generally Chapter 11.
4. See [1206].
5. See further [1208], [2303].

contractual assent, so that the 'contract' is void. Today, at least as a matter of logic, this can be the case only if there is no agreement to contract, because the mistake caused offer and acceptance, both properly construed, not to coincide, or because the objective theory of contract is displaced.[6] These are very rare occurrences. Although in a handful of cases contracts have been held void on the ground of unilateral mistake,[7] cases in which a contract has been held void on the ground of common or mutual mistake are virtually unknown, at least in Australian law.[8]

If offer and acceptance coincide it is difficult to see how the agreement so constituted can be void. If the parties have agreed (expressly or impliedly) that the contract is not to bind them unless a certain circumstance exists or a certain assumption is correct, effect will be given to this term, as creating a condition precedent. However, it is incorrect to call the initial agreement 'void' when it transpires that the circumstance does not exist or the assumption was incorrect.

In any event, it would be an error to regard voidness as the only possible consequence of mistake at common law. The common law recognised that mistake might provide one party with a right of rescission, at least if it arose from a misrepresentation by the other. Thus, in *Kennedy v Panama New Zealand and Australian Royal Mail Co Ltd*[9] Blackburn J said:[10]

> There is, however, a very important difference between cases where a contract may be rescinded on account of fraud, and those in which it may be rescinded on the ground that there is a difference in substance between the thing bargained for and that obtained. It is enough to show that there was a fraudulent representation as to *any part* of that which induced the party to enter into the contract which he seeks to rescind; but where there has been an innocent misrepresentation or misapprehension, it does not authorise a rescission, unless it is such as to shew that there is a complete difference in substance between what was supposed to be and what was taken, so as to constitute a failure of consideration. For example, where a horse is bought under a belief that it is sound, if the purchaser was induced to buy by a fraudulent misrepresentation as to the horse's soundness, the contract may be rescinded. If it was induced by an honest misrepresentation as to its soundness, though it may be clear that both vendor and purchaser thought that they were dealing about a sound horse and were in error, yet the purchaser must pay the whole price, unless there was a warranty ...

This aspect of mistake at common law is now of merely historical interest because of the more expansive rights of rescission available under equitable principles.[11]

[1207] Equity. Courts of equity have relieved against mistake where the common law courts could not. This is true to the origin and nature of equitable jurisdiction as a supplement to the common law. Thus, in respect of a valid contract, equity could intervene on the ground of mistake in three ways:

6. See [1213].
7. See [1241], [1245].
8. See [1216], [1234].
9. (1867) LR 2 QB 580.
10. (1867) LR 2 QB 580 at 587.
11. See [1037]–[1038], [1207], [1208].

[1207]

- to refuse specific performance;[12]
- to rectify the contract;[13] or
- to set the contract aside.

It is the third possibility, in effect a right of rescission under equitable principles similar to those which operate in the context of misrepresentation, which is the law's main concern.[14] However, even today, an equitable approach to mistake cannot be relevant where the effect of mistake is to deny that the contract exists.

[1208] Remedies for mistake. The narrowness of the common law approach to mistake is largely explained by the limited remedies available. Treating a contract as void relegates the parties to restitutionary remedies.[15] An award of damages for breach of contract is not possible: damages are only available under tort law or statute.[16] It is due to equity's wider range of remedies, and its ability to take into account and deal with all aspects of a dispute, that mistake could, in equity, be treated as a broader concept than the common law would allow. Today, where equitable relief is available in all superior courts, a wide range of possibilities exists.

First, a litigant may seek a declaration that mistake prevented a contract from coming into being.

Second, and at the other extreme, is the discretion to withhold the remedy of specific performance, on the basis that the contract was entered into under the influence of mistake. However, it must be emphasised that all the circumstances of a case must be taken into account, and it must not be readily assumed, where specific performance is refused against a mistaken party, that the refusal is based on the mistake alone or at all. Moreover, such a refusal says nothing as to the status of the 'contract', and the court may or may not be prepared to take the further step of setting aside the contract, so as to prevent the plaintiff enforcing it by an action for damages based on the defendant's failure to perform.[17]

Third, there may be a right of rescission, or a right to approach the court for an order setting the contract aside or upholding the validity of a rescission. There is undoubtedly an equitable right of rescission in some cases at least.[18]

[1209] Mistake must relate to factual matter. The traditional view is that, just as a statement or other conduct, in order to amount to actionable misrepresentation, must generally be as to past or existing fact,[19] so must mistake. So it is usually said that a mistake of law is no ground for relief

---

12. See [1237], [2411].
13. See [1256]–[1266].
14. See [1226]–[1232], [1236], [1252]–[1254].
15. See further [1215] and generally Chapter 23.
16. See generally Chapter 10.
17. In some cases a court refusing specific performance has acknowledged that the contract remains available for the purpose of common law remedies: see, eg *Cochrane v Willis* (1865) LR 1 Ch App 58 at 64; *Dell v Beasley* [1959] NZLR 89.
18. The high water mark is the judgment of Denning LJ in *Solle v Butcher* [1950] 1 KB 671 (see [1229]).
19. See [1006]–[1012].

whereas a mistake of fact is.[20] Although courts of equity have been readier than courts of common law to relieve against mistakes of law,[21] a contracting party's mistaken construction of a contract is not a ground for affording relief,[22] unless it was caused by the other party.[23] However, two points may be made in this connection.

First, the distinction between a mistake of law and a mistake of fact is not clearly defined by the cases.[24] As with misrepresentation, 'law' is used in this context to refer to the general law of the land and not to private rights. Private rights usually arise from the operation of the general law on particular facts. The hybrid result, a legal right or lack of it, tends to be treated as a matter of fact rather than of law. In *Cooper v Phibbs*,[25] in which the subject matter of the contract was a private title to a salmon fishery,[26] Lord Westbury affirmed that the expression 'ignorantia juris non excusat' (ignorance of the law does not excuse), relates to 'the general law, the ordinary law of the country' and that a private right of ownership is a matter of fact.[27]

Second, the idea that a mistake cannot ground a claim for restitutionary relief unless one of fact has been rejected.[28] It is at least arguable that the same approach should be taken where other forms of relief are at issue in the context of mistake.[29]

Mistake and Other Doctrines

[1210] Frustration and mistake. The relationship between mistake and frustration is considered later.[30] It is sufficient at this stage to point out that issues of mistake arise, if at all, in respect of matters occurring prior to entry into the contract, whereas frustration is concerned with subsequent events. For example, although most of the cases which arose from the postponement of Edward VII's coronation concerned frustration, *Griffith v Brymer*[31] was a case of mistake. The plaintiff hired a room from the defendant to view the coronation procession on 26 June 1902. The contract was verbal and was made at 11 am on 24 June. Unbeknown to the parties, the decision to operate on the King had been taken at 10 am. The

---

20. See *Rogers v Ingham* (1876) 3 Ch D 351.
21. See, eg *Lansdown v Lansdown* (1730) Mos 364; 25 ER 441; *Allcard v Walker* [1896] 2 Ch 369; *Re Roberts* [1905] 1 Ch 704; *Solle v Butcher* [1950] 1 KB 671; *Davidson v Atlas Assurance Co Ltd* [1932] NZLR 1163.
22. *Powell v Smith* (1872) LR 14 Eq 85; *Dowsett v Reid* (1912) 15 CLR 695.
23. *Wilding v Sanderson* [1897] 2 Ch 534; *Easyfind (NSW) Pty Ltd v Paterson* (1987) 11 NSWLR 98 at 107.
24. See *Avon County Council v Howlett* [1983] 1 WLR 605 at 620.
25. (1867) LR 2 HL 149.
26. See [1227].
27. (1867) LR 2 HL 149 at 170. And see *Earl of Beauchamp v Winn* (1873) LR 6 HL 223; *Eaglesfield v Marquis of Londonderry* (1876) 4 Ch D 693 at 703 where a similar approach was taken. But note the dissenting judgment of Jenkins LJ in *Solle v Butcher* [1950] 1 KB 671.
28. See [1010], [2301], [2318].
29. See also [1010].
30. See [2055].
31. (1903) 19 TLR 434. See also *William Sindall Plc v Cambridgeshire County Council* [1994] 1 WLR 1016 at 1039, 1040 (tests the same). Contrast *Krell v Henry* [1903] 2 KB 740 (see [2018]).

plaintiff's action to recover the amount (£100) paid by him succeeded. Wright J said[32] there was a 'missupposition of the state of facts which went to the whole root of the matter'.

[1211] Misrepresentation and mistake. There is an obvious connection between mistake and misrepresentation, since mistake may be induced by misrepresentation. This can be seen most clearly in cases of unilateral mistake as to identity.[33] The mistake arises from the fact that one party has made a fraudulent misrepresentation to the other. But even a case of common mistake may arise from a misrepresentation, since where A believes that a fact is true, and represents the truth of the fact to B, both A and B are under a mistake. The fact that the mistake of B arose from a misrepresentation by A implies that the parties' rights and liabilities are to be resolved under the rubric of misrepresentation.[34] This is because[35] a misrepresentation, whether fraudulent or innocent, will be found to give rise to greater rights and liability and more ample and flexible remedies than mere mistake as such.

However, it is not difficult to see why in some cases of induced mistake a party may be dissatisfied by the remedies available for misrepresentation. For example, assume that C sells goods to D, in the mistaken belief (induced by D) that D was in fact E. The fraudulent misrepresentation by D provides C with a right to rescind the contract and to sue (in tort) for damages. But D may have no assets and C may be more concerned to regain the goods. If the goods have already been sold to F, an innocent purchaser, this will only be possible if the contract between C and D had no validity at all, by reason of C's mistake.[36]

[1212] Mistake and warranty. The law of contract is designed to give effect to the intentions of the parties. The terms of their agreement are paramount. So, most disputes said to involve questions of mistake will be resolved by the process of construction of the contract and the implication of terms. Similarly, a mistake as to a term of the contract is distinguishable from a mistake as to collateral matters. So, a misguided motive for making a contract is normally without legal consequences.

The important distinction between a contractual term (a 'warranty' in the broad sense) and a mere representation was explained earlier.[37] Where a statement of fact is made which induces a party to enter into a contract, the statement will give rise to a right to rescind the contract, assuming falsity and reliance: the representor may rely on the false inducement to rescind the contract. However, damages for breach of contract are only available if the truth of the statement was guaranteed.[38] It is, of course, tempting to say that a person cannot guarantee the impossible, so that where a mistake arises by reason of ignorance[39] as to the truth of a

32. (1903) 19 TLR 434 at 434.
33. See generally [1240]–[1248].
34. See Chapter 10.
35. Subject to what is said in [1245] concerning the suggested possibility that contracts can be 'void' for mistake.
36. It is assumed that there is no rescission prior to the sale to F. See [1053].
37. See [602]–[610].
38. The relevant factors were considered [606]–[610].

statement or the accuracy of a term of the contract, there can be no contractual liability. However, the common law does not work in this way. Whether a person has guaranteed the truth of a fact depends on the construction placed on the words used in the circumstances of the case. A person may guarantee the truth of a fact which is false, and be responsible in damages even though the very subject matter of the contract never existed.[40] The guarantee of the truth of a fact amounts to an assumption of contractual responsibility for the truth of the statement, and the acceptance of the risk of error. Once it is found that one party has accepted the risk vis-à-vis the other party, of the existence of facts, it is simply not open to the promisor to plead the mistake as a defence. The warranty is all that matters.[41]

[1213] **Mistake and objective theory of contract.** The primary emphasis of the law of contract in common law systems is on how one party's words and conduct ought reasonably to have been understood by the other, rather than their subjective states of mind.[42] It would be unjust for one contracting party to be detrimentally affected by what was actually in the mind of the other when unaware of that person's state of mind. This injustice does not exist where the other party knew or should have known of the other's actual state of mind.

In other legal systems there may be a greater emphasis on subjective intention. However, as Dixon and Fullagar JJ said in *McRae v Commonwealth Disposals Commission*:[43]

> When once the common law had made up its mind that a promise supported by consideration ought to be performed, it was inevitable that the theorisings of the civilians about 'mistake' should mean little or nothing to it. On the other hand, the question whether a promisor was excused from performance by existing or supervening impossibility without fault on his part was a practical every-day question of which the common law has been vividly conscious ... But here too the common law has generally been true to its theory of simple contract, and it has always regarded the fundamental question as being: 'What did the promisor really promise?' Did he promise to perform his part at all events, or only subject to the mutually contemplated original or continued existence of a particular subject matter? So questions of intention or 'presumed intention' arise, and these must be determined in the light of the words used by the parties and reasonable inferences from all the surrounding circumstances.

McRae's case concerned an allegation that the contract was void on account of mistake, but the inability to rely on subjective mistake extends

---

39. 'Ignorance' is, however, a broader concept. See D W McLauchlan and C E F Rickett, 'Mistake and Ignorance Under the New Zealand Contractual Mistakes Act 1977' (1995) 8 *JCL* 193.
40. See, eg *McRae v Commonwealth Disposals Commission* (1951) 84 CLR 377 (see [1217]). Contrast *Cox v Prentice* (1815) 3 M & S 344; 105 ER 641; *Jeffries v Fairs* (1876) 4 Ch D 448.
41. Contrast a pre-contractual misrepresentation which may continue to be available as a source of rights even though incorporated as a term of the contract; see [1057].
42. See, eg *Taylor v Johnson* (1983) 151 CLR 422; 45 ALR 265 (see [1254]). See also [110], [206], [703].
43. (1951) 84 CLR 377 at 407–8.

further. Subjective mistake cannot be used as a defence to specific performance[44] or as a basis for rescission of the contract.[45]

Common Mistake

[1214] General. In the following discussion it is assumed that, although agreement has been reached, (because offer and acceptance coincide or otherwise) both parties share the same mistake. This is not to say that their 'shared' or 'common' mistake is of equal significance to both parties. Given that only one party seeks to be relieved of the contract, the other apparently finds the mistake made not disadvantageous. Nor is it implicit in common mistake that the parties had equal access to the means of knowing the truth: one may have had readier access than the other.

Almost certainly, at the time of contracting the parties will not have directed their minds equally to the matter in respect of which the mistake was made. One may have thought about it seriously and been prepared to make an assumption (since proved mistaken) whereas the other may not have given it a passing thought. It follows that the dividing line between common mistake and unilateral (albeit spontaneous) mistake may sometimes be a thin one.

Common Mistake Rendering Contract Void

Absence of subject matter of contract

[1215] Failure of consideration. *Absence* of consideration signifies that a 'contract' is void for failure to satisfy the law's requirements for the existence of a contract but *failure* of consideration does not require that a contract be held void. The concept of 'total failure of consideration'[46] is the basic notion which underlies the treatment of mistake at common law. If the consideration for a payment fails totally it may be recovered by the payer, because it would unjustly enrich the payee to retain the payment in the circumstances.[47] What the common law courts could not readily do was order the repayment of money where the consideration only partially failed. Therefore, the contract could not be treated as void in cases where the failure of consideration was partial rather than total.

The mere fact that the consideration for a payment has failed does not indicate that the contract was void from its inception. Accordingly, whether or not mistake is present, not all cases in which the consideration for a payment fails are cases involving void contracts. It is clearly incorrect to treat cases in which money has been held recoverable on the ground of total failure of consideration, in circumstances where there may have been a common mistake between the parties,[48] as justifiable only on the basis that

---

44. See [2411].
45. See, eg [1213].
46. See [2229], [2306].
47. See [2306] and generally Mason and Carter, *Restitution Law in Australia*, 1995, paras 1017, 1311, 1320.
48. See, eg *Cox v Prentice* (1815) 3 M & S 344; 105 ER 641; *Strickland v Turner* (1852) 7 Ex 208; 155 ER 919. Contrast *Clare v Lamb* (1875) LR 10 CP 334.

the contract was void for mistake. Indeed, many of the cases may be justified on equitable grounds,[49] or the terms of the contract, express or implied.[50] However, the limitations on common law relief in the context of mistake implies that a contract cannot be regarded as void for mistake unless there was *at least* a combination of mistake and total failure of consideration.[51]

[1216] Sale of specific goods which have ceased to exist. Under the sale of goods legislation,[52] a contract for the sale of specific goods is void if the goods have, without the knowledge of the seller, 'perished at the time when the contract is made'.

This provision is thought to be derived from *Couturier v Hastie*,[53] a case which has given rise to much debate. The plaintiffs were the consignors of a cargo of corn. The buyer failed to pay. They sued their British del credere commission agents.[54] Unbeknown to these parties, a few days before the contract and the sending of the bought note to the buyer, the vessel carrying the corn had put into harbour (following tempestuous weather and resultant heating and fermenting of the cargo) where the cargo was surveyed, found unfit to be carried further, and sold. On his discovery of these facts the buyer repudiated his contract.

At the trial, Martin B construed the contract as one for the sale of a cargo supposed to exist and to be capable of transfer to the buyer, and so found for the agents. The Court of Exchequer, by majority, construed the contract of sale as one by which the buyer bought the cargo if it existed, but otherwise the benefit of the insurance, so that the buyer was liable to pay under his contract and the agents were, when the buyer defaulted, liable to the plaintiffs in his place. On further appeal, the Court of Exchequer Chamber emphasised that the case turned on the construction of the contract. Coleridge J (for the court) agreed with the trial judge's construction, then referred to the plaintiffs' contention that some consideration had passed to the buyer, namely, the benefit of the shipping documents:[55]

> If the contract for sale of the cargo was valid the shipping documents would pass as accessories to it; but if, in consequence of the previous sale of the cargo, the contract failed as to the principal subject matter of it, the shipping documents would not pass ... For these reasons, it appears to us that the basis of the contract in this case was the sale and purchase of goods, and that all the other terms in the bought note were dependent upon that, and that we cannot give to it the effect of a contract for goods lost or not lost.

---

49. Cf *Bingham v Bingham* (1748) 1 Ves Sen 126; 27 ER 934; *Cooper v Phibbs* (1867) LR 2 HL 149 (see [1227]).
50. See further [1216], [1217].
51. See [1206], [1208]. See also [1023].
52. See **ACT**: *Sale of Goods Act* 1954, s 11; **NT**: *Sale of Goods Act* 1972, s 10; **NSW**: *Sale of Goods Act* 1923 s 11; **Qld**: *Sale of Goods Act* 1896, s 9; **SA**: *Sale of Goods Act* 1895, s 6; **Tas**: *Sale of Goods Act* 1896, s 11; **Vic**: *Goods Act* 1958, s 11; **WA**: *Sale of Goods Act* 1895, s 6.
53. (1856) 5 HLC 673; 10 ER 1065. See Louis Proksch, 'Couturier v Hastie and the Indian Corn Trade' (2000) 15 *JCL* 268. Cf *Barr v Gibson* (1838) 3 M & W 390; 150 ER 1196.
54. That is, commission agents on sale who guarantee that the buyer will pay.
55. Sub nom *Hastie v Couturier* (1853) 9 Ex 102 at 109–10; 156 ER 43 at 46–7.

The House of Lords took the opinion of the judges which was unanimously in accord with the judgment of the Exchequer Chamber. Lord Cranworth LC also emphasised that the whole question turned on the construction of the contract, and gave as the true construction that the contract showed that the parties contemplated 'an existing something to be sold and bought'[56] and that *if* that something was sold and bought, *then* the benefit of the insurance should go with it. Nowhere did the court use the term 'void' or suggest that the contract was void. The holding was that the contract of sale could not have been enforced against the buyer. This would have been obvious and unarguable but for the possible construction that the buyer had bought 'goods lost or not lost', that is, had bought an 'adventure'.

The case also leaves untouched the possibility of an action for damages by the buyer for breach by the seller of a warranty that the goods existed.

[1217] Scope of the sale of goods rule. Given that the sale of goods legislation provides that a contract in relation to specific goods which perished prior to entry into the contract is void, one might expect similar treatment of a contract in relation to goods which *never existed*. However, in *McRae v Commonwealth Disposals Commission*[57] the High Court held that this is not so. The Commission accepted the plaintiffs' tender for the purchase of an 'oil tanker lying on Jourmaund Reef, which is approximately 100 miles north of Samarai'. The plaintiffs were sent a 'sales advice note' in respect of 'one (1) oil tanker including contents wrecked on Jourmaund Reef approximately 100 miles north of Samarai'. The plaintiffs could not locate Jourmaund Reef on a map and the Commission supplied them with the latitude and longitude at which the tanker was alleged to be lying. At considerable expense the plaintiffs fitted out a salvage expedition but found no tanker at the locality given and in fact there was none in the locality at any material time. They sued the Commission for damages for breach of contract and the torts of deceit and negligence.

The Commission contended that the contract was void for common mistake and the trial judge, Webb J,[58] so held in reliance on *Couturier v Hastie*.[59] However, his judgment in this respect was reversed on appeal. In the leading judgment, Dixon and Fullagar JJ (with whom McTiernan J agreed) analysed *Couturier v Hastie* and concluded that the question whether a contract is void for common mistake is primarily one of construction of the contract to ascertain 'whether the contract was subject to an implied condition precedent that the goods were in existence. Prima facie, one would think, there would be no such implied condition precedent, the position being simply that the vendor *promised* that the goods *were* in existence'.[60] They concluded:[61]

---

56. (1856) 5 HLC 673 at 681; 10 ER 1065 at 1069.
57. (1951) 84 CLR 377.
58. Webb J's judgment in favour of the plaintiffs on the ground of deceit is also reported (1950) 84 CLR 377.
59. (1856) 5 HLC 673; 10 ER 1065 (see [1216]).
60. (1951) 84 CLR 377 at 407.
61. (1951) 84 CLR 377 at 409–10.

Whatever might then have been held on the facts of *Couturier v Hastie*, it is impossible in this case to imply any such term. The terms of the contract and the surrounding circumstances clearly exclude any such implication. The buyers relied upon, and acted upon, the assertion of the seller that there was a tanker in existence. It is not a case in which the parties can be seen to have proceeded on the basis of a common assumption of fact so as to justify the conclusion that the correctness of the assumption was intended by both parties to be a condition precedent to the creation of contractual obligations. The officers of the Commission made an assumption, but the plaintiffs did not make an assumption in the same sense. They knew nothing except what the Commission had told them. If they had been asked, they would certainly not have said: 'Of course, if there is no tanker, there is no contract'. They would have said: 'We shall have to go and take possession of the tanker. We simply accept the Commission's assurance that there is a tanker and the Commission's promise to give us that tanker'. The only proper construction of the contract is that it included a promise by the Commission that there was a tanker in the position specified. The Commission contracted that there was a tanker there.

They pointed out that the meaning of *Couturier's* case was merely that since the contract was construed as one for the sale of specific goods, there was a total failure of consideration so far as the buyer was concerned, with the result that he was not liable for the price. Dixon and Fullagar JJ considered that the Commission had warranted the existence of an oil tanker at the locality specified and was liable in damages for breach of this warranty.[62]

[1218] Sale of land. A vendor of land who is unable to make out title will not in all cases be liable in damages for the purchaser's loss of bargain, but this is not because the contract is void, or because there is no breach of contract. It arises from a particular rule of damages rather than the mistake doctrine.[63] Apart from this special rule, such contracts commonly provide that errors or misstatements in the contract description of the property do not annul the sale, but shall be the subject of compensation.[64]

In *Svanosio v McNamara*[65] a contract was entered into for the purchase by the plaintiff of the 'Bull's Head' hotel and the land on which it stood together with the licence and goodwill of the hotel. The price had been paid and the plaintiff entered into possession. After title was conveyed it was discovered that the hotel stood partly on the land conveyed and partly on Crown land to which the vendor did not have title. There was, however, no suggestion of fraud on the part of the vendor, and so the plaintiff relied on common mistake as to a fundamental fact, in that the parties believed that the hotel stood wholly on the land sold. Dixon CJ and Fullagar J said that neither the contract nor the conveyance of the property was void. So far as the contract was concerned, they said:[66]

> [I]t may be assumed that all parties believed that the hotel stood wholly on the land sold. In that sense there was a 'common mistake'. It may also be assumed that the [plaintiff], if he had known that a considerable part of the

---

62. See further [2111].
63. See [2165]–[2166].
64. See [759].
65. (1956) 96 CLR 186.
66. (1956) 96 CLR 186 at 195.

[1218] Contract Law in Australia

building stood on Crown land, would not have entered into the contract. But these facts do not make the contract void.

Accordingly, it was held that the contract was not void.[67]

[1219] **Partial absence of subject matter.** *Svanosio v McNamara*[68] illustrates the difficulties which confront a party who argues that a partial absence of subject matter has the effect of rendering the contract void where both parties believed that the entire subject matter existed.[69] Dixon CJ and Fullagar J approved[70] the following passage in the judgment of Denning LJ in *Solle v Butcher*:[71]

> [O]nce a contract has been made, that is to say, once the parties, whatever their inmost states of mind, have to all outward appearances agreed with sufficient certainty in the same terms on the same subject matter, then the contract is good unless and until it is set aside for failure of some condition on which the existence of the contract depends, or for fraud, or on some equitable ground. Neither party can rely on his own mistake to say it was a nullity from the beginning, no matter that it was a mistake which to his mind was fundamental, and no matter that the other party knew that he was under a mistake. A fortiori, if the other party did not know of the mistake, but shared it.

[1220] **Ability to rely on common mistake.** In *McRae v Commonwealth Disposals Commission*[72] the High Court, as an alternative ground for its decision, held that if there was an element of mistake, the Commission could not rely on it because it arose from the fault of its own servants in recklessly, and without reasonable grounds, asserting the existence of the tanker at the specified locality. Thus, it seems that there is a general principle prohibiting reliance on common mistake where there is an element of fault.[73]

Common mistake as to quality of subject matter

[1221] **Introduction.** There is considerable support, particularly in the English cases,[74] for a distinction between cases where the failure to answer to the contract description is a mere breach of contract and those where the thing delivered is of a different 'kind' from that to which the contract referred. In the latter case, the courts have treated the contract as void or

---

67. For the treatment of equitable relief see [1230].
68. (1956) 96 CLR 186 (see [1218]). See also *Bligh v Martin* [1968] 1 All ER 1157. Compare cases in which the subject matter was found to be a 'chance': *Cochrane v Willis* (1865) LR 1 Ch App 58; *Jeffries v Fairs* (1876) 4 Ch D 448. And cf *Re Roberts* [1905] 1 Ch 704; *Veitch v Sinclair* [1975] 1 NZLR 264.
69. Care must be taken in relying on English cases in this area since there is some evidence of a tendency to adopt a wider view of mistake than is tenable under Australian law. See, eg *Barrow Lane & Ballard Ltd v Phillip Phillips & Co Ltd* [1929] 1 KB 574 (sale of goods).
70. (1956) 96 CLR 186 at 195–6.
71. [1950] 1 KB 671 at 691.
72. (1951) 84 CLR 377 (see [1217]).
73. See also *Associated Japanese Bank (International) Ltd v Credit du Nord SA* [1989] 1 WLR 255 at 268–9 and cf [2043]–[2048] (self-induced frustration).
74. See, eg *Gompertz v Bartlett* (1853) 2 E & B 849; 118 ER 985; *Gurney v Wormersley* (1854) 4 E & B 133; 119 ER 51; *Scott v Coulson* [1903] 1 Ch 453 (affirmed [1903] 2 Ch 249).

allowed an action for money had and received based on total failure of consideration. It may be that some of these cases are based on the view that common mistake renders a contract void where the subject matter is different in kind.[75]

[1222] *Bell v Lever Bros.* The House of Lords reviewed the common law principles relating to common mistake in *Bell v Lever Bros Ltd*[76] but the judgments did little to clarify the law.

Lever Brothers had a subsidiary, Niger Co Ltd, of whose board Bell and Snelling were members for a term of five years not yet expired under service agreements with Lever Bros. These obliged Bell and Snelling to devote the whole of their time to the company's business. The contract in respect of which the common mistake was alleged was one by which they resigned immediately (and thus prematurely) in consideration of payments totalling £50,000 by Lever Bros. In fact, Bell and Snelling had, while holding office, engaged in some private transactions resulting in secret profits to themselves. This was a breach of fiduciary duty which would have entitled their employers to terminate the service agreements immediately and without compensation. Bell and Snelling admitted that they were liable to account for their secret profits, but denied liability to repay the £50,000. Lever Bros claimed damages for fraudulent misrepresentation and breach of contract. The jury negatived the allegation of fraud, found that the defendants had committed breaches of their service agreements which would have justified their immediate termination, found that Lever Bros did not know of Bell and Snelling's private trading and found that they did not have the trading in mind when the termination contract was negotiated.

The English Court of Appeal (affirming Wright J) held the termination contract void for common mistake, so that the payments made by Lever Bros under it could be recovered. A majority of the House of Lords (Lord Warrington, with whom Lord Hailsham agreed, dissented) allowed Bell and Snelling's appeal. The ground of the decision was that the parties' erroneous assumption that the service agreements were not terminable (except by consent) did not involve the actual subject matter of the contract but a mere quality thereof or motive therefor, and so were not of a sufficiently fundamental character.[77] The case was, perhaps, a difficult one, although it is supposed to be a watershed, and later cases, at least in England, are to be read in the light of it.

In considering whether the termination contract was vitiated by common mistake, Lord Atkin first referred to whether there was an implied term to the effect that it would be void if the parties' assumption — that the service agreements could not be terminated without payment — proved to be incorrect. He referred to the danger of reconstructing contracts to make them more businesslike, or more 'just', and said that a condition

---

75. See *Galloway v Galloway* (1914) 30 TLR 531; *Law v Harrigan* (1917) 33 TLR 381. Cf *Sherwood v Walker* 33 NW 919 (1887) in which seller and buyer of a cow for a price of $80 both believed she was barren. In fact she was in calf. Such a breeding cow would have brought the seller from $750 to $1000. The court sustained the seller's rescission and refusal to deliver.
76. [1932] AC 161.
77. Cf *Robert A Munro & Co Ltd v Meyer* [1930] 2 KB 312.

discharging the consensus should not be implied 'unless the new state of facts makes the contract something different in kind from the contract in the original state of facts'.[78] In his view, the test was: 'Does the state of the new facts destroy the identity of the subject matter as it was in the original state of facts?'[79] Clearly, this test makes everything hinge on construction of the contract and identification of its subject matter. Applying this approach to the facts, Lord Atkin concluded that the subject matter of the contract was the same:[80]

> But, on the whole, I have come to the conclusion that it would be wrong to decide that an agreement to terminate a definite specified contract is void if it turns out that the agreement had already been broken and could have been terminated otherwise. The contract released is the identical contract in both cases, and the party paying for release gets exactly what he bargains for. It seems immaterial that he could have got the same result in another way, or that if he had known the true facts he would not have entered into the bargain.
>
> - A buys B's horse; he thinks the horse is sound, and he pays the price of a sound horse; he would certainly not have bought the horse if he had known as the fact that the horse is unsound. If B has made no representation as to soundness and has not contracted that the horse is sound, A is bound and cannot recover back the price.
> - A buys a picture from B; both A and B believe it to be the work of an old master, and a high price is paid. It turns out to be a modern copy. A has no remedy in the absence of representation or warranty.
> - A agrees to take on lease or to buy from B an unfurnished dwelling-house. The house is in fact uninhabitable. A would never have entered into the bargain if he had known the fact. A has no remedy, and the position is the same whether B knew the facts or not, so long as he made no representation or gave no warranty.
> - A buys a roadside garage business from B abutting on a public thoroughfare: unknown to A, but known to B, it has already been decided to construct a bypass road which will divert substantially the whole of the traffic from passing A's garage. Again A has no remedy.
>
> All these cases involve hardship on A and benefit B, as most people would say, unjustly. They can be supported on the ground that it is of paramount importance that contracts should be observed, and that if parties honestly comply with the essentials of the formation of contracts — ie, agree in the same terms on the same subject matter — they are bound, and must rely on the stipulations of the contract for protection from the effect of facts unknown to them.

Lord Thankerton said:[81]

> The phrase 'underlying assumption by the parties', as applied to the subject matter of a contract, may be too widely interpreted so as to include something which one of the parties had not necessarily in his mind at the time of the contract; in my opinion it can only properly relate to something which both must necessarily have accepted in their minds as an essential and

---

78. [1932] AC 161 at 226.
79. [1932] AC 161 at 227.
80. [1932] AC 161 at 223–4. The bullet points have been inserted to highlight the examples given by Lord Atkin.
81. [1932] AC 161 at 235–6.

integral element of the subject matter. In the present case, however probable it may be, we are not necessarily forced to that assumption.

He thought that, in the present case, it was not an inevitable inference that Lever Bros 'regarded the indefeasibility of the service agreements as an essential and integral element in the subject matter of the bargain'.[82]

[1223] Identifying the subject matter. The test of identification of the contract's 'subject matter' is one which reserves considerable latitude to the judge. For example, in *Scott v Coulson*,[83] which involved a contract for the sale of a life policy, both parties mistakenly believed that the assured was still alive but he had died. Although the contract and assignment were set aside in equity, Vaughan Williams LJ suggested that the vendor might have contented himself with proceedings at law, and that recourse to equity was unnecessary. Apparently, the insurer's promise to pay a sum when a death should occur in the future, and an existing liability to pay the sum were regarded as totally different in kind. However, it might be argued that the subject matter was simply the insurer's contract to pay a specified sum, and the fact that the life assured had already dropped might, like the defeasibility of the service agreements in *Bell v Lever Bros Ltd*,[84] have been left out of account. In that case, Lord Thankerton thought it clear that the subject matter in *Scott v Coulson* was 'a policy still current with a surrender value',[85] but it is doubtful whether the assumed indefeasibility of the service agreements in that case was any less influential in the formation of the termination contract, than was the assumed currency of the policy in *Scott v Coulson*.

[1224] Impact of *Bell v Lever Bros*. Cases and academic writings since *Bell v Lever Bros Ltd*[86] show that it has not greatly elucidated the nature and effect of operative common mistake at common law. Although the case recognised that in some cases a contract might be void for common mistake in relation to the quality of the subject matter, the bulk of the cases deal with the possibility of equitable relief.[87] In *Taylor v Johnson*[88] the High Court recognised the authority of Lord Atkin's speech[89] in *Bell v Lever Bros*, for the proposition that the *formation* of contracts is to be determined objectively, with the consequence that, until the objective approach is displaced, there is a contract which remains binding unless and until it is set aside for fraud, failure of an agreed condition precedent or on some equitable ground. The theme of the Australian cases, beginning with *McRae v Commonwealth Disposals Commission*,[90] is that although the speech

---

82. [1932] AC 161 at 236. Lord Blanesburgh stressed that a case of voidness for common mistake on which Lever Bros had succeeded in the lower courts was not open on the pleadings and considered that an amendment should not be allowed, but in any event expressed agreement with the 'conclusions' of Lords Atkin and Thankerton.
83. [1903] 1 Ch 453 (affirmed [1903] 2 Ch 249). Contrast *Veitch v Sinclair* [1975] 1 NZLR 264.
84. [1932] AC 161 (see [1222]).
85. [1932] AC 161 at 236.
86. [1932] AC 161 (see [1222]).
87. See [1226]–[1232].
88. (1983) 151 CLR 422 (see [1254]).
89. [1932] AC 161 at 217–27.

of Lord Atkin is a correct statement of the law, the test stated is so rarely satisfied as to be of marginal significance. Nevertheless, there are English cases, the application of which in Australia must be regarded as doubtful, where the test in *Bell v Lever Bros* has been satisfied.

In *Associated Japanese Bank (International) Ltd v Credit du Nord SA*[91] one Bennett, acting fraudulently, purported to sell four non-existent machines to the bank. The bank leased the machines back to Bennett and Credit du Nord (the guarantors) guaranteed Bennett's performance of the lease. When Bennett defaulted the bank sought to enforce the guarantee. The existence of the machines was an important matter for the guarantors, who would not have entered into the contract if they had known the true position. Relying on a clause which required the guarantors' consent to any substitution of the goods comprised in the lease, Steyn J held that there was an express condition precedent in the contract of guarantee that the machines existed. Alternatively, he held that this was an implied term of the guarantee. There is considerable difficulty in supporting either basis. The express term did not state that it was a condition precedent that the goods existed. And, if it is accepted that there was an implied term that the machines existed, *McRae* suggests that the term was a promise rather than a condition precedent to the existence of the contract. As a third ground for his decision, Steyn J held that the contract of guarantee was void for mistake. Although he accepted that the mere fact that the guarantors would not have entered into the contract had they known the true position was not enough to make the contract void, he said[92] the 'subject matter of the *guarantee* … was essentially different from what it was reasonably believed to be'. The conclusion is surprising, particularly in view of the fact that he did not consider that the lease contract was void for mistake. The guarantors' mistake would seem to have related to a purely collateral matter, namely, the value of their rights against the goods on meeting Bennett's liability to the bank. What the guarantors guaranteed was Bennett's promise to pay. That promise existed and was enforceable, although the lease contract was voidable by the bank for fraud. The fact that the guarantors entered into the contract in the mistaken belief that the goods existed would not, under Australian law, render the contract void. Following *McRae*, we would approach the matter by asking whether the guarantors could defend the claim by relying on a breach by the bank of an (express or) implied promise that the machines existed.

[1225] One party's mistaken motive. The subject matter of a mistake may be so much the concern of one party only that it may be, although vaguely assumed to be correct by the other party insofar as it was thought

---

90. (1951) 84 CLR 377 (see [1217]).
91. [1989] 1 WLR 255 (see G H Treitel, (1988) 104 *LQR* 501; Geoffrey Marston, [1989] *CLJ* 173; J W Carter, (1991) 3 *JCL* 237). See also *Norwich Union Fire Insurance Society v William H Price Ltd* [1934] AC 455 (on appeal from (1933) 33 SR (NSW) 196); *Nicholson and Venn v Smith Marriott* (1947) 177 LT 189; *William Sindall Plc v Cambridgeshire County Council* [1994] 1 WLR 1016 at 1039. Contrast *Upton-on-Severn RDC v Powell* [1942] 1 All ER 220; *Citibank NA v Brown Shipley & Co Ltd* [1991] 2 All ER 690 (see A H Hudson, [1991] *LMCLQ* 291; Andrew Phang, (1992) 5 *JCL* 69).
92. [1989] 1 WLR 255 at 269.

about at all (and to this extent 'common' rather than 'unilateral'), categorised as a mere mistake as to the motive or reason of one party for contracting. A mistake so viewed affords no ground for relief.[93] Indeed, it could be said that in *Bell v Lever Bros Ltd*[94] the presumed inability to terminate the service agreements unilaterally was only the motive or reason which caused Lever Bros to make the contract.

Similarly, common mistake as to the meaning of an express contractual term (including the description of the contract's subject matter) will not render the contract void.[95]

Rescission for Common Mistake

[1226] Void and voidable contracts distinguished. The analysis above has been concerned with the circumstances in which a contract may be regarded as void on the ground of common mistake. A 'void' contract is a nullity. The theme which we have tried to develop is that a mistake, although common to both parties, does not render a contract void at common law.[96] It remains to consider whether the contract is 'voidable', that is, liable to be rescinded or set aside by the court. Under the modern law this must in most cases be the crucial issue.

At common law a contract can be regarded as voidable if the common mistake of the parties has also been the subject of a representation by one of the parties. In such cases the mistake of the other party is induced. Now that equitable rules govern rescission for innocent misrepresentation, 'voidability' is a creature of equity. These cases were dealt with under the heading of misrepresentation.[97] More relevant to the present context are suggestions that mistake may render a contract voidable on equitable grounds even though there is no misrepresentation.

[1227] Origin of the modern law. There is, superficially at least, respectable authority for a jurisdiction to set aside a contract on the ground of common mistake as to a substantial matter. In *Cooper v Phibbs*[98] there was a lease of a salmon fishery which the parties believed to belong to the lessor, but which was subsequently discovered to belong already to the lessee.[99] It was ordered that the lease be set aside on the ground of the parties' common mistake. Although the lease document had been incapable of conveying any interest to the lessee, the lessee had had the

---

93. Cf *Pope & Pearson v The Buenos Ayres New Gas Co* (1892) 8 TLR 758; *Subdivisions Ltd v Payne* [1934] SASR 214.
94. [1932] AC 161 (see [1222]).
95. *Frederick E Rose (London) Ltd v William H Pim Junior & Co Ltd* [1953] 2 QB 450; *Harrison & Jones Ltd v Bunten & Lancaster Ltd* [1953] 1 QB 646.
96. It would follow from this that we favour amendment of the sale of goods legislation (see [1216]) to provide merely that where there is a contract for the sale of specific goods which have, without the seller's knowledge or fault, perished at the time of contract, the contract is void only if there is an express or implied term to this effect.
97. See especially [1037]–[1038].
98. (1867) LR 2 HL 149. Cf *Bettyes v Maynard* (1882) 46 LT 766; *Huddersfield Banking Co Ltd v Henry Lister & Son Ltd* [1895] 2 Ch 273; *Allcard v Walker* [1896] 2 Ch 369.
99. The mistake was treated as one of fact, not of law.

[1227]

benefit of a period of occupation of a small piece of land owned by the lessor, and the lessor had improved the premises. Accordingly, rescission was on terms as to payment of an occupation rent to the lessor and a lien to the lessor for the improvements. Another ground for the rescission was that the lessee had been led into the lease by a pre-contract misrepresentation.

The general test as to the nature and quality of the mistake which will ground intervention is less stringent than that applicable at common law.[100]

[1228] Justification for relief. The jurisdiction predicates the existence of a valid contract. Although it has been enlarged as the common law doctrine of common mistake has been narrowed, it cannot be compelled to be exercised and will not be exercised where the rights of innocent third parties have intervened, where restitutio in integrum is no longer possible, or where there has been an affirmation of the contract or even delay by the mistaken party.[101] However, mere 'difficulty' in restoring the parties exactly to their original condition, and acquiescence where the acquiescing party was ignorant of the mistake, will not preclude rescission.[102]

The assumption of this jurisdiction was justified by reference to equity's established role of relieving against fraud in the broadest sense. In the contemplation of equity it would be 'fraud' in the case of an executory contract, to allow the contract to remain enforceable at law,[103] and in the case of an executed contract to allow one party to retain the benefit of the other's performance.[104] It is easier for a court to intervene where the contract is still executory than where, for example, it has been executed by a conveyance of property and payment of price.[105]

The jurisdiction to set aside, like the discretion to refuse specific performance,[106] is large and flexible, and based on the 'injustice' or 'inequity' which would occur if the court did not intervene.[107] But this makes it difficult to define and to exercise with consistency.

[1229] Modern reformulation in *Solle v Butcher*. In *Solle v Butcher*[108] Lord Denning attempted to synthesise the authorities. The case concerned a lease of a flat and garage. The flat had been let at a 'standard rent' of £140 per year in 1939. Because the flat had been reconstructed by the landlords and the lease included the garage, the parties believed that the lease would be unaffected by the *Rent Restriction Acts*. Even on the assumption that it was still 'rent-controlled', it could be lawfully let for

---

100. See *Huddersfield Banking Co Ltd v Henry Lister & Son Ltd* [1895] 2 Ch 273; *Hudson v Jope* (1914) 14 SR (NSW) 351.
101. Cf *Huddersfield Banking Co Ltd v Henry Lister & Son Ltd* [1895] 2 Ch 273; *Hudson v Jope* (1914) 14 SR (NSW) 351; *Whitelaw v Delaney* [1914] AC 131; *Leaf v International Galleries* [1950] 2 KB 86 esp at 92-3, 94.
102. *Earl of Beauchamp v Winn* (1873) LR 6 HL 223.
103. *Hitchcock v Giddings* (1817) 4 Price 135; 146 ER 418; *Jones v Clifford* (1876) 3 Ch D 779; *Bettyes v Maynard* (1882) 46 LT 766.
104. *Bingham v Bingham* (1748) 1 Ves Sen 126; 27 ER 934.
105. See *Allen v Richardson* (1879) 13 Ch D 524; *Brownlie v Campbell* (1880) 5 App Cas 925.
106. See [2411].
107. *Mills v Fox* (1887) 37 Ch D 153; *Allcard v Walker* [1896] 2 Ch 369; *Robert A Munro & Co Ltd v Meyer* [1930] 2 KB 312.
108. [1950] 1 KB 671.

£250 per year, provided the landlords first gave notice of increases based on improvements. The subject lease was indeed at a rental of £250 but notices of increase were not given first since the parties assumed that the landlords' structural work made the flat not the same dwelling as that which had been rent-controlled. Subsequently, the tenant sought a declaration that the standard rent of the flat was £140 and that he should get a refund of all rent which he had paid in excess of the amount.

The English Court of Appeal held unanimously that the identity of the premises had not changed and that the tenant was not precluded from relying on the Act. But the parties had addressed their minds to the identity question, and since Denning and Bucknill LJJ held[109] that it was a material issue, the landlords were entitled to have the lease set aside upon such terms as the court thought fit. Bucknill LJ observed that there was no merit in the tenant's case and that since the lease was for a period of seven years, it involved considerable hardship to the landlords. Denning LJ said:[110]

> In order to see whether the lease can be avoided for this mistake it is necessary to remember that mistake is of two kinds: first, mistake which renders the contract void, that is, a nullity from the beginning, which is the kind of mistake which was dealt with by the courts of common law; and, secondly, mistake which renders the contract not void, but voidable, that is, liable to be set aside on such terms as the court thinks fit, which is the kind of mistake which was dealt with by the courts of equity. Much of the difficulty which has attended this subject has arisen because, before the fusion of law and equity, the courts of common law, in order to do justice in the case in hand, extended this doctrine of mistake beyond its proper limits and held contracts to be void which were really only voidable, a process which was capable of being attended with much injustice to third persons who had bought goods or otherwise committed themselves on the faith that there was a contract ... Since the fusion of law and equity there is no reason to continue this process, and it will be found that only those contracts are now held void in which the mistake was such as to prevent the formation of any contract at all.

In Denning LJ's view:[111]

> A contract is ... liable in equity to be set aside if the parties were under a common misapprehension either as to facts or as to their relative and respective rights, provided that the misapprehension was fundamental and that the party seeking to set it aside was not himself at fault.

Denning LJ, with whom Bucknill LJ agreed in this respect, proposed giving the tenant a choice between submitting to rescission or having a lease at the rental of £250 which would have been payable if the landlords had given the necessary notices. Other orders required that if the tenant accepted the alternative of rescission, he would pay a reasonable sum for use and occupation and mesne profits.

The equitable doctrine of common mistake, broadly as formulated by Denning LJ, has been recognised or accepted in several other English cases.[112] There are also cases in New Zealand and Canada in which it has been applied.[113] It has also received some measure of support in

---

109. Jenkins LJ dissented.
110. [1950] 1 KB 671 at 690–1.
111. [1950] 1 KB 671 at 693.

Australia.[114] The fact that there appear to be many authorities supporting the approach of Denning LJ in *Solle v Butcher* should not be taken as implying that the law is settled. There are at least three very significant points. First, many of the English cases in which *Solle* has been treated as good law involved Lord Denning.[115]

Second, it is difficult to reconcile these cases with *Bell v Lever Bros Ltd*,[116] unless it is assumed that the case was solely concerned with the issue of voidness.[117] There is, for example, a strong similarity between the facts of *Bell v Lever Bros* and those of *Magee v Pennine Insurance Co Ltd*.[118] In that case an insured and his insurer agreed to compromise a claim under the policy, overlooking that the policy was voidable for non-disclosure by the insured in the proposal form. The English Court of Appeal held that the compromise contract could be set aside on the ground of common mistake as to a matter fundamental to that contract. It seems that the two cases can be reconciled only on the view that the House of Lords was confining its attention to the common law relating to operative mistake. Yet several dicta in the opinions suggest otherwise.[119]

Third, although we can now accept that there are cases in which rescission may be obtained on the ground of common mistake in relation to a fundamental matter, it is by no means clear that the formulation of Lord Denning in *Solle* is an accurate statement of the legal requirements.[120]

[1230] Requirement of fundamental mistake. *Solle v Butcher*[121] relies on a concept of fundamental mistake. Although it is clear that this is broader than the common law concept, since where mistake is operative at common law the contract is void, it is doubtful whether the mere fact of fundamental mistake is sufficient. For example, the courts are reluctant to

---

112. See, eg *Magee v Pennine Insurance Co Ltd* [1969] 2 QB 507 (see [1229]); *Associated Japanese Bank (International) Ltd v Credit du Nord SA* [1989] 1 WLR 255 (see [1224]); *William Sindall Plc v Cambridgeshire County Council* [1994] 1 WLR 1016 at 1042.
113. See *Dell v Beasley* [1959] NZLR 89; *Waring v S J Brentnall Ltd* [1975] 2 NZLR 401; *Ivanochko v Sych* (1967) 60 DLR (2d) 474.
114. See [1254].
115. See, eg *Leaf v International Galleries* [1950] 2 KB 86; *Oscar Chess Ltd v Williams* [1957] 1 WLR 370; *Magee v Pennine Insurance Co Ltd* [1969] 2 QB 507.
116. [1932] AC 161 (see [1217]).
117. See *Associated Japanese Bank (International) Ltd v Credit du Nord SA* [1989] 1 WLR 255 at 266. As a further ground for his decision in that case (see [1224]) Steyn J said the contract of guarantee could have been set aside on equitable grounds. But see John Cartwright, 'Solle v Butcher and the Doctrine of Mistake in Contract' (1987) 103 *LQR* 594.
118. [1969] 2 QB 507.
119. There is an additional difficulty, namely, that the law on compromises of disputed claims (see N H Andrews, 'Mistaken Settlements of Disputed Claims' [1989] *LMCLQ* 431 at 437–8 and generally [350]–[355]) proceeds on the basis that the fact that the disputed claim would have failed does not vitiate the compromise if bona fide, as seems to have been the case in *Magee*. See *Prudential Assurance Co Ltd v C M Breedon Pty Ltd* [1994] 2 VR 452. Cf *Huddersfield Banking Co Ltd v Henry Lister & Son Ltd* [1895] 2 Ch 273 at 282, 283, 285–6.
120. See further [1230], [1231].
121. [1950] 1 KB 671. Cf *Earl of Beauchamp v Winn* (1873) LR 6 HL 223 at 233 (mistake affecting 'essence'); *Huddersfield Banking Co Ltd v Henry Lister & Son Ltd* [1895] 2 Ch 273 at 284 ('material').

relieve a purchaser of land in view of the express contractual provisions for investigation of, requisitions on and acceptance of the vendor's title prior to conveyance.[122] Certainly this was the view of the High Court in *Svanosio v McNamara*.[123] However, that case has peculiar features which render it something less than a comprehensive statement of the Australian law.

It will be recalled[124] that the hotel which was the subject of the transaction stood partly on adjoining Crown land. Apart from relief based on the allegation that the contract was void, the purchaser sought orders setting aside the agreements and conveyance, and for repayment of the price. If the circumstance of the vendor's lack of title had been discovered before conveyance, the purchasers might not have been compelled to accept the title.[125] Similarly, the purchasers might not have obtained a decree for specific performance requiring the vendors to obtain and convey that title which they did not have,[126] unless, perhaps, compensation was provided by the vendor. But as the contract had been completed, there was no question of the vendor seeking relief to enforce the contract. The conveyance and the transfer of the liquor licence were both effective, neither was void.

Equitable principles may in certain circumstances be relied upon to set aside a conveyance and transfer. However, the cases involving contracts for the sale of land in which relief is granted after conveyance were, in *Svanosio v McNamara*, limited to cases in which the vendor had no title at all. The advantage of being able to invoke equitable principles is that orders for adjustments and allowances can be made in addition to the recovery of money paid. The court held that there was no basis for setting aside the conveyance. In the joint judgment of McTiernan, Williams and Webb JJ it is said that the only authority for the proposition that *any* executed contract for the sale of property could be rescinded for innocent misrepresentation or material common mistake is *Solle v Butcher*, but the judgments had there expressly excluded contracts for the sale of land. Dixon and Fullagar JJ deduced from the cases the principle that equity will not grant relief after conveyance unless there has been fraud or 'a total failure of consideration or what amounts practically to a total failure of consideration'.[127]

Svanosio v McNamara was distinguished in *Lukacs v Wood*.[128] Land was described in a contract of sale and in a transfer of land. The purchaser, for

---

122. See *William Sindall Plc v Cambridgeshire County Council* [1994] 1 WLR 1016 (contractual allocation of risk left no room for rescission on the ground of mistake). Cf *Soper v Arnold* (1887) 37 Ch D 96; *Debenham v Sawbridge* [1901] 2 Ch 98.
123. (1956) 96 CLR 186. See also *Cousins v Freeman* (1957) 58 WALR 79.
124. See [1218].
125. Indeed, they would have been entitled to damages for breach of warranty, although the *amount* of damages would have been limited by the rule in *Bain v Fothergill* (1874) LR 7 HL 158, as to which see [2165].
126. See *Perrin v Reynolds* (1886) 12 VLR 440.
127. (1956) 96 CLR 186 at 198. This may be the explanation for *Cooper v Phibbs* (1867) LR 2 HL 149 (see [1227]); see Paul Matthews, 'A Note on *Cooper v Phibbs*' (1989) 105 *LQR* 599) A peculiar feature of contracts for the sale of land which reinforces this position is that a purchaser has ample opportunity to discover defects of title before completion. Moreover, a particular reason for not holding the contract void (or voidable) for mistake was that the contract provided expressly for the circumstance of a deficiency of title (the 'error or misdescription' clause).
128. (1978) 19 SASR 520.

the price of three vacant allotments, became the registered proprietor of two of the vacant lots and a fourth lot on which was erected a block of residential flats. Jacobs J held that there had been a common mistake as to the substance of what was purchased, and ordered the purchaser to execute and deliver a transfer of the improved parcel in exchange for delivery of an executed transfer of the third vacant allotment.

[1231] **Requirement of equitable fraud.** A right to approach the court for an order rescinding the contract relies on an element of 'equitable fraud'. The question that arises is when that will be present in mistake cases in the absence of misrepresentation. In *Svanosio v McNamara*[129] Dixon and Fullagar JJ observed[130] that it was because 'there was no fraud or misrepresentation', that the position of the parties depended on the terms of the contract. After citing *Solle v Butcher*,[131] they said:[132]

> 'Mistake' might, of course, afford a ground on which equity would refuse specific performance of a contract, and there may be cases of 'mistake' in which it would be so inequitable that a party should be held to his contract that equity would set it aside. No rule can be laid down a priori as to such cases: see an article by Professor R A Blackburn in (1955) 7 *Res Judicatae* 43. But we would agree with Professor Shatwell (1955) 33 *Can Bar Rev* 164 at 186, 187 that it is difficult to conceive any circumstances in which equity could properly give relief by setting aside the contract unless there has been fraud or misrepresentation or a condition can be found expressed or implied in the contract.

This passage denies that relief may be granted in the absence of fraud. What did they mean by 'fraud'? Any argument that they intended to exclude the broad concept of fraud in equity, which includes unconscionable dealing, is precluded by *Taylor v Johnson*[133] where Mason ACJ, Murphy and Deane JJ said[134] that if Dixon and Fullagar JJ did not intend to include unconscionable dealing, 'we do not share the difficulty to which they referred. To the contrary, it seems to us that the reported cases, including *Solle v Butcher* ... readily provide concrete examples of such circumstances'. Therefore, not only is it clear that there is a jurisdiction in Australia to set aside a contract on the ground of common mistake, but also *Solle v Butcher* can be taken as a valid illustration of the jurisdiction. However, in order for the contract to be liable to be set aside there must be circumstances which render it *unconscionable* for the party who seeks to uphold the contract to have it enforced.

[1232] **Relevance of 'fault'.** Lord Denning's formulation in *Solle v Butcher*[135] requires not only that the parties' common mistake be 'fundamental' but also that the party seeking to have the contract set aside not be 'at fault'. Something less than great care on the part of at least one party will characterise most instances of common mistake, but apparently

---

129. (1956) 96 CLR 186.
130. (1956) 96 CLR 186 at 195.
131. [1950] 1 KB 671.
132. (1956) 96 CLR 186 at 196.
133. (1983) 151 CLR 422 (see [1254]).
134. (1983) 151 CLR 422 at 431. See also *Earl of Beauchamp v Winn* (1873) LR 6 HL 223 at 233.
135. [1950] 1 KB 671.

this will not defeat that party.[136] In the New Zealand case, *Waring v S J Brentnall Ltd*,[137] Chilwell J suggested that 'unconscionable' should be substituted for 'at fault'. It may be, however, that the concept is broader than this, including some cases of carelessness.[138]

Mutual Mistake

Mutual Mistake Rendering Contract Void

[1233] Concordance of offer and acceptance. Where offer and acceptance are literally and in their true meanings different, no contract is concluded. But it is their significations — the one to the other — that are essential. If these coincide there is a contract notwithstanding any literal discrepancy. More importantly for present purposes, if they do not coincide, there is no contract though they may literally correspond.

[1234] Illustrations. In *Raffles v Wichelhaus*[139] A agreed to buy and B agreed to sell cotton to arrive 'ex *Peerless* from Bombay'. In fact there were two ships named '*Peerless*' due to sail from Bombay: one to sail in October, the other in December. The goods were shipped on the December ship but the buyer refused to accept them, contending that he had meant to buy cotton via the earlier ship. The seller sued for damages for non-acceptance and argued that it was not open to the buyer to adduce evidence of his actual intention: that all that mattered was that the seller had performed in accordance with the literal wording of the contract. The court rejected the seller's argument.

This case does not contradict the objective theory of contract for the important reason that it was not possible to say that the only reasonable interpretation to be placed upon the words used by one party was that advanced by one party or the other. Where there is insoluble ambiguity and the evidence shows that both parties meant different things, there is no contract. On the other hand, the evidence may show that the only reasonable construction to be placed on words or conduct was that contended for by one party and in this event there will be a contract conforming to that construction. In the context of the facts in *Raffles v Wichelhaus*, if the evidence had shown that a reasonable person in the buyer's position *should* have construed the seller's offer as referring to the December *Peerless*, the buyer would be bound accordingly even though subjectively he intended by his acceptance to buy cotton via the earlier ship.[140] This is the objective theory of contract at work.[141] It is not clear that

---

136. Cf *Bingham v Bingham* (1748) 1 Ves Sen 126; 27 ER 934; *Earl of Beauchamp v Winn* (1873) LR 6 HL 223.
137. [1975] 2 NZLR 401. Cf *Huddersfield Banking Co Ltd v Henry Lister & Son Ltd* [1895] 2 Ch 273 at 277.
138. *Earl of Beauchamp v Winn* (1873) LR 6 HL 223 at 234 ('wilful ignorance or culpable neglect'). But this does not imply that there must be a breach of some duty of care.
139. (1864) 2 H & C 906; 159 ER 375.
140. For a case similar to *Raffles v Wichelhaus* and with the same result, see *Smidt v Tiden* (1874) LR 9 QB 446.
141. See [206].

the court actually held the contract to be void for mutual mistake. Although the case is certainly open to this interpretation,[142] a better rationale may be that there was no contract, since the agreement was void for uncertainty. An alternative argument is that the contract was not void at all, because the construction of the contract showed that the seller had agreed to sell cotton via the earlier ship, and the buyer was entitled to sue for breach of contract. It was not necessary for the court to decide this issue: all that was in question was whether the seller could sue.

A second case is *Scriven Bros & Co v Hindley & Co*.[143] The plaintiff instructed an auctioneer to sell a number of bags of hemp and tow. Although the goods were described in the auction catalogue, it did not disclose which lot comprised hemp and which comprised tow. Moreover, the same shipping mark (the mark of the ship which had brought the bales to England) was entered against both lots. Samples of both lots were on view but the defendants did not examine them and relied on their earlier inspection of the samples of the hemp in the plaintiff's show room. When the lots representing tow were put up, their buyer made a bid, intending to bid for hemp. The amount of the bid was an extravagant price for tow. The lots were knocked down to the defendants, whom the plaintiff sued for the price. The jury's findings were that (1) the auctioneer intended to sell tow; (2) the defendants' buyer intended to bid for hemp; (3) the auctioneer believed that the bid had been made under the influence of a mistake but had reasonable grounds for believing that the mistake was as to the value of the goods rather than as to their identity; (4) the form of the catalogue and a careless inspection by the defendants' manager had both contributed to the mistake. A T Lawrence J found simply that findings (2) and (3) showed that the parties were never ad idem as to the subject matter of the sale and that therefore there was no contract. He also said that the plaintiffs could succeed only if they could show that the defendants were, in the circumstances, estopped from setting up their true state of mind.

The result can be supported on the ground that it was not possible to say which of the two commodities was the subject of the 'sale'. In such cases of true ambiguity, it is proper to say that offer and acceptance do not coincide, notwithstanding appearances to the contrary. It is for a person seeking to enforce a contract to show that the terms contracted for were so clear and unambiguous that the other party cannot be heard to say that there was a mistake.[144]

[1235] Mistake as to legal effect. It is important to distinguish from cases of the type discussed above[145] those where neither the subject matter nor the terminology of the contract is in dispute, the sole question being 'the legal effect of the mutually agreed words in their accepted

---

142. See *Sharp v Thomson* (1915) 20 CLR 137 at 142; *R W Cameron & Co v L Slutzkin Pty Ltd* (1923) 32 CLR 81 at 90, 93; *Life Insurance Co of Australia Ltd v Phillips* (1925) 36 CLR 60 at 79–80.
143. [1913] 3 KB 564.
144. See *Falck v Williams* [1900] AC 176. Cf *Henkel v Pape* (1870) LR 6 Ex 7.
145. See [1234].

signification'.[146] There is neither operative common mistake nor operative mutual mistake in such cases.

In *Goldsbrough Mort & Co Ltd v Quinn*[147] a contract for the sale and purchase of 2590 acres of land comprising freehold, conditional purchase and conditional lease was agreed for a price of £1.10.0 an acre 'calculated on a freehold basis'. The purchaser sought specific performance on the basis that out of the sum of £1.10.0 an amount necessary to convert the conditional purchase and conditional lease lands to freehold would be paid to the Crown. The vendor gave evidence that he had contracted on the footing of his understanding that the price meant that he would receive £1.10.0 cash per acre. The High Court held that the expression 'calculated on a freehold basis' was plain and unambiguous and that there was a binding contract importing the construction advanced by the purchaser. This would provide the basis on which the purchaser might obtain damages for the vendor's wrongful repudiation but the court went further and held that there was no reason why it should, in the exercise of its discretion, decline to grant the discretionary equitable remedy of specific performance of the contract as sought by the purchaser. In particular, there was no evidence of fraud, misleading conduct or hardship.

Cases of the *Goldsbrough Mort* type have been common. These are cases in which a party has contracted under an erroneous understanding of the meaning (or effect) of contractual words or even of the impact of the contract as a whole. Since, ex hypothesi, the court in such a case is holding that the other party's construction is the only right one, the case does not involve mutual mistake. Rather, one party only is mistaken. In such cases the mistaken party must, in order to establish that the mistake affected the validity or enforceability of the contract, prove that the other party knew or had reason to suspect that there was mistake, or contributed to the mistake.[148]

Rescission for Mutual Mistake

[1236] Introduction. In considering the question of rescission, in order that the circumstances should not be categorised as operative unilateral mistake, it must be assumed that the unmistaken party:

- did not know or have reason to suspect that the other party was mistaken; and
- did not contribute to the mistake.

These elements of themselves imply that mutual mistake is unlikely to give rise to issues to be determined by equitable principles of rescission.

[1237] Equitable relief for mutual mistake. If mutual mistake prevents a contract from coming into existence,[149] no remedy is available to enforce the contract. Thus, where appropriate, orders may be made declaring that no contract was formed and giving consequential relief, such as setting

---

146. See *Life Insurance Co of Australia Ltd v Phillips* (1925) 36 CLR 60 at 80.
147. (1910) 10 CLR 674.
148. See [1239], [1254].
149. See [1233]–[1235].

aside documents and awarding restitution of money paid. Where mutual mistake does not render a contract void, there are suggestions of an ability to refuse specific performance. However, these statements have referred, if not to the necessity of outright ambiguity, at least to a requirement that the mistake must have been a reasonable one.[150]

For example, in *Swaisland v Dearsley*[151] Sir John Romilly MR, in refusing to grant a vendor specific performance, said:[152]

> [I]f it appears upon the evidence that there was, in the description of the property, a matter on which a person might bona fide make a mistake, and he swears positively that he did make such mistake, and his evidence is not disproved, this court cannot enforce the specific performance against him. If there appear on the particulars no ground for the mistake, if no man with his senses about him could have misapprehended the character of the parcels, then I do not think it is sufficient for the purchaser to swear that he made a mistake, or that he did not understand what he was about.

It is doubtful whether such cases involve anything other than common or unilateral mistake. The better view is that mutual mistake has no operation in equity beyond that at law, and that cases where one party's construction is upheld by the court as correct are to be dealt with under the rubric of unilateral mistake.

Unilateral Mistake

General

[1238] Introduction. The circumstance that one party — but not the other — is mistaken is not of itself a reason for saying that the contract is void or that a right of rescission is available. Some additional factor must be shown. That factor will be the combination of knowledge that the other is mistaken and an element of responsibility for that mistake.

The analysis below draws on two perspectives:

(1) whether the effect is to make the contract void or voidable; and
(2) whether the mistake relates to the identity of the other party or the terms of the contract.

[1239] Relationship between mutual and unilateral mistake. In cases of operative mutual mistake the parties are at cross-purposes and neither can be blamed for this: because of ambiguity neither party's construction can be held to be 'the correct one'.

Once one party's construction is held correct, the unmistaken party can insist on performance unless the case is one of unilateral mistake, that is, there was knowledge of the mistake, reasons for suspecting that the other party was mistaken or contribution to the mistake.[153] It is one party's 'involvement' that displaces the normal operation of the contract.

---

150. Cf *Goldsbrough Mort & Co Ltd v Quinn* (1910) 10 CLR 674 at 683, 688–9, 695.
151. (1861) 29 Beav 430; 54 ER 694.
152. (1861) 29 Beav 430 at 433–4; 54 ER 694 at 695.
153. See also [1235].

Unilateral Mistake Rendering Contract Void[154]

Mistake as to identity — parties at a distance

[1240] General. Not every unilateral mistake relating to a contracting party will render the contract void. Just as a buyer's mistake as to the quality and value of the goods bought will normally be inconsequential, so will a seller's mistake as to the character and creditworthiness of the buyer. It matters not that the buyer or seller would not have contracted but for the mistake.

Mistake as to the identity of a contracting party will be unilateral, and arise as a result of a fraudulent misrepresentation. Given those circumstances, there is no reason to doubt the ability of the mistaken party to rescind the contract. What is in issue is whether the mistake makes the contract void.

[1241] Offer can only be accepted by offeree. A's offer to B cannot be accepted by C so as to create a contract between A and C. In *Boulton v Jones*[155] an action was brought for the price of goods sold. The defendants had been in the habit of dealing with one Brocklehurst. Indeed, he owed them money. They sent a written order for goods, addressed expressly to Brocklehurst. But, unbeknown to the defendants, he had sold his business to the plaintiff (an employee) the very same day. The plaintiff struck out Brocklehurst's name on the order and substituted his own. He then purported to fulfil the order without advising the defendants that the goods had been supplied by himself rather than by Brocklehurst. When the plaintiff asked for payment, the defendants said they knew nothing of him. His action for the price failed, notwithstanding that in the result the defendants were not contractually bound to pay anyone for the goods.[156]

Pollock CB said:[157]

> It is a rule of law, that if a person intends to contract with A, B cannot give himself any rights under it. Here the order in writing was given to Brocklehurst. Possibly Brocklehurst might have adopted the act of the plaintiff in supplying the goods, and maintained an action for their price. But since the plaintiff has chosen to sue, the only course the defendants could take was to plead that there was no contract with him.

The difficulty with the case is why the offer was interpreted as being personal to Brocklehurst, since it would normally be a reasonable construction of an offer made to a business that it is open for acceptance by whoever carries on the business. The case would have been different if it had been addressed to 'the proprietor' (of the business) or to the business itself or to whom it might concern or to no-one in particular. There is, in other words, a tension with the objective approach to contract formation. Bramwell B said:[158] 'When a contract is made, in which the personality of

---

154. See Esther Stern, 'Objectivity, Legal Doctrine and the Law of Mistaken Identity' (1995) 8 *JCL* 154, esp at 168ff.
155. (1857) 2 H & N 564; 157 ER 232. See also *Hardman v Booth* (1863) 1 H & C 803; 158 ER 1107.
156. On whether a claim in restitution should have succeeded see Mason and Carter, *Restitution Law in Australia*, 1995, para 1038.
157. (1857) 2 H & N 564 at 565–6; 157 ER 232 at 233. Martin B concurred.

the contracting party is or may be of importance, as a contract with a man to write a book, or the like, or where there might be a set-off, no other person can interpose and adopt the contract.' This approach, which requires a consideration of whether the contract was of such a kind that the identity of the other party could be expected to be an important consideration to the offeror, treats the defendants' entitlement to a set-off against Brocklehurst as crucial in the interpretation of the offer. The availability of a set-off against Brocklehurst may explain why the defendants addressed their order to him expressly. And it may be that the plaintiff knew or ought to have known of the set-off. Given an objective approach to contract formation, without that knowledge the case would have been differently decided.[159]

The leading case is *Cundy v Lindsay*.[160] One Blenkarn ordered in writing goods from Lindsays. On the order he gave his identity as 'Blenkarn & Co, 37 Wood St and 5 Little Love Lane, Cheapside' and signed so that his name appeared as 'Blenkiron & Co'. There was in fact a respectable firm by that name which carried on business at 123 Wood Street, Cheapside. Lindsays knew their name and believed that they were dealing with them. Lindsays dispatched the goods, without checking the address, to 'Blenkiron & Co, 37 Wood Street'. The goods were received by the rogue Blenkarn at that address and he sold some of them to an unsuspecting third party, Cundy. Blenkarn did not pay for the goods and was indeed convicted of obtaining them by false pretences. In the result, Lindsays sued Cundy in tort for conversion of their goods, and the argument was that the alleged contract with the rogue was void, so that Cundy did not obtain ownership of the goods.

The jury found that the mode of the letter led and was intended to lead Lindsays to believe that they were dealing with Blenkiron & Co. As to Blenkarn, in the emphatic words of Lord Cairns:[161]

> Of him they knew nothing, and of him they never thought. With him they never intended to deal. Their minds never, even for an instant of time rested upon him, and as between him and them there was no consensus of mind which could lead to any agreement, or to any contract whatever.

Lords Hatherley and Penzance observed that cases of personal dealing, that is, cases where a rogue deals face to face with the other party but misrepresents himself or herself, were different. Lord Penzance added that the mere fact that the goods were addressed to No 37 was not enough, in the light of the other facts, to show an offer to deal with whoever might be at that address. There being no contract, Lindsays were successful.

Cundy v Lindsay is not a satisfactory decision. The House of Lords did not adequately dispose of the argument that Lindsays intended to deal with the person doing business — whoever it was — at 37 Wood St. It may be suggested that undue prominence was given to the subjective intention of

---

158. (1857) 2 H & N 564 at 566; 157 ER 232 at 233.
159. The case would certainly have been different if the defendants had retained and consumed the goods *after* receiving the plaintiff's invoice. This might have been construed as an acceptance of a counter-offer by the plaintiff to sell to them.
160. (1878) 3 App Cas 459. See also *Re International Society of Auctioneers and Valuers (Baillie's Case)* [1898] 1 Ch 110.
161. (1878) 3 App Cas 459 at 465.

Lindsays. There is no analysis of whether they should have taken steps to verify the address, and the result was that a party took advantage of its own mistake to defeat the rights of an innocent third party.

[1242] **Self-styled agent.** Having some similarity with *Cundy v Lindsay*,[162] but determinable on the simple ground of lack of authority, are cases where there is a fraudulent misrepresentation by a rogue, not as a known existing entity, but as the agent of such an entity authorised to contract on its behalf.[163] There is no contract in such a case, whether the parties are at a distance or face to face.[164]

[1243] **Non-existent party.** In the cases already referred to, there was in existence a firm with which the mistaken party thought it was dealing. So it could be said that the offer was addressed to that firm and could not be accepted by anyone else. The facts were otherwise in *King's Norton Metal Co Ltd v Edridge Merrett & Co Ltd*.[165] One Wallis sent a letter to the plaintiffs who were metal manufacturers at King's Norton seeking a quotation for the supply of metal. The letter purported to come from 'Hallam & Co' on a letterhead with a representation of a large factory with a number of chimneys and a statement in one corner that Hallam & Co had branches and depots at certain places. The quotation was sent, an order was lodged, and the goods were dispatched but their price was never paid. However, Wallis sold them to the defendants whom the plaintiffs sued for damages for conversion of what was allegedly still the plaintiffs' property. The English Court of Appeal held that the plaintiffs had intended to contract with 'the writer of the letters', whoever that might be, so that a contract existed between them and Wallis. The court noted that the result might have been different, and governed by *Cundy v Lindsay*,[166] if it could have been shown that there were two separate entities called respectively 'Wallis' and 'Hallam & Co'.

It is scarcely satisfactory from either the defrauded party's or the innocent third party's viewpoint that their rights should depend on the precise form which the rogue's misrepresentation takes. A possible answer to the question, which of these two innocent parties should suffer, would be to provide by legislation for their sharing of the loss on an equitable basis having regard to the extent to which, by their carelessness, they may have facilitated the fraud.[167]

---

162. (1878) 3 App Cas 459.
163. Contrast cases where there is an aversion to contracting with a particular party, eg *Archer v Stone* (1898) 78 LT 34; *Said v Butt* [1920] 3 KB 497; *Dyster v Randall & Sons* [1926] 1 Ch 932; *Williams v Bulat* [1992] 2 Qd R 566 (see Amanda Milin, (1994) 7 JCL 76).
164. Cf *Higgons v Burton* (1857) 26 LJ Ex 342; *Morrison v Robertson* 1908 SC 332; *Roache v Australian Mercantile Land & Finance Co Ltd* (1964) 64 SR (NSW) 307. And see *Lake v Simmons* [1927] AC 487.
165. (1897) 14 TLR 98.
166. (1878) 3 App Cas 459 (see [1241]).
167. But see the approach taken in s 8 of New Zealand's *Contractual Mistakes Act* 1977, which prevents any order under the Act from affecting innocent third party purchasers for value or their successors in title.

Mistake as to identity — parties face to face

[1244] General. Mistake as to identity can occur not only where a contract is made by correspondence, or on the telephone, but also where it is made inter praesentes, that is, in the presence of each other. In such cases a rogue deals face to face with the plaintiff, misrepresenting his or her identity, or his or her qualifications or characteristics. A distinction has been suggested between these two classes of misrepresentations, the suggestion being that the former will prevent the victim's offer from being accepted by the rogue so as to create a contract, whereas the latter will merely render the contract voidable. A distinction has also been made between misrepresentations which induce the victim to contract and those which merely induce the victim to extend credit terms to the rogue, or to give the rogue immediate possession of goods.

The cases are impossible to reconcile, but it is suggested that since it is the victim's apparent intention to contract with the person physically present, there exists a sufficient element of assent on which a contract can come into being, albeit a contract voidable at the instance of the representee.

A starting point for analysis of these cases is the undoubted presumption that where parties appear to contract, there is a contract between the parties. In order for that presumption to be rebutted there must be admissible evidence that there was no such intention.

[1245] Cases in which the 'contract' has been held void. The decision in *Lake v Simmons*[168] turned on whether a jeweller had 'entrusted' necklets to a 'customer', as those words were used in an exception clause in the jeweller's insurance policy. The person who obtained the necklets was a woman who claimed to represent her husband (he had no knowledge of the matter) and her sister's husband (sister and husband were fictitious). It was held by the House of Lords that the jeweller's intention was not to entrust to or deal *with her as his customer* and that there was no contract between them.[169]

In *Ingram v Little*[170] two sisters, Elsie and Hilda Ingram, and a Miss Badger with whom they lived, advertised their car for sale. A swindler called on the sisters. After a drive in the car they agreed on a price of £717. Elsie declined to accept payment by cheque and would only sell for cash. She said that the deal was finished and made as to walk out of the room. The man said he was 'Mr P G M Hutchinson' and lived at Stanstead House, Stanstead Road, Caterham. While the others continued talking, Hilda went to the local post office and returned saying that she had checked that name and address in the phone directory. Elsie then agreed to accept payment by cheque and the car was handed over. Within a few days the rogue sold the car to the defendant, who purchased in good faith. The

---

168. [1927] AC 487.
169. Viscount Haldane quoted from the French jurist Pothier ([1927] AC 487 at 501) and application of the civil law principle led to a strange result in *Sowler v Potter* [1940] 1 KB 271. See also *Dennant v Skinner & Collom* [1948] 2 KB 164, where the sale was by auction.
170. [1961] 1 QB 31.

rogue's cheque was dishonoured, and as he could not be found the plaintiffs sued the defendant to recover the car or its value.

There was a division of opinion in the English Court of Appeal which held (Devlin LJ dissenting) that there was no contract with the rogue. The majority acknowledged that in the case of contracts made face to face there is a presumption that each intends to deal with the person physically present, and that the presumption can be rebutted only by clear evidence. Reference was made to the fact that any agreement to sell which may have been made immediately after the drive in the car was expressly repudiated by Elsie when the rogue showed his intention not to pay by cash, and that the subsequent discussion and agreement proceeded only on the footing that the sisters were dealing with P G M Hutchinson. Both inquired whether the rogue should have understood the plaintiffs as intending to sell to him and, as was inevitable, answered in the negative.

[1246] Cases in which the contract has been held to be voidable. In *Phillips v Brooks Ltd*,[171] one North visited the plaintiff jeweller's shop and selected pearls and an emerald ring. While writing out his cheque he said, 'You will see who I am: I am Sir George Bullough' and gave his address as in St James' Square. The plaintiff had heard of Sir George Bullough as a man of means and checked in a directory that the address given was correct. The plaintiff allowed North to take the ring away. North pledged the ring with the unsuspecting defendant pawnbrokers.

The cheque was returned by the bank marked 'no account' and North was convicted of obtaining the ring from the plaintiff by false pretences. The plaintiff sued the pawnbrokers for the return of the ring or its value, and claimed damages in tort for its detention. He gave evidence that he thought he was contracting with Sir George Bullough, that if he had known who the man really was he would not have let him have the ring, and that he did not intend to deal with anyone other than Sir George Bullough. However, Horridge J held that this uncontradicted evidence of the plaintiff's subjective intention did not conclude the matter. He inferred that the plaintiff intended to deal with the person physically present in his shop, but that he would not have done so but for the fraudulent misrepresentations. The contract was voidable only, and the property in the ring passed to North who could effectively pass it on to anyone who acquired the ring in good faith, for value and without notice of the fraud, before any attempt by the plaintiff to avoid the contract.[172]

In *Lewis v Averay*[173] a swindler, after inspecting and driving the plaintiff's car which had been advertised for sale in the newspaper, identified himself to the plaintiff and his fiancée as Richard Greene, star of the television series 'Robin Hood'. After a price of £450 was agreed, he wrote out a cheque for that amount and signed it, 'R A Green'. He wanted to take the

---

171. [1919] 2 KB 243. See also *Fawcett v Star Car Sales Ltd* [1960] NZLR 406.
172. In *Lake v Simmons* [1927] AC 487 Viscount Haldane distinguished *Phillips v Brooks Ltd* as a case in which the jeweller intended to deal with the person whom he identified by sight and hearing in his shop, the rogue's misrepresentation being only as to payment and merely rendering voidable the right to delivery in advance of payment.
173. [1972] 1 QB 198.

car at once. The plaintiff asked for proof of identity. The rogue produced a special admission pass to Pinewood Studios with an official stamp on it. It bore the name 'Richard A Green', an address and a photograph of the rogue. Lewis handed over the car, the log book, a Ministry of Transport test certificate and a receipt for £450 in favour of 'Richard A Green'.

The rogue sold the car to an unsuspecting Averay. After the bank told Lewis that the cheque was worthless (the rogue had stolen a cheque book and written on a cheque from it) Lewis sued Averay in tort for conversion of the car. The English Court of Appeal unanimously held that there was a contract, albeit a voidable one. Since it had not been avoided prior to the time of the contract between the rogue and Averay, the latter obtained a good title to the vehicle.[174] Lord Denning MR and Phillimore LJ thought that there was nothing to rebut the presumption of an intention to deal with the person physically present. Megaw LJ decided for the defendant on the ground that Lewis had failed to prove that he had regarded the identity of the person before him as a matter of vital importance: he viewed the mistake as one going to a mere attribute of the rogue, namely, his creditworthiness.

In a forthright manner, the Master of the Rolls condemned fine distinctions between fraudulent misrepresentations which induce the making of a contract and those made after contract which induce a seller to part with possession; and between mistakes as to identity and those as to attributes. He said:[175]

> As I listened to the argument in this case, I felt it wrong that an innocent purchaser (who knew nothing of what passed between the seller and the rogue) should have his title depend on such refinements. After all, he has acted with complete circumspection and in entire good faith: whereas it was the seller who let the rogue have the goods and thus enabled him to commit the fraud. I do not, therefore, accept the theory that a mistake as to identity renders a contract void. I think the true principle is that which underlies the decision of this court in *King's Norton Metal Co Ltd v Edridge Merrett & Co Ltd*[176] and of Horridge J in *Phillips v Brooks Ltd*[177] which has stood for these last 50 years. It is this: When two parties have come to a contract — or rather what appears, on the face of it, to be a contract — the fact that one party is mistaken as to the identity of the other does not mean that there is no contract, or that the contract is a nullity and void from the beginning. It only means that the contract is voidable, that is, liable to be set aside at the instance of the mistaken person, so long as he does so before third parties have in good faith acquired rights under it.

[1247] Australian cases. There have been surprisingly few Australian cases on mistake as to identity. In *Porter v Latec Finance (Qld) Pty Ltd*,[178] Kitto J touched on the matter inconclusively. Windeyer J referred to the 'now somewhat shaky' authority[179] of *Phillips v Brooks Ltd*,[180] to 'the real or

---

174. Contrast *Car and Universal Finance Co Ltd v Caldwell* [1965] 1 QB 525 (see [1040], [1053]).
175. [1972] 1 QB 198 at 207.
176. (1897) 14 TLR 98.
177. [1919] 2 KB 243.
178. (1964) 111 CLR 177.
179. Presumably in the light of the then recent English Court of Appeal decision in *Ingram v Little* [1961] 1 QB 31.

supposed distinction between a unilateral mistake as to the identity of a person and a unilateral mistake as to his attributes' as lying 'at the root of the matter',[181] and to *Ingram v Little*[182] as showing how readily the same facts in this area may be susceptible of more than one interpretation. Three points must be made:

(1) the judgments of Kitto and Windeyer JJ were dissenting judgments;

(2) they were delivered before Lord Denning, at least, had cast doubt on the correctness of *Ingram v Little* in *Lewis v Averay*;[183] and

(3) the facts were not in the mould of the three English cases.

[1248] **Reconciling the cases — the search for a principle.** A distinction based on the termination of the initial dealing is too fine to be a satisfactory ground for decision in such cases. All the cases have too much in common. What is necessary is a principle that embraces the facts that the victim always has the intentions *both* of dealing with the person identified by sight and hearing *and* of dealing with the person whose identity that person has appropriated.

There is much force in Lord Denning's criticism of *Ingram v Little*[184] in *Lewis v Averay*.[185] The process of categorising a contract according to whether the identity of the other contracting party enters as an element and then inquiring into the deceived party's subjective state of mind is foreign to the mainstream of the common law and is inconsistent with most of the other English cases studied, such as *King's Norton Metal Co Ltd v Edridge Merrett & Co Ltd*.[186] Indeed, if it is correct to have regard to whether the representor is telling the truth, it is difficult to see why other forms of fraud do not render contracts void. The answer, of course, is that the representor's fraud is merely a proper basis for rescission of the contract, and not a sufficient ground for concluding that the contract was void. Moreover, in *Lewis v Averay* Megaw LJ did not accept the test propounded by the majority in *Ingram v Little*, that is, whether the rogue ought to have interpreted the promise as addressed to him or her. But he did accept the distinction between a mistake as to the rogue's *identity* made when the offer was made which the victim at that time regarded as of vital importance, and a mistake as to the rogue's *attributes*, such as creditworthiness. Although we agree with his criticism of *Ingram v Little*, we do not regard Megaw LJ's distinction as helpful.

Bearing in mind that there is no authoritative decision of the High Court in this area we accept, but with one qualification, Lord Denning's analysis in *Lewis v Averay* as correct. It is consistent with Australian cases in the context of rescission for unilateral mistake as to terms.[187] The one qualification is that the mere 'appearance' of a contract is not sufficient if

---

180. [1919] 2 KB 243.
181. (1964) 111 CLR 177 at 200.
182. [1961] 1 QB 31 (see [1245]).
183. [1972] 1 QB 198 (see [1246]).
184. [1961] 1 QB 31 (see [1245]).
185. [1972] 1 QB 198 at 207 (see [1246]). See also his deprecation (at 206) of reliance on principles of the civil law (but cf *Smith v Wheatcroft* (1878) 9 Ch D 223 at 230).
186. (1897) 14 TLR 98 (see [1243]).
187. See [1254].

there is in fact no agreement. In other words, the perspective of an impartial bystander looking down from above cannot be applied to impose a contract where none otherwise exists.

Unilateral mistake as to terms

[1249] General. It is not every unilateral mistake of which the other party is aware that will entitle the mistaken party to relief. A seller of goods may know that the buyer is mistaken as to their qualities and value, yet is entitled to remain silent and, since no representation has been a cause of the mistake, enforce the contract.[188] The proposition that one contracting party cannot rely on the other to look after his or her interests, suggested by the maxim caveat emptor ('buyer beware'), is of general application.

Assume that A sells a motor car to B, knowing that it is a 1999 model. If B buys believing that it is a 2000 model, B's mistake will not affect the validity of the contract whether it was known to A or not. What was sold and bought was 'A's motor car'. If the car had been bought and sold as 'A's 2000 model motor car' once again the validity of the contract would not have been affected but A would have breached a term of it by tendering in performance a car which did not correspond to the contract description.

[1250] Smith v Hughes. *Smith v Hughes*[189] is an important illustration of the early common law's treatment of unilateral mistake which, however, may need to be reconsidered in Australia in the light of the High Court's decision in *Taylor v Johnson*.[190]

A seller sued his buyer for the price of oats sold and also for damages for non-acceptance of other oats. The seller was a farmer and the defendant an owner and trainer of racehorses. The plaintiff offered to sell oats and exhibited a sample. The defendant took the sample, and wrote saying that he would take the oats at 34 shillings per quarter. Afterwards he refused to accept the oats tendered on the ground that they were 'new', whereas he thought he was buying 'old' oats. The price was high for new oats, but oats were scarce at the time. The county court judge left two questions to the jury. First, was the word 'old' used in the conversation between the plaintiff and the defendant's manager? Second, if not, did the plaintiff believe that the defendant believed, or was under the impression that he was contracting to purchase, old oats? In either of these cases he directed the jury to find for the defendant. The jury gave a general verdict for the defendant rather than specific answers to these two questions. The issue on the appeal was whether the judge's direction was correct.

Insofar as it related to the first ground, the direction was held correct, but it could not be known that the jurors had all proceeded on this ground. The question therefore was whether the direction was also correct in relation to the second ground. The Court of Queen's Bench held that it was not. Cockburn CJ considered that the passive acquiescence of the seller in the

---

188. Subject, as always, to the impact of statutory prohibitions discussed in Chapter 11.
189. (1871) LR 6 QB 597. See also *London Holeproof Hosiery Co v Padmore* (1928) 44 TLR 499.
190. (1983) 151 CLR 422 (see [1222], [1231], [1254]).

self-deception of the buyer did not entitle the latter to avoid the contract. He said:[191]

> If, indeed, the buyer, instead of acting on his own opinion, had asked the question whether the oats were old or new, or had said anything which intimated his understanding that the seller was selling the oats as old oats, the case would have been wholly different; or even if he had said anything which shewed that he was not acting on his own inspection and judgment, but assumed as the foundation of the contract that the oats were old, the silence of the seller, as a means of misleading him, might have amounted to a fraudulent concealment, such as would have entitled the buyer to avoid the contract. Here, however, nothing of the sort occurs. The buyer in no way refers to the seller, but acts entirely on his own judgment.

In dealing with the contention that the plaintiff intended to sell new oats and the defendant to buy old oats, so that there was no consensus ad idem, the Chief Justice added:[192]

> This argument proceeds on the fallacy of confounding what was merely a motive operating on the buyer to induce him to buy with one of the essential conditions of the contract. Both parties were agreed as to the sale and purchase of this particular parcel of oats. The defendant believed the oats to be old, and was thus induced to agree to buy them, but he omitted to make their age a condition of the contract. All that can be said is, that the two minds were not ad idem as to the age of the oats; they certainly were ad idem as to the sale and purchase of them. Suppose a person to buy a horse without a warranty, believing him to be sound, and the horse turns out unsound, could it be contended that it would be open to him to say that, as he had intended to buy a sound horse, and the seller to sell an unsound one, the contract was void, because the seller must have known from the price the buyer was willing to give, or from his general habits as a buyer of horses, that he thought the horse was sound? The cases are exactly parallel.

In similar vein, and in an important passage, Blackburn J said in relation to the second direction:[193]

> I doubt whether the direction would bring to the minds of the jury the distinction between agreeing to take the oats under the belief that they were old, and agreeing to take the oats under the belief that the plaintiff contracted that they were old.
>
> The difference is the same as that between buying a horse believed to be sound, and buying one believed to be warranted sound; but I doubt if it was made obvious to the jury, and I doubt this the more because I do not see much evidence to justify a finding for the defendant on the latter ground if the word 'old' was not used.

Hannen J's judgment was similar. He said:[194]

> In order to relieve the defendant it was necessary that the jury should find not merely that the plaintiff believed the defendant to believe that he was buying old oats, but that he believed the defendant to believe that he, the plaintiff was contracting to sell old oats.

---

191. (1871) LR 6 QB 597 at 605.
192. (1871) LR 6 QB 597 at 606.
193. (1871) LR 6 QB 597 at 608.
194. (1871) LR 6 QB 597 at 611.

[1250]

He thought that although the direction in relation to the second ground was correct in its terms, the jury did not understand it in the sense which he described in the passage quoted.

The importance of *Smith v Hughes* lies in the distinction drawn between unilateral mistake as to the offer or acceptance intended, and unilateral mistake as to collateral, albeit fundamental, matters.

[1251] **'Snapping up offer'.** A particular class of case which illustrates unilateral mistake as to the terms intended, known to the other party, is that in which an offer which would be very advantageous to the offeree is 'snapped up' by the offeree.[195] In such cases, the terms of the offer are clear and unambiguous and the offeree accepts the offer according to its true sense. The difficulty is that it must have been obvious that the offeror did not intend to make an offer in those terms. In *Hartog v Colin & Shields*[196] there was a contract to sell 30,000 Argentine hare skins. The offer was mistakenly stated as being at a price *per pound*, the sellers' intention having been to offer at the same price *per piece*. The value of a pound of the skin was approximately three times that of a piece. Moreover, the preliminary negotiations had proceeded on the footing that the price would be at so much per piece and there was evidence of a trade custom to fix the price by reference to a piece. In the buyer's action for damages for non-delivery, the judge found that the buyer could not reasonably have supposed that the offer expressed the sellers' intention, and so his snapping up their offer did not create a contract: 'The offer was wrongly expressed, and the defendants by their evidence, and by the correspondence, have satisfied me that the plaintiff could not reasonably have supposed that that offer contained the offerors' real intention.'[197]

It is not a necessary element that the party seeking to enforce the contract has actively contributed to the mistake. Rather, the knowledge that the offer is not meant according to its literal terms simply displaces the rationale of the objective theory of contract, and allows the absence of a subjective consensus to prevent contract formation. In contrast to situations of common mistake, the invalidity cannot be explained on the ground of an implied term based upon the imputed intention of the parties, since the unmistaken party is actually seeking to take advantage of the other's mistake and cannot realistically be taken as agreeing that it is a condition precedent to the contract's effectiveness that the position is as understood by the mistaken party.

A mistaken party will not often be able to discharge the onus of showing that the other party knew or must have known that he or she intended terms different from the terms of the offer or acceptance.[198]

---

195. The expression 'snapped at an offer' comes from James LJ in *Tamplin v James* (1880) 15 Ch D 215 at 221.
196. [1939] 3 All ER 566.
197. [1939] 3 All ER 566 at 568.
198. It is, moreover, not easy to reconcile these cases with *Taylor v Johnson* (1983) 151 CLR 422 (see [1254]).

Rescission for Unilateral Mistake

[1252] General. Equitable principles and remedies may be used to give effect to the treatment of a contract void (or avoided) for unilateral mistake, for example, by declaration and consequential orders by way of adjustment. It is also possible, in cases where the contract is neither void nor voidable, that an order for specific performance would be refused on equitable grounds.[199]

The important question is whether there are circumstances, falling short of those which would render a contract void or voidable under the principles discussed above, but which might induce equity to grant relief by setting the contract aside on the basis of a unilateral mistake.

[1253] Knowledge of the mistake. A contract may be set aside for a unilateral mistake which was not effective to render the contract void or voidable at common law if the plaintiff contributed to the mistake.[200]

There is also a line of authority, suggesting that the unmistaken party may be given the choice between suffering a rescission and having the contract rectified so as to accord with the mistaken party's understanding.[201]

[1254] Unconscionable conduct. If the cases are based on a general principle it is that a mistaken party may be accorded the right of rescission, or at least an ability to approach the court for an order setting aside the contract, even though the contract is neither void nor voidable under the principles derived from the common law, where it would be unconscionable for the other party to enforce the contract according to its terms. Knowledge of the mistake, contribution to the mistaken party's belief (falling short of misrepresentation), or steps by which the party with knowledge deprives the mistaken party of the opportunity to discover the true facts may, depending on the circumstances, be sufficient grounds for setting aside the contract.

In *Taylor v Johnson*[202] the High Court had to deal with a written contract for the sale of some ten acres of land. The price stated was $15,000. The vendor gave evidence that she believed and contracted on the basis that the contract provided for a price of $15,000 per acre ($150,000 in total). There was evidence that under its zoning at the time of contract, the value of the land was approximately $65,000 and that if a proposed rezoning became effective, its value would be approximately $195,000. Since the purchasers sought specific performance, and the vendor sought rectification, alternatively an order setting aside the contract of sale, the issues between the parties fell to be decided on equitable rather than common law

---

199. See [2411]. In some cases where the mistake goes to the defendant's ability to perform the contract according to its terms, the court has ordered performance to the extent possible. See *Burrows v Scammell* (1881) 19 Ch D 175; *Preston v Luck* (1881) 27 Ch 497.
200. See *Torrance v Bolton* (1872) 8 Ch App 118; *Australia Hotel Co Ltd v Moore* (1899) 20 LR (NSW) Eq 155; *Riverlate Properties Ltd v Paul* [1975] Ch 133; *Trans Realties Pty Ltd v Grbac* [1975] 1 NSWLR 170. But cf *Hickman v Berens* [1895] 2 Ch 638.
201. See [1266].
202. (1983) 151 CLR 422.

principles. In their joint judgment, Mason ACJ, Murphy and Deane JJ accepted that it is the objective rather than the subjective theory of contract which properly determines whether a contract has been made, with the consequence that a contracting party cannot rely on his or her own mistake to say that the contract was void ab initio, even if the fact in question was fundamental, and if the other party knew of the mistake.

In saying this, they adopted[203] dicta in the judgment of Denning LJ in *Solle v Butcher*.[204] As they noted, Lord Denning's judgment had been referred to with approval in earlier High Court cases concerning common mistake. They were prepared to apply it to a unilateral mistake in relation to the terms of a formal contract of sale.[205] Having held that the contract was valid, Mason ACJ, Murphy and Deane JJ had to consider 'the basis upon which relief in equity is available from the contractual consequences of unilateral mistake'.[206] They accepted that the basis of equity's jurisdiction to set aside a contract for unilateral mistake was equity's ordinary jurisdiction to deal with any instrument or other transaction in which enforcement of a party's legal rights would be 'unconscientious'. In their view, where one party to a contract is under a mistake as to the terms or subject matter of the contract, 'special circumstances' would ordinarily need to be shown before the requisite unconscientiousness could be established.[207]

Mason ACJ, Murphy and Deane JJ stated the following proposition as appropriate and adequate for disposing of the case:[208]

> [A] party who has entered into a written contract under a serious mistake about its contents in relation to a fundamental term will be entitled in equity to an order rescinding the contract if the other party is aware that circumstances exist which indicate that the first party is entering the contract under some serious mistake or misapprehension about either the content or subject matter of that term and deliberately sets out to ensure that the first party does not become aware of the existence of his mistake or misapprehension.

They thought that the proposition had a broad basis of support in the authorities and was 'calculated to do justice' between contracting parties. They added that, for present purposes, their proposition could be limited to cases where there has been no material alteration of position by the non-mistaken party and where the rights of third parties had not intervened. On the facts, the contract could be rescinded because of the nature of the vendor's mistake *and* the purchasers' unconscionable conduct in deliberately ensuring that the vendor did not become aware of her mistake.[209]

---

203. (1983) 151 CLR 422 at 429.
204. [1950] 1 KB 671 at 691 (see [1218]).
205. (1983) 151 CLR 422 at 430. It would seem to follow that where a written offer is snapped up (see [1251]) the contract is not void.
206. (1983) 151 CLR 422 at 431.
207. Cf *Logwon Pty Ltd v Warringah Shire Council* (1993) 33 NSWLR 13 at 32.
208. (1983) 151 CLR 422 at 432. In his dissenting judgment, Dawson J referred (at 444) to 'fraud, misrepresentation or, perhaps, sharp practice, falling short of actual fraud' as a sufficient basis for rescission in equity, but thought that this was not established by the trial judge's findings. See also *Easyfind (NSW) Pty Ltd v Paterson* (1987) 11 NSWLR 98.

Since Mason ACJ, Murphy and Deane JJ 'left to another day' the question whether Lord Denning's dictum applied to informal contracts such as those involved in *Smith v Hughes*[210] and *Hartog v Colin & Shields*,[211] their judgment does not touch on the correctness of the position at common law as expounded in those cases. Moreover, *Taylor v Johnson* was not a mistake of identity case, and the correctness of cases such as *Cundy v Lindsay*[212] and *Ingram v Little*[213] is also unresolved. It might also be mentioned that although the particular species of objective contract theory[214] which characterised Lord Denning's judgments was given prominence, an integral part of the decision in *Taylor v Johnson* was that it was open to the vendor to gave evidence of (and to rely upon) her subjective belief.

Restrictions on Rescission for Mistake

[1255] **Applicability of the rules of misrepresentation.** We saw in Chapter 10 that there are certain restrictions on the right of a person to rescind a contract for misrepresentation.[215] By and large the same restrictions apply to cases of rescission for mistake.[216]

Both judgments in *Svanosio v McNamara*[217] noted that even if the case had otherwise been a proper one for the exercise of equitable jurisdiction, there was a question whether restitutio in integrum was still possible. In *Solle v Butcher*[218] the English Court of Appeal set aside an executed lease for common mistake and Denning LJ suggested that the observations of Joyce J in *Seddon v North Eastern Salt Co Ltd*[219] that an executed contract could not be rescinded for innocent misrepresentation had lost authority since Scrutton LJ had cast doubt on them in *Lever Bros Ltd v Bell*.[220] The High Court did not have to deal with this matter in *Svanosio v McNamara* but considered that at least an ordinary contract for the *sale* of land, once executed, cannot be rescinded either for misrepresentation or for mistake in the absence of fraud, or (in effect) a total failure of consideration.

---

209. Dawson J, who dissented, would have held that the finding of the trial judge (Powell J) that the purchaser's belief at the time of contracting was that the vendor intended to sell for a total price of $15,000, should have been accepted by the New South Wales Court of Appeal, with the consequential making of an order for specific performance.
210. (1871) LR 6 QB 597 (see [1250]).
211. [1939] 3 All ER 566 (see [1251]).
212. (1878) 3 App Cas 459 (see [1241]).
213. [1961] 1 QB 31 (see [1245]).
214. See [112] ('fly on the wall' theory).
215. See generally [1042]–[1062].
216. As to partial rescission (see [1045]) see *Tutt v Doyle* (1997) 42 NSWLR 10 at 12–13.
217. (1956) 96 CLR 186 (see [1218]).
218. [1950] 1 KB 671.
219. [1905] 1 Ch 326 (see [1054]).
220. [1931] 1 KB 557 at 588.

Rectification

General

[1256] Equitable remedy for correction of instruments. The common law courts had no power to order that errors in instruments be rectified, but the courts of equity took to themselves such a jurisdiction. Assume that A contracts to sell land to B and that due to an oversight by the parties the instrument of conveyance which they execute to give effect to the contract erroneously contains or omits some words or figures with the result that it does not accord with the contract. On the application of one party rectification of the instrument will be ordered, notwithstanding opposition from the party benefited by the error. This example shows that rectification is not concerned solely with contracts: the remedy is concerned with *documents*, not contracts. Of course, our concern is with contract documents and contract related instruments.

Rectification refers to mistakes in instruments and is an order that an instrument be 'rectified' or 'reformed' so that the mistake in it will be eliminated. Rectification is available to reform the parties' document, and not to reform the parties' bargain. It is an equitable remedy which has, until quite recently, been associated exclusively with cases of common mistake. Certainly mistake by one party, without more, will not be a ground for rectification: some implication of the unmistaken party is necessary. On this basis, however, the remedy now extends to some cases of unilateral mistake.[221]

Rectification is retrospective in effect. Therefore, the instrument is to be read as if originally executed in its rectified form.[222]

[1257] Dangers associated with rectification. If rectification were available only where there was a legally enforceable contract antecedent to the defective instrument, the jurisdiction would be a limited one. On the other hand, there are dangers in ordering rectification too readily.

First it seems reasonable that the court should not give one party legally enforceable rights against the other which the former did not previously have.

Second, often an instrument sought to be rectified will not merely be a formal expression or outworking of legal rights which have themselves been deliberately and carefully reduced to writing (as in the contract-conveyance illustration above), but will mark, for the first time, the reaching of agreement itself. In these circumstances it can reasonably be contended that apart from the instrument there is no enforceable agreement and so no standard against which it can be determined whether the instrument is erroneous.

---

221. See [1264]–[1266].
222. *Malmesbury (Earl) v Malmesbury (Countess)* (1862) 31 Beav 407 at 418; 54 ER 1196 at 1200; *Walker v Armstrong* (1856) 8 De G M & G 531 at 544; 44 ER 495 at 500; *Issa v Berisha* [1981] 1 NSWLR 261.

[1258] Bars to rectification. Rectification and specific performance of a contract as rectified may be sought in the one proceeding;[223] and an order for rectification can justify a prior discharge of the contract for breach of the contractual terms as rectified.[224]

The usual discretionary bars to equitable remedies such as laches are available in respect of rectification. Other bars to rectification are acquisition of rights for value by an innocent third party under the contract in its original form,[225] and that the contract is no longer capable of being performed.[226] Apparently, it is no bar that the party seeking rectification had sought to enforce the contract in its original form.[227]

Nature of Agreement Relied Upon and Relevant Intention

[1259] Continuing common intention sufficient. It used to be said that there must have been a concluded and binding contract antecedent to execution of the instrument sought to be rectified.[228] It is understandable that the courts have referred to the heavy onus on a plaintiff seeking rectification, but the law is not now so stringent.

First, if the prior agreement is a contract, it need not be enforceable as such. For example, in *United States v Motor Trucks Ltd*[229] the Privy Council ordered rectification of a deed from a schedule to which certain lands and buildings were omitted, notwithstanding that the agreement was *unenforceable* insofar as it related to those lands for lack of a written memorandum satisfying the *Statute of Frauds* 1677 (Imp).

Second, it is now established that there need be no prior agreement, so long as there is a continuing common intention. *Shipley UDC v Bradford Corp*[230] concerned an alleged contract between two bodies corporate which could not make a contract of the type in question except under seal, yet Clauson J ordered rectification.[231] He was followed in *Crane v Hegeman-Harris Co Inc*[232] by Simonds J who observed that the opposing view would produce the strange result that the parties would be bound to an instrument by a mistake to which they had equally contributed. In *Slee v Warke*[233] the High Court adopted his view that rectification can be ordered

---

223. *Craddock Bros v Hunt* [1922] 2 Ch 809; [1923] 2 Ch 136; *United States v Motor Trucks Ltd* [1924] AC 196.
224. *Tydhof v Miethke* (1982), unreported, SC (Qld) (Connolly J), 3 June.
225. *Garrard v Frankel* (1862) 30 Beav 445; 54 ER 961; *Smith v Jones* [1954] 2 All ER 823; *J J Leonard Properties Pty Ltd v Leonard (WA) Pty Ltd (No 2)* (1987) 13 ACLR 77.
226. *Borrowman v Rossel* (1864) 16 CB (NS) 58; 143 ER 1045.
227. *Market Terminal Pty Ltd v Dominion Insurance Co of Australia* [1982] 1 NSWLR 105.
228. See *Mackenzie v Coulson* (1869) LR 8 Eq 368 at 375; *United States v Motor Trucks Ltd* [1924] AC 196 at 200; *Australian Gypsum Ltd v Hume Steel Ltd* (1930) 45 CLR 54 at 63, 64.
229. [1924] AC 196.
230. [1937] Ch 375.
231. Cf *Issa v Berisha* [1981] 1 NSWLR 261 (contract void for uncertainty).
232. [1939] 1 All ER 662 at 664 (affirmed [1939] 4 All ER 68).
233. (1949) 86 CLR 271.

of an instrument which does not give effect in some respect to 'the concurrent intention of the parties existing at the date of its execution',[234] even though a previously existing binding contract cannot be proved. The test of 'common intention continuing down to execution of the contract' has been adopted by the High Court.[235]

[1260] Intention that instrument express whole agreement. Assume that the parties have agreed on points 1 to 9, and that the instrument contains only points 1 to 7. In order to obtain rectification the plaintiff must show that the parties intended by the instrument to give effect to points 8 and 9 of the antecedent agreement in respect of which rectification is sought.[236] There may, in fact, be a number of objections to a conclusion that the instrument should be rectified to include those points. It may not have been intended that points 8 and 9 be legally binding at all. It may have been intended that they be legally binding but not by reason of being included in the instrument in question.

[1261] Intention must be as to content of instrument. The common intention which must be proved is usually expressed in terms requiring that the instrument take a certain form, as distinct from a common understanding that it would have a certain effect. In *Pukallus v Cameron*[237] a contract for the sale of land described the land as 'subdivision 1 of Portion 1154'. The parties believed that an area of some 27 acres containing a bore and cultivation lay within the land so described, but in truth it lay within the remainder of Portion 1154 which was being retained by the vendor. The contract was completed by conveyance and the purchasers took possession of the disputed area. The truth was not discovered until some 20 months later when a survey was carried out. The High Court held that the purchasers had not established a common intention that the instrument should provide for anything other than a sale of subdivision 1 of Portion 1154. There was no evidence of an intention to contract for the sale of the bore and cultivated area; rather the intention was to contract for the sale of subdivision 1 of Portion 1154 which the parties erroneously believed included the bore and cultivated area.

The high water mark of the thesis that the relevant intention is that the instrument take a certain form, rather than achieve a certain effect or result is *Frederick E Rose (London) Ltd v William H Pim Junior & Co Ltd*.[238] The parties made an oral agreement for the sale of 'horsebeans', and the subsequent written contract used the same word. The parties mistakenly believed that 'horsebeans' were 'feveroles'. This was a fundamental mistake as to the nature of the subject matter of the contract, yet the court declined

---

234. (1949) 86 CLR 271 at 280.
235. See *Hooker Town Developments Pty Ltd v Director of War Service Homes* (1973) 47 ALJR 320 at 323–4; *Maralinga Pty Ltd v Major Enterprises Pty Ltd* (1973) 128 CLR 336 at 350; 1 ALR 169; *Pukallus v Cameron* (1982) 180 CLR 447 at 452, 456; 43 ALR 243. See also *Australasian Performing Right Association Ltd v Austarama Television Pty Ltd* [1972] 2 NSWLR 467 at 472–5; *Bishopsgate Insurance Australia Ltd v Commonwealth Engineering (NSW) Pty Ltd* [1981] 1 NSWLR 429.
236. *Maralinga Pty Ltd v Major Enterprises Pty Ltd* (1973) 128 CLR 336. See also *RACV Investment Co Pty Ltd v Silbury Pty Ltd* (1986) 13 ACLR 555 at 558–9.
237. (1982) 180 CLR 447.
238. [1953] 2 QB 450.

to rectify the contract, by making it refer to 'horsebeans of the feverole type', because the written contract did not depart at all from the oral agreement. Denning LJ said that rectification is 'concerned with contracts and documents, not with intentions. In order to get rectification it is necessary to show that the parties were in complete agreement on the terms of their contract, but by an error wrote them down wrongly'.[239]

Although these cases, particularly *Rose v Pim*, show that 'common intention as to what an instrument shall say' is not to be equated with 'common belief or understanding as to what effect an instrument shall produce', the more recent cases indicate that rectification may sometimes be ordered where the relevant mistake is as to the legal effect of the agreed terms, rather than their form.[240] Thus, in *Winks v W H Heck & Sons Pty Ltd*[241] the parties to a contract for the sale of land intended that the purchaser's ownership should be subject to the rights of a third party to whom the vendor had sold timber growing on the land. The contract contained a term acknowledging that the purchaser was aware of the third party's interest. The parties believed that this was effective to preserve the third party's rights. In law it did not have this effect. The person who drafted the contract did not give effect to the common intention of the parties and rectification was ordered, even though (as was conceded) the parties' mistake was as to the meaning of the words used.[242] The position would have been different if the document had been adopted as superseding or overriding their original intention.[243] More recently, in *Commissioner of Stamp Duties (NSW) v Carlenka Pty Ltd*[244] the New South Wales Court of Appeal held that where it was intended that an amendment to a deed should achieve a particular legal effect, but the instrument by inadvertence achieved an unintended result, the fact that there was an intention to execute the deed as drafted did not prevent rectification being ordered.

Proof of Intention

[1262] Standard of proof. The courts have often emphasised that the plaintiff's onus of proving that an instrument assented to which differs from the form which, according to the parties' common intention, it was meant to take, is a heavy one. Various expressions have been used in the cases, including:[245]

---

239. [1953] 2 QB 450 at 461.
240. The requirements for rectification may be more difficult to satisfy in such a case. See *Bush v National Australia Bank Ltd* (1992) 35 NSWLR 390 at 406–8 per Hodgson J (expressing the view that rectification will not be refused merely because the mistake is as to legal effect).
241. [1986] 1 Qd R 226. See also *NSW Medical Defence Union Ltd v Transport Industries Insurance Co Ltd* (1986) 6 NSWLR 740.
242. But cf *Bacchus Marsh Concentrated Milk Co Ltd v Joseph Nathan & Co Ltd* (1919) 26 CLR 410 at 451 (dictum questioning such an approach).
243. See *Maralinga Pty Ltd v Major Enterprises Pty Ltd* (1973) 128 CLR 336.
244. (1995) 41 NSWLR 329 at 332, 335, 344. See also *Permanent Trustee Australia Ltd v FAI General Insurance Co Ltd* (1998) 44 NSWLR 186 at 231; 153 ALR 529 per Hodgson CJ in Eq (substance must dominate form).

- 'irrefragable';
- 'beyond all reasonable doubt';
- 'convincing proof';
- 'very strong proof'; and
- 'clear proof'.

However, it is a 'question of fact and degree what weight of evidence is needed to overcome the inherent probability that the parties meant what they wrote and to establish that contrary to it the parties did not mean what they wrote'.[246] For example, rectification will be more readily ordered if it was the duty of the defendant rather than the plaintiff to draw up the instrument.[247]

[1263] External manifestation of intention not required. In several cases the courts have said that there must have been some 'manifestation or disclosure by words or conduct' or 'outward expression' of the accord which the subsequent instrument fails to express.[248] But the view that, as a matter of law, the parties' common intention must have been outwardly manifested has been challenged.[249]

In view of the clear and convincing evidence which a plaintiff seeking rectification must adduce,[250] lack of any outward manifestation of the required common intention may well signify that the party seeking rectification will not be able to discharge the onus of proof. Although in most cases it is difficult to see how a plaintiff can succeed without evidence of a manifested common intention, there are distinctions between what must be proven, how proof is adduced and how convincingly the common intention must be proved. The existence of an antecedent contract is no longer required.[251] It is suggested that the law does not require an outward manifestation of accord, and that it suffices that the plaintiff proves, even

---

245. See, eg *Australian Gypsum Ltd v Hume Steel Ltd* (1930) 45 CLR 54 at 64; *Slee v Warke* (1949) 86 CLR 271 at 281; *Maralinga Pty Ltd v Major Enterprises Pty Ltd* (1973) 128 CLR 336 at 349; *Bishopsgate Insurance Australia Ltd v Commonwealth Engineering (NSW) Pty Ltd* [1981] 1 NSWLR 429 at 431; *Pukallus v Cameron* (1982) 180 CLR 447 at 452, 456. See also *Restatement (2d) Contracts* (1979), § 155, com c ('clear and convincing evidence').
246. *Earl v Hector Whaling Ltd* [1961] 1 Lloyd's Rep 459 at 468 per Pearce LJ.
247. *Moses v Northern Assurances Co* (1856) 1 VLT 114.
248. See *Frederick E Rose (London) Ltd v William H Pim Junior & Co Ltd* [1953] 2 QB 450 at 461, 462; *Re Streamline Fashions Pty Ltd* [1965] VR 418; *Johnstone v Commerce Consolidated Pty Ltd* [1976] VR 463 at 467 (affirmed [1976] VR 469); *Joscelyne v Nissen* [1970] 2 QB 86 at 98; *Australasian Performing Right Association Ltd v Austarama Television Pty Ltd* [1972] 2 NSWLR 467 at 473; *Hooker Town Developments Pty Ltd v Director of War Service Homes* (1973) 47 ALJR 320 at 323–4; *Maralinga Pty Ltd v Major Enterprises Pty Ltd* (1973) 128 CLR 336 at 349–50.
249. See *Bishopsgate Insurance Australia Ltd v Commonwealth Engineering (NSW) Pty Ltd* [1981] 1 NSWLR 429 at 431; *Pukallus v Cameron* (1982) 180 CLR 447 at 452; *Commissioner of Stamp Duties (NSW) v Carlenka Pty Ltd* (1995) 41 NSWLR 329 at 336. See also Leonard Bromley, 'Rectification in Equity' (1971) 87 *LQR* 532; Meagher, Gummow and Lehane, *Equity: Doctrines and Remedies*, 3rd ed, 1992, para 2606.
250. See [1262].
251. But cf *Olympia Sauna Shipping Co SA v Shinwa Kaiun Kaisha Ltd (The Ypatia Halcoussi)* [1985] 2 Lloyd's Rep 364 at 370.

out of the mouths of the witnesses at the hearing, that both parties had the necessary common intention.[252]

Rectification for Unilateral Mistake

[1264] Knowledge of the mistake. In *A Roberts & Co Ltd v Leicestershire County Council*,[253] rectification was granted where a construction company tendered to perform construction work for a council specifying a certain period of completion in its tender and the council's officers inserted a different period in the formal contract which they caused to be prepared. The formal contract was submitted to the company for execution and its attention was not drawn to the time for completion specified in the contract. The company unwittingly executed it. The tender price would have been higher if it had been based on the period specified in the contract. The council's officers knew that the company mistakenly believed that the period specified in the tender had been repeated in the contract.

Although the case was not one of common mistake, Pennycuick J ordered rectification, on the basis that where one contracting party knows that an instrument contains a mistake in its favour but does nothing to correct it, the party with knowledge will be precluded from resisting rectification on the ground that the mistake was unilateral and not common.

[1265] Equitable fraud. The relevant criterion here, as in other areas of mistake where equitable relief is sought,[254] is 'equitable fraud'. Equity has a well established jurisdiction to order rectification in cases where the non-mistaken party is guilty of unconscionable conduct.[255]

In *Riverlate Properties Ltd v Paul*[256] in which a lease did not express what the lessor had intended it to express, the case was treated as one of a lessor's unilateral mistake *not known to or in any way attributable to anything said or done by* the other party. The English Court of Appeal held that the lessor was not entitled to rectification or rescission. Russell LJ (for the court) emphasised that:

- the defendant did not share the plaintiff's mistake;
- the defendant did not know that the document did not give effect to the plaintiff's intention; and
- the plaintiff's mistake was not attributable to the defendant.

Russell LJ said:[257]

> If reference be made to principles of equity, it operates on conscience. If conscience is clear at the time of the transaction, why should equity disrupt the transaction? If a man may be said to have been fortunate in obtaining a property at a bargain price, or on terms that make it a good bargain, because the other party unknown to him has made a miscalculation or other mistake,

---

252. See *NSW Medical Defence Union Ltd v Transport Industries Insurance Co Ltd* (1986) 6 NSWLR 740 at 753.
253. [1961] Ch 555. See also *Johnston v Arnaboldi* [1990] 2 Qd R 138 at 144.
254. See Chapter 15.
255. See *The Ypatia Halcoussi* [1985] 2 Lloyd's Rep 364 at 371; Meagher, Gummow and Lehane, *Equity: Doctrines and Remedies*, 3rd ed, 1992, para 2615.
256. [1975] Ch 133.
257. [1975] Ch 133 at 141.

some high-minded men might consider it appropriate that he should agree to a fresh bargain to cure the miscalculation or mistake, abandoning his good fortune. But if equity were to enforce the views of those high-minded men, we have no doubt that it would run counter to the attitudes of much the greater part of ordinary mankind (not least the world of commerce), and would be venturing upon the field of moral philosophy in which it would soon be in difficulties.

The court expressed the view that before rectification will be ordered in a case of unilateral mistake, the evidence must show that the non-mistaken party was involved in 'a degree of sharp practice'.[258] In Australia, the Full Court of the Victorian Supreme Court has accepted that the law on rectification for unilateral mistake is correctly stated in the *Riverlate* case.[259] However, whether actual knowledge is required and whether the mistake must operate to the benefit of the unmistaken party, or merely prejudice the mistaken party are unclear.[260]

[1266] Option of rescission or rectification. Assume that A contracts to sell land to B, and that due to inadvertence the description of the land includes more land than A intended to include. Should B be given the option of submitting to rescission of the contract ab initio or to rectification of the description to make it accord with what A intended? There have been cases in which courts have made such orders for rescission *or* rectification at the 'option' or 'election' of the unmistaken party.[261] These cases have been criticised.[262] In *Riverlate Properties Ltd v Paul*[263] Russell LJ (for the court) raised the following question:[264]

> What is there in principle, or in authority binding upon this court, which requires a person who has acquired a leasehold interest on terms upon which he intended to obtain it, and who thought when he obtained it that the lessor intended him to obtain it on those terms, either to lose the leasehold interest, or, if he wished to keep it, to submit to keep it only on the terms which the lessor meant to impose but did not?

What should be emphasised is that normally unilateral mistake will not be a basis for judicial intervention, and in particular, that mere unilateral mistake as to the effect of words agreed to has been rejected as a basis for rectification.[265] It seems clear that rescission is not now awarded for *unilateral* mistake unless the unmistaken party knows or has reason to suspect that the other party is mistaken or has contributed to the mistake.

---

258. [1975] Ch 133 at 140.
259. *Commerce Consolidated Pty Ltd v Johnstone* [1976] VR 724. It has also been applied in New Zealand. See *Leighton v Parton* [1976] 1 NZLR 165.
260. See *Commission for the New Towns v Cooper (Great Britain) Ltd* [1995] Ch 259 (actual knowledge not required) (see David Mossop, (1996) 10 *JCL* 259); *Leibler v Air New Zealand Ltd (No 2)* [1999] 1 VR 1 at 14, 24 (questions not decided).
261. See, eg *Paget v Marshall* (1884) 28 Ch D 255; *May v Platt* [1900] 1 Ch 616. Cf *Solle v Butcher* [1950] 1 KB 671; *Joscelyne v Nissen* [1970] 2 QB 86.
262. See Meagher, Gummow and Lehane, *Equity: Doctrines and Remedies*, 3rd ed, 1992, para 2615.
263. [1975] Ch 133.
264. [1975] Ch 133 at 140–1. Cf *Australia Hotel Co Ltd v Moore* (1899) 20 LR (NSW) Eq 155.
265. *Powell v Smith* (1872) LR 14 Eq 85; *Stewart v Kennedy* (1890) 15 App Cas 108.

Non Est Factum

[1267] **Introduction.** The Latin expression non est factum ('it is not my deed') signifies a plea by a person who seeks to disown a deed or other document which it is alleged he or she sealed or signed. The plea is available where the defendant did not sign at all. It is also available in a limited range of circumstances where the document was signed. When the plea is established, the contract in which the document is expressed is void.[266]

The plea served a useful purpose at a time when most people could not read, and had to rely on others to explain documents to them. The proportion of the community that is illiterate has decreased and the importance of the plea has therefore diminished. The law has, in general, developed in the context of a contest between the rights of a signer who has been misled as to what the signer was signing and those of an innocent third party who has acted in reliance on the signature.

[1268] **Non est factum and mental incapacity.** A plea that a deed is voidable for mental incapacity[267] is incompatible with the plea of non est factum. The former admits signature but denies capacity to *understand*, whereas the latter denies signature.[268] Mental incapacity could, however, support a plea of non est factum if it went not merely to the victim's capacity to judge, assess and evaluate, but also to the capacity to understand what was being signed so that the mind of the person signing did not go with the signature.[269]

[1269] **History.** The plea has experienced a rise and fall. Its rise took place in the 19th century when it became available to persons other than illiterates, and also in respect of documents other than deeds. Its fall has occurred as the courts have shown reluctance to allow persons — neither blind nor illiterate — to disown documents which they have foolishly signed without reading. Since, typically, non est factum is pleaded by the signer as against an unsuspecting third party who acted in reliance on the signature, the cases resemble the mistaken identity cases in which an imposter tricks the victim into handing over property then disposes of it for value to an innocent third party. Both raise the question: which of two innocent parties is to suffer from the fraudulent act of a third?

Thoroughgood's Case[270] is a good illustration of the early operation of the plea. The illiterate Thoroughgood executed what John Ward told him was a release of arrears of rental in favour of William Chicken. It was in truth a release of Thoroughgood's entire estate and interest in the land to Chicken. The Court of Common Pleas held that a deed executed by an illiterate was not binding if it had been falsely explained, whether by the grantee or by a

---

266. See, eg *Petelin v Cullen* (1975) 132 CLR 355; 6 ALR 129; *PT Ltd v Maradona Pty Ltd* (1991) 25 NSWLR 643.
267. See [842].
268. *Gibbons v Wright* (1954) 91 CLR 423 at 442, 443, 444, 446; *PT Ltd v Maradona Pty Ltd* (1991) 25 NSWLR 643 at 673.
269. *Crago v McIntyre* [1976] 1 NSWLR 729 at 737.
270. (1584) 2 Co Rep 9a; 76 ER 408.

stranger to the deed. What was overlooked in later cases is the dictum that if even a blind or illiterate person signs without desiring the deed to be read at all, it is binding.

The plea was given its most liberal scope in *Carlisle and Cumberland Banking Co v Bragg*.[271] Bragg signed, without reading, a banker's continuing guarantee in respect of the account of one Rigg. Rigg had fraudulently represented to Bragg that the document was an insurance paper which Bragg had signed the previous day and which had got wet and blurred in the rain and needed to be re-signed. The English Court of Appeal held that the jury's finding of 'negligence' on Bragg's part was immaterial since it was only in respect of negotiable instruments that a signer owed such a duty of care to others as might form the basis of 'negligence' which would estop Bragg. The judgments suggested that the only relevant consideration is the nature and extent of the mistake actually made. This would make innocent third parties' rights dependent exclusively upon the subjective state of mind of the signer, an improbable position for the common law to take. The case was overruled in *Saunders v Anglia Building Society*,[272] where the House of Lords restated the principles governing the availability of non est factum, in a manner favouring the innocent third party as against the signer.

[1270] ***Saunders v Anglia Building Society.*** In *Saunders v Anglia Building Society*[273] the plaintiff, 78-year-old Mrs Gallie, executed what proved to be an assignment, expressed to be for consideration, of her leasehold interest in her home to the first defendant, Lee. Her intention had been to execute a deed of *gift* of that interest to her nephew, Parkin, knowing that he intended, with his business associate Lee, to raise money on the security of the property. They both attended upon her to have her sign the document. At the time her spectacles were broken. She could not read without them and so did not read the document. Lee mortgaged the property for £2000 to a building society which acted in reliance on Mrs Gallie's signature on the deed of assignment. She sought a declaration that the deed of assignment was void not only as against Lee but also as against the building society.

Mrs Gallie succeeded before the trial judge. The building society appealed and in the English Court of Appeal[274] the majority held that the plea failed because the mistake related not to the essential character of the document but merely to its contents. Lord Denning MR also held that the plea failed, but on a different basis. He exposed unsatisfactory aspects of the character-contents distinction and simply applied the rule that a person who does not take the trouble to read a legal document must accept the consequences which flow from an innocent third party's reliance on the document, for example, in advancing money on the faith of the document.

The House of Lords agreed that the plea must be closely confined and can only rarely be sustained by a person of full capacity.[275] Lord Reid

---

271. [1911] 1 KB 489.
272. [1971] AC 1004 (see [1270]).
273. [1971] AC 1004.
274. Sub nom *Gallie v Lee* [1969] 2 Ch 17.

suggested that the plea is available to 'those who are permanently or temporarily unable through no fault of their own to have without explanation any real understanding of the purport of a particular document, whether that be from defective education, illness or innate incapacity'[276] and perhaps, where the document has been misrepresented as not affecting the signer's legal rights, even to a person of full capacity.

[1271] **Proof of non est factum.** In *Saunders v Anglia Building Society*[277] the House of Lords said that the plea of non est factum requires clear and positive evidence before it can be established. It was also held that the onus of proof lies on a party seeking to disown the signature.

It was also accepted that three requirements, explained below,[278] are relevant to the plea:

(1) that the signer is under a disability;
(2) that there is a sufficient difference between the document as it is and as the signer believed it to be; and
(3) that the signer should not have been careless.

[1272] **Necessary difference and relevant disability.** The nature and extent of the necessary difference between what the signed document is and what it was believed by the signer to be were redefined in *Saunders v Anglia Building Society*.[279] The character-contents formulation was thought unsatisfactory and a number of their Lordships proposed that the difference must be 'radical or fundamental'. The High Court in *Petelin v Cullen*[280] has since used the expression 'radically different'.

In *Petelin v Cullen* the High Court formulated what was decided in *Saunders* in the following terms:[281]

> The class of persons who can avail themselves of the defence is limited. It is available to those who are unable to read owing to blindness or illiteracy and who must rely on others for advice as to what they are signing; it is also available to those who through no fault of their own are unable to have any understanding of the purport of a particular document. To make out the defence a defendant must show that he signed the document in the belief that it was radically different from what it was in fact and that, at least as against innocent persons, his failure to read and understand it was not due to carelessness on his part. Finally, it is accepted that there is a heavy onus on a defendant who seeks to establish the defence.

It has been suggested that where the actual and supposed documents are both legal documents dealing with the same property or rights, the difference (which will be between actual and supposed effect) will not suffice.[282] It would be open to a court to hold that such a difference is not 'radical' or 'fundamental'. Thus, in *O'Brien v Australia and New Zealand*

---

275. Between the hearings in the English Court of Appeal and House of Lords Mrs Gallie died and Saunders, her executor, took the appeal to the House.
276. [1971] AC 1004 at 1016.
277. [1971] AC 1004.
278. See [1272]–[1274]. See also [1275] (filling in blanks).
279. [1971] AC 1004.
280. (1975) 132 CLR 355 at 360.
281. (1975) 132 CLR 355 at 359–60.

Bank Ltd[283] Zelling J held that the difference between a guarantee of any future indebtedness and a guarantee and indemnity as to both existing and future indebtedness was not sufficiently 'fundamental' to sustain a plea of non est factum.

[1273] Carelessness in signing. The importance of carelessness seems to have been most obvious in relation to cheques and other negotiable instruments because of their wide circulation, and the commercial necessity that signatures on them be trustworthy. Yet ex hypothesi the signer did not know that the instrument was a negotiable instrument and so it is not rational to look for the exercise of special and additional care towards others just because the document being signed turns out to be a negotiable instrument. In the earliest of the reported negotiable instrument cases, *Foster v Mackinnon*,[284] the defendant was induced to endorse a bill of exchange by a fraudulent misrepresentation that the document was a guarantee. He was subsequently sued by a bona fide holder for value. The jury was directed that the plea of non est factum would be made out, and the defendant entitled to a verdict, if he:

(1) signed as a result of that fraudulent misrepresentation;

(2) believed that the instrument was not a bill but was a guarantee; and

(3) was not guilty of 'negligence'.

The Court of Common Pleas upheld this direction, although Byles J (for the court) considered that when applied to negotiable instruments the plea must be closely confined in order to protect innocent transferees for value.

Foster v Mackinnon would be decided differently today, not because a negotiable instrument proved to be involved, but because the notion of 'estoppel by careless signature' in favour of unsuspecting third parties has become dominant in this area. Today, 'negligence' sufficient to defeat the signer is presumed unless the signer was under a disability which forced reliance on another for an explanation of the document. In *Hunter v Walters*[285] Sir George Mellish LJ said:[286]

> When a man knows that he is conveying or doing something with his estate but does not ask what is the precise effect of the deed, because he is told it is a mere form, and has such confidence in his solicitor as to execute the deed in ignorance, then, in my opinion, a deed so executed, although it may be voidable upon the ground of fraud, it is not a void deed ...
>
> [T]he parties who signed the receipt are guilty of such negligence that they ought to be postponed in equity to Mr Curling, who had a perfectly equitable title without any notice, and who advanced his money on the faith of the representation contained in that instrument.

---

282. Cf *Howatson v Webb* [1908] 1 Ch 1 (affirming [1907] 1 Ch 537); *Blay v Pollard and Morris* [1930] 1 KB 628; *Mercantile Credit Co Ltd v Hamblin* [1965] 2 QB 242. But cf *Muskham Finance Ltd v Howard* [1963] 1 QB 904.
283. (1971) 5 SASR 347.
284. (1869) LR 4 CP 704.
285. (1871) LR 7 Ch App 75.
286. (1871) LR 7 Ch App 75 at 88 and 89. See also *Howatson v Webb* [1908] 1 Ch 1, where Farwell LJ questioned whether a person who is not blind or illiterate is not always estopped by a signature.

In *Saunders v Anglia Building Society*[287] it was held that the carelessness or 'negligence' referred to in this context is not based on a specific duty of care owed to individuals of the kind which founds an action in tort, and that the defeat of the plea by the signer's carelessness is not truly an instance of estoppel by negligence but of the principle that persons may not take advantage of their own wrong. *Foster v Mackinnon*[288] was approved in this respect.[289] Some of the earlier cases dealing with the issues of the negligence of the signer[290] are now doubtful in the light of this more expansive concept. There are also cases,[291] which although correct in their findings of 'estoppel by negligence' would be reasoned along different lines.

[1274] Absence of innocent third party. Where no innocent third party is involved, and the binding effect of a signature is in issue only as between the signer and the other party to the document, considerations different from those discussed above apply. In particular, the issue of negligence does not arise.[292]

The signing will be merely one factor, albeit a most important and persuasive factor, on which the objective theory of contract will operate. But factors at work as between the parties may displace the theory. Examples are that the other party misrepresented the nature of the document to the signer, or that that party knew that the signer intended to sign a document of a fundamentally or radically different nature from that signed in fact.[293] Such cases are dealt with under the rubric of unilateral mistake as to the terms of the offer or promise.[294]

[1275] Filling in blanks. Where a person signs a document containing blanks, intending that they be filled in by someone else, the mere fact that the latter fills them in in an unauthorised and improper manner will not render the document void.[295] However, the document may be rectified if by an honest mistake incorrect material is inserted.[296]

---

287. [1971] AC 1004. See also *Avon Finance Co Ltd v Bridger* (1979) [1985] 2 All ER 281.
288. (1869) LR 4 CP 704.
289. *Carlisle and Cumberland Banking Co v Bragg* [1911] 1 KB 489 (see [1269]) was overruled.
290. See, eg *National Provincial Bank of England v Jackson* (1886) 33 Ch D 1.
291. See, eg *King v Smith* [1900] 2 Ch 425; *Howatson v Webb* [1908] 1 Ch 1.
292. See *Petelin v Cullen* (1975) 132 CLR 355.
293. Cf *Lee v Ah Gee* [1920] VLR 278; *Taylor v Smith* [1926] VLR 100 (affirmed (1926) 38 CLR 48); *Nemtsas v Nemtsas* [1957] VR 191; *Petelin v Cullen* (1975) 132 CLR 355.
294. See [1252]–[1254].
295. *United Dominions Trust Ltd v Western* [1976] 1 QB 513 (not following *Campbell Discount Co Ltd v Gall* [1961] 1 QB 431). See also *Egan v Ross* (1928) 29 SR (NSW) 382. See Bob Allcock, 'Documents Signed in Blank' (1982) 45 *MLR* 18.
296. See *Warburton v National Westminster Finance Australia Ltd* (1988) 15 NSWLR 238.

Chapter 13

Duress

General..1301
    Introduction *1301*
    Effect of Duress..................................... *1302*

Forms of Duress......................................1307
    Introduction *1307*
    Duress to the Person or Goods *1308*
    Economic Duress.................................... *1311*

Elements of Duress...................................1314

Illegitimate Pressure.................................1317

Duress By and Against Third Parties 1324

Remedies for Duress..................................1326

General

Introduction

[1301] Duress and undue influence. In the discussion of misrepresentation (Chapter 10) and mistake (Chapter 12) we were concerned with the impact of misinformation on contractual assent.[1] In this chapter and the next (concerned with 'undue influence') the concern is with situations in which contractual assent of one of the parties is affected by pressure. A third category of case is the subject of Chapter 15, in which the focus is not the assent of the party seeking relief from the contract so much as the 'advantage-taking' involved in unconscionable conduct.

Since pressure may be associated with misinformation or unconscionable conduct, these are overlapping categories. Indeed, the distinction between undue influence and unconscionable conduct is now often difficult to draw.[2] It is, however, clear that duress (sometimes termed 'compulsion') is a distinct category. In any civilised legal system contracts entered into by a

---

1. Chapter 11, in analysing the impact of the breach of statutory prohibitions on conduct, was more general.
2. Cf Ross McKeand, 'Economic Duress — Wearing the Clothes of Unconscionable Conduct' (2001) 17 *JCL* 1. See further [1416].

party in consequence of serious threats, such as death or physical injury, must be treated as either nullities or, at the least, unenforceable. The only problem, apart from determining the precise consequences of such duress, lies in working out a definition of the scope of the concept. Duress and undue influence have generally been treated as distinct forms of pressure.[3] Thus, whereas 'duress' signifies a procuring of contractual assent by an illegitimate threat, 'undue influence' signifies an influence which may fall short of that compulsion, and not associated with any illegitimate threat,[4] but which is deemed 'undue' nonetheless.

Effect of Duress

[1302] Contract voidable not void. Where the elements of a binding contract are present, and the parties appear to have had an intention to contract, the courts are reluctant to treat the contract as void merely because some vitiating factor, such as mistake or misrepresentation, has impaired the decision of one party (or both) to contract.[5]

Accordingly, most judicial pronouncements favour the view that a contract procured by duress is not void, but merely 'voidable'.[6] Thus, although in *Barton v Armstrong*[7] a declaration was made that the subject deed was 'void' between the parties to the litigation, this should be interpreted as a reference to the effectiveness of Barton's supervening election to rescind the contract.[8]

[1303] Basis on which contract voidable. Notwithstanding that an element of duress is present, there is, ex hypothesi, an element of 'willingness to contract'. That is to say, acts which normally give rise to a binding contract have occurred with knowledge that a contract is being entered into and of what it says. It is therefore difficult to say that there is an absence of contractual intent sufficient to make the contract void.

Instead, because one party's contractual assent was procured by pressure which the law regards as improper, that party has a right to rescind the contract. Since there is, as in the case of misrepresentation, an ability to rescind the contract, it is open to the party imposed upon to enforce the contract and to become bound unconditionally by it. This is the effect of an

---

3. But cf I J Hardingham, 'Unconscionable Dealing' in Finn, ed, *Essays in Equity*, 1985, pp 19–24.
4. The terms are taken from the judgment of Isaacs J in *Smith v William Charlick Ltd* (1924) 34 CLR 38 at 56. See also [1401].
5. See, eg [1002]; [1206].
6. *Sternbeck v Sternbeck* (1968) 11 FLR 360 at 363–4; *Barton v Armstrong* [1973] 2 NSWLR 598 at 615, 617 (on appeal [1976] AC 104); *DPP for Northern Ireland v Lynch* [1975] AC 653 at 680, 695; *North Ocean Shipping Co Ltd v Hyundai Construction Co Ltd (The Atlantic Baron)* [1979] 1 QB 705 especially at 720–1; *Pao On v Lau Yiu Long* [1980] AC 614 at 634; *Dimskal Shipping Co SA v International Transport Workers Federation (The Evia Luck)* [1992] 2 AC 152 at 167, 168, 169, 171. But see D J Lanham, 'Duress and Void Contracts' (1966) 29 *MLR* 615.
7. [1976] AC 104 at 120 per Lord Cross (delivering the advice of the majority of the Judicial Committee).
8. In the *Restatement (2d) Contracts* (1979), §§174, 175 a contrast is drawn between cases of physical compulsion (void) and cases where the manifestation of assent is induced by an improper threat (voidable).

election to affirm the contract. The opportunity to make the choice between rescission and affirmation is beneficial. It also assists in the protection of third parties, and is moreover an important element by which the concept has in recent years been extended.

[1304] Duress and the overborne will. Because a contract affected by duress is not regarded as void, the contract will be binding until set aside by an election on the part of the victim or by court order. Nevertheless, there is an element of controversy in the cases which arises from the way in which many definitions of duress talk in terms of an effect on a person's 'will', 'consent' or 'assent'. For example, in *Occidental Worldwide Investment Corp v Skibs A/S Avanti (The Siboen and The Sibotre)*,[9] Kerr J said that the court must 'at least be satisfied that the consent of the other party was overborne by compulsion so as to deprive him of any animus contrahendi'. And in *Pao On v Lau Yiu Long*[10] the Privy Council said that 'duress, whatever form it takes, is a coercion of the will so as to vitiate consent'. Although the paradigm case of duress, involving threats to the person, seems to have been allowed to denote a requirement of total control over the mind affected, this does not justify the adoption of a general theory in which duress is only present if the will of the person relying on the concept is 'overborne'.

Reliance on an 'overborne will theory' for duress is not consistent with *DPP for Northern Ireland v Lynch*,[11] and that case became a stimulus for a lively academic debate.[12] In *Lynch*, a decision on the criminal law, it was accepted that the availability of duress as a defence to a criminal charge did not depend on absence of 'intention', 'will' or 'choice'. The case was not cited in the contract cases until *Crescendo Management Pty Ltd v Westpac Banking Corp*,[13] where the New South Wales Court of Appeal rejected the overborne will as a theory of duress.

Expressions such as 'overborne', 'will', 'voluntarily', 'vitiate', 'consent', 'compulsion', 'coercion', and 'intention' are notoriously difficult and can reduce the debate to one of semantics. However, it can now be accepted:

(1) it is inherent in the nature of a threat that alternative courses of action be open to the victim, even if one may be at the cost of the victim's life;

(2) that of the alternatives, the victim chose that of entering into the contract;

(3) if the expression 'overborne will' is used to indicate a total absence of intention to make the particular contract, it is inconsistent with the act of contracting and must result in voidness ab initio; and

---

9. [1976] 1 Lloyd's Rep 293 at 336.
10. [1980] AC 614 at 635. See also *Syros Shipping Co SA v Elaghill Trading Co (The Proodos C)* [1981] 3 All ER 189 at 192.
11. [1975] AC 653, especially at 680, 695.
12. See P S Atiyah, 'Economic Duress and the Overborne Will' (1982) 98 *LQR* 197; David Tiplady, 'Concepts of Duress' (1983) 99 *LQR* 188; P S Atiyah 'Duress and the Overborne Will Again' (1983) 99 *LQR* 353.
13. (1988) 19 NSWLR 40 (see Peter Birks, [1990] *LMCLQ* 342). See also *Equiticorp Finance Ltd v Bank of New Zealand* (1993) 32 NSWLR 50 at 149–150.

(4) the illegitimate pressure on which the claim of duress is based need not have been the sole cause of the decision to contract.

[1305] Causation. The fourth of the points made above is most significant. It is inconsistent with an overborne will theory that a party can rely on duress where the pressure complained against is not the sole or at least principal cause of the decision to contract. It was accepted in *Barton v Armstrong*[14] that it is sufficient for the pressure to be *a* cause of the decision to contract. The majority in the Privy Council thought[15] that there was 'an obvious analogy between setting aside a disposition for duress or undue influence and setting it aside for fraud'. The New South Wales Court of Appeal, when rejecting the overborne will theory in *Crescendo Management Pty Ltd v Westpac Banking Corp*,[16] treated this idea as applicable to all forms of duress. On the facts in that case, there was no duress because the element of causation was lacking.

This brings the law of duress into line with other areas where a right of rescission arises, such as fraud and mistake, in that it is sufficient for the misrepresentation, mistake or duress to be *an inducement* to enter into the contract.

[1306] Burden of proof. An initial burden of proof rests on the person who alleges that the contract was entered into as a result of duress, to prove the making of the appropriate kind of threat and unlawful pressure directed to the procuring of contractual assent.[17]

In *Barton v Armstrong*[18] it was held that once the party seeking relief establishes these matters, the onus shifts to the other party to show that this 'contributed nothing' to the decision to contract. In *Crescendo Management Pty Ltd v Westpac Banking Corp*[19] this analysis was treated as applicable to all forms of duress.

Forms of Duress

Introduction

[1307] Overall development. The development of the law relating to duress has been concerned with defining the kinds of conduct allowed to form the basis of duress and of the necessary effect on the party threatened. However, the cases have witnessed a process of simplification. Thus, it is no longer required that the conduct constituting the threat should fit into a

---

14. [1976] AC 104. See also *Dimskal Shipping Co SA v International Transport Workers Federation (The Evia Luck)* [1992] 2 AC 152 at 165.
15. [1976] AC 104 at 118 per Lord Cross (applying a dictum of Lord Cranworth LC in *Reynell v Sprye* (1852) 1 De GM & G 660 at 708; 42 ER 710 at 728 (see [1042])).
16. (1988) 19 NSWLR 40. See also *Magnacrete Ltd v Douglas-Hill* (1988) 48 SASR 565 (no causal connection).
17. See generally [1317]–[1323].
18. [1976] AC 104 at 120.
19. (1988) 19 NSWLR 40 at 46.

preconceived category other than the general requirement of 'illegitimacy'.[20]

Money paid under duress is recoverable under the principle of restitution for unjust enrichment.[21] To this extent, there is no requirement that the duress lead to a contract. However, our main concern[22] is with the impact of duress in the contract context, and in that context restitution is not available until the contract has been rescinded.

Duress to the Person or Goods

[1308] **Duress to the person.** It has long been a principle of the common law that a contract is not enforceable against a party whose assent was procured by actual or threatened violence to his or her person.[23] This includes actual or threatened deprivation of liberty.[24]

It is not, however, essential that the threat be to the person who seeks to avoid the contract: a threat to the person's parent, spouse or child is sufficient.[25]

[1309] **Duress of goods.** Violence to or confinement of the person or a threat thereof is a narrow category. However, the common law also recognised a form of duress involving goods. Duress of goods involves an unlawful taking, detention, damaging or destruction of a person's goods. Money paid for the release of the payer's goods unlawfully detained by another, or to avoid the wrongful seizure of goods, is recoverable in an action for restitution.[26]

A person detaining goods will virtually always do so under a claim of right. So, the possibility is available that an agreement to pay for their release constitutes a final compromise or settlement of a bona fide claim.[27] However, the cases on duress of goods acknowledged the possibility that if the claim to retain them was known to be bad, the contract to pay for their

---

20. See [1317]–[1323].
21. See generally Mason and Carter, *Restitution Law in Australia*, 1995, Chapter 5.
22. See further [1328].
23. *Cumming v Ince* (1847) 11 QB 112 at 120; 116 ER 418 at 421. For a more recent example see *Barton v Armstrong* [1976] AC 104.
24. *McLarnon v McLarnon* (1968) 112 Sol J 419.
25. Cf *Saxon v Saxon* [1976] 4 WWR 300 (husband's threat to kill children unless wife executed deed of separation).
26. *Astley v Reynolds* (1731) 2 Str 915; 93 ER 939; *Valpy v Manley* (1845) 1 CB 594; 135 ER 673; *Green v Duckett* (1883) 11 QBD 275; *Maskell v Horner* [1915] 3 KB 106; *Mason v New South Wales* (1959) 102 CLR 108 at 144. See Mason and Carter, *Restitution Law in Australia*, 1995, para 526. Money paid to release goods from the custody of the law may form an exception. See, eg *Liverpool Marine Credit Co v Hunter* (1868) 3 Ch App 479 at 487–8. However, such cases do not state any general principle: *J & S Holdings Pty Ltd v NRMA Insurance Ltd* (1982) 41 ALR 539 at 557.
27. Cf *Atlee v Backhouse* (1838) 3 M & W 633; 113 ER 1298; *Valpy v Manley* (1845) 1 CB 594; 135 ER 673. See Jack Beatson, 'Duress as a Vitiating Factor in Contract' [1974] *CLJ* 97. And see [1320].

release would not be enforceable.[28] By contrast, duress of the person will virtually always be wrongful.

[1310] The payment/agreement distinction. Where money is paid without contract it is recoverable on proof of duress to the person or goods.[29] But the scope of duress was originally limited by a distinction between a payment for the release of goods and an *agreement to pay* for the release of goods. This arose from an alleged distinction between duress of the person and duress of goods. It was stated in *Skeate v Beale*:[30]

> The former is a constraining force, which not only takes away the free agency, but may leave no room for appeal to the law for a remedy: a man, therefore, is not bound by the agreement which he enters into under such circumstances: but the fear that goods may be taken or injured does not deprive any one of his free agency who possesses that ordinary degree of firmness which the law requires all to exert.

This reasoning is psychologically unrealistic. As Collins MR observed in a different context in *Kaufman v Gerson*,[31] '... what does it matter what particular form of coercion is used, so long as the will is coerced? Some persons would be more easily coerced by moral pressure ... than by the threat of physical violence'. Once it is conceded that violence or a threat of violence to an individual *other than the contracting party* can be within the common law notion of duress to the contracting party,[32] there is no reason to insist that duress of a contracting party's goods lies outside it. Given the development of a general doctrine of economic duress,[33] relief cannot be refused simply on the basis that the case involved payment pursuant to contract, rather than a simple payment of money. It was therefore acknowledged in *Hawker Pacific Pty Ltd v Helicopter Charter Pty Ltd*[34] that the distinction drawn in *Skeate v Beale* is no longer good law. Accordingly, where it is established that conduct amounting to duress contributed to entry into a contract, that conduct justifies rescission of the contract by the other party even if there is no duress to the person.[35]

Economic Duress[36]

[1311] Payments made under compulsion. Any general distinction between payment and agreement to pay is impossible to maintain today in the light of the development of a concept of economic duress. The first step

---

28. See further [1310]. Cf *Smith v Monteith* (1844) 13 M & W 427; 153 ER 178 (agreement to pay in order to obtain release of a person imprisoned).
29. See [1309] and further [1328].
30. (1841) 11 Ad & E 983 at 990; 113 ER 688 at 690.
31. [1904] 1 KB 591 at 597.
32. See [1308].
33. See [1311]–[1313]. But cf *Atlas Express Ltd v Kafco (Importers and Distributors) Ltd* [1989] QB 833 at 839.
34. (1991) 22 NSWLR 298 at 302, 306. See also *Occidental Worldwide Investment Corp v Skibs A/S Avanti (The Siboen and The Sibotre)* [1976] 1 Lloyd's Rep 293 (see Jack Beatson, (1976) 92 *LQR* 496); *Magnacrete Ltd v Douglas-Hill* (1988) 48 SASR 565 at 590; *Dimskal Shipping Co SA v International Transport Workers Federation (The Evia Luck)* [1992] 2 AC 152 at 165.
35. See Mason and Carter, *Restitution Law in Australia*, 1995, paras 532, 1312.
36. See A J Stewart, 'Economic Duress — Legal Regulation of Commercial Pressure' (1984) 14 *MULR* 410.

is to see how payments made under compulsion — where there is no pretence of contract — are prima facie recoverable.[37]

In *Smith v William Charlick Ltd*,[38] a flour miller yielded to a demand from the Wheat Harvest Board of South Australia for additional payment in respect of wheat sold to him by the Board. The Board was his sole source of supply. The Board was not (and did not claim to be) legally entitled. It claimed to be 'morally' entitled to the further payment, and intimated that unless payment was made it would not supply the plaintiff with any more wheat. The plaintiff sued to recover the payment. On the facts, the High Court held that the claim failed. Knox CJ said:[39]

> In the present case there was no mistake of fact, no threat of unauthorised interference with the person or the property or any legal right of the respondent, and no demand made under colour of office. The payment was made with full knowledge of all material facts. The respondent knew that the Board was not, and did not claim to be, legally entitled to demand the money. It was paid, not in order to have that done which the Board was legally bound to do, but in order to induce the Board to do that which it was under no legal obligation to do.

Isaacs J observed:[40]

> It is conceded that the only ground on which the promise to repay could be implied is 'compulsion'. The payment is said by the respondent not to have been 'voluntary' but 'forced' from it within the contemplation of the law.
>
> Leaving aside, for the present, the question whether in law the payment was 'forced' from the respondent by some undue advantage taken of its situation having regard to the Wheat Harvest legislation, the point is whether the Board's insistence was what is regarded as 'compulsion' from the simple standpoint of common law. 'Compulsion' in relation to a payment of which refund is sought, and whether it is also variously called 'coercion', 'extortion', 'exaction', or 'force', includes every species of duress or conduct analogous to duress, actual or threatened, exerted by or on behalf of the payee and applied to the person or the property or any right of the person who pays or, in some cases, of a person related to or in affinity with him. Such compulsion is a legal wrong, and the law provides a remedy by raising a fictional promise to repay.
>
> Apart from any additional feature presented by the relevant legislation, it is plain that a mere abstention from selling goods to a man except on condition of his making a stated payment cannot, in the absence of some special relation, answer the description of 'compulsion', however serious his situation arising from other circumstances may be ...

[1312] Claim for restitution. The importance of *Smith v William Charlick Ltd*[41] lies in the recognition of a plaintiff's right of recovery in cases where the payment is made under compulsion.[42] The second step is to illustrate that where a payment is made under illegitimate economic pressure, pursuant to an agreement which is not in point of law supported

---

37. See [1307].
38. (1924) 34 CLR 38.
39. (1924) 34 CLR 38 at 51.
40. (1924) 34 CLR 38 at 56.
41. (1924) 34 CLR 38 (see [1311]).
42. See also *Mason v New South Wales* (1959) 102 CLR 108.

by consideration, the payment is also recoverable in restitution for unjust enrichment.

In *TA Sundell & Sons Pty Ltd v Emm Yannoulatos (Overseas) Pty Ltd*,[43] there was a contract for the purchase by the plaintiff-buyer from the defendant-seller of galvanised iron at £109.15.0 a ton and the buyer established a letter of credit accordingly. Some months later the seller told the buyer that an increase in the price of the iron (which was to come from France) was inevitable and requested that the amount of the letter of credit be increased, in default of which the plaintiff would not be supplied. The buyer ordered the same quantity of iron afresh at £140 per ton, at the same time asking the seller to acknowledge that the buyer should have the right to contend that the original contract required the defendant to supply at £109.15.0 a ton. The plaintiff amended and increased the letter of credit accordingly. The seller utilised the increased letter of credit. However, there was no consideration to support the variation of the original contract of sale, due to the fact that the seller did no more than perform an existing contractual obligation.[44] The buyer successfully sued to recover the excess as money paid under 'duress' or 'compulsion'. The Full Court of the Supreme Court of New South Wales rejected a contention that recoverability as for payment made 'under compulsion' should not be allowed where all that is proved is that 'a compulsive threat has been made to refrain from performing merely a contractual duty as distinct from a threat to refrain from performing a statutory duty or a threat to interfere with a proprietary right of the payer'.[45]

[1313] Contracts supported by consideration. Lord Scarman for the Privy Council in *Pao On v Lau Yiu Long*[46] (which involved a threat of breach of contract) expressed the view obiter, that 'there is nothing contrary to principle in recognising economic duress as a factor which may render a contract voidable, provided always that the basis of such recognition is that it must amount to a coercion of will, which vitiates consent' and that the victim 'must have entered the contract against his will, must have had no alternative course open to him'[47] and that 'the pressure must be such that the victim's consent to the contract was not a voluntary act on his part'.[48] In *Universe Tankships Inc of Monrovia v International Transport Workers Federation (The Universe Sentinel)*[49] Lord Diplock identified the rationale of the development of the common law in relation to a party's contractual assent procured by duress in these terms:[50]

43. (1955) 56 SR (NSW) 323. Cf *Atlas Express Ltd v Kafco (Importers and Distributors) Ltd* [1989] QB 833.
44. See generally [341]–[364].
45. (1955) 56 SR (NSW) 323 at 328. The court cited references to the application of 'duress or conduct analogous to duress' to 'any right' of the payer by Isaacs J in *Smith v William Charlick Ltd* (1924) 34 CLR 38 at 56. See also *Nixon v Furphy* (1925) 25 SR (NSW) 151 at 160 (affirmed sub nom *Furphy v Nixon* (1925) 37 CLR 161); *Re Hooper & Grass' Contract* [1949] VLR 269 at 272–3.
46. [1980] AC 614 at 636.
47. [1980] AC 614 at 636. But cf [1322].
48. [1980] AC 614 at 636.
49. [1983] 1 AC 366.
50. [1983] 1 AC 366 at 384.

The rationale is that his apparent consent was induced by pressure exercised upon him by that other party which the law does not regard as legitimate, with the consequence that the consent is treated in law as revocable unless approbated either expressly or by implication after the illegitimate pressure has ceased to operate on his mind. It is a rationale similar to that which underlies the avoidability of contracts entered into and the recovery of money exacted under colour of office, or under undue influence or in consequence of threats of physical duress.

Leaving aside the terminological difficulties in these statements, they clearly recognise a category of economic duress at a very high level of authority. And the early Australian authorities referred to above[51] have justifiably been treated in the recent Australian cases[52] as anticipating the recognition of a general concept of economic duress in England. Thus, in *North Ocean Shipping Co Ltd v Hyundai Construction Co Ltd (The Atlantic Baron)*,[53] which involved a shipowner-payer's claim to recover an extra payment that it agreed to make and did make in order to avoid the shipbuilder-payee's threat to break a shipbuilding contract between them, Mocatta J applied the view that duress is not limited to duress to the person and goods. He held that 'economic duress' may suffice. In his view a threat to break an existing contract can constitute such economic duress, and on the facts did amount to duress. Accordingly, the contract — tainted by economic duress — was voidable.

These authorities therefore support a third step in our analysis, since they recognise the ability to recover payments made pursuant to a contract supported by consideration. Nevertheless, until the contract has been rescinded, money paid under the contract is 'irrecoverable in restitution'.[54] Although there is therefore no direct right to claim restitution for unjust enrichment, the importance of economic duress is that it gives rise to a right to rescind the contract. Once the contract has been rescinded, any payment made can be recovered, 'on the ground either of duress or possibly of failure of consideration'.[55]

Elements of Duress[56]

[1314] Introduction. In *Universe Tankships Inc of Monrovia v International Transport Workers Federation (The Universe Sentinel)*[57] Lord Scarman noted 'two elements in the wrong of duress', namely pressure and the illegitimacy of the pressure. He explained:[58]

---

51. See [1311].
52. See, eg *J & S Holdings Pty Ltd v NRMA Insurance Ltd* (1982) 41 ALR 539; *Crescendo Management Pty Ltd v Westpac Banking Corp* (1988) 19 NSWLR 40.
53. [1979] QB 705 (see also [1321]).
54. *Dimskal Shipping Co SA v International Transport Workers Federation (The Evia Luck)* [1992] 2 AC 152 at 165.
55. *Dimskal Shipping Co SA v International Transport Workers Federation (The Evia Luck)* [1992] 2 AC 152 at 165. See generally Mason and Carter, *Restitution Law in Australia*, 1995, paras 1319–1322, 1326–1327.
56. See Nicholas Seddon, 'Compulsion in Commercial Dealings' in Finn, ed, *Essays on Restitution*, 1990, p 138.
57. [1983] 1 AC 366 at 400.
58. [1983] 1 AC 366 at 400.

There must be pressure, the practical effect of which is compulsion or the absence of choice. Compulsion is variously described in the authorities as coercion or the vitiation of consent. The classic case of duress is, however, not the lack of will to submit but the victim's intentional submission arising from the realisation that there is no other practical choice open to him. This is the thread of principle which links the early law of duress (threat to life or limb) with later developments when the law came also to recognise as duress first the threat to property and now the threat to a man's business or trade.

This may be expanded to an approach having three elements. First, and fundamentally, there must be an element of wrongful conduct or unlawful demand constituting *illegitimate* pressure. Second, there must be an analysis of why the victim has chosen to enter into the contract rather than to pursue a claim in respect of the pressure. Third, it must be considered whether the contract relied upon by the party who exerted the threats is in fact valid under the requirement of consideration. Analysis of these three elements will give rise to a decision that there was or was not a contract affected by duress. That will leave a fourth issue for analysis, namely whether relief is available to the victim.

Although rare, there is no rule that duress cannot occur where the suggestion of an alteration to contractual relations comes first from the party who subsequently seeks to rely on duress. Thus, in *B & S Contracts and Design Ltd v Victor Green Publications Ltd*[59] the plaintiffs agreed to prepare a hall for an exhibition. They were experiencing industrial difficulties with employees who had been made redundant and were seeking payment. The defendants said they would pay money to the plaintiffs to pay the employees. It was held that this payment was made under duress even though there was merely a veiled threat and no demand. The clear inference was that unless the payment was made the plaintiffs would not perform the contract.

[1315] **Analysis.** In the cases, the four elements, particularly the first two, are so bound up together that it is difficult to justify a detailed separate treatment of each.

A separate analysis of the third and fourth issue is justifiable,[60] because we need to examine the way in which general principles of rescission apply to contracts affected by economic duress.

We deal in detail with the other elements under the general heading 'illegitimate pressure'.[61]

[1316] **Duress and consideration.** There are three fundamental points about the element of consideration. First, cases such as *T A Sundell & Sons Pty Ltd v Emm Yannoulatos (Overseas) Pty Ltd*[62] indicate that the victim will find it relatively easy to recover payments made under duress where the 'contract' on which the other person relies is not supported by consideration. As we have seen,[63] the law allows a person to recover money

---

59. [1984] ICR 419 (see N E Palmer and Louise Catchpole, (1985) 48 *MLR* 102). Contrast *Williams v Roffey Bros & Nicholls (Contractors) Ltd* [1991] 1 QB 1 (see [348]).
60. See [1316], [1326]–[1330].
61. See [1317]–[1323].
62. (1955) 56 SR (NSW) 323 (see [1312]).

paid under duress in an action in restitution. Thus, once a case was perceived to be a 'payment' case rather than an 'agreement' case, it is sufficient to characterise such payments as having been not 'voluntary' and as having been made under 'compulsion' or 'practical compulsion'.[64]

Second, recent developments indicate that the presence of consideration does not necessarily bar the victim's claim. It is, however, required that the contract be rescinded on the basis of the duress.[65]

Third, the fact that there has been illegitimate pressure does not mean that consideration otherwise sufficient to give rise to a contract, is somehow obliterated by the duress.[66] This follows from, or helps to justify, the conclusion that a contract affected by duress is not void but merely voidable.

Illegitimate Pressure[67]

[1317] Introduction. The concern of the law of duress should now be with identifying 'those forms of pressure which the law should regard as legitimate',[68] rather than improper and unacceptable. Or, to put the matter from a wider perspective, it is concern with the permissible limits of coercion in our society, and 'the extent to which society can legitimately require people to stand up to threats when they are made, rather than to submit and litigate afterwards'.[69]

Factual matters such as the nature of the threat, the demand made, the presence or absence of protest by the victim and the courses open to the victim, will be relevant to the effect produced by a threat found to be wrongful and to that extent at least illegitimate.

[1318] Mere commercial pressure. A threat may affect the victim's mind yet not constitute duress. As Lords Wilberforce and Simon observed in *Barton v Armstrong*,[70] 'the pressure must be one of a kind which the law does not regard as legitimate'. On this basis, 'mere commercial pressure' as such, even of an extreme kind, is not duress. So, in *Smith v William Charlick Ltd*,[71] a threat by a Wheat Board which was a monopolist supplier of wheat to flour millers not to make new contracts, or have any future business dealings with a particular miller unless he paid it money which he was not legally liable to pay, was held not to be illegitimate in a context where the

---

63. See [1307], [1311]. See further [1328].
64. Cf *Valpy v Manley* (1845) 1 CB 594; 135 ER 673; *Green v Duckett* (1883) 11 QBD 275; *White Rose Flour Milling Co Pty Ltd v Australian Wheat Board* (1944) 18 ALJ 324; *Re Hooper & Grass' Contract* [1949] VLR 269; *J & S Holdings Pty Ltd v NRMA Insurance Ltd* (1982) 41 ALR 539.
65. See [1313], [1327].
66. Contrast the position where there is no consideration but promissory estoppel is relied on. See *D & C Builders Ltd v Rees* [1966] 2 QB 617 (see [381]).
67. See R C Nicholls, 'Conduct after Breach: The Position of the Party in Breach — Part II' (1991) 3 *JCL* 163.
68. David Tiplady, 'Concepts of Duress' (1983) 99 *LQR* 188 at 194.
69. P S Atiyah, 'Duress and the Overborne Will Again' (1983) 99 *LQR* 353 at 356.
70. [1976] AC 104 at 121.
71. (1924) 34 CLR 38 (see [1311]). Cf John Adams, 'The Economics of Good Faith in Contract' (1995) 8 *JCL* 126 at 127.

relevant legislation did not oblige the Board to supply. The case may be contrasted with *White Rose Flour Milling Co Pty Ltd v Australian Wheat Board*,[72] in which there was a subsisting contract and the threat was not to supply in breach of that contract.

In seeking to mark off those agreements which are the result of unacceptable pressure and those which, although negotiated as a result of pressure, ought not to be regarded as within the purview of duress, an element of uncertainty is inevitable. It is, nevertheless, a cause for concern.[73] Moreover, since it is recognised that the exertion of pressure is not intrinsically wrong, that is, that the law permits some pressure to be brought to bear, it is essential that the concept of economic duress not be made so broad that it impedes the renegotiation of contracts.[74]

[1319] Lawful threats. Prima facie, a threat to do something the actual doing of which would be lawful, is legitimate.[75] But lawfulness cannot be conclusive. For example, a lawful threat may be accompanied by an unlawful demand. Thus, in *Kaufman v Gerson*[76] the English Court of Appeal accepted that blackmail, in that case a threat to prosecute the victim's husband for a crime if she would not undertake to pay his debt, was duress.

It is not unlawful to threaten legal proceedings, and such a threat will not normally constitute illegitimate pressure. But *Kaufman v Gerson* illustrates that such a threat may in exceptional cases be illegitimate. In *J & S Holdings Pty Ltd v NRMA Insurance Ltd*[77] the Full Federal Court stated that an illegitimate threat does not become legitimate because the person making the threats states that proceedings may be brought. Thus, if the victim, a debtor who is threatened with legal proceedings to recover an amount in excess of the creditor's entitlement, succumbs to a demand for the excessive amount in order to prevent the proceedings being brought, the debtor may recover the amount of the excess. In *J & S Holdings Pty Ltd v NRMA Insurance Ltd* a debtor was threatened with proceedings which would lead to a winding up order, and it was said that this may be regarded as illegitimate pressure even though the creditor is entitled to sue for the amount actually owing, and to put the debtor into liquidation for nonpayment of that sum.

---

72. (1944) 18 ALJ 324.
73. See *Equiticorp Finance Ltd v Bank of New Zealand* (1993) 32 NSWLR 50 at 107–9 and the discussion by Andrew Phang, 'Whither Economic Duress? Reflections on Two Recent Cases' (1990) 53 *MLR* 107. Cf *Deemcope Pty Ltd v Cantown Pty Ltd* [1995] 2 VR 44 at 47.
74. See J W Carter, 'Problems in Enforcement — Part I' (1992) 5 *JCL* 199 at 201–2 (tension between 'strategic behaviour' and 'efficient' renegotiation). See also J W Carter, 'The Renegotiation of Contracts' (1998) 13 *JCL* 185.
75. Cf *Hardie and Lane Ltd v Chilton* [1928] 2 KB 306.
76. [1904] 1 KB 591. Cf *Thorne v Motor Trade Association* [1937] AC 797 at 820–2; *CTN Cash and Carry Ltd v Gallaher Ltd* [1994] 4 All ER 714 (see J W Carter and Gregory Tolhurst, (1996) 9 *JCL* 220). See also *Universe Tankships Inc of Monrovia v International Transport Workers Federation (The Universe Sentinel)* [1983] 1 AC 366 at 401.
77. (1982) 41 ALR 539 at 556.

[1320] Bona fide conduct. A person's conduct may be bona fide, that is, in good faith, and yet not legally justifiable. For example, a person may honestly believe that a particular course of conduct is lawful even though it is not. This idea has its main application in cases where a threat not to perform the contract leads to a contract of compromise or settlement.[78] By definition, one of the parties (perhaps both) is wrong in the claim made. Even if it is the party making a threat not to perform who is wrong, the contract is not usually regarded as entered into under duress.[79] It would throw that area of the law into profound confusion if a threat not to perform were to be regarded as illegitimate pressure merely because of an error in assessment of contractual obligation or liability. An inquiry into duress is, however, justified if the party making the threat expresses it in the form 'whether or not I am correct in my assessment of obligation or liability, I do not intend to perform unless you enter into a contract by which you abandon your rights against me'.[80]

It will be explained later[81] that where a party is bound by a contract, a statement that it will not be performed may amount to a repudiation of the contract. Although such conduct is not in itself a breach of contract,[82] it is generally accepted that for the purposes of duress the conduct may be wrongful even though the promisee acquiesces, and does not take the step of terminating the performance of the contract. Conversely, a statement that the promisor will not perform, in the bona fide belief that the contract does not require performance, although not constituting a repudiation, may be wrongful for the purposes of duress.[83]

[1321] Wrongful conduct. The illegitimacy of the pressure or threat may be obvious. In *Occidental Worldwide Investment Corp v Skibs A/S Avanti (The Siboen and The Sibotre)*,[84] Kerr J instanced a threat to burn down the house or slash a valuable picture of the contracting party. Equally, however, it is clear that less extreme forms of conduct will constitute duress. An obvious starting point is wrongful conduct. But what does 'wrongful' mean? In *Crescendo Management Pty Ltd v Westpac Banking Corp*[85] McHugh JA, speaking for the New South Wales Court of Appeal, said that pressure will be illegitimate if it 'consists of unlawful threats or amounts to unconscionable conduct'. This should not be taken as implying that every unlawful threat will constitute illegitimate pressure: it is too simplistic to say that any wrongful conduct is sufficient to justify a claim of duress.[86] Similarly, conduct is 'unconscionable' only if there is an exploitation by one party of another's position of disadvantage, and McHugh JA's reference to

---

78. See generally [350]–[355].
79. Cf N E Palmer and Louise Catchpole, (1985) 48 *MLR* 102 at 107.
80. See, eg *Vantage Navigation Corp v Suhail and Saud Bahwan Building Materials LLC (The Alev)* [1989] 1 Lloyd's Rep 138 (see [1322]).
81. See [1928]–[1947].
82. There is a requirement that the repudiation be 'accepted': see [1945].
83. See *Nixon v Furphy* (1925) 25 SR (NSW) 151 (affirmed sub nom *Furphy v Nixon* (1925) 37 CLR 161); Jones, *Anglo-American Trends in Restitution*, 1978, p 11.
84. [1976] 1 Lloyd's Rep 293 at 335.
85. (1988) 19 NSWLR 40 at 46.
86. *Pao On v Lau Yiu Long* [1980] AC 614.

'unconscionable conduct' should not be taken as saying that every instance of unfair conduct involves duress.[87]

It is nevertheless true that where a person enters into a new contract in order to avoid the carrying out of the threat, it may be appropriate to conclude that economic duress is present and that the contract is voidable. Thus, in *North Ocean Shipping Co Ltd v Hyundai Construction Co Ltd (The Atlantic Baron)*[88] a shipbuilding contract was agreed between North Ocean and Hyundai for the vessel subsequently known as the *Atlantic Baron*. The contract was to build a tanker for a fixed price (in United States dollars), payable in five instalments. In order to secure the repayment of the price should the contract not be fulfilled, Hyundai was required to open a letter of credit in favour of North Ocean. After the first instalment was paid the dollar was devalued by 10 per cent. Hyundai then demanded that the amount of all outstanding instalments be increased by 10 per cent. North Ocean's legal advisers informed them that there was no obligation to pay any such sum and so North Ocean initially refused to pay. This advice was correct. Hyundai said that unless the increased payment was made the contract would be cancelled. Since Hyundai did not have a bona fide belief that it was entitled to the extra payments, its demand was a repudiation. But North Ocean paid the extra amounts, and Hyundai provided consideration for the payments by increasing the amount of the letter of credit. Nevertheless, Mocatta J held that the contract under which North Ocean paid the extra amounts was voidable for duress.[89]

[1322] Consequences if threat carried out. In *Universe Tankships Inc of Monrovia v International Transport Workers Federation (The Universe Sentinel)*[90] it was conceded that a contribution which shipowners had made to a welfare fund had been exacted by economic duress by an international federation of trade unions. Lord Diplock expressed this as a concession 'that the financial consequences to the shipowners ... were so catastrophic as to amount to a coercion of the shipowners' will which vitiated their consent to those agreements' and to the payments made by them.[91] The shipowners had, in response to the duress, entered into two agreements in writing as well as paying the money sought to be recovered.

More recently, in *Vantage Navigation Corp v Suhail and Saud Bahwan Building Materials LLC (The Alev)*[92] the plaintiffs chartered their vessel the *Alev* to charterers who later became insolvent. At the first loading port steel was loaded and freight pre-paid bills of lading were issued. These provided for the steel to be carried to Muscat. The defendants had purchased the steel for a price of about $US3.3 million and property in the steel had passed to them. Because of their difficulty in obtaining payment of the carriage charges from the charterers, the plaintiffs sought direct financial

---

87. Cf *Equiticorp Finance Ltd v Bank of New Zealand* (1993) 32 NSWLR 50 at 149–150. See further [1416].
88. [1979] 1 QB 705 (see Brian Coote, [1980] *CLJ* 40).
89. See further [1322].
90. [1983] 1 AC 366.
91. [1983] 1 AC 366 at 383. It was held by a three to two majority that the demand was not protected by a statutory provision.
92. [1989] 1 Lloyd's Rep 138 (see P A Chandler, [1989] *LMCLQ* 270).

assistance from the defendants, who became increasingly concerned because the delay to the cargo was seriously dislocating their business. There was little scope for mitigating their position by buying in steel from elsewhere. It was made clear to them that the cargo was not going to be delivered. Although the plaintiffs fully appreciated that they were contractually bound to deliver the defendants' cargo, they retained control. The defendants were aware that on occasions shipowners faced with this situation had sometimes simply dumped cargo at some port convenient to themselves, or even sold it. An agreement was signed which stated that in consideration of the plaintiffs refraining from arresting or detaining the cargo, and further agreeing to abandon any claim against the cargo arising out of the charterers' failure to fulfil their contractual obligations, the defendants would pay the port expenses and discharge costs and abandon any claims against the plaintiffs or the ship. The defendants paid the sums stipulated. Subsequently, the vessel arrived and discharged its cargo. During discharge, the defendants rescinded the agreement, arrested the vessel and recovered the money paid in a local court. The plaintiffs then sued in England to recover damages for breach of contract. They failed because the agreement under which the money was paid to the plaintiffs was vitiated by duress. The principal reason given was that the defendants had no real option, if they were to get their cargo, but to enter into the agreement and pay the money.

Nevertheless, since litigation is always open, the crucial question is not whether the victim had an alternative. Rather, it is whether the choice between the alternatives was made freely or under pressure.[93] A threat of a breach of contract will not suffice if the victim makes a 'commercial decision' to submit rather than to litigate, or if the threat to breach is commercially reasonable because of unexpected difficulties encountered by the threatening party in performing the contract.[94] However, in *North Ocean Shipping Co Ltd v Hyundai Construction Co Ltd (The Atlantic Baron)*,[95] the fact that North Ocean had agreed a charterparty with Shell was regarded as significant even though, allowing for the increased price of the vessel, a substantial profit would be made on the charter with Shell. The point seems to be that, on the facts, the option of terminating the contract with Hyundai, and looking for an alternative vessel, was not a viable one.[96] Such a vessel may not have been obtainable. Moreover, it could not be argued against North Ocean that it could have recovered damages for breach of that charterparty from Hyundai, because full compensation might not have been obtainable under the contract rules,[97] and because the damage to its commercial reputation implicit in breaching a contract with Shell might have far outweighed any sum which could have been recovered from Hyundai.

---

93. *Mason v New South Wales* (1959) 102 CLR 108 at 128. Cf *Restatement (2d) Contracts* (1979), §175 ('no reasonable alternative').
94. Cf *Chitty on Contracts*, 28th ed, 1999, Vol 1, para 7-024.
95. [1979] QB 705 (see [1321]). See also *B & S Contracts and Design Ltd v Victor Green Publications Ltd* [1984] ICR 419 at 428 (consequences must be 'serious and immediate').
96. Cf *Atlas Express Ltd v Kafco (Importers and Distributors) Ltd* [1989] QB 833.
97. See generally [2123]–[2128].

[1323] **Protest.** Many of the cases refer to the relevance of protest by the victim to the course of conduct required by the threatening party. The relevance of this can easily be overstated. In *Mason v New South Wales*[98] Windeyer J said that the presence (or absence) of protest is relevant to the question whether the victim acted freely or under compulsion. But he also recognised that it is not conclusive.[99]

Duress By and Against Third Parties

[1324] **Duress by third parties.** Although less common than duress exercised by one contracting party against the other, duress may be exercised by a third party or against a third party. In such a case, a contracting party seeking to rescind on the ground of duress must show that the other contracting party knew of the duress,[100] or that the person who exercised the duress was an agent in connection with the making of the contract.[101]

[1325] **Duress against third parties.** Consideration of duress against a third party requires us to distinguish three situations.

First, a threat may be made to a contracting party that an evil will befall another. An example would be a threat to shoot a hostage. There is no à priori rule that the threat cannot qualify as duress applied to the contracting party: the closer the relationship between the latter and the potential sufferer, the stronger will be the presumption that the threat was a reason for the making of the contract.

Second, there is the special case of a threat to a contracting agent that an evil will befall the agent's principal who is a party to the contract. For example, in *Cumming v Ince*[102] an agreement entered into by the plaintiff's attorney, at a time when the plaintiff was confined in a lunatic asylum, to the effect that the deeds to the plaintiff's property would be deposited with the solicitors for the defendants if the defendants would not, as they would otherwise have done, seek the continued confinement of the plaintiff, was held not binding on the plaintiff.

Third, a threat may be made to a third party that an evil will befall that person or some other non-contracting party. For example, in the case of a contract of guarantee, there might be a threat to the person whose liability is being guaranteed. It is difficult to accept that a guarantor would be liable where the debtor had incurred the principal liability under duress,[103] although the position might differ according to whether the principal debtor had rescinded or affirmed the principal contract.[104]

---

98. (1959) 102 CLR 108 at 142. Cf *Universe Tankships Inc of Monrovia v International Transport Workers Federation (The Universe Sentinel)* [1983] 1 AC 366 at 400.
99. See also [1317].
100. *Kesarmal S/O Letchman Das v NKV Valliappa Chettiar S/O Nagappa Chettiar* [1954] 1 WLR 380.
101. Cf [1405].
102. (1847) 11 QB 112; 116 ER 418.
103. But *Huscombe v Standing* (1607) Cro Jac 187; 79 ER 163 is an early authority to the contrary.
104. Cf [826] (guarantees of minors' contracts).

Remedies for Duress

[1326] Introduction. It is sufficient to give a brief description of the remedies available for duress. Assuming that a contract was induced by duress,[105] the primary remedy is rescission.[106] Thus, the party affected is entitled to rescind the contract in accordance with general principles of election between rights.

In cases where no benefit was conferred under the contract rescission will be sufficient protection for the plaintiff. However, the plaintiff may seek a formal order confirming rescission or setting aside the contract. Rescission will not be sufficient where a benefit was conferred under the contract. The plaintiff's claim to recover the benefit (usually money) is governed by principles of restitution.[107]

Generally, there seems no right to damages.[108] However, certain statutory provisions must also be noticed under which damages may be claimed.[109]

[1327] Rescission. Particularly in the economic duress cases, rescission assumes a significant position in determining the remedial position of the plaintiff. As indicated above,[110] rescission is the step which must precede the action to recover money or the monetary value of a benefit conferred. Accordingly, if rescission is not available, the plaintiff will fail in the action for recovery. Thus, in *North Ocean Shipping Co Ltd v Hyundai Construction Co Ltd (The Atlantic Baron)*,[111] although the vessel was delivered on 27 November 1974 it was not until 30 July 1975 that North Ocean claimed repayment of the money paid. Mocatta J decided in favour of Hyundai on the basis that North Ocean had affirmed the contract. This was an application of the general rule[112] that rescission ceases to be available once the contract has been affirmed.

[1328] Restitution. In most of the duress cases the plaintiff seeks no more than the return of money paid. Whether paid under contract or not, the basis for recovery is the restitutionary right to recover in reliance on the unjust enrichment of the defendant. Duress being a species of compulsion recognised by Australian law as coming within the unjust enrichment concept, the plaintiff's argument is that the defendant has obtained a benefit which it was unjust for the defendant to receive.[113]

However, the general rule[114] is that where a payment is made under a contract, restitution is not available until the contract has been rescinded. Once rescission has occurred, restitution will usually be awarded.[115] For

---

105. The element of causation required is that applied to cases of fraud. See [1020], [1027].
106. See [1327].
107. See [1328].
108. See [1329].
109. See [1330].
110. See [1326]. See further [1328].
111. [1979] QB 705 (see [1321]). Contrast *Hawker Pacific Pty Ltd v Helicopter Charter Pty Ltd* (1991) 22 NSWLR 298.
112. See, eg [1047].
113. See [1307].
114. See [2303].

example, in *Dimskal Shipping Co SA v International Transport Workers Federation (The Evia Luck)*[116] contracts made with unions who had threatened to 'blacklist' a vessel were lawfully rescinded for economic duress, and payments made under employment contracts with the crew were then recoverable in restitution.

[1329] Damages for duress. Dicta as to whether duress is actionable as a tort are inconsistent.[117] In *Universe Tankships Inc of Monrovia v International Transport Workers Federation (The Universe Sentinel)*[118] Lord Diplock explained that although the form that the duress takes 'may, or may not, be tortious', the 'use of economic duress to induce another person to part with property or money is not a tort per se'. He thus explained that it is only 'where the particular form taken by the economic duress used is itself a tort' that an action for damages (in tort) is available.[119] However, in the same case Lord Scarman, without qualification, said that it is established law that duress is actionable as a tort if it causes damage or loss.[120]

In the older cases[121] referring to duress as a 'wrong' the purpose seems to have been the justification of the fictional promise to repay money, required under the now discarded implied contract theory of restitution.[122] Today, it is perhaps arguable that where duress induces the making of a disadvantageous contract it ought, so far as an action for damages is concerned, to be treated as analogous to fraud. But the fact that the victim is not in any way misled makes the analogy doubtful.[123] Although the matter is not entirely free from debate, Lord Diplock's view appears to be correct, and is important in showing that 'conduct does not have to be tortious to constitute duress'.[124]

---

115. See Mason and Carter, *Restitution Law in Australia*, 1995, para 1326 and further [2306]. In so far as the requirement of restitutio in integrum (see generally [1043]–[1046], [2336]) applies, the applicable principles are those governing adjustment following rescission of a contract induced by fraudulent misrepresentation.
116. [1992] 2 AC 152. See Richard O'Dair, [1992] *LMCLQ* 145; Andrew Phang, 'Economic Duress — Uncertainty Confirmed' (1992) 5 *JCL* 147.
117. And see the exchange between R A Conti, 'Economic Duress' (1985) 1 *Aust Bar Rev* 106 and D A Staff, (1985) 1 *Aust Bar Rev* 122.
118. [1983] 1 AC 366 at 385. See also *Dimskal Shipping Co SA v International Transport Workers Federation (The Evia Luck)* [1992] 2 AC 152 at 166.
119. If the duress takes the form of a threat not to perform a contract unless the plaintiff agrees to enter into a second contract, the plaintiff may claim damages in contract only if the plaintiff did not succumb to the duress, but instead elected to terminate the contract. See [1945], [2102].
120. [1983] 1 AC 366 at 400 (citing *Barton v Armstrong* [1976] AC 104 and *Pao On v Lau Yiu Long* [1980] AC 614). See also *Alec Lobb (Garages) Ltd v Total Oil (Great Britain) Ltd* [1985] 1 WLR 173 at 177 (the 'tort of economic duress').
121. See, eg *Smith v William Charlick Ltd* (1924) 34 CLR 38 at 56.
122. See [2301], [2307]. It is a separate question whether duress is a wrong on which the plaintiff may rely for the purpose of recovering a benefit obtained by the defendant, but not amounting to a loss suffered by the plaintiff. See generally [2326]–[2329].
123. Another argument is that where what is threatened is an unlawful act, an analogy with the tort of intimidation, for which damages are available (see *Rookes v Barnard* [1964] AC 1129), ought to be applied.
124. See *Dimskal Shipping Co SA v International Transport Workers Federation (The Evia Luck)* [1992] 2 AC 152 at 169. See also at 171.

[1330] Statute. The impact of statute on the law of duress is varied. One possibility, illustrated by the *Contracts Review Act* 1980 (NSW),[125] is the relaxation of the common law rules. Section 9(2)(j) allows a court to have regard to 'whether any undue influence, unfair pressure or unfair tactics' was exerted on or used against the party seeking relief under the Act when deciding whether the contract was unjust. Unfair pressure, whether amounting to duress at common law or not, may justify a conclusion that the contract was unjust,[126] and permit, for example, an order for rescission of the contract.

A second possibility is legislation dealing with particular forms of duress. It is a question of interpretation whether the word is used in its common law sense, or has a broader or narrower meaning.[127] Section 60 of the *Trade Practices Act* 1974 (Cth) provides that:

> A corporation shall not use physical force or undue harassment or coercion in connection with the supply or possible supply of goods or services to a consumer or the payment for goods or services by a consumer.

Section 53A(2) prohibits the same kind of conduct in connection with the sale or grant, or the possible sale or grant, of an interest in land or the payment for an interest in land. The context indicates that 'coercion' as used in these sections has a wider connotation than duress under the general law. Corresponding provisions, not limited to conduct by corporations against consumers, are to be found in the fair trading legislation.[128] The same is true of the remedial provisions attracted by contravention. There is power to grant a wide range of remedies,[129] in respect of, for example, a disadvantageous contract procured by the contravening conduct.

These provisions also illustrate a third possibility, namely, the conferral of remedies not available under the common law. Thus, notwithstanding the uncertainty in relation to damages at common law for duress,[130] damages may be obtained for contravention of the *Trade Practices Act* 1974 (Cth).

---

125. See generally [1517]–[1522].
126. See *St Clair v Petricevic* (1988) ANZ Conv R ¶105.
127. See *Schanka v Employment National (Administration) Pty Ltd* (2000) 170 ALR 42 at 46.
128. **NSW**: *Fair Trading Act* 1987, ss 55, 45(2); **ACT**: *Fair Trading Act* 1992, ss 15(2), 26; **NT**: *Consumer Affairs and Fair Trading Act* 1990, ss 55, 45; **Qld**: *Fair Trading Act* 1989, ss 50, 40a; **SA**: *Fair Trading Act* 1987, ss 69, 59(2); **Tas**: *Fair Trading Act* 1990, ss 26, 17(2); **Vic**: *Fair Trading Act* 1999, s 21; **WA**: *Fair Trading Act* 1987, ss 23, 12(2)(d).
129. *Trade Practices Act* 1974 (Cth), ss 80, 82, 87 and corresponding provisions in the fair trading legislation discussed [1111]–[1121].
130. See [1329].

Chapter 14

Undue Influence

General	1401
Concerns and Categories of Undue Influence	1403
Presumed Undue Influence	1406
General	1406
Raising the Presumption	1408
Rebutting the Presumption	1411
Actual Undue Influence	1413
Undue Influence, Non Est Factum and Unconscionable Bargains	1415

General

[1401] Influence and 'undue influence'. It is common in the negotiation of a contract for one party to seek to persuade the other to make the contract. Such 'influence' without more does not prevent the contract from being fully enforceable. But some situations of influence have long been regarded as 'undue' and liable to be set aside by the court. Moreover, once it is proved that the parties stood in a 'relationship of influence', undue influence is presumed, though the presumption is rebuttable by evidence.[1]

The doctrine of undue influence is equitable in origin. It is broader than the common law's concern with the reality and motive for contractual assent.[2] Equity, true to its origins, had regard to the conscience of the party seeking to enforce a contract, with a view to ensuring that a position of influence should not be 'abused', and that confidence 'reposed' should not be 'betrayed'.[3] Now that common law and equity have been fused, at least in their administration, it is a little anachronistic to speak in terms of an 'equitable doctrine' of undue influence. However, in determining its scope it is crucial to bear in mind its origins, and the concern for the 'conscience' of the party who is claimed to have exercised undue influence.

1. See generally [1406]–[1412].
2. See [1301].
3. *Smith v Kay* (1859) 7 HLC 750 at 779; 11 ER 299 at 311.

[1401]   Contract Law in Australia

Although the brief description above refers to contracts, the concept of undue influence is not limited to such transactions. It also extends to transactions by way of contract, gift or otherwise.[4] Thus, while the leading case of *Allcard v Skinner*[5] concerned a *gift* (from a member of a religious sisterhood to the lady superior of the sisterhood and in trust for it) the principles enunciated apply equally to a *contract* procured by undue influence. Accordingly, it is appropriate, even in a discussion of contractual undue influence, to rely on cases on transactions such as gifts. Although the mere presence of consideration cannot, in a system concerned with justice, be allowed to exclude the equitable jurisdiction, lack or inadequacy of consideration has characterised many of the cases.

[1402] **Remedies for undue influence.** Where a contract is affected by undue influence, the party influenced may approach the court for an order setting aside the contract.[6] Therefore, the remedy for undue influence is an order for rescission with consequential adjustments. The essence of the consequential relief is restitutio in integrum, that is, orders for restitution in favour of both parties.[7] Although the relief is equitable in origin, it gives effect to the principle of unjust enrichment.[8] Undue influence is neither a tort nor a breach of contract, and does not per se give rise to a claim for damages in contract or tort.[9] However, undue influence may in some cases be associated with tortious conduct,[10] or conduct constituting the breach of a statutory prohibition.[11] In these cases damages in tort or under statute may be available.

Relief for undue influence may include equitable compensation[12] or an account of profits if a fiduciary relationship has been breached, or as an incident of equitable relief when having the contract set aside. For example, in *O'Sullivan v Management Agency and Music Ltd*[13] the English Court of Appeal, in setting aside contracts affected by undue influence, awarded an account of the profits that had been made from the contracts. This was, however, subject to a just allowance of 'reasonable remuneration' for the work which the defendants did under the contracts, to the benefit of the plaintiff. These orders were necessary to do what was 'practically just as between the parties'[14] in setting aside the contracts.

---

4. For a recent illustration see *Louth v Diprose* (1992) 175 CLR 621; 110 ALR 1.
5. (1887) 36 Ch D 145.
6. The defences discussed [1039]–[1062] apply.
7. The principles stated [1043]–[1046], [2336] apply.
8. See generally Chapter 23.
9. It has been held in Canada that if rescission is no longer an appropriate remedy, damages may be awarded in respect of a disadvantageous contract induced by undue influence. See *Treadwell v Martin* (1977) 13 NBR (2d) 137.
10. Cf [1329] (duress).
11. See generally Chapter 11.
12. See J D Heydon, 'Equitable Compensation for Undue Influence' (1997) 113 *LQR* 8.
13. [1985] QB 428 (see [1410]). See also *Vadasz v Pioneer Concrete (SA) Pty Ltd* (1995) 184 CLR 102 at 112–13; 130 ALR 570.
14. [1985] QB 428 at 466 per Fox LJ. Compare the unusual application in *Cheese v Thomas* [1994] 1 WLR 129 (see M Chen-Wishart, (1994) 110 *LQR* 173; Martin Dixon, [1994] *CLJ* 232; John Mee, [1994] *LMCLQ* 330). See generally Mason and Carter, *Restitution Law in Australia*, 1995, paras 1437, 1736.

Concerns and Categories of Undue Influence

[1403] Concerns of undue influence. The name 'undue influence' given to the equitable doctrine suggests a concern with, first, the precise causal relation between the influence and the decision to contract; and second, a requirement that the influence should warrant the epithet 'undue'. But the former concern has not characterised the cases and the reason is not far to seek. Generally, it is of the essence that 'undue influence' arises from an antecedent relationship between the parties. This is 'such a relation that while it continues, confidence is necessarily reposed by one, and the influence which naturally grows out of that confidence is possessed by the other'.[15] Once some influence so arising is found to have existed, equity will not be careful to protect the person who exercised it by an inquiry into its effectuality in relation to the particular contract.

The justification for the presumption in both the familiar classes of relationship,[16] as well as in the special fiduciary relationships noted later,[17] is 'to prevent victimisation by influence over the mind of another in circumstances where proof of the exercise of such influence may be impossible'.[18] More generally, the justification is to guard against one party taking advantage of a superior position.

[1404] Categories of undue influence. In *Allcard v Skinner*[19] Cotton LJ classified the undue influence cases as instances of 'actual' or 'presumed' undue influence in the following terms:[20]

> First, where the court has been satisfied that the gift was the result of influence expressly used by the donee for the purpose; second, where the relations between the donor and donee have at or shortly before the execution of the gift been such as to raise a presumption that the donee had influence over the donor. In such a case the court sets aside the voluntary gift, unless it is proved that in fact the gift was the spontaneous act of the donor acting under circumstances which enabled him to exercise an independent will and which justifies the court in holding that the gift was the result of a free exercise of the donor's will. The first class of cases may be considered as depending on the principle that no one shall be allowed to retain any benefit arising from his own fraud or wrongful act.
>
> In the second class of cases the court interferes, not on the ground that any wrongful act has in fact been committed by the donee, but on the ground of public policy, and to prevent the relations which existed between the parties and the influence arising therefrom being abused.

The duality of this treatment of the topic, according to whether undue influence (in the present context, on contractual assent) is proved as a fact or is presumed where an antecedent special relationship is shown to have existed between the parties, is well accepted in Australia.[21] Therefore:

---

15. *Tate v Williamson* (1866) LR 2 Ch App 55 at 61.
16. See [1408].
17. See [1410].
18. *Re Craig deceased; Meneces v Middleton* [1971] Ch 95 at 104.
19. (1887) 36 Ch D 145.
20. (1887) 36 Ch D 145 at 171.
21. See, eg *Johnson v Buttress* (1936) 56 CLR 113 at 119, 134; *Louth v Diprose* (1992) 175 CLR 621.

- in the first category of case (actual undue influence) this is the nature and extent of influence which must be proved; and
- in the second category of case (presumed undue influence) there is a rebuttable presumption that influence of this nature and extent existed.

The question is not whether the person seeking relief understood the transaction but whether it was the result of a free exercise of the will,[22] and it is influence, not complete domination, that is necessary.[23]

We deal first with the second category.[24]

[1405] Third party situations. The possibility must be considered that undue influence, like duress,[25] may emanate from a third party. For example, in *Powell v Powell*,[26] a voluntary settlement procured by the undue influence of a stepmother/guardian and her solicitor in favour of the former *and her two children* was set aside in toto. Moreover, the claim to have a contract set aside for undue influence may be available against a third party who enters into a transaction with the influencer. In *Bainbrigge v Browne*,[27] Fry J explained that undue influence operated against the actual influencer, 'against every volunteer who claimed under him, and also against every person who claimed under him with notice of the equity thereby created, or with notice of the circumstances from which the court infers the equity' but no further.

It follows that a guarantee or security, provided to a *creditor* for the benefit of a debtor, may be set aside for the undue influence of the *debtor*. The modern decisions focus on the position of a bank (creditor) which obtains a guarantee or security from the person influenced. There are two types of case.[28] First, the creditor may have left the obtaining of the guarantee or security in the hands of the influencer in such a way as to make that person the agent of the creditor.[29]

Second, more commonly, the creditor may have been put on notice (or known) of facts indicative of impropriety. For example, in *Bank of New South Wales v Rogers*[30] a bank's awareness of the close relationship between an uncle and his niece amounted to notice of a (presumed) relationship of

---

22. *Adenan v Buise* [1984] WAR 61 (approved *Bridgewater v Leahy* (1998) 194 CLR 457 at 477; 158 ALR 66).
23. *Tufton v Sperni* [1952] 2 TLR 516 at 519–25. Suggestions in *National Westminster Bank Plc v Morgan* [1985] 1 AC 686 at 706–7 of domination as an essential ingredient are not supported by Australian authority.
24. See [1406]–[1412].
25. See [1324]. See also [1028] (fraud by agent).
26. [1900] 1 Ch 243. Contrast *Wright v Carter* [1903] 1 Ch 27.
27. (1881) 18 Ch D 188 at 197. See also *Barclays Bank Plc v Boulter* [1999] 1 WLR 1919 at 1925 (onus of proof).
28. See generally N Y Chin, 'Undue Influence and Third Parties' (1992) 5 *JCL* 108. The reasoning in the cases is applicable also to cases of misrepresentation and duress: *Barclays Bank Plc v O'Brien* [1994] 1 AC 180.
29. See Meagher, Gummow and Lehane, *Equity: Doctrines and Remedies*, 3rd ed, 1992, para 1530.
30. (1941) 65 CLR 42. See also *Barclays Bank Plc v O'Brien* [1994] 1 AC 180 (see Martin Dixon, [1994] *CLJ* 21; John Mee, [1995] *CLJ* 330); *CIBC Mortgages Plc v Pitt* [1994] 1 AC 200 (see J R F Lehane, (1994) 110 *LQR* 167; A G J Berg, [1994] *LMCLQ* 34); *Tresize v National Australia Bank Ltd* (1994) 122 ALR 185 at 188 (cf at 197–8).

undue influence, and gave rise to a duty to prove that her actions were voluntary and understood when she transferred most of her property to the bank as security for the uncle's overdraft.

In *Yerkey v Jones*[31] the High Court held that a wife stands in a special position where she acts as a guarantor for her husband's debt. If she signs a written guarantee, 'which the creditor accepts without dealing directly with her personally, she has a prima facie right to have it set aside', if her consent was 'procured by the husband' and she did not understand its effect 'in essential respects'. In *Garcia v National Australia Bank Ltd*[32] a majority of the High Court (Kirby J dissenting) confirmed the *Yerkey* principle. Gaudron, McHugh, Gummow and Hayne JJ explained that *Yerkey* distinguished between situations where the transaction is set aside because of actual undue influence, and situations in which the transaction is set aside because the guarantor does not understand the effect of the document or the nature of the transaction. Of course, the mere fact that a guarantor does not understand the effect of the document or the nature of the transaction would not normally be a sufficient basis for having the transaction set aside. However, according to Gaudron, McHugh, Gummow and Hayne JJ,[33] it may be unconscionable for the creditor to enforce a guarantee by a wife of her husband's debts in such a case, because of the 'trust and confidence, in the ordinary sense of those words' which exists 'between marriage partners'.

The facts were that Ms Garcia signed a guarantee to secure the debts of a company of which she and her husband were directors. There was no explanation of the transaction by the creditor to Ms Garcia, who did not fully understand the nature of the guarantee, and believed that it was a 'risk proof' transaction. Moreover, although the company benefited from the giving of the guarantee, Ms Garcia obtained no personal benefit from the transaction. Accordingly, the guarantee was set aside. Gaudron, McHugh, Gummow and Hayne JJ expressed the principle in these terms:[34]

> [W]hat makes it unconscionable to enforce [the guarantee] is the combination of circumstances that:
>
> (a) in fact the surety did not understand the purport and effect of the transaction;
>
> (b) the transaction was voluntary (in the sense that the surety obtained no gain from the contract the performance of which was guaranteed);
>
> (c) the lender is to be taken to have understood that, as a wife, the surety may repose trust and confidence in her husband in matters of business and therefore to have understood that the husband may not fully and accurately explain the purport and effect of the transaction to his wife; and yet
>
> (d) the lender did not itself take steps to explain the transaction to the wife or find out that a stranger had explained it to her.

---

31. (1939) 63 CLR 649 at 683.
32. (1998) 194 CLR 395; 155 ALR 614 (see Andrew Phang and Hans Tjio, (1999) 14 *JCL* 72; Robyn Baxendale, (1999) 21 *Syd LR* 313); Simon Gardner, (1999) 115 *LQR* 1.
33. See (1998) 194 CLR 395 at 404.
34. See (1998) 194 CLR 395 at 409.

The practical impact of the case is that it is essential for a creditor who takes the benefit of a guarantee from a wife in respect of her husband's debts, or the debts of the husband's company, to 'take steps to explain the transaction to the wife or find out that a stranger had explained it to her'.[35] The creditor may therefore enforce the transaction against the surety, even though the surety is a volunteer who later claims to have been mistaken, if the creditor explained the transaction sufficiently, or knew that the surety received competent, independent and disinterested advice from a third party.[36]

Several further points can be made about the application of the *Yerkey* principle in *Garcia* and its scope.

First, Gaudron, McHugh, Gummow and Hayne JJ also stated[37] that the principles applied in *Yerkey* 'do not depend upon the creditor having, at the time the guarantee is taken, notice of some unconscionable dealing between the husband as borrower and the wife as surety'. Therefore, the creditor need have no notice of impropriety.[38]

Second, the guarantee related to the company of which both parties to the marriage were directors. Thus, the principle is not limited to guarantees given in respect of a husband's personal debts.

Third, although the principle was expressed in terms of a transaction which is 'voluntary', this must be understood in a broader sense than whether contractual consideration is present. Thus, the principle applies unless there is a benefit to the guarantor which is substantial, or at least not negligible.

Fourth, the rationale for the principle is not to be found in notions based on the subservience or inferior economic position of women, or their vulnerability to exploitation because of their emotional involvement.[39]

Fifth, although the High Court expressly left open for later consideration the question whether the principle applies to other relationships,[40] it is difficult to see why it would not apply, for example, where a husband is a surety for his wife, or the domestic relationship is between unmarried partners or between same sex partners.

---

35. See (1998) 194 CLR 395 at 409 per Gaudron, McHugh, Gummow and Hayne JJ.
36. See (1998) 194 CLR 395 at 411 (approving *Yerkey v Jones* (1939) 63 CLR 649 at 686).
37. (1998) 194 CLR 395 at 409. See also at 409. English law takes a different approach. See *Barclays Bank Plc v O'Brien* [1994] 1 AC 180 at 195 (see J R F Lehane, (1994) 110 *LQR* 167).
38. Analysis based on notice may be required in ordering the priority of competing interests in property. See *Garcia v National Australia Bank Ltd* (1998) 194 CLR 395 at 411.
39. See (1998) 194 CLR 395 at 404 (save to the extent that a case may be concerned with actual undue influence).
40. See (1998) 194 CLR 395 at 404.

Presumed Undue Influence

General

[1406] Introduction. Within the category of presumed undue influence it is necessary to deal with two sub-categories. In the first, the relationship of the parties belongs to a class in which, according to established practice, undue influence must be presumed.

In the second, although the relationship does not come within a class in which influence has traditionally been presumed, the factual relationship is such that the court will presume undue influence to be present.

[1407] Relationship between established classes and special relations. In *Johnson v Buttress*,[41] Dixon J considered the relationship between the established familiar classes of relationship and the special relations of influence directed to the particular transaction at issue. After noting that 'because of the presence of circumstances which might be regarded as presumptive proof of express influence', factual situations outside the list of established classes 'but nevertheless importing a special relationship of influence sometimes are treated as if they were not governed by the presumption but depended on an inference of fact', he said:[42]

> Further, when the transaction is not one of gift but of purchase or other contract, the matters affecting its validity are necessarily somewhat different. Adequacy of consideration becomes a material question. Instead of inquiring how the subordinate party came to confer a benefit, the court examines the propriety of what wears the appearance of a business dealing. These differences form an additional cause why cases which really illustrate the effect of a special relation of influence in raising a presumption of invalidity are often taken to decide that express influence which is undue should be inferred from the circumstances.

Raising the Presumption

[1408] Established classes of relationship. Common experience has led the courts to accept that certain commonly occurring personal relationships are likely to give rise to influence of the nature and extent mentioned above. Relationships between the following classes of persons have been judicially recognised as falling within this category:

- parent (or person in loco parentis)[43] and child;[44]
- guardian and ward;[45]
- solicitor and client;[46]
- trustee and beneficiary;[47]

---

41. (1936) 56 CLR 113.
42. (1936) 56 CLR 113 at 135–6.
43. *Bank of New South Wales v Rogers* (1941) 65 CLR 42 at 52.
44. See, eg *Bainbrigge v Browne* (1881) 18 Ch D 188 at 196; *London and Westminster Loan and Discount Co Ltd v Bilton* (1911) 27 TLR 184.
45. See, eg *Powell v Powell* [1900] 1 Ch 243.
46. See, eg *Re P's Bill of Costs* (1982) 45 ALR 513 at 521–5; *Westmelton (Vic) Pty Ltd v Archer and Shulman* [1982] VR 305.

- physician and patient;[48] and
- religious adviser and advisee.[49]

A notable omission from this list is the relationship of husband and wife.[50]

Questions are raised by the simple proposition that any one of these relationships, irrespective of features peculiar to the particular instance of it, gives rise to the presumption. Must the relationship (such as between solicitor and client) subsist down to the moment of contracting, and if so, with what (if any) 'characteristics', 'strength' or 'intensity'? Does a short temporal hiatus between termination of the relationship and the making of the contract signify that the presumption does not arise? Does the presumption arise, to take extreme examples, between a young recently admitted solicitor who is the junior partner in a firm which represents a large public company and that company, or between an aged, ill and poorly educated parent with little business experience and a well-educated and prosperous adult child?

[1409] **Scope of the established classes.** The answers given to the questions stated above[51] may make little difference in the deciding of cases because, in a particular case where the presumption is held to arise, it may be that little evidence is required to rebut it.[52] Similarly, in *Westmelton (Vic) Pty Ltd v Archer and Shulman*[53] it was held that the established presumption applied to all instances of the solicitor–client relationship but that the extent of the evidence required to rebut it varied from one case to another.

In any case where it is held that the presumption does not arise, there always remains scope for the evidence to show actual undue influence or a special fiduciary relationship on the facts giving rise to a presumption of undue influence.[54] In *Avon Finance Co Ltd v Bridger*[55] a majority of the English Court of Appeal held, without reference to the established converse presumption of undue influence by parent over child, that there was a presumption of undue influence on the facts of the case by a chartered accountant in a good practice over his parents who were aged, in humble circumstances and inexperienced in business, and who had, at his instance, unwittingly executed a second mortgage over their home to secure his borrowing.

There is authority for the rejection of the following relationships as giving rise to the presumption:

- husband and wife;[56]
- dentist and patient;[57]

---

47. See, eg *Wheeler v Sargeant* (1893) 69 LT 181.
48. See, eg *Dent v Bennett* (1839) 4 My & Cr 269; 41 ER 105; *Williams v Johnson* [1937] 4 All ER 34.
49. See, eg *Allcard v Skinner* (1887) 36 Ch D 145.
50. See, eg *Colonial Bank of Australasia v Kerr* (1889) 15 VLR 314; *Yerkey v Jones* (1939) 63 CLR 649. See further [1409].
51. See [1408].
52. See [1405].
53. [1982] VR 305.
54. See [1410].
55. (1979) [1985] 2 All ER 281.

- master and servant;[58] and
- government monopolist supplier and retailer.[59]

This is not to say, however, that on the facts of particular cases there cannot be either actual undue influence or even a presumption of undue influence[60] between the parties to such relationships. The categories of relationship which yield a presumption of undue influence are not closed.[61]

[1410] Special relationships giving rise to the presumption. Where the relationship between the parties in a particular case does not fall within one of the familiar classes, the court may be asked to find either that the parties' antecedent relationship was such that undue influence should, as a matter of law, be presumed unless rebutted, or that there was actual undue influence.[62] The reason for the presumption in the established categories, and what must be established by evidence if an *ad hoc special relation of influence* is to give rise to the same presumption, was explained by Dixon J in *Johnson v Buttress*:[63]

> [O]ne party occupies or assumes towards another a position naturally involving an ascendancy or influence over that other, or a dependence or trust on his part. One occupying such a position falls under a duty in which fiduciary characteristics may be seen. It is his duty to use his position of influence in the interest of no one but the man who is governed by his judgment, gives him his dependence and entrusts him with his welfare.

It is neither possible nor desirable to attempt to categorise the special relationships which, in particular cases, have been held to give rise to the presumption. However, it is perhaps noteworthy that some have concerned persons, accustomed to rely on a spouse or other person for business and financial advice, who have, following the death of that person, become dependent on the alleged influencer.

In *Lloyds Bank Ltd v Bundy*[64] the defendant was an elderly farmer. His only asset was his farm which had been in his family for generations. His son's company was in financial difficulty. On 16 September 1966 he guaranteed its bank overdraft up to £1500 and charged his house to the bank as security. He, his son and the company banked at the same bank. On 27 May 1969, he executed a further guarantee for £5000 and a further charge for £6000. This time the assistant branch manager left the documents with the defendant overnight and before he executed them the defendant was advised by a solicitor that £5000 was the furthest extent to

---

56. See [1408]. See, however, [1405] (position where wife is guarantor of husband's debts).
57. *Brooks v Alca* (1976) 60 DLR (3d) 577.
58. *Mathew v Bobbins* [1980] EG Dig 421 (see (1980) 54 *ALJ* 744).
59. *Eric Gnapp Ltd v Petroleum Board* [1949] 1 All ER 980.
60. See [1404].
61. *Allcard v Skinner* (1887) 36 Ch D 145 at 158; *Johnson v Buttress* (1936) 56 CLR 113 at 119; *Louth v Diprose* (1992) 175 CLR 621 at 628.
62. See *Johnson v Buttress* (1936) 56 CLR 113 at 119, 134; *Re Brocklehurst deceased; Hall v Roberts* [1978] Ch 14.
63. (1936) 56 CLR 113 at 134–5. See also *Union Fidelity Trustee Co v Gibson* [1971] VR 573 and further [1412].
64. [1975] 1 QB 326.

which he should commit himself and his home to the company's business. The house was now charged for £7500.

The company's difficulties continued and in December 1969 a new assistant branch manager told the son that something must be done. The son said his father would help. The new assistant branch manager went to see the defendant at his farmhouse. He took further forms of guarantee for £11,000 and a charge for a further £3500 (which would bring the amount secured by charges up to £11,000), both completed and ready for execution. He told the defendant that the bank could continue to support the company only if the documents were executed. The defendant executed them at the farm in the presence of his wife, his son, his son's wife and the assistant branch manager. The farmhouse was worth about £10,000.

In May 1970 a receiver was appointed in respect of the company. The bank, as plaintiff, sought possession to enforce the guarantee and charge but the defendant successfully applied to have both set aside. All three members of the English Court of Appeal favoured this result. The special relationship in question was regarded from the viewpoint of the influencer's duty to ensure that the other party contracted free from the influence. Sir Eric Sachs (with whose reasons Cairns LJ agreed) said[65] that the special relationship tends to arise 'where someone relies on the guidance or advice of another, where the other is aware of that reliance and where the person upon whom reliance is placed obtains, or may well obtain, a benefit from the transaction or has some other interest in it being concluded' and where an element of 'confidentiality' is present.

More recently, in *O'Sullivan v Management Agency and Music Ltd*[66] the plaintiff, who became a famous singer and songwriter under the name 'Gilbert O'Sullivan', placed total confidence in one Mills, who controlled the defendant companies, and trusted him to look after his interests. O'Sullivan lived in a cottage in the grounds of Mills's house and was given £10 per week 'pocket money'. Subsequently, there were changes in the contractual relationships and, on Mills's advice, O'Sullivan signed various agreements without reading them or taking independent advice. The English Court of Appeal held that the close confidential relation between Mills and O'Sullivan gave rise to a presumption of undue influence in relation to the transactions.

Rebutting the Presumption

[1411] **Onus.** Clearly, the onus of rebutting (displacing) the presumption of undue influence rests on the party supporting the transaction. It must be established that the transaction 'was the result of a free exercise of the ... will'.[67] If the onus is not discharged, the transaction is voidable.

A common way of attempting to rebut the presumption is by the tender of evidence that the person said to have been influenced received competent independent advice and, in particular, advice from a duly

---

65. [1975] 1 QB 326 at 341.
66. [1985] QB 428.
67. *Allcard v Skinner* (1887) 36 Ch D 145 at 171 per Cotton LJ. Cf *Johnson v Buttress* (1936) 56 CLR 113 at 120, 138, 143.

qualified legal practitioner employed independently of the other contracting party. Independent advice is not, however, essential as a matter of law.[68] Moreover, the mere giving of some such advice is not necessarily sufficient.[69]

[1412] Transaction need not be disadvantageous. Since what is required is evidence displacing the presumption, the strength of the evidence required will vary according to the strength of the presumption. So, where the transaction is a gift or disposition for inadequate consideration by an illiterate or weakminded person of all or virtually all of that person's property, the presumption is more difficult to rebut than where a person not subject to personal disabilities has entered into an agreement for full value extending to only an insubstantial part of his or her property.[70]

But the question arises whether the transaction must be disadvantageous to the party seeking relief. In *Blomley v Ryan*,[71] an 'unconscionable bargain' case, Fullagar J said:[72]

> It does not appear to be essential in all cases that the party at a disadvantage should suffer loss or detriment by the bargain … But inadequacy of consideration, while never of itself a ground for resisting enforcement, will often be a specially important element in cases of this type. It may be important in either or both of two ways — firstly as supporting the inference that a position of disadvantage existed, and secondly as tending to show that an unfair use was made of the occasion

It was on account of public policy directed against the risk of abuse of influence, not disadvantage actually suffered, that equity relieved.[73] Accordingly, under Australian law[74] it is not essential to relief on the ground of undue influence that the contract was disadvantageous to the person who has the benefit of the presumption.[75] Similarly, the

---

68. *Inche Noriah v Shaik Allie Bin Omar* [1929] AC 127; *Re P's Bill of Costs* (1982) 42 ALR 513.
69. *Powell v Powell* [1900] 1 Ch 243; *Inche Noriah v Shaik Allie Bin Omar* [1929] AC 127; *Westmelton (Vic) Pty Ltd v Archer and Shulman* [1982] VR 305.
70. See *Johnson v Buttress* (1936) 56 CLR 113 at 120.
71. (1956) 99 CLR 362.
72. (1956) 99 CLR 362 at 405. See also *Tate v Williamson* (1866) LR 2 Ch App 55 at 66. But cf *Fry v Lane* (1888) 40 Ch D 312.
73. *Allcard v Skinner* (1887) 36 Ch D 145 at 171. See also *Maguire v Makaronis* (1997) 188 CLR 449 at 467; 144 ALR 729 (equity to a decree of rescission will be generated by a prior breach of fiduciary duty).
74. But see *James v Australian and New Zealand Banking Group Ltd* (1986) 64 ALR 347 at 390.
75. Although in *National Westminster Bank Plc v Morgan* [1985] 1 AC 686 at 704 (see Neil Andrews, [1985] *CLJ* 193) the House of Lords appeared to take a different view, by treating as a requirement of relief on the ground of undue influence that the contract 'must constitute a disadvantage sufficiently serious to require evidence to rebut the presumption that in the circumstances of the relationship between the parties it was procured by the exercise of undue influence' (see Malcolm Cope, 'Undue Influence and Alleged Manifestly Disadvantageous Transactions: *National Westminster Bank Plc v Morgan*' (1986) 60 *ALJ* 87) this was explained in *Royal Bank of Scotland v Etridge (No 2)* [2001] 3 WLR 1021 as referring simply to evidence showing that the transaction is not 'reasonably accounted for on the ground of friendship, relationship, charity or other ordinary motives' (*Allcard v Skinner* (1887) 36 Ch D 145 at 185 per Lindley LJ).

presumption of undue influence is not displaced merely by proof that the transaction was advantageous.

Actual Undue Influence

[1413] Actual undue influence distinct from presumptions. There is a thin dividing line between actual undue influence and special relationships which give rise to a presumption of undue influence. In each case the onus of proof rests on the person setting up the undue influence. Typically, it will be argued that a finding of undue influence is, on the facts, supported on both bases.

In the case of a special relationship of influence or duty of fiduciary care, the emphasis is on the antecedent relationship from which the court will be asked to infer that undue influence continued down to the time of contract. On the other hand, in the case of *actual* undue influence without the benefit of any presumption, the evidence must establish the actual influence on the mind at the time of contract. Inevitably the latter will involve evidence of the genesis of the influence, and the former will usually involve some evidence of actual influence.

[1414] Adequacy or inadequacy of consideration. Commonly, where undue influence is relieved against, the weaker party has received no consideration or inadequate consideration. This may explain the sense of grievance, and will also be relevant to issues of opportunity to influence, actual influence and rebuttal of the presumption of undue influence.

The presence of consideration will require the court to examine the propriety of what wears the appearance of a business dealing.[76] However, as we have seen,[77] in Australia the absence or inadequacy of consideration is not essential to the availability of relief.

Undue Influence, Non Est Factum and Unconscionable Bargains

[1415] Undue influence and non est factum. Non est factum[78] is a plea 'that the mind of the signer did not accompany the signature'.[79] It is concerned with signatures, the nature and effect of the document signed and the state of mind and conduct of the signer at the time in relation to the document. The focus of attention is not the other party, although any role played in procuring the signature and/or in the signer's lack of understanding of the document will be relevant, for example, to the issue of the signer's negligence. By contrast, in undue influence the relationship between the contracting parties and the conduct of the alleged influencer are essential matters.

---

76. See *Johnson v Buttress* (1936) 56 CLR 113 at 136; *Maguire v Makaronis* (1997) 188 CLR 449 at 465.
77. See [1412].
78. 'It is not my deed', see generally [1267]–[1275].
79. *Foster v Mackinnon* (1869) LR 4 CP 704 at 711.

The effect of the non est factum plea, if successful, is that the document is void ab initio. By contrast, undue influence is relevant to oral and to written contracts, and such influence renders a contract not void but liable to be set aside under equitable principles.

[1416] Undue influence, unconscionable conduct and duress. Since both are species of equitable fraud,[80] undue influence may be a form of unconscionable conduct by the person seeking to retain the benefit of a transaction and to resist equitable intervention. But the expression 'unconscionable conduct' is sometimes used to designate not merely a common characteristic of equitable grounds of relief, but that more specific class of case discussed in Chapter 15 where the reason for setting aside the transaction is not the existence of undue influence, but the unconscionable nature of the transaction or the conduct of one party to the transaction. Intervention is justified in such cases because the contract is due to the combination of the 'disadvantageous position' in which the party seeking relief is placed and the fact that the other party 'unconscientiously [takes] advantage of that position'.[81] And the common law concept of duress[82] may operate in situations where undue influence does not.

In *Commercial Bank of Australia Ltd v Amadio*[83] Deane J expressed the difference between the concepts in this way:[84]

> Undue influence, like common law duress, looks to the quality of the consent or assent of the weaker party ... Unconscionable dealing looks to the conduct of the stronger party in attempting to enforce, or retain the benefit of, a dealing with a person under a special disability in circumstances where it is not consistent with equity or good conscience that he should do so.

On this basis, the jurisdictions in relation to unconscionable conduct and undue influence are 'distinct'.[85] Moreover, the continued reliance on presumptive relationships in the undue influence context itself implies a significant practical difference between establishing undue influence and proving unconscionable conduct. Although it has been doubted whether there are many cases of undue influence which cannot be brought within the unconscionable conduct concept,[86] it seems important to acknowledge the difference in focus emphasised by Deane J.[87]

---

80. See [1501]. And note the relevance of undue influence to the jurisdiction exercised under the *Contracts Review Act* 1980 (NSW) (see [1520]).
81. *Commercial Bank of Australia Ltd v Amadio* (1983) 151 CLR 447 at 461; 46 ALR 402 per Mason J.
82. See Chapter 13.
83. (1983) 151 CLR 447.
84. (1983) 151 CLR 447 at 474.
85. *Louth v Diprose* (1992) 175 CLR 621 at 627. Contrast David Capper, 'Undue Influence and Unconscionability: A Rationalisation' (1998) 114 *LQR* 479.
86. See I J Hardingham, 'Unconscionable Dealing' in Finn, ed, *Essays in Equity*, 1985, pp 17–19. See also Anthony Mason, 'The Place of Equity and Equitable Remedies in the Contemporary Common Law World' (1994) 110 *LQR* 238 at 249 (undue influence now in a 'position of relative unimportance'). Cf J R F Lehane, (1994) 110 *LQR* 167 at 173 ('conjunction' with *actual* undue influence).
87. See Peter Birks and Chin Nyuk Yin, 'On the Nature of Undue Influence' in Beatson and Friedmann, eds, *Good Faith and Fault in Contract Law*, 1995, p 57. Cf *Bridgewater v Leahy* (1998) 194 CLR 457 at 478. See also Anne Finlay, 'Can We See the Chancellor's Footprint?: Bridgewater v Leahy' (1999) 14 *JCL* 265.

On the other hand, notwithstanding Deane J's statement that undue influence is like common law duress, because it looks to the 'quality of the consent or assent of the weaker party', it is important to acknowledge that undue influence differs from duress because it is no defence to show that the plaintiff's decision to contract was made freely.[88]

---

88. See P J Millett, 'Equity's Place in the Law of Commerce' (1998) 114 *LQR* 214 at 219.

Chapter 15

Unconscionability

General	1501
Equitable Principles	1504
Catching Bargains	1504
Modern Case Law	1507
Unfair Contracts Legislation	1515
Introduction	1515
Legislation Dealing with Particular Kinds of Contracts	1516
Legislation of More General Application	1517
Towards a System of Abstract Control of Unfair Contracts?	1529

General

[1501] **Relevance of unconscionability.** In the past 15 years the concept of unconscionability has become a significant theme in the Australian law of contract.[1] In nearly every area of the law unconscionability has been treated as having relevance in one way or another. To appreciate its relevance, a number of focal points may be distinguished.

First, a person may unconscionably seek to depart from a promise, representation or assurance made, but which has no contractual significance. Second, unconscionability may be relevant to the decision to contract. That is to say, a contract may be entered into because one party has engaged in unconscionable conduct in order to influence the other to enter into the contract. Third, the terms of a contract may be unconscionable in the sense of being unfair to one of the parties. Fourth, enforcement of a contract (or the rights which it creates) may, in particular circumstances, be unconscionable. Finally, unconscionability may be a statutory justification for re-opening a contract.

---

1. Cf [113]. See generally D Harland, 'Unconscionable and Unfair Contracts: An Australian Perspective' in Brownsword, Hird and Howells, eds, *Good Faith in Contract*, 1999, Chapter 11; J W Carter and A Stewart, 'Commerce and Conscience: the High Court's Developing View of Contract' (1993) 23 *UWALR* 49; P Finn, 'Unconscionable Conduct' (1994) 8 *JCL* 37; G Dal Pont, 'The varying shades of unconscionable conduct — same term, different meaning' (2000) 19 *Aust Bar Rev* 135.

It follows from the situations referred to above that the concept of unconscionability has been referred to in several places in this book. Thus, we dealt with unconscionable departure from non-contractual promises, representations and assurances in the context of estoppel.[2] And we shall later deal with the unconscionable exercise of contractual rights in the context of termination[3] and the recovery of sums fixed by the contract.[4] Again, much of what was said in the discussion of mistake[5] illustrates the operation of an unconscionability concept.

The significant feature of most of the other discussions of unconscionability is that the concept in those contexts does not operate as a separate doctrine so much as a criterion or factor leading to interference with the terms of a bargain not itself procured by unconscionable conduct. Thus, for example, where the exercise of a right of termination deprives the other party of an interest in property, the court may exercise a jurisdiction to grant relief against forfeiture if the conduct of the first party is, in the circumstances, unconscionable. However, the particular concern of the present chapter is whether, and in what circumstances, a contract may be set aside by the court on the ground that it is an unconscionable contract. In one sense this is a residual class of case in which there is equitable jurisdiction to relieve from a contract. From a broader — and more accurate — perspective the discussion can be seen as defining the limits of a jurisdiction which courts undoubtedly possess to relieve against fraud in the widest sense. The jurisdiction encompasses misrepresentation, mistake, undue influence and, in limited cases, unconscionable conduct. These do not amount to a general jurisdiction to intervene, based on some indefinable concept of 'unfairness'.[6]

[1502] Limits on general law relief against harsh contracts. The courts have no general supervisory jurisdiction over the making of contracts and there is no shortage of judicial warning against assuming to the contrary. Thus, Lord Radcliffe, in *Bridge v Campbell Discount Co Ltd*[7] said:

> 'Unconscionable' must not be taken to be a panacea for adjusting any contract between competent persons when it shows a rough edge to one side or the other, and equity lawyers are, I notice, sometimes both surprised and discomfited by the plenitude of jurisdiction and the imprecision of rules that are attributed to 'equity' by their more enthusiastic colleagues ... Even such masters of equity as Lord Eldon and Sir George Jessel, it must be remembered, were highly sceptical of the court's duty to apply the epithet 'unconscionable' or its consequences to contracts made between persons of full age in circumstances that did not fall within the familiar categories of fraud, surprise, accident, etc ...

For example, although in *South Australian Railways Commissioner v Egan*[8] Menzies J stated[9] that the court was concerned with 'perhaps the most

---

2. See [365]–[387]. Cf [521] (part performance); [2309] (restitution).
3. See [1979], [1983]. See also [2332] (relief against forfeiture).
4. See, eg [2212].
5. See, eg [1231], [1254], [1265]. Cf [1321] (duress), [1416] (undue influence).
6. See [1502].
7. [1962] AC 600 at 626.
8. (1973) 130 CLR 506.
9. (1973) 130 CLR 506 at 512. Cf *Hart v O'Connor* [1985] AC 1000 at 1018.

wordy, obscure and oppressive contract' that he had come across, he had to resist the temptation presented by such a contract to go outside his function and 'attempt to relieve against the harshness of, rather than give effect to, what has been agreed by the parties'.

[1503] Basis of relief. Probably every contract involves some disparity between the parties in terms of bargaining power, needs, means and business acumen. Certainty of contract would be destroyed if courts were to relieve merely upon proof of some such disparity. Moreover, it would be inconsistent with the philosophy of a free enterprise system to attempt to eliminate all negotiating advantage. Finally, a concern with fine differences between the parties' respective negotiating positions would give rise to protracted and costly hearings and great evidentiary difficulties.

The history of the topic certainly illustrates the development of a basis for relief which may be described as 'unconscionability' or 'unconscionable conduct'.[10] Following the decision of the High Court in *Commercial Bank of Australia Ltd v Amadio*[11] and the enactment of legislation controlling unconscionable conduct,[12] relief on the basis of unconscionability has been sought in the Australian courts far more frequently than was traditionally the case, and the question of how far statements such as those cited above[13] should now be qualified is an important and developing issue in the contemporary Australian law of contract.

Another interesting issue for the future is how unconscionability will develop as more Australian contract cases are considering the notion of 'good faith'.[14] Currently the two concepts are regarded separately. Yet, perhaps as 'unconscionability' expands in common law and statutory provisions make reference to 'good faith' as a factor in deciding whether there has been unconscionable conduct,[15] in the future the distinction may become less apparent.[16]

Equitable Principles

Catching Bargains[17]

[1504] Catching bargains with 'expectants'. Equity has a long established jurisdiction to relieve from transactions on account of equitable fraud.[18] Many of the early cases were concerned with catching bargains

10. See generally Chen-Wishart, *Unconscionable Bargains*, 1989; D C Ford, 'Unconscionable Conduct — A Matter for the Courts or the Legislatures?' (1985) 13 *ABLR* 307. Cf Garry Muir, 'Contract and Equity: Striking A Balance' (1985) 10 *Adel LR* 153.
11. (1983) 151 CLR 447 (see [1512]).
12. See L J Priestley, 'Contract — The Burgeoning Maelstrom' (1988) 1 *JCL* 15 and [1515]ff.
13. [1502]
14. See, eg Elisabeth Peden, 'Incorporating Terms of Good Faith in Contract Law in Australia' (2001) 23 *Syd LR* 222.
15. See, eg ss 51AC(3)(k), 51AC(4)(k) *Trade Practices Act*; [1524]ff.
16. See also [1809].
17. See Meagher, Gummow and Lehane, *Equity: Doctrines and Remedies*, 3rd ed, 1992, Chapter 16.

with 'expectants'. These were members of the English upper class, often young and certainly not accustomed to possessing and dealing with wealth, who were about to inherit property or to become entitled to property upon the cessation of an estate or interest vested in someone else. As an illustration of the latter, such a person might be entitled to property which was leased to another and the period of the lease might be about to end so that the right to possession would revert to the person ('reversioner') who would then suddenly be entitled to dispose of valuable property.[19]

Catching bargains with expectant heirs and reversioners of young age was the most common class of contract with which equity interfered in the 19th century.[20] In *Nevill v Snelling*[21] Denman J thought the principle of the cases applicable to 'the case of an improvident young man who falls into the hands of a professional moneylender and gets deeper and deeper into debt, the moneylender trading upon the probable unwillingness of the young man's relations to let him and his family be exposed by bankruptcy'. They were easily exploited. If they needed or thought they needed money, they would find it all too easy to pledge, or otherwise rely on, their expectancy in order to satisfy (perhaps 'gratify') that need. Thus, imprudent transactions were inevitable and expectancies were lost through 'catching bargains' made by the avaricious and calculating.

Earl of Chesterfield v Janssen[22] concerned an expectant heir's bond to pay, for a present loan of £5000, £10,000 if he survived his grandmother, which he did six years and three months later. Lord Hardwicke referred to equity's 'undoubted jurisdiction to relieve against every species of fraud'[23] including the fraud 'which infects catching bargains with heirs, reversioners, or expectants, in the life of the father etc' and said of such cases, 'there is always fraud presumed or inferred from the circumstances or conditions of the parties contracting: weakness on one side, usury on the other, or extortion or advantage taken of that weakness. There has been always an appearance of fraud from the nature of the bargain ... '.[24]

In *Earl of Aylesford v Morris*,[25] relief was granted to a 22-year-old nobleman who, being heavily in debt but entitled to a large estate if he should survive his father, in response to his creditor's pressure and recommendation, borrowed from a moneylender at an effective interest rate of 60 per cent per annum. The young man had no professional advice and no advice from his father or his father's solicitors. Wickens V-C restrained proceedings by the moneylender and ordered discharge of the securities which had been given, on payment of the sum actually advanced and interest at only five per cent per annum. In the course of the moneylender's unsuccessful appeal, Lord Selborne LC said:[26]

18. See J L Barton, 'The Enforcement of Hard Bargains' (1987) 103 *LQR* 118.
19. A similar situation was that of persons entitled to property in remainder upon the death of an aged life tenant.
20. See, eg *Fry v Lane* (1888) 40 Ch D 312; *O'Rorke v Bolingbroke* (1877) 2 App Cas 814.
21. (1880) 15 Ch D 679 at 696.
22. (1751) 2 Ves Sen 125; 28 ER 82.
23. (1751) 2 Ves Sen 125 at 155; 28 ER 82 at 100.
24. (1751) 2 Ves Sen 125 at 157; 28 ER 82 at 101.
25. (1873) LR 8 Ch App 484.

fraud does not here mean deceit or circumvention; it means an unconscientious use of the power arising out of these circumstances and conditions; and when the relative position of the parties is such as prima facie to raise this presumption, the transaction cannot stand unless the person claiming the benefit of it is able to repel the presumption by contrary evidence, proving it to have been in point of fact fair, just and reasonable.

After observing that there was present no 'element of personal influence' of the kind that forms the basis of 'undue influence',[27] his Lordship said that it sufficed:[28]

> ... for the application of the principle, if the parties meet under such circumstances as, in the particular transaction, to give the stronger party dominion over the weaker, and such power and influence are generally possessed, in every transaction of this kind, by those who trade upon the follies and vices of unprotected youth, inexperience, and moral imbecility.

His Lordship concluded that the circumstances coupled with the terms of the bargain threw the onus of proof on the defendant and that no evidence had been given to discharge that burden.

[1505] Statutory intervention. As Meagher, Gummow and Lehane observe:[29]

> So tender was the concern of equity that by the mid-nineteenth century the position had been reached that inadequacy of price alone was sufficient ground for setting aside such transactions; there was no necessity to show other badges of fraud usually associated with unconscionable bargains ...

The consequent vulnerability of bona fide transactions in which it happened that consideration did not equal value, led to legislative intervention in England[30] which has been followed in Australia.[31] The New South Wales section reads:

> (1) No acquisition made in good faith, without fraud or unfair dealing, of any reversionary interest in real or personal property for money or money's worth, shall be liable to be opened or set aside merely on the ground of under value. In this sub-section 'reversionary interest' includes an expectancy or possibility.
>
> (2) This section does not affect the jurisdiction of the court to set aside or modify unconscionable bargains.

The section displaces the presumption that arose from inadequacy of consideration in the case of transactions with expectants, leaving them to be treated according to the same principles as other allegedly unconscionable transactions, with inadequacy of consideration as a matter relevant to be regarded.

---

26. (1873) LR 8 Ch App 484 at 490–1.
27. See Chapter 14.
28. (1873) LR 8 Ch App 484 at 491.
29. *Equity: Doctrines and Remedies*, 3rd ed, 1992, para 1608.
30. *Sale of Reversions Act* 1867 (UK); see now *Law of Property Act* 1925 (UK), s 174.
31. **ACT**: *Conveyancing and Law of Property Act* 1898, s 30; *Imperial Acts (Substituted Provisions) Act* 1986, s 3 and Sch 2, Pt 7, cll 5, 6; **NSW**: *Conveyancing Act* 1919, s 37C; **NT**: *Law of Property Act* 2000, s 210; **Qld**: *Property Law Act* 1974, s 230; **SA**: *Law of Property Act* 1936, s 88; **Tas**: *Conveyancing and Law of Property Act* 1884, s 42; **Vic**: *Property Law Act* 1958, s 175; **WA**: *Property Law Act* 1969, s 92.

[1506] **Catching bargains with other persons at a disadvantage.** An analogous class of case was that of the catching bargain with persons disadvantaged by one, or more often several, of the following: poverty, age, youth, inexperience, illiteracy, ill health, lack of education, eccentricity, isolation. Expectation of wealth was no ingredient of this second class of case. In a much cited passage in *Fry v Lane*,[32] Kay J enunciated[33] the principle established by the 19th century cases in these terms:

> The result of the decisions is that where a purchase is made from a poor and ignorant man at a considerable undervalue, the vendor having no independent advice, a court of equity will set aside the transaction.
>
> This will be done even in the case of a property in possession, and à fortiori if the interest be reversionary.
>
> The circumstances of poverty and ignorance of the vendor, and absence of independent advice, throw upon the purchaser, when the transaction is impeached, the onus of proving ... that the purchase was 'fair, just and reasonable'.

Equity relieved with caution: it often did not award costs in favour of the party granted relief.[34]

In *Cresswell v Potter*[35] Megarry J regarded Kay J's dictum as laying down three requirements: first, that the plaintiff must be 'poor and ignorant'; second, that the sale challenged must be 'at a considerable undervalue'; and third, that the vendor must have had no independent advice. He treated the first and second requirements as referring, in modern terms, to a 'less highly educated member of the lower income group'. However, Megarry J's following of *Fry v Lane* was in our view inappropriately mechanistic in that the ground of intervention is the broad concept of fraud in equity. The three factors referred to by Kay J constitute a common manifestation of this rather than an exhaustive definition of 'unconscionable transactions'.[36] It is thought that while Kay J had purported to describe what were, on the authorities, 'sufficient' grounds for equitable intervention, he did not make or purport to make a comprehensive statement of the 'necessary elements' of such grounds.

---

32. (1888) 40 Ch D 312. Earlier cases included *Evans v Llewellin* (1787) 1 Cox 333; 29 ER 1191; *Longmate v Ledger* (1860) 2 Giff 157; 66 ER 67; *Clark v Malpas* (1862) 31 Beav 80; 54 ER 1067 (affirmed 4 De GF & J 401; 45 ER 1238); and *Baker v Monk* (1864) 33 Beav 419; 55 ER 430 (affirmed 4 De GJ & S 388; 46 ER 968).
33. (1888) 40 Ch D 312 at 322.
34. See *Evans v Llewellin* (1787) 1 Cox 333; 29 ER 1191; *Earl of Aylesford v Morris* (1873) LR 8 Ch App 484; *Fry v Lane* (1888) 40 Ch D 312.
35. (1968) [1978] 1 WLR 255 at 257.
36. Cf *Commercial Bank of Australia Ltd v Amadio* (1983) 151 CLR 447 at 460, 479.

Modern Case Law[37]

[1507] Illustrations. In *Harrison v National Bank of Australasia Ltd*[38] a 64-year-old lady, inexperienced in business, had reluctantly, and without independent advice or time for reflection, given a letter of lien to a bank in respect of advances to her son-in-law on the security of uncompleted brickworks which, as the bank knew, lacked good financial prospects. She was granted relief from the security which she had given.

In *Blomley v Ryan*[39] the court upheld the trial judge's rescission of a contract for the sale of a grazing property at the instance of the vendor, an old and uneducated man, mentally and physically weak from the effects of intoxication and lacking in independent advice.

[1508] Variety of circumstances. In *Blomley v Ryan*[40] Fullagar J said:[41]

> The circumstances adversely affecting a party, which may induce a court of equity either to refuse its aid or to set a transaction aside, are of great variety and can hardly be satisfactorily classified. Among them are poverty or need of any kind, sickness, age, sex, infirmity of body or mind, drunkenness, illiteracy or lack of education, lack of assistance or explanation where assistance or explanation is necessary. The common characteristic seems to be that they have the effect of placing one party at a serious disadvantage vis à vis the other. It does not appear to be essential in all cases that the party at a disadvantage should suffer loss or detriment by the bargain ... But inadequacy of consideration, while never of itself a ground for resisting enforcement, will often be a specially important element in cases of this type. It may be important in either or both of two ways — firstly as supporting the inference that a position of disadvantage existed, and secondly as tending to show that an unfair use was made of the occasion.

McTiernan J described the species of equitable fraud referred to by Lord Hardwicke in *Earl of Chesterfield v Janssen*[42] as 'getting bargains by taking surreptitious advantage of persons unable to judge for themselves by reason of weakness, necessity or ignorance' and thought that the word 'surreptitious' implied that the bargain was 'snatched'.[43] And Kitto J, who dissented on the facts, thought that the head of equity applied 'whenever one party to a transaction is at a special disadvantage in dealing with the other party because illness, ignorance, inexperience, impaired faculties, financial need or other circumstances affect his ability to conserve his own interests, and the other party unconscientiously takes advantage of the opportunity thus placed in his hands'.[44] His Honour described the

---

37. See, eg A H Angelo and E P Ellinger, 'Unconscionable Contracts: A Comparative Study' (1979) 4 *Otago L Rev* 300; Malcolm Cope, 'The Review of Unconscionable Bargains in Equity' (1983) 57 *ALJ* 279; I J Hardingham, 'Unconscionable Dealing' in Finn, ed, *Essays in Equity*, 1985, pp 1–29; K E Lindgren, 'Unconscionable Dealing' in *Laws of Australia*, 1993, Chapter 35.
38. (1928) 23 Tas LR 1.
39. (1956) 99 CLR 362. See also *Johnson v Buttress* (1936) 56 CLR 113; *Yerkey v Jones* (1939) 63 CLR 649; *Wilton v Farnworth* (1948) 76 CLR 646.
40. (1956) 99 CLR 362.
41. (1956) 99 CLR 362 at 405. The reference to sex in the list of circumstances of disadvantage is quite anachronistic: see *European Asian of Australia Ltd v Kurland* (1985) 8 NSWLR 192 at 200 per Rogers J.
42. (1751) 2 Ves Sen 125; 28 ER 82 (see [1504]).
43. (1956) 99 CLR 362 at 385.

'essence' of the ground as 'unconscientiousness on the part of the party seeking to enforce the contract' which, in the instant case, would necessitate proof that the defendant was in such a debilitated condition that there was not 'a reasonable degree of equality between the contracting parties'[45] and that this was sufficiently evident to the plaintiffs' representatives to make it prima facie unfair for them to take up his decision to sell. According to his Honour, if these two matters were established, the burden of proving 'that the transaction was nevertheless fair'[46] would rest on the plaintiff.

[1509] **The search for a guiding principle.** Three elements have traditionally been present before equity would relieve against a contract on the ground that it was unconscionable. First, one party has been at a serious disadvantage to the other of which unfair advantage might be taken. Second, exploitation of this weakness was in a morally culpable manner. And, third, a transaction resulted which is overreaching and oppressive rather than merely hard or improvident.[47]

Is it possible to find a single guiding principle or controlling factor in cases of unconscionability? One suggestion is a general doctrine based on inequality of bargaining power. Inequality of bargaining power is present in instances of duress, undue influence and the two classes of unconscionable transactions just mentioned.

[1510] **Suggestions of inequality of bargaining power as basis.** For a time the English cases suggested the view that inequality of bargaining power is an independent ground for relief. In *Lloyds Bank Ltd v Bundy*,[48] the defendant successfully applied to have a guarantee contract and charge over his property set aside. The majority of Cairns LJ and Sir Eric Sachs so decided on the ground that in having the defendant execute the documents without independent advice, the bank had been in breach of a 'duty of fiduciary care' owed to the defendant.[49] However, Lord Denning MR espoused a broader principle. His Lordship reviewed the categories of situation in which a contracting party has been relieved from his or her bargain and concluded that a characteristic of them all was inequality of bargaining power, which he deduced was the essential and general ground for relief. By virtue of this 'single thread' of 'inequality of bargaining power' his Lordship said:[50]

> English law gives relief to one who, without independent advice, enters into a contract upon terms which are very unfair or transfers property for a consideration which is grossly inadequate, when his bargaining power is grievously impaired by reason of his own needs or desires, or by his own

44. (1956) 99 CLR 362 at 415.
45. (1956) 99 CLR 362 at 428.
46. (1956) 99 CLR 362 at 428–9, citing Sir John Stuart V-C in *Longmate v Ledger* (1860) 2 Giff 157 at 163; 66 ER 67 at 69.
47. Cf *Alec Lobb (Garages) Ltd v Total Oil (Great Britain) Ltd* [1985] 1 WLR 173 at 182–3.
48. [1975] 1 QB 326.
49. See [1410].
50. [1975] 1 QB 326 at 339. See Philip Slayton, 'The Unequal Bargain Doctrine: Lord Denning in *Lloyds Bank v Bundy*' (1976) 22 *McGill LJ* 94.

ignorance or infirmity, coupled with undue influences or pressures brought to bear on him by or for the benefit of the other.

During the 1970s the suggested general doctrine based on inequality of bargaining power was discussed in a number of English cases. And it seemed at one time that it might take hold.[51]

Indirect support was gained for the principle in cases involving one-sided standard form agreements from which young musicians sought relief. In *A Schroeder Music Publishing Co Ltd v Macaulay*[52] an unknown songwriter Macaulay entered into a contract with a music publishing company on the latter's standard form. Lord Diplock (with whom Lords Simon and Kilbrandon agreed) said that in refusing to enforce a restraint of trade, the public policy which the courts are implementing is 'the protection of those whose bargaining power is weak against being forced by those whose bargaining power is stronger to enter into bargains that are unconscionable'.[53] Lord Reid (with whom Viscount Dilhorne and Lords Simon and Kilbrandon agreed) accepted that well-established standard form restraint contracts may no longer need to be justified by the public policy test of reasonableness[54] but also that this concession applied only where the contract had been 'made freely by parties bargaining on equal terms' or 'moulded under the pressures of negotiation, competition and public opinion'. *Lloyds Bank Ltd v Bundy* was not cited in either speech.

In *Clifford Davis Management Ltd v WEA Records Ltd*[55] the Court of Appeal relieved two young musicians, members of a 'pop group' named 'Fleetwood Mac', from one-sided cyclostyled publishing agreements with the group's manager, the plaintiff company ('Davis'). In interlocutory proceedings by Davis to restrain two other publishers from infringing its copyright (assigned to it by the agreement) in the compositions and writings of the two musicians, Lord Denning MR (with whom Browne LJ agreed) found in *Macaulay's* case support for 'the principles' which his Lordship had stated in *Bundy's* case about inequality of bargaining power. Without arriving at a final opinion (the proceedings were only interlocutory), his Lordship found indicia of a case of 'inequality of bargaining power' and thought that Davis had driven 'so unconscionable a bargain' as to incur an obligation to see that the composers had independent advice.[56]

The restraint of trade element[57] and consequential concern with the fairness of the bargain from the perspective of public policy obscures their significance as authorities on inequality of bargaining power. But Lord Denning MR felt free to refer to a supposed principle of the inequality of

---

51. For discussion see P H Clarke, 'Unequal Bargaining Power in the Law of Contract' (1975) 49 *ALJ* 229; Christopher Carr, 'Inequality of Bargaining Power' (1975) 38 *MLR* 463; M J Trebilcock, 'The Doctrine of Inequality of Bargaining Power: Post-Benthamite Economics in the House of Lords' (1976) 26 *Univ Toronto LJ* 359; S M Waddams, 'Unconscionability in Contracts' (1976) 39 *MLR* 369.
52. [1974] 3 All ER 616. See also *Mountford v Scott* [1974] 1 All ER 248 at 252 (affirmed on other grounds [1975] Ch 258).
53. [1974] 3 All ER 616 at 623. See further [1646], [1653].
54. Cf [1645].
55. [1975] 1 All ER 237.
56. [1975] 1 All ER 237 at 241.
57. See generally [1634]–[1654].

bargaining power in *Mathew v Bobbins*[58] in which a protected tenant of a house owned by his employer, upon a takeover of his employer, surrendered his tenancy in return for a gratuitous (rent free and rates free) licence to occupy, terminable at the will of the licensor. After enjoying these conditions for five years, the tenant was made redundant and his licence was terminated by his employer. Lord Denning MR said, 'It does seem sensible nowadays to hold that any abuse of a dominant position (which one person has in relation to another) is contrary to law if and in so far as it grossly contravenes ordinary principles of fair dealing',[59] but held that while the employers were in a dominant position, the dealing was not 'grossly unfair'. Waller and Dunn JJ agreed.

[1511] **Rejection of inequality of bargaining power as basis.** There is no English support, Lord Denning apart, for a proposition that inequality of bargaining power is either a general independent ground for relief, or itself the pervasive and unifying explanation of other established general grounds for relief. Indeed, it may be questioned whether there is any need in the modern law to erect a general principle of relief against inequality of bargaining power in the field of contract. Such inequality is, as we have seen,[60] relevant to the reasonableness of contractual promises in restraint of trade. The availability of undue influence, particularly the presumption of undue influence arising from an ad hoc duty of fiduciary care,[61] and the two classes of 'unconscionable bargain' noted above,[62] have reduced the need for a general law principle of inequality of bargaining power. So has the legislation discussed below,[63] though it will be seen that such legislation commonly adopts inequality of bargaining power as one matter relevant to the exercise of the discretion to grant relief.

In *National Westminster Bank Plc v Morgan*[64] the House of Lords rejected the general principle developed by Lord Denning,[65] and the case also confined unconscionability to the recognised classes of case referred to earlier.[66] It does not suffice that the parties were of unequal bargaining power and that the stronger does not show that the contract was fair; rather, the stronger party's conduct must (at least) be shown to be unconscionable or oppressive.[67]

[1512] **Commercial Bank of Australia Ltd v Amadio.** The equitable jurisdiction to relieve against transactions unconscionably obtained from persons at a disadvantage[68] has long been exercised by Australian courts,

---

58. [1980] EG Dig 421. See also *Avon Finance Co Ltd v Bridger* (1979) [1985] 2 All ER 281 at 285; and cases involving exclusion clauses: see [765].
59. [1980] EG Dig 421 at 425.
60. See [1510].
61. See [1409], [1410].
62. See [1504], [1506].
63. See [1515]–[1528].
64. [1985] 1 AC 686 (see [1412]).
65. *Lloyds Bank Ltd v Bundy* [1975] 1 QB 326 was approved on the majority basis of undue influence; but see Paul Finn, 'Contract and the Fiduciary Principle' (1989) 12 *UNSWLJ* 76 at 96.
66. See [1504], [1506].
67. *Alec Lobb (Garages) Ltd v Total Oil (Great Britain) Ltd* [1985] 1 WLR 173.
68. See [1504], [1505].

and is far more liberally exercised than under English law as stated in *National Westminster Bank Plc v Morgan*.[69] Indeed, one commentator has argued that in England the unconscionability doctrine has been 'virtually dead for almost a century'.[70] However, there are signs that that may be changing.[71]

In *Commercial Bank of Australia Ltd v Amadio*,[72] Amadio Builders (the company) had an overdraft account with the Commercial Bank of Australia Ltd (the bank). Vincenzo Amadio was the managing director of the company and met regularly with the bank's branch manager. It was clear to the manager that the company was insolvent, but he agreed to assist Vincenzo in maintaining an apparent prosperity, for example, by the selective dishonour of the company's cheques. In March the account was so overdrawn that the bank closed it. The account was re-opened on condition that the overdraft was secured by a mortgage on property owned by Vincenzo's parents (the Amadios). The deed of mortgage was executed at their home in the presence of the branch manager. They were quite old and had only a limited knowledge of written English. The deed secured, by way of guarantee, all sums which might be owed by the company to the bank. There was no limit as to time or amount, notwithstanding that, prior to their signing the deed, Vincenzo had informed them that the guarantee would be for six months and have an upper limit of $50,000. The branch manager did in fact inform them that it was not limited to a six month period, but they received no independent advice at all. When the company went into liquidation it owed the bank nearly $240,000. The bank demanded payment from the Amadios who sued in the Supreme Court of South Australia for a release from the deed. The bank counter-claimed for a declaration of validity and an order for payment. Wells J dismissed the claim and gave judgment for the bank on the counter-claim. An appeal to the Full Court was successful and the bank appealed to the High Court. That court dismissed the appeal.

Gibbs CJ, who decided in favour of the Amadios on the ground of misrepresentation, said[73] that 'a transaction will be unconscientious within the meaning of the relevant equitable principles only if the party seeking to enforce the transaction has taken unfair advantage of his own superior bargaining power, or of the position of disadvantage in which the other party was placed' and would have held that the bank did not take unfair advantage of any disabilities of the parents. In one of only three references to *Lloyds Bank Ltd v Bundy*[74] in the judgments, Gibbs CJ noted[75] that Lord

---

69. [1985] 1 AC 686.
70. S R Enman, 'Doctrines of Unconscionability in Canadian, English and Commonwealth Contract Law' (1987) 16 *Anglo-American LR* 191 at 217.
71. See, eg *Portman Building Society v Dusangh* (2000) 80 P & CR 20; *Credit Lyonnais Bank Nederland NV v Burch* [1997] 1 All ER 144 per Nourse LJ; *Boustany v Pigott* (1993) 69 P & CR 298.
72. (1983) 151 CLR 447 (see Ashley Black, (1986) 11 *Syd LR* 134). Compare *Micarone v Perpetual Trustees Australia Ltd* (1999) 75 SASR 1.
73. (1983) 151 CLR 447 at 459.
74. [1975] 1 QB 326 (see [1410]).
75. (1983) 151 CLR 447 at 459.

Denning had observed[76] that the mere fact that contracting parties did not meet on equal terms did not call for the intervention of equity.

Mason J referred[77] to 'an underlying general principle which may be invoked whenever one party by reason of some condition of [sic — or] circumstance is placed at a special disadvantage vis à vis another and unfair or unconscientious advantage is then taken of the opportunity thereby created' and emphasised that the disabling condition or circumstance must 'seriously' affect the innocent party's ability to judge his or her own best interests and that the other party must know of that condition or circumstance and its effect. And according to his Honour the equity may extend further:[78]

> if A having actual knowledge that B occupies a situation of special disadvantage in relation to an intended transaction, so that B cannot make a judgment as to what is in his own interests, takes unfair advantage of his (A's) superior bargaining power or position by entering into that transaction, his conduct in so doing is unconscionable. And if, instead of having actual knowledge of that situation, A is aware of the possibility that that situation may exist or is aware of facts that would raise that possibility in the mind of any reasonable person, the result will be the same.

Deane J, with whose reasons and conclusion Wilson J agreed, said:[79]

> The jurisdiction is long established as extending generally to circumstances in which (i) a party to a transaction was under a special disability in dealing with the other party with the consequence that there was an absence of any reasonable degree of equality between them and (ii) that disability was sufficiently evident to the stronger party to make it prima facie unfair or 'unconscientious' that he procure, or accept, the weaker party's assent to the impugned transaction in the circumstances in which he procured or accepted it. Where such circumstances are shown to have existed, an onus is cast upon the stronger party to show that the transaction was fair, just and reasonable ...

He compared the relative positions of the bank and the Amadios and concluded that the latter's 'weakness' constituted a 'special disability' in their dealing with the bank of the type required to attract the equitable principles governing relief against unconscionable dealing. In his view this was sufficiently evident to the bank through its branch manager to make it 'unconscientious' for the bank to procure the execution of the deed which had occurred. It was because the bank had not discharged the onus thus lying upon it of showing 'that the transaction was "in point of fact fair, just and equitable"'[80] that the appeal had to fail.

Dawson J dissented on the basis that the trial judge's findings did not support a conclusion that the parents 'were in any position of disadvantage which was used by the bank for its benefit'.[81]

---

76. [1975] 1 QB 326 at 336.
77. (1983) 151 CLR 447 at 462.
78. (1983) 151 CLR 447 at 467. Cf D K Malcolm, 'The Penetration of Equitable Principles into Modern Commercial Law — Part I' (1987) 3 *Aust Bar Rev* 185 at 213.
79. (1983) 151 CLR 447 at 474.
80. (1983) 151 CLR 447 at 479. There is a difference of judicial opinion as to the onus of proof point: compare eg Deane J in *Amadio* at 474 and in *Louth v Diprose* (1992) 175 CLR 621 at 637 with Brennan J in the latter case at 631–2.

[1513] **Application of the concept.** The concept of unconscionability as a basis for relief may be established by evidence of, inter alia, inequality of bargaining power in particular cases but unconscionability does not lend itself to specification. Unconscionability is a concept better described than defined.[82] It is an error to circumscribe equity's jurisdiction by supposing that equitable fraud can be specifically defined, or that classes of case in which it has been found to exist are mutually exclusive, or by concluding that an element such as inadequacy of consideration or disadvantage resulting from a transaction which influenced a court to relieve in a particular case, is always essential, or that any one element, such as the absence of independent advice, which supported a refusal of relief in a particular case, will always be decisive.[83] The prescription of certain elements, proof of which by the plaintiff is to place an 'onus of justification' of the transaction on the defendant cannot make predictable decisions which depend on all the circumstances of the particular case and which necessarily involve an element of impression. It therefore seems more profitable, outside the statutory contexts in which unconscionability is made a specific ground for relief, to approach unconscionability as a component of the general jurisdiction of the courts to grant relief in cases of equitable fraud, and to see unconscionable conduct as a circumstance which may attract the exercise of that jurisdiction.[84]

An important factor in many cases of an allegedly unconscionable transaction is whether or not the disadvantaged party received independent advice. The provision of such advice may help to establish that the weaker party's position of disadvantage was in the circumstances overcome, or that no unconscientious advantage of that position was taken by the stronger party. Despite the importance of the notion of independent legal advice there is a curious uncertainty as to the nature of the advice which should be given, especially when given by a legal practitioner.[85]

Although cases where a contract is set aside on the ground of unconscionability will frequently involve a significant inadequacy of consideration or disadvantageous terms of contract, this is not essential.[86] Thus, if a person in a situation of disadvantage is prevailed upon to sell his or her home the fact that the market (or greater) price is obtained does not necessarily prevent the application of the doctrine to a contract which

---

81. (1983) 151 CLR 447 at 490.
82. *Antonovic v Volker* (1986) 7 NSWLR 151 at 165 per Mahoney JA.
83. Cf *National Westminster Bank Plc v Morgan* [1985] 1 AC 686 at 709.
84. Cf *Hart v O'Connor* [1985] AC 1000 at 1024, 1028; *Antonovic v Volker* (1986) 7 NSWLR 151 at 163–5; *Commonwealth of Australia v Verwayen* (1990) 170 CLR 394 at 440–1. As to the position where a creditor leaves it to the debtor to obtain the signing of a guarantee by a third party, and as to the special rule where a wife guarantees her husband's debts, see [1405] (a discussion of undue influence, but the principles there discussed seem equally applicable in the present context).
85. See M Sneddon, 'Unfair Conduct in Taking Guarantees and the Role of Independent Advice' (1990) 13 *UNSWLJ* 302; M Sneddon, 'Lenders and Independent Solicitors' Certificates for Guarantors and Borrowers: Risk Minimisation or Loss Sharing?' (1996) 24 *ABLR* 5; Phillips, Horrigan and Collier, *Guarantees and solicitors' certificates — Guidelines for lawyers, financiers and guarantors*, 1999.
86. See, eg *Commercial Bank of Australia v Amadio* (1983) 151 CLR 447 at 475 per Deane J; *Antonovic v Volker* (1986) 7 NSWLR 151 at 165 per Mahoney JA.

would not have been entered into had unconscionable advantage not been taken of that person's disability. Many cases have involved, as did *Amadio*[87] itself, persons giving a guarantee (often secured by a mortgage over the family home) of a loan made to a business owned by a spouse, relative or friend. Although there is in such cases sufficient consideration to make the contract between the lender and the guarantor prima facie binding,[88] the fact that the guarantor receives no personal benefit from the transaction is an important factor.

When considering the concept of 'special disadvantage' courts look at whether the weaker party was able to make a judgment in his or her own best interests.[89] It is noticeable that the circumstances of disadvantage which may lay the foundation of a case for relief are often considerably less extreme than would have previously been thought to be necessary. The circumstances in which a situation of special disadvantage will arise may be 'matters arising ... from the context and circumstances surrounding the transaction'.[90] Recent cases emphasise the idea of the weaker party being unable to make a judgment in his or her own best interests.[91] Thus, for example, a mortgage and guarantee were set aside as unconscionable where a widow in her late 40s, with more than average experience in land dealings, was taken advantage of by a man to whom she was attracted and who misled her about his property affairs.[92] In that case the judge held that the special disability depended on 'an objective comparison of the relative positions of the respective parties and of their ability to protect their own interests'.[93] In the circumstances she was held to be under a relevant disadvantage vis-à-vis the bank with which the man had dealt, the disparity in knowledge between herself and the bank as to the man's intentions as to the use of funds loaned by the bank preventing her making a judgment as to her own best interests concerning the provision of security for the loan.[94]

Where a contract is found to be unconscionable, the normal remedy is an order for rescission. A court, in granting this remedy, has some flexibility in setting the contract aside only in part or in making its order subject to conditions to avoid injustice to the party against whom the order is made,[95]

---

87. *Commercial Bank of Australia v Amadio* (1983) 151 CLR 447.
88. See [321].
89. See, eg *Begbie v State Bank of New South Wales* (1994) ATPR 41-288; *Geelong Building Society (in liq) v Thomas* (1996) V Conv R 54-545 at 66,477; *Teachers Health Investments Pty Ltd v Wynne* [1996] ASC 56-356.
90. *Geelong Building Society (in liq) v Thomas* (1996) V Conv R 54-545 at 66,477.
91. See, eg *Geelong Building Society (in liq) v Thomas* (1996) V Conv R 54-545; *Teachers Health Investments Pty Ltd v Wynne* (1996) ASC 56-356. But see *ACCC v Samton Holdings Pty Ltd* (2000) ATPR 41-791.
92. *Begbie v State Bank of New South Wales* (1994) ATPR 41-288.
93. *Begbie v State Bank of New South Wales* (1994) ATPR 41-288 at 41,897.
94. See also *Familiar Pty Ltd v Samarkos* (1994) 115 FLR 443; *Bridgewater v Leahy* (1998) 194 CLR 457; 158 ALR 66. See also *Asia Pacific International Pty Ltd v Dalrymple* [2000] 2 Qd R 229 where it was held an agreement of a loan providing for the capitalisation of interest and interest payable at the rate of 20 per cent per month, compounding monthly, was unconscionable. This was so despite the other party receiving independent advice and possessing knowledge of business.
95. See *Commercial Bank of Australia v Amadio* (1983) 151 CLR 447 at 480–1 (per Deane J); *Bridgewater v Leahy* (1998) 194 CLR 457; 158 ALR 66. See also *Vadasz v Pioneer Concrete (SA) Pty Ltd* (1995) 184 CLR 102; 130 ALR 570.

but the limits of this power have not been explored and a feature of the statutory provisions discussed below is the apparently greater flexibility afforded to the courts in framing orders to meet the needs of the particular case.[96] Affirmation or delay in seeking relief may be a bar to relief being ordered.[97]

[1514] **The future of unconscionability in Australia.** The decision of the High Court in *Commercial Bank of Australia v Amadio*[98] was obviously important in restating the principles relating to unconscionable contracts, and also in making it clear that actual knowledge by the superior party of the disability of the other is not essential. However, it is suggested that the significance of the decision goes far beyond this. Traditionally the jurisdiction was (apart from the rather special cases of so-called expectant heirs, which have lost contemporary relevance and were in any event probably never of real significance in Australian social conditions) exercised only in cases of quite extreme disadvantage and unfairness. One experienced judge has said that *Amadio* would probably have been decided differently on the unconscionability point 30 years previously[99] and indeed since *Amadio's* case Australian courts have become considerably more willing to set aside contracts on the ground of unconscionability than would previously have been the case.[100] Defences based on *Amadio* are now regularly raised in the courts and are quite often successful,[101] whereas previously unconscionability cases featured only relatively rarely in the law reports. (It should be noted that the High Court has rejected the suggestion that a wife's special equity based on *Yerkey v Jones*[102] could come within the 'special disability' principle of *Amadio*.[103]) This expansion of the jurisdiction has no doubt been at least partly influenced (as was probably *Amadio's* case itself) by recent statutory developments to which we must now turn.

---

96. See [1522], [1526].
97. See *Baburin v Baburin* [1991] 2 Qd R 240.
98. (1983) 151 CLR 447.
99. L J Priestley, 'Unconscionability as a Restriction on the Exercise of Contractual Rights' in Carter, ed, *Rights and Remedies for Breach of Contract*, 1986, pp 80–1. See also Sir Anthony Mason, 'The Place of Equity and Equitable Remedies in the Contemporary Common Law World' (1994) 110 *LQR* 238 at 248–9.
100. See in particular *Baburin v Baburin* [1990] 2 Qd R 101, affirmed [1991] 2 Qd R 240; *Louth v Diprose* (1992) 175 CLR 621. (The latter case involved a gift rather than a contract but the *Amadio* principles were applied.) See also *George T Collings (Aust) Pty Ltd v H F Stevenson (Aust) Pty Ltd* (1991) ATPR 41–104.
101. For recent examples see *Commonwealth Bank of Australia v Oberdan* (2000) 211 LSJS 330; [2000] SASC 428; *Child v Commonwealth Development Bank of Australia Ltd* (2000) AustContractR 90-118; *National Australia Bank Ltd v Starbronze Pty Ltd* [2001] ANZConvR 247; *Edmunds v Pickering (No 4)* (2000) 77 SASR 381; *Project Blue Moon Pty Ltd v Fairway Trading Pty Ltd* [2000] ANZConvR 628; *Grineff v Chusov* [2000] ANZConvR 212.
102. (1939) 63 CLR 649.
103. See *Garcia v National Australia Bank* (1998) 194 CLR 395; 155 ALR 614, discussed at [1405].

Unfair Contracts Legislation

Introduction

[1515] Types of unfair contracts legislation. Legislation providing for relief from unfair contracts falls into two classes: that dealing with particular kinds of contracts which have been shown, by experience, to be themselves frequently characterised by harshness, unconscionability and injustice or to contain unfair terms; and that which addresses this problem in contracts generally or at least in contracts of a 'consumer' kind generally. Our main concern is with the second class of legislative intervention.

During the 1970s an increasing number of suggestions were made for the enactment of legislation enabling courts to give relief in respect of unconscionable contracts. There had indeed been examples of such power being given in earlier legislation relating to specific types of contracts (particularly moneylending and hire purchase contracts) but the critics felt that generally speaking such powers had had little impact and that the courts had been unable themselves to develop a doctrine of general application, suitable to modern marketplace conditions, to establish minimum standards of contractual fairness, especially in consumer contracts.[104]

Legislation Dealing with Particular Kinds of Contracts

[1516] Illustrations. Many illustrations could be given of legislation dealing with particular kinds of contracts. For example, under s 70 of the Consumer Credit Code, relief may be given from certain unjust contracts, mortgages or guarantees in respect of the provision of consumer credit.[105] And s 106 of the *Industrial Relations Act* 1996 (NSW) provides for relief in respect of 'unfair' contracts or arrangements whereby a person performs work in any industry.

Legislation of More General Application

The **Contracts Review Act *1980 (NSW)***

[1517] Generally. Pursuant to a reference from the Minister for Consumer Affairs and Co-operative Societies, the late Professor John R Peden submitted a Report to that Minister and to the Attorney-General for New South Wales on harsh and unconscionable contracts.[106] In due course the *Contracts Review Act* 1980 (NSW) was enacted.[107] The preamble to the

---

104. For a discussion of the background see Peden, *The Law of Unjust Contracts*, 1982, Chapter 3.
105. 'Unjust' is defined in s 70(7) to include 'unconscionable, harsh or oppressive', which is the same as the definition in the *Contracts Review Act* (NSW) 1980. The *Consumer Credit (Queensland) Act* 1994 was passed on 2 September 1994. All other Australian States and Territories have introduced legislation adopting the Queensland Code, except Western Australia, which has passed consistent legislation. See *Consumer Credit (NSW) Act* 1995; *Consumer Credit (Vic) Act* 1995; *Consumer Credit (SA) Act* 1995; *Consumer Credit (WA) Act* 1996; *Consumer Credit (NT) Act* 1995; *Consumer Credit (ACT) Act* 1995; *Consumer Credit (Tas) Act* 1996.

Act describes it as an 'Act with respect to judicial review of certain contracts and the grant of relief in respect of harsh, oppressive, unconscionable or unjust contracts'. By and large then[108] the Act is a means by which persons can seek relief in respect of unjust contracts,[109] or contracts containing unjust terms, notwithstanding that they have been entered into in circumstances which might not justify relief under the general principles considered in this chapter.[110] The Act has been described as 'revolutionary legislation whose evident purpose is to overcome the common law's failure to provide a comprehensive doctrinal framework to deal with "unjust" contracts'.[111]

[1518] **Unjust contracts and consumers.** It was originally intended that the *Contracts Review Act* should be of application to all contracts, but following claims that this would result in unacceptable uncertainty in commercial transactions, a provision was introduced which in effect means that only consumers can apply for relief under the Act. In the result the Act applies to contracts generally in the sense that, unlike the legislation referred to above,[112] the subject matter of the contract is irrelevant, but its scope is restricted in that commercial parties to a contract may not be granted relief under its provisions.

Sections 4(2), 5 and 6 of the *Contracts Review Act* 1980 (NSW) define its scope. The Act draws a distinction between persons bound by the Act and persons entitled to relief. Thus, although the Act binds the Crown,[113] the Crown may not be granted relief under the Act.[114] Nor is a corporation[115] entitled to relief. It follows that the small family company may not be granted relief whereas the wealthy individual may be![116] Section 6(2) provides for a 'business contracts' exception:

> A person may not be granted relief under this Act in relation to a contract so far as the contract was entered into in the course of or for the purpose of a trade, business or profession carried on by the person or proposed to be carried on by the person, other than a farming undertaking (including, but not limited to, an agricultural, pastoral, horticultural, orcharding or viticultural undertaking) carried on by the person or proposed to be carried on by the person wholly or principally in New South Wales.

---

106. See Peden, *The Law of Unjust Contracts*, 1982; J Goldring, J L Pratt and D E J Ryan, 'The *Contracts Review Act* (NSW)' (1981) 4 *UNSWLJ* 1; A L Terry, 'Unconscionable Contracts in NSW — the *Contracts Review Act* 1980' (1982) 10 *ABLR* 311.
107. Cf *Unconscionable Transactions Relief Act* RSO, Ontario 1970, c 472.
108. But see s 10 (general orders) and *Minister for Consumer Affairs v W W Vallack Real Estate Pty Ltd* (1986) ASC §55–478, see further [1530].
109. This includes deeds: *Toscano v Holland Securities Pty Ltd* (1985) 1 NSWLR 145 at 149.
110. Or, for that matter, the principles discussed in Chapters 13 and 14.
111. *West v AGC (Advances) Ltd* (1986) 5 NSWLR 610 at 621 per McHugh JA.
112. [1515].
113. Section 5.
114. Section 6(1). This includes a public or local authority. The Act also does not apply to certain contracts of service: s 21.
115. Other than as described in s 4(2).
116. See *Australian Bank Ltd v Stokes* (1985) 3 NSWLR 174 at 176.

Section 6(2) refers to a contract entered into (a) 'in the course of' or (b) 'for the purpose of' a trade, business or profession carried on or proposed to be carried on by a person. So, neither a contract entered into for the purpose of a trade, business or profession carried on by another, such as a guarantee of another's business debts or liabilities,[117] nor a borrowing where the borrower intends to use the amount borrowed to invest in a business conducted by another in which the borrower would acquire an interest,[118] is excepted from the Act's scope.[119] It has been held that where a person sells his or her business the contract of sale is not one 'in the course of' or 'for the purpose of' that business and that the Act is therefore applicable.[120] This rather literal interpretation of s 6(2) has been doubted[121] and seems difficult to reconcile with the apparent policy basis of the provision.

[1519] Section 7. The pivotal provision of the *Contracts Review Act* is s 7(1):

> Where the court finds a contract or a provision of a contract to have been unjust in the circumstances relating to the contract at the time it was made, the court may, if it considers it just to do so, and for the purpose of avoiding as far as practicable an unjust consequence or result, do any one or more of the following—
>
> (a) It may decide to refuse to enforce any or all of the provisions of the contract;
>
> (b) It may make an order declaring the contract void, in whole or in part;
>
> (c) It may make an order varying, in whole or in part, any provision of the contract;
>
> (d) It may, in relation to a land instrument,[122] make an order[123] for or with respect to requiring the execution of an instrument that —
>
> (i) varies, or has the effect of varying, the provisions of the land instrument; or
>
> (ii) terminates or otherwise affects, or has the effect of terminating or otherwise affecting, the operation or effect of the land instrument.

This provision does two things. First, it describes the criterion by which the operation of the Act is activated, namely, a contract or a provision of a contract which is 'unjust'. 'Unjust' includes 'unconscionable, harsh or oppressive' and 'injustice' is construed in a corresponding way (s 4(1)). Second, it sets out the relief which may be granted in respect of an unjust contract or provision.[124] It is not possible for people to waive, or contract out of their rights under the Act: ss 17, 18.

---

117. Cf *Beaumont v Helvetic Investment Corp Pty Ltd* (1982) ASC §55–194.
118. Cf *Collins v Parker* (1984) NSW Conv R §55–212.
119. Cf *Toscano v Holland Securities Pty Ltd* (1985) 1 NSWLR 145 at 149.
120. *Coombs v Bahama Palm Trading Pty Ltd* (1991) ASC 56–097.
121. *Bosnjak v Farrow Services Pty Ltd (in liq)* (1993) ASC 56–225 per Cripps JA.
122. By s 4(1) of the *Contracts Review Act* 1980 (NSW) 'land instrument' means an instrument that transfers title to land, creates an estate or interest in land or is a dealing within the meaning of the *Real Property Act* 1900 (NSW).
123. See *Toscano v Holland Securities Pty Ltd* (1985) 1 NSWLR 145.
124. And note [1521] (ancillary relief).

The term 'unjust' was selected in preference to 'harsh and unconscionable' in order to avoid any suggestion that the Act should be interpreted narrowly or in accordance with previous case law on that expression in earlier legislation.[125] (We must recall in this context that the Act was passed three years before *Amadio's*[126] case was decided.) Whether a contract or a provision is unjust must be decided in relation to the circumstances relating to the contract at the time it was made.

[1520] Relevant considerations. Section 9(1) of the *Contracts Review Act* 1980 (NSW)[127] provides as follows:

> In determining whether a contract or a provision of a contract is unjust in the circumstances relating to the contract at the time it was made, the court shall have regard to the public interest and to all the circumstances of the case, including such consequences or results as those arising in the event of:—
>
> (a) compliance with any or all of the provisions of the contract; or
>
> (b) non-compliance with, or contravention of, any or all of the provisions of the contract.

Section 9, referring to 'all the circumstances of the case', is clearly very wide. Significantly, it also recognises the public interest in contracts not being unjust or containing unjust terms and requires the court to have regard not merely to the interest of the party who complains but also the public at large.

Section 9(2), without in any way affecting the generality of s 9(1), requires the court to have regard, to the extent that they are relevant to the circumstances of the case, to the matters specified in its 12 paragraphs. The following are some, perhaps the more important, of these:

> (a) whether or not there was any material inequality in bargaining power between the parties to the contract;
>
> (b) whether or not prior to or at the time the contract was made its provisions were the subject of negotiation;
>
> ...
>
> (d) whether or not any provisions of the contract impose conditions which are unreasonably difficult to comply with or not reasonably necessary for the protection of the legitimate interests of any party to the contract;
>
> (e) whether or not—
>
> (i) any party to the contract (other than a corporation) was not reasonably able to protect his or her interests; or
>
> (ii) any person who represented any of the parties to the contract was not reasonably able to protect the interests of any party whom he or she represented,
>
> because of his or her age or the state of his or her physical or mental capacity;

---

125. See Peden, *The Law of Unjust Contracts*, 1982, pp 94–6.
126. *Commercial Bank of Australia Ltd v Amadio* (1983) 151 CLR 447, discussed [1512]–[1514].
127. For a discussion see Ben Zipser, 'Unjust Contracts and the Contracts Review Act 1980 (NSW)' (2001) 17 *JCL* 76; T Carlin, 'The *Contracts Review Act* 1980 (NSW) — 20 years on' (2001) 23 *Syd LR* 125.

(f) the relative economic circumstances, educational background and literacy of—

  (i) the parties to the contract (other than a corporation); and

  (ii) any person who represented any of the parties to the contract;

...

(h) whether or not and when independent legal or other expert advice was obtained by the party seeking relief under this Act; ...

(j) whether any undue influence, unfair pressure or unfair tactics were exerted on or used against the party seeking relief under this Act—

  (i) by any other party to the contract;

  (ii) by any person acting or appearing or purporting to act for or on behalf of any other party to the contract;[128] or

  (iii) by any person to the knowledge (at the time the contract was made) of any other party to the contract or of any person acting or appearing or purporting to act for or on behalf of any other party to the contract;

... and

(l) the commercial or other setting, purpose and effect of the contract.

This list of factors to which the court is to have regard (often referred to as the 'shopping list') was intended to guide the judges in the exercise of their new powers. This approach was taken partly because of a fear that in the absence of such guidance the courts might be unduly cautious in their application of the Act.

It will be noticed that s 9 refers both to circumstances which make the contract (or provision) unjust in its operation — for example, an unreasonable term — and to circumstances which make the contract (or provision) unjust in the way it was made: for example, unfair pressure.[129]

The question of whether a contract (or a provision of it) is unjust must be determined as at the time when the contract was made. It is specifically provided (s 9(4)) that in determining this issue the court shall not have regard to any injustice arising from circumstances that were not reasonably foreseeable when the contract was made,[130] though in determining whether it is just to grant relief the court may have regard to the conduct of the parties in relation to the performance of the contract since it was made (s 9(5)).

[1521] Relief. Section 11 of the *Contracts Review Act* 1980 (NSW) provides for the making of 'applications' to the court for relief under the Act. It seems that the Act may be set up merely by way of defence and without the necessity of an application for relief.[131]

Section 8 empowers the court to grant ancillary relief in accordance with Schedule 1. It applies where the court makes a decision or order under s 7.

---

128. See *Antonovic v Volker* (1986) 7 NSWLR 151.
129. See *Dillon v Charter Travel Co Ltd* (1989) 92 ALR 331 at 367.
130. As to 'reasonably foreseeable' see *Morlend Finance Corp (Vic) Pty Ltd v Westendorp* [1993] 2 VR 284; *Custom Credit Corp Ltd v Lupi* [1992] 1 VR 99.
131. *Commercial Banking Co of Sydney Ltd v Pollard* [1983] 1 NSWLR 74. But see *Beaumont v Helvetic Investment Corp Pty Ltd* (1982) ASC §55-194.

Various possibilities are listed, including such orders as may be 'just in the circumstances'.[132]

[1522] Interpretation. In *S H Lock (Australia) Ltd v Kennedy*[133] the New South Wales Court of Appeal held that under s 7 of the *Contracts Review Act* 1980 (NSW), whether a contract or a provision of it is unjust is a separate question from what relief should be granted in respect of the contract. This interpretation was based on the fact that s 7 provides that the order must be made for the purpose of avoiding as far as practicable an unjust consequence or result. The effect is that there are two steps in granting relief. First, the court must decide by reference to the matters set out in the Act and the circumstances of entry into the contract, that the contract or a provision was unjust. Second, the order made must relate back to the ground of injustice, so that if there is no unjust consequence or result no order can be made.

In *West v AGC (Advances) Ltd*[134] AGC sought to enforce a deed of loan and guarantee against Mrs West, her husband, a company ('Quiche') and three directors of that company. By virtue of the deed Mrs West had borrowed $68,000 from AGC. She saw the loan as having a twofold purpose: to discharge an existing mortgage on her home; and to lend money to Quiche, where her husband was a part-time employee. The husband had suggested the loan as a way of profiting from Quiche's expansion, and he guaranteed payment by Mrs West. In order to secure the loan Mrs West gave AGC a mortgage over her home and in these proceedings AGC sought to obtain possession after default on the loan. She had, however, received no independent legal advice: she had no solicitor (one of the directors acted for her). However, her son had advised her against the transaction and a barrister friend had told her to obtain more substantial guarantees from Quiche's directors than she actually obtained. She knew, moreover, that the wives of the directors had refused to put their own homes up as security and was well aware that she was giving a mortgage and that AGC could have recourse to the property in the event of default.[135] She also had some experience with business practice and concepts, and was not, in McHugh JA's words,[136] merely an ordinary home owner or suburban housewife.

The arrangement between Mrs West and Quiche was that the latter would pay the instalments due under the loan in return for what was an interest free loan from Mrs West. AGC knew of this arrangement, and from their possession of Quiche's accounts could reasonably have foreseen that the company would be wound up. In fact, but unknown to AGC, Quiche was insolvent even with the loan — nearly $40,000 — from Mrs West. After making some payments Quiche was wound up in 1982. Although Hodgson J[137] granted certain equitable relief to Mrs West, he refused to

---

132. As to orders in favour of or against persons who are not a party to the contract see s 12 and Schedule 1. See also s 16 (time limit on applications for relief).
133. (1988) 12 NSWLR 482.
134. (1986) 5 NSWLR 610.
135. Contrast *Robinson v ANZ Banking Group Ltd* (1990) Unreported, SC (NSW) (Hodgson J), 16 May.
136. (1986) 5 NSWLR 610 at 631.

grant her relief under the *Contracts Review Act* 1980 (NSW). Her appeal was dismissed by a majority of the New South Wales Court of Appeal. McHugh JA (with whom Hope JA agreed) said:[138]

> The *Contracts Review Act* 1980 is beneficial legislation. It must be interpreted liberally. But it operates within and not outside the domain of the law of contract, except for one form of ancillary relief available for the benefit of a person not a party to the contract.

He emphasised the knowledge of Mrs West that AGC could (if necessary) sell her house; her business experience (admittedly fairly limited); the fact that she had received independent expert advice and that the loan was on ordinary commercial rates, and that the Act regulates contracts not investments.

Kirby P, dissenting, thought that relief should be granted. He emphasised the need to approach the Act as a departure from the old common law and equitable principles. The court should not begin by asking how the facts would be viewed under those principles. Rather, the court should go straight to the Act. In his view, given the absence of independent legal advice, Mrs West was entitled to relief.

It is clear that there are cases where a contract will not be 'unconscionable' under the *Amadio* doctrine but will be 'unjust' for the purposes of the *Contracts Review Act*.[139] One relevant factor is that under the general law the superior party must know of, or at least have notice of, the other's situation of special disadvantage,[140] whereas it seems that under the Act knowledge or notice is not essential, though it is very relevant to the court's exercise of discretion as to whether to grant relief.[141] It would appear to follow from this approach that the element of moral blameworthiness which seems inherent in the application of the general law doctrine[142] is not essential when the *Contracts Review Act* is being applied.[143]

As we have seen[144] the traditional form of relief under the general law has been to rescind contracts, sometimes on conditions, and it is generally thought that the remedies available under the statute are wider and more flexible. For example, in one case involving a mortgage by an elderly mother of her home in order to guarantee a loan to her son's business, the

---

137. See *AGC (Advances) Ltd v West* (1984) 5 NSWLR 590.
138. (1986) 5 NSWLR 610 at 631. See also *Sharman v Kunert* (1985) 1 NSWLR 225 at 231.
139. For examples see *Melverton v Commonwealth Development Bank of Australia* (1989) ASC 55–921; *Robinson v ANZ Banking Group Ltd* (1990) ASC 55–979.
140. See [1512]–[1514].
141. See in particular *Collier v Morlend Finance Corp (Victoria) Pty Ltd* (1989) ASC 55–716. See also *Elders Rural Finance Ltd v Smith* (1996) 41 NSWLR 296; *Esanda Finance Corporation Ltd v Tong* (1997) 41 NSWLR 482.
142. But see *Commercial Bank of Australia Ltd v Amadio* (1983) 151 CLR 447 at 478 per Deane J.
143. See in particular *Baltic Shipping Co v Dillon (The Mikhail Lermontov)* (1991) 22 NSWLR 1 at 20 per Kirby P (on appeal (1993) 176 CLR 344). The frequently cited judgment of McHugh JA in *West v AGC (Advances) Ltd* (1986) 5 NSWLR 610 is rather ambiguous on this point. Contrast the approach which was taken on this point under the similar but differently worded provisions of the *Credit Act* 1984 (Vic): *Morlend Finance Corp (Vic) Pty Ltd v Westendorp* [1993] 2 VR 284.
144. [1513].

judge felt that some relief was in the circumstances appropriate, and indicated that, subject to any further argument by the parties' lawyers, he proposed to make orders limiting the bank to its security interest in the property (that is, she was not to be personally liable for the debt) and preventing the bank selling the house during her lifetime without her consent.[145]

The general law unconscionability doctrine deals essentially with (to use what has become the accepted American terminology) 'procedural' rather than 'substantive' unconscionability.[146] The former refers to elements in the process of formation of the contract, the latter to the contents of the transaction itself. Under the unconscionability provision of the *Uniform Commercial Code* in the United States, courts will at least usually require some elements of both types of unconscionability to be present before relief is given.[147] It would seem that although both elements will usually be present before courts will intervene under the *Contracts Review Act* provisions, this is not essential and that in some cases extreme substantive unfairness alone will suffice.[148] This is a point of significance in the context of 'abstract' control of unfair contracts, discussed below. Whether so-called 'price unconscionability' alone would justify relief under the American provision has given rise to much debate.

Whether or not a particular contract is to be treated as unjust depends very much on the particular facts and it is impossible to lay down definite rules as to when relief will be given. There is a conflict of authority on the issue of the extent to which decisions under ss 7 and 9 are to be given the comparative immunity from review on appeal which is conferred on decisions which are treated as exercises of judicial discretion.[149]

The Trade Practices Act *1974 (Cth) and Fair Trading legislation*

[1523] Federal legislation. The New South Wales example was not followed by the other States (although the consumer credit legislation of the States has important provisions on unjust contracts.)[150] However, in 1986 an important new provision dealing with unconscionable conduct was

---

145. *Melverton v Commonwealth Development Bank of Australia* (1989) ASC 55–921. For further examples see *Bridge Wholesale Acceptance (Australia) Ltd v GVS Associates Pty Ltd* (1991) ASC 56–105; *National Australia Bank Ltd v Hall* (1993) ASC 56–234; *O'Brien v Hooker Homes Pty Ltd* (1993) ASC 56–217, but contrast *Advance Bank of Australia Ltd v Hartshorn* (1993) ASC 56–216.
146. But see Chen-Wishart, *Unconscionable Bargains*, 1989, especially pp 104–19, arguing that judges have in fact been far more concerned with substantive factors than they have generally articulated. See also *Asia Pacific International Pty Ltd v Dalrymple* [2000] 2 Qd R 229, which seems very close to a decision based on substantive unconscionability.
147. See Deutch, *Unfair Contracts — the Doctrine of Unconscionability*, 1977. For a criticism that the Act lacks a coherent philosophy, partly because no guidance is given as to the extent to which the legislature was concerned with the latter regardless of the former see A J Duggan, 'Trade Practices Act 1974 (Cth), Section 52A and the Law of Unjust Contracts' (1991) 13 *Syd LR* 138.
148. See in particular the judgment of McHugh JA in *West v AGC (Advances) Ltd* (1986) 5 NSWLR 610.
149. See in particular *Antonovic v Volker* (1986) 7 NSWLR 151; *Beneficial Finance Corp Ltd v Karavas* (1991) 23 NSWLR 256.
150. See [1516].

inserted in the *Trade Practices Act*.[151] The new provision, influenced in part by American and Canadian legislation,[152] followed the recommendation of a committee appointed to review the operation of the *Trade Practices Act*.[153] (It should be remembered that the provision had a long gestation period, the review committee's report having been published some 10 years earlier, that is, before both *Amadio* and the New South Wales Act.) This provision supplements a previous provision of the *Trade Practices Act* containing a general prohibition on 'misleading or deceptive' conduct.[154]

Section 51AB (originally s 52A) was introduced to give consumers greater protection against unconscionable conduct than the general law doctrine of unconscionable conduct. This was only three years after *Amadio* and before the impact of that decision was fully felt. But continuing governmental concern to protect small business, which was regarded as often being in little better position than private consumers, led to the introduction of s 51AA in 1992. But, largely because of a general belief (possibly, in light of some later decisions, incorrect) that s 51AA required an *Amadio* situation of special disadvantage, the view gained ground that, because special disadvantage was very difficult to prove between commercial parties, s 51AA was of little assistance to small business. In the result in 1998 s 51AC was inserted and sought to give small business protection similar to that afforded to consumers by s 51AB. Although all three sections refer, without definition, to unconscionable conduct, it is generally thought that the concept in ss 51AB and 51AC is wider than that in s 51AA.

In respect of unconscionable conduct in relation to financial services one must look to the *Australian Securities and Investments Commission Act* 2001 (which replaced the 1989 Act of the same name). Section 12CA corresponds to s 51AA while s 12CB corresponds to s 51AB. As a result of amending legislation expected to commence on 11 March 2002 a new s 12CC will correspond to s 51AC. As a result of the same amending legislation all sections will apply to persons generally.[155]

[1524] *Trade Practices Act* 1974 (Cth). Section 51AB of the *Trade Practices Act* 1974 (Cth)[156] provides that a corporation[157] shall not, 'in trade or commerce',[158] in connection with the supply or possible supply of goods or services of a kind ordinarily acquired for personal, domestic or household use or consumption,[159] engage in conduct that is 'unconscionable'.[160] Section 51AB(2) states the factors to which regard

---

151. Section 52A. This provision was in 1992 repealed but re-enacted, as s 51AB, as part of a new Pt IVA entitled 'Unconscionable Conduct'.
152. See D J Harland, 'The Legal Concept of Unfairness and the Economic and Social Environment: Fair Trade, Market Law and the Consumer Interest' in Balate, ed, *Unfair Advertising and Comparative Advertising*, 1988, pp 25, 32–3.
153. Trade Practices Act Review Committee, *Report to the Minister for Business and Consumer Affairs*, 1976.
154. Section 52, discussed in Chapter 11.
155. *Financial Services Reform (Consequential Provisions) Act* 2001.
156. See A J Duggan, '*Trade Practices Act* 1974 (Cth), Section 52A and the Law of Unjust Contracts' (1991) 13 *Syd LR* 138.
157. In certain circumstances the provision will apply also to unincorporated traders: see [1102].
158. As to the meaning of this phrase see [1104].

may be had[161] in determining whether a corporation has contravened s 51AB in connection with the supply or possible supply of goods or services to a person described in s 51AB(2) as a 'consumer'. Section 51AB(3) refers to:

(a) the relative strengths of the bargaining positions of the corporation and the consumer;

(b) whether, as a result of conduct engaged in by the corporation, the consumer was required to comply with conditions that were not reasonably necessary for the protection of the legitimate interests of the corporation;

(c) whether the consumer was able to understand any documents relating to the supply or possible supply of the goods or services;

(d) whether any undue influence or pressure was exerted on, or any unfair tactics were used against, the consumer or a person acting on behalf of the consumer by the corporation or a person acting on behalf of the corporation in relation to the supply or possible supply of the goods or services; and

(e) the amount for which, and the circumstances under which, the consumer could have acquired identical or equivalent goods or services from a person other than the corporation.

In 1992 the *Trade Practices Act* was amended with the introduction of s 51AA, which provides courts with statutory power to intervene in at least some commercial transactions. Section 51AA enables the courts to apply to conduct generally, when engaged in by corporations in trade or commerce, the rules of the general law as to unconscionable conduct.[162] The section provides that 'a corporation must not, in trade or commerce, engage in conduct that is unconscionable within the meaning of the unwritten law, from time to time, of the States and Territories' (s 51AA(1)). While this may seem at first a strangely paradoxical provision, in that the substantive rules as to when unconscionability has occurred remain unchanged, the new provision is in fact quite significant because the courts now have available to them the range of remedial orders available under the Act, those orders being apparently wider in scope than those which have been made under the general law.[163] The Australian Competition and Consumer Commission may also now take action in appropriate cases where unconscionable conduct affects, for example, small business persons such as franchisees or lessees in shopping centres.[164]

Section 51AC extends the scope of the statutory prohibition of unconscionable business transactions involving the supply or acquisition of goods or services of $3 million or less[165] by a person or corporation, other

---

159. Other than, in the case of goods, for the purpose of resupply or for the purpose of using them up or transforming them in trade or commerce (s 51AB(6)). 'Goods' and 'services' are defined in s 4(1). See, eg *Begbie v State Bank of New South Wales* (1994) ATPR 41-288; *Leitch v Natwest Australia Bank Ltd* (1995) ATPR (Digest) 46-153.

160. See, eg *Dai v Telstra Corp Ltd* (2000) 171 ALR 348.

161. 'Have regard to' simply means 'to take into account' or 'to consider': *A v Pelekanakis* (1999) 91 FCR 70; *ACCC v Leelee Pty Ltd* (2000) ATPR 41-742.

162. See D Healey, 'Unconscionable Conduct in Commercial Dealings' (1993) 1 *TPLJ* 169; Trade Practices Commission, *Unconscionable Conduct in Commercial Dealings*, 1993.

163. As to this see [1526].

164. See [1527] as to the meaning of 'unconscionability' in s 51AA.

than a listed public company. The section was intended to help small businesses dealing with larger corporations.[166] Section 51AC(3) contains the 'shopping list' of factors to which the court may have regard when determining whether a corporation or person (the supplier) has contravened s 51AC in connection with the supply or possible supply of goods or services to a person or a corporation (the 'business consumer'). And s 51AC(4) lists the same factors as s 51AC(3) in relation to the behaviour of the 'acquirer' who acquires or might acquire goods or services from the 'small business supplier'. Factors (a)–(e) in the lists in ss 51AC(3) and (4) are equivalent to those in s 51AB. However, there are some additional factors. Subsection 51AC(3) further provides:

> (f) the extent to which the supplier's conduct towards the business consumer was consistent with the supplier's conduct in similar transactions between the supplier and other like business consumers; and
>
> (g) the requirements of any applicable industry code;[167] and
>
> (h) the requirements of any other industry code, if the business consumer acted on the reasonable belief that the supplier would comply with that code; and
>
> (i) the extent to which the supplier unreasonably failed to disclose to the business consumer:
>
>> (i) any intended conduct of the supplier that might affect the interests of the business consumer; and
>>
>> (ii) any risks to the business consumer arising from the supplier's intended conduct (being risks that the supplier should have foreseen would not be apparent to the business consumer); and
>
> (j) the extent to which the supplier was willing to negotiate the terms and conditions of any contract for supply of the goods or services with the business consumer; and
>
> (k) the extent to which the supplier and the business consumer acted in good faith.

Subsection 51AC(4)(f)–(k) provide equivalent factors for an acquirer and small business supplier.

However, by virtue of ss 51AB(3) and 51AC(5) the mere instituting of legal proceedings or referral of disputes or claims to arbitration is not to be taken as engaging in unconscionable conduct. And, although the court may have regard to conduct engaged in, or circumstances existing, before the commencement of this section, it must not have regard to any

---

165. However, s 51AC(10) has the effect that some contracts at a price of over $3 million can have the price notionally apportioned so that in respect of at least some goods and services the threshold is not exceeded. Originally the limit was $1 million, and was increased from 1 July 2000 to $3 million.
166. The section came into effect in July 1998 following the Reid Report, *Finding a Balance: Towards Fair Trading in Australia*. For a discussion of this relatively new section see, eg Jade Harkness, 'New Law of Unconscionability' (2000) 14 *CLQ* 11; Philip Tucker, 'Too Much Concern Too Soon? Rationalising the Elements of Section 51AC of the Trade Practices Act' (2001) 17 *JCL* 120; A Finlay, 'Unconscionable Conduct and the Business Plaintiff: has Australia gone too far?' (1999) 28 *Anglo-American L Rev* 470.
167. See also Pt IVB — Industry Codes, which permits industry codes to be prescribed and enforced and prohibits corporations from contravening applicable industry codes.

circumstances that were not reasonably foreseeable at the time of the alleged contravention (s 51AB(4)). Subsection 51AC(6) is slightly different from s 51AB(4) as the court can have regard to 'circumstances existing' but not to 'conduct' engaged in before the commencement.[168]

Subsection 51AC(2) further distinguishes s 51AC from ss 51AA and 51AB. It provides that a *person* must not engage in unconscionable conduct 'in connection with': (a) the supply or possible supply of goods or services to a corporation; or (b) the acquisition or possible acquisition of goods or services from a corporation.

[1525] **Fair trading legislation.** A corresponding provision to s 51AB is contained in the fair trading legislation of the States.[169] However, as yet, no State has an equivalent of s 51AC.[170] A very significant point to be made is that although the 'in trade or commerce' requirement of ss 51AB of the *Trade Practices Act* 1974 (Cth) is reproduced, the conduct need not be engaged in by a corporation. The reason for this is the same as in the case of the statutory prohibition on misleading conduct and was explained earlier.[171]

[1526] **Rights and remedies.** The usual context of unconscionability in the general contract setting is the ability of a party to enforce the contract, or the entitlement of the party subjected to the unconscionable conduct to an order setting aside the contract. But the provisions of ss 51AA, 51AB and 51AC are not limited in their impact to contractual situations. Rather, they prohibit a particular kind of conduct in particular contexts, and a person may obtain an injunction to prevent contravention.[172]

Although ss 51AA, 51AB and 51AC of the *Trade Practices Act* prohibit unconscionable conduct, a contravention (or threatened contravention) of either section does not result in a pecuniary penalty becoming payable by the corporation. In many cases, the person who seeks relief will do so as a defence to an action to enforce a contract. But, assuming that a contract is entered into as a result of conduct infringing ss 51AA, 51AB or 51AC of the *Trade Practices Act* 1974 (Cth), the Act, in s 87, does allow for an approach to the court which may make a wide range of orders which may be made not only against any person who contravened the section, but also

---

168. The distinction between the two words was considered in *ACCC v Leelee Pty Ltd* (2000) ATPR 41-742.
169. See **ACT**: *Fair Trading Act* 1992, s 13; **NSW**: *Fair Trading Act* 1987, s 43; **NT**: *Consumer Affairs and Fair Trading Act* 1990, s 43; **Qld**: *Fair Trading Act* 1989, s 39; **SA**: *Fair Trading Act* 1987, s 57; **Tas**: *Fair Trading Act* 1990, s 15; **Vic**: *Fair Trading Act* 1999, s 8; **WA**: *Fair Trading Act* 1987, s 11. Those States and Territories that have a limitation period for unconscionable conduct now vary. As to the fair trading legislation see [1103] and note that the Queensland provisions on private remedies are more restricted than those of the other jurisdictions.
170. This may well change following the enactment of s 51ACAA *Trade Practices Act*, inserted by *Trade Practices Amendment Act (No 1)* 2001, which provides: '51ACAA Concurrent operation of State and Territory laws. It is the Parliament's intention that a law of a State or Territory should be able to operate concurrently with this Part unless the law is directly inconsistent with this Part'. Victoria does currently have an equivalent of s 51AA: see *Fair Trading Act* 1999, s 7.
171. See [1103]–[1104].
172. See *Trade Practices Act* 1974 (Cth), s 80.

against any person 'involved in' that contravention.[173] Although conferring no positive right of rescission on a party, a court may under s 87 make a declaration that any contract entered into be set aside.[174] There is also power to order the payment of monetary compensation, which, unlike the remedy of damages under s 82,[175] is discretionary. It should be noted that whereas damages under s 82 were originally not available in respect of contraventions of ss 51AA and AB, such damages are now available as a result of amendments to the Act coming into force on 26 July 2001; s 82 damages were always available in respect of contraventions of s 51AC. The courts under these provisions have a flexibility in framing relief similar to that enjoyed by courts applying the *Contracts Review Act* 1980 (NSW).[176]

[1527] Different meanings of 'unconscionable conduct'. It has been generally assumed that 'unconscionable conduct' in s 51AA referred to the relatively narrow doctrine of unconscionable contracts under *Amadio*. However, it is possible that it extends further and refers to other equitable doctrines (such as equitable estoppel and relief against forfeiture) where unconscionable conduct is an element, or even that it applies wherever the judge concludes that the conduct attacked was against conscience according to ordinary standards.[177]

The fact that s 51AA contains no 'shopping list' of factors to guide the courts now adds force to the argument that the inclusion of the 'shopping lists' in ss 51AB and 51AC[178] implies that, despite the use in all sections of the familiar and traditional expression 'unconscionable', ss 51AB and 51AC are intended to apply to a wider range of conduct than is s 51AA.[179] It seems that the meaning of 'unconscionable' in ss 51AB and 51AC is

---

173. For the purpose of determining whether to make an order under s 87 in relation to a contravention of Pt IVA, the court may have regard to the conduct of the parties since the contravention occurred (s 87(1D)). See also s 87(1CA) (special limitation period of six years for subs (1A) applications; this period was prior to 26 July 2001, two years). As to the significance of the liability of persons 'involved in' a contravention see [1114], [1121].
174. This is subject to the possible implications of *Webb Distributors (Aust) Pty Ltd v Victoria* (1993) 179 CLR 15; 117 ALR 321, discussed [1116]. As to further limitations under the Queensland *Fair Trading Act* 1989 see [1103]. In some jurisdictions no order may be made in respect of a contravention in relation to certain contracts of insurance.
175. Section 82 is available for breaches of ss 51AA, 51AB by virtue of *Trade Practices Amendment Act (No 1)* 2001. Section 82 is discussed [1112]–[1114].
176. See [1522].
177. For discussions, so far inconclusive see, eg *Australian Competition & Consumer Commission v Chats House Investments Pty Ltd* (1996) 142 ALR 177; *Pritchard v Racecage Pty Ltd* (1997) 72 FCR 203; *Olex Focas Pty Ltd v Skodaexport Co Ltd* [1998] 3 VR 380; *Hurley v McDonald's Australia Ltd* (2000) ATPR 41-741; *ACCC v CG Berbatis Holdings Pty Ltd (No 2)* (2000) 96 FCR 491.
178. See [1524].
179. See discussion in *Australian Competition & Consumer Commission v Simply No-Knead (Franchising) Pty Ltd* (2000) 104 FCR 253, at paras 31–7 per Sundberg J, *ACCC v Berbatis Holding Pty Ltd (No 2)* (2000) 96 FCR 491. But see *Hurley v McDonald's Australia Ltd* (2000) ATPR 41-741. However, conduct by one party is not 'unconscionable' within s 51AA merely because the other made a bad business decision: *Australian Competition & Consumer Commission v Samton Holdings Pty Ltd* (2000) ATPR 41-791.

probably not exactly the same, as s 51AC has a much longer 'shopping list'.[180]

[1528] Application of ss 51AA, 51AB and 51AC. The *Trade Practices Act* is wider than the *Contracts Review Act* in that it is not limited to unconscionable contracts but speaks more generally of unconscionable conduct. It therefore applies to unconscionable promotional conduct as well as to post-contractual conduct (for example, certain enforcement practices). It may well extend to such matters as unconscionable exercise of rights.[181]

On the other hand ss 51AA, 51AB and 51AC are not as extensive in scope as the *Contracts Review Act* in that ss 51AA, 51AB and 51AC apply only to 'unconscionable' conduct whereas as we have seen,[182] the *Contracts Review Act* extends also to 'unjust' contracts. 'Unconscionable' is not defined in the *Trade Practices Act*. In principle the threshold concept for plaintiffs proceeding under the *Trade Practices Act* is harder to establish than that for those proceeding under the *Contracts Review Act*; put another way, 'unconscionable' is narrower than 'unjust'. In practice the difference is probably slight.[183] Yet it should be noted that the 'shopping lists' of factors to be taken into account in ss 51AB and 51AC are, while shorter than that under the New South Wales Act, wider in one important respect, namely, that they include 'the amount for which, and the circumstances under which, the consumer could have acquired identical or equivalent goods or services from a person other than the corporation'.

In the result it is unclear how far ss 51AA, 51AB and 51AC may be used to attack contracts which might be vulnerable under the *Contracts Review Act*. 'Unconscionable conduct' under ss 51AB and 51AC requires 'something clearly unfair or unreasonable' or action that shows no regard for conscience and imports a 'pejorative moral judgment'.[184] As we have seen,[185] this element of blameworthiness which seems inherent in the *Amadio* doctrine (and also, because of the use without definition of the concept of unconscionability, in s 51AA of the *Trade Practices Act*) is not

---

180. See *Australian Competition & Consumer Commission v Simply No-Knead (Franchising) Pty Ltd* (2000) 104 FCR 253, at para 35 per Sundberg J; *Hurley v McDonald's Australia Ltd* (2000) ATPR 41-741 at 40,585, Full Federal Court. See further [1528].
181. See *Olex Focas Pty Ltd v Skodaexport Co Ltd* (1997) ATPR (Digest) 46-163 (a decision on s 51AA, discussed below). Compare *Tri-Global (Aust) Pty Ltd v Colonial Mutual Life Assurance Society Ltd* (1992) ATPR 41-174 at 40,382 per Spender J and see Sandra Welsman, 'Commercial Power and Competitor Litigation' (1996) 24 *Australian Business Law Review* 85.
182. See [1519].
183. See Anthony Mason, 'The Place of Equity and Equitable Remedies in the Contemporary Common Law World' (1994) 110 *LQR* 238 at 242, 256 but see *Burt v Australia and New Zealand Banking Group Ltd* (1994) ATPR (Digest) 46-123; A Mason, 'Contract, Good Faith and Equitable Standards in Fair Dealing' (2000) 116 *LQR* 66 at 89–90.
184. *Hurley v McDonald's Australia Ltd* (2000) ATPR 41-741 at 40,585 (Full Federal Court), approving *Cameron v Qantas Airways Ltd* (1994) 55 FCR 147 at 179; *Qantas Airways Ltd v Cameron* (1996) 66 FCR 246 at 262, 283–4, 298. See also *Micarone v Perpetual Trustees Australia Ltd* (1999) 75 SASR 1; *Australian Competition & Consumer Commission v Samton Holdings Pty Ltd* (2000) ATPR 41-791.
185. See [1522].

essential under the *Contracts Review Act*.[186] Despite the 'transparent moral dimension'[187] in the unconscionability doctrine and in the insistence in many elaborations of it that there be a degree of exploitation, there is some ambiguity as to how far reprehensible conduct is essential,[188] especially as in some cases passive acceptance or retention of a benefit may in the circumstances suffice. At this point the place of the unconscionability doctrine as a species of equitable fraud[189] raises issues as to how far what is seen as an unfair result produced without deliberately unfair behaviour comes within the scope of the doctrine.

On the other hand, the elements in ss 51AB and 51AC's 'shopping lists' place somewhat more emphasis on substantive matters than does that in the *Contracts Review Act*.[190] In particular, the *Trade Practices Act* does, while the *Contracts Review Act* does not, expressly refer to the amount of the price payable under the contract. Whether so-called 'price unconscionability' alone would justify relief under the American law has given rise to much debate. In many countries legislation dealing with unfair contract terms expressly excludes the contract price from the scheme of control.[191] Also, some factors in ss 51AC(3) and (4) describe conduct that goes beyond what would constitute unconscionability in equity. For example, factor (j) directs attention to the extent to which the supplier/acquirer was willing to negotiate the terms and conditions of any contract for supply of the goods or services with the business consumer/small business supplier. Factor (g) relates to the requirements of any applicable industry code,[192] and factor (k) relates to the extent to which the supplier and the business consumer, or the acquirer and small business supplier acted in good faith.[193]

One limiting factor of s 51AB is that, for reasons which are not readily apparent, it applies only to the supplier of goods or services, and thus would not, for example, apply to unconscionable conduct by a purchaser.[194]

---

186. See in particular *Baltic Shipping Co v Dillon (The Mikhail Lermontov)* (1991) 22 NSWLR 1 at 20 per Kirby P (on appeal (1993) 176 CLR 344). See also *Jedda Investments Pty Ltd v Krambousanos* (1997) 72 FCR 138. Contrast the approach taken under similar but differently worded provisions of the *Credit Act* 1984 (Vic): *Morlend Finance Corp (Vic) Pty Ltd v Westendorf* [1993] 2 VR 284. The frequently cited judgment of McHugh JA in *West v AGC (Advances) Ltd* (1986) 5 NSWLR 610 is rather ambiguous on this point.
187. P Finn, 'Commerce, the Common Law and Morality' (1989) 17 *Melb ULR* 87 at 87.
188. See *Commercial Bank of Australia Ltd v Amadio* (1983) 151 CLR 447 at 478 per Deane J, and Peter Birks and Chin Nyuk Yin, 'On the Nature of Undue Influence' in Beatson and Friedmann, eds, *Good Faith and Fault in Contract Law*, 1995, pp 57 at 60.
189. See Patrick Parkinson, 'The Conscience of Equity' in Parkinson, ed, *The Principles of Equity*, 1996, pp 28–52.
190. See [1522].
191. See, eg European Community Directive of 1993 on Unfair Terms in Consumer Contracts, Art 4.
192. *Australian Competition & Consumer Commission v Simply No-Knead (Franchising) Pty Ltd* (2000) 104 FCR 253, at para 31 per Sundberg J.
193. See *Australian Competition & Consumer Commission v Simply No-Knead (Franchising) Pty Ltd* (2000) 104 FCR 253.
194. See G Taperell, 'Unconscionable Conduct and Small Business' (1990) 18 *ABLR* 370.

As happened in New South Wales, complaints by business concerns as to the uncertainty which it was felt would otherwise arise in commercial transactions led to s 51AB being in effect limited to conduct directed at consumers. This was done by providing that references in the section to goods or services are taken to be references to goods or services of a kind ordinarily acquired for personal, domestic or household use or consumption and that a reference to the supply or possible supply of goods does not include a reference to such supply or possible supply for the purpose of resupply or for the purpose of using them up or transforming them in trade or commerce.[195] This limitation in s 51AB to goods or services 'of a kind ordinarily acquired for personal, domestic or household use or consumption' causes considerable difficulties of interpretation in the context of the making of loans and the giving of guarantees[196] and may, indeed, paradoxically mean that in a situation such as occurred in *Amadio* the section would be inapplicable.[197]

Damages have always been available under s 82 for breaches of s 51AC and, since 26 July 2001,[198] s 82 also applies to breaches of ss 51AA and 51AB.

Towards a System of Abstract Control of Unfair Contracts?

[1529] The concept of abstract control. Provisions of the substantive law of the kind described in this chapter are obviously very important in providing a means of achieving justice for individuals, particularly consumers, trying to enforce their contractual rights. This, however, may have limited effect in providing control in the interests of consumers generally. This is partly because of cost and other factors, increasingly discussed recently in public debate in Australia on 'access to justice' problems, making resort to the courts to resolve their disputes quite beyond the reach of most individuals. Moreover, even in those relatively rare cases which are brought to court, the decision in any individual case directly binds only the parties to the contract being sued on. The mere fact that a particular provision is likely to be held to be ineffective if litigation does arise does not necessarily deter enterprises from continuing to use such provisions in their contracts. Accordingly, many jurisdictions have experimented with a variety of techniques designed to provide a more generalised or 'abstract' control of unfair contracts. This can take various forms, but typically a public authority or an organisation of consumers or traders will be empowered to seek an injunction or similar order prohibiting the continued use by a trader of a contract term that is unfair to consumers.[199]

195. See s 51AB(5), (6). See *Comco Constructions Pty Ltd v Westminster Properties Pty Ltd* (1990) 2 WAR 335.
196. See *Begbie v State Bank of New South Wales* (1994) ATPR 41-288. See also *George T Collings (Aust) Pty Ltd v H F Stevenson (Aust) Pty Ltd* (1991) ATPR 41-104.
197. G Taperell, 'Unconscionable Conduct and Small Business' (1990) 18 *ABLR* 370; M Sneddon, 'Unfair Conduct in Taking Guarantees and the Role of Independent Advice' (1990) 13 *UNSWLJ* 302.
198. See *Trade Practices Amendment Act (No 1)* 2001.

Abstract control of unfair contracts almost of necessity concentrates on the substantive terms of contracts against which complaint is made. Many reform statutes in Europe follow a pattern of combining a general prohibition on unfair contracts with the setting out of certain types of clauses which are to be regarded as unfair. For example, the German *Law Governing Standard Business Conditions* of 1976 provides that, in contracts with consumers, certain specified types of clause are presumed to be invalid unless the business party can show they are reasonably justified in the circumstances (the 'grey' list) and others are always invalid (the 'black' list).[200] The European Directive of 1993 on unfair terms in consumer contracts contains an 'indicative and non-exhaustive' list of the terms which may be regarded as unfair.[201]

[1530] Abstract control in Australia.[202] There has been very little reference in the Australian literature to approaches towards the abstract control of unfair contracts, and so it is something of a paradox that provisions do exist which permit such an approach, but they have in fact been little utilised. Although the *Contracts Review Act* 1980 (NSW) focuses principally upon the enforcement of individual contracts, s 10 empowers the court, on the application of the Minister, to grant an order prescribing the terms on which a person may enter into contracts of a specified class. Such an order may be made where 'a person has embarked, or is likely to embark, on a course of conduct leading to the formation of unjust contracts'. A similar result is possible under the provisions of the *Trade Practices Act* enabling injunctions to be granted to restrain, inter alia, contraventions of the provisions of the Act on unconscionable conduct. (In this case the injunction may be obtained not only by the Minister or the Australian Competition and Consumer Commission, but also by 'any other person'; this has the effect of abolishing traditional requirements of locus standi for the obtaining of an injunction.)[203] In what appears to be the only reported case where such an order was obtained, the New South Wales Minister for Consumer Affairs proceeded against a real estate agency in respect of its standard form of agency contract with vendor clients. This included an unusual clause giving the agent an interest in the property being sold as security for any unpaid commission. This clause was held to be unjust under the *Contracts Review Act* and the agent was ordered not to use it in future contracts.[204]

---

199. See E Hondius, 'Unfair Contract Terms: New Control Systems' (1978) 26 *Amer J of Comp L* 525; Hondius, *Unfair Terms in Consumer Contracts*, 1987.
200. For a description see Reich and Micklitz, *Consumer Legislation in the Federal Republic of Germany*, 1981, Chapter 7.
201. For a description of the Directive see E Hondius, 'EC Directive on Unfair Terms in Consumer Contracts' (1994) 7 *JCL* 34. For the United Kingdom implementation of the principles of the Directive see Unfair Terms in Consumer Contracts Regulations 1994.
202. See further David Harland, 'The Regulation of Unfair Contracts in Australia' in Rachagan, ed, *Developing Consumer Law in Asia*, 1994, pp 89–103.
203. *Tobacco Institute of Australia Ltd v Australian Federation of Consumer Organisations Inc* (1989) 84 ALR 337.
204. *Minister for Consumer Affairs v W W Vallack Real Estate Pty Ltd* (1986) ASC 55-478.

The general law doctrine of unconscionability has traditionally focused attention on procedural unconscionability[205] (although in *Amadio's* case Mason CJ seems to have thought that the doctrine may in future have a wider application than previously to standard form contracts).[206] It is probably true to say that at the time the *Contracts Review Act* 1980 (NSW) was enacted there was an expectation that it would have a significant impact on substantively unfair terms in one-sided standard form contracts used by businesses in dealings with consumers. However, it is very noticeable that to date the reported cases under the Act have been principally concerned with procedural unfairness. No doubt the very existence of the legislation has affected the way in which some contracts are drafted, and it is of course possible that there are significant numbers of cases involving substantively unfair terms which are settled or which are, because of relatively small amounts involved, litigated in the lower courts and thus not reported. It may be that as more experience is gained under the legislation more problems of substantive unfairness will come before the courts. Certainly a case can be made that somewhat greater certainty would be created if, following the European example, the existing 'shopping lists' of relevant factors appearing in the State and federal legislation[207] were to be supplemented by lists of types of clauses which are to be (absolutely or presumptively) ineffective, at least in consumer transactions.

---

205. See [1522].
206. *Commercial Bank of Australia Ltd v Amadio* (1983) 151 CLR 447 at 462–3.
207. See [1520], [1524].

PART VI
Illegality

Chapter 16

Illegal Contracts

General..1601
    Introduction.. 1601
    Basic Rules and Distinctions............................ 1603
Contracts Illegal by Statute..........................1607
    Contracts Prohibited by Statute......................... 1607
    Contracts Affected But Not Prohibited by Statute............. 1616
Contracts which Infringe Public Policy..................1619
    General.. 1619
    Contracts to Commit a Legal Wrong..................... 1621
    Contracts Injurious to Public Life or Foreign Relations......... 1624
    Contracts Purporting to Oust the Jurisdiction of the Courts..... 1626
    Contracts Prejudicial to the Administration of Justice.......... 1628
    Immoral Contracts and Contracts Prejudicial to the
       Status of Marriage............................... 1631
    Contracts in Restraint of Trade......................... 1634

General

Introduction

[1601] Scope of this chapter. Whether a contract is illegal, or simply void[1] or unenforceable[2] must depend on the circumstances of the case. In this chapter we deal with contracts which are illegal and/or contrary to public policy. The concern is with illegality existing at the time of the contract.[3] The consequences of such illegality are discussed in Chapter 17.

A contract may be illegal because it is prohibited by statute, or because it infringes a rule of public policy. It should not, however, be thought that wherever statutory requirements are not fulfilled the resulting contract, if indeed one results, is necessarily illegal or affected by illegality. For example, where the parties to a contract fail to comply with a requirement

---

1. For discussion of the concept of 'voidness' see [1215].
2. For discussion of the concept of 'unenforceable' see [519].
3. For supervening illegality see [2021]–[2024].

[1601] of writing,[4] the contract (although unenforceable) is not illegal. Similarly, although it might be said, in a very general sense, that it is 'illegal' for a person (or corporation) who lacks full contractual capacity to enter into a contract except in accordance with the applicable statutory or common law rules,[5] this is not what is ordinarily understood by the concept of illegality.

In relation to statutes the concern is with situations where contravention amounts to an offence, for which a penalty is imposed. The issue is whether, in the circumstances, the contract is prohibited by statute. This depends on the intention of the legislature. Similarly, the relevant public policy is that concerned with the upholding of community standards, rather than the protection of disadvantaged persons such as minors. The contract will only be illegal if it is of a sufficiently heinous nature.

[1602] State of the law. The topic of illegality is one of the least satisfactory branches of contract law. This is perhaps more true of the consequences of illegality than the issue of when a contract is in fact illegal or contrary to public policy,[6] but it is also true of the concept of illegality itself. It is frequently said that some contracts are illegal and void, whereas others are simply void; and that illegality or 'voidness' may be the result of statute or a rule of public policy. However, it has also been suggested that when a contract is affected by illegality it is usually merely unenforceable. Not surprisingly, when attempts are made to analyse the law there is little agreement on how it should be discussed.[7] Therefore, the analysis made in this book is simply one way of examining the topic.

It also seems to be generally accepted that it is impossible to reconcile all the cases on illegality.[8] To some extent this is understandable because views on the contravention of public policy are likely to change over time. But there are substantive inconsistencies, not all of which can be explained simply by saying that public policy has changed. Inconsistencies are particularly in evidence where the consequences of illegality are in issue.[9] Although these comments do little to engender the confidence of students trying to come to grips with the topic, it is in our view appropriate to warn the reader that disagreements are very frequent in this area.

Basic Rules and Distinctions

[1603] Illegality need not always be pleaded. In the vast majority of cases the issue of illegality is raised when one party to a contractual dispute pleads illegality as a defence to a claim arising out of the contract or its performance. However, because of the nature of illegality — the contravention of statute or a rule of public policy — the court may be obliged to have regard to illegality even if it has not been pleaded.

---

4. See generally Chapter 5.
5. See generally Chapter 8.
6. See generally Chapter 17.
7. See M P Furmston, 'The Analysis of Illegal Contracts' (1966) 16 *Univ of Toronto LJ* 267 and the discussion in Treitel, *The Law of Contract*, 10th ed, 1999, pp 392–3.
8. See *Fitzgerald v F J Leonhardt Pty Ltd* (1997) 189 CLR 215 at 231–2; 143 ALR 569 at 580.
9. See, eg [1721]–[1724]. It is also difficult to reconcile all the cases on statutory illegality. See generally [1607]–[1618].

In *Knowles v Fuller*[10] Jordan CJ said that a court 'will not entertain a defence of illegality which has not been pleaded', unless:

- the contract giving rise to the plaintiff's claim was on its face ('ex facie') illegal;[11]
- the plaintiff is unable to prove the case without relying on an illegal transaction;[12] or
- the fact of illegality comes to light at the trial of the action and it is clear from the circumstances that there is no way in which the illegality could have been cured.[13]

Jordan CJ regarded the third case as an exceptional one, and if there is the possibility that what appears to be a case of illegality might be explained or cured, for example, by the admission of further evidence or the operation of an exempting provision to a statutory prohibition, the court will not allow the defendant to raise illegality as a defence. Thus, the defendant in *Knowles v Fuller* was not permitted to rely on a defence of illegality based on the failure to obtain prior approval of building work under s 311 of the *Local Government Act* 1919 (NSW), because the plaintiff might have adduced additional evidence to negative the contravention of the statute or have obtained a certificate of compliance, under s 317A of the Act.[14]

[1604] Contracts to do an illegal act. Perhaps the most basic general principle is that a contract entered into with the object of committing an illegal act will not be enforced.[15] As Devlin J explained in *St John Shipping Corp v Joseph Rank Ltd*,[16] the 'application of this principle depends upon proof of the intent, at the time the contract was made, to break the law'. This principle applies not only to a contract entered into with the object of infringing a statute, but also to a contract to infringe a common law rule. If both parties possess the intent the contract is in fact a criminal conspiracy. Such a contract is clearly illegal.

[1605] Varying impacts of statutes on contracts. The effect of statute law on contracts varies as between statutes. What must be emphasised is that each Act raises its own issues of construction.[17]

---

10. (1947) 48 SR (NSW) 243 at 245. See also *North Western Salt Co Ltd v Electrolytic Alkali Co Ltd* [1914] AC 461 at 469, 475–6, 477; *Gozzard v McKell* (1931) 32 SR (NSW) 39; *Varley v Spatt* [1955] VLR 403; *Re Rosemac Pty Ltd's Caveat* (1992) [1994] 1 Qd R 137.
11. See, eg *Re Mahmoud and Ispahani* [1921] 2 KB 716; and [1622].
12. See [1705].
13. Cf *Bank of India v Trans Continental Commodity Merchants Ltd* [1982] 1 Lloyd's Rep 427 at 434.
14. See also *North Western Salt Co Ltd v Electrolytic Alkali Co Ltd* [1914] AC 461 at 477–8; *G C Dickson & Yorston (Builders) Pty Ltd v Hattam* [1935] VLR 168; *Ford v Bartley* (1956) 57 SR (NSW) 281; *United City Merchants (Investments) Ltd v Royal Bank of Canada* [1983] 1 AC 168.
15. See further [1621]–[1623].
16. [1957] 1 QB 267 at 283 (approved *Yango Pastoral Co Pty Ltd v First Chicago Australia Ltd* (1978) 139 CLR 410 at 413, 423; 21 ALR 585).
17. See also *Nelson v Nelson* (1995) 184 CLR 538 at 552, 611; 132 ALR 133 (classifications also applicable to express trusts).

(1) An Act may *prohibit* the making of contracts of a particular description or (more broadly) 'agreements', 'arrangements' or 'understandings'.[18] Many Acts which, while lacking language of express prohibition, penalise the making of contracts of a particular description, fall within this first class.

(2) Parliament may, while stopping short of express or implied prohibition, declare contracts of a particular description to be null and void.

(3) Parliament may merely declare void a particular class of contractual provision, such as an exclusion clause.[19]

(4) Parliament may render them void in whole or in part as against a third party only, while not touching the validity of contracts as between the parties.[20]

Contracts within (1) are examples of illegal contracts. They are expressly or impliedly prohibited. The making of the contracts within the other classes is lawful, but legal enforcement is withheld.[21]

[1606] **Public policy.** Similarly, not all contracts which are contrary to public policy are illegal. In some such cases a contract may be rendered void, or merely unenforceable, without actually being illegal. For example, a contract provision which is in restraint of trade[22] is considered to be unenforceable (or perhaps void) on the ground of public policy, but not illegal.

This distinction may be important when the consequences of illegality are being considered.[23]

Contracts Illegal by Statute

Contracts Prohibited by Statute

General

[1607] **Issue of legislative intention.** Whether a contract is prohibited by statute depends on the intention of the legislature as expressed in the statute, and principles governing the interpretation of statutes must be applied.[24] The recent decisions indicate that a legislative intention to prohibit a contract is not to be inferred except in the clearest cases.[25]

In *St John Shipping Corp v Joseph Rank Ltd*[26] Devlin J stated, as a general principle, that a court 'will not enforce a contract which is expressly or

---

18. See [1607]–[1615].
19. See [1617].
20. See [1618].
21. See [1616].
22. See generally [1634]–[1653].
23. See generally Chapter 17.
24. See, eg *Yango Pastoral Co Pty Ltd v First Chicago Australia Ltd* (1978) 139 CLR 410 at 414.
25. See *Nelson v Nelson* (1995) 184 CLR 538 at 552, 554, 581, 594; *Fitzgerald v F J Leonhardt Pty Ltd* (1997) 189 CLR 215 at 218–19, 227, 242–5.
26. [1957] 1 QB 267 at 283.

impliedly prohibited by statute'. He went on to explain: 'if the contract is of this class it does not matter what the intent of the parties is; if the statute prohibits the contract it is unenforceable whether the parties meant to break the law or not'. In distinguishing a contract entered into with the intention of breaking a statute from a contract expressly or impliedly prohibited by statute, Devlin J said:[27]

> In the former class you have only to look and see what acts the statute prohibits; it does not matter whether or not it prohibits a contract; if a contract is deliberately made to do a prohibited act, that contract will be unenforceable. In the latter class, you have to consider not what acts the statute prohibits, but what contracts it prohibits; but you are not concerned at all with the intent of the parties; if the parties enter into a prohibited contract, that contract is unenforceable.

[1608] **Concept of 'statute'.** The concept of statutory prohibition extends beyond Acts of parliament and therefore includes, for example, regulations made under statutes. Thus, in *Re Mahmoud and Ispahani*[28] a contract which contravened an Order issued by the Food Controller under the *Defence of the Realm Regulations* (UK) (called the Seeds, Oils and Fats Order 1919) was held to be illegal and prohibited.

[1609] **Commission of offence not conclusive.** In considering whether a contract is prohibited by statute it is always material to consider whether an offence has been (or may have been) committed by either or both the parties. Although a contract may be void where the statute does not make contravention an offence, such a contract would not be illegal.[29] Illegality is more likely if an offence has been committed.

If the contract is not expressly prohibited, the court must consider what consequences flow from the offence. There is, for example, a certain reluctance to treat a contract as prohibited where the offence is committed during the performance of the contract rather than at the time of its formation.[30] It follows that the commission of an offence is not conclusive. For example, in *Dalgety and New Zealand Loan Ltd v C Imeson Pty Ltd*[31] a diseased animal was sold in contravention of the *Cattle Slaughtering and Diseased Animals and Meat Act* 1902 (NSW), and an offence committed under s 47 of the Act. Nevertheless, the court held that the contract in issue was not illegal because it was not prohibited by the Act.

[1610] **Illegality in formation or performance.** The main examples of illegal contracts prohibited by statute are those which are illegal in formation. For example, in *George v Greater Adelaide Land Development Co Ltd*[32] s 23(c) of the *Town Planning and Development Act* 1920 (SA) made it

---

27. [1957] 1 QB 267 at 283.
28. [1921] 2 KB 716 (see further [1611]).
29. See, eg *Australian Broadcasting Corp v Redmore Pty Ltd* (1989) 166 CLR 454 at 462; 84 ALR 199.
30. The leading case is *St John Shipping Corp v Joseph Rank Ltd* [1957] 1 QB 267 (see [1615]).
31. [1964] NSWR 638 (see further [1614]). For other illustrations see *Bassin v Standen* (1945) 46 SR (NSW) 16 at 18; *Yango Pastoral Co Pty Ltd v First Chicago Australia Ltd* (1978) 139 CLR 410 at 413.
32. (1929) 43 CLR 91.

unlawful for a person, 'to offer for sale, or to sell, or to convey, transfer or otherwise dispose of any existing allotment or parcel of land', except in accordance with the Act. Section 44 imposed a penalty on any person who contravened certain sections of the Act, including s 23. A contract for the sale of certain allotments of land was held to be illegal because it contravened the Act, and was expressly prohibited, even though the parties had in the contract expressed an intention that performance was not to take place until the Act had been complied with. The position would have been different had the statute merely prohibited the disposition.[33]

On the other hand, where the illegality arises in the course of performance it will be more difficult to establish that a contract is prohibited.[34] Nevertheless, the issue is the same as that applied to contracts illegal in formation, namely, whether the contract was expressly or impliedly prohibited by the statute.

Express provisions

[1611] **Express prohibition.** In order for the prohibition of a contract to be express it is not necessary for the statute to say 'and any contract entered into in contravention of this statute is illegal'. If the substance of the relevant provision is sufficiently clear the contract will be regarded as expressly prohibited. Generally, if the statute prohibits certain conduct, and entry into a contract constitutes such conduct, the contract will be regarded as expressly prohibited.

Re Mahmoud and Ispahani[35] is frequently cited[36] as an example of express prohibition. The relevant provision prohibited persons from buying or selling or otherwise dealing in, any of the articles specified in a schedule, 'except under and in accordance with the terms of a licence issued by or under the authority of the Food Controller'. Linseed oil, which was an article specified in the schedule, was the subject matter of a contract for the sale of goods between the parties. The contract was held to be prohibited, even though the plaintiff possessed a licence, because the contract provided for sale to a person (the defendant) who did not possess a licence. The prohibition was regarded as express because the contract could not be entered into, or performed, without infringing the legislation.

[1612] **Express permission.** In view of the importance of the issue of prohibition it is unfortunate that there is frequently no express statement that a contract infringing a legislative provision is (or is not) illegal. Where it is clear that there is no express prohibition, the issue of implied prohibition is, as we shall see,[37] often difficult to resolve. Certainty would

---

33. See *Braham v Walker* (1961) 104 CLR 366; *Gaye (No 1) Pty Ltd v Allan Rowlands Holdings Pty Ltd* (1993) 114 ALR 341.
34. It may also be difficult to determine whether the issue is illegality or frustration of contract. Cf *Gamerco SA v ICM/Fair Warning (Agency) Ltd* [1995] 1 WLR 1226 (see [2021]).
35. [1921] 2 KB 716. Cf *Metcalf v Permanent Building Society* (1993) 10 WAR 145.
36. See, eg *Archbolds (Freightage) Ltd v S Spanglett Ltd* [1961] 1 QB 374 at 385; Salahuddin Ahmed, 'Consequences of Illegality on Contracts in Contravention of Statutes' (1984) 13 Uni of Qld LJ 219 at 223–4. But see *Ross v Ratcliff* (1988) 91 FLR 66 at 67.
37. See [1613]–[1615].

therefore be more easily obtained by a general use of express statements of the kind found in s 116(1) of the *Goods Act* 1958 (Vic) which states that a 'sale or a lease is not illegal, void or unenforceable by reason only that the seller or lessor is guilty of an offence' under Pt IV of the Act.[38]

Implied prohibition

[1613] Object of statute. By far the most important consideration in cases where there is no express prohibition is the object of the statute. If the object of the statute can only be attained by holding that a particular class of contract is prohibited then prohibition must necessarily have been intended in respect of any contract within the class.

In cases where prohibition is consistent with the object of the statute the contract will usually be prohibited, although it may be necessary to consider other factors as well. But if prohibition is *not necessary* in order to further the object of the statute, the court will be reluctant to hold the contract illegal.[39] As Pearce LJ explained in *Archbolds (Freightage) Ltd v S Spanglett Ltd*:[40]

> If the court too readily implies that a contract is forbidden by statute, it takes it out of its own power (so far as that contract is concerned) to discriminate between guilt and innocence. But if the court makes no such implication, it still leaves itself with the general power, based on public policy, to hold those contracts unenforceable which are ex facie unlawful, and also to refuse its aid to guilty parties in respect of contracts which to the knowledge of both can only be performed in contravention of the statute ... or which though apparently lawful are intended to be performed illegally or for an illegal purpose ...

In focussing on the object of the statute, it may be important whether there is an intention to protect the public or merely to exact a penalty for the benefit of the revenue.[41] If the statute is designed to protect the public a contract in contravention of it will generally be regarded as prohibited. Thus, in *Bradshaw v Gilbert's (Australasian) Agency (Vic) Pty Ltd*,[42] s 25(1) of the *Prices Regulation Act* 1948 (Vic) prohibited the sale of declared goods at a price greater than the maximum fixed by regulation. This was held to make illegal a contract for the sale of goods at a price greater than that fixed, even though the goods were destined for export, because the policy of the legislation (to keep prices below a predetermined level) might be thwarted by international sales at a higher price. However, the fact that the statute protects the public is merely a factor to be considered, and is not necessarily conclusive.[43]

---

38. Cf *S C F Finance Co Ltd v Masri (No 2)* [1987] 1 QB 1002 (contravention not to 'affect any civil liability').
39. See *PT Ltd v Maradona Pty Ltd* (1991) 25 NSWLR 643 at 652. Contrast *Hurst v Vestcorp Ltd* (1988) 12 NSWLR 394.
40. [1961] 1 QB 374 at 387.
41. See, eg *Marks v Jolly* (1938) 38 SR (NSW) 351 at 357; *Yango Pastoral Co Pty Ltd v First Chicago Australia Ltd* (1978) 139 CLR 410 at 414, 431.
42. (1952) 86 CLR 209. See also *Pretorius Pty Ltd v Muir & Neil Pty Ltd* [1976] 1 NSWLR 213; *Australian Broadcasting Corp v Redmore Pty Ltd* (1989) 166 CLR 454 at 462.
43. See, eg *Shaw v Groom* [1970] 2 QB 504; *Yango Pastoral Co Pty Ltd v First Chicago Australia Ltd* (1978) 139 CLR 410 at 414.

Many statutes have as their object the implementation of planning and building requirements or the promotion of safe and efficient transport. For example, in *Hayes v Cable*[44] a contract for the construction of a swimming pool was not prohibited even though neither party obtained council approval for the work prior to commencement.[45] The contract was not illegal in formation — since subsequent approval could be applied for — and if the work was found not to comply with the statutory requirements the council was empowered to order the work to be done again. In fact, the approval of the council was obtained after the builder had issued his proceedings. The policy of the Act did not require the contract to be regarded as prohibited. In the instant case a certificate of compliance was subsequently obtained and it would have provided the defendant with an unmerited windfall if the contract had been held illegal.

Similarly, in *Archbolds (Freightage) Ltd v S Spanglett Ltd*[46] the *Road and Rail Traffic Act* 1933 (UK) required a private carrier to hold an 'A' licence for the carriage of goods for reward, and a 'C' licence for the carriage of goods for or in connection with any trade or business carried on by the carrier not being carriage for reward. The defendants agreed to carry whisky for the plaintiffs for reward, but the vehicle which carried the goods had in fact only a 'C' licence. The plaintiffs did not know that this was the case and there was no evidence that they ought to have known that the defendants' vehicle had only a 'C' licence. The contract was not expressly prohibited, and the court refused to hold that the contract was impliedly prohibited. Pearce LJ described[47] the object of the Act as 'not (in this connection) to interfere with the owner of goods or his facilities for transport; but to control those who provided the transport, with a view to promoting its efficiency ... to provide an orderly and comprehensive service'. This object did not require the contract to be held to be prohibited and the object was sufficiently served by the imposition of penalties on offenders.[48]

[1614] Penalty and the conduct prohibited. In *Dalgety and New Zealand Loan Ltd v C Imeson Pty Ltd*[49] the Full Court of the Supreme Court of New South Wales said that the imposition of a penalty for the failure to observe the terms of a statute creates a presumption of prohibition. The case nevertheless illustrates the displacement of the presumption. Section 47 of the *Cattle Slaughtering and Diseased Animals and Meat Act* 1902 (NSW) made it an offence for any person to sell, consign or expose for sale, or supply for rations any diseased animal. A penalty, not exceeding £20, was imposed for an offence under this section. The plaintiffs conducted an auction at which, unknown to either the plaintiffs or defendants, a diseased animal was sold to the defendants. The defendants sought to withhold from the plaintiffs a sum of money equal to its price.

44. (1962) 62 SR (NSW) 1; [1961] NSWR 610. See also *Doug Rea Enterprises Pty Ltd v Hymix Australia Pty Ltd* [1987] 2 Qd R 495.
45. As required by the *Local Government Act* 1919 (NSW).
46. [1961] 1 QB 374.
47. [1961] 1 QB 374 at 386.
48. Contrast *Buckland v Massey* [1985] 1 Qd R 502 (statute concerned with road-worthiness of motor vehicles).
49. [1964] NSWR 638.

Their defence of illegality failed. The court found no express prohibition, but held that the presumption of implied prohibition was displaced by a consideration of the absence of guilty intent and the policy of the statute. The offence under s 47 was one of strict liability, that is, it could be committed even though there was no means of knowing that the animal was diseased. The only way a seller could be sure of not committing an offence was not to sell cattle at all. The Act was designed for the protection of the public, but it did not contemplate the termination of cattle sales generally. Moreover, in a case such as the present, where there was no guilty intent and where the parties could not reasonably know in advance of the disease, a finding that the contract was prohibited would have imposed an additional penalty. In this respect the form of the legislation was important. For persons convicted who knew, or ought to have known, that the animal dealt with was diseased, the maximum penalty was *mandatory* under s 48. The presence of a discretion under s 47 was an indication that the absence of knowledge (or means of knowledge) was relevant to the impact of the Act on the contract.

The form of penalty was also relied on by the High Court in *Yango Pastoral Co Pty Ltd v First Chicago Australia Ltd*.[50] Section 8 of the *Banking Act* 1959 (Cth) prohibited a body corporate from carrying on 'banking business in Australia' unless in possession of an authority under the Act to carry on such business. A penalty of $10,000 was payable 'for each day during which the contravention' continued. It was assumed that the plaintiffs contravened this section, and the issue was whether this prevented the recovery of $132,600 from the defendants. This was a sum which the plaintiffs had lent to the defendants on the security of a mortgage. In addition, a guarantee had been given in respect of the mortgage. Both were assumed to have occurred in the course of banking business. The issue of illegality depended on whether the mortgage (or guarantee) was prohibited by the Act. There was no express prohibition, and the main factor which led the court to conclude that there was no implied prohibition was that the statutory penalty was quite independent of the number of banking transactions entered into on any day. Thus, the penalty was directed to the carrying on of banking business, and not imposed in respect of each banking transaction. This conclusion was equally justified if the conduct of the plaintiffs was examined from the viewpoint of performance. Section 8 did not proscribe any manner of performance for mortgage transactions and the fact that the plaintiffs had contravened the Act by entering into the mortgage in the course of banking business did not mean that it was impliedly prohibited.

The decision was distinguished in *Phoenix General Insurance Co of Greece SA v Halvanon Insurance Co Ltd*[51] where, although the issue of statutory illegality did not in fact arise for decision, the English Court of Appeal considered two conflicting first instance judgments[52] on the impact of legislation imposing a penalty on anyone who carried on insurance business

---

50. (1978) 139 CLR 410. Contrast *Cornelius v Phillips* [1918] AC 199; *Ambassador Refrigeration Pty Ltd v Trocadero Building and Investment Co Pty Ltd* [1968] 1 NSWR 75.
51. [1988] 1 QB 216. See also *Farrow Mortgage Services Pty Ltd v Edgar* (1993) 114 ALR 1 at 18.

without authority to effect or carry out contracts of insurance of designated classes. The court said that, in order to give effect to the policy of the legislation in protecting persons who dealt with unauthorised insurers, common sense and public policy would justify a conclusion that contracts entered into with such persons were not illegal. Unfortunately, it was said that the legislation left no room for such a conclusion. Because the legislation prohibited both the effecting and carrying out of such contracts it was, in the court's view, necessary to conclude that the contracts were impliedly prohibited, since otherwise a court order requiring performance would force the insurer to do an act prohibited by statute.[53] The court was satisfied that reputable insurers would not rely on the prohibition.[54] It has been forcefully argued[55] that the approach taken was erroneous, and also unduly optimistic of the conduct of insurers. In view of the form of the prohibition, the better view is that the contracts were, in the circumstances assumed, *expressly prohibited*, so that the issue of implied prohibition could not have arisen.[56]

[1615] Reasonableness of result. One theme of the cases on statutory illegality is that the court should not find an implied prohibition if this would lead to an unreasonable or inconvenient result, or to an absurd conclusion. The leading case is *St John Shipping Corp v Joseph Rank Ltd*,[57] where the plaintiffs sought to recover the balance of freight due on the carriage of a quantity of wheat from Mobile, Alabama to Birkenhead, England. The defence of illegality was raised because the plaintiffs had contravened the *Merchant Shipping (Safety and Load Line Conventions) Act 1932* (UK) by so loading the vessel which carried the wheat that the vessel's loadline was submerged by about 11 inches. The Act provided for a penalty and the master of the vessel was fined £1200. The amount of the fine was in fact less than the freight earned by overloading the vessel and the defendants, in concert with another receiver of cargo, withheld a sum equal to the freight earned. Clearly, the legislature had imposed an insufficient penalty which had not deterred contravention of the Act, but was the contract of affreightment prohibited? Devlin J held that there was no express prohibition. Nor could he find an implied prohibition in the statute.

Devlin J was impressed by how unreasonable it would have been to reach a contrary conclusion. If the defendants were right, their ability to withhold freight extended to the entire freight earned by the plaintiffs. Therefore, in a case of minor contravention, for example, if the loadline were submerged

---

52. *Stewart v Oriental Fire and Marine Insurance Co Ltd* [1985] QB 988 (overruled); *Bedford Insurance Co Ltd v Instituto de Resseguros do Brasil* [1985] QB 966 (approved).
53. See [1988] 1 QB 216 at 274.
54. [1988] 1 QB 216 at 275. The court left open the possibility that an insured might be able to sue on a collateral contract that the insurer was authorised. See also *Re Cavalier Insurance Co Ltd* [1989] 2 Lloyd's Rep 430 at 448 where there was held to be no 'separate discernible collateral contract' and further [1726].
55. Andrew Stewart, 'Insurance Contracts and Illegality' (1988) 1 *ILJ* 63.
56. See *Permanent Building Society v Wheeler* (1992) 10 WAR 109 at 137 (but cf on appeal sub nom *Metcalf v Permanent Building Society* (1993) 10 WAR 145 at 163).
57. [1957] 1 QB 267. See also *Shaw v Groom* [1970] 2 QB 504.

by a matter of one inch, all the cargo owners could withhold payment and the carrier would suffer an enormous penalty additional to that actually imposed by the Act. Devlin J also thought it relevant to consider the connection between the contract and the offence. A contract which had the result of submerging the loadline, for example, in loading extra cargo or stores when the vessel's loadline was already at the water line, might well be prohibited. But a contract for carriage by a vessel which was subsequently overloaded was one step removed from the offence which had been committed, the plaintiffs having committed their offence during the performance of the contract.[58]

The approach is confirmed in recent decisions of the High Court which have emphasised that in many cases the appropriate conclusion will be that the statutory penalty is a sufficient penalty.[59]

Contracts Affected But Not Prohibited by Statute

[1616] **Void contracts.** Gaming or wagering contracts were valid at common law. However, they now illustrate classes of contract made void (but not prohibited) by statute. In *Carlill v Carbolic Smoke Ball Co*[60] Hawkins J, after acknowledging that it is not easy to define wagering contracts nor the dividing line between them and other contracts, described a wagering contract as[61]

> one by which two persons, professing to hold opposite views touching the issue of a future uncertain event, mutually agree that, dependent upon the determination of that event, one shall win from the other, and that other shall pay or hand over to him, a sum of money or other stake; neither of the contracting parties having any other interest in that contract than the sum or stake he will so win or lose, there being no other real consideration for the making of such contract by either of the parties. It is essential to a wagering contract that each party may under it either win or lose, whether he will win or lose being dependent on the issue of the event, and, therefore, remaining uncertain until that issue is known. If either of the parties may win but cannot lose, or may lose but cannot win, it is not a wagering contract.

Legislation in Australia provides that, subject to certain exceptions, a contract or agreement by way of gaming or wagering is null and void.[62]

---

58. In *Yango Pastoral Co Pty Ltd v First Chicago Australia Ltd* (1978) 139 CLR 410 at 414–15 it was pointed out that it would have been inconvenient and unreasonable to treat all banking contracts as impliedly prohibited by the Act in issue since that might have resulted in depositors being unable to recover their money from a corporation carrying on banking business in contravention of the Act. Recent developments in the law of restitution (see [1727]) suggest that lenders would probably have been entitled to recover their money.
59. See *Nelson v Nelson* (1995) 184 CLR 538 at 570, 613, 616; *Fitzgerald v F J Leonhardt Pty Ltd* (1997) 189 CLR 215 at 227, 246, 251.
60. [1892] 2 QB 484 (affirmed [1893] 1 QB 256).
61. [1892] 2 QB 484 at 490. See also *Morley v Richardson* (1942) 65 CLR 512 at 522–3, 524; *Petranker v Brown* [1984] 2 NSWLR 177 at 194; *National Mutual Holdings Pty Ltd v Sentry Corp* (1989) 87 ALR 539 at 572.
62. **ACT:** *Games Wagers and Betting-houses Act* 1901, s 13; **NSW:** *Unlawful Gambling Act* 1998, s 56; **NT:** *Racing and Betting Act* 1983, s 135; **Qld:** *Racing and Betting Act* 1980, s 248; **SA:** *Lottery and Gaming Act* 1936, ss 50, 50A; **Tas:** *Racing and Gaming Act* 1952, s 114; **Vic:** *Lotteries, Gaming and Betting Act* 1966, s 15; **WA:** *Gaming and Betting (Contracts and Securities) Act* 1985, s 4.

However, certain gaming and wagering contracts may be prohibited, such as those involving the use of prohibited gaming devices, or betting in special circumstances, for example, betting in the streets or on sportsgrounds and with persons known to be under the age of 18 years. In certain cases, criminal penalties will be imposed for contravention. The same (or related) legislation regulates matters such as unlawful games and gaming and betting houses, poker machines, lotteries and art unions, pool betting, totalisator betting, lotto and so on. The exceptions include:

- contributions to winners' prizes, that is, where contestants contribute to the prizes to be awarded to the winners of the contest; and
- betting on a licensed racecourse with a bookmaker in the course of his or her business.

The effect of the general nullifying provision on wagering contracts was described by Rich J in *Defina v Kenny*[63] by saying that 'the legality of wagering contracts was not affected, but the law was no longer available for their enforcement and the parties to them were left to pay wagers or not as their sense of honour might dictate'. Accordingly, where an agent was employed but failed to bet on commission, he was not liable in damages for the amount of the prospective gains, less the prospective losses and his commission, since the wagering contracts (if made) would have been void.[64] But since performance of a void contract is lawful, if the loser of a bet pays the winner by cash or a negotiable instrument (such as a cheque) which is later honoured, title to the money or negotiable instrument passes and the loser cannot recover the money.[65] Moreover, if a commission agent places bets as instructed, thereby incurring personal responsibility (though not legal liability) for them, the agent's principal is liable to reimburse the agent once the amount of the lost bet is paid.[66] A negotiable instrument given or endorsed in payment of a bet arising out of a void contract is not given for an 'illegal' consideration but is given for a 'void' consideration (that is, for no consideration at all) and cannot be sued on.[67]

[1617] Particular contractual provisions declared void. A familiar example of statutory avoidance of particular contractual terms relates to 'exclusion clauses' and other forms of 'contracting out'. For example, s 68 of the *Trade Practices Act* 1974 (Cth) declares void clauses which 'exclude, restrict or modify' the application of the provisions of Div 2 of Pt V of the Act, the exercise of a right conferred, or any 'liability' for breach of a condition or warranty implied by such a provision, or the application of s 75A of the Act.[68]

The *Consumer Credit Code* contains several examples. Thus, s 40(1) provides that a mortgage which does not describe or identify the property

---

63. (1946) 72 CLR 164 at 171. See also *Lipkin Gorman v Karpnale Ltd* [1991] 2 AC 548.
64. *Cohen v Kittell* (1889) 22 QBD 680. An argument that the losers would probably have paid them as debts of honour was described (at 683) by Huddlestone B as 'wholly immaterial'.
65. *Bridger v Savage* (1885) 15 QBD 363 at 367.
66. *Read v Anderson* (1882) 10 QBD 100 (affirmed (1884) 13 QBD 779).
67. *Fitch v Jones* (1855) 5 E & B 238; 119 ER 470.
68. See also [770].

which is subject to the mortgage is void; and s 44(3) states that a mortgage which does not comply with s 44 is unenforceable. Similarly, under s 21(2) a term is void if it imposes a monetary obligation prohibited by s 21(1). Again, s 169 renders void a provision by which a person seeks to avoid or modify the effect of the Code.[69]

[1618] Voidness as against a third party only. Section 122(1) of the *Bankruptcy Act* 1966 (Cth) illustrates voidness against a third party. It declares 'void as against the trustee in the debtor's bankruptcy', that is, the person appointed trustee of the bankrupt's estate, a 'transfer of property by a person who is insolvent in favour of a creditor' where the transfer 'had the effect of giving the creditor a preference, priority or advantage over other creditors' where the transfer occurs within a period specified in a table to the section.

Although the section limits[70] the preferential transactions to conveyances or transfers of property, this includes a payment of money. A preferential transaction will often be a contract. Indeed, property is transferred, principally, by contracts. Subject to the exceptions allowed in s 122(2), the trustee of the bankrupt's property is entitled to recover that which passed under the transaction to the preferred creditor. The property becomes available to creditors on avoidance of the transaction.[71]

Contracts which Infringe Public Policy

General

[1619] The concept of public policy. The refusal to enforce such contracts has been described[72] as a 'striking illustration of the subordination of private right to public interest'. A contract may be void and/or illegal if it infringes public policy.[73] Some contracts, such as contracts in restraint of trade,[74] are not illegal even though they may be rendered void by a rule of public policy. Other contracts, such as contracts prejudicial to the administration of justice,[75] are often said to be not only void but also illegal. It is frequently unclear whether the effect of public policy is voidness alone or illegality as well because the degree of impropriety may be difficult to gauge.[76] However, a contract can only be described as 'illegal' if the degree of impropriety is great, generally shown by the commission of a criminal offence.

---

69. See also *Caltex Oil (Australia) Pty Ltd v Best* (1990) 170 CLR 516; 97 ALR 217 (effect of *Petroleum Retail Marketing Franchise Act* 1980 (Cth), s 7).
70. See also *Bankruptcy Act* 1966 (Cth), ss 120 (undervalued transactions), 121 (transfers to defeat creditors).
71. See *Cannane v J Cannane Pty Ltd (In Liq)* (1998) 192 CLR 557 at 566, 574; 153 ALR 163 at 168, 174.
72. *A v Hayden* (1984) 156 CLR 532 at 559; 56 ALR 82.
73. See further on the appropriate description [1702].
74. See generally [1634]–[1653].
75. See generally [1628]–[1630].
76. See [1702].

In *Wilkinson v Osborne*[77] Isaacs J explained the public policy which a court is 'entitled to apply as a test of validity to a contract is in relation to *some definite and governing principle which the community as a whole has already adopted either formally by law or tacitly by its general course of corporate life*'. It is therefore appropriate for the court to take judicial notice of what standards of behaviour are accepted in the community.[78] The relevant public policy is, of course, the public policy of Australia (or perhaps more accurately that of the jurisdiction in which the dispute is adjudicated), and it should not be assumed that all the decisions reached by (for example) the English courts are applicable in Australia.

It is arguable that the implied prohibition of contracts by statute, considered earlier,[79] is based on public policy. In *Vita Food Products Inc v Unus Shipping Co Ltd*[80] Lord Wright (for the Privy Council) said[81] that the 'rule by which contracts not expressly forbidden by statute or declared to be void are in proper cases nullified for disobedience to a statute is a rule of public policy only'. On the other hand, as a matter of analysis it is helpful to keep the cases in which a contract is impliedly prohibited by statute distinct from the common law on public policy and, in any event, even though a contract is not prohibited by statute it may still be contrary to public policy.[82]

[1620] **The changing face of public policy.** It is sometimes said[83] that the courts have no power to create new heads of public policy. Even accepting such statements as correct, it is important to see that, because public policy is not fixed and stable,[84] whether a contract is contrary to public policy depends on the circumstances existing at the time when the contract is entered into. Therefore, it is not to be resolved purely by reference to, for example, a case decided 100 years previously.[85]

The heads of public policy considered in this chapter represent most of the main heads, but it is not intended to be an exhaustive description of the possible situations in which a contract may be affected by public policy.

Contracts to Commit a Legal Wrong

[1621] **Requirement of intent.** A contract which involves the commission of a legal wrong will be illegal if entered into with the intent of committing the wrong.[86] This rule of public policy extends to the

77. (1915) 21 CLR 89 at 97 (italics supplied). See also *A v Hayden* (1984) 156 CLR 532 at 571.
78. The court may have regard to legislation; see *Seidler v Schallhofer* [1982] 2 NSWLR 80 (see [1632]); *Gollan v Nugent* (1988) 166 CLR 18 at 49; 82 ALR 193; *Green v Green* (1989) 17 NSWLR 343 at 358.
79. See [1607]–[1615].
80. [1939] AC 277.
81. [1939] AC 277 at 293.
82. See further [1622].
83. See, eg *Wilkinson v Osborne* (1915) 21 CLR 89 at 96–7. But cf *Fender v St John-Mildmay* [1938] AC 1 at 11.
84. See *Fitzgerald v F J Leonhardt Pty Ltd* (1997) 189 CLR 215 at 248–9.
85. See, eg *Shaw v Groom* [1970] 2 QB 504 at 523; *Seidler v Schallhofer* [1982] 2 NSWLR 80.
86. See [1604].

commission of a common law or statutory crime or a civil wrong. For example, a contract to defraud a third party is contrary to policy. If the necessary intent is present it matters not that the contract, as formed, was capable of being performed in a legal manner. But if there is no guilty intent, the fact that the contract is not totally effective, for example, because of noncompliance with statute, does not render it illegal on the ground of public policy. Thus, in *Hutchinson v Scott*[87] an agreement was reached for the purpose of searching for gold and other minerals on certain land. This agreement purported to be a lease made under s 33 of the *Mining on Private Lands Act* 1894 (NSW), which dealt with the right to mine on private property. However, the *Crown Lands Act* 1884 (NSW) applied to the land and prohibited the conferment of any right to remove material from the land in question. It was contended that the agreement was totally void as it was executed for an illegal purpose, namely, to mine for gold on private land. However, even on the assumption that there was an unlawful purpose, the High Court held that the agreement was not unlawful because there was no evidence of an intention to break the law. In fact, the parties had expressly stated that the lease was made under the provisions of the *Mining on Private Lands Act* 1894, 'so that the parties far from evincing an intention to break the law ... clearly indicated their intention to abide by the law'.[88]

In deciding whether there is an intention to break the law, the knowledge of the parties is an important element where the unlawful act occurs in the performance of the contract. If the parties know the law and perform the contract in an illegal way it is far easier to infer that their intention was to break the law. On the other hand, if they had no such knowledge it may be possible to say that the contract is not illegal even though the contract is performed in the way intended and notwithstanding that the law is infringed by performance of the contract.[89] However, where the contract is such that it cannot be performed without a violation of the law, it would seem that the contract is illegal whether the parties knew the law or not.[90] Such a contract is usually described as being *ex facie illegal*.

[1622] Intention of one party to break the law. If one party only has the intention of committing a legal wrong, or knows that the contract will be performed in an illegal way, the contract will be unenforceable by that party and, to that extent at least, also illegal by reason of public policy. For example, in *Alexander v Rayson*[91] the plaintiff agreed to let a flat to the defendant at a rent of £1200 per year. Two documents were prepared, and

87. (1905) 3 CLR 359.
88. (1905) 3 CLR 359 at 369. See also *Holidaywise Koala Pty Ltd v Queenslodge Pty Ltd* [1977] VR 164 at 176–7.
89. See Treitel, *The Law of Contract*, 10th ed, 1999, pp 396–8. Cf *Fire and All Risks Insurance Co Ltd v Powell* [1966] VR 513 at 520, 525, 527–8.
90. See *Waugh v Morris* (1873) LR 8 QB 202 at 208; *J M Allan (Merchandising) Ltd v Cloke* [1963] 2 QB 340; *Holidaywise Koala Pty Ltd v Queenslodge Pty Ltd* [1977] VR 164 at 174–5.
91. [1936] 1 KB 169. See also *McCarthy Bros (Milk Vendors) Pty Ltd v Dairy Farmers' Co-operative Milk Co Ltd* (1945) 45 SR (NSW) 266; *T P Rich Investments Pty Ltd v Calderon* [1964] NSWR 709. Contrast *Gray v Pastorelli* [1987] WAR 174; *Yaroomba Beach Development Co Pty Ltd v Coeur de Lion Investments Pty Ltd* (1989) 18 NSWLR 398.

signed. The first was a lease, providing also for the provision of certain services, showing a rent of £450; and the second a service agreement requiring the defendant to pay £750. To an action for £300 due under the two documents the defendant pleaded that as the documents had been prepared to effect a legal wrong they were illegal. It was established that the documents had been prepared in order to defraud the Westminster City Council by obtaining a lower valuation of the property for rating purposes. The plaintiff had disclosed only the lease and succeeded, initially at least, in having the valuation of the flat reduced by reference to the defendant's agreement to pay £450. The court held that because the plaintiff had prepared the documents in order to commit a legal wrong he could not enforce the lease.[92]

Intention will, it seems, be irrelevant in cases where the contract is on its face illegal. This issue may arise, for example, where a statutory offence is committed but it is not immediately clear whether the contract is prohibited by statute. Thus, in *Archbolds (Freightage) Ltd v S Spanglett Ltd*[93] the carriage contract was neither expressly nor impliedly prohibited by the statute, but as an offence had been committed it was also asked whether the contract was ex facie illegal on the ground of public policy. Pearce LJ framed[94] the issue as follows: 'Must any reasonable person on hearing the terms of the contract ([with] presumed knowledge of the law) realise that it was illegal?' Because there was nothing illegal in the terms of the contract, further knowledge, namely, knowledge that the vehicle was not properly licensed, was necessary. Because the plaintiffs were ignorant of that fact, the contract was not illegal.

[1623] **Contract to commit a crime or tort.** It is assumed in cases such as *Alexander v Rayson*[95] that, as a matter of general principle, a contract to commit a crime or tort is illegal. The court will concentrate on the central purpose of the contract. It will, as Dixon and Evatt JJ said in *Neal v Ayers*,[96] be reluctant to hold the contract illegal if the legal wrong is 'extrinsic to the dealing which forms the foundation of the contract and of the inducing causes'. The case illustrates just such a situation. The plaintiff brought an action for deceit arising out of the plaintiff's purchase of the lease, licence, goodwill, stock-in-trade and furniture of a hotel. During the course of negotiations the defendant represented that about £15 to £20 of the weekly takings of the hotel came from after-hours trading in contravention of the *Liquor Act* 1912 (NSW). In fact, of the weekly takings of £100, about £40 was taken during illegal trading. The defendant argued that the purpose or object of the contract of purchase was to break the law and illegal on that ground. However, the High Court held that the real purpose or object was the purchase of a hotel in the ordinary course of business. It could not be said that the plaintiff purchased the hotel in order to violate the law even though the plaintiff admitted that she did intend, for a time, to carry on

92. But cf *Iannotti v Corsaro* (1984) 36 SASR 127 (see Neil Francey, (1986) 60 *ALJ* 637).
93. [1961] 1 QB 374 (see [1613]).
94. [1961] 1 QB 374 at 387. See also *Waugh v Morris* (1873) LR 8 QB 202.
95. [1936] 1 KB 169 (see [1622]). See also *Scott v Brown Doering McNab & Co* [1892] 2 QB 724.
96. (1940) 63 CLR 524 at 532.

unlawful trading. The decision should not be seen as qualifying the law stated in *Alexander v Rayson* in any general way.[97] For example, the position might have been different had the plaintiff entered into the contract in order to break the law and to take advantage of the illegal trading.

Where the contract is entered into with the object of committing a minor statutory offence there may be room for inquiry whether the contract is necessarily contrary to public policy, particularly where it is common for the law not to be observed.[98] For example, if A, who is in a hurry to get to the airport, contracts with B to be driven there at a speed five kilometres per hour above the legal speed limit, can A refuse to pay for the journey because the contract is illegal? Public policy may not require the conclusion of illegality to be drawn, assuming that B has not contracted to drive in an unsafe manner. In such a case it must be asked whether the act 'is of such an anti-social character that the interests of the public require that the courts should for their protection decline to enforce the contract'.[99]

Contracts Injurious to Public Life or Foreign Relations

[1624] **Promotion of corruption in public life.** In *Wilkinson v Osborne*[100] the plaintiffs sued to recover the commission alleged to be due in connection with the sale of a tract of land to the New South Wales Government. The action failed as the plaintiffs, who were land agents in partnership, were also members of the Legislative Assembly and had agreed with the owner's agent to use their positions to influence the government to purchase the land. The contract was contrary to public policy because of the clear conflict of interest and duty. The plaintiffs, as members of the Legislative Assembly, owed a duty to the public and ought to have maintained their impartiality. The effect of their contract with the defendant was to provide an incentive to see that the government reached (and the Legislative Assembly supported) a decision which might not have been in the public interest.

In cases of this kind the court does not inquire into the extent of conflict, or whether the contract has in fact resulted in the placement of private interest in front of the public duty. It is therefore enough that the conflict of interest and duty may arise. An extreme example is *Wood v Little*[101] where land belonging to the defendant was sold to the Closer Settlement Board of Victoria and the plaintiff, a land agent, sought to recover commission which the defendant had agreed to pay him on the sale. At the time when the defendant placed the property in the plaintiff's hands for sale he (the plaintiff) was a shire councillor and, by virtue of s 35 of the *Discharged Soldiers Settlement Acts* 1917 and 1919 (Vic), became a member of an advisory committee to the Board on matters relating to the selection and

---

97. See *McCarthy Bros (Milk Vendors) Pty Ltd v Dairy Farmers' Co-operative Milk Co Ltd* (1945) 45 SR (NSW) 266 at 269.
98. Cf *St John Shipping Corp v Joseph Rank Ltd* [1957] 1 QB 267 at 292.
99. *Fire and All Risks Insurance Co Ltd v Powell* [1966] VR 513 at 523.
100. (1915) 21 CLR 89.
101. (1921) 29 CLR 564. Cf *Horne v Barber* (1920) 27 CLR 494 on the authority of which *Wood v Little* was decided, but which was doubted by Higgins J and perhaps also by Starke J.

purchase of land. The plaintiff might, therefore, have misused his position by ensuring that the Board purchased the land, and his public duty was in conflict with his private interest. The contract was, on that basis, illegal irrespective of whether there was in fact any corrupt or sinister intent.

Further examples can be found in cases dealing with the exercise of electoral franchise and election to public offices. For example, in *Taylor v Taylor*[102] the plaintiff sued on a promise that in consideration that the plaintiff would retire from being a candidate at an election for a seat to the Parliament of New South Wales, in favour of another candidate, and would support that other candidate, the defendant promised to pay the expenses which the plaintiff had incurred in his candidature. The court held that the contract was contrary to public policy, even though the payment was to be made by a person who was not himself a candidate for election, because it was opposed to the public good by having a tendency to be injurious to the public.

[1625] **Injuries to foreign relations.** A contract which has as its object the assistance of persons acting (or intending to act) against the government of a state in friendly relations with Australia is contrary to public policy.[103] Similarly, a contract which involves trading with the enemy in time of war infringes public policy and is illegal on that basis.[104]

Contracts Purporting to Oust the Jurisdiction of the Courts

[1626] **Ouster of common law jurisdiction.** Although a contract which purports to oust the jurisdiction of the courts is probably not illegal, it is contrary to public policy and therefore void or unenforceable.[105] However, an agreement which is binding in honour only, and which therefore does not contemplate legal relations, does not come within the rule.[106]

Subject to statute,[107] it is not contrary to public policy for the parties to a contract to agree to submit disputes under the contract to arbitration. The High Court said in *Dobbs v National Bank of Australasia Ltd*[108] that a distinction must be drawn between a restriction on the right to invoke the jurisdiction of the courts and contractual provisions which give efficacy to the award of an arbitrator when made. The effect of such an ordinary submission to arbitration is merely to make the action of a party in going to court rather than arbitration a breach of contract.[109] If the contract

---

102. (1890) 11 NSWR 323.
103. See, eg *Foster v Driscoll* [1929] 1 KB 470. And see *Defence Act* 1903 (Cth), s 118. For discussion from the broader perspective of contracts illegal in a foreign country see, eg *Lemenda Trading Co Ltd v African Middle East Petroleum Co Ltd* [1988] 1 QB 448; *Euro-Diam Ltd v Bathurst* [1990] 1 QB 1.
104. See, eg *Ertel Bieber & Co v Rio Tinto Co Ltd* [1918] AC 260 (see [2023]).
105. See *Halsbury's Laws of England*, 4th ed, 1974, Vol 9, para 405. But a contract which ousts the jurisdiction of a foreign court may be valid: *Addison v Brown* [1954] 2 All ER 213.
106. See *Rose & Frank Co v J R Crompton & Bros Ltd* [1925] AC 445; *Dobbs v National Bank of Australasia Ltd* (1935) 53 CLR 643 at 652 and generally Chapter 4.
107. See, eg *Insurance Contracts Act* 1984 (Cth), s 43.
108. (1935) 53 CLR 643 at 652, 656.

contains an arbitration clause which requires any action to be brought on the arbitrator's award, prior arbitration is made a condition precedent to any action on the contract. Nevertheless, in *Scott v Avery*[110] the House of Lords decided that an arbitration clause of this type does not infringe public policy even if it enables the arbitrator to determine whether any liability has been incurred under the contract. This suggests a general principle that a provision which makes the ability to invoke a court's jurisdiction dependent on the occurrence of an event (such as default), will not usually be contrary to public policy.[111]

Unincorporated associations may be governed by rules which make the decision of an elected committee binding on the members. The jurisdiction of the committee is conferred by the rules which themselves express the contract between the members of the association. If the rules make the decision of the committee 'final and conclusive' this may be effective to make the committee the final arbiter of factual issues which arise for decision. But the rules cannot make the decision final and conclusive on matters of law,[112] because that would be an ouster of the courts' jurisdiction. Therefore, any rules which purport to be conclusive on matters of law, such as construction of the contract between the members of the association, will be void.[113] Similarly, the certificate of a third person may be conclusive on factual matters, and an agreement to this effect does not purport to oust the jurisdiction of the courts. Thus, in *Dobbs*' case, the certificate of a bank officer was conclusive as to the customer's indebtedness to the bank pursuant to the parties' agreement to that effect.[114]

The inability of the parties to a contract to oust the jurisdiction of the courts does not preclude the compromise of a contractual dispute.[115] Assuming that consideration for the compromise can be found,[116] it will be binding on the parties and may therefore prevent the previous contractual dispute being the subject of a decision by the courts.

---

109. A liability in damages may therefore result; see *Doleman & Sons v Ossett Corp* [1912] 3 KB 257 at 267–8, 270–1; *Mantovani v Carapelli SpA* [1980] 1 Lloyd's Rep 375. In addition, the court may, in the exercise of a statutory discretion, order a stay of the proceedings. See **ACT:** *Commercial Arbitration Act* 1986, ss 53, 55; **NSW:** *Commercial Arbitration Act* 1984, ss 53, 55; **NT:** *Commercial Arbitration Act* 1985, ss 53, 55; **Qld:** *Commercial Arbitration Act* 1990, ss 53, 55; **SA:** *Commercial Arbitration Act* 1986, ss 53, 55; **Tas:** *Commercial Arbitration Act* 1986, ss 53, 55; **Vic:** *Commercial Arbitration Act* 1984, ss 53, 55; **WA:** *Commercial Arbitration Act* 1985, ss 53, 55.
110. (1856) 5 HLC 811; 10 ER 1121. For the history see D Rhidian Thomas, '*Scott v Avery* Agreements' [1991] *LMCLQ* 508. On international arbitration see *Bulk Chartering & Consultants Australia Pty Ltd v T & T Metal Trading Pty Ltd (The Krasnogrosk)* (1993) 31 NSWLR 18 at 33ff.
111. See *Hong Kong Bank of Australia Ltd v Larobi Pty Ltd* (1991) 23 NSWLR 593.
112. See, eg *Lee v Showmen's Guild of Great Britain* [1952] 2 QB 329 at 343.
113. See, eg *Baker v Jones* [1954] 2 All ER 553.
114. Other, more common, examples include certificates of accountants, architects and engineers, assessing matters such as work done under building contracts and the valuation of assets. See, eg *South Australian Commissioner for Railways v Egan* (1973) 47 ALJR 140; *Jones v Sherwood Computer Services Plc* [1992] 1 WLR 277.
115. See, eg *Lieberman v Morris* (1944) 69 CLR 69 at 80.
116. See generally [350]–[355].

[1627] **Ouster of statutory jurisdiction.** What is the position where a statute confers rights on an individual but does not expressly preclude that person from bargaining away his or her rights? In *Re Morris*[117] Jordan CJ stated the issue as being whether it is contrary to public policy for a person to 'surrender' by contract those rights which are conferred or vested in persons of one category against persons of another when the person is a member of the first category. To a large extent the resolution of this issue will depend on the nature and subject matter of the statute. In *Re Morris*[118] the *Testator's Family Maintenance and Guardianship of Infants Act* 1916 (NSW) was in issue, and a majority of the court decided that the terms of the Act, conferring power to make orders in favour of particular categories of persons, and providing for their maintenance out of the estate of a testator (and thereby overriding the testator's will), were for the *public* benefit by preventing persons, such as the spouse or child of the testator, being a charge on the public. Therefore, it was contrary to public policy for the Act to be excluded by contract. This indicates that for the parties to a contract to exclude a statutory jurisdiction the rights conferred must be of a private, rather than public, kind.

Many of the cases decided in the present context have concerned contracts dealing with the maintenance payable pursuant to statute to a wife (or husband or child), following divorce. In *Brooks v Burns Philp Trustee Co Ltd*[119] a deed was made between husband and wife shortly before the hearing of a petition by the wife for dissolution of the marriage. Clause 1 provided for the payment to the wife of weekly sums and for the assignment to her of certain insurance policies and other property; and cl 2 contained a promise by the wife to accept the terms of the deed 'in full settlement of all claims against the husband for alimony and maintenance of any description'. Because cl 2 was intended to operate immediately, and to bind the wife not to ask the court for more than was provided for by the deed, it was held by a majority of the High Court to be contrary to public policy as extinguishing her statutory rights to maintenance and ousting the jurisdiction of the court to award a greater sum than that provided for.[120]

One feature of *Brooks v Burns Philp Trustee Co Ltd*, which illustrates a controversy which can be found more particularly in the subsequent cases, is the failure of the court to refer in detail to the legislation governing alimony and maintenance rights. Clearly, the court proceeded on the basis that because there was no express statement in the legislation that the wife could not contract out of her statutory rights, the decision depended merely on the application of public policy as derived from the general nature of the Act. Although they placed more emphasis on the public nature of the rights being bargained away, a similar approach was adopted by Starke J in *Lieberman v Morris*[121] and by Windeyer J in *Felton v Mulligan*.[122] On the other hand, Latham CJ in *Lieberman* felt it necessary to

117. (1943) 43 SR (NSW) 352 at 356.
118. Approved in *Lieberman v Morris* (1944) 69 CLR 69.
119. (1969) 121 CLR 432.
120. See further [1730]. See also *O'Loughlin v O'Loughlin* [1958] VR 649.
121. See (1944) 69 CLR 69 at 86–7. Cf *Commonwealth of Australia v Verwayen* (1990) 170 CLR 394 at 404–5, 456; 95 ALR 321.
122. (1971) 124 CLR 367, especially at 390.

consider[123] not only the 'general character of the Act' but also its 'particular provisions'; and in *Felton v Mulligan* Barwick CJ said[124] that the ability to agree not to enforce a statutory right depends on a 'consideration of the statute itself'. However, there is no reason why the adoption of one approach in preference to the other should produce a different result, and it seems fair to say that where the right in issue is of a public rather than a private kind, contracting out will not be permitted unless the terms of the statute clearly indicate that that was the intention of the legislature.

Contracts Prejudicial to the Administration of Justice

[1628] Contracts to stifle a prosecution. At least where the prosecution is of a public rather than private nature, it is contrary to public policy for a contract to be made to stifle or withdraw a prosecution. For example, in *Callaghan v O'Sullivan*[125] the plaintiff sought to recover money which he had paid to the defendants, four police constables, in return for their promise not to prosecute the plaintiff and his daughter for the possession of uncustomed stolen goods. They did not prosecute him, but once it became clear that an inquiry was to be held based on some unrevealed source of information, he sued to recover the money paid. Irvine CJ held that the consideration for the payment of the money was illegal as it had been paid to stifle a prosecution. The contract was therefore contrary to public policy and the money could not be recovered.

One basis for this rule of public policy is the interest of the public in the prosecution of criminals. Where the act in question infringes a private right, as in the case of common assault, there is scope for a contract to compromise that private right.[126] For example, in *Kerridge v Simmonds*[127] a deed included an agreement by the plaintiff to withdraw from proceedings pending in the Laverton Police Court against the defendant in consideration of a promise to pay to the plaintiff £13 per month for an unspecified period. The summons had been issued in respect of the publication of oral defamatory matter about the plaintiff. Although the proceedings were for an indictable misdemeanour, the High Court held that the agreement in issue was not contrary to public policy. Griffith CJ said[128] that the injury complained of was a 'purely personal injury'; Barton J said[129] that by no possible construction of the proceedings could they be 'called matters in which the public had an interest'; and Higgins J said[130] that he could find no 'legal or ... moral duty to prosecute or to proceed with a prosecution'.

---

123. See (1944) 69 CLR 69 at 79.
124. See (1971) 124 CLR 367 at 377. Cf *In The Marriage of Burge* (1985) 10 Fam LR 514.
125. [1925] VLR 664. See also *Clegg v Wilson* (1932) 32 SR (NSW) 109; *Public Service Employees Credit Union Co-operative Ltd v Campion* (1984) 75 FLR 131; 56 ACTR 39.
126. Cf *P T Garuda Indonesia Ltd v Grellman* (1992) 107 ALR 199 at 216 (uncertainty in relation to embezzlement).
127. (1906) 4 CLR 253.
128. (1906) 4 CLR 253 at 260.
129. (1906) 4 CLR 253 at 262.
130. (1906) 4 CLR 253 at 264.

The line between public and private rights is not always easy to draw and the distinction is therefore not always clear.

[1629] Maintenance. 'Maintenance' is the 'giving of assistance or encouragement to one of the parties to litigation by a person who has neither an interest in the litigation nor any other motive recognised by the law as justifying his interference'.[131] At one time, maintenance was a civil wrong and also a crime.[132] Although it is by no means clear that this is the position today,[133] the public policy rule continues to apply.[134]

If justified, maintenance is not regarded as contrary to public policy. The main justification is the existence of an interest in the subject matter of the litigation as, for example, where an insurer, having a potential liability to the insured, provides an insured with funds to defend a claim by a third party.[135] But a potential liability to the other litigant is not an essential requirement.[136] Moreover, today the courts are more willing to countenance maintenance than their 19th century counterparts. As Lord Roskill said in *Trendtex Trading Corp v Credit Suisse*,[137] the courts now adopt 'an infinitely more liberal attitude towards the supporting of litigation by a third party'.

The policy against maintenance has been given as an explanation of the rule of law which precludes the assignment of a 'bare right of action'[138] in contract or tort. Such an assignment has traditionally been regarded as savouring of maintenance, or as likely to lead to maintenance.[139] But it is now clear that the assignment is valid if, on analysis of the whole transaction, the assignee has a genuine commercial or proprietary interest in the success of the proceedings.[140] It follows that suing for an assigned debt raises no question of maintenance.[141]

---

131. *Halsbury's Law of England*, 4th ed, 1974, Vol 9, para 400.
132. See *Neville v London 'Express' Newspaper Ltd* [1919] AC 368 at 386, 398; *Magic Menu Systems Pty Ltd v AFA Facilitation Pty Ltd* (1997) 142 ALR 198 at 205–6.
133. See *Clyne v New South Wales Bar Association* (1960) 104 CLR 186 at 203; *Brew v Whitlock* [1967] VR 449; *Roux v Australian Broadcasting Commission* [1992] 2 VR 577 at 605–6. For an illustration of statutory abolition see *Maintenance, Champerty and Barratry Abolition Act* 1993 (NSW), ss 3, 4.
134. Generally, where the offence and the tortious liability have been abolished by statute the public policy rule has been preserved. See, eg *Maintenance, Champerty and Barratry Abolition Act* 1993 (NSW), s 6.
135. See *Schultz v Ocean Accident & Guarantee Corp Ltd* (1923) 23 SR (NSW) 153; *Halliday v High Performance Personnel Pty Ltd* (1993) 113 ALR 637 at 640.
136. *Roux v Australian Broadcasting Commission* [1992] 2 VR 577 at 607. Thus, another justification is the poverty of the person maintained. See *Stevens v Keogh* (1946) 72 CLR 1 (libel action).
137. [1982] AC 679 at 702.
138. 'No single phrase', said Lloyd LJ in *Brownton Ltd v Edward Moore Inbucon Ltd* [1985] 3 All ER 499 at 506–7, 'has given rise to greater confusion'.
139. See *Glegg v Bromley* [1912] 3 KB 474 at 489–90; *Re Kenneth Wright Distributors Pty Ltd; W J Vine Pty Ltd v Hall* [1973] VR 161 at 165, 166. See Y L Tan, 'Champertous Contracts and Assignments' (1990) 106 *LQR* 656.
140. See, eg *Beard v Baulkham Hills Shire Council* (1986) 7 NSWLR 273 at 281. It follows that suing for an assigned debt raises no question of maintenance. The fact that a 'profit' is made on the assignment does not mean that it is invalid: *Brownton Ltd v Edward Moore Inbucon Ltd* [1985] 3 All ER 499. In *Giles v Thompson* [1994] 1 AC 142, the view is expressed that the rule ought now to be regarded as an independent one.

[1630] Champerty. 'Champerty' is a particular form of maintenance, 'namely maintenance of an action in consideration of a promise to give the maintainer a share in the proceeds or subject matter of the action'.[142] Thus, if A agrees to lend $5000 to B to finance litigation by B against C, in consideration of a promise by B to pay A a sum equal to 50 per cent of the damages recovered, the contract between A and B infringes public policy and is unenforceable. The rule extends to proceedings to establish a right to recover money on the liquidation of a company, and generally to all contentious proceedings where property which is in dispute becomes the subject of a contract to share in the proceeds of the proceedings. However, in *Giles v Thompson*[143] the House of Lords suggested that an agreement for maintenance should be treated as infringing public policy on the basis that it is champertous only if there is a wanton and officious intermeddling with the disputes of others.[144]

In *Re Trepca Mines Ltd (No 2)*[145] a solicitor brought an action to recover fees and disbursements from his client. The client had been unsuccessful in a claim to recover a debt in the liquidation of a company, but successfully appealed with the help of finance from a third person in return for a promise to pay the third person 25 per cent of any sums recovered. The agreement between the client and the third party was clearly champertous and the issue was whether the solicitor was implicated in the agreement. The court said that to disentitle the solicitor it had to be established that he had actively participated in the champertous agreement. On the facts he was found to have been aware of the agreement. Moreover, the solicitor agreed to receive the proceeds of the action in order to distribute them in accordance with the champertous agreement. In these circumstances the contract of retainer, between the solicitor and his client, was contrary to public policy because it was an agreement to abet the doing of a series of illegal acts.

In *Clyne v New South Wales Bar Association*[146] the High Court explained[147] that a solicitor:

> may with perfect propriety act for a client who has no means, and expend his money in payment of counsel's fees and outgoings, although he has no prospect of being paid either fees or outgoings except by virtue of a judgment or order against the other party to the proceedings.

The court said that this proposition is subject to two requirements: the solicitor must believe that the client has a reasonable cause of action; and the solicitor must not bargain with the client for an interest in the subject

---

141. See *Camdex International Ltd v Bank of Zambia* [1998] QB 22. In *Giles v Thompson* [1994] 1 AC 142, the view is expressed that the rule ought now to be regarded as an independent one.
142. *Halsbury's Laws of England*, 4th ed, 1974, Vol 9, para 400 (approved *Trendtex Trading Corp v Credit Suisse* [1982] AC 679 at 694). See also *Giles v Thompson* [1994] 1 AC 142; Meagher, Gummow and Lehane, *Equity: Doctrines and Remedies*, 3rd ed, 1992, para 694.
143. [1994] 1 AC 142.
144. But cf NSW Law Reform Commission, *Barratry, Maintenance and Champerty*, Discussion Paper No 36, 1994.
145. [1962] Ch 511. But see *In the Marriage of Sheehan* (1991) 104 FLR 57 at 65–6.
146. (1960) 104 CLR 186.
147. (1960) 104 CLR 186 at 203.

matter of the litigation, or for a remuneration in proportion to the amount which may be recovered by the client. However, the common law rule must be considered in conjunction with statutory provisions regulating professional conduct and contractual arrangements for the payment of fees.[148]

Immoral Contracts and Contracts Prejudicial to the Status of Marriage

[1631] Sexual immorality. The classic illustration of the proposition that a contract is void and illegal if sexually immoral is *Pearce v Brooks*.[149] The plaintiffs supplied the defendant with a new miniature brougham[150] pursuant to a contract of hire. The defendant returned the vehicle and failed to pay a forfeit pursuant to the contract. The defence to the action was illegality, namely, that to the knowledge of the plaintiffs the defendant was a common prostitute, and the brougham was to be used to assist her in carrying out her immoral vocation. The jury found that the carriage was used by the defendant as part of her display to attract men. Moreover, although there was no direct evidence that the plaintiffs knew that the brougham was to be used by the defendant to prosecute her trade, and no evidence that they expected payment to be made out of her earnings, the jury found that the plaintiffs knew of the defendant's purpose. The court held the contract to be illegal, on the ground of sexual immorality, and said that it was of no moment whether the plaintiffs expected to be paid out of the proceeds of the defendant's trade. The jury's finding on the plaintiffs' knowledge could be sustained. Bramwell B said[151] in argument that the: 'inference that a prostitute ... required an ornamental brougham for the purposes of her calling, was as natural a one as that a medical man would want a brougham for the purpose of visiting his patients'.

It would seem that the rule of public policy against immoral contracts does not extend beyond sexual immorality.[152] Most of the modern cases involve an alleged illicit cohabitation.

[1632] Illicit cohabitation. The courts have, traditionally at least, treated as contrary to public policy a contract providing for or relating to illicit cohabitation. Although it may be true to say that a contract to pay money in consideration of an immoral association is still contrary to public policy,[153] the recent cases indicate that a contract is not to be regarded as contrary to public policy merely because the parties to the contract are living together in a de facto relationship.

---

148. See *Mohamed v Alaga & Co (a firm)* [2000] 1 WLR 1815; *Awwad v Geraghty (a firm)* [2000] 3 WLR 1041 (see Neil Andrews, [2000] *CLJ* 265; Adrian Walters, (2000) 116 *LQR* 371; Nelson Enonchong, (2000) 116 *LQR* 377). Cf *Thai Trading Co (a firm) v Taylor* [1998] QB 781.
149. (1866) LR 1 Ex 213.
150. A one horse closed carriage with two or four wheels, for two or four persons (*OED*).
151. See (1866) LR 1 Ex 213 at 215.
152. Cf *Barac v Farnell* (1994) 125 ALR 241.
153. See, eg *Fender v St John-Mildmay* [1938] AC 1 at 42.

In *Andrews v Parker*[154] the plaintiff and defendant lived together as man and wife in a house owned by the plaintiff. When they met the plaintiff was a widower aged 55 and the defendant a married woman aged about 41. Subsequently, a de facto relationship commenced. A few months later the plaintiff agreed to transfer title in his house to the defendant. This agreement was subject to certain terms including a requirement that the defendant reconvey the title to the house if she returned to her husband. After another four months the plaintiff signed a memorandum of transfer. Although this expressed as consideration the payment of $6000, the plaintiff did not in fact receive any such sum. A few months later the defendant was reunited with her husband and asked the plaintiff to leave the house. The defendant and her husband expressed a willingness to pay $4000 for the house. The plaintiff left the house, and opened a bank account for payment of the money, but the defendant and her husband paid only an initial sum of $10.

Stable J held that the original agreement to transfer the house was not contrary to public policy; it did not bring about a state of extramarital cohabitation because one already existed. That agreement provided for the retransfer of the title to the house in certain events and, as one of those events had occurred, the plaintiff was entitled to enforce the contract.[155] In addition, Stable J said that the court was not to judge the actions of the parties in the light of 19th century cases. Rather, the court was bound to apply the public policy of the day and to consider contemporary moral standards. Stable J said that, if there was an immoral consideration, judged by today's standards the immorality was not such as to deprive the plaintiff of his right to enforce the contract.

If the parties to a de facto relationship contemplate the termination of that relationship, by marriage or formal separation, an agreement between them may be enforced. Thus, in *Seidler v Schallhofer*[156] the plaintiff and defendant, although unmarried, commenced living together in 1974. Early in 1978 it was agreed that they would buy a house and live in it in order to enable them to decide whether marriage should take place. They executed a detailed agreement in March 1978 and the purchase of the house which they had agreed to buy was completed in May. Title to the property was then registered in their names as joint tenants. As part of the purchase the plaintiff had mortgaged her interest to the defendant to secure the repayment of $20,000. Of the purchase price of $49,500, all was furnished by the defendant except $4640, which the plaintiff had contributed. The $20,000 was, in effect, lent by the defendant in order to ensure that the respective contributions were equal. In January 1979 the plaintiff left the house. The issue was whether the 1978 agreement was void as being contrary to public policy.

On the assumption that the agreement provided for the continuance of an existing and illicit cohabitation, the court held that the agreement did not infringe public policy. Hope JA relied on the fact that the agreement

---

154. [1973] Qd R 93.
155. See further [1712].
156. [1982] 2 NSWLR 80. See Frank Bates, 'Private Law and Public Policy: An Extrapolation from *Seidler v Schallhofer*' (1983) 57 *ALJ* 460.

was reached long after the illicit cohabitation had commenced, and the fact that the agreement contemplated the termination of that cohabitation (by marriage or separation) after six months. In addition, Hope JA pointed out[157] that the 'agreement did not involve meretricious sexual services, but a sexual relationship as part only of a wider relationship'. Having regard to the recognition and acceptance by the community and the legislature of de facto relationships, it would have been wrong to hold the present agreement to be contrary to public policy. Reynolds JA agreed. Hutley JA, while reasoning along slightly different, and at times broader lines, reached the same conclusion.

In several jurisdictions the rule of public policy has been abrogated.[158] Thus, in New South Wales it is now provided that, notwithstanding any rule of public policy to the contrary, two persons who are not married to each other may enter into a domestic relationship agreement or termination agreement.[159] Such an agreement is enforceable in accordance with the law of contract.[160]

[1633] Contracts prejudicial to the status of marriage. A contract infringes public policy if it is prejudicial to the status of marriage. The marital relationship is the concern of the public because of the legal status attached to it, the obligation of loyalty between the spouses, the public interest in the status of children and the fact that the rules for its dissolution have been expressed by statutory enactments. This head of public policy is related to the prohibition on immoral contracts but distinguishable from it on the ground that a contract may be prejudicial to the status of marriage even though it does not involve the encouragement of sexual immorality.[161]

An agreement for the future separation of husband and wife is contrary to the public policy of the common law.[162] However, if the parties have already separated, or have determined to separate at once, the agreement is valid[163] as it deals with the consequences of separation and does not itself provide for separation. As with other heads of public policy, the recent cases adopt a more lenient attitude reflecting the changing nature of public policy. Moreover, the impact of legislation such as the *Marriage Act* 1961 (Cth) and the *Family Law Act* 1975 (Cth) must be borne in mind, particularly when the old cases are being considered.

---

157. [1982] 2 NSWLR 80 at 88–9.
158. **ACT:** *Domestic Relationships Act* 1994, Pt IV; **NSW:** *Property (Relationships) Act* 1984, Part 4; **NT:** *De Facto Relationships Act* 1991, s 44; **SA:** *De Facto Relationships Act* 1996, Pt 2.
159. See *Property (Relationships) Act* 1984 (NSW), s 45(1). The Act defines 'domestic relationship' to include a de facto relationship.
160. See *Property (Relationships) Act* 1984 (NSW), s 46. This is subject to the provisions of Part 4.
161. See, eg *Hermann v Charlesworth* [1905] 2 KB 123; *Minister for Education v Oxwell* [1966] WAR 39 at 42.
162. See *Halsbury's Laws of England*, 4th ed, 1974, Vol 9, para 413.
163. See, eg *Fender v St John-Mildmay* [1938] AC 1 at 24, 44; *Money v Money (No 2)* [1966] 1 NSWR 348. If necessary, a short period of time between the agreement and separation will be ignored: *Re Field and the Conveyancing Act* [1968] 1 NSWR 210.

A contract by a married person to marry was formerly contrary to public policy if the person to whom the promise was made knew the first person to be married even if the parties merely contemplated that marriage would take place after dissolution of the existing marriage by death or divorce decree.[164] However, in *Fender v St John-Mildmay*[165] a majority of the House of Lords held that a promise by the defendant, a married person, to marry the plaintiff was valid as it had been made after a decree nisi for the dissolution of the defendant's marriage had been pronounced. For all practical purposes the marriage had come to an end, and since the promise was to take effect after the divorce decree had become absolute, that is, made final, it was not contrary to the status of marriage for the promise to be enforced. The decision was applied by the High Court in *Psaltis v Schultz*[166] where the promise was again made after the decree nisi. The promise was enforceable for that reason, even though it was not expressly stated that the marriage would be postponed until the decree became absolute. The abolition of actions for breach of a promise to marry[167] makes the actual decisions in these cases largely of historical interest. The lasting value of the cases lies in the way they illustrate the changing face of public policy.

Contracts in Restraint of Trade

General principles

[1634] **Definition.** In *Petrofina (Gt Britain) Ltd v Martin*,[168] Diplock LJ defined a contract in restraint of trade as 'one in which a party (the covenantor) agrees with any other party (the covenantee) to restrict his liberty in the future to carry on trade with other persons not parties to the contract in such manner as he chooses'. Although this description received a measure of support in *Esso Petroleum Co Ltd v Harper's Garage (Stourport) Ltd*,[169] Lord Wilberforce pointed out[170] that often in the cases the words 'restraint of trade' are used 'indifferently to denote, on the one hand in a broad popular sense, any contract which limits the free exercise of trade or business, and, on the other hand, as a term of art covering those contracts which are to be regarded as offending a rule of public policy'. As we shall see,[171] Diplock LJ's definition may be too broad if understood as a description of the latter.

The following examples may be given in order to indicate, in a general way, the types of contracts involved:

- A partnership deed between the members of a medical practice might include an agreement that any partner leaving the practice is not to practise within a five kilometre radius of the existing surgery for a period of three years.

---

164. See, eg *Psaltis v Schultz* (1948) 76 CLR 547 at 558.
165. [1938] AC 1.
166. (1948) 76 CLR 547.
167. *Marriage Act* 1961 (Cth), s 111A.
168. [1966] 1 Ch 146 at 180.
169. [1968] AC 269 at 307, 317.
170. [1968] AC 269 at 331.
171. See [1637], [1638].

- The vendor of a business might contract not to set up the same (or a similar) business within a ten kilometre radius of the location of the business sold.
- A garage proprietor might agree to take supplies of petroleum products exclusively from one supplier for a period of five years.
- An employee might contract to give his or her services exclusively to an employer, and not to work for a rival employer within a five kilometre radius for a period of one year after termination of the employment.

Although it is convenient to speak of a 'contract' in restraint of trade, it is more accurate to speak in terms of a *covenant*[172] in restraint of trade. So, the definition stated above applies to any contractual term amounting to a restriction of the type referred to. However, the restraint of trade doctrine may apply even though the 'covenantee' has promised to do an act, for example to pay pension benefits, provided the 'covenantor' does not do an act, such as entering a particular trade. Although in such a case there is no promise by the 'covenantor' not to enter the trade, a restraint may still be found due to the contingency.[173] Moreover, the restraint need not be found in a contract between the covenantor and covenantee. Thus, in *Buckley v Tutty*[174] the plaintiff, a professional footballer under contract with the Balmain District Rugby League Football Club, was subject to a restraint contained in the rules of the New South Wales Rugby League, an unincorporated association. It was because those rules operated in unreasonable restraint of trade that the High Court held the restraint to be unenforceable, and not because there was no contract between the plaintiff and the League.

Buckley v Tutty also illustrates the width of the concept of 'trade' in the context of employment. The doctrine applies to employment generally and, as the High Court said,[175] the 'fact that football is a sport does not mean that a man paid to play football is not engaged in employment'.

[1635] Contract in restraint of trade prima facie void. In *Nordenfelt v Maxim Nordenfelt Guns and Ammunition Co Ltd*[176] Lord Macnaghten expressed the 'general rule' as being that a contract in restraint of trade is void. This statement of principle has been accepted in the subsequent cases,[177] with the result that a covenant which operates in restraint of trade

---

172. That word is most accurately applied to a restraint contained in a deed, but the courts speak generally in terms of 'covenants' in restraint of trade rather than 'clauses', 'terms' or 'promises' in restraint of trade.
173. See *Wyatt v Kreglinger* [1933] 1 KB 793; *Howard F Hudson Pty Ltd v Ronayne* (1972) 126 CLR 449. Cf *Marshall v NM Financial Management Ltd* [1997] 1 WLR 1527 at 1533.
174. (1971) 125 CLR 353. See also *Pharmaceutical Society of Great Britain v Dickson* [1970] AC 403 (pharmacist); *Barnard v Australian Soccer Federation* (1988) 81 ALR 51 (professional soccer player); *Adamson v New South Wales Rugby League Ltd* (1991) 103 ALR 319, see Kim Baumeler and Lynden Griggs, (1993) 6 *JCL* 275; Andrew Humphreys, (1993) 15 *Syd LR* 92 (professional footballer).
175. (1971) 125 CLR 353 at 372.
176. [1894] AC 535 at 565.
177. See, eg *Esso Petroleum Co Ltd v Harper's Garage (Stourport) Ltd* [1968] AC 269 at 295, 299, 307, 318; *Buckley v Tutty* (1971) 125 CLR 353 at 376; *Amoco Australia Pty Ltd v Rocca Bros Motor Engineering Co Pty Ltd* (1973) 133 CLR 288 at 306–7, 315; 1 ALR 385.

is presumed to be void. The presumption can, however, be rebutted; that is, the restraint may be justified.

[1636] Justification of a restraint. The way in which a restraint is to be justified was explained by Lord Macnaghten in *Nordenfelt v Maxim Nordenfelt Guns and Ammunition Co Ltd*:[178]

> [R]estraints of trade and interferences with individual liberty of action may be justified by the special circumstances of a particular case. It is a sufficient justification, and indeed it is the only justification, if the restriction is reasonable — reasonable, that is, in reference to the interests of the parties concerned and reasonable in reference to the interests of the public, so framed and so guarded as to afford adequate protection to the party in whose favour it is imposed, while at the same time it is in no way injurious to the public.

Lord Macnaghten described this as the 'fair result' of the prior authorities, and the subsequent decisions have endorsed his statement of the law.[179] The distinction between 'reasonable' restraints and 'unreasonable' restraints is therefore that a reasonable restraint will be enforced, while a restraint which is unreasonable will not. Thus, if the restraint is found to be unreasonable, the clause imposing the restraint is unenforceable and (perhaps) void. But the contract is not thereby rendered illegal, and the contract as a whole is not unenforceable or void if the infringing clause is severable.[180] However, no issue of reasonableness arises if the person bound by the restraint chooses not to object to it: it is not unlawful for the parties to keep to their contract.[181]

Like the other public policy rules, the restraint of trade rule represents a restriction on the general rule of freedom of contract. A contract in restraint of trade is prima facie void, notwithstanding the general principle of freedom of contract, because of the public interest in freedom of competition and trade. On the other hand, the ability to justify a contract which is otherwise contrary to public policy sets this head of public policy apart from those previously considered. It is probably true to say that the courts find the tension between freedom of contract and considerations of public policy more acute in this area, and correspondingly more difficult to resolve, than in respect of the other heads of public policy. The cases indicate that the decision whether to enforce a contract in restraint of trade will depend not only on the nature of the restraint, but also on the nature of the contract. Thus, the rule of public policy is weaker in respect of contracts for the sale of a business than in employment contracts.[182] In the former context there is a tendency to allow a greater freedom of contract than in the latter, and a restraint clause in an employment contract is more likely to be held to be unjustified, particularly if it is found to be 'penal' in nature.[183]

---

178. [1894] AC 535 at 565.
179. See, eg *Esso Petroleum Co Ltd v Harper's Garage (Stourport) Ltd* [1968] AC 269 at 295, 307, 318–19; *Buckley v Tutty* (1971) 125 CLR 353 at 376; *Amoco Australia Pty Ltd v Rocca Bros Motor Engineering Co Pty Ltd* (1973) 133 CLR 288 at 306–7, 315.
180. See generally on severance [1729]–[1739].
181. See *Esso Petroleum Co Ltd v Harper's Garage (Stourport) Ltd* [1968] AC 269 at 297.
182. See further [1648].

At common law,[184] a covenant in restraint of trade which is found to be unreasonable is not enforceable even though the covenantor has acted in a way which could have been the subject of a valid restraint. For example, in *Papastravou v Gavan*[185] the plaintiffs purchased the defendants' hairdressing business under a contract which contained an undertaking that the defendants would not, for a period of three years, be employed, interested or directly or indirectly concerned, whether as proprietors or otherwise, in a hairdressing business within a radius of three miles of the premises sold. After about eight months the defendants opened a hairdressing business only about 350 yards away from the business sold. Because the undertaking went beyond what was reasonable, the plaintiffs were unable to obtain relief,[186] even though, had the restraint been limited to, say, a 500 yard radius, it would undoubtedly have been enforceable.

[1637] **Existence of restraint.** In *Esso Petroleum Co Ltd v Harper's Garage (Stourport) Ltd*[187] Lord Wilberforce emphasised the need to segregate two issues when applying the rule of public policy. The first issue is whether a restraint actually exists. The second issue, which need only be resolved if a restraint has been found, is whether the restraint is reasonable. This may sound obvious enough, but Lord Wilberforce saw a danger of fusing the two issues, by speaking of a clause which is in 'undue restraint of trade'. In fact, in some cases, deciding whether a restraint exists is the most difficult of the many issues raised by the restraint of trade doctrine.[188]

Generally, the courts have said that for a restraint to be found the covenantor must have given up some pre-existing freedom.[189] Thus, in the *Esso* case Lord Reid said[190] that a 'restraint of trade' implies that a person has contracted 'to give up some freedom which otherwise he would have had'. And in the same case Lord Pearce said[191] it would be 'intolerable' for a person who buys or leases land subject to a restraint, on terms which are 'more favourable' because of the restraint, to be able to 'repudiate' the restraint while retaining the benefit of the purchase or lease. In the final analysis, whether a restraint exists depends on the 'practical working'[192] of the contract rather than the form of the clauses in issue. Thus, although in

---

183. See, eg *Mason v Provident Clothing and Supply Co Ltd* [1913] AC 724 at 738, 739, 746. See also *Buckley v Tutty* (1971) 125 CLR 353 at 381; *Hughes v Western Australian Cricket Association (Inc)* (1986) 69 ALR 660 at 703–4. But the suggestion (see *Nagle v Feilden* [1966] 2 QB 633) that a person's 'right to work' is an independent basis for decision has been rejected. See, eg *Curro v Beyond Productions Pty Ltd* (1993) 30 NSWLR 337 at 346.
184. Subject to the rules on severance discussed [1729]–[1739].
185. [1968] 2 NSWR 286.
186. But see now the *Restraints of Trade Act* 1976 (NSW) (see [1738]–[1739]).
187. [1968] AC 269 at 331.
188. The issue dealt with in [1638] is closely related to this issue.
189. See, however, *Australian Capital Territory v Munday* (2000) 173 ALR 1 at 14, where it is suggested that there is no High Court authority to support this approach.
190. [1968] AC 269 at 298; cf at 309.
191. [1968] AC 269 at 325; cf at 316–17. See also *Foley v Classique Coaches Ltd* [1934] 2 KB 1, especially at 7–8; *Amoco Australia Pty Ltd v Rocca Bros Motor Engineering Co Pty Ltd* (1973) 133 CLR 288 at 313; *Quadramain Pty Ltd v Sevastapol Investments Pty Ltd* (1976) 133 CLR 390; 8 ALR 555; J D Heydon, 'Restraint of Trade in the High Court' (1976) 50 *ALJ* 290.

the *Esso* case Lord Reid said[193] that 'no one has ever suggested' that exclusive service contracts are in restraint of trade 'except in very unusual circumstances', subsequent decisions such as *A Schroeder Music Publishing Co Ltd v Macaulay*[194] indicate that those circumstances sometimes exist.

[1638] Contracts to which the principles apply. As the discussion in the previous paragraph indicates, there is debate as to the contracts which are subject to the restraint of trade doctrine. In *Esso Petroleum Co Ltd v Harper's Garage (Stourport) Ltd*[195] Lord Wilberforce said the doctrine is 'to be applied to factual situations with a broad and flexible rule of reason'. He refused to accept that any exhaustive test could be stated to define or identify the contracts to which the doctrine applies.

In the *Esso* case it was argued that the doctrine applies only to 'personal' restraints and does not apply to a restriction on the use of a particular piece of land. However, as a general proposition, this argument was rejected and the doctrine applied to a mortgage of land.[196] Similarly, in *Amoco Australia Pty Ltd v Rocca Bros Motor Engineering Co Pty Ltd*[197] the High Court rejected an argument that the doctrine does not apply to a lease of land. Nevertheless, it would seem that where a purchaser or lessee of land acquires rights and takes possession for the first time under a sale of land contract or lease which imposes a restriction on, say, the use to which the land can be put, the purchaser or lessee is not able to invoke the doctrine because a new right — to an extent defined by the restraint — is acquired by virtue of the contract or lease.[198]

There may, as the Privy Council explained in *Bridge v Deacons*,[199] be certain types of contract which, although imposing a 'measure of interference with the freedom of trade', are not to be treated as 'within the field of restraint of trade, provided that the degree of interference does not exceed the accepted standard'. On the other hand, it may be preferable to regard such contracts as within the doctrine, but as expressing only reasonable restraints. In fact, virtually any contract is likely to impose a restraint of some kind. For example, an agreement to sell specific goods implies a restraint, namely, that the seller will not sell them to another person. The doctrine is never applied to contracts where the restraint is merely incidental to the contract.

---

192. *Howard F Hudson Pty Ltd v Ronayne* (1972) 126 CLR 449 at 467 per Gibbs J. See also *Pharmaceutical Society of Great Britain v Dickson* [1970] AC 403 at 440; *Stenhouse Australia Ltd v Phillips* [1974] AC 391 at 402.
193. [1968] AC 269 at 294; cf at 307. See also *Curro v Beyond Productions Pty Ltd* (1993) 30 NSWLR 337 at 341–2.
194. [1974] 1 WLR 1308 (see [1653]). See also *Watson v Prager* [1991] 1 WLR 726, especially at 742–7.
195. [1968] AC 269 at 331, 332; see also at 306.
196. Cf *Queensland Co-operative Milling Association Ltd v Pamag Pty Ltd* (1973) 133 CLR 260; 1 ALR 47 (bill of sale).
197. (1973) 133 CLR 288. Compare *Cleveland Petroleum Co Ltd v Dartstone Ltd* [1969] 1 WLR 116; and contrast *Alec Lobb (Garages) Ltd v Total Oil (Great Britain) Ltd* [1985] 1 WLR 173.
198. See *Cleveland Petroleum Co Ltd v Dartstone Ltd* [1969] 1 WLR 116; *Quadramain Pty Ltd v Sevastapol Investments Pty Ltd* (1976) 133 CLR 390.
199. [1984] AC 705 at 713.

[1639] **Onus of proof.** In *Herbert Morris Ltd v Saxelby*[200] Lord Atkinson expressed the onus of proof in the following terms:[201]

> If the restraint affords to the person in whose favour it is imposed nothing more than reasonable protection against something which he is entitled to be protected against, then as between the parties concerned the restraint is to be held to be reasonable in reference to their respective interests, but notwithstanding this the restraint may still be held to be injurious to the public and therefore void; the onus of establishing to the satisfaction of the judge who tries the case facts and circumstances which show that the restraint is of the reasonable character abovementioned resting upon the person alleging that it is of that character, and the onus of showing that, notwithstanding that it is of that character, it is nevertheless injurious to the public and therefore void, resting, in like manner, on the party alleging the latter.

This contrast, between reasonableness in the parties' interests and reasonableness in the public interest, was confirmed by the subsequent authorities.[202] Since, in most cases,[203] it is the person who obtained the restraint (the covenantee) who seeks to have it enforced, the onus is on the covenantee to prove that the restraint is reasonable as between the parties. But the burden is on the covenantor to show that the restraint is against the public interest.

[1640] **Two questions of reasonableness not one.** As can be implied from the preceding paragraph, there are two issues of reasonableness, not just one.[204] Thus, in theory, the two issues of reasonableness are distinct. It follows that Lord Pearce's suggestion in *Esso Petroleum Co Ltd v Harper's Garage (Stourport) Ltd*,[205] that there is 'one broad question: is it in the interests of the community that this restraint should, as between the parties, be held to be reasonable and enforceable?' does not accurately express the law. However, in practice they overlap.[206] This is hardly surprising. Because public policy is the dominant consideration, and relevant to both,[207] the second issue of reasonableness tends to merge with the first.[208]

So far as the parties' interest is concerned, Lord Parker said in *Herbert Morris Ltd v Saxelby*[209] that the restraint 'must afford *no more than* adequate protection to the party in whose favour it is imposed'. He thought this test

---

200. [1916] 1 AC 688.
201. [1916] 1 AC 688 at 700. See also at 707, 708.
202. See, eg *Esso Petroleum Co Ltd v Harper's Garage (Stourport) Ltd* [1968] AC 269 at 319; *Amoco Australia Pty Ltd v Rocca Bros Motor Engineering Co Pty Ltd* (1973) 133 CLR 288 at 315–16.
203. But not all; see *Wyatt v Kreglinger* [1933] 1 KB 793.
204. See, eg *Esso Petroleum Co Ltd v Harper's Garage (Stourport) Ltd* [1968] AC 269 at 299, 307, 319; *Amoco Australia Pty Ltd v Rocca Bros Motor Engineering Co Pty Ltd* (1973) 133 CLR 288 at 307–8.
205. [1968] AC 269 at 324.
206. See *Herbert Morris Ltd v Saxelby* [1916] 1 AC 688 at 699; *Amoco Australia Pty Ltd v Rocca Bros Motor Engineering Co Pty Ltd* (1973) 133 CLR 288 at 307–8.
207. *Esso Petroleum Co Ltd v Harper's Garage (Stourport) Ltd* [1968] AC 269 at 301, 321.
208. *Amoco Australia Pty Ltd v Rocca Bros Motor Engineering Co Pty Ltd* (1973) 133 CLR 288 at 307–8.
209. [1916] 1 AC 688 at 707. See also *Lindner v Murdock's Garage* (1950) 83 CLR 628 at 645, 654; *Bridge v Deacons* [1984] AC 705 at 713.

valid as regards both covenantor and covenantee. Thus, although in one sense it is contrary to the covenantor's interests to be subject to *any* restraint, it may, as Lord Parker explained, 'be for his advantage to be able so to subject himself in cases where, if he could not do so he would lose other advantages'. He gave as examples the 'best terms' on the sale of an existing business, and the possibility of obtaining employment or training under 'competent employers'.

If the court is satisfied that the restraint confers greater protection than can be justified, there is no further issue of reasonableness and it is unnecessary to consider separately the public interest.[210] On the other hand, if no more than adequate protection is achieved by the clause, public interest must be further considered, and the restraint found not to be 'injurious to the public'.[211] One feature of the modern cases is to give more prominence to the public interest than was formerly overtly in evidence, and in the *Esso* case Lord Hodson[212] held one of the restrictive covenants in issue to be unreasonable on the basis that it was injurious to the public. Traditionally, there has been a tendency for the courts to assume that a restraint reasonable as between the parties is not injurious to the public.

[1641] Time of inquiry. The relevant time for examining the reasonableness of a restraint is the time of entry into the contract.[213] Although the court must construe the contract, in order to reach a conclusion on its scope, duration and so on, reasonableness does not depend on the intention of the parties. The fact that they regarded the restraint as reasonable, although relevant, cannot be conclusive because of the overriding importance of public policy.[214]

In practice, it is difficult for the court to disregard totally events between formation and enforcement, and such events may sometimes be useful in determining whether the restraint was reasonable.[215] But in *Shell UK Ltd v Lostock Garage Ltd*[216] Lord Denning MR went further, suggesting that the court should not enforce the clause where a subsequent event, unforeseen when the contract was entered into, proves the restraint to be unreasonable. The rationale for such an approach is that, since the court is required to uphold public policy, an agreement which operates in a way which is contrary to public policy should not be enforced even if that was not the position when the contract was agreed. However, the other members of the

---

210. See *Amoco Australia Pty Ltd v Rocca Bros Motor Engineering Co Pty Ltd* (1973) 133 CLR 288 at 306.
211. *Herbert Morris Ltd v Saxelby* [1916] 1 AC 688 at 707. See also *Amoco Australia Pty Ltd v Rocca Bros Motor Engineering Co Pty Ltd* (1973) 133 CLR 288 at 307–8.
212. [1968] AC 269 at 321.
213. See, eg *Nordenfelt v Maxim Nordenfelt Guns and Ammunition Co Ltd* [1894] AC 535 at 573–4; *Lindner v Murdock's Garage* (1950) 83 CLR 628 at 653; *Amoco Australia Pty Ltd v Rocca Bros Motor Engineering Co Pty Ltd* (1973) 133 CLR 288 at 318; *Bridge v Deacons* [1984] AC 705 at 718–19.
214. See *Amoco Australia Pty Ltd v Rocca Bros Motor Engineering Co Pty Ltd* (1973) 133 CLR 288 at 308. But see [1652].
215. See *Adamson v New South Wales Rugby League Ltd* (1991) 103 ALR 319 at 360.
216. [1977] 1 All ER 481 at 488–9.

court did not agree, and in *Geraghty v Minter*[217] Gibbs J left the issue open for future consideration.

Relevant factors

[1642] Protectable interests. At the heart of the justification of a restraint of trade is the idea that a covenantee is entitled to protect certain interests. If there is no such interest the covenant will be regarded as unreasonable. For example, a restriction on competition per se is unenforceable.[218] It is therefore important to know what interests may legitimately be the subject of protection.

The main justification for a restraint is the protection of an interest in property, typically the goodwill[219] of a business. This can be seen most clearly in the sale of business cases where the purchaser is entitled to obtain a restraint covenant from the vendor in order to protect the goodwill transferred by the sale.[220] Goodwill is relevant in other cases as well, as where an employer obtains a restraint from an employee to prevent solicitation of clients of the business on termination of the employment.[221] The concept of proprietary interest is not a narrow one; it includes, for example, confidential information and trade secrets.[222]

One important feature of the modern law is the extension of protectable interests beyond proprietary rights, so as to include matters such as economies of trade by manufacturers and suppliers of goods.[223] Thus, in *Queensland Co-operative Milling Association Ltd v Pamag Pty Ltd*[224] a restraint clause in a contract between a baker and flour miller, obliging the baker to use the miller's products, was justified by reference to the 'commercial interest' of the miller in obtaining customers and maximising sales. In the case of professional sportsmen (and sportswomen) the courts are even prepared to allow such matters as the concern of a governing body to ensure that teams competing do so on an equal footing to be a justification for a restraint on members of the teams.[225]

[1643] Scope and duration of restraint. It will always be material to consider the scope and duration of the restraint. So far as scope is

---

217. (1979) 142 CLR 177 at 188; 26 ALR 141. But cf (1979) 142 CLR 177 at 199–200.
218. See, eg *Vancouver Malt and Sake Brewing Co Ltd v Vancouver Breweries Ltd* [1934] AC 181 (see [1647]). But the description is not in itself particularly helpful: *Esso Petroleum Co Ltd v Harper's Garage (Stourport) Ltd* [1968] AC 269 at 301.
219. For the meaning of 'goodwill' see *Bacchus Marsh Concentrated Milk Co Ltd v Joseph Nathan & Co Ltd* (1919) 26 CLR 410 at 438; *FCT v Murry* (1998) 193 CLR 605; 155 ALR 67.
220. See [1647].
221. See, eg *Fitch v Dewes* [1921] 2 AC 158; *Marion White Ltd v Francis* [1972] 3 All ER 857, and generally [1648]–[1649]. See also *Peters American Delicacy Co Ltd v Patricia's Chocolates and Candies Pty Ltd* (1947) 77 CLR 574 (see [1652]).
222. See *Bacchus Marsh Concentrated Milk Co Ltd v Joseph Nathan & Co Ltd* (1919) 26 CLR 410 at 441; *K A & C Smith Pty Ltd v Ward* (1998) 45 NSWLR 702 at 723.
223. See, eg *Esso Petroleum Co Ltd v Harper's Garage (Stourport) Ltd* [1968] AC 269 (see [1652]).
224. (1973) 133 CLR 260.
225. See *Buckley v Tutty* (1971) 125 CLR 353. See K E Lindgren, 'Sport and the Law: The Players Contract' (1991) 4 *JCL* 135.

concerned, the court is looking for a definite connection between the restraint and the covenantee's business, trade or profession. If the restraint goes beyond the covenantee's business[226] it will almost invariably be unreasonable by reason of its width.[227] There are three things to be considered.

First, if relevant, there is the geographical area covered by the restraint clause. For example, it may be relevant to consider whether an employer, vendor of a business or partnership carries on business in the areas covered by a restraint clause in the contract.

Second, there are the acts covered by the restraint. It must be asked what the covenantor is restrained from doing, and whether the covenantor must refrain from doing all the acts referred to, for the covenantee to be adequately protected.

Third, duration must be taken into account. The longer the restraint the less likely it is that the restraint will be held to be reasonable. Of course, area and time are frequently related: the more limited the area the longer the period which will be justifiable, and vice versa.[228] Although duration is necessarily relative to the facts of each case, long restraints are generally held to be unreasonable.[229] Two further points about duration may be noted.

One is that it is sometimes possible to lay down guidelines for parties to particular types of contracts. For example, in *Esso Petroleum Co Ltd v Harper's Garage (Stourport) Ltd*[230] a restriction on the freedom of the proprietors of a petrol service station, obliging them for a period not exceeding five years to purchase their petroleum supplies from the one supplier, was said, as a general rule, not to be unreasonable.[231]

The other point is whether the restraint is to operate after the termination of the contract. Generally, a restraint is more likely to be regarded as reasonable where it operates for no longer than the duration of the contract,[232] and in the *Esso* case Lord Pearce said[233] that in some cases the question of reasonableness will not arise in respect of a restraint so limited. Of course, frequently the restriction of a restraint to such a period would be of little value, as in the case of the sale of a business,[234] and even in employment contracts, where one might expect a restraint on the employee's activities to be limited to the duration of employment, the court may find a restraint extending beyond that period to be reasonable.[235]

[1644] Benefits derived by the parties. Particularly where reasonableness between the parties is in issue, the court will place emphasis

---

226. See, eg [1647].
227. Subject to issues of severance dealt with [1729]–[1739].
228. See, eg *Fitch v Dewes* [1921] 2 AC 158 at 162–3.
229. For an extreme illustration of enforcement see *Fitch v Dewes* [1921] 2 AC 158 (lifetime restraint on solicitor).
230. [1968] AC 269 (see [1652]).
231. For enforcement of a longer restraint see *Alec Lobb (Garages) Ltd v Total Oil (Great Britain) Ltd* [1985] 1 WLR 173.
232. See, eg *Buckenara v Hawthorn Football Club Ltd* [1988] VR 39.
233. [1968] AC 269 at 328.
234. See generally [1647].
235. See generally [1648]–[1649].

on the benefits derived by the parties from the contract. But, if the restraint affords more than adequate protection to the covenantee, it will be immaterial 'whether the covenantor has received much or little by way of benefits from entering into the transaction'.[236]

Frequently, there will be a relationship between the restraint and the benefits derived by the covenantor. Perhaps the best illustration is in respect of contracts for the sale of a business.[237] The fact that the vendor is prepared to agree to a restraint, and so ensure that the purchaser obtains the full benefit of the goodwill sold, enhances the price of the business and so benefits the vendor.[238] Indeed, a vendor who is unwilling to agree to a restraint may find it difficult to sell. In this sense it is in the vendor's interest to agree to a restraint. The court will be reluctant to hold the restraint unreasonable if that would enable the vendor to obtain (or retain) the purchase price without providing the whole of the consideration bargained for by the purchaser.[239] Thus, the benefits to be taken into account are, as Walsh J said in *Amoco Australia Pty Ltd v Rocca Bros Motor Engineering Co Pty Ltd*,[240] 'not limited' to what the covenantor 'receives in money or other property'. Walsh J went on to explain, in the context of an exclusive dealing contract, that a covenantor may be regarded 'as obtaining, in return for a restraint, a benefit which consists simply in being able by this means to procure an agreement in aid of his trading'. He gave as an example an agreement for the regular supply of goods which the covenantor would not be able to obtain but for an agreement to sell only those goods supplied by the covenantee.

The effect of having regard to benefits obtained under the contract is to make the 'quantum',[241] and perhaps even the 'adequacy',[242] of the consideration received by the covenantor relevant to the issue of reasonableness.

[1645] Commercial setting of contract. From what has already been said it is obvious that the issue of reasonableness, whether between the parties or in respect of the public interest, is not considered in the abstract. The commercial setting of the contract is therefore important. For example, in *Esso Petroleum Co Ltd v Harper's Garage (Stourport) Ltd*[243] there was evidence that of about 36,000 petrol filling stations in Britain some 35,000 were tied to particular petrol companies, such as Esso. Having regard to the general acceptance of such restrictions in the industry the House of Lords was reluctant to reach a decision which would outlaw all

---

236. *Amoco Australia Pty Ltd v Rocca Bros Motor Engineering Co Pty Ltd* (1973) 133 CLR 288 at 306.
237. See generally [1647].
238. See, eg *Bridge v Deacons* [1984] AC 705 at 713.
239. See *Esso Petroleum Co Ltd v Harper's Garage (Stourport) Ltd* [1968] AC 269 at 335–6.
240. (1973) 133 CLR 288 at 306.
241. See, eg *Nordenfelt v Maxim Nordenfelt Guns and Ammunition Co Ltd* [1894] AC 535 at 565; *Esso Petroleum Co Ltd v Harper's Garage (Stourport) Ltd* [1968] AC 269 at 300, 323 (cf at 318); *Amoco Australia Pty Ltd v Rocca Bros Motor Engineering Co Pty Ltd* (1973) 133 CLR 288 at 305–6, 316.
242. See *Bridge v Deacons* [1984] AC 705 at 718; *Alec Lobb (Garages) Ltd v Total Oil (Great Britain) Ltd* [1985] 1 WLR 173 at 185.
243. [1968] AC 269 (see [1652]).

these trade ties. Accordingly, a decision was reached which gave judicial acceptance to the practice of the trade, but which indicated that an unreasonably long restraint would be treated as contrary to public policy. Similarly, in *Bridge v Deacons*[244] the Privy Council thought it relevant to the reasonableness of a restraint in a solicitors' partnership agreement that the agreement had been drawn up by solicitors, and represented the view of persons experienced in the field.

In *Texaco Ltd v Mulberry Filling Station Ltd*[245] Ungoed-Thomas J said that the court should not, in considering the reasonableness of a restraint, attempt to promote any general economic theory. That could, he said,[246] involve 'balancing a mass of conflicting economic, social and other interests which a court of law might be ill-adapted to achieve', notwithstanding that the public interest might in fact be prejudiced (or promoted) by the decision of the court. Legislation such as the *Trade Practices Act* 1974 (Cth) has been passed to promote economic theories favouring competition and such evidence is relevant to contracts within the Act, some of which would formerly have been governed by the common law.[247] In effect parliament has made the point that the common law approach is too narrow.

[1646] **Bargaining position of the parties.** There are many decisions in which the courts have referred to the relevance of inequality of bargaining power to contracts in restraint of trade.[248] Thus, whatever view should be taken about the relevance of inequality of bargaining power and unconscionability to contracts generally,[249] when considering whether a restraint is reasonable it may be relevant to examine the relative bargaining positions of the parties to the contract. In *A Schroeder Music Publishing Co Ltd v Macaulay*[250] Lord Diplock said[251] that it is

> salutary to acknowledge that in refusing to enforce provisions of a contract whereby one party agrees for the benefit of the other party to exploit or to refrain from exploiting his own earning power, the public policy which the court is implementing is not some 19th-century economic theory about the benefit to the general public of freedom of trade, but the protection of those whose bargaining power is weak against being forced by those whose bargaining power is stronger to enter into bargains that are unconscionable ... If one looks at the reasoning of 19th-century judges in cases about contracts in restraint of trade one finds lip service paid to current economic theories, but if one looks at what they said in the light of what they did, one finds that they struck down a bargain if they thought it was unconscionable as between the parties to it and upheld it if they thought it was not.

244. [1984] AC 705 at 717.
245. [1972] 1 WLR 814.
246. [1972] 1 WLR 814 at 827.
247. See generally [1655].
248. See, eg *Queensland Co-operative Milling Association Ltd v Pamag Pty Ltd* (1973) 133 CLR 260 at 268; *Curro v Beyond Productions Pty Ltd* (1993) 30 NSWLR 337 at 345. And cf *Potato Producers Co-operative Ltd v Pavone* [1962] VR 231.
249. See generally Chapter 15.
250. [1974] 1 WLR 1308.
251. [1974] 1 WLR 1308 at 1315. For a criticism, principally from an economic theory perspective, see M J Trebilcock, 'The Doctrine of Inequality of Bargaining Power: Post-Benthamite Economics in the House of Lords' (1976) 26 *Univ of Toronto LJ* 359. See also B A Leon, B J Reiter and C L Waldrum, 'Fairness Issues in Employment Contracts' (1993) 6 *JCL* 189.

Where inequality of bargaining power is present the court will, as the passage quoted above indicates, hold the restraint to be unreasonable if the party with the stronger position used that position to extract an unconscionable restraint. The fact that the parties bargained on equal terms, or that there is no evidence of abuse of a superior position, while not conclusive,[252] is given considerable weight.[253] And there are some industries and markets where restraints are so well established and widely practised that acceptance of some restraint is in effect part of the price of entry into the industry or market.[254] In such cases, acceptance of the restraint — and entry into the industry or market — may well advance trade.[255]

Particular contracts

[1647] Sale of business. In *Nordenfelt v Maxim Nordenfelt Guns and Ammunition Co Ltd*[256] Nordenfelt had been very successful in the munitions industry and carried on a very substantial business until the business was purchased in 1886 by the Nordenfelt Guns and Ammunition Co. Nordenfelt was held to be bound by a restraint clause which precluded his involvement in the munitions industry for a period of 25 years. There was no limitation placed on the geographical scope of the clause, although it was subject to provisos exempting explosives, other than gunpowder and submarines and torpedoes. The 25-year period commenced from the time of incorporation of the defendant company which was formed to amalgamate the Nordenfelt Guns and Ammunition Co and the Maxim Gun Co. Although the restraint clause was in fact obtained pursuant to the amalgamation agreement, the House of Lords considered that the case had to be treated as if the restraint clause had been agreed in consideration of a direct transfer by Nordenfelt of the goodwill of his business, and taken by the plaintiffs with the object of protecting it from derogation by Nordenfelt. Now, it may seem surprising that a restraint unlimited in scope should have been upheld, but the point was that Nordenfelt had comparatively few customers, but a world-wide trade so that, by reason of the nature of the business, the restraint could be justified. In any event, it was hardly contrary to the public policy of England for an individual to be restrained from doing munitions business in foreign countries.

Time and again in the sale of business cases the courts have said that the sale of the goodwill of the business provides a justification for and measure of the enforceability of a restraint.[257] But if the restraint is not ancillary to the sale of the goodwill of a business it will be struck down. Thus, in *Vancouver Malt and Sake Brewing Co Ltd v Vancouver Breweries Ltd*[258] an

---

252. See *Queensland Co-operative Milling Association Ltd v Pamag Pty Ltd* (1973) 133 CLR 260 at 268; *Amoco Australia Pty Ltd v Rocca Bros Motor Engineering Co Pty Ltd* (1973) 133 CLR 288 at 306–7, 316–17.
253. See further [1652].
254. See, eg *Esso Petroleum Co Ltd v Harper's Garage (Stourport) Ltd* [1968] AC 269.
255. See *Bacchus Marsh Concentrated Milk Co Ltd v Joseph Nathan & Co Ltd* (1919) 26 CLR 410 at 441.
256. [1894] AC 535.
257. See, eg *Esso Petroleum Co Ltd v Harper's Garage (Stourport) Ltd* [1968] AC 269 at 335–6.
258. [1934] AC 181.

agreement was reached in 1927 for the sale by the Malt and Sake company (the vendor) of the goodwill of their brewers' licence, except insofar as it related to sake, to the Breweries company (the purchaser). The agreement contained a covenant by the vendor not to engage in the business of manufacturing, brewing, selling or disposing of beer or similar products other than sake. But the vendor had no goodwill relating to beer, as its sole business was the brewing of sake. In fact, the Privy Council was satisfied that there was no sale of anything, just a facade of a sale invented to give respectability to a promise by the vendor not in future to compete with the purchaser. In addition, the covenant was too wide: if interpreted literally it covered the whole world; whereas any goodwill of the vendor was limited to Vancouver where it carried on business, or perhaps to British Columbia. Thus, the restraint clause was contrary to public policy and the purchaser was unsuccessful in seeking to enforce it.

[1648] Employment contracts: matters to be considered. Employment contracts are subject to a stricter approach than contracts for the sale of a business. It is quite common for a restraint clause in an employment contract to fail to pass the test of reasonableness on the ground that it is too wide, or for too long a period. Gibbs J explained in *Geraghty v Minter*[259] that the courts 'in general take a stricter and less favourable view of covenants in restraint of trade entered into between employer and employee than of similar covenants between vendor and purchaser'. This is because a restraint is likely to have more impact in the employment context, and because there is a greater danger of abuse of a superior bargaining position. The proper approach is as follows.[260]

First, the properly protectable interests of the employer must be identified. The nature and geographical spread of the employer's operations, the location of clients and the goodwill of the business, are relevant.

Second, the status, functions and duties of the particular employee must be determined. The degree of contact between the particular employee and the clients, the level of seniority and responsibility within the structure of the employer's operations and possession of (or access to) trade secrets and confidential information belonging to the employer are all relevant factors.

Third, a decision must be made as to whether, in the light of these matters, the particular restraint imposed goes no further than to safeguard the employer's protectable interest.

[1649] Employment contracts: illustrations. In *Lindner v Murdock's Garage*[261] the defendant was employed as a mechanic by the plaintiffs who carried on a business as motor and general engineers in Crystal Brook and Wirrabara, two towns in South Australia about 30 miles apart. There was no fixed term of employment, and either party could terminate the

---

259. (1979) 142 CLR 177 at 185. See also *Mason v Provident Clothing and Supply Co Ltd* [1913] AC 724 at 738.
260. See generally *Brightman v Lamson Paragon Ltd* (1914) 18 CLR 331; *Fitch v Dewes* [1921] 2 AC 158; *Lindner v Murdock's Garage* (1950) 83 CLR 628; *A Buckle & Son Pty Ltd v McAllister* (1986) 4 NSWLR 426.
261. (1950) 83 CLR 628.

relationship on giving 21 days' notice. After the defendant had been employed for more than three years at Crystal Brook he left the plaintiffs' employment and obtained work at a garage located two or three hundred yards from the plaintiffs' garage. When the plaintiffs sought an injunction to enforce the restraint clause in the contract, the defendant argued that the clause was unreasonable. So far as is material the clause provided that the defendant would not, for the term of his employment or within a period of one year from the termination thereof 'in any way carry on or be engaged concerned or interested ... in the business of garage proprietors, motor and general engineers ... or in any similar business now and hereafter carried on' by the plaintiffs in the same area.

A majority of the High Court held the restraint to be unreasonable because it extended not only to Crystal Brook, where the plaintiff had to some extent come into contact with the plaintiffs' customers, but also to Wirrabara where the defendant had never been employed. To use Kitto J's words,[262] a restraint which applied 'indiscriminately', to all the areas in which the plaintiffs carried on business, went beyond what was 'reasonably necessary' to prevent the injury to their business, because of the limited extent of the defendant's employment.[263]

Notwithstanding the general reluctance to enforce restraints contained in employment contracts, the courts are sometimes prepared to enforce a restraint, particularly if the only basis for invalidity is an improbable application of the clause. Thus, in *Home Counties Dairies Ltd v Skilton*[264] the defendant was employed as a milkman under a contract which contained a covenant not to 'serve or sell milk or dairy produce to, or solicit orders for milk or dairy produce from any person or company who at any time during the last six months of his employment shall have been a customer' of the plaintiffs, and served by the defendant in the course of his employment. This restraint was for a period of one year after the termination of the defendant's employment. The restraint was held to be valid notwithstanding that, literally interpreted, it might have prevented the defendant from working in a grocery shop or restaurant where dairy produce was sold or served to a customer of the plaintiffs. The court emphasised that a period of one year was reasonable, and also that the clause was limited in its operation to customers of the plaintiffs with whom the defendant had dealt in the course of his employment. The court's interpretation of the restraint clause was reinforced by another restraint clause, which applied during the term of the defendant's employment and was expressly limited to dairy businesses. So far as the wide application of the restraint relied on by the defendant was concerned:

- Harman LJ said[265] that the clause was as a matter of construction 'an agreement not to serve an employer as a milk roundsman';

---

262. (1950) 83 CLR 628 at 656.
263. For further illustrations see *Attwood v Lamont* [1920] 3 KB 571; *Herbert Morris Ltd v Saxelby* [1916] 1 AC 688. Cf *Heine Bros (Aust) Pty Ltd v Forrest* [1963] VR 383.
264. [1970] 1 WLR 526.
265. [1970] 1 WLR 526 at 533.

- Salmon LJ said[266] that the clause did not 'purport' to prevent the defendant 'from selling cheese or butter in a grocery business; nor ... from doing anything in any business other than a dairy business' and rejected[267] the argument that it was invalid because 'it might cover circumstances' which were, in fact, 'so "extravagant", "fantastical", "unlikely or improbable" that they must have been entirely outside the contemplation of the parties'; and

- Cross LJ, agreeing, said[268] that the restraint clause had to be construed 'as applying only to the event' of the defendant 'engaging himself in or being employed by someone engaged in the business of a dairyman', and did not think that the court should pay regard to 'improbable contingencies' which were not within the contemplation of the parties.[269]

[1650] **Partnership agreements: general.** In *Geraghty v Minter*[270] a deed of partnership stated the business of the partnership as being 'that of insurance loss adjusting investigations and allied business activities'. Clause 21 stated that in the event of dissolution of the partnership certain of its members, including the defendants, should 'not exercise or carry on or be in any manner whatsoever either directly or indirectly concerned or interested ... in the trade or business of a similar nature' within a radius of 20 miles for a period of three years. When the defendants breached this clause the plaintiffs sought an injunction to restrain further breaches. The defendants' argument that the restraint clause was unreasonable was rejected by a majority of the High Court.

Gibbs J said[271] that it was 'probably right to regard partnership agreements as sui generis ... and to treat some cases where there is in fact a sale of goodwill as different from those in which an employee is taken into partnership'. In the present case the plaintiffs had retained a substantial interest in the goodwill and the restraint clause was intended to protect that interest. The partnership had a comparatively small number of clients, each of whom was likely to be valuable, and dependent to a large extent on personal contact with the partners. The defendants had been admitted as partners, rather than mere employees, and the only basis on which the restraint could have been said to be unreasonable was its application to 'allied business activities'. In fact, no such activities were carried on by the partnership and the majority of the court took the view that the restraint was not intended to extend beyond businesses of the same character as those actually carried on by the partnership.[272]

[1651] **Partnership agreements: solicitors.** Some of the recent cases have concerned solicitors' partnerships and the applicable principles were

---

266. [1970] 1 WLR 526 at 535.
267. [1970] 1 WLR 526 at 536.
268. [1970] 1 WLR 526 at 527.
269. See also *Marion White Ltd v Francis* [1972] 3 All ER 857. Query whether this approach was taken too far in *Littlewoods Organisation Ltd v Harris* [1978] 1 All ER 1026 (see *Talk of the Town Pty Ltd v Hagstrom* (1990) 99 ALR 130 at 134).
270. (1979) 142 CLR 177.
271. (1979) 142 CLR 177 at 185.
272. Cf *Lu v Lim* (1993) 30 NSWLR 332 at 335.

stated by the Privy Council in *Bridge v Deacons*.[273] The plaintiffs, a Hong Kong firm of solicitors, sought to enforce a restraint clause contained in a partnership agreement to which the defendant was a party. He had been a partner between 1974 and 1982. The relevant clause provided, in part, that a person who ceased to be a partner would not 'for a period of five years thereafter act as a solicitor, notary, trade mark or patent agent or in any similar capacity' in Hong Kong for 'any person, firm or company who was at the time of his ceasing to be a partner or had during the period of three years prior thereto been a client of the partnership'.

In rejecting the defendant's contention that the restraint was unreasonable, the Board considered relevant prior decisions in both sale of business cases and employment contracts. This was because the partnership agreement bore some resemblance to both. The evidence established that the defendant had been mainly concerned with a specialised area of the plaintiffs' business (the intellectual and industrial property department): he had had no connection or dealings with over 90 per cent of the plaintiffs' clients. If this had been a simple employment contract there would have been a strong case for saying that the restriction on the defendant's activities after he had left the firm was too wide. However, this was not the position and, while a partner, the defendant was owner of a share in the most valuable asset of the partnership, namely, its goodwill. Once he ceased to be a partner the plaintiffs owned the whole of the assets and they were therefore entitled to some protection against appropriation by the defendant of any part of the goodwill. In this respect the position was analogous to a sale of business case. Five specific factors were referred to:

(1) the protection did not extend beyond the clients of the plaintiffs' practice;

(2) the restraint applied equally to all partners — the defendant had not been singled out for special treatment and the partners' interests were not separated in a way which made the restraint unreasonable;

(3) the five-year period was not unreasonably long;

(4) the quantum of consideration provided for by the partnership agreement, while perhaps a little on the low side, was not insignificant and could be justified;

(5) there was a 'clear public interest in facilitating the assumption by established solicitors' firms of younger men as partners',[274] and a decision that the restraint was unreasonable might have discouraged the introduction of young solicitors, such as the defendant, to established firms.

In reaching this decision the Privy Council expressly disapproved[275] a statement by Lord Denning MR in *Oswald Hickson Collier & Co v Carter-Ruck*[276] where he accepted an argument that, because the relationship between solicitor and client is of a fiduciary nature, a restraint clause

---

273. [1984] AC 705.
274. [1984] AC 705 at 718.
275. [1984] AC 705 at 719.
276. (1982) [1984] AC 720n at 723.

precluding a solicitor from acting for a client who wanted the solicitor to act is necessarily contrary to public policy. The idea that it is impossible to have a 'reasonable' restraint where a fiduciary relationship exists is difficult to accept as a general proposition. In *Sharah v Healey*[277] McLelland J said that the existence of such a relationship is not a sufficient reason for creating a special rule

> since it is often the position of confidence or influence giving rise to the fiduciary character of the relationship which a solicitor or other professional has with clients of the relevant business that justifies a contractual restraint to protect the legitimate interests of those interested in the goodwill of the business.

Accordingly, he rejected the argument that a restraint placed on a solicitor is necessarily contrary to public policy. And in *Edwards v Worboys*[278] the English Court of Appeal said that there is no special rule of law applicable to restraints of trade on the part of persons who occupy a fiduciary position in relation to their clients.

[1652] Exclusive dealing and other commercial transactions. Where a manufacturer and retailer reach an agreement under which the retailer agrees to take all requirements exclusively from the manufacturer,[279] the approach of the courts has generally been to regard the parties as the best judges of what is reasonable between them. Thus, assuming the parties have in fact bargained at arm's length, the court will be slow to hold the restraint unreasonable.

For example, in *Peters American Delicacy Co Ltd v Patricia's Chocolates and Candies Pty Ltd*[280] a contract between a retailer and manufacturers of ice cream provided that the retailer would not for a period of 60 months sell ice cream, other than that manufactured by the manufacturers, from certain premises or at any other place within a radius of five miles. The period of 60 months was fixed by reference to cl 1 of the agreement which stated an obligation to supply quantities of ice cream ordered by the retailer. In addition, the restraint clause was prefaced by an agreement that its operation was contingent on the manufacturers being able to supply ice cream at prices specified, or agreed from time to time. The High Court, by majority, held that the restraint clause was valid. The parties had bargained on equal terms, the manufacturers were entitled to protect their business reputation and goodwill, the agreement did not operate unfairly against the retailer and there was no evidence that it was injurious to the public. Accordingly, the manufacturers obtained an injunction preventing the sale of ice cream other than that manufactured or supplied by them.

The same approach has been taken:

- to restraints in contracts between traders and trading associations, entered into for the purpose of orderly marketing and price protection;[281]

---

277. [1982] 2 NSWLR 223 at 227.
278. (1982) [1984] AC 724n at 726, 728. See also *Kerr v Morris* [1987] Ch 90 (National Health Service doctor); *Watson v Prager* [1991] 1 WLR 726 (manager of boxer occupied fiduciary position).
279. See [223].
280. (1947) 77 CLR 574.

- to restraints in contracts for the distribution of products, between agents and combinations of producers, aimed at regulating supply and maintaining prices;[282] and
- to exclusive dealing contracts between manufacturers and suppliers of raw materials.

For example, in *Queensland Co-operative Milling Association Ltd v Pamag Pty Ltd*[283] the plaintiffs, flour millers in Queensland, sought to enforce a restraint clause against the defendants who carried on a bakery business in that State. As part of a loan agreement for $4500, the defendants agreed, for a maximum period of seven years, to purchase 'all flour wheatmeal or other commodities' which they might require for their bakery business, so long as the plaintiffs were 'ready to supply the same at fair and reasonable prices'. In breach of this covenant the defendants purported to grant the right of exclusive supply to another supplier. The High Court held that the restraint was valid, and restrained the defendants from purchasing their flour in breach of the covenant given to the plaintiffs.

In justification of this decision it was pointed out that the parties had bargained at arm's length, and that the covenant was simply part of the price of financial assistance. The covenant was reasonable because the obligation to charge a fair and reasonable price protected the defendants, and helped to overcome the matter most likely to prejudice them, namely, the supply of inferior grades of flour and other materials. There was no restriction on sales by the defendants of their products, and no requirement that they purchase a minimum quantity of raw materials. Moreover, the plaintiffs were major grain producers and the prospect of them refusing to supply was remote. Judged at the time when the agreement was reached, it could not be said that a period of seven years was excessive. The defendants had in fact expressed a willingness to agree to a much longer restraint, and the commercial interest of the plaintiffs, in selling as large a quantity of their goods as possible, was legitimately protected by the covenant.

The basic principles governing the restraint of trade doctrine were restated in two important cases in the context of exclusive dealing ('solus') arrangements between garage proprietors and petrol companies. Under these arrangements, proprietors of petrol filling stations agree to take their supplies exclusively from one supplier. In the first case, *Esso Petroleum Co Ltd v Harper's Garage (Stourport) Ltd*,[284] two contracts were in issue: one related to the Corner Garage and was for a period of 21 years; the other, which related to the Mustow Green Garage, was for a period of four years and five months. Both garages were owned by the defendants, who undertook to purchase their 'total requirements of motor fuels' from Esso. The period of the first restraint depended on the repayment of a loan from the plaintiffs, and the period of the second was fixed by reference to the unexpired period of an earlier agreement. The defendants had also promised to grant security to the plaintiffs for a loan of £7000 by giving a

---

281. See, eg *English Hop Growers Ltd v Dering* [1928] 2 KB 174, especially at 180, 192.
282. See, eg *North Western Salt Co Ltd v Electrolytic Alkali Co Ltd* [1914] AC 461, especially at 471.
283. (1973) 133 CLR 260.
284. [1968] AC 269.

mortgage over the Corner Garage. The mortgage was subsequently granted and the mortgage deed also contained an exclusive dealing covenant by the defendants as mortgagors. The plaintiffs had agreed to lend the £7000 and to supply all the defendants' motor fuel requirements at the plaintiffs' wholesale schedule price. Subsequently, the defendants found that they could purchase their petrol requirements elsewhere at a lower price and they ceased to sell Esso petrol. Accordingly, the plaintiffs sought injunctions to restrain the defendants from buying petrol other than from the plaintiffs.

The House of Lords held that both agreements were in restraint of trade but that the shorter restraint, in respect of the Mustow Green Garage, had been shown to be reasonable. Apart from the loan, the benefits to the defendants consisted mainly in the ability to purchase Esso petrol at the discounted wholesale price; and the main benefits for the plaintiffs were economies in distribution costs and a degree of certainty in purchases. A tie of less than five years did not afford more than adequate protection[285] whereas a tie of 21 years went far beyond what was commercially necessary. Leaving aside the loan, the defendants obtained no greater advantage than they would have obtained from agreeing to a five-year tie.

The second case is *Amoco Australia Pty Ltd v Rocca Bros Motor Engineering Co Pty Ltd*,[286] where the High Court followed the *Esso* case. The facts were complicated but, essentially, were as follows. Rocca owned land in Para Hills, South Australia. On 19 June 1964 an agreement was reached with Amoco under which, with the assistance of Amoco, Rocca was to develop the land and erect a service station. It was also agreed that a lease of the premises would be granted to Amoco for a period of 15 years, and that Amoco would then grant Rocca an underlease for a term of 15 years less one day. The lease and underlease were executed in May 1966, but commenced on 30 November 1964. The underlease obliged Rocca to purchase stated minimum quantities of petrol and motor oil from Amoco each month. In addition, Rocca covenanted to purchase exclusively from Amoco all the petroleum products required for sale on the premises, and not to buy petroleum products from anyone else, provided that Amoco was able to supply such products. The underlease precluded Rocca from ceasing to carry on business without the consent of Amoco. In 1971 Rocca wished to renegotiate the arrangements and, when Amoco refused, began negotiations with another oil company. Subsequently, Rocca began to replace the Amoco equipment with that of another oil company and Amoco then commenced proceedings for an injunction to restrain breaches of the underlease.

A majority of the High Court held the 15-year restraint to be too long and unreasonable. Moreover, the terms of the underlease were quite stringent from Rocca's point of view. In particular, Rocca was bound to purchase the minimum quantities of petrol and oil regardless of the state of

---

285. But there was no undertaking by the plaintiffs to supply at a reasonable price and they retained a discretion to withhold supplies if, for example, there was insufficient petrol to supply all their outlets.
286. (1973) 133 CLR 288.

trade and the market conditions.[287] The restraint covenants in the underlease were therefore held to be unenforceable.[288]

[1653] Exclusive service contracts. An exclusive service contract obliges a person to provide a service exclusively to the other party to the contract. Many such contracts are not considered to be in restraint of trade. For example, an executive employee's undertaking to serve only one employer may merely be an incident of the contract, necessary to ensure that the employer gets the full benefit of the employee's services. But the agreement may go too far. Thus, in *A Schroeder Music Publishing Co Ltd v Macaulay*[289] the defendants, music publishers, engaged the exclusive services of the plaintiff for a period of at least five years, and possibly 10, under an agreement which contained provisions capable of operating unfairly against the plaintiff. By virtue of the contract the plaintiff assigned to the defendants the full copyright for the whole world in each and every composition written by the plaintiff either alone or in collaboration with any other person. In the event of royalties being received, 50 per cent was to go to the defendants. A clause in the contract gave the defendants the right to terminate the agreement on giving one month's notice. Although the plaintiff could not assign his rights under the contract without the defendants' consent, the defendants had an unfettered right of assignment. The House of Lords had little difficulty in holding that the contract was in restraint of trade, and that it could not be justified:

- there was no obligation on the defendants to publish the plaintiff's works — the plaintiff could not even recover the copyright in a work which the defendants refused to publish;
- the agreement was unreasonably long in its duration; and
- the bargain was an unfair one from the plaintiff's point of view, the defendants having used their superior bargaining position to obtain an unconscionable contract.

Impact of the Trade Practices Act 1974 (Cth)

[1654] Introduction. The *Trade Practices Act* 1974 (Cth) prohibits 'Restrictive Trade Practices' (Pt IV) and 'Unfair Practices' (Div 1 of Pt V). Most of the prohibitions are against the various defined forms of conduct 'in trade or commerce' by 'corporations'.[290] Wide as the operation of the Act may be, it does not apply as generally as the common law restraint of trade doctrine.[291]

Whether a contract is unenforceable by reason of a contravention of a particular provision of the Act may be a difficult question. Defences of illegality based on alleged contraventions of provisions of Pt IV have been entertained in several cases.[292] State courts have jurisdiction to entertain

---

287. Cf *Shell UK Ltd v Lostock Garage Ltd* [1977] 1 All ER 481.
288. See further [1733].
289. [1974] 1 WLR 1308.
290. Defined in s 4(1). The Act is also given an operation against non-corporate entities, such as natural persons, when any one of several other specified constitutional bases of legislative power is present: s 6.
291. For the impact of the *Restraints of Trade Act* 1976 (NSW) see [1738]–[1739].

such defences: a defence of illegality is not a matter arising under the Act in respect of a civil proceeding instituted under Pt VI of the Act, jurisdiction to hear and determine which is vested by s 86(1) in the Federal Court of Australia.[293] State courts have jurisdiction in relation to matters arising under Pt V.[294]

[1655] Contrast with common law. There are also differences between the common law doctrine and the substantive aspects of the practices outlawed by Pt IV of the Act.

First, s 51 excepts from Pt IV (among other things) three classes of restraint which had dominated the cases on the common law doctrine:[295]

- restraints on employees as to their post-employment work;
- restraints on partners; and
- provisions in contracts for the sale of a business or shares in a company carrying on a business, protecting the purchaser in respect of the goodwill of the business.

Second, the requirements in s 45, that a contract, arrangement or understanding should contain an exclusionary provision,[296] or a provision having the purpose or effect of substantially lessening competition, have no counterpart in the common law doctrine.

Third, it was explained earlier[297] that although a reasonable restraint is unenforceable against a party who has chosen not to observe it, voluntary observance is lawful notwithstanding any conflict with the public interest involved. At common law restraints are unenforceable but not illegal.[298] Although the common law doctrine is expressed in terms of both inter-party and public interests, once a restraint is held to give no more than reasonable protection as between the parties, independent questions of 'the public interest' rarely arise.[299] The public interest is not conceived of as entitling the courts to legislate for society's economic welfare.[300] But the scheme of the *Trade Practices Act* 1974 (Cth) is radically different. On the basis of the legislature's concept of the public interest, the Act, within its field of operation, prohibits certain practices and provides for enforcement remedies of various kinds by the Australian Competition and Consumer Commission and by private persons, including persons who were not subject to any restraint of trade.

---

292. *Hollywood Premiere Sales Pty Ltd v Faberge Australia (Pty) Ltd* (1976) 11 ALR 18; *W R Carpenter Finance Corp Ltd v Moloney* (1979) 6 TPC 17; *Westco Motors Distributors Pty Ltd v Palmer* [1979] 2 NSWLR 93; *Bestoys Pty Ltd v George Wills & Co Ltd* (1981) 36 ALR 366.
293. See *Bestoys Pty Ltd v George Wills & Co Ltd* (1981) 36 ALR 366; *Stack v Coast Securities (No 9) Pty Ltd* (1983) 154 CLR 261; 49 ALR 193; *Carlton and United Breweries Ltd v Castlemaine Tooheys Ltd* (1986) 161 CLR 543; 66 ALR 347.
294. See s 86(2). Note also s 86A, providing for the transfer of certain matters to State or Territory courts.
295. See also s 4M (preservation of common law restraint of trade).
296. Defined in s 4D.
297. See [1636].
298. See [1636].
299. Cf [1640].
300. And the onus of establishing that a restraint is contrary to the public interest rests on the party asserting this. See [1639].

[1656] **Contraventions and remedies.** It is convenient to consider the provisions of Pt IV and Pt V separately. The position is straightforward in the case of sections in Pt IV which declare particular contractual provisions 'unenforceable'[301] or prohibit the making of 'contracts' falling within a particular description.[302] But it is more complex where, for example, a particular contract merely happens to constitute, in whole or in part, a 'practice' defined otherwise, such as 'the practice of exclusive dealing'.[303] Most of Pt IV's prohibitions are of this class[304] and so are not aimed at the making of contracts as such.

Section 76 provides for payment of a pecuniary penalty to the Commonwealth by a person in contravention of a Pt IV prohibition, and also by other persons, such as aiders and abettors and persons who have been in any way, directly or indirectly, knowingly concerned in, or party to, a contravention. Section 78 provides that criminal proceedings do not lie against those liable to pay the pecuniary penalties. It can reasonably be argued that ss 87(1) and (2)(a) of the Act, which empower the court to declare contracts void ab initio, indicate a legislative intention that contracts which constitute contraventions of Pt IV provisions should not, generally, be illegal or void.[305]

Division 1 of Pt V contains many prohibitions of 'unfair practices'. The conduct prohibited may, in a particular case, be conduct which affects a contract; for example, a pre-contract misrepresentation,[306] or 'physical force or undue harassment or coercion' in connection with the supply of goods or services to a consumer.[307] With one exception, contravention of any of the Div 1 provisions is punishable under s 79 by a fine. Contravention of these provisions may well imply that any resulting contract is illegal. But it is not an offence to contravene the prohibition stated in s 52,[308] and contravention of that provision does not of itself make a contract illegal or void.[309]

Generally, contravening conduct will not consist in the making of a contract. But special mention may be made of the provisions in Pt V, Div 1A. For example, ss 65C and 65D prohibit the supply of consumer goods in respect of which there is a prescribed consumer product safety standard or a prescribed consumer product information standard respectively, unless the standard is complied with.[310] If performance of a contract to supply goods would inevitably constitute a contravention of

---

301. See ss 45(1), 45B(1).
302. See, eg ss 45(2), 45E(1).
303. Section 47.
304. See, eg ss 46, 47, 48, 50.
305. Further difficult questions would arise as to the legality of a contract which did not itself constitute a contravention of a prohibition in Pt IV, but which constituted one of the classes of conduct described in s 76 as giving rise to the same liability, ie to a pecuniary penalty under that section.
306. See, eg ss 52, 53, 53A.
307. Section 60. Section 53A(2) prohibits the same kind of conduct in relation to land transactions. See [1330] for corresponding State provisions.
308. For corresponding State provisions see [1103].
309. *S H Lock (Australia) Ltd v Kennedy* (1988) 12 NSWLR 482 at 494; *Bank of America Australia Ltd v Ceda Jon International Pty Ltd* (1988) 17 NSWLR 290.

such a section, the contract would not be enforced and may be illegal or void.

By reference to similar reasoning, provisions in Pt V, Div 1 might also render particular contracts illegal. An example would be the prohibition against referral selling contained in s 57.[311]

---

310. Section 65C also extends to goods in respect of which there is a notice declaring the goods unsafe or banning the goods. And see **NSW:** *Fair Trading Act* 1987, s 27, 29; **NT**: *Consumer Affairs and Fair Trading Act* 1990, ss 26, 31; **WA:** *Fair Trading Act* 1987, ss 51, 52, 60.
311. See also **ACT:** *Fair Trading Act* 1992, s 23; **NSW:** *Fair Trading Act* 1987, s 52; **NT:** *Consumer Affairs and Fair Trading Act* 1990, 53; **Qld:** *Fair Trading Act* 1989, s 47; **SA:** *Fair Trading Act* 1987, s 66; **Vic:** *Fair Trading Act* 1999, s 18; **WA:** *Fair Trading Act* 1987, s 20.

Chapter 17

The Effects of Illegality

Introduction 1701
Actions Dependent on Illegality for Success 1705
Relevance of Fault. 1710
   Action by a Party Not in Pari Delicto. 1711
   Performance and Repentance. 1715
   Equitable Relief. 1719
   Statute 1720
Independent Causes of Action. 1721
   The Bowmakers *Principle* 1721
   Cause of Action Based on Statute or Collateral Contract 1725
   Restitution 1727
Severance 1729
   General. 1729
   Severance at Common Law 1732
   Severance Under Statute 1738

Introduction

[1701] Effect on what? It might well be argued that the effects of illegality have already been dealt with, because in Chapter 16 we considered the ways in which statutes and rules of public policy affect contracts. On more than one occasion, for example, it was said that a particular contract was 'void' on the ground that public policy had been contravened.[1] Thus, to the extent that the effects of illegality include the status of an agreement as an illegal or void contract, 'effects' *on the contract* have been dealt with.[2]

There is, however, a second dimension to the problem of the effects of illegality, namely, its effect on causes of action, rights and remedies. In essence, the primary question is: 'To what extent (and in respect of what) is one party to an illegal contract entitled to sue the other?'

1. See, eg [1626]. See further [1702].
2. It has, moreover, been said that one way of determining whether a contract is contrary to public policy is by examining the impact of enforcement of the contract by the court. See, eg *A v Hayden* (1984) 156 CLR 532 at 557; 56 ALR 82.

A third issue to be dealt with is the effect of illegality on contract performance, that is, the impact of illegality in relation to the consequences which would otherwise flow from performance of the contract. The fact that performance of the contract has taken place may be indicative of the existence of, say, property rights in the subject matter of the contract which are enforceable independently of the contract. For example, delivery of goods under an illegal sale of goods contract may be effective to transfer title in the goods to the buyer.

In dealing with the effects of illegality it may be necessary to draw on all three aspects of the problem. Consider, then, the following statement by Devlin LJ in *Archbolds (Freightage) Ltd v S Spanglett Ltd*:[3]

> The effect of illegality upon a contract may be threefold. If at the time of making the contract there is an intent to perform it in an unlawful way, the contract, although it remains alive, is unenforceable at the suit of the party having that intent; if the intent is held in common, it is not enforceable at all. Another effect of illegality is to prevent a plaintiff from recovering under a contract if in order to prove his rights under it he has to rely upon his own illegal act; he may not do that even though he can show that at the time of making the contract he had no intent to break the law and that at the time of performance he did not know that what he was doing was illegal. The third effect of illegality is to avoid the contract ab initio and that arises if the making of the contract is expressly or impliedly prohibited by statute or is otherwise contrary to public policy.

In Devlin LJ's analysis the first two issues described above are, to some extent, bound together; but his statement clearly indicates that the effects of illegality do not depend solely on an ability to label the contract as 'illegal'. If the contract is void and/or illegal this will preclude any action on the contract. However, we must also take into account the intention of the plaintiff and the means by which the plaintiff establishes a cause of action. Devlin LJ's statement is important in another respect. It is an acknowledgment that the effects of illegality where the contract is expressly or impliedly prohibited by statute may differ from those which attach in other cases. This contrast reflects a distinction which has, unfortunately, been blurred in recent cases.

The contrast is between, on the one hand, cases where (whether or not the contract is illegal), public policy may operate to deny a plaintiff's entitlement to bring a contractual claim and, on the other hand, cases where the contract is expressly or impliedly prohibited.[4] In other words, we must distinguish cases where illegality is present, for example, because the plaintiff has committed a statutory offence public policy may require the court to refuse to assist the plaintiff, from cases where, because *the contract* is prohibited no contractual claim arise. The significance of the contract being prohibited (particularly by statute) is shown by the traditional refusal of the courts to deny other non-contractual claims as well, subject only to certain narrow exceptions.

[1702] **Terminology.** There is no shortage of confusing terminology in the area of illegality. Descriptions such as 'void', 'void and illegal',

---

3. [1961] 1 QB 374 at 388.
4. See further [1705].

'unenforceable' and so on pervade the cases. There is frequently disagreement as to whether a rule of public policy should be seen as rendering a contract 'void', 'void and illegal' or merely 'unenforceable'. For example, a contract in restraint of trade was said by Lord Denning MR in *Shell UK Ltd v Lostock Garage Ltd*[5] to be merely unenforceable, whereas the Australian cases[6] usually express the view that the contract is 'void'.

The High Court found a similar type of disagreement in the context of contracts prejudicial to the administration of justice in *A v Hayden*.[7] This prompted Mason J to say:[8]

> The true position, as I see it, is that some contracts are void whereas others are valid, though the court will decline to enforce the particular provision in a valid contract in particular circumstances where enforcement of that provision would have an adverse effect on the administration of justice. Thus, a simple agreement not to disclose the existence of a serious criminal offence, which has been, or is about to be, committed in consideration of the payment of a sum of money may well be void because it is illegal. However, it will be otherwise with a contract which is in all respects lawful but nevertheless contains a provision which, if enforced according to its terms, will result in an interference with the administration of justice. Take a contract which contains a minor or subsidiary provision which, though not directed to non-disclosure of criminal offences, imposes an obligation of confidentiality in sweeping terms. If those terms are not susceptible of being read down, the court will refuse to lend its aid to the enforcement of the provision if enforcement would result in the non-disclosure of a criminal offence adversely affecting the administration of justice. In such a case the contract is not void; nor is it unenforceable in the sense in which that term is customarily used in the law of contracts. The case is one in which the court refuses a remedy on the ground of public policy.

He referred to *Beresford v Royal Insurance Co*[9] as an example of a case in which the court refused a remedy on the ground of public policy (although the contract was not void) because a term of it was contrary to public policy. In that case a term in an insurance contract created an obligation to pay money on the death of the insured, except by suicide occurring within one year from the commencement of the assurance. The insured committed suicide outside the one-year period but the House of Lords refused to enforce the policy, even though on its proper construction it imposed an obligation to pay, because enforcement of the term would have been contrary to public policy.[10]

The fact that a particular (specific) description has been chosen gives the impression that the description has a predictive value. In fact, the precise

---

5. [1977] 1 All ER 481 at 489. He cited *Esso Petroleum Co Ltd v Harper's Garage (Stourport) Ltd* [1968] AC 269 at 297, 304, 321, 324, 333 in support. See also *Stenhouse Australia Ltd v Phillips* [1974] AC 391 at 403.
6. See, eg *McFarlane v Daniell* (1938) 38 SR (NSW) 337 at 349. But see *Buckley v Tutty* (1971) 125 CLR 353 at 379–80 where the point was left open by the High Court.
7. (1984) 156 CLR 532.
8. (1984) 156 CLR 532 at 557.
9. [1938] AC 586. Cf *Davitt v Titcumb* [1989] 3 All ER 417.
10. Query whether the decriminalisation of suicide implies that the decision would be different today. See *Kirkham v Chief Constable of the Greater Manchester Police* [1990] 2 QB 283.

meaning of a word such as 'void' depends, as always, on the intention of the user. As Windeyer J said in his dissenting judgment in *Brooks v Burns Philp Trustee Co Ltd*:[11]

> The words used do not matter if the actual legal result they are used to express be not in doubt or debate. But it has always seemed to me likely to lead to error, in matters such as this, to adopt first one of the familiar legal adjectives — 'illegal', 'void', 'unenforceable', 'ineffectual', 'nugatory' — and then having given an act a label to deduce from that its results in law. That is to invert the order of inquiry, and by so doing to beg the question, and allow linguistics to determine legal rights.

The approach which Windeyer J criticises has undoubtedly been used in many of the cases, and may explain some of the inconsistencies and difficulties in the law. For example, the cases give conflicting guidance on whether an illegal contract is effective to transfer proprietary rights and this is, perhaps, due to indiscriminate use of words such as 'void' to describe the contract.[12] However, the recent cases[13] emphasise that, in the final analysis, it is whether the court will assist the plaintiff that matters, not whether the description of the contract, as void, unenforceable or illegal, is accurate.

[1703] Policy considerations. Policy considerations have an important role to play even after it has been decided that the contract is illegal. For example, if A has transferred land to B pursuant to a contract prohibited by statute, whether B should be entitled to keep the land without paying for it is an issue of policy, and is not to be determined simply by saying that the contract was illegal but nevertheless effective to pass title.[14] Whether public policy is better served by allowing A to recover the land, or by allowing B to retain it without paying for it, remains an important question.[15]

Conversely, a contract which is otherwise valid should not be enforced if that would be contrary to public policy or statute. It might be objected that placing emphasis on policy considerations when deciding whether rights should be enforced places the courts in the position of meting out penalties for illegal acts. The fact that the plaintiff has already incurred a criminal penalty, by, for example, contravening statute, may influence the decision on whether to grant the civil relief claimed. A refusal by the court to assist the plaintiff may be a greater penalty than that imposed by the statute. This may influence the court, in cases where the illegality is not of a particularly heinous nature, to reach a decision in the plaintiff's favour on the basis that the statutory penalty is sufficient. This is a valid approach.[16] However, it should not be taken so far that it encourages the commission of illegal acts. Thus, it would frequently be wrong for the court to endeavour to achieve any substantial *restitutio in integrum*,[17] because this might encourage illegality, or involve further illegal acts.

---

11. (1969) 121 CLR 432 at 458. Cf *A v Hayden* (1984) 156 CLR 532 at 596.
12. See, eg [1721].
13. See *Nelson v Nelson* (1995) 184 CLR 538; 132 ALR 133; *Fitzgerald v F J Leonhardt Pty Ltd* (1997) 189 CLR 215; 143 ALR 569.
14. Cf *Andrews v Parker* [1973] Qd R 93 (see [1712]).
15. See further [1721].

Because it is impossible for a court to enforce a contract which is prohibited by statute, one way to bring policy to bear on the effects of illegality is to have regard to the likely consequences of illegality when deciding whether the contract is prohibited by statute or is contrary to public policy.[18] For example, in *Vita Food Products Inc v Unus Shipping Co Ltd*[19] in the context of statutory illegality, Lord Wright, in delivering the advice of the Privy Council, said that 'the rule by which contracts not expressly forbidden by statute or declared to be void' are found to be prohibited is a 'rule of public policy only, and public policy understood in a wider sense may at times be better served by refusing to nullify a bargain save on serious and sufficient grounds'. Therefore, given the severe consequences of prohibition,[20] it may be more consonant with public policy to hold that the contract is not prohibited.[21]

[1704] Relevant considerations. A number of considerations are relevant to the effects of illegality, or may be relevant depending on the circumstances of the case. First, what is the source of the illegality? As has been explained, the contract may have been prohibited by statute,[22] or have infringed a rule of public policy.[23]

Second, if a public policy rule has been infringed, does the rule make the contract illegal, as in a case where the contract is to stifle a prosecution,[24] or is there merely an element of unenforceability or 'voidness', as in the case of a covenant in restraint of trade?[25]

Third, did the plaintiff (or defendant) in the action know of the illegality? The court is less likely to assist a party who has such knowledge than a party who is 'innocent' in the matter.[26] Their relative positions may be important: are the parties equally implicated in the illegality or is one more guilty than the other? Generally speaking, the court will not assist either party where they are equally in the wrong (in pari delicto) but a party who is not equally implicated is more likely to be successful when attempting to enforce a right or remedy.[27]

16. The broader suggestion made in some English cases (see *Thackwell v Barclays Bank Plc* [1986] 1 All ER 676; *Saunders v Edwards* [1987] 1 WLR 1116; *Euro-Diam Ltd v Bathurst* [1990] 1 QB 1 at 35; *Howard v Shirlstar Container Transport Ltd* [1990] 1 WLR 1292) that a 'conscience test' should be applied, to permit relief unless success by the plaintiff would be an affront to the public conscience, was disapproved in *Tinsley v Milligan* [1994] 1 AC 340. Although that case was itself disapproved by the High Court in *Nelson v Nelson* (1995) 184 CLR 538 at 593, 605–8, 612, the conscience test has not (at least in the terms expressed in the English cases) been adopted in Australia. See generally Andrew Phang, 'Of Illegality and Presumptions — Australian Departures and Possible Approaches' (1996) 11 *JCL* 53.
17. For the meaning of this expression see [1045], [1982]. See further [1720], [1727].
18. See also [1619].
19. [1939] AC 277 at 293. See also *Farrow Mortgage Services Pty Ltd v Edgar* (1993) 114 ALR 1 at 10–11.
20. See, eg [1706].
21. Such an approach would have helped to avoid the problems to which *Hurst v Vestcorp Ltd* (1988) 12 NSWLR 394 has given rise. See further [1727].
22. See generally [1607]–[1615].
23. See generally [1619]–[1653].
24. See [1628].
25. See generally [1634]–[1653].
26. See, eg [1711].

Fourth, has the illegal purpose of the contract been carried into effect? Again a court is more likely to assist a plaintiff (or defendant) where the illegality has not been carried out.[28] This may involve a consideration of whether the plaintiff (or defendant) repented, and sought to avoid the contract, before or after any illegal purpose was carried out.[29]

Fifth, and perhaps most importantly, is the plaintiff (or defendant) seeking to enforce the contract or relying on some independent cause of action? It is rare for a party to be able to enforce the contract, but sometimes possible for an independent cause of action (for example, in tort) to be successful.[30]

Sixth, is the illegal portion of the contract severable from the remainder? If severance is possible the illegal part of the contract can be ignored.[31]

Finally, there is the overriding consideration of public policy itself.[32]

Actions Dependent on Illegality for Success

[1705] The ex turpi maxim. The basic maxim of the common law is *ex turpi causa non oritur actio*, that is, *no cause of action arises out of illegality*. Lord Mansfield said in *Holman v Johnson*:[33]

> The principle of public policy is this; *ex dolo malo non oritur actio*. No court will lend its aid to a man who founds his cause of action upon an immoral or an illegal act. If, from the plaintiff's own stating or otherwise, the cause of action appears to arise ex turpi causa, or the transgression of a positive law of this country, there the court says he has no right to be assisted. It is upon that ground the court goes; not for the sake of the defendant, but because they will not lend their aid to such a plaintiff.

Strictly speaking, this maxim is, at least in Australia, limited to causes of action which depend for their enforcement on an illegal contract.[34] However, the maxim can be seen as stating one aspect of a broader principle of public policy[35] under which the plaintiff, as the person invoking the aid of the court, may be refused relief if reliance is placed on an illegal act to establish the cause of action. This is true even if the defendant has not specifically pleaded illegality.[36] As explained by Lord Mansfield, the maxim is applied not for the benefit of the defendant, but to protect the public by refusing to allow the machinery of the courts to be used to assist the commission (or furtherance) of illegal acts, which might be achieved by the enforcement of rights arising from illegal acts.[37] Assuming that the

---

27. See [1711]–[1720].
28. See [1715]–[1716].
29. See, eg [1718].
30. See generally [1721]–[1728].
31. See generally [1729]–[1739].
32. See [1703].
33. (1775) 1 Cowp 341 at 343; 98 ER 1120 at 1121.
34. See *Smith v Jenkins* (1970) 119 CLR 397 at 410ff; *Gollan v Nugent* (1988) 166 CLR 18; 82 ALR 193. Contrast *Hardy v Motor Insurers' Bureau* [1964] 2 QB 745 at 767.
35. Cf *Pitts v Hunt* [1991] 1 QB 24.
36. *Scott v Brown Doering McNab & Co* [1892] 2 QB 724 at 728, 732; *Noble v Maddison* (1912) 12 SR (NSW) 435 at 436; *Knowles v Fuller* (1947) 48 SR (NSW) 243 at 245.

contract is not illegal, or contrary to public policy, the fact that the plaintiff has committed an unlawful act is not conclusive. The court must inquire whether the public interest dictates a conclusion adverse to the plaintiff. The nature of the unlawful act, the degree of knowledge and the likelihood that enforcement of the contract would encourage the repetition of the act are factors to be considered.[38]

To this extent, the application of the ex turpi maxim does not depend on whether the illegality in question rendered the contract void.[39] Thus, a plaintiff who has committed some illegal act when performing the contract may find that relief is refused even though the contract is not void. In such a case, because the contract is not illegal it may be enforceable by the other party. Care must, however, be taken not to extend the maxim too far. For example, in *Hardy v Motor Insurers' Bureau*[40] the English Court of Appeal allowed the plaintiff to recover compensation from the defendants in respect of serious personal injuries suffered when he was injured by a van bearing a stolen road fund licence. Although s 203(3)(a) of the *Road Traffic Act* 1960 (UK) required a policy of insurance covering liability in respect of the death or bodily injury to any person caused by or arising out of the use of a vehicle on the road to be taken out by the driver of a vehicle, the driver of the van was not insured. An agreement between the Minister of Transport and the Motor Insurers' Bureau provided for the payment to an injured person in respect of the liability of an uninsured driver. The plaintiff relied on this agreement as the basis for his claim.[41] The court held that although the ex turpi maxim would have applied to prevent the driver recovering an indemnity if he had paid damages to the plaintiff, the fact that the driver was guilty of criminal offences was not a bar to the claim by the plaintiff against the defendants because he himself committed no antisocial act, and because it was not contrary to public policy for his claim to be enforced.

[1706] No action for damages or debt. A plaintiff is not entitled to recover contract damages or a contract debt if the cause of action depends on an illegal contract. For example, an employee cannot recover wages earned in performing an illegal employment contract.[42] Similarly, a creditor will fail to recover money lent if the money was lent pursuant to an illegal contract.[43] But the mere fact that the plaintiff is able to frame the claim on

---

37. See, eg *Chai Sau Yin v Liew Kwee Sam* [1962] AC 304 at 311.
38. See, eg *Fire and All Risks Insurance Co Ltd v Powell* [1966] VR 513 and generally on the effect of criminality on contractual remedies, John Shand, 'Unblinkering the Unruly Horse: Public Policy in the Law of Contract' [1972A] *CLJ* 144.
39. See, eg *T P Rich Investments Pty Ltd v Calderon* [1964] NSWR 709 at 716; *North v Marra Developments Ltd* (1981) 148 CLR 42 at 60; 37 ALR 341.
40. [1964] 2 QB 745.
41. No point of privity of contract (see generally Chapter 9) was taken by the Motor Insurers' Bureau, and to do so would have been contrary to its agreement with the Ministry of Transport.
42. See, eg *Wild v Simpson* [1912] 2 KB 544. Cf *North v Marra Developments Ltd* (1981) 148 CLR 42; 37 ALR 341.
43. See, eg *Dressy Frocks Pty Ltd v Bock* (1951) 51 SR (NSW) 390.

some other basis, such as in tort,[44] makes no difference if the plaintiff is forced to rely on the illegal contract in order to make out the claim.

For example, in *Nicholls v Stanton*[45] an action for damages for deceit in respect of a fraudulent misrepresentation made by the defendant which induced the plaintiff to purchase a motor car was unsuccessful because the contract itself was illegal by statute. The court held that in order to prove that damage had been suffered, that is, in order to establish his cause of action, the plaintiff had to prove and rely on the contract. Again, in *Thomas Brown & Sons Ltd v Fazal Deen*[46] an action was brought to recover damages for the defendants' failure to return a quantity of gold which the plaintiff had deposited with the defendants. This bailment contract contravened the *National Security (Exchange Control) Regulations* (Cth) and was held to be illegal. As it was necessary for the plaintiff to rely on the bailment contract in order to recover damages, the High Court held that the action could not be maintained.

However, the ex turpi maxim will not apply if the contract is not illegal and there is no reliance on any illegal act. Thus, in *Fitzgerald v F J Leonhardt Pty Ltd*[47] the plaintiff in no way relied on illegality to establish a cause of action in contract for a debt arising from the performance of a drilling contract in the course of which the defendant committed a statutory offence.

[1707] No recovery of money paid or property transferred. The ex turpi rule has also been applied to actions for restitution, to recover money paid or property transferred, at least where the claim depends, as a matter of substance, on proof of an illegality. Thus, in *Kearley v Thomson*[48] the plaintiff paid £40 to the defendants, a firm of solicitors, who undertook not to appear at the public examination of a bankrupt. The court held that the contract was illegal as it had a tendency to pervert the course of justice. The defendants, although not obliged to appear, were subject to a duty not to contract out of the opportunity of appearing. The plaintiff failed in his action to recover the money because, in order to enforce his claim, he relied on the illegality. The court expressed[49] the 'general rule' as being that the 'plaintiff cannot get at the money which he seeks to recover' when forced to prove the illegal contract. The rule also applies, indeed the position is a fortiori, where the contract is prohibited by statute.[50]

So far as the recovery of property is concerned, *M'Cahill v Henty*[51] provides an illustration of a case where the court clearly proceeded on the view that no order for reconveyance of land will be made when the transferee received title pursuant to an illegal contract — in that case an agreement which was illegal under the *Land Act* 1865 (Vic).

---

44. For independent claims in tort see [1721]–[1724]. For restitutionary claims see [1707], [1727]–[1728].
45. (1915) 15 SR (NSW) 337. See also *Bradshaw v Gilbert's (Australasian) Agency (Vic) Pty Ltd* (1952) 86 CLR 209 (see [1613]).
46. (1962) 108 CLR 391 (see further [1723], [1724]).
47. (1997) 189 CLR 215 at 220.
48. (1890) 24 QBD 742.
49. (1890) 24 QBD 742 at 745.
50. See further [1727]–[1728].
51. (1878) 4 VLR (E) 68. See also *Taylor v Chester* (1869) LR 4 QB 309 (see [1724]).

[1708] Other remedies. The equitable remedies of specific performance[52] and injunction[53] are not available where a contract is illegal. It is, for example, impossible for a court to order the specific performance of a contract for the sale of land prohibited by statute and the court would deny any jurisdiction to do so.[54] We have also seen,[55] when examining the restraint of trade cases, that no relief by way of injunction will be given to enforce a restraint clause which is contrary to public policy and void or unenforceable on that ground.

Other equitable remedies, such as rectification[56] or an account of profits,[57] will also be refused in most cases.

[1709] Generally no estoppel. As can be implied from the above, there is generally no estoppel[58] operating to prevent a defendant setting up illegality as a defence to an action framed in reliance on illegality. In *Holman v Johnson*[59] Lord Mansfield said:[60]

> The objection, that a contract is immoral or illegal as between plaintiff and defendant, sounds at all times very ill in the mouth of the defendant. It is not for his sake, however, that the objection is ever allowed; but it is founded in general principles of policy, which the defendant has the advantage of, contrary to the real justice, as between him and the plaintiff, by accident, if I may so say.

For example, the seller in *Re Mahmoud and Ispahani*[61] could not, in an action for damages for breach of contract,[62] rely on the buyer's representation that he possessed the necessary licence as creating an estoppel precluding reliance by the buyer on statutory illegality. In some cases, however, there may be scope for estoppel. For example, in *Psaltis v Schultz*[63] Dixon J acknowledged that the rule of public policy against contracts prejudicial to the status of marriage[64] did not preclude an action for breach of promise if, at the time when the promise was made, the promisee was ignorant of the fact that the promisor was married. One possible explanation of the availability of the action is that the promisor is estopped from setting up illegality as a defence to the action. But the inquiry can be relevant only where there is scope for considering whether the plaintiff was 'at fault'.

---

52. See generally [2401]–[2412].
53. See generally [2413]–[2420].
54. See, eg *Chapman v Wade* [1939] SASR 298 at 302–4.
55. See [1634]–[1653].
56. See, eg *DJE Constructions Pty Ltd v Maddocks* [1982] 1 NSWLR 5; and see generally on rectification [1256]–[1266].
57. See, eg *Noble v Maddison* (1912) 12 SR (NSW) 435.
58. See generally on estoppel [365]–[387], [1974]–[1976].
59. (1775) 1 Cowp 341; 98 ER 1120.
60. (1775) 1 Cowp 341 at 343; 98 ER 1120 at 1121.
61. [1921] 2 KB 716 at 729, 732. See also *Day Ford Pty Ltd v Sciacca* [1990] 2 Qd R 209 at 216.
62. The court did not consider whether any damages would have been available against the buyer for deceit; but see [1713].
63. (1948) 76 CLR 547 at 558.
64. See [1633].

Relevance of Fault

[1710] Introduction. It is sometimes relevant to consider whether either (or both) of the parties to the contract knew of the illegality or possessed a sinister intent when entering into the contract. It is clear, however, that the mere fact of 'innocence' does not necessarily entitle a party to enforce the contract, and a party will not be so entitled where the making of the contract is prohibited in the public interest.[65] If the parties are equally at fault the plaintiff will fail as the court will consider that the condition of the defendant is better. This is the meaning of the maxim *in pari delicto potior est conditio defendentis*. As Lord Mansfield explained in *Holman v Johnson*:[66]

> So if the plaintiff and defendant were to change sides, and the defendant was to bring his action against the plaintiff, the latter would then have the advantage of [the ex turpi maxim]; for where both are equally in fault, *potior est conditio defendentis*.

The traditional approach to the maxim has been to look for circumstances which displace the maxim because they fall within a specific exception to the rule. However, in the recent cases this approach has been questioned, on the basis that relief may be available under the modern law even though the case does not fall within any such category. Thus, in the context of illegality resulting from a failure to comply with statute, McHugh J suggested in *Nelson v Nelson*[67] that:

> courts should not refuse to enforce legal or equitable rights simply because they arose out of or were associated with an unlawful purpose unless: (a) the statute discloses an intention that those rights should be unenforceable in all circumstances; or (b)(i) the sanction of refusing to enforce those rights is not disproportionate to the seriousness of the unlawful conduct; (ii) the imposition of the sanction is necessary, having regard to the terms of the statute, to protect its objects or policies; and (iii) the statute does not disclose an intention that the sanctions and remedies contained in the statute are to be the only legal consequences of a breach of the statute or the frustration of its policies.

With respect, this statement creates many difficulties. First, McHugh J's reference to 'legal or equitable rights' needs some qualification since, if read literally, this might imply that a claim in contract could be brought in respect of a contract prohibited by statute. However, that could not have been his intention[68] that these principles do not apply to cases where the contract is prohibited by statute.

Second, the words 'arose out of or were associated with an unlawful purpose' are both too broad and too narrow. They are too broad in the sense that they beg the question of what 'unlawful purpose' was involved. They are too narrow in the sense that it has never been the law that an 'association' with an 'unlawful purpose' is enough to bar a plaintiff's claim.

---

65. See, eg *Re Mahmoud and Ispahani* [1921] 2 KB 716 (see [1611], [1709]); *Thackwell v Barclays Bank Plc* [1986] 1 All ER 676.
66. (1775) 1 Cowp 341 at 343; 98 ER 1120 at 1121. See also *Smith v Bromley* (1760) 2 Doug 696n at 697; 99 ER 441 at 443.
67. See *Nelson v Nelson* (1995) 184 CLR 538 at 613.
68. (1997) 189 CLR 215 at 229, 249.

Indeed, in some contexts it is clear that an unlawful purpose will not prevent a claim being brought in contract.

Third, the shift from specific exceptions to general principle creates major analytical problems. It is by no means certain that the law is advanced by the approach suggested by McHugh J, which is in terms limited to cases of illegality arising from the operation of statute.

It is therefore still appropriate to consider the categories of case in which the maxim will not apply. These comprise:

- since innocence may arise from matters such as mistake, or the fraud or duress of the defendant, account must be taken of the knowledge of the plaintiff, the conduct of the defendant and the relationship between the parties;[69]
- the fact that the plaintiff has repented of the illegal purpose may need to be considered;[70]
- there is sometimes the possibility of equitable relief; and[71]
- in the case of statutory illegality, there may be an implied right to sue operating for the benefit of persons protected by the statute.[72]

Action by a Party Not in Pari Delicto[73]

[1711] No knowledge of illegality. In some cases the plaintiff has succeeded, notwithstanding an element of illegality in the contract or its performance, because of the absence of knowledge of the illegality. Thus, in *Archbolds (Freightage) Ltd v S Spanglett Ltd*[74] the plaintiffs succeeded in their action for damages in respect of the loss of goods the subject of a contract of carriage even though the defendants had contravened the *Road and Rail Traffic Act* 1933 (UK) by carrying goods for reward without possessing the appropriate licence for carriage. The plaintiffs did not know that the defendants did not have the necessary licence and there was no evidence that they ought to have known. They were therefore not in pari delicto. The position would, however, have been different had the making of the contract been prohibited by statute or had it been ex facie illegal.[75]

[1712] Oppression and duress. The parties are not considered in pari delicto if one has entered into the contract as the result of oppression or duress by the other party.[76] Oppression has, however, rarely been established and the exception has traditionally been treated as a narrow one.[77] A wider view was perhaps taken in *Andrews v Parker*.[78] Stable J did not regard the contract as contrary to public policy by being immoral.[79]

---

69. See [1711]–[1714].
70. See [1715]–[1718].
71. See [1719].
72. See [1720]. Cf [1725].
73. See J K Grodecki, 'In Pari Delicto Potior Est Conditio Defendentis' (1955) 71 *LQR* 254.
74. [1961] 1 QB 374 (see [1613]).
75. See, eg [1610].
76. See, eg *Kearley v Thomson* (1890) 24 QBD 742 at 745–6; *George v Greater Adelaide Land Development Co Ltd* (1929) 43 CLR 91 at 99, 101; *Re Ferguson* (1969) 14 FLR 311 at 316. See generally on duress Chapter 13.

However, he found that the plaintiff entered into the contract in issue as a result of the pressure of a 'strong-willed' and 'ruthless' woman. Therefore, on the assumption that the contract did contravene public policy, the plaintiff was not in pari delicto and was entitled to reconveyance of the property which he had transferred to the defendant.

A plaintiff who can show that the contract was entered into as a result of oppression or duress may be entitled to equitable relief in the form of an order declaring the contract void and cancelling it.[80]

[1713] **Mistake and fraud.** Where money has been paid under a mistake which would have made the contract legal, a plaintiff may be able to rely on an exception to the in pari delicto rule. The plaintiff will not be considered in pari delicto with the defendant if the defendant made a fraudulent misrepresentation as to the legality of the contract. Thus, if the defendant fraudulently concealed the nature of the transaction or the misrepresentation was of a fact which, if it had been true, would have made the contract legal, the plaintiff may succeed.[81] Since the traditional insistence on a mistake of fact rather than law can no longer be maintained, a representation of legality is sufficient.[82]

In *Hatcher v White*[83] the defendant represented to the plaintiff that he held a permit under the *Building Operations and Building Materials Control Act* 1945 (NSW), and thereby induced the plaintiff to do certain construction work pursuant to a contract between the parties. In fact the defendant had no such permit and was guilty of fraud. The plaintiff suffered damage by expending money in doing the work and brought the present action to recover damages. Street CJ stated[84] the 'general principle' as being that a 'claim may be made in fraud by an innocent person' who has entered into a contract as a result of a fraudulent misrepresentation that the 'agreement could lawfully be entered into, if it was not on its face one which was obviously unlawful'. The plaintiff was innocent, and it was only the performance of the contract, not its making, which was illegal. Had the permit existed the contract would have been valid, but the contract was not on its face obviously illegal. Accordingly, a majority of the court held that the plaintiff was entitled to retain the damages which had been awarded in his favour in the District Court. There was no doubt that the plaintiff was unable to sue on the contract: the defendant would not have been estopped from setting up a defence of illegality to such a claim; but the action brought in deceit was independent of the contract and illegality was not

---

77. See, eg *Callaghan v O'Sullivan* [1925] VLR 664 (exception not applicable where contract to stifle prosecution (see [1628]) entered into as a result of oppression). But cf *Clegg v Wilson* (1932) 32 SR (NSW) 109 (see [1718]).
78. [1973] Qd R 93.
79. See [1632].
80. See *Jones v Bouffier* (1911) 12 CLR 579 at 621.
81. See, eg *Nicholls v Stanton* (1915) 15 SR (NSW) 337; *George v Greater Adelaide Land Development Co Ltd* (1929) 43 CLR 91 at 101. Cf *Radford v Ferguson* (1947) 50 WALR 14 (money paid to unregistered builder for building of house held recoverable where he had fraudulently misrepresented that he was registered).
82. See Mason and Carter, *Restitution Law in Australia*, 1995, para 2637.
83. (1953) 53 SR (NSW) 285. See also *Quin v Mutual Acceptance Co Ltd* [1968] 1 NSWR 122.
84. (1953) 53 SR (NSW) 285 at 288–9.

available as a defence to the claim based on the fraudulent misrepresentation.

[1714] **Fiduciary relationship.** The authorities support the existence of another reason for saying that the parties to an illegal contract may not be in pari delicto, namely, the abuse of a fiduciary position by one of the parties.[85] Thus, in *Re Ferguson*[86] Gibbs J explained that a person, such as a director of a company, 'who is under a fiduciary duty to the plaintiff cannot retain moneys which he has received pursuant to an illegal arrangement'; and so a director who has abused a position of confidence cannot keep an illegal payment procured from his or her company.[87]

Performance and Repentance[88]

[1715] **Illegal purpose not carried out.** If the contract is fully performed in a way which involves no illegality, the plaintiff's claim may succeed. An example is *Payne v McDonald*.[89] The plaintiff brought an action for a declaration that the defendant held land as trustee for her because it had been purchased with money which she provided. The defence was that the plaintiff had procured the certificate of title to the land to be issued in the name of Ellen Payne in order to defeat the plaintiff's creditors, and that this unlawful purpose meant that no order should be made against the defendant who was the executor of Ellen Payne's will. In fact, no creditors were defeated or defrauded because the plaintiff never found herself in the position where she could not pay her debts. In deciding in favour of the plaintiff, the High Court emphasised that the existence of an unlawful or sinister intent in the transaction was irrelevant as no part of the intent had been effectuated.

It is a more difficult case where the contract is not performed fully because the plaintiff rescinds the contract and repents of the illegality. If no part of the illegal purpose has been carried out the Australian authorities support the proposition that a plaintiff who has paid money or transferred property to the defendant is entitled on rescission to restitution of the money paid or property transferred,[90] provided the contract is not prohibited by statute.[91]

---

85. See, eg *Harse v Pearl Life Assurance Co* [1904] 1 KB 558 at 563; *George v Greater Adelaide Land Development Co Ltd* (1929) 43 CLR 91 at 101.
86. (1969) 14 FLR 311 at 317. See also *Sykes v Stratton* [1972] 1 NSWLR 145 at 163–4.
87. See also *Abdurahman v Field* (1987) 8 NSWLR 158; *Weston v Beaufils* (1994) 122 ALR 240.
88. See J Beatson, 'Repudiation of Illegal Purpose as a Ground for Restitution' (1975) 91 *LQR* 313; Robert Merkin, 'Restitution by Withdrawal from Executory Illegal Contracts' (1981) 97 *LQR* 420.
89. (1908) 6 CLR 208. Cf *Symes v Hughes* (1870) LR 9 Eq 475. See also *Perpetual Executors and Trustees Association of Australia Ltd v Wright* (1917) 23 CLR 185; *Donaldson v Freeson* (1934) 51 CLR 598.
90. See, eg *Payne v McDonald* (1908) 6 CLR 208 at 212, 213. Suggestions that a different view is perhaps the law in England (see *Martin v Martin* (1959) 110 CLR 297 at 305; *Donaldson v Freeson* (1934) 51 CLR 598 at 617) must now be read in light of *Tribe v Tribe* [1996] Ch 107 (reliance on Australian cases applicable where the unlawful purpose has not been carried into effect).
91. See [1718].

There are, obviously, numerous reasons why an illegal purpose might not have been carried out. The particular reason may be material when considering whether the parties are in pari delicto. For example, if the reason the purpose has not been carried out is the frustration of that illegal purpose by a third party (or the defendant) the courts have been reluctant to allow that to be a basis for saying that the plaintiff was not in pari delicto. Thus, in *Alexander v Rayson*[92] although the plaintiff's efforts to defraud the Westminster City Council were thwarted by the council's discovery of the fraud, the court nevertheless refused to permit the enforcement of the contract by which the plaintiff had sought to perpetrate the fraud.

[1716] Partially executed contracts. To what extent must the contract be executory, when the plaintiff repents, in order to entitle the plaintiff to recover money or property transferred? In *Clegg v Wilson*[93] Long Innes J concluded that a plaintiff is entitled to recover if rescission of the contract has occurred while the illegal purpose is still wholly executory and the defendant has not given legal consideration, even if the contract was itself partially performed. He explained[94] that the court should grant such a plaintiff equitable relief in the form of orders for the 'repayment of money paid, goods delivered, or property transferred to the defendant pursuant to the contract, notwithstanding that there is an element of turpitude in the contract, and that both parties are in pari delicto'.

It is not easy to reconcile Long Innes J's conclusion with the prior authorities. For example, in *George v Greater Adelaide Land Development Co Ltd*[95] Knox CJ treated *Harse v Pearl Life Assurance Co*[96] as deciding that partial execution of the contract is fatal to a claim for money paid where the parties were in pari delicto at the time of payment. Similarly, in *Kearley v Thomson*[97] the English Court of Appeal disapproved a statement made by Mellish LJ in *Taylor v Bowers*[98] similar in effect to that expressed by Long Innes J in *Clegg v Wilson*.

In support of Long Innes J's statement of the law in *Clegg v Wilson* it can be said, first, that if repentance is to be encouraged the payment of money under a contract should not be regarded as necessarily involving the execution of the illegal purpose. Indeed, if it is always to be so regarded it might as well be said that repentance can never be a basis for the recovery of money paid. Second, in *George v Greater Adelaide Land Development Co Ltd* the contract was prohibited by statute, and illegality based on public policy, as was in issue in *Clegg v Wilson*, has usually been treated more generously.[99] Third, in *Kearley v Thomson* the illegal purpose was, it seems, substantially achieved,[100] whereas Mellish LJ (in *Taylor v Bowers*) and Long

---

92. [1936] 1 KB 169 (see [1622]). See also *Bigos v Bousted* [1951] 1 All ER 92; *Euro-Diam Ltd v Bathurst* [1990] 1 QB 1 at 35–6.
93. (1932) 32 SR (NSW) 109 at 125.
94. (1932) 32 SR (NSW) 109 at 125.
95. (1929) 43 CLR 91 at 100, 101.
96. [1904] 1 KB 558.
97. (1890) 24 QBD 742 at 746.
98. (1876) 1 QBD 291 at 300; cf at 295.
99. See *Marks v Jolly* (1938) 38 SR (NSW) 351 at 358, and further [1718].
100. The facts were stated in [1707].

Innes J were describing situations in which the purpose had not been carried into effect.[101]

[1717] Payments made to stakeholders. Even if Long Innes J's statement in *Clegg v Wilson*[102] is wrong as regards payments made to another party to the contract, restitution is available from a third party who has received it as a stakeholder or quasi-stakeholder, provided that the illegal purpose has not otherwise been carried out.[103] This is a claim against a person who has received money under instructions to pay it to one or other of the parties in certain defined circumstances. As Knox CJ said in *George v Greater Adelaide Land Development Co Ltd*,[104] 'where the action is to recover money deposited with a stakeholder to abide the event of an illegal contract the money can be recovered if notice be given to the stakeholder at any time before he has actually paid it over in pursuance of the contract'.

[1718] Scope of the repentance exception. Three further matters touching the repentance exception should be mentioned. First, as can be implied from the discussion in the previous paragraph, repentance is of no relevance if the illegal purpose has been carried out wholly or substantially.[105]

Second, the exception does not apply if the making of the contract is prohibited by statute. For example, repentance would not have assisted the plaintiffs in *George v Greater Adelaide Land Development Co Ltd*.[106] It may be, however, that the basis of this qualification is again the fact that the illegal purpose of the contract is regarded as having been carried out. Thus, in *Marks v Jolly*[107] Jordan CJ said:[108]

> Where, however, the contract is illegal because a statute prohibits the making of the contract, the illegal purpose is regarded as having been effected to some extent by the mere making of the contract; and hence money paid pursuant to such a contract cannot be recovered ... unless it can be established that there is a special right to recover it arising out of some fraud, duress or undue influence which has been practised to induce the payment ...

Finally, there is the issue of whether the motive for repentance is relevant. In *Clegg v Wilson*[109] the plaintiff transferred her interest in certain property to the defendant, pursuant to a contract whereby the defendant promised to see that a criminal charge brought against the plaintiff's son would be withdrawn and the prosecutions discontinued. It was conceded that this

---

101. See *Hermann v Charlesworth* [1905] 2 KB 123 at 134–5; *Bigos v Bousted* [1951] 1 All ER 92 at 97–8.
102. (1932) 32 SR (NSW) 109.
103. See, eg *Hermann v Charlesworth* [1905] 2 KB 123. Cf *Taylor v Bowers* (1876) 1 QBD 291. And see Mason and Carter, *Restitution Law in Australia*, 1995, para 2634.
104. (1929) 43 CLR 91 at 100–1. See also *Clegg v Wilson* (1932) 32 SR (NSW) 109 at 122–4.
105. See, eg *Kearley v Thomson* (1890) 24 QBD 742; *Chettiar v Chettiar* [1962] AC 294.
106. (1929) 43 CLR 91 (see [1707]).
107. (1938) 38 SR (NSW) 351.
108. (1938) 38 SR (NSW) 351 at 358.
109. (1932) 32 SR (NSW) 109.

contract was an illegal attempt to stifle a prosecution.[110] In an action to recover the property transferred, the plaintiff asserted that she had repented of the transaction and that the transfer should be set aside on that basis. The charge in question had in fact been withdrawn, not by reason of the defendant's performance of the contract but, instead, because a number of other charges were brought. In respect of these charges the defendant had expressed a willingness to give evidence against the plaintiff's son. The plaintiff was aware of the contract's illegal element, and Long Innes J found the plaintiff's prompt repentance to have been due to a realisation that, owing to the imminence of other charges, the contract would not achieve the desired result, namely, her son's freedom from imprisonment. Nevertheless, he held that the plaintiff was entitled to the relief claimed. Although it is difficult to accept the view that the court should assist a party who repents on unmeritorious grounds, particularly where (as in *Clegg v Wilson*), the reason for repentance is the realisation that the illegal purpose has been frustrated,[111] in *Tribe v Tribe*[112] Millett LJ (with whom Otton LJ agreed) said that because restitution is not confined to the penitent, voluntary repentance at the appropriate time is sufficient.

Equitable Relief

[1719] Equitable relief to protect public. An exception to the common law rule against the assistance of a party in pari delicto operates where equitable relief in favour of one party to an illegal contract is necessary to secure the protection of the public.

For example, in *Money v Money (No 2)*[113] a memorandum of transfer was executed by a husband with the object of transferring title to land owned by him to his wife. The consideration for this transfer was a promise by the wife, defendant in the action, not to take proceedings for maintenance against her husband, the plaintiff in the action. Alternatively, it was alleged that the consideration was the future separation of the parties. On either basis the agreement was contrary to public policy. Jacobs J found that there had been a partial execution of the contract and that the plaintiff was in pari delicto with the defendant. Therefore, relief in favour of the plaintiff, who sought a declaration that the defendant had no estate or interest in the land, would normally have been denied. However, Jacobs J thought[114] it appropriate to invoke the equitable jurisdiction of the court, 'to order delivery up of instruments such as bonds, negotiable instruments, or deeds upon which a party could sue at [common] law, where there [is] an illegal consideration and such consideration [does] not appear on the face of the document' because the continued existence of the memorandum of transfer was a 'source of possible confusion and fraud'. Moreover, any court which came to deal with an application by the defendant for maintenance would, in Jacobs J's words,[115] 'be fettered in its approach by the illegal transaction

---

110. See [1628].
111. See *Berg v Sadler* [1937] 2 KB 158. Cf *Sykes v Stratton* [1972] 1 NSWLR 145.
112. [1996] Ch 107 at 135; [1995] 3 WLR 913 at 938 (see Graham Virgo, [1996] *CLJ* 23; Peter Creighton, (1997) 60 *MLR* 102).
113. [1966] 1 NSWR 348.
114. [1966] 1 NSWR 348 at 351.

itself'. Since the illegal purpose was not substantially complete, it was appropriate to exercise the jurisdiction to order delivery up and cancellation of the memorandum of transfer, and delivery up of the certificate of title for the land.

Although the equitable exception applied in *Money v Money (No 2)* has traditionally been regarded as a special one, there are indications in *Fitzgerald v F J Leonhardt Pty Ltd*[116] of a more general jurisdiction justifying the imposition of terms where the 'plaintiff seeks equitable relief, whether in aid of a legal or equitable right'.

Statute

[1720] **Statute protective of a class.** A well-accepted basis[117] for the recovery of money or property paid or transferred under a contract applies if:[118]

(1) the contract is contrary to statute (rather than public policy); and

(2) the statute has as its object the protection of a particular class of persons (of which the plaintiff is a member) rather than some other objective.

As Lord Mansfield said in *Browning v Morris*:[119]

> [W]here contracts or transactions are prohibited by positive statutes, for the sake of protecting one set of men from another set of men, the one, from their situation and condition, being liable to be oppressed or imposed upon by the other; there the parties are not in pari delicto; and in furtherance of these statutes, the person injured, after the transaction is finished and completed, may bring his action and defeat the contract.

Thus, the exception will not apply where the statute is for the protection of the public generally, rather than a particular class of the public. For example, in *South Australian Cold Stores Ltd v Electricity Trust of South Australia*[120] electricity was supplied by the trust at prices in excess of those which were the maximum permitted under the *Prices Act* 1948–1951 (SA). South Australian Cold Stores sought restitution of the amount paid in excess of the lawful prices. Napier CJ's judgment in the Supreme Court of South Australia for the trust was upheld by the High Court on the basis that the Act was directed to the regulation of prices generally.

However, it is not necessary to show that a party relying on the exception was in fact oppressed or exploited by the other party to the contract.[121] Nor does the exception depend on the statute expressly making provision for a claim by a member of the class.[122] For example, in *Kiriri Cotton Co Ltd v Dewani*[123] the plaintiff paid a sum of money (a 'premium') to the

---

115. [1966] 1 NSWR 348 at 352.
116. (1997) 189 CLR 215 at 231 per McHugh and Gummow JJ. See also *Nelson v Nelson* (1995) 184 CLR 538 at 562–7, 617.
117. See, eg *Kearley v Thomson* (1890) 24 QBD 742 at 746; *South Australian Cold Stores Ltd v Electricity Trust of South Australia* (1965) 115 CLR 247 at 256, 257–8, 263; *Re Ferguson* (1969) 14 FLR 311 at 316–17.
118. See *Smith v Bromley* (1760) 2 Doug 696n at 697; 99 ER 441 at 443.
119. (1778) 2 Cowp 790 at 792; 98 ER 1364 at 1364.
120. (1965) 115 CLR 247.
121. *Re Cavalier Insurance Co Ltd* [1989] 2 Lloyd's Rep 430.

defendants in order to secure the lease of a flat. This payment contravened the *Rent Restriction Ordinance* 1949 (Uganda) and was therefore illegal. The lease was subsequently executed and the plaintiff became lessee of the flat. The issue before the Privy Council was whether the plaintiff could recover the premium as restitution. Neither party knew that there was any illegality involved in the payment and receipt of the money, and the amount paid was not extortionate. But the payment was nevertheless illegal. The statute conferred no express right of recovery. Nor could it be argued that repentance had taken place since the money had been paid and the lease executed. However, the Board did not consider that the plaintiff was in pari delicto with the defendants. Section 3(2) of the Ordinance provided for the imposition of penalties on the person who 'asks for, solicits or receives' a premium. Thus, the duty of observing the law was placed on the defendants and the statutory penalty was imposed on lessors such as the defendants, for the protection of lessees, such as the plaintiff. Therefore, the fact that there was no express right of recovery did not preclude implication by the Board of a right of restitution based on common law principles.[124]

Independent Causes of Action

The Bowmakers *Principle*[125]

[1721] The decision in the *Bowmakers* case. One of the most controversial and difficult aspects of illegality is the so-called '*Bowmakers* principle', derived from the decision of the English Court of Appeal in *Bowmakers Ltd v Barnet Instruments Ltd*.[126] The plaintiffs sued to recover damages for the conversion[127] of certain machine tools which were the subject of three contracts of hire-purchase, the plaintiffs having purchased the goods from one Smith and hired them to the defendants under three hire-purchase agreements. The acts amounting to conversion were alleged to have occurred prior to the payment of the money due under the agreements. The defence of illegality arose from the fact that Orders made by the Ministry of Supply, applicable to the goods comprised in the agreements, were alleged to have been contravened. The court assumed that all three agreements were affected by illegality, but held that the plaintiffs' claim was not brought in reliance on the agreements. The plaintiffs were enforcing their right to possession: they owned the machine

---

122. The extent to which a plaintiff, entitled to relief under this exception, must make restitution is uncertain. See *Mayfair Trading Co Pty Ltd v Dreyer* (1958) 101 CLR 428 at 451ff; *Farrow Mortgage Services Pty Ltd v Edgar* (1993) 114 ALR 1 at 19 and the discussion in Mason and Carter, *Restitution Law in Australia*, 1995, para 2639.
123. [1960] AC 192.
124. See further [1727]–[1728] and generally Chapter 23.
125. See Brian Coote, 'Another Look at *Bowmakers v Barnet Instruments*' (1972) 35 *MLR* 38; Andrew Stewart, 'Contractual Illegality and the Recognition of Proprietary Interests' (1988) 1 *JCL* 134. See also Nelson Enonchong, 'Title Claims and Illegal Transactions' (1995) 111 *LQR* 135.
126. [1945] 1 KB 65.
127. See further [1723].

tools because the sale by Smith had been effective to transfer title to the plaintiffs. The court explained the law as follows:[128]

> Prima facie, a man is entitled to his own property, and it is not a general principle of our law (as was suggested) that when one man's goods have got into another's possession in consequence of some unlawful dealings between them, the true owner can never be allowed to recover those goods by an action. The necessity of such a principle to the interests and advancement of public policy is certainly not obvious. The suggestion that it exists is not, in our opinion, supported by authority.
>
> In our opinion, a man's right to possess his own chattels will as a general rule be enforced against anyone who, without any claim of right, is detaining them, or has converted them to his own use, even though it may appear either from the pleadings, or in the course of the trial, that the chattels in question came into the defendant's possession by reason of an illegal contract between himself and the plaintiff, provided that the plaintiff does not seek, and is not forced, either to found his claim on the illegal contract or to plead its illegality in order to support his claim.

Because the plaintiffs were able to assert their ownership of the goods, and to prove a cause of action in conversion without relying on the illegal contracts, they were able to succeed. Although the decision has twice been approved by the High Court,[129] the case creates several difficulties.

It seems clear that the court adopted the position that it was necessary, but sufficient, for the plaintiff to establish the right to possession independently of the contract. The independent cause of action could then be enforced. Thus, in conceiving exceptions to the principle, for example, in respect of goods with which it is unlawful to deal at all, the court referred to situations where the plaintiff is unable to establish the proprietary right. In *Gollan v Nugent*[130] the High Court approved this limited exception.

The difficulty most relevant to the present discussion is how the plaintiffs were able to assert their ownership without relying on the hire-purchase contracts. This is not clearly explained and it can be argued, for example, that in order to prove a right to possession the plaintiffs had to show a right to terminate the contracts, and an exercise of that right. That would, of course, have involved reliance on the agreements. It appears that the court took the view that where an action is brought by the owner of goods, and the defendant has possession pursuant to an illegal contract, it will be the defendant who is forced to set up the illegal contract.

A second problem is this. If, as was conceded, and the court allowed, the sale by Smith to the plaintiffs was effective to transfer ownership, the hire-purchase agreements must have been effective to transfer a limited form of ownership, namely, a right to possession. Again the issue arises: how did the plaintiffs establish that the defendants ceased to have a right of possession without relying on the hire-purchase agreements to prove that the defendants had acted wrongfully? In respect of two agreements (numbered one and three by the court) the act of conversion was the sale of the goods and that might conceivably be regarded as having conferred a

---

128. [1945] 1 KB 65 at 70–1.
129. See *Thomas Brown & Sons Ltd v Fazal Deen* (1962) 108 CLR 391; *Gollan v Nugent* (1988) 166 CLR 18. Contrast *Nelson v Nelson* (1995) 184 CLR 538 at 557, 592–3.
130. (1988) 166 CLR 18 at 38, 49.

right to possession independently of the bailment contracts, it being presumed that a bailee would have no right to sell the bailor's goods. But that argument was not available in respect of the other agreement, and it is clear that the commission of a breach under that contract, for example, by non-payment of hire, would not itself have terminated the contractual relationship.[131] Surprisingly, the court does not appear to have regarded the point as significant.

These and other problems have given rise to difficulty in the subsequent cases. For example, in *Bassin v Standen*,[132] the Full Court of the Supreme Court of New South Wales cited *Bowmakers* for the propositions that no property in goods is transferred by virtue of a contract of sale which is prohibited by statute, and that the seller is entitled to assert title in an action in conversion. That court later said, in *Newcastle District Fishermen's Co-Operative Society v Neal*,[133] that a proviso must be added to the proposition, to the effect that the plaintiff's claim must be independent of the contract. On the other hand, in *Leonard v Booth*[134] Taylor J cited *Bowmakers* as an authority for the proposition that title to goods may be acquired in the course of dealings or activities which are unlawful. Superficially at least, it would appear that the *Bowmakers* case can be cited for two contradictory general propositions of law.

We investigate below the scope of the *Bowmakers* decision by considering its operation in the context of the personal actions of trespass, conversion and detinue in relation to contracts dealing with goods[135] and affected by illegality.[136]

[1722] **Trespass.** A person in possession of goods, or entitled to their immediate possession, has the right to recover damages for trespass against a person who unlawfully interferes with the goods by taking them out of the possession of the person legally in possession of the goods.[137] Such a cause of action was relied upon by the plaintiff in *Singh v Ali*.[138] The plaintiff was a lorry driver in need of a lorry and haulage permit to carry goods for reward. However, he had no prospect of obtaining such a permit. The defendant, on the other hand, had every chance of obtaining a permit and an agreement was reached that the defendant would acquire a second-hand lorry, register it and obtain a permit in his own name. However, the lorry was to belong to the plaintiff and be used by him on his own account. Accordingly, a vehicle was purchased by the defendant, and registered in

---

131. See [1967].
132. (1945) 46 SR (NSW) 16 at 19.
133. (1950) 50 SR (NSW) 237 (see [1723]).
134. (1954) 91 CLR 452 at 483. See also *Ayerst v Jenkins* (1873) LR 16 Eq 275 (gift); *Alexander v Rayson* [1936] 1 KB 169 at 186 (lease); *Ison v Australian Wheat Board* (1967) 68 SR (NSW) 102 (sale). But see M J Higgins, 'The Transfer of Property Under Illegal Transactions' (1962) 25 *MLR* 149.
135. That is not to say that the principle is inapplicable to land (see *Chettiar v Chettiar* [1962] AC 294; *McKenna v Perecich* [1973] WAR 56; *Munro v Morrison* [1980] VR 83 (see J C Phillips, (1981) 55 *ALJ* 292)). However, given the disapproval of *Tinsley v Milligan* [1994] 1 AC 340 in *Nelson v Nelson* (1995) 184 CLR 538, it will rarely apply.
136. See [1722]–[1724].
137. See, eg *Penfolds Wines Pty Ltd v Elliott* (1946) 74 CLR 204 at 226.
138. [1960] AC 167.

his name, but paid for by the plaintiff. A document was signed stating that the defendant had sold the vehicle to the plaintiff. For some time the plaintiff operated the vehicle in the name of the defendant and this operation was illegal because the plaintiff did not possess a permit as required by statute. Subsequently, the parties fell out and the defendant removed the vehicle from the plaintiff's possession.

Before the Privy Council the plaintiff sought to assert his ownership and to claim damages in detinue or for trespass by the defendant in wrongfully removing the vehicle from the plaintiff's possession and refusing to return it. The Board was satisfied that the document referred to above was genuine and that the *transaction* was effective to transfer title in the vehicle to the plaintiff, notwithstanding the illegality, because it was fully carried out by sale and delivery to the plaintiff. The plaintiff had been in possession of the vehicle at the time of its seizure by the defendant, and the plaintiff had an immediate right to possession when the action was brought. Therefore, he was entitled to succeed in both trespass and detinue.[139] On the other hand, had the plaintiff been forced to prove his title otherwise than by possession, he would have been in difficulty because of the absence of registration in his name.

[1723] Conversion. An action in conversion, sometimes referred to as trover, is brought by a person entitled to the immediate possession of goods in respect of an act of conversion, such as a wrongful sale, by the defendant. The 'essence of conversion' Dixon J explained in *Penfolds Wines Pty Ltd v Elliott*,[140] is a 'dealing with a chattel in a manner repugnant to the immediate right of possession of the person who has the property or special property in the chattel'.

The plaintiffs' action in *Bowmakers Ltd v Barnet Instruments Ltd*[141] was based on conversion of the machine tools. The success of the claim in that case can be contrasted with its failure in two Australian cases. The first is *Thomas Brown & Sons Ltd v Fazal Deen*.[142] In 1943 the plaintiff deposited gold with the general manager of the defendants under an illegal bailment contract. When the plaintiff demanded the return of the goods they could not be found, the gold having disappeared from the defendants' custody no later than April 1953. Actions were then brought in detinue[143] and conversion. Although the bailment imposed an obligation on the defendants to keep the gold safe and to return it on demand, because it was an illegal arrangement the plaintiff could not succeed if it was necessary for him to rely on the contract. The High Court took the view that the facts of *Bowmakers* differed materially. In that case the title of the plaintiffs, as well as the defendants' act of conversion, had been conceded, and the plaintiffs were able to make out their claim without relying on the hire-purchase contracts. In *Fazal Deen* there were no such concessions and the action in conversion was barred by the *Statute of Limitations*. However, it is unclear

---

139. See further [1724].
140. (1946) 74 CLR 204 at 229.
141. [1945] 1 KB 65 (see [1721]).
142. (1962) 108 CLR 391.
143. See [1724].

whether the High Court would have decided in the plaintiff's favour had the action not been statute barred.

The second case is *Newcastle District Fishermen's Co-operative Society v Neal*,[144] decided prior to *Fazal Deen* but not referred to by the High Court in that case. The plaintiff sued to recover damages for the conversion of a quantity of fish sold to the defendants in contravention of the *Fisheries and Oyster Farms Act* 1935 (NSW). The act of conversion relied on was the sale by the defendants without payment to the plaintiff. Because the contract was illegal it was essential for the plaintiff to establish his cause of action without relying on the contract. The Full Court of the Supreme Court of New South Wales held he was unable to do so. Street CJ said that, in order for the plaintiff to prove that the defendants' act was wrongful, reliance on the contract was necessary. Merely proving that the fish had been delivered by the plaintiff was not sufficient because that would be consistent with a gift having been made. Thus, the act of the defendants was only wrongful if the plaintiff could rely on non-payment under the contract of sale. Street CJ distinguished *Bowmakers* on the basis of the concessions of ownership and conversion in that case. Maxwell J and Owen J, in separate judgments, by similar reasoning concluded that the plaintiff had to fail because it was necessary for him to disclose the illegal nature of the transaction and to rely on it.

Leaving aside the concessions made in *Bowmakers*, why was it that property in the fish never passed to the defendants in the *Newcastle* case? There are two possible reasons to be considered. First, the contract, unlike that in *Singh v Ali*,[145] was not fully executed. Second, property does not pass under a contract of sale affected by illegality. The first reason seems somewhat technical and the second is inconsistent with the *Bowmakers* case. However, if property did pass, the case is clearly distinguishable from *Bowmakers* since the plaintiff could show that the defendants' act was wrongful only by relying on nonperformance of the contract. It is suggested that this is the better explanation of the *Newcastle* case.

Although the principle stated in *Bowmakers* has been accepted as correct,[146] *Fazal Deen* and the *Newcastle* case indicate that there is little scope for the application of the case in Australia. To some extent this is because of the importance attached to the concessions made in the *Bowmakers* case. The defendants certainly conceded that the general property (that is, ownership) in the machine tools rested with the plaintiffs at the time of the conversion. However, the purpose of that concession was probably to reinforce the argument that the defendants had obtained special property (their right to possession) in the goods by virtue of the illegal hire-purchase agreements. The real difficulty of the case lies in explaining how the plaintiffs were able to assert their ownership, and it is arguable that this issue was not fully dealt with in the *Newcastle* case. Moreover, even if the defendants in *Bowmakers* conceded that their actions amounted to conversion, they did not concede that the plaintiffs were entitled to maintain their cause of action without relying on the illegal

---

144. (1950) 50 SR (NSW) 237.
145. [1960] AC 167 (see [1722]).
146. See *Gollan v Nugent* (1988) 166 CLR 18.

contracts. The plaintiffs were successful because the defendants had to defend the action by relying on the illegal nature of the hire-purchase agreements. In *Fazal Deen* the position was different since it was the plaintiff who was relying on the illegal bailment contract.

[1724] **Detinue.** Unlike the other actions referred to, the gist of detinue is not the wrongful taking of goods. Rather, it is the wrongful detention of goods after the plaintiff's lawful request for their return.[147] Thus, in *Singh v Ali*[148] the plaintiff was able to recover in detinue because he was the owner of the lorry and had, in the Board's view, made a lawful demand for its return without relying on the illegal contract for sale. However, because the vehicle was registered in the defendant's name, it is difficult to see how the defendant's detention of the lorry could be regarded as wrongful unless the plaintiff was permitted to rely on the terms under which the sale took place.

The mere intention to engage in criminal conduct is not enough to deny the plaintiff the right to possession.[149] On the other hand, in *Taylor v Chester*[150] an action in respect of half of a £50 Bank of England note in the defendant's possession failed because the half-note had been pledged as security for the payment of a debt arising out of the supply to the defendant, the keeper of a brothel and disorderly house, of wine and suppers for the purpose of being consumed in a debauch in the brothel. To succeed in detinue it was necessary for the plaintiff to show the illegal and immoral character of the contract. He could not rely solely on his title to the half-note because the pledge was effective to transfer a limited (possessory) title to the half-note, and the plaintiff could only avoid the defendant's title by relying on the illegal nature of the contract. Thus, the plaintiff sought to rely on the illegality in order to establish that the defendant's possession of the half-note was wrongful, and this was not permissible.[151]

A claim in detinue was also unsuccessful in *Thomas Brown & Sons Ltd v Fazal Deen*.[152] Because the claim in conversion was barred by the *Statute of Limitations*, the plaintiff argued that a fresh cause of action arose when the return of the gold was demanded in 1959. The refusal to hand over the gold occurred six years later than the act of conversion, and was not statute barred as the action was commenced in 1960. However, the High Court said that, in order to succeed, the plaintiff had to invoke the bailment contract. In other words, the plaintiff was required to show that the defendants had failed to comply with an obligation imposed by the bailment contract, namely, to redeliver the goods on demand, and as the bailment contract was illegal the plaintiff failed. Thus, he could not invoke the *Bowmakers* principle because his right to possession depended on proof of the terms of the bailment, whereas in *Bowmakers* it was possible for the plaintiffs to assert their ownership without reliance on the illegal hire-purchase agreements.

---

147. See, eg Fifoot, *History and Sources of the Common Law*, 1949, pp 24–34.
148. [1960] AC 167 (see [1722]). See also *Taylor v Bowers* (1876) 1 QBD 291.
149. *Gollan v Nugent* (1988) 166 CLR 18.
150. (1869) LR 4 QB 309.
151. See *Gollan v Nugent* (1988) 166 CLR 18 at 30.
152. (1962) 108 CLR 391 (see [1723]).

Cause of Action Based on Statute or Collateral Contract

[1725] Statute. Occasionally a plaintiff is presented with the opportunity of basing an independent cause of action on a statutory provision. In *Ison v Australian Wheat Board*[153] the plaintiff, a grain dealer, purchased wheat from growers and received possession of it in contravention of the *Wheat Industry Stabilization Act* 1958 (NSW). Subsequently, the defendants obtained possession and the plaintiff was convicted of an offence under the Act. The plaintiff alleged that he was entitled under ss 11 and 12 of the Act to the price of the wheat. Section 11 stated the rules applicable in determining payments which the defendants were required to make when wheat was delivered to them pursuant to the Act. Section 12 provided that the amount payable under the Act was 'payable to the person who would have been entitled to receive the price of the wheat if the wheat had been lawfully sold' to the defendants at the time of the delivery of the wheat. There was no doubt that the (antecedent) contracts between the plaintiff and the wheat growers were illegal, and also that the plaintiff was in pari delicto. But those transactions were completely executed and title had passed under them to the plaintiff. Therefore, if the plaintiff could establish ownership and possession without relying on those transactions he would be entitled to recover payment under the Act.

Possession was a merely factual matter. At the time the defendants demanded the wheat, the plaintiff and his agents were in actual possession and so the plaintiff did not need to rely on the illegal contracts to establish possession. But could the plaintiff lawfully have sold the wheat? The court took the view that the plaintiff could also establish an affirmative answer to this question without reliance on the illegal transactions. Had those transactions not been performed the plaintiff would have failed because he would have been required to establish rights under the contracts. His right to sell did not depend on an ability to enforce the transactions because they were fully executed. In the result the plaintiff was able to assert his statutory right. Additionally, the plaintiff had given evidence, which was not objected to, that he was the owner of the wheat and that no other person had any interest in the wheat.

[1726] Collateral contract. If the defendant has promised that a contract will be performed legally, and the plaintiff entered into the contract in consideration of that promise being given, the plaintiff may be able to enforce the guarantee as a collateral contract.[154] Thus, in *Strongman (1945) Ltd v Sincock*[155] the defendant, an architect, undertook that he would obtain the licences which might be needed for building work being done by the plaintiffs, a firm of builders. In fact, the builders did work in excess of the amounts for which licences had been obtained and the excess work was therefore illegal under the *Defence (General) Regulations* 1939 (UK). When the builders sued to recover the balance due under the building contract, the architect raised the defence of illegality. It was clear that the plaintiffs

---

153. (1967) 68 SR (NSW) 102.
154. See generally [611]–[614].
155. [1955] 2 QB 525. See also *Quin v Mutual Acceptance Co Ltd* [1968] 1 NSWR 122. Cf *Brownett v Newton* (1941) 64 CLR 439.

could not recover on the building contract for anything in excess of that authorised by the licence, but the plaintiffs argued that the excess work had been done because of a promise by the defendant to obtain a supplementary licence and that as this promise (contract) was collateral to the illegal contract an action for damages was available when the defendant failed to obtain the licence as promised.

The English Court of Appeal agreed that a case for relief on that basis had been made out and that the illegality of the main contract was no bar to an action on the collateral contract. However, it was also said that the plaintiffs would have been denied relief had they been guilty of 'culpable negligence'. There was no evidence of this, that is, there were no circumstances from which it could be implied that the plaintiffs were grossly careless in not asking to inspect the defendant's licence. Had the defendant been an ordinary home owner having building work done, and not an architect, it might have been open to the court to deny relief on the basis of culpable negligence because in such a case the primary duty of obtaining the licence would rest on the builder, who ought to inspect the licence and not rely on the word of the home owner.

As a matter of policy there is a great deal to be said for holding a defendant liable on an undertaking that a contract will be performed in a legal way. However, there may be technical objections to the collateral contract device and the qualification relating to negligence. For example, if the consideration for the main contract is illegal, or if the main contract is void rather than merely unenforceable, what is the consideration for the defendant's promise? Is entry into a void contract a sufficient consideration? It is also unclear whether the absence of negligence is a qualification for enforcement of the collateral contract, or an element of proof of the collateral contract.

Restitution[156]

[1727] Restitution as an independent basis for recovery. An action for restitution may be brought in respect of a benefit conferred on the defendant if the elements of unjust enrichment are established.[157] In some cases, conduct which is illegal may be a basis for restitution. For example, where a plaintiff pays money to a defendant as a result of the latter's fraud, the fact that the defendant engaged in criminal conduct cannot be a defence to the claim. The contract is not illegal, and may be rescinded for fraud. Following rescission, the defendant's fraud is treated as the basis upon which the plaintiff is entitled to restitution.

Although this illustration shows that proof that a contract is ineffective may be an element of a claim in restitution, it is facile to say that the fact that a contract is ineffective is of itself a sufficient basis for allowing a claim in restitution. Thus, in cases where reliance on an illegal contract is necessary to establish the claim, it will normally fail and the usual context

---

156. See Brice Dickson, 'Restitution and Illegal Transactions', in Burrows, ed, *Essays on the Law of Restitution*, 1991, p 171; Aleco Vrisakis and J W Carter, 'Restitution of Payments Made Under Contracts Prohibited by Statute' (2000) 15 *JCL* 228.
157. See generally Chapter 23.

for the discussion of illegality in the law of restitution is as a defence to an otherwise valid claim.[158] For example, in *George v Greater Adelaide Land Development Co Ltd*[159] a purchaser paid part of the purchase price under a contract for the sale of certain allotments of land which contravened the *Town Planning and Development Act* 1920 (SA). The court held[160] the money to be irrecoverable because it was paid to a party to the contract pursuant to the contract. The impact of this approach is to restrict restitutionary claims to situations where the parties were not in pari delicto.[161]

However, a broader approach has been taken in the more recent cases. Thus, McHugh and Gummow JJ said in *Fitzgerald v F J Leonhardt Pty Ltd*:[162]

> [A]s was pointed out in *Hurst v Vestcorp Ltd* (1988) 12 NSWLR 394 at 445–6, what may now be classified as restitutionary remedies may be available to assist in the striking of a balance. For example, it was held long ago that where a borrower had paid interest in excess of the rate permitted by statute, whilst the debtor could not recover the whole back, an action would lie to recover the surplus. (*Smith v Bromley*, reported as a Note to *Jones v Barkley* (1781) 2 Dougl 684 at 697; 99 ER 434 at 444 ... .) The use of the *quantum meruit* in *Pavey & Matthews Pty Ltd v Paul* (1987) 162 CLR 221; 69 ALR 577 may be seen as another example. Set-off may also have a role to play in adjusting the respective final positions of the parties.

[1728] Claims for restitution. The two principal claims in restitution are to recover money paid and to recover the reasonable value of services rendered or goods supplied. The former usually depends on proof of total failure of consideration,[163] and the latter on 'acceptance' of the benefit.[164]

Restitution will be available where the illegality was just an historical fact. For example, in *Strang v Owens*[165] the plaintiff, who owned a 'disorderly house and sly grog shop', sought to recover £500 from the defendant. It was established that the money had been earned in the plaintiff's illegal and immoral business and that it was deposited with the defendant's father (who assisted the plaintiff in the business) as trustee for the plaintiff. The defendant's father had wrongfully withdrawn the money and placed it in a joint bank account in the names of himself and the defendant. The plaintiff was not seeking to enforce a right arising out of the illegal business or an agreement between herself and the defendant. In fact, she was merely asserting that money belonging to her had been appropriated by the defendant's father and was now in the possession of the defendant.

Restitution is also available where the parties are not in pari delicto. Indeed, in that context money paid may be recovered whether or not there

---

158. See generally Mason and Carter, *Restitution Law in Australia*, 1995, Chapter 26.
159. (1929) 43 CLR 91 (see [1610]).
160. Applying *Harse v Pearl Life Assurance Co* [1904] 1 KB 558 (non-recoverability of premiums paid under illegal insurance policy). See also *Cheers v Pacific Acceptance Corp Ltd* (1959) 60 SR (NSW) 1.
161. See [1711]–[1718].
162. (1997) 189 CLR 215 at 231.
163. See [2306], [2318], [2321].
164. See [2307].
165. (1925) 42 WN (NSW) 183.

was a total failure of consideration.[166] However, the fact that there was a total failure of consideration is not of itself a sufficient justification for the recovery of money paid if the court is being asked to reopen an illegal transaction: illegality will be a valid defence.[167]

A claim to recover as on a quantum meruit must usually fail if there was an illegal contract, because some reference to and reliance on the illegality is inevitable and necessary. For example, in *Wild v Simpson*[168] Atkin LJ said that if an employment contract is illegal the employee is not entitled to recover a reasonable sum for services rendered. Again, where a contract between solicitor and client is illegal by reason of champerty,[169] the solicitor cannot recover ordinary costs as on a quantum meruit.[170] There is, however, some support for a distinction between common law illegality and illegality under statute. In the latter context, authority is against the success of a claim as on a quantum meruit;[171] whereas in the case of contracts illegal at common law the possibility of the claim being successful is less remote.[172]

Because a restitutionary claim depends on proof of an unjust enrichment it is not a claim in contract.[173] The controversial point is whether there is a more general basis for recovery of restitution, arising from the fact that it is not contractual. As already indicated,[174] traditionally it has not been regarded as sufficiently independent of the contract to form a distinct exception to the ex turpi rule. However, in *Hurst v Vestcorp Ltd*[175] McHugh JA stated, as a general principle, that restitution for unjust enrichment may be available even where a contract is prohibited by statute, provided there is no legislative intent to deny the claim, if the defendant would otherwise obtain an 'unmerited benefit'. Although it is not easy to reconcile this principle with the approach traditionally taken to restitution in the context of statutory illegality, it was approved by McHugh and Gummow JJ in *Fitzgerald v F J Leonhardt Pty Ltd*.[176] This would seem to imply that, under the guidance of unjust enrichment, courts should always inquire whether a prohibition on claims in contract was intended to extend to claims in restitution. The policy which prohibits a claim in contract may in particular cases not extend to claims in restitution.[177]

---

166. See, eg *Kiriri Cotton Co Ltd v Dewani* [1960] AC 192 (see [1720]).
167. See, eg *George v Greater Adelaide Land Development Co Ltd* (1929) 43 CLR 91 (see [1727]).
168. [1919] 2 KB 544 at 565.
169. See [1630].
170. Cf *Mohamed v Alaga & Co (a firm)* [2000] 1 WLR 1815.
171. See, eg *Newton v Brownett* (1940) 41 SR (NSW) 1 (quantum valebat) (affirmed without reference to the point sub nom *Brownett v Newton* (1941) 64 CLR 439); *Re Central Queensland Leather Industries Ltd* [1969] QWN 26; *Williamson v Diab* [1988] 1 Qd R 210. For the position where the contract is merely void see [2318].
172. See *Newton v Brownett* (1940) 41 SR (NSW) 1 at 6 (affirmed without reference to the point sub nom *Brownett v Newton* (1941) 64 CLR 439).
173. See [2307].
174. See [1727].
175. (1988) 12 NSWLR 394 at 445–6. Kirby P agreed.
176. (1997) 189 CLR 215 at 231 (see [1727]).

Severance[178]

General

[1729] **Forms of severance.** There are two main forms of severance. First, a term[179] of a contract which is itself invalid may be severable from the rest of the contract so as to permit enforcement of the remainder. This form of severance cannot occur if all the promises by one party are invalid, since in such a case no consideration is provided for the enforcement of the valid promises.[180] The second form of severance arises if a term is partially invalid and the invalid part can be severed so as to permit enforcement of the remainder of the term.

In addition to these cases of severance *within the contract*[181] there is a third form of severance relating to *associated transactions*.[182] An invalid contract may be associated with one or more other contracts and the issue may arise whether the other contracts are also invalid or, instead, severable from the invalid contract.

[1730] **Test of severance.** The cases on severance in the context of uncertainty[183] emphasise the intention of the parties as the key to severance. For example, in *Fitzgerald v Masters*[184] a contract for the sale of an interest in land purported to incorporate the 'usual conditions of sale in use or approved of by the Real Estate Institute of New South Wales relating to sales by private contract of lands held under the *Crown Lands Act*'. There were in fact no such 'usual conditions of sale'. This raised the issue of severance. Did the parties *intend* to contract otherwise than by reference to the terms which were referred to but did not exist? Since the parties had reached agreement on all the essential matters there was no justification for imputing an intention which would have brought down the whole contract on the failure of the clause in issue. Accordingly, severance took place.

Intention is also emphasised in most of the cases on illegality. For example, in *Brooks v Burns Philp Trustee Co Ltd*[185] Taylor J said that 'fundamentally the question is one of intention to be gathered from the instrument itself'. The fact that each case is likely to turn so much on terms of the contract, their relationship to one another and the parties' choice of words, gives some support to the view that it is difficult to adopt a single formula to all cases of severance.[186] Because every contract is different, and

---

177. Thus, because the parties were not equally at fault in *Hatcher v White* (1953) 53 SR (NSW) 285 (see [1713]), the claim for work done and materials supplied ought to have succeeded. See Mason and Carter, *Restitution Law in Australia*, 1995, para 2637.
178. See R E McGarvie, 'Illegality and Severability in Contracts' (1977) 13 *UWALR* 1. For the history see N S Marsh, 'The Severance of Illegality in Contract' (1948) 64 *LQR* 230 and 347.
179. We use this word generally, to include promise and covenant.
180. See *McFarlane v Daniell* (1938) 38 SR (NSW) 337 at 344.
181. See [1734]–[1739].
182. See [1732]–[1733].
183. See [272].
184. (1956) 95 CLR 420.
185. (1969) 121 CLR 432 at 442.

because the parties do not foresee the possibility that invalidity will affect the contract,[187] it is usually necessary to impute an intention to the parties. Tests for severance are therefore essential. Moreover, in the present context, intention cannot be the sole criterion.[188]

In *McFarlane v Daniell*[189] Jordan CJ stated:[190]

> When valid promises supported by legal consideration are associated with, but separate in form from, invalid promises, the test of whether they are severable is whether they are in substance so connected with the others as to form an indivisible whole which cannot be taken to pieces without altering its nature ... If the elimination of the invalid promises changes the extent only but not the kind of the contract, the valid promises are severable ... If the substantial promises were all illegal or void, merely ancillary promises would be inseverable.

This test, which has been approved and applied on a number of occasions,[191] focuses on the effect of severance and asks whether the nature of the contract will be changed. If it would alter only the 'extent' of the contract, severance can take place; but altering the 'nature' of the contract is not permitted under the guise of severance. It is, of course, far easier to state a test of severance than to apply it. As Kitto J observed in *Brooks v Burns Philp Trustee Co Ltd*,[192] 'questions of severability are often difficult'. The formulation of Jordan CJ is not an exclusive test.[193] In *Carney v Herbert*[194] the Privy Council said there are two matters to be considered: first, whether 'as a matter of construction' or intention the lawful part can be severed from the unlawful part; and, second, 'whether, despite severability, there is a bar to enforceability' arising out of the illegality.

[1731] **Relevant considerations.** The process of severance requires the court to draw on a number of considerations. First, and at the most general level, there is the issue of whether severance must be decided by reference to the common law or under statute.[195] For example, the *Restraints of Trade Act* 1976 (NSW) provides a statutory form of severance which is much more generous than the common law.

Second, as explained above,[196] it is necessary to take account of the intention of the parties. Severance cannot occur if it would be inconsistent with the parties' intention.

---

186. See, eg *O'Loughlin v O'Loughlin* [1958] VR 649 at 652; *Carney v Herbert* [1985] AC 301 at 309–10. And see *Sydney City Council v Ilenace Pty Ltd* [1984] 3 NSWLR 414 at 422 (tests 'various and difficult to reconcile').
187. See *Amoco Australia Pty Ltd v Rocca Bros Motor Engineering Co Pty Ltd [No 2]* [1975] AC 561 at 578; 133 CLR 331; 5 ALR 65.
188. Cf *Brew v Whitlock (No 2)* [1967] VR 803 at 806, where the court could see no distinction between the test applicable in cases of uncertainty and cases of illegality.
189. (1938) 38 SR (NSW) 337.
190. (1938) 38 SR (NSW) 337 at 345.
191. See, eg *Thomas Brown & Sons Ltd v Fazal Deen* (1962) 108 CLR 391 at 411.
192. (1969) 121 CLR 432 at 438.
193. *Humphries v Proprietors 'Surfers Palms North' Group Titles Plan 1955* (1994) 179 CLR 597 at 619; 121 ALR 1.
194. [1985] AC 301 at 311.
195. See [1738]–[1739].
196. See [1730].

Third, the reason for invalidity is important. The courts have been slow to apply the principles of severance to contracts which are illegal in the strictest sense, as in the case of a contract to commit a serious crime.[197] For example, in *McFarlane v Daniell*[198] Jordan CJ said it could 'hardly be imagined' that a court would enforce a promise 'however inherently valid and however severable, if contained in a contract one of the terms of which provided for assassination'.

Fourth, the type of contract may be relevant. For example, in the context of contracts in restraint of trade, the courts have shown a greater willingness towards severing covenants in cases involving contracts for the sale of businesses than in cases involving contracts of employment. It is unusual for severance to take place where an employment contract contains a covenant in restraint of trade.[199] On the other hand, although the necessity for consideration in a simple contract may 'introduce an additional element to be taken into account',[200] severance in the context of a deed is no different from severance in the context of a simple contract.[201]

Fifth, there is the factor which is the main basis for the mode of analysis adopted below, namely, the form of severance. It is probably easier to establish that transactions are severable than to establish that terms in a single contract are severable. Similarly, it is easier to establish that terms in a contract are severable than to establish that part of a term is severable.

Severance at Common Law

Severance of associated transactions

[1732] Transactions associated with illegal contracts. The mere fact that a contract is to some extent connected or associated with an illegal contract is not a sufficient basis for saying that it must also be regarded as invalid. For example, in *Dalgety and New Zealand Loan Ltd v C Imeson Pty Ltd*[202] the court considered that the statutory prohibition of a contract of sale between A and B did not necessarily imply that a contract between B and C, under which C provided B with finance, was also invalid. In such a case the validity of the related contract can be approached either from the point of view of the scope of the statutory prohibition or the degree of connection between the illegal contract and the related transaction. If the statutory prohibition extends to the related transaction no question of severance can arise. But, if the prohibition does not extend so far, the degree of connection becomes the measure of severance.

In *Noble v Maddison*[203] the plaintiff was a partner with the defendant in a series of contracts. Some of these contracts were illegal because the plaintiff occupied a government post and had placed himself in the position where

---

197. See further [1737].
198. (1938) 38 SR (NSW) 337 at 346.
199. See, eg *Attwood v Lamont* [1920] 3 KB 571. This reflects the distinction drawn in [1648].
200. *Brooks v Burns Philp Trustee Co Ltd* (1969) 121 CLR 432 at 442, and see [1736].
201. For the distinction between simple contracts and deeds see [312].
202. [1964] NSWR 638 at 646.
203. (1912) 12 SR (NSW) 435.

his public duty conflicted with his private interest in the contracts.[204] In respect of one contract there was no conflict of interest and duty and that contract was not illegal. The question then arose whether this contract could be enforced. Rich J held that a separate partnership existed in respect of each contract, and also that the illegality of the other contracts was no bar to the enforcement of the associated transaction.[205]

[1733] **Transactions associated with contracts in restraint of trade.** In *Amoco Australia Pty Ltd v Rocca Bros Motor Engineering Co Pty Ltd*[206] the High Court held void certain provisions in an underlease from Amoco to Rocca. The question then arose whether the whole of the underlease was 'void' and, if so, whether the head lease, from Rocca to Amoco, was also void. In *Amoco Australia Pty Ltd v Rocca Bros Motor Engineering Co Pty Ltd [No 2]*[207] the Privy Council held first, that the whole of the underlease was void because the covenants which were in restraint of trade could not be severed; and, second, that the underlease was not severable from the lease. The Board said that no distinction was to be drawn between the consequences of invalidity in contracts generally and covenants in leases.[208]

As to the severability of the two transactions, Lord Cross, delivering the Board's advice, said[209] it was impossible 'to regard the two leases as separate dispositions of property': the two transactions (lease and underlease) were very closely connected; in reality there was a 'single commercial transaction' under which Rocca was 'to get a supply of petrol at an agreed rebate' and Amoco a 'trade tie with security for its investment in the station'. Severance was not made possible by cl 18 of the lease which stated that the lease was 'not in consideration for or dependent or contingent in any manner upon any other contract' and that its provisions were 'entirely and completely independent of any other transaction or relationship between the parties'. Lord Cross said that these statements were 'untrue' and may have been inserted in order to place Amoco in a stronger bargaining position in any challenge by Rocca to the validity of the underlease. In reaching this conclusion, however, it was necessary for the Board to invoke public policy because, in the absence of public policy considerations, Rocca would have been precluded by the express provision from denying that the lease and underlease were independent.

Severance within the contract

[1734] **Court will not rewrite the contract.** Time and time again the courts have said that they will not rewrite the contract for the parties, in order to achieve severability.[210] Accordingly, the court will not reduce the

---

204. See [1624].
205. Cf *Subdivisions Ltd v Payne* [1934] SASR 214. Contrast *Re Trepca Mines Ltd (No 2)* [1962] Ch 511 (see [1630]) where a solicitor was unable to recover costs from his clients when he gave advice about, and participated in, a champertous agreement between his clients and a third party.
206. (1973) 133 CLR 288; 1 ALR 385 (see [1652]).
207. [1975] AC 561.
208. But cf *Esso Petroleum Co Ltd v Harper's Garage (Stourport) Ltd* [1968] AC 269 at 299.
209. [1975] AC 561 at 580. Contrast *Alec Lobb (Garages) Ltd v Total Oil (Great Britain) Ltd* [1985] 1 WLR 173.

length or scope of a covenant in restraint of trade except by the excision of words. And even then the substance of the contract must remain unchanged. For example, in *Lindner v Murdock's Garage*[211] the restraint clause in the defendant's employment contract was held to be invalid because it applied not only to Crystal Brook, where the defendant was employed, but also to Wirrabara where the defendant had not been employed. The High Court rejected an argument that the restraint clause should be seen as embodying two severable restrictions. Kitto J said[212] it was 'quite consistent with the agreement' that he might be employed at either place and that 'in order to be valid' the clause should 'have been so limited in respect of each area as not to operate therein unless' the defendant was employed 'in that area within some specified reasonable period preceding the termination of his service'.

[1735] **Severance of part of a term.** In some of the cases a term which, taken as a whole, infringes public policy, has been severed so as to permit enforcement of a valid part of the term. The criterion to apply was stated by Lord Moulton in *Mason v Provident Clothing and Supply Co Ltd*[213] as being whether the 'excess is of trivial importance, or merely technical, and not a part of the main purport and substance' of the term. Although this form of severance is the most difficult to establish, the courts are a little more flexible in their approach today than when Lord Moulton stated the test. Most cases have concerned covenants in restraint of trade.[214]

Before severance within a term can become an issue for decision, the term must be of a severable nature. For example, in *Attwood v Lamont*,[215] where the defendant was employed as a cutter and head of the tailoring department of the plaintiff, it was argued that the term in issue was severable to the extent that the enumerated trades, other than that of a tailor, could be struck out and the covenant enforced to prohibit the defendant being concerned in the tailoring trade. The English Court of Appeal rejected this argument. Lord Sterndale MR said[216] that severance would 'alter entirely the scope and intention of the agreement'. Atkin LJ agreed with Younger LJ, whose judgment has ever since been regarded as expressing the proper approach. He rejected a mechanical approach to severance accomplished by striking a blue pencil through the infringing parts of the clause, and said[217] that the doctrine of severance has not 'gone further than to make it permissible in a case where the covenant is not really a single covenant but is in effect a combination of several distinct covenants'. Severance was not possible, even though it was possible to strike a blue pencil through the entire covenant except that part relating to tailoring, because there was in fact one covenant for the protection of the plaintiff's entire business. It was impossible to say that the plaintiff was

210. See, eg *Esso Petroleum Co Ltd v Harper's Garage (Stourport) Ltd* [1968] AC 269 at 295.
211. (1950) 83 CLR 628 (see [1649]).
212. (1950) 83 CLR 628 at 659.
213. [1913] AC 724 at 745.
214. See, eg *Nordenfelt v Maxim Nordenfelt Guns and Ammunition Co Ltd* [1894] AC 535.
215. [1920] 3 KB 571.
216. [1920] 3 KB 571 at 580.
217. [1920] 3 KB 571 at 593.

carrying on several businesses, and therefore impossible to treat the covenant as stating several covenants for the protection of several businesses. Accordingly, the court could not sever that part of the covenant which related to tailoring. In any event the covenant was held to be too wide in its application to the tailoring trade.

[1736] Severance of a whole term. One way in which the issue of severance within a contract can be decided is by reference to the relationship of the term sought to be severed with other important terms of the contract. If the remaining terms are dependent on the term which is sought to be severed, severance is not possible; whereas if the terms are independent severance can take place.

Dependency occurs if the obligation to perform one term is dependent (or contingent) on the validity or performance of another,[218] and implies that the parties intended performance to take place only if the invalid term was valid or performed. The effect of severance in such a case would be to alter the nature and effect of the contract. For example, in *Brooks v Burns Philp Trustee Co Ltd*[219] the plaintiffs sought determination of the question whether the defendant was entitled to £25 per week under a deed between the defendant and her husband. Clause 1 was a covenant by the husband which entitled her to receive such payments, but cl 2 was invalid as purporting to oust the jurisdiction of the courts. The issue was whether cl 2 could be severed, so as to permit enforcement of the covenant in cl 1. A majority of the High Court decided that severance was not possible because the covenant sought to be enforced was dependent on the invalid covenant.[220] Kitto J said[221] the 'intended reciprocity of obligation' between the covenants was sufficiently clear 'to necessitate an inference that the legal validity' of each covenant was a 'condition of the operation of the other'. Similarly, Windeyer J, who dissented on whether cl 2 purported to oust the jurisdiction of the courts, said[222] that the covenants were 'dependent, not independent, covenants'.

Another approach, favoured to some extent by Taylor J in *Brooks*' case, is to ask whether the term held to be invalid is the sole or main consideration for the term sought to be enforced. Severance may take place if the invalid term is not the sole or main consideration for the term sought to be enforced. Thus, in *Alec Lobb (Garages) Ltd v Total Oil (Great Britain) Ltd*[223] covenants in a lease which were in restraint of trade were severable from the remainder of the lease. If it is clear that this is the case, severance will not take place. In *Brooks*' case Windeyer J said the issue is not easily resolved 'because, for more than three hundred years, courts of common law have said that they will not inquire into the adequacy of a consideration or weigh the inducements of a promise'.[224] In fact, the cases illustrating this

---

218. See generally [1805]–[1808].
219. (1969) 121 CLR 432 (see [1627]).
220. Contrast *Stenhouse Australia Ltd v Phillips* [1974] AC 391.
221. See (1969) 121 CLR 432 at 438.
222. (1969) 121 CLR 432 at 464. Owen J expressed (at 479) the same conclusion, whereas Menzies J expressed no opinion.
223. [1985] 1 WLR 173. See also *Marshall v NM Financial Management Ltd* [1997] 1 WLR 1527 at 1532.
224. (1969) 121 CLR 432 at 463. And see [325]; but cf [1644].

approach look more to the effect on the contract as a whole than to one party's consideration so that, in effect, 'consideration' in the present context means 'performance of the contract', and the issue is whether the parties will receive the performance for which they bargained.[225]

[1737] Position where contract illegal. Nearly all the cases on severance within an illegal contract have involved contracts in restraint of trade or those which purport to oust the jurisdiction of the courts. The courts have been reluctant to sever a contract which is prohibited by statute or is contrary to public policy because it involves particularly wicked conduct, such as the commission of a serious crime. Thus, in *McFarlane v Daniell*[226] Jordan CJ considered it 'difficult to see how, in principle, a legal promise associated with an illegal promise can ever be enforceable unless it is supported solely by a separate consideration so exclusively attributable to it that there are in substance two independent contracts and not one composite contract'. For example, in *DJE Constructions Pty Ltd v Maddocks*[227] a provision for payment was not severable where it was an integral part of an agreement which (if it existed) was illegal by virtue of a prohibition in the companies legislation on the giving of financial assistance to enable the purchase of its shares. Street CJ said[228] the 'principles relating to severability were developed in connection with contractual clauses void for uncertainty and for restraint of trade, and not in cases involving contracts *illegal* and void'.

It is, however, clear from the High Court's decision in *Thomas Brown & Sons Ltd v Fazal Deen*[229] that severance of an illegal contract is sometimes possible. It was explained earlier[230] that the plaintiff had deposited a quantity of gold with the defendants in contravention of the *National Security (Exchange Control) Regulations* (Cth). In addition, the plaintiff had deposited a quantity of gems and this did not contravene the Regulations. However, in form there was one contract of bailment and, given the reluctance to sever illegal contracts, one might have expected the court to decide that the illegality affected the bailment of the gems and to deny the plaintiff relief on that basis. However, the court severed the bailment contract, and permitted enforcement of that part which related to the gems, because the 'contractual obligation' of the defendants 'as to the return of the plaintiff's property on demand applied to every part of the property deposited whether demanded together with the rest of it or separately'.[231] This suggests that because the plaintiff could demand the return of any other part of the property bailed, the bailment of the gems was in effect distinct from the bailment of the gold.

225. See *O'Loughlin v O'Loughlin* [1958] VR 649. Cf *Howard F Hudson Pty Ltd v Ronayne* (1972) 126 CLR 449. Contrast *Re Field and the Conveyancing Act* [1968] 1 NSWR 210 at 216–17.
226. (1938) 38 SR (NSW) 337 at 346.
227. [1982] 1 NSWLR 5. See also *Electric Acceptance Pty Ltd v Doug Thorley Caravans (Aust) Pty Ltd* [1981] VR 799 at 812.
228. [1982] 1 NSWLR 5 at 10. For a similar statement see *Halsbury's Laws of England*, 4th ed, 1974, Vol 9, para 430.
229. (1962) 108 CLR 391.
230. See [1706], [1723].
231. See (1962) 108 CLR 391 at 411.

In *Electric Acceptance Pty Ltd v Doug Thorley Caravans (Aust) Pty Ltd*[232] Brooking J explained *Fazal Deen* as illustrating the relevance of the character of the illegality. In his view severance was possible because the offence committed was not of a sufficiently heinous character to be a bar. Although the High Court did not expressly refer to such a consideration, it is one way of explaining the case. However, a wider view was taken by the Privy Council in *Carney v Herbert*.[233] The illegal term was that payment of the purchase price for shares in a company would be secured by mortgages to be provided by a subsidiary company of the company whose shares were the subject of the sale. The mortgages were void and illegal by reason of s 67 of the *Companies Act* 1961 (NSW).[234] The buyers contended that because of this, and notwithstanding that the shares had been transferred to them, they could not be compelled to pay the outstanding price.

While acknowledging that it was undesirable, if not impossible, to lay down principles to cover all severance problems, Lord Brightman (delivering the advice) suggested[235] that:

> [A]s a general rule, where parties enter into a lawful contract of, for example, sale and purchase, and there is an ancillary provision which is illegal but exists for the exclusive benefit of the plaintiff, the court may and probably will, if the justice of the case so requires, and there is no public policy objection, permit the plaintiff if he so wishes to enforce the contract without illegal provision.

The Privy Council said the contract was, basically, one for the sale of shares to which the mortgages were ancillary. The buyers wanted the shares, the sellers the purchase money and, only incidentally to the latter, adequate security for payment thereof. The sellers were therefore held to be entitled to enforce the contract of sale without the illegal mortgages.

Severance Under Statute

[1738] The *Restraints of Trade Act* 1976 (NSW).[236] In New South Wales the severance of covenants in restraint of trade created on or after 15 November 1976 is governed by the *Restraints of Trade Act* 1976 (NSW).[237] It seems clear that the Act was intended to overcome at least one feature of the common law governing the restraint of trade doctrine,[238] a feature which was criticised by the New South Wales Law Reform Commission in its *Report on Covenants in Restraint of Trade*.[239] This is the fact that the

---

232. [1981] VR 799 at 818.
233. [1985] AC 301 (see Jennifer Hill and J W Carter, 'Severance, Illegal Contracts and Company Law' (1986) 4 *Companies and Securities Law Journal* 183). Contrast *Hurst v Vestcorp Ltd* (1988) 12 NSWLR 394.
234. See also *Hurst v Vestcorp Ltd* (1988) 12 NSWLR 394; *Australian Breeders Co-operative Society Ltd v Jones* (1997) 150 ALR 488.
235. [1985] AC 301 at 317. See also *South Western Mineral Water Co Ltd v Ashmore* [1967] 1 WLR 1110.
236. For severance under the *Trade Practices Act* 1974 (Cth) (see [1654]) see Taperell, Vermeesch and Harland, *Trade Practices and Consumer Protection*, 3rd ed, 1983, paras 593–98.
237. See s 3(1). The Act applies notwithstanding any stipulation to the contrary: s 3(2); but does not affect the operation of enactments set out in s 3(3). For the policy perspective see *Wright v Gasweld Pty Ltd* (1991) 22 NSWLR 317 at 337.
238. See generally [1634]–[1653].

reasonableness of a restraint is determined by its widest possible application (consistent with the intention of the parties),[240] rather than its application to the conduct in respect of which the covenantee seeks relief. For example, if a restraint covenant in a partnership deed prohibits competition by a retiring partner within a radius of 10 kilometres from the partnership business, the covenant's validity is determined at the boundary of the restraint. Thus, even if a retiring partner sets up a competing business which is, say, 50 metres from the partnership's place of business, the restraint will be invalid if a 10 kilometre restraint is unreasonable, notwithstanding that the same restraint, extending to a 50 metre radius, would be reasonable between the parties and not injurious to the public.[241] Moreover, such a restraint would not be saved by the common law rules on severance[242] because the court will not rewrite the covenant so as to make it extend only to a radius of 50 metres from the partnership business.

The central provision is s 4(1) which states, simply, that a 'restraint of trade is valid to the extent to which it is not against public policy, whether it is in severable terms or not'.[243] This allows the court to ignore the fact that the restraint goes beyond what is reasonable if it can be enforced to an extent which is reasonable. If it stood alone s 4(1) would provide no incentive for the parties to try to arrive at a reasonable restraint. In *Mason v Provident Clothing and Supply Co Ltd*[244] Lord Moulton deprecated the application by the courts of their 'ingenuity and knowledge of the law' in order to 'carve out' of a void covenant the 'maximum' of what might 'validly' have been required in cases where the covenant is deliberately framed in unreasonably wide terms with the object of oppressing, say, an employee, by the fear of expensive litigation. Thus, s 4(1) is qualified by s 4(3) which allows a person subject to a restraint to apply to the court in circumstances where the restraint is against public policy as regards its application to the applicant, 'by reason of, or partly by reason of, a manifest failure by a person who created or joined in creating the restraint to attempt to make the restraint a reasonable restraint'.[245] Once such a failure is established, the court is empowered to order that the restraint be 'altogether invalid' as against the applicant. Alternatively, the court may order that the restraint be valid 'to such extent only (not exceeding the extent to which the restraint is not against public policy) as the court thinks fit'. Regard must be had to the circumstances in which the restraint was created.[246] Therefore, if the court finds that the covenant is unreasonable it may, in the exercise of its discretion, refuse to enforce it at all if it is satisfied that there was a 'manifest failure' to make the restraint reasonable.

239. LRC 9, 1970.
240. See [1649].
241. See [1636].
242. See [1729]–[1737].
243. This does not affect the invalidity of a restraint of trade by reason of any matter other than public policy: s 4(2). See *Austra Tanks Pty Ltd v Running* [1982] 2 NSWLR 840 (uncertainty).
244. [1913] AC 724 at 745. See also *K A & C Smith Pty Ltd v Ward* (1998) 45 NSWLR 702 at 728.
245. Where, under the rules of an association, a person who is a member of the association is subject to the restraint, the association is deemed to have created or joined in creating the restraint: s 4(4).

The onus of proof is on the applicant for relief under s 4(1).[247] On the other hand, the onus is on the defendant to establish that the qualification in s 4(3) applies.[248]

[1739] Interpretation of the Act. A broad interpretation to the *Restraints of Trade Act* 1976 (NSW) was given by McLelland J in *Orton v Melman*,[249] where the plaintiffs sought an injunction to restrain the defendant from carrying on the practice of a medical practitioner at either Toronto or Teralba (two suburbs of Lake Macquarie), contrary to cl 24 of a partnership deed between the parties entered into on 1 July 1977. Clause 24 imposed a restraint for a period of three years on an outgoing member of the partnership. It extended to medical practice within a radius of eight miles by road from the two surgeries operated by the partnership, at Toronto and Teralba. There was no doubt that the defendant breached cl 24 by leaving the partnership in June 1980 and practising as a general practitioner at a surgery in Toronto about six months later. But the defendant sought relief under s 4(3) of the Act. McLelland J's approach to the Act can be summarised as follows.

First, the court must decide *independently of public policy*, whether the restraint has been (or will be) breached by the covenantor.

Second, assuming that a breach has been established, the court must decide whether the restraint *in its application to that breach*, is contrary to public policy. If the restraint does not, in its application to the breach, infringe public policy, it should be enforced unless the defendant successfully makes an application under s 4(3).

Applying this approach, McLelland J held that cl 24 had been breached, but that it was not contrary to public policy in its application to the defendant's breach. It was, in other words, reasonable for an outgoing member of the medical partnership to be subject to a restraint on medical practice in the same suburbs as the practice of the partnership. Therefore, subject to the issues of duration and s 4(3), McLelland J was satisfied that the plaintiffs were entitled to relief. On duration, he concluded that three years was not an unreasonably long period for the breaches which had been established. As to s 4(3), McLelland J considered[250] it was a 'condition precedent of the power of the court to grant relief under this provision that there be found to be "a manifest failure by a person who created or joined in creating the restraint to attempt to make the restraint a reasonable restraint"'. He placed the onus of proof on the applicant, that is, the defendant in this case. However, there was no evidence which justified a conclusion in favour of the defendant.

McLelland J's approach in *Orton v Melman* has been followed in the subsequent cases.[251] However, it is not readily applied to cases where no

---

246. The order has effect from such date, not being earlier than the day on which the order is made, as is specified in the order. The order does not affect any right (including any right to damages) which accrued before the day on which the order takes effect: s 4(5).
247. *ICT Pty Ltd v Sea Containers Ltd* (1995) 39 NSWLR 640.
248. *Orton v Melman* [1981] 1 NSWLR 583.
249. [1981] 1 NSWLR 583.
250. [1981] 1 NSWLR 583 at 589.

breach has been established. In that context the court must be able to define a valid restraint within the clause before it can restrain future breaches, and it cannot do so if there is no evidence establishing the limits of a valid restraint. Thus, in *ICT Pty Ltd v Sea Containers Ltd*,[252] the New South Wales Court of Appeal quoted with apparent approval a statement by Needham J in *A Buckle & Son Pty Ltd v McAllister*:[253]

> Whatever may be the proper interpretation of the (NSW) *Restraints of Trade Act* 1976, s 4(1) I do not think it empowers the court to create a valid restraint out of an invalid one unless that can be done by a reading down process.

---

251. See, eg *IRAF Pty Ltd v Graham* [1982] 1 NSWLR 419; *Fleming Bros (Monaro Agencies) Pty Ltd v Smith* (1983) ATPR ¶40-389; *Knogo Corp v Halligan* (1984) ATPR ¶40-460.
252. (1995) 39 NSWLR 640 at 674.
253. (1986) 4 NSWLR 426 at 434. See also *Wright v Gasweld Pty Ltd* (1991) 22 NSWLR 317 at 329.

PART VII
Performance and Breach

Chapter 18

Performance and Breach

Introduction 1801
Performance 1802
   Time and Order of Performance 1802
   Discharge by Performance 1812
   Enforcement of the Promisee's Obligations 1819
   Suspension and Termination of Performance 1839
Breach 1841
   General 1841
   Failure to Perform 1844
   Standards of Contractual Duty 1853
   Consequences of Breach 1858

Introduction

[1801] Issues. In *McRae v Commonwealth Disposals Commission*,[1] Dixon and Fullagar JJ described as a 'fundamental question' of contract law, the question 'What did the promisor really promise?'. This has two aspects. The first is the scope of the promisor's promise. It may be expressed in terms: in what circumstances will a promisor be obliged to perform? Approached from the perspective of the law on performance,[2] the concern is with three main issues:[3]

- the time and order of performance required by the contract;
- the performance which must be rendered in order to discharge the parties; and
- the performance which each party must render in order to be entitled to enforce the obligations of the other.

The second aspect relates to the standard of care which a promisor must exercise when performing its promises. Failure to perform a promise in accordance with the applicable standard of care is a breach of contract.[4]

---

1. (1951) 84 CLR 377 at 407–8.
2. See further Chapters 19 and 20 (perspective of discharge).
3. See [1802]–[1852].
4. See [1853]–[1859].

Although both aspects of the question depend on the construction of the contract, the courts have developed and applied rules to govern them. These rules are in the nature of 'default rules', that is, rules which apply where the parties have not expressed an intention on the matter. In practice they take the form of presumptions about the parties' intention.

Performance

Time and Order of Performance

[1802] Issues of construction. The time and order of performance under a contract are decided by reference to the intention of the parties as expressed in the contract. Intention is an issue of construction.[5] Assuming that the contract is in writing, these are issues of law not fact.[6]

Time of performance

[1803] Express provision. The parties may expressly provide for the time at which their obligations are to be performed. Thus, the time of performance may be fixed by a term ('time stipulation') by reference to a specified date or time period. Alternatively, time may be fixed by reference to an event, such as the arrival of goods the subject of a contract of sale at the buyer's place of business.

However, the event need not be an element of either party's performance. For example, the commission payable to an agent under an agency contract may become due when payment is received by the principal under a contract entered into with a third party.

[1804] Performance within a reasonable time. Generally, where a contract does not specify the time of performance, the obligation in question must be performed within a 'reasonable' time.[7] What constitutes a reasonable time is a question of fact to be determined at the time when performance is alleged to be due rather than at the moment of contractual formation.[8] For example, where a contract for the sale of goods states no time for delivery, a reasonable time expires when, in the actual circumstances, the seller has had sufficient time to make delivery. Because the period is not to be regarded as fixed at the moment the contract is agreed, matters such as the nature of the goods, weather conditions, and so on may be relevant.

Order of performance

[1805] Relation between obligations. Unless the parties, in fixing the time of performance, have also expressly agreed on the order in which they

---

5. See [703].
6. See [702].
7. *Hick v Raymond* [1893] AC 22 at 32; *Canning v Temby* (1905) 3 CLR 419 at 424. The principle also applies where the time stipulated for performance expires without either party being in breach: *Electronic Industries Ltd v David Jones Ltd* (1954) 91 CLR 288.
8. See, eg *Postlethwaite v Freeland* (1880) 5 App Cas 599 at 608, 621; *Perri v Coolangatta Investments Pty Ltd* (1982) 149 CLR 537 at 567–8; 41 ALR 441.

are to perform, the order of performance depends on the relation between the parties' obligations, that is, whether one party's obligation to perform is dependent on or independent of the other party's obligation to perform.[9] Classification depends on the intention of the parties, and is therefore decided by construing the contract.[10]

[1806] **Independent obligations.** Where the parties' obligations are independent of one another the order of performance is immaterial. Thus, if A's obligation to perform is independent of performance by B, B may call upon A to perform without first performing. If the contract does not specify the time of performance, A must perform within a reasonable time, but if the contract specifies a time for performance it is sufficient that that time has arrived: A cannot refuse to perform on the ground that B has not performed.

Originally, obligations were treated as independent in the absence of words linking the parties' obligations. For example, in the absence of a provision stating that a buyer of goods was to pay *for* the goods, the buyer's obligation was construed as independent of performance by the seller.[11] Accordingly, at that time, but not today, the seller could recover the price of goods without first delivering them. Even the use of a linking word might not rebut the presumption of independency if a time for performance was named. Thus, in the famous case of *Pordage v Cole*[12] a purchaser's promise to pay for land 'before Midsummer' was construed as independent in character. Therefore, the vendor could recover the price of the land by an action commenced after Midsummer even though he had not transferred title to the land.

The rationale for construing promises as independent was that, in the absence of clear words to the contrary, the court would presume that each party had bargained for the other party's promise, rather than the performance of the promise. This meant that if either party failed to perform the other would have a remedy, in damages, on the promise. But reliance could not be placed on the other party's failure to perform as a ground for not performing. However, towards the end of the 18th century the courts took a more practical approach and were less willing to apply a presumption of independency. Accordingly, the existence of a relation of independency of obligation was said to depend on the 'good sense of the case'[13] and not on 'any formal arrangement of the words'.[14] The more practical approach prevailed, with the result that, today, the presumption is that obligations are dependent in character.[15]

Nevertheless, even today an independent relationship between promises may be found. Thus, there is a present day reminder of the decision in

---

9. S J Stoljar, 'Dependent and Independent Promises' (1957) 2 *Syd LR* 217.
10. *Burton v Palmer* [1980] 2 **NSWLR** 878 at 895. See also *Newcombe v Newcombe* (1934) 34 SR (NSW) 446 at 450 (implied term).
11. *Nichols v Raynbred* (1615) Hob 88; 80 ER 238. Contrast *Peeters v Opie* (1677) 2 Wms Saund 346; 85 ER 1141.
12. (1669) 1 Wms Saund 319; 85 ER 449.
13. *Campbell v Jones* (1796) 6 TR 570 at 572; 101 ER 708 at 709.
14. *Ritchie v Atkinson* (1808) 10 East 295 at 306; 103 ER 787 at 791.
15. See [1807]–[1808].

Pordage v Cole in a provision of the sale of goods legislation which permits a seller to recover the price of goods without making delivery if the buyer's promise is to pay for the goods on a day certain irrespective of delivery.[16]

[1807] Dependent obligations. Where a contract between A and B makes A's obligation to perform dependent on B's performance, B must perform first unless it has been agreed that the parties are to perform at the same time.[17] For example, under a lump sum employment contract the employee must perform first because the courts now apply a presumption of dependency of obligation between the employer's obligation to pay wages and the employee's obligation to work.[18]

Where dependency of obligation exists, one party's obligation to perform is dependent on the occurrence of an event termed a 'condition precedent'. Thus, if a party's obligation to perform is dependent on prior performance by the other party, full performance by that party is fulfilment of the condition precedent.[19] In theory this means that the first party's performance obligation cannot be enforced unless and until the other party has fully performed. However, in practice the condition precedent may be treated as fulfilled by substantial performance.[20]

Strictly speaking, a 'condition precedent' is a contingency which must be fulfilled before performance of a dependent obligation can be called for, rather than a term of the contract. Nevertheless, it has been common practice to refer to conditions precedent as terms.[21] At times this is confusing, particularly where a party's obligation to perform depends on an event which is not the subject of a promise, such as a Ministerial consent which neither party has promised to obtain.

[1808] Concurrent performance. Towards the end of the 18th century it was established that in contracts for the sale of land or goods which contemplate concurrent performance, the parties' obligations are dependent in character.[22] However, dependency in this context does not refer to actual performance. Rather, it refers to the obligation of the parties to be ready and willing to perform.[23] Thus, the sale of goods legislation states that the seller must be ready and willing 'to give possession of the

---

16. **ACT**: *Sale of Goods Act* 1954, s 52(2); **NSW**: *Sale of Goods Act* 1923, s 51(2); **NT**: *Sale of Goods Act* 1972, s 51(2); **Qld**: *Sale of Goods Act* 1896, s 50(2); **SA**: *Sale of Goods Act* 1895, s 48(2); **Tas**: *Sale of Goods Act* 1896, s 53(2); **Vic**: *Goods Act* 1958, s 55(2); **WA**: *Sale of Goods Act* 1895, s 48(2).
17. See [1808].
18. *Automatic Fire Sprinklers Pty Ltd v Watson* (1946) 72 CLR 435 at 465; *Graham v Baker* (1961) 106 CLR 340 at 345. See further [1824]. For the position in respect of periodic payments see [1826].
19. See further [1820].
20. See [1809], [1810], [1830]–[1832]. See also [1947].
21. See [742].
22. The main authorities were *Kingston v Preston* (1773) 2 Doug 689; 99 ER 437; *Jones v Barkley* (1781) 2 Doug 684; 99 ER 434. For a more recent case see *Foran v Wight* (1989) 168 CLR 385; 88 ALR 413.
23. *Morton v Lamb* (1797) 7 TR 125 at 129; 101 ER 890 at 892; *Foran v Wight* (1989) 168 CLR 385. Readiness and willingness includes an ability to perform. See [1929].

goods in exchange for the price', and that the buyer must be ready and willing 'to pay the price in exchange for possession'.[24]

In the absence of agreement to the contrary, a sale of goods contract will be taken to require concurrent performance. Thus, payment of the price (and acceptance of the goods) takes place, normally, at the time of delivery. Accordingly, the rule stated in the legislation refers to 'concurrent' obligations of delivery and payment.[25] Although the concept of dependency of obligation in cases of concurrent performance is expressed in terms of readiness and willingness to perform, this does not imply that a buyer of goods can be held liable to pay their price merely because the seller was ready and willing to deliver. Except in the situation referred to above,[26] the seller must rely on *performance*, that is, the transfer of ownership.[27] The same is true in sale of land transactions, where the vendor's right to the price depends on conveyance of title.[28]

[1809] Co-operation and good faith in performance. In many contracts the ability of one party to perform will depend on the co-operation of the other. An express term requiring co-operation may be present.[29] If there is no such term, the duty may be inferred from the nature of the parties' performance obligations, as where the contract requires concurrent performance.[30] Similarly, in a contract of employment the ability of the employee to perform depends on co-operation by the employer, for example, in allowing access to the place of employment. Such situations are obvious examples that construing a contract may indicate the presence of a duty to co-operate. As was said by Lord Blackburn in *Mackay v Dick*:[31]

> [Where] it appears that both parties have agreed that something shall be done, which cannot effectually be done unless both concur in doing it, the construction of the contract is that each agrees to do all that is necessary to be done on his part for the carrying out of that thing, though there may be no express words to that effect. What is the part of each must depend on [the] circumstances.

In other situations, the requirement of co-operation may be established by the implication of terms. Thus, in *Secured Income Real Estate (Australia)*

---

24. **ACT**: *Sale of Goods Act* 1954, s 32; **NSW**: *Sale of Goods Act* 1923, s 31; **NT**: *Sale of Goods Act* 1972, s 31; **Qld**: *Sale of Goods Act* 1896, s 30; **SA**: *Sale of Goods Act* 1895, s 28; **Tas**: *Sale of Goods Act* 1896, s 33; **Vic**: *Goods Act* 1958, s 35; **WA**: *Sale of Goods Act* 1895, s 28.
25. The expression 'concurrent conditions' is, however, apt to cause confusion; see [742].
26. See [1806].
27. See [2204].
28. See, eg *Harry Davies & Co Pty Ltd v East* [1925] VLR 681; *McDonald v Dennys Lascelles Ltd* (1933) 48 CLR 457; and [2221].
29. See *Insurance Co of Africa v Scor (UK) Reinsurance Co Ltd* [1985] 1 Lloyd's Rep 312; *Trans-Pacific Insurance Co (Australia) Ltd v Grand Union Insurance Co Ltd* (1989) 18 NSWLR 675.
30. See Elisabeth Peden, 'Co-operation in English Contract Law: to Construe or Imply' (2000) 16 *JCL* 56. See further [1808].
31. (1881) 6 App Cas 251 at 263. See also *Thompson v ASDA-MFI Group Plc* [1988] Ch 241 at 253; and generally J F Burrows, 'Contractual Co-operation and the Implied Term' (1968) 31 *MLR* 390.

Ltd v St Martins Investments Pty Ltd[32] Mason J approved the following statement by Griffith CJ in *Butt v M'Donald*:[33]

> It is a general rule applicable to every contract that each party agrees, by implication, to do all such things as are necessary on his part to enable the other party to have the benefit of the contract.

The term may require active co-operation, or create an obligation not to prevent the other party performing the contract.[34] For example, in *Fitzgerald v F J Leonhardt Pty Ltd*[35] a land owner was subject to an implied obligation to obtain a licence for the drilling of a bore. Failure to co-operate will in these cases be a breach of contract.[36] Further consequences depend on the precise circumstances of the case. There are several possibilities.

First, where co-operation is essential to performance, a promisor who does not perform because of the other party's failure to co-operate will have a valid excuse for not performing.

Second, sometimes the promisor can be treated as having fully performed. Thus, in *Mackay v Dick* the plaintiff, who sued to recover the price of a digging machine, was met by the defence that the machine had not passed performance tests required by the contract. Because the machine had not been properly tested due to the failure of the defendant to co-operate, the House of Lords treated the requirements of the contract as having been fulfilled. The plaintiff was then entitled to recover the price of the machine without proving that it would have performed satisfactorily had it been properly tested. In such a case the doctrinal basis appears to be estoppel:[37] the defendant was, by his conduct, estopped from relying on the term in question as a defence to the action. But if the term is not solely for the benefit of the party who has failed to co-operate, the failure to co-operate will not be treated as equivalent to performance.[38]

This leads to a third possibility. Unless co-operation may be compelled by an order for specific performance,[39] as where the court orders a purchaser to sign a document required for performance of a contract for the sale of land, the plaintiff will generally be restricted to a claim for compensation. For example, where a buyer under an FOB contract of sale fails to co-operate with the seller by refusing to name an effective ship to carry the goods, the buyer will not be held liable for the price. The buyer's failure provides the seller with a defence to any action for breach, and also with a cause of action in damages, but the court cannot treat the buyer as liable to pay the price unless title to the goods has been received.[40] This shows that *Mackay v Dick* was a rather special case. The defendant's failure to co-operate there led to liability to pay a liquidated sum (the purchase

---

32. (1979) 144 CLR 596 at 607; 26 ALR 567.
33. (1896) 7 QLJ 68 at 70–1.
34. See [1810].
35. (1997) 189 CLR 215 at 219; 143 ALR 569 at 570–1.
36. See *Luxor (Eastbourne) Ltd v Cooper* [1941] AC 108 at 148–9.
37. See *Sprague v Booth* [1909] AC 576 at 580.
38. *Newmont Pty Ltd v Laverton Nickel NL* (1982) 44 ALR 598 at 606.
39. See generally [2401]–[2412].
40. *Colley v Overseas Exporters* [1921] 3 KB 302. See also *Plaimar Ltd v Waters Trading Co Ltd* (1945) 72 CLR 304 (CIF contract). Contrast *Martin v Hogan* (1917) 24 CLR 234, the decision in which depended on the pleadings.

price) on the basis that ownership of the goods had already passed to the buyer.[41]

The willingness of Australian courts to imply a duty of co-operation signifies that in many cases each party will be required to act in good faith towards the other.[42] However, a good faith duty, which at least requires that each party consider the interests of the other when performing the contract, is more general than a requirement of co-operation, and is not a general incident of contracts. Under §205 of the *Restatement (Second) Contracts* (1979) every contract is regarded as including a duty of good faith and fair dealing in performance. In *Hospital Products Ltd v United States Surgical Corp*[43] Dawson J referred without disapproval to the finding of the trial judge in that case that the contract contained a good faith obligation to the same effect. However, notwithstanding the many situations in which the good faith duty will be implied,[44] this will not always be the case.[45] Where the duty is implied, the consequences of breach will depend on the circumstances. Thus, the breach may disentitle a party to rely on a term of the contract,[46] prevent the exercise of a particular right against the other party,[47] or give rise to a liability in damages.[48]

The duty of good faith must not be confused with the more onerous duty which is owed by a fiduciary. A person who occupies a fiduciary position is not merely required to consider the interests of the other party: there is a positive duty to act in the other's interests. Sometimes (but not usually) a contracting party will occupy a fiduciary position. For example, under a contract of partnership the partners owe fiduciary duties to one another. It is always necessary to determine the scope of the relationship and it should not be assumed that every breach of contract will also be a breach of fiduciary duty.[49]

[1810] Prevention of performance. Even if the contract does not involve active co-operation between the parties, one party's ability to

---

41. See further [2204].
42. For an argument that good faith may be based simply on the construction of the contract, without the need for implication of a term, see Elisabeth Peden, 'Incorporating Terms of Good Faith in Contract Law in Australia' (2001) 23 *Syd LR* 222.
43. (1984) 156 CLR 41 at 137–8; 55 ALR 417. See further H O Hunter, 'The Duty of Good Faith and Security of Performance' (1993) 6 *JCL* 19.
44. See, eg *Shepherd v Felt and Textiles of Australia Ltd* (1931) 45 CLR 370 (see [1921]); *Renard Constructions (ME) Pty Ltd v Minister for Public Works* (1992) 26 NSWLR 234 per Priestley JA. See E A Farnsworth, 'Good Faith in Contract Performance' in Beatson and Friedmann, eds, *Good Faith and Fault in Contract Law*, 1995, p 153 and further [1842]. Cf Hugh Collins, 'Implied Duty to Give Information During Performance of Contracts' (1992) 55 *MLR* 556.
45. See *Service Station Association Ltd v Berg Bennett & Associates Pty Ltd* (1993) 117 ALR 393 at 401–3. Cf *GSA Group Pty Ltd v Siebe Plc* (1993) 30 NSWLR 573 at 579–80. Such a term would be implied in law rather than implied in fact. For this distinction see [620]. See also *Australian Mutual Provident Society v 400 St Kilda Road Pty Ltd* [1991] 2 VR 417 (implied term would have been inconsistent with express term).
46. See, eg *Lock v Westpac Banking Corp* (1991) 25 NSWLR 593 at 607–8.
47. See [1983].
48. See [1842].
49. See *Breen v Williams* (1996) 186 CLR 71; 138 ALR 259 (see J W Carter and G J Tolhurst, (1997) 12 *JCL* 152; Jane Swanton and Barbara McDonald, (1997) 71 *ALJ* 332).

perform may depend on the other not preventing that performance. In such cases the court may be prepared to imply a term in accordance with the principle stated by Cockburn CJ in *Stirling v Maitland*:[50]

> [I]f a party enters into an arrangement which can only take effect by the continuance of a certain existing state of circumstances, there is an implied engagement on his part that he shall do nothing of his own motion to put an end to that state of circumstances, under which alone the arrangement can be operative.

Thus, where a contract between A and B requires A to perform first, A will usually have an excuse for not performing if B has prevented performance. As in the case of a failure to co-operate,[51] there may be additional consequences. Any breach of contract occurring by reason of prevention will give rise to a liability in damages, and may also amount to a repudiation of the contract.[52]

In some of the older cases there was a tendency to treat prevention as equal to performance.[53] Although this is still the case in some situations, for example, where the conduct in question prevents the fulfilment of a contingency which was to operate for the benefit of the party who prevented performance,[54] usually the party whose performance has been prevented will simply have a claim for damages for breach of contract. For example, where an employer prevents an employee from performing an employment contract, the employee will be entitled to recover damages for breach but not the wages which the employer agreed to pay for services rendered.[55]

[1811] Plea of performance implied. Under modern Supreme Court pleading rules[56] a plaintiff (or defendant) need not expressly plead that conditions precedent have been fulfilled, since this will be implied under rules of court.[57] This can be contrasted with the position which formerly obtained and is important when considering the older cases on dependent and independent promises. For example, at the time when *Pordage v Cole*[58] was decided, a party seeking to enforce the other party's obligations had specifically to aver fulfilment of any condition precedent on which the obligation of that party to perform depended.

---

50. (1864) 5 B & S 840 at 852; 122 ER 1043 at 1047. See also *CSS Investments Pty Ltd v Lopiron Pty Ltd* (1987) 76 ALR 463 at 479–80.
51. Arguably a failure to co-operate must also prevent performance: *Sametiet M/T Johs Stove v Istanbul Petrol Rafinerisi A/S (The Johs Stove)* [1984] 1 Lloyd's Rep 38 at 40.
52. See generally on repudiation [1928]–[1947].
53. See, eg *Hotham v East India Co* (1787) 1 TR 638 at 645; 99 ER 1295 at 1299. See further [2202].
54. Cf *Mackay v Dick* (1881) 6 App Cas 251 (see [1809]).
55. Cf *Bolwell Fibreglass Pty Ltd v Foley* [1984] VR 97 (building contract).
56. See, eg Supreme Court Rules (NSW), Pt 15, r 11. Cf *Bahr v Nicolay (No 2)* (1988) 164 CLR 604; 78 ALR 1.
57. See *Australian National Airlines Commission v Robinson* [1977] VR 87 at 91; *Foran v Wight* (1989) 168 CLR 385 at 393.
58. (1669) 1 Wms Saund 319; 85 ER 449 (see [1806]). The averment was not material where an independent obligation was in issue: *Graves v Legg* (1854) 9 Ex 709 at 716; 156 ER 304 at 307. Later, a plaintiff (or defendant) was required to aver generally the performance or fulfilment of all conditions precedent; see *Maynard v Goode* (1926) 37 CLR 529 at 540.

It follows that a party who claims that the other has not performed must in the pleadings put performance in issue in order to oblige the other party to provide evidence of performance.[59] Similarly, if a plaintiff (or defendant) relies on some excuse for a failure to perform, such as a prevention of performance, this should be stated. If it is claimed that a breach of contract has occurred this must be alleged and, if disputed, proved.[60]

Discharge by Performance

General

[1812] Performance must be exact. For a party to be discharged by performance the performance must correspond exactly to the requirements of the contract. However, minute failures and insignificant defects in performance will be excused.[61]

Where both parties have fully performed their contractual obligations, the *contract* is discharged by performance.

[1813] Discharge by substantial performance. The rule stated above will be excluded if the parties have expressed an intention that a performance which is not exact is nevertheless to discharge a party. Sometimes this can be implied from the nature of the obligations. For example, in *Luna Park (NSW) Ltd v Tramways Advertising Pty Ltd*[62] an advertising contract required the contractors to display advertisements for 'at least eight hours per day'. The High Court interpreted this as requiring display for 'substantially' eight hours. Usually, however, the courts will not accept the argument that obligations in commercial contracts are discharged by substantial performance.[63]

Method of performance

[1814] Demand of performance. As a general rule, once performance is due there is no requirement that the promisee demand performance from the promisor, and so a promisor (debtor) must pay a debt due under the contract even though the promisee (creditor) has made no demand for payment.[64]

The parties may reach a contrary agreement, by providing that performance is not to become due until demanded, and there are also statutory exceptions to the general rule.[65] If performance — such as the payment of a debt — is due 'on demand' the debtor is entitled to a reasonable period of time to comply with the demand.[66] In cases where the

---

59. *Cooper v Australian Electric Co (1922) Ltd* (1922) 25 WALR 66 at 67.
60. See [1843].
61. Under the rule de minimis non curat lex. See, eg *Shipton Anderson & Co v Weil Bros & Co* [1912] 1 KB 574.
62. (1938) 61 CLR 286. See also *Bowes v Chaleyer* (1923) 32 CLR 159.
63. See, eg *Arcos Ltd v E A Ronaasen & Son* [1933] AC 470 at 479.
64. See *M S Fashions Ltd v Bank of Credit and Commerce International SA* [1993] Ch 425 at 446; [1993] 3 WLR 220 at 237.
65. *Bills of Exchange Act* 1909 (Cth), s 50.
66. *Bunbury Foods Pty Ltd v National Bank of Australasia Ltd* (1984) 153 CLR 491; 51 ALR 609.

contract requires a demand for performance to be made, a repudiation by the promisor may eliminate the requirement, and in such cases an action may be brought by the promisee without any prior demand.[67]

Whether or not a demand is required, performance cannot be demanded prior to the time specified by the contract. Similarly, under Australian law, a promisee is not usually entitled to an assurance from the promisor that he or she will perform when the time for performance arrives, even if there are reasons for doubting the promisor's ability to perform.[68]

[1815] **Tender of performance.** The promisor must tender performance, that is, offer it to the promisee, within the time required by the contract unless the promisee has dispensed with the requirement. The dispensation may be express or implied. A request not to perform is an example of the former[69] and a repudiation of obligation may be treated as an implied dispensation.[70] Thus, if a buyer has intimated that performance will not be accepted, the seller is absolved from the requirement of making what would be a formal tender,[71] but is not entitled to recover the price of the goods.[72]

A promisee is not obliged to accept an early tender. However, since the promisor has until the expiry of the time specified by the contract to tender performance, the fact that a bad tender is made prior to the expiry of the time for performance, for example, of goods which do not conform with the contract, does not prevent a fresh tender being made of goods which do conform.[73] The promisee (buyer) must accept such a tender unless the first tender was a repudiation of obligation which has been accepted as an anticipatory breach. For example, if a seller tenders unsuitable goods, and also states that no other goods are available for delivery, the buyer may be entitled to treat the statement as a repudiation of obligation.

The sale of goods legislation provides that a demand or tender of goods must be made at a reasonable hour; and that what constitutes a reasonable hour is a question of fact.[74] These rules appear to be of general application. In the case of a tender of money, the tender must be a legal tender, that is, of notes or coin issued by the Reserve Bank[75] of the correct amount and in accordance with the requirements of s 16 of the *Currency Act* 1965 (Cth).

67. *Short v Stone* (1846) 8 QB 358; 115 ER 911.
68. See, eg *Universal Cargo Carriers Corp v Citati* [1957] 2 QB 401. For an exception see [1839]. See further [1944].
69. *Electronic Industries Ltd v David Jones Ltd* (1954) 91 CLR 288 at 295.
70. *M'Clure v Ripley* (1850) 5 Ex 140; 155 ER 60; *Foran v Wight* (1989) 168 CLR 385.
71. *Sinason-Teicher Inter-American Grain Corp v Oilcakes and Oilseeds Trading Co Ltd* [1954] 2 All ER 497 (affirmed [1954] 3 All ER 468). See also, in the sale of land context, *Kershaw v Forster Pastoral Pty Ltd* (1985) 3 BPR 9515; *Beard v Wratislaw* (1991) [1993] 2 Qd R 494 (see Scott Atkins, (1995) 8 *JCL* 275).
72. Cf *Sunbird Plaza Pty Ltd v Maloney* (1988) 166 CLR 245; 77 ALR 205 (land).
73. *Borrowman v Free* (1878) 4 QBD 500; *Motor Oil Hellas (Corinth) Refineries SA v Shipping Corp of India (The Kanchenjunga)* [1990] 1 Lloyd's Rep 391 at 399.
74. **ACT**: *Sale of Goods Act* 1954, s 33(5); **NSW**: *Sale of Goods Act* 1923, s 32(4); **NT**: *Sale of Goods Act* 1972, s 32(5); **Qld**: *Sale of Goods Act* 1896, s 31(4); **SA**: *Sale of Goods Act* 1895, s 29(4); **Tas**: *Sale of Goods Act* 1896, s 34(4); **Vic**: *Goods Act* 1958, s 36(4); **WA**: *Sale of Goods Act* 1895, s 29(4).
75. Section 36(1) of the *Reserve Bank Act* 1959 (Cth) provides that Australian notes are legal tender throughout Australia.

The effect of a refusal to accept a valid tender may depend on the nature of the contract. If A owes money to B under a contract and B refuses to accept a legal tender, A is not discharged from the obligation to pay the debt. If B brings an action to recover the money due, A should pay the debt into court so as to avoid being held liable to pay the costs of the proceedings. On the other hand, where a seller tenders goods to a buyer, and the buyer rejects the tender, and without justification refuses to accept delivery, the seller is entitled to bring an action for damages — for non-acceptance — and is not liable in respect of the failure to deliver.[76] Usually, however, the buyer is not obliged to pay the price of the goods unless property passed to the buyer under the contract.[77] Moreover, even if property did pass, if the seller has exercised the statutory right of resale the seller's right will be to recover only damages.[78]

[1816] **Payment.** Where a contract requires payment in cash, the promisee (creditor) is not bound to accept a negotiable instrument, such as the promisor's (debtor's) personal cheque, since this is not payment in cash.[79] It is, however, extremely common for a creditor to accept a bill of exchange as payment. Where this occurs the consequences depend on the intention of the parties. There are two possibilities: the cheque may be accepted as conditional payment; or as a discharge of the debtor's obligations.[80] In the former case the debtor will be discharged only if the bill is honoured on presentation, and, if it is not, the creditor has the choice of suing on the original contract or on the separate contract evidenced by the bill. On the other hand, if the intention was for the debtor to be treated as discharged under the contract, the creditor is restricted to an action on the bill of exchange. In the absence of indications to the contrary, payment will be presumed to be conditional on the bill being met.[81]

Where the contract expressly provides that payment need not be made in cash, or may be made alternatively in cash or some other form, the problem discussed above also arises. For example, if a contract for the sale of goods provides for payment by 'banker's confirmed credit', the fact that a credit has been opened in favour of the seller does not necessarily mean that the buyer has discharged the obligation to pay. This may be the intention of the parties, but usually the credit is to be taken as a conditional discharge, in which case the seller may sue the buyer, under the contract of sale, or bring an action against the banker, under the credit.[82] For example, in *Saffron v*

76. *Startup v Macdonald* (1843) 6 Man & G 593; 134 ER 1029.
77. See [2204].
78. *R V Ward Ltd v Bignall* [1967] 1 QB 534.
79. See, eg *Stirling Properties Ltd v Yerba Pty Ltd* (1987) 74 ACTR 1. On the other hand, in commercial transactions a bank cheque is equivalent to cash. See *Perel v Australian Bank of Commerce* (1923) 24 SR (NSW) 62 at 75 (on appeal sub nom *Australian Bank of Commerce Ltd v Perel* [1926] AC 737).
80. This analysis is not applicable to the deposit of a cheque in a bank account: *National Australia Bank Ltd v KDS Construction Services Pty Ltd* (1987) 163 CLR 668; 76 ALR 27.
81. See, eg *Tilley v Official Receiver* (1960) 103 CLR 529; *W J Alan & Co Ltd v El Nasr Export and Import Co* [1972] 2 QB 189 at 210. For the effect of payment by credit card see *Re Charge Card Services Ltd* [1989] Ch 497.
82. This was the position in *W J Alan & Co Ltd v El Nasr Export and Import Co* [1972] 2 QB 189.

Société Minière Cafrika[83] the High Court held that a seller was entitled to maintain an action for the price of goods accepted by the buyer when, through no fault of his own, the seller was unable to recover on a letter of credit.

[1817] **Alternative methods of performance.** Where a contract may be performed in two or more different ways the contract may or may not provide who has the power to make the choice. If it does so provide, the party entitled to make the choice does so by electing in favour of one method,[84] for example, by actually performing in one of the permitted ways.

If there is no express provision, the court must decide who has the benefit of the choice and the decision may seem quite arbitrary. For example, in *Reed v Kilburn Co-operative Society*,[85] the plaintiff lent £50 to the defendants under a contract which provided that the plaintiff had agreed to lend the money for a 'term of nine or six months'. The plaintiff made a demand after six months but the court decided that the choice lay with the defendants, as borrowers. During argument, Blackburn J expressed the rule as being that the party who is to do the first act has the choice, and in this case it was the defendants. Cockburn CJ said, also in argument, that the contract conferred the benefit on the defendants who were the masters of the situation.

[1818] **Vicarious performance.** A promisor performs a contract vicariously where it performs through a third party. The most common example is subcontracting of a building contract. Two issues arise:

- whether the promisor is permitted to perform through a third party; and
- the effect of vicarious performance.

Generally, subcontracting is permitted unless the nature or terms of the contract show that the contract is personal to the promisor. If an element of personal skill or expertise or personal confidence exists, vicarious performance will not be permitted.[86] To take an obvious example, if A agrees to paint B's portrait the contract is personal to A, and A cannot subcontract for another person, C, to do the work. On the other hand, in *British Waggon Co v Lea & Co*,[87] the plaintiffs hired certain railway wagons to the defendants and agreed to keep the wagons in repair for the term of the contracts. It was held that there was no element of skill or expertise sufficient to make performance of the contract personal to the plaintiffs. The defendants were therefore bound to pay the hire due under the contracts even though the plaintiffs had assigned the benefit of the contracts to a third party and had not personally carried out the repairs.

Whatever the nature of the contract, it may provide, expressly or impliedly, that vicarious performance is not permitted. For example, in

---

83. (1958) 100 CLR 231.
84. See, eg *Timmerman v Nervina Industries (International) Pty Ltd* [1983] 2 Qd R 261.
85. (1875) LR 10 QB 264. See also *Head v Kelk* (1963) 63 SR (NSW) 340 at 345–6.
86. *Bruce v Tyley* (1916) 21 CLR 277.
87. (1880) 5 QBD 149.

Davies v Collins[88] the plaintiff entrusted his army uniform to the defendant for cleaning and repair. The uniform was not returned and, for the purposes of the case, was taken to have been lost. The defendant had in fact delivered the uniform to a subcontractor to have the work done. The court held that the terms of the contract impliedly prohibited vicarious performance. The contract provided:

> Whilst every care is exercised in cleaning and dyeing all garments, all orders are accepted at owner's risk entirely and we are unable to hold ourselves responsible for damage, shrinkage, colour or defects developed in necessary handling.

Because it was impossible for the defendant to exercise 'every care' in cleaning and dyeing while the work was being done by a third party, and since the subcontract could not be described as 'necessary handling', the defendant had no right to subcontract the work.

As a general rule, where the promisor performs the contract through a third party (subcontractor) the promisor remains liable on the contract and may therefore be sued in contract if the (vicarious) performance is not in accordance with the contract.[89] However, if the promisee agrees to accept performance by a third party (or subsequently ratifies what has been done by the promisor) the promisee must accept the performance, even though it may differ from that required by the agreement. For example, if a creditor agrees to accept payment from a third party in discharge of a debt, the creditor will be bound to accept payment, and once the payment has been accepted the debtor is discharged, even if the creditor agreed to accept less than the full amount due.[90]

Vicarious performance — which relates to the burden of a contract — must be distinguished from assignment. Assignments relate to the right to receive the benefit of performance which, as a chose in action, is assignable to a third party in accordance with the rules governing assignment.[91] Although in many cases a promisor can subcontract for a third party to perform its obligations vicariously, on behalf of the promisor, a promisor cannot assign the burden of a contract.

Enforcement of the Promisee's Obligations

[1819] Entitlement to enforce. A promisor who is discharged by performance may enforce the promisee's obligations. It is also clear, however, that even a promisor who is not discharged by performance is generally entitled to enforce the promisee's obligations even though

---

88. [1945] 1 All ER 247.
89. *Stewart v Reavell's Garage* [1952] 2 QB 545.
90. *Hirachand Punamchand v Temple* [1911] 2 KB 330. But it must be made clear to the creditor that the offer of a smaller sum is being made to satisfy the whole amount of the debt: *Waghorn v Linden Manufacturing Pty Ltd* [1970] 3 NSWR 559. Cf [359].
91. A contract may prohibit assignment: *Linden Gardens Trust Ltd v Lenesta Sludge Disposal Ltd* [1994] 1 AC 85. Alternatively, the right to receive performance may be personal to the promisee, so that in practice whether or not the benefit of a contract is assignable depends on factors similar to those discussed in the text. See Meagher, Gummow and Lehane, *Equity: Doctrines and Remedies*, 3rd ed, 1992, paras 688–92.

performance is not exactly that required, provided the performance is a substantial performance by the promisor.

In considering the position of a promisor who has not fully performed, regard must be to:

- the nature of the contract, and the claim made by the promisor; and
- whether the promisee is discharged, by termination for breach or repudiation or under the doctrine of frustration.

[1820] **Nature of the claim and contract.** A party who seeks to enforce the other party's obligations may be seeking to recover damages, claiming the contract price or some other liquidated sum, or pursuing an equitable remedy such as specific performance. In this chapter we deal with claims to recover the 'contract price', that is, the money sum which the other party has promised to pay as the price of performance. Other types of claim are discussed elsewhere.[92]

Where the contract price is sought the courts have generally treated the nature of the contract as crucial, and drawn a distinction between entire and severable contracts.[93]

[1821] **Contract price not recoverable after discharge by termination.** Almost invariably, a party who has been discharged by reason of termination of the performance of the contract for breach or repudiation by the other party,[94] will not be liable to pay the contract price.[95] Similarly, if the contract has been discharged under the doctrine of frustration,[96] the contract price is not usually recoverable.[97]

Entire contracts

[1822] **Definition.** An entire contract is one in which the parties have agreed, expressly or impliedly, that complete performance by the promisor is a condition precedent to enforcement of the contract. A contract may be entire if it provides for the payment of a lump sum and 'no provision is made for setting off a portion of this consideration against a portion of the performance'.[98] Most of the cases concern this type of contract, under which complete performance is a condition precedent to recovery of the lump sum.

[1823] **Contracts within the definition.** Whether or not a contract is entire depends on the construction of the contract.[99] However, the fact that the contract provides for a lump sum payment is not conclusive.[100] In other words, a contract which provides for a lump sum payment will not be entire

---

92. See Chapter 21; [2401]–[2412]. Cf [2218]–[2224].
93. See [1822]–[1835].
94. See generally Chapter 19.
95. But see *Westralian Farmers Ltd v Commonwealth Agricultural Service Engineers Ltd* (1936) 54 CLR 361 at 369.
96. See generally Chapter 20.
97. But cf [2073].
98. G L Williams, 'Partial Performance of Entire Contracts' (1941) 57 *LQR* 373.
99. *Purcell v Bacon* (1914) 19 CLR 241 at 249 (reversed on other grounds sub nom *Bacon v Purcell* (1916) 22 CLR 307).
100. *William Thomas & Sons v Harrowing SS Co* [1915] AC 58 at 63.

unless the parties have agreed that the sum is to be payable only in the event of complete performance.

The main example of an entire contract is a lump sum building contract, where performance by the builder in accordance with the contract is usually a condition precedent to the recovery of payment.[101] However, it is common for a contract to be treated as entire for some purposes, but not for others. Thus, an employment contract is entire with respect to time of service: the employee must serve for the entire term as this is a condition precedent to recovery of wages by the employee. However, the contract is not entire from the point of view of the quality of service. Therefore, even though a lump sum payment is provided for, the failure of the employee to serve to the best of his or her ability does not necessarily mean that wages cannot be recovered. The only explanation for this confusing approach is that, in most cases at least, the expression 'entire obligation' should be substituted for 'entire contract'.[102]

[1824] Failure of condition precedent precludes enforcement. Where a contract is entire, and the condition precedent has not been fulfilled, the contract price will not be recoverable.[103] This is the 'doctrine' of the entire contract. However, substantial performance by the promisor is usually sufficient to enable recovery of the contract price;[104] and certain statutory exceptions must also be considered.[105]

The doctrine of the entire contract does not depend on the existence of a breach of contract: recovery will be refused even if the promisor has an excuse in respect of the failure of the condition precedent. For example, in *Cutter v Powell*[106] a seaman died before he completed the voyage in respect of which he was to be paid. The court took it for granted that, as the seaman had not served for the entire voyage, his executrix could not recover his wages even though there was no breach by the seaman. Nor could she recover a proportionate part of the wages, since the contract did not provide for payment pro rata. The case also illustrates another important feature of the doctrine, namely, that where the condition precedent fails the court will not award a reasonable sum in respect of benefits conferred. Thus, in *Cutter v Powell* the court refused to allow restitution (a quantum meruit claim), in respect of the services actually rendered by the seaman.[107]

On the other hand, where the condition precedent fails because the promisee has prevented the promisor performing, the doctrine does not apply[108] and the promisor may bring an action to recover the value of any

---

101. *Sumpter v Hedges* [1898] 1 QB 673.
102. See *Baltic Shipping Co v Dillon (The Mikhail Lermontov)* (1993) 176 CLR 344 at 350, 384; 111 ALR 289.
103. *Phillips v Ellinson Bros Pty Ltd* (1941) 65 CLR 221.
104. See [1830]–[1832].
105. See [1827]–[1829].
106. (1795) 6 TR 320; 101 ER 573. See S J Stoljar, 'The Great Case of *Cutter v Powell*' (1956) 34 *Can B Rev* 288; Martin Dockray, 'Cutter v Powell: a Trip Outside the Text' (2001) 117 *LQR* 664.
107. See further [2066].
108. *Forman & Co Pty Ltd v The Ship 'Liddesdale'* [1900] AC 190 at 202.

work done,[109] or an action for damages if the conduct of the promisee was a breach of contract.[110]

Severable contracts

[1825] Definition. A contract which is not entire is usually referred to as a 'severable' or 'divisible' contract. However, the description is most appropriately used to describe contracts in which the parties have divided the contract price into a number of instalments, each corresponding to a definite proportion of the other party's performance. For example, where A agrees to make instalment deliveries of goods to B, and B agrees to pay for each instalment when delivered, the contract is severable.[111]

The mere fact that the contract provides for progress payments towards a lump sum price does not make the contract severable.[112]

[1826] Enforcement of a severable part. Where a contract is severable, a promisor may be able to recover in respect of a severable part of the contract, notwithstanding a failure to discharge obligations under the contract. Thus, in *Government of Newfoundland v Newfoundland Railway Co*[113] the Newfoundland Government agreed, as part of its obligations under a railway construction contract, to grant the Railway Co title to 5000 acres of land for each mile of railway constructed, on completion of each five-mile section. The Railway Co promised to complete the construction in five years, but completed only 17 of the 68 five-mile sections. One of the issues before the Privy Council was whether the Railway Co was entitled to receive title to the land. It was held that the Government was bound to grant title to 25,000 acres once each section was completed, because each claim to a grant was independent or severable and earned when each section of the railway was completed.

The entitlement of a promisor to recover in respect of a severable part nevertheless depends on similar considerations to those applicable to entire contracts. For example, if a seller of goods agrees to make four instalment deliveries and the buyer accepts the first two deliveries but rejects the third, the seller is entitled to the agreed price for the deliveries made (and accepted) because property in the goods delivered will have passed to the buyer. Similarly, if an employer agrees to make monthly payments to an employee, the latter's right to recover wages in respect of each month depends, at common law,[114] on the performance rendered during that month. If the employee resigns during the second week of a month, the employee will not be entitled to wages for that month because the employer's obligation to pay is entire with respect to that severable part.[115]

---

109. See [2322].
110. See generally Chapter 21.
111. *Mersey Steel and Iron Co Ltd v Naylor Benzon & Co* (1884) 9 App Cas 434.
112. See *Gilbert-Ash (Northern) Ltd v Modern Engineering (Bristol) Ltd* [1974] AC 689 at 717.
113. (1888) 13 App Cas 199.
114. For the position under statute see [1827], [1828].
115. *Steele v Tardiani* (1946) 72 CLR 386.

Statutory exceptions

[1827] The apportionment legislation. Under the apportionment legislation, 'all rents, annuities, dividends and other periodical payments in the nature of income' are considered as accruing from day to day and are 'apportionable in respect of time accordingly'.[116] Superficially, the legislation looks to assist a promisor who would otherwise fail in an action to enforce the other party's obligation to pay money because of a failure to discharge contractual obligations. However, the legislation is fairly narrow in scope. Thus, it will not apply if the parties have 'expressly stipulated'[117] that no apportionment is to occur. The legislation has also been restrictively interpreted.

The legislation applies to 'periodical' payments and this is not an appropriate description of sums payable under entire contracts. Accordingly, it would not have assisted the executrix in *Cutter v Powell*.[118] However, it might assist a lessor to recover a proportion of the rent which a lessee has agreed to pay and it might assist a salaried employee. The legislation defines[119] 'annuities' as including 'salaries' and an employee whose contract provides for monthly payments of salary might be able to recover, say, three quarters of a promised payment, if three out of the four weeks were completed.[120]

It is uncertain whether the legislation applies where the promisor is in breach of contract. In principle, the legislation should apply, for example, if the salaried employee in the example just given has been lawfully dismissed by the employer. The cases do not give any clear guidance on the point.[121]

[1828] State and Federal awards. The remuneration of a large number of employees is governed by State and Federal awards made under statute.[122] When considering the performance of employment contracts, and in particular the employee's right to recover wages, the effect of such awards must be taken into account.[123] The awards are important, for

---

116. **ACT**: *Apportionment Act* 1905, s 4; **NSW**: *Conveyancing Act* 1919, s 144(1); **NT**: *Law of Property Act* 2000, s 212(1); **Qld**: *Property Law Act* 1974, s 232; **SA**: *Law of Property Act* 1936, s 64; **Tas**: *Apportionment Act* 1871, s 2; **Vic**: *Supreme Court Act* 1986, s 54; **WA**: *Property Law Act* 1969, s 131.
117. **ACT**: *Apportionment Act* 1905, s 8; **NSW**: *Conveyancing Act* 1919, s 144(5); **NT**: *Law of Property Act* 2000, s 213(2); **Qld**: *Property Law Act* 1974, s 233(2); **SA**: *Law of Property Act* 1936, s 68; **Tas**: *Apportionment Act* 1871, s 7; **Vic**: *Supreme Court Act* 1986, s 53(4); **WA**: *Property Law Act* 1969, s 134(2).
118. (1795) 6 TR 320; 101 ER 573 (see [1824]).
119. **ACT**: *Apportionment Act* 1905, s 2; **NSW**: *Conveyancing Act* 1919, s 142; **NT**: *Law of Property Act* 2000, s 211; **Qld**: *Property Law Act* 1974, s 231; **SA**: *Law of Property Act* 1936, s 63; **Tas**: *Apportionment Act* 1871, s 5; **Vic**: *Supreme Court Act* 1986, s 53(1); **WA**: *Property Law Act* 1969, s 130(1).
120. But see Paul Matthews, '"Salaries" in the *Apportionment Act* 1870' (1982) 2 *Legal Studies* 302.
121. Doubts were expressed in *Moriarty v Regent's Garage and Engineering Co Ltd* [1921] 1 KB 423 at 434 (reversed without reference to the point [1921] 2 KB 766). Contrast *Sim v Rotherham MBC* [1987] Ch 216 and see S M Waddams, 'Restitution for the Part Performer', in Reiter and Swan, eds, *Studies in Contract Law*, 1980, p 162.
122. See **Cth**: *Industrial Relations Reform Act* 1993; **NSW**: *Industrial Relations Act* 1996; **Qld**: *Industrial Relations Act* 1999; **SA**: *Industrial and Employee Relations Act* 1994; **Tas**: *Industrial Relations Act* 1984; **Vic**: *Long Service Leave Act* 1992; **WA**: *Industrial Relations Act* 1979.

example, in guaranteeing minimum wages and in regulating other matters such as dismissal. However, an award employee's right to recover wages does not depend solely on the award, since the relationship between the employer and employee is one created by contract.[124]

In the present context, the main relevance of the existence of an award is that the payment terms of the contract are not conclusive. Thus, an award specification for payment at a daily or hourly rate may assist an employee who would fail at common law because of the rules governing performance. For example, if the contract provides for payment at fortnightly intervals, but the employee is lawfully dismissed in the middle of one of these periods, the employee would fail at common law in an action for a fortnightly wage payment. Since under the award the employee's wages may accrue daily (or hourly), recovery for the days (or hours) actually worked may be permitted. In this respect the award substitutes a different (and obligatory) method for determining wages from that applicable at common law.[125]

[1829] **Frustrated contracts legislation.** Where a contract is frustrated after partial performance by the promisor, legislation in New South Wales, Victoria and South Australia confers a right to recover a sum of money, independently of the terms of the contract, in respect of benefits conferred. The legislation is considered in Chapter 20.[126]

The doctrine of substantial performance

[1830] **Origin of the doctrine.** The origin of the modern doctrine of substantial performance is Lord Mansfield's famous statement in *Boone v Eyre*:[127]

> The distinction is very clear, where mutual covenants go to the whole of the consideration on both sides, they are mutual conditions, the one precedent to the other. But where they go only to a part, where a breach may be paid for in damages, there the defendant has a remedy on his covenant, and shall not plead it as a condition precedent.

The proceedings in *Boone v Eyre* were by way of demurrer on a deed whereby the plaintiff conveyed to the defendant the equity of redemption of a plantation in the West Indies, together with its stock of Negroes. He covenanted that he had good title to the plantation, and also that he was lawfully possessed of the Negroes. In consideration of this, the defendant had paid £5000 and covenanted that if the plaintiff 'well and truly' performed his side of the bargain he would pay the plaintiff an annuity of £160 per annum. When the plaintiff alleged a breach by nonpayment of the

---

123. See G J McCarry, 'No Work, No Pay' (1983) 57 *ALJ* 378.
124. *Amalgamated Collieries of WA Ltd v True* (1938) 59 CLR 417 at 423 (and on appeal sub nom *True v Amalgamated Collieries of WA Ltd* [1940] AC 537 at 546); *Byrne v Australian Airlines Ltd* (1995) 185 CLR 410 at 419–20; 131 ALR 422.
125. See *Mallinson v Scottish Australian Investment Co Ltd* (1920) 28 CLR 66 at 72–3; *Byrne v Australian Airlines Ltd* (1995) 185 CLR 410 at 419–20. See also *Huskisson RSL Sub-Branch Club Ltd v Sullivan* (1990) 20 NSWLR 332 at 343ff; *Ansett Transport Industries (Operations) Pty Ltd v Australian Federation of Air Pilots (No 2)* [1991] 2 VR 636 at 638.
126. See [2068]–[2098].
127. (1777) 1 H Bl 273n; 126 ER 160.

annuity, the defendant pleaded that the plaintiff was not lawfully possessed of the Negroes. The purport of Lord Mansfield's statement was that the plea was not a good plea because, 'if it were to be allowed, any one Negro not being the property of the plaintiff would bar the action'. Therefore, the plaintiff was successful even though the defendant's obligation to pay the annuity was, arguably, expressly dependent[128] on full performance by the plaintiff. The conclusion would presumably have been different had a serious breach been alleged,[129] or if the defendant had not received substantial benefits under the deed.[130]

[1831] **Effect of substantial performance.** Except in that limited class of cases where substantial performance is the extent of performance required by the contract,[131] substantial performance will not discharge the promisor. Moreover, if there is no excuse for the failure to perform, the promisor will be in breach of contract, and liable in damages. However, unless the promisor breached a condition, the promisee will not be entitled to terminate the performance of the contract.

Under the doctrine of substantial performance, the promisee may be held liable to pay the contract price.[132] For example, in *Hoenig v Isaacs*[133] a contractor was able to recover the balance payable under a contract for work and labour and materials supplied notwithstanding that his work did not correspond exactly to the requirements of the contract. The court found that the cost of remedying the defects in the work was relatively small in proportion to the work that the contractor had agreed to do, and his performance was therefore substantial enough to justify holding the defendant liable to pay the balance of the contract price.

In cases where a promisee is held liable to pay the contract price by reason of the promisor's substantial performance, the former will retain the right to claim compensation in respect of the latter's failure to perform and this claim may, depending on the circumstances, be pursued as a cross claim or counterclaim for damages or by the enforcement of a right of set-off.[134]

[1832] **Scope of the doctrine.** The scope of the doctrine of substantial performance is to some extent uncertain. It has been said that the doctrine does not apply unless the promisor's failure constitutes a breach of contract.[135] The rationale for this restriction is that the promisee must be in a position to claim compensation, and the presence of an excuse for the

---

128. See [1807].
129. See *Glazebrook v Woodrow* (1799) 8 TR 366 at 374; 101 ER 1436 at 1441.
130. See *Ellen v Topp* (1851) 6 Ex 424 at 442; 155 ER 609 at 616; *Graves v Legg* (1854) 9 Ex 709 at 717; 156 ER 304 at 307. But cf *Wallis v Pratt* [1911] AC 394 at 400.
131. See [1813].
132. The action is on the contract, not for restitution. A contrary statement in *Connor v Stainton* (1924) 27 WALR 72 at 73–4 is incorrect: *Simpson Steel Structures v Spencer* [1964] WAR 101 at 104.
133. [1952] 2 All ER 176. See also *Lemura v Coppola* [1960] Qd R 308; *Zamperoni Decorators Pty Ltd v Lo Presti* [1983] VR 338. Cf *Williamson v Murdoch* (1912) 14 WALR 54.
134. See *Bolton v Mahadeva* [1972] 1 WLR 1009 at 1015.
135. *O'Sullivan v O'Leary* [1955] VLR 52 at 58. But see *William Thomas & Sons v Harrowing SS Co* [1915] AC 58.

failure to perform will prevent any such claim being made. However, the position is far from clear and it seems more just to hold the promisee liable to pay the whole sum than to deny the promisor any right of recovery at all.[136]

A second area of uncertainty is what constitutes substantial performance. Although this is essentially a question of fact, the cases illustrate inconsistent approaches. In *Hoenig v Isaacs*[137] the court said the performance can be considered as substantial unless the promisor's failure goes to the 'root' of the contract. On the other hand, in *Bolton v Mahadeva*[138] a contractor agreed to install a heating and hot water system in return for a promised payment of £560. The work was defectively done, and a sum of £174 was required to make the work comply with the requirements of the contract. The court held that the performance rendered was not substantial and restricted the application of the doctrine to cases where a small expenditure by the promisee will make the work conform.

A third area of uncertainty is whether the doctrine applies to entire contracts. Generally the view has been taken that it does, and the English Court of Appeal certainly proceeded on this basis in *Bolton v Mahadeva*. On the other hand, in *Hoenig v Isaacs* the court appears to have taken the view that had the contract been entire the doctrine would not have been applicable. As a matter of strict logic the latter view is correct since, if the parties have agreed that complete performance by the plaintiff is a condition precedent to recovery, it is difficult to see how the promisee can be required to pay for performance which is not complete. The law was indeed stated in these terms in *Mondel v Steel*,[139] where, referring to a building contract, the court said that 'the law appears to have construed the contract as not importing that the performance of every portion of the work should be a condition precedent to the payment of the stipulated price'. It seems more realistic to recognise that the contract is not entire than to engraft an inconsistent requirement of substantial performance on an 'entire' contract. Accordingly, the proper approach is to identify the term breached, and to consider its nature and the consequences of the breach.

The doctrine applies to severable contracts. For example, in *Steele v Tardiani*[140] an employment contract, which provided for remuneration of employees per ton of firewood cut by them, was construed as a severable contract requiring substantial performance in respect of 'each divisible application of the contract'. This is, however, difficult to reconcile with reasoning in recent English cases on employment contracts. In *Miles v Wakefield MDC*[141] an employee, as part of industrial action, refused to carry out some of his normal Saturday duties. It was held that the employee had no right to wages for weeks in which the conduct took place, because he

---

136. Query the position where the claim is for restitution in respect of an unenforceable contract. See Mason and Carter, *Restitution Law in Australia*, 1995, para 1031.
137. [1952] 2 All ER 176.
138. [1972] 1 WLR 1009.
139. (1841) 8 M & W 858 at 870; 151 ER 1288 at 1293.
140. (1946) 72 CLR 386 at 401.
141. [1987] AC 539. Cf *Csomore v Public Service Board of New South Wales* (1986) 10 NSWLR 587.

had not fulfilled the condition precedent to payment — full performance — and had not shown readiness and willingness to work. The employer had deducted only three hours' pay, and this was regarded as an appropriate (proportionate) deduction.[142] The reference to readiness and willingness seems beside the point,[143] and upholding the employer's conduct in making small deductions from wages directs attention away from the gravity of the decision, since the employee, on the House of Lords' analysis, was not entitled to any payment at all.[144] Subsequently, in *Wiluszynski v Tower Hamlets London BC*,[145] the English Court of Appeal rejected an approach based on substantial performance under an entire contract analysis for two reasons. First, the doctrine of substantial performance does not apply to a severable contract. Second, the failure in performance in the case was not insubstantial.

It seems unrealistic to deny that the rationale for *Miles v Wakefield* is a policy concern, namely, to discourage industrial action of the type encountered. But, as a matter of contract doctrine the reasoning in that case, and *Wiluszynski*, leaves a lot unexplained. First, there is little analysis of whether the performance was substantial. The idea that substantial performance does not apply to severable contracts is untenable in Australia. However, in cases where performance is not substantial, a sound justification exists for denying that the employee is entitled to payment. Second, in most cases the employee will be engaging in conduct which is repudiatory, and the general approach to such conduct is to treat the employer as faced with a choice between terminating and affirming the contract.[146] Yet, in these cases the employer does not terminate performance and the courts have struggled to explain how the employer is able to deny the contractual obligation to pay for the services rendered.[147] Third, if the employee merely performs the contract defectively, the employer must pay full wages (subject to a right to claim damages for loss caused by the employee's breach of contract),[148] with the result that a formalistic distinction is drawn between incomplete performance and defective performance. It is doubtful whether an Australian court would accept that distinction. The proper analysis relies in all cases on whether performance is substantially in accordance with the contract. The employee is entitled to be paid for substantial performance, subject, of course, to the employer's claim to damages for breach.[149]

---

142. Cf *Sim v Rotherham MBC* [1987] Ch 216 (equitable set-off) (see B W Napier, [1987] *CLJ* 44).
143. See [1808].
144. See further [2325].
145. [1989] ICR 493.
146. *Fercometal SARL v Mediterranean Shipping Co SA* [1989] AC 788 at 805. But cf [1947].
147. One suggestion is that it is impossible in large organisations to know which employees are working in accordance with their contracts. Although this may be true, it is difficult to see why it should disentitle the employee to reliance on normal contract principles.
148. Presumably this would also be subject to the substantial performance doctrine.
149. B W Napier, 'Aspects of the Wage-Work Bargain' [1984] *CLJ* 337 at 342, 348; J W Shaw and Robert McClelland, 'Selective Work Bans: "No Work No Pay" Revisited' (1986) 3 *Aust Bar Rev* 250 at 256–7. See also G F Smith, 'Part Work No Pay?' (1989) 2 *AJLL* 91. Contrast Greg McCarry, (1987) 3 *Aust Bar Rev* 174 at 177.

Finally, there is the problem of reconciling this area of the law with the law applicable to termination for breach. In *H Dakin & Co Ltd v Lee*[150] a Divisional Court approached the doctrine of substantial performance from the point of view of termination for breach, and said that where a builder's performance is not strictly in accordance with the contract it will nevertheless be regarded as substantial unless the work done is of no value to the other party, is entirely different from that provided for by the contract or the conduct of the builder constitutes a repudiation ('abandonment') of the contract. Although this approach has been the subject of criticism,[151] it is consistent with *Hoenig v Isaacs*[152] and also the doctrine later developed by the courts in reliance on *Hongkong Fir Shipping Co Ltd v Kawasaki Kisen Kaisha Ltd*.[153]

The need for consistency was arguably ignored[154] by the court in *Bolton v Mahadeva*.[155] Under the *Hongkong Fir* doctrine the issue is whether the promisee has a right to terminate, whereas under the entire contract doctrine the issue is whether the promisor has performed sufficiently. The effect of cases such as *Dakin v Lee* and *Hoenig v Isaacs* is to treat the issues as two sides of the same coin.[156] This seems logical enough, although difficult to reconcile with the older cases. The doctrine of the entire contract evolved out of the distinction between dependent and independent promises.[157] However, the concept of termination did not emerge until the middle of the 19th century.[158] This was because if, by reason of a failure in performance, a dependent obligation could not be enforced, it remained unenforceable until the condition precedent had been fulfilled and so there was no need to ask whether the performance of the contract was terminated. The procedural reforms begun in England in the middle of the 19th century, which made precise pleading less important,[159] may well have encouraged a focus on the issue of termination rather than dependency of obligation, and perhaps explains the development of two different approaches.

Criticism

[1833] Entire contract terminology. The law governing the enforcement of contractual obligations can be criticised on a number of grounds, one of which is that the terminology is confusing and unhelpful. Although it may be helpful to speak in terms of a distinction between entire and severable obligations, it is not helpful to distinguish entire and

---

150. [1916] 1 KB 566.
151. See *Vigers v Cook* [1919] 2 KB 475 at 483–4; *Eshelby v Federated European Bank Ltd* [1932] 1 KB 423 at 431.
152. [1952] 2 All ER 176 (see [1831]). See also *Lemura v Coppola* [1960] Qd R 308 at 314.
153. [1962] 2 QB 26 (see [1922]–[1927]).
154. See Carter, *Breach of Contract*, 2nd ed, 1991, para 694.
155. [1972] 1 WLR 1009 (see [1832]).
156. Cf *Baltic Shipping Co v Dillon (The Mikhail Lermontov)* (1993) 176 CLR 344 at 350.
157. See [1805]–[1808].
158. *Glaholm v Hays* (1841) 2 Man & G 257 at 265; 133 ER 743 at 746, is an early example.
159. See Carter, *Breach of Contract*, 2nd ed, 1991, para 115.

severable contracts.[160] For example, a contract for the sale of goods is entire with respect to the quantity to be delivered, but not entire in the sense that every breach by the seller precludes recovery of the price of the goods.

It has also been shown that interpreting a contract as severable does not necessarily place the promisor in a better position, because the contract may be 'entire' with respect to each severable part.[161] This reinforces the view that the distinction drawn is between entire and severable obligations not contracts.

[1834] Uncertainty of substantial performance doctrine.[162] The second criticism concerns the uncertain nature and scope of the substantial performance doctrine.[163] It would seem that two quite different approaches are to be found in the cases. The first, typified by Denning LJ's judgment in *Hoenig v Isaacs*,[164] treats the right to recover the contract price as determined by the right of the promisee to terminate for breach or repudiation. If there is a right to terminate, because the promisor has breached a condition, repudiated the contract or committed a breach which renders the performance of the contract substantially different, the promisor cannot recover the contract price. The second approach, exemplified by *Bolton v Mahadeva*,[165] conceives of the doctrine applying even though the contract is entire, that is to say, even though the condition precedent of complete performance has not been fulfilled.

The divergence of approach indicates that it is difficult to find an acceptable basis for the doctrine. The doctrine may be based on the 'presumed intention'[166] of the parties. However, this is difficult to reconcile with its application in cases where the contract is entire, since ex hypothesi the parties have expressed their intention that complete performance is required. In cases where the contract is entire the true basis has been described as the prevention of unjust enrichment.[167] However, this ought to lead to recovery on a restitutionary claim rather than an action on the contract. But it is clear that for substantial performance the liability is to pay the contract price rather than the reasonable value of services rendered. The statement in *O'Sullivan v O'Leary*,[168] that the doctrine must rest 'either upon a benevolent construction of the contract or on some special rule of equity applicable to the relief of specific performance' is perhaps the best indication of uncertainty generated by the doctrine since it treats the

---

160. See G H Treitel, 'Some Problems of Breach of Contract' (1967) 30 *MLR* 139. See also [1823].
161. See [1826].
162. See Anthony Beck, 'The Doctrine of Substantial Performance: Conditions and Conditions Precedent' (1975) 38 *MLR* 413.
163. See [1832].
164. [1952] 2 All ER 176 (see [1831]).
165. [1972] 1 WLR 1009 (see [1832]). But cf *O'Sullivan v O'Leary* [1955] VLR 52 at 58.
166. *Corio Guarantee Corp v McCallum* [1956] VLR 755 at 760.
167. See S J Stoljar, 'Substantial Performance in Building Contracts' (1954–56) 3 *UWALR* 293 at 307.
168. [1955] VLR 52 at 58 per Gavan Duffy J. Cf *Simpson Steel Structures v Spencer* [1964] WAR 101 at 105 ('equity relieving against forfeiture').

promisor's action for the contract price as being one for specific performance, which it clearly is not.[169]

[1835] Unjust enrichment. The final criticism of the law is the way in which it encourages unjust enrichment. Where a promisor confers benefits on the promisee, but obtains no payment at all, the promisee may be unjustly enriched. In *Bolton v Mahadeva*[170] the result was that the defendant paid nothing for the work, and therefore effectively obtained the system for £174, that is, the sum which was (presumably) paid to a third party to remedy the defects in the system. As the law currently stands,[171] the plaintiff would almost certainly have failed in a claim for restitution. It is by no means clear that this is a fair result.

There are two possible conclusions. One is that the doctrine of substantial performance does not go far enough, and that (for example) a more flexible approach should be taken to the assessment of what constitutes substantial performance.[172] In cases such as *Bolton v Mahadeva* there is too much stress on the cost of remedying the defects of the promisor's performance. A substantial benefit was obtained and in such cases it is appropriate to use the value of the work done as the guide.[173]

The second is that reform of the law of restitution is required, since application of the principle of unjust enrichment is the better approach to the problems which arise on partial (but not substantial) performance of a contract.[174]

Unilateral contracts, options and aleatory contracts

[1836] Unilateral contracts. The feature which characterises unilateral contracts is that there is only one promisor, whose obligation to perform arises on the occurrence of an event in respect of which no promise has been made.[175] For example, if A promises to pay B $100 if B locates A's lost dog, and B, although making no promise, finds the animal in reliance on A's promise, B will be entitled to recover payment under the contract. The applicable rule is clear: performance must conform exactly with the requirements of the contract; there is no room for a doctrine of substantial performance.

In some cases it may be doubtful whether a bilateral or unilateral relation exists between the parties. For example, in *United Dominions Trust (Commercial) Ltd v Eagle Aircraft Services Ltd*,[176] A sold two aircraft to B who then let them out on hire-purchase to C. An agreement between A and B provided that A would repurchase the aircraft when called upon by B to do so. C defaulted under the hire-purchase contracts and these were

---

169. See [2203].
170. [1972] 1 WLR 1009 (see [1832]).
171. *Sumpter v Hedges* [1898] 1 QB 673 still governs the position. See [2325].
172. A flexible approach has been part of US law for some time. See *Jacob & Youngs, Inc v Kent* 129 NE 889 (1921).
173. There is support for this in *Finlayson v James* [1986] BTLC 163; *Ruxley Electronics and Constructions Ltd v Forsyth* [1996] AC 344 at 367.
174. See [2325].
175. See [249].
176. [1968] 1 All ER 104 (see P S Atiyah, (1968) 31 *MLR* 332).

terminated by B. However, B did not call upon A to repurchase the aircraft under the agreement until more than six months later. The English Court of Appeal held that B could not enforce A's obligation to repurchase because the latter's obligation was subject to a contingency that B would call upon A to repurchase within a reasonable time which had, in the circumstances, expired. Had the court interpreted the contract as containing a promise by B to call upon A within a reasonable period of time the contract would have been bilateral, and some inquiry would have been made into the nature of B's breach. This inquiry was not possible, or relevant, because the contract was unilateral.

[1837] **Options.** An option is like a unilateral contract in that the optionee, that is, the person to whom the option is granted, does not promise to exercise it.[177] The optionor's obligation to perform, for example, to sell land, becomes enforceable on the fulfilment of a contingency, namely, exercise of the option. The requirements of the option must be strictly complied with. For example, in *Hare v Nicoll*[178] an option relating to shares required the optionee to pay their price before 1 June 1963. When the optionee failed to pay before that date the court held that he was unable to enforce the optionor's obligation as he had not exercised the option according to its terms.

The requirements of the option may include the due performance of another contract. For example, a lease which includes an option to purchase the land or to renew the lease may state, as one of its requirements, that the optionee fulfil its obligations under the lease. At common law the optionee (lessee) will be precluded from exercising the option if in breach of the lease.[179]

[1838] **Aleatory contracts.** In aleatory contracts the promisor's obligation to perform becomes enforceable on the occurrence of a fortuitous event. The event is fortuitous because neither party desires it to occur, and neither makes any promise that it will occur. For example, if A contracts with B that B will insure A's house against fire, B's obligation to perform becomes enforceable once the house has been damaged or destroyed by fire. Such contracts are distinguishable from ordinary bilateral contracts because enforcement depends on a fortuitous event rather than performance by the other party. Thus, once the premium has been paid it is not appropriate to ask whether A has performed, or substantially performed, the question is simply whether fire has occurred.

Of course, the promisor's obligation to perform may be subject to qualifications or provisos. For example, an insurance contract may require

---

177. On the nature of option contracts see [248].
178. [1966] 2 QB 130. Cf *Lewes Nominees Pty Ltd v Strang* (1983) 49 ALR 328.
179. *Gilbert J McCaul (Aust) Pty Ltd v Pitt Club Ltd* (1957) 59 SR (NSW) 122. See also *Traywinds Pty Ltd v Cooper* [1989] 1 Qd R 222; *B S Stillwell & Co Pty Ltd v Budget Rent-A-Car System Pty Ltd* [1990] VR 589. However, relief against forfeiture may be available under statute. See **NSW:** *Conveyancing Act* 1919, s 133E; **Qld:** *Property Law Act* 1974, s 128; **WA:** *Property Law Act* 1969, s 83C. See Peter Butt, 'A Lessor's Rights and Obligations on Exercise of an Option to Renew' (1994) 68 *ALJ* 217.

a claim to be made within a specified period of time. In relation to such matters three questions may be relevant:

- what constitutes compliance;
- whether compliance is the subject of a promise; and
- whether strict compliance is a condition precedent to enforcement of the promise.

The contract in *United Dominions Trust (Commercial) Ltd v Eagle Aircraft Services Ltd*[180] was aleatory in nature, and the case illustrates a tendency to treat compliance as a non-promissory matter, with the result that strict compliance is a condition precedent. This may have severe consequences for the party seeking to enforce the contract. Thus, in *Tricontinental Corp Ltd v HDFI Ltd*[181] the ability to enforce a promise analogous to a guarantee of a debtor's obligations was subject to formal requirements, including sending a notice of demand to a particular address. It was held that the requirements were non-promissory conditions precedent, not subject to implied requirement of substantial fulfilment. Accordingly, whether or not there was any prejudice to the promisor, the failure to give a proper notice meant that the promise was not enforceable.

The aleatory nature of a contract of guarantee explains one special rule applicable to such contracts. An agreement between the debtor and a creditor, which varies the debtor-creditor contract, will discharge the guarantor, unless the variation is insubstantial or to the benefit of the guarantor.[182]

Suspension and Termination of Performance[183]

[1839] **Suspension of performance.** In certain circumstances a party may suspend the performance of a contract. It is important, however, to distinguish the right of a party to refuse to perform or suspend the performance of his or her own obligations from the right to suspend performance by the other party *as well*. To avoid confusion the former will be referred to as a right to withhold performance.

An ability to withhold performance is fairly common.[184] This may be conferred by the contract, as where a party's obligation to perform is expressly made 'subject to' performance by the other party. It may also be conferred by statute. For example, under the sale of goods legislation an unpaid seller of goods may be entitled to withhold delivery from the buyer until payment or tender of the price.[185] More generally, where one party's obligation to perform is dependent on the other party's performance (or readiness and willingness to perform), the first party is entitled to withhold

---

180. [1968] 1 All ER 104 (see [1836]).
181. (1990) 21 NSWLR 689. See also *Bond v Hongkong Bank of Australia Ltd* (1991) 25 NSWLR 286. For discussion see J W Carter, 'Conditions and Conditions Precedent' (1991) 4 *JCL* 90; Lee Aitken, [1992] *LMCLQ* 177.
182. See *Ankar Pty Ltd v National Westminster Finance (Australia) Ltd* (1987) 162 CLR 549; 70 ALR 641.
183. See J W Carter, 'Suspending Contract Performance for Breach', in Beatson and Friedmann, eds, *Good Faith and Fault in Contract Law*, 1995, p 485.
184. See Beale, *Remedies for Breach of Contract*, 1980, pp 16–49.

performance until the second party has performed (or shown readiness and willingness). In other words, until the condition precedent has been fulfilled the party for whose benefit it operates is under no obligation to perform.[186] For example, an employer is entitled to withhold wages until the employee has performed, and in a case where the employer is obliged to provide work,[187] is entitled to withhold performance by not providing work for an employee who is not ready and willing to work.[188]

It was explained earlier[189] that under Australian law, a promisee is not usually entitled to an assurance from the promisor that he or she will perform when the time for performance arrives. It follows that a promisee cannot usually demand an assurance from the promisor and withhold performance if none is given. However, under Art 71 of the *United Nations Convention on Contracts for the International Sale of Goods* 1980, which applies to international contracts for sale of goods, a party is entitled to withhold ('suspend') its own performance if it becomes apparent that the other party will not perform a substantial part of that party's obligations as a result of (1) a serious deficiency in ability or in creditworthiness; or (2) that party's conduct in performing or preparing to perform. The party who withheld its performance must continue with performance if the other party provides an adequate assurance of performance.[190]

A contract may expressly suspend the parties' performance until the occurrence of a stated event, as where the obligation to perform a contract for the sale of land is 'subject to' the execution of a formal document.[191] Sometimes a right to withhold or suspend performance is associated with a right of termination, but a right to suspend does not generally arise unless expressly conferred by the contract.[192] Thus, the conferral of an express right to terminate does not of itself provide the party with a choice between terminating[193] and withholding or suspending performance, and the courts have been reluctant to imply either right.[194] Whatever the source of the right to terminate, it is usually said that there is no 'half-way house'[195]

---

185. See **ACT**: *Sale of Goods Act* 1954, s 44; **NSW**: *Sale of Goods Act* 1923, s 43; **NT**: *Sale of Goods Act* 1972, s 43; **Qld**: *Sale of Goods Act* 1896, s 42; **SA**: *Sale of Goods Act* 1895, s 40; **Tas**: *Sale of Goods Act* 1896, s 45; **Vic**: *Goods Act* 1958, s 47; **WA**: *Sale of Goods Act* 1895, s 40.
186. Subject to the substantial performance doctrine discussed [1830]–[1832].
187. See, eg *Curro v Beyond Productions Pty Ltd* (1993) 30 NSWLR 337 at 343.
188. See *Australian National Airlines Commission v Robinson* [1977] VR 87.
189. See [1814].
190. For discussion of the similar right under the UNIDROIT Principles For International Commercial Contracts (1994) see J W Carter, 'Adequate Assurance of Due Performance' (1996) 11 *JCL* 1.
191. See [273] (it is assumed that execution is not a condition precedent to contract formation).
192. See, eg *Gilbert-Ash (Northern) Ltd v Modern Engineering (Bristol) Ltd* [1974] AC 689.
193. For the distinction between withholding performance and terminating performance see [1840].
194. *Steelwood Carriers Inc of Monrovia Liberia v Evimeria Compania Naviera SA of Panama (The Agios Giorgis)* [1976] 2 Lloyd's Rep 192.
195. *Tankexpress A/S v Compagnie Financière Belge des Petroles SA (The Petrofina)* [1949] AC 76 at 91. See also *Fercometal SARL v Mediterranean Shipping Co SA* [1989] AC 788 at 805; *Channel Tunnel Group Ltd v Balfour Beatty Construction Ltd* [1992] 1 QB 656 at 666 (affirmed without reference to the point [1993] AC 334).

between termination and the obligation to perform. Thus, an employer cannot suspend an employee — and so suspend the performance of the contract — merely because the employee has repudiated contractual obligations:[196] the employer must be able to point to an express (or implied) term giving the right. Nevertheless, in practice a repudiation of obligation effectively confers on the other party a right to withhold performance, at least for a reasonable period of time. This is the period allowed for exercise of the right to terminate[197] and this implies that he or she is not obliged to perform during this period.[198]

[1840] Termination of performance. Termination of performance refers to the termination of a promisor's obligation to perform contractual duties.[199] Termination may occur:

- as the result of an express agreement;[200]
- on the exercise of a right to terminate for breach or repudiation;[201]
- on the exercise of a statutory right;[202] or
- (automatically) by reason of the 'frustration' of a contract.[203]

Termination differs from suspension by reason of its finality. If the performance of a contract is merely suspended the parties can resume performance of the original contract. Where performance is terminated, any resumption of performance must be considered as occurring under a new contract.[204] The distinction is, however, sometimes difficult to maintain. For example, where a seller of goods, in breach of condition, tenders goods which are not of merchantable quality, the buyer's decision to withhold performance, by not accepting the goods, will usually constitute a termination by rejection. For the buyer's action *not* to amount to termination the buyer must indicate that the rejection is not final, that is, indicate that the seller is being provided with an opportunity to deliver conforming goods at a later stage.

---

196. See, eg *Hanley v Pease & Partners Ltd* [1915] 1 KB 698. A contrary statement by Fullagar J in *Welbourne v Australian Postal Commission* (1983) 52 ALR 669 at 688 is difficult to follow, in view of the acceptance (at 685) of *Hanley* as good law; see G J McCarry, (1984) 58 *ALJ* 226. Cf *Csomore v Public Service Board of New South Wales* (1986) 10 NSWLR 587.
197. See [1984].
198. But withholding performance may be interpreted as an election to terminate; see [1970]. In fact, the distinction is frequently difficult to maintain; see [1840].
199. See [1985].
200. See [526].
201. See generally Chapter 19.
202. See, eg *Trade Practices Act* 1974 (Cth), s 75A.
203. See generally Chapter 20.
204. *Newbon v City Mutual Life Assurance Society Ltd* (1935) 52 CLR 723 at 733. Exceptionally, the court may order specific performance after termination, or reinstate the contract, when giving relief against forfeiture; see [1979].

Breach

General

[1841] Forms of breach. There are two forms of breach of contract: failure to perform; and anticipatory breach. A failure to perform occurs if a promisor, without lawful excuse, fails to discharge a contractual obligation.

An anticipatory breach arises where, prior to the time appointed for performance by the promisor, the promisee justifiably terminates the performance of the contract. The promisee's termination will be justified if the words or conduct of the promisor, or the promisor's actual position, give rise to a repudiation of obligation[205] or indicate that the promisor was wholly and finally disabled[206] from performing the contract.

The basic distinction between the two forms of breach is the time of occurrence:

- a failure to perform can only occur after the time for performance has expired;
- an anticipatory breach precedes the time of performance.

A breach may, however, be of a hybrid kind, for example, where the promisor not only fails to perform but also repudiates future contractual obligations.[207]

There is one other distinction between the two forms of breach: a failure to perform need not give rise to a right to terminate whereas an anticipatory breach arises, if at all, on termination of the performance of the contract.[208] Thus, if, prior to the time for performance, a promisor repudiates contractual obligations the breach only occurs if the promisee terminates performance. If there is no termination, but the promisor continues to repudiate, a breach will arise once the promisor fails to perform, but this breach is a failure to perform rather than an anticipatory breach.

[1842] Bad faith performance.[209] In some situations performance which is not in good faith will constitute a breach of contract. But it is not meaningful to speak of 'bad faith performance' unless there is a duty to act in good faith. Such a duty may arise for a number of reasons. First, there are some contracts of a fiduciary nature which necessarily create a relationship under which one party is expected to act in good faith towards the other. Thus, an agency contract requires the agent to exercise good

---

205. See generally [1937]–[1941].
206. See generally [1942]–[1943].
207. Occasionally, the expression 'anticipatory breach' is used to describe a failure to perform which gives rise to a right to terminate, or to describe a breach of the hybrid kind. The former is an erroneous usage and the latter somewhat confusing. See Carter, *Breach of Contract*, 2nd ed, 1991, paras 708–9. See further [1930].
208. *Ogle v Comboyuro Investments Pty Ltd* (1976) 136 CLR 444 at 450; 9 ALR 309.
209. See Raphael Powell, 'Good Faith in Contracts' [1956] *CLP* 16; S J Burton, 'Breach of Contract and the Common Law Duty to Perform in Good Faith' (1980) 94 *Harv L Rev* 369; H K Lücke, 'Good Faith and Contractual Performance' in Finn, ed, *Essays on Contract*, 1987, p 155; Mr Justice T R H Cole, 'Law — All in Good Faith' (1994) 10 *Building and Construction Law* 18.

faith when performing the contract. Therefore, performance in a way which indicates bad faith, such as dealing with a third party on behalf of the principal but with the object of imposing onerous and unprofitable obligations on the principal, will amount to a breach.[210] Alternatively, the relationship may be such that both parties are subject to good faith obligations, as under a partnership contract.[211]

Second, a contract may include an express term requiring good faith performance.[212]

Third, there may be an implied term to the same effect. Breach of the duty of co-operation[213] will frequently occur by reason of a failure to act in good faith. Because of the general willingness to imply that duty, relief will often be available against a party who has acted in bad faith. Indeed, it is not inappropriate to say that the content of the duty to co-operate is informed by a desire to police bad faith.

It follows that performance which discharges a party does not amount to a breach of contract merely because a reasonable person would consider that a party has not acted in good faith.[214] Therefore, the general rule is that performance complying with the contract is not converted into a breach merely by reference to the intention of the promisor.[215] In *Secretary of State for Employment v ASLEF (No 2)*,[216] there was an industrial dispute in which the employees had engaged in 'work to rule' conduct with the object of disrupting the employer's business. A majority of the court held that this was a breach of an implied term that the employees would not perform their contractual obligations in a way which made it impossible for the employers to carry on their business.[217] Although Lord Denning MR may have gone further,[218] and suggested that there can be a breach of contract by bad faith performance even though no term of the contract has been breached, the subsequent cases have not taken that approach.

[1843] Onus of proof. Where a promisee alleges that the promisor has breached the contract the onus of proof rests on the promisee.[219] The rule holds true not only in the case of failure to perform but also in cases of anticipatory breach.

---

210. Cf *Shepherd v Felt and Textiles of Australia Ltd* (1931) 45 CLR 359 (see [630]).
211. *Service Station Association Ltd v Berg Bennett & Associates Pty Ltd* (1993) 117 ALR 393 at 401. See also [1809].
212. Cf [1809].
213. See [1809].
214. The conduct may amount to breach of the statutory prohibition on misleading and deceptive conduct, but this is a distinct question. See generally Chapter 11. On whether a tortious liability may arise see *Gibson v Parkes District Hospital* (1991) 26 NSWLR 9; *Gimson v Victorian Workcover Authority* [1995] 1 VR 209.
215. See *Secretary of State for Employment v ASLEF (No 2)* [1972] 2 QB 455 at 506 per Roskill LJ ('in the law of contract, questions of intent are usually irrelevant in determining whether or not there has been a breach of contract').
216. [1972] 2 QB 455.
217. [1972] 2 QB 455 at 498, 508–9.
218. [1972] 2 QB 455 at 491–2.
219. *Commonwealth Portland Cement Co Ltd v Weber Lohmann & Co Ltd* [1905] AC 66; *Hobbs v Petersham Transport Co Ltd* (1971) 124 CLR 220 at 230. See also [1969] (justification of termination); [2043] (self-induced frustration).

Failure to Perform

[1844] Scope of the concept. The failure to perform concept embraces three types of breach:

- nonperformance;
- defective performance; and
- late performance.

However, the concept is not limited to failures in respect of promises to do things in the future or to bring about results. Accordingly, contractual undertakings ('warranties')[220] as to the truth or reliability of statements may, if terms of the contract, be the subject of a failure to perform.[221]

Nonperformance and defective performance

[1845] Nonperformance. Superficially, the most straightforward type of failure to perform is nonperformance. A promisor who makes no attempt to perform is guilty of nonperformance. But a case of nonperformance may also arise even though the promisor has attempted to perform. The supply of a different article is a clear example of nonperformance. The time-honoured example of this is the seller who sends beans when the contract requires the delivery of peas.[222]

A case of nonperformance may also arise as the result of the termination of the performance of a contract. For example, assume that a seller agrees to sell a specific motor vehicle to a buyer, but, because it is not fit for the buyer's purposes, the buyer rejects the vehicle and announces that the contract is terminated because of the seller's breach. If the buyer's termination is justified, because the seller has breached an express or implied condition, and property in the goods has not passed to the buyer, the effect of termination is to render the seller guilty of nonperformance, and liable in damages for non-delivery.

[1846] Defective performance. A promisor's performance is defective where it is not of the quality or quantity required by the contract, or not fit for the purpose required. For example, if a builder agrees to build a house but does the work negligently, so that repair work is needed to make the work done conform with the contract, the breach arises from defective performance of the contract.

In order to find a true case of defective performance the promisee must receive and retain the performance. The seller in the example given above[223] is guilty of nonperformance because the buyer rejected the performance when tendered. On the other hand, if the buyer 'accepts' the vehicle, the seller's breach is a defective performance.

---

220. See [728].
221. For example, a shipowner may be in breach of a voyage charterparty which states the location of the vessel if the vessel was not, at the time of the contract, located as stated. See *Behn v Burness* (1863) 3 B & S 751; 122 ER 281.
222. *Chanter v Hopkins* (1838) 4 M & W 399 at 404; 150 ER 1484 at 1486–7.
223. See [1845].

Late performance[224]

[1847] General. Breach by defective performance arguably includes breach by late performance. However, for the purposes of exposition it is convenient to deal with them separately.

Where performance is tendered late, and not accepted, valid termination by the promisee (for example, because timely performance was of the essence),[225] means that the promisor's breach amounts to nonperformance.

[1848] Common law rule. The original rule at common law was that time was considered to be 'of the essence' of the contract unless the parties had expressed a contrary agreement. The consequence of this was that a failure by a promisor to perform at the appointed time not only meant that the promisor was liable to pay damages, but also that enforcement of the promisee's obligations was not permitted. Timely performance was therefore a condition precedent to the promisor's ability to enforce the promisee's obligations.

Such bald statements of the common law rule are, however, open to criticism since until about the middle of the 18th century many contractual obligations were construed as independent[226] with the result that a failure to perform on time did not preclude enforcement. In truth, the common law treatment of time stipulations as essential was not established until the beginning of the 19th century. Even then it was applied chiefly to conveyancing and mercantile transactions,[227] and time was not necessarily essential in other contexts.[228]

[1849] Equitable rule. The general rule in equity was that time was not essential. Therefore, a promisor's failure to perform at the appointed time was not usually a bar to the enforcement of the contract in the equity court, although the promisor remained liable to pay damages.

Again, however, such an unqualified statement of the rule is open to criticism.[229] In equity, a distinction was drawn between form and substance.[230] Provided the object of the contract was still obtainable, equity would usually (but not invariably) order specific performance at the promisor's behest. The equity court did not apply its rule in disregard of the parties' intentions, and an express statement that time was to be of the essence of the contract was sufficient to oust the equitable rule. Nor would the rule apply if the nature of the subject matter, or the circumstances surrounding the contract, indicated that time was of the essence, for example, because of the perishable nature of the subject matter. Moreover, the intervention of the equity court was a matter of discretion and if, for example, the plaintiff was not ready and willing to perform the court might

---

224. Lindgren, *Time in the Performance of Contracts*, 2nd ed, 1982.
225. See generally [1950]–[1953].
226. See [1806].
227. See, eg *Busk v Spence* (1815) 4 Camp 329; 171 ER 105; *Coddington v Paleologo* (1867) LR 2 Ex 193.
228. See, eg *Bettini v Gye* (1876) 1 QBD 183 (employment contract).
229. See S J Stoljar, 'Untimely Performance in the Law of Contract' (1955) 71 *LQR* 527 at 560–1.
230. *Parkin v Thorold* (1852) 16 Beav 59; 51 ER 698.

not assist the plaintiff to enforce the contract. Again, the fact that the equitable rule operated in the context of equitable claims, for specific performance or injunction, meant that it would not usually be relevant to, for example, a commercial contract for the sale of goods.

Equity also recognised a procedure under which time could be made of the essence, by the promisee serving notice on the promisor, after breach on the promisor's part, requiring performance within a specified period of time. If the promisor failed to perform within the period specified, and the court found a 'reasonable' time to have been allowed, the court would not usually come to the promisor's aid.

[1850] **Area of conflict.** The area of conflict between the rules stated above is, obviously, where a failure to perform on time would be a good defence at common law but not in equity. For example, if a contract for the sale of land did not expressly make time of the essence, there would be a conflict between equity and common law. Thus, a purchaser in breach of contract by not tendering the purchase money on the day named for completion would be unable to enforce the contract at common law but not necessarily barred from relief in equity.

The conflict between law and equity did not concern the construction of the contract:[231] the equity court did not deny that at common law time was of the essence, or that the promisor's failure to perform constituted a breach of contract entitling the promisee to claim damages. However, acting by analogy with the principles governing relief against forfeiture,[232] the court would deny the full legal effect of the promisor's breach, that is, an inability to enforce the contract.

[1851] **Position under statute.** The statutory resolution of the conflict between law and equity is in favour of the equitable rule. Section 13 of the *Conveyancing Act* 1919 (NSW) provides:[233]

> Stipulations in contracts, as to time or otherwise, which would not before the commencement of this Act have been deemed to be or to have become of the essence of such contracts in a court of equity, shall receive in all courts the same construction and effect as they would have heretofore received in such court.

This provision is derived from s 25(7) of the *Judicature Act* 1873 (UK) and has counterparts in most Australian jurisdictions.[234] Although the wording of some of these is based on s 41 of the *Law of Property Act* 1925 (UK) (which replaced the *Judicature Act* provision) they are to the same effect. Therefore, where a stipulation as to time would not be of the essence in equity it must be so treated by the court notwithstanding that, at common law, the stipulation might have been regarded as essential.

---

231. *Tilley v Thomas* (1867) LR 3 Ch App 61 at 67.
232. *Seton v Slade* (1802) 7 Ves Jun 265 at 273–4; 32 ER 108 at 111.
233. The reference to time being 'deemed ... to have become' of the essence is a reference to the notice procedure referred to in [1849] and discussed [1959]–[1964].
234. **ACT:** *Law of Property (Miscellaneous Provisions) Act* 1958, s 4; **NT:** *Law of Property Act* 2000, s 65; **Qld:** *Property Law Act* 1974, s 62; **SA:** *Law of Property Act* 1936, s 16; **Tas:** *Supreme Court Civil Procedure Act* 1932, s 11(7); **Vic:** *Property Law Act* 1958, s 41; **WA:** *Property Law Act* 1969, s 21.

[1852] **Impact of the statutory provision.** Although the provision is relevant to both legal and equitable proceedings,[235] the scope of the provision in respect of the former has traditionally been regarded as quite narrow. The traditional view was stated as follows by Kitto J in *Holland v Wiltshire*:[236]

> The qualification thus made upon the rule to be applied in the exercise of common law jurisdiction is, however, of limited application. It applies only in cases which are appropriate for the granting of equitable remedies by way of relief against the loss by a party of his contractual rights by reason of a failure on his part to perform the contract in precise accordance with its provisions as to time. This is so because only in such cases do the rules of equity treat as not of the essence of the contract stipulations which are of the essence according to the traditional view of the common law ...

The provision does not operate to relieve the plaintiff from liability in damages in respect of the breach. However, one impact is to permit a plaintiff in breach to obtain damages for breach of contract. Prior to the enactment of the provision the plaintiff would have been unable to enforce the claim by reason of the breach.[237] A failure to perform a time stipulation is still a breach of contract, and in this respect the statutory provision does not alter the legal construction of the contract.[238] Nor does it prevent the parties from agreeing, expressly or impliedly, that time is to be essential.[239]

In *United Scientific Holdings Ltd v Burnley BC*[240] the House of Lords appeared to take a wider view, namely, that the statutory provision is relevant to the construction of the contract and requires the court to apply a *general* presumption that time is not of the essence. Although this may be the position in practice, particularly in conveyancing transactions, the view was influenced by a wider interpretation of the scope of the provision than has traditionally been taken. Briefly, the facts were that certain leases provided for rent reviews. However, the leases specified dates for initiating the review procedure. The lessors failed to comply with the time stipulations but the House of Lords held that time was not of the essence. It was said that in determining whether time was of the essence the court should not go back to the old equity cases but, instead, should look to see whether there is anything in the contract to rebut the presumption that time is not essential. In the instant case there was no such indication, and the lessors' breach did not preclude them from invoking the review procedure. However, equitable relief was not claimed by the lessors and could not have been claimed by them.

---

235. *Canning v Temby* (1905) 3 CLR 419 at 426.
236. (1954) 90 CLR 409 at 418–19. See also *Stickney v Keeble* [1915] AC 386 at 417; *Citicorp Australia Ltd v Hendry* (1985) 4 NSWLR 22 at 27; *G R Mailman & Associates Pty Ltd v Wormald (Aust) Pty Ltd* (1991) 24 NSWLR 80 at 99.
237. *Howe v Smith* (1884) 27 Ch D 89 at 103; *Stickney v Keeble* [1915] AC 386 at 404.
238. *Canning v Temby* (1905) 3 CLR 419 at 426; *Raineri v Miles* [1981] AC 1050; *Louinder v Leis* (1982) 149 CLR 509; 41 ALR 187.
239. See [1950]–[1953].
240. [1978] AC 904. See also *Amherst v James Walker Goldsmith & Silversmith Ltd* [1983] Ch 305.

The main[241] difficulty created by the *United Scientific* case is the view, apparently expressed, that the statutory provision is relevant to all time stipulations. If the view taken in *Holland v Wiltshire* is applied to the facts of *United Scientific*, the statutory provision would not be relevant. The result would be the same because of the absence of any express or implied agreement that time was of the essence. However, the result would not be achieved by application of the statutory provision for the simple reason that no equitable remedies were relevant to the proceedings in issue. Rather, the conclusion would flow from the interpretation of the rent review provisions in accordance with general commercial principles. Therefore, although the actual decision in the case is consistent with Australian law, and indeed has been approved by the High Court,[242] the reasoning is difficult to reconcile with the Australian cases. In any event, the English courts reverted to the traditional view of the impact of the statutory provision in *Bunge Corp New York v Tradax Export SA Panama*,[243] where the House of Lords held that time was of the essence of a commercial contract for the sale of goods, and treated the position as governed entirely by the parties' agreement. Since no equitable relief was claimed, or relevant, this was the appropriate course to take.

There is one other limitation on the scope of the statutory provision: it does not apply to time stipulations which state contingencies.[244] Thus, if A grants to B an option to purchase real estate, and the option provides for exercise by, say, 1 March, B's failure to exercise the option in time does not attract the statutory provision. Various reasons have been given for this, but the fundamental reason is that the option is a species of privilege which, as was explained earlier,[245] must be exercised according to its terms. There is no promise by the optionee (B) to exercise the option and no question of the optionor (A) being compensated by damages in respect of B's failure.

Standards of Contractual Duty[246]

[1853] **Relevance of standard of duty.** The relevance of the standard of contractual duties to breach of contract is straightforward. In order to establish a breach by failure to perform, the promisee must establish that the promisor has failed to perform a contractual obligation in accordance with the standard of duty applicable to that obligation. In cases of anticipatory breach the promisee must establish, by reference to the promisor's words or conduct or actual position, that the promisor would have failed to perform in accordance with the applicable standard of duty.[247]

---

241. For discussion see P V Baker, 'The Future of Equity' (1977) 93 *LQR* 530; Carter, *Breach of Contract*, 2nd ed, 1991, para 546.
242. *Gollin & Co Ltd v Karenlee Nominees Pty Ltd* (1983) 153 CLR 455; 49 ALR 135.
243. [1981] 1 WLR 711 (see [1952]).
244. See Carter, *Breach of Contract*, 2nd ed, 1991, para 548. Rent review clauses give rise to particular problems. See *G R Mailman & Associates Pty Ltd v Wormald (Aust) Pty Ltd* (1991) 24 NSWLR 80 (see Diane Skapinker and J W Carter, (1992) 5 *JCL* 136).
245. [1837].
246. See Carter, *Breach of Contract*, 2nd ed, 1991, Chapter 2.
247. See further [1935].

What then do we mean by 'standard of duty'? In essence the concept refers to the *degree of care* which the promisor must exercise in performing contractual obligations.[248]

[1854] **Types of standards.** Broadly speaking there are two types of standard:

(1) a standard of absolute or strict liability; and

(2) a standard requiring the exercise of care.

Obviously the first imposes a higher standard of duty than the second, and is correspondingly more onerous for the promisor.

[1855] **Determining the standard.** The standard of duty applicable to a contractual obligation depends on the construction of the contract.[249] In some cases it is possible to find express terms stating the standard of duty. For example, a sale of goods contract might provide for the seller to use its 'best endeavours' to obtain a licence for the export of the goods. An exclusion clause[250] may achieve the same result, by providing that the promisor is liable to the promisee unless the promisor has failed to exercise 'due diligence'. Subject to statute,[251] such express terms will govern the standard of duty.

Usually, however, the contract will contain no express statement of the standard of duty. The court must then decide what standard the parties impliedly agreed to.[252] It is helpful to distinguish contracts under which the promisor agrees to produce a result from contracts under which the only reasonable interpretation is that the promisor has agreed to use care to bring about a result. In this way the obligation of, say, a lessee to pay rent is distinguished from the obligation of, say, a solicitor in the conduct of a client's litigation. The lessee's obligation is a strict one, to see that the lessor is paid; but because a solicitor does not normally promise to win a client's case, the standard is one of (professional) care.

In informal contracts the standard of duty problem will usually be solved by the implication of a term.[253] For example, in the absence of an express term to the contrary a court will imply a term into an employment contract requiring the exercise of 'proper or reasonable' care on the part of the employee.[254] An implied term need not, however, impose a standard requiring the exercise of care. For example, if a contract for the hire of goods attracts an implied term requiring the goods to be fit for the hirer's purpose, the standard of duty is strict.[255] In some contracts both types of standard will be present in the terms implied. For example, in a building

---

248. This is the second aspect of the 'fundamental question' stated by Dixon and Fullagar JJ in *McRae v Commonwealth Disposals Commission* (1951) 84 CLR 377 at 407–8 (see [1801]).
249. *McRae v Commonwealth Disposals Commission* (1951) 84 CLR 377 at 407.
250. See generally [748]–[772].
251. See [769], [1515]–[1530].
252. See [703].
253. See, eg *Lloyd v Citicorp Australia Ltd* (1986) 11 NSWLR 286. Cf *Hawkins v Clayton* (1988) 164 CLR 539; 78 ALR 69.
254. *Lister v Romford Ice and Cold Storage Co Ltd* [1957] AC 555.
255. *Derbyshire Building Co Pty Ltd v Becker* (1962) 107 CLR 633. This is the position under s 71(2) of the *Trade Practices Act* 1974 (Cth) (see [639]).

contract there are normally implied terms requiring the builder to perform the work in a good and workmanlike manner, using good quality materials fit for the purpose of the work.[256] The work element is subject to a standard of duty requiring the exercise of care, whereas the builder is strictly liable for the quality and fitness of the materials used.[257]

[1856] **Absolute and strict liability.** Where a promisor's standard of duty is absolute or strict the promisee makes out a prima facie case simply by proving that the performance contracted for has not been received. Since a promisor's obligation to pay money is usually strict, the promisor cannot escape liability merely by proving that impecuniosity arose despite the exercise of care. The promisee does not need to establish want of care on the part of the promisor: a failure to perform occurs even if the promisor has used reasonable care. The strict liability standard is most common in commercial contracts,[258] but it may also apply in the consumer context. For example, in *Grant v Australian Knitting Mills Ltd*,[259] a purchaser of woollen underwear brought an action against a retailer. The court said that no question of negligence was 'relevant to the liability in contract' for the breach of terms implied by the sale of goods legislation.[260]

So far no attempt has been made to distinguish between absolute and strict liability. In fact, when courts speak of absolute liability they usually mean strict liability. An obligation to perform can certainly be strict without being absolute. For example, a buyer's obligation to pay for goods is strict but not absolute if it is dependent on the transfer of ownership of the goods. If it were absolute the buyer would be required to pay in any event, as is the position where the buyer promises to pay on a day certain irrespective of delivery.[261] Indeed, the presumption of dependency, and the development of the doctrine of frustration, mean that there are very few absolute obligations under the modern law of contract.[262] Of course, the further the performance of a contract has proceeded the more absolute a strict liability becomes. Thus, once a buyer has obtained title to goods complying with the requirements of the contract, the seller's side of the bargain has been performed and the range of possible excuses for the buyer is so diminished that the obligation to pay the price is, for all practical purposes, absolute in nature.

[1857] **Liability for failure to exercise care.** Most contracts of a personal nature, such as employment contracts, contain obligations attracting a standard requiring the exercise of care, skill or diligence.[263] The nature of the ordinary employee's duty is that proper or reasonable care must be exercised.[264] Where an element of special skill is present, as in

---

256. See [633].
257. *Reg Glass Pty Ltd v Rivers Locking Systems Pty Ltd* (1968) 120 CLR 516.
258. There is support for a movement towards the lesser standard. See Lord Devlin, 'The Treatment of Breach of Contract' [1966] *CLJ* 192 at 209. Cf *Pagnan SpA v Tradax Ocean Transportation SA* [1987] 3 All ER 565 (see David Yates and J W Carter, (1988) 1 *JCL* 57).
259. [1936] AC 85.
260. [1936] AC 85 at 100. Contrast the position of the manufacturer sued in tort.
261. See [1806].
262. See [2003].

contracts with solicitors, engineers, doctors and so on, the duty is to exercise the degree of care expected of the 'ordinary skilled [person] exercising and professing to have that special skill'.[265] It is, of course, open to a professional person to agree to a higher standard of duty.[266]

In all these cases the promisee establishes a breach of contract by proving that the promisor has not exercised the requisite degree of care. If there is no evidence the plaintiff will fail,[267] but what the promisee must prove will depend on the facts: there is no single criterion, and the amount of evidence required will vary from contract to contract. If an element of special skill is present, evidence of practice in the industry will be a useful guide to whether the promisor has done what an ordinary skilled person exercising and professing to have that special skill would have done,[268] but it is not conclusive that the promisor has behaved in accordance with industry practice.[269]

A very common type of contract, that of bailment, requires the bailee to exercise reasonable care in relation to the goods.[270] However, a bailee is in a less favourable position than other promisors subject to a duty requiring the exercise of care. Where negligence, or 'breach of bailment' as it is sometimes termed, is alleged by a bailor, a prima facie case is established simply by proving that the goods have not been returned, or have been returned in a damaged condition.[271] The onus then shifts to the bailee (promisor) to establish that the loss or damage occurred despite the exercise of reasonable care.

Consequences of Breach

[1858] Right to damages. The commission of a breach of contract by a promisor provides the promisee with a right to claim damages.[272] Although a purely nominal sum will be awarded in the absence of proof that loss or damage was caused by the breach, the relevance of such evidence is to the recovery of a substantial sum.[273] Moreover, except in cases of anticipatory breach, the promisee need not establish termination of the performance of the contract.[274]

---

263. The result, in cases of proved breach, will be for the promisor to be subject to concurrent liabilities in tort and contract; see, eg *Pullen v Gutteridge Haskins & Davey Pty Ltd* [1993] 1 VR 27 at 39; *Breen v Williams* (1996) 186 CLR 71; *Astley v Austrust Ltd* (1999) 197 CLR 1; 161 ALR 155. See also [635].
264. See [1855].
265. *Bolam v Friern Hospital Management Committee* [1957] 1 WLR 582 at 586 (the case was disapproved on another ground in *Rogers v Whitaker* (1992) 175 CLR 479; 109 ALR 625). See also [642].
266. See, eg *Greaves & Co (Contractors) Ltd v Baynham Meikle & Partners* [1975] 1 WLR 1095 at 1100–1.
267. *Max Garrett (Distributors) Pty Ltd v Tobias* (1975) 50 ALJR 402.
268. *Fanhaven Pty Ltd v Bain Dawes Northern Pty Ltd* [1982] 2 NSWLR 57 at 63.
269. See *Rogers v Whitaker* (1992) 175 CLR 479. See also *Naxakis v Western General Hospital* (1999) 197 CLR 269 at 275–6; 162 ALR 540.
270. See Palmer, *Bailment*, 2nd ed, 1991, pp 45–61.
271. See *Hobbs v Petersham Transport Co Pty Ltd* (1971) 124 CLR 220 at 233, 240.
272. See [2101].
273. See [2106].
274. See [2102].

The assessment of damages for breach of contract is dealt with in Chapter 21.

[1859] **No automatic termination.** No matter how serious, a breach of contract does not automatically terminate its performance unless the parties have clearly expressed an intention that this is to be the result.[275]

The rule against automatic termination applies where the breach gives rise to a right to terminate. As will be explained,[276] termination is a matter of election on the part of the promisee. This implies that a promisee entitled to terminate for breach (or repudiation) by the promisor may continue with the performance of the contract. The consequences of such an election are discussed later.[277]

---

275. See [1967].
276. See [1968].
277. See [1971] and [2218]–[2224].

PART VIII
Termination

Chapter 19

Termination for Breach and Repudiation

General 1901
   The Right to Terminate *1901*
   Terminology *1905*
Termination for Breach 1909
   Contractual and Statutory Rights *1909*
   Breach of Condition *1911*
   Breach of Intermediate Term *1922*
Termination for Repudiation 1928
   General *1928*
   Repudiation Based on Words or Conduct *1937*
   Repudiation Based on Inability *1942*
   The Acceptance Requirement *1945*
Termination for Delay 1948
   General *1948*
   Breach of Essential Time Stipulation *1950*
   Breach of Non-essential Time Stipulation *1954*
   Delay as Consequence of Breach *1957*
   Failure to Comply with Notice *1959*
Unilateral and Partially Executed Contracts 1965
Restrictions on the Right to Terminate 1967
   Principles of Election *1967*
   Estoppel *1974*
   Exclusion Clauses and Breach by Terminating Party *1977*
   Relief Against Forfeiture *1979*
   Other Possible Restrictions *1981*
Consequences of Termination 1985
   Discharge of the Parties *1985*
   Accrued Rights Not Divested *1988*
   Restitutionary Claims *1990*
   Terms Operating After Termination *1992*

General

The Right to Terminate[1]

[1901] Nature of the right. The right to terminate, which flows from some breaches of contract and a repudiation of obligation, is a right to terminate the obligation of the parties to perform their contractual duties. After termination the parties are *discharged* from the obligation to perform (or to be ready and willing to perform) their respective contractual duties.[2]

Whether a right to terminate exists is an issue of law.

[1902] Onus of proof. The onus of proving the existence and exercise of a right to terminate for breach or repudiation rests on the party who claims that the right existed or has been exercised.[3] That party is usually described as the promisee, the 'innocent' party or the 'party not in breach'.

[1903] Relevant situations. The basic distinction is between a right to terminate expressly conferred by the contract ('contractual' right to terminate), and a right to terminate which is conferred by law ('implied' right to terminate). The concept of a right conferred by law embraces both a right of termination conferred by a common law and one conferred by statute. We are mainly concerned with the former.

There are three situations in which the right will be implied, unless the parties have expressly or impliedly agreed that the right should not be implied:

- for breach of condition;
- for a sufficiently serious breach of an intermediate term; and
- in respect of an absence of readiness or willingness to perform constituting a repudiation or capable of being treated as an anticipatory breach of contract.

Any given fact situation may be such that the right to terminate is available on more than one ground, for example, because breach of condition amounts to a repudiation.

It is analytically convenient to deal separately with the situations in which a right to terminate arises from delay in performance.[4]

[1904] Generally no right to rescind. A right to rescind the contract *ab initio* (from the beginning) is distinguishable from a right to terminate the performance of the contract *in futuro*.[5] Generally, the existence of a breach of contract does not confer on the promisee a right to rescind the contract.[6] Although there is some support for the view that a right to rescind is conferred by the common law in cases of repudiation resulting from an

---

1. See generally Carter, *Breach of Contract*, 2nd ed, 1991, Chapter 3.
2. See further [1985]–[1987].
3. See, eg *Southern Foundries (1926) Ltd v Shirlaw* [1940] AC 701 at 729.
4. See [1948]–[1964].
5. See [1988].
6. See, eg *Johnson v Agnew* [1980] AC 367. See generally Michael Albery, 'Mr Cyprian Williams' Great Heresy' (1975) 91 *LQR* 337. See further [1982].

express refusal to perform,[7] this seems anomalous and the cases may need to be reconsidered. However, the contract,[8] or a statutory provision may expressly confer a right to rescind for breach. But the use of the word 'rescind' is not conclusive as it is frequently used as a synonym for 'terminate'.[9]

A breach of contract may be associated with a right to rescind, but not be the source of the right. Thus, where a false statement of fact by A induces B to contract with A, the misrepresentation entitles B to rescind the contract. This is true even if the misrepresentation is repeated as a term of the contract.[10] Because the misrepresentation is also a term of the contract, A is also in breach of contract. However, B's right to rescind arises because of the misrepresentation rather than the breach.

Terminology

[1905] Contractual terms. The various types of contractual terms were described earlier.[11] For the purpose of the right to terminate, only those terms which state promises or undertakings are relevant and, in particular, terms which are conditions or intermediate in character.

[1906] Repudiation and anticipatory breach. The expressions 'repudiation' and 'anticipatory breach' are used in various senses.[12] For the purpose of the right to terminate, 'repudiation' means 'repudiation of obligation' and describes a situation in which a promisor's absence of readiness or willingness to perform gives rise to a right to terminate.

The expression 'anticipatory breach' also concentrates on the absence of readiness or willingness to perform. Generally, the expression is restricted to an absence of readiness or willingness preceding the time for performance by the promisor which can be treated as a ground for termination by the promisee.[13] For example, a repudiation which precedes the time of performance may be 'accepted' by the promisee as an anticipatory breach. The concept of anticipatory breach is therefore part of the wider concept of repudiation.[14]

[1907] Fundamental and total breach. The concepts of 'fundamental' and 'total' breach were considered earlier in the context of exclusion clauses.[15] Either type of breach will give rise to a right to terminate.

The expression 'fundamental breach' is usually used to describe the type of breach which must be established where the promisee is relying on the

7. See *Brooks Robinson Pty Ltd v Rothfield* [1951] VLR 405. Cf *Moschi v Lep Air Services Ltd* [1973] AC 331 at 356.
8. Cf [2408] (equitable right of 'rescission' may arise out of a want of mutuality in the remedy of specific performance).
9. This is the position under: **Cth:** *Trade Practices Act* 1974, s 75A; **NT:** *Consumer Affairs and Fair Trading Act* 1990, s 67(1); **WA:** *Fair Trading Act* 1987, s 41.
10. See [1058].
11. See [724]–[747].
12. See *Heyman v Darwins Ltd* [1942] AC 356; *Satellite Estate Pty Ltd v Jaquet* (1968) 71 SR (NSW) 126.
13. See [1841].
14. *Afovos Shipping Co SA v Pagnan* [1983] 1 WLR 195 at 203. But cf [1934].
15. See [754], [757].

breach of an intermediate term.[16] The expression has also been used to describe the type of breach which the promisee must establish under the anticipatory breach concept,[17] or to describe a failure to comply with a notice served after delay in performance.[18] Sometimes, but unhelpfully, it is used as a general description of any breach which gives rise to a right to terminate.[19]

[1908] **Repudiatory breach.** The phrase 'repudiatory breach' is often employed to describe any breach which gives rise to a right to terminate the performance of a contract, on the basis that any such breach may be treated by the promisee as a repudiation of the whole contract.[20] It is difficult, however, to describe every breach of condition as 'repudiatory' in any objective sense and a repudiation of obligation — which gives rise to a right to terminate — may not of itself amount to a breach of contract, because it precedes the time of performance.

Termination for Breach[21]

Contractual and Statutory Rights

[1909] **Contractual rights.** Whether a contract expressly confers a right to terminate for breach depends, of course, on the construction of the contract. Whether the right can be exercised in the circumstances which have occurred also depends on the construction of the express term. Generally, construction is also the basis upon which it is determined whether the promisee has exercised the right according to its terms.[22]

A right to terminate may be general, and arise on a breach of any term of the contract, or specific, and arise only on the breach of a particular term or a particular kind of breach.[23] Sometimes it is difficult to classify the right, but the court must do its best to arrive at an interpretation which corresponds with the parties' intentions.[24]

Since rights must be exercised according to their terms, if the right is to come into operation at a particular time, the right cannot be exercised in advance by the promisee.[25] Similarly, a party may not act on the clause prior to the expiry of the notice given under it.[26] On the other hand, the

---

16. *Direct Acceptance Finance Ltd v Cumberland Furnishing Pty Ltd* [1965] NSWR 1504 at 1511; *Photo Production Ltd v Securicor Transport Ltd* [1980] AC 827 at 849.
17. *Afovos Shipping Co SA v Pagnan* [1983] 1 WLR 195 at 201; but see [1935].
18. *Ciavarella v Balmer* (1983) 153 CLR 438 at 446; 48 ALR 407.
19. *Suisse Atlantique Société d'Armement Maritime SA v NV Rotterdamsche Kolen Centrale* [1967] 1 AC 361 at 397.
20. *Bremer Vulkan Schiffbau und Maschinenfabrik v South India Shipping Corp Ltd* [1981] AC 909 at 980, 981.
21. See Jane Swanton, 'Discharge of Contracts for Breach' (1981) 13 *MULR* 69.
22. See [1970].
23. See further [1912], [1924].
24. See, eg *Antaios Compania Naviera SA v Salen Rederierna AB* [1985] AC 191.
25. See, eg *Rawson v Hobbs* (1961) 107 CLR 466; *Afovos Shipping Co SA v Pagnan* [1983] 1 WLR 195. See also *Sanders v Snell* (1998) 196 CLR 329; 157 ALR 491 (no entitlement to make payment to employee in lieu of notice).
26. *Eriksson v Whalley* [1971] 1 NSWLR 397.

mere existence of a contractual right, not applicable to the circumstances which have occurred, generally does not preclude reliance on a common law right, such as the right to terminate for repudiation, which is applicable.[27]

[1910] **Statutory rights.** No Australian statute confers a general right to terminate for breach or repudiation. There are, however, statutes which confer the right to terminate in specified situations. Generally, these acknowledge rights which would be conferred by the common law. Thus, the sale of goods legislation confers a right to terminate for breach of condition in a contract for the sale of goods and in respect of the repudiation of a contract for the sale of goods by instalments.[28] There is a more sophisticated statutory regime in the *United Nations Convention on Contracts for the International Sale of Goods* 1980 which, although using some of the terminology of the common law, does not revolve around the distinction between conditions and warranties.[29]

Although it is convenient to term these rights of termination 'statutory' rights, exercise of the right by the promisee is in fact the exercise of an implied contractual right. Therefore, unless the statute prohibits its exclusion,[30] the parties may agree that the right is not to be available.

Breach of Condition[31]

[1911] **Types of conditions.** Conditions have been classified in two main ways. The first classification depends on whether a breach of the term is likely to cause serious loss or detriment to the promisee. If every breach of a term is likely to be serious it will generally be a condition;[32] but if some breaches will probably not be serious the term is less likely to be construed as a condition. However, a term may be a condition even though its breach is not likely to be a serious matter for the promisee. In the latter case the term is a condition if the parties have accounted the breach a serious matter, either by an express agreement that *any* breach is to give rise to a right to terminate,[33] or by reason of an implied agreement between the parties that the term is to be so treated.

The second classification distinguishes cases in which precise or literal compliance with the term is essential from cases in which substantial performance is essential. The importance of the distinction was explained by Jordan CJ in *Tramways Advertising Pty Ltd v Luna Park (NSW) Ltd*:[34]

27. See, eg *Rawson v Hobbs* (1961) 107 CLR 466. Cf [1970].
28. **ACT:** *Sale of Goods Act* 1954, ss 16(2), 35(2); **NSW:** *Sale of Goods Act* 1923, ss 16(2), 34(2); **NT:** *Sale of Goods Act* 1972, ss 16(2), 34(2); **Qld:** *Sale of Goods Act* 1896, ss 14(2), 33(2); **SA:** *Sale of Goods Act* 1895, ss 11(2), 31(2); **Tas:** *Sale of Goods Act* 1896, ss 16(2), 36(2); **Vic:** *Goods Act* 1958, ss 16(2), 38(2); **WA:** *Sale of Goods Act* 1895, ss 11(2), 31(2).
29. See J W Carter, 'Party Autonomy and Statutory Regulation: Sale of Goods' (1993) 6 *JCL* 93; R E Speidel, 'Buyer's Remedies of Rejection and Cancellation under the UCC and the Convention' (1993) 6 *JCL* 131.
30. See [770].
31. See Carter, *Breach of Contract*, 2nd ed, 1991, Chapter 5.
32. *Wallis v Pratt* [1910] 2 KB 1003 at 1012 (adopted [1911] AC 394).
33. See, eg *Mardorf Peach & Co Ltd v Attica Sea Carriers Corp of Liberia* [1977] AC 850. For problems with this usage see [1912].

If the innocent party would not have entered into the contract unless assured of a strict and literal performance of the promise, he may in general treat himself as discharged upon any breach of the promise, however slight. If he contracted in reliance upon a substantial performance of the promise, any substantial breach will ordinarily justify a discharge.

However, if the definition of condition stated in the sale of goods legislation[35] is accepted as a general definition, the second class of conditions referred to by Jordan CJ should now be described as intermediate terms. This is certainly the effect of decisions applying *Hongkong Fir Shipping Co Ltd v Kawasaki Kisen Kaisha Ltd*.[36] But the matter is one of terminology, not substance.

Express agreement

[1912] Ways of indicating express agreement. Perhaps surprisingly, it is difficult to find words which will expressly make a term a condition. The expression 'time is of the essence of this contract' is effective to make the time stipulations conditions.[37] But the mere use of the word 'condition' is not conclusive, due to its inherent ambiguity. For example, in *L Schuler AG v Wickman Machine Tool Sales Ltd*,[38] a term in a distributorship agreement made visits by Wickman to Schuler's clients a 'condition' of the contract. Schuler argued that as the term was a condition any breach by Wickman would give rise to a right to terminate the performance of the contract. The House of Lords rejected the argument: the use of so ambiguous a word as 'condition' was not conclusive, and when regard was had to the other terms of the contract it was clear that the term in issue was intermediate in character.

The decision in *Schuler v Wickman* does not mean that the parties can only establish an express agreement by expressly providing that every breach of the term is to give rise to a right to terminate. Nevertheless, given the ambiguity of the word, the only sure way to express agreement is to state the consequence which is to flow. Indeed, if the consequence — a right to terminate in respect of *any* breach — is expressly stated, the word 'condition' need not be used by the parties. Moreover, since the effect of such a provision is the conferral of a contractual right to terminate, the character of the term becomes irrelevant to the promisee's right to terminate.[39]

Implied agreement

[1913] Establishing an implied agreement. Most terms which are conditions are found to be such by reason of an implied agreement between the parties. Whether such an agreement exists depends, of course, on the construction of the contract. Assuming that the contract is in writing, and

---

34. (1938) 38 SR (NSW) 632 at 642 (reversed on other grounds sub nom *Luna Park (NSW) Ltd v Tramways Advertising Pty Ltd* (1938) 61 CLR 286).
35. See [727].
36. [1962] 2 QB 26. And see *Ankar Pty Ltd v National Westminster Finance (Australia) Ltd* (1987) 162 CLR 549; 70 ALR 641.
37. See [1950].
38. [1974] AC 235 (see Roger Brownsword, (1974) 37 *MLR* 104).
39. *Honner v Ashton* (1979) 1 BPR 9478 at 9483.

that the parol evidence rule[40] applies, the court cannot have regard to the prior negotiations of the parties, or their subsequent conduct, when deciding the issue. This means, for example, that the seriousness of an established breach of the term in question cannot be used as a basis for saying that the term was, or was not, a condition.[41] Again, the fact that the parties, when performing the contract, did not treat the term as a condition cannot be used as a guide on construction,[42] although it may be significant for another purpose, such as establishing an election to continue performance or estoppel.[43]

[1914] **Prior decisions.** Where a standard form contract is in issue, such as the New South Wales Law Society's Standard Conditions of Sale, the New York Produce Exchange time charterparty, or one of the many GAFTA forms frequently encountered in English commodity contract cases, it may be important to know whether the term alleged to be a condition has been the subject of a prior decision. If the term has been interpreted, the parties are presumed to have agreed to be bound by the prior decision unless they have expressly agreed to a contrary result. Moreover, if a term has been the subject of an authoritative interpretation by the High Court the decision will bind the lower courts and, in the absence of a contrary agreement between them, be conclusive between the parties.

It is not, however, necessary for a term to be precisely the same as one which has been the subject of a prior decision. If the term is similar the court may feel bound, in the interests of uniformity of decision, to construe the term in accordance with the earlier decision. For example, in *Maredelanto Compania Naviera SA v Bergbau-Handel GmbH (The Mihalis Angelos)*,[44] an expected ready to load clause in a charterparty was construed as a condition because it had been interpreted as such in earlier sale of goods cases.

[1915] **Motivation for entry into contract.** Jordan CJ stated the following test in *Tramways Advertising Pty Ltd v Luna Park (NSW) Ltd*:[45]

> The test of essentiality is whether it appears from the general nature of the contract considered as a whole, or from some particular term or terms, that the promise is of such importance to the promisee that he would not have entered into the contract unless he had been assured of a strict or a substantial performance of the promise, as the case may be, and that this ought to have been apparent to the promisor ...

Although the Full Court's decision in the *Tramways* case was reversed on appeal,[46] Jordan CJ's statement was approved and applied by the High

---

40. See [705]–[723].
41. But see *Cehave NV v Bremer Handelsgesellschaft mbH (The Hansa Nord)* [1976] QB 44 at 58.
42. See [718].
43. See generally [1967]–[1973], [1974]–[1976]. And see [712].
44. [1971] 1 QB 164. See D W Greig, 'Condition — Or Warranty?' (1973) 89 *LQR* 93.
45. (1938) 38 SR (NSW) 632 at 641–2.
46. Sub nom *Luna Park (NSW) Ltd v Tramways Advertising Pty Ltd* (1938) 61 CLR 286.

Court in *Associated Newspapers Ltd v Bancks*.[47] Bancks agreed to prepare and furnish weekly a full page drawing which Associated Newspapers promised to publish on the front page of the comic section of their newspaper. Their breach of this obligation was held to constitute a breach of condition. The term was so construed because it must have been apparent to Associated Newspapers that Bancks would not have entered into the contract unless assured of a strict or at least a substantial compliance with the term. On the facts a substantial breach was established as Associated Newspapers committed three successive breaches of their promise.

Because the prior negotiations of the parties are not usually admissible as evidence on the construction of a contract, a promisee cannot rely on such negotiations when seeking to establish the motivation for entry into the contract. Jordan CJ's test is therefore objective.[48] For example, where a contract for the sale of land specifies that a deposit must be paid on entry into the contract, the term will usually be construed as a condition[49] because a deposit payment is so important that a vendor would not be prepared to enter into the contract without an assurance that the payment will be made strictly in accordance with the contract. On the other hand, if there is nothing to indicate that the promisee's entry was motivated by an assurance of strict (or substantial) compliance,[50] the term cannot be construed as a condition in reliance on the test. However, this does not necessarily mean that the term will not be a condition since there are other factors to be considered. In other words, although satisfaction of the test stated by Jordan CJ is sufficient, it may not be necessary, provided there is some other basis for saying that the term was intended to be a condition.

[1916] **Structure of term and contract.** Where a term states the promisor's obligation in clear and precise words it is more likely to be a condition than a term couched in general words. Thus, in *Luna Park (NSW) Ltd v Tramways Advertising Pty Ltd*[51] a contract under which advertisements were to be displayed on boards placed on Sydney trams contained a promise by the advertisers in the following terms: 'We guarantee that these boards will be on the tracks at least eight hours per day throughout your season'. The fact that the parties had chosen words of guarantee, and also stated a definite time duration, were good indications that the term in question was a condition, even though this construction imposed a very onerous obligation on the advertisers. When the advertisers breached the term the High Court held that the promisees were entitled to terminate the performance of the contract.

The term in issue must, however, be construed as a whole, and even a promise expressed in definite terms may not be construed as a condition if

---

47. (1951) 83 CLR 322.
48. See *Tramways Advertising Pty Ltd v Luna Park (NSW) Ltd* (1938) 38 SR (NSW) 632 at 641 (reversed on other grounds sub nom *Luna Park (NSW) Ltd v Tramways Advertising Pty Ltd* (1938) 61 CLR 286).
49. At least as regards time; see [1951].
50. As in *DTR Nominees Pty Ltd v Mona Homes Pty Ltd* (1978) 138 CLR 423; 19 ALR 223.
51. (1938) 61 CLR 286.

it expressly confers a right on either or both parties to terminate in defined circumstances which is inconsistent with the existence of a right in respect of *any* breach of the term.[52] The structure of the contract may be relevant to the issue, and there is obviously a need to construe the whole contract when considering whether a particular term is a condition. For example, one reason for saying that the term considered in *L Schuler AG v Wickman Machine Tool Sales Ltd*[53] was not intended to be a condition was that another term of the distributorship agreement conferred a right to terminate in the event of a 'material' breach of the contract not being remedied within a certain time. Although the presence of a contractual right does not necessarily prevent another term being a condition, in *Schuler v Wickman* the House of Lords took the view that the presence of the express provision was a good indication that the parties did not intend that every breach by Wickman of its obligation to make weekly visits to Schuler's client would give rise to a right to terminate independently of the procedure which the parties had laid down.

Construction of the whole contract may indicate an interrelation between the obligations of the parties. Thus, in *Associated Newspapers Ltd v Bancks*,[54] the court considered that Bancks's obligation to furnish the drawing was a condition, and since there was a direct relation between his obligation and the obligation of Associated Newspapers to publish the drawing in the way described, it was logical to construe the latter obligation as a condition as well.

[1917] **Likely consequences of breach.** In *Bettini v Gye*[55] the court applied, as a test for determining whether a term is a condition, whether the term 'goes to the root of the matter', on the basis that a 'failure to perform it would render the performance of the rest of the contract by the plaintiff a thing different in substance from what the defendant has stipulated for'. Similarly, in *Hongkong Fir Shipping Co Ltd v Kawasaki Kisen Kaisha Ltd*,[56] Diplock LJ said that a term will be a condition if it can be said that every breach of the term will give rise to an 'event which will deprive the party not in default of substantially the whole benefit which it was intended that he should obtain from the contract'.

Under these formulations, the fact that the breach of a term will give rise to serious consequences for the promisee is a good indication that the parties must have intended the term to be a condition. On the other hand, where a term can be breached in various ways, some of which will have serious consequences and others only minor effects on the performance of the contract, the term is not likely to be a condition.[57] Thus, in *Cehave NV v Bremer Handelsgesellschaft mbH (The Hansa Nord)*,[58] a term stating that goods, the subject of a sale of goods contract, would be shipped 'in good

---

52. See *DTR Nominees Pty Ltd v Mona Homes Pty Ltd* (1978) 138 CLR 423.
53. [1974] AC 235 (see also [1912]).
54. (1951) 83 CLR 322 (see [1915]). See also *Bunge Corp New York v Tradax Export SA Panama* [1981] 1 WLR 711 (see [1952]).
55. (1876) 1 QBD 183 at 188.
56. [1962] 2 QB 26 at 69.
57. See, eg *Hongkong Fir Shipping Co Ltd v Kawasaki Kisen Kaisha Ltd* [1962] 2 QB 26 (see [1958]).
58. [1976] QB 44.

condition' by the seller was not a condition because of the range of possible breaches of the term.

Two important points need to be made about the seriousness of breach consideration. First, regard cannot be had to the actual breach which has occurred because that would be to construe the contract *ex post facto*, that is, in the light of subsequent events. Thus, regard should be had not to the 'effect of the breach which has in fact taken place; but the effect likely to be produced ... by any such breach'[59] of the term. Second, although it is sufficient for serious consequences to be found as the likely effect of the breach, it is not essential, in order for a term to be a condition, that every breach must produce substantial loss or detriment.[60] Other factors must be considered, and a term may be a condition, particularly in a commercial contract, even though its breach is not likely to cause substantial loss or detriment to the promisee.

[1918] **Assessment of damages and reasonableness of result.**[61] If damages would be an adequate remedy for the promisee in respect of a breach of the term alleged to be a condition then this is an indication that the term was not intended to be a condition,[62] on the basis that the promisee is adequately protected from the consequences of the promisor's breach without being accorded the right to terminate performance. On the other hand, if damages would not be an adequate remedy, for example, because their assessment would be extremely difficult, this is an indication that the term was intended to be a condition. For example, in *Ankar Pty Ltd v National Westminster Finance (Australia) Ltd*[63] a security deposit agreement secured the obligations of a lessee under a goods lease. Two terms required the promisor to notify the promisee of defaults by the lessee, and to consult with the promisee with a view to determining the appropriate course of action to take when defaults occurred. The High Court construed both terms as conditions, partly on the ground that the promisee would not be adequately protected from the consequences of breach by an award of damages.

Where construing a term as a condition would achieve an unreasonable result the court will presume that the parties did not intend that construction to be placed on the contract.[64] For example, in *Hongkong Fir Shipping Co Ltd v Kawasaki Kisen Kaisha Ltd*,[65] Upjohn LJ said that it would have been 'contrary to common sense' to construe the seaworthiness term as a condition. Of course, the court does not have a discretion to construe contracts reasonably. Therefore, if the parties have sufficiently indicated their intention that the term is to be construed as a condition the

---

59. *Bentsen v Taylor Sons & Co (No 2)* [1893] 2 QB 274 at 281. And see *Ankar Pty Ltd v National Westminster Finance (Australia) Ltd* (1987) 162 CLR 549.
60. *Bunge Corp New York v Tradax Export SA Panama* [1981] 1 WLR 711 (see [1952]).
61. See Roger Brownsword, 'Retrieving Reasons, Retrieving Rationality? A New Look at the Right to Withdraw for Breach of Contract' (1992) 5 *JCL* 83.
62. *Friedlander v Bank of Australasia* (1909) 8 CLR 85 at 96.
63. (1987) 162 CLR 549 (see J W Carter and J C Phillips, (1988) 1 *JCL* 70). See also *Bunge Corp New York v Tradax Export SA Panama* [1981] 1 WLR 711 at 720.
64. *L Schuler AG v Wickman Machine Tool Sales Ltd* [1974] AC 235 (see [1912], [1916]).
65. [1962] 2 QB 26 at 62.

court cannot reject that construction merely because it produces what is, in the opinion of the court, an unreasonable result.

[1919] Nature of the term, subject matter and contract. It is always important to consider the nature of the term alleged to be a condition, and the subject matter of the contract. Some terms have, over the years, achieved a particular status. For example, terms dealing with documentary credits,[66] and also time stipulations,[67] to some extent at least, attract special rules.

Other types of terms may be conditions because of their intrinsic importance. For example, terms relating to a perishable subject matter[68] are more likely to be regarded as conditions than those dealing with permanent subject matter such as land. Generally, terms descriptive of the subject matter of a contract are usually construed as conditions,[69] although there is some evidence of a tendency to adopt a more discerning approach and to treat such terms as conditions only where an item in the description of the subject matter constitutes a 'substantial ingredient' of the 'identity' of the subject matter.[70] On the other hand, if a term is essentially procedural in character it will be difficult to establish that the term is a condition in the absence of some special factor.[71]

In *Bentsen v Taylor Sons & Co (No 2)*[72] Bowen LJ said[73] that there is 'no way of deciding' whether a term is a condition

> except by looking at the contract in the light of the surrounding circumstances, and then making up one's mind whether the intention of the parties, as gathered from the instrument itself, will best be carried out by treating the promise as a warranty sounding only in damages, or as a condition precedent by the failure to perform which the other party is relieved of his liability.

Recent decisions have relied on this statement to justify construing important terms in commercial contracts as conditions, on the basis of a need for certainty.[74] Although this assists in ensuring that parties know their positions without first going to court for a ruling on the construction of the contract, the emphasis is by no means a recent development. For example, in *Bowes v Chaleyer*[75] Starke J said that the court is not in as good a position as the parties to a commercial contract when the 'value and importance' of a term must be estimated, and he put forward the view that

---

66. See, eg *Trans Trust SPRL v Danubian Trading Co Ltd* [1952] 2 QB 297.
67. See generally [1948]–[1964].
68. See, eg *Harrington v Browne* (1917) 23 CLR 297.
69. *Bowes v Shand* (1877) 2 App Cas 455; *Bowes v Chaleyer* (1923) 32 CLR 159. See also [638] (implied condition).
70. See *Reardon Smith Line Ltd v Yngvar Hansen-Tangen* [1976] 1 WLR 989 at 998.
71. See, eg *Bremer Handelsgesellschaft mbH v Vanden Avenne-Izegem PVBA* [1978] 2 Lloyd's Rep 109.
72. [1893] 2 QB 274 (see [1975]).
73. [1893] 2 QB 274 at 281.
74. See, eg *Bunge Corp New York v Tradax Export SA Panama* [1981] 1 WLR 711 (see [1952]); *Ankar Pty Ltd v National Westminster Finance (Australia) Ltd* (1987) 162 CLR 549 (see [1917]); *Compagnie Commerciale Sucres et Denrées v C Czarnikow Ltd* [1990] 1 WLR 1337 (see G H Treitel, [1991] *LMCLQ* 147; Malcolm Clarke, [1991] *CLJ* 29; J W Carter, (1992) 5 *JCL* 60).
75. (1923) 32 CLR 159 at 196.

it is 'far safer ... to treat as conditions substantial and important provisions in a mercantile contract relating to the time, place or mode of shipment of goods' the subject of the contract 'unless the contrary intention is manifest'.

Implied terms

[1920] Statutory classification. As was explained earlier,[76] where a statute implies a term into a contract it will almost invariably classify that term. If the term is classified as a condition the term will be so construed unless the parties have expressed an agreement that the term is to be classified in another way, for example, as a warranty. However, where the contract is made with a consumer the ability of the parties to re-classify the term may be restricted, if not altogether prohibited, by the statute.[77]

[1921] Express and implied agreement. Where an implied term is not classified by statute, for example, because it is implied at common law, the character of the term depends on the construction of the contract and the term may be a condition as a result of express or implied agreement.

Having regard to the difficulties encountered in making express terms conditions, cases in which an implied term is a condition by reason of express agreement are rare indeed. Probably the only situation in which an express agreement is likely to extend to an implied term is where a general agreement, created by words such as 'time shall be of the essence of this contract' is found. Even then the question may be raised whether the agreement was intended to extend to implied terms as well as express terms.

Usually, if an implied term is a condition this will be because of the implied agreement of the parties. In deciding whether this is the case the court will have regard to considerations similar to those referred to above. For example, in *Shepherd v Felt and Textiles of Australia Ltd*[78] the High Court implied a term into an agency contract requiring the agent to render faithful service to his principal and construed the term as a condition, on the basis that the breach of such a term was likely to have serious consequences for the principal, for example, by damaging his commercial reputation, and because faithful service is important to the relation of confidence which must exist between principal and agent.

Breach of Intermediate Term[79]

Terms which are intermediate in character

[1922] Express terms. Cases such as *Cehave NV v Bremer Handelsgesellschaft mbH (The Hansa Nord)*[80] justify the general proposition if an express term is not a condition it will be presumed to be intermediate

---

76. See [737].
77. See [737], [769]–[772].
78. (1931) 45 CLR 370.
79. See Carter, *Breach of Contract*, 2nd ed, 1991, Chapter 6; Lord Devlin, 'The Treatment of Breach of Contract' [1966] *CLJ* 192.
80. [1976] QB 44.

in character, and construed as such unless the parties have clearly expressed an intention that the term is a warranty. This is particularly true if the term is capable of being breached in various ways. Nevertheless, in the final analysis the issue must be decided by reference to the express or implied agreement of the parties. An express agreement may be found even though the parties have not used the intermediate term terminology. For example, if the parties have expressed agreement that a particular type of breach, such as a 'serious', 'substantial' or 'material' breach is to give rise to a right to terminate, the term is intermediate in character.

More commonly, intermediate terms result from implied agreement:
- on the basis of the presumption explained above;
- because of the presence of an exclusion clause which restricts the right to terminate to particular types of breach;[81] or
- because the parties have not expressed an intention to depart from the construction previously adopted in a standard form contract.[82]

As was explained earlier,[83] where a term is intermediate in character not every breach of the term will give rise to a right to terminate: the breach must be 'sufficiently serious'[84] before the right will accrue to the promisee.

[1923] Implied terms. An implied term may be intermediate in character. The implied term commonly found in employment contracts, requiring the employee to exercise proper or reasonable care in the performance of duties,[85] must usually be intermediate because it can be breached in various ways.

There are no examples of intermediate terms implied by statute.

Degree of seriousness required

[1924] Express provision. If a term is intermediate, and the parties have specified the type of breach which is to be regarded as sufficiently serious to give rise to a right to terminate, then the express provision governs the promisee's right to terminate. For example, if the contract provides that a 'material' breach is to give rise to a right to terminate, the court must decide whether the breach which has occurred is 'material' within the meaning of the contract.[86] However, strictly speaking, if the parties have expressly conferred the right to terminate for a material breach the occurrence of such a breach activates a contractual right rather than an implied right.

[1925] Criterion at common law. The criterion to be applied at common law has been stated in various ways, such as by requiring the

---

81. For example, a no-rejection clause in a contract for the sale of goods which requires the buyer to accept deductions from the price in respect of quality defects up to, say, 15 per cent of the goods.
82. See, eg *Bunge SA v Kruse* [1980] 2 Lloyd's Rep 142.
83. See [732].
84. See further [1924], [1925].
85. See [1855].
86. Cf *L Schuler AG v Wickman Machine Tool Sales Ltd* [1974] AC 235 (see [712], [1912], [1916]).

breach to go to the 'root'[87] of the contract, or to be 'fundamental'[88] in character. The actual description does not matter so long as the following points are taken into account.

First, the seriousness of the breach depends not only on the breach itself but also on the consequences of the breach, both actual and foreseeable, for the promisee.[89]

Second, it is the effect of the breach on the contract as a whole which matters: as a consequence of the promisor's breach the performance of the contract must be rendered substantially different from that intended by the parties.

Third, the assessment of the consequences of the breach is essentially a factual matter on which opinions are likely to differ.

Fourth, there is a link with the doctrine of frustration in that, in commercial contracts at least, the degree of seriousness required is the same as that applied under the doctrine of frustration.[90] This is why, in *Hongkong Fir Shipping Co Ltd v Kawasaki Kisen Kaisha Ltd*,[91] the English Court of Appeal adopted the criterion of commercial frustration in the context of breach. Because the 'frustrating' event is caused by the promisor's breach of contract, the distinguishing features are: that the promisor is liable in damages; and that the contract is not automatically discharged.[92]

Actual and foreseeable consequences

[1926] Actual consequences. In cases where the promisee relies on the actual consequence of the breach to establish substantially different performance, the court will concentrate on the detriment suffered by the promisee as a consequence of the breach. The promisee must establish deprivation of 'substantially the whole benefit which it was the intention of the parties as expressed in the contract that he should obtain as the consideration'[93] for the performance of the promisee's own obligations. For example, where the contract relates to a specific subject matter the breach is sufficiently serious if the promisor delivers something which is, in substance, a thing different from that contracted for.[94] Other situations in which the promisee may be regarded as having been deprived of substantially the whole benefit of the contract include:

---

87. See, eg *Decro-Wall International SA v Practitioners in Marketing Ltd* [1971] 1 WLR 361 at 368.
88. See, eg *Direct Acceptance Finance Ltd v Cumberland Furnishing Pty Ltd* [1965] NSWR 1504 at 1511. Although this is the criterion stated in *United Nations Convention on Contracts for the International Sale of Goods* 1980, Art 25, the expression has a broader meaning there (and is more easily satisfied) than under the general law.
89. See [1926]–[1927].
90. But cf Beale, *Remedies for Breach of Contract*, 1980, p 45.
91. [1962] 2 QB 26.
92. See [2043]–[2048] (self-induced frustration).
93. *Hongkong Fir Shipping Co Ltd v Kawasaki Kisen Kaisha Ltd* [1962] 2 QB 26 at 66; *Direct Acceptance Finance Ltd v Cumberland Furnishing Pty Ltd* [1965] NSWR 1504 at 1511.
94. *Lion White Lead Ltd v Rogers* (1918) 25 CLR 533 at 55. See also *W & S Pollock & Co v Macrae* 1922 SC (HL) 192 at 200.

- the breach will deprive the promisee of the profit which was expected from performance of the contract;[95]
- performance is so defective that damages would not be adequate compensation in respect of loss caused by the promisor's breach, for example, because the performance has no value at all;[96]
- the breach will substantially injure professional or commercial reputation;[97]
- where substantial expenditure would be required to make the performance rendered by the promisor conform with the requirements of the contract;[98]
- where the promisee's burden of performance is substantially increased by the promisor's breach.[99]

In many cases detailed examination of the facts will be required to establish whether performance is in fact substantially different from that intended by the parties. For example, in *Cehave NV v Bremer Handelsgesellschaft mbH (The Hansa Nord)*[100] buyers of citrus pulp pellets on terms CIF Rotterdam sought to justify their rejection of the goods on the ground that the sellers had breached a term requiring the shipment to be made 'in good condition'. Some 3400 tonnes of pellets were in dispute and on arrival in Rotterdam 1300 tonnes were found to have been substantially affected by heat. Minor damage (between two and five per cent) had occurred to the remainder, and the entire shipment had been resold by the sellers for only £33,700. Although the contract price for the goods had been about £100,000 the court found that the sellers' breach was not sufficiently serious. The diminution in value of the goods could be explained, not only on the basis that the sellers had breached the contract but also on the ground that the market price of sound goods had fallen, and that the goods in question had been resold in suspicious circumstances, for less than their true value. It transpired that the damaged condition of the goods did not prevent them being used as an ingredient in the manufacture of *animal* feed, a purpose not substantially different from that intended by the buyers, namely, *cattle* feed. When all these factors are taken into account the court's decision seems justified. However, it also indicates that a very serious breach is required.

[1927] Foreseeable consequences. Even if the actual consequences of the breach of an intermediate term are not sufficiently serious, the promisee may be able to establish a right to terminate by reference to the

---

95. *Carr v J A Berriman Pty Ltd* (1953) 89 CLR 327.
96. The promisee may be in a stronger position if the contract is construed as 'entire'; see [1824], [1832].
97. *Federal Commerce and Navigation Co Ltd v Molena Alpha Inc* [1979] AC 757, a case of anticipatory breach (see [1935]).
98. Compare the facts in *Harbutt's 'Plasticine' Ltd v Wayne Tank and Pump Co Ltd* [1970] 1 QB 447 (overruled in *Photo Production Ltd v Securicor Transport Ltd* [1980] AC 827).
99. Contrast the fact situation in *Hongkong Fir Shipping Co Ltd v Kawasaki Kisen Kaisha Ltd* [1962] 2 QB 26 (see [1958]).
100. [1976] QB 44 (see F M B Reynolds, (1976) 92 *LQR* 17; Tony Weir, [1976] *CLJ* 33 and [736]).

foreseeable consequences of the breach.[101] Moreover, a promisee is permitted to combine actual and foreseeable consequences, and the promisor's breach may, in some cases, achieve the significance required only as the result of the combined consequences. The promisee must, however, establish that any foreseeable consequences relied on were reasonably foreseeable at the time of termination.[102]

In considering the effect of foreseeable consequences it is important to have regard to the types of consequences which are reasonably foreseeable. If the breach is likely to cause physical injury to the promisee, for example, because a repairer has negligently repaired a motor vehicle so that it is dangerous to drive, then the consequences can be regarded as serious.[103] On the other hand, if the only likely consequence is delay, there is clearly a need to consider not only the period of delay but also its effect on the object of the contract.[104]

It may also be relevant to consider the conduct of the promisor if informed of the breach. A promisor who is informed of the consequences which are likely to occur as the result of the breach may offer to remedy its breach, for example, by doing repair work again.[105] The promisor's offer is relevant to the consequences of the breach, because, assuming the offer to be genuine and feasible, it may operate to remove the element of foreseeable loss or damage.

A promisee is not obliged to terminate in respect of foreseeable events, and does not necessarily lose the right to terminate merely by waiting for them to occur. The promisee may, however, find that the foreseeable consequences do not occur. If that is the position the promisee will cease to be entitled to terminate. Of course, even if the reason for their non-occurrence is the fact that the promisor has remedied the breach, the promisee may claim damages for breach of contract.[106] However, in exceptional cases the right to terminate may be lost by waiting on events, for example, because the delay amounts to an election to continue performance; but since election depends on knowledge of the circumstances a party who does not know of the consequences which were likely to have resulted can hardly be denied the right to rely on consequences which do occur.[107]

---

101. *Hongkong Fir Shipping Co Ltd v Kawasaki Kisen Kaisha Ltd* [1962] 2 QB 26 at 38, 57, 64, 72.
102. Cf *United Nations Convention on Contracts for the International Sale of Goods* 1980, Art 25 ('unless the party in breach did not foresee and a reasonable person of the same kind in the same circumstances would not have foreseen such a result').
103. Cf *Farnworth Finance Facilities Ltd v Attryde* [1970] 1 WLR 1053.
104. See [1958].
105. Cf *Astley Industrial Trust Ltd v Grimley* [1963] 1 WLR 584 at 599. An express term may oblige the promisee to provide an opportunity to remedy the breach (eg *L Schuler AG v Wickman Machine Tool Sales Ltd* [1974] AC 235) or the promisee may be obliged to do so by statute (see [1970]). See also [1959] (delay).
106. *Carr v J A Berriman Pty Ltd* (1953) 89 CLR 327 at 349.
107. See [1971].

Termination for Repudiation[108]

General[109]

[1928] Focus of the repudiation concept. The focus of the concept of repudiation of obligation is on the readiness and willingness of a promisor to perform contractual obligations. If the promisor is not ready and willing, or will not, at the appointed time, be ready and willing to perform, the law treats the promisee as possessing the right to terminate the performance of the contract under the doctrine of repudiation, provided that the absence of readiness or willingness satisfies a *requirement of seriousness*.

The focal point of the repudiation concept distinguishes it from termination for breach, where the focus is on the promisor's breach and its consequences. However, there is considerable overlap between the two bases for termination because an absence of readiness or willingness may manifest itself in a breach of contract.

An *anticipatory breach* of contract occurs if a repudiation and exercise of the right of termination take place prior to the time appointed for performance by the promisor.

[1929] Readiness and willingness. The following features of the concept of readiness and willingness may be noted.

First, the concept includes an ability to perform. Thus, a promisor is ready and willing to perform only if ready, willing and able to perform.[110]

Second, whether a promisor is ready and willing to perform is a question of fact.[111]

Third, since a promisor must be both ready *and* willing to perform, an absence of either (or ability) may amount to a repudiation.

Fourth, the extent of readiness and willingness required is determined by the terms of the contract. Therefore, a promisor must be ready and willing to perform in accordance with the standard of contractual duty imposed by the contract[112] at the time when performance is due.

Fifth, although a promisor need not be ready and willing to perform until performance is due, the striking feature of the doctrines of repudiation and anticipatory breach is that they permit a promisee to terminate on the basis of an anticipated absence of readiness or willingness.

Sixth, a plaintiff (or defendant) is not obliged to plead expressly readiness and willingness to perform, this being implied by rules of court.[113]

---

108. For analysis of the development of the law see Samuel Williston, 'Repudiation of Contracts' (1901) 14 *Harv LR* 317 and 421; Sir Michael Mustill, 'Anticipatory Breach', *Butterworth Lectures 1989–90*, 1990. See also P W Young, 'Repudiation' (1985) 1 *Aust Bar Rev* 21.
109. See Carter, *Breach of Contract*, 2nd ed, 1991, Chapter 7.
110. *British & Beningtons Ltd v North Western Cachar Tea Co Ltd* [1923] AC 48 at 63; *Peter Turnbull & Co Pty Ltd v Mundus Trading Co (Australasia) Pty Ltd* (1954) 90 CLR 235 at 253; *Foran v Wight* (1989) 168 CLR 385; 88 ALR 413.
111. See, eg *English and Australian Copper Co Ltd v Johnson* (1911) 13 CLR 490 at 497; *Dainford Ltd v Smith* (1985) 155 CLR 342 at 366; 58 ALR 623.
112. See generally [1853]–[1857].

Accordingly, if one party wishes to contest the readiness or willingness of the other, that party must expressly do so in order to oblige the other party to produce evidence of readiness and willingness to perform.[114]

Seventh, proof that a promisor was not ready and willing to perform at the time when performance was due will generally be sufficient proof of a breach of contract by failure to perform. However, proof that a promisor will not be ready and willing when performance falls due is not sufficient proof of an anticipatory breach. As explained below,[115] two further elements must be established: a right to terminate the performance of the contract; and an election to terminate on the part of the promisee.

[1930] **Anticipatory breach.**[116] The expression 'repudiation of obligation' includes words or conduct which can be treated by a promisor as an anticipatory breach. For the breach to be anticipatory in character there must be a prospective element.[117] The clearest case of this is where a promisor repudiates obligations at a time which precedes the earliest date for performance on the promisor's part, as where a seller, obliged to deliver by 1 March, repudiates on 1 February. It is nevertheless fairly common for a breach to be described as anticipatory even though performance by the promisor has commenced, and notwithstanding that he or she may have committed an actual breach by failure to perform.[118]

For an anticipatory breach to occur the promisee must terminate the performance of the contract,[119] and a repudiation, standing alone, does not have this effect.[120] Because of the requirement of termination, it is not, strictly speaking, correct to describe a repudiation as itself an anticipatory breach of contract.[121]

Where the promisee's right to terminate is based on an inability to perform, the promisor may not, in fact, be repudiating his or her obligations. However, because the concept of readiness and willingness embraces an ability to perform, it is appropriate to deal with inability under the heading of 'repudiation'.

[1931] **Ways of proving repudiation.** There are two ways of establishing repudiation: by reference to the promisor's words and conduct; and by reference to the promisor's actual position. In the latter situation the existence of repudiation depends on the promisor being unable to perform, although, as we shall see, the words or conduct of the promisor may also have relevance to inability. The distinction between the two ways of proving

---

113. See [1811].
114. *Hensley v Reschke* (1914) 18 CLR 452 at 467; *Foran v Wight* (1989) 168 CLR 385.
115. See [1930].
116. See J W Carter, 'Anticipatory Breach' in *Current Developments in International Transfers of Goods and Services*, 1994, p 227.
117. See [1906]. See also [1841].
118. See, eg *Universal Cargo Carriers Corp v Citati* [1957] 2 QB 401; *Progressive Mailing House Pty Ltd v Tabali Pty Ltd* (1985) 157 CLR 17; 57 ALR 609.
119. *Heyman v Darwins Ltd* [1942] AC 356 at 382; *Peter Turnbull & Co Pty Ltd v Mundus Trading Co (Australasia) Pty Ltd* (1954) 90 CLR 235. Cf *Martin v Stout* [1925] AC 359 at 368.
120. *Automatic Fire Sprinklers Pty Ltd v Watson* (1946) 72 CLR 435; *White and Carter (Councils) Ltd v McGregor* [1962] AC 413.
121. See also [1841]. But see *Michael v Hart & Co* [1902] 1 KB 482 at 490.

repudiation is important because the law permits the promisee to terminate in respect of words or conduct amounting to repudiation even if the promisor is in fact able to perform. Thus, where the promisee justifiably terminates in respect of words or conduct, the promisee is not required to prove that the promisor was unable to perform.

Obviously, the first mode of proof is more appealing to the promisee, but in either case the promisee must establish that the absence of readiness or willingness is, or will be, a serious matter.

[1932] The requirement of seriousness. Superficially the requirement of seriousness is extremely straightforward: the promisee must prove either[122] that the absence of readiness or willingness relied on extends to all the promisor's obligations[123] or that it clearly indicates that the promisor will breach the contract in a way which gives rise to a right to terminate for breach.[124] In the first situation the only difficulty likely to confront the promisee is the relevance, in some cases, of the bona fides of the promisor. In cases where the absence of readiness or willingness does not extend to all the promisor's obligations further difficulties are likely to be encountered.

First, there may be a problem of classification. If the time for performance has arrived, and a case of actual breach established, the court may approach the issue of termination either from the point of view of the nature of the promisor's breach or by reference to the repudiation doctrine.

Second, where the time for performance by the promisor has not arrived, that is, a case of *prospective* breach, it may be difficult to prove that the requirement of seriousness is satisfied.

[1933] Basis of the right to terminate. Before discussing the problems referred to above it is appropriate to consider the basis of the promisor's right to terminate in cases of repudiation.

Various bases have been suggested for the right to terminate which exists under the repudiation doctrine,[125] including:

- the repudiation is an 'offer' of a breach that the promisee is entitled to accept;[126]
- the repudiation is a present breach which gives rise to a right to terminate;[127]
- the existence of an implied term prohibiting repudiation;[128]
- impossibility or prevention of performance;[129]

---

122. *Honner v Ashton* (1979) 1 BPR 9478 at 9492.
123. See, eg *Hochster v De la Tour* (1853) 2 E & B 678; 118 ER 922 (see [1937]).
124. See, eg *Federal Commerce and Navigation Co Ltd v Molena Alpha Inc* [1979] AC 757 at 779, 783, 785.
125. See the discussion by McHugh JA in *Wight v Foran* (1987) 11 NSWLR 470 at 487–8 (reversed without reference to the point sub nom *Foran v Wight* (1989) 168 CLR 385).
126. *Denmark Productions Ltd v Boscobel Productions Ltd* [1969] 1 QB 699 at 731.
127. *Maredelanto Compania Naviera SA v Bergbau-Handel GmbH (The Mihalis Angelos)* [1971] 1 QB 164 at 196.
128. *Bradley v H Newsom Sons & Co* [1919] AC 16 at 33; *Larratt v Bankers and Traders Insurance Co Ltd* (1941) 41 SR (NSW) 215 at 222. But see Lawrence Vold, 'Withdrawal of Repudiation after Anticipatory Breach of Contract' (1926) 5 *Texas LR* 9.

- protection of the promisee's expectations;[130]
- convenience;[131] and
- the existence of an 'inevitable' breach of contract.[132]

Although a particular fact situation may justify the application of any of these theories, the offer and acceptance theory has been discredited as a general explanation.[133] Anglo-Australian law provides little support for the present breach view in cases where the absence of readiness or willingness precedes the time of performance.[134] To the extent that the doctrine is a means to an end, the right to terminate is largely a matter of convenience, although this hardly provides a conceptual framework.

In order to explain the existence of a right to terminate in cases where the repudiation precedes the time of performance, the courts frequently rely on the inevitable breach theory. Thus, if it is clear that the promisor will not (or cannot) perform, the right to terminate exists because the law permits the promisee to anticipate a breach which is, for practical purposes, inevitable. In cases where the promisor is wholly and finally disabled from performing contractual obligations it would be pointless to require the promisee to wait, so the law treats the promisor's breach as inevitable.

Where the repudiation arises merely from the promisor's words or conduct it might be objected that the breach cannot be regarded as inevitable for the simple reason that the promisor might change his or her mind and actually perform. However, the doctrine of repudiation permits the promisee to take the promisor at his or her word, and the promisor cannot retract the repudiation once the performance of the contract has been terminated.[135] Accordingly, damages are generally assessed on the basis of a breach at the time when performance would have been due, rather than at the time of the promisor's repudiation or the promisee's election to terminate.[136] Because the breach is regarded as inevitable, the promisor is not permitted to defeat the promisee's claim by proving, for example, that he or she would have been able to perform had there been no repudiation, or that the contract would have been frustrated,[137] or that a contractual right to terminate would have been exercised.[138]

---

129. *Cort v Ambergate Nottingham and Boston and Eastern Junction Railway Co* (1851) 17 QB 127 at 145; 117 ER 1229 at 1236; Francis Dawson, 'Metaphors and Anticipatory Breach of Contract' [1981] *CLJ* 83.
130. *Frost v Knight* (1872) LR 7 Ex 111 at 114. See J C Vyn, 'Anticipatory Repudiation Under the Uniform Commercial Code: Interpretation, Analysis, and Problems' (1976) 30 *Southwestern LJ* 601.
131. *Woodar Investment Development Ltd v Wimpey Construction UK Ltd* [1980] 1 WLR 277 at 296–7.
132. *Maredelanto Compania Naviera SA v Bergbau-Handel GmbH (The Mihalis Angelos)* [1971] 1 QB 164.
133. See *Moschi v Lep Air Services Ltd* [1973] AC 331 at 349–50.
134. Except, perhaps, in cases where the repudiation makes performance impossible; see, eg *Southern Foundries (1926) Ltd v Shirlaw* [1940] AC 701 at 717.
135. *Martin v Stout* [1925] AC 359 at 364; *Ogle v Comboyuro Investments Pty Ltd* (1976) 136 CLR 444 at 451; 9 ALR 309.
136. See [2148].
137. See [2063].
138. *Maredelanto Compania Naviera SA v Bergbau-Handel GmbH (The Mihalis Angelos)* [1971] 1 QB 164.

One criticism of the inevitable breach theory is that it tends to explain the consequences of termination rather than the existence of the right to terminate. Another is that in some cases the inevitability of breach is largely fictional, and nice questions can arise in the assessment of damages.[139]

[1934] The problem of classification. The problem of classification is largely, but not entirely, academic. Differing views have been expressed as to the scope of the repudiation doctrine. Lord Denning MR[140] once suggested that the concept should be utilised only in cases of anticipatory breach. This supports the view that where an absence of readiness or willingness involves an actual failure to perform, the right to terminate must be based on the character of the term breached and the consequences of the breach. On the other hand, in *Shevill v Builders Licensing Board*,[141] Gibbs CJ considered that there was 'high authority' to support the proposition that, except in cases where the absence of readiness or willingness involves a breach of condition, or triggers a contractual right to terminate, the existence of a right to terminate depends on the application of the repudiation doctrine. The solution would seem to lie somewhere between these opposing views.

Where an absence of readiness or willingness involves a breach of condition there is no need, so far as the right to terminate is concerned, to invoke the repudiation concept. Breach of condition may in some cases amount to a repudiation, and the presence or absence of repudiation may be important to other matters, such as the assessment of damages; but, since the right to terminate necessarily follows from the promisor's failure to perform, the repudiation doctrine is irrelevant to that right. On the other hand, if the promisor has merely breached a warranty the repudiation concept will be relevant since no right to terminate will accrue to the promisee unless it can be established that the absence of readiness or willingness is so serious as to amount to a repudiation of substantially the whole contract.[142]

If the absence of readiness or willingness causes the promisor to breach an intermediate term, and a right to terminate arises, the distinction between termination for breach and termination for repudiation is admittedly subtle. The right to terminate should, as was explained earlier, be seen as stemming from the breach if the consequences are sufficiently serious.[143] However, a right to terminate may arise under the repudiation doctrine even though the consequences are not particularly serious if, for example, it is 'unjust' or 'unfair'[144] to hold the promisee to the contract, for example, because the absence of readiness or willingness implies a fundamental disregard of the contract. The two concepts merge if it is established that the foreseeable consequences of a promisor's breach are

---

139. See [2147], [2149], [2161].
140. *Cehave NV v Bremer Handelsgesellschaft mbH (The Hansa Nord)* [1976] QB 44 at 59.
141. (1982) 149 CLR 620 at 626; 42 ALR 305.
142. See also [738].
143. See [1926], [1927].
144. *Decro-Wall International SA v Practitioners in Marketing Ltd* [1971] 1 WLR 361 at 380 (approved *Federal Commerce and Navigation Co Ltd v Molena Alpha Inc* [1979] AC 757); *Honner v Ashton* (1979) 1 BPR 9478 at 9491.

further breaches on the promisor's part, and the accumulation of breaches would be seriously detrimental to the promisee. The reason the concepts merge is that the consequences of the promisor's breach — the focal point of the intermediate term concept — are synonymous with a serious absence of readiness or willingness to perform on the part of the promisor.

The classification problem is not entirely academic because the nature of the evidence required under the intermediate term concept differs from that required under the repudiation concept. Under the latter the emphasis is on the words and conduct of the promisor and evidence of what has been said and done may differ quite substantially from evidence directed to the impact of a breach on the promisee. The choice of evidence is important because the extent of the absence of readiness or willingness, and the impact of the breach, are both largely factual issues.[145]

[1935] **The problem of prospective breach.** The main problem of prospective breach is the conception of a breach without a failure to perform. Out of the conceptual problem at least three legal difficulties emerge.

(1) How certain must it be that the promisor will breach the contract?
(2) How serious must the breach be?
(3) In cases where the seriousness of a breach depends on its consequences, how are the consequences established?

The general approach to the problem of prospective breach is illustrated by *Federal Commerce and Navigation Co Ltd v Molena Alpha Inc*,[146] which concerned three time charterparties. Notwithstanding cl 9 of these contracts, which provided that the masters of the vessels were to be under the orders of the charterers as regards employment of the vessels, the owners threatened to instruct the masters not to sign any bill of lading endorsed 'freight prepaid'. The House of Lords held that such conduct would involve a breach of cl 9, but that such a breach would not necessarily justify termination by the charterers since the term was not a condition. The charterers' right to terminate depended on the consequences which would flow from the breach which the owners had threatened. The umpire had found that, had the owners actually breached the contract, the consequences for the charterers would have been very serious indeed; for example, the vessels in question would have been barred from the CIF trade which, as the owners well knew, was essential to the charterers. It did not matter that the owners had acted bona fide[147] on legal advice that cl 18 of the charters justified their conduct since it was clear, to any reasonable person in the position of the charterers that, if the owners carried out the threat, the charterers would suffer great loss. There was, therefore, a repudiation by the shipowners, based on proof of a sufficiently serious breach of an intermediate term.

Under the *Federal Commerce* case, it is sufficient for it to be 'clear'[148] that the breach will occur, provided the prospective breach is of a kind that

---

145. *Direct Acceptance Finance Ltd v Cumberland Furnishing Pty Ltd* [1965] NSWR 1504 at 1510; *Walters v Cooper* [1967] VR 583 at 587.
146. [1979] AC 757 (see J W Carter, [1979] *CLJ* 270).
147. See [1941].

would, on its occurrence, give rise to a right to terminate for breach. If the promisee is forced to rely on the (hypothetical) consequences of the breach it is sufficient that serious consequences would, in the opinion of informed persons, flow from the breach. It can also be inferred from the *Federal Commerce* case that, had cl 9 been classified as a condition, the charterers could have justified their termination without proving that serious consequences would have resulted from the breach, on the basis that where a term is classified as a condition any (prospective) breach of it is a sufficient justification for termination.[149]

[1936] Scope of the doctrine. The doctrine of repudiation can be excluded by the parties. Such exclusion must be expressly stated or arise by necessary implication from the terms of the contract. Express exclusion is rare, but the possibility of implied exclusion is not so remote.[150] For example, in *Amann Aviation Pty Ltd v The Commonwealth*[151] a clause (cl 2.24) conferred a right of termination on the Commonwealth 'Whenever and so often as the Contractor fails to carry out the contract or comply with a condition of the contract to the satisfaction of the Secretary' of the Department of Transport, and imposed a show cause procedure under which the Secretary could call upon the contractor to show cause 'in writing to the satisfaction of the Secretary, why the contract or any specified portion thereof should not be cancelled'. The court considered the termination clause to be a more or less exclusive code for termination. Davies J said that all that was left of the common law bases for termination was 'repudiation ... in its strict sense' of anticipatory breach.[152]

From time to time it has been suggested that particular types of contracts are excluded from the repudiation doctrine. Consideration will be given later to the treatment of unilateral and partially executed contracts.[153] At this stage it is sufficient to note that leases, bills of exchange, arbitration clauses and partnership agreements have given rise to controversy.

A contract to enter into a lease is subject to the doctrines of repudiation and anticipatory breach.[154] Moreover, although on the grant of the lease an interest in the land arises, it is now clear that the doctrines of repudiation

---

148. See also *Forslind v Bechely-Crundall* 1922 SC (HL) 173 at 179; *Stevenson v Hook* (1956) 73 WN (NSW) 307 at 313. See also [1938].
149. See [1979] AC 757 at 778, 783, 785. See also *Universal Cargo Carriers Corp v Citati* [1957] 2 QB 401; *Foran v Wight* (1989) 168 CLR 385 at 395, 416, 441. A contrary dictum in *Afovos Shipping Co SA v Pagnan* [1983] 1 WLR 195 at 203 is best explained by the fact that the term was a 'condition' merely in the sense that there was an express (contractual) right to terminate in respect of any breach of the term.
150. Statutes such as the *Contracts Review Act* 1980 (NSW) may apply if the parties have excluded the doctrine. See generally Chapter 15.
151. (1990) 92 ALR 601 (affirmed on other grounds sub nom *Commonwealth of Australia v Amann Aviation Pty Ltd* (1991) 174 CLR 64; 104 ALR 1). Contrast *Leslie Shipping Co v Welstead* [1921] 3 KB 420; *Concut Pty Ltd v Worrell* (2000) 176 ALR 693 at 699–700.
152. However, when analysing whether such a repudiation had occurred Davies J does seem to have considered conduct after the arrival of the time for performance, which suggests that the clause did not go quite so far as he had indicated.
153. See [1965]–[1966].
154. See, eg *Diamond v Moore* (1931) 45 CLR 159; *Laurinda Pty Ltd v Capalaba Park Shopping Centre Pty Ltd* (1989) 166 CLR 623; 85 ALR 183. Cf *Leitz Leeholme Stud Pty Ltd v Robinson* [1977] 2 NSWLR 544.

and anticipatory breach apply to the lease itself.[155] In *Progressive Mailing House Pty Ltd v Tabali Pty Ltd*[156] the lessor leased factory premises to the lessee for a period of five years. Clause 10.1 provided that in the event of any rent payable under the lease remaining unpaid for 14 days, or the lessee's failure to perform any term of the lease (and failure to remedy same after 30 days' notice to rectify), the lessor could re-enter the land. Rent was unpaid for a number of months and the lessee failed to remedy breaches of other terms of the lease pursuant to a notice served by the lessor. These events were held to give rise to a right to terminate the lease and to re-enter the land pursuant to cl 10.1. The High Court made it clear that the general principles of repudiation apply to leases, and used those principles to justify an award of substantial damages in favour of the lessor.[157]

Nevertheless, apart from the general difficulty of proving that the requirement of seriousness has been satisfied, a number of problems still arise. It may be that satisfaction of the statutory requirements for forfeiture[158] is a prerequisite to invocation of the repudiation doctrine, at least where the repudiation is based on breach by failure to perform the lease. Difficulties may also arise where damages are claimed following termination. If the election to terminate is based solely on a contractual right to terminate, damages for loss of the bargain may not be available.[159]

In at least three Australian cases[160] it has been stated that the doctrine of repudiation does not apply to bills of exchange, at least in so far as it would create an anticipatory breach in advance of actual dishonour of the bill. It may be that application of the doctrine depends on whether the bill has been taken as absolute or conditional payment.[161] If the creditor has agreed to accept the bill as an absolute payment there is something to be said for the view that the creditor is required to give whatever credit the bill allows, even though the debtor has repudiated his or her obligation under the bill. On the other hand, if the bill was taken as conditional payment there seems to be no reason, in principle, for not allowing the creditor to proceed for the recovery of the money in reliance on the contractual obligation to pay in respect of which the bill was given. However, since the action is for anticipatory breach, the creditor cannot recover the payment as a debt due;

---

155. See J W Carter and Jennifer Hill, 'Repudiation of Leases: Further Developments' [1986] *Conv* 262; Ken Mackie, 'Repudiation of Leases' (1988) 62 *ALJ* 53.
156. (1985) 157 CLR 17. See also *NLS Pty Ltd v Hughes* (1966) 120 CLR 583; *Shevill v Builders Licensing Board* (1982) 149 CLR 620; *Ripka Pty Ltd v Maggiore Bakeries Pty Ltd* [1984] VR 629 (see J W Carter, [1985] *Conv* 289). The position in England is not entirely clear. See *Total Oil Great Britain Ltd v Thompson Garages (Biggin Hill) Ltd* [1972] 1 QB 318; *National Carriers Ltd v Panalpina (Northern) Ltd* [1981] AC 675 at 703. But cf [2035]–[2036] (frustration).
157. See [2159].
158. See [1980]. See also [1979] (relief under equitable principles).
159. See further [2159]. Where the conduct of the lessor is interpreted as a surrender of the lease, the lessor may not be able to claim damages. See *Buchanan v Byrnes* (1906) 3 CLR 704 (as interpreted in *Tabali*); *Wood Factory Pty Ltd v Kiritos Pty Ltd* (1985) 2 NSWLR 105; Carter, *Breach of Contract*, 2nd ed, 1991, para 784. Cf *Konica Business Machines Australia Pty Ltd v Tizine Pty Ltd* (1992) 26 NSWLR 687.
160. *Pennicott v Pennicott* (1936) 30 Tas LR 111 at 116; *Mackenzie v Rees* (1941) 65 CLR 1 at 15 (see [1965]); *Geo Thompson (Aust) Pty Ltd v Vittadello* [1978] VR 199 at 202.
161. See [1816].

the creditor must recover it by way of damages, and some discount may be necessary to take account of recovery in advance of the time when the bill would have fallen due for payment.[162]

The doctrine of repudiation, like that of the intermediate term,[163] gives rise to a right to terminate all, but not part, of the parties' contractual obligations unperformed at the time of termination. This limitation on the scope of the doctrine does not apply to an arbitration clause, and the doctrine can be applied to permit termination of the parties' obligations under the clause. One explanation is that an arbitration clause 'constitutes a self-contained contract collateral or ancillary'[164] to the contract in which it is found.

In *Hurst v Bryk*[165] Lord Millett suggested[166] that it was 'doubtful' whether the doctrine of repudiation applies to a partnership relationship. Although the House of Lords was able to dismiss the appeal without having to decide the point, the English Court of Appeal had taken the view[167] that the doctrine does apply to partnership contracts. Lord Millett reasoned that because the partnership legislation, in setting out the circumstances in which a relationship might be dissolved, does not refer to repudiation it would be inconsistent with that legislation to apply the doctrine of repudiation. With respect, dissolution differs from termination. The former may only be achieved through court orders, whereas the latter merely depends on whether a partner has validly elected to terminate for breach or repudiation. It is difficult to see why partners should not (subject to the terms of the partnership contract) enjoy normal rights of termination in relation to their contract of partnership. Thus, if a partnership has two members and one of the partners repudiates the contract, it should be open to the other to terminate the contract so as, for example, to ensure that no further partnership liabilities are incurred. In other words, termination for repudiation may be a legitimate step which precedes a petition to have the partnership dissolved.

Repudiation Based on Words or Conduct[168]

[1937] Express refusal to perform. The clearest case of a repudiation of obligation is an express refusal to perform. For example, in the landmark case of *Hochster v De la Tour*,[169] the defendant agreed to employ the plaintiff for a specified period as a courier. Before the employment was due to commence the defendant repudiated his obligations by telling the plaintiff that his services were not required. The plaintiff having accepted the repudiation, the court held that the plaintiff was entitled to succeed in an action for damages for anticipatory breach.

---

162. See generally [2160].
163. See *Direct Acceptance Finance Ltd v Cumberland Furnishing Pty Ltd* [1965] NSWR 1504 at 1511.
164. *Bremer Vulkan Schiffbau und Maschinenfabrik v South India Shipping Corp Ltd* [1981] AC 909 at 980.
165. [2000] 2 WLR 740 (see Elisabeth Peden and J W Carter, (2000) 16 *JCL* 275).
166. [2000] 2 WLR 740 at 747. The other members of the House of Lords agreed.
167. See [1999] Ch 1 at 9.
168. See Carter, *Breach of Contract*, 2nd ed, 1991, Chapter 8.
169. (1853) 2 E & B 678; 118 ER 922.

[1937]

The principle applies even though the promisor's obligation to perform is subject to a contingency which has not been fulfilled. Thus, in *Frost v Knight*,[170] the plaintiff successfully sued for anticipatory breach of a promise to marry, even though the marriage was to take place on the death of the defendant's father and notwithstanding that the repudiation occurred (and proceedings were commenced) prior to the fulfilment of that contingency.

Two points should be noted about the cases considered above. First, although both concerned refusals to perform prior to the time of performance, there is no doubt that an express refusal after the arrival of the time of performance also gives rise to a right to terminate.[171] Second, although the defendant in each case repudiated all his contractual obligations, a repudiation may arise in less extreme cases, provided that the requirement of seriousness is satisfied. In this respect it is important to appreciate that a wilful, but partial, refusal to perform is not necessarily a repudiation. Even if a wilful refusal constitutes a breach of contract there is no rule of law that the refusal amounts to a repudiation.[172] It may be easier to establish repudiation where the refusal is wilful,[173] but the requirement of seriousness must still be satisfied. Similarly, a repudiation may occur where the promisor merely refuses to perform in accordance with the contract. The decision in *Federal Commerce and Navigation Co Ltd v Molena Alpha Inc*[174] provides an example of this in the context of anticipatory breach. *Associated Newspapers Ltd v Bancks*[175] is an example in the context of refusal after the arrival of the time of performance. The promisor's breach was there held to amount to a repudiation even if the term breached was a warranty rather than a condition.

[1938] **Implied refusal to perform.** Even if there is no express refusal to perform, a promisee may establish repudiation if a refusal can be inferred from the promisor's words or conduct. Lord Coleridge CJ formulated the test, in *Freeth v Burr*,[176] as being 'whether the acts or conduct ... amount to an intimation of an intention to abandon and altogether to refuse performance of the contract'. Such an 'intimation' will be established if the words or conduct of the promisor make it 'quite plain'[177] that the promisor

---

170. (1872) LR 7 Ex 111. See also *Psaltis v Schultz* (1948) 76 CLR 547 but note that the action for breach of promise was abolished by s 111A of the *Marriage Act* 1961 (Cth).
171. See, eg *Mersey Steel and Iron Co Ltd v Naylor Benzon & Co* (1884) 9 App Cas 434.
172. See, eg *Adami v Maison de Luxe Ltd* (1924) 35 CLR 143 at 151; *Mathieson v Sunshine Wrappings Pty Ltd* (1962) 80 WN (NSW) 1312.
173. See *Suisse Atlantique Société d'Armement Maritime SA v NV Rotterdamsche Kolen Centrale* [1967] 1 AC 361 at 394, 429, 435.
174. [1979] AC 757 (see [1935]).
175. (1951) 83 CLR 322 (see [1915]).
176. (1874) LR 9 CP 208 at 213 (approved *Mersey Steel and Iron Co Ltd v Naylor Benzon & Co* (1884) 9 App Cas 434). See also *Laurinda Pty Ltd v Capalaba Park Shopping Centre Pty Ltd* (1989) 166 CLR 623 at 647–8.
177. *Spettabile Consorzio Veneziano di Armamento e Navigazione v Northumberland Shipbuilding Co Ltd* (1919) 121 LT 628 at 635 per Atkin LJ. See also *Contractual Remedies Act* 1979 (NZ), s 7; *Restatement (2d) Contracts* (1979), §250; *United Nations Convention on Contracts for the International Sale of Goods* 1980, Art 72; [1935].

will not perform, or not perform in accordance with the contract. Of course, the requirement of seriousness must also be satisfied.

Cases on contracts for the sale of goods by instalments frequently provide examples of implied refusals to perform. Under the sale of goods legislation[178] the court must have regard to the terms of the contract and the 'circumstances of the case' in deciding whether a breach by either the seller or the buyer amounts to a repudiation. An express refusal to perform is sufficient to establish a repudiation, but an implied refusal will also be sufficient. As Bigham J explained in *Millars' Karri and Jarrah Co (1902) v Weddel Turner & Co*,[179] if a buyer fails to pay for one delivery, or the seller delivers goods differing from the requirements of the contract, a repudiation may occur if the circumstances lead to the inference future breaches will occur. This does not mean that where the promisee reasonably infers (from the existence of a breach) that further breaches will occur, there is necessarily a repudiation. The breaches, even when added together, may not satisfy the requirement of seriousness.[180] But if the accumulated breaches are sufficiently serious the other party is entitled to terminate the contract. Thus, in *Warinco AG v Samor SpA*,[181] buyers under a contract for the sale of rapeseed oil of good, wholesome, merchantable quality rejected the first of the two instalments deliverable under the contract, claiming it was not in accordance with the contract. In fact it was in accordance with the contract requirements and the sellers drew the inference, from communications with the buyers, that the second instalment would also be rejected. They therefore terminated the performance of the contract. The court held that the sellers were, in the circumstances, entitled to draw the inference and justified in terminating on the ground of repudiation because the refusal of the buyers related to all their outstanding obligations.[182]

In *Maple Flock Co Ltd v Universal Furniture Products (Wembley) Ltd*[183] the court said that apart from the probability that the breach will be repeated it may be relevant to consider the ratio, quantitatively, which the 'breach bears to the contract as a whole'. The contract in issue related to 'rag flock' and provided for the delivery of 100 tons at a rate of three loads, each of one ton, per week. Of the first 19 deliveries one was found to be defective and the buyers relied on this as a repudiation by the sellers. However, the chances of the breach being repeated were found to be 'practically negligible' and a breach in relation to one ton, out of a contract for 100 tons, was not a serious matter. There was, therefore, no repudiation by the sellers.[184]

---

178. **ACT:** *Sale of Goods Act* 1954, s 35(2); **NSW:** *Sale of Goods Act* 1923, s 34(2); **NT:** *Sale of Goods Act* 1972, s 34(2); **Qld:** *Sale of Goods Act* 1896, s 33(2); **SA:** *Sale of Goods Act* 1895, s 31(2); **Tas:** *Sale of Goods Act* 1896, s 36(2); **Vic:** *Goods Act* 1958, s 38(2); **WA:** *Sale of Goods Act* 1895, s 31(2).
179. (1908) 14 Com Cas 25 at 29.
180. See *Shevill v Builders Licensing Board* (1982) 149 CLR 620 at 630.
181. [1979] 1 Lloyd's Rep 450. See also *International Leasing Corp (Vic) Ltd v Aiken* [1967] 2 NSWR 427 (persistent breach by lessee of goods).
182. Contrast *Mersey Steel and Iron Co Ltd v Naylor Benzon & Co* (1884) 9 App Cas 434 (see [1941]).
183. [1934] 1 KB 148 at 157. See also *Hammer v Coca-Cola* [1962] NZLR 723 at 725–6.

[1939] **Erroneous construction of the contract.** Where a promisor adopts an erroneous construction of the contract a repudiation may occur if the promisor acts on the construction by breaching one or more terms, or by evincing an intention to perform only in accordance with his or her construction.

Performance in accordance with an erroneous construction will not discharge the promisor, and will amount to a breach of contract, but a repudiation will not occur unless the requirement of seriousness is satisfied, for example, because the promisor is not ready and willing to perform major contractual obligations.[185] It does not matter that the promisor has done his or her best to perform, since the obligation may be strict in nature. For example, a repudiation was established in *Luna Park (NSW) Ltd v Tramways Advertising Pty Ltd*[186] even though the advertisers had no control over the movement of the trams carrying the advertisements. They had construed the contract in such a way that they would be discharged by their performance if, taken overall, the advertisements were displayed for an average of eight hours per day. However, the contract actually required them to display *each* advertisement for substantially eight hours per day. It was no defence that they did not control the movements of the trams as their standard of duty was strict.

If the promisor evinces an intention to perform in accordance with an erroneous construction the promisor may be found to have refused to perform in accordance with the contract, even though not actually intending to repudiate. Thus, Lord Wright said in *Ross T Smyth & Co Ltd v T D Bailey Son & Co*[187] that it is not

> necessary to show that the party alleged to have repudiated should have an actual intention not to fulfil the contract. He may be determined to do so only in a manner substantially inconsistent with his obligations, and not in any other way.

An example is *Federal Commerce and Navigation Co Ltd v Molena Alpha Inc*,[188] where, because of their erroneous construction of the contract, the shipowners threatened to act in a way which was substantially inconsistent with their contractual obligations. There was no subjective intention to repudiate, but a repudiation nevertheless occurred even though the shipowners had acted bona fide.

[1940] **Wrongful termination.** The general rule is that a wrongful termination of the performance of a contract constitutes a repudiation.[189] Thus, if a promisor purports to 'cancel', 'end', 'terminate', 'rescind' or 'determine' the contract or its performance in circumstances in which there is no right to do so, the promisor's conduct may generally be treated by the promisee as a repudiation.[190] Since the promisor's 'termination' is wrongful

---

184. Contrast *Simpson v Surman* (1922) 24 WALR 79; *Robert A Munro & Co Ltd v Meyer* [1930] 2 KB 312.
185. See, eg *Summers v The Commonwealth* (1918) 25 CLR 144 (affirmed (1919) 26 CLR 180).
186. (1938) 61 CLR 286.
187. [1940] 3 All ER 60 at 72.
188. [1979] AC 757 (see [1935]).
189. *Ogle v Comboyuro Investments Pty Ltd* (1976) 136 CLR 444 at 453.

it is not effective as such, and the promisee is not obliged to accept it by terminating the performance of the contract.[191]

It makes no difference whether the wrongful termination takes place before or after the arrival of the time for performance by the promisor, and the requirement of seriousness is satisfied because the promisor is repudiating all outstanding contractual obligations.

[1941] Bona fides and absoluteness. There is no doubt that, in considering whether a repudiation has taken place, it is legitimate to have regard to whether the promisor has acted bona fide, and whether the words or conduct are absolute in character.[192] However, since the test of repudiation is objective, and based mainly on considerations of fact, a repudiation can be established even though the promisor has acted bona fide and notwithstanding that the words or conduct do not amount to an absolute refusal to be bound by the contract. As Asprey JA said in *Satellite Estate Pty Ltd v Jaquet*:[193]

> Moreover, where the conduct of one of the parties ... has been such as would lead a reasonable person to the conclusion that he does not intend to fulfil his part of the obligation, the other party to the contract, whatever in fact may have been the actual intention of the former, may treat such conduct as an intimation that the contract has been repudiated ...

It may be necessary to inquire into the bona fides of the promisor where termination in reliance on a contractual right to terminate is not justified by the circumstances. The issue is whether the promisor can be found to have repudiated where termination, though wrongful, was based on a bona fide belief in its validity. For example, in *Woodar Investment Development Ltd v Wimpey Construction UK Ltd*,[194] purchasers of land purported to exercise a contractual right to 'rescind' because of the commencement of procedures for compulsory acquisition of the property. Although they acted bona fide in the belief that they could rescind, there was in fact no right to do so because no acquisition procedures on which they could rely had been commenced. The purchasers' termination was wrongful, but held by a majority of the House of Lords not to constitute a repudiation. Because the purchasers had acted bona fide there was no repudiation and the vendors should have approached the court, by way of a construction summons, to obtain a declaration vindicating their view before taking the step of terminating the performance of the contract. Alternatively, they should have sought specific performance.

---

190. See, eg *White Trucks Pty Ltd v Riley* (1948) 66 WN (NSW) 101.
191. *White and Carter (Councils) Ltd v McGregor* [1962] AC 413 (see [2220]).
192. See, eg *Ross T Smyth & Co Ltd v T D Bailey Son & Co* [1940] 3 All ER 60 at 72; *Laurinda Pty Ltd v Capalaba Park Shopping Centre Pty Ltd* (1989) 166 CLR 623 at 647–8.
193. (1968) 71 SR (NSW) 126 at 150. See also *Carr v J A Berriman Pty Ltd* (1953) 89 CLR 327 at 351; *Dainford Ltd v Smith* (1985) 155 CLR 342 at 366; *Laurinda Pty Ltd v Capalaba Park Shopping Centre Pty Ltd* (1989) 166 CLR 623 at 633–4, 644, 657–8.
194. [1980] 1 WLR 277 (see J W Carter, [1980] *CLJ* 256; Andrew Nicol and Rick Rawlings, (1980) 43 *MLR* 696; Peter Butt, (1981) 55 *ALJ* 231). For discussion from the renegotiation perspective see J W Carter, 'The Renegotiation of Contracts' (1998) 13 *JCL* 185. See also H O Hunter, 'Commentary on "The Renegotiation of Contracts"' (1998) 13 *JCL* 205.

The relevance of bona fides is not restricted to cases of wrongful termination in purported reliance on a contractual right. For example, in *Mersey Steel and Iron Co Ltd v Naylor Benzon & Co*[195] buyers under an instalment goods contract refused to pay for goods delivered by the sellers because of a bona fide, but erroneous, belief that the presentation of a petition to wind up the sellers meant that payment could only be made with the court's sanction. The House of Lords held that there was no repudiation by the buyers since they had acted bona fide and the only effect of their conduct would be to delay payment for a short period of time. Bona fides is also relevant to cases where the words or conduct of the promisor involve the maintenance of an erroneous construction of the contract. A court will be reluctant to infer repudiation where there is a bona fide mistake as to the legal effect of the contract.[196]

The emphasis on a promisor's bona fides can be overstated and may cause difficulties. For example, in the *Mersey Steel* case the sellers had reacted to the buyers' conduct by terminating the performance of the contract. Applying the general rule that a wrongful termination is a repudiation the House of Lords awarded the buyers damages for repudiation;[197] yet in some cases the bona fides of the *promisee* may also be relevant and there is certainly a risk of the objectivity of the repudiation concept being lost in the search for the parties' actual intentions. However, bona fides can have no relevance at all where the promisor's conduct involves a serious breach of contract, as was the position in *Luna Park (NSW) Ltd v Tramways Advertising Pty Ltd*.[198] Similarly, if the promisor embarks on a course of conduct which will be seriously prejudicial to the promisee, the promisee should be permitted to terminate for repudiation, even though the promisor has acted bona fide, unless the circumstances of the case clearly suggest that the appropriate course for the promisee is to take out a construction summons. For example, in *Federal Commerce and Navigation Co Ltd v Molena Alpha Inc*,[199] the bona fides of the shipowners did not prevent them repudiating their obligations because the consequences of what they had threatened to do would have been disastrous for the charterers and a construction summons was clearly not the appropriate way to deal with the parties' dispute.

Repudiation Based on Inability[200]

[1942] Declared inability and disabling conduct. The clearest case of repudiation based on an inability to perform is where the promisor expressly declares that it is unable to perform all contractual obligations.[201]

---

195. (1884) 9 App Cas 434.
196. *Dainford Ltd v Smith* (1985) 155 CLR 342 at 365–6. See also *Green v Sommerville* (1979) 141 CLR 594; 27 ALR 351; *Haneet Chandru Vaswani v Italian Motors (Sales and Services) Ltd* [1996] 1 WLR 270 at 276, 277. Cf *Nina's Bar Bistro Pty Ltd v MBE Corp (Sydney) Pty Ltd* [1984] 3 NSWLR 613 at 615. And see R B S Macfarlan, (1985) 1 *Aust Bar Rev* 37.
197. Contrast *DTR Nominees Pty Ltd v Mona Homes Pty Ltd* (1978) 138 CLR 423.
198. (1938) 61 CLR 286 (see [1916]).
199. [1979] AC 757 (see [1935]).
200. See Carter, *Breach of Contract*, 2nd ed, 1991, Chapter 9.
201. See, eg *Hoad v Swan* (1920) 28 CLR 258 at 264.

However, the declaration need not be express and may, therefore, be inferred from conduct. As Devlin J said in *Universal Cargo Carriers Corp v Citati*,[202] 'a profession by words or conduct of inability is by itself enough to constitute renunciation'. Thus, even if a promisor does not expressly state an inability to perform, a repudiation will occur if the only reasonable inference from the promisor's words or conduct is an inability to perform the contract.

Where the contract relates to a specific subject matter, or if there is a personal element in performance, a disabling act by the promisor will amount to a repudiation. For example, if A agrees to convey a particular piece of land to B, but instead conveys it to C, A's act can be treated by B as a repudiation because the conduct is a disabling act which is manifestly inconsistent with the obligation to convey the land to B.[203] Similarly, the voluntary liquidation of an employer-company may amount to a repudiation of a contract of employment.[204]

In order to establish repudiation a promisor must be able to prove that the requirement of seriousness is satisfied. In the examples given above the requirement is satisfied because the words or conduct relate to all, or substantially all, of the promisor's obligations. However, the words or conduct need not go so far. For example, in *Foran v Wight*[205] a contract for the sale of land dated 24 December 1982 fixed completion for 22 June 1983. The vendors told the purchasers on 20 June that they would be unable to settle on time because a right of way which the vendors were required to provide had not been registered. This was a repudiation by the vendors because time was of the essence.

[1943] **Factual inability.** Where the promisor's inability results from words or conduct the promisee need not prove that the promisor was in fact unable to perform. For example, if A agrees to convey land to B but instead conveys it to C, B can establish repudiation without proving that A was unable to repurchase the land from C. Once B has terminated the performance of the contract the law treats B's cause of action as complete. In cases of factual inability the position is different since, in order to rely on the promisor's inability, the promisee must prove that the promisor was in fact 'wholly and finally disabled'[206] from performing the contract. The emphasis, therefore, is on the promisor's actual *position* rather than on what the promisor has said or done. For example, in *Universal Cargo Carriers Corp v Citati*[207] Devlin J held that shipowners could succeed on the ground of factual inability when the charterer under a voyage charterparty was so placed as to be unable to find and load a cargo before the expiry of a period of time sufficient to frustrate the commercial purpose of the contract. Again, in *Rawson v Hobbs*[208] the High Court held that the purchaser of a

---

202. [1957] 2 QB 401 at 437. See also *Bell v Scott* (1922) 30 CLR 387 at 395–6.
203. *Synge v Synge* [1894] 1 QB 466; *Schaefer v Schuhmann* [1972] AC 572.
204. *Brace v Calder* [1895] 2 QB 253. See also *Ogdens Ltd v Nelson* [1905] AC 109. Cf *Re Palmdale Insurance Ltd* [1982] VR 921.
205. (1989) 168 CLR 385 (see [1947]). Cf *Ellen v Topp* (1851) 6 Ex 424; 155 ER 609.
206. *British & Beningtons Ltd v North Western Cachar Tea Co Ltd* [1923] AC 48 at 72; *Honner v Ashton* (1979) 1 BPR 9478 at 9494. See Francis Dawson, 'Waiver of Conditions Precedent on a Repudiation' (1980) 96 *LQR* 239.
207. [1957] 2 QB 401.

grazing property could rely on the vendor's inability to convey title when it was clear that the vendor would not be able to obtain the consent of a government Minister, required by the contract, to the transfer of title.

Factual inability is very difficult to prove,[209] and usually a matter of last resort. Thus, the usual case is where a ground stated at the time of termination turns out to be unfounded and the promisee seeks to justify termination by reference to factual inability on the part of the promisor. It is a general principle of termination that a promisee may rely on a valid ground even though not stated at the time of termination.[210] But the promisor in such a case may seek to argue that the erroneous ground given shows that the promisee's termination was itself a wrongful repudiation of the contract. Notwithstanding suggestions in some of the cases[211] that this argument may be made against the promisee, it is now clear that these suggestions are wrong in principle.[212] Therefore, if a promisee who terminates is able to show, at the time of termination, that the promisor was wholly and finally disabled from performing, the promisee's termination will be regarded as valid.[213]

[1944] **Inferred inability.**[214] The extent to which a promisee is permitted to rely on inferred inability, that is, is entitled to terminate the performance of a contract on the ground that a reasonable person in the promisee's position would draw the inference that the promisor is wholly and finally disabled from performing, is uncertain. It seems that where there is conduct, such as a breach of contract by the promisor, the promisee is permitted to terminate (assuming that the requirement of seriousness is satisfied), if the circumstances would suggest to a reasonable person that the promisor will be unable to perform in the future.[215]

It is important to know whether the principle of inferred inability extends to other situations because a promisee who validly terminates on the ground of inferred inability will be protected from an action for wrongful termination if it transpires, when all the facts are ascertained, that the promisor would in fact have been able to perform. In the context of frustration it is clear that a principle of inferred inability is of general application, that is to say, it operates irrespective of whether the

---

208. (1961) 107 CLR 466. Contrast *Bell v Scott* (1922) 30 CLR 387.
209. See, eg *Winterton Constructions Pty Ltd v Hambros Australia Ltd* (1992) 111 ALR 649. For a suggestion that the test is too strict see *Foran v Wight* (1989) 168 CLR 385 at 425.
210. See [1969].
211. See *Braithwaite v Foreign Hardwood Co* [1905] 2 KB 543; *Taylor v Oakes Roncoroni & Co* (1922) 27 Com Cas 261; M C Lloyd, 'Ready and Willing to Perform: The Problem of Prospective Inability in the Law of Contract' (1974) 37 *MLR* 121.
212. *British & Beningtons Ltd v North Western Cachar Tea Co Ltd* [1923] AC 48 at 70; *Sunbird Plaza Pty Ltd v Maloney* (1988) 166 CLR 245 at 278; 77 ALR 205; *Fercometal SARL v Mediterranean Shipping Co SA* [1989] AC 788; *Foran v Wight* (1989) 168 CLR 385.
213. *Sunbird Plaza Pty Ltd v Maloney* (1988) 166 CLR 245 (see John Harris, (1988) 1 *JCL* 177). On the question of damages see [2161].
214. See J W Carter, 'The Embiricos Principle and the Law of Anticipatory Breach' (1984) 47 *MLR* 422.
215. See *Millars' Karri and Jarrah Co (1902) v Weddel Turner & Co* (1908) 14 Com Cas 25 at 29 (see [1938]).

performance of the contract has actually commenced.[216] There is some support for the same approach to anticipatory breach in the context of contracts for the sale of land.[217] However, the value of the principle is its commercial convenience and the real issue is whether it applies in that context.

In *Universal Cargo Carriers Corp v Citati*[218] Devlin J took the view that the principle does not apply to cases of anticipatory breach, at least where the only basis for the inference of inability is the promisor's position. Devlin J's opinion was based on a fear that a promisee entitled to terminate on the ground of inferred inability might receive substantial damages even if it turned out that the promisor would have been able to perform. His fear stemmed from a view of the consequences of the inevitable breach basis[219] of the doctrine of anticipatory breach. However, the fact that the law permits a promisee to anticipate a breach, and so regards the promisor's breach as inevitable, tells us only that the promisee is entitled to recover nominal damages.[220] Any right to substantial damages depends on proof of actual loss or damage.

In so far as Devlin J's views about the principle of inferred inability depended on the conclusions he drew from the inevitable breach basis for the doctrine of anticipatory breach, subsequent decisions require the matter to be reconsidered[221] and a strong argument can be made for the application of the principle of inferred inability in the context of anticipatory breach. An alternative approach would be to permit the promisee to demand an assurance of performance where there is doubt as to the promisor's ability to perform. A right to terminate could then be based on the failure to provide an adequate assurance.[222] But under Australian[223] law there is no general right for a promisee to demand an assurance of due performance.[224] At best an unfulfilled assurance is some evidence of repudiation.[225]

The Acceptance Requirement[226]

[1945] **'Acceptance' of a repudiation.** The word 'acceptance' is used in the context of repudiation to describe the promisee's decision ('election') to terminate the performance of the contract.

Therefore, acceptance of a repudiation is necessary if the promisee wishes to terminate the performance of the contract.[227] Acceptance is also

---

216. See [2025]–[2027].
217. See *Bell v Scott* (1922) 30 CLR 387 at 392 (termination justified if it is 'quite clear' that the vendor has no title).
218. [1957] 2 QB 401 at 449.
219. See [1933].
220. See [2161].
221. See [2161].
222. This is the approach under *Uniform Commercial Code* (US), §2-609(1).
223. But see J W Carter, 'Suspending Contract Performance for Breach', in Beatson and Friedmann, eds, *Good Faith and Fault in Contract Law*, 1995, p 485.
224. See [1839].
225. See *Laurinda Pty Ltd v Capalaba Park Shopping Centre Pty Ltd* (1989) 166 CLR 623 (see Peter Butt, (1989) 63 *ALJ* 773).
226. See Carter, *Breach of Contract*, 2nd ed, 1991, paras 750–74.

required to complete the promisee's cause of action for damages in cases where the repudiation precedes the time for performance.[228] For example, if frustration occurs prior to acceptance, damages cannot be claimed.[229]

Acceptance is also important to the *locus poenitentiae* ('time for repentance') afforded by the repudiation doctrine. This is the idea that, generally, a promisor may retract a verbal repudiation which has not been accepted, and call upon the promisee to perform.[230] Therefore, acceptance by the promisee will prevent the promisor retracting the repudiation.[231] However, the promisor's power to retract a repudiation at any time prior to acceptance is subject to an important qualification. If the repudiation has been relied upon by the promisee, for example, in not performing obligations because of the belief, induced by the promisor's repudiation, that performance would be futile, the promisor must give notice of retraction and allow the promisee time to perform.[232]

[1946] Position where repudiation accepted. The consequences of acceptance do not differ from those attributable to an election to terminate for breach by failure to perform.[233] The general propositions stated later[234] apply to the acceptance of a repudiation. Therefore, although both parties are discharged from the obligation to perform (or to be ready and willing to perform) their respective contractual duties, accrued rights and liabilities are not affected.[235]

[1947] Position where repudiation not accepted.[236] Where the promisor's repudiation is not accepted by the promisee, the question may arise whether, and to what extent, the promisee is discharged by the unaccepted repudiation.

Generally speaking a repudiation continues to operate as such until it has been retracted by the promisor. In *Foran v Wight*[237] the vendors were regarded as continuing to repudiate when they failed to settle the transaction after their statement of inability. However, the vendors sought to treat the failure of *the purchasers* to tender the purchase price on the day for settlement as the breach of an essential time stipulation. The High Court said that the repudiation by the vendors meant that the purchasers

---

227. See [1930].
228. See [2102].
229. See [2063].
230. See *Frost v Knight* (1872) LR 7 Ex 111 at 112. See further [1947].
231. *Guy-Pell v Foster* [1930] 2 Ch 169.
232. *Cohen & Co v Ockerby & Co Ltd* (1917) 24 CLR 288 at 298. The basis would seem to be estoppel or change of position in reliance on the repudiation. See *Foran v Wight* (1989) 168 CLR 385; *Austral Standard Cables Pty Ltd v Walker Nominees Pty Ltd* (1992) 26 NSWLR 524 at 533, 540; *Restatement (2d) Contracts* (1979), §256(1); A M Squillante, 'Anticipatory Repudiation and Retraction' (1973) 7 *Valparaiso ULR* 373.
233. *Heyman v Darwins Ltd* [1942] AC 356 at 399.
234. See [1985]–[1989].
235. See further [2157], [2225].
236. See J W Carter, 'The Higher Altitudes of Contract Law' [1989] *LMCLQ* 81.
237. (1989) 168 CLR 385 (see also [1942]). See J W Carter, (1990) 3 *JCL* 70; Andrew Beech, 'Terminating a Contract: Dispensing with the Requirement of Readiness and Willingness' (1992) 5 *JCL* 47. See also *Sibbles v Highfern Pty Ltd* (1987) 164 CLR 214; 76 ALR 13.

were not in breach by failing to tender the purchase price. There will, however, be cases in which a repudiation is nullified by the promisee's actions notwithstanding the absence of retraction by the promisor. For example, in *Bowes v Chaleyer*,[238] a seller of silk elected to continue performance after repudiation by the buyer, and tendered goods to the buyer. The buyer's decision to reject the goods was upheld by the High Court on the ground that by failing to ship the goods in accordance with the contract the seller had breached a condition. The buyer's repudiation did not preclude his later rejection of the goods because the seller had elected to continue with the contract.

As can be inferred from the above, an unaccepted repudiation is not without legal effect. Most important is the idea that an unaccepted repudiation may absolve a promisee from the consequences which would otherwise attach to a failure on the promisee's part to discharge contractual obligations. The leading case is *Peter Turnbull & Co Pty Ltd v Mundus Trading Co (Australasia) Pty Ltd*,[239] where a sale of goods contract required the buyers to nominate a vessel which could load at Sydney in January or February. No nomination was made by the buyers because the sellers repudiated their contractual obligations. However, that repudiation was not accepted by the buyers prior to the time at which they should (under the contract) have nominated a vessel, and when they eventually brought their action for damages the sellers' defence was that the buyers had breached a condition by not making a nomination. A majority of the High Court held that the buyers were entitled to succeed in their action because the sellers' repudiation 'dispensed' with the nomination. The case indicates that it is a little misleading to say, as is commonly done, that a repudiation has no effect 'until'[240] acceptance has occurred. Although the buyers were not fully discharged until they accepted the sellers' repudiation, the buyers were in the meantime absolved from any adverse consequences which would otherwise have attached to their failure to nominate the vessel.

The *Peter Turnbull* case has been followed on a number of occasions.[241] There are also similar English authorities.[242] What these cases did not settle is whether a promisee may rely on the unaccepted repudiation as a basis for saying that there is no obligation to remain ready and willing to perform. Normally termination is required for this consequence.[243] Some of the English cases nevertheless suggested that a promisee would not be required to remain ready and willing to perform, even in cases where the contract is affirmed after the repudiation.[244] This is difficult to justify since it is acceptance of the repudiation which absolves the promisee from the

---

238. (1923) 32 CLR 159.
239. (1954) 90 CLR 235 (see R A Blackburn, (1955) 71 *LQR* 473).
240. See, eg *Woodar Investment Development Ltd v Wimpey Construction UK Ltd* [1980] 1 WLR 277 at 290. Cf *Fullers' Theatres Ltd v Musgrove* (1923) 31 CLR 524 at 549.
241. See, eg *Mahoney v Lindsay* (1980) 33 ALR 601 (see J W Carter, (1982) 56 *ALJ* 251); *Nina's Bar Bistro Pty Ltd v MBE Corp (Sydney) Pty Ltd* [1984] 3 NSWLR 613; *Austral Standard Cables Pty Ltd v Walker Nominees Pty Ltd* (1992) 26 NSWLR 524; *Murphy v Zamonex Pty Ltd* (1993) 31 NSWLR 439 at 454.
242. They begin with *Jones v Barkley* (1781) 2 Doug 684; 99 ER 434.
243. See [1985].
244. See, eg *Braithwaite v Foreign Hardwood Co* [1905] 2 KB 543. Contrast *Moschi v Lep Air Services Ltd* [1973] AC 331 at 356.

obligation to remain ready and willing to perform. In *Fercometal SARL v Mediterranean Shipping Co SA*[245] the House of Lords indicated that there is no such principle, and that an unaccepted repudiation will not usually absolve the promisee from *both* the obligation to perform and also from the obligation to remain ready and willing. This is consistent with the *Turnbull* case which clearly proceeded on the basis that the buyers remained ready and willing to perform.

This issue was the subject of much discussion in *Foran v Wight*, where the trial judge had found that the purchasers were unable to prove their ability to perform. The High Court was unanimous in holding that this finding was not fatal to the purchasers' claim to have validly terminated the contract after the date for settlement, there being no evidence of inability at the time of the vendors' declaration of inability to perform. Conflicting views were, however, expressed on why this was so, and application of the law produced a difference of opinion on the facts. Mason CJ dissented because, treating estoppel[246] as the basis for the absolving effects of an unaccepted repudiation, he could find no evidence of detriment, that is, there was no causal connection between the purchasers' inability to find finance and the vendors' repudiation. Brennan J and Dawson J did not regard the finding of the trial judge as equivalent to a finding that the purchasers could not perform. The purchasers could succeed because the vendors had not proved the purchasers to have been wholly and finally disabled from performing the contract. For Deane J the purchasers did not need to show that, but for the vendors' repudiation, they would have been able to perform. In so far as they relied on estoppel, the majority judges were satisfied that the purchasers had, to some extent at least, refrained from taking steps to obtain finance because of the vendors' repudiation.[247]

The discussion above indicates that Asquith LJ's colourful statement in *Howard v Pickford Tool Co Ltd*,[248] that an unaccepted repudiation is a 'thing writ in water and of no value to anybody: it confers no legal rights of any sort or kind' is a misleading, unhelpful and gross oversimplification of the law.

Termination for Delay

General

[1948] Relevance of delay. Delay may be relevant in two ways. First, there may be delay in the sense that the promisor does not perform at the appointed time. Second, delay may be a consequence of breach, as in *Hongkong Fir Shipping Co Ltd v Kawasaki Kisen Kaisha Ltd*,[249] where a shipowner's breach of the obligation to provide a seaworthy vessel caused the vessel to be laid up while repairs were carried out. In the first situation

---

245. [1989] AC 788 (see Geoffrey Marston, [1988] *CLJ* 340).
246. See [1945].
247. Gaudron J was of the view that the purchasers had not by their conduct lost the right to rely on the essentiality of the time set for completion.
248. [1951] 1 KB 417 at 421.
249. [1962] 2 QB 26 (see [1958]).

delay involves the breach of a time stipulation, whereas in the second situation delay is a consequence of the breach of some other type of term.

Sometimes it is difficult to distinguish the two. For example, if A agrees to hire a motor car to B, but tenders a defective vehicle in breach of contract, the rights of the hirer may be approached from the point of view of the time required to remedy the breach, that is, by reference to the delay in performance. Alternatively, the position of the hirer may be tested by the loss or damage likely to be suffered as a consequence of the vehicle not being available for use.

[1949] Treatment of time stipulations. As was explained in the previous chapter, the courts of common law and equity differed in their treatment of time stipulations, the common law courts taking a stricter view and treating failure to perform on time as a serious breach. The more liberal view of the equity court now prevails as a result of statutory provisions such as s 13 of the *Conveyancing Act* 1919 (NSW).[250] However, the distinction between essential and non-essential time stipulations is still very important.

Using the terminology of the tripartite classification,[251] essential time stipulations are conditions, and non-essential time stipulations either warranties or intermediate terms. Whether or not time is essential depends on the construction of the contract.

It is arguable that the separate treatment of time stipulations is unnecessary for two reasons. First, the rules on termination for breach can generally be applied to time stipulations.[252] Second, where a promisor 'breaches' a time stipulation the breach is arguably merely the defective performance of a substantive obligation.[253] As against these reasons there is the simple fact that historically the courts have preferred to give time stipulations a distinct operation and are likely to continue to do so. It can also be said that the time stipulation concept is necessary to explain why the breach of a fundamental obligation, such as that of a purchaser of land to pay the agreed price, does not necessarily give rise to a right to terminate. An obligation may be essential or fundamental — the purchaser must pay for the land — even though timely performance (payment at the agreed time) is not essential. Thus, the courts inquire into whether the term stating the time for performance is essential.

Breach of Essential Time Stipulation[254]

[1950] Express agreement. The parties may expressly agree that time is essential, with respect to a particular time stipulation or with regard to all time stipulations appearing in the contract. Thus, it is quite common in contracts for the sale of land to find provisions stating that time is 'of the essence' of the contract.[255] Breach of such a time stipulation gives rise to a right to terminate.[256]

---

250. See [1851].
251. See [725].
252. *United Scientific Holdings Ltd v Burnley BC* [1978] AC 904.
253. *Ciavarella v Balmer* [1983] 2 NSWLR 439 at 450 (affirmed (1983) 153 CLR 438).
254. Lindgren, *Time in the Performance of Contracts*, 2nd ed, 1982, Chapter 3.

It is not necessary for the parties to use the words 'time is of the essence of this contract', an express agreement to make time essential may be stated in other ways, for example, by a term stating that any failure to perform at the time appointed is a repudiation of the contract.[257]

[1951] **Implied agreement.** Even if time is not expressly made essential, a right to terminate will arise on the breach of a time stipulation if the construction of the contract indicates an implied agreement that time of performance is essential.

In deciding whether, as a matter of construction, the parties reached an implied agreement, particular regard will be had to the nature of the subject matter and the circumstances surrounding the contract.[258] Thus, time may be regarded as essential because of the perishable, fluctuating or wasting nature of the subject matter, such as the stock of a business sold under a contract for the sale of a business as a going concern.[259] However, this does not mean that the factors referred to in the discussion of termination for breach of condition are irrelevant. For example, it may be important to consider the nature of the term and the nature of the contract. In this way time stipulations dealing with deposits are often interpreted[260] as essential terms, notwithstanding that, generally, time of payment is not essential.[261]

Outside the context of standard form commercial contracts there is, and has always been, a reluctance to treat time stipulations as conditions in the absence of express agreement. For example, in *Bettini v Gye*[262] it was alleged that an opera singer had breached his contract to arrive in London 'without fail at least six days before the commencement of his engagement'. The court, assuming the allegation to be proved, held that it was not a sufficient justification for the employer's decision to terminate as the term was not a condition. Notwithstanding the clear and somewhat emphatic words ('without fail') the court said that as the term did not go 'to the root of the matter' it was not a condition.

[1952] **Commercial contracts.** In order to promote certainty in commercial matters, time stipulations dealing with substantive obligations are usually treated as conditions.[263] For example, with respect to contracts for the sale of goods, the times for shipment, delivery and acceptance of the

---

255. In *Citicorp Australia Ltd v Hendry* (1985) 4 NSWLR 22 at 27 Mahoney JA suggested that this expression does not define the nature of the terms to which it extends so much as exclude the equitable treatment (see [1847]–[1852]) of time stipulations.
256. Exercise of the right may, however, be affected by a purchaser's ability to apply for relief against forfeiture; see [1979].
257. See *Lombard North Central Plc v Butterworth* [1987] 1 QB 527.
258. See *United Scientific Holdings Ltd v Burnley BC* [1978] AC 904; *Raineri v Miles* [1981] AC 1050 (approving *Halsbury's Laws of England*, 4th ed, 1974, Vol 9, para 481).
259. See, eg *Lock v Bell* [1931] 1 Ch 35.
260. *Brien v Dwyer* (1978) 141 CLR 378; 22 ALR 485; *Damon Compania Naviera SA v Hapag-Lloyd International SA (The Blankenstein)* [1985] 1 WLR 435.
261. See, eg *Shevill v Builders Licensing Board* (1982) 149 CLR 620 at 627.
262. (1876) 1 QBD 183.
263. See *Bunge Corp New York v Tradax Export SA Panama* [1981] 1 WLR 711 at 720, 727 (approving *Halsbury's Laws of England*, 4th ed, 1974, Vol 9, para 482).

goods have been held to be essential.[264] However, the basis for such decisions is the presumed intention of the parties: the courts do not apply a rule that all time stipulations in commercial contracts are conditions. For example, time of payment is not usually essential where a sale of goods contract provides for payment in exchange for the goods.[265] On the other hand, where payment is by way of a banker's confirmed credit, the time for opening the credit will usually be essential because the credit operates as a guarantee of payment.[266]

The doctrine of the intermediate term has not had much impact on time stipulations in commercial contracts, partly for the reason that there is only one type of breach, namely, 'to be late',[267] and partly because of the need for certainty. In *Bunge Corp New York v Tradax Export SA Panama*[268] a term in an FOB contract for the sale of goods required the buyers to give at least 15 days' notice of the probable readiness of the vessel which was to receive the goods. The buyers' notice was not given in time to allow the full period and the House of Lords held that the buyers had breached a condition. Apart from a general concern with certainty, the relationship which existed between the nomination term and the obligation of the sellers to nominate the loading port was emphasised. Since the term stating the latter obligation was a condition there was a sound basis for saying that the former was also a condition. It did not matter whether breach of the term would cause serious loss or damage to the sellers because their right to terminate stemmed from the essential nature of the term.

Nevertheless, a time stipulation may be treated as intermediate in character, at least in the sense that the gravity of a breach may depend on the length of delay.[269] Thus, notwithstanding that a term is usually construed as intermediate on the basis that its breach may take various forms, the intermediate term terminology is legitimately applied to cases where, although there is only one form of breach, the degree of seriousness will depend on how long the breach lasts.[270] Procedural terms in commercial contracts fall into this category. Where a term is procedural the court will not reach the conclusion that time is essential unless an express agreement is present or some peculiar feature of the contract justifies the conclusion that the parties impliedly agreed that time was essential.[271]

---

264. *Bowes v Shand* (1877) 2 App Cas 455; *Harrington v Browne* (1917) 23 CLR 297; *Bowes v Chaleyer* (1923) 32 CLR 159.
265. See **ACT:** *Sale of Goods Act* 1954, s 15(1); **NSW:** *Sale of Goods Act* 1923, s 15(1); **NT:** *Sale of Goods Act* 1972, s 15(1); **Qld:** *Sale of Goods Act* 1896, s 13(1); **SA:** *Sale of Goods Act* 1895, s 10(1); **Tas:** *Sale of Goods Act* 1896, s 15; **Vic:** *Goods Act* 1958, s 15; **WA:** *Sale of Goods Act* 1895, s 10(1).
266. *Pavia & Co SpA v Thurmann-Nielsen* [1952] 2 QB 84.
267. *Bunge Corp New York v Tradax Export SA Panama* [1981] 1 WLR 711 at 715 per Lord Wilberforce.
268. [1981] 1 WLR 711 (see F M B Reynolds, (1981) 97 *LQR* 541; J W Carter, [1981] *CLJ* 219).
269. Cf *Ankar Pty Ltd v National Westminster Finance (Australia) Ltd* (1987) 162 CLR 549 at 562.
270. See *Phibro Energy AG v Nissho Iwai Corp (The Honam Jade)* [1991] 1 Lloyd's Rep 38, where delay had a fundamental effect on the contract (see J W Carter, (1992) 5 *JCL* 60). Contrast *Torvald Klaveness A/S v Arni Maritime Corp* [1994] 1 WLR 1465 at 1476.
271. See, eg *United Scientific Holdings Ltd v Burnley BC* [1978] AC 904 (see [1852]).

[1953] **Implied time stipulations.** An implied time stipulation may be essential, as where a contract for the sale of goods specifies no time for delivery, or for the opening of a letter of credit, and the court implies a term requiring delivery within a reasonable time, or a term requiring the opening of the credit by the beginning of the shipment period.[272] On the other hand, where a contract for the sale of land specifies no time for settlement, and the court implies that settlement must occur within a reasonable time, time is unlikely to be essential.

Breach of Non-essential Time Stipulation

[1954] **Generally no right to terminate without notice.** The general rule where time is not essential is that the promisor's failure to perform on time does not give rise to a right to terminate unless the promisee first serves a notice requiring performance within a reasonable time.[273]

There are, however, two exceptions to this rule:[274]

(1) unreasonable delay in performance may amount to a repudiation or frustrate the commercial purpose of the contract; or

(2) the promisee may be entitled to anticipate failure to comply with a notice to perform.

[1955] **Unreasonable delay.** Although, in one sense, 'unreasonable delay' is simply a failure to perform on time, it follows from the general rule stated in the previous paragraph that a promisee is not entitled to treat any delay as unreasonable, and to claim to be entitled to terminate. Therefore, when it is said that unreasonable delay may of itself give rise to a right of termination,[275] the expression is being used in a special sense. There are two possibilities. First, delay may be unreasonable because it amounts to a repudiation of obligation.[276]

Second, delay may be unreasonable because the breach has had serious consequences for the promisee. Thus, by way of analogy with the right of termination which may arise if the promisor breaches an intermediate term, a promisee will be entitled to terminate for unreasonable delay where there is a 'frustrating' delay, that is, where the delay is so serious as to frustrate the commercial purpose of the contract.[277]

---

272. *McDougall v Aeromarine of Emsworth Ltd* [1958] 1 WLR 1126. But see *British and Commonwealth Holdings Plc v Quadrex Holdings Inc* [1989] QB 842 at 857 (dictum that an implied time stipulation can never be essential) (not followed on another point in *Behzadi v Shaftesbury Hotels Ltd* [1992] Ch 1).
273. See *Rian Financial Services Ltd v Alfred Investments Projects Pty Ltd* (1988) NSW Conv R ¶55-400 at 57,698 and [1959]–[1964].
274. See [1955]–[1956].
275. See, eg *Geipel v Smith* (1872) LR 7 QB 404 at 411, 413, 414; *Louinder v Leis* (1982) 149 CLR 509 at 526. See also *Neeta (Epping) Pty Ltd v Phillips* (1974) 131 CLR 286 at 302; 3 ALR 151 ('gross and protracted').
276. For example, because it indicates a refusal to perform the contract: *Howe v Smith* (1884) 27 Ch D 89; *Satellite Estate Pty Ltd v Jaquet* (1968) 71 SR (NSW) 126 at 150.
277. *MacAndrew v Chapple* (1866) LR 1 CP 643 at 648; *Universal Cargo Carriers Corp v Citati* [1957] 2 QB 401 (a case of anticipatory breach).

In some cases delay in remedying the breach of a contractual term may be so unreasonable as to give rise to a right to terminate.[278] For example, where A, in breach of contract, tenders defective goods to B under a contract of hire, and B asks A to remedy the defects, unreasonable delay on A's part gives rise to a right to terminate, either on the ground of repudiation or because the delay renders the performance of the contract substantially different.[279]

Whether delay is unreasonable is a question of fact[280] depending, for example, on the nature of the contract and the detriment, loss or disadvantage suffered by the promisee.

Where the time stipulation is implied, two periods of unreasonable delay must be established. The first period is necessary to establish a breach, and the second period required to establish a sufficiently serious breach or a repudiation.

[1956] Anticipated failure to comply with notice. In some situations a promisee may be able to terminate the performance of a contract on the ground that, had a notice been served on the promisor requiring performance within a reasonable time, the promisor would not have been able to comply with the notice.[281]

The principle was established by the decision of Devlin J in *Etablissements Chainbaux SARL v Harbormaster Ltd*,[282] which concerned a contract for the sale of goods. The sellers 'cancelled' the contract on the ground that the buyers had not opened a letter of credit as required by the contract. Devlin J found a breach of the obligation but held that the sellers had 'waived' their right to terminate. Therefore, although the time stipulation was originally essential, it ceased to be available to the sellers as a condition. Nevertheless, Devlin J held that the sellers could justify what they had done on the ground that if they had taken the course of serving a notice requiring the letter of credit to be opened within a reasonable time the buyers would not have been able to comply.

A decision to terminate without notice for breach of a non-essential time stipulation certainly exposes the promisee to considerable risks, since it must be difficult to prove that the promisor was so placed that compliance with a reasonable notice would not have been possible. It is therefore a 'perilous'[283] course to take. The suggestion has also been made that the course is only available in respect of time stipulations which were originally essential.[284] However, it is difficult to find any logical basis for this suggestion; and the only restriction which can logically be applied is that the breach by the promisor must be of such a nature that it would, at the

---

278. See *Stanton v Richardson* (1872) LR 7 CP 421 (affirmed (1874) LR 9 CP 390; (1875) 45 LJ CP 78).
279. It is arguable, however, that this is merely an instance of the notice procedure considered [1959]–[1964].
280. *Universal Cargo Carriers Corp v Citati* [1957] 2 QB 401 at 435.
281. Cf [1943].
282. [1955] 1 Lloyd's Rep 303.
283. Lindgren, *Time in the Performance of Contracts*, 2nd ed, 1982, para 424.
284. *Michael Realty Pty Ltd v Carr* [1977] 1 NSWLR 553 at 567. But see *Universal Cargo Carriers Corp v Citati* [1957] 2 QB 401 at 448.

time of its occurrence, have justified service of a notice requiring performance within a reasonable time.

Delay as Consequence of Breach

[1957] Criterion for delay. Assuming that the promisor has not breached a condition, the criterion to be applied where a breach of contract causes delay is the same as that applicable to the breach of a non-essential time stipulation. Therefore, the delay must be unreasonable, that is, so serious as to render the performance of the contract substantially different, or indicative of a repudiation. In the context of commercial contracts, 'unreasonable' delay again means delay sufficient to 'frustrate' the performance of the contract.[285]

[1958] Actual and foreseeable delay. When deciding whether the criterion of unreasonable delay has been satisfied regard may be had to both actual and foreseeable delay. For example, in *Hongkong Fir Shipping Co Ltd v Kawasaki Kisen Kaisha Ltd*,[286] shipowners breached cl 1 of a charterparty contract by delivering an unseaworthy vessel. The charter was for a period of 24 calendar months and the breach had caused a delay of nearly seven weeks when the charterers purported to terminate the performance of the contract, this being the period of time the vessel was off hire waiting for repairs. A foreseeable delay of nearly 13 weeks was also established, but the English Court of Appeal held that even when the actual delay which had occurred was added to the delay which was likely to occur, the performance of the contract could not be regarded as substantially different from that intended by the parties. The case at first sight seems hard on the charterers, but it must be remembered that they were under no obligation to pay hire during the period in question, so that the delay did not substantially increase their burden of performance. It was also important that the charter had a considerable period of time to run at the time of the charterers' wrongful termination. A different result would be reached in a short-term contract for the hire of a motor vehicle which is delivered in a defective condition, particularly if the contract requires the hirer to pay hire while the vehicle is off the road for repairs.[287]

Failure to Comply with Notice[288]

[1959] The notice procedure. Where the promisor breaches a non-essential time stipulation the law usually permits the promisee to serve a notice the effect of which is expressed by saying that time becomes essential. This is the way in which the procedure is acknowledged, and preserved, by statutory provisions such as s 13 of the *Conveyancing Act 1919* (NSW).[289]

---

285. *Hongkong Fir Shipping Co Ltd v Kawasaki Kisen Kaisha Ltd* [1962] 2 QB 26.
286. [1962] 2 QB 26.
287. See *Astley Industrial Trust Ltd v Grimley* [1963] 1 WLR 584 at 598–9.
288. See Lindgren, *Time in the Performance of Contracts*, 2nd ed, 1982, Chapter 4; Peter Butt, 'The Modern Law of Notices to Complete' (1985) 59 *ALJ* 260.
289. See [1851].

The ability of a promisee to dispense with the notice in some cases was explained earlier.[290]

[1960] Time of service. The promisee, in order to rely on the notice procedure, must establish that the promisor has breached the contract. In cases where there is no express time stipulation there is no delay until a reasonable time has expired, because the law allows the promisor a reasonable time to perform. The promisee must wait for that period to expire before serving the notice.[291]

On the other hand, where an express time stipulation is present the mere fact of breach is sufficient.[292] Thus, so far as proof of breach is concerned, no question of unreasonable delay arises.[293]

Breach of one obligation does not entitle the promisee to serve notice requiring the performance of another obligation, distinct from the first, which has not been breached.[294]

[1961] Requirements of the notice. The three basic requirements of the procedure are that the notice must:

(1) inform the promisor of the obligation which is to be performed;[295]

(2) fix a period of time which is, in the circumstances, a reasonable time for performance;[296] and

(3) clearly indicate, either that it makes time essential, or that failure to comply with the notice will give rise to a right to terminate.[297]

However, unless the contract specifies the form which the notice must take, no particular form is required, and it is the substance of the notice which counts.[298]

[1962] Ability to make time essential. Three issues arise with respect to the promisee's ability to make time essential by notice. First, to what terms and contracts does the procedure apply? Although the notice procedure is most frequently applied to conveyancing transactions, it is of general application and can be applied to any type of contract.[299] It may not be practicable to apply it to some contracts, such as some commodity contracts, where the parties must make their decisions within short periods.

---

290. See [1955]. For the ability to rely on unreasonable delay where the notice procedure fails see Angela Sydenham, 'Unreasonable Delay — Something of a Long-Stop on the Failure of a Notice to Complete?' [1980] *Conv* 19.
291. *Green v Sevin* (1879) 13 Ch D 589 at 599; *Louinder v Leis* (1982) 149 CLR 509.
292. *Louinder v Leis* (1982) 149 CLR 509. See also *Neeta (Epping) Pty Ltd v Phillips* (1974) 131 CLR 286 at 299; *Behzadi v Shaftesbury Hotels Ltd* [1992] Ch 1 (see Charles Harpum, [1991] *CLJ* 40; Diane Skapinker, (1992) 5 *JCL* 67).
293. See *Raineri v Miles* [1981] AC 1050.
294. *Louinder v Leis* (1982) 149 CLR 509.
295. *Falconer v Wilson* [1973] 2 NSWLR 131 at 145; *Laurinda Pty Ltd v Capalaba Park Shopping Centre Pty Ltd* (1989) 166 CLR 623.
296. *Stickney v Keeble* [1915] AC 386; *Wendt v Bruce* (1931) 45 CLR 245 at 253; *Sindel v Georgiou* (1984) 154 CLR 661; 55 ALR 1; *Laurinda Pty Ltd v Capalaba Park Shopping Centre Pty Ltd* (1989) 166 CLR 623.
297. See *Laurinda Pty Ltd v Capalaba Park Shopping Centre Pty Ltd* (1989) 166 CLR 623. Cf *O'Brien v Dawson* (1941) 41 SR (NSW) 295 at 304 (affirmed on other grounds (1942) 66 CLR 18).
298. *Balog v Crestani* (1975) 132 CLR 289; 6 ALR 29.

But it is important to see that the notice procedure is not restricted to situations in which the statutory provisions dealing with the treatment of time stipulations have relevance. On the other hand, a term which merely provides for a contingency, and cannot be breached, is not subject to the procedure for the simple reason that there is no obligation to be performed.[300]

Second, what type of breach must be established? Any type of breach, in theory at least, gives rise to a right to serve a notice to perform.[301] There is obviously no requirement that the breach be such as to give rise to a right to terminate without notice. Nor need the promisor's breach be wilful in character. However, the contract may itself lay down a notice procedure restricted to such cases and to be applied accordingly.

Third, must the *promisee* be ready and willing to perform and not in breach of contract at the time of service? It is frequently said that the promisee must be ready and willing to perform at the time when the notice is served.[302] But, strictly speaking, the requirement is that the person serving the notice be ready and willing to perform in accordance with the contract. This means that the promisee need not be (presently) ready and willing to perform obligations to be discharged in the future.[303] Consistently with this, a promisee in breach of contract is generally denied the right to serve a notice requiring the promisor to perform.[304] However, it may be that the breach of a purely 'collateral' stipulation would not debar the promisee.[305] It might even be argued that provided the promisee is ready and willing to perform at the time of service, an earlier breach should be disregarded.

[1963] **Parties bound by the notice.** Obviously the promisor is bound by the notice; but in many cases the promisee will also be bound.[306] For example, where a vendor of land serves a notice to complete, both the purchaser and the vendor are bound by the notice; and a *purchaser* who is ready and willing to perform at the time specified in the notice may rely on a failure by the vendor to comply with its terms.[307]

[1964] **Effect of failure to comply.** Where a promisor fails to comply with a notice to perform, the failure gives rise to a right to terminate

---

299. See *Carr v J A Berriman Pty Ltd* (1953) 89 CLR 327 at 348–9; *United Scientific Holdings Ltd v Burnley BC* [1978] AC 904 at 928. Cf *United Nations Convention on Contracts for the International Sale of Goods* 1980, Arts 49, 64.
300. *Perri v Coolangatta Investments Pty Ltd* (1982) 149 CLR 537; 41 ALR 441.
301. See *Louinder v Leis* (1982) 149 CLR 509.
302. See, eg *Halkidis v Bugeia* [1974] 1 NSWLR 423. There may be an express provision to this effect in the contract; see, eg *Re Barr's Contract* [1956] 1 Ch 551 (not followed on another point in *British and Commonwealth Holdings Plc v Quadrex Holdings Inc* [1989] QB 842).
303. *McNally v Waitzer* [1981] 1 NSWLR 294. See Peter Butt, 'Notices to Complete: "Ready, Able and Willing"' [1982] *Conv* 62.
304. *Neeta (Epping) Pty Ltd v Phillips* (1974) 131 CLR 286 at 299.
305. See *Ciavarella v Balmer* [1983] 2 NSWLR 439 at 451. On appeal ((1983) 153 CLR 438), the High Court found it unnecessary to decide the matter. An even more lenient approach is suggested by Francis Dawson, (1979) 8 *NZULR* 281 at 287.
306. *Halfpenny v Wilson* (1967) 87 WN (Pt 1) (NSW) 547; *Balog v Crestani* (1975) 132 CLR 289 at 298.
307. See *Dainford Ltd v Yulora Pty Ltd* [1984] 1 NSWLR 546.

because this can generally be regarded as a repudiation of obligation.[308] In cases where noncompliance occurs despite the promisor's willingness to perform it may be preferable to refer to the failure as a 'fundamental' breach, because the word 'repudiation' generally connotes an express or implied refusal to perform.[309]

However, the right to terminate cannot be ascribed to the breach of an essential contractual term. Strictly speaking, it is compliance with the notice which is essential. The notice procedure is evidentiary in character: the promisor's failure to comply provides the promisee with evidence of a repudiation of obligation or fundamental breach.[310] The notice does not have the effect of converting a non-essential term into an essential term because this would effectively permit a unilateral variation of the contract.[311]

Unilateral and Partially Executed Contracts[312]

[1965] Principles applicable to unilateral contracts. Where a unilateral contract exists there is only one promisor and therefore the issue of termination can only arise with respect to a breach or repudiation on his or her part. Generally, however, the issue of termination does not in fact arise: usually a unilateral contract raises an issue of formation or performance. If a contract is established,[313] and the promisee seeks to recover payment as a debt due[314] there is no issue of termination.

One situation where a right to terminate may exist in the case of a unilateral contract is where the promisor becomes unable to perform the promise.[315] For example, where an optionor sells land to which the option relates to a third party, the conduct may be treated as a repudiation by the optionee.[316] And where the promisor's obligation requires the payment of money over time, a repudiation or serious breach on the promisor's part may give rise to a right to terminate notwithstanding that the promisee has no obligations from which to be discharged.

[1966] Principles applicable to partially executed contracts. Where one party to a bilateral contract has fully performed his or her contractual obligations, the contract can be described as 'partially executed'. Such a contract resembles a unilateral contract in one respect, namely, that one only of the parties has outstanding ('executory') obligations. Accordingly, the promisee has no further obligations to be discharged from.

---

308. *Louinder v Leis* (1982) 149 CLR 509; *Ciavarella v Balmer* (1983) 153 CLR 438.
309. See *Ciavarella v Balmer* [1983] 2 NSWLR 439 at 450 (affirmed (1983) 153 CLR 438).
310. *Ciavarella v Balmer* (1983) 153 CLR 438 at 446.
311. *Neeta (Epping) Pty Ltd v Phillips* (1974) 131 CLR 286 at 299.
312. See J W Carter, 'The Breach of Unilateral Contracts' (1982) 11 *Anglo-American L Rev* 169.
313. See generally [249]–[250].
314. See [1836].
315. See *United Dominions Trust (Commercial) Ltd v Eagle Aircraft Services Ltd* [1968] 1 WLR 74 at 83.
316. See *Wright v Dean* [1948] Ch 686. Cf *Alpha Trading Ltd v Dunnshaw-Patten Ltd* [1981] QB 290.

In *Mackenzie v Rees*[317] Dixon J said that there was 'no English decision which applies the doctrine of anticipatory breach to contracts completely executed on one side'. Nevertheless, the English Court of Appeal would seem to have applied the anticipatory breach doctrine to a partially executed contract as long ago as the decision in *Synge v Synge*,[318] where the defendant, by conveying the property to a third party, repudiated his contractual obligation to leave an interest in property to his wife. The contract had originally been executory, the plaintiff having promised to marry the defendant, but once marriage had taken place it was completely executed on the plaintiff's side. Perhaps Dixon J intended to confine himself to obligations to pay money, as his statement was made in the context of a bill of exchange. It is certainly arguable that there can be no anticipatory breach of the contract contained in the bill,[319] but it is impossible to exclude all contracts to pay money from the doctrines of repudiation and anticipatory breach. For example, in *Moschi v Lep Air Services Ltd*[320] the House of Lords saw no difficulty in applying the doctrine of repudiation to a partially executed contract under which the only outstanding obligation was to pay money. It was conceded that a repudiation had occurred, but Lord Diplock said that the consequences of the promisor's breach would in any event have justified termination by the promisee.

That the position in Australia is still uncertain is indicated by the fact that in *Wigan v Edwards*[321] the High Court left open for future decision the question whether Dixon J's statement is of general application.

Restrictions on the Right to Terminate[322]

Principles of Election[323]

[1967] **Termination not automatic.** In the 19th century it was reasonably common for the courts to say that where a condition precedent failed by reason of a breach of contract (or repudiation) the contract was 'void' or 'at an end'.[324] However, it is now clearly established that, unless the parties have expressly agreed to a contrary result, a breach of contract or repudiation of obligation does not automatically terminate the obligation of the parties to perform.[325] Termination is a matter of election, to be made by the promisee.[326]

---

317. (1941) 65 CLR 1 at 15. See also *Pennicott v Pennicott* (1936) 30 Tas LR 111. American law generally favours the view that termination is not permitted. See *Restatement (2d) Contracts* (1979), §243 (no damages for total breach).
318. [1894] 1 QB 466.
319. See [1936].
320. [1973] AC 331.
321. (1973) 1 ALR 497; 47 ALJR 586. See also *Progressive Mailing House Pty Ltd v Tabali Pty Ltd* (1985) 157 CLR 17 at 44–6 (repudiation).
322. J W Carter, 'Problems in Enforcement — Part I' (1992) 5 *JCL* 199.
323. See Carter, *Breach of Contract*, 2nd ed, 1991, Chapter 10.
324. See, eg *Chanter v Leese* (1838) 4 M & W 295 at 311; 150 ER 1440 at 1447 (affirmed (1839) 5 M & W 698; 151 ER 296). Contrast *Behn v Burness* (1863) 3 B & S 751 at 754, 759; 122 ER 281 at 283, 284.

The contract of employment has been the subject of considerable discussion on this issue. In Australia the law has been settled for some time that a serious breach or repudiation, while frequently destructive of the master–servant relationship, does not automatically terminate the parties' obligations.[327] In England there was, until recently, support for the view that the contract of employment is exceptional in that either party may terminate the parties' obligations by committing a serious breach or repudiation.[328] And even in *Gunton v Richmond-upon-Thames London BC*,[329] where a majority of the English Court of Appeal rejected the automatic termination theory, one member of the court suggested that termination occurs unless the other party can obtain the remedy of specific performance.[330] In many cases this may be the practical result[331] since, for example, a wrongfully dismissed employee cannot obtain specific performance, or convert an action for damages into a claim to recover wages merely by refusing to accept the employer's repudiation.[332] However, this restriction on remedies does not justify special treatment of the contract of employment.[333]

An express provision for automatic termination which may operate on the occurrence of a breach or repudiation is usually interpreted as giving rise to a right to terminate if and when the event occurs.[334] And a party who has the right to terminate may choose to ignore any breach (or repudiation) and continue with the contract. Moreover, in Australia, clauses which provide for automatic termination in respect of events which may or may not, depending on the circumstances, be caused by one of the parties, are given a uniform treatment, with the result that termination is not automatic even if the clause is triggered by an event which does not involve a breach.[335]

---

325. *Photo Production Ltd v Securicor Transport Ltd* [1980] AC 827. The House of Lords overruled *Harbutt's 'Plasticine' Ltd v Wayne Tank and Pump Co Ltd* [1970] 1 QB 447 on this basis (see [1993]). The reference to that case in *Lombok Pty Ltd v Supetina Pty Ltd* (1987) 71 ALR 333 at 344 is therefore difficult to understand.
326. See [1968].
327. *Automatic Fire Sprinklers Pty Ltd v Watson* (1946) 72 CLR 435; *Byrne v Australian Airlines Ltd* (1995) 185 CLR 410 at 427–8; 131 ALR 422. Cf *Macksville & District Hospital v Mayze* (1987) 10 NSWLR 708 at 730.
328. See, eg *Marriott v Oxford and District Co-operative Society Ltd (No 2)* [1970] 1 QB 186. Cf *Vine v National Dock Labour Board* [1957] AC 488 at 500.
329. [1981] Ch 448. See also *Decro-Wall International SA v Practitioners in Marketing Ltd* [1971] 1 WLR 361 (agency).
330. [1981] Ch 448 at 460.
331. *Southern Foundries (1926) Ltd v Shirlaw* [1940] AC 701 at 722.
332. See [2403] and [2221].
333. *Decro-Wall International SA v Practitioners in Marketing Ltd* [1971] 1 WLR 361 at 376. But there may be express agreement to the contrary, or statute may provide for automatic termination. See K D Ewing, 'Remedies for Breach of the Contract of Employment' [1993] *CLJ* 405 at 409–15.
334. See *New Zealand Shipping Co Ltd v Société des Ateliers et Chantiers de France* [1919] AC 1; *Newbon v City Mutual Life Assurance Society Ltd* (1935) 52 CLR 723 at 732–3.
335. *Suttor v Gundowda Pty Ltd* (1950) 81 CLR 418 at 441–2; *Meehan v Jones* (1982) 149 CLR 571 at 591–2; 42 ALR 463. But see *Rudi's Enterprises Pty Ltd v Jay* (1987) 10 NSWLR 568.

The restrictive treatment of automatic termination clauses is based on a rule of construction, namely, that the parties are presumed not to have intended the clause to operate so as to allow a promisor to rely on his or her own breach of duty, whether express or implied,[336] as terminating the performance of the contract. The presumption will not apply if the clause can only operate in circumstances which do not involve a breach of contract, for example, a force majeure clause. Such a clause can be literally interpreted. Similarly, if the duty is owed to a third party the clause may be literally interpreted because the presumption will not apply.[337] If the parties have expressly agreed for automatic termination in the case of breach, the presumption may be rebutted.[338] But even here there may be scope for saying that the clause infringes a rule of public policy.

[1968] **Election to terminate required.** Because of the rule against automatic termination, the obligation of the parties to perform is not terminated unless and until the promisee elects to terminate the performance of the contract.[339] No such right of election lies with the promisor, and the promisor cannot compel the promisee to exercise the right of election.[340]

Unless the contract or a statutory provision provides to the contrary, the promisee may terminate at once; there is no obligation to allow the promisor further time in which to perform, or to afford the promisor an opportunity to remedy the breach.[341]

[1969] **Alternative grounds for termination.** Although the promisee must justify termination, by reference to a legal right to do so, the promisee is not usually required to justify it on any ground given at the time of the election, provided that a valid ground then existed.[342] If no ground was stated, the promisee may generally rely on any available ground. For example, in *Rawson v Hobbs*[343] purchasers of a grazing property were unable to rely on a contractual right to terminate, but permitted to rely on the vendors' inability to perform even though this had not initially been put forward as a ground for termination. Again, in *Maredelanto Compania Naviera SA v Bergbau-Handel GmbH (The Mihalis Angelos)*,[344] the fact that charterers had relied on force majeure as a basis for termination did not

---

336. *Thompson v ASDA-MFI Group Plc* [1988] Ch 241.
337. *Cheall v APEX* [1983] 2 AC 180; *Alghussein Establishment v Eton College* [1988] 1 WLR 587 at 593–4. Cf *Westralian Farmers Ltd v Commonwealth Agricultural Service Engineers Ltd* (1936) 54 CLR 361 (see [2226]).
338. See *Cheall v APEX* [1983] 2 AC 180 at 188–9.
339. *Heyman v Darwins Ltd* [1942] AC 356; *Holland v Wiltshire* (1954) 90 CLR 409.
340. *R v Paulson* [1921] 1 AC 271 at 277; *Dyke v McLeish Estates Ltd* (1927) 27 SR (NSW) 74 at 76; *White and Carter (Councils) Ltd v McGregor* [1962] AC 413.
341. *Loughridge v Lavery* [1969] VR 912 at 922; *Bunge Corp New York v Tradax Export SA Panama* [1981] 1 WLR 711 at 725. The decision to the contrary in *Millichamp v Jones* [1982] 1 WLR 1422 is difficult to justify; see J W Carter, (1983) 99 LQR 504.
342. *Shepherd v Felt and Textiles of Australia Ltd* (1931) 45 CLR 359; *Sunbird Plaza Pty Ltd v Maloney* (1988) 166 CLR 245; *Concut Pty Ltd v Worrell* (2000) 176 ALR 693.
343. (1961) 107 CLR 466.
344. [1971] 1 QB 164 (see [1914]).

prevent them justifying their election to terminate by reference to the shipowners' breach of condition.

There are restrictions on the ability to rely on an alternative ground for termination. If a statutory provision precludes reliance on an alternative ground;[345] or the promisee tries to invoke a contractual right, but has not complied with its requirements;[346] or has failed to allow the promisor an opportunity to perform in accordance with the contract,[347] the promisee will not be permitted to justify the election by reference to the alternative ground. Principles of estoppel[348] may also operate to restrict the promisee's rights, as may the approach taken in *Panchaud Frères SA v Etablissements General Grain Co.*[349]

[1970] **Requirements of election to terminate.** Basically, the requirements of election depend on the source of the right to terminate:

- if the right to terminate is conferred by the common law the common law requirements apply;
- if the right is conferred by the terms of the contract the requirements stated in the contract apply; and
- if the right is conferred by statute the requirements are those stated in the legislation.

Where the right is conferred by an express term, or by statute, and no specific requirements are stated, the common law rules apply. However, whatever the source of the right to terminate, the terms of the contract, or a statutory provision, may have relevance. Whether the promisee has complied with the applicable requirements of election is an issue of fact.[350]

At common law the requirements of election involve unequivocal words or conduct evincing an election to terminate the performance of the contract. Generally, the promisee should communicate the election to the promisor,[351] for example, by saying that the contract is being terminated on the ground of the promisor's breach, or by issuing and serving a writ alleging termination.[352] However, communication need not be by the promisee personally,[353] and in some cases an act may be regarded as

---

345. Compare and contrast *W Devis & Sons Ltd v Atkins* [1977] AC 931 and *West Midlands Co-operative Society Ltd v Tipton* [1986] AC 536 (see Simon Deakin, [1986] CLJ 214).
346. See [1970].
347. See *Heisler v Anglo-Dal Ltd* [1954] 1 WLR 1273.
348. See [1974]–[1976]. See also [1943] and *Bowes v Chaleyer* (1923) 32 CLR 159 at 184, 191, 197 ('waiver' of the right to terminate on any other ground).
349. [1970] 1 Lloyd's Rep 53 (see [1983]).
350. *Hoad v Swan* (1920) 28 CLR 258, unless the evidence of election is documentary in character: *Larratt v Bankers and Traders Insurance Co Ltd* (1941) 41 SR (NSW) 215 at 225.
351. *Car and Universal Finance Co Ltd v Caldwell* [1965] 1 QB 525 at 550; *Lakshmijit v Sherani* [1974] AC 605 at 616. But see *Poort v Development Underwriting (Victoria) Pty Ltd (No 2)* [1977] VR 454 at 459 and cf *Zucker v Straightlace Pty Ltd* (1986) 11 NSWLR 87 at 95.
352. *Heyman v Darwins Ltd* [1942] AC 356 at 362; *International Leasing Corp (Vic) Ltd v Aiken* [1967] 2 NSWR 427. Query the position where the writ is not served; see *Garnac Grain Co Inc v HMF Faure & Fairclough Ltd* [1968] AC 1130n at 1140.
353. *Wood Factory Pty Ltd v Kiritos Pty Ltd* (1985) 2 NSWLR 105 at 146; *Vitol SA v Norelf Ltd (The Santa Clara)* [1996] AC 800 at 810–11; [1996] 3 WLR 105 at 113.

unequivocal even though there is no communication, as where a vendor of land resells to a third party after a repudiation by the purchaser of his or her obligations under the contract.[354] However, equivocal words or conduct, even if communicated, will not amount to an election to terminate. For example, if the vendor in the example just given serves a writ on the purchaser which states alternative claims for (1) specific performance and (2) damages based on termination, there is no election because the vendor has not communicated any choice to the purchaser.[355]

Where the right to terminate is expressly conferred by the terms of the contract it will frequently require the promisee to give notice to the promisor. It would be wrong to say that the courts adopt a rigidly strict approach to contractual termination clauses.[356] It is the substance of such a notice — what it conveys to the reasonable person in the position of the promisor — which matters. On this basis, the House of Lords held in *Mannai Investments Co Pty Ltd v Eagle Star Life Assurance Co Ltd*[357] in the context of a break clause in a lease that even if a termination notice contains errors (and therefore does not strictly comply with the requirements of the clause under which it is given) it may nevertheless be effective to terminate the contract. Thus, if the notice is clear, or so plain that a reasonable person would not be misled by it, the notice will not be vitiated by errors which it contains.[358] Ultimately, the relevant test is, in Lord Steyn's words,[359] whether a reasonable person in the position of the recipient is 'left in no doubt' that the right has been exercised.

The term may go further than this and require the promisee to allow the promisor an opportunity to remedy the breach within a specified time.[360] Where such a requirement exists the promisee must follow the procedure, and any termination before the expiry of the notice will be ineffective.[361] Alternatively, the contract may oblige the promisee to give the promisor an opportunity to explain the breach, that is, to show cause why the contract should not be terminated for breach.[362] The existence of such contractual requirements may preclude the promisee justifying the election by reference to an alternative ground, based on a common law and arising from the facts which also activate the contractual right. However, unless the contract

---

354. *Holland v Wiltshire* (1954) 90 CLR 409. See also *Vitol SA v Norelf Ltd* [1996] AC 800 (see J W Carter, (1997) 11 *JCL* 255).
355. *Ogle v Comboyuro Investments Pty Ltd* (1976) 136 CLR 444 at 452, 460–1. See further [1972].
356. See, eg *Sullivan v Glennon* (1986) 68 ALR 399; 61 ALJR 63.
357. [1997] AC 749 (see P V Baker, (1998) 114 *LQR* 55).
358. See [1997] AC 749 at 768, 780, 782.
359. [1997] AC 749 at 768. The factual matrix (see [713]–[715]) can be taken into account.
360. See, eg *L Schuler AG v Wickman Machine Tool Sales Ltd* [1974] AC 235.
361. *Eriksson v Whalley* [1971] 1 NSWLR 397.
362. See, eg *Amann Aviation Pty Ltd v The Commonwealth* (1990) 92 ALR 601 (affirmed without reference to the point sub nom *Commonwealth of Australia v Amann Aviation Pty Ltd* (1991) 174 CLR 64). Although the clause may itself introduce requirements analogous to public law notions of natural justice, this is not a necessary consequence of a notice procedure: *Hounslow London BC v Twickenham Garden Developments Ltd* [1971] 1 Ch 233.

constitutes an exhaustive code for termination,[363] contractual rights are treated as *additional* bases for termination.

Although there are relatively few statutes conferring a right to terminate for breach of contract, in many situations statutory provisions impinge on common law and contractual rights. For example, the forfeiture of a lease may be subject to a statutory requirement that the lessee be allowed to make reasonable compensation for the breach, and, if it is capable of remedy, to a reasonable time in which to remedy the breach.[364] Other examples of statutory requirements can be found in the consumer protection legislation, such as s 75A of the *Trade Practices Act* 1974 (Cth).[365] One feature of statutory requirements is worthy of note: they frequently prohibit the parties reaching any agreement by which the protection conferred by the statute could be avoided. The regulation of public sector employees' contracts by statute frequently involves the presence of statutory codes governing dismissal. These may impose specific requirements for termination (dismissal) and public law concepts of natural justice, such as the right to a hearing before dismissal. For example, in *O'Rourke v Miller*[366] the High Court held that the dismissal of a probationary constable pursuant to statutory regulations was subject to the requirements of natural justice.

[1971] Election to continue performance. So far we have been concerned with what the promisee must do in order to exercise the right to terminate. However, a promisee may find that the right to terminate has been lost because the promisee has elected to pursue an alternative right, namely, to continue performance. Once a party is faced with a choice between terminating the contract and continuing with its performance,[367] continuation is regarded as inconsistent with termination. As Lord Atkin explained in *United Australia Ltd v Barclays Bank Ltd*:[368]

> [I]f a man is entitled to one of two inconsistent rights it is fitting that when with full knowledge he has done an unequivocal act showing that he has chosen the one he cannot pursue the other, which after the first choice is by reason of the inconsistency no longer his to choose.

It can be seen from this statement that a promisee must have knowledge, and also do some unequivocal act indicating a choice. 'Knowledge', in the context of breach, means that the promisee has *at least* knowledge of the circumstances which in law give rise to the right to terminate.[369] However,

---

363. See [1936].
364. See **ACT:** *Forfeiture of Leases Act* 1901, s 1(1); **NSW:** *Conveyancing Act* 1919, s 129(1); **NT:** *Law of Property Act* 2000, s 137; **Qld:** *Property Law Act* 1974, s 124(1); **SA:** *Landlord and Tenant Act* 1936, s 10; **Tas:** *Conveyancing and Law of Property Act* 1884, s 15(1); **Vic:** *Property Law Act* 1958, s 146(1); **WA:** *Property Law Act* 1969, s 81(1).
365. See also *Property Law Act* 1974 (Qld), s 72 (instalment contract for sale of land).
366. (1985) 156 CLR 342; 58 ALR 269. See also *Ridge v Baldwin* [1964] AC 40; *O'Reilly v Mackman* [1983] 2 AC 237; *Macksville & District Hospital v Mayze* (1987) 10 NSWLR 708. Compare and contrast *Sibbles v Highfern Pty Ltd* (1987) 164 CLR 214; *Braidotti v Queensland City Properties Ltd* (1991) 172 CLR 293; 100 ALR 1 (impact of *Property Law Act* 1972 (Qld), s 72).
367. *Immer (No 145) Pty Ltd v Uniting Church in Australia Property Trust (NSW)* (1993) 182 CLR 26; 112 ALR 609 (see Diane Skapinker, (1994) 7 JCL 86).
368. [1941] AC 1 at 30. See also *Wendt v Bruce* (1931) 45 CLR 245 at 257.

it is sometimes said that the promisee must *also* have knowledge of his or her rights;[370] and in *Coastal Estates Pty Ltd v Melevende*,[371] in the context of *misrepresentation*, a distinction was drawn between rights implied at common law (or equity) and express contractual rights. The sufficiency of knowledge of the circumstances was limited to the latter.

In *Sargent v ASL Developments Ltd*[372] the High Court adopted Lord Atkin's statement of principle and did not decide whether the distinction drawn in *Melevende* should be followed in cases of breach. However, in *Khoury v Government Insurance Office of NSW*[373] it was noted that where alternative rights 'arise under the terms of one contract, a party may be held to have elected to affirm it, notwithstanding that he was unaware of the actual right to avoid it'. Given that *Khoury* involved election in respect of a common law right it is arguable that the case has settled the position. However, there are cases which suggest a contrary approach.[374]

Whether a promisee's words or conduct amount to an election to continue performance is a question of fact.[375] They may take a variety of forms, but must be inconsistent with the exercise of the right to terminate. An express communication to the promisor, or the voluntary receipt of the promisor's performance, such as the rent payable under a lease, will usually be regarded as unequivocal.[376] But an extension of the time for performance by the promisor which is for a specified period, and coupled with a warning that failure to perform within the extended time will lead to termination, is generally not an election to continue performance unless the promisor actually performs.[377]

[1972] **Finality of election.** Generally, an election by the promisee, whether to terminate,[378] or to continue performance,[379] is final. Therefore, an election to continue performance is a permanent restriction on the right to terminate. However, an election in respect of one breach does not preclude reliance on an unknown or later breach by the promisor, provided, of course, that the other breach gives rise to a right to terminate.[380] In order to do that it must be distinguishable from the first breach, and the failure to remedy a breach does not give rise to a second right to terminate unless it

---

369. *Fuller's Theatre and Vaudeville Co Ltd v Rofe* [1923] AC 435; *Elder's Trustee and Executor Co Ltd v Commonwealth Homes and Investment Co Ltd* (1941) 65 CLR 603 at 617–18; *Wallace v Hermans* (1974) 131 CLR 672; 4 ALR 285.
370. See, eg *Owendale Pty Ltd v Anthony* (1967) 117 CLR 539 at 556, 601.
371. [1965] VR 433 (see [1048]).
372. (1974) 131 CLR 634; 4 ALR 257.
373. (1984) 165 CLR 622 at 633–4; 54 ALR 639. See also *Champtaloup v Thomas* [1976] 2 NSWLR 264 at 274–5; *Zucker v Straightlace Pty Ltd* (1986) 11 NSWLR 87 at 93; *Motor Oil Hellas (Corinth) Refineries SA v Shipping Corp of India (The Kanchenjunga)* [1990] 1 Lloyd's Rep 391 at 398–9.
374. See, eg *Peyman v Lanjani* [1985] Ch 457.
375. *Larratt v Bankers and Traders Insurance Co Ltd* (1941) 41 SR (NSW) 215 at 227.
376. *Davenport v R* (1877) 3 App Cas 115; *Wendt v Bruce* (1931) 45 CLR 245. Contrast *International Leasing Corp (Vic) Ltd v Aiken* [1967] 2 NSWR 427.
377. *Barclay v Messenger* (1874) 30 LT 351; *Tropical Traders Ltd v Goonan* (1964) 111 CLR 41.
378. *Ogle v Comboyuro Investments Pty Ltd* (1976) 136 CLR 444 at 451; *Meng Leong Development Pte Ltd v Jip Hong Trading Co Pte Ltd* [1985] AC 511.
379. *Central Estates (Belgravia) Ltd v Woolgar (No 2)* [1972] 1 WLR 1048 at 1054; *Sargent v ASL Developments Ltd* (1974) 131 CLR 634 at 655–6.

was a continuing, as distinct from a 'once and for all', breach.[381] An election to continue performance does not prevent reliance on a subsequent repudiation by the promisor.[382] Nor does the election prevent the promisee claiming damages for the breach.

An election to continue performance is sometimes described as 'waiver' of the breach.[383] Although the word is used in other senses as well,[384] it does not usually signify that the promisee has waived all rights.[385] Therefore, waiver does not prevent the promisee claiming damages in respect of the breach.[386]

[1973] **Equitable relief in favour of terminating party.**[387] A promisee may pursue alternative and inconsistent remedies without being held to have elected in favour of either, since, as Lord Atkin stated in *United Australia Ltd v Barclays Bank Ltd*,[388] 'no question of election [between remedies] arises until one or other claim has been brought to judgment'. Therefore, if the promisee pursues alternative claims of, say, damages based on termination and specific performance, and the court indicates that the promisee has made out a case for both remedies, the promisee must elect between them.

Assuming that the promisee elects for the equitable remedy (specific performance in the example just given), the subsequent control of the dispute will be in the hands of the court. This constitutes a restriction on the promisee's right to terminate arising from any failure by the promisor to comply with the court's order.[389]

Estoppel

[1974] **Estoppel as a restriction on the right to terminate.** Estoppel may operate as a restriction on the right to terminate by precluding the promisee from setting up an election to terminate as a ground for

---

380. *Tramways Advertising Pty Ltd v Luna Park (NSW) Ltd* (1938) 38 SR (NSW) 632 at 645 (reversed on other grounds sub nom *Luna Park (NSW) Ltd v Tramways Advertising Pty Ltd* (1938) 61 CLR 286).
381. *Larking v Great Western (Nepean) Gravel Ltd* (1940) 64 CLR 221.
382. *Ogle v Comboyuro Investments Pty Ltd* (1976) 136 CLR 444.
383. See, eg *Matthews v Smallwood* [1910] 1 Ch 777 at 786; *Craine v Colonial Mutual Fire Insurance Co Ltd* (1920) 28 CLR 305 at 326 (affirmed sub nom *Yorkshire Insurance Co Ltd v Craine* [1922] 2 AC 541).
384. See, eg *Larratt v Barkers and Traders Insurance Co Ltd* (1941) 41 SR (NSW) 215 at 227; *Kammins Ballrooms Co Ltd v Zenith Investments (Torquay) Ltd* [1971] AC 850. See also [390]–[393].
385. See *Mulcahy v Hoyne* (1925) 36 CLR 41 at 55, 56; *Kwei Tek Chao v British Traders and Shippers Ltd* [1954] 2 QB 459 at 477. And see [393].
386. *Hain SS Co Ltd v Tate & Lyle Ltd* [1936] 2 All ER 597 at 608. But see *Banning v Wright* [1972] 1 WLR 972 at 990–1.
387. For criticism see Marion Hetherington, 'He Who Comes to Common Law Must Come with Clean Hands' (1980) 9 *Syd LR* 71; Marion Hetherington, 'Keeping the Plaintiff Out of His Contractual Remedies: the Heresies that Survive *Johnson v Agnew*' (1980) 96 *LQR* 403; but cf Dirik Jackson, (1981) 97 *LQR* 26.
388. [1941] AC 1 at 30. See also *Ciavarella v Balmer* (1983) 153 CLR 438 at 449.
389. *Facey v Rawsthorne* (1925) 35 CLR 566; *Johnson v Agnew* [1980] AC 367 (see [2173]); *Sunbird Plaza Pty Ltd v Maloney* (1988) 166 CLR 245 (see W D Duncan, (1988) 62 *ALJ* 804).

discharge. The general purpose of estoppel,[390] as Dixon J explained in *Thompson v Palmer*,[391] is to prevent 'an unjust departure by one person from an assumption adopted by another as the basis of some act or omission which, unless the assumption be adhered to, would operate to that other's detriment'. Usually, in the context of the right to terminate for breach or repudiation, the assumption arises from a representation made by the promisee and acted on by the promisor. The representation need not be express, it may sometimes be implied from the promisee's conduct.[392]

In the present context the effect of estoppel is procedural: it does not result in loss of the right to terminate.[393] Thus, unlike an election not to terminate, estoppel may be purely temporary. It follows that the estoppel may sometimes be avoided by notice by the promisee, advising the promisor of an intention to insist on its strict legal rights.[394] Assuming that it has been validly given, but the requirements of the notice are not complied with, the promisee can insist on the right of termination in reliance on the promisor's original breach or repudiation. There is no need to prove the existence of a fresh right to terminate unless the circumstances in which the estoppel occurred also involved an election by the promisee to continue performance. Two other important distinctions between principles of election and estoppel are that:

(1) estoppel does not require knowledge of the right or the circumstances which gave rise to the right to terminate;[395] and

(2) detriment to the promisor, although essential to estoppel, is not an element of election.[396]

The word 'waiver' is sometimes used to describe the effect of estoppel,[397] and the promisee regarded as having, temporarily at least, waived the right to terminate. The fact that the word is used in the context of both election and estoppel indicates that it has no fixed meaning. It does not appear to operate as a separate (distinct) doctrine.[398]

[1975] Estoppel based on representation of fact. One form of estoppel relies on a factual representation to the promisor.[399] The representation

---

390. See generally on the forms of estoppel [366].
391. (1933) 49 CLR 507 at 547.
392. *Maclaine v Gatty* [1921] 1 AC 376 at 386; *Western Australian Insurance Co Ltd v Dayton* (1924) 35 CLR 355 at 374. Although silence on the part of the promisee will not usually amount to an implied representation (see [379]), unreasonable delay in the exercise of a right to terminate may sometimes create an estoppel. See [1984].
393. But see *Charles Rickards Ltd v Oppenhaim* [1950] 1 KB 616 at 623.
394. See *Hughes v Metropolitan Railway Co* (1877) 2 App Cas 439.
395. *Sargent v ASL Developments Ltd* (1974) 131 CLR 634 at 642.
396. *Turner v Labafox International Pty Ltd* (1974) 131 CLR 660; 4 ALR 277. But cf C J Rossiter, 'The Doctrine of Election and Contracts for the Sale of Land' (1986) 60 *ALJ* 563 at 571.
397. See, eg *Bremer Handelsgesellschaft mbH v Vanden Avenne-Izegem PVBA* [1978] 2 Lloyd's Rep 109 at 127; *Société Italo-Belge pour le Commerce et l'Industrie v Palm and Vegetable Oils (Malaysia) Sdn Bhd (The Post Chaser)* [1981] 2 Lloyd's Rep 695 at 700. See also [390]–[393].
398. See, eg *Freshmark Ltd v Mercantile Mutual Insurance (Australia) Ltd* [1994] 2 Qd R 390 at 404.
399. See [382].

must come from the promisee and be inconsistent with exercise of the right to terminate. The representation must be unequivocal in nature, and reasonably relied upon by the promisor to its detriment.[400] Injustice must also be established by the promisor,[401] who must show that departure by the promisee from the assumption generated by the representation would, in the circumstances of the case, be unjust, unfair or unconscionable.

The decision in *Bentsen v Taylor Sons & Co (No 2)*[402] may be an example of estoppel by representation, although the court based its decision on 'waiver' and the facts are consistent with election, on the part of the promisees, to continue performance. The case concerned a voyage charterparty. A breach of condition was established because the vessel had not, at the time of the contract, sailed 'from a pitch pine port to the United Kingdom'. When they discovered the breach the charterers did not terminate the performance of the contract. Instead, they told the shipowner that when the vessel arrived at the port of loading they would protest and claim damages. This amounted to a representation to the shipowner that he was obliged to perform and that the contract was not discharged by termination for breach. However, on arrival the charterers refused to load and the shipowner claimed damages in respect of this refusal. The court held that the shipowner was entitled to succeed and refused to allow the charterers to set up termination as a defence to the claim. It would clearly have been unjust to permit the charterers to rely on their election after the shipowner had relied on their representation by proceeding to the port of loading.

Since estoppel may arise despite the absence of knowledge, a promisee may be unable to assert a right to terminate even though there was no knowledge of the circumstances which gave rise to the right. For example, if a seller tenders shipping documents under a sale of goods contract, and these are taken up by the buyer, the buyer may be estopped from setting up a defect in the documents as a ground for termination even though the buyer did not know of it. The seller would need to establish that it would be unjust for the buyer to go back on the representation implied by the latter's conduct in accepting the documents.[403]

[1976] **Promissory estoppel.**[404] Because of the traditional requirement that the representation be one of fact,[405] estoppel by a representation (or promise) as to future conduct is less common. The principle of promissory estoppel is founded on words or conduct amounting to a representation, promise or assurance that the promisee will not at a future time exercise the right to terminate. If such words or conduct have been relied on by the promisor to its detriment, so that it would be inequitable for the promisee

---

400. *Newbon v City Mutual Life Assurance Society Ltd* (1935) 52 CLR 723 at 738; *Evans v Bartlam* [1937] AC 473 at 483.
401. *Maclaine v Gatty* [1921] 1 AC 376 at 386; *Grundt v Great Boulder Pty Gold Mines Ltd* (1937) 59 CLR 641 at 674–5.
402. [1893] 2 QB 274.
403. The inability to reject the documents in *Panchaud Frères SA v Etablissements General Grain Co* [1970] 1 Lloyd's Rep 53 (see [1983]) can be supported on this basis.
404. See K E Lindgren and K G Nicholson, 'Promissory Estoppel in Australia' (1984) 58 *ALJ* 249 and [365]–[387].
405. See *Yorkshire Insurance Co Ltd v Craine* [1922] 2 AC 541 at 553.

to contradict the representation, promise or assurance, the promisee will be precluded from electing to terminate.[406]

The words or conduct said to give rise to the estoppel must be clear and unequivocal. For example, in *Legione v Hateley*[407] purchasers of land breached an essential time stipulation and the vendors, in accordance with the contract, served a notice requiring completion within 15 days and advising that the contract would be 'rescinded' on a failure to comply with the notice. Prior to the expiry of the notice the purchasers asked whether a further seven days would be allowed for completion. The vendors' solicitors replied that this would be 'all right', but that they would 'have to get instructions'. There was no further communication, and on the expiry of the notice the vendors advised that the contract was rescinded pursuant to the contract. The High Court, by majority, held that there was no estoppel because there was only an equivocal reply to the purchasers' inquiry.

The element of inequity is also essential, and in the present context requires proof of unconscionable conduct by the party who would otherwise be entitled to terminate. For example, if a seller tenders documents under a sale of goods contract and the buyer takes these up notwithstanding the presence in the documents of a clear indication that the goods were shipped late, the buyer may be treated as having impliedly represented (by conduct) that the goods will not be rejected when they arrive. If it would be unconscionable to allow contradiction of the (earlier) representation, for example, because the seller has tendered the goods in reliance,[408] the buyer will be precluded from terminating the contract on the ground of late shipment,[409] and any termination based on that ground will be ineffective.

Exclusion Clauses and Breach by Terminating Party

[1977] **Exclusion clauses.** As has been explained,[410] the application of an exclusion clause depends on the construction of the contract save only to the extent that a statutory provision may render an exclusion clause, which might otherwise apply, void or inoperative.

Although the seriousness of the promisor's breach is relevant to the construction of exclusion clauses,[411] the mere fact that a breach would, but for the clause, give rise to a right to terminate does not mean that the clause does not apply. However, where a breach is serious an exclusion may be

---

406. In *W J Alan & Co Ltd v El Nasr Export and Import Co* [1972] 2 QB 189 at 213 Lord Denning MR suggested that detriment is not required. The House of Lords left the matter open for future consideration in *Bremer Handelsgesellschaft mbH v Vanden Avenne-Izegem PVBA* [1978] 2 Lloyd's Rep 109 at 127. See also *Foran v Wight* (1989) 168 CLR 385 at 413 and [380].
407. (1983) 152 CLR 406; 46 ALR 1 (see also [373]). Contrast *Strada Estates Pty Ltd v Harcla Hotels Pty Ltd* (1980) 25 SASR 284.
408. Contrast *Société Italo-Belge pour le Commerce et l'Industrie v Palm and Vegetable Oils (Malaysia) Sdn Bhd (The Post Chaser)* [1981] 2 Lloyd's Rep 695, where after breach by the sellers the buyers called for the documents but rejected them. It was not inequitable for the buyers to rely on the sellers' breach.
409. See *Kwei Tek Chao v British Traders and Shippers Ltd* [1954] 2 QB 459 at 481.
410. See [750].
411. See [753] et seq.

construed as inapplicable. For example, in *Robert A Munro & Co Ltd v Meyer*,[412] an exclusion clause in a sale of goods contract provided: 'The goods to be taken with all faults and defects; damaged or inferior, if any, at valuation to be arranged mutually or by arbitration.' Wright J held that this no-rejection clause did not preclude termination where the sellers were in breach by tendering goods which did not match the description required by the contract. He reasoned that a breach in relation to the description of the goods was too severe to be covered by the clause, and effectively restricted it to defects in the quality or condition of the goods.

Because the right to terminate is distinct from the right to damages, the fact that a clause excludes the right to damages does not of itself imply that the right to terminate is also excluded.[413]

[1978] **Breach by terminating party.** The general rule, it seems, is that a breach by the terminating party does not preclude termination unless it was so serious as to give the other party the right to terminate the performance of the contract.[414] For example, in *Hongkong Fir Shipping Co Ltd v Kawasaki Kisen Kaisha Ltd*,[415] the shipowners' breach of the seaworthiness clause did not preclude their termination of the performance of the contract on the ground of the charterers' repudiation by wrongful termination. Similarly, where, at the time of termination, the promisee is not ready and willing to perform, the absence of readiness or willingness does not restrict termination in respect of a breach or repudiation by the promisor, unless the promisor was entitled to terminate the performance of the contract.[416]

Where both parties are in breach, complicated fact situations frequently arise, and it may be impossible to apportion blame with any degree of certainty. For example, where a contract creates concurrent obligations, and both parties are guilty of delay, it may be that neither party is in a position to terminate performance, because both have contributed to the delay. In theory, they remain bound by their contractual obligations. The English courts have held this to be the position where parties to a submission to arbitration are both guilty of delay.[417] Some dissatisfaction with the result in that context has been registered,[418] because it is unrealistic to expect a respondent to arbitration proceedings to wake up a

---

412. [1930] 2 KB 312.
413. Even if there is no breach: *Jackson v Union Marine Insurance Co Ltd* (1874) LR 10 CP 125 (see [2042]); see Brian Coote, 'Discharge for Breach and Exception Clauses Since Harbutt's "Plasticine"' (1977) 40 *MLR* 31 at 35–6. See also *Ernest Beck & Co v K Szymanowski & Co* [1924] AC 43 at 52 (exclusion of the right to terminate need not prevent a claim for damages being made).
414. See *Roadshow Entertainment Pty Ltd v ACN 053 006 269 Pty Ltd Receiver & Manager Appointed (formerly CEL Home Video Pty Ltd)* (1997) 42 NSWLR 462 at 479–80.
415. [1962] 2 QB 26 (see [1958]). See also *Murphy v Zamonex Pty Ltd* (1993) 31 NSWLR 439 at 454.
416. See *Foran v Wight* (1989) 168 CLR 385. Cf *Morris v Baron & Co* [1918] AC 1 at 9. Where the absence of readiness or willingness precedes the time of performance there is no breach by the promisee unless the promisor has terminated the contract for anticipatory breach. See [1930].
417. *Bremer Vulkan Schiffbau und Maschinenfabrik v South India Shipping Corp Ltd* [1981] AC 909.

sleeping arbitration, and in Australia a different result is possible in this context due to a power to approach the court.[419] However, the general principle remains valid that delay in performance may prevent a party successfully terminating the contract. And breach by both parties may signify that the contract has been abandoned.[420]

Relief Against Forfeiture[421]

[1979] Inherent jurisdiction. Termination of the performance of a contract will deprive the promisor of the benefits which were expected from future performance by the promisee. It may also enable the promisee to retain money paid under the contract, since the contract may provide that the money is to be *forfeited* if the contract is discharged. Alternatively, termination may lead to a forfeiture of the promisor's proprietary interest in land or goods. Although it is clear that the courts do not have a general jurisdiction to relieve against the loss of the benefit of the contract, there is undoubtedly an inherent jurisdiction to grant relief against the forfeiture of money or property.

Whether under the 'special heads' of fraud, accident, surprise or mistake, or otherwise, a court exercising equitable jurisdiction may grant relief to the promisor against the forfeiture in 'appropriate and limited cases'.[422] The relief granted may take various forms, but the main examples are:

- an order for the repayment of money;
- an injunction preventing the promisee from terminating the performance of the contract;
- an order allowing the promisor further time to pay; or
- an order for specific performance of the contract.

This inherent jurisdiction is relevant to an election by the promisee to terminate the performance of the contract in two distinct situations.[423]

---

418. See *Allied Marine Transport Ltd v Vale do Rio Doce Navegacao SA (The Leonides D)* [1985] 1 WLR 925 at 928; *Food Corp of India v Antclizo Shipping Corp* [1988] 1 WLR 603 at 605–6.
419. See **ACT:** *Commercial Arbitration Act* 1986, s 46; **NSW:** *Commercial Arbitration Act* 1984, s 46; **Qld:** *Commercial Arbitration Act* 1990, s 46; **NT:** *Commercial Arbitration Act* 1985, s 46; **SA:** *Commercial Arbitration Act* 1986, s 46; **Tas:** *Commercial Arbitration Act* 1986, s 46; **Vic:** *Commercial Arbitration Act* 1984, s 46; **WA:** *Commercial Arbitration Act* 1985, s 46.
420. See, eg *DTR Nominees Pty Ltd v Mona Homes Pty Ltd* (1978) 138 CLR 423.
421. See K G Nicholson, 'Breach of an Essential Time Stipulation and Relief Against Forfeiture' (1983) 57 *ALJ* 632; W M C Gummow, 'Forfeiture and Certainty: The High Court and the House of Lords' in Finn, ed, *Essays in Equity*, 1985, p 30; Charles Harpum, 'Relief Against Forfeiture and the Purchaser of Land' [1984] *CLJ* 134; Rossiter, *Penalties and Forfeiture*, 1992; J W Carter, 'Problems in Enforcement — Part II' (1993) 6 *JCL* 1; Hossein Abedian and M P Furmston, 'Relief Against Forfeiture After Breach of Essential Time Stipulation in the Light of *Union Eagle Ltd v Golden Achievement Ltd*' (1998) 12 *JCL* 189; Lionel Smith, 'Relief Against Forfeiture: A Restatement' [2001] *CLJ* 89.
422. *Shiloh Spinners Ltd v Harding* [1973] AC 691 at 723. See also *Legione v Hateley* (1983) 152 CLR 406 at 424.
423. For relief against the forfeiture money see [2239]–[2240], [2331]–[2334].

First, there is the situation explained by Lord Wilberforce in *Shiloh Spinners Ltd v Harding*.[424] Where the 'primary object' of the contract is to secure a stated result, and an express provision for forfeiture of an interest in property was inserted in the contract 'by way of security for the production' of the result, the promisor may be entitled to relief against forfeiture if, notwithstanding the promisor's breach, the result can 'effectively be attained', when the case comes before the court. For example, the object of the clause might be to secure payment of a debt due under the contract. But the provision must effect the forfeiture of an interest in property, and relief must be 'appropriate' in the circumstances. In *Scandinavian Trading Tanker Co AB v Flota Petrolera Ecuatoriana*,[425] a time charterparty provided for termination in the event of default by the charterers in their obligation punctually to pay hire under the contract. Following termination for default, the charterers sought relief against forfeiture. The House of Lords held that even if the termination provision was intended to secure the production of a stated result, namely, punctual payment of hire, there was no case for relief. The charterers had no property interest in the vessel: the contract being one for the provision of services, their interest was purely contractual. The court was also influenced by:

(1) the uncertainty which would be created by the granting of relief in a commercial contract;[426]

(2) the fact that the contract had been freely entered into by parties with equal bargaining power;

(3) the absence of unconscionable conduct; and

(4) the fact that relief by way of injunction against the shipowners would have been tantamount to specific performance of a contract for the provision of services.[427]

The case does not, however, stand for the proposition that relief will never be granted in the context of a commercial contract. For example, in *BICC Plc v Burndy Corp*[428] the English Court of Appeal said that relief may be granted against the forfeiture of an interest in a patent, by allowing further time for performance. And, in *On Demand Information Plc v Michael Gerson Finance Plc*,[429] the same court acknowledged that in an appropriate case relief may be granted against forfeiture of a lessee's possessory interest under a commercial chattel lease which has been terminated for non-payment of hire.

Second, under Australian law, relief may be granted where a sale of land contract is terminated, in order to prevent the forfeiture of the purchaser's equitable interest in the land.[430] In these cases forfeiture is a consequence of termination rather than the effect of an express provision designed to

---

424. [1973] AC 691 at 723. See also *Legione v Hateley* (1983) 152 CLR 406 at 424; *Minister for Lands and Forests v McPherson* (1991) 22 NSWLR 687.
425. [1983] 2 AC 694.
426. See also *Sport Internationaal Bussum BV v Inter-Footwear Ltd* [1984] 1 WLR 776 at 788–9, 794 (see Charles Harpum, [1984] *CLJ* 369).
427. Such orders are rarely made in that context. See further [2403].
428. [1985] Ch 232 (see Charles Harpum, [1985] *CLJ* 204).
429. [2001] 1 WLR 155.

secure a stated result. Although it may be relevant to consider whether the forfeiture operates as a penalty for non-observance of the contract,[431] this is not an essential requirement. In *Legione v Hateley*[432] a majority of the High Court held that in extreme cases it may be appropriate for the court to give relief by decreeing specific performance of the contract. In that case termination would have been particularly hard on the purchasers as they had been let into possession and effected a substantial improvement to the land by erecting a dwelling. Since there was nothing in the contract to entitle them to compensation in respect of this improvement, the vendors would have received what Gibbs CJ and Murphy J described[433] as 'an ill-merited windfall'. Mason and Deane JJ said[434] that it was relevant to consider factors such as the following:

(1) Did the conduct of the vendor contribute to the purchaser's breach? (2) Was the purchaser's breach (a) trivial or slight, and (b) inadvertent and not wilful? (3) What damage or other adverse consequences did the vendor suffer by reason of the purchaser's breach? (4) What is the magnitude of the purchaser's loss and the vendor's gain if the forfeiture is to stand? (5) Is specific performance with or without compensation an adequate safeguard for the vendor?

The court may intervene even though the right to terminate has been exercised.[435] For example, in *Stern v McArthur*[436] a contract for the sale of land provided for the payment of the price by instalments over a number of years, and the High Court (by majority) held that the purchaser was entitled to relief against the forfeiture of the interest which arose on entry into the contract when the vendor acted unconscionably in exercising an express right of termination for non-payment of instalments of the price. Nevertheless, relief is rarely granted, and will be refused if there is no evidence of unconscionable conduct by the vendor. Thus, in *Ciavarella v Balmer*,[437] the High Court refused to entertain a claim for relief against forfeiture as there was no evidence of unconscionability.

Relief against forfeiture is not relevant to cases where the forfeiture results from the failure of a contingency which is not the subject of an express (or implied) obligation on the promisor.[438] For example, where A grants an option to B, B's failure to exercise it in time is not a breach of

---

430. Contrast *Union Eagle Ltd v Golden Achievement Ltd* [1997] AC 514 (see Peter Butt, (1997) 71 *ALJ* 410; J D Heydon, (1997) 113 *LQR* 385.)
431. On relief against penalties see [2207]–[2217], [2332]–[2333].
432. (1983) 152 CLR 406.
433. (1983) 152 CLR 406 at 429.
434. (1983) 152 CLR 406 at 449. The case was remitted to the Supreme Court of Victoria to decide whether it was appropriate to grant relief, and the terms on which relief — in the form of specific performance — might be granted.
435. Provided that there will be no prejudice to a third party who acted bona fide and without notice.
436. (1988) 165 CLR 489; 81 ALR 463 (see Kevin Nicholson, (1989) 2 *JCL* 148 and (1990) 106 *LQR* 39).
437. (1983) 153 CLR 438. See also *Sunbird Plaza Pty Ltd v Maloney* (1988) 166 CLR 245 at 263 ('exceptional circumstances'); *P C Developments Pty Ltd v Revell* (1991) 22 NSWLR 615 (unconscionable conduct essential). Whether the *vendor* may invoke the principle was raised but not decided in *Dainford Ltd v Yulora Pty Ltd* [1984] 1 NSWLR 546.
438. See *United Scientific Holdings Ltd v Burnley BC* [1978] AC 904 at 929, 951. See also [1837], [1853].

contract and, although the effect of the failure is a forfeiture of an interest in the land, the court's inherent jurisdiction to grant relief against forfeiture does not become relevant.

[1980] Statutory jurisdiction. Some statutes confer a jurisdiction to grant relief against forfeiture. Two examples may be given in order to indicate the main contexts of relief. First, where a lessor is proceeding, by action or otherwise, to enforce a right of re-entry or forfeiture under any 'proviso or stipulation' in a lease for a breach of any 'covenant or condition' (not involving the payment of rent) the lessee may apply to the court which may, having regard to the proceedings and conduct of the parties, and to such other circumstances as it thinks fit, grant relief, on such terms (if any) as are appropriate.[439]

Second, in some jurisdictions there is a power to grant relief against the forfeiture of an option to purchase contained in a lease.[440]

Other Possible Restrictions

[1981] Statute. Although there is no example in Australia of a general statutory provision applying in all cases of termination, there are instances of restrictions operating in specific contexts and for specific purposes. For example, in the context of commercial leases[441] statutory restrictions on termination are present for the purpose of allowing the court to grant relief against forfeiture. Under the *Consumer Credit Code* (NL) detailed provisions can be found regulating the exercise by a credit provider of rights under contracts regulated by the Acts. More generally, under the *Contracts Review Act* 1980 (NSW),[442] the court may grant relief in respect of 'unjust' contracts or provisions.

Two provisions in the sale of goods legislation restrict termination.[443]

First, under the legislation of all Australian jurisdictions, 'acceptance' of goods (or part thereof) by the buyer prevents rejection of the goods and termination of the performance of the contract.[444] This restriction does not apply where the buyer has accepted part of the goods and the contract is

---

439. **ACT:** *Forfeiture of Leases Act* 1901, s 1(2); **NSW:** *Conveyancing Act* 1919, s 129(2); **NT:** *Law of Property Act* 2000, s 137; **Qld:** *Property Law Act* 1974, s 124(2); **SA:** *Landlord and Tenant Act* 1936, s 11; **Tas:** *Conveyancing and Law of Property Act* 1884, s 15(2); **Vic:** *Property Law Act* 1958, s 146(2); **WA:** *Property Law Act* 1969, s 81(2). See also *Supreme Court Act* 1986 (Vic), s 85 (non-payment of rent).
440. See [1837].
441. See [1980].
442. See generally [1517]–[1522].
443. See also **ACT:** *Sale of Goods Act* 1954, s 16(1); **NSW:** *Sale of Goods Act* 1923, s 16(1); **NT:** *Sale of Goods Act* 1972, s 16(1); **Qld:** *Sale of Goods Act* 1896, s 14(1); **SA:** *Sale of Goods Act* 1895, s 11(1); **Tas:** *Sale of Goods Act* 1896, s 16(1); **Vic:** *Goods Act* 1958, s 16(1); **WA:** *Sale of Goods Act* 1895, s 11(1) which preserve 'waiver' of condition and 'election' by the seller to treat a breach of condition as a breach of warranty as restrictions on the right to terminate. 'Waiver' must here mean something more than an election against termination. For waiver and election see [1972], [1974].
444. **ACT:** *Sale of Goods Act* 1954, s 16(4); **NSW:** *Sale of Goods Act* 1923, s 16(3); **NT:** *Sale of Goods Act* 1972, s 16(4); **Qld:** *Sale of Goods Act* 1896, s 14(3); **SA:** *Sale of Goods Act* 1895, s 11(3); **Tas:** *Sale of Goods Act* 1896, s 16(3); **Vic:** *Goods Act* 1958, ss 16(3); 99(1); **WA:** *Sale of Goods Act* 1895, s 11(3).

'severable'.⁴⁴⁵ The legislation deems acceptance to have occurred in three situations:⁴⁴⁶

(1) where the buyer intimates acceptance to the seller;
(2) where the buyer does an act in relation to the goods which is inconsistent with the ownership of the seller; and
(3) where the buyer does not reject the goods within a reasonable period of time.

In the Australian Capital Territory[447] each of the three cases of acceptance is subject to the buyer's right to a reasonable opportunity of examining the goods. In some jurisdictions[448] the description of acceptance by an act in relation to the goods which is inconsistent with the ownership of the seller is subject to the buyer's right to a reasonable opportunity of examining the goods. In the other jurisdictions the relation between acceptance and the right to examine is governed by the general law and is unclear.[449]

The second restriction is that the passing of property in specific goods bars rejection — and therefore prevents termination — unless there is a term in the contract providing for a contrary result.[450] This unfair restriction of the buyer's right of rejection, which confuses termination with rescission ab initio,[451] does not apply in the Australian Capital Territory, New South Wales or South Australia.[452] And in Victoria[453] it does not apply to consumer sales to which Pt IV of the *Goods Act* 1958 (Vic) applies. Moreover, s 75A of the *Trade Practices Act* 1974 (Cth)[454] permits termination — described as 'rescission' — in respect of contracts to which the provision applies even if property has passed, provided that the buyer follows the procedure stated in the section.[455]

[1982] Impossibility of restitutio in integrum. Where a contract is rescinded ab initio, for example, for misrepresentation, the parties must be

---

445. See, eg *Rosenthal & Sons Ltd v Esmail* [1965] 1 WLR 1117.
446. **ACT:** *Sale of Goods Act* 1954, s 39; **NSW:** *Sale of Goods Act* 1923, s 38; **NT:** *Sale of Goods Act* 1972, s 38; **Qld:** *Sale of Goods Act* 1896, s 37; **SA:** *Sale of Goods Act* 1895, s 35; **Tas:** *Sale of Goods Act* 1896, s 40; **Vic:** *Goods Act* 1958, s 42; **WA:** *Sale of Goods Act* 1895, s 35.
447. *Sale of Goods Act* 1954 (ACT), s 39.
448. **NSW:** *Sale of Goods Act* 1923, s 38; **SA:** *Sale of Goods Act* 1895, s 35; **Vic:** *Goods Act* 1958, s 42 (see also s 99(2), (3) (consumer sales)). See Peter Kincaid, 'Acceptance and Examination under the Amended Sale of Goods Acts' (1994) 68 *ALJ* 515.
449. See *J S Robertson (Aust) Pty Ltd v Martin* (1956) 94 CLR 30 at 44, 51–2, 59–60.
450. **NT:** *Sale of Goods Act* 1972, s 16(4); **Qld:** *Sale of Goods Act* 1896, s 14(3); **Tas:** *Sale of Goods Act* 1896, s 16(3); **Vic:** *Goods Act* 1958, s 16(3); **WA:** *Sale of Goods Act* 1895, s 11(3).
451. The restriction is derived from *Street v Blay* (1831) 2 B & Ad 456; 109 ER 1212, where restitutio in integrum was stated to be a requirement of termination. For the present position see [1982], [2306], [2336].
452. A similar reform is recommended by the Law Reform Commission of Western Australia, *Report on the Sale of Goods Act* 1895, Project No 89, 1998.
453. See *Goods Act* 1958 (Vic), ss 99, 118(1).
454. See also **NT:** *Consumer Affairs and Fair Trading Act* 1990, s 67(1); **WA:** *Fair Trading Act* 1987, s 41.
455. See generally Taperell, Vermeesch and Harland, *Trade Practices and Consumer Protection*, 3rd ed, 1983, paras 1762–65.

restored, substantially at least, to the positions which they occupied prior to entry into the contract.[456] Since termination for breach or repudiation merely operates in futuro, this requirement of restitutio does not apply as a general restriction on an election to terminate.[457] That restitutio may be required by the *particular facts* of a case is illustrated by *Rawson v Hobbs*.[458] Title to the sheep and cattle on the grazing property had passed to the purchasers who had, for a period of time, occupied the land. Dixon CJ said that on the facts the purchasers' termination could not 'amount to a rescission ab initio with complete restitutio in integrum'. However, in order for termination by the purchasers to be effective, restitution in respect of the benefits received was required, and the court declared that the purchasers were discharged from the contract of sale but entitled to a refund of the money which they had paid, subject to a deduction to take account of the benefits which they had obtained under the contract.

[1983] **Unconscionability, good faith and reasonableness.** On one view, statute, as well as concepts such as election and estoppel, provide sufficient protection against the unfair or unjust exercise of termination rights. However, from time to time suggestions are made that additional restrictions operate, either generally or in specific contexts. For example, in *Panchaud Frères SA v Etablissements General Grain Co*,[459] a buyer of goods was held not to be entitled to terminate the performance of the contract on the ground that the seller had breached a condition by late shipment. Lord Denning MR said[460] they were estopped by their conduct in accepting shipping documents, a close examination of which would have disclosed the sellers' breach. Winn LJ based his decision on a broader 'requirement of fair conduct'.[461] However, in *Glencore Grain Rotterdam BV v Lebanese Organisation for International Commerce*[462] the English Court of Appeal has explained the case, on narrow grounds, and rejected the idea that the *Panchaud Frères* decision stands for any principle of 'fair conduct' independent of waiver and estoppel.

Although it is therefore clear that there is no general requirement that contractual rights, particularly those conferred by the common law, must be exercised reasonably,[463] in particular contexts requirements of reasonableness and good faith have been applied. Thus, in the context of express termination rights in building contracts a requirement of reasonableness has been applied,[464] and in some contracts it may be implied that rights are to be exercised in good faith.[465] It is also arguable

---

456. See [1045]; [2336].
457. *McDonald v Dennys Lascelles Ltd* (1933) 48 CLR 457 at 477; *Johnson v Agnew* [1980] AC 367. Any suggestions to the contrary in *Fullers' Theatres Ltd v Musgrove* (1923) 31 CLR 524 at 539–44 must be regarded as incorrect or restricted to the particular circumstances of that case. See further [1988].
458. (1961) 107 CLR 466 (see [1969]).
459. [1970] 1 Lloyd's Rep 53. See Tony Dugdale and David Yates, 'Variation, Waiver and Estoppel — A Re-appraisal' (1976) 39 *MLR* 680.
460. [1970] 1 Lloyd's Rep 53 at 57.
461. [1970] 1 Lloyd's Rep 53 at 59.
462. [1997] 4 All ER 514 (see J W Carter, (1999) 14 *JCL* 239).
463. See *White and Carter (Councils) Ltd v McGregor* [1962] AC 413 at 430; *Vroon BV v Foster's Brewing Group Ltd* [1994] 2 VR 32 at 95–7. Cf *Alcatel Australia Ltd v Scarcella* (1998) 44 NSWLR 349 at 369.

that cases such as *Legione v Hateley*[466] have a more general basis, namely, that the court may grant relief against the termination of any contract where the promisee is guilty of unconscionable conduct.[467]

[1984] **Delay.** Generally, an election to terminate the performance of a contract must be made within a reasonable time.[468] The basis for this restriction on the right to terminate can be seen as an implied term of the contract[469] or (preferably) a requirement of election itself.[470] In some cases a failure to elect within a reasonable time will give rise to estoppel,[471] and there are statutes which fix a reasonable time for election.[472]

What constitutes a reasonable time is an issue of fact depending on the circumstances of the case at the time when the period is alleged to have expired.[473] The mere fact that there has been some delay does not mean that it is unreasonable since there is no requirement that the promisee elect immediately.[474] Moreover, delay is not unreasonable merely because the promisor has had sufficient time to tender performance to the promisee.[475]

It is open to the parties to fix a maximum period for termination, for example, by requiring rejection of goods under a sale of goods contract within a specified period of time. And in some cases the maximum period of time allowed to the promisee is the subject of statutory determination.[476]

---

464. See *Renard Constructions (ME) Pty Ltd v Minister for Public Works* (1992) 26 NSWLR 234; *Hughes Bros Pty Ltd v Trustees of the Roman Catholic Church for the Archdiocese of Sydney* (1993) 31 NSWLR 91 and the discussion by Hon Mr Justice T R H Cole, 'The Concept of Reasonableness in Construction Contracts' (1994) 10 *Building and Construction Law* 7. Cf *Amann Aviation Pty Ltd v The Commonwealth* (1990) 92 ALR 601, and on appeal sub nom *Commonwealth of Australia v Amann Aviation Pty Ltd* (1991) 174 CLR 64 (impact of show cause procedure). But contrast *Canberra Advance Bank Ltd v Benny* (1992) 115 ALR 207 (appointment of receiver).
465. See *Imperial Group Pension Trust Ltd v Imperial Tobacco Ltd* [1991] 1 WLR 589 at 597 (exercise of rights under employment contract or pension scheme); *Service Station Association Ltd v Berg Bennett & Associates Pty Ltd* (1993) 117 ALR 393 at 401 (exercise of mortgagee's power of sale).
466. (1983) 152 CLR 406.
467. See *CSS Investments Pty Ltd v Lopiron Pty Ltd* (1987) 76 ALR 463 at 472, 482; *Sunbird Plaza Pty Ltd v Maloney* (1988) 166 CLR 245 at 263; *Federal Airports Corp v Makucha Developments Pty Ltd* (1993) 115 ALR 679. But cf F M B Reynolds, 'Discharge by Breach as a Remedy', in Finn, ed, *Essays on Contract*, 1987, pp 194ff.
468. *Champtaloup v Thomas* [1976] 2 NSWLR 264 at 273; *China National Foreign Trade Transportation Corp v Evlogia Shipping Co SA of Panama (The Mihalios Xilas)* [1979] 1 WLR 1018 at 1023.
469. See the discussion in *Antaios Compania Naviera SA v Salen Rederierna AB* [1983] 1 WLR 1362 (affirmed without reference to the point [1985] AC 191).
470. See, eg *Carter v Scargill* (1875) LR 10 QB 564; *Majik Markets Pty Ltd v S & M Motor Repairs Pty Ltd (No 1)* (1987) 10 NSWLR 49 at 54.
471. See *Mardorf Peach & Co Ltd v Attica Sea Carriers Corp of Liberia* [1977] AC 850 at 871, 880.
472. See [1981].

Consequences of Termination[477]

Discharge of the Parties

[1985] Discharge of contractual duties. An election to terminate the performance of a contract, whether for breach or repudiation, discharges the parties from the obligation to perform (or to be ready and willing to perform) their respective contractual duties.[478] It is sometimes said that such an election 'rescinds' or 'terminates' the contract. However, it is clear that termination affects the parties' duties rather than the contract itself.

The classic statement of this fundamental point is contained in Lord Porter's speech in *Heyman v Darwins Ltd*:[479]

> To say that the contract is rescinded or has come to an end or has ceased to exist may in individual cases convey the truth with sufficient accuracy, but the fuller expression that the injured party is thereby absolved from future performance of his obligations under the contract is a more accurate description of the position. Strictly speaking to say that on acceptance of the renunciation of a contract the contract is rescinded is incorrect. In such a case the injured party may accept the renunciation as a breach going to the root of the whole consideration. By that acceptance he is discharged from further performance and may bring an action for damages, but the contract itself is not rescinded.

Although Lord Porter's statement refers only to discharge of the promisee, in most cases *both* parties will be discharged by the promisee's election to terminate.[480] It is also clear that although the statement refers only to repudiation ('renunciation'), it applies generally to all bases for termination.

[1986] Time and scope of discharge. Discharge of a contract, by a promisee's election to terminate, takes effect from the time of the promisee's election: it is not retrospective to the time of the promisor's breach or repudiation.[481]

Although discharge is effective from the time of termination, most statements apply the discharging effect to all the *unperformed* primary

---

473. See [1804]. The decision in *Bernstein v Pamson Motors (Golders Green) Ltd* [1987] 2 All ER 220, interpreting the sale of goods provision (see [1981]), seems unduly restrictive (see F M B Reynolds, (1988) 104 *LQR* 16).
474. A contrary statement in *Pennicott v Pennicott* (1936) 30 Tas LR 111 at 116 is based on a misinterpretation of *Halkett v Earl of Dudley* [1907] 1 Ch 590 at 597 (equitable right of 'rescission').
475. See, eg *Mardorf Peach & Co Ltd v Attica Sea Carriers Corp of Liberia* [1977] AC 850.
476. See *Consumer Transactions Act* 1972 (SA), s 12(1) (seven days).
477. See Carter, *Breach of Contract*, 2nd ed, 1991, Chapter 12; A M Shea, 'Discharge from Performance of Contracts by Failure of Condition' (1979) 42 *MLR* 623.
478. *McDonald v Dennys Lascelles Ltd* (1933) 48 CLR 457 at 469-70, 476-7; *Heyman v Darwins Ltd* [1942] AC 365 at 367, 373, 379, 399; *Walters v Cooper* [1967] VR 583 at 587; *Bank of Boston Connecticut v European Grain & Shipping Ltd* [1989] AC 1056 at 1098-9.
479. [1942] AC 356 at 399.
480. *Holland v Wiltshire* (1954) 90 CLR 409 at 416; *Johnson v Agnew* [1980] AC 367 at 392.

obligations of the parties.[482] In other words, it is not restricted to those obligations which would have fallen due for performance after termination. A narrower statement in *Hyundai Heavy Industries Co Ltd v Papadopoulos*,[483] restricting discharge to such obligations, may be explained by the fact that an accrued right to receive performance was being considered. In the absence of an accrued right, the promisee can only enforce the promisor's obligations by way of a claim for damages.[484] The narrower statement, if generally applied, would lead to absurd results. For example, if a vendor of land terminated performance after the time for payment had arrived he or she would, prima facie, be entitled to recover the price of the land on the ground that it should have been paid prior to termination. The true position is that the purchaser is discharged from the obligation to pay the price, but liable in damages for breach.[485]

[1987] **Finality of discharge.** Once the promisee has exercised a right to terminate and the parties have been discharged, the promisee cannot go back on the election.[486] Neither party is permitted to reinstate the contractual obligations of the parties unilaterally. The parties may agree for reinstatement, but this involves the formation of a new contract.[487]

An exception to the general rule of finality arises if the court, in granting relief against forfeiture, orders specific performance notwithstanding the promisee's election to terminate the performance of the contract.[488]

Accrued Rights Not Divested[489]

[1988] **Termination distinguished from rescission.** The fact that a contract is not rescinded when it is discharged for breach or repudiation is very significant where accrued rights are in issue. In *McDonald v Dennys Lascelles Ltd*[490] Dixon J explained the significance in the following words:[491]

> When a party to a simple contract, upon a breach by the other contracting party of a condition of the contract, elects to treat the contract as no longer binding upon him, the contract is not rescinded as from the beginning. Both parties are discharged from the further performance of the contract, but rights are not divested or discharged which have already been

---

481. *Boston Deep Sea Fishing & Ice Co v Ansell* (1888) 39 Ch D 339 at 365; *Larratt v Bankers and Traders Insurance Co Ltd* (1941) 41 SR (NSW) 215 at 226. Compare the position where an insurance contract is discharged: see *Bank of Nova Scotia v Hellenic Mutual War Risks Association (Bermuda) Ltd* [1992] 1 AC 233 (see Malcolm Clarke, [1991] *LMCLQ* 437; Mark Leeming, (1992) 5 *JCL* 163).
482. See, eg *McDonald v Dennys Lascelles Ltd* (1933) 48 CLR 457 at 469–70; *Photo Production Ltd v Securicor Transport Ltd* [1980] AC 827 at 849; *Re Dingjan; Ex parte Wagner* (1995) 183 CLR 323 at 341; 128 ALR 81.
483. [1980] 1 WLR 1129 at 1141. See further [2229] and generally on recovery of liquidated sums after termination [2225]–[2241].
484. See [1993].
485. *Laird v Pim* (1841) 7 M & W 474; 151 ER 852.
486. See [1972].
487. *Newbon v City Mutual Life Assurance Society Ltd* (1935) 52 CLR 723 at 733.
488. See [1979]–[1980].
489. See J W Carter and J C Phillips, 'The Liability of Debtors and Guarantors Under Contracts Discharged for Breach' (1992) 22 *UWALR* 338.
490. (1933) 48 CLR 457.
491. (1933) 48 CLR 457 at 476–7 (adopted *Johnson v Agnew* [1980] AC 367 at 396).

unconditionally acquired. Rights and obligations which arise from the partial execution of the contract and causes of action which have accrued from its breach alike continue unaffected. When a contract is rescinded because of matters which affect its formation, as in the case of fraud, the parties are to be rehabilitated and restored, so far as may be, to the position they occupied before the contract was made. But when a contract, which is not void or voidable at law, or liable to be set aside in equity, is dissolved at the election of one party because the other has not observed an essential condition or has committed a breach going to its root, the contract is determined so far as it is executory only and the party in default is liable for damages for its breach.

Of course, Dixon J was using the word 'rescinded', in the sense of 'terminated'. As already mentioned, in the context of breach, it is preferable to use the terminology of termination or discharge.[492]

[1989] Types of accrued rights. There are two types of rights either (or both) of which may survive termination: the right to damages; and the right to receive performance of a contractual obligation. If an accrued right exists, it is not divested by termination even if it exists for the benefit of the party whose breach or repudiation led to termination.[493]

The assessment of damages is considered in detail later.[494] At this stage it is sufficient to say that because termination discharges the unperformed obligations of a promisor, the promisor may be held liable to pay damages not only in respect of the obligations which fell due for performance prior to termination, but also in respect of obligations which would have fallen due for performance after termination.

When it is said that the right to receive performance of a contractual obligation may survive termination, the reference is usually to obligations to pay sums fixed by the contract. These may be enforced by way of an action in the nature of debt. Other types of obligations may be enforceable by way of injunction, but specific performance is not available. However, the fact that an obligation to pay a fixed sum should have been discharged prior to termination does not necessarily imply that an accrued right exists in respect of the obligation. As Dixon J explained in *McDonald v Dennys Lascelles Ltd*,[495] the right must have been 'unconditionally' acquired by reason of the 'partial execution' of the contract.[496]

The survival of accrued rights, and the effects of termination, have sometimes been explained in terms of a distinction between primary and secondary obligations.[497] Although termination discharges the primary obligations of the parties, that is, those obligations expressly or impliedly created by the contract, it does not discharge the secondary obligations of the parties, that is, those obligations which arise by operation of law on the breach of primary contractual obligations. The chief secondary obligation is a promisor's obligation to pay damages for breach. This is not discharged

---

492. *Photo Production Ltd v Securicor Transport Ltd* [1980] AC 827 at 844; Mr Justice McGarvie, 'Contractual Concepts of the Credit Bills' (1979) 53 *ALJ* 687.
493. See [2157]; [2225].
494. See especially [2157]–[2161].
495. (1933) 48 CLR 457 at 477 (see [1988]).
496. See [2228]–[2238].
497. See A L Corbin, 'Conditions in the Law of Contract' (1919) 28 *Yale LJ* 739 at 745; *Photo Production Ltd v Securicor Transport Ltd* [1980] AC 827 at 848–50.

by termination even though the primary obligation breached by the promisor is discharged so that, in most cases, the secondary obligation is *substitutive* in character.

However, some primary obligations do survive termination, because of the express or implied intention of the parties. In these cases the secondary obligation is *additional* to the primary obligation. It is because termination usually discharges all 'unperformed' primary obligations that the promisee is so frequently unable to enforce a primary obligation after termination.

Restitutionary Claims

[1990] Restitutionary claim for benefit conferred. A restitutionary claim may be enforceable after termination to recover in respect of a benefit conferred prior to termination. The benefit may be money paid prior to termination, or goods or services supplied.

[1991] Termination a requirement for restitution. Restitutionary claims of the type referred to in the preceding paragraph can only be pursued after the performance of the contract has been terminated.[498] They are distinguishable from claims for damages, and actions to recover liquidated sums due under the contract.

Restitutionary claims are based on the principle of unjust enrichment. They depend on elements of injustice and benefit rather than the presence of breach. Moreover, although termination is essential there is no requirement that the claim be pursued by the party who elected to terminate. This means that, for example, a promisor may claim restitution of a monetary payment on the basis of a total failure of consideration even though a breach or repudiation on the promisor's part led to termination.[499]

Terms Operating After Termination

[1992] Operation of terms a question of construction. Whether or not a contractual term operates after termination is a question of construction.[500] If the parties expressly provide that a particular term is (or is not) to be enforceable after termination the construction question presents no great difficulties. Usually, however, there is no express agreement on the matter and the court is left to decide what the parties must, as reasonable persons, have intended.

If the court decides that a term was intended to survive termination, two further questions may arise for decision. First, if the term operates in favour of the party whose breach or repudiation led to termination, was the intention of the parties contingent on that party not being in breach of contract?[501]

---

498. *McDonald v Dennys Lascelles Ltd* (1933) 48 CLR 457; *Update Constructions Pty Ltd v Rozelle Child Care Centre Ltd* (1990) 20 NSWLR 251. In the 19th century *rescission* (ab initio) was treated as a necessary requirement for restitutionary claims. See, eg *De Bernardy v Harding* (1853) 8 Ex 822; 155 ER 1586. See further [2339].
499. See further [2324].
500. See *Photo Production Ltd v Securicor Transport Ltd* [1980] AC 827.

Second, is the term unenforceable, by reason of a legal restriction based on public policy or statute?[502]

[1993] Types of terms likely to survive termination. Where there is no express agreement, in order to decide whether a term was intended to survive termination regard will be had, mainly, to the nature of the term sought to be enforced. Some terms, such as exclusion clauses[503] and agreed damages clauses,[504] deal with the consequences of breach and must usually be intended to operate after termination.

The decision in *Harbutt's 'Plasticine' Ltd v Wayne Tank and Pump Co Ltd*,[505] which suggested that termination for fundamental breach necessarily precludes the enforcement of an exclusion clause, was overruled by the House of Lords in *Photo Production Ltd v Securicor Transport Ltd*;[506] and in *Port Jackson Stevedoring Pty Ltd v Salmond & Spraggon (Aust) Pty Ltd*[507] the Privy Council found no difficulty in applying *Securicor*, when giving its advice on an appeal from the High Court. The Privy Council said that the basis for applying the exclusion clause in question after termination was that it regulated the 'manner in which liability'[508] was to be established.

A term regulating liability, such as the exclusion clause in the *Port Jackson* case, is quite different from a term creating a primary contractual obligation. Generally, a term creating a primary obligation is not enforceable after termination except by way of a claim for damages.[509] However, some such terms are intended to operate after termination. For example, a term requiring an employee not to disclose confidential information, or a term restraining an employee from competing with his or her employer may be intended to operate after termination.

A further distinction can be drawn between procedural and substantive contractual terms. A substantive primary obligation, such as that created by a term requiring the payment of interest on unpaid sums payable to the promisee, will not usually be enforceable after termination except by way of a claim for damages.[510] On the other hand, a procedural term, such as an agreement to submit disputes to arbitration, is generally intended by the parties to be enforceable notwithstanding termination.[511]

[1994] Enforcement by party in breach. The fact that the party seeking to enforce a term after termination breached the contract should be

---

501. See [1994].
502. See [1995].
503. See Brian Coote, 'The Effect of Discharge by Breach on Exception Clauses' [1970] *CLJ* 221.
504. See generally [2207]–[2217]. For a specific statement on the effect of termination see *International Leasing Corp (Vic) Ltd v Aiken* [1967] 2 NSWR 427 at 440.
505. [1970] 1 QB 447.
506. [1980] AC 827.
507. [1981] 1 WLR 131 (see [349], [925]).
508. [1981] 1 WLR 131 at 145.
509. See *Moschi v Lep Air Services Ltd* [1973] AC 331 at 345, 350.
510. *F J Bloemen Pty Ltd v Gold Coast City Council* [1973] AC 115.
511. See *Photo Production Ltd v Securicor Transport Ltd* [1980] AC 827 at 850 and further [1994]. Even a *Scott v Avery* clause (see [1626]) may be enforceable for this reason (see *Woolf v Collis Removal Service* [1948] 1 KB 11) although it is perhaps better regarded as enforceable on the basis that it regulates rights and liabilities.

irrelevant to its enforcement, unless it can be implied that the right to enforce was conditional on the absence of breach. Obviously this implication will not be applicable to exclusion clauses since, by definition, they operate to protect a party in breach. However, statute or a public policy rule may apply.

Where a term is substantive in nature it will usually be unenforceable after termination except by way of a claim for damages.[512] Procedural clauses, on the other hand, are frequently intended to operate notwithstanding termination and are usually enforceable on that basis. For example, in *Heyman v Darwins Ltd*[513] the House of Lords held that the arbitration clause was enforceable even though the party who was seeking its enforcement was alleged to be in breach of contract.

Employment contracts sometimes contain restraint clauses intended to operate after termination. A restraint clause does not fit neatly into the distinction between substantive and procedural terms. A claim for damages against the employee will be available, but the employer is usually more concerned with injunctive relief, ideally before the term has been breached. Assuming that the clause does not infringe public policy[514] it will be enforceable according to its terms if the employer was not in breach at the time of termination.[515] In *General Billposting Co Ltd v Atkinson*[516] the employers claimed both damages and an injunction but were refused relief because they had wrongfully dismissed the employee. Notwithstanding that the restraint clause imposed a restriction on the employee's right to trade after termination, the House of Lords held that the discharge of the contract precluded enforcement. Lord Robertson said[517] that the clause was 'germane' to the contract of service and unenforceable after the contract of service was 'rescinded'. Lord Collins said[518] that the employee was entitled to consider himself 'absolved' from further performance of the contract, including the restraint clause.

The same approach was taken by the High Court in *Kaufman v McGillicuddy*.[519] However, the view that a restraint clause is not enforceable following termination because it is a material term of the contract looks to contradict the general approach, outlined above, emphasising the intention of the parties. The decisions would be more compelling if they had been based on the view that the parties must have intended the restraint clause to be enforceable only if the employers were not in breach.[520]

[1995] Public policy and statute. Even if the parties intended certain terms of the contract to be enforceable after termination, public policy or statute may intervene to make the terms unenforceable or void. For

---

512. See [1993].
513. [1942] AC 356.
514. See [1634]–[1654].
515. See, eg *Home Counties Dairies Ltd v Skilton* [1970] 1 WLR 526 (see [1649]).
516. [1909] AC 118.
517. [1909] AC 118 at 121.
518. [1909] AC 118 at 122. The Earl of Halsbury agreed.
519. (1914) 19 CLR 1.
520. The court may, in the exercise of its discretion (see [2416]), refuse to grant relief on the basis of the employer's breach. See *Geraghty v Minter* (1979) 142 CLR 177 at 187; 26 ALR 141.

example, an agreed damages clause may infringe the rule against penalties,[521] and a restraint clause may infringe public policy.[522] Thus, an alternative (and perhaps more compelling) basis for cases such as *General Billposting Co Ltd v Atkinson*[523] is that it is against public policy to permit an employer to enforce a restraint clause where the employer's breach has led to termination.[524]

The statutory restrictions on the use of exclusion clauses were explained earlier[525] and an exclusion clause caught by the restrictions will not be enforceable after termination even if the parties have indicated a contrary intention. And a general statute, such as the *Contracts Review Act* 1980 (NSW) will preclude the enforcement of an 'unjust' term.[526]

---

521. See [2207].
522. See [1634]–[1654].
523. [1909] AC 118 (see [1994]).
524. See *Rock Refrigeration Ltd v Jones* [1997] 1 All ER 1, CA (see Charles Wynn-Evans, (1997) 113 *LQR* 377).
525. See [769]–[772].
526. See [1515]–[1530].

Chapter 20

Termination by Frustration

The Doctrine of Frustration 2001
   General 2001
   Law or Fact? 2005
   Evidence of Frustration 2007

Scope of the Doctrine 2011
   Impossibility of Performance 2011
   Frustration of Purpose 2018
   Illegality 2021
   Delay 2025
   War 2028
   Contracts Involving Land 2031

Foresight and Terms Dealing with Frustration 2038
   Foresight of the Event 2038
   Terms Dealing with Frustration 2040

Self-induced Frustration 2043

Basis of the Doctrine 2049

Consequences of Frustration 2057
   Common Law Principles 2057
   Under Statute 2068

The Doctrine of Frustration

General

[2001] The concept. The modern concept of frustration was stated in the following terms by Lord Radcliffe in *Davis Contractors Ltd v Fareham UDC*:[1]

---

1. [1956] AC 696 at 729 (adopted *Codelfa Construction Pty Ltd v State Rail Authority of New South Wales* (1982) 149 CLR 337; 41 ALR 367).

[F]rustration occurs whenever the law recognises that without default of either party a contractual obligation has become incapable of being performed because the circumstances in which performance is called for would render it a thing radically different from that which was undertaken by the contract. Non haec in foedera veni. It was not this that I promised to do.

The statement indicates that the concept of frustration is concerned with the position of the parties to a contract when, without default of either party, performance of the contract has been radically changed. Where the concept operates, the event which brings about the 'radical' change is usually referred to as a 'frustrating' event.[2]

[2002] **Frustrating events.** Since frustration necessarily depends on the terms of the contract and the circumstances of the particular case, it is not possible to define, except in general terms, what constitutes a frustrating event. However, it is clear that the event must have severe consequences.

Under Lord Radcliffe's formulation[3] the event must not merely alter the circumstances in which performance is called for; there must be a 'radical' change. Other formulations of the concept also emphasise the strictness of the requirement, by referring:

- to an event which would make further performance 'a thing different in substance'[4] from that contracted for;
- to an event which creates a 'fundamentally'[5] different situation; or
- to an event which deprives a party with further obligations to perform of 'substantially the whole benefit which it was the intention of the parties as expressed in the contract that he should obtain'[6] from performing those obligations.

[2003] **Absolute contracts.** The mere fact that an event deprives a party to a contract of benefits which were expected from its performance, or even renders performance physically impossible, does not imply that the doctrine of frustration can be used as an excuse for not performing, since a party may be found to have taken the risk of such an eventuality,[7] or undertaken an absolute promise to perform. A distinction must therefore be drawn between absolute obligations on the one hand, and conditional (or dependent), obligations on the other. If an obligation is absolute, the promisor must perform, if that is physically possible, and if not pay damages for breach of contract.[8] Whether or not a party to a contract has undertaken an absolute obligation depends on the construction of the

---

2. See *Qantas Airways Ltd v Christie* (1998) 193 CLR 280 at 317; 152 ALR 365 at 393 per Gummow J. The concept may also operate if a series of events combine to make performance radically different. See, eg *Pioneer Shipping Ltd v BTP Tioxide Ltd* [1982] AC 724 at 738, 744.
3. See [2001].
4. *Metropolitan Water Board v Dick Kerr & Co Ltd* [1917] 2 KB 1 at 30 (affirmed [1918] AC 119).
5. *British Movietonews Ltd v London and District Cinemas Ltd* [1952] AC 166 at 185.
6. *Hongkong Fir Shipping Co Ltd v Kawasaki Kisen Kaisha Ltd* [1962] 2 QB 26 at 66 per Diplock LJ.
7. *Horlock v Beal* [1916] 1 AC 486 at 525.
8. *Taylor v Caldwell* (1863) 3 B & S 826 at 833; 122 ER 309 at 312. See, eg *Ockerby & Co Ltd v Watson* (1918) 25 CLR 431; *Re De Garis and Rowe's Lease* [1924] VLR 38.

contract.[9] The question which then arises is whether an obligation, absolute in terms, must necessarily be construed as such.

In the 17th century a literal approach was taken to this question of construction. Thus, in *Paradine v Jane*[10] it was said that when 'a party by his own contract creates a duty or charge upon himself, he is bound to make it good, if he may, notwithstanding an accident by inevitable necessity, because he might have provided against it by his contract'. Although there are statements in some of the modern cases which assume that this dictum is still applicable,[11] it is generally accepted that a contract framed in absolute terms need not be construed as absolute in effect.[12] For example, if a promisor agrees to allow the promisee to stage a play at his or her theatre, destruction of the theatre will frustrate the contract, and excuse the promisor, even though the promise was made in absolute terms. In truth, the unqualified statement in *Paradine v Jane* is not consistent with the modern law of frustration.[13]

[2004] Contracts to which the doctrine applies. The doctrine has been applied, and the following kinds of contracts held to be frustrated:

- construction contracts;[14]
- contractual licences;[15]
- employment contracts;[16]
- contracts for the sale of goods;[17]
- voyage and time charterparties;[18]
- trading agreements;[19] and
- contracts between the members of an unincorporated association.[20]

Although this list does not purport to be exhaustive, it does indicate the variety of contexts in which the doctrine has been applied. It also illustrates

---

9. See [1855].
10. (1647) Aleyn 26 at 27; 82 ER 897. The court was prepared to adopt a more lenient view in cases where the duty was implied by law and the promisor had 'no remedy over'. Although this type of distinction was referred to in later cases (eg *Connor v Spence* (1878) 4 VLR (L) 243 at 258) it is seldom applied today.
11. See, eg *Matthey v Curling* [1922] 2 AC 180 at 235; *Scanlan's New Neon Ltd v Tooheys Ltd* (1943) 67 CLR 169 at 198.
12. *Joseph Constantine SS Line Ltd v Imperial Smelting Corp Ltd* [1942] AC 154 at 184.
13. *Cricklewood Property and Investment Trust Ltd v Leighton's Investment Trust Ltd* [1945] AC 221 at 237; *National Carriers Ltd v Panalpina (Northern) Ltd* [1981] AC 675 at 706. But see *F C Shepherd & Co Ltd v Jerrom* [1987] QB 301 at 321. See also Barry Nicholas, 'Fault and Breach of Contract' in Beatson and Friedmann, eds, *Good Faith and Fault in Contract Law*, 1995, p 337. Cf A J Morris, 'Practical Reasoning and Contract as Promise: Extending Contract-Based Criteria to Decide Excuse Cases' [1997] *CLJ* 147.
14. *Metropolitan Water Board v Dick Kerr & Co Ltd* [1918] AC 119; *Codelfa Construction Pty Ltd v State Rail Authority of New South Wales* (1982) 149 CLR 337.
15. *Krell v Henry* [1903] 2 KB 740.
16. See, eg *Simmons Ltd v Hay* (1964) 81 WN (Pt 1) (NSW) 358.
17. See, eg *Comptoir d'Achat et de Vente du Boerenbond Belge SA v Luis de Ridder Limitada (The Julia)* [1949] AC 293.
18. See, eg *Jackson v Union Marine Insurance Co Ltd* (1874) LR 10 CP 125; *Bank Line Ltd v Arthur Capel & Co* [1919] AC 435.
19. *Denny Mott & Dickson Ltd v James B Fraser & Co Ltd* [1944] AC 265.
20. *Re The Unley Democratic Association* [1936] SASR 473.

the 'flexibility'[21] of the doctrine. Therefore, although contracts involving land still give rise to certain difficulties,[22] the general principle, undoubtedly, is that prima facie the doctrine is applicable to any type of contract.

Law or Fact?

[2005] Frustration a conclusion of law. Where a court or commercial arbitrator concludes that a particular contract has (or has not) been frustrated, that conclusion is one of law.[23] There are two reasons for this. First, the conclusion always involves a consideration of the terms of the contract, and the proper construction of contractual documents is an issue of law, not fact.[24]

Second, the application of the concept of frustration to the circumstances relied upon as frustrating the contract involves the application of a legal principle.[25]

[2006] Factual elements. Where an event is relied upon as frustrating the contract, the event is 'something which happens in the world of fact'.[26] This factual element explains why the question of frustration is sometimes said to be a 'mixed' question of law and fact.[27] In other words, in reaching the conclusion of law, due regard must be had to the evidence relied upon as frustrating the contract.

Sometimes the factual element of frustration will be extremely important, for example, in cases where an event has caused delay in performance.[28] The factual element is emphasised in English cases where a marked reluctance has been shown to interfere with the conclusions of commercial arbitrators. Because the assessment of matters such as delay is often largely a matter of impression on which opinions are likely to differ, the view has been taken that it is wrong to interfere with the arbitrator's conclusion unless the wrong test has been applied, or a perverse or unreasonable conclusion was reached.[29]

Because of the factual element, the relevant conclusion of law will, in many cases, be 'almost completely determined'[30] by what the judge or

---

21. *Cricklewood Property and Investment Trust Ltd v Leighton's Investment Trust Ltd* [1945] AC 221 at 235, 241; *National Carriers Ltd v Panalpina (Northern) Ltd* [1981] AC 675 at 701, 712.
22. See [2031]–[2037].
23. *Tsakiroglou & Co Ltd v Noblee Thorl GmbH* [1962] AC 93. Cf *Scanlan's New Neon Ltd v Tooheys Ltd* (1943) 67 CLR 169 at 222–3.
24. See [701].
25. *National Carriers Ltd v Panalpina (Northern) Ltd* [1981] AC 675 at 717.
26. *Denny Mott & Dickson Ltd v James B Fraser & Co Ltd* [1944] AC 265 at 276. See also *Universal Cargo Carriers Corp v Citati* [1957] 2 QB 401 at 435; *F C Shepherd & Co Ltd v Jerrom* [1987] QB 301 at 316.
27. See, eg *Davis Contractors Ltd v Fareham UDC* [1956] AC 696 at 735.
28. See [2025].
29. See *Pioneer Shipping Ltd v BTP Tioxide Ltd* [1982] AC 724; *Kodros Shipping Corp of Monrovia v Empresa Cubana de Fletes (The Evia (No 2))* [1983] 1 AC 736. See also *F C Shepherd & Co Ltd v Jerrom* [1987] QB 301 (industrial tribunal's error in interpreting rules governing a contract of employment).
30. *Tsakiroglou & Co Ltd v Noblee Thorl GmbH* [1962] AC 93 at 124.

arbitrator determines as the commercial significance of the event relied upon as frustrating the contract. Nevertheless, as Lord Diplock said in *Pioneer Shipping Ltd v BTP Tioxide Ltd*,[31] no matter how closely the conclusion of law may seem to follow from findings about the commercial significance of differences found to exist between what the parties bargained for and their position after the occurrence of the event relied upon as frustrating the contract, frustration is 'never a pure question of fact'.

Evidence of Frustration

[2007] Data for decision. In *Denny Mott & Dickson Ltd v James B Fraser & Co Ltd*[32] Lord Wright explained that where frustration is alleged to have taken place the data for reaching a decision on the issue are:

(1) the terms and construction of the contract; and

(2) the events which have occurred.

[2008] Construction of the contract. Assuming that the contract is in or evidenced by writing, construction of the contract involves the interpretation of a written document and is a question of law to which the parol evidence rule applies.[33] If the parties have expressly dealt with the event relied upon as frustrating the contract then the position is, subject to considerations of public policy in the case of illegality, governed by the express terms.[34]

Assuming that the parties have not expressly dealt with the event, or not dealt with it sufficiently, the contract must be construed in the light of the circumstances existing at the time when it was made.[35] It is legitimate to have regard to the circumstances surrounding the contract, that is, the 'factual matrix' against which it was entered into.[36] Such evidence may enable the court to identify a common assumption of the parties which was essential to the contract,[37] or the 'foundation', 'substance' or 'basis' of the contract.[38]

[2009] Evidence of the event. Evidence of the event relied upon as frustrating the contract is not admitted for the purpose of construing it and the parol evidence rule has no relevance. The purpose of the evidence is to show that the contract cannot be performed in the way contemplated by the parties.

---

31. [1982] AC 724 at 738. See also *Simmons Ltd v Hay* (1964) 81 WN (Pt 1) (NSW) 358 at 361.
32. [1944] AC 265 at 274–5.
33. See generally [705]–[712].
34. See further [2040]–[2042].
35. *F A Tamplin SS Co Ltd v Anglo-Mexican Petroleum Products Co Ltd* [1916] 2 AC 397 at 403.
36. See *F A Tamplin SS Co Ltd v Anglo-Mexican Petroleum Products Co Ltd* [1916] 2 AC 397 at 403; *Scanlan's New Neon Ltd v Tooheys Ltd* (1943) 67 CLR 169 at 222 and generally [713]–[715].
37. *Codelfa Construction Pty Ltd v State Rail Authority of New South Wales* (1982) 149 CLR 337.
38. *Krell v Henry* [1903] 2 KB 740 at 749.

Generally, the question of frustration must be considered at the time when the event relied upon as frustrating the contract occurred.[39] Later events, such as conduct of the parties, may be some evidence of the view to be taken by 'informed minds',[40] but is not conclusive. Thus, in cases where a party to the contract has acted on the basis that the contract was frustrated, and behaved as an 'informed' commercial person would, that party is generally permitted to invoke the doctrine even though subsequent events show that the contract would not have been frustrated.

[2010] **Relevance of prior cases.** Although it may be helpful, when considering whether a given event has frustrated a particular contract, to look at the impact of similar events on similar types of contracts, each fact situation must be considered on its own merits and the conclusion to be reached will seldom, if ever, be dictated by an earlier decision.

Even where a particular event, such as the closure of the Shatt-al-Arab waterway by the war between Iran and Iraq, is likely to frustrate a large number of contracts, no two cases will be identical. Thus, the House of Lords in *Kodros Shipping Corp of Monrovia v Empresa Cubana de Fletes (The Evia (No 2))*[41] saw no conflict between the decision of the commercial arbitrator in that case and earlier decisions in which arbitrators had found similar charterparty contracts in respect of vessels trapped in the waterway to have been frustrated on a different date from that chosen by the arbitrator, because the charterparties in question may well have been of 'differing characteristics and of different lengths'. The question, therefore, is not whether one case resembles another but whether, applying the test of frustration, the particular circumstances of the case justify the invocation of the doctrine.[42]

Scope of the Doctrine

Impossibility of Performance

[2011] **Scope of impossibility.** Most cases of frustration involve an element of impossibility. Apart from the obvious cases where performance by either (or both) of the parties is physically impossible, for example, because the subject matter of the contract has been destroyed, the legal concept of impossibility encompasses situations where performance is not literally impossible, but is 'impracticable in a commercial sense'.[43]

[2012] **Destruction of subject matter.** The doctrine of frustration first emerged in cases where specific subject matter had been destroyed (or perished) without the fault of either party. For example, in *Taylor v Caldwell*[44] the defendants agreed to allow the plaintiffs to use the Surrey

---

39. *Scanlan's New Neon Ltd v Tooheys Ltd* (1943) 67 CLR 169 at 184; *National Carriers Ltd v Panalpina (Northern) Ltd* [1981] AC 675 at 706. For the position in cases of delay see [2026].
40. *Hirji Mulji v Cheong Yue SS Co Ltd* [1926] AC 497 at 509.
41. [1983] 1 AC 736 at 768.
42. See *Pioneer Shipping Ltd v BTP Tioxide Ltd* [1982] AC 724 at 752.
43. *Horlock v Beal* [1916] 1 AC 486 at 492.

Gardens and Music Hall for four days in July and August 1861 for the purpose of concerts and fetes. On 11 June the Music Hall was destroyed by fire and the court held that the contract was discharged by this event as the Music Hall was essential to the performance of the contract.

It is important to identify the subject matter of the contract. For example, in *Turner v Goldsmith*[45] the defendants employed the plaintiff to sell goods 'manufactured or sold' by them. The contract was not frustrated by the destruction of the defendants' factory because the subject matter was not confined to goods which they manufactured.

The fact that the subject matter of the contract has been destroyed will not amount to frustration if either party has agreed, expressly or impliedly, to bear the risk of destruction, or guaranteed that the subject matter will remain in existence.[46] For example, under the sale of goods legislation[47] an agreement to sell specific goods is 'avoided' if the goods 'perish before the risk passes to the buyer'. Although the risk of destruction frequently passes at the time when property in the goods is transferred to the buyer, this is not necessarily the case. However, once the risk has passed, destruction of the goods does not frustrate the contract and the buyer will be liable to the seller.

[2013] Availability of subject matter. Even if the subject matter of the contract remains in existence, the contract may be frustrated if it ceases to be available to the parties. For example, in *Hirji Mulji v Cheong Yue SS Co Ltd*[48] a time charterparty entered into on 17 November 1916 provided that the vessel should be placed at the charterers' disposal for 10 months from 1 March 1917. Shortly before that date the vessel was requisitioned, and it continued in government service until late in February 1919. At the latest the contract was frustrated in the latter part of 1917, when it was clear that the vessel could not be made available to the charterers.[49]

The fact that the subject matter will not be available for the entire period of the contract need not frustrate its performance: regard must be had to the delay which is likely to occur.[50] Where the contemplated duration of the contract is long, a temporary unavailability will not amount to frustration. For example, in *F A Tamplin SS Co Ltd v Anglo-Mexican Petroleum Products Co Ltd*[51] a five-year time charterparty was not frustrated when requisition caused the vessel to be unavailable. The charter had nearly three years to run, and release of the vessel might well take place in time to allow performance of a significant proportion of the contract.

---

44. (1863) 3 B & S 826; 122 ER 309.
45. [1891] 1 QB 544. Contrast *Reilly v R* [1934] AC 176 (abolition of statutory office).
46. See *Goldsbrough Mort & Co Ltd v Carter* (1914) 19 CLR 429 at 437–8, 443–4, 446–9.
47. See **ACT:** *Sale of Goods Act* 1954, s 12; **NSW:** *Sale of Goods Act* 1923, s 12; **NT:** *Sale of Goods Act* 1972, s 12; **Qld:** *Sale of Goods Act* 1896, s 10; **SA:** *Sale of Goods Act* 1895, s 7; **Tas:** *Sale of Goods Act* 1896, s 12; **Vic:** *Goods Act* 1958, s 12; **WA:** *Sale of Goods Act* 1895, s 7.
48. [1926] AC 497.
49. Cf *Austin v Sheldon* [1974] 2 NSWLR 661 (see [2033]).
50. See also [2025]–[2027].
51. [1916] 2 AC 397.

[2014] Availability of source of supply. Where a supplier's source is not available to satisfy the requirements of a contract, the question of frustration depends on two matters:

(1) the reason the source is not available; and

(2) the scope of the supplier's promise.

If a supplier's source is not available because of external events, such as government prohibition or destruction by fire, flood and so on, the supplier may be in a position to invoke the doctrine of frustration. On the other hand, if the failure is due simply to a decision to supply another person who has offered a higher price, the doctrine will not be applicable because the 'frustration' is 'self-induced'.[52]

A supplier who has expressly or impliedly agreed to bear the risk of a particular source not being available will be unable to invoke the doctrine, should that source not be available to satisfy the contract. For example, if a seller has agreed to sell 'New South Wales wheat' of a specified quality, with the intention of obtaining a supply of goods from a contract with a particular dealer, acquisition of that dealer's wheat by the government does not constitute frustration.[53] On the other hand, where the contract identifies a particular source, such as the crop to be grown on the seller's land, frustration will occur if, through no fault of the seller, the crop fails.[54]

[2015] Death and incapacity. Where the performance of a contract has a personal element, death or incapacity may frustrate its performance. For example, the death of an employee frustrates a contract of employment.[55] Similarly, frustration will occur if an artist engaged to prepare a drawing is 'attacked with blindness'.[56] Similarly, in *Simmons Ltd v Hay*[57] a printery engineer was permanently incapacitated by illness, so that he was not able to discharge his contractual duties, and the contract of employment was frustrated.

In cases of temporary incapacity, the issue of frustration will depend on the kind of contract, the extent of incapacity and its expected duration. For example, if a pianist is unable to give a concert because of illness, the contract will be discharged if only one concert is anticipated. Thus, the pianist will not be liable to pay damages for breach and the employer is entitled to cancel the concert.[58] In *Horlock v Beal*[59] the detention of a vessel by German authorities in the First World War was held to frustrate the

---

52. See further [2043]–[2048].
53. *Gelling v Crespin* (1917) 23 CLR 443. See also *J Lauritzen AS v Wijsmuller BV (The Super Servant Two)* [1990] 1 Lloyd's Rep 1 (see [2043]). Cf *Universal Cargo Carriers Corp v Citati* [1957] 2 QB 401 (see [1943]).
54. Cf *Howell v Coupland* (1876) 1 QBD 258. Contrast *Sharp v Batt* (1930) 25 Tas LR 33 (source not identified).
55. *Taylor v Caldwell* (1863) 3 B & S 826 at 835–7; 122 ER 309 at 313. Cf *Cutter v Powell* (1795) 6 TR 320; 101 ER 573 (see [1824]). See also *Lobb v Vasey Housing Auxiliary (War Widows Guild)* [1963] VR 239 (agreement for lease or licence).
56. *Jackson v Union Marine Insurance Co Ltd* (1874) LR 10 CP 125 at 145.
57. (1964) 81 WN (Pt 1) (NSW) 358.
58. See *Robinson v Davison* (1871) LR 6 Ex 269.
59. [1916] 1 AC 486. See also *Whim Well Copper Mines Ltd v Pratt* (1910) 12 WALR 166.

contract of employment between a member of the crew and the owner of the vessel because it made it impossible for the crew members to perform their duties.

Where the contract does not involve a specific task, but instead envisages a long-term relationship, it will be more difficult to establish that the contract has been frustrated by a temporary incapacity. Apart from the difficulty of identifying the period of the incapacity, and its impact on the contract, modern contracts of employment frequently contain provisions dealing with sickness benefits. Moreover, superannuation schemes frequently provide for retirement in the event of permanent medical incapacity. These may leave little room for discharge under the doctrine of frustration.[60] But if an employee is incapacitated for what will, in all probability, be an unreasonably long period of time, the contract must usually be frustrated.

If the contract is frustrated the parties are discharged and, for example, an employee is not to be regarded as in breach of contract by not turning up for work. However, it should not be assumed that a conclusion that the contract has *not* been frustrated necessarily means the incapacitated party is liable in damages. In fact, almost invariably the party in question, for example, an incapacitated employee, is temporarily excused from performance.[61]

[2016] Contemplated method of performance not possible. Where parties contract on the basis that their bargain will be performed in a particular way, and that method of performance is not possible, the contract may be discharged under the doctrine of frustration. For example, in *Cornish & Co v Kanematsu*[62] a contract for the sale of goods provided that shipment was to be made 'per P & O steamer sailing from Japan about the 7 September and coming direct to Sydney'. However, no such vessel was despatched and so the mode of performance contemplated became impossible. The court held that the contract was frustrated.[63]

The decision can be contrasted with that in *Tsakiroglou & Co Ltd v Noblee Thorl GmbH*,[64] where a CIF contract for the sale of Sudanese groundnuts, to be delivered at Hamburg, was not frustrated by closure of the Suez Canal. The parties contemplated shipment from Port Sudan, and the seller intended to send the goods through the Canal. After its closure the performance of the contract was still possible since the goods could have been sent via the Cape of Good Hope. The court held that this change in the method of performance was not so material as to frustrate the contract. The position might have been different had the goods been of a more perishable kind.

---

60. *Finch v Sayers* [1976] 2 NSWLR 540 at 558. But cf *Notcutt v Universal Equipment Co (London) Ltd* [1986] 1 WLR 641 (see John McMullen, (1986) 49 *MLR* 785; G J McCarry, (1987) 61 *ALJ* 35; David Howarth, [1987] *CLJ* 47).
61. See further [2061] (force majeure clauses).
62. (1913) 13 SR (NSW) 83.
63. See also *Codelfa Construction Pty Ltd v State Rail Authority of New South Wales* (1982) 149 CLR 337.
64. [1962] AC 93.

[2017] **Increased burden of performance.** Generally, the fact that the performance of a contract has become more onerous because of the occurrence of an event not contemplated by the parties to the contract does not amount to frustration. For example, in another of the Suez Canal cases, *Ocean Tramp Tankers Corp v V/O Sovfracht (The Eugenia)*,[65] the closure of the Canal did not frustrate a charterparty even though a voyage from Odessa to India around the Cape would have taken 138 days, and a voyage through the Canal some 30 days less.

On the other hand, in *Codelfa Construction Pty Ltd v State Rail Authority of New South Wales*,[66] an increase in the burden of performance did amount to frustration. The contractors' burden of performance was increased when the issue of an injunction delayed the carrying out of excavation work required by the contract. The High Court considered that the situation created by the injunction was radically different from anything contemplated by the parties.[67] The parties had fixed a specific period of time within which the work was to be completed while labouring under the misapprehension that the contractors would have the benefit of the Rail Authority's statutory immunity from injunction for nuisance. The lack of immunity severely disrupted the parties' calculations. Performance had not simply become more onerous, performance in the way contemplated by the parties had become impossible.

Frustration of Purpose

[2018] **The principle of *Krell v Henry*.** An extension of the doctrine of frustration was made in *Krell v Henry*,[68] one of the 'Coronation Cases'. The plaintiff hired a flat in Pall Mall to the defendant for 26 and 27 June 1902. Although not mentioned in the contract, its purpose was to enable the defendant to view the Royal Coronation procession of Edward VII, a point reflected by the fact that the hire was for the days 'but not the nights'. The procession was cancelled owing to the King's illness and the court held that this frustrated the contract. The basis for the decision was that the procession was 'regarded by both contracting parties as the foundation of the contract'.[69] The decision did not therefore depend on impossibility, there was nothing impossible in doing what the parties had agreed to do; rather, performance was rendered 'pointless'.[70]

For a time *Krell v Henry* was viewed with suspicion. Although it is now accepted as correct, care must be taken not to treat every change in

---

65. [1964] 2 QB 226. See also *Scottish Halls Ltd v The Minister* (1915) 15 SR (NSW) 81 at 89–90.
66. (1982) 149 CLR 337. See Jane Swanton, 'Discharge of Contracts by Frustration: *Codelfa Construction Pty Ltd v State Rail Authority of New South Wales*' (1983) 57 *ALJ* 201. See also *Scottish Halls Ltd v The Minister* (1915) 15 SR (NSW) 81 (resumption of land). Contrast *Davis Contractors Ltd v Fareham UDC* [1956] AC 696 (labour shortage).
67. The case was remitted to the arbitrator for his decision on the issue.
68. [1903] 2 KB 740.
69. [1903] 2 KB 740 at 750.
70. *Empresa Exportadora de Azucar v Industria Azucarera Nacional SA (The Playa Larga)* [1983] 2 Lloyd's Rep 171 at 187 per Ackner LJ.

circumstances as frustration, even if the expectation of one of the parties is to some extent 'frustrated' by an extraneous event.

[2019] Uncontemplated turn of events not necessarily sufficient. The mere fact that an event which was not contemplated by the parties when they entered into the contract has occurred does not amount to frustration.[71] The purpose of the contract must be frustrated, that is, the facts must involve the 'cessation or non-existence of an express condition or state of things going to the root of the contract, and essential to its performance'.[72] The point is illustrated by *Herne Bay Steam Boat Co v Hutton*,[73] another of the Coronation Cases. The plaintiffs agreed to place one of their vessels at the defendant's disposal on 28 and 29 June 1902 'for the purpose of seeing the naval review and for a day's cruise round the fleet'. Owing to the King's illness the review was cancelled and the defendant argued that this frustrated the purpose of the contract. However, the court held that as the review was not the foundation of the contract it was not frustrated by the cancellation of the review. The event which had happened did not make the contract pointless and the defendant could still employ the vessel in a cruise around the fleet.

[2020] Disappointed expectations. Events frequently occur which cause the expectations of contracting parties to be disappointed. However, disappointment is not synonymous with frustration, and the purpose of a contract is not frustrated merely because the benefits which a party expected to obtain from its performance are not realised in full.[74] For example, in *Scanlan's New Neon Ltd v Tooheys Ltd*[75] two contracts for the hire of neon signs were not frustrated when governmental orders prohibited the signs being illuminated. The orders were made as security measures during the Second World War and were indefinite in duration. No doubt the hirers' expectations were to some extent disappointed, but the owners did not guarantee that the signs could be illuminated and the orders did not interfere with the performance of the contracts. The hirers were taken to have agreed to bear the risk that the use of the signs might be affected.[76]

Illegality

[2021] Concern with supervening illegality. The topic of illegality was dealt with earlier[77] from the point of view of contracts void or unenforceable at the time of formation. The present concern is with *supervening illegality*, that is, cases in which the performance of the contract becomes illegal after formation but before it has been discharged by performance.

---

71. *British Movietonews Ltd v London and District Cinemas Ltd* [1952] AC 166 at 185.
72. *Krell v Henry* [1903] 2 KB 740 at 748.
73. [1903] 2 KB 683.
74. *Davis Contractors Ltd v Fareham UDC* [1956] AC 696 at 715.
75. (1943) 67 CLR 169.
76. See also *Consolidated Neon (Phillips System) Pty Ltd v Tooheys Ltd* (1942) 42 SR (NSW) 152; *Claude Neon Ltd v Hardie* [1970] Qd R 93.
77. Chapters 16 and 17.

The distinction between the two cases cannot always be maintained. For example, a contract may require a government consent or licence and be perfectly legal because of a term in the contract requiring one of the parties to obtain the consent or licence. If the consent or licence cannot be obtained or is revoked, the performance of the contract becomes illegal, and may therefore be frustrated. Thus, in *Gamerco SA v ICM/Fair Warning (Agency) Ltd*[78] the plaintiffs — concert promoters in Spain — obtained a permit to stage the defendants' concert at a particular stadium in Madrid. The venue was found to be unsafe and the permit was revoked. Garland J held that the contract was frustrated when the use of the stadium was banned. It is not clear whether this was a decision that frustration occurred because performance at the agreed venue had become impossible, or a decision that frustration occurred because performance became illegal. The better view is that the contract was frustrated by subsequent illegality rather than the construction defect.

Nevertheless, a contract is not necessarily void for illegality or frustrated if a valid licence cannot be obtained, since the party who promised to obtain the consent or licence may have taken the risk of that eventuality.[79]

[2022] Impossibility and illegality. Discharge by supervening illegality, while frequently dealt with under the heading 'frustration', is a common law rule of general application[80] and much wider than the doctrine of frustration.[81]

In cases where the illegality results from the application of a foreign law the discharge of the parties arises because of impossibility. For example, if A, in country X, agrees to sell goods to B, in country Y, and the contract provides for delivery at a port in Y, frustration by illegality may occur if the government of Y prohibits importation of goods of the kind dealt with by the contract. Although in all other cases the discharge has a wider basis than impossibility, the legal consequences of the discharge are, at common law, the same as under the doctrine of frustration.[82]

[2023] Contracts with the enemy. Where the performance of a contract involves trading with the enemy during war-time the contract will be regarded as illegal and frustrated. For example, in *Fibrosa Spolka Akcyjna v Fairbairn Lawson Combe Barbour Ltd*[83] an English company agreed to sell machinery to a Polish company and to deliver the machinery at Gdynia, Poland. When Poland was occupied by German forces during the course of the Second World War prior to delivery, the contract became illegal and its performance was regarded as frustrated. The decision can be contrasted with *Cooper & Sons v Neilson & Maxwell Ltd*,[84] where a contract for the sale

---

78. [1995] 1 WLR 1226 (see J W Carter and Gregory Tolhurst, (1996) 10 *JCL* 264).
79. See *Bangladesh Export Import Co Ltd v Sucden Kerry SA* [1995] 2 Lloyd's Rep 1.
80. *Joseph Constantine SS Line Ltd v Imperial Smelting Corp Ltd* [1942] AC 154 at 163.
81. See Treitel, *The Law of Contract*, 10th ed, 1999, p 826 ('the court has to take into account, not only the relative interests of the parties, but also the interests of the public in seeing that the law is observed').
82. See *Consolidated Neon (Phillips System) Pty Ltd v Tooheys Ltd* (1942) 42 SR (NSW) 152 at 157.
83. [1943] AC 32. See also [1625].
84. [1919] VLR 66.

of 'Continental steel shoeing bars' was not frustrated by illegality even though the seller had intended to obtain the goods from Germany. The seller could obtain the goods from another country without trading with a German supplier since the contract did not require the seller to obtain the goods from any particular source.

[2024] Disappearance of the foundation of the contract. In cases which do not involve trading with the enemy it may be difficult to decide whether the contract is frustrated when affected by illegality. Decisions such as *Scanlan's New Neon Ltd v Tooheys Ltd*[85] illustrate the obvious point that the mere fact that a party cannot enjoy the full benefit of the contract because of supervening illegality does not give rise to frustration. On the other hand, if the foundation of the contract disappears because of illegality it must be regarded as frustrated. For example, in *Denny Mott & Dickson Ltd v James B Fraser & Co Ltd*[86] a trading agreement provided, inter alia, for the purchase of pine wood. Subsequently, an order was made under the *Defence Regulations* (UK) which had the effect of making it illegal for the sellers to supply the timber at the price stipulated, and a later order prevented the importation of timber as contemplated by the contract. The House of Lords held that as the trading in timber was the 'main object' of the contract it was frustrated once trading became illegal.

The *Denny Mott* case also illustrates that illegality which may be only temporary can frustrate a contract. Where the contract requires work to be done, or the provision of services, frustration will occur if the interruption to the contract will in all probability be so long as to destroy the identity of the work or service when resumed, with the work or service when interrupted.[87]

Delay[88]

[2025] The criterion for delay. The fact that an event not contemplated by the parties causes some delay in performance, or renders impossible performance at the appointed time, need not amount to frustration. In order for the delay to give rise to frustration it must be such as radically to alter the performance of the contract. For example, in *Jackson v Union Marine Insurance Co Ltd*[89] a charterparty provided that the vessel would proceed with all possible dispatch from Liverpool to Newport for the purpose of loading a cargo of iron rails which were to be transported to San Francisco. On its way to Newport the vessel ran aground. The delay involved in repairing the vessel would have been prolonged, and the jury found that the time taken would have been so long as to make it unreasonable to require the charterers to supply the agreed cargo. The Exchequer Chamber held that this finding justified a decision that the contract was frustrated, because the delay would have made the venture one entirely different from that contemplated by the contract.

---

85. (1943) 67 CLR 169 (see [2020]).
86. [1944] AC 265.
87. *Metropolitan Water Board v Dick Kerr & Co Ltd* [1918] AC 119 at 128; *Ringstad v Gollin & Co Pty Ltd* (1924) 35 CLR 303 at 315.
88. See J E Stannard, 'Frustrating Delay' (1983) 46 *MLR* 738.
89. (1874) LR 10 LP 125.

Although the court in *Jackson v Union Marine Insurance* spoke in terms of 'unreasonable' delay[90] it is now accepted, in commercial contracts at least, that it is preferable to speak in terms of 'frustrating' delay.[91] Whether the criterion is satisfied is a question of fact.[92]

[2026] Time for assessment. The general rule of frustration, that the impact of an event relied on as a frustrating event must be assessed at the time of its occurrence,[93] although relevant to cases of delay,[94] gives rise to difficulty since it will rarely be certain how long the interruption to performance will last. In commercial contracts, where certainty is essential, the parties must be entitled to act when they come to know of the delay.[95] In such contracts the applicable principle is that stated by Scrutton J in *Embiricos v Sydney Reid & Co*:[96]

> Commercial men must not be asked to wait till the end of a long delay to find out from what in fact happens whether they are bound by a contract or not; they must be entitled to act on reasonable commercial probabilities at the time when they are called upon to make up their minds.

This statement, which has been approved on a number of occasions,[97] indicates that a party is entitled to consider itself discharged by an event which has caused delay before the delay actually frustrates the contract. This indicates the relevance of prospective delay.[98]

[2027] Prospective delay. In *Jackson v Union Marine Insurance Co Ltd*[99] it was acknowledged that reliance may be placed on prospective delay. This is obvious enough in cases where some delay has actually occurred; but reliance may also be placed on delay which is entirely prospective.

This was established in *Embiricos v Sydney Reid & Co*.[100] The plaintiff chartered a vessel (sailing under the Greek flag) to the defendants to proceed to a port in the Sea of Azoff and there to load a cargo of grain for any direct port to the United Kingdom. The vessel passed through the Dardanelles into the Black Sea and on arrival at her loading port received some cargo. Loading was discontinued, and never resumed, when the shippers learned that Greek vessels were being seized and detained at the Dardanelles by Turkish authorities. Later, the Turkish Government allowed laden Greek vessels to pass through the Dardanelles until 24 October 1912. Although lay days were not due to expire until 22 October, it would not have been possible for the defendants to load a complete cargo and to pass through the Dardanelles within the period of the permission. The defendants therefore cancelled the charterparty. However, the period of

---

90. See also *Geipel v Smith* (1872) LR 7 QB 404 at 411; *Nobel's Explosives Co v Jenkins & Co* [1896] 2 QB 326 at 331.
91. *Universal Cargo Carriers Corp v Citati* [1957] 2 QB 401 at 434–5.
92. *Dahl v Nelson* (1881) 6 App Cas 38 at 48; *Universal Cargo Carriers Corp v Citati* [1957] 2 QB 401 at 435.
93. See [2009].
94. See *National Carriers Ltd v Panalpina (Northern) Ltd* [1981] AC 675 at 706.
95. *Bank Line Ltd v Arthur Capel & Co* [1919] AC 435 at 454.
96. [1914] 3 KB 45 at 54.
97. See, eg *Watts Watts & Co Ltd v Mitsui & Co Ltd* [1917] AC 227 at 246.
98. See [2027].
99. (1874) LR 10 CP 125 (see [2025]).
100. [1914] 3 KB 45.

permission was unexpectedly extended, and had the defendants waited they would have been able to load a complete cargo. Scrutton J held that even though the delay would not in fact have frustrated the contract, the defendants could invoke the doctrine of frustration. At the time of their cancellation of the charterparty reasonable commercial probabilities pointed to a frustrating delay: it did not matter that no delay had actually occurred, and the subsequent events could not be used to exclude the defendants' defence.

These cases show that a contract may be treated as discharged by frustration, on account of delay, before the frustrating delay actually occurs. However, there will be cases in which it is necessary to wait upon events in order to see whether delay will make performance radically different.[101] For example, where a strike delays the performance of a contract the court may say that the parties should wait, to see how long the strike is likely to last and to determine the prospects for an early settlement of the labour dispute. Accordingly, the event relied upon must reasonably — objectively — give rise to the inference that it will cause such delay as will frustrate the contract.[102] If the court decides that a reasonable person would not have drawn the inference of frustration, the contract is not frustrated, and a party who has treated the contract as frustrated will be regarded as having repudiated its obligation to perform the contract.

War

[2028] Outbreak of war may frustrate contract. The outbreak of war is capable of by itself frustrating a contract,[103] as the cases involving trading with the enemy[104] clearly indicate. However, the fact that a declaration of war impinges on performance does not necessarily indicate that frustration has occurred.[105] For example, the effect may be simply to make performance more onerous,[106] without making it radically different.

Unless the contract involves trading with the enemy, it is usually the acts done in furtherance of war, rather than the declaration itself, which frustrates the contract. This was the position in the cases involving charterparties which were frustrated because of the trapping of vessels in the Shatt-al-Arab waterway. Frustration occurred, not because of the war between Iran and Iraq per se, but because the fighting made leaving the waterway too dangerous.[107]

[2029] Impossibility and illegality. Clear cases of frustration by war involve illegality or impossibility of performance. If performance of the

---

101. See *Pioneer Shipping Ltd v BTP Tioxide Ltd* [1982] AC 724 at 752, 754.
102. Cf *Dahl v Nelson* (1881) 6 App Cas 38 at 54. Subsequent events may assist in showing what the probabilities actually were. See *Bank Line Ltd v Arthur Capel & Co* [1919] AC 435 at 454; *Denny Mott & Dickson Ltd v James B Fraser & Co Ltd* [1944] AC 265 at 277–8.
103. *Horlock v Beal* [1916] 1 AC 486 at 507, 508.
104. See [2023].
105. *Finelvet AG v Vinava Shipping Co Ltd* [1983] 1 WLR 1469.
106. See, eg *Cooper & Sons v Neilson & Maxwell Ltd* [1919] VLR 66.
107. See, eg *Kodros Shipping Corp of Monrovia v Empresa Cubana de Fletes (The Evia (No 2))* [1983] 1 AC 736.

contract involves trading with the enemy it will be illegal.[108] In *Metropolitan Water Board v Dick Kerr & Co Ltd*[109] a construction contract was frustrated, when the Ministry of Munitions lawfully ordered the work to cease, because legal performance of the contract then became impossible.

It is because the illegality must go further than merely making performance of the contract less beneficial to one of the parties that the contracts in *Scanlan's New Neon Ltd v Tooheys Ltd*[110] were not frustrated. The illumination of the signs had become illegal, but the signs had advertising value during daylight hours, and no impossibility of performance could be established. The position in *Dick Kerr* was different because the interruption to the work was of such a nature as radically to alter the contract.

[2030] Contracts entered into in time of war. Where a contract is entered into after war has been declared it may be difficult to establish frustration because the parties may be assumed to have accepted the risk that the war will disrupt the contract. For example, contracts for the sale of goods made during time of war are not likely to be frustrated when the war causes delivery to be delayed.[111] And in *British Movietonews Ltd v London and District Cinemas Ltd*[112] an agreement for the supply of newsreels was not frustrated when *Defence Regulations* (UK) had the effect of reducing the consumption of raw film stock even though the regulations continued to operate after the war had ended.

There are, however, quite a few cases in which frustration has occurred. For example, in *Comptoir d'Achat et de Vente du Boerenbond Belge SA v Luis de Ridder Limitada (The Julia)*[113] a contract for the sale of goods between an Argentine company and Belgian sellers was frustrated by occupation of the port of delivery by German forces. Again, in *Bank Line Ltd v Arthur Capel & Co*[114] a charterparty entered into during the First World War was frustrated by requisition of the vessel even though the parties foresaw the possibility of requisition.[115] In both cases war interfered with the performance of the contracts. In *The Julia* the port was invaded while the goods were in transit, so that the contract became illegal. In *Bank Line* the requisition was for an indefinite duration.

Contracts Involving Land

General

[2031] The problem. The courts have been reluctant to extend the contractual doctrine of frustration to contracts involving land because of the distinction between property and contract. A contract involving land will frequently confer a proprietary interest on one of the parties. The

---

108. See [2023].
109. [1918] AC 119.
110. (1943) 67 CLR 169 (see [2020]).
111. Cf *Ringstad v Gollin & Co Pty Ltd* (1924) 35 CLR 303.
112. [1952] AC 166.
113. [1949] AC 293.
114. [1919] AC 435.
115. See further [2040].

interest may be equitable, as where a vendor agrees to sell land to a purchaser, or legal, as is conferred by the execution (and registration) of a lease. Allied to the theoretical problem there are at least three practical problems. First, such contracts are so common that the incidence of risk between the parties was worked out long ago, and application of the doctrine might upset this.

Second, land is much more permanent than the subject matter of most other contracts.

Third, discharge, when frustration occurs, is automatic[116] and independent of the volition of the parties,[117] so that application of the doctrine to a contract involving land may transfer the proprietary interest irrespective of the knowledge or wishes of the parties.

Options and sale of land contracts

[2032] Options. Although there appears to be little authority on the point, it would seem that an option to purchase or lease land is subject to the frustration doctrine. For example, the trading agreement which was held to be frustrated by illegality in *Denny Mott & Dickson Ltd v James B Fraser & Co Ltd*[118] contained an option to purchase (or take on long lease) a timber yard. The court did not see the existence of the option as an impediment to application of the frustration doctrine.

[2033] Sale of land. The doctrine of frustration is not likely to apply to many sale of land cases. For example, destruction of the buildings on the land by fire will not work a frustration because the risk of such destruction rests with the purchaser[119] who, in any event, still has unimproved land to build on. However, there is authority to support the proposition that the doctrine of frustration applies to an executory contract, notwithstanding that the contract confers an equitable interest on the purchaser. For example, in *Wong Lai Ying v Chinachem Investment Co Ltd*,[120] contracts for the sale of flats in two tower blocks were frustrated by an unforeseen (and unforeseeable) landslip which 'seriously interrupted' the building of the blocks after building had commenced. The Privy Council emphasised that after the landslip the earliest date for completion was nearly 30 months after the latest date for completion specified by the contract.

Generally speaking, in the absence of a specific provision dealing with the event, a purchaser is taken to have assumed the risk of not being able to develop or use the land in a particular way. Thus, the occurrence of an event which prevents the purchaser developing the land in the way intended does not amount to frustration.[121] However, in *Austin v Sheldon*,[122] where six out of the seven acres which the vendor had agreed to sell were resumed, Mahoney J held that frustration had occurred.[123] Since the

---

116. See [2058].
117. See [2059].
118. [1944] AC 265 (see [2024]).
119. *British Traders' Insurance Co Ltd v Monson* (1964) 111 CLR 86. Cf *Scottish Special Housing Association v Wimpey Construction UK Ltd* [1986] 1 WLR 995 (construction contract). See also *Fletcher v Manton* (1940) 64 CLR 37 (demolition pursuant to government order).
120. (1979) 13 Build LR 81.

purchaser was also held to be entitled to the compensation payable in respect of the resumption the result seems rather peculiar.[124]

Leases[125]

[2034] Agreement for lease. In *National Carriers Ltd v Panalpina (Northern) Ltd*[126] the House of Lords accepted as correct the proposition that the doctrine of frustration applies to an agreement to execute a lease of land. Although there is no Australian authority directly supporting this,[127] there is indirect support in cases on the frustration of contracts for the sale of land, and the application of the doctrine of *repudiation* to an agreement to execute a lease.[128] In principle, if the repudiation of an agreement to execute a lease is a basis for termination by the other party, termination by frustration is a legal possibility.

[2035] Leases: English law. Until the decision of the House of Lords in *National Carriers Ltd v Panalpina (Northern) Ltd*[129] the prevailing view in England[130] was that the doctrine of frustration did not apply to leaseholds. However, in the *Panalpina* case the majority (Lord Russell dissenting) took a contrary view, and the position in England is now settled. In reaching its decision, the majority gave the following reasons to justify the application of the doctrine.

First, the distinction between land and other types of property should not be overdone; the doctrine of frustration is flexible and capable of being applied to new situations.

Second, it is wrong to say that a lessee takes the risk of frustration unless the lessee has expressly agreed that a particular event, which would frustrate the lease, is to terminate the lease.

Third, it is also wrong to compartmentalise contracts in a way which restricts the application of general contractual principles. For example, the

---

121. *Meriton Apartments Pty Ltd v McLaurin & Tait (Developments) Pty Ltd* (1976) 133 CLR 671. Cf *Amalgamated Investment & Property Co Ltd v John Walker & Sons Ltd* [1976] 3 All ER 509. See also *E Johnson & Co (Barbados) Ltd v NSR Ltd* [1997] AC 400 (see Peter Butt, (1996) 70 *ALJ* 795).
122. [1974] 2 NSWLR 661.
123. Cf *SJR Investment Co Pty Ltd v Housing Commission of Victoria* (1970) 22 LGRA 318. See also *McMahon v Sydney County Council* (1940) 40 SR (NSW) 427. Contrast *Scanlan's New Neon Ltd v Tooheys Ltd* (1943) 67 CLR 169 at 229.
124. Mahoney J took the view (see [1974] 2 NSWLR 661 at 667) that the issue of frustration was independent of the entitlement to compensation.
125. See J T Robertson, 'Frustrated Leases: "No to Never — But Rarely if Ever"' (1982) 60 *Can B Rev* 619.
126. [1981] AC 675 at 690, 694, 705, 715.
127. Cf *Lobb v Vasey Housing Auxiliary (War Widows Guild)* [1963] VR 239.
128. *Dimond v Moore* (1931) 45 CLR 159.
129. [1981] AC 675 (see Donald Robertson, (1984) 9 *Syd LR* 674).
130. As expressed by the Court of Appeal in *Leighton's Investment Trust Ltd v Cricklewood Property and Investment Trust Ltd* [1943] KB 493. On appeal, sub nom *Cricklewood Property and Investment Trust Ltd v Leighton's Investment Trust Ltd* [1945] AC 221, although the decision was unanimously affirmed, the House was evenly divided on the issue whether the doctrine applies to leaseholds.

doctrine applies to contractual licences[131] and it is often difficult to distinguish a licence from a lease.

Fourth, the distinction between the equitable interest conferred by an agreement for a lease and the legal estate transferred by the grant of a lease does not justify the non-application of the doctrine to leases.

[2036] Leases: Australian law. The Australian authorities are in a confused state. In *Halloran v Firth*[132] the court said that the 'present state of the authorities shows a considerable body of legal authority in support of the proposition that the doctrine of "frustration" does not apply to a demise by which an estate in land is created and passed to the lessee'. On appeal to the High Court[133] Knox CJ and Gavan Duffy J said that they agreed with the decision of the Supreme Court and the reasons given to support the conclusion that there was no frustration of the lease in issue. Although Isaacs J agreed with the Supreme Court's decision, he rejected the proposition that the doctrine can never be applied to leases.

As a matter of precedent one would have thought that the High Court's decision in *Firth* would be conclusive against the application of the doctrine in Australia.[134] However, the decision did not achieve any prominence in the subsequent decisions. For example, in *Scanlan's New Neon Ltd v Tooheys Ltd*[135] Williams J said that the doctrine is only excluded by the lessee taking possession, and in *Minister of State for the Army v Dalziel*[136] he relied on English authority[137] for the proposition that the 'doctrine of frustration does not apply to leases'. More puzzling still is the fact that Ligertwood J, in *Shiell v Symons*,[138] and McClemens J in *Robertson v Wilson*,[139] should consider themselves free from any binding authority and justified in treating the leases there in issue as frustrated. And, when Walsh J in *Thearle v Keeley*[140] considered himself bound by authority to hold that the doctrine does not apply, he relied principally on English cases.

Notwithstanding the uncertainty apparent in the cases referred to above, the State and Territory Supreme Courts remain bound by *Firth*. However, for two reasons it is suggested that when the High Court considers this issue it will decide that the doctrine applies to leases. First, there is the fact that in *Codelfa Construction Pty Ltd v State Rail Authority of New South Wales*[141] the court approved certain passages in *National Carriers Ltd v Panalpina (Northern) Ltd*.[142]

---

131. See, eg *Krell v Henry* [1903] 2 KB 740 (see [2018]).
132. (1926) 26 SR (NSW) 183 at 187.
133. Sub nom *Firth v Halloran* (1926) 38 CLR 261. But see [1936] (repudiation).
134. See *Re The Equity Trustees Executor & Agency Co Ltd and Considine's Contract* [1932] VLR 137 at 144.
135. (1943) 67 CLR 169 at 228.
136. (1944) 68 CLR 261 at 302. Contrast *Scanlan's New Neon Ltd v Tooheys Ltd* (1943) 67 CLR 169 at 202.
137. *Matthey v Curling* [1922] 2 AC 180.
138. [1951] SASR 82 at 88. Contrast *Re De Garis and Rowe's Lease* [1924] VLR 38, where an argument based on impossibility was rejected because the lease was construed as absolute in character.
139. (1958) 75 WN (NSW) 503.
140. (1958) 76 WN (NSW) 48 at 50.
141. (1982) 149 CLR 337.
142. [1981] AC 675.

Second, it is now clear that the doctrine of repudiation applies to leases.[143]

[2037] Circumstances in which the doctrine might apply. Accepting the argument that ultimately the doctrine of frustration will be applied to leaseholds in Australia, the circumstances in which the doctrine might apply may be considered, always bearing in mind the opinion of the majority in *National Carriers Ltd v Panalpina (Northern) Ltd*[144] that the doctrine will rarely operate to frustrate a lease. In *Cricklewood Property and Investment Trust Ltd v Leighton's Investment Trust Ltd*[145] Viscount Simon said that, in a simple lease for a term of years under which the lessee is free to use the land as the lessee wishes, he could not imagine frustration occurring unless some 'vast convulsion of nature swallowed up the property altogether, or buried it in the depths of the sea'. However, less catastrophic events may frustrate a lease. In the *Panalpina* case Lord Hailsham LC and Lord Simon said[146] that coastal erosion would do equally as well.

When considering the impact of any event, consideration must be given to the duration of the lease and its object. The longer the term of the lease the more serious must be the event. For example, a long lease is not likely to be frustrated by requisitioning of the property, if it will keep the lessee out of possession for only a few years. A 'singularly harsh decision'[147] from the lessee's point of view was reached in *Matthey v Curling*.[148] Possession of demised premises was taken by military authorities towards the end of a 21-year lease and the lessee kept out of possession until after the expiry of the term. The lessee was held bound by his covenant to rebuild when the premises were destroyed by fire during the occupation, notwithstanding that their destruction was not his fault, because the temporary occupation did not frustrate the lease.

In commercial and building leases it is, theoretically at least, 'less difficult'[149] to establish a case of frustration. However, in the *Cricklewood* case a 99-year building lease was not frustrated by war-time building restrictions. And in *Panalpina* a 10-year lease of warehouse premises was not frustrated when the only access to the warehouse ceased to be available due to a road closure, notwithstanding that it was of a 'sort that might be frustrated',[150] because on the facts the interruption was only likely to last about 20 months and the lessees would be able to use the warehouse for nearly three years after the interruption ceased.

---

143. See [1936] and *Progressive Mailing House Pty Ltd v Tabali Pty Ltd* (1985) 157 CLR 17 esp at 28; 57 ALR 609, where reference is made to the English frustration cases. But note Brennan J's statement ((1985) 157 CLR 17 at 41) that frustration and repudiation are distinct modes of termination to which different consequences attach.
144. [1981] AC 675.
145. [1945] AC 221 at 229.
146. [1981] AC 675 at 691, 700–1.
147. *National Carriers Ltd v Panalpina (Northern) Ltd* [1981] AC 675 at 715.
148. [1922] 2 AC 180.
149. *Cricklewood Property and Investment Trust Ltd v Leighton's Investment Trust Ltd* [1945] AC 221 at 229.
150. [1981] AC 675 at 706.

The type of lease most likely to be frustrated is a short-term residential lease where the main purpose of the demise is habitation of the buildings on the land. For example, demolition of the premises pursuant to the order of a health authority as part of a slum clearance program would in all likelihood frustrate the lease.[151]

Foresight and Terms Dealing with Frustration

Foresight of the Event[152]

[2038] Event must generally be unforeseen. Although not reproduced in Lord Radcliffe's statement of the concept of frustration in *Davis Contractors Ltd v Fareham UDC*,[153] it is usually said that the event relied upon as frustrating the contract must not have been foreseen by the parties.[154] In fact, he said[155] that one reason why a shortage of labour did not frustrate the construction contract being considered was that the 'possibility of enough labour and materials not being available was before their eyes and could have been the subject of special contractual stipulation'. Therefore, if the event was foreseen, and the contract contains no provision covering the event, the inference will usually be drawn that the parties agreed to bear the risk of the occurrence of the event. The contract will not be frustrated.

As against the body of authority supporting the general proposition stated above, there is a statement by Lord Denning MR in *Ocean Tramp Tankers Corp v V/O Sovfracht (The Eugenia)*:[156]

> It has frequently been said that the doctrine of frustration only applies when the new situation is 'unforeseen' or 'unexpected' or 'uncontemplated', as if that were an essential feature. But it is not so. The only thing that is essential is that the parties should have made no provision for it in their contract. The only relevance of it being 'unforeseen' is this: If the parties did not foresee anything of the kind happening, you can readily infer they have made no provision for it: whereas, if they did foresee it, you would expect them to make provision for it.

However, this statement arguably confuses the question of construction to be dealt with shortly,[157] namely, whether the parties have dealt with the event relied upon as frustrating the contract, with the issue of whether the absence of a specific provision implies that either (or both) of the parties agreed to bear the risk of the event. It is also arguable that Lord Denning assumed too wide a criterion of foresight. The mere fact that the parties

---

151. See *Shiell v Symons* [1951] SASR 82 at 88; *Robertson v Wilson* (1958) 75 WN (NSW) 503.
152. Cf C G Hall, 'Frustration and the Question of Foresight' (1984) 4 *Legal Studies* 300.
153. [1956] AC 696 at 729 (see [2001]).
154. See, eg *Krell v Henry* [1903] 2 KB 740 at 751; *Paal Wilson & Co A/S v Partenreederei Hannah Blumenthal* [1983] 1 AC 854 at 909. See also [2039].
155. [1956] AC 696 at 731. See also *Silva v Tarval Pty Ltd* (1986) 4 BPR 9101.
156. [1964] 2 QB 226 at 239.
157. See [2040].

foresaw an event of the same kind as that relied upon is not a sufficient ground for saying that the event was foreseen.[158]

[2039] Extent of foresight required. The extent of foresight required has not been the subject of detailed discussion in the authorities. Three points are, however, consistent with the authorities. First, the fact that the parties foresaw the possibility of the *cause* of the frustrating event occurring is not sufficient. For example, the parties to a charterparty might foresee the possibility of the vessel being delayed by hostilities, and make provision for an alternative loading port. The fact that the same hostilities prevent loading at the alternative port does not necessarily mean that the doctrine is excluded, since the parties may not have foreseen the possibility of delay at the alternative port for a long period of time.

Second, it would seem that a fairly strict standard of foreseeability applies. The parties must be found to have foreseen the occurrence of the event as a serious possibility. The fact that the event was *reasonably* foreseeable is not sufficient to exclude the doctrine. For example, in *Simmons Ltd v Hay*[159] the employers knew, at the time when the plaintiff was employed as a printery engineer, that he was not a well man, but they could not reasonably have contemplated that he would suffer a disease of a permanently incapacitating character.

Third, the fact that the parties have foreseen the possibility that performance might be interfered with or interrupted, for example, by war or illness, does not necessarily prevent the contract being discharged by frustration, because the extent of the interference or interruption may be much greater than anything contemplated. For example, in *W J Tatem Ltd v Gamboa*[160] the defendant chartered a ship from the plaintiffs during the Spanish Civil War for 30 days. It was assumed that the parties contemplated the possibility of the vessel being seized and detained by the Nationalists, but the occurrence of this event was nevertheless held to frustrate the contract because the vessel had been detained for a period of time which was much longer than anything contemplated.

Terms Dealing with Frustration

[2040] Scope of contractual provisions. Whether or not a contractual provision deals with the event relied upon as frustrating the contract in such a way as to prevent the parties being discharged under the doctrine of frustration depends on the construction of the contract.[161]

If the contract contains express provisions which indicate sufficiently the consequences which are to result from the occurrence of the event the parties' rights will be regulated by the express terms, and there will be no room for the operation of the doctrine.[162] For example, in *Claude Neon Ltd v Hardie*[163] a contract for the hire of a neon sign was not frustrated by the

---

158. Cf *Beaton v McDivitt* (1987) 13 NSWLR 162 at 176–7.
159. (1964) 81 WN (Pt 1) (NSW) 358 (see [2015]). But cf *Krell v Henry* [1903] 2 KB 740 at 751–2.
160. [1939] 1 KB 132. See also *Metropolitan Water Board v Dick Kerr & Co Ltd* [1918] AC 119; *Simmons Ltd v Hay* (1964) 81 WN (Pt 1) (NSW) 358.
161. *Bank Line Ltd v Arthur Capel & Co* [1919] AC 435 at 455–6.

resumption of the premises on which the sign was erected because of a term in the contract providing that the hirer was to be 'deemed to have made default' under the contract in the event of, inter alia, his 'interest' in the premises being 'extinguished or transferred'. The resumption was held to be an event within the clause, and since the parties had clearly indicated the result which was to flow, namely, default under the contract, there was no room for discharge under the doctrine of frustration.

More frequently, however, the courts have found contractual provisions to be incomplete or insufficient. For example, in *Bank Line Ltd v Arthur Capel & Co*[164] a vessel the subject of a time charterparty was requisitioned by the British Government prior to its delivery to the charterers. Two clauses were relied on as indicating that the requisition did not frustrate the charter. Clause 26 conferred on the charterers an option to cancel if the vessel was not delivered before a certain date. Clause 31 gave the charterers an option to cancel if the vessel was commandeered by the government. The House of Lords held that these provisions did not deal completely with the event relied on (by the owners) as frustrating the contract. Clause 26 was not inconsistent with the owners being automatically discharged by an event which produced a radical change in the nature of the contract, and since it dealt only with the position of the charterers, cl 31 did not exclude the possibility of a radical change resulting from a requisition of the vessel. Clause 31 gave the charterers an option to cancel in the event of requisition. For the owners to rely on frustration they had to prove more than requisition per se: it was also necessary for the requisition to be such as radically to change the nature of the contract.

A similar result was reached in *Metropolitan Water Board v Dick Kerr & Co Ltd*[165] where the construction contract was frustrated when the Minister of Munitions ordered work to cease and directed the contractors to sell a large portion of their plant. Although there was a possibility that the work might be resumed at a later date, the stoppage was likely to continue for an unreasonably long period of time. A term in the contract providing for the engineer to extend the time for completion was inadequate to deal with the delay which was likely to occur. The decision was reached notwithstanding that the term purported to deal with 'any difficulties or impediments ... whatsoever or howsoever occasioned', because the term could not be read literally. In all likelihood the interruption to the work would render the contractual obligations of the parties radically different from those contemplated.

[2041] Public policy. A contractual provision which would otherwise be effective to exclude the operation of the doctrine of frustration is not enforceable if contrary to public policy. This is clearly the case where a contract involves trading with the enemy.[166] For example, in *Ertel Bieber &*

---

162. *Empresa Exportadora de Azucar v Industria Azucarera Nacional SA (The Playa Larga)* [1983] 2 Lloyd's Rep 171 at 188; *Thors v Weekes* (1989) 92 ALR 131 at 142. Cf *Re Comptoir Commercial Anversois v Power Son & Co* [1920] 1 KB 868.
163. [1970] Qd R 93.
164. [1919] AC 435. See also *Wong Lai Ying v Chinachem Investment Co Ltd* (1979) 13 Build LR 81.
165. [1918] AC 119. See also *Simmons Ltd v Hay* (1964) 81 WN (Pt 1) (NSW) 358.

Co v Rio Tinto Co Ltd[167] contracts for the supply of sulphur contained terms providing for the suspension of the parties' obligations in the event of prevention of performance by, inter alia, war. The suppliers were an English company and the buyers German companies. Once war between England and Germany was declared the contracts became illegal because performance would involve trading with the enemy. The illegality frustrated the contracts, notwithstanding the suspensory terms, either because the terms did not extend to the event which had occurred or because, if they did, were contrary to public policy and unenforceable.

[2042] **Frustration under a contractual term.** Even if the occurrence of an event does not frustrate a contract under the common law, the event may bring into play an express term providing for the discharge of the parties. For example, a contract for the sale of goods might provide for its cancellation in the event of shipment of the goods proving to be impossible during the contract period by reason of a government prohibition.[168] An event within such a clause provides a defence for failure to perform irrespective of whether the event would also have frustrated the contract.

Where an express term merely protects one of the parties, the doctrine of frustration, if applied, will excuse or discharge the other. For example, in *Jackson v Union Marine Insurance Co Ltd*[169] the failure of the vessel to arrive in time for the voyage was caused by an excepted peril and the charterers therefore had no cause of action against the shipowner. The court held that the charterers were discharged, not by any express term of the contract, but, instead, under the doctrine of frustration.

Self-induced Frustration[170]

[2043] **No frustration where event self-induced.** Lord Radcliffe's statement of the frustration[171] concept posits the absence of 'default' by either of the parties. Where the event relied on as frustrating the contract occurs because of 'blame', 'fault' or 'default', the contract is not frustrated because reliance cannot be placed on self-induced frustration. Frustration may be regarded as self-induced by reason of default arising from an act or an omission by the parties. For example, in the leading case on the topic, *Maritime National Fish Ltd v Ocean Trawlers Ltd,*[172] charterers of a steam trawler sought to rely on the failure of a Minister to license the vessel's use of an otter trawl as frustrating their contract with the owners of the vessel. Because the vessel was fitted with a trawl the licence was essential to its use, as required by the contract, in the fishing industry. However, the Privy Council held that any frustration of the contract had been self-induced. The Minister had granted three licences for the charterers' five trawlers and

---

166. See [2023].
167. [1918] AC 260.
168. Cf *Bremer Handelsgesellschaft mbH v Vanden Avenne-Izegem PVBA* [1978] 2 Lloyd's Rep 109.
169. (1874) LR 10 CP 125 (see [2025]).
170. See Jane Swanton, 'The Concept of Self-Induced Frustration' (1990) 2 *JCL* 206.
171. *Davis Contractors Ltd v Fareham UDC* [1956] AC 696 at 729 (see [2001]).
172. [1935] AC 524. Contrast *Re The Unley Democratic Association* [1936] SASR 473.

it was their decision not to apply one of these licences to the vessel under the charterparty.

A more recent illustration is provided by *J Lauritzen AS v Wijsmuller BV (The Super Servant Two)*,[173] where a contract for the carriage of a large and heavy drilling rig provided for carriage of the rig by either the *Super Servant One* or the *Super Servant Two*, at the carriers' option.[174] Prior to carriage of the goods the *Super Servant Two*, on which the defendants intended to transport the rig, became a total loss. Although there had been no intimation to the plaintiffs of the intention to use the vessel (the carriers' option was not exercised), the defendants contended that the loss of the *Super Servant Two*, and the unavailability of the other vessel due to commitments to other persons, frustrated the contract of carriage. The argument was rejected by the court since the contract did not oblige them to use the *Super Servant Two*, and their inability to use the other vessel was, for the purposes of self-induced frustration, their own fault.

[2044] Must the act or omission be deliberate? Although there is no doubt that a deliberate act by one of the parties is sufficient to constitute self-induced frustration[175] (assuming that the act involves default), it is doubtful whether this is necessary. In *Joseph Constantine SS Line Ltd v Imperial Smelting Corp Ltd*[176] Viscount Simon LC said that 'default' is a 'much wider term and in many commercial cases dealing with frustration is treated as equivalent to negligence'. However, he left open the question whether, in a contract for personal services, personal incapacity arising from want of care would be sufficient.[177]

In *J Lauritzen AS v Wijsmuller BV (The Super Servant Two)*[178] the English Court of Appeal treated negligence as sufficient to prevent reliance on frustration, at least where it is a cause of the event alleged to constitute frustration.

[2045] Must the act or omission involve a breach of contract? The clearest case of self-induced frustration is where a party's default not only causes the frustrating event to occur but also amounts to a breach of contract. In *Scanlan's New Neon Ltd v Tooheys Ltd*[179] Latham CJ inclined to the view that there could be 'no default or fault in relation to any contract without a breach of the contract'. However, a deliberate act which frustrates the contract, by preventing performance, is usually within the ambit of the 'default' concept even if not a breach of an express term of the contract.[180] And in *Paal Wilson & Co A/S v Partenreederei Hannah*

---

173. [1990] 1 Lloyd's Rep 1, affirming [1989] 1 Lloyd's Rep 148 (see Ewan McKendrick, [1990] *LMCLQ* 153).
174. See generally on the impact of optional and alternative performances and obligations G H Treitel, 'Alternatives and Frustration' in Beatson and Friedmann, eds, *Good Faith and Fault in Contract Law*, 1995, p 377.
175. *Cricklewood Property and Investment Trust Ltd v Leighton's Investment Trust Ltd* [1945] AC 221 at 228. See, eg *Brace v Calder* [1895] 2 QB 253.
176. [1942] AC 154 at 166; see also at 192.
177. See also [1942] AC 154 at 204.
178. [1990] 1 Lloyd's Rep 1.
179. (1943) 67 CLR 169 at 186.
180. Cf *Denmark Productions Ltd v Boscobel Productions Ltd* [1969] 1 QB 699.

Blumenthal[181] Lord Diplock said that an omission not amounting to a breach of contract can be sufficient to preclude reliance by that party on frustration.

[2046] Onus of proof. On whom does the onus of proof lie in cases where frustration is alleged to be self-induced? Is it on the party who makes the allegation, or must the party who relies on the doctrine prove that there was no default on his or her part? In *Joseph Constantine SS Line Ltd v Imperial Smelting Corp Ltd*[182] the House of Lords held that the onus is on the party who makes the allegation that frustration was self-induced. In that case a vessel the subject of a charterparty was damaged by an explosion which rendered it impossible for the vessel to perform under the charterparty. The cause of the explosion could not be established, and the owners were able to invoke the doctrine of frustration because the charterers could not establish that the explosion occurred by reason of the owners' default.

The upshot of the *Constantine* case is that a party is not disentitled to rely on the doctrine by the mere possibility that the event alleged to frustrate the contract occurred as a result of its default. The placement of the onus of proof seems both logical and satisfactory. Usually, the allegation of self-induced frustration is made to support a claim of damages for breach of contract, and since the onus of proving the existence of a breach is on the party who makes the allegation,[183] it is logical to require that party to prove the existence of default where the defence of frustration is raised. It is notoriously difficult to prove a negative, and therefore satisfactory that the party who relies on frustration should not be required to prove the absence of default.

It is doubtful, however, whether the *Constantine* case supports the view that an allegation of frustration is of itself sufficient to require the other party to prove that frustration was self-induced. In some cases a prima facie case of breach will be established simply by proving that a promisor has not performed. In these cases the promisor must produce evidence of frustration in order to require the other party to prove that any 'frustration' was self-induced.[184]

One other point about the onus of proof deserves mention as it was to some extent relied upon in the *Constantine* case. Most descriptions of the concept of frustration refer to the absence of default by *either* party.[185] If the onus were on the party invoking the doctrine to prove that frustration was not self-induced there would, logically, be a need to prove not only the absence of default by that party but also by the other party.[186] This would be unreasonable and unduly restrictive. A party may rely on frustration, even if the other party is at fault, where the claim is to be discharged from

---

181. [1983] 1 AC 854 at 920.
182. [1942] AC 154. See also *Allied Mills Ltd v Gwydir Valley Oilseeds Pty Ltd* [1978] 2 NSWLR 26 at 30. But cf *F C Shepherd & Co Ltd v Jerrom* [1987] QB 301 at 319.
183. See [1843].
184. This may be the explanation for *Sharp v Batt* (1930) 25 Tas LR 33, although a statement (at 44) is difficult to reconcile with the decision in the *Constantine* case.
185. In *J Lauritzen AS v Wijsmuller BV (The Super Servant Two)* [1990] 1 Lloyd's Rep 1 at 8 the statement of the principle refers simply to the person relying on frustration.
186. See [1942] AC 154 at 199, 200.

the contract. Proof of the existence of fault should be required only if a claim for damages is also made, in which case it is necessary to establish that default amounted to a breach of contract. This analysis is supported by *F C Shepherd & Co Ltd v Jerrom*[187] where it was held that the sentencing of an employee to a custodial term for criminal conduct may be relied on by the employer as frustrating the contract, even though the delay in performance is in a sense caused by wrongful conduct on the part of the employee.

[2047] **Causation.** There must be an element of causation between the default of the promisor and the 'frustration' of the contract. For example, in *Ocean Tramp Tankers Corp v V/O Sovfracht (The Eugenia)*[188] the charterers could not rely on the closure of the Suez Canal, even if it had frustrated the contract, as they had ordered the vessel to enter it and breached a term of the contract in doing so. It is clear, however, that the default need not be the sole cause of frustration.[189]

Where there is no element of causation between the default of the promisor and the frustration of the contract, frustration cannot be regarded as self-induced and the parties will be discharged.[190]

[2048] **Both parties in default.** If both parties are in default, because each has contributed to the occurrence of the event relied on as frustrating the contract, neither may rely on it and the contract is not frustrated.[191]

Basis of the Doctrine

[2049] **Construction.** The acceptance of Lord Radcliffe's formulation of the concept of frustration[192] implies that the doctrine is primarily based on the construction of the contract.[193] The court can only decide what a party promised to do by construing the contract and the modern cases emphasise construction as the most satisfactory basis for the doctrine.[194]

It is nevertheless still useful to consider some of the other theories put forward over the years, and to ask whether the choice of theory actually has any significance.

[2050] **Implied term.** Initially, the implied term theory was adopted as the basis of the doctrine, so that whenever the doctrine operated it was

---

187. [1987] QB 301.
188. [1964] 2 QB 226 (see [2017]).
189. See *Monarch SS Co Ltd v A/B Karlshamns Oljefabriker* [1949] AC 196.
190. For the assessment of damages see [2063].
191. *Paal Wilson & Co A/S v Partenreederei Hannah Blumenthal* [1983] 1 AC 854.
192. *Davis Contractors Ltd v Fareham UDC* [1956] AC 696 at 729 (see [2001]).
193. Lord Radcliffe's theory is sometimes referred to as the 'change of obligation theory'. See *National Carriers Ltd v Panalpina (Northern) Ltd* [1981] AC 675 at 702, although, in the same case (at 717) Lord Roskill appears to have drawn a distinction between them.
194. *National Carriers Ltd v Panalpina (Northern) Ltd* [1981] AC 675 at 688, 717; *Pioneer Shipping Ltd v BTP Tioxide Ltd* [1982] AC 724 at 744, 751–2; *Codelfa Construction Pty Ltd v State Rail Authority of New South Wales* (1982) 149 CLR 337 at 357, 376, 408. See also *Brisbane City Council v Group Projects Pty Ltd* (1979) 145 CLR 143 at 159–163; 26 ALR 525 (see Julie Ward, (1984) 9 *Syd LR* 461).

because the court could imply a term into the contract providing for the discharge of the parties.[195]

The implied term theory has been attacked on a number of grounds. In *Hongkong Fir Shipping Co Ltd v Kawasaki Kisen Kaisha Ltd*[196] Diplock LJ said that once the event has occurred, and the parties have been discharged, it is unnecessary to say that, in addition, there was an implied term to this effect. The theory also smacks of fiction[197] since it is difficult to conceive of an officious bystander[198] being suppressed in relation to a matter which the parties did not have in their contemplation.[199] In *Denny Mott & Dickson Ltd v James B Fraser & Co Ltd*[200] Lord Wright said that the theory does not explain why the term is implied. Finally, there is the problem that at common law the consequences of frustration are often very severe on one of the parties[201] and it is by no means clear that the parties, as reasonable persons, would both have agreed to the term finally implied.[202]

[2051] **Just solution.** In *Hirji Mulji v Cheong Yue SS Co Ltd*,[203] Lord Sumner (for the Privy Council), described the frustration doctrine as 'really a device, by which the rules as to absolute contracts are reconciled with a special exception which justice demands'. Lord Wright accepted this as the best theory for the doctrine in *Joseph Constantine SS Line Ltd v Imperial Smelting Corp Ltd*,[204] and said that the 'doctrine is invented by the court in order to supplement the defects of the actual contract'.[205]

Although it might seem strange that the theory preferred by two of the greatest authorities on the law of contract is not applied today, the just solution theory is not supported as the basis of the doctrine. In *Scanlan's New Neon Ltd v Tooheys Ltd*[206] Latham CJ objected to its uncertainty. More recently, in *National Carriers Ltd v Panalpina (Northern) Ltd*[207] Lord Hailsham LC said that although the formulation of Lord Sumner 'admirably expresses the purpose of the doctrine, it does not provide it with

---

195. See, eg *Taylor v Caldwell* (1863) 3 B & S 826; 122 ER 309; *Scanlan's New Neon Ltd v Tooheys Ltd* (1943) 67 CLR 169.
196. [1962] 2 QB 26 at 71.
197. See L E Trakman, 'Frustrated Contracts and Legal Fictions' (1983) 46 *MLR* 39.
198. See [628].
199. Cf *Davis Contractors Ltd v Fareham UDC* [1956] AC 696 at 728.
200. [1944] AC 265 at 275. In *Scanlan's New Neon Ltd v Tooheys Ltd* (1943) 67 CLR 169 at 223 Williams J put it on the basis of the achievement of justice. It was on this ground that Lord Wright was prepared to accept the implied term theory in *Fibrosa Spolka Akcyjna v Fairbairn Lawson Combe Barbour Ltd* [1943] AC at 70, although he usually adopted (see [2051]) the 'just solution' theory. See also *Hirji Mulji v Cheong Yue SS Co Ltd* [1926] AC 497 at 510.
201. See, eg [2066].
202. See *Davis Contractors Ltd v Fareham UDC* [1956] AC 696 at 720. Cf *Ocean Tramp Tankers Corp v V/O Sovfracht (The Eugenia)* [1964] 2 QB 226 at 238–9.
203. [1926] AC 497 at 510.
204. [1942] AC 154 at 184, 186. See also at 171 and *Denny Mott & Dickson Ltd v James B Fraser & Co Ltd* [1944] AC 265 at 275; *Cricklewood Property and Investment Trust Ltd v Leighton's Investment Trust Ltd* [1945] AC 221 at 237. Cf *Ocean Tramp Tankers Corp v V/O Sovfracht (The Eugenia)* [1964] 2 QB 226 at 239.
205. Contrast *F A Tamplin SS Co Ltd v Anglo-Mexican Petroleum Products Co Ltd* [1916] 2 AC 397 at 404 ('no court has an absolving power').
206. (1943) 67 CLR 169 at 187–8.
207. [1981] AC 675 at 687.

any theoretical basis at all'. In any event, if the contract is absolute in character, the doctrine does not apply,[208] and the doctrine is more concerned with whether an obligation which is framed in unconditional terms should be interpreted as absolute in character. In other words, although the court may be searching for a just construction which accords with the intention of the parties,[209] there is no requirement that it be 'just' to apply the doctrine.[210]

[2052] **Disappearance of foundation.** 'Disappearance of the foundation of the contract' is sometimes put forward as *the* basis for frustration.[211] This idea finds two different expressions in the cases. The first is where 'foundation' refers to commercial purpose.[212] Thus, in *Jackson v Union Marine Insurance Co Ltd*[213] the event frustrated the commercial purpose of a charterparty contract.

The second is where 'foundation' refers to an assumption on the basis of which the contract was agreed. This is supported by decisions such as *Krell v Henry*.[214]

However, the theory cannot explain all cases of frustration, and really begs the question of how one decides what is the 'foundation' of the contract. Logically, it must be construction of the contract. In fact, *Jackson v Union Marine Insurance* was decided on the basis of an implied term. This formulation therefore tends to merge with the construction and implied term theories.[215] But, in so far as it has an independent existence, it is 'too vague'[216] to be a satisfactory explanation.

[2053] **Impossibility of performance.** It seems never to have been seriously suggested that impossibility of performance is the basis of the doctrine of frustration, notwithstanding that many of the cases have been decided on the ground of impossibility. There are at least two reasons for saying that impossibility is not a general explanation. First, in some cases there is no impossibility, discharge being based on, for example, frustration of purpose.

Second, impossibility really only explains why one of the parties is discharged. For example, in *Taylor v Caldwell*[217] although the destruction of the music hall made it impossible for the performances to be staged, it did not make it impossible for the hirer to pay the agreed rent. In such situations the explanation of discharge is impossibility on the one side and deprivation of benefit or failure of consideration on the other.[218] The

---

208. See [2003]. But see *Kawasaki Steel Corp v Sardoil SpA (The Zuiho Maru)* [1977] 2 Lloyd's Rep 552 at 554 and cf *J Lauritzen AS v Wijsmuller BV (The Super Servant Two)* [1990] 1 Lloyd's Rep 1 at 8, 9.
209. *British Movietonews Ltd v London and District Cinemas Ltd* [1952] AC 166 at 185–6.
210. *Notcutt v Universal Equipment Co (London) Ltd* [1986] 1 WLR 641 at 647.
211. See *W J Tatem Ltd v Gamboa* [1939] 1 KB 132 at 137.
212. See *National Carriers Ltd v Panalpina (Northern) Ltd* [1981] AC 675 at 687–8.
213. (1874) LR 10 CP 125 (see [2025]).
214. [1903] 2 KB 740 (see [2018]). See also *Scanlan's New Neon Ltd v Tooheys Ltd* (1943) 67 CLR 169 at 188.
215. See, eg *F A Tamplin SS Co Ltd v Anglo-Mexican Petroleum Products Co Ltd* [1916] 2 AC 297 at 404.
216. *National Carriers Ltd v Panalpina (Northern) Ltd* [1981] AC 675 at 703.
217. (1863) 3 B & S 826; 122 ER 309 (see [2012]).

appeal of the construction theory is then its simplicity in providing a comprehensive explanation of the discharge of *both parties*.

[2054] Failure of consideration. At one time it was thought that the doctrine of frustration applied only to executory contracts, where the doctrine could be based on a total failure of consideration caused by the frustrating event. However, the doctrine has been applied to partially executed contracts,[219] and a theory based on failure of consideration cannot be applied to such cases because of the general rule[220] that a failure of consideration must be total.[221] The theory also has the same defect as a theory based on impossibility, namely, that it does not explain why both parties are discharged.

[2055] Mistake.[222] It is sometimes said that the concepts of common mistake[223] and frustration are related.[224] Clearly, both deal with the impact of events which were unknown to the parties when they entered into the contract. In *Bank Line Ltd v Arthur Capel & Co*[225] Viscount Haldane considered common mistake to be a possible basis for the frustration doctrine. On the other hand, in *Joseph Constantine SS Line Ltd v Imperial Smelting Corp Ltd*[226] Lord Wright said that mistake could only explain those cases in which specific subject matter perished. His view, that frustration and mistake are different juristic concepts, seems correct.

There is, in principle, an important difference between factual errors made by both parties when they enter into an agreement and the impact of subsequent events. The law responds to this difference. Indeed, the structure of this book assumes that there is a significant contrast between cases where the intention to contract was to some extent vitiated and the (subsequent) failure of one party to discharge its contractual obligations.

Although it may seem (factually) fortuitous where neither party is at fault, the same contrast informs the classification of factual circumstances as mistake or frustration. For example, in *Amalgamated Investment & Property Co Ltd v John Walker & Sons Ltd*[227] the effect on a contract for the

---

218. See McElroy and Williams, *Impossibility of Performance*, 1941, p xxvii.
219. See, eg *Bensaude v Thames and Mersey Marine Insurance Co Ltd* [1897] AC 609; *Horlock v Beal* [1916] 1 AC 436 at 496.
220. See [2067].
221. *National Carriers Ltd v Panalpina (Northern) Ltd* [1981] AC 675 at 687. It may be more difficult to establish frustration where the contract is partially executed: *Scanlan's New Neon Ltd v Tooheys Ltd* (1943) 67 CLR 169 at 230.
222. See Sir Anthony Mason and S J Gageler, 'The Contract' in Finn, ed, *Essays on Contract*, 1987, pp 21–4; Andrew Kull, 'Mistake, Frustration and the Windfall Principle of Contract Remedies' (1991) 43 *Hastings LJ* 1; Andrew Phang, 'Common Mistake and Frustration in Hong Kong' [1991] *LMCLQ* 297; J C Smith, 'Contracts — Mistake, Frustration and Implied Terms' (1994) 110 *LQR* 400.
223. See generally Chapter 12.
224. See, eg *Codelfa Construction Pty Ltd v State Rail Authority of New South Wales* (1982) 149 CLR 337 at 360 per Mason J ('closely related'); *William Sindall Plc v Cambridgeshire County Council* [1994] 1 WLR 1016 at 1039 per Evans LJ ('same concept').
225. [1919] AC 435 at 444–5.
226. [1942] AC 154 at 186. An example, in a case of partial discharge by frustration (see [2060]) is *Goldsbrough Mort & Co Ltd v Carter* (1914) 19 CLR 429.
227. [1976] 3 All ER 509.

sale of land of inclusion of the property in a statutory list of properties of special architectural or historical interest was said to depend on when inclusion took place. If it was before the contract was entered into an issue of mistake would have arisen; but as it took place on a later date the issue was one of frustration. The facts disclosed an element of misprediction rather than mistake. The case illustrates that mistake and misprediction are different legal concepts, with different consequences. Mistake — if it has any impact — operates from the time of entry into the contract. It either renders the contract void or gives rise to a right to rescind, whereas misprediction can only be shown by a subsequent event which — if it amounts to frustration — discharges the parties from their respective contractual duties.[228]

[2056] **Does it matter?** Although the cases contain a good deal of discussion of the basis of the doctrine of frustration, they do not provide much support for the view that the choice of basis has substantive significance. For example, the fact that the construction theory has displaced the earlier theories does not imply that any of the earlier cases were wrongly decided.[229]

In *Joseph Constantine SS Line Ltd v Imperial Smelting Corp Ltd*[230] Lord Wright doubted whether the choice made would affect the decision reached in any case. Again, all the theories have been based on the presumed intention of the parties,[231] or been said to depend on the 'true meaning' of the contract.[232] Since the true meaning of any contract depends on its construction,[233] construction of the contract is relevant to all theories.[234] It is therefore hardly surprising that in *National Carriers Ltd v Panalpina (Northern) Ltd*[235] Lord Wilberforce should express the view that the various bases 'shade into one another and that a choice between them is a choice of what is most appropriate to the particular contract under consideration'. Thus, in *Panalpina* itself, Lord Simon[236] pointed out that application of the total failure of consideration theory would have been 'incompatible' with the application of the doctrine to a lease. And in *Codelfa Construction Pty Ltd v State Rail Authority of New South Wales*[237] the High Court held that a construction contract was frustrated even though no term, dealing with the situation created by the events which had occurred, could be implied.

---

228. See [2058]–[2061].
229. *Codelfa Construction Pty Ltd v State Rail Authority of New South Wales* (1982) 149 CLR 337 at 357.
230. [1942] AC 154 at 186; see also at 163 per Viscount Simon LC.
231. See, eg *Dahl v Nelson* (1881) 6 App Cas 38 at 59; *Hirsch v The Zinc Corp Ltd* (1917) 24 CLR 34 at 62; *Joseph Constantine SS Line Ltd v Imperial Smelting Corp Ltd* [1942] AC 154 at 159, 185. Cf *Davis Contractors Ltd v Fareham UDC* [1956] AC 696 at 720, 728.
232. *F A Tamplin SS Co Ltd v Anglo-Mexican Petroleum Products Co Ltd* [1916] 2 AC 397 at 404; *Joseph Constantine SS Line Ltd v Imperial Smelting Corp Ltd* [1942] AC 154 at 187.
233. *National Carriers Ltd v Panalpina (Northern) Ltd* [1981] AC 675 at 688.
234. See also *Gelling v Crespin* (1917) 23 CLR 443 at 454; *Bank Line Ltd v Arthur Capel & Co* [1919] AC 435 at 444; *British Movietonews Ltd v London and District Cinemas Ltd* [1952] AC 166 at 184.
235. [1981] AC 675 at 693. Cf *Brisbane City Council v Group Projects Pty Ltd* (1979) 145 CLR 143 at 161.
236. [1981] AC 675 at 702.

On the other hand, in *Davis Contractors Ltd v Fareham UDC*[238] Lord Reid thought the choice between the foundation of the contract theory and the construction theory to be important. His view was that on the foundation theory the issue would 'largely' be one of fact and permit the admission of evidence not admissible on the construction theory, where the issue is one of law. However, this is difficult to maintain because the foundation of the contract can only be established by construction. Similarly, Lord Reid's contrast of the implied term theory and the construction theory, from the point of view of the difficulty in formulating the implied term, does not arise if the implied term theory predicates a term implied in law on the basis of construction.[239]

Consequences of Frustration[240]

Common Law Principles

[2057] **Relevance of the common law.** The principles governing the consequences of termination are those of the common law, except in New South Wales, Victoria and South Australia[241] where statutory provisions apply. However, the common law is still relevant even in these jurisdictions for three reasons. First, the statutes do not apply to all contracts.

Second, the statutes can be excluded by the parties, and where not excluded may not cover all the consequences which result.

Third, the legislation was intended to fill certain gaps in the common law and can best be understood in the light of these principles.

Discharge of parties

[2058] **Discharge automatic.** When frustration occurs it *automatically* discharges the parties from the obligation to perform their contractual duties.[242] This is distinguishable from discharge following breach or repudiation which requires an election (by the promisee), to terminate the performance of the contract.[243]

Where frustration is self-induced[244] the parties are not discharged, although the default of one of the parties may give rise to a right to terminate the performance of the contract, for example, because the default

---

237. (1982) 149 CLR 337. The case is hardly conclusive against the implied term theory because the term sought to be implied would have dealt with more than the automatic discharge of the parties.
238. [1956] AC 696 at 719; cf at 728.
239. See *Shell UK Ltd v Lostock Garage Ltd* [1977] 1 All ER 481 at 487; E W Patterson, 'Constructive Conditions in Contracts' (1942) 42 *Col LR* 903 at 947–8.
240. See Andrew Stewart and J W Carter, 'Frustrated Contracts and Statutory Adjustment: The Case for a Reappraisal' [1992] *CLJ* 66.
241. See [2069]–[2098].
242. *Hirji Mulji v Cheong Yue SS Co Ltd* [1926] AC 497 at 509; *Scanlan's New Neon Ltd v Tooheys Ltd* (1943) 67 CLR 169 at 203; *J Lauritzen AS v Wijsmuller BV (The Super Servant Two)* [1990] 1 Lloyd's Rep 1 at 8.
243. See *Denny Mott & Dickson Ltd v James B Fraser & Co Ltd* [1944] AC 265 at 274 and [1968].
244. See [2043]–[2048].

amounts to repudiation.[245] If the fact that frustration is self-induced does give rise to a right to terminate, and the promisee elects to terminate the performance of the contract, the consequences are governed by the principles applicable to termination for breach or repudiation.[246]

The rule of automatic discharge has been criticised[247] and gives rise to a slight difficulty in cases where frustration results from delay in performance. As was explained earlier,[248] a party who reasonably infers that a frustrating delay would have occurred will usually be protected even though he or she has treated the contract as discharged prior to the frustrating delay and notwithstanding that, had the party waited, frustration would not in fact have occurred. In these cases it is arguably more appropriate to ask whether the party was justified in considering the contract as discharged than to inquire whether frustration automatically discharged the parties to the contract.[249] Nevertheless, even in cases of delay, discharge does not depend on election by either of the parties.[250]

[2059] Election and estoppel after frustration.[251] Where the performance of a contract is terminated for breach or repudiation neither party is able, unilaterally, to reinstate the obligations of the parties.[252] The position is similar where frustration occurs: one party, acting alone, cannot reinstate the obligations of the parties. Thus, it has been said that frustration operates for the 'good or ill'[253] of both parties. However, there is nothing to prevent the parties entering into a fresh contract,[254] and it is not uncommon, when an event interferes with the performance of the contract, for the parties to come to an agreement in order to avoid litigation on whether frustration has occurred.

It has also been suggested that although a party may be estopped from setting up any of the rights which may flow from frustration, there can be no estoppel in relation to the discharge which takes place on the occurrence of the event.[255] However, this distinction does not appear to be fully established by the authorities. For example, in *Black-Clawson International*

---

245. *Bank Line Ltd v Arthur Capel & Co* [1919] AC 435 at 452. In some cases of self-induced frustration it may be possible to infer that the parties have abandoned the contract. See *André et Compagnie SA v Marine Transocean Ltd* [1981] QB 694.
246. See [1985]–[1995]. If abandonment occurs, the consequences depend on the terms of the contract of abandonment inferred from the parties' conduct. See *Paal Wilson & Co A/S v Partenreederei Hannah Blumenthal* [1983] 1 AC 854 at 915.
247. See McElroy and Williams, *Impossibility of Performance*, 1941, pp 221 et seq.
248. See [2026]–[2027].
249. *Dahl v Nelson* (1881) 6 App Cas 38 at 53; *Bensaude v Thames and Mersey Marine Insurance Co Ltd* [1897] AC 609 at 613. Cf *Poussard v Spiers* (1876) 1 QBD 410; *Notcutt v Universal Equipment Co (London) Ltd* [1986] 1 WLR 641 at 648.
250. *Bank Line Ltd v Arthur Capel & Co* [1919] AC 435 at 459. But cf *Finch v Sayers* [1976] 2 NSWLR 540 at 547, 548.
251. See Andrew Rogers, 'Frustration and Estoppel' in McKendrick, ed, *Force Majeure and Frustration of Contract*, 2nd ed, 1995, p 245.
252. See [1987].
253. *Joseph Constantine SS Line Ltd v Imperial Smelting Corp Ltd* [1942] AC 154 at 171 per Viscount Maugham.
254. *Bank Line Ltd v Arthur Capel & Co* [1919] AC 435 at 455.
255. See *BP Exploration Co (Libya) Ltd v Hunt (No 2)* [1979] 1 WLR 783 at 810, 811–12 (affirmed [1981] 1 WLR 232; [1983] 2 AC 352 but without reference to this point).

Ltd v Papierwerke Waldhof-Aschaffenburg AG[256] Mustill J considered that unequivocal acts recognising the 'existence' of the contract would have precluded reliance on frustration. In principle, there is no reason a party should not be estopped, by words or conduct, from relying on the doctrine, at least where no element of illegality or public policy is involved.

[2060] Partial discharge. Since frustration, when it operates, discharges the whole contract, a party cannot rely on frustration as a ground for partial discharge.[257] There are, however, four exceptions to this rule.

The first exception is more apparent than real. Where the contract was partially executed prior to frustration, discharge extends only to the executory part of the contract.[258] Frustration never operates to rescind a contract.[259]

Second, where a contract relating to a specific subject matter, or subject matter to be obtained from a particular source, is frustrated because the subject matter substantially perishes, or the source substantially fails, the promisor is discharged to the extent that the subject matter has perished,[260] or the source has failed,[261] but not as to the balance.[262]

The third exception arises where an event occurs which does not frustrate the performance of the contract, but, instead, provides the promisor with an excuse for not performing. For example, where a lessee's obligation to build under a building lease is affected by a government order prohibiting building, the lessee may be able to rely on the order as an excuse for not performing the obligation to build, but remain liable to pay the rent reserved by the lease.[263] Since the excuse may be only temporary, and not actually amount to discharge,[264] the exculpation does not in fact occur under the doctrine of frustration. Thus, the lessee is excused because of illegality in performance, not frustration.

Fourth, partial frustration will occur if a part of the contract is so distinct from the remainder as to be, for all practical purposes, a separate contract. For example, a submission to arbitration may be frustrated even though the contract in which it is contained is not.[265] However, the mere fact that a

---

256. [1981] 2 Lloyd's Rep 446 at 457.
257. *Aurel Forras Pty Ltd v Graham Karp Developments Pty Ltd* [1975] VR 202; *Nelson v Kimberley Homes Pty Ltd* (1988) 4 BCL 289 at 291.
258. See, eg *Hirsch v The Zinc Corp Ltd* (1917) 24 CLR 34.
259. See [2062]. However, supervening illegality (see [2021]) may sometimes have this effect.
260. *Goldsbrough Mort & Co Ltd v Carter* (1914) 19 CLR 429.
261. *Howell v Coupland* (1876) 1 QBD 258.
262. *H R and S Sainsbury Ltd v Street* [1972] 1 WLR 834 (see J W A Thornely, [1973] *CLJ* 15). In cases where more than one contract exists there may be an entitlement to pro rata performance; see A H Hudson, 'Pro-rating in the English Law of Frustrated Contracts' (1968) 31 *MLR* 535.
263. See *Cricklewood Property and Investment Trust Ltd v Leighton's Investment Trust Ltd* [1945] AC 221 at 244. Cf *Gerraty v McGavin* (1914) 18 CLR 152. Contrast *Re De Garis and Rowe's Lease* [1924] VLR 38, where the lessee was not discharged from his building covenant because it was construed as absolute. The case seems a doubtful one.
264. See further [2061].
265. *Bremer Vulkan Schiffbau und Maschinenfabrik v South India Shipping Corp Ltd* [1981] AC 909 at 980.

contract contains severable obligations need not imply that part of the contract can be discharged by frustration,[266] although the parties can expressly provide for this.[267]

[2061] Suspension of performance. Frustration does not merely suspend the parties' obligations, it discharges them.[268] However, an event which does not frustrate the contract may effectively suspend the performance of an obligation. For example, supervening illegality, not amounting to frustration, may suspend performance.[269] Similarly, an employer's obligation to pay wages (and the employee's duty to serve) may be suspended by the employee's illness, not because the illness frustrates the contract but because the employee is not entitled to wages which have not been earned.[270] The illness may also provide a situation where the employer's (and employee's) obligation is suspended for a time and then discharged, because it is so prolonged as to frustrate the performance of the contract.[271]

The parties may expressly provide that the occurrence of a particular event is to suspend performance.[272] Force majeure clauses are frequently used to suspend performance on the occurrence of an event for which neither party is responsible, such as an act of God affecting a building contract.[273] Because of the express clause, it is not material to consider whether the event in question would operate to suspend performance under the common law.

Accrued rights and liabilities

[2062] Contract not rescinded. Frustration discharges the parties' obligations *in futuro*, it does not rescind the contract *ab initio*.[274] Because there is no rescission it is misleading to speak of the contract as being 'void': the contract remains alive as the measure of the rights and liabilities of the parties. Accordingly, accrued rights and liabilities are not divested by frustration.[275]

In this respect, the consequences of frustration more closely resemble those applicable when a contract is discharged for breach or repudiation

---

266. *Ertel Bieber & Co v Rio Tinto Co Ltd* [1918] AC 260 at 270.
267. See, eg *Bremer Hardelsgesellschaft mbH v Vanden Avenne-Izegem PVBA* [1978] 2 Lloyd's Rep 109.
268. *Cricklewood Property and Investment Trust Ltd v Leighton's Investment Trust Ltd* [1945] AC 221 at 232.
269. *Cricklewood Property and Investment Trust Ltd v Leighton's Investment Trust Ltd* [1945] AC 221 at 239–40; *Libyan Arab Foreign Bank v Bankers Trust Co* [1989] QB 728 at 772.
270. *Finch v Sayers* [1976] 2 NSWLR 540.
271. *Carmichael v Colonial Sugar Refining Co Ltd* (1944) 44 SR (NSW) 233 at 235–6. Cf *Finch v Sayers* [1976] 2 NSWLR 540 at 547.
272. See, eg *Tennants (Lancashire) Ltd v C S Wilson & Co Ltd* [1917] AC 495. For the relevance of public policy issue see [2041].
273. See David Yates, 'Drafting Force Majeure and Related Clauses' (1991) 3 *JCL* 186; M P Furmston, 'Drafting Force Majeure Clauses' in McKendrick, ed, *Force Majeure and Frustration of Contract*, 2nd ed, 1995, p 57.
274. *Hirsch v The Zinc Corp Ltd* (1917) 24 CLR 34 at 64; *Fibrosa Spolka Akcyjna v Fairbairn Lawson Combe Barbour Ltd* [1943] AC 32; *Bank of Boston Connecticut v European Grain and Shipping Ltd* [1989] AC 1056 at 1108.

than those applicable where a contract is rescinded for misrepresentation.[276]

[2063] Recovery of damages. The occurrence of an event which frustrates a contract does not give rise to any right to claim damages. The fact that damages may be recoverable where 'frustration' is self-induced, because the default in question amounted to a breach of contract, does not constitute an exception to this rule, because self-induced frustration does not automatically discharge the parties' obligations.

However, if a cause of action in damages accrued prior to the frustrating event, this is not divested by frustration. There must, of course, be an accrued right. For example, if a seller delivers defective goods under an instalment goods contract which is *subsequently* frustrated, the buyer will possess an accrued right to claim damages which is not divested by frustration. But in some cases frustration will prevent the right accruing. For example, if, prior to the time for performance, a promisor repudiates contractual obligations, but the promisee does not accept this as an anticipatory breach of contract, frustration of the contract will prevent the promisee claiming damages.[277]

Where a cause of action in damages exists at the time of frustration, the fact of frustration may be relevant to the assessment of damages, because it may decrease the plaintiff's loss. Moreover, the fact that the contract has been discharged for breach or repudiation prior to the occurrence of the event which would have frustrated the contract does not necessarily prevent the court having regard to later events when assessing damages. Thus, if the evidence shows that the contract *would have been frustrated* the court may take this into account and, if appropriate, reduce the plaintiff's damages.[278] But even if frustration of the contract (or the fact that it would have been frustrated) indicates that the plaintiff has suffered no loss at all by reason of the defendant's breach, the plaintiff retains a right to claim nominal damages.

[2064] Terms operating after frustration. The general rule is that once frustration has occurred the terms of the contract cease to operate and neither party may claim to enforce its terms.[279] Accordingly, for a term to operate after frustration the parties must clearly have intended this to be the case.[280]

An obvious case is where the parties expressly provide for what is to happen in the event of frustration. However, in some cases it may be

---

275. See, eg *Re Continental C & G Rubber Co Pty Ltd* (1919) 27 CLR 194 at 201; *Joseph Constantine SS Line Ltd v Imperial Smelting Corp Ltd* [1942] AC 154 at 170; *C T Bowring Reinsurance Ltd v Baxter (The M Vatman and M Ceyhan)* [1987] 2 Lloyd's Rep 416 at 424.
276. *Hirji Mulji v Cheong Yue SS Co Ltd* [1926] AC 497 at 510. However, where frustration occurs through illegality, the right to sue in respect of accrued rights may be suspended. See *Ertel Bieber & Co v Rio Tinto Co Ltd* [1918] AC 260 at 269.
277. *Avery v Bowden* (1856) 6 E & B 953; 119 ER 1119.
278. *Watts Watts & Co Ltd v Mitsui & Co Ltd* [1917] AC 227. See also [2161].
279. See, eg *Metropolitan Water Board v Dick Kerr & Co Ltd* [1918] AC 119.
280. *BP Exploration Co (Libya) Ltd v Hunt (No 2)* [1979] 1 WLR 783 at 829 (affirmed [1981] 1 WLR 232; [1983] 2 AC 352).

possible to infer such an intention, for example, in respect of a term requiring the parties to submit a dispute under the contract to arbitration,[281] or in respect of an employee's promise not to divulge confidential information obtained in the course of employment. In all cases it is a question of construction whether the parties intended the term to operate.

[2065] **Accrued liabilities.** The principle stated above does not apply to a term stating a liability which accrued prior to frustration. For example, where a contract for the sale of goods is discharged by frustration after deliveries have been made under the contract, the seller will be entitled to payment in respect of the deliveries made, if payment was due prior to frustration, unless payment by the buyer to the seller has become illegal.[282] And there is no reason, in principle, why an accrued liability should not be enforced *after* frustration even if payment would have fallen due after the frustrating event.[283]

Where a contract is discharged for breach or repudiation, a liability which accrued due prior to termination is not enforceable unless it was *unconditional* in character. For example, if a vendor agrees to convey title to land but terminates the performance of the contract for breach or repudiation after the time for payment has passed, the vendor cannot recover the price of the land because the right is conditional on transfer of title. In such cases the purchaser is permitted to rely on the total failure of consideration, which would occur if the obligation to pay were enforced, as a defence to the vendor's claim so as to avoid circuity of action.[284] In *Fibrosa Spolka Akcyjna v Fairbairn Lawson Combe Barbour Ltd*[285] the House of Lords considered the same reasoning to be applicable in cases of frustration.

Restitution after frustration

[2066] **No restitution for partial performance.** At common law[286] partial performance of the contract *prior* to frustration does not give rise to a restitutionary claim in respect of that performance, and so a plaintiff cannot recover, as on a quantum meruit, the reasonable value of such performance.

For example, in *Appleby v Myers*[287] the plaintiffs agreed to erect certain machinery at the defendant's premises. After the work had been partially completed, the premises, together with the partially erected machinery, were destroyed by fire without default by either party. The Exchequer

---

281. *Codelfa Construction Pty Ltd v State Rail Authority of New South Wales* (1982) 149 CLR 337; *State Rail Authority of New South Wales v Codelfa Construction Pty Ltd* (1982) 150 CLR 29; 42 ALR 289; *Paal Wilson & Co A/S v Partenreederei Hannah Blumenthal* [1983] 1 AC 854 at 917.
282. *Hirsch v The Zinc Corp Ltd* (1917) 24 CLR 34.
283. See *Westralian Farmers Ltd v Commonwealth Agricultural Service Engineers Ltd* (1936) 54 CLR 361 (express provision for termination — see [2226]). But see *Re Continental C & G Rubber Co Pty Ltd* (1919) 27 CLR 194.
284. *McDonald v Dennys Lascelles Ltd* (1933) 48 CLR 457 at 477; and see [2238].
285. [1943] AC 32 at 53 (see [2067]).
286. See Mason and Carter, *Restitution Law in Australia*, 1995, paras 1228–31.
287. (1867) LR 2 CP 651.

Chamber held that this frustrated the contract. However, the plaintiffs could not recover anything in respect of the work done. The contract provided for payment on completion of the work and the fact that the defendant had received some performance prior to frustration did not imply a right to restitution on a quantum meruit. This was said to be because the plaintiffs contracted to do 'an entire work for a specific sum'.[288] Similarly, where an employment contract is frustrated prior to the completion of the period of employment in respect of which the employee would be entitled to wages, under the common law the employee is not entitled to restitution for the work done.[289]

It might be thought that these cases are unjust, and that under the principle of unjust enrichment which now governs restitution[290] reasonable remuneration should be recoverable. It is certainly true that the reasoning in the cases themselves is outmoded. However, the unjust enrichment principle requires proof of benefit and it is not clear that the defendant in *Appleby v Myers* did receive a benefit. The court took the view that the plaintiff had accepted the risk that part performance would not be paid for, and the benefit of that performance was received (as a matter of obligation) under the contract and on the assumption that the work would be completed. Moreover, whatever value was received, it was destroyed by the frustrating event. On the other hand, in *Cutter v Powell*[291] the defendant did receive something of value, namely, the work which was done prior to the death of the seaman.[292] The benefit of this was not affected by the seaman's death, and it may well be that such a defendant should now be regarded as having received a benefit, to be paid for under the principle of unjust enrichment.[293] If a party incurs expenses, for example, in preparing for performance, no claim in restitution is available in respect of the wasted expenditure, because the expenditure does not benefit the other party.

Where benefits are conferred *after* frustration the plaintiff is more likely to be entitled to recover the reasonable value (or price) of the benefits conferred.[294] Thus, the contractors in *Codelfa Construction Pty Ltd v State Rail Authority of New South Wales*[295] were assumed to be entitled to recover in respect of the work done after the contract had been frustrated. And in *Société Franco Tunisienne D'Armement v Sidermar SpA*[296] Pearson J held that quantum meruit was available to a carrier who was forced by the closure of the Suez Canal to take the longer voyage around the Cape.

---

288. (1867) LR 2 CP 651 at 661.
289. *Cutter v Powell* (1795) 6 TR 320; 101 ER 573; *Horlock v Beal* [1916] 1 AC 486.
290. See [2308].
291. (1795) 6 TR 320; 101 ER 573 (see [1824]).
292. Cf *Independent Grocers Co-operative Ltd v Noble Lowndes Superannuation Consultants Ltd* (1993) 60 SASR 525.
293. For discussion see Mason and Carter, *Restitution Law in Australia*, 1995, para 1231.
294. On whether the right of recovery is restitutionary or contractual see Mason and Carter, *Restitution Law in Australia*, 1995, para 1232.
295. (1982) 149 CLR 337 (see [2017]). But see *Davis Contractors Ltd v Fareham UDC* [1956] AC 696 at 722–4.
296. [1961] 2 QB 278 at 312–15 (overruled in *Ocean Tramp Tankers Corp v V/O Sovfracht (The Eugenia)* [1964] 2 QB 226 on the basis that the contract was not frustrated). Contrast *Adelfamar SA v Silos E Mangimi Martini SpA (The Adelfa)* [1988] 2 Lloyd's Rep 466.

[2067] Recovery of money paid. Where money is paid prior to the frustration of the contract, the right to recover restitution of the amount paid depends on the terms under which the money was paid and the effect of frustration.

The terms of the contract (express and implied) may indicate that, no matter what transpires, the money may be retained by the payee. On the other hand, payment may be made on terms that it is recoverable unless the payer is in default under the contract. For example, a deposit payment made under a contract for the sale of land may be made on terms that it is to be repaid if the contract does not proceed to completion unless the purchaser defaults. If the contract is frustrated prior to completion, and the purchaser is not in default, the purchaser can recover the payment, either on the basis of the parties' intention or by application of the unjust enrichment principle.

The time and effect of frustration may be important. Frustration of the contract will have no impact at all on a payment made under the contract if it was *earned* prior to frustration. In *Re Continental C & G Rubber Co Pty Ltd*[297] cl 22 of a contract for the construction and installation of machinery provided that payments were to be made at the rate of 90 per cent 'on the value of the machinery in progress', as certified by an engineer. Payments totalling £6000 (for which certificates were given) were made, but the contract was frustrated prior to delivery of the machinery. The High Court held that the payments could not be recovered. Isaacs and Rich JJ said[298] cl 22 indicated that the contractors had earned the payment. An even clearer case is where the contract is severable. For example, if a contract for the sale of goods provides for delivery and payment by instalments, frustration after payment has been made for deliveries received does not impact on the payments and they cannot be recovered by the buyer.

On the other hand, if the impact of frustration is to cause a total failure of consideration the payer will be entitled to restitution. This was established in *Fibrosa Spolka Akcyjna v Fairbairn Lawson Combe Barbour Ltd*.[299] The buyers of machinery to be manufactured by the suppliers made a payment on account of the purchase price at the time when the order for the machinery was placed. Although the contract was frustrated prior to delivery, the buyers' action to recover the payment made failed before the English Court of Appeal[300] which held[301] that the right to recover the payment depended on rescission ab initio which, of course, had not occurred. But the House of Lords held[302] that the buyers' right to recover the money merely depended on whether the consideration for their payment had totally failed, not whether the contract had been rescinded. Because the payment was a conditional payment on account of the price of

---

297. (1919) 27 CLR 194.
298. (1919) 27 CLR 194 at 204.
299. [1943] AC 32 (see [2023]).
300. Sub nom *Fibrosa Société Anonyme v Fairbairn Lawson Combe Barbour Ltd* [1942] 1 KB 12.
301. Applying *Chandler v Webster* [1904] 1 KB 493.
302. Overruling *Chandler v Webster* [1904] 1 KB 493.

the machinery there was a total failure of consideration and restitution was ordered.[303]

There is an intermediate case: frustration may result in a failure of consideration which is merely partial. Although unsatisfactory, the law is (at present) clear that on a partial failure there is no restitution of payments made.[304] For example, if A pays in advance for services to be rendered by B, frustration of the contract after the services have been rendered in part results in only a partial failure of consideration, and A cannot recover any portion of the payment made. However, the fact that the payee has incurred expenses for the purpose of performing a contract does not prevent the failure of consideration being total. In other words, the restitutionary principle depends on proof that the payer has not obtained a benefit and it is irrelevant whether the payee has sustained a loss.[305]

Until recently it was not entirely clear that the principles stated in the *Fibrosa* case formed part of Australian law.[306] This was because in *Re Continental* the High Court had adopted the same reasoning as the English Court of Appeal in *Fibrosa*. However, in a footnote to his judgment in *Baltic Shipping Co v Dillon (The Mikhail Lermontov)*[307] Mason CJ stated[308] that *Fibrosa* 'correctly reflects the law in Australia and, to the extent that it is inconsistent, should be preferred to the decision' in *Re Continental*. Moreover, as indicated above, the decision in *Re Continental* was dictated by the terms of the contract. Thus, Isaacs and Rich JJ emphasised that the contract excluded the total failure of consideration concept.

Under Statute[309]

[2068] Defects of the common law. Four defects of the common law stand out. First, there is the restriction on the ability to recover money paid prior to frustration imposed by the requirement of a *total* failure of consideration. There is obvious injustice if a substantial sum has been paid and a relatively small benefit obtained by performance prior to frustration.

Second, from the other party's point of view, it will frequently be unjust for nothing to be recovered in respect of performance rendered (but not paid for) prior to frustration.

---

303. Similarly a buyer under a sale of goods contract may recover a pre-paid price if frustration prevents delivery, title to the goods not having been transferred to the buyers. See *Comptoir d'Achat et de Vente du Boerenbond Belge SA v Luis de Ridder Limitada (The Julia)* [1949] AC 293.
304. *Whincup v Hughes* (1871) LR 6 CP 78; *Re Palmdale Insurance Ltd* [1982] VR 921 at 931; *Bank of Boston Connecticut v European Grain and Shipping Ltd* [1989] AC 1056 at 1108. See further [2306].
305. See *Fibrosa Spolka Akcyjna v Fairbairn Lawson Combe Barbour Ltd* [1943] AC 32 at 49–50, 54–5, 71–2 (cf at 76).
306. But cf *Westralian Farmers Ltd v Commonwealth Agricultural Service Engineers Ltd* (1936) 54 CLR 361 at 371–2; *Lobb v Vasey Housing Auxiliary (War Widows Guild)* [1963] VR 239 at 246; *Aurel Forras Pty Ltd v Graham Karp Developments Pty Ltd* [1975] VR 202 at 207; *Re Palmdale Insurance Ltd* [1982] VR 921 at 931; *Muschinski v Dodds* (1985) 160 CLR 583 at 618; 62 ALR 429.
307. *Baltic Shipping Co v Dillon* (1993) 176 CLR 344; 111 ALR 289.
308. (1993) 176 CLR 344 at 355 n 55. Brennan and Toohey JJ agreed. See also (1993) 176 CLR 344 at 375 (obligation to make restitution prima facie imposed where there has been a total failure of consideration).
309. See Mason and Carter, *Restitution Law in Australia*, 1995, paras 1236–68.

Third, the inability to recover anything in respect of expenditure incurred prior to frustration, without regard to whether any performance was received prior to frustration, is unsatisfactory if the expenditure is entirely wasted.

Fourth, the ability to enforce a cause of action which accrued due prior to frustration may be unsatisfactory because of the absence of adjustment mechanisms other than the total failure of consideration concept.

The statutes[310] enacted in Victoria, New South Wales and South Australia attempt to overcome the shortcomings of the common law. It will be seen that the solutions offered by the statutes differ markedly. It is by no means clear that any is a significant improvement on the common law.

New South Wales

[2069] Position governed by *Frustrated Contracts Act* 1978. In New South Wales the consequences of frustration are regulated by the *Frustrated Contracts Act* 1978 (NSW),[311] the substantive sections of which came into force on 1 May 1979. For the purposes of the Act,[312] frustration includes the 'avoidance' of an agreement under s 12 of the *Sale of Goods Act* 1923 (NSW). The Act attempts to provide a scheme for the apportionment of loss caused by frustration. It is an attempt to state a scheme which can be applied by the parties without resorting to litigation.

Generally, the Act applies only to things done, or required by the contract to be done, before frustration. However, s 5(4) provides that anything 'which is done or suffered under the contract' after the time of frustration by a party before the party 'knows or ought to know' of the circumstances — whether of law or fact — giving rise to frustration is to have 'effect as if done or suffered before the time of frustration'.

The Act binds the Crown: s 4.

[2070] Contracts to which the Act does not apply. Certain contracts are excluded from the Act by s 6.

Under s 6(1), the Act does not apply to:

- a contract made before 1 May 1979;
- a charterparty which is not a time or demise charterparty;
- a contract (other than a charterparty) for the carriage of goods by sea;
- a contract of insurance; or
- any other contract 'in so far as the parties thereto have agreed' that the Act is not to apply.

In addition, under s 6(2), the Act does not apply to a contract 'embodied in or constituted by the memorandum or articles of association or rules or other instrument or agreement constituting, or regulating the affairs of', certain enumerated bodies such as companies and partnerships, 'in any

---

310. The legislation discussed [1827]–[1828] may also apply. For other relevant statutory provisions see Mason and Carter, *Restitution Law in Australia*, 1995, para 1235.
311. See NSW Law Reform Commission, *Report on Frustrated Contracts*, LRC 25, 1976.
312. Contrast *Law Reform (Frustrated Contracts) Act* 1943 (UK), s 2(5)(c).

case in which the circumstances alleged to give rise to frustration of the contract furnish a case for the winding up or dissolution of the body'.

Finally, under s 6(3), where a contract which is severable into parts is partially frustrated, the Act does not apply to the part (or parts) not frustrated.

[2071] Extent of discharge under the Act. At common law[313] discharge by frustration operates in futuro and does not therefore affect, directly at least, any promise due for performance prior to frustration. However, under s 7 of the Act a promise due for performance prior to frustration which was not performed before the time of frustration is discharged, except to the extent necessary to support a claim for damages, unless the promise would not have been discharged had it fallen due for performance after the time of frustration. For example, if A promises to build machinery for B, but the contract is frustrated, A's promise is discharged by frustration even if it fell due for performance prior to frustration, except to the extent that B may claim damages for A's breach of contract. On the other hand, an employee's promise not to divulge the secrets of the employer may not be discharged, even though the contract is frustrated, if, no matter at what time the promise was due to be performed, it would not be discharged by frustration at common law.

[2072] Damages after frustration. Section 8 of the Act provides that, when damages are assessed in respect of a liability which accrued prior to frustration, regard must be had to the fact that the contract has been frustrated. The section says nothing about the assessment of damages where a contract which would have been frustrated was discharged by termination for breach or repudiation prior to the occurrence of the event which would have frustrated the contract.[314]

[2073] Full performance prior to frustration. Section 10 deals with the situation where full performance, which does not involve (either wholly or in part) the payment of money,[315] is received prior to the time of frustration.[316] The position of a plaintiff who fully performed prior to frustration could be solved in at least three ways. First, the defendant could be required to pay the agreed sum, or, if the defendant's performance was to take some other form, the money value of the defendant's performance. Second, the defendant could be held liable to pay the market value of the plaintiff's performance. Third, the plaintiff might be entitled to recover the market value of the performance which the defendant promised to render.

---

313. See [2062].
314. The common law (see [2063]) applies, since a contract which has already been discharged cannot be frustrated and is therefore not within the ambit of the Act.
315. Section 9 qualifies the general meaning in s 5(1). A reference to the 'performing party' is a reference to the party to the contract by whom the performance was given or intended to be given: s 5(2)(a).
316. A reference to the 'other party' is a reference to the party 'by whom performance is contemplated by the contract as consideration for the performance'. Under s 5(3) performance is deemed to be given and received if 'received as contemplated by the contract', whether received by a party or not.

In fact, s 10 provides for payment, to the party who performed, of an amount equal to the 'value of the agreed return for the performance'. The 'agreed return' of one party's performance is defined by s 5(1) of the Act as the performance by the other party 'contemplated by the contract as consideration for the first-mentioned performance'. Although the position is far from clear, it appears that s 10 adopts the third solution. This is the logical implication of the reference to the 'value of the agreed return for performance', rather than the 'value of the performance rendered by the defendant' (first solution), or the 'value of the performance received by the plaintiff' (second solution). This creates two problems. To begin with, it is difficult to see how a promise to pay money can have any value other than the sum promised, so that it would have been simpler to adopt the first solution. Given that s 10 applies only where the plaintiff's performance did not involve the payment of money, the 'agreed return' will almost invariably take a monetary form. It was perhaps thought that such an approach would have been inconsistent with the idea that the parties are discharged from their contractual obligations.

The second problem is that the defendant bears the whole loss caused by frustration, since there is no indication that regard may be had to any diminution in value caused by the event which frustrates the contract. Although the justice of this is not readily apparent, it seems that the drafters considered that the only diminution to be taken into account on frustration is the fact of discharge itself.[317] Since discharge does not impact on the value of what was promised by the defendant, no diminution is permitted.

[2074] Partial performance prior to frustration. Section 11 of the Act deals with *partial performance*, that is, situations in which part, but not all, of the performance to be given by one party was received by the other before frustration. It is therefore, like s 10, concerned with frustration occurring after the receipt by the other party of a non-monetary performance.

Under s 11(2) the amount payable by the party who received performance depends on whether what the Act terms the 'attributable cost' of performance is greater than the 'attributable value' of performance. If attributable cost does exceed attributable value, the performing party is entitled to an amount equal to the sum of attributable value and one-half of the amount by which attributable cost exceeds attributable value. In all other cases the performing party is entitled to receive the attributable value of performance. Thus, in symbolic terms:

P is entitled to av, unless—

ac > av

in which case P receives

$$av + \frac{(ac - av)}{2}$$

where:
  P is the performing party
  ac means attributable cost
  av means attributable value

---

317. See [2074].

The concepts of attributable cost and attributable value are defined by s 11(1). It is an indication of the complexity of the section that four more concepts, namely, 'incidental gain', 'lost value', 'proportionate allowance' and 'reasonable cost' have to be defined in order to define the two basic concepts. 'Lost value' refers to the impact of discharge of the contract on the value of the performance received, rather than the physical effect of the event giving rise to frustration on the benefits conferred. It therefore appears that *Appleby v Myers*[318] would be decided differently. However, at this stage the lawyer passes the file on to an accountant.[319]

[2075] Recovery of money paid. Section 12, dealing with the return of money paid prior to frustration, is thankfully more straightforward than s 11. The party who received the money must pay an equal sum to the party who made the payment. However, this is subject to an important refinement, in that the money must have been paid 'as, or as part of, an agreed return for performance of the contract by the other party'. Recalling the definition in s 5(1),[320] there will be no obligation to repay if the money was not paid as consideration for performance. Therefore, a payment made in consideration of performance will be recoverable. For example, if A agrees to design, build and deliver machinery to B for $100,000, and B pays A $50,000 in anticipation of installation by A, but the contract is frustrated after partial installation, B is entitled to receive $50,000.

On the other hand, if a buyer of goods agrees to pay on a day certain irrespective of delivery,[321] the buyer may be unable to recover the payment if the contract is subsequently frustrated, because the payment was not the agreed return for the seller's performance. This seems an odd result.

[2076] Wasted expenditure. Expenditure prior to the frustration is not recoverable at common law even though the expenditure may be entirely wasted because of frustration. Section 13 of the Act is intended to provide a solution to this.

Under s 13(1), a party who suffers detriment 'by reasonably paying money, doing work or doing or suffering any act or thing for the purpose of giving performance under the contract' is entitled to receive 'an amount equal to one-half of the amount that would be fair compensation for the detriment suffered'. For example, if A agrees to design, build and deliver machinery to B for $100,000, and A spends $10,000 in doing the design and preliminary construction work for *machinery not delivered*, A would be entitled to receive $5000, assuming $10,000 to be 'fair compensation' for the work done. If, as in an earlier version of this example,[322] B paid $50,000 in advance, B would be entitled to recover $45,000 ($50,000 − $5000). The manufacturer (A) may be able to salvage something from the partially completed machinery, and it might be thought that this is relevant to the assessment of the 'fair compensation'. However, this is not the

---

318. (1867) LR 2 CP 651 (see [2066]).
319. For analysis see Mason and Carter, *Restitution Law in Australia*, 1995, paras 1249–51.
320. See [2073].
321. See [1806].
322. See [2075].

position. Instead, there is an express provision in s 13(2), which provides that where the performing party has, as a 'consequence' of doing or suffering the act or things that caused that party to suffer the detriment, 'acquired or derived any property or improvement to property', that party must pay to the other party 'one-half of the value of the property or improvement so acquired or derived'. Thus, if we assume that the partially completed machinery had a value of $2000, B would be entitled to receive $1000. The end result would be the receipt by A of a sum of $46,000. In effect, therefore, the net loss of $8000 is apportioned equally between the parties.

[2077] **Basis of recovery.** Where money is payable as a result of the application of ss 9 to 13, it is recoverable *as a debt* in a court of competent jurisdiction: s 14.

[2078] **Adjustment by court.** In three situations the court may, by order, exclude a contract from the operation of ss 9 to 13, and substitute such adjustments 'in money or otherwise' as it considers proper (s 15(1)). The court must be satisfied that the 'terms of the contract or the events which have occurred' are such that, in relation to the contract, ss 9 to 13:

- are 'manifestly inadequate or inappropriate';
- cause 'manifest injustice' in their application; or
- would be 'excessively difficult or expensive' to apply.

By virtue of s 15(2), the orders which a court may make under s 15(1) include orders for the payment of interest, and orders as to the time when money shall be paid.[323]

Having regard to the novelty of the concepts stated, for example, in s 11, and the likelihood that the parties will disagree on the sums payable after frustration, it may be that the Act will not achieve its intended function of allowing the parties to fix their respective entitlements after frustration without resorting to litigation. Section 15 will come into play in all but the most straightforward cases. It is difficult to believe that the *Frustrated Contracts Act* 1978 (NSW) is, in the majority of cases, an improvement on the common law.

Victoria[324]

[2079] **Position governed by *Frustrated Contracts Act* 1959.** In Victoria the consequences of frustration are regulated by the *Frustrated Contracts Act* 1959 (Vic), which came into force on 29 September 1959. The Act is modelled on the *Law Reform (Frustrated Contracts) Act* 1943 (UK).

The Act applies not only where a 'contract has become impossible of performance or been otherwise frustrated', but also to cases where a sale of

---

323. Additional jurisdiction to make orders is conferred by s 15(3); but s 15(7) states that ss 15(2) to (6) do not limit the generality of s 15(1). Sections 15(4)–(6) deal with the application of certain sections of the *Trustee Act* 1925 (NSW).
324. See Williams, *The Law Reform (Frustrated Contracts) Act 1943*, 1944; Ewan McKendrick, 'Frustration, Restitution, and Loss Apportionment' in Burrows, ed, *Essays on the Law of Restitution*, 1991, p 147.

goods contract has been 'avoided' under s 12 of the *Goods Act* 1958 (Vic): s 3(1).

It has been suggested,[325] rightly in our view, that the 'fundamental principle' underlying the legislation is 'prevention of the unjust enrichment of either party to the contract at the other's expense'.

[2080] Discharge under the Act. Section 2 provides that the 'time of discharge' is the time at which the contract becomes impossible of performance, or is otherwise frustrated, or avoided by s 12 of the *Goods Act* 1958 (Vic).

The discharging effect of frustration is acknowledged in s 3(1), by reference to the 'further performance of the contract'. The discharging effect is extended a little by s 3(2), which provides that money payable prior to the 'time of discharge' ceases to be payable.[326] Although it has been suggested that the effect of this is that non-monetary obligations are not discharged,[327] because specific performance will not be ordered after frustration the better view is that such obligations are also discharged.

Although s 3(2) does not expressly say that an accrued right to damages remains enforceable, it would seem that this is the case. Therefore, although the fact of breach does not prevent a party enforcing rights under the Act, it may have the effect of reducing the sum payable.

[2081] Recovery of money paid. Under s 3(2) all sums paid before the time of discharge are recoverable by the party who made the payment. There is a proviso, which applies also to cases where money was due to be paid, but was not paid, prior to discharge. The proviso operates if the party to whom the money was paid (or payable) incurred expenses before the time of discharge 'in, or for the purpose of, the performance of the contract'. The proviso confers on the court a power to allow the party to whom the money was paid (or payable) to retain (or recover) all or part of the amount paid (or payable). Where no allowance for expenses is claimed, an award under s 3(2) is not subject to any deduction.[328]

Where an allowance is sought, the court must consider it 'just' to make the deduction, and have regard to all the circumstances of the case. The onus rests on the party to whom the money was paid (or payable) to establish that the expenses were in fact incurred in or for the purpose of performance.[329] Moreover, the amount which can be retained (or recovered) is not to exceed the expenses incurred; and if the expenses incurred exceeded the amount paid (or payable) the court cannot increase the liability of the defendant.

[2082] Expenses incurred. As explained above, the court may allow a party to retain (or recover) a just sum where expenses were incurred prior

---

325. See *BP Exploration Co (Libya) Ltd v Hunt (No 2)* [1979] 1 WLR 783 at 799. On appeal see [1981] 1 WLR 232 at 243; [1983] 2 AC 352.
326. The provision is subject to a proviso; see [2081].
327. See Treitel, *The Law of Contract*, 10th ed, 1999, p 854.
328. *BP Exploration Co (Libya) Ltd v Hunt (No 2)* [1979] 1 WLR 783 at 800 (affirmed on other grounds [1981] 1 WLR 232; [1983] 2 AC 352).
329. See *Lobb v Vasey Housing Auxiliary (War Widows Guild)* [1963] VR 239.

to the time of frustration if the contract stipulated that a sum would be paid prior to the time of frustration. Therefore, although there is no obligation to make an allowance,[330] s 3(2) may result in a party, such as the suppliers in *Fibrosa Spolka Akcyjna v Fairbairn Lawson Combe Barbour Ltd*[331] retaining (or recovering) something to cover wasted expenditure.

However, unlike the position in other jurisdictions, the court will have no jurisdiction to award a just sum in respect of wasted expenditure where:

(1) the contract did not provide for pre-payment;

(2) the contract provided for pre-payment but the time for payment had not arrived at the time of discharge; or

(3) the contract provided for performance in a non-monetary form.

This may be explained by the unjust enrichment perspective: there is no justification for allowing expenses to be claimed unless the other party is entitled to make a claim for restitution, or entitled to rely on discharge as a defence to a claim for payment of a sum of money which ought to have been paid prior to frustration.

[2083] **Benefits obtained.** Sections 3(3), (4) and (5) deal with restitution in respect of benefits obtained by one party to the contract[332] as a result of anything done by any other party to the contract 'in, or for the purpose of, the performance of the contract'. Under s 3(3) the benefit must be a 'valuable benefit' (other than the payment of money to which s 3(2) applies) and the benefit must have been obtained prior to frustration. The court may award such sum, not exceeding the 'value' of the benefit, as it considers just, having regard to all the circumstances of the case, and, in particular:

(1) to the amount of any expenses incurred before the time of discharge by the benefited party, including any sums paid or payable to any other party in pursuance of the contract and retained or recoverable by virtue of s 3(2); and

(2) to the effect in relation to the benefit of the circumstances giving rise to the frustration or avoidance of the contract.

There are 'two distinct stages'[333] in the assessment of an award under s 3(3), namely: identification and valuation of the benefit; and calculation of the just sum. Where the plaintiff's performance required work to be done or services to be provided, it seems that it is the end product of the work or services that has to be identified,[334] and valued at the moment before frustration. The court must then decide what, in the circumstances of the case, it is just to award to the plaintiff. What is the effect of requiring the court to have regard to two matters in particular? Paragraph (1) is

---

330. See *Gamerco SA v ICM/Fair Warning (Agency) Ltd* [1995] 1 WLR 1226 where Garland J declined to make any allowance even though expenses were proved.
331. [1943] AC 32 (see [2067]).
332. For the position with respect to benefits conferred on third parties see [2086].
333. *BP Exploration Co (Libya) Ltd v Hunt (No 2)* [1979] 1 WLR 783 at 801 (affirmed [1981] 1 WLR 232; [1983] 2 AC 352).
334. *BP Exploration Co (Libya) Ltd v Hunt (No 2)* [1979] 1 WLR 783 at 801 (affirmed [1981] 1 WLR 232; [1983] 2 AC 352).

relatively straightforward: its purpose is to prevent double counting of expenses incurred.[335] Paragraph (2) is more difficult.

Consider, for example, a contract for the construction of machinery on the defendant's premises which is frustrated by the destruction of the premises after the machinery has been partially constructed. Assume that the contract price was $5000 and that a sum of $1000 was paid to the contractor prior to frustration. Assume also that the contractor incurred expenses of $3000 in designing and building the machinery and that its value, the moment before frustration, was $1500. The maximum which the court may award under s 3(3) is the value of the benefit,[336] that is, $1500. However, the court must take three other considerations into account:[337]

- the expenses incurred by the contractor;
- any sum retained under s 3(2); and
- the effect of the circumstances which gave rise to frustration.

The contractor's expenses were $3000 and, for the purposes of argument it can be assumed that having regard to these expenses, it would be just to allow the contractor to retain the $1000 pre-payment under s 3(2). That assumption reduces the amount which may be recovered under s 3(3) to $500. Whether the court should award the contractor this sum, or any part of it, depends mainly on how the court interprets the requirement that it have regard to the effect of the circumstances which frustrated the contract.

One view is that because destruction of the defendant's premises destroyed the machinery there is no benefit at all if regard is had to the circumstances.[338] The alternative view is that the benefit must be valued prior to the event, and the event taken into account when assessing the sum which the court in its discretion considers just.[339] Although the alternative view might appear more logical, it amounts to a reversal of *Appleby v Myers*,[340] and is therefore controversial. If the Act said that account must be taken of the discharge of the contract,[341] the alternative view would be correct. But because the reference is to the 'circumstances giving rise to the frustration', the first view is to be preferred, at least as a matter of statutory interpretation.

[2084] Overhead expenses and work done. Section 3(4) of the Act provides that in estimating for the purposes of ss 3(2) and (3) the amount of any expenses incurred by any party to the contract, the court may include 'such sum as appears to be reasonable in respect of overhead

---

335. See *BP Exploration Co (Libya) Ltd v Hunt (No 2)* [1979] 1 WLR 783 at 808 (affirmed [1981] 1 WLR 232; [1983] 2 AC 352). See also *Libyan Arab Foreign Bank v Bankers Trust Co* [1989] QB 728 at 772.
336. See *BP Exploration Co (Libya) Ltd v Hunt (No 2)* [1979] 1 WLR 783 at 799 (affirmed [1981] 1 WLR 232; [1983] 2 AC 352).
337. See also [2084], [2085], [2087].
338. *BP Exploration Co (Libya) Ltd v Hunt (No 2)* [1979] 1 WLR 783 at 801 (affirmed [1981] 1 WLR 232; [1983] 2 AC 352 but without reference to this point).
339. See Birks, *An Introduction to the Law of Restitution*, 1985, p 253; Treitel, *The Law of Contract*, 10th ed, 1999, pp 853.
340. (1867) LR 2 CP 651 (see [2066]).
341. As in New South Wales; see [2074].

expenses' and any 'work or services performed personally' by the party. This is without prejudice to the generality of the earlier provisions.

[2085] Money payable under insurance contract. Under s 3(5) the court must not take into account, when considering whether a sum is to be recovered or retained by a party under ss 3(2), (3) and (4), any sums which have, by reason of the circumstances giving rise to the frustration or avoidance of the contract, become payable to that party under any contract of insurance. The provision is subject to a qualification that the court may have regard to an *obligation* to insure imposed by an express term of the contract or under any enactment.

It is perhaps significant that s 3(5) does not refer to money payable under a contract for insurance to a party who obtains a valuable benefit before the time of discharge. Thus, when considering the effect of frustration on the benefit, it may be that the court can have regard to the fact that frustration gives rise to a claim under an insurance contract.

[2086] Benefits conferred on third parties. Section 3(6) extends the operation of s 3(3) to the following situation. Assume that A is subject to obligations under a contract in consideration of the performance of a promise by B and undertakes to confer benefits on a third party (C). Section 3(6) provides that, irrespective of whether C is a party to the contract, the court may treat any benefit conferred on C as a benefit obtained by A. The court must consider whether the circumstances of the case are such that it is just so to treat the benefit.

[2087] Terms dealing with frustration. Section 4(3) provides that where a term, on its 'true construction' is intended to have effect in the circumstances which have occurred, the court must apply the provision, and only give effect to s 3 to such extent as is consistent with the provision.[342] This applies irrespective of whether the circumstances which have occurred operate, or would but for the contractual provision operate, to frustrate or avoid the contract. It also applies if the contractual provision was intended to have effect irrespective of the circumstances which have in fact arisen.

[2088] Contracts to which the Act applies. The Act applies to contracts whenever made, in respect of which the time of discharge was on or after 29 September 1959: s 4(1).

The Act also applies to contracts to which the Crown is a party: s 4(2).

[2089] Contracts to which the Act does not apply. Section 4(5) excludes from the operation of the Act:

- a charterparty, other than a time charterparty or one by way of demise;
- a contract for the carriage of goods by sea other than a charterparty; and
- a contract of insurance.

In addition, the Act may be expressly excluded by the parties' contract.

---

342. *BP Exploration Co (Libya) Ltd v Hunt (No 2)* [1979] 1 WLR 783 at 806–7 (affirmed [1981] 1 WLR 232; [1983] 2 AC 352).

[2090] Contracts severable into parts. Where it appears to the court that a part of a contract to which the Act applies can be severed from the remainder, s 4(4) may apply and require the severable parts to be treated as separate contracts.

For s 4(4) to operate, the portion of the contract which is severed must have been 'wholly performed' before the time of discharge, or wholly performed except for the payment of sums 'which are or can be ascertained under the contract'. The court is then required to treat the part which has been performed as not subject to the Act, and to apply the Act only to the severed part.

[2091] Basis of recovery. Section 5 provides that all actions to recover money payable under the Act are deemed to be 'founded on simple contract'.[343]

South Australia[344]

[2092] Position governed by *Frustrated Contracts Act* 1988. In South Australia the consequences of frustration are regulated by the *Frustrated Contracts Act* 1988 (SA). The Act came into force on April Fools Day 1988, a not inappropriate date for any legislation dealing with the consequences of frustration.

Section 7(1) provides for an 'adjustment between the parties so that no party is unfairly advantaged or disadvantaged in consequence of the frustration'. The Act sets out to achieve, broadly, the same goal as that underlying the New South Wales Act, namely, restitution of benefits plus an element of apportionment of net loss suffered.[345]

[2093] Application of the Act. The Act applies to contracts avoided under s 7 of the *Sale of Goods Act* 1895 (SA) (s 3(1)), and binds the Crown (s 4(3)).

However, the Act may also be excluded by a term of the contract (s 4(1)(b)) and certain contracts are excluded from the operation of the Act by s 4(2). The main exclusions are:

- contracts made before the commencement of the Act;
- charterparties, other than time charterparties or charterparties by way of demise; and
- any other contracts for the carriage of goods by sea and insurance contracts.

[2094] Extent of discharge. Sections 5 and 6 regulate the extent and effect of discharge. In providing that a contract is not wholly frustrated by the frustration of a particular part of the contract if that part is severable

---

343. Contrast the position under *Law Reform (Frustrated Contracts) Act* 1943 (UK), s 1(2).
344. We are grateful to Andrew Stewart, Professor of Law at Flinders University, for providing material from which the paragraphs below are derived. See also Andrew Stewart, 'The South Australian Frustrated Contracts Act' (1992) 5 *JCL* 220.
345. See further [2095].

from the remainder of the contract,[346] s 5 appears to do no more than restate the common law position.[347]

Under s 6(1), frustration has the effect of discharging all obligations that remain unperformed, whether or not performance had fallen due. However, s 6(2) exempts any 'obligation that is, according to the proper construction of the contract, to survive frustration', thus ensuring that obligations intended to operate *after* frustration remain enforceable.[348] Section 6(2) also states that an action for damages may be maintained in respect of loss suffered as a result of any breach prior to frustration, but requires assessment of damages to take account not only of the fact that frustration has occurred, but also of any adjustment or right to an adjustment under the Act.[349]

[2095] **Adjustment under the Act.** The adjustment is to be effected, according to s 7(2), in four steps.[350] First, the aggregate value of *contractual benefits* received up to the date of frustration by each party[351] is assessed as at the date of frustration.

Second, the aggregate value of the *contractual performance* of each party to the contract is calculated up to the date of frustration.

Third, the second sum is subtracted from the first sum, and the remainder notionally divided between the parties in equal shares.

Fourth, an adjustment is made between the parties so that there is an equalisation of the contractual return of each at the figure attributed under the third step.

Section 7(6) applies where a party to a contract purportedly performs a contractual obligation, or an act preparatory to performance, after frustration of the contract. Provided that the party did not know and could not reasonably be expected to have known that the contract had been frustrated, the value of the performance (and of any consequent contractual benefits) is brought into account for the purposes of any adjustment as if it had occurred prior to frustration.

A broad discretion is conferred on the court by s 7(4), to make the necessary adjustment on a 'more equitable basis' than that of s 7(2). No guidance is given as to how this discretion is to be exercised, but presumably regard would be had to the basic aim of an adjustment laid down in s 7(1). That still leaves the object of the provision unclear. Is the intention that any adjustment conform to the basic premise of restitution plus apportionment of loss? Or are the details of the scheme merely one way of preventing unfair advantage or disadvantage, so that it would be quite acceptable for a court to achieve what it considers to be a more 'equitable' adjustment?

---

346. Cf [2070], [2090].
347. See [2060].
348. See [2064].
349. Cf *Frustrated Contracts Act* 1978 (NSW), s 8 (see [2071]); *Frustrated Contracts Act* 1959 (Vic), s 4(3) (see [2087]).
350. Expansive powers for the purpose of giving effect to this adjustment are conferred by s 7(5).
351. For the position of guarantors and persons who are jointly parties to a contract see ss 3(1) and 7(7) respectively.

The 'integrated' approach produces a return for each party after a single calculation. The Act does not deal separately with different types of performance, and it looks at the net positions of all parties collectively and then allocates a return, as opposed to looking at each party individually. These features make the Act considerably simpler than the New South Wales legislation. However, the provision for a residual discretion, when added to the ambiguities surrounding issues of valuation,[352] has the unfortunate consequence of precluding any certainty that legal advisers might have in predicting the outcome of the Act's application.

[2096] Valuation of benefits. In s 3(1) of the Act, 'contractual benefit' is defined as:

(1) a benefit received by a party under the contract;
(2) a benefit that is received by a party otherwise than under the contract but:
   (i) at a cost to the party that is taken into account under the Act in calculating the value of the contractual performance of that party; or
   (ii) in circumstances in which the receipt of the benefit constitutes part of the contractual performance of that party.

Under s 7(2), benefits are to be assessed 'as at the date of frustration'. But s 3(3) provides that the effect of frustration is to be taken into account in making a valuation. This must, however, be read together with s 3(4), which provides that where an event occurring before, or resulting in the frustration of a contract, diminishes the value of a contractual benefit, a party is in certain circumstances deemed to have received a benefit equivalent to that diminution. The circumstances described in s 3(4) are:

(1) where the event consists of, or arises from, a negligent act or omission for which that party is responsible;
(2) where the risk of the event occurring is, by law or custom, to be borne by that party or is a risk against which that party should, in accordance with ordinary prudence or good business practice, have insured; or
(3) where the event consists of, or arises from, an act or omission for which that party is responsible but which is 'extraneous' to the contract.

The effect is to discount any loss in value caused by the frustrating event in any of the three situations, placing the burden on one party rather than apportioning it.

Paragraph (1) appears to be largely misconceived. Since a negligent act or omission causing what would otherwise be 'frustration' will constitute 'self-induced frustration', and prevent discharge under the doctrine of frustration,[353] the paragraph can only apply to events occurring before frustration which do not contribute to the occurrence of the event.

---

352. See [2096]–[2098].
353. See [2043]–[2048].

Paragraph (2) will rarely apply, since there will usually be no frustration if the risk is of a type to be 'borne by that party or is a risk against which that party should, in accordance with ordinary prudence or good business practice, have insured'. It is difficult to know quite what to make of para (3). It seems intended to apply to an act or omission which contributes to the occurrence of the event which has frustrated the contract, but which does not constitute a breach of contract. Perhaps there is an idea that, although not debarred from relying on frustration, such a party should still be held responsible for the act or omission. This responsibility is expressed in terms of a notional benefit. If so, its effect is to restrict unduly the 'lost value' provision in s 3(3).

By applying to 'an event occurring before' the frustration of a contract, s 3(4) also attempts to deal with the situation where a party who has initially derived a benefit from performance has lost all or part of the value of that benefit by the date of frustration. The effect is that the apportionment exercise is not distorted by losses being counted which have nothing to do with the transaction. The combined result is that a party will only be able to have a benefit calculated at a figure reduced from its original value where neither party has caused the loss, and neither would have been expected to bear the risk of the loss.[354]

[2097] Valuation of performance. Just as the valuation of benefit provisions in the Act are somewhat problematic, so also is the other preliminary calculation necessary for an adjustment to be made under s 7, that of the cost that each party has incurred in relation to performance. 'Performance' here includes anything done by way of preparation, as well as the actual fulfilment of an obligation: s 3(1).[355]

Section 3(2) sets out how performance is valued. First, the value of a monetary payment is the amount of the payment.

Second, if performance is valued by the contract, (or such a value can be deduced from the contract) that value applies. This is presumably intended to cover the situation where full or part performance has been rendered, and the value of the agreed counter-performance appears on the face of the contract. Allowing value to be deduced raises the possibility of pro-rating of the agreed return or contract price where partial performance is rendered. It is, however, far from easy to calculate the appropriate rateable proportion of the contract price in many instances, particularly when the precise basis for pro-rating is not specified. This explains why there is a third case.

Third, in any other case, value is determined by first calculating the costs incurred by the party in carrying out, or preparatory to carry out, contractual obligations.[356] This figure is increased (or reduced) by the percentage profit (or loss) which the party in question would have made from full performance of the contract. This allows for purely preparatory work which results in no performance actually being rendered. But in other

---

354. Section 3(4) does not allow for the possibility of a rise in value of a benefit between the dates of receipt and frustration.
355. Where a party's performance is referable to a number of separate contracts, the court may apportion the value of the performance between the contracts as it thinks just: s 4(3).
356. This includes a reasonable allowance for work done by the party.

situations it is difficult to see how this provision can work alongside the second case. In what circumstances is it intended that pro-rating is *not* to be used under the second case?

The general intent of s 3(2) is plainly to value performance not according to its actual cost, but according to what the contract price would have allowed for it, whether higher under a 'good' bargain or lower under a 'bad' one. Unfortunately, that intent is fatally flawed. In implementing the principle that the profit/loss component of the original bargain is to be respected in making the necessary adjustment, s 3(2) will, leaving aside the difficulties in making the necessary calculations, operate appropriately in the situation where one party makes a profit and the other a corresponding loss — in other words where *one's good bargain is the other's bad bargain*. This may occur where, for instance, one party agrees to pay the other more (or less) than the 'market rate' applicable to the type of performance in question. But many contracts envisage *both* parties making a profit; and correspondingly may, if fully performed, prove to be bad bargains for both. Section 3(2) has no means of allowing for these situations, because it looks solely at the strength of the performer's bargain. Whichever formula is used, the performer's actual cost is inflated to allow a profit component, which is then built into the calculation of the final aggregate return. But no account is taken of the other party's profit expectation.

Similarly, the performer may have made a bad bargain (anticipated expenditure exceeds the contract price) and this will effectively depreciate the cost figure, to the other's benefit. Yet the latter may also have made a poor bargain, if the market for the benefit required has subsequently fallen. The only extent to which the Act will bring a non-performing party's profit/loss into account will be where the benefit created by performance is still realisable. Frequently, however, the benefit is destroyed by the frustration or diminished to such an extent that only a slight residual value remains. In these circumstances the assessment of the performer's cost under s 3(2) will dominate the calculation of the aggregate return and hence the adjustment between the parties. This scarcely seems satisfactory.

[2098] **Basis of recovery.** Any action seeking an adjustment, or the exercise of the court's consequential powers under the Act, may be commenced before a court as if it were an action under the contract that arose at the time of frustration: s 8.

PART IX
Remedies

Chapter 21

Damages

General 2101
    Right to Damages 2101
    Purpose of a Damages Award 2103
    Proof of Loss 2105
    Rule in Hadley v Baxendale 2108
    Bases of Assessment 2110
    Date for Assessment 2114
    Difficulty of Assessment 2117

Causation and Remoteness 2119
    Causation 2120
    Remoteness of Damage 2123

Contributory Negligence 2129

Mitigation of Loss 2133

Sale of Goods 2138

Particular Issues 2145
    Pre-contract Expenditure 2145
    Anticipatory Breach 2146
    Delay in Performance 2150
    Injured Feelings, Disappointment and Loss of Reputation 2152
    Reinstatement Costs 2155
    Termination 2157
    Alternative Methods of Performance 2162
    Loss of Chance 2163
    Rule in Bain v Fothergill 2165
    Taxation and Inflation 2167
    Lord Cairns' Act 2169

General

Right to Damages

[2101] Existence of breach. Where a breach of contract occurs, whether by failure to perform or by anticipatory breach, the party not in breach ('the plaintiff') is entitled to recover damages. The right to claim damages is implied by law.[1] One explanation of this is the general idea that whenever the law recognises or creates a *primary* obligation (or duty), a *secondary* obligation (or duty) is implied by law if the primary obligation is breached.[2] In the present context, this secondary obligation is to pay damages for the breach of a primary contractual obligation. This secondary obligation will be implied in the absence of a term to the contrary.

It is open to the parties to exclude, restrict or qualify the secondary obligation. However, such provisions are subject to the rules governing exclusion clauses.[3] Similarly, although it is open to parties to quantify the secondary obligation in advance, provisions having this effect are subject to the rules on penalty clauses.[4] More generally, any terms dealing with rights flowing from breach are affected by restrictions on the use of unjust or unconscionable contractual terms.[5]

Although it is quite legitimate to speak of a plaintiff having the *right* to claim damages from a defendant in breach of contract, it is more accurate to say that following a breach of contract a plaintiff is entitled to pursue a remedy. This establishes a contrast between a claim for damages and termination of a contract for breach or repudiation.[6] Unlike claims for damages, which generally depend on the existence of a court order in favour of the plaintiff, a right of termination may be exercised, in most cases at least, without going to court. From this technical perspective, if we describe termination as a 'remedy' it is a form of self-help remedy, whereas damages is a curial one.

Although the concern is with claims in contract, there are situations (some of which are considered) where, because the breach amounts to tortious conduct, damages will be recoverable in tort. However, it is not a general feature that breach of contract amounts to a tort.[7]

[2102] Right to terminate not required. Except in one situation, a plaintiff need not prove the exercise of a right to terminate the performance of a contract in order to claim damages for breach.[8] The one exception is in cases of anticipatory breach, where termination is necessary to complete

---

1. *Photo Production Ltd v Securicor Transport Ltd* [1980] AC 827 at 849.
2. See Tilbury, *Civil Remedies*, 1990, Vol 1, paras 1002–4. See also [1989] and further [2302], [2326].
3. See [769]–[772].
4. See [2207]–[2217].
5. See Chapter 15.
6. See F M B Reynolds, 'Discharge by Breach as a Remedy', in Finn, ed, *Essays on Contract*, 1987, p 183; J W Carter and M J Tilbury, 'Remedial Choice and Contract Drafting' (1998) 13 *JCL* 5. Cf S M Waddams, 'Remedies as a Legal Subject' (1983) 3 *OJLS* 113.
7. The conduct may also amount to breach of the statutory prohibition on misleading and deceptive conduct. See generally Chapter 11.

the plaintiff's cause of action.[9] For example, if prior to the time for delivery of goods, a seller repudiates the obligation to deliver, no breach occurs unless and until the buyer accepts the repudiation as an anticipatory breach. Of course, the buyer may wait until the time appointed for delivery, to see whether the seller delivers, in which case no right to damages accrues[10] unless the seller fails to deliver.[11] Therefore, if the seller does in fact deliver in accordance with the contract, or the contract is frustrated prior to the time for delivery, no right to damages will have accrued to the buyer.[12]

Purpose of a Damages Award

[2103] The compensation principle. The fundamental principle governing the award of damages is that they are compensatory.[13] In other words, the object of the award is to compensate the plaintiff rather than to penalise the defendant. This is true even if the breach is intentional or accompanied by an element of malice, the guiding principle being that the measure of damages is 'not affected'[14] by considerations such as the motive or intention of the defendant in breaching the contract. For example, in *Addis v Gramophone Co Ltd*[15] the plaintiff claimed damages for wrongful dismissal and the jury awarded two sums: £600 and £340. The latter sum covered extra commission due to the plaintiff and there was evidence which justified the award of this amount. However, the former sum could only cover wages which the plaintiff had lost by reason of the dismissal, and as the plaintiff had been employed under a contract providing for the payment of £15 per week, there was no basis for the award of such a large sum, even allowing the plaintiff wages for the full period of notice to which he was entitled under the contract, a period of six months. The House of Lords took the view that the jury must have included a sum to mark their disapproval of the manner of dismissal. Therefore, the jury's verdict could not be sustained.

It follows that exemplary or punitive damages — sometimes awarded in tort[16] to punish a defendant — will not be awarded in contract.[17] It also follows that, where a defendant makes a profit as a result of its breach of

---

8. *Luna Park (NSW) Ltd v Tramways Advertising Pty Ltd* (1938) 61 CLR 286 at 300. Nevertheless, termination may affect the quantification of damages. See [2157]–[2161].
9. *Ogle v Comboyuro Investments Pty Ltd* (1976) 136 CLR 444 at 450; 9 ALR 309.
10. *Huppert v Stock Options of Australia Pty Ltd* (1965) 112 CLR 414.
11. See [2142].
12. See [2063].
13. *Whitfeld v De Lauret & Co Ltd* (1920) 29 CLR 71 at 80; *Johnson v Perez* (1988) 166 CLR 351 at 355, 386; 82 ALR 587; *Ruxley Electronics and Constructions Ltd v Forsyth* [1996] AC 344.
14. *Butler v Fairclough* (1917) 23 CLR 78 at 89 per Griffith CJ (approved *Gray v Motor Accident Commission (formerly State Government Insurance Commission)* (1998) 196 CLR 1 at 6; 158 ALR 485).
15. [1909] AC 488. Cf *Malik v Bank of Credit and Commerce International SA* [1998] AC 20 (financial loss arising from breach of an implied obligation of trust and confidence). Contrast *Burazin v Blacktown City Guardian Pty Ltd* (1997) 142 ALR 144 (statutory provision permitted award for shock, humiliation and distress suffered by employee following wrongful dismissal).

contract, the court has no jurisdiction to award the defendant's profit to the plaintiff unless the plaintiff has sustained a corresponding loss. On the other hand, according to the decision of the House of Lords in *Attorney-General v Blake*,[18] a court may in some cases make such award.

[2104] Contract and tort. Damages in contract and tort generally have one thing in common: the court awards a sum which places the plaintiff in the position which would have been occupied had the wrong (breach of contract or tort) not occurred.[19] However, if matters are looked at more closely, there will usually be a difference in the basis of the award made. In contract 'where a party sustains a loss by reason of a breach of contract, he is, so far as money can do it, to be placed in the same situation, with respect to damages, as if the contract had been performed'.[20] The object is thus to place the plaintiff in the position which would have been occupied had the defendant performed the obligation breached. On the other hand, in tort, placing the plaintiff in the position which would have been occupied but for the legal wrong usually involves restoring the plaintiff to his or her former position, for example, to the position occupied prior to the defendant's fraudulent misrepresentation or negligence.[21]

At one time it seems to have been thought that the principles of law governing remoteness of damage are the same in tort and contract.[22] However, in *Koufos v C Czarnikow Ltd*[23] the House of Lords decided that the test of remoteness in contract is narrower than that applied in tort. Nevertheless, in situations where a breach of contract also involves the commission of a tort, for example, the tort of negligence, the plaintiff will not, it seems, be prejudiced by the choice of cause of action and can normally recover under the wider concept of remoteness even if the action is framed in contract.[24]

---

16. For a list of the categories see *Gray v Motor Accident Commission (formerly State Government Insurance Commission)* (1998) 196 CLR 1 at 27–8 (see Jane Swanton and Barbara McDonald, (1999) 73 *ALJ* 402).
17. See [2103].
18. [2001] 1 AC 268. See further [2107], [2112], [2329].
19. *Monarch SS Co Ltd v A/B Karlshamns Oljefabriker* [1949] AC 196 at 220; *Wenham v Ella* (1972) 127 CLR 454 at 466; *Johnson v Perez* (1988) 166 CLR 351 at 355, 371.
20. *Robinson v Harman* (1848) 1 Ex 850 at 855; 154 ER 363 at 365 per Parke B (approved *Commonwealth of Australia v Amann Aviation Pty Ltd* (1991) 174 CLR 64 at 80, 98, 117, 134, 148, 161; 104 ALR 1).
21. See [1069]. The suggestion in *Junior Books Ltd v Veitchi Co Ltd* [1983] 1 AC 520 that expectation loss may be recovered in tort has not been taken up in the subsequent cases which have shown little inclination towards extending liability in tort for pure economic loss; see, eg *Candlewood Navigation Corp Ltd v Mitsui OSK Lines Ltd* [1986] AC 1. See also *Marks (in a Representative Capacity) v GIO Australia Holdings Ltd* (1998) 196 CLR 494; 158 ALR 333 (expectation damages are not generally available for breach of the statutory prohibition on misleading or deceptive conduct).
22. *Addis v Gramophone Co Ltd* [1909] AC 488 at 498.
23. [1969] 1 AC 350. See also *Astley v Austrust Ltd* (1999) 197 CLR 1 at 23, 28; 161 ALR 155 and generally on remoteness [2123]–[2128].
24. See *Koufos v C Czarnikow Ltd* [1969] 1 AC 350 at 411. Cf *Pennant Hills Restaurants Pty Ltd v Barrell Insurances Pty Ltd* (1981) 145 CLR 625 at 637; 34 ALR 162. See further [2126].

Proof of Loss

[2105] Onus of proof. Where a plaintiff claims to have suffered loss or damage by reason of the defendant's breach, the onus of proving the extent of loss or damage rests on the plaintiff.[25] It must be established:

- that the loss or damage was caused by the defendant's breach[26] and
- that the loss or damage was not too remote.[27]

[2106] Nominal and substantial damages. A distinction is drawn between nominal damages and substantial damages. The former is awarded where, for one reason or another, the plaintiff proves no more than the defendant's breach. For example, in *Luna Park (NSW) Ltd v Tramways Advertising Pty Ltd*,[28] a breach of condition was proved by Luna Park, but because no evidence of loss or damage occasioned by the breach was produced only a nominal sum (one shilling) was awarded under the cross-claim against Tramways.[29] The case illustrates the point that a nominal sum is awarded to indicate the 'infraction of a legal right'.[30]

On the other hand, a plaintiff who proves quantifiable loss or damage will not be restricted to a nominal sum and in this sense is entitled to recover a 'substantial' sum. However, until the loss or damage is actually quantified the plaintiff's damages are 'at large' and the word 'substantial' does not signify that a large sum is always awarded.

[2107] Identifying the loss.[31] Generally speaking, in actions for breach of contract, the court will identify the plaintiff's loss or damage by reference to the position of the *plaintiff* following the defendant's breach. Thus, the plaintiff must establish what has been lost, not what the defendant has saved or gained as a result of the breach.[32] For example, if a buyer of unascertained goods establishes a breach by non-delivery, but the market price of goods of the type which the seller agreed to deliver has fallen, the buyer is, prima facie, limited to the recovery of transaction costs because the buyer can go into the market and purchase equivalent goods for a lower price. The buyer does not displace the prima facie rule merely by establishing that the seller has sold goods to a third party at a higher price, even if this looks to enable the seller to profit from the breach of contract.[33]

---

25. *Luna Park (NSW) Ltd v Tramways Advertising Pty Ltd* (1938) 61 CLR 286.
26. See [2120]–[2122].
27. See [2123]–[2128].
28. (1938) 61 CLR 286.
29. See also *Dyke v McLeish Estates Ltd* (1927) 27 SR (NSW) 74; *Berger v Boyles* [1971] VR 321; *Biotechnology Australia Pty Ltd v Pace* (1988) 15 NSWLR 130 at 156.
30. See *Owners of SS 'Mediana' v Owners etc of SS 'Comet'* [1900] AC 113 at 116 where it is pointed out, in the context of an action in tort, that 'nominal' is a technical expression and does not mean 'small'. See also *Baume v The Commonwealth* (1906) 4 CLR 97 at 116–17.
31. See J L R Davis, 'Damages' in Finn, ed, *Essays on Contract*, 1987, p 200; Daniel Friedmann, 'The Performance Interest in Contract Damages' (1995) 111 *LQR* 468; Brian Coote, 'The Performance Interest, *Panatown*, and the Problem of Loss' (2001) 117 *LQR* 81.
32. See *Tito v Waddell (No 2)* [1977] Ch 106; *Alucraft Pty Ltd v Grocon Ltd* (1994) [1996] 2 VR 386 at 400–1.

There will, however, be cases where a benefit obtained by the defendant does in fact represent the plaintiff's loss.[34]

Rule in Hadley v Baxendale

[2108] Statement of the rule. The basic rule governing the law of remoteness of damage in contract was stated by Alderson B in *Hadley v Baxendale*:[35]

> Where two parties have made a contract which one of them has broken, the damages which the other party ought to receive in respect of such breach of contract should be *such as may fairly and reasonably be considered either arising naturally, ie, according to the usual course of things, from such breach of contract itself,* OR *such as may reasonably be supposed to have been in the contemplation of both parties, at the time they made the contract, as the probable result of the breach of it.*

Italics have been supplied to show the 'rule in *Hadley v Baxendale*'. Although it might appear that there are two rules stated, separated by the capitalised 'or', the better view is that there is a single rule with two branches or limbs.[36]

[2109] General and special damages. Damages under the first limb of the rule in *Hadley v Baxendale*[37] are sometimes described as 'general' damages, and those awarded under the second limb 'special' damages. Accordingly, 'general' damages are those which the law presumes to flow 'naturally' from the breach, whereas 'special' damages are of an exceptional nature and only recoverable where the defendant had prior knowledge of the likelihood that the loss would be suffered.[38]

Bases of Assessment

[2110] Protection of expectation. It is common, when damages are awarded in contract cases, for assessment to protect the plaintiff's expectation of receiving the defendant's performance.[39] Thus, the idea[40] that the plaintiff is entitled to be placed in the same situation as if the contract had been performed usually means that the plaintiff will recover an 'expectation loss'.[41] This does not, however, entail specific performance of

---

33. See also [2107] and further [2329].
34. See [2112].
35. (1854) 9 Ex 341 at 354; 156 ER 145 at 151.
36. See further [2123]–[2128].
37. (1854) 9 Ex 341 at 354; 156 ER 145 at 151.
38. Although the terminology of 'special' damages is employed in the sale of goods legislation (see [2144]) the division has been said to be more appropriate to cases of tort than cases of contract. See *Ströms Bruks Aktie Bolag v Hutchison* [1905] AC 515 at 525. See also *International Minerals & Chemical Corp v Helm* [1986] 1 Lloyd's Rep 81 at 103 (ambiguity). But cf *President of India v La Pintada Compania Navigacion SA* [1985] AC 104 at 115.
39. See generally M G Bridge, 'Expectation Damages and Uncertain Future Losses', in Beatson and Friedmann, eds, *Good Faith and Fault in Contract Law*, 1995, p 427.
40. See [2104].
41. See also *Koufos v C Czarnikow Ltd* [1969] 1 AC 350 at 414, 420; *Wenham v Ella* (1972) 127 CLR 454 at 471; *Burns v MAN Automotive (Aust) Pty Ltd* (1986) 161 CLR 653 at 667, 672; 69 ALR 11.

the contract,[42] even where the defendant has promised to pay money. For example, if V agrees to sell land to P for $100,000, and P fails to attend for settlement, V cannot recover by way of damages the price of the land.[43] Assuming that V has validly terminated the performance of the contract, V is entitled to compensation for the loss of the bargain[44] and if land prices have fallen, so that the land is worth, say $80,000, V is entitled to recover $20,000 on the basis that if P had performed V would have received $100,000 whereas V can now only obtain $80,000 on the market.[45]

The influence of the expectation approach is shown by the fact that in commonly recurring situations, such as non-acceptance and non-delivery of goods, a particular expectation will be presumed to apply.[46] Thus, in cases of non-acceptance and non-delivery of goods the plaintiff will almost invariably recover the difference between market price and the contract price.

Damages are not invariably awarded to protect a plaintiff's expectation interest, and other bases for assessing the plaintiff's loss may be considered. These bases protect a plaintiff's reliance or restitution interest. However, in all situations the guiding principle is simply that the plaintiff is entitled to be placed in the same situation as if the contract had been performed.[47]

[2111] Reliance damages. It is not at all uncommon for a plaintiff to expend money in the performance[48] of a contract. If the defendant breaches the contract the plaintiff may find that the expenditure is wasted and may therefore seek to recover the wasted expenditure as damages.[49]

Usually, the claim for reliance damages does not form the main basis for an award.[50] However, in *McRae v Commonwealth Disposals Commission*[51] the plaintiff was awarded a contract for the salvage of an oil tanker 'said to contain oil' and 'lying on Jourmaund Reef ... approximately 100 miles north of Samarai'. The plaintiffs equipped a vessel and sent it from Sydney to where the vessel should have been found — some distance from Port Moresby. It transpired that no such tanker existed and the High Court held the Commonwealth had breached an implied promise that the tanker existed.[52] The court also held that the appropriate way to compensate the plaintiffs was to award damages based on the money thrown away in searching for the tanker. As Dixon and Fullagar JJ said[53] in their joint

42. See *Marks (in a Representative Capacity) v GIO Australia Holdings Ltd* (1998) 196 CLR 494 at 502.
43. See [2238].
44. See further [2158].
45. Cf *Mallick v Parish* (1916) 16 SR (NSW) 305.
46. See [2140], [2142].
47. See *Commonwealth of Australia v Amann Aviation Pty Ltd* (1991) 174 CLR 64.
48. For the case of pre-contractual expenditure see [2145].
49. Subject to rules preventing double recovery: [2113].
50. The emphasis on reliance loss in the seminal article by L L Fuller and W R Perdue, 'The Reliance Interest in Contract Damages' (1936, 1937) 46 *Yale LJ* 52 and 373 is not fully supported by Australian law. See also H K Lücke, 'Two Types of Expectation Interest in Contract Damages' (1989) 12 *UNSWLJ* 98, where the neglect of damages in respect of consequential loss is noted. See also M A Eisenberg, 'The Emergence of Dynamic Contract Law' (2000) *California Law Review* 1743.
51. (1951) 84 CLR 377.
52. See [1210].

[2111]

judgment: in the 'waste of their considerable expenditure seems to lie the real and understandable grievance of the plaintiffs'. Accordingly, the court awarded the costs of setting up and sending out the salvage expedition. Expenses incurred must be 'reasonable'. In *McRae's* case the plaintiffs had in fact grossly exaggerated their claim. However, the court was able to arrive at a reasonable sum, on the basis of the evidence produced by the plaintiffs, and the Commonwealth could not prove that, had the tanker existed, the expenditure would have been wasted in any event.

The main reason that the concept of reliance damages does not figure prominently in the cases is that generally a plaintiff is adequately compensated by damages awarded on an expectation basis, for loss of the bargain. In *McRae's* case there was no basis for quantifying loss of bargain damages. Another situation in which the plaintiff may claim reliance damages is where no profit would have been made on the transaction. For example, if A agrees to sell goods to B on a constant market, the goods can be sold for the same price if the buyer refuses to accept the goods. In such a case A may claim any money thrown away in sending the goods to the buyer. On the other hand, if it is established that the plaintiff has in fact made a bad bargain, a claim to recover the full amount of any expenditure wasted will be rejected by the court on the ground that awarding the full amount would place the plaintiff in a better position than if the contract had been performed.[54] In *Commonwealth of Australia v Amann Aviation Pty Ltd*[55] Amann agreed to provide aerial surveillance of Australia's northern coastline for three years. Amann incurred substantial expenditure in acquiring aircraft, and other costs and expenses. The Commonwealth repudiated the contract. Since, had it run for its full term, Amann's income under the contract would not have exceeded the contract price, the Commonwealth contended that Amann was not entitled to recover its reliance loss as damages. However, although there was no contractual right of renewal, Amann could legitimately say that it would occupy a negotiating position superior to that of its competitors when the contract expired. The High Court held that, because Amann had established that the Commonwealth's breach deprived it of the chance[56] of obtaining a renewal, the onus was on the Commonwealth to prove that the contract was in fact an unprofitable one. Since this onus was not discharged, Amann recovered its reliance loss.[57]

---

53. (1951) 84 CLR 377 at 412.
54. Cf *C & P Haulage v Middleton* [1983] 1 WLR 1461 (see A S Burrows, (1984) 100 *LQR* 27).
55. (1991) 174 CLR 64 (see G H Treitel, (1992) 108 *LQR* 226). See also S M Waddams, 'Damages: Assessment of Uncertainties' (1998) 13 *JCL* 55; Nick Seddon, 'Contract Damages Where Both Parties Are at Fault' (2000) 15 *JCL* 207 where *Amann* is discussed from broader perspectives.
56. See generally [2163]–[2164].
57. This was also the position in *McRae's* case where, because there was no tanker in existence, it was impossible to prove the plaintiffs would not have recouped their expenditure. See also *Goldburg v Shell Oil Of Australia Ltd* (1990) 95 ALR 711 at 720. Cf *CCC Films (London) Ltd v Impact Quadrant Films Ltd* [1985] QB 16.

Where the rule in *Bain v Fothergill*[58] applies, the plaintiff is, by an arbitrary rule of the common law, restricted to reliance damages and cannot claim damages for loss of the bargain.

[2112] Restitution damages. Where a plaintiff confers benefits on the defendant, but is unable to claim the contract price because, for example, the defendant has prevented completion of performance,[59] the plaintiff may recover damages assessed by reference to the value of the benefit obtained from the plaintiff's partial performance, as where an employee is unlawfully dismissed after partial performance of an employment contract.[60] Similarly, where a buyer of goods pays the price in advance of delivery, but the seller does not deliver, or delivers worthless goods, the buyer is entitled to recover a sum equal to the amount paid, less the value of any benefit in fact obtained.[61] In such cases the plaintiff's loss simply represents the value of the benefit which the defendant obtained.

Such claims are relatively rare under Australian law. Usually, damages in protection of the plaintiff's restitution interest are simply an element of a general damages award, as where the claim includes money paid to the defendant which is effectively lost or thrown away because of the defendant's breach.[62] It is, moreover, difficult to draw a sharp distinction between restitution and reliance damages, because the former arises out of reliance on the contract. The difference is more marked where reliance does not involve the conferral of any benefit on the defendant but the plaintiff is able to recover money thrown away.[63]

In many cases where damages assessed to protect a restitution interest might be sought, the plaintiff may prefer to present the claim as one for restitution not damages. Thus, where a total failure of consideration occurs, for example, on the termination of a contract for the sale of land, money paid is recoverable by the purchaser as restitution and there is no need to claim damages. Such a claim invokes the principle of unjust enrichment.[64] A more controversial question is whether a plaintiff can recover damages based on a benefit obtained by the defendant which does not represent a loss to the plaintiff.[65]

[2113] Combined claims. The method for assessing damages is, ultimately, a matter for the court: a plaintiff cannot claim an entitlement to elect between the bases of assessment considered above.[66] Moreover, where it is appropriate to do so, a court may assess damages on more than one basis. However, since the plaintiff is not entitled to recover an amount which exceeds the loss actually suffered, care must be taken to ensure both

---

58. (1874) LR 7 HL 158. See [2165]–[2166].
59. See [1810].
60. See *Automatic Fire Sprinklers Pty Ltd v Watson* (1946) 72 CLR 435 at 451, 452, 461, 465, 476.
61. See, eg *Beale v Taylor* [1967] 1 WLR 1193.
62. See, eg *Aerial Advertising Co v Batchelors Peas Ltd (Manchester)* [1938] 2 All ER 788.
63. See, eg *CCC Films (London) Ltd v Impact Quadrant Films Ltd* [1985] QB 16.
64. See [2306].
65. See [2329]. See also [2107], [2112].
66. *Commonwealth of Australia v Amann Aviation Pty Ltd* (1991) 174 CLR 64.

that damages are not awarded on mutually inconsistent bases, and that the plaintiff does not recover the same loss twice over. Two cases may be contrasted.

In *Cullinane v British 'Rema' Manufacturing Co Ltd*[67] the plaintiff purchased a clay pulverising and drying plant from the defendants at a price of £6578. The defendants guaranteed that the machinery would produce dry clay at a rate of six tons per hour, but the machine was found to be incapable of producing clay at that rate. Accordingly, the plaintiff claimed damages under five heads. Heads A, B and C represented capital expenditure; head D covered interest on A, B and C; and head E represented lost profit. Therefore, the plaintiff was claiming not only his reliance loss (heads A, B and C) but also his expectation loss (head E). The court rejected the claim to recover both the whole of the plaintiff's capital loss as well as the whole of the profit which the plaintiff would have made, because the plaintiff could not have earned the profit without incurring capital expenditure. The plaintiff was found to have conceded that he was only entitled to recover up to the date of the trial which effectively limited the claim to profits to three years even though the machinery had an expected life of 10 years. A majority of the court held that the plaintiff was entitled to recover lost profit for the three-year period, but not his loss of capital as well.

The *British 'Rema'* case was distinguished by the High Court in *TC Industrial Plant Pty Ltd v Robert's Queensland Pty Ltd*.[68] The plaintiff purchased a machine known as a 'Hazemag' Impeller Breaker, designed to crush stone and gravel, in order to fulfil a contract entered into with the Commonwealth for the supply of crushed stone. The machine was found to be unsuitable for the plaintiff's purpose and it was able to establish that this constituted a breach of a term of the contract. The machine was rejected and the plaintiff claimed damages. The trial judge awarded £15,889 to cover wasted expenditure and £12,000 to represent the profit lost by reason of the plaintiff's inability to fulfil its contract with the Commonwealth. The defendants argued that these heads of damage could not be combined. The court said, first, that the justification of the court's refusal in the *British 'Rema'* case to award the capital outlay lay in the failure to claim profits for the final seven years of the machine's life. Second, in the instant case, since the machine had been rejected by the plaintiff there was no 'residual value' to be allowed for. In other words, there was no need for the plaintiffs to give credit for the depreciated value of the machine. The plaintiff was therefore able to recover the costs incurred in purchasing the machine and trying to employ it in the contract with the Commonwealth, less payments received from the Commonwealth. The trial judge had assessed this sum as £15,889. Third, however, the court was not satisfied that £12,000 was the correct figure to award for loss of profit. The case was therefore remitted to the Supreme Court of Queensland for damages to be re-assessed.

The *TC Industrial Plant* case expresses the view that expectation damages, in the form of lost profit, can be recovered in addition to reliance

---

67. [1954] 1 QB 292.
68. (1963) 180 CLR 130. See also *Wenham v Ella* (1972) 127 CLR 454 at 463–4, 465–6, 473.

damages — wasted expenditure — provided that the award does not allow the plaintiff to recover profit without spending the money required to make that profit. Thus, if the plaintiff spends $X on a machine in the expectation of making $Z (a sum found by adding $X (the price) to $Y (the profit to be obtained by working it)), the plaintiff is entitled to recover what the machine would have been worth had it complied with the contract, presumably $X, minus the actual value of the machine. Alternatively, the plaintiff can recover $X plus $Y minus $X (in the form of depreciation) and, in addition, the capital outlay ($X).[69]

Date for Assessment[70]

[2114] General rule. The general rule in contract is that damages are assessed, on a once and for all basis,[71] at the date of breach.[72] For example, a buyer's damages for non-delivery are assessed as at the time appointed for delivery or, if there is no time appointed, the time of the seller's refusal or failure to deliver.[73] There are, however, exceptions to the general rule.

Given that inflation is generally not taken into account when assessing damages,[74] and that damages are assessed on a once and for all basis, the choice of date for assessment may have considerable impact. The earlier the date chosen the more that the plaintiff bears the risk of inflation. This provides some incentive for the courts to treat the choice of date as a matter of judgment rather than an inflexible rule.[75] Although the general rule is still frequently applied in contract cases, probably more so than in tort, it might well be a more accurate description of the choice of date process in the recent cases to say that the appropriate date is when the plaintiff's loss crystallises.[76]

[2115] Exceptions. In *Johnson v Agnew*[77] Lord Wilberforce stated that, even in contracts of sale where the general rule is most frequently applied, it will not be applied if to do so 'would give rise to injustice', in which case the court has the power to 'fix such other date as may be appropriate in the circumstances'. For example, in *Radford v De Froberville*[78] the defendant purchased land from the plaintiff under a contract which provided that she would 'forthwith erect ... a brick wall' separating the land from that owned by the plaintiff. The contract specified the height and minimum thickness of the wall and the materials to be used. In fact, the wall was never built

---

69. See (1963) 180 CLR 130 at 141.
70. See S M Waddams, 'The Date for the Assessment of Damages' (1981) 97 *LQR* 445.
71. See *Johnson v Perez* (1988) 166 CLR 351 at 355, 367, 370, 380, 386.
72. See, eg *Wenham v Ella* (1972) 127 CLR 454 at 473; *Smith New Court Securities v Citibank NA* [1997] AC 254 at 265, 282. For application to cases of anticipatory breach see [2148], [2158].
73. See [2142].
74. See [2168].
75. See *Johnson v Perez* (1988) 166 CLR 351 at 355–6.
76. At least in cases of negligence: *Johnson v Perez* (1988) 166 CLR 351.
77. [1980] AC 367 at 401. See also *Domb v Isoz* [1980] Ch 548; *Johnson v Perez* (1988) 166 CLR 351 at 386–9.
78. [1978] 1 All ER 33. See also *Miliangos v George Frank (Textiles) Ltd* [1976] AC 443 (foreign currency award); *Johnson v Perez* (1988) 166 CLR 351 at 357–8, 386.

and the plaintiff claimed damages for breach of the building covenant. Oliver J concluded that the correct measure of damages was the cost to the plaintiff in carrying out the work on his own land,[79] and that these damages had to be assessed as at the date of the hearing so as to place the plaintiff in as good a position as if the defendant had performed. He also said that this sum might be reduced if the plaintiff ought reasonably to have mitigated his loss by seeking 'an alternative performance at an earlier date'.[80]

[2116] Period covered by the award. The plaintiff's cause of action in damages for breach must be complete at the time when the action is brought and the plaintiff cannot, for example, recover as damages money which would have been payable at a later date.[81] However, the rule only restricts recovery where a future sum depends on a fresh cause of action. For example, if a lessee is late in paying rent, future rental payments cannot be recovered as damages if there is no breach by the lessee of the obligation to pay the future sums. On the other hand, in cases where the plaintiff has terminated the performance of the contract for repudiation by the defendant, there is no objection to future sums being awarded, because the breach is regarded as extending further than the obligations which have fallen due for performance.[82] In such cases a discount may be necessary to take account of future contingencies,[83] but no discount will be necessary in respect of sums which would have been payable after the repudiation but which would have accrued due prior to judgment being given.[84]

Difficulty of Assessment

[2117] No bar to recovery. At times the assessment of damages is extremely difficult, particularly where a speculative claim is in issue.[85] But it is well established that difficulty of assessment is not a bar to recovery,[86] provided, of course, that the difficulty does not arise from the fact that the plaintiff has produced no evidence of loss or damage. As was explained earlier,[87] the absence of such evidence means that the plaintiff will be restricted to a nominal sum. Where damages are difficult to assess because the plaintiff has produced evidence which, while establishing some loss or damage, does not permit the court to make as reliable an assessment as should have been possible, the plaintiff cannot complain if the award is not as high as it would have been had reliable information been produced.[88]

[2118] Relevance to basis of assessment. The fact that damages are difficult to assess on one basis may lead the court to award a sum on some other basis. For example, in *McRae v Commonwealth Disposals Commission*[89]

---

79. See further [2156].
80. [1978] 1 All ER 33 at 56–7. See generally on mitigation [2133]–[2137].
81. *Mann v Capital Territory Health Commission* (1982) 148 CLR 97; 42 ALR 46.
82. *De Soysa v De Pless Pol* [1912] AC 194. See generally [2157]–[2161].
83. See [2160].
84. *Moschi v Lep Air Services Ltd* [1973] AC 331.
85. See further [2118], [2163]–[2164].
86. *Fink v Fink* (1946) 74 CLR 127 at 143.
87. See [2106].
88. *Aerial Advertising Co v Batchelors Peas Ltd (Manchester)* [1938] 2 All ER 788.
89. (1951) 84 CLR 377 (see [2111]).

it was impossible for the court to place any value on what the Commission had purported to sell and the plaintiff's claim for loss of bargain damages would have been restricted to the recovery of the price paid (£285) plus nominal damages, because the subject matter was impossible to value. Accordingly, the court awarded damages on a reliance (rather than expectation) basis.

Causation and Remoteness

[2119] **Methods of limiting the award.** The view is taken, in the law of contract as well as tort, that a defendant should not be held responsible for every loss suffered by a plaintiff and in some way associated with the defendant's wrong. There are two main ways by which the court's award is limited, namely, requirements of causation and remoteness. Other factors, such as mitigation[90] of loss, also operate, in most cases, to reinforce the requirements of causation and remoteness and to keep the defendant's responsibility within acceptable bounds.

Causation

[2120] **Causal connection required.** Causation is a question of fact[91] not law. As Lord Wright said in *Monarch SS Co Ltd v A/B Karlshamns Oljefabriker*[92] causation does not 'depend on remoteness or immediacy in time'. Causation refers to the connection between the breach and the loss suffered. The law is 'not concerned with philosophic speculation, but is only concerned with ordinary everyday life and thoughts and expressions'.[93] Therefore, rather than making a scientific or philosophical inquiry, the relevant question is whether the defendant's breach was so connected with the plaintiff's loss or damage that, 'as a matter of ordinary common sense and experience it should be regarded as a cause of it'.[94]

A sufficient connection will be established if the plaintiff proves[95] that the loss or damage in question would not have been suffered but for the defendant's breach. For example, in *Reg Glass Pty Ltd v Rivers Locking Systems Pty Ltd*[96] the defendants agreed to supply and install a burglar-proof door. A breach of contract was established by proof that the door, when locked, was not reasonably fit to keep burglars out. Therefore, when burglars broke in through the door and stole stock from their premises the plaintiffs were able to recover damages. The position would have been different if it had been proved that the burglars would have gained entry through a door which was reasonably fit.

---

90. See [2133]–[2137].
91. *Bennett v Minister for Community Welfare* (1992) 176 CLR 408 at 412–13; 107 ALR 617. Cf *Environment Agency (formerly National Rivers Authority) v Empress Car Co (Abertillery) Ltd* [1999] 2 AC 22 at 30–2 (scope of the relevant duty must first be identified).
92. [1949] AC 196 at 227 per Lord Wright.
93. *Monarch SS Co Ltd v A/B Karlshamns Oljefabriker* [1949] AC 196 at 228. See also *Alexander v Cambridge Credit Corp* (1987) 9 NSWLR 310 at 315, 350, 351.
94. *March v E & M H Stramare Pty Ltd* (1991) 171 CLR 506 at 522; 99 ALR 423.
95. The onus is on the plaintiff: *Wilsher v Essex Area Health Authority* [1988] AC 1074.
96. (1968) 120 CLR 516.

Although the breach must cause the plaintiff's loss, so that, metaphorically, there is a chain of causation between the breach and the loss, satisfaction of the 'but for' test is not always essential.[97] Indeed, in so far as the test requires the absence of any other cause, it is not satisfactory. In both tort and contract a loss may be regarded as having been caused by a breach even though the test is not satisfied.[98] Account must therefore be taken of the possibility that:[99]

- multiple causes contributed to the loss; and
- the chain of causation may be broken.

[2121] Multiple causes. Difficulties of causation may arise where the plaintiff's loss or damage occurs partly as a result of the defendant's breach and partly as a result of some other factor. Nevertheless, if there are concurrent causes it is sufficient that one of these is the defendant's breach.[100]

In cases where one factor has more relevance than others it is sufficient for the defendant's breach to be the 'decisive' or 'dominant' cause.[101] However, the object of such descriptions is to exclude cases where the contribution of the breach is minimal and they should not be taken as requiring the breach to be the dominant cause of the loss or damage.[102] Thus, most formulations of causation now accept that it is sufficient for the breach to be a cause of the loss or damage.[103] Because the 'but for' test is not an exclusive test of causation, where damages are claimed for negligence, the law in both tort and contract is that a loss may be regarded as having been caused by a breach even though the test is not satisfied because of the presence of some other factor.[104] But if the loss or damage is, as a matter of common sense, caused by factors for which the defendant is not responsible, the causation requirement will not be satisfied.[105]

Although what was reasonably contemplated as the consequence of breach is a criterion for remoteness not causation, it may sometimes be relevant to consider the knowledge of the parties. For example, in *Owners of the Dredger Liesbosch v Owners of SS Edison*[106] the plaintiffs were forced to buy a second dredger to complete work on a dredging contract when the defendants sunk the dredger employed by the plaintiffs. The defendants conceded liability, in tort, and the plaintiffs' claim included expenses which

---

97. *Smith New Court Securities v Citibank NA* [1997] AC 254 at 284–5; *Chappel v Hart* (1998) 195 CLR 232 at 255; 156 ALR 517 at 534; *Kenny & Good Pty Ltd v MGICA (1992) Ltd* (1999) 199 CLR 413 at 426; 163 ALR 611 at 619.
98. See *March v E & M H Stramare Pty Ltd* (1991) 171 CLR 506.
99. See [2121], [2122].
100. *Simonius Vischer & Co v Holt* [1979] 2 NSWLR 322 at 346. Cf *Alexander v Cambridge Credit Corp* (1987) 9 NSWLR 310 at 351.
101. *Monarch SS Co Ltd v A/B Karlshamns Oljefabriker* [1949] AC 196 at 227.
102. *Alexander v Cambridge Credit Corp* (1987) 9 NSWLR 310 at 352.
103. See, eg *Simonius Vischer & Co v Holt* [1979] 2 NSWLR 322 at 346; *Alexander v Cambridge Credit Corp* (1987) 9 NSWLR 310 at 315, 353–8.
104. See, eg *Unity Insurance Brokers Pty Ltd v Rocco Pezzano Pty Ltd* (1998) 192 CLR 603 at 607, 612, 650–1; 154 ALR 361 at 363, 367, 397–8.
105. Cf *Alexander v Cambridge Credit Corp* (1987) 9 NSWLR 310 (auditors of the plaintiff not responsible for downturn in the property market caused by economic conditions).
106. [1933] AC 449.

arose from their lack of money. The House of Lords held that the plaintiffs' financial embarrassment was an independent cause of their loss and could not be the subject of compensation. However, in *Monarch SS Co Ltd v A/B Karlshamns Oljefabriker*[107] it was explained that damages consequent on impecuniosity can be recovered where they were in the contemplation of the parties as likely to flow from the breach.

[2122] **Breaks in the chain.** If an extraneous event, or the conduct of the plaintiff or a third party, intervenes in such a way as to break the chain of causation between the defendant's breach and the plaintiff's loss or damage, the plaintiff will be restricted to a claim for a nominal sum. For example, in *Lexmead (Basingstoke) Ltd v Lewis*[108] the purchaser of a coupling claimed damages from the suppliers and relied on the fact that the coupling — used to join his Land Rover to a trailer — had a design defect. The trailer became detached and a serious accident resulted, but the House of Lords found that the cause of the accident was really the purchaser's negligence in continuing to use the coupling for a considerable period after he had noticed that the handle which operated the locking mechanism was broken. On the other hand, in *Monarch SS Co Ltd v A/B Karlshamns Oljefabriker*[109] a vessel's voyage to a port in Sweden was protracted because of its unseaworthiness and, during the course of the voyage, the vessel was ordered by the British Admiralty to discharge her cargo at Glasgow. Had the vessel not been delayed the indorsees of the bills of lading relating to the cargo would not have been required to forward the goods in neutral ships to Sweden. The House of Lords held that as the orders of the Admiralty were a foreseeable consequence of delay during war there was no break in the chain of causation.

The fact that damage is suffered as a result of a *wrongful* act of a third party does not necessarily break the chain of causation between breach and loss. This is because in some situations the duty of the defendant extends to prevention of a wrong by a third party.[110]

Remoteness of Damage[111]

[2123] **The remoteness concept.** The plaintiff's loss or damage, even if caused by the defendant's breach, must not be too remote. Although the question whether or not a particular item of loss or damage is capable of coming within the concept of remoteness is probably a question of law,[112] once this has been established remoteness becomes a question of fact.[113]

---

107. [1949] AC 196 at 224. Cf *Fox v Wood* (1981) 148 CLR 438; 35 ALR 607. See also *Burns v MAN Automotive (Aust) Pty Ltd* (1986) 161 CLR 653 at 658, 674–5; *March v E & M H Stramare Pty Ltd* (1991) 171 CLR 506 at 518 and [2137].
108. [1982] AC 225. Cf *Quinn v Burch Bros (Builders) Ltd* [1966] 2 QB 370.
109. [1949] AC 196.
110. See, eg *Commonwealth Trading Bank of Australia v Sydney Wide Stores Pty Ltd* (1981) 148 CLR 304; 35 ALR 513. See also *March v E & M H Stramare Pty Ltd* (1991) 171 CLR 506 (tort). But cf *Medlin v State Government Insurance Commission* (1995) 182 CLR 1 at 6; 127 ALR 180 at 183. Contrast *Norton Australia Pty Ltd v Streets Ice Cream Pty Ltd* (1968) 120 CLR 635 at 647 (tort).
111. See Francis Dawson, 'Reflections on Certain Aspects of the Law of Damages for breach of Contract' (1995) 9 *JCL* 125.
112. Cf *H Parsons (Livestock) Ltd v Uttley Ingham & Co Ltd* [1978] QB 791 at 801.

It is necessary to distinguish the test of remoteness under the first limb of the rule in *Hadley v Baxendale*[114] from that applied under the second limb. Although the second limb of the rule is usually concerned with knowledge which *increases* the defendant's liability, there is no reason the defendant's knowledge should not be used to reduce the award to the plaintiff.[115]

Remoteness under the first limb of Hadley v Baxendale

[2124] **How remote?** Under the first limb of the rule in *Hadley v Baxendale*[116] the damages claimed must flow 'according to the usual course of things' from the defendant's breach. But what degree of certainty is actually required? Over the years the courts have tried to reformulate (or at least paraphrase) Alderson B's statement, but without any obvious success. For example, in *Monarch SS Co Ltd v A/B Karlshamns Oljefabriker*[117] Lord du Parcq put the test in terms of what would have been foreseen as a 'serious possibility' and Lord Morton spoke of a 'grave risk'.[118] On the other hand, in *Victoria Laundry (Windsor) Ltd v Newman Industries Ltd*[119] the English Court of Appeal expressed the criterion in terms of 'reasonably foreseeable' losses, and losses 'likely to result' or even those which are 'on the cards'.

In *Koufos v C Czarnikow Ltd*,[120] where the House of Lords reviewed the authorities, the view was taken that 'reasonably foreseeable' is more appropriate to tort than contract cases,[121] and that 'on the cards' is far too imprecise. However, there was no real agreement on the proper criterion to be applied:

- Lord Reid preferred the criterion of 'not unlikely' to result;[122]
- Lord Morris did not dissent from that view but he indicated that 'liable to result' was also acceptable;[123]
- Lord Hodson indicated a preference for 'liable to result';[124] and
- Lord Pearce found 'liable to result' somewhat ambiguous[125] and, like Lord Upjohn,[126] preferred to state the criterion in terms of 'serious possibility' or 'real danger'.

Nevertheless, Lord Reid said[127] that it has 'never been held to be sufficient in contract that the loss was foreseeable as "a serious possibility"

---

113. See *Burns v MAN Automotive (Aust) Pty Ltd* (1986) 161 CLR 653 at 675; *Malik v Bank of Credit and Commerce International SA* [1998] AC 20 at 49–50.
114. (1854) 9 Ex 341 at 354; 156 ER 145 at 151 (see [2108]).
115. *Koufos v C Czarnikow Ltd* [1969] 1 AC 350 at 416.
116. (1854) 9 Ex 341 at 354; 156 ER 145 at 151 (see [2108]).
117. [1949] AC 196 at 233.
118. [1949] AC 196 at 235.
119. [1949] 2 KB 528 at 539, 540.
120. [1969] 1 AC 350.
121. See further [2126].
122. [1969] 1 AC 350 at 388.
123. [1969] 1 AC 350 at 406.
124. [1969] 1 AC 350 at 410–11.
125. [1969] 1 AC 350 at 415.
126. [1969] 1 AC 350 at 425.
127. [1969] 1 AC 350 at 390.

or "a real danger"' and the preponderance of Australian authority would seem to accept Lord Reid's approach.[128]

The discussion in the *Koufos* case is hardly conclusive in favour of any one of the various expressions used. It does, however, indicate that a fairly high degree of probability is required in contract, certainly higher than that applied to damages claims in tort.[129]

[2125] Losses in the 'usual course of things'. Because each contract is unique, in one sense only limited assistance can be gained from previous cases on what is, or is not, to be regarded as in the usual course of things. In *Hadley v Baxendale*[130] itself, the plaintiffs, owners of a flour mill, contracted with the defendants, who were common carriers, to have a broken crankshaft conveyed to engineers for the purpose of manufacturing a new shaft. Delivery of the shaft was delayed and the consequence for the plaintiffs was that the mill was stopped for five days longer than it should have been and profits which would otherwise have accrued were lost. The court held that the defendants were not liable for the lost profits. They were merely carriers who did not know that the mill would be stopped. The plaintiffs might, for example, have had a spare shaft in their possession, and the plaintiffs' loss of profit was not something which the defendants should have contemplated as occurring in the usual course of things.

From a broader perspective, *Hadley v Baxendale* illustrates a general approach under which the first limb reflects a 'conventional' measure of loss. This is highlighted by the presumptive measures applicable to the breach of sale of goods contracts.[131] These and other similar measures give content to the 'usual course of things', so that a plaintiff who seeks to recover on a different basis must justify the claim by reference to the second limb. However, the fact that a presumptive measure of loss is displaced does not mean that the plaintiff is required to rely on the second limb. Thus, in *Koufos v C Czarnikow Ltd*[132] what was previously thought to be the prima facie measure applicable to contracts of carriage by sea was displaced in favour of the prima facie measure analogous to that applicable to late delivery under a contract of sale.[133] The defendants, owners of the vessel *Heron II*, were thus held liable for profit lost by the plaintiffs, charterers of the vessel. The defendants had agreed to carry sugar from Constanza to Basrah but deviated during the course of the voyage, with the result that it took nine or 10 days longer than it should have to reach Basrah. Sugar prices fell on the Basrah market and the plaintiffs suffered loss of profit by selling at a lower price than would have been obtained had the vessel not deviated. The House of Lords held that the loss occurred in the 'usual course of things' because the defendants knew (1) that the plaintiffs were

---

128. See, eg *Wenham v Ella* (1972) 127 CLR 454 at 471–2; *Burns v MAN Automotive (Aust) Pty Ltd* (1986) 161 CLR 653 at 667; *Alexander v Cambridge Credit Corp* (1987) 9 NSWLR 310 at 363–4; Tilbury, *Civil Remedies*, 1990, Vol 1, para 3077. See also *Baltic Shipping Co v Dillon (The Mikhail Lermontov)* (1993) 176 CLR 344 at 365, 368, 370; 111 ALR 289.
129. See also *Astley v Austrust Ltd* (1999) 197 CLR 1 at 23, 28. But see [2126].
130. (1854) 9 Ex 341; 156 ER 145.
131. See generally [2138]–[2144].
132. [1969] 1 AC 350.
133. See [2141].

sugar merchants; and (2) that there was a market for sugar at Basrah. It did not matter that they had no actual knowledge of the plaintiffs' intention to sell because they ought to have contemplated that the plaintiffs would, under the criteria applied, suffer the loss in question.

[2126] Causes of action in both contract and tort. If, as has been suggested,[134] the remoteness test in contract differs from that in tort, what is the position where a plaintiff has concurrent causes of action in contract and tort? The decision in *H Parsons (Livestock) Ltd v Uttley Ingham & Co Ltd*[135] seems to indicate that, whether the plaintiff frames the action in contract or tort, damages will be assessed on the more favourable test. However, the reasoning in the case is not always easy to follow. The plaintiffs, owners and managers of a pig farm, purchased a bulk feed storage hopper from the defendants, who were the manufacturers. Unknown to the plaintiffs, when the hopper was delivered the ventilator lid on the top of the hopper was not opened. The plaintiffs used the hopper to feed pig nuts to their herd, but because of the absence of proper ventilation the nuts became mouldy and eating the mould caused the pigs to become ill. In fact, a large number of pigs died and the plaintiffs suffered a very large financial loss. The trial judge found that at the time of purchase neither party could 'reasonably have contemplated that there was either a very substantial degree of possibility or a real danger or serious possibility' that feeding the pigs mouldy nuts would cause illness. But he also found that the 'natural result of feeding toxic food to animals is damage to their health and maybe death, which is what occurred, albeit from a hitherto unknown disease and to particularly susceptible animals'. In the result he upheld the plaintiffs' claim and left damages to be assessed by an official referee.

In the English Court of Appeal, Lord Denning MR drew a distinction between, on the one hand, claims for loss of profit consequent on breach and, on the other, claims for compensation for physical damage caused by a breach of contract. He said that in the former case the strict criteria discussed in *Koufos v C Czarnikow Ltd*[136] apply, whereas in the latter case the criterion applied to tortious claims is relevant so that the defendant is liable for 'any loss or expense which he ought reasonably to have *foreseen* at the time of the breach as a possible consequence'.[137] In the instant case he had no doubt that the type or kind of damage suffered by the plaintiffs was reasonably foreseeable and held[138] that the defendants were liable in respect of the pigs which died and for veterinary expenses and so on, but not for the profit lost on future sales.

Scarman LJ, with whom Orr LJ agreed, rejected the distinction drawn by Lord Denning. He took the view that, generally, the test for remoteness

---

134. See [2104].
135. [1978] QB 791.
136. [1969] 1 AC 350 (see [2104]).
137. [1978] QB 791 at 803.
138. Applying *Hughes v Lord Advocate* [1963] AC 837 (liability in tort for burns suffered by plaintiff where the defendant could foresee type of injury suffered, even though the injury was caused by an unforeseeable event). Cf *Vacwell Engineering Co Ltd v BDH Chemicals Ltd* [1971] 1 QB 88.

should not differ between contract and tort according to the classification of the plaintiff's cause of action, and said[139] that 'the law is not so absurd as to differentiate between contract and tort save in situations where the agreement, or the factual relationship, of the parties with each other requires it in the interests of justice'. Having regard to this statement, and his inclination towards the view that the difference between the contract test and the tort test is 'semantic, not substantial'[140] one might have expected analysis of the plaintiffs' claim by reference to the test applied in tortious actions. However, Scarman LJ was concerned to show that the defendants were liable under a contract criterion of 'serious possibility' and this resulted in some minute, and not entirely convincing, discussion of the trial judge's findings of fact. He said that the first of the two findings was not conclusive against the plaintiffs because it was not a finding that the defendants 'could not reasonably have had in contemplation that a hopper unfit for its purpose of storing food in a condition suitable for feeding to the pigs might well lead to illness'.[141] He was then able to treat the second finding as establishing, as a serious possibility, that if the hopper proved to be unsuitable by reason of the lack of ventilation, the pigs would become ill. Moreover, once illness was foreseeable as a serious possibility it did not matter that the degree of illness suffered could not have been contemplated.[142]

Remoteness under the second limb of Hadley v Baxendale

[2127] **Degree of knowledge required.** A plaintiff who claims in respect of loss or damage which does not arise in the 'usual course of things' must bring the claim within the second limb of the rule stated in *Hadley v Baxendale*,[143] by relying on knowledge actually possessed by the defendant. For example, in *McRae v Commonwealth Disposals Commission*[144] the court took the view that the plaintiffs' expenditure fell within the second limb, presumably on the basis that the defendants, having promised that a tanker existed, had actual knowledge of the need for salvage operations. On the other hand, in *Victoria Laundry (Windsor) Ltd v Newman Industries Ltd*[145] the requisite degree of knowledge was lacking. The plaintiffs, who carried on business as launderers and dyers, purchased a boiler of considerable capacity from the defendants for the purpose of expanding their operations. The plaintiffs sent a lorry to take delivery but found that the boiler had been damaged. They therefore refused to take delivery until repairs had been carried out and this caused a delay of some five months. The issue before the English Court of Appeal was whether, in addition to a sum of £110 awarded by the trial judge, the plaintiffs were entitled to claim in respect of the business profits which they would have made had the boiler been delivered punctually. They relied on the defendants' knowledge that

---

139. [1978] QB 791 at 806.
140. [1978] QB 791 at 807. Contrast *Alexander v Cambridge Credit Corp* (1987) 9 NSWLR 310 at 365.
141. [1978] QB 791 at 811.
142. See also *Alexander v Cambridge Credit Corp* (1987) 9 NSWLR 310 at 365-6.
143. (1854) 9 Ex 341 at 354; 156 ER 145 at 151 (see [2108]).
144. (1951) 84 CLR 377 (see [2111]).
145. [1949] 2 KB 528.

the plaintiffs were launderers and dyers who needed the boiler for use in their business, and the fact that during negotiations the defendants had been informed of the plaintiffs' intention 'to put it into use in the shortest space of time'. The court held the plaintiffs entitled to recover something for lost profits but not necessarily the profits actually lost. The defendants did not know the precise role of the boiler, that is, whether it was to be an extra unit or to operate in substitution for another boiler. It was, therefore, important to consider how the profits claimed had been calculated. The plaintiffs said a very large number of new customers could have been served and that a number of highly lucrative dyeing contracts for the Ministry of Supply would have been available to them. The court held that the judge was wrong not to award some 'general (and perhaps conjectural) sum for loss of business in respect of dyeing contracts to be reasonably expected';[146] but it rejected the claim to recover specifically the profit on contracts with the Ministry for the reason that the defendants had no knowledge of this business.

[2128] Acceptance of the risk. The most difficult aspect of the second limb of the rule stated in *Hadley v Baxendale*[147] is the extent to which the defendant must have agreed to accept the risk of the damage. At one time it seems to have been thought that there must be a term of the contract indicating the defendant's acceptance of the risk.[148] Although this view has been rejected,[149] there is, of course, nothing to stop the parties expressing their agreement on what is to be regarded as foreseeable.[150] Where there is no express agreement it has been said[151] that the

> basis of the defendant's liability ... is his implied undertaking to the plaintiff to bear it. His actual knowledge of the special circumstances is relevant as *one* of the factors from which his undertaking can be implied. The second factor is also necessary, viz, that he should have acquired this knowledge from the plaintiff, or at least that he should know that the plaintiff knew that he was possessed of it at the time the contract was entered into and so could reasonably foresee at that time that an enhanced loss was liable to result from a breach. Where both these factors are present, the defendant's conduct in entering into the contract without disclaiming liability for the enhanced loss which he can foresee gives rise to the implication that he undertakes to bear it.

On this view the court will, as a matter of law, draw the inference that the defendant has accepted responsibility if the defendant acquired the necessary information from the plaintiff and took no steps to disclaim liability, for example, by having a clause limiting liability in damages inserted in the contract. Thus, in *Gull v Saunders*[152] the plaintiffs purchased an engine and pump from the defendants for the purpose of irrigating their farm. The engine did not prove to be suitable for the plaintiffs' purpose and

---

146. [1949] 2 KB 528 at 543.
147. (1854) 9 Ex 341 at 354; 156 ER 145 at 151 (see [2108]).
148. See *British Columbia etc Saw-Mill Co Ltd v Nettleship* (1868) LR 3 CP 499 at 509.
149. See, eg *Koufos v C Czarnikow Ltd* [1969] 1 AC 350 at 422.
150. Provided it is not a penalty the parties may agree in advance the sum to be recoverable on breach. See M P Furmston, 'Contract Planning: Liquidated Damages, Deposits and the Foreseeability Rule' (1991) 3 *JCL* 11 and further [2207]–[2217].
151. *Robophone Facilities Ltd v Blank* [1966] 1 WLR 1428 at 1448.
152. (1913) 17 CLR 82.

they suffered loss to their crops. In deciding that the defendants were responsible under the second limb, the High Court pointed out that during negotiations the defendants were told:

- that the engine had to be of sufficient power to do work of a special kind;
- that the engine was to be used for irrigation;
- the nature of the crop; and
- that failure by the plaintiffs in their irrigation project would in all probability result in the loss of their crop.

Clearly, on these facts it was just to hold the defendants responsible for the risk in the absence of disclaimer on their part.

In order to rebut the presumption implied by actual knowledge the defendant must show that there was no acceptance of the risk of liability for the damage. In commercial contracts this may be achieved by a suitably drafted exclusion clause.[153] In respect of other types of contracts the defendant may perhaps rely on the fact that the price for performance is out of all proportion with the risk implied by the knowledge obtained.

Contributory Negligence

[2129] Introduction. 'Contributory negligence' does not refer to the breach of a duty of care. Rather, it refers to a careless act or omission of the plaintiff which contributes to the loss or damage which forms the subject of the plaintiff's claim for damages. At common law, the contributory negligence of the plaintiff is not a defence to a claim for breach of contract. In other words, unless the contract provides to the contrary, it is not a defence to a claim for breach of contract for a defendant to show that the plaintiff's carelessness contributed to the loss or damage which forms the subject of the plaintiff's claim.[154]

Nevertheless, as we have seen,[155] the requirement that a plaintiff prove that its loss or damage was caused by the defendant's breach of contract necessarily means that if the plaintiff's own carelessness breaks the chain of causation between the breach and the loss or damage the plaintiff will fail, not on the basis of contributory negligence but on the basis that the loss or damage was not caused by the breach. For example, in *Lexmead (Basingstoke) Ltd v Lewis*[156] the supplier of the coupling was in breach of contract by reason of the defect in the goods even though there was no negligence on his part. But the fact that the plaintiff continued to use it after it had become broken constituted conduct which broke the chain of causation between the supplier's breach and the plaintiff's loss.

The position in tort was somewhat different. At least in relation to the tort of negligence, at common law a plaintiff would fail completely in relation to any claim relying on loss or damage resulting in part from the

---

153. See [769]–[772].
154. See *Astley v Austrust Ltd* (1999) 197 CLR 1.
155. See [2122].
156. [1982] AC 225 (see [2122]).

[2129] plaintiff's own carelessness. This defence of contributory negligence operated in addition to the causation requirement. However, the law was modified by the apportionment legislation,[157] under which contributory negligence ceased to be a total defence. In place of the all or nothing approach of the common law, the apportionment legislation requires the court to reduce the plaintiff's claim to reflect the plaintiff's degree of responsibility for the loss or damage.

Until the decision of the High Court in *Astley v Austrust Ltd*[158] there was considerable doubt whether that legislation, as originally enacted, applied to claims in contract.[159] However, in *Astley* the High Court held that the legislation does not apply to claims in contract. The effect of that decision was soon reversed by legislation amending the apportionment legislation in most jurisdictions.[160] However, *Astley* continues to govern the matter in Western Australia and also in situations to which the amended legislation does not apply.

[2130] Apportionment legislation. Apportionment legislation has been enacted in all jurisdictions,[161] and in all jurisdictions other than Western Australia the legislation will apply to certain claims for breach of contract.

Section 9(1) of the *Law Reform (Miscellaneous Provisions) Act* 1965 (NSW)[162] provides:

> If a person (the claimant) suffers damage as the result partly of the claimant's failure to take reasonable care (contributory negligence) and partly of the wrong of any other person:
>
> (a) a claim in respect of the damage is not defeated by reason of the contributory negligence of the claimant, and

---

157. For the legislation see [2130].
158. (1999) 197 CLR 1 (see Jane Swanton and Barbara McDonald, (1999) 73 *ALJ* 541; Jane Swanton, (1999) 14 *JCL* 251). See generally Michael Tilbury and J W Carter, 'Converging Liabilities and Security of Contract: Contributory Negligence in Australian Law' (2000) 16 *JCL* 78. See also *Scott v Davis* (2000) 175 ALR 217 at 285.
159. See N E Palmer and P J Davies, 'Contributory Negligence and Breach of Contract — English and Australasian Attitudes Compared' (1980) 29 *ICLQ* 415; Jane Swanton, 'Contributory Negligence as a Defence to Actions for Breach of Contract' (1981) 55 *ALJ* 278.
160. See **ACT:** *Law Reform (Miscellaneous Provisions) Amendment Act* 2001; **NSW:** *Law Reform (Miscellaneous Provisions) Amendment Act* 2000; **NT:** *Law Reform (Miscellaneous Provisions) Amendment Act* 2001; **Qld:** *Law Reform (Contributory Negligence) Amendment Act* 2001; **SA:** *Law Reform (Miscellaneous Provisions) Act* 2001; **Tas:** *Tortfeasors and Contributory Negligence Amendment Act* 2000; **Vic:** *Wrongs (Amendment) Act* 2000.
161. See: **ACT:** *Law Reform (Miscellaneous Provisions) Act* 1955; **NSW:** *Law Reform (Miscellaneous Provisions) Act* 1965; **NT:** *Law Reform (Miscellaneous Provisions) Act* 1956; **Qld:** *Law Reform Act* 1995; **SA:** *Law Reform (Miscellaneous Provisions) Act* 2001; **Tas:** *Wrongs Act* 1954; **Vic:** *Wrongs Act* 1958; **WA:** *Law Reform (Contributory Negligence and Tortfeasors' Contribution) Act* 1947.
162. See also **ACT:** *Law Reform (Miscellaneous Provisions) Act* 1955, s 15(1); **NT:** *Law Reform (Miscellaneous Provisions) Amendment Act* 2001, s 16; **Qld:** *Law Reform Act* 1995, s 10(1); **SA:** *Law Reform (Miscellaneous Provisions) Act* 2001, s 7; **Tas:** *Wrongs Act* 1954, s 4; **Vic:** *Wrongs Act* 1958, s 26(1).

(b) the damages recoverable in respect of the wrong are to be reduced to such extent as the court thinks just and equitable having regard to the claimant's share in the responsibility for the damage.

Section 8 of the Act[163] defines 'wrong' as an act or omission that:

(a) gives rise to a liability in tort in respect of which a defence of contributory negligence is available at common law, or

(b) amounts to a breach of a contractual duty of care that is concurrent and co-extensive with a duty of care in tort.

Therefore, if a plaintiff claims damages for the 'breach of a contractual duty of care', and that duty is 'concurrent and co-extensive with a duty of care in tort', the plaintiff's claim must be reduced 'to such extent as the court thinks just and equitable' having regard to the plaintiff's 'share in the responsibility for the damage'.[164]

In Western Australia, and in all other jurisdictions in situations to which the legislation is not applicable, the common law applies and the court will have no jurisdiction to apportion loss or damage by reducing an award in contract, unless the contract provides the contrary, even in cases where the defendant is liable in both tort and contract. In these jurisdictions, the position summarised by Manning JA in *Harper v Ashtons Circus Pty Ltd*[165] will be applicable. He explained that a plaintiff, entitled to sue in contract or tort, may avoid apportionment by abandoning the claim in tort (to which the apportionment legislation would apply) and electing to sue in contract.

The common law position will apply in all jurisdictions in cases where the defendant's breach does not involve the breach of a contractual duty of care,[166] or where application of the apportionment legislation would defeat a defence arising under a contract.[167] Moreover, if the contract (or statute) provides for a limitation of liability which is applicable to the claim, the amount of damages recoverable by the plaintiff (as determined by the court) must not exceed that limitation.[168]

[2131] Breach of concurrent duty. In jurisdictions other than Western Australia the apportionment legislation will be relevant to a claim for

---

163. See also **ACT:** *Law Reform (Miscellaneous Provisions) Act* 1955, s 14; **NT:** *Law Reform (Miscellaneous Provisions) Amendment Act* 2001, s 15; **Qld:** *Law Reform Act* 1995, s 5; **SA:** *Law Reform (Miscellaneous Provisions) Act* 2001, s 3; **Tas:** *Wrongs Act* 1954, s 2; **Vic:** *Wrongs Act* 1958, s 25.
164. See further [2131].
165. [1972] 2 NSWLR 395 at 399.
166. See further [2131], [2132].
167. See **ACT:** *Law Reform (Miscellaneous Provisions) Act* 1955, s 15(4); **NSW:** *Law Reform (Miscellaneous Provisions) Act* 1965, s 9(2) **NT:** *Law Reform (Miscellaneous Provisions) Amendment Act* 2001, s 16(2); **Qld:** *Law Reform Act* 1995, s 10(2); **SA:** *Law Reform (Miscellaneous Provisions) Act* 2001, s 7(3); **Tas:** *Tortfeasors and Contributory Negligence Act* 1954, s 4(1)(a); **Vic:** *Wrongs Act* 1958, s 26(1A).
168. See **ACT:** *Law Reform (Miscellaneous Provisions) Act* 1955, s 15(3); **NSW:** *Law Reform (Miscellaneous Provisions) Act* 1965, s 9(3); **NT:** *Law Reform (Miscellaneous Provisions) Amendment Act* 2001, s 16(2A); **Qld:** *Law Reform Act* 1995, s 10(2A); **SA:** *Law Reform (Miscellaneous Provisions) Act* 2001, s 7(3); **Tas:** *Tortfeasors and Contributory Negligence Act* 1954, s 4(1)(b); **Vic:** *Wrongs Act* 1958, s 26(1B).

damages for breach of contract, if the breach by the defendant amounts to the 'breach of a contractual duty of care that is concurrent and co-extensive with a duty of care in tort'.[169] This has three elements:

(1) the defendant has undertaken a contractual duty of care;

(2) under common law principles of negligence the defendant is also subject to a tortious duty of care; and

(3) the contractual duty is concurrent and co-extensive with the tortious duty.

As a general rule, where the defendant owes a contractual duty of care, a breach of that duty[170] will give rise to concurrent liability in tort and contract. The contractual duty undertaken by the defendant may be express. However, there is no reason to doubt that the implied duty may arise under the general law of implied terms or by reason of statute. The three elements serve to capture situations in which, prior to *Astley v Austrust Ltd*,[171] some courts had held the apportionment legislation to apply. Although the reasoning in those cases must now be seen as based on an erroneous interpretation of the legislation, they may be of some assistance in the application of the recently enacted provisions.

The most likely context in which the contributory negligence of the plaintiff will be relevant is where a professional person such as a doctor, solicitor or engineer breaches an express or implied duty to exercise care in the performance of services, and the carelessness of the client contributes to the loss.[172] For example, the view that negligence by a solicitor in the conduct of a client's affairs gives rise to a liability in contract, but not tort,[173] has been exploded.[174] However, it will depend on the circumstances whether the duty in contract is co-extensive with a common law duty of care. In cases where the duties differ, the apportionment legislation will not apply.

[2132] Cases of strict liability. In cases of strict liability, a defendant who has exercised reasonable care may nevertheless be found to be in breach of contract.[175] For example, a seller who supplies goods which are not fit for the buyer's purpose is in breach of contract even if reasonable care has been exercised. The apportionment legislation is not relevant to such cases.[176]

---

169. For the provisions see [2130].
170. Sometimes termed 'negligent breach of contract', an expression which has, however, been criticised; see *Quinn v Burch Bros (Builders) Ltd* [1966] 2 QB 370 at 378, 379; *Read v Nerey Nominees Pty Ltd* [1979] VR 47 at 51.
171. (1999) 197 CLR 1.
172. See, eg *Queen's Bridge Motors and Engineering Co Pty Ltd v Edwards* [1964] Tas SR 93 (repairer); *Forsikringsaktieselskapet Vesta v Butcher* [1989] 1 AC 852 at 858ff, affirmed by the House of Lords without reference to the point (quantity surveyor).
173. *Groom v Crocker* [1939] 1 KB 194.
174. See, eg *Swain v The Law Society* [1982] 1 WLR 17; *Macpherson v Kevin J Prunty & Associates* [1983] VR 573; *Brickhill v Cooke* [1984] 3 NSWLR 396 at 400–1; *Johnson v Perez* (1988) 166 CLR 351 at 363; *Waimond Pty Ltd v Byrne* (1989) 18 NSWLR 642 and generally J L Dwyer, 'Solicitor's Negligence — Tort or Contract?' (1982) 56 *ALJ* 524. See also on concurrent duties [635], [1857].
175. See generally [1856].

This remains true even if the plaintiff has in fact been negligent, because the *defendant's* breach does not amount to the 'breach of a contractual duty of care that is concurrent and co-extensive with a duty of care in tort'.[177] Thus, the only relevance of the negligence of the plaintiff in such cases is whether it breaks the chain of causation between the defendant's breach and the loss or damage.[178]

Mitigation of Loss

[2133] **The mitigation concept.** The concept of mitigation cannot be defined with any real precision. Nevertheless, it is usually used in connection with:

(1) steps which the plaintiff has taken which do, in fact, operate to minimise loss; and

(2) steps which the plaintiff ought — acting reasonably — to have taken so as to minimise loss or at least so as not to increase it.

In cases where it is contended that the plaintiff should have taken steps to mitigate its loss, the onus of proof is on the defendant to prove this contention.[179]

[2134] **Benefits obtained.** Where, as a consequence of the defendant's breach, the plaintiff obtains benefits which would not otherwise have been available, the plaintiff is usually required to bring these into account, so as to reduce the amount recoverable from the defendant. For example, when an employee is wrongfully dismissed by an employer, the employee must give credit for sums earned from another employer.[180] Thus, assuming that the employee has not been out of work for any time, damages will be expressed as the difference between the sum which the first employer agreed to pay and that received from the second employer.

A more complex illustration is *Lavarack v Woods of Colchester Ltd*.[181] The plaintiff was employed by the defendants in a senior position for a five-year period. A little over two years later the plaintiff was wrongfully dismissed. The plaintiff took up alternative employment and it was held that he had to give credit for this. Thus, the salary which he received had to be deducted from the salary which he would have received from the defendants. But he had also taken a financial interest in his new employers — by the purchase of shares — and in a new company to which he had lent money. Did the

---

176. See, eg *A S James Pty Ltd v Duncan* [1970] VR 705; *Basildon DC v J E Lesser (Properties) Ltd* [1985] QB 839 (see A S Burrows, (1985) 101 *LQR* 161); *Barclays Bank Plc v Fairclough Building Ltd* [1995] QB 214 (see C A Hopkins, [1995] *CLJ* 21).
177. This was also the position prior to the recent amendment of the apportionment legislation. See *Quinn v Burch Bros (Builders) Ltd* [1966] 2 QB 370 at 379 (affirmed at 381); *Barclays Bank Plc v Fairclough Building Ltd* [1995] QB 214.
178. See *O'Connor v BDB Kirby & Co* [1972] 1 QB 90. See also [2122], [2129].
179. *Roper v Johnson* (1873) LR 8 CP 167; *TC Industrial Plant Pty Ltd v Robert's Queensland Pty Ltd* (1963) 180 CLR 130 at 138; *Metal Fabrications (Vic) Pty Ltd v Kelcey* [1986] VR 507; *TCN Channel 9 Pty Ltd v Hayden Enterprises Pty Ltd* (1989) 16 NSWLR 130 at 158.
180. See, eg *Lucy v The Commonwealth* (1923) 33 CLR 229.
181. [1967] 1 QB 278.

plaintiff have to give credit for these investments? The court held that although the investments would not have been possible but for the termination of his employment with the defendants, the plaintiff was only required to give credit for the first investment. Lord Denning MR described[182] the second as an 'entirely collateral benefit'.

Lavarack illustrates that benefits obtained must be attributable to the breach, and not merely collateral. The leading case is *British Westinghouse Electric and Manufacturing Co Ltd v Underground Electric Railways Co of London Ltd*.[183] A contract for the sale of steam turbines and alternators required British Westinghouse to deliver and erect the machinery in accordance with a specification annexed to the contract. Disputes arose and the Railways Co claimed that the machines provided did not satisfy the terms of the contract with regard to economy and steam consumption. They claimed £280,000, which was their estimate of the loss caused by excessive coal consumption for the life of the machines, estimated to be 20 years. Alternatively, a claim was made for the cost of installing new machines of greater capacity which had in fact been purchased. This cost was a little over £78,000, to which the Railways Co added £42,000 representing the loss caused by excess coal consumption while British Westinghouse's machines were in operation and before the new machines could be installed.

The arbitrator found that the installation of the new machines mitigated or prevented the loss or damage which would have occurred had the Railways Co continued to use the defective machinery. He also found that, since the new machines were superior, had the machines of British Westinghouse complied with the contract it would still have been to the advantage of the Railways Co to have replaced them. The House of Lords held that the benefits obtained by the Railways Co were not collateral but were, at least in part, attributable to the breach of contract which had taken place. The case was therefore remitted to the arbitrator for an assessment of damages on the basis that the benefits of the purchase of the new machines had to be taken into account.

Where a plaintiff has suffered loss or damage by reason of the defendant's breach, but has received benefits which are taken into account as mitigation of the loss or damage, the plaintiff need only give credit for the '*net* gain accruing to him'.[184] For example, a wrongfully dismissed employee who recovers damages from the employer, but is required to account for the wages received from a new employer by way of mitigation, is entitled to recover as damages the cost of obtaining new employment. Therefore, in arriving at a net figure, the employee's travelling, advertising expenses and so on may be deducted from the wages received from the new employer.

[2135] Failure to minimise loss. The second aspect of mitigation concerns the failure of a plaintiff to take steps which would operate to decrease loss. In this context it is frequently said that there is a 'duty' to

---

182. [1967] 1 QB 278 at 290. Contrast *Levison v Farin* [1978] 2 All ER 1149.
183. [1912] AC 673. See also *Gardner v Marsh & Parsons (a firm)* [1997] 1 WLR 489.
184. *Westwood v Secretary of State for Employment* [1985] AC 20 at 44. Cf *Hoad v Scone Motors Pty Ltd* [1977] 1 NSWLR 88 (tort).

mitigate. However, it is a little misleading to speak in terms of a 'duty'.[185] To begin with there is no positive duty to take steps to minimise loss, rather it is a duty not to act unreasonably.[186] Second, if the duty is not discharged there is no liability in damages,[187] the 'breach' being reflected in the reduction of the plaintiff's award. In effect, therefore, the plaintiff is 'debarred' from claiming some or all of its loss.[188]

Whether the plaintiff has acted reasonably or unreasonably must depend on the circumstances of the case, and the authorities are of limited guidance. Typically, the issue arises in contracts for the sale of goods in cases of anticipatory breach.[189] But it can also arise with respect to other contracts. For example, in *Shindler v Northern Raincoat Co Ltd*[190] the plaintiff, a company director wrongfully dismissed by the defendants, refused to accept employment by a company related to the defendants, who therefore contended that the plaintiff had acted unreasonably. Diplock J held otherwise. Having regard to the senior position occupied by the plaintiff, the fact that litigation had commenced between the plaintiff and the defendants, and the friction which existed between the plaintiff and executives in the company, it was, 'as a matter of common sense',[191] not right to say that the plaintiff had acted unreasonably.

On the other hand, in *Brace v Calder*[192] the plaintiff was employed by the defendants, who carried on business in partnership, as a manager for a period of two years. Six months later the partnership was dissolved and this was held by a majority of the court to constitute a wrongful dismissal of the plaintiff. But the business had been transferred to two of the original partners who offered to retain the plaintiff's services on the same terms as he had been employed by the defendants. The plaintiff refused this offer and the court said that he had acted unreasonably in doing so. Consequently, only nominal damages were awarded. The position might have been different had the offer been for employment with a reduced salary or status.

Generally speaking it will be unreasonable to require a plaintiff, in the name of mitigation, to take steps which would injure the plaintiff's commercial reputation.[193]

[2136] Increasing the loss. The mere fact that the conduct of the plaintiff has *increased* the loss which would otherwise have flowed from the

---

185. See *TCN Channel 9 Pty Ltd v Hayden Enterprises Pty Ltd* (1989) 16 NSWLR 130 at 162. Contrast the position where there is an express term requiring mitigation. See *Stocznia Gdanska SA v Latvian Shipping Co* [1998] 1 WLR 574.
186. *Sotiros Shipping Inc v Sameiet Solholt (The Solholt)* [1983] 1 Lloyd's Rep 605 at 608. But cf *Falko v James McEwan & Co Pty Ltd* [1977] VR 447 at 452.
187. See *Empresa Cubana Importada de Alimentos 'Alimport' v Iasmos Shipping Co SA (The Good Friend)* [1984] 2 Lloyd's Rep 586 at 597.
188. See *Kaines (UK) Ltd v Osterreichische Warrenhandelsgesellschaft Austrowaren Gesellschaft mbH* [1993] 2 Lloyd's Rep 1 at 10 per Bingham LJ.
189. See [2149].
190. [1960] 1 WLR 1038. See also *Challenge Bank Ltd v V L Cooper & Associates Pty Ltd* [1996] 1 VR 220 at 232.
191. [1960] 1 WLR 1038 at 1049.
192. [1895] 2 QB 253.
193. *James Finlay & Co Ltd v NV Kwik Hoo Tong Handel Maatschappij* [1929] 1 KB 400; *Metal Fabrications (Vic) Pty Ltd v Kelcey* [1986] VR 507.

defendant's breach does not necessarily mean that the plaintiff is unable to recover the increased loss. The plaintiff will be unable to recover the increased loss if the conduct is unreasonable. For example, in *Ardlethan Options Ltd v Easdown*[194] the plaintiff claimed damages for the defendant's refusal to issue share certificates or scrip. Had he gone to the office of the company he would have obtained the certificates. But, instead of doing so, he stood by and allowed the shares to dwindle in value. This was described by Isaacs J[195] as 'most unbusinesslike and unreasonable', and the plaintiff's damages were therefore reduced.

On the other hand, a plaintiff who has acted reasonably may be entitled to recover the increased loss. Thus, in *Banco de Portugal v Waterlow & Sons Ltd*[196] the defendants agreed to print bank notes for the plaintiffs. They printed, and delivered to the plaintiffs, 600,000 Vasco da Gama 500 escudo notes which were put into circulation in Portugal. The defendants then breached their contract by delivering 580,000 of the same type of notes to the head of a band of criminals, in the belief that he had the plaintiffs' authority to receive them. The reaction of the plaintiffs was to withdraw the whole issue from circulation. They also agreed to exchange on presentation *all* 500 escudo notes for their face value. A majority of the House of Lords held that the proper measure of the plaintiffs' loss was the exchange value of the genuine currency given for the Vasco da Gama 500 escudo notes, plus the cost of printing the genuine Vasco da Gama 500 escudo notes which had been withdrawn. It was emphasised that the plaintiffs were not bound to do any act which would have injured their commercial reputation, and that the failure to take the steps which had been taken would have involved a breach of the plaintiffs' duty to their shareholders, customers and country. It was therefore reasonable for the plaintiffs to exchange the forged notes for valid notes of equal value.[197]

[2137] Scope of the mitigation principles. There are three important limitations on the scope of the mitigation principles. First, no question of mitigation can arise until a breach has taken place.[198] Thus, in *Shindler v Northern Raincoat Co Ltd*[199] the plaintiff was entitled to disregard offers of employment made between the time when the defendants first repudiated their obligations and the termination of his office as director.

Second, in cases where a repudiation precedes the time for performance, it is not part of the mitigation rules to consider whether the plaintiff behaved reasonably in deciding to terminate[200] or to continue with performance.[201]

---

194. (1915) 20 CLR 285.
195. (1915) 20 CLR 285 at 296.
196. [1932] AC 452. See John Tillotson, 'The Portuguese Bank Note Case: Legal, Economic and Financial Approaches to the Measure of Damages in Contract' (1994) 68 *ALJ* 93.
197. See also *Simonius Vischer & Co v Holt* [1979] 2 NSWLR 322 at 355–6; *London and South of England Building Society v Stone* [1983] 1 WLR 1242 at 1263.
198. See further [2149].
199. [1960] 1 WLR 1038 (see [2135]).
200. See, eg *Sotiros Shipping Inc v Sameiet Solholt (The Solholt)* [1983] 1 Lloyd's Rep 605 and further [2149].
201. *White and Carter (Councils) Ltd v McGregor* [1962] AC 413.

Third, the principles do not apply unless damages are actually being claimed. Thus, if the plaintiff is able to frame the claim as one for the recovery of a liquidated sum, no question of mitigation will arise.[202]

A quite different issue is the relationship between the rule of remoteness and the mitigation concept. It seems fairly clear that in some respects the former embodies the latter. Thus, the prima facie rules in sale of goods contracts,[203] which rely on a comparison of market price and contract price assume that the plaintiff will (or should) mitigate loss by going into the market.[204] It is therefore hardly surprising that in some cases the result achieved under remoteness may be obtained by reference to mitigation (and vice versa).

This process may explain the decision of the High Court in *Burns v MAN Automotive (Aust) Pty Ltd*.[205] The defendant sold a prime mover to a finance company, having warranted to the plaintiff that the vehicle's engine had previously been reconditioned. It knew that the plaintiff would acquire the vehicle and use it in an interstate haulage business and should also have known that the plaintiff was not financially well off. Unfortunately, the vehicle had not been reconditioned. Although in June 1978 the plaintiff realised that the vehicle could not be used for the purpose intended, he continued to use it for carriage in Queensland. The breach of warranty caused the plaintiff loss, principally by reason of carrying on an unprofitable business. In fact, the plaintiff was unable to keep up the payments to the finance company and the vehicle was repossessed at the end of 1979. We need only be concerned with the claim for lost profits which (from the date of contract until July 1981) were assessed at $131,000.

The Full Court of the Supreme Court of Queensland allowed $34,000 for lost profits in the period to June 1978, but held that lost profits could not be recovered after July 1978. Although this decision was affirmed by a majority of the High Court, conflicting views were expressed on whether the reduction was justified by mitigation or remoteness. It was said that the plaintiff was not 'locked in' to an unprofitable business, since he was not compelled to go on losing money. The problem for the plaintiff, however, was that he did not have sufficient funds to have the vehicle reconditioned, or to purchase a replacement. Wilson, Deane and Dawson JJ, in a joint judgment, said that loss of profits after June 1978 was too remote. They emphasised the need to identify the point in time beyond which the plaintiff's claim had to be regarded as too remote. In their view the plaintiff's loss crystallised in July 1978 and the plaintiff was not entitled to recover beyond that time.

On the other hand, Gibbs CJ said that the plaintiff should have mitigated his loss by terminating the agreement. He did not consider the plaintiff's impecuniosity a shield from the mitigation principles, but took the view that because the defendant's breach was the very reason why the plaintiff

---

202. *White and Carter (Councils) Ltd v McGregor* [1962] AC 413. See further [2218]–[2224].
203. See [2140], [2142].
204. Cf *Hussey v Eels* [1990] 2 QB 227 at 233.
205. (1986) 161 CLR 653 (see Robyn Carrol, (1989) 2 *JCL* 171).

had insufficient funds, it would have been wrong to deny his claim by reference to that lack of funds. Gibbs CJ said that, allowing four years as the effective life of a reconditioned vehicle, losses beyond June 1978 could not be recovered because it was unreasonable to continue using the vehicle at a loss.[206]

Sale of Goods

[2138] **Breach of warranty.** Section 54 of the *Sale of Goods Act* 1923 (NSW)[207] deals with the damages recoverable by a buyer for breach of warranty on the part of the seller. Section 54(2) reproduces the first limb of the rule in *Hadley v Baxendale*[208] by stating: 'The measure of damages for breach of warranty is the estimated loss directly and naturally resulting in the ordinary course of events from the breach of warranty'. Section 54(3) provides further guidance. This states as a prima facie measure of damages applicable to breach of a warranty of quality, 'the difference between the value of the goods at the time of delivery to the buyer and the value they would have had if they had answered to the warranty'.

Therefore, at least in a case of a breach of warranty of quality, only if the prima facie rule does not give a satisfactory result need there be a general consideration of the first limb of the rule in *Hadley v Baxendale*. An obvious example where the prima facie measure will not usually apply is where the breach of warranty causes physical injury to the plaintiff.[209] And, treating the breach in *H Parsons (Livestock) Ltd v Uttley Ingham & Co Ltd*[210] as a breach of warranty of quality, the case illustrates the rejection of the prima facie rule in a case of damage to a plaintiff's property.[211]

Section 54(1) makes it clear that the provision extends not only to the breach of a term classified by construction (or implication) as a warranty, but also to the breach of a term classified as a condition, where the buyer has accepted the goods or otherwise lost the right to reject them. It also applies to breach by the seller of an intermediate term if there is no right to reject, or the right of rejection has been lost. However, as an alternative to maintaining an action for damages, the buyer is entitled, by virtue of s 54(1), to set up the seller's breach in 'diminution or extinction' of the price of the goods if this has not been paid.[212]

---

206. Brennan J, who dissented, and would have remitted the case for reassessment of damages, said that remoteness expresses the same limitation as mitigation where an act on the part of the plaintiff is needed to put an end to the losses resulting from breach of warranty (cf *TCN Channel 9 Pty Ltd v Hayden Enterprises Pty Ltd* (1989) 16 NSWLR 130). In his view neither mitigation nor remoteness operated to restrict the plaintiff to profits lost prior to July 1978.
207. For corresponding provisions see **ACT:** *Sale of Goods Act* 1954, s 56; **NT:** *Sale of Goods Act* 1972, s 54; **Qld:** *Sale of Goods Act* 1896, s 54; **SA:** *Sale of Goods Act* 1895, s 52; **Tas:** *Sale of Goods Act* 1896 s 57; **Vic:** *Goods Act* 1958, s 59; **WA:** *Sale of Goods Act* 1895, s 52.
208. (1854) 9 Ex 341 at 354; 156 ER 145 at 151 (see [2108]).
209. *Andrews v Hopkinson* [1957] 1 QB 229.
210. [1978] QB 791 (see [2126]).
211. Cf *Bostock & Co Ltd v Nicholson & Sons Ltd* [1904] 1 KB 725.
212. See also s 54(4) (further damage).

Section 54 is not concerned with cases where the buyer has validly rejected the goods, because the buyer is then entitled to damages for non-delivery.

[2139] Delay in acceptance. Section 40 of the *Sale of Goods Act* 1923 (NSW)[213] provides that where a seller is ready and willing to make delivery, and requests the buyer to take the goods, the failure by the buyer to take delivery of the goods within a reasonable time subjects the buyer to a liability 'for any loss occasioned' by the 'neglect or refusal to take delivery'. The seller is entitled to recover a 'reasonable charge for the care and custody of the goods'.

Section 40 is concerned with situations in which the goods are delivered, albeit late. If the buyer has wrongly refused to accept the goods, the seller will be entitled to terminate the contract and claim damages for non-acceptance.

[2140] Non-acceptance. Under s 52 of the *Sale of Goods Act* 1923 (NSW),[214] where a buyer wrongfully neglects or refuses to accept and pay for goods, the seller may maintain an action for non-acceptance. Section 52(2) provides a general rule that the measure of damages is the estimated loss directly and naturally resulting in the ordinary course of events from the buyer's breach of contract. This is, of course, the first limb of the rule in *Hadley v Baxendale*.[215]

However, s 52(3) states a prima facie measure, applicable where there is an available market[216] for the goods in question, namely, 'the difference between the contract price and the market or current price at the time or times when the goods ought to have been accepted, or if no time was fixed for acceptance, then at the time of the refusal to accept'. Thus, in cases where there is an available market the prima facie measure will apply. If, for example, A agrees to sell B 100 tonnes of wheat at $100 per tonne, but B refuses to take delivery, A's damages will be assessed as the difference between the contract price ($100) and the market price. Assuming that the market price is only $90 per tonne, A will be entitled to recover $1000. If, however, the market price of the goods has risen, or remained constant, because A can go into the market and sell for a higher price than B agreed to pay, or the same price, A will be restricted to a claim for transaction costs.

In cases where there is no available market, or the prima facie rule is not, in the circumstances, a satisfactory rule to apply, the court must apply s 52(2). If, for example, a seller wishes to recover loss of profit on the sale, the seller must displace the prima facie rule. Thus, in *W L Thompson Ltd v*

---

213. For corresponding provisions see **ACT:** *Sale of Goods Act* 1954, s 41; **NT:** *Sale of Goods Act* 1972, s 40; **Qld:** *Sale of Goods Act* 1896, s 39; **SA:** *Sale of Goods Act* 1895, s 37; **Tas:** *Sale of Goods Act* 1896, s 42; **Vic:** *Goods Act* 1958, s 44; **WA:** *Sale of Goods Act* 1895, s 37.
214. For corresponding provisions see **ACT:** *Sale of Goods Act* 1954, s 53; **NT:** *Sale of Goods Act* 1972, s 52; **Qld:** *Sale of Goods Act* 1896, s 51; **SA:** *Sale of Goods Act* 1895, s 49; **Tas:** *Sale of Goods Act* 1846, s 54; **Vic:** *Goods Act* 1958, s 56; **WA:** *Sale of Goods Act* 1895, s 49.
215. (1854) 9 Ex 341 at 354; 156 ER 145 at 151 (see [2108]).
216. See [2143].

Robinson (Gunmakers) Ltd[217] a seller of a new motor car was able to recover the profit lost on the sale to the defendant, when he refused to accept the vehicle, because the demand for new cars of that type was exceeded by supply. On the other hand, the seller's claim failed in *Charter v Sullivan*,[218] where demand exceeded supply. In *Thompson* the seller must be regarded as having lost the opportunity to make an extra sale, since there were fewer customers than cars, whereas in *Charter* the seller suffered no loss because there were more customers than cars to sell.

Where the goods are second-hand, supply and demand are generally irrelevant because each item is regarded as unique. Thus, if a buyer of a second-hand motor car refuses to accept delivery, and the seller resells the car at a profit, the seller will be restricted to the recovery of a nominal sum (or transaction costs) from the original buyer.[219]

[2141] Late delivery. Usually, where a seller tenders goods after the time appointed by the contract, the buyer is under no obligation to accept the goods, time of delivery being of the essence in commercial contracts at least.[220] But what if time is not essential, or if the seller decides to accept the goods so as to be able, for example, to honour a contract with a third party? In *Wertheim v Chicoutimi Pulp Co*[221] a contract between the plaintiff and the defendants provided for the delivery of 3000 tons of wood pulp. The defendants were manufacturers of wood pulp and agreed to make delivery, at Chicoutimi, between 1 September and 1 November 1900. Delivery was delayed until June 1901 and the plaintiffs claimed to recover the difference between the market price of the goods at Manchester (which was the ultimate destination of the goods) at the time when the pulp ought to have been delivered and when in fact it was delivered. The Privy Council held that this sum could be recovered but that the plaintiff had to give credit for the price received under subcontracts.

As *Wertheim's* case illustrates, the prima facie rule in the case of late delivery is the difference between the *market price* of the goods at the time and place of actual delivery and the market price when the goods ought to have been delivered.[222]

[2142] Non-delivery. Section 53 of the *Sale of Goods Act* 1923 (NSW)[223] provides that the buyer may claim damages for non-delivery where the seller fails to deliver the goods. The provisions parallel those applicable to cases of non-acceptance. Thus, s 53(2) provides a general rule that the measure of damages is the 'estimated loss directly and naturally resulting in

---

217. [1955] Ch 177.
218. [1957] 2 QB 117. See also *Shearson Lehman Hutton Inc v Maclaine Watson & Co Ltd (No 2)* [1990] 1 Lloyd's Rep 441.
219. *Lazenby Garages Ltd v Wright* [1976] 2 All ER 770.
220. See [1952].
221. [1911] AC 301. See also *Linnett Bay Shipping Co Ltd v Patraicos Gulf Shipping Co SA (The Al Tawfiq)* [1984] 2 Lloyd's Rep 598.
222. However, the deduction made in respect of the plaintiff's subcontracts has been criticised. See *Benjamin's Sale of Goods*, 5th ed, 1997, para 17-38.
223. For corresponding provisions see **ACT:** *Sale of Goods Act* 1954, s 54; **NT:** *Sale of Goods Act* 1972, s 53; **Qld:** *Sale of Goods Act* 1896, s 52; **SA:** *Sale of Goods Act* 1895, s 50; **Tas:** *Sale of Goods Act* 1896, s 55; **Vic:** *Goods Act* 1958, s 57; **WA:** *Sale of Goods Act* 1895, s 50.

the ordinary course of events from the seller's breach of contract', that is, the first limb of the rule in *Hadley v Baxendale*.[224]

Section 52(3) then states a prima facie measure, applicable where there is an available market[225] for the goods, namely, 'difference between the contract price and the market or current price of the goods at the time or times when they ought to have been delivered, or if no time was fixed, then at the time of the refusal to deliver'. Where the prima facie rule applies, the calculation of damages is relatively straightforward. For example, if A agrees to sell 100 tonnes of corn to B at a price of $100 per tonne, but A refuses to deliver the goods, B's damages are represented by the difference between the contract price ($100) and the market price at the time stipulated for delivery, or if no time was fixed, at the time of A's refusal. Therefore, if the market price is $110, B recovers $1000; but if the market price is $100 or less, B will be restricted to transaction costs.

The prima facie rule may be displaced by the circumstances of the case, or there may be no available market. In either case the court must apply s 53(2). For example, in *Hasell v Bagot Shakes & Lewis Ltd*[226] the plaintiff agreed to sell a quantity of Japanese superphosphates to the defendants at a price of 71s 6d. Some 3000 tons were not delivered and the plaintiff claimed damages. There was no market for the goods and Griffith CJ stated[227] that the court was required to ascertain 'what a reasonable man, acting sensibly on his own behalf and at his own risk, would be willing to pay in order to get the goods at the place and at the time stipulated'. He went on to explain that this amount was to be ascertained by taking the price at the place of manufacture or other source, together with the cost of carriage and a reasonable sum for the profit of the importer. The plaintiff had purchased goods through an importer at 78s when the market price of superphosphates in Japan was about 72s 10d. An issue could have been raised as to whether the plaintiff had allowed the importer too much profit, but it was not, and the court accepted the difference between the price paid and the contract price as the appropriate measure of the plaintiff's loss.

[2143] Available market concept. The concept of an 'available market' for goods is relevant to both non-acceptance and non-delivery. In *Francis v Lyon*[228] Griffith CJ said that he understood the term to mean that the 'circumstances, including conditions of time and place, are such that a purchaser having money in his hands can, then and there, if he so desires, buy other goods of the same quality'. To this must be added a requirement that the goods be of the same description. From the seller's perspective, for there to be an available market the circumstances must be such that the seller can sell goods of the description and quality provided for by the contract.

There is probably no available market for second-hand goods,[229] because none of the other goods available will be of the same quality and

---
224. (1854) 9 Ex 341 at 354; 156 ER 145 at 151 (see [2108]).
225. See [2143].
226. (1911) 13 CLR 374.
227. (1911) 13 CLR 374 at 381.
228. (1907) 4 CLR 1023 at 1036.
229. *Lazenby Garages Ltd v Wright* [1976] 2 All ER 770.

description. It has also been doubted whether there is an available market where the retail price of goods is fixed,[230] for example, by government regulations, because the price of the goods is not regulated by market forces.

[2144] Special damages. Section 55[231] of the *Sale of Goods Act* 1923 (NSW) preserves the right of a buyer or seller to recover 'special' damages where these would be recoverable. This allows recovery of damages under the second limb of the rule in *Hadley v Baxendale*.[232]

Particular Issues

Pre-contract Expenditure

[2145] Not generally recoverable. Normally, expenditure incurred prior to the contract being entered into is not recoverable by a plaintiff as a distinct head of damages. Of course, damages do frequently compensate the plaintiff for expenditure incurred before the contract is entered into. For example, where a purchaser of land receives damages to cover expenses in investigating title and executing the contract there is an element of pre-contract expenditure in the award. But it is exceptional for pre-contract expenditure to be the main basis for assessment.

That damages in respect of pre-contract expenditure are sometimes recoverable is illustrated by *Anglia Television Ltd v Reed*.[233] The defendant agreed to play the leading role in a play which the plaintiffs intended to produce for television. However, a few days later he repudiated his obligations and the plaintiffs brought an action for damages. Because the plaintiffs had no way of estimating the profit they would have made on the production, they claimed in respect of the money they had spent on the production. Their claim (£2750) was made up, in part, of director's and designer's fees and so on, incurred prior to the contract being entered into. The basis for claiming this pre-contract expenditure was that the defendant's breach had caused the benefit of such expenditure to be lost. The English Court of Appeal held that the £2750 was recoverable because it was in the contemplation of the parties as likely to be lost if the contract was not performed. On the facts it does not appear that the defendant actually knew that the expenditure was likely to be lost, but the court said that such knowledge could reasonably be imputed to him.

Two features of *Anglia Television v Reed* require explanation.[234] First, was the court justified in imputing to the defendant knowledge that if his

---

230. *Charter v Sullivan* [1957] 2 QB 117.
231. For corresponding provisions see **ACT**: *Sale of Goods Act* 1954, s 57; **NT**: *Sale of Goods Act* 1972, s 55; **Qld**: *Sale of Goods Act* 1896, s 55; **SA**: *Sale of Goods Act* 1896, s 53; **Tas**: *Sale of Goods Act* 1896, s 58; **Vic**: *Goods Act* 1958, s 60; **WA**: *Sale of Goods Act* 1895, s 53.
232. (1854) 9 Ex 341 at 354; 156 ER 145 at 151 (see [2108]).
233. [1972] 1 QB 60. See also *Lloyd v Stanbury* [1971] 1 WLR 535.
234. In *Commonwealth of Australia v Amann Aviation Pty Ltd* (1991) 174 CLR 64 the High Court disagreed with Lord Denning MR's view that a plaintiff is entitled (or required) to elect between reliance and expectation loss.

contract was not performed the whole production would be cancelled? The basis for saying that it was justified is that he contracted to play the leading role and must have known that it would be very difficult, if not impossible, for the plaintiffs to replace him at short notice. As against this, the court was applying the second limb of the rule in *Hadley v Baxendale*[235] and actual knowledge is generally taken to be the basis for its application.

Second, there appears to have been no evidence before the court that the expenditure incurred would have been recouped, either in whole or in part, had the production gone ahead. Nevertheless, the court was entitled to assume, in the absence of evidence to the contrary, that the play would have brought in revenue, if not necessarily profit.[236]

Anticipatory Breach

[2146] Termination required. For a plaintiff's cause of action to be complete in cases of anticipatory breach the obligation of the parties to perform must have been terminated.[237] Therefore, it is essential for a plaintiff who claims damages for anticipatory breach to prove that performance has been validly terminated.[238]

[2147] Problems created by anticipatory breach. The assessment of damages in cases of anticipatory breach creates a number of problems:
- determining the impact of termination of the contract on damages assessment;[239]
- determining the date at which damages are to be assessed;[240]
- applying mitigation principles;[241] and
- dealing with the fact that the plaintiff may recover damages prior to performance by the defendant falling due.[242]

To a large extent these problems arise because of the way the law interprets the plaintiff's cause of action, namely, as damages for what is conceived of as an 'inevitable' breach.[243] In cases where the breach is wholly anticipatory the court must treat the defendant's breach by nonperformance as inevitable and assess damages without necessarily having all the information required to assess the plaintiff's loss accurately.

[2148] Date for assessment. Application of the general rule,[244] that damages are assessed at the time of breach, gives rise to two possible dates:
- the date of the plaintiff's election to terminate; and
- the date fixed in the contract for performance by the defendant.

---

235. (1854) 9 Ex 341 at 354; 156 ER 145 at 151 (see [2108]).
236. See *CCC Films (London) Ltd v Impact Quadrant Films Ltd* [1985] QB 16.
237. See [1933].
238. *Ogle v Comboyuro Investments Pty Ltd* (1976) 136 CLR 444 at 450.
239. See [2157]–[2161].
240. See [2148].
241. See [2149].
242. See [2160].
243. See [1933].
244. See [2114].

Although in one sense the defendant's breach occurs at the time of termination by the plaintiff, the plaintiff's cause of action arises in respect of obligations which would have been due for performance at a later date.[245] The later date is generally chosen as the date for assessment because choice of the earlier date would, in effect, accelerate performance by the defendant.

Cases where the contract states a time for performance are relatively straightforward. Assume, for example, that a buyer wrongfully repudiates its obligations prior to the time for performance, and the seller terminates performance prior to the date for payment. Damages are assessed on the basis of market values existing at the time when performance would have been due.[246] Thus, the earlier date — the date of termination — is rejected. If the case happens to come to trial before the contractual date, the court must determine the market price 'as best it can'.[247]

Although conceptually more difficult, the position is the same where no time is fixed for performance. Thus, in *Tai Hing Cotton Mill Ltd v Kamsing Knitting Factory*,[248] the Privy Council decided that a buyer was entitled to damages for anticipatory breach equal to the difference between the contract price and the market price on the last day on which the buyers could have given reasonable notice requiring delivery of the goods.[249]

[2149] **Mitigation.**[250] Where A repudiates obligations under a contract with B prior to performance falling due, there is no breach of contract. Therefore no question of mitigation on the part of B can arise until the repudiation has been accepted as an anticipatory breach. Disagreements frequently arise on the market price to be taken in sale of goods cases. One reason for the general rule that damages are assessed as at the date specified for performance is to avoid the possibility that, on a falling (or rising) market, a plaintiff might recover a substantial sum simply by terminating the contract at an early date. But it is also clear that any reasonable opportunity for mitigation must be taken. Thus, if a seller repudiates its obligations, and the buyer accepts the seller's repudiation on a rising market, the buyer should buy in against the contract with the seller if there is a reasonable opportunity to do so.[251] If the buyer fails to do so, and the market price continues to rise until the date for delivery, the buyer will find it difficult to have damages assessed as at the time for delivery.[252] On the other hand, if the buyer, acting reasonably, does buy in, damages are

---

245. Cf *SIB International SRL v Metallgesellschaft Corp (The Noel Bay)* [1989] 1 Lloyd's Rep 361 (breach followed by repudiation).
246. *Millet v Van Heck & Co* [1920] 3 KB 535 at 542–3.
247. *Melachrino v Nickoll* [1920] 1 KB 693 at 699.
248. [1979] AC 91. See further [2150].
249. The Hong Kong equivalent to s 53(2) of the *Sale of Goods Act* 1923 (NSW) (see [2142]) was applied. However, since this was, in effect, the time when the goods ought to have been delivered the same result would have flowed from application of s 53(3).
250. See W E D Davies, 'Anticipatory Breach and Mitigation of Damages' (1960–62) 5 *UWALR* 576; M G Bridge, 'Mitigation of Damages in Contract and the Meaning of Avoidable Loss' (1989) 105 *LQR* 398.
251. *Garnac Grain Co Inc v HMF Faure & Fairclough Ltd* [1968] AC 1130n at 1140.
252. *Kaines (UK) Ltd v Osterreichische Warrenhandelsgesellschaft Austrowaren Gesellschaft mbH* [1993] 2 Lloyd's Rep 1.

assessed at the date of repurchase[253] even if the buyer has paid a higher price than that which (later) rules at the date fixed for delivery.

The same principles apply where the defendant's breach is not wholly anticipatory. In *Payzu Ltd v Saunders*[254] a contract for the sale of two instalments of crepe de chine provided for delivery between January and September 1918. Payment was to be made for each instalment within one month of delivery. The seller repudiated her obligations in January 1918 and the buyers claimed damages. But the seller had been ready and willing to supply goods for cash and argued that the buyers should have accepted this offer in order to mitigate their loss. The English Court of Appeal agreed; Scrutton LJ said[255] that 'in commercial contracts it is generally reasonable to accept an offer from the party in default'.

The idea that it may be unreasonable for a plaintiff not to accept a defendant's offer to enter into a subsequent contract is of general application and therefore applies to termination for actual breach. Indeed, it was taken a step further by the 'quite extraordinary'[256] decision of the English Court of Appeal in *Sotiros Shipping Inc v Sameiet Solholt (The Solholt)*.[257] Buyers cancelled a contract for the sale of a ship pursuant to an express right of termination when the vessel was not delivered on time. The contract price was for $US5 million, but at the time of cancellation the vessel was worth $US5.5 million. The buyers sought to recover the $US0.5 million loss, but went away empty handed. It was held that the failure to make an offer to buy the vessel for $US5 million was a failure to mitigate. The court affirmed the decision of Staughton J who had said:[258] 'The test is: Did the innocent party act reasonably in mitigating his loss? That must include consideration of any opportunity he had to make a fresh bargain.' While it is easy to agree that a plaintiff should accept a reasonable offer of a substitute contract, it is not so easy to see why a plaintiff should be regarded as failing to mitigate merely because the defendant would probably have accepted an offer to perform the contract at the contract price.

Delay in Performance

[2150] Damages for delay. It is now clearly established that a failure to perform on time is a breach of contract even if the time stipulation is not essential.[259] Accordingly, damages for delay may be available to a plaintiff. For example, in *Oakacre Ltd v Claire Cleaners (Holdings) Ltd*[260] it was held that delay in completion of a contract for the sale of land could be relied upon by purchasers as a ground for claiming damages.[261]

---

253. *Melachrino v Nickoll* [1920] 1 KB 693 at 697.
254. [1919] 2 KB 581.
255. [1919] 2 KB 581 at 589.
256. M G Bridge, 'Mitigation of Damages in Contract and the Meaning of Avoidable Loss' (1989) 105 *LQR* 398 at 418.
257. [1983] 1 Lloyd's Rep 605.
258. [1981] 2 Lloyd's Rep 574 at 580.
259. See [1852].
260. [1982] Ch 197. See also [2139].
261. Because the writ was issued prior to the completion date, damages were awarded in substitution for specific performance.

[2151] Delay in the payment of money. The traditional approach of the common law has been to deny the recovery of damages, whether in the form of interest or otherwise, for the mere failure to pay money. It mattered not whether the money was a debt due under the contract, money which the plaintiff was denied by the breach or the money value of the loss caused by the defendant's breach.[262] The major problem created is that a plaintiff entitled to receive payment of a debt, such as rent due under a lease, was by this rule deprived of the right to claim compensation for the loss suffered in not receiving the money on the due date. The common law rule is based on the unreal assumption that the value of money does not change, and that inflation should be disregarded when assessing damages. It is, however, qualified in several ways. First, at the very specific level, it is always open to parties to insert terms in the contract by which they agree that interest is to be payable.

Second, and more generally, courts have a *discretionary* power to order the payment of interest in defined circumstances.[263] Interest is recoverable on all claims for breach of contract (or tort) that give rise to a money judgment. Since the award of the court occurs after the loss is suffered, this power provides a measure of protection against the loss suffered on the (subsequent) conversion of the plaintiff's loss into a money sum. However, it is principally because: (1) the power is discretionary; and (2) it does not cover all the situations in which a plaintiff in a breach of contract case may wish to claim compensation for the late payment of money that it is important to consider the common law approach.

Third, the common law rule is not as broad as it sounds. Thus, the rule is not relevant where a contract is terminated for repudiation. The defendant becomes liable to pay loss of bargain damages even if its principal obligation was to pay money. For example, if a buyer of goods is guilty of non-acceptance, the seller's claim for general damages is not based on a failure to pay money. Similarly, if a buyer of goods fails to open a letter of credit in the seller's favour, the seller's claim is not conceived of as being for the failure to pay money in accordance with the contract. The credit operates as a guarantee of performance and it is for breach of the obligation to provide the guarantee that the seller may claim damages.[264]

Fourth, in recent years the courts have reconsidered the common law rule, and sought to confine its operation, in order to achieve flexibility and lessen the injustices of the rule. In *Trans Trust SPRL v Danubian Trading Co Ltd*[265] Denning LJ said that it was too 'rigid' a proposition to say that damages can never be recovered for the failure to pay money. The English courts[266] have confined the common law rule by recourse to the second

---

262. See, eg *London Chatham and Dover Railway Co v South Eastern Railway Co* [1893] AC 429; *Shevill v Builders Licensing Board* (1982) 149 CLR 620 at 637; 42 ALR 305; *Norwest Refrigeration Services Pty Ltd v Bain Dawes (WA) Pty Ltd* (1984) 157 CLR 149 at 162; 55 ALR 509; *President of India v La Pintada Compania Navigacion SA* [1985] AC 104.
263. See, eg *Supreme Court Act* 1970 (NSW), s 94.
264. *Trans Trust SPRL v Danubian Trading Co Ltd* [1952] 2 QB 297.
265. [1952] 2 QB 297 at 306. See also *Wenham v Ella* (1972) 127 CLR 454 at 463.

limb of the rule in *Hadley v Baxendale*.[267] However, in Australia a more direct attack has been made on the rule.

In *Hungerfords v Walker*[268] the defendants were accountants engaged to prepare tax returns for the plaintiffs who carried on business as a partnership. For a number of years an error was made in preparing returns which resulted in the overpayment of tax. This error arose due to the defendants' negligent breach of contract. Ultimately, the error was discovered and the plaintiffs were able to recover some of the overpaid tax from the taxation authorities. The plaintiffs sought to recover the balance of overpaid tax, together with damages for the loss of use of the money. The High Court took the view that the plaintiffs had suffered an economic loss: they had been deprived of the use of the money which was paid away due to the defendants' breach, and thereby had been deprived of the opportunity to invest. Alternatively, they had incurred a borrowing cost, that is, suffered loss by having to borrow money to pay their tax.[269] Damages were therefore recovered by the plaintiffs, and the court made it clear that recovery was based on the first limb of the rule in *Hadley v Baxendale*. This amounts to a proposition that the defendant was regarded as having contemplated such loss 'according to the usual course of things' by reason of the defendant's breach. Of course, the second limb of the rule will be relevant in cases where the plaintiff's claim is for an exceptional economic loss, for example, a claim that a particularly lucrative investment was lost.

It follows that the statutory provisions allowing the recovery of interest are not exhaustive codes governing the award of interest. However, two points are important. First, a plaintiff is still required to establish (and ultimately quantify) a loss which was not only caused by the defendant's failure to pay money but which is also not too remote. In other words, the recovery of damages in the form of interest is a matter of proof not assumption.[270]

Second, the fact that a liability to pay damages accrues on the occurrence of a breach of contract does not entitle the plaintiff to say that there was from that time a sum of money (the sum ultimately awarded) which is being detained by the defendant. In *Hungerfords v Walker* the court took the view that the case involved more than a claim for damages for the late payment of damages. However, the High Court approved *President of India v Lips Maritime Corp*[271] where the House of Lords affirmed the view that there is 'no such thing as a cause of action in damages for late payment of damages. The only remedy that the law affords for delay in paying damages is the discretionary award of interest pursuant to statute'. That principle

---

266. See *Wadsworth v Lydall* [1981] 1 WLR 598 (approved *President of India v La Pintada Compania Navigacion SA* [1985] AC 104). See F A Mann, 'On Interest, Compound Interest and Damages' (1985) 101 *LQR* 30.
267. (1854) 9 Ex 341 at 354; 156 ER 145 at 151.
268. (1989) 171 CLR 125; 84 ALR 119. Contrast *Pooraka Holdings Pty Ltd v Participation Nominees Pty Ltd* (1991) 58 SASR 184. Cf *F A Pidgeon & Son Pty Ltd v Danehurst Investments Pty Ltd* [1986] 1 Qd R 448.
269. See also *Sanrod Pty Ltd v Dainford Ltd* (1984) 54 ALR 179 at 191.
270. See *Hobartville Stud Pty Ltd v Union Insurance Co Ltd* (1991) 25 NSWLR 358 at 364.
271. [1988] AC 395 at 425.

also applies to a failure to pay *liquidated damages*,[272] on the basis that liquidation of damages in the contract does not alter the character of the defendant's liability.

Injured Feelings, Disappointment and Loss of Reputation

[2152] General. Damages claims for injured feelings, disappointment, distress or vexation raise a number of difficulties. We have already seen[273] that punitive damages are not awarded in contract. In *Addis v Gramophone Co Ltd*[274] it was decided that it was not competent for the jury to award a sum in respect of the harsh and humiliating manner of the plaintiff's dismissal. Thus, the manner of breach is not a basis for increasing the defendant's liability. Moreover, distinguishing manner of breach from damage in the form of injured feelings or disappointment in performance may not be easy. Most breaches of contract are likely to cause some disappointment to a plaintiff. If causation and remoteness were the only criteria, claims for disappointment would nearly always be successful, although quantification would present real difficulties because of the non-pecuniary nature of the loss.

Therefore, although it would be wrong to deny damages in all cases, there must be some (additional) justification, beyond mere disappointment. It is accordingly quite clear that, where the contract is a standard transaction, damages for disappointment will not be awarded. For example, in *Falko v James McEwan & Co Pty Ltd*[275] Anderson J refused to award damages for disappointment when the defendants breached a contract to supply and install an oil heater in the plaintiff's home. The consequence of the defendants' breach was for the plaintiff to be without adequate heating and this certainly caused some inconvenience and disappointment. But the disappointment was minimal and the contract was in the nature of an ordinary commercial transaction for sale and supply and the defects in the heater could have been remedied by the plaintiff at a small cost. Recovery was limited to pecuniary loss on that ground.

In *Hobbs v London and South Western Railway Co*[276] the plaintiffs took tickets for conveyance by train from Wimbledon to Hampton Court. In breach of contract the plaintiffs were taken to Esher and it was therefore necessary for them to walk the remaining distance to their home. The night was a wet one and the plaintiffs were awarded £8 for the inconvenience which they suffered. The award was upheld on the basis that damages are recoverable for physical inconvenience.[277] However, Mellor J said[278] that

---

272. See generally [2207]–[2217].
273. See [2103].
274. [1909] AC 188 (see [2103]).
275. [1977] VR 447. See also *Allison v Hewitt* (1974) 3 DCR (NSW) 193 (purchaser of land cannot usually recover damages for disappointment if the vendor refuses to convey title).
276. (1875) LR 10 QB 111.
277. See also *Boncristiano v Lohmann* [1998] 4 VR 82 at 94; *Johnson v Gore Wood & Co (A firm)* [2001] 2 WLR 73 at 108.
278. (1875) LR 10 QB 111 at 122.

'for the mere inconvenience, such as annoyance and loss of temper, or vexation, or for being disappointed in a particular thing which you have set your mind upon, without real physical inconvenience resulting, you cannot recover damages'. The court denied recovery of damages as compensation for illness suffered as a consequence of having to walk home in the rain on the ground that it was too remote. However, the decision indicates that physical inconvenience or suffering is a sufficient justification for an award where it is not too remote.

In *Cox v Phillips Industries Ltd*[279] the plaintiff recovered damages — for injured feelings — when he was removed by his employers to a position of lesser responsibility in the company. The employers' conduct was a breach of contract, and Lawson J said that vexation, distress and general disappointment and frustration were within the contemplation of the parties. Notwithstanding that the decision might be justified on the basis that the plaintiff's depression had led to physical ill health, Lawson J was, it seems, content merely to apply a criterion of remoteness. Damages for vexation, distress and general disappointment and frustration cannot be awarded merely on the basis that these matters were within the contemplation of the parties, since that would treat remoteness as a criterion for increasing (rather than reducing) damages liability.[280] Lawson J's broad approach has therefore not been followed, and *Cox* was disapproved by the English Court of Appeal in *Bliss v Southeast Thames Regional Health Authority*,[281] a decision which was approved by the High Court in *Baltic Shipping Co v Dillon (The Mikhail Lermontov)*.[282]

On the other hand, in *Bliss* it was recognised[283] that a plaintiff is entitled to recover 'where the contract which has been broken was itself a contract to provide peace of mind or freedom from distress'. Thus, in *Heywood v Wellers*[284] the plaintiff recovered damages from a firm of solicitors when their breach of contract caused upset and distress. The solicitors had been engaged to take proceedings to protect the plaintiff from molestation by one Morrison, but owing to their negligence, in not obtaining a final injunction against Morrison when the plaintiff was entitled to the order, the molestation continued.

[2153] Breach of a contract to provide entertainment or enjoyment. In *Jarvis v Swans Tours Ltd*[285] the plaintiff booked a skiing holiday in Zurich with the defendants and paid a sum of £63.45. The holiday was a great disappointment, mainly due to absence of proper facilities for skiing and

---

279. [1976] 3 All ER 161. See also *Watts v Morrow* [1991] 1 WLR 1421 (see M P Furmston, (1993) 6 *JCL* 64).
280. See Coote, *Contract — An Underview*, 1995, p 25.
281. [1987] ICR 700.
282. (1993) 176 CLR 344 (see [2153]).
283. [1987] ICR 700 at 718 per Dillon LJ.
284. [1976] 1 QB 446. See also *Perry v Sidney Phillips & Son* [1982] 1 WLR 1297; *Calabar Properties Ltd v Stitcher* [1984] 1 WLR 287. Cf *Thake v Maurice* [1986] QB 644.
285. [1973] 1 QB 233. See also *Wings Ltd v Ellis* [1985] AC 272 at 287. For an early Australian authority see *Athens-MacDonald Travel Service Pty Ltd v Kazis* [1970] SASR 264 where Zelling J awarded damages for disappointment, discomfort and inconvenience against a travel agency.

the failure of the defendants to provide the services promised. On this basis, a sum of £125 was awarded and the court said that the general rule against the award of damages for injured feelings or disappointment does not apply where there is a breach of a contract to provide entertainment or enjoyment.[286]

Jarvis v Swans Tours was approved by the High Court in *Baltic Shipping Co v Dillon (The Mikhail Lermontov)*.[287] In that case Ms Dillon, a passenger on a cruise ship, sued to recover compensation when the voyage was dramatically cut short half way through a 14-day cruise when the vessel sank as a result of negligent navigation. Ms Dillon lost items of personal property, she suffered physical injuries and emotional trauma and severe tension of mind. She was also disappointed and distressed. The contract was naturally characterised as one the object of which was to provide for enjoyment and relaxation. Clearly, she was entitled to an award of damages for the loss of her property, for her injuries, inconvenience and emotional trauma. All these matters were caused by the breach of contract and not too remote. But since the contract was one for enjoyment she was also entitled to say that damages were recoverable for her disappointment and distress.

[2154] **Loss of reputation or publicity.** Damages for loss of reputation or publicity are recoverable where the contract expressly or impliedly promises publicity or enhancement to reputation. Thus, in *Marbe v George Edwardes (Daly's Theatre) Ltd*[288] Barnes LJ stated:[289]

> [I]t is sufficiently established that where there has been a breach of a contract to employ an actress, whose reputation depends on the continued and successful practice of her art, and where the engagement is accompanied by promises of widespread publicity and advertisement which will probably lead to future opportunities following on successful performance, the court recognises that the damages for that breach may properly include such a sum as a jury may award to compensate the plaintiff for the loss of the reputation which would have been acquired, or damage to reputation already acquired, or, to use another expression, for loss of publicity.

For example, in *Herbert Clayton and Jack Waller Ltd v Oliver*[290] the plaintiff was an American actor engaged by the defendants to play one of the three leading roles in a musical for six weeks at a salary of £55 per week. In breach of contract the defendants assigned to the plaintiff a role which was not one of the three leading parts and the plaintiff declined to appear. The jury awarded £1000 damages for loss of publicity. The House

---

286. It was unnecessary to decide whether statements made by the defendants in their brochures were terms or representations because the *Misrepresentation Act* 1967 (UK) (see [1076]) provided a remedy in damages even if there was no breach of contract. The principle applies to claims in tort. See *Archer v Brown* [1985] QB 401; *Dillon v Charter Travel Co Ltd* (1989) 92 ALR 331; *Graham v Voigt* (1989) 89 ACTR 11. See also [1113] (damages for breach of statutory prohibition on misleading and deceptive conduct).
287. (1993) 176 CLR 344. See Elizabeth Macdonald, 'Contractual Damages for Mental Distress' (1994) 7 *JCL* 134; Jane Swanton, (1993) 67 *ALJ* 379; Stuart Hetherington, [1993] *LMCLQ* 289.
288. [1928] 1 KB 269.
289. [1928] 1 KB 269 at 281.
290. [1930] AC 209.

of Lords held that the plaintiff was entitled to damages for loss of publicity, and although the damages awarded by the jury were probably extravagant, they were not so extravagant as to require a fresh assessment.

Reinstatement Costs[291]

[2155] Diminished value or reinstatement cost? In cases where the defendant breaches a promise to build or to do repair work the courts generally award the cost of remedying any defects in the work done, in preference to an award of the difference between the value of the work done and the value the work would have had if it been in accordance with the contract. Similarly, where the defendant has done nothing at all, a court will award the cost of doing the work. Thus, in *Bellgrove v Eldridge*[292] a builder sued to recover £400 alleged to be due under a building contract by which he undertook to build for the defendant a two storey 'villa' for £3500. The defendant, who had paid £3100, was dissatisfied with the building erected. She brought a cross-action for damages. O'Bryan J found substantial departures from the contract in the composition of the concrete in the foundations of the building and in the mortar used to cement the brick walls and awarded £4950 on the cross-action. That sum represented the cost of demolishing the building and re-erecting it in accordance with the contract. The decision was upheld in the High Court.

The general rule in other cases where the defendant's breach relates to the quality or condition of goods or services supplied, is that the plaintiff is limited to the difference in value measure.[293] However, reinstatement costs may be recoverable in cases where the defendant's breach causes damage to the plaintiff's property,[294] although in that context as well it is perhaps more common to award the difference between the value of the property before and after breach.

[2156] Relevance of plaintiff's intention and mitigation. In *Bellgrove v Eldridge*[295] the High Court said:[296]

> It was suggested during the course of argument that if the respondent retains her present judgment and it is satisfied, she may or may not demolish the existing house and re-erect another. If she does not, it is said, she will still have a house together with the cost of erecting another one. To our mind this circumstance is quite immaterial and is but one variation of a feature which

---

291. See Ewan McKendrick, 'Promises to Perform: How Valuable?' (1992) 5 *JCL* 6; Brian Coote, 'Contract Damages, Ruxley and the Performance Interest' [1997] *CLJ* 537; F H Loke, 'Cost of Cure or Difference in Market Value? Toward a Sound Choice in the Basis for Quantifying Expectation Damages' (1996) 10 *JCL* 189.
292. (1954) 90 CLR 613. See also *Perry v Sidney Phillips & Son* [1982] 1 WLR 1297 at 1301.
293. See, eg [2138].
294. See *Harbutt's 'Plasticine' Ltd v Wayne Tank and Pump Co Ltd* [1970] 1 QB 447 (overruled on another point *Photo Production Ltd v Securicor Transport Ltd* [1980] AC 827); see P N Legh-Jones and M A Pickering, '*Harbutt's "Plasticine" Ltd v Wayne Tank and Pump Co Ltd*: Fundamental Breach and Exemption Clauses, Damages and Interest' (1970) 86 *LQR* 513.
295. (1954) 90 CLR 613.
296. (1954) 90 CLR 613 at 620.

so often presents itself in the assessment of damages in cases where they must be assessed once and for all.

Thus, under Australian law it is not essential for the plaintiff to have an intention to use the award to carry out the reinstatement.

The cost of reinstatement may, of course, be more than the value of the property after it has been reinstated, in which case an issue of mitigation may arise. Or the property may cost more to reinstate than its current value. In *Bellgrove v Eldridge*[297] the High Court said that there is a qualification to the rule expressed, namely, 'that, not only must the work undertaken be necessary to produce conformity, but that also, it must be a reasonable course to adopt'.[298] This presented no difficulty because the defect in the foundations seriously threatened the stability of the house, and could be remedied only by demolition and re-erection.[299] On the other hand, in *Ruxley Electronics and Constructions Ltd v Forsyth*[300] the House of Lords refused to award reinstatement damages where a swimming pool was not built to the depth required by the contract. There was no substantial loss of amenity, and the pool was (as built) quite safe for swimming and diving. Moreover, the cost of rebuilding was out of all proportion to the value which would be added by doing the work. It was therefore thought to be unreasonable for the customer to insist on rebuilding. An award was, however, made by way of compensation for loss of amenity.

It is unclear whether a plaintiff should be entitled to recover reinstatement costs if the property of the plaintiff will diminish in value by virtue of reinstatement.[301] In principle this should depend on whether, notwithstanding the diminution of value, it is reasonable for the plaintiff to reinstate the property. But it would be wrong to take a narrow and materialistic view.[302]

Termination[303]

[2157] Accrued right to damages not divested. Where the plaintiff's right to recover damages accrued prior to termination of the performance

---

297. (1954) 90 CLR 613 at 618–19.
298. Reference was made to the expression of the qualification in terms of a concept of 'economic waste' in the *Restatement of the Law of Contracts* (1932), §346. But the High Court preferred to use expressions such as 'necessary' and 'reasonable' so as not to deny a building owner 'the right to demolish a structure which, though satisfactory as a structure of a particular type, is quite different in character from that called for by the contract'. See (1954) 90 CLR 613 at 619. See also *Parramatta City Council v Lutz* (1988) 12 NSWLR 293 at 335. In the *Restatement (2d) Contracts* (1979), §348, com c the expression 'economic waste' is described as 'misleading'.
299. Contrast *Pantalone v Alaouie* (1989) 18 NSWLR 119 (tort).
300. [1996] AC 344 (see Gerard McMeel, [1995] *LMCLQ* 356; Janet O'Sullivan, [1995] *CLJ* 496; Jane Swanton and Barbara McDonald, (1996) 70 *ALJ* 444; Jill Poole, (1996) 59 *MLR* 272).
301. See *Radford v De Froberville* [1978] 1 All ER 33, a case which (wrongly) treats the plaintiff's intention to reinstate the property as a major consideration.
302. Cf *Ruxley Electronics and Constructions Ltd v Forsyth* [1996] AC 344 at 360.
303. See J W Carter, 'The Effect of Discharge of a Contract on the Assessment of Damages for Breach or Repudiation' (1988) 1 *JCL* 113 and 249; B R Opeskin, 'Damages for Breach of Contract Terminated Under Express Terms' (1990) 106 *LQR* 293.

of the contract, the right survives termination.[304] The plaintiff's accrued right to damages may be additional to other accrued rights, such as a right to receive performance.[305]

Although the claimant will usually be the party who terminated the performance of the contract, the accrued right will survive termination even if it was the other party who validly terminated performance.[306]

[2158] Loss of bargain damages. The expression 'loss of bargain damages' describes damages which represent the difference between the market value of the contract or its subject matter and the price (or monetary equivalent) expressed in the contract.[307] Discharge of the contract, by termination for repudiation or breach, is necessary before such damages can be recovered.[308]

As we saw earlier,[309] in cases of anticipatory breach, the general approach is to treat the time for performance as the date for assessment, even if the contract did not expressly fix a time for performance. Thus, in *Hoffman v Cali*[310] a contract for the purchase of a home unit for $89,000 did not fix a time for completion. Performance was therefore required within a reasonable time. Before that time had expired the vendors repudiated the contract and the purchaser terminated the contract and sought damages for anticipatory breach. Although completion would not have been due until about September 1982, the contract was terminated sometime between the end of November 1981 and 26 February 1982. The value of the unit between December 1981 and February 1982 was $130,000. From the middle of 1982 prices fell, so that in September 1982 the market price of the unit was $104,000. The court assessed damages at $15,000, that is, the difference between the contract price and the market price in September 1982, when the contract ought to have been completed.

[2159] Relevance of basis for termination. Where the plaintiff's termination is based on repudiation or breach of an essential term there is a presumption that the plaintiff can recover loss of bargain damages.[311] The same is true where termination is based on a sufficiently serious breach of an intermediate term. Moreover, for the purpose of this analysis, where termination is based on the breach of a term classified as a condition, it does not matter whether this classification is made on the ground of

---

304. *McDonald v Dennys Lascelles Ltd* (1933) 48 CLR 457 at 477; *Financings Ltd v Baldock* [1963] 2 QB 104 at 121.
305. *Larratt v Bankers and Traders Insurance Co Ltd* (1941) 41 SR (NSW) 215 at 225; *Hyundai Heavy Industries Co Ltd v Papadopoulos* [1980] 1 WLR 1129 at 1141.
306. *Ettridge v Vermin Board of the District of Murat Bay* [1928] SASR 124 at 128; *Hyundai Heavy Industries Co Ltd v Papadopoulos* [1980] 1 WLR 1129 at 1136. An accrued right to damages is not divested on termination by frustration; see [2063].
307. Cf *Lombard North Central Plc v Butterworth* [1987] 1 QB 527 at 535 (loss of opportunity to receive performance).
308. *Sunbird Plaza Pty Ltd v Maloney* (1988) 166 CLR 245; 77 ALR 205. Cf *Couglin v Blair* 262 P 2d 305 at 311 (1953); *Photo Production Ltd v Securicor Transport Ltd* [1980] AC 827 at 849.
309. See [2148].
310. [1985] 1 Qd R 253.
311. Cf *Buchanan v Byrnes* (1906) 3 CLR 704 at 715; *Sunbird Plaza Pty Ltd v Maloney* (1988) 166 CLR 245 at 260.

commercial convenience or because breach of the term is likely to have serious consequences.[312] We have already seen how a prima facie measure of this kind is used in sale of goods transactions.[313] Thus, where time of delivery is essential, a buyer is entitled to reject the goods, if tendered late, and to terminate the contract. The buyer can then recover loss of bargain damages — for non-delivery — whether or not a loss would have been suffered on acceptance of the late delivery.

A much debated question is how to deal with termination pursuant to a clause expressly conferring a right to terminate for what may (and usually will) be a minor breach. Although such a clause may also contain an agreed damages provision,[314] it is not the function of such clauses to express agreement on the damages recoverable. Rather, they are inserted to provide a means of termination which depends on proof of nothing more than that an event within the purview of the clause has occurred.[315] In *Shevill v Builders Licensing Board*[316] a lessor claimed loss of bargain damages on the termination of a commercial lease of land pursuant to an express contractual right. Rent had been outstanding for a period of 14 days, an event which triggered the lessor's right of termination, and the lessor complied with the formal requirements for valid termination. However, as there was no breach of any essential term, and no repudiation or serious breach by the lessee, the lessor was restricted to the recovery of a nominal sum.[317]

Subsequent cases[318] have justified the decision in *Shevill* on the basis that the loss which the lessor suffered, by renting the property to a third party at a lower rent, was caused by the decision to terminate in the face of the lessee's ability to pay. On this approach, a plaintiff who seeks loss of bargain damages following exercise of a contractual right to terminate must show that, as a matter of construction, the term breached was an essential term.[319] Alternatively, where the term breached was not essential, the plaintiff will need to prove a repudiation or serious breach on the defendant's part. Thus, in *Progressive Mailing House Pty Ltd v Tabali Pty Ltd*[320] a lessor leased factory premises to the lessee for a period of five years.

---

312. See [1917].
313. See [2140], [2142].
314. See [2217]. The agreed damages provision may, of course, be in another term of the contract.
315. See generally J W Carter, 'Termination Clauses' (1990) 3 *JCL* 90.
316. (1982) 149 CLR 620. See also *Yeoman Credit Ltd v Waragowski* [1961] 1 WLR 1124; *Financings Ltd v Baldock* [1963] 2 QB 104.
317. The claim was in fact brought against a guarantor, but this was said to make no difference to the analysis.
318. See, eg *Progressive Mailing House Pty Ltd v Tabali Pty Ltd* (1985) 157 CLR 17; 57 ALR 609.
319. See, eg *Lombard North Central Plc v Butterworth* [1987] 1 QB 527; *Citicorp Australia Ltd v Hendry* (1985) 4 NSWLR 1 at 28–9 where the contracts made time of the essence and deemed every breach to be a repudiation by the defendant. There is a suggestion in *Shevill* (1982) 149 CLR 620 at 629 that such a provision might be regarded as inequitable, although it is not clear that the defendant would be given relief against the operation of the clause. See also *Esanda Finance Corp Ltd v Plessnig* (1989) 166 CLR 131 at 147–8; 84 ALR 99.
320. (1985) 157 CLR 17 (see J W Carter and J Hill, 'Repudiation of Leases: Further Developments' [1986] *Conv* 262). See also *Nangus Pty Ltd v Charles Donovan Pty Ltd* [1989] VR 184. Cf *W & J Investments Ltd v Bunting* [1984] 1 NSWLR 331.

As in *Shevill*, the lease provided for a right of termination in respect of a number of events, including 'rent or other moneys payable' under the lease remaining unpaid for 14 days, or the lessee failing 'to perform or observe any one or more of the covenants or provisions' of the lease and failing to remedy same after 30 days' notice. No rent was paid for a period of four months, and the lessor validly terminated the lease and sought as compensation the difference between the rent reserved by the lease for its total term and that which would be received on a reletting of the premises. The lessee had done more than merely fail to pay rent. There were breaches which, when combined with the failure to pay rent, enabled the High Court to find repudiation or serious ('fundamental') breach on the part of the lessee. Accordingly, the lessor was successful.

For a number of reasons the reasoning in *Shevill* is not satisfactory. First, the idea that the plaintiff causes the loss suffered seems commercially unreal. Second, and more significantly, the effect is to require a plaintiff who seeks compensation to do the very thing that the clause was intended to avoid, namely, to prove a breach which would, apart from the clause, have justified termination. Third, the result creates a tension between form and substance when efforts are made to avoid the result.[321] Fourth, it might be suggested that a better approach was put forward by Jordan CJ in *Larratt v Bankers and Traders Insurance Co Ltd*[322] when he said that the 'consequences which flow' from termination by virtue of an express right[323]

> depend on the intention of the parties, actual or imputed and, in the absence of some express or implied indication of intention to the contrary, are governed by the ordinary law applicable to the avoidance of contracts for breaches of essential promises.

On this view, the right to recover loss of bargain damages is not affected by the causation problem exposed in *Shevill*, since the loss of the bargain is regarded as having been caused by the defendant's breach. Thus, in *Sotiros Shipping Inc v Sameiet Solholt (The Solholt)*[324] Sir John Donaldson MR said[325] it is 'trite law' that in deciding whether to exercise a contractual right to cancel the plaintiff need have 'no regard to the fact that in the absence of cancellation he would suffer no loss'. There is recent support for Jordan CJ's approach in preference to *Shevill*.[326] However, it is a matter which can only be resolved by the High Court.

[2160] Discounting the award. Termination, particularly in the case of anticipatory breach, may raise the issue of whether the plaintiff's award should be discounted. The most obvious case for discount is where the award is a lump sum representing money which the defendant promised to pay at a future date. Since there is an element of acceleration, the plaintiff will be awarded the present value of the sum which the defendant agreed to

---

321. See [2217].
322. (1941) 41 SR (NSW) 215.
323. (1941) 41 SR (NSW) 215 at 225–6.
324. [1983] 1 Lloyd's Rep 605.
325. [1983] 1 Lloyd's Rep 605 at 607. See also J S Ziegel, [1988] *LMCLQ* 276 at 279–80.
326. See, eg *Progressive Mailing House Pty Ltd v Tabali Pty Ltd* (1985) 157 CLR 17 at 55; *AMEV-UDC Finance Ltd v Austin* (1986) 162 CLR 170 at 205–7, 216–20; 68 ALR 185.

pay.[327] For example, if the plaintiff is a creditor suing the guarantor of a debtor who promised to pay the debt by instalments over time, discount will be necessary in respect of sums which had not fallen due for payment by the debtor at the time of termination. The need for discount will not arise if the court delivers judgment after the time when payment was due[328] because there is then no acceleration of the defendant's promise to pay.

[2161] Subsequent events and accrued rights. Subsequent events sometimes need to be taken into account when assessing damages. This is mainly true in cases where there is an anticipatory element in termination, that is, where some or all of the defendant's obligations had not fallen due for performance at the time of termination, but it may also apply to termination for breach of a term. Since damages must be assessed by reference to the realities of the situation, account must be taken of events which have in fact occurred and which indicate that the plaintiff's award should be reduced.[329]

Where an event might have occurred had the contract run its course, this may be taken into account even though the contract has been terminated.[330] There are three points. First, the clearest case is where the event was certain to occur. It was explained earlier[331] that in *Maredelanto Compania Naviera SA v Bergbau-Handel GmbH (The Mihalis Angelos)*[332] the charterers' termination was justified because of the shipowners' breach of condition. However, Mocatta J had held that the charterers were guilty of anticipatory breach and awarded the shipowners substantial damages even though, had the charter run its course, the charterers would have been able to cancel the contract pursuant to a cancellation clause. Mocatta J relied on the inevitable breach basis for the doctrine of anticipatory breach[333] and said that he was not entitled to reduce the award to take account of events which would have occurred. Having reversed Mocatta J's decision on the interpretation of the expected readiness clause, it was not strictly necessary to consider the damages point, because there was no anticipatory breach by the charterers. However, the English Court of Appeal said that the inevitable breach basis for the doctrine does not prevent the court having regard to subsequent events. Accordingly, because the charterers would undoubtedly have exercised their right of cancellation, the shipowners would only have recovered a nominal sum. In other words, the shipowners would not have suffered any loss had the charterers been guilty of anticipatory breach.[334]

---

327. See, eg *Robophone Facilities Ltd v Blank* [1966] 1 WLR 1428; *W & J Investments Ltd v Bunting* [1984] 1 NSWLR 331.
328. See [2116].
329. See [2063], [2072], [2080] (frustration).
330. See also [2162]. Normally damages are assessed by reference to the plaintiff's position on the assumption that the defendant's breach had not occurred: *Proctor & Gamble Philippine Manufacturing Corp v Kurt A Becher GmbH & Co KG* [1988] 2 Lloyd's Rep 21 at 28.
331. See [1914].
332. [1971] 1 QB 164.
333. See [1933].
334. Cf *Reigate v Union Manufacturing Co (Ramsbottom) Ltd* [1918] 1 KB 592 at 597, 602, 604, 607.

Second, where the defendant's obligation to perform was subject to a contingency which might not have been fulfilled, the possibility of its non-occurrence may need to be taken into account even if the defendant did not promise that it would occur. For example, in *Frost v Knight*[335] the defendant's promise to marry was contingent on the death of his father and there was the possibility that the plaintiff (or defendant) might not outlive the father. Therefore, although the plaintiff's acceptance of the defendant's repudiation meant that her cause of action was complete, some discount in her award was appropriate.

Third, if there is evidence that the defendant might subsequently have been in a position to terminate for breach by the plaintiff, the court may take this into account, and discount the award to reflect the possibility.[336] However, because the plaintiff is entitled to be placed in the position which would have been occupied had the contract been performed, a discount is rarely appropriate.

These situations illustrate that once the plaintiff has a cause of action for damages, it may be reduced, but is not divested, by subsequent events. It also follows that reduction may be necessary in order to take account of a *defendant's* pre-existing cause of action. For example, where a buyer rejects documents tendered under a CIF contract, and the seller terminates performance, for example, for breach of condition, the buyer may set up any cause of action for damages for breach of warranty which accrued prior to termination. Thus, if the buyer proves that the seller shipped goods which were not of the quality provided for by the contract, the seller's damages must be reduced. Prima facie the seller would recover the difference between the contract price of the goods and the price obtainable on the market for the documents representing the goods. However, this would, to use Lord Diplock's words in *Berger & Co Inc v Gill & Duffus SA*,[337] 'fall to be reduced by the sum' which the buyer 'would have been entitled to set up in diminution of the contract price by reason of the breach of warranty as to ... quality'.

Alternative Methods of Performance

[2162] Assessment on basis beneficial to defendant. Where the defendant could have performed the contract in alternative ways, damages are assessed, at least in the case of nonperformance, on the basis of the performance least onerous to the defendant.[338] For example, where a contract for the sale of goods provides that the seller may deliver '1000 tonnes, five per cent more or less at seller's option', damages will, in a case of non-delivery, be assessed on the basis of non-delivery of 950 tonnes.[339]

---

335. (1872) LR 7 Ex 111 (see [1937]). See also *Synge v Synge* [1894] 1 QB 466 (see [1966]) where the defendant's obligation to perform was contingent on the plaintiff not predeceasing him.
336. See the discussion in *Commonwealth of Australia v Amann Aviation Pty Ltd* (1991) 174 CLR 64 at 117, 122, 132, 144, 177.
337. [1984] 1 AC 382 at 392 (see G H Treitel, 'Rights of Rejection Under CIF Sales' [1984] *LMCLQ* 565; J W Carter, (1985) 101 *LQR* 167). Cf [2138].
338. *Abrahams v Herbert Reiach Ltd* [1922] 1 KB 477 at 480; *Biotechnology Australia Pty Ltd v Pace* (1988) 15 NSWLR 130 at 156. See also *Commonwealth of Australia v Amann Aviation Pty Ltd* (1991) 174 CLR 64 at 91, 102, 133.

To the extent that cancellation under an express clause may be seen as performance of a contract, the discussion in *Maredelanto Compania Naviera SA v Bergbau-Handel GmbH (The Mihalis Angelos)*,[340] deals with an analogous situation. In *TCN Channel 9 Pty Ltd v Hayden Enterprises Pty Ltd*,[341] two contracts were entered into in 1985 between TCN and the plaintiff companies. Those contracts were repudiated by TCN and the plaintiffs terminated performance. Clause 10 of one of the contracts conferred on TCN the right to terminate by giving three months' notice, and one argument by which it sought to limit its damages was by alleging that it would have exercised this right. However, termination would have involved ceasing transmission of a television programme to which the agreement related and which was regarded as a profitable enterprise. Since the evidence showed that this was not TCN's intention, the course of conduct alleged could not be regarded as the performance least onerous to the company.

Loss of Chance

[2163] The concept. In some cases it may be clear that the defendant's breach has caused loss to the plaintiff, but be very difficult to quantify that loss. As was explained earlier,[342] difficulty in assessing damages is not a basis for a refusal to make an award in the plaintiff's favour. The concept of damages for loss of a chance frequently operates where damages in contract are difficult to assess and involves the court in estimating the plaintiff's chance of obtaining benefits from the defendant's performance. The fact that the defendant has not performed means that the plaintiff's chance of obtaining the benefit has been lost, but may make it very difficult to determine what the plaintiff would have gained. Where, as in *McRae v Commonwealth Disposals Commission*,[343] the element of chance lies in the nature of the thing contracted for, in that case a stranded tanker which did not in fact exist, there is no ground for awarding damages on a loss of chance basis. The position would have been different had the tanker existed and the defendants' breach involved, say, the refusal to supply correct information as to its location. Similarly, where the loss suffered is so dependent on the exercise of a person's discretion in the plaintiff's favour that it is impossible to say there has been any assessable loss, only nominal damages will be awarded.[344]

[2164] Principles. There are three categories of case in which damages for breach of contract may be awarded on a loss of chance basis:

(1) where the principal object of the contract, from the plaintiff's perspective, was to provide the chance of obtaining a benefit;

---

339. See *Benjamin's Sale of Goods*, 5th ed, 1997, para 17-02.
340. [1971] 1 QB 164 (see [2161]). See also *Commonwealth of Australia v Amann Aviation Pty Ltd* (1991) 174 CLR 64 at 95, 113, 132–3.
341. (1989) 16 NSWLR 130. Cf *Santa Martha Baay Scheepvart v Scanbulk A/S (The Rijn)* [1981] 2 Lloyd's Rep 267 at 270.
342. See [2117].
343. (1951) 84 CLR 377 (see [2111]).
344. *Fink v Fink* (1946) 74 CLR 127.

(2) where an express or implied term of the contract amounted to a promise by the defendant of a chance to obtain a benefit; and

(3) in any other case where a business opportunity is lost as a consequence of the defendant's breach and the loss of the opportunity is within the rules on remoteness of damage.

Even if it has a less than 50 per cent chance of obtaining the benefit which is the subject of the chance, the plaintiff will be entitled to recover something. Thus, in *Sellars v Adelaide Petroleum NL*[345] Mason CJ, Dawson, Toohey and Gaudron JJ said:

> In the realm of contract law, the loss of a chance to win a prize in a competition resulting from breach of a contract to provide the chance is compensable, notwithstanding that, on the balance of probabilities, it is more likely than not that the plaintiff would not win the competition ...

A leading case on loss of chance, which illustrates the first category, is *Chaplin v Hicks*[346] where the defendant's breach of contract deprived the plaintiff of the opportunity of competing in a contest. There was, of course, no certainty that the plaintiff would have won a prize in the contest, but the defendant's breach deprived her of the chance of doing so and she was entitled to receive an award on that basis.

Commonwealth of Australia v Amann Aviation Pty Ltd[347] illustrates the second category. It was there held that although the Commonwealth had not guaranteed the plaintiff a renewal of the contract which it repudiated, it did have the benefit of an implied promise which Brennan J formulated[348] in terms of a 'promise to give the plaintiff an opportunity to acquire the unexpressed benefit'. Since that promise was breached, the plaintiff was entitled to an award, apparently as a distinct head of loss, which represented the value of the chance.

In *David Securities Pty Ltd v Commonwealth Bank of Australia*[349] the Full Federal Court referred to *Chaplin v Hicks* as a 'classic case providing a source for development of the law to provide recovery in respect of lost business opportunities'. There are, therefore, situations in which a loss of chance award — for lost business opportunities — may be made although there was no promise of a chance. In such a case, damages for lost business opportunity are recovered for *consequential* loss.[350]

Assuming that damages for loss of a chance are recoverable, the question of assessment will arise. Damages are 'ascertained by reference to the court's assessment of the prospects of success of that opportunity had it been pursued'.[351] For example, in *Howe v Teefy*[352] the defendant leased a

---

345. (1994) 179 CLR 332 at 349; 120 ALR 16.
346. [1911] 2 KB 786.
347. (1991) 174 CLR 64.
348. See (1991) 174 CLR 64 at 102.
349. (1990) 93 ALR 271 at 295 (reversed on other grounds (1992) 175 CLR 353; 109 ALR 57).
350. On this basis, damages for the loss of a chance may be recovered in claims in tort or for breach of statutory provisions such as s 52 of the (Cth) *Trade Practices Act* 1974. See, eg *Sellars v Adelaide Petroleum NL* (1994) 179 CLR 332. See also [1069], [1113].
351. See *Sellars v Adelaide Petroleum NL* (1994) 179 CLR 332 at 354 per Mason CJ, Dawson, Toohey and Gaudron JJ.

racehorse to the plaintiff, who was a trainer, for a period of three years. After about three months the defendant, in breach of contract, removed the horse from the plaintiff thereby depriving him of the chance of recouping the cost of training the horse out of the prize money which the horse might have earned, and from the money which he might have made in betting on the horse and supplying information to other people. The defendant had certainly lost something of value, but the loss was extremely difficult to assess. Street CJ said[353] that the 'calculation ... to make was not how much he would probably have made in the shape of profit out of his use of the horse, but how much his chance of making that profit, by having the use of the horse, was worth in money'. A sum of £250 had been awarded by the jury and the Full Court considered that it was impossible to interfere with that award.

Rule in Bain v Fothergill

[2165] **Common law.** In 1874 the House of Lords expressed its approval of a rule which severely restricts the damages payable by a defendant who is unable to transfer a good title to land. The 'rule in *Bain v Fothergill*',[354] as it has been termed, denies the plaintiff the right to recover loss of bargain damages and restricts the claim to the recovery of the deposit (if paid), expenses in investigating title and interest. In other words, there is a measure of compensation for reliance loss but no damages in protection of the plaintiff's expectation loss. The rationale for this anomalous rule was said to be the uncertainty and difficulty involved in establishing good title to land. This might have been true in England in the 19th century, but it is not the position today. In *Sharneyford Supplies Ltd v Edge*[355] Balcombe LJ said that the rule is 'today impossible to justify'. It was, indeed, open to Australian courts to say that the rule in *Bain v Fothergill* is not applicable to land held under the Torrens system, where the title to land is established by a search of registered interests. Nevertheless, when the Australian courts adopted the rule it was not restricted to land being held under old system title.[356]

When approving the rule, the House of Lords excepted the case of fraud. Therefore, a vendor who knowingly misrepresents the existence of a clear title to land the subject of an agreement to sell must pay damages to the purchaser. Presumably, however, these damages would, at common law, be based on the tort of deceit and therefore not lead to the recovery of loss of bargain damages in contract.[357] It is hardly surprising that the courts have

---

352. (1927) 27 SR (NSW) 301.
353. (1927) 27 SR (NSW) 301 at 307 (Gordon and Campbell JJ concurred).
354. (1874) LR 7 HL 158. For more recent illustrations see *Ray v Druce* [1985] Ch 437; *Seven Seas Properties Ltd v Al-Essa* [1988] 1 WLR 1272.
355. [1987] 1 Ch 305 at 318. See also at 325 per Kerr LJ.
356. See, eg *Powys v Brown* (1924) 25 SR (NSW) 65 at 74; *Boardman v McGrath* [1925] QWN 14.
357. There may be a statutory right to claim damages (see generally [1076], [1182]) or, possibly, a claim under the common law, in cases of negligence (see [1065]). Query the position with regard to damages awarded under *Lord Cairns' Act* (see [2169]–[2173]).

engrafted further exceptions on the rule, and that it has been abolished in some jurisdictions.[358]

An important qualification is that the rule applies only to title defects and not matters of conveyancing.[359] The rule will therefore not apply where the vendor is at fault, in the sense that the vendor has refrained from taking steps to secure a good title. For example, in *Malhotra v Choudhury*[360] the English Court of Appeal held that the rule did not apply where the defect in title was the refusal of a co-owner (who was not a party to the contract) to join in the conveyance of the property and the vendor had made no efforts to get her co-operation in the matter. Stephenson LJ went so far as to say:[361]

> But I conclude ... that to come within this anomalous exception a vendor must prove his inability to carry out his contractual obligations. And if the evidence leaves the court in the position where the right inference is that inability is not proved, then, even where there is no allegation of the duty to use his best endeavours to carry out his contractual obligations and of a breach of that duty, as in this case, it is open to the court to hold that the ordinary principle of damages, putting a victim of a breach of contract in the position in which he would have been if the contract had been performed, applies ...

In *Wroth v Tyler*[362] Megarry J held that the rule in *Bain v Fothergill* does not apply where the defect in the vendor's title is not present at the time the contract is entered into, but arises subsequently, prior to completion of the contract. In such a case loss of bargain damages are available. Again, in *ASA Constructions Pty Ltd v Iwanov*,[363] Needham J held that the rule did not apply where the defect in title arose from the vendor's reckless decision to enter into a contract of sale after he had already agreed to sell the property to another purchaser.

[2166] Statute. Section 68(1) of the *Property Law Act* 1974 (Qld) and s 70 of the *Law of Property Act* 2000 (NT) abolish the rule in *Bain v Fothergill* except in its application to contracts for the sale of 'unregistered' land. These provisions state that a purchaser is entitled to recover damages to cover the loss which was 'liable to result' and in fact sustained by reason of the vendor's breach. Unless the contract provides to the contrary, the vendor is not relieved from the obligation to compensate the purchaser by reason only of an inability to make title to the land the subject of the

---

358. See *Property Law Act* 1974 (Qld), s 68(1) (see [2166]); and see Law Reform Commission of Victoria, *Sale of Land*, Report No 20, 1989; NSW Law Reform Commission, *Damages for Vendor's Inability to Convey Good Title*, LRC 64, 1990 and the discussion by Peter Butt, 'The Gentle Demise of *Bain v Fothergill*' (1991) 65 *ALJ* 285; J W Carter, 'Reform of the Rule in Bain v Fothergill' (1991) 4 *JCL* 230. See also *Law of Property (Miscellaneous Provisions) Act* 1989 (UK), s 3 (adopting Law Commission, *Transfer of Land, The Rule in Bain v Fothergill*, Law Com No 166, 1987).
359. *Sharneyford Supplies Ltd v Edge* [1987] 1 Ch 305 (see Charles Harpum, [1987] *CLJ* 212).
360. [1980] Ch 52 (see David Hayton, [1979] *CLJ* 35). See also *Noske v McGinnis* (1932) 47 CLR 563.
361. [1980] Ch 52 at 71.
362. [1974] Ch 30.
363. [1975] 1 NSWLR 512. See also *Allison v Hewitt* (1974) 3 DCR (NSW) 193.

contract of sale, whether or not such inability was occasioned by the vendor's own default.

In New South Wales, the rule has been abolished both in relation to registered land and in relation to unregistered land by s 54B of the *Conveyancing Act* 1919 (NSW). Moreover, the parties to the contract may not reinstate the rule by express contractual provision.[364] However, since there is nothing in the provision to indicate the criterion of remoteness which governs damages recovery, general principles apply.[365]

Taxation and Inflation

[2167] **Taxation.** In *British Transport Commission v Gourley*[366] the House of Lords, in the context of an action for damages in tort, held that the tax position of the plaintiff was relevant to the assessment of damages. A majority of the High Court held[367] in *Cullen v Trappell*[368] that *Gourley* should be followed in Australia.

For the court to take taxation into account when assessing the plaintiff's damages two circumstances must generally be found. First, the award of damages must not be taxable. Second, the earnings or profit which the plaintiff has lost, and in respect of which the damages are awarded, must have been such that they would have been taxable had they been received. Assuming that these requirements are met the court will assess the tax notionally payable by the plaintiff and deduct this from the award.[369] But the court will strive for 'substantial fairness rather than precise accuracy'[370] when arriving at a figure.

In most actions for damages in contract the damages will not be subject to a deduction for taxation for the simple reason that the plaintiff either suffers a capital loss or the sum awarded will itself be taxable. However, taxation may be relevant to an action for damages for wrongful dismissal,[371] and an action to recover damages for personal injury, at least where there is an element to cover loss of earnings.[372]

[2168] **Inflation.** The courts have generally adhered to the view that no account should be taken of the likelihood of inflation in assessing damages, whether in tort or contract[373] even though, at times, inflation rates are high. But the rule is really only relevant to inflation during the period subsequent to the court's award, and inflation will in effect be taken into account where

---

364. See *Conveyancing Act* 1919 (NSW), s 54B(3).
365. See *Conveyancing Act* 1919 (NSW), s 54B(2).
366. [1956] AC 185.
367. Overruling *Atlas Tiles Ltd v Briers* (1978) 144 CLR 202; 21 ALR 129.
368. (1980) 146 CLR 1; 29 ALR 1 (overruled on another point *MBP (SA) Pty Ltd v Gogic* (1991) 171 CLR 657; 98 ALR 193).
369. For the position where the award is taxable see *Gill v Australian Wheat Board* [1980] 2 NSWLR 795.
370. *Atlas Tiles Ltd v Briers* (1978) 144 CLR 202 at 236.
371. *Atlas Tiles Ltd v Briers* (1978) 144 CLR 202 (dissenting judgments). See also *Parsons v BNM Laboratories Ltd* [1964] 1 QB 95.
372. See *British Transport Commission v Gourley* [1956] AC 185 (tort); *Pennant Hills Restaurants Pty Ltd v Barrell Insurances Pty Ltd* (1981) 145 CLR 625 at 645.
373. See *O'Brien v McKean* (1968) 118 CLR 540 (tort).

damages are assessed at the date of the award rather than the time of breach. This is the position in personal injury cases, and in *Johnson v Perez*[374] Mason CJ was in favour of approaching in the same way an action against solicitors for negligence which, although brought in tort could have been brought in contract. The cause of action arose when negligence on the part of the solicitors caused the plaintiffs' actions for damages for personal injury against their employers to be dismissed for want of prosecution. However, a majority of the court thought that the appropriate date was when the personal injury claims were dismissed for want of prosecution. In *Perry v Sidney Phillips & Son*[375] Lord Denning MR said that where the defendant is in breach of a promise to build or repair, and the court assesses damages on the basis of the cost of doing the work, increases in the cost due to inflation between the date of breach and the date of award are recoverable. If the plaintiff has acted unreasonably in not carrying out the work, principles of mitigation may reduce the award.

In contract cases the possibility of prejudice to the plaintiff, due to the failure to take account of inflation, occurs where the defendant's breach gives rise to a loss of future income, for example, because of personal injury being suffered by the plaintiff. Wage rates can be expected to rise, and if the plaintiff is compensated by reference to present wage rates the plaintiff is to some extent prejudiced. But in *Pennant Hills Restaurants Pty Ltd v Barrell Insurances Pty Ltd*[376] the court reduced the discount rate normally applied to awards made in actions for personal injury because the plaintiff was, as a result of the defendants' breach, liable to make payments in accordance with the *Workers' Compensation Act* 1926 (NSW). The Act expressly provided for periodic adjustment in accordance with average weekly wage rate changes. The defendants had failed, in breach of contract, to arrange insurance cover on the plaintiffs' liability and in view of the fact that average weekly wages would undoubtedly rise in the future because of inflation it would have been wrong to ignore the effects of inflation. In other words, an award which took no account of inflation would not have been equivalent to the periodic sums which would, but for the defendants' breach, have been payable under the *Workers' Compensation Act*.

Lord Cairns' Act[377]

[2169] **Damages in equity.** Prior to the passing of the *Chancery Amendment Act* 1858 (UK),[378] commonly referred to as *Lord Cairns' Act*, the power of the Court of Chancery to award damages was uncertain.[379] One object of the Act, and that most relevant to this work, was to confer jurisdiction to award damages in addition to or in substitution for the

---

374. (1988) 166 CLR 351. See also *Nikolaou v Papasavas Phillips & Co* (1988) 166 CLR 394; 82 ALR 617 (date when claim statute barred).
375. [1982] 1 WLR 1297 at 1301.
376. (1981) 145 CLR 625. And see *Todorovic v Waller* (1981) 150 CLR 402; 37 ALR 481.
377. See generally Meagher, Gummow and Lehane, *Equity: Doctrines and Remedies*, 3rd ed, 1992, paras 2306–21.
378. 21 & 22 Vic c 27.
379. For the early history see P M McDermott, 'Jurisdiction of the Court of Chancery to Award Damages' (1992) 108 *LQR* 652.

remedies of specific performance and injunction. In New South Wales s 68 of the *Supreme Court Act* 1970 provides:

> Where the court has power —
>
> (a) to grant an injunction against the breach of any covenant, contract or agreement, or against the commission or continuance of any wrongful act; or
>
> (b) to order the specific performance of any covenant, contract or agreement,
>
> the court may award damages to the party injured either in addition to or in substitution for the injunction or specific performance.

Similar provisions are to be found in most other Australian jurisdictions.[380] And in those jurisdictions in which there is no direct counterpart, the power can be implied from the statutory provisions conferring power to make appropriate orders, and those dealing with the administration of law and equity.[381]

In order for damages to be awarded at common law the plaintiff's cause of action must have arisen by the time proceedings are commenced. A feature of damages in equity is that damages may be awarded in cases in which a legal wrong, such as the commission of a breach of contract, is merely threatened. If there is jurisdiction to grant an injunction to prevent a breach of contract, damages may be awarded under *Lord Cairns' Act*, for example, in substitution for the injunction, even though no breach has been committed. Damages may also be awarded in lieu of specific performance, although there is no remedy at common law because of a failure to comply with a requirement of writing,[382] provided acts of part performance are proved which are sufficient to take the case outside the statute,[383] or an estoppel precludes reliance on the statute.[384] But, once a breach of contract is established, it has been doubted whether the *assessment* of damages under the Act differs from the common law.[385]

Is it sufficient for the plaintiff to show that the contract is of its nature susceptible to the equitable relief claimed, or must the position also be that the court has not refused the plaintiff equitable relief on discretionary grounds?[386] Conflicting views can be found in the cases.[387] In *Wentworth v*

---

380. **SA:** *Supreme Court Act* 1935, s 30; **Tas:** *Supreme Court Civil Procedure Act* 1932, s 11(13); **Vic:** *Supreme Court Act* 1986, s 38; **WA:** *Supreme Court Act* 1935, s 25(10). In Queensland it has been held that the repeal of the section in question does not affect the power to award damages in equity. *Conroy v Lowndes* [1958] Qd R 375. See also *Leeds Industrial Co-operative Society Ltd v Slack* [1924] AC 851 (but see now *Supreme Court Act* 1981 (UK), s 50). Cf *Corporations Act* 2001 (Cth), s 1324(10).
381. See **Cth:** *Judiciary Act* 1903, ss 31, 32 (High Court); *Federal Court of Australia Act* 1976, ss 21–33 (Federal Court); **ACT:** *Supreme Court Act* 1933, ss 20, 25–34; **NT:** *Supreme Court Act* 1979, Pt IV (see *Brooks v Wyatt* (1994) 99 NTR 12).
382. Imposed by, or derived from, the *Statute of Frauds* 1677 (Imp), 29 Car II c 3; see generally Chapter 5.
383. See *Price v Strange* [1978] Ch 337. Cf *Ellul v Oakes* (1972) 3 SASR 377 at 395; and generally on part performance see [521]–[524].
384. *Waltons Stores (Interstate) Ltd v Maher* (1988) 164 CLR 387; 76 ALR 513 (see [376]).
385. See, eg *Johnson v Agnew* [1980] AC 367 (see [2172]); *William Sindall Plc v Cambridgeshire County Council* [1994] 1 WLR 1016 at 1037; Tilbury, *Civil Remedies*, 1990, Vol 1, para 3266. But cf *Jaggard v Sawyer* [1995] 1 WLR 269 (see [2171]).
386. See generally [2407]–[2412].

Woollahra Municipal Council[388] the High Court said it 'conforms to the main object of the statute if damages ... are awarded under the section, even though the claim for equitable relief is defeated by a discretionary defence such as laches, acquiescence or hardship'. Although this suggests that the matter is still open in the High Court,[389] the recent authorities support the view that the existence of a discretionary defence does not bar a claim for equitable damages.[390] On the other hand, if the case for relief is not made out there is no basis for ordering the payment of damages.[391]

[2170] Damages in substitution. In *Norton v Angus*[392] an action for specific performance of a contract for the sale of land failed because a majority of the High Court, in the exercise of its discretion, did not consider it fair to a purchaser of land to make the order. Knox CJ said[393] that the 'best justice' of which the case was capable could be done by an inquiry into damages in substitution for specific performance. The contract provided for the sale of two selections under the *Land Acts* 1910–24 (Qld). But it would have been illegal for the purchaser to take a transfer of both selections, and the effect of an order for specific performance would have been to compel the purchaser to find some person willing to accept a transfer of one of the selections, to reside on the land transferred and to pay rent to the Crown. If the purchaser transferred the land to a trustee it would be liable to forfeiture. These circumstances, and in particular the serious risk of forfeiture, justified the decision to award damages rather than specific performance. Again, in *Biggin v Minton*[394] damages were awarded in substitution when a decree for specific performance proved useless because the purchaser under a contract for the sale of land failed to carry out the court's order.[395]

On the other hand, in *Jaggard v Sawyer*[396] damages were sought in lieu of injunction. The English Court of Appeal held that where the defendant failed to observe a restrictive covenant attaching to a residential property, and placed itself in the position where it would regularly trespass on the plaintiff's land, it was appropriate to award as damages in lieu of an injunction a sum which was a fair and proper price for release of the covenant. Although the award was rationalised on a compensatory basis, the award was based on the value to the plaintiff of the covenant breached. Since its value was enhanced by the ability to claim an injunction, this was taken into account in the award.

---

387. Compare *Goldsbrough Mort & Co Ltd v Quinn* (1910) CLR 674 at 701 and *J C Williamson Ltd v Lukey* (1931) 45 CLR 282 at 295 with *King v Poggioli* (1923) 32 CLR 222 at 250.
388. (1982) 149 CLR 672 at 679; 42 ALR 69.
389. But see *Norton v Angus* (1926) 38 CLR 523 (see [2170]).
390. See, eg *Price v Strange* [1978] Ch 337 at 358; *Madden v Kevereski* [1983] 1 NSWLR 305; *McMahon v Ambrose* [1987] VR 817 at 842, 848. Cf Tilbury, *Civil Remedies*, 1990, Vol 1, para 3260.
391. See, eg *McMahon v Ambrose* [1987] VR 817.
392. (1926) 38 CLR 523.
393. (1926) 38 CLR 523 at 530.
394. [1977] 2 All ER 647.
395. See further [2173].
396. [1995] 1 WLR 269.

[2171] **Damages in addition.** Where a court orders specific performance or grants an injunction after the defendant has breached the contract, there would, even apart from *Lord Cairns' Act*, be a power to order the payment of damages in addition to the equitable relief. The fact that the defendant subsequently complies with the court's order does not negate the earlier breach. However, the jurisdiction conferred by *Lord Cairns' Act* will be relevant if there would be no power to award damages at common law, for example, because the plaintiff commenced proceedings prior to the defendant's breach of contract.[397]

Damages in addition to specific performance were awarded by Goff J in *Grant v Dawkins*.[398] A contract for the sale of land provided for the transfer of title free from encumbrances. However, the land was subject to two mortgages the redemption of which would cost more than the purchase money. Damages in addition to specific performance were ordered so as to bridge the gap between the amount of the purchase price and the cost of redeeming the mortgages.

[2172] **Date for assessment.** The flexibility in the choice of the date for the assessment of damages, noted earlier,[399] is most evident in the award of damages under *Lord Cairns' Act*. In *Wroth v Tyler*[400] damages were awarded in substitution for specific performance of a contract for the sale of land. The land had appreciated in value and was worth £1500 more than the contract price at the date of the vendor's breach. However, by the time of the hearing the difference was £5500 and Megarry J reasoned that for the award to be truly substitutionary in character a later date than the time of breach had to be chosen. Accordingly, damages were assessed on the basis of the higher valuation of the property. When *Wroth v Tyler* was considered by the House of Lords in *Johnson v Agnew*[401] the view was expressed that the decision should not be considered as laying down a basis for assessment different from that applicable at common law. Therefore, although the ability of the court to choose a date later than the date of breach was acknowledged, this cannot be justified on the ground that damages have to be 'truly substitutionary'. The position is simply that a later date may be chosen if this is necessary to achieve justice. Accordingly, the reasoning of Megarry J in *Wroth v Tyler* is not to be followed and the fact that damages are given in lieu of specific performance is not, of itself, a sufficient justification for rejecting the date of breach as the proper date for assessment.

Madden v Kevereski[402] again concerned a contract for the sale of land. Helsham CJ in Eq chose the date of the hearing of the action as the

---

397. Cf *Oakacre Ltd v Claire Cleaners (Holdings) Ltd* [1982] Ch 197 (see [2150]).
398. [1973] 1 WLR 1406. It may be that Goff J was wrong to accept that the purchaser's damages were limited to the difference between the value of the property and the purchase price; see P H Pettit, (1974) 90 *LQR* 297.
399. See [2115].
400. [1974] Ch 30. See also *Malhotra v Choudhury* [1980] Ch 52 (date of judgment); *Suleman v Shahsavari* [1988] 1 WLR 1181 (date of hearing). Cf *Grant v Dawkins* [1973] 1 WLR 1406 (see [2171]).
401. [1980] AC 367.
402. [1983] 1 NSWLR 305.

appropriate date for assessment. The contract price of the land was $33,500 and at the date of the hearing the land was valued at $55,000. The only complication in the case was that the matter had been before the Master after the date of the original hearing, and sent back to Helsham CJ in Eq for a decision on the date of assessment. The land had fallen in value to $47,000 but $55,000 was accepted as the basis for assessment, because the contract had been 'lost' at the date of the original judgment for damages in substitution for specific performance.

It follows that there is no special rule applicable to damages awarded under *Lord Cairns' Act*. The normal rule in contract cases — assessment as at the time of breach — will be applied unless the circumstances indicate that that is not the appropriate date.[403] Moreover, as explained below, in cases where damages are awarded after an order for specific performance, a date later than the date of the defendant's breach is usually more appropriate because when the order becomes incapable of enforcement there is, in effect, a subsequent breach.

[2173] **Damages after specific performance.** Where damages are awarded after a decree for specific performance has been made, for example, because the order has not been complied with by the defendant, there are, as in cases where specific performance is declined, alternative bases for the award. First, as we have seen, the court may award damages under the legislative power, in substitution for the order for specific performance. Alternatively, the award may be under the common law, on the basis that the defendant's breach (or repudiation) has, with the leave of the court,[404] been treated as a basis for termination. The question then arises whether any difference is likely in the assessment, depending on the basis for the award. In *Johnson v Agnew*[405] the House of Lords decided that no distinction is to be drawn. Except to the extent that the Act creates a power to award damages which did not exist at common law, damages under *Lord Cairns' Act* are to be assessed in the same way as damages at common law. A similar view had been expressed by O'Bryan J in *McKenna v Richey*.[406]

Where damages are awarded after the failure of an order for specific performance, *Johnson v Agnew* indicates that, generally, the date for assessment will be the date when the contract is lost. Therefore, if, as in that case, the plaintiff has reasonably tried to have the contract completed and is pursuing the remedy of specific performance, the date for assessment will be pushed forward. There is, however, no rule that damages must in such a case be assessed as at the date of the court's judgment in the plaintiff's favour, because the contract may be found to have been lost at an earlier date. In *Johnson v Agnew* the date chosen was the date on which the mortgagees of the vendor first contracted to sell the property. The sale occurred after the order for specific performance had been made, but before it had been carried out. In effect, the date of the sale was the date

---

403. See *ASA Constructions Pty Ltd v Iwanov* [1975] 1 NSWLR 512.
404. See [1973].
405. [1980] AC 367. See also *Attorney-General v Blake* [2001] 1 AC 268 at 286.
406. [1950] VLR 360 at 376. But see *Madden v Kevereski* [1983] 1 NSWLR 305 at 306–7; and cf *Wenham v Ella* (1972) 127 CLR 454 at 460.

when, without the default of the vendor, the order for specific performance was aborted.

Chapter 22

Recovery of Sums Fixed by the Contract

Debt and Damages 2201
Agreed Damages Clauses 2207
    General 2207
    Factors to be Considered 2212
    Scope of the Distinction 2216
Recovery after Election to Continue Performance 2218
    Position Where Co-operation Required 2221
    Absence of Legitimate Interest in Continuing Performance 2223
Recovery after Termination 2225
    Introduction 2225
    Termination following Breach or Repudiation 2228
    Restrictions on Recovery 2238

Debt and Damages[1]

[2201] Reasons for distinguishing debt and damages. The action to recover a debt due for payment has a longer history than the action to recover damages for breach of contract.[2] Moreover, although development of the action for breach has made the distinction between debt and damages less important than formerly, for two main reasons it is still important.

First, there are procedural advantages in recovering a sum payable as a debt due.[3] Generally, a plaintiff can invoke a procedure under which judgment can be obtained with a minimum of supporting evidence. A writ is issued specifying the amount claimed and advising the defendant that judgment will be signed by default if the defendant fails to defend the

---

1. See J W Carter and M J Tilbury, 'Remedial Choice and Contract Drafting' (1998) 13 *JCL* 5.
2. See [105].
3. These advantages extend to claims for sums which, although not fixed by the contract, are liquidated at the time of suit.

matter. By contrast, if a plaintiff wishes to recover more than a nominal sum by way of damages, the plaintiff must often produce detailed evidence of loss, which may include evidence of market values and so on.[4] There is also a difference in the onus of proof. Where a plaintiff alleges that a debt is due, but the defendant denies this and pleads a defence of payment, the onus is on the defendant.[5] On the other hand, a plaintiff who seeks damages for breach bears the onus of proving the breach and the loss in respect of which compensation is sought.[6] It was also explained earlier that a plea of tender may answer, that is, provide a defence to, the claim that there was a breach on the part of the defendant,[7] but the plea of tender does not answer the plaintiff's claim in debt.[8]

Second, as the High Court explained in *Young v Queensland Trustees Ltd*,[9] the common law 'does not and never did conceive of indebtedness in a sum certain for an executed consideration as a mere breach of contract: it is rather the detention of a sum of money and that was so whether the creditor enforced his demand by an action of debt or by indebitatus assumpsit'. This means, for example, that the rules dealing with the mitigation of loss are not relevant where the plaintiff is seeking to recover a debt due under the contract, whereas they are frequently relevant to an action for damages.

[2202] Characteristics of liquidated sums. In the present context a liquidated sum has two essential characteristics: it is fixed by the contract; and due for payment by the defendant.[10] Where the sum is not due for payment it cannot usually be recovered as a debt due: unless there is a clause accelerating the time for payment[11] applicable to the events which have occurred, or the contract has been terminated for breach or repudiation by the defendant,[12] the plaintiff must wait until the payment actually falls due.[13]

The idea that a debt has fallen due for payment usually assumes that it has been earned by the plaintiff, by performance of the contract. If the parties have agreed that the payment must be earned, the fact that a breach on the part of the defendant has prevented performance by the plaintiff does not permit the plaintiff to ignore the requirement of performance.[14] On the other hand, once the payment has been earned, the fact that the performance of the contract is terminated by the plaintiff on account of the defendant's breach does not divest the plaintiff of the cause of action.[15] The

---

4. See [2106].
5. *Young v Queensland Trustees Ltd* (1956) 99 CLR 560.
6. See [2105]. Generally, where the defendant raises a defence, such as frustration of the contract, the onus remains with the plaintiff. Cf [2046] (self-induced frustration).
7. See [1815].
8. *Young v Queensland Trustees Ltd* (1956) 99 CLR 560 at 568.
9. (1956) 99 CLR 560 at 567.
10. Cf *Coast Securities No 9 Pty Ltd v Alabac Pty Ltd* [1984] 2 Qd R 25. If no sum is fixed but is capable of being liquidated, it may, if subsequently fixed, be recovered in contract or under principles of restitution. See generally Chapter 23.
11. See further [2231], [2240].
12. The claim is for damages for anticipatory breach; see [2146]–[2149].
13. *P v D1 and D2 (The C & J)* [1984] 2 Lloyd's Rep 601; *Zea Star Shipping Co SA v Parley Augustsson (Invest) A/S* [1984] 2 Lloyd's Rep 605n. But see [2026].

defendant may, however, be entitled to set-off that claim against the plaintiff's claim.[16]

In some cases a plaintiff who looks to have earned the right to recover a sum fixed by the contract will be restricted to a claim for damages because the defendant has prevented the occurrence of the event on which the obligation to pay depends. For example, in *Alpha Trading Ltd v Dunnshaw-Patten Ltd*[17] an agency agreement provided for the payment of commission out of the proceeds of a contract of sale entered into by the principals with buyers introduced by the agents. The principals breached the *contract of sale* and did not receive payment. It was held by the English Court of Appeal that the principals had breached an implied term of the agency contract. Therefore, although there was no entitlement to claim the sum fixed by the contract as a debt, they were entitled to damages which, on the facts, were equal to the commission which the principals had agreed to pay.[18]

[2203] **Nature of the action.** Historically, the action to recover a liquidated sum under the contract was framed at common law in debt. The disappearance of the 'forms of action',[19] and the fusion of law and equity, makes it a little anachronistic to speak today of an action 'in debt'.

Nevertheless, it remains true that an action to recover a contract debt due is not a claim for breach of contract. Nor does it involve specific performance of the contract. Therefore, the claim is not subject to the exercise of a judicial discretion in favour of the plaintiff based on equitable considerations.[20] For example, where a seller of goods recovers the price due under the contract, the order of the court is not one for specific performance, and equitable defences, such as laches, are not relevant. In some cases an order for specific performance may lead to the recovery of a liquidated sum, as where the court orders specific performance of a contract for the sale of land. However, recovery of the liquidated sum is here merely an incident of the decree.

[2204] **Illustrating the debt/damages distinction.** A good illustration of the distinction between debt and damages can be found in the context of a seller's action to recover the price of goods sold to a buyer. Under s 51(1) of the *Sale of Goods Act* 1923 (NSW),[21] the seller may recover the price once property has passed to a buyer who has refused to pay for the goods according to the terms of the contract. The requirement that property must

---

14. Cases in which prevention is said to be 'equal' to performance (see, eg *Hotham v East India Co* (1787) 1 TR 638 at 645; 99 ER 1295 at 1299) must be taken as referring to an ability to claim damages even though the plaintiff has not performed. See, eg *Peter Turnbull & Co Pty Ltd v Mundus Trading Co (Australasia) Pty Ltd* (1954) 90 CLR 235 (see [1947]). But note the difference of opinion in *City Motors (1933) Pty Ltd v Southern Aerial Super Service Pty Ltd* (1961) 106 CLR 477 at 484, 488, 489–90.
15. See [2225].
16. *Mondel v Steel* (1841) 8 M & W 858; 151 ER 1288.
17. [1981] QB 290.
18. See also [628].
19. See [105].
20. See also S M Waddams, 'The Choice of Remedy for Breach of Contract', in Beatson and Friedmann, eds, *Good Faith and Fault in Contract Law*, 1995, p 479 (different consequences on failure to comply with the orders).

have passed emphasises the importance of performance by the seller, and the Act draws a clear distinction between this situation and the seller's cause of action for damages where property has not passed to the buyer but the buyer refuses to accept delivery of the goods.[22]

In practice, the seller's right depends, almost invariably, on performance of the contract. However, under s 51(2) of the *Sale of Goods Act* 1923 (NSW),[23] if the price is payable on a 'day certain irrespective of delivery' the seller can maintain the action for the price, assuming that the day certain has passed, even though property has not been transferred to the buyer. Here the seller's right to the price does not depend on the seller's performance of the contract. However, the day certain must be fixed by the contract and not left to be determined by later events.[24]

[2205] **Entire contracts.** Full performance of an entire contract will lead to the recovery of a liquidated sum, that is, the contract price. Moreover, in most cases substantial performance of the contract will have this effect, subject to the right of the other party to claim damages.[25]

[2206] **Instalment payments.** Contracts frequently provide for the payment of money by instalments. For example, A might lend $1000 to B and B might promise to pay a specified amount, say $110 per month, for 10 months. Another form of instalment payment is found in severable contracts.[26] For example, a buyer may agree to pay a specified amount for each delivery made by the seller under an instalment goods contract. Other examples can be found in leases, time charterparties, and so on, where the contract fixes an amount to be paid at specified intervals. In respect of these contracts the plaintiff is able to recover each instalment payment, as a debt, when it falls due for payment.[27]

Two features of contracts which provide for instalment payments deserve emphasis. First, the plaintiff may sue for and recover each payment as it falls due without waiting for all payments to become due. Even if the defendant has repudiated all liability under the contract, the plaintiff is not conceived as 'splitting' a cause of action by claiming each payment as it falls due. Accordingly, an action for one instalment does not bar a subsequent claim in respect of a later instalment.

Second, in the absence of a clause accelerating payment, the plaintiff is not entitled to recover future payments as debts due. If the defendant commits a serious breach, or repudiates the contract, and the plaintiff terminates the performance of the contract, instalments which had not fallen due for payment can only be recovered as damages. The defendant's

---

21. See **ACT:** *Sale of Goods Act* 1954, s 52(1); **NT:** *Sale of Goods Act* 1972, s 51(1); **Qld:** *Sale of Goods Act* 1896, s 50(1); **SA:** *Sale of Goods Act* 1895, s 48(1); **Tas:** *Sale of Goods Act* 1896, s 53(1); **Vic:** *Goods Act* 1958, s 55(1); **WA:** *Sale of Goods Act* 1895, s 48(1).
22. See *Colley v Overseas Exporters* [1921] 3 KB 302 at 306–10; *Plaimar Ltd v Waters Trading Co Ltd* (1945) 72 CLR 304. On damages for non-acceptance see [2140].
23. For the corresponding provisions see [1806].
24. *Martin v Hogan* (1917) 24 CLR 234 at 261, 267.
25. See [1822]–[1824].
26. See [1825]–[1826].
27. See, eg *Workman Clark & Co Ltd v Brazileno* [1908] 1 KB 968.

conduct does not bring forward the time for payment and the court will discount an award of future payments to take account of premature recovery.[28]

Agreed Damages Clauses[29]

General

[2207] Liquidated damages distinguished from penalty. The function of an agreed damages clause is to overcome a problem referred to earlier,[30] namely, the requirement of proof of loss in a claim for damages. If damages have been liquidated by the parties, there is no requirement that the plaintiff prove loss or damage, and recovery of compensation is thereby facilitated. In *Boucaut Bay Co Ltd v The Commonwealth*[31] Isaacs ACJ said that an agreed damages clause serves its function by being an 'admitted ... pre-assessment'. That being the case, unless the defendant denies that the contract has been breached, the clause fixes the amount recoverable by the plaintiff without the need for litigation.[32] Subject to statute,[33] such clauses are enforceable.

However, some agreed damages clauses have a different function, that of fixing a sum which is payable as a penalty for breach. Such a sum is not fixed as a genuine pre-estimate of loss or damage but is stipulated 'as in terrorem'[34] of the defendant. Such clauses are not enforceable. Although the basis for the rule has been debated, as a restriction on freedom of contract[35] it is best understood as based on public policy.[36]

Two issues arise in relation to the distinction between liquidated damages and penalties:

(1) Having regard to the nature of the clause, and the circumstances in which it is activated, is the clause one to which the distinction applies?

---

28. See [2160]. Specific performance may be a more appropriate remedy in some cases; see [2406].
29. See Meagher, Gummow and Lehane, *Equity: Doctrines and Remedies*, 3rd ed, 1992, Chapter 18; E V Lanyon, 'Equity and the Doctrine of Penalties' (1996) 9 *JCL* 234.
30. See [2106].
31. (1927) 40 CLR 98 at 106.
32. *Robophone Facilities Ltd v Blank* [1966] 1 WLR 1428 at 1447.
33. Alternatively, the court may by virtue of statutes such as the *Contracts Review Act 1980* (NSW), have jurisdiction to grant relief against the clause. See generally [1517]–[1528]. Note also [2240], [2331]–[2333] (relief against forfeiture).
34. *Dunlop Pneumatic Tyre Co Ltd v New Garage and Motor Co Ltd* [1915] AC 79 at 86.
35. On the economic efficiency of the rule see E L Talley, 'Contract Renegotiation, Mechanism Design, and the Liquidated Damages Rule' (1994) 46 *Stanford LR* 1195.
36. *Robophone Facilities Ltd v Blank* [1966] 1 WLR 1428 at 1446. On whether the basis is an equitable jurisdiction, see *Citicorp Australia Ltd v Hendry* (1985) 4 NSWLR 1 at 40; Meagher, Gummow and Lehane, *Equity: Doctrines and Remedies*, 3rd ed, 1992, para 1801. Cf *International Leasing Corp (Vic) Ltd v Aiken* [1967] 2 NSWR 427 at 442. But see *AMEV-UDC Finance Ltd v Austin* (1986) 162 CLR 170 at 191; 68 ALR 185; *P C Developments Pty Ltd v Revell* (1991) 22 NSWLR 615.

(2) Assuming that the distinction applies, is the clause to be classified as a valid and enforceable liquidated damages provision, or an invalid and unenforceable penalty?

[2208] Time and basis for classification. An agreed damages clause must be classified, as either a penalty or a liquidated damages clause, by reference to the circumstances which existed at the *time the contract was entered into*, rather than at the time of breach.[37]

The basis for classification is usually said to be the 'construction' of the contract.[38] However, as Deane J pointed out in *O'Dea v Allstates Leasing System (WA) Pty Ltd*,[39] the question of construction must be determined as a matter of 'substance' rather than form, and on the basis of the 'operation' of the clause rather than its description by the parties.[40]

The onus of proving that the clause is a penalty rests on the defendant.[41]

[2209] Description by the parties. Where the parties have described the sum payable as a 'penalty' or 'liquidated damages', this may create a presumption in favour of that classification, but it is not conclusive.[42]

For example, in *Clydebank Engineering and Shipbuilding Co Ltd v Don Jose Ramos Yzquierdo y Castaneda*[43] the Clydebank Engineering Co agreed to build four torpedo boats and to deliver them within various periods specified by the contract. It was expressly provided that in the event of 'later delivery' the 'penalty' was to be 'at the rate of £500 per week for each vessel not delivered by the contractors in the contract time'. The vessels were a number of weeks late and £500 was claimed for each week in reliance on the express provision. It was held by the House of Lords that the clause was not accurately described as a penalty, but was in effect a provision for the payment of a liquidated sum. On the other hand, there are many examples of cases in which a payment described as 'damages' has been construed as a penalty.[44]

[2210] Effect of termination.[45] The fact that the performance of the contract has been terminated, and the parties discharged from the obligation to perform their contractual duties, does not itself prevent the operation of an agreed damages clause.[46] This can be justified on the basis that the clause is intended to regulate the rights and liabilities of the parties

---

37. *Public Works Commissioner v Hills* [1906] AC 368.
38. See, eg *Dunlop Pneumatic Tyre Co Ltd v New Garage and Motor Co Ltd* [1915] AC 79 at 86; *Western Electric Co (Australia) Ltd v Ward* (1933) 51 WN (NSW) 19 at 20.
39. (1983) 152 CLR 359 at 400; 45 ALR 632. See also *Acron Pacific Ltd v Offshore Oil NL* (1985) 157 CLR 514; 61 ALR 245.
40. For the evidence admissible see *Multiplex Constructions Pty Ltd v Abgarus Pty Ltd* (1992) 33 NSWLR 504 at 508. See further [2209].
41. *Robophone Facilities Ltd v Blank* [1966] 1 WLR 1428 at 1447; *Multiplex Constructions Pty Ltd v Abgarus Pty Ltd* (1992) 33 NSWLR 504 at 527.
42. *Dunlop Pneumatic Tyre Co Ltd v New Garage and Motor Co Ltd* [1915] AC 79 at 86; *Boucaut Bay Co Ltd v The Commonwealth* (1927) 40 CLR 98 at 107.
43. [1905] AC 6.
44. See, eg *Bridge v Campbell Discount Co Ltd* [1962] AC 600 ('agreed compensation').
45. See J W Carter, 'Termination Clauses' (1990) 3 JCL 90.
46. See, eg *Boucaut Bay Co Ltd v The Commonwealth* (1927) 40 CLR 98; *Bridge v Campbell Discount Co Ltd* [1962] AC 600.

on breach, or because the clause quantifies the defendant's secondary obligation to pay compensation. It was explained earlier[47] that terms regulating rights and liabilities generally survive termination because this is presumed to be the intention of the parties, and the (quantified) secondary obligation to pay damages, unlike the parties' primary obligations, is not discharged by termination.[48]

Termination does, however, create two difficulties.

(1) It is more difficult to quantify in advance the liability of the defendant following termination.[49]

(2) There may be an additional obstacle for the plaintiff to overcome, namely, the possibility of the court granting relief against forfeiture in favour of the defendant.[50]

[2211] Effect of clause being penalty. Five questions are raised by the interpretation of the agreed damages clause as a penalty. First, is the plaintiff able to claim damages under the general law? Where a clause is construed as a penalty the plaintiff is able to claim damages for breach of contract.[51] Of course, it will be necessary for the plaintiff to produce evidence of loss or damage since otherwise the plaintiff will be restricted to a nominal sum.[52]

Second, is the clause void for all purposes, even in relation to breaches in respect of which the clause would not have been construed as a penalty? In *Pigram v Attorney-General (NSW)*[53] Barwick CJ explained that a term which is a penalty vis-à-vis one type of breach is unenforceable in respect of a breach the damages for which have been genuinely pre-estimated by the clause. This emphasises that the decision is not based on the particular breach or breaches on which the plaintiff's claim is based.[54] It may also provide a reason for having more than one agreed damages clause.[55]

Third, is the plaintiff entitled to sue on the clause to the extent that it is valid? It might be implied from the description of the invalid penalty clause as being unenforceable or void[56] that it cannot be sued upon at all. In fact, there is considerable authority for saying that the clause is enforceable to the extent of its validity.[57] Whether this is still the law is, however, largely a theoretical issue since, as Nicholls LJ said in *Jobson v Johnson*,[58] a penalty clause is 'in practice a dead letter'. The cold reality for the plaintiff is that compensation (rather than a liquidated sum) must be sought and proved.

---

47. See [1993].
48. *Robophone Facilities Ltd v Blank* [1966] 1 WLR 1428 at 1446.
49. See [2217].
50. See [2240].
51. See, eg *Scandinavian Trading Tanker Co AB v Flota Petrolera Ecuatoriana* [1983] 2 AC 694 at 702; *W & J Investments Ltd v Bunting* [1984] 1 NSWLR 331 at 335–6.
52. See [2101].
53. (1975) 132 CLR 216 at 221; 6 ALR 15.
54. *Cooden Engineering Co Ltd v Stanford* [1953] 1 QB 86 at 94.
55. See further [2214].
56. See, eg *Citicorp Australia Ltd v Hendry* (1985) 4 NSWLR 1 at 39–40.
57. See the discussion in *AMEV-UDC Finance Ltd v Austin* (1986) 162 CLR 170 at 192–3, 201–3, 212.
58. [1989] 1 WLR 1026 at 1039.

The fourth question, which arises when damages are claimed under the general law, is whether the amount fixed by the penalty is relevant to the assessment of the claim, in showing the intention of the parties with respect to the amount contemplated as the plaintiff's loss. The general answer is that the clause is not relevant.[59] Thus, in *AMEV-UDC Finance Ltd v Austin*[60] a contract for the lease of certain printing equipment stated that on default in the payment of rent, the lessor could terminate and recover the whole unpaid balance of the total rent. This was a penalty[61] and the lessor was relegated to its common law right to damages, which it sought to have assessed on a loss of bargain basis. However, a majority of the High Court, applying common law principles,[62] had no hesitation in saying that such damages were not recoverable. For the majority, the minor nature of the breach meant that there was no causal connection between the breach and the loss suffered, and the fact that the parties had indicated by their agreed damages clause that a substantial sum would be payable had to be ignored. However, Deane J (dissenting) considered that the clause could be enforced to the extent that it allowed recovery of damages for loss of the bargain. And Dawson J, who also dissented, said that the clause could not be ignored for the simple reason that it was indicative that the parties did not intend a purely nominal sum to be recovered. There is much to be said for the views of the minority in *Austin*. Given that the penalty rules are today rather strictly applied, it seems commercially naive to hold that a plaintiff should recover only a nominal sum when the clause shows an intention that the defendant was to pay substantial compensation on termination for breach.

Fifth, does the clause, although invalid, constitute the upper limit of the defendant's liability? It may be that the preferred answer to this question is that the penalty does not operate to limit an award under the common law.[63] However, the High Court has indicated that the question awaits authoritative resolution.[64]

Factors to be Considered

[2212] Magnitude of payment. It has never been the law that the mere fact that a clause stipulates for payment of a sum which exceeds what would be recoverable under common law principles governing the award of damages is enough to indicate that the sum is penal.

In *Dunlop Pneumatic Tyre Co Ltd v New Garage and Motor Co Ltd*[65] Lord Dunedin said that the clause will be a penalty 'if the sum stipulated for is extravagant and unconscionable in amount in comparison with the greatest loss that might conceivably be proved to have followed from the breach'. He referred to an example, given by Lord Halsbury LC in *Clydebank*

---

59. See Treitel, *Remedies for Breach of Contract*, 1988, p 217.
60. (1986) 162 CLR 170 (see J W Carter, (1987) 1 *Com LQ* 9; R M Goode, (1988) 104 *LQR* 25).
61. See [2217].
62. See [2159].
63. *W & J Investments Ltd v Bunting* [1984] 1 NSWLR 331 at 335 (see A H Hudson, (1985) 101 *LQR* 480).
64. *AMEV-UDC Finance Ltd v Austin* (1986) 162 CLR 170 at 192–3, 201–3, 212.
65. [1915] AC 79 at 87. The rules set out in this case seem now quite dated.

Engineering and Shipbuilding Co Ltd v Don Jose Ramos Yzquierdo y Castaneda,[66] of a builder who promises to build a house for £50, but agrees to pay a million pounds on breach of the contract. As Lord Halsbury said, the 'extravagance' would be at once apparent. Although the example is an extreme one, it does suggest that, the concern is with bona fide, rather than accurate, assessments, so that only where the amount recoverable is manifestly in excess of what might be expected to be recoverable under common law principles should the sum be regarded as penal. Nevertheless, it seems clear that the evolution of the law since the *Dunlop* case has included a shift from a requirement of genuineness in assessment to substantial accuracy in assessment. Accordingly, the disparity permitted today is much less than at the turn of the century.[67]

A valid agreed damages clause may in practice operate to the defendant's advantage, since the amount fixed may be less than the amount which would have been recoverable under damages rules. Thus, in *Cellulose Acetate Silk Co Ltd v Widnes Foundry (1925) Ltd*[68] contractors agreed to pay to the purchasers of an acetone recovery plant the sum of £20 per week 'by way of penalty' if the plant was not erected and delivered within a specified period. The contractors were 30 weeks late in finishing the work. Although the sum was not a pre-estimate of the purchaser's loss — delay was likely to cause damage in excess of £20 per week — the House of Lords said that the clause provided the maximum amount for which the contractors could be held liable and it was therefore enforceable as a liquidated damages clause.

[2213] Nature of the defendant's obligation. It is relevant to consider the nature of the defendant's obligations under the contract, and in particular whether the agreed damages clause comes into operation on the failure to pay a sum of money. In *Dunlop Pneumatic Tyre Co Ltd v New Garage and Motor Co Ltd*[69] Lord Dunedin said the clause 'will be held to be a penalty if the breach consists only in not paying a sum of money, and the sum stipulated is a sum greater than the sum which ought to have been paid'. For example, if B owes A $100 payable on 1 March, a clause of the agreement providing for the payment of $1000 as damages for default in payment would clearly be a penalty.[70]

[2214] Circumstances in which sum payable. The scope of the clause, that is, the circumstances in which it will apply and require the defendant to pay, is sometimes relevant to the distinction between liquidated damages and penalties. For example, in *Pigram v Attorney-General (NSW)*[71] a teacher was granted financial assistance by the government to enable him to study at the University of New England. A deed was executed which

---

66. [1905] AC 6 at 10.
67. See, eg *Photo Production Ltd v Securicor Transport Ltd* [1980] AC 827 at 850. For criticism see G D Muir, 'Stipulations for the Payment of Agreed Sums' (1985) 10 Syd LR 503. Cf *Multiplex Constructions Pty Ltd v Abgarus Pty Ltd* (1992) 33 NSWLR 504 at 513.
68. [1933] AC 20.
69. [1915] AC 79 at 87.
70. Cf *Jobson v Johnson* [1989] 1 WLR 1026; and see further [2217].
71. (1975) 132 CLR 216.

obliged the defendant to pay 'as and for liquidated damages' the 'cost incurred' by the government in providing financial assistance, in the event of the defendant failing to resume his duties as a teacher. The High Court considered that there was a clear attempt to provide a pre-estimate of the damage likely to result from a breach on the defendant's part because the clause was limited to a failure to resume duties. If it had also applied in the event of a failure to serve his employers 'faithfully and diligently' it would have been a penalty. Such an event would occur, if at all, after the resumption of service and be quite unrelated to the government's expenditure in providing financial assistance.

In *Dunlop Pneumatic Tyre Co Ltd v New Garage and Motor Co Ltd*[72] Lord Dunedin said[73] that there is a 'presumption (but no more)' that the term 'is a penalty "if a single sum is made payable ... on the occurrence of one or more or all of several events, some of which may occasion serious and others but trifling damage"'. The facts of the *Dunlop* case provide an illustration of the rebuttal of the presumption. The plaintiffs manufactured motor tyres and sold them under terms which required the defendants, as purchasers:

- not to alter or tamper with the markings on tubes or tyre covers;
- not to sell or offer for sale at prices below list prices;
- not to supply goods to suspended customers of the plaintiffs or to exhibit the goods without their consent; and
- not to export without the plaintiffs' consent.

The agreement further provided for the payment of £5 in respect of each and every 'tyre, cover or tube sold or offered in breach of this agreement'. The House of Lords held that, having regard to the difficulty in assessing damages,[74] the term was not a penalty. It was assumed that the stipulated sum applied to any breach of the agreement, but because the damage caused by every breach was of an uncertain nature the presumption was rebutted.

[2215] Difficulty in estimating loss. The consideration which formed the basis for the decision in *Dunlop Pneumatic Tyre Co Ltd v New Garage and Motor Co Ltd*[75] was that the damages for breach by the defendants would have been difficult to assess and the sum stipulated (£5) was not an extravagant pre-estimate of the plaintiffs' loss. Lord Dunedin said:[76]

> It is no obstacle to the sum stipulated being a genuine pre-estimate of damage, that the consequences of the breach are such as to make precise pre-estimation almost an impossibility. On the contrary, that is just the situation when it is probable that pre-estimated damage was the true bargain between the parties.

---

72. [1915] AC 79 at 87. See also *O'Dea v Allstates Leasing System (WA) Pty Ltd* (1983) 152 CLR 359 at 399–400.
73. Quoting *Lord Elphinstone v Monkland Iron and Coal Co Ltd* (1886) 11 App Cas 332 at 342 per Lord Watson.
74. See further [2215].
75. [1915] AC 79.
76. [1915] AC 79 at 87–8.

In *Waterside Workers' Federation of Australia v Stewart*[77] a bond between the Waterside Workers' Federation of Australia and the Industrial Registrar of the Commonwealth Court of Conciliation and Arbitration provided for the payment of £50 in the event of, among other things, a strike by two or more members of the Federation. The court said[78] it would have been practically 'impossible' to calculate with any degree of certainty or accuracy the loss suffered by any of the plaintiffs on breach by the defendants. The sum was not extravagant and was therefore treated as providing for liquidated damages.

Damages for delay are frequently difficult to assess, and this consideration therefore has particular relevance in that context.[79]

Scope of the Distinction[80]

[2216] Penalty must be payable on breach. For a sum to be classified under the liquidated damages/penalty distinction it must be payable on breach.[81] However, the sum need not be payable exclusively on breach. This was established by *Bridge v Campbell Discount Co Ltd*,[82] where the defendant acquired possession of a motor car pursuant to a hire-purchase contract with the plaintiffs, but found himself unable to meet his obligations under the agreement. He communicated this to the plaintiffs, saying that he was 'very sorry'. He later returned the vehicle. Clause 9 of the contract provided for the payment, as 'agreed compensation for depreciation' of a sum equal to two-thirds of the hire-purchase price less the instalments paid by the hirer. Clause 9 operated if the agreement was for any reason terminated and the defendant contended that it provided for a penalty. The position was complicated by cl 6, which deemed the provisions of cl 9 to apply if the hirer gave notice of early termination. Early termination was a right conferred on the hirer and would not involve a breach on his part. A majority of the House of Lords held that the hirer had not exercised his option of early termination under cl 6 and that the sum in question was payable, under cl 9, on breach by the defendant. Moreover, the House was unanimous in holding that the amount stipulated could not be regarded as a genuine pre-estimate of the plaintiffs' loss, primarily because the amount described as 'depreciation' would become progressively less the longer the vehicle was used. In other words, the sliding scale went the wrong way.

However, Viscount Simonds expressed the view that the defendant had exercised his rights under cl 6 so that the distinction between penalties and liquidated damages did not apply. Lord Morton agreed that had the defendant exercised his option the distinction could not have applied. Lord Radcliffe, on the other hand, refused to decide the issue, whereas Lord

---

77. (1919) 27 CLR 119.
78. (1919) 27 CLR 119 at 128, 133.
79. See *Clydebank Engineering and Shipbuilding Co Ltd v Don Jose Ramos Yzquierdo y Castaneda* [1905] AC 6 at 11.
80. See M P Furmston, 'Contract Planning: Liquidated Damages, Deposits and the Foreseeability Rule' (1991) 4 *JCL* 1.
81. See, eg *Export Credits Department v Universal Oil Products Co* [1983] 1 WLR 399.
82. [1962] AC 600 (see G H L Fridman, (1963) 26 *MLR* 198).

Denning and Lord Devlin concluded that the defendant would still have been entitled to relief. In Lord Denning's view[83] equity could not commit itself to the 'absurd paradox' that the defendant would have been beyond the court's assistance had he performed, rather than breached, the contract. He considered the 'minimum payment' to be a sum payable on the failure of a contingency, that is, the payment of two-thirds of the hire-purchase price. A narrower approach was taken by Lord Devlin, who said that if cl 9 provided for a penalty it made no difference whether it was activated by cl 6 or by an event within the clause itself: once it was a penalty it was so for all purposes. The decision in *Bridge* was approved (and applied) by the High Court in *O'Dea v Allstates Leasing System (WA) Pty Ltd*.[84] However, it was unnecessary to consider which of the conflicting opinions expressed in *Bridge* should be applied in the event of termination without breach.[85]

Although the vast bulk of the cases on the distinction between liquidated damages and penalties have concerned promises to pay money, there are cases in which the distinction has been applied to promises to confer non-monetary benefits.[86]

[2217] Acceleration clauses and loss of bargain damages. It is common for contracts for the lease of goods to contain terms which accelerate the payment of rent by the lessee on the occurrence of specified events. The terms vary somewhat and the distinction between liquidated damages and penalties may not apply to all such provisions. The leading case is *O'Dea v Allstates Leasing System (WA) Pty Ltd*,[87] where Gibbs CJ said[88] that the cases in which the distinction has been held *not* to apply fall into two classes.

In the first, where the contract provides for the payment of money by instalments and it is provided that the whole sum is to become payable immediately on the lessee's failure to make punctual payment, the distinction does not apply because there is a 'present debt, which, by reason of the indulgence given by the creditor, is payable either in the future, or in a lesser amount, provided that certain conditions are met'.[89]

In the second, the parties have agreed that 'a sum shall be payable on a certain event which, although brought about by the party required to make the payment, does not involve a breach of contract'. For example, the sum

---

83. [1962] AC 600 at 629.
84. (1983) 152 CLR 359 (see [2217]).
85. But see *Associated Distributors Ltd v Hall* [1938] 2 KB 83; *International Leasing Corp (Vic) Ltd v Aiken* [1967] 2 NSWR 427 at 442. And cf *United Dominions Trust (Commercial) Ltd v Ennis* [1968] 1 QB 54.
86. See, eg *Jobson v Johnson* [1989] 1 WLR 1026 (see Charles Harpum, [1989] *CLJ* 370; D R Harris, [1990] *LMCLQ* 158); *P C Developments Pty Ltd v Revell* (1991) 22 NSWLR 615; *Wollondilly Shire Council v Picton Power Lines Pty Ltd* (1994) 33 NSWLR 551 at 555. But cf *CRA Ltd v NZ Goldfields Investments* [1989] VR 870.
87. (1983) 152 CLR 359. See R P Meagher, 'Penalties in Chattel Leases' in Finn, ed, *Essays in Equity*, 1985, p 46; D S K Ong, 'Chattel Leasing: Indulgences, Liquidated Damages and Penalties' (1986) 60 *ALJ* 272.
88. (1983) 152 CLR 359 at 366-8.
89. See also *Thompson v Hudson* (1869) LR 4 HL 1. Cf *Acron Pacific Ltd v Offshore Oil NL* (1985) 157 CLR 514 (moratorium deed).

may be payable where a lessee of goods requests the lessor to retake possession. The distinction may not apply here because there is no breach.

It may be, however, that in respect of the first class of case the lessee can apply for relief against forfeiture if deprived of the use of the goods, and the principles applicable to the second class of case are not entirely settled.[90]

O'Dea in fact illustrates that there is frequently room for debate on the application of the distinction between liquidated damages and penalties to an acceleration clause. The contract provided for the lease for a period of 36 months of a 'Mercedes Benz' prime mover. Although cl 1(a) stated that the rent for the period of the lease was to be 'due and payable' by the lessee on the signing of the agreement, it permitted the lessee to pay the rent by instalments. Clause 6(a) contained a promise of due and punctual payment by the lessee, and cl 12 stated that, in the event of default in punctual payment, the lessor could retake possession without notice to the lessee and thereby terminate the lessee's right to retention and use of the vehicle. Clause 12 further provided that all money due for 'unexpired terms' should 'become immediately due and payable' by the lessee, plus 'reasonable costs of repossession'. On the same day as the lease was signed a guarantee of performance by the lessee was given by M G O'Dea Pty Ltd.

When default occurred the vehicle was repossessed and sold. In proceedings against the lessee and the guarantor the claim was for the difference between the instalments paid and those payable under the agreement, together with interest and the costs of repossession. Alternatively, damages were claimed. It was conceded that the repossession costs were recoverable, but the defendants alleged that the other sum claimed was a penalty. The court was unanimous in holding that the sum which the lessor sought was in the nature of a penalty. In the result the case was remitted to the Supreme Court of Western Australia for an assessment of the amount of damages recoverable by the plaintiffs.

The decision illustrates that the law is excessively technical, and that anyone drafting an acceleration clause must be particularly astute.[91] Subsequent cases[92] confirm that recovery of instalment payments as damages will not be permitted after termination. However, an agreed damages clause which quantifies loss of bargain damages, as the difference between the rental payable and the sum of rent paid, the value of the goods and a rebate which expresses an appropriate discount for early recovery of instalments will be valid.[93] In one sense this is surprising. As a matter of strict logic such a clause ought to be invalid, because of the possibility that it will apply where only a minor breach on the part of the lessee leads to termination. In such a case[94] a plaintiff would recover only a nominal sum

---

90. See [2240] and [2216] respectively.
91. For suggestions of a need for reform in the law see *Citicorp Australia Ltd v Hendry* (1985) 4 NSWLR 1 at 22–4, 29–30; *AMEV-UDC Finance Ltd v Austin* (1986) 162 CLR 170 at 190.
92. See, eg *AMEV-UDC Finance Ltd v Austin* (1986) 162 CLR 170. See also *Financings Ltd v Baldock* [1963] 2 QB 104.
93. *IAC (Leasing) Ltd v Humphrey* (1972) 126 CLR 131; *Esanda Finance Corp Ltd v Plessnig* (1989) 166 CLR 131; 84 ALR 99 (see J W Carter, (1989) 2 *JCL* 78; John Wilkin, [1990] *LMCLQ* 16); *AMEV Finance Ltd v Artes Studios Thoroughbreds Pty Ltd* (1989) 15 NSWLR 564.

as damages on termination. The rationalisation for enforcing such clauses is that the court may take into account termination of the contract — and the consequent loss of bargain — notwithstanding that, in a claim for damages, the loss of the bargain would be regarded as having been caused by the election to terminate rather than the breach.[95]

Recovery after Election to Continue Performance[96]

[2218] **Right to continue performance.** It was explained earlier[97] that a breach or repudiation does not operate to terminate the performance of a contract automatically. If there is a right to terminate, the promisee may choose to exercise the right. However, as Jordan CJ said in *Tramways Advertising Pty Ltd v Luna Park (NSW) Ltd*,[98] a 'party by committing a breach of an essential promise cannot thereby compel the innocent party to put an end to the contract: the latter may go on with the performance of the contract if he chooses'. If follows that a plaintiff is not compelled to terminate the contract and claim damages for breach: it may, at least in theory,[99] continue to perform and earn the sum which the defendant had agreed to pay.

[2219] **Recovery through specific performance.** A plaintiff may be able to give substance to an election to continue performance by obtaining an order for specific performance. Thus, a vendor of land may elect to continue performance, notwithstanding the purchaser's breach of an essential time stipulation, and recover the contract price through a court order for specific performance. Although most frequently applied to such contracts, the remedy of specific performance is not restricted to contracts for the sale of land.[100] It may, for example, be available to assist a plaintiff who has fully performed to recover a liquidated sum if the defendant has promised to make instalment payments.[101]

[2220] **The *White and Carter* case.** In *White and Carter (Councils) Ltd v McGregor*[102] the House of Lords pushed the two principles emphasised

---

94. See [2159].
95. Cf *Capital Finance Co Ltd v Donati* (1977) 121 SJ 270. The problem is avoided if the contract makes every breach the breach of an essential term or a repudiation: *Lombard North Central Plc v Butterworth* [1987] 1 QB 527 (see Hugh Beale, (1988) 104 *LQR* 355).
96. Carter, *Breach of Contract*, 2nd ed, 1991, paras 1107–1130; L J Priestley, 'Conduct after Breach: The Position of the Party Not in Breach' (1991) 3 *JCL* 218 (and commentary thereon by Keith Mason, (1991) 3 *JCL* 232); J W Carter, Andrew Phang and Sock-Yong Phang, 'Performance Following Repudiation: Legal and Economic Interests' (1999) 15 *JCL* 97.
97. See [1967].
98. (1938) 38 SR (NSW) 632 at 645 (reversed on other grounds sub nom *Luna Park (NSW) Ltd v Tramways Advertising Pty Ltd* (1938) 61 CLR 286).
99. For qualifications see [2221]–[2224].
100. See generally [2401]–[2412].
101. See [2406].
102. [1962] AC 413 (see K Scott, [1962] *CLJ* 12; M P Furmston, (1962) 25 *MLR* 364; Note, (1963) 2 *Adel LR* 103).

above, namely (1) the distinction between debt and damages and (2) the plaintiff's right to continue performance, to their logical, but (to some) objectionable, conclusion. The case concerned an advertising contract between White and Carter and McGregor, who owned a garage business at Clydebank. White and Carter agreed to advertise the business for 156 weeks. The contract obliged McGregor to pay a weekly sum and to make an annual payment towards the cost of the advertising plates which were to be placed on litter bins in fixed positions in Clydebank. McGregor purported to cancel the contract on the very day it was signed. He had no right to do so and the contract specifically stated that it was not subject to 'countermand'. Now, White and Carter's reaction was not, as might have been expected, to claim damages for breach. Instead, they manufactured the plates, advertised the business and claimed payments from McGregor.

By the time the House of Lords delivered judgment in their favour, White and Carter had advertised the business for the full period.[103] They therefore recovered the total of the sums which McGregor had agreed to pay under the contract. It was irrelevant, so the majority thought, to consider whether White and Carter had acted reasonably, as a plaintiff is not bound by any requirement of reasonableness when making an election.[104] Nor was it relevant to consider whether they had mitigated their loss, because the claim was for a debt due under the contract, not damages.[105]

The decision in the *White and Carter* case was not well received, either by commentators[106] or the courts. There is, however, nothing in the Australian cases to suggest that a contrary result would be reached here. And nothing turns on the fact that the *White and Carter* case was a Scottish appeal. Nevertheless, as will appear from the discussion below, in most situations the reasoning of the case will not enable a plaintiff to recover a liquidated sum rather than damages for breach.

Position Where Co-operation Required

[2221] Effect of failure to co-operate. In *White and Carter (Councils) Ltd v McGregor*[107] there was no requirement of co-operation between the parties, since White and Carter could perform their obligations without McGregor's assistance: all he had to do was to pay money. But it was recognised that where co-operation is required a plaintiff's ability to claim the contract price depends on whether specific performance is available.[108]

---

103. Initially their claim was based on an acceleration clause in the contract, but this played no part in the proceedings before the House of Lords.
104. But cf [1983].
105. White and Carter had, in fact, made no attempt to minimise their loss; see Alan Rodger, (1977) 93 *LQR* 168.
106. See A L Goodhart, 'Measure of Damages when a Contract is Repudiated' (1962) 78 *LQR* 263; S J Stoljar, 'Some Problems of Anticipatory Breach' (1974) 9 *MULR* 355. Contrast P M Nienaber, 'The Effect of Anticipatory Repudiation: Principle and Policy' [1962] *CLJ* 213.
107. [1962] AC 413.
108. See also *City Motors (1933) Pty Ltd v Southern Aerial Super Service Pty Ltd* (1961) 106 CLR 477 at 489.

Co-operation is required in a great many contracts to which the remedy of specific performance is not generally applicable. Chief among these are employment contracts and most contracts for the sale of goods or supply of services. In an employment contract the employee's performance normally takes place at the employer's place of business, and if the employer refuses to co-operate, and excludes the employee from the work place, the employee will be unable to complete performance. Similarly, if a buyer refuses to accept goods the seller will usually be unable to make delivery. Again, where a contract for the supply of services requires co-operation, the supplier will usually be unable to earn the price of the services if co-operation is not forthcoming.

What, then, is the effect of a failure to co-operate? In *Tramways Advertising Pty Ltd v Luna Park (NSW) Ltd*,[109] Jordan CJ explained that where the

> participation of the defaulting party is necessary to enable the innocent party to perform the contract on his part, and this participation is withheld, the innocent party is necessarily prevented and absolved from performance so long as participation is withheld.

Therefore, although not in breach of contract by not performing, because the plaintiff has not earned the payment the plaintiff is not entitled to recover the sum which the defendant agreed to pay. Accordingly, the general rule in cases where co-operation is required is that the plaintiff is entitled to recover damages or restitution, if the failure to co-operate amounts to a breach of contract,[110] but not the contract sum. For example, an employee who is prevented from working is not usually entitled to wages, and a supplier of goods or services who is prevented from making delivery or rendering the services is not entitled to the price of the goods or services.[111] Of course, in all these cases even though unable to recover the sum which the defendant agreed to pay, the plaintiff is entitled to compensation. For example, a seller is entitled to recover the difference between the contract price and the market price if the buyer refuses to accept delivery of the goods.

At first sight *Mackay v Dick*[112] appears to contradict the principles stated above. A contract for the sale of a machine required the machine to be put through performance tests. The understanding of the parties was that if the machine did not perform satisfactorily the buyer would be under no liability to pay the price. As the buyer refused to co-operate with the seller the machine was not properly tested. Nevertheless, the House of Lords held that the buyer was liable to pay. The explanation for this decision is that the property in the goods had passed to the buyer by virtue of the

---

109. (1938) 38 SR (NSW) 632 at 645 (reversed on other grounds sub nom *Luna Park (NSW) Ltd v Tramways Advertising Pty Ltd* (1938) 61 CLR 286).
110. See [1809], [2322].
111. See, eg *Martin v Hogan* (1917) 24 CLR 234 at 264; *Automatic Fire Sprinklers Pty Ltd v Watson* (1946) 72 CLR 435 at 451, 452, 461, 465, 476; *Byrne v Australian Airlines Ltd* (1995) 185 CLR 410 at 428; 131 ALR 422. For the same reasons a vendor of land who makes no claim for specific performance will be unable to recover the price of the land if the purchaser refuses to co-operate in the performance of the contract; see [2238].
112. (1881) 6 App Cas 251.

contract.[113] The requirement that the machine pass performance tests was simply a safeguard for the buyer. If the tests showed the machine to be unsatisfactory, title to the goods would have passed back to the seller and the buyer would not have been liable to pay. However, as the buyer prevented tests being carried out he could not take advantage of the contingency and his obligation to pay became absolute.

[2222] **Scope of the co-operation limitation.** In the situations considered above the co-operation required by the contract might be described as 'active'. However, the co-operation concept may have a wider significance, and include what might be termed 'passive' co-operation. The expression has been used to describe cases in which the plaintiff must use the defendant's land or goods in order to complete performance.[114] The plaintiff will be able to complete performance if the defendant remains passive, and does not take steps to remove the plaintiff from the land or to obtain possession of the goods. However, a defendant who has repudiated the contract will usually have indicated to the plaintiff an intention not to remain passive. For example, the defendant may have revoked a contractual licence and barred the plaintiff's entry to the land.

In order for the plaintiff to complete performance the plaintiff must be in a position to prevent the defendant taking possession of the land or goods. The measure of the plaintiff's ability to complete performance can then be expressed in terms of whether an injunction can be obtained to restrain the defendant from breaching the contract. Accordingly, and taking again the example of a contractual licence to enter land, the plaintiff will be unable to complete performance — and claim a liquidated sum under the contract — unless the court grants an injunction to the plaintiff.[115]

Absence of Legitimate Interest in Continuing Performance

[2223] **Lord Reid's statement.** In *White and Carter (Councils) Ltd v McGregor*[116] Lord Reid stated a limitation, which possibly applies to the principles applied in that case, in the following terms:

> It may well be that, if it can be shown that a person has no legitimate interest, financial or otherwise, in performing the contract rather than claiming damages, he ought not to be allowed to saddle the other party with an additional burden with no benefit to himself. If a party has no interest to enforce a stipulation, he cannot in general enforce it: so it might be said that, if a party has no interest to insist on a particular remedy, he ought not to be allowed to insist on it. And, just as a party is not allowed to enforce a penalty, so he ought not to be allowed to penalise the other party by taking one course when another is equally advantageous to him.

In the *White and Carter* case itself this limitation did not apply because, as Lord Reid said,[117] McGregor 'did not set out to prove' that White and

---

113. *Colley v Overseas Exporters* [1921] 3 KB 302; and see [1809].
114. *Hounslow London BC v Twickenham Garden Developments Ltd* [1971] 1 Ch 233 at 253–4.
115. Contrast the decision in *Larking v Great Western (Nepean) Gravel Ltd* (1940) 64 CLR 221.
116. [1962] AC 413 at 431.

Carter 'had no legitimate interest in completing the contract and claiming the contract price rather than claiming damages'. By way of contrast, Lord Reid referred to the following hypothetical situation. Assume that a company commissions an expert (E) to go abroad to prepare a report but decides, prior to E's departure, that the report will be of no value. Lord Reid said that if the company then repudiates its obligations, but E goes abroad and prepares the report, E might be denied the right to claim the promised payment as a debt due if the company could prove that E had no legitimate interest in claiming the debt rather than damages. On such proof Lord Reid said that there might be a 'proper case for the exercise of the general equitable jurisdiction of the court'.[118]

[2224] Status of the legitimate interest concept. There appears to be no Australian decision in which the legitimate interest concept has been applied and its status in Australia is uncertain. Guidance on the legitimate interest concept can be found in the English cases, where the concept has been adopted as a restriction on a plaintiff's right to recover the sum due under the contract after performance on his or her part. To some extent this is surprising. Lord Reid's formulation was particularly tentative and although he delivered one of the two majority speeches in *White and Carter (Councils) Ltd v McGregor*,[119] it is difficult to reconcile with the opinion of Lord Hodson,[120] who delivered the other majority speech (with which Lord Tucker agreed), that to deny a plaintiff who has fully performed the debt due under the contract would be to 'introduce a novel equitable doctrine' and make the 'action for debt a claim for a discretionary remedy'.

The English cases indicate that the onus of proof is on the defendant, who must establish that the plaintiff had no legitimate interest in claiming the liquidated sum rather than damages.[121] However, if the plaintiff establishes a legitimate interest, such as the conversion of an unsecured claim to recover damages into a secured claim against property in the possession of the defendant, the plaintiff will obviously succeed in the action for the liquidated sum.[122] Similarly, if it is established that termination of performance would damage the plaintiff's commercial reputation, or expose the plaintiff to claims for damages by third parties, a legitimate interest will be present.[123] Performance by the plaintiff may, for example, prevent the plaintiff breaching a related contract with another person. In other cases the courts have concentrated on the assessment of damages in respect of the plaintiff's claim. Thus, in *Gator Shipping Corp v*

---

117. [1962] AC 600 at 431.
118. [1962] AC 600 at 431.
119. [1962] AC 413.
120. [1962] AC 600 at 445. Nevertheless, the suggestion by two members of the English Court of Appeal in *Decro-Wall International SA v Practitioners in Marketing Ltd* [1971] 1 WLR 361, that Lord Reid was merely formulating an argument of counsel, was rejected in *Hounslow London BC v Twickenham Garden Developments Ltd* [1971] 1 Ch 233 at 253, 254.
121. See *Clea Shipping Corp v Bulk Oil International Ltd (The Alaskan Trader)* [1984] 1 All ER 129 at 133, 135.
122. See *George Barker (Transport) Ltd v Eynon* [1974] 1 WLR 462.
123. See *Anglo-African Shipping Co of New York Inc v J Mortner Ltd* [1962] 1 Lloyd's Rep 81 at 91 (affirmed without reference to the point at 610). Cf *Ahmed v Estate and Trust Agencies (1927) Ltd* [1938] AC 624 at 639–40.

Trans-Asiatic Oil Ltd SA (The Odenfeld)[124] Kerr J said that the absence of any legitimate interest in continuing performance could not be established when the assessment of damages would have been extremely difficult. By way of contrast, in *Attica Sea Carriers Corp v Ferrostaal Poseidon Bulk Reederei GmbH*[125] and *Clea Shipping Corp v Bulk Oil International Ltd (The Alaskan Trader)*[126] an absence of any legitimate interest was established, mainly on the basis that there was no difficulty in assessing damages.

One problem with these cases is that they provide little by way of doctrinal basis for the legitimate interest concept. Lord Reid drew an analogy with penalties, and invoked the court's equitable jurisdiction when stating how the concept might be applied. But, if the plaintiff has earned the contract price, how is the sum agreed upon by the parties converted to a penalty? A penalty, as was explained earlier,[127] is a sum payable on breach, and the amount payable by the defendant as the price of the plaintiff's performance does not become due as the consequence of a breach of contract. And, if the concept is exercised according to equitable principles, more attention should be paid to whether the plaintiff has acted unconscionably in completing performance. It should, for example, be explained that performance without any legitimate interest is unconscionable conduct. This leads to two further difficulties.

First, most of the cases have concerned time charterparties and it is doubtful whether the concept should be applied to such commercial contracts where certainty is so important. The House of Lords has warned of the dangers in applying equitable concepts to commercial contracts where it would engender uncertainty.[128]

Second, the English cases in effect deny the plaintiff the right to continue performance, rather than the remedy to which the plaintiff is otherwise entitled. The majority in the *White and Carter* case rejected the view that a plaintiff is bound to exercise the right to continue performance reasonably, yet the effect of the subsequent decisions is to subject the right of election to some such requirement.

Nevertheless, the presence of some sort of qualification on the right of a party to continue to perform seems desirable. Whether it is best expressed in terms of 'legitimate interest' of the promisee, the 'reasonableness' of the promisee's conduct or some other criterion may of course be debated, but it would be inconsistent with the current concern to promote good faith in contract law to treat the promisee as having an unfettered right.[129]

---

124. [1978] 2 Lloyd's Rep 357.
125. [1976] 1 Lloyd's Rep 250.
126. [1984] 1 All ER 129 (see A S Taylor, (1984) 128 *Sol J* 843; J W Carter and Geoffrey Marston, [1985] *CLJ* 21).
127. See [2216].
128. *Scandinavian Trading Tanker Co AB v Flota Petrolera Ecuatoriana* [1983] 2 AC 694.
129. See *Stocznia Gdanska SA v Latvian Shipping Co* [1996] 2 Lloyd's Rep 132 at 139 (see J W Carter, (1998) 12 *JCL* 247) (reversed without reference to the point [1998] 1 WLR 574).

Recovery after Termination[130]

Introduction

[2225] **Accrued right not divested.** Where the performance of a contract is terminated the contract is not rescinded. As was explained earlier,[131] this distinguishes termination for breach or repudiation, or by frustration, from rescission for misrepresentation or mistake. Because the contract is not rescinded, the accrued rights of the parties may remain enforceable after termination. The present concern is with a plaintiff's accrued right to recover a sum fixed by the contract.

[2226] **Time for recovery.** A liquidated sum is recoverable after termination if the right to recover it from the defendant unconditionally accrued to the plaintiff prior to termination. As Dixon and Evatt JJ explained in *Westralian Farmers Ltd v Commonwealth Agricultural Service Engineers Ltd*:[132]

> In general the termination of an executory agreement out of the performance of which pecuniary demands may arise imports that, just as on the one side no further acts of performance can be required, so, on the other side, no liability can be brought into existence if it depends on a further act of performance. If the title to rights consists of vestitive facts which would result from the further execution of the contract but which have not been brought about before the agreement terminates, the rights cannot arise. But if all the facts have occurred which entitle one party to such a right as a debt, a distinct chose in action which for many purposes is conceived as possessing proprietary characteristics, the fact that the right to payment is future or is contingent upon some event, not involving further performance of the contract, does not prevent it maturing into an immediately enforceable obligation.

This passage is also important because it indicates that an accrued right may exist in respect of a liquidated sum due for payment *after* termination. Thus, in the *Westralian Farmers* case itself, agents were entitled to recover the commission payable on the sale of certain tractors even though the performance of the contract with their principals terminated prior to the time for payment. The contract provided for payment after the arrival of the tractors in Australia, and termination occurred while the goods were in transit. Because the commission had been earned, and payment was merely contingent on the arrival of the tractors, a majority of the court held that the commission could be recovered.[133] The position would have been different had some further act of performance by the agents been required. Of course, the agents had to wait for the arrival of the tractors before bringing their action; termination did not bring forward the time for payment.

---

130. See Jack Beatson, 'Discharge for Breach: The Position of Instalments, Deposits and Other Payments Due Before Completion' (1981) 97 *LQR* 389.
131. See [1989].
132. (1936) 54 CLR 361 at 379–80.
133. See also *George Mountreas & Co SA v Navimpex Centrala Navala* [1985] 2 Lloyd's Rep 515; *Bank of Boston Connecticut v European Grain and Shipping Ltd* [1989] AC 1056. Cf *Torminster Properties Ltd v Green* [1982] 1 WLR 751.

[2227] **Position where contract frustrated.** The position of a plaintiff with respect to liquidated sums due prior to termination by frustration was considered earlier.[134]

Termination following Breach or Repudiation[135]

[2228] **Intention of the parties.** Whether an accrued right exists in relation to a liquidated sum payable prior to termination depends on the intention of the parties as expressed by the contract. It is, therefore, an issue of construction. If the parties have expressly agreed that a sum is to remain payable after termination this expression of intention governs the rights of the parties subject only to the restrictions considered later.[136]

Usually, however, the parties do not deal expressly with the recovery of liquidated sums after termination, and the court must decide what the parties, as reasonable persons, impliedly agreed on the matter. The court will have regard to the terms of the contract, the performance rendered by the plaintiff and the extent to which the plaintiff is discharged by termination.[137] Dixon J explained in *McDonald v Dennys Lascelles Ltd*,[138] the right must have 'unconditionally' accrued to the plaintiff from the 'partial execution' of the contract. One way of testing whether a right to payment has unconditionally accrued is to consider whether the payment could be recovered by the payee in a claim for restitution on the basis of a total failure of consideration.

[2229] **Contractual right to terminate.** Where termination occurs pursuant to a contractual right, the parties are more likely to have expressed an intention on the recovery of liquidated sums. For example, a contract of hire (or lease) might provide that termination for breach by the hirer is to leave intact the hirer's (or lessee's) liability in respect of payments due prior to termination.[139]

The contract may, however, do no more than expressly preserve the plaintiff's common law rights. This was the position in *Hyundai Heavy Industries Co Ltd v Papadopoulos*,[140] which concerned a contract for the construction of a ship. The price was payable in instalments, representing agreed proportions of the total price, and due on dates specified by the contract. The builders agreed to design the vessel, to supply all necessary drawings, and to build, launch, equip and complete the vessel. The first payment due from the buyers was paid, but the second, representing 2.5 per cent of the purchase price, was not. The builders then exercised a contractual right to terminate and sought to recover the overdue payment from Papadopoulos and others who guaranteed the builders' performance of the construction contract. The House of Lords was unanimous in

---

134. See [2065], [2071], [2080].
135. See Carter, *Breach of Contract*, 2nd ed, 1991, Chapter 12; J W Carter and J C Phillips, 'The Liability of Debtors and Guarantors Under Contracts Discharged for Breach' (1992) 22 *UWALR* 338.
136. See [2238]–[2241].
137. See also [1986].
138. (1933) 48 CLR 457 at 477 (see [1988]).
139. See, eg *Shevill v Builders Licensing Board* (1982) 149 CLR 620; 42 ALR 305.
140. [1980] 1 WLR 1129.

holding that the guarantors were liable.[141] The present concern, however, is with the position of the buyers.

Would the builders have been entitled to recover the overdue payment from the buyers? Three members of the House of Lords gave an affirmative answer to this question.[142] They regarded the case as involving no more than the recovery of a sum which should have been paid prior to termination. It did not matter that the builders had produced no evidence of performance because the contract did not make their right to sue dependent on any performance by the builders. Their Lordships conceded that had the contract been simply one of sale the buyers would probably have had a defence based on failure of consideration.[143] However, in their view the contract more closely resembled one for the provision of services,[144] so that there was no total failure of consideration[145] on termination even though no performance had been received by the buyers. Viscount Dilhorne went so far as to say that *because* the payment should have been made prior to termination the obligation to pay was not affected by termination. This is a little misleading. As Dixon J explained in *McDonald v Dennys Lascelles Ltd*,[146] it is the fact of partial execution, that is, performance, which gives rise to an accrued right. To take a fairly straightforward example, if A employs B under a contract of employment providing for monthly payments, but A repudiates his or her obligations, termination by B after a payment date does not preserve an accrued right to wages unless these were earned prior to termination. In the *Hyundai* case the builders did not prove that they had performed, but the buyers may be taken to have admitted performance by not putting it in issue. Alternatively, the buyers' obligation to pay may have been wholly independent of performance by the builders, which seems to have been the view applied by Viscount Dilhorne and Lord Edmund-Davies. There was, in other words, no total failure of consideration because the buyers had agreed to pay in return for a promise to perform (that is, to design the vessel), rather than in return for performance of the promise.

The views expressed in the *Hyundai* case were approved in another shipbuilding case *Stocznia Gdanska SA v Latvian Shipping Co*.[147] Six shipbuilding contracts were terminated by the builder for the buyer's repudiation. The House of Lords held that *Hyundai* was applicable even though there was no contract provision expressly preserving the builders' rights following termination. The builders were thus held to be entitled to recover overdue instalments of the contract price which had been earned prior to termination. These represented the amounts due following

---

141. See also *Hyundai Shipbuilding & Heavy Industries Co Ltd v Pournaras* [1978] 2 Lloyd's Rep 501; *Nangus Pty Ltd v Charles Donovan Pty Ltd* [1989] VR 184. Contrast *Sunbird Plaza Pty Ltd v Maloney* (1988) 166 CLR 245; 77 ALR 205.
142. Lord Russell and Lord Keith did not consider the issue in detail.
143. See [2238].
144. But see *Rover International Ltd v Cannon Film Sales Ltd* [1989] 1 WLR 912 at 931 (more appropriate analogy was with a building contract providing for progress payments).
145. See further [2238].
146. (1933) 48 CLR 457 at 477 (see [1988]).
147. [1998] 1 WLR 574 (see J Beatson and G Tolhurst, [1998] *CLJ* 253; J W Carter, (1998) 13 *JCL* 156; Gerard McMeel, [1998] *LMCLQ* 308).

completion of keel laying for two of the vessels to which the contracts related.

[2230] Recovery by party in breach. Any discussion of the recovery of liquidated sums after termination for breach or repudiation must necessarily concentrate on the position of the terminating party. However, termination does not divest the party in breach of a right to recover a liquidated sum, provided that it accrued unconditionally prior to termination.[148] For example, where a seller has delivered conforming goods under an instalment goods contract, termination by the buyer after acceptance of a delivery does not preclude recovery by the seller of the price of the goods delivered, even though termination by the buyer was based on a repudiation by the seller.[149] Similarly, an agent may be able to recover commission earned prior to termination of the agency relation for breach by the agent;[150] and an employee may recover wages which accrued due prior to lawful dismissal.[151]

Recovery of the contract price

[2231] Contract price not generally recoverable. Generally, the contract price will not be recoverable as a liquidated sum after termination for the simple reason that it is unlikely to have been earned. For example, if a builder terminates the performance of a building contract for repudiation by the other party before the completion of the work, the builder will be restricted to the recovery of damages or restitution. If progress payments have been earned these may be recovered, but the balance, or the total price if there is no provision for progress payments, will not be recoverable as a liquidated sum. And, if the contract specifies a date for payment of the price, the builder's position is not improved merely by delaying termination until the date for payment has passed.

There are three common law exceptions to the general rule stated above. First, if the contract price was earned prior to termination it will be recoverable. For example, if a seller terminates a sale of goods contract after the price was earned by delivery of conforming goods, the seller can recover the price.[152] However, generally speaking, a plaintiff who has fully performed does not terminate performance.

Second, if the contract price is payable independently of performance, termination after the day when payment was due will not affect the plaintiff's right of recovery. Such situations are, however, rare since most contracts make recovery of the price dependent on performance.[153]

---

148. *Ettridge v Vermin Board of the District of Murat Bay* [1928] SASR 124 at 128; *Elkoury v Farrow Mortgage Services Pty Ltd* (1993) 114 ALR 541.
149. *Mersey Steel and Iron Co Ltd v Naylor Benzon & Co* (1884) 9 App Cas 434.
150. *Boston Deep Sea Fishing & Ice Co v Ansell* (1888) 39 Ch D 339 at 352, 360, 366–7.
151. *Automatic Fire Sprinklers Pty Ltd v Watson* (1946) 72 CLR 435 at 461; and see [2233]. Cf *Bank of Boston Connecticut v European Grain and Shipping Ltd* [1989] AC 1056 (shipowner may recover advance freight under a voyage charterparty).
152. *Westralian Farmers Ltd v Commonwealth Agricultural Service Engineers Ltd* (1936) 54 CLR 361 at 369. For recovery of instalment payments see [2234].
153. See [1806]–[1807].

Third, the contract may contain a clause accelerating payment in the event of termination. However, when activated by breach on the defendant's part, acceleration clauses are usually subjected to the distinction between liquidated damages and penalties.[154]

Recovery of instalment payments

[2232] Hire and hire-purchase contracts, charterparties and leases. The feature common to hire and hire-purchase contracts is that the hirer agrees to make periodic payments for the use of goods. Termination for breach or repudiation on the part of the hirer does not remove any accrued liability to pay for use prior to termination, even if the goods have been repossessed by the owner. For example, in *Brooks v Beirnstein*,[155] it was held that the hirer was liable for hire due prior to repossession, pursuant to a contractual right, on breach by the hirer. Bigham J said[156] that the hirer had 'enjoyed' the use of the goods which was the 'consideration for the rent' and there was no reason 'why he should not be liable to pay the arrears claimed'.

The basis for recovery by a shipowner under a time charterparty is the enjoyment by the charterer of the services provided by the shipowner. Therefore, withdrawal of the vessel after the charterer has had the benefit of the services does not prevent recovery of the agreed hire as a liquidated sum,[157] and difficulty is only likely to arise in respect of a payment due prior to termination but covering, in whole or part, a later period.[158]

Leases frequently contain express provisions dealing with the recovery of rent after re-entry by the lessor.[159] However, even without such a provision, the lessee's liability to pay rent due prior to termination survives the lessor's termination of the lease. The lessor may, therefore, recover the rent as a liquidated sum.[160] Again, dispute is only likely to arise in respect of advance payments.

[2233] Employment and construction contracts. Whether an employee can recover wages after termination for breach or repudiation by the employer, for example, in wrongfully dismissing the employee, depends on a number of factors. At common law the time of termination is crucial. For example, if the employer agrees to pay wages monthly, and the employee terminates performance after six weeks, wages can be recovered in respect of the first month, but not the second.[161] Wages for the first month are recoverable as a liquidated sum. Under statute the time of termination may not be crucial, and it is necessary to have regard to the

---

154. See [2217].
155. [1909] 1 KB 98.
156. [1909] 1 KB 98 at 102. See also *Chatterton v Maclean* [1951] 1 All ER 761.
157. *Leslie Shipping Co v Welstead* [1921] 3 KB 420.
158. See *China National Foreign Trade Transportation Corp v Evlogia Shipping Co SA of Panama (The Mihalios Xilas)* [1979] 1 WLR 1018 at 1025, 1026. Cf *Pan Ocean Shipping Co Ltd v Creditcorp Ltd (The Trident Beauty)* [1994] 1 WLR 161.
159. *Shevill v Builders Licensing Board* (1982) 149 CLR 620.
160. See *Canas Property Co Ltd v KL Television Services Ltd* [1970] 2 QB 433.
161. See *Goodman v Pocock* (1850) 15 QB 576; 117 ER 577; *Lucy v The Commonwealth* (1923) 33 CLR 229.

possible application of the apportionment legislation and the employee's rights under any applicable industrial award.[162]

Construction contracts frequently provide for progress payments and these are recoverable, even after termination, if the builder has completed a designated portion of the work.[163] And *Hyundai Heavy Industries Co Ltd v Papadopoulos*[164] and *Stocznia Gdanska SA v Latvian Shipping Co*[165] illustrate that a shipbuilder may recover payments which were earned prior to termination of the contract even though the vessel is never completed.

[2234] **Sale of goods.** A contract for the sale of goods which requires the buyer to make instalment payments may take two forms. First, the contract may provide for the goods to be delivered by instalments and require the buyer to pay for each instalment on or after delivery. This creates few difficulties. If the seller terminates for breach or repudiation by the buyer, the seller is entitled to recover as a liquidated sum the price of all goods delivered to, and accepted by, the buyer.

Second, the contract may provide for a single delivery but entitle the buyer to pay for the goods by instalments. Here termination will lead to difficulties unless title to the goods has passed to the buyer and the buyer retains the goods. If the seller terminates the contract and retakes possession of the goods there may be a total failure of consideration, which would be a good defence to the claim.[166] And if property in the goods originally passed to the buyer, but is divested by the seller's termination of the contract, there is an element of forfeiture which may also be a good defence.[167]

[2235] **Sale of land.** Where a contract for the sale of land provides for instalment payments of the price, the transfer of title to the land will usually be postponed until the final instalment is paid by the purchaser. An action to recover an overdue instalment payment can be based on the vendor's promise to convey title.[168] However, if the vendor terminates the contract prior to payment of the final instalment, the vendor's right to recover an overdue instalment depends, in the first instance, on the terms of the contract. If it expressly provides that payment must be made, recovery is subject to the restrictions imposed by the court's jurisdiction to grant relief against forfeiture.[169]

If the contract does not expressly provide for recovery, the decision in *McDonald v Dennys Lascelles Ltd*[170] applies unless the court can imply a right of recovery. In the *Dennys Lascelles* case it was said that termination causes a total failure of consideration, on which the purchaser is entitled to

---

162. See [1827]–[1828].
163. Cf *Government of Newfoundland v Newfoundland Railway Co* (1888) 13 App Cas 199 (see [1826]).
164. [1980] 1 WLR 1129 (see [2229]).
165. [1998] 1 WLR 574 (see [2229]).
166. See [2238].
167. See [2240].
168. *Reynolds v Fury* [1921] VLR 14. For the position where termination subsequently occurs see [2324].
169. See [2240].
170. (1933) 48 CLR 457 (see [2238]).

rely as a defence to any action to recover an overdue payment. The vendor may, of course, claim damages[171] and also recover any deposit payment not paid by the purchaser.[172]

Recovery of deposit payments[173]

[2236] Basis of recovery. A 'deposit' is a payment which the contract requires the defendant ('payer') to make, usually on entry into the contract, to signify genuineness. In this respect a deposit is a payment in earnest. Deposit payments also provide security for the plaintiff ('payee') in that the payee is entitled to keep ('forfeit') the payment if the contract goes off on account of the payer's default under the contract.

Contracts for the sale of land almost invariably provide for deposit payments, and also contain express provisions for forfeiture. But they are also found in other types of contracts, such as sale of goods. However, whatever the nature of the contract, the payee's right of forfeiture in the event of default is implied unless the contract contains an express provision to the contrary.[174]

Assuming that the deposit is not paid, but the payee subsequently terminates the performance of the contract for breach or repudiation on the part of the payer, the basis on which the deposit may be recovered as a liquidated sum is the express or implied right of forfeiture. In other words, the payer cannot be in a better position, by reason of not having paid the deposit, than if the deposit had been paid. Since there is a right to forfeit payments made, logic dictates that the payee be entitled to recover an unpaid deposit.[175]

A deposit payment usually bears a third characteristic, namely, that it represents a portion of the contract price which on completion of the contract is credited towards the contract price. The proportion will, in the context of a sale of land contract, usually be 10 per cent. Although this is a fairly small proportion, as a sum of money it is, in fact, frequently quite large. For example, contracts for the sale of land at a price in excess of $400,000 are quite common. Since a 10 per cent deposit amounts to more than $40,000, the forfeiture provision subjects the purchaser to a substantial financial risk. Moreover, the vendor's right to forfeit the deposit does not depend on the purchaser's breach having caused an equivalent loss. Therefore, it can be forfeited even if the vendor subsequently sells the property to a third party for a higher price than the first purchaser agreed to pay.

---

171. If interest was payable during a period of occupation by the purchaser, this may be recovered for the period until termination: *Tropical Traders Ltd v Goonan* (1964) 111 CLR 41 at 56.
172. See [2236]–[2237].
173. See K E Lindgren and K G Nicholson, 'The Problem of Recovery of an Unpaid Deposit' (1985) 59 *ALJ* 11.
174. *Howe v Smith* (1884) 27 Ch D 89 at 101. See further [2333].
175. *Dewar v Mintoft* [1912] 2 KB 373 at 387. And where the defendant has given a cheque or some other form of bill of exchange in payment, the plaintiff may be able to sue on the bill if it has not been met. See *Pollway Ltd v Abdullah* [1974] 1 WLR 493. Cf *Hinton v Sparkes* (1868) LR 3 CP 161 (IOU).

[2237] **The authorities.** The recovery of unpaid deposits has been considered in a number of authorities. It is, however, difficult to find any authoritative statement is favour of the views expressed above. In fact, there are three quite distinct lines of authority.

One view is that the failure to pay a deposit prevents any contract coming into existence. In other words, the existence of a binding contract is contingent on the payment being made. As a general proposition this view cannot be supported.[176] There is abundant authority for the proposition that, generally, the failure to pay a deposit is simply a breach of contract,[177] and this is entirely at odds with the view that a failure to pay prevents any binding agreement being reached. On the other hand, where an option relating to land requires a deposit to be paid on the exercise of the option, a failure to pay may amount to noncompliance with the requirements of the option. No binding contract for the sale of land will result if the deposit is not paid.[178]

The second view is that recovery is precluded by the fact of termination. However, the main authority here, *Lowe v Hope*,[179] is difficult to support because it proceeds on the basis that termination requires restitutio in integrum. There is, in other words, a confusion between rescission and termination. Decisions such as *McDonald v Dennys Lascelles Ltd*[180] indicate that this line of authority cannot be supported.[181]

The third view is that explained above, namely, that the deposit is recoverable as a liquidated sum due for payment prior to termination and recoverable afterwards on the basis of an accrued right. Most of the recent decisions apply this view.[182] As against these cases it might be argued that a deposit payment is a security which comes from possession,[183] rather than a right of action, so that if the plaintiff has entered into the contract without obtaining the payment the express or implied right of forfeiture is irrelevant.[184] However, the argument based on accrued rights can withstand this line of reasoning. The right to payment is 'unconditionally acquired' by the plaintiff because termination does not cause a total failure

---

176. The main authority, *Myton Ltd v Schwab-Morris* [1974] 1 WLR 331 was overruled on this point in *Damon Compania Naviera SA v Hapag-Lloyd International SA (The Blankenstein)* [1985] 1 WLR 435. But cf *Brien v Dwyer* (1978) 141 CLR 378 at 386; 22 ALR 485.
177. See, eg *Pollway Ltd v Abdullah* [1974] 1 WLR 493 (see Note, (1975) 39 *Conv (NS)* 313 at 315); *Brien v Dwyer* (1978) 141 CLR 378.
178. See *Lewes Nominees Pty Ltd v Strang* (1983) 49 ALR 328; see also [1837]. The nature of an option may be relevant; see generally [248]. However, the particular terms of the option may indicate that punctual payment is not a condition precedent to the existence of a binding contract. See *Millichamp v Jones* [1982] 1 WLR 1422.
179. [1970] 1 Ch 94. See also *Lyon v Magnet Nominees Pty Ltd* [1978] VR 673; *Kathopoulos v Bjelica Investments Pty Ltd* (1979) 25 NTR 309.
180. (1933) 48 CLR 457. See also *Johnson v Agnew* [1980] AC 367.
181. See [1988], [1989].
182. See *Farrant v Leburn* [1970] WAR 179; *Bot v Ristevski* [1981] VR 120; *Millichamp v Jones* [1982] 1 WLR 1422 (see David Hayton, [1983] *CLJ* 197); *Damon Compania Naviera SA v Hapag-Lloyd International SA (The Blankenstein)* [1985] 1 WLR 435 (affirming and approving [1983] 2 Lloyd's Rep 522 at 531).
183. A M Shea, 'Discharge from Performance of Contracts by Failure of Condition' (1979) 42 *MLR* 623 at 643.

of consideration.[185] Therefore, although the obligation to pay is not entirely independent of the plaintiff's obligation to perform, it is sufficiently independent to say that the payment remains recoverable after termination.

Restrictions on Recovery

Common law

[2238] **Total failure of consideration.** If termination causes a total failure of consideration, a promisor who has paid money under the contract is entitled to recover it from the promisee.[186] This principle is relevant to the present context because of a defendant's ability to set up total failure of consideration as a defence to an action by the plaintiff to recover money which should have been paid prior to termination. In this way circuity of action is avoided.[187] For example, assume that V agrees to sell land to P and that P breaches an essential time stipulation. If V terminates performance of the contract V will be discharged from the obligation to convey title. Therefore, in any action to recover an overdue payment towards the price V must fail,[188] because the consideration for the payment has failed. V 'cannot have the land and its value'[189] as well. However, V is entitled to claim compensation.

The principle also applies to contracts which provide for the payment of the price by instalments. Thus, if V terminates performance of a sale of land contract because P failed to pay an instalment and breached an essential time stipulation, P may rely on total failure of consideration in an action to recover the outstanding payment,[190] because the law regards V's title to payment as conditional upon the ultimate completion of the contract.[191]

Although the principles stated above are not restricted to contracts for the sale of land, and can, for example, be applied to contracts for the sale of goods,[192] the failure of consideration must be *total*, not partial. Thus, the principles will not apply to a contract of hire where the hirer has had the use of the goods.[193] Nor will they apply to restrict a plaintiff's right to

---

184. This argument would justify a refusal to award the amount of the deposit as damages in a case where the deposit was not due at the time of termination. It is therefore difficult to support the decision of the majority of the English Court of Appeal in *Damon Compania Naviera SA v Hapag-Lloyd International SA (The Blankenstein)* [1985] 1 WLR 435, holding that the deposit can be recovered as damages because of the right of forfeiture in cases where the deposit has been paid; see J W Carter, (1988) 104 *LQR* 207.
185. See [2238].
186. See [2306].
187. See *McDonald v Dennys Lascelles Ltd* (1933) 48 CLR 457 at 481; *Rover International Ltd v Cannon Film Sales Ltd* [1989] 1 WLR 912. See also [2065].
188. Assuming that the price is not payable on a day certain irrespective of conveyance; see [1806].
189. *Laird v Pim* (1841) 7 M & W 474 at 478; 151 ER 852 at 854; *McDonald v Dennys Lascelles Ltd* (1933) 48 CLR 457 at 470, 477–8.
190. Even if P has been let into possession: see [2324].
191. *McDonald v Dennys Lascelles Ltd* (1933) 48 CLR 457; and see [2235].
192. See *McEntire v Crossley Bros Ltd* [1895] AC 457 at 464.
193. See, eg *O'Dea v Allstates Leasing System (WA) Pty Ltd* (1983) 152 CLR 359 at 392–3.

recover an unpaid deposit since the consideration for the payment (or promise of payment) is almost invariably the plaintiff's entry into the contract.[194]

A court's refusal to allow the recovery of a liquidated sum on the ground of a total failure of consideration, does not prevent the plaintiff claiming damages for the defendant's breach of contract.[195]

Equitable relief against penalties and forfeiture

[2239] **Deposits.** An agreed damages clause is not enforceable.[196] That distinction is, however, only applicable if the money is payable on breach.[197] Accordingly, a sum fixed by the contract will not fall within the distinction if it is simply the price of the plaintiff's performance. The fact that a deposit payment does not become payable by reason of a breach of contract looks, at first blush, to exclude it from the distinction. A liquidated damages clause quantifies the plaintiff's damages even if the defendant has committed a serious breach or repudiation and the plaintiff has terminated performance of the contract.[198] On the other hand, a plaintiff can claim damages *and* forfeit a deposit in the event of default by the defendant. Even if the plaintiff has suffered no loss, a nominal sum is recoverable as damages in addition to the deposit. However, a deposit is liable to forfeiture on breach and the plaintiff's right to retain the deposit, in cases where the performance of the contract has been terminated, has been held to be sufficient to make the distinction between liquidated damages and penalties relevant to the sum to be forfeited on breach,[199] but not determinative.

In *NLS Pty Ltd v Hughes*[200] Barwick CJ explained the relationship between the plaintiff's rights of forfeiture and damages, and the distinction drawn between liquidated damages and penalties. He said[201] that the 'question whether there is an implied limitation upon the amount of the damages recoverable does not arise for discussion' where the plaintiff is 'content to forfeit the amount of the money'. Although in such a case it can be assumed that the loss is less than the amount of the payment, treatment of the 'money [as] a genuine pre-estimate of the damages does involve an implied limitation upon the liability to pay damages'. Nevertheless, in his view[202] it is not correct to say that if the amount agreed is not a penalty 'it must be a pre-estimate of damages'. The reason for this conclusion was that a deposit may be 'neither a penalty nor a pre-estimate of damages but an earnest of performance which, on default, may be retained and credited against the damage suffered'.

The fact that a deposit which is not a penalty is not necessarily a pre-estimate of damages implies that the distinction between liquidated

---

194. *Farrant v Leburn* [1970] WAR 179 at 184; *Bot v Ristevski* [1981] VR 120 at 123.
195. *McDonald v Dennys Lascelles Ltd* (1933) 48 CLR 457 at 479.
196. See [2207]–[2217].
197. See [2216].
198. *Suisse Atlantique Société d'Armement Maritime SA v NV Rotterdamsche Kolen Centrale* [1967] 1 AC 361.
199. *Boucaut Bay Co Ltd v The Commonwealth* (1927) 40 CLR 98. See further [2333].
200. (1966) 120 CLR 583.
201. (1966) 120 CLR 583 at 589.
202. (1966) 120 CLR 583 at 589.

damages and penalties is applied to deposit payments in a way which differs from its application to agreed damages clauses. In fact, it may be better to treat the jurisdiction of the court as based on an ability to relieve against the unconscionable forfeiture of payments made by a defendant, with the result that the factors referred to earlier[203] are not determinative.[204] There is, however, authority for the proposition that where a deposit is so extravagant as to be in the nature of a penalty the court may permit the defaulting party to recover part of the deposit if forfeiture would be unconscionable.[205]

If the court should decide to grant relief against the forfeiture of the deposit the plaintiff can claim damages in respect of the defendant's breach.[206]

[2240] **Part payments.** The law with respect to part payments is complicated. If the contract expressly provides for forfeiture this provision will prevent the defendant relying on total failure of consideration as a defence to an action to recover an overdue payment. The defendant must defend the action by seeking relief against forfeiture.

Consider, for example, a contract for the sale of land which provides for the payment of the price by instalments and contains a clause which, in the event of default in punctual payment by the defendant-purchaser (P), confers on the plaintiff-vendor (V) the right to terminate the performance of the contract, and to forfeit payments made under the contract. Assume that V exercises the right to terminate on default by P. Relief against forfeiture may be relevant in any of three ways.

First, as has already been explained,[207] P may apply for relief against the forfeiture of the interest in the land obtained on entry into the contract and (at least in extreme cases) obtain specific performance of the contract.

Second, the decision in *Kilmer v British Columbia Orchard Lands Ltd*[208] supports the view that specific performance may also be obtained so as to provide relief against the forfeiture of the *payments* actually made under the contract. Therefore, if V seeks to recover an overdue instalment, and P establishes that the forfeiture clause is in the nature of a penalty designed to secure payment, the readiness and willingness of P to pay may provide P with a case for specific performance of the contract.

A third approach is for P to invoke relief against forfeiture as a ground for restitution of the money which has been paid, on the basis that the forfeiture provision is in the nature of a penalty.[209] This might, for example, assist a defendant who is not ready and willing to perform. However, there

---

203. See [2212]–[2215].
204. See *Yardley v Saunders* [1982] WAR 231 at 237.
205. See [2332]. It may be that in cases where the deposit has not been paid the defendant can defend the action on the basis that the sum in question is a penalty.
206. See *Smyth v Jessep* [1956] VLR 230.
207. See [1979].
208. [1913] AC 319. See also *Re Dagenham (Thames) Dock Co* (1873) LR 8 Ch App 1022; *McDonald v Dennys Lascelles Ltd* (1933) 48 CLR 457 at 470; *Legione v Hateley* (1983) 152 CLR 406 at 426–8; 46 ALR 1; *Stern v McArthur* (1988) 165 CLR 489; 81 ALR 463.
209. Cf *Steedman v Drinkle* [1916] 1 AC 275.

is no case in which this line of defence has been used in an action for a liquidated sum and it is more appropriately discussed in the context of restitution.[210]

An acceleration clause in a contract, which is not construed as a penalty under the rules discussed earlier,[211] might possibly provide a case for relief against forfeiture. In *O'Dea v Allstates Leasing System (WA) Pty Ltd*,[212] in the context of a lease of goods, Brennan J said:[213]

> By conferring on the lessor the right in the event of the lessees' default to recover both possession of the vehicle hired and the entire price of the hiring before the hiring period expires, cl 12 provides an incentive for the due and punctual performance of the lessee's obligations — pecuniary and other — by imposing a liability to forfeiture. The lessees may lose both possession and use of the vehicle for the remaining period of 36 months and that proportion of the entire rental which is attributable to the hiring period remaining after repossession. Although a stipulation as to the price payable for the sale or hiring of goods is not itself in the nature of a penalty, a stipulation which provides for the forfeiture on breach by the buyer or hirer of both the price and the consideration for which it is payable is in the nature of a penalty and equity will relieve against it. The foundation of the jurisdiction to relieve against forfeiture is that the stipulation for the forfeiture is really in the nature of a penalty ...

As he went on to point out, the principle could only apply in respect of the money payable for the period after repossession of the vehicle.

Assuming that the defendant makes out a defence to the plaintiff's action to recover a part payment, the plaintiff is entitled to recover damages for breach notwithstanding the relief granted to the defendant.[214]

Statute

[2241] Examples of statutory restrictions. A defendant may be granted relief in respect of the recovery of a liquidated sum if the provision, or the conduct of the plaintiff, falls within a statutory provision relating to unjust or unconscionable contracts and provisions.[215] Other examples of statutory restrictions are more specific.

In New South Wales and Victoria there is power to order the return of a deposit paid under a contract for the sale of land.[216] There is no reason, in principle, why a purchaser of land should not be permitted to defend an action for payment by proving that, if payment were ordered, he or she would be entitled to the return of the money. That is not to say, however, that the defendant is likely to succeed; the jurisdiction is a fairly narrow one.

---

210. See [2332].
211. See [2217].
212. (1983) 152 CLR 359 (see [2217]).
213. (1983) 152 CLR 359 at 391. Cf *IAC (Leasing) Ltd v Humphrey* (1972) 126 CLR 131 at 145; *Forestry Commission of New South Wales v Stefanetto* (1976) 133 CLR 507 at 524; 8 ALR 297; *Jobson v Johnson* [1989] 1 WLR 1026; *On Demand Information Plc v Michael Gerson Finance Plc* [2001] 1 WLR 144.
214. *Real Estate Securities Ltd v Kew Golf Links Estate Pty Ltd* [1935] VLR 114.
215. See generally Chapter 15.
216. See [2334].

Under the *Consumer Credit Code* ('the Code'), a credit contract must not impose a monetary liability on a debtor in respect of a fee or charge which is prohibited by the Code or in respect of a fee, charge or interest charge which exceeds that which may be charged under the Code;[217] and where a court re-opens a credit transaction, it may relieve a debtor from the payment of any amount in excess of what the court considers to be reasonably payable.[218] These provisions may also apply in favour of a defendant who is defending a plaintiff's claim to recover a liquidated sum.

---

217. See *Consumer Credit Code*, s 21.
218. See *Consumer Credit Code*, s 71(b).

Chapter 23

Restitution

Claims for Restitution 2301
  General *2301*
  Quasi-contract *2305*
  Unjust Enrichment *2308*
Benefit 2310
  Types of Benefits *2310*
  Inherently Ineffective Contracts *2316*
  Contracts Discharged after Partial Performance *2320*
At the Expense of the Plaintiff 2326
Injustice 2330
Adjustment and Valuation Issues 2335
  General *2335*
  Relevance of Contract Price *2337*

Claims for Restitution

General

[2301] Introduction. The law of restitution is concerned with the situations in which a plaintiff may recover a money sum equal in value to a benefit obtained by the defendant at the expense of the plaintiff. Although having a long history,[1] restitution 'has recently awakened from [a] long slumber'.[2] In Australia today the whole subject is still in the process of development. The structure of this chapter relies heavily on the principle of unjust enrichment, yet that principle has only recently achieved respectability in the common law.[3]

Most of the instances of restitution discussed below have traditionally been described as *quasi-contractual*, and based on an implied contract between the parties to the action.[4] Thus, where it is held that a defendant is

---

1. See [2305].
2. Sir Anthony Mason, 'Book Review' (1989) 1 *JCL* 265.
3. See [2308].
4. See, eg *Sinclair v Brougham* [1914] AC 398.

liable to make restitution to the plaintiff, the old approach was to treat the liability as based on a notional or *fictional* promise analogous to a contractual promise.[5] The promise is fictional where — as in all cases of genuine restitutionary liability — there is no contractual promise. The courts recognised this, but continued, for historical reasons, to treat the promise as an essential element of recovery.[6] In truth, the concept is a legacy of the time when the plaintiff had to plead one of the forms of action, such as indebitatus assumpsit or debt.[7] Or, to put the same point in a less technical way, the assumption that all liability is either contractual or tortious requires the basis for recovery to be in the nature of contract.

Nevertheless, as Lord Atkin explained in *United Australia Ltd v Barclays Bank Ltd*,[8] these 'fantastic resemblances of contracts invented in order to meet requirements of the law as to forms of action which have now disappeared should not in these days be allowed to affect actual rights'. Accordingly, in the context of an action to recover money after a total failure of consideration, Lord Wright said in *Fibrosa Spolka Akcyjna v Fairbairn Lawson Combe Barbour Ltd*,[9] that the 'gist of the action is a debt or obligation implied, or, more accurately, imposed, by law in much the same way as the law enforces as a debt the obligation to pay a statutory or customary impost'. Griffith CJ had expressed the same idea in *R v Brown*,[10] when he said that an action lies 'whenever the defendant had received money which in justice and equity belonged to the plaintiff'. This invokes the famous statement of Lord Mansfield in *Moses v Macferlan*[11] that liability in restitution is ultimately based on 'the ties of natural justice and equity'. Although Lord Mansfield's statement sounds vague and imprecise, it is the origin of the modern law.

It is neither necessary nor appropriate to give an exhaustive account of the principles of restitution in this chapter. It is unnecessary because many examples of situations in which restitution may be sought have already been referred to.[12] It is inappropriate because restitutionary claims often have no connection with contract. For example, the claim may be based simply on the receipt of money paid under a mistake,[13] where there is no suggestion that the money was paid pursuant to a contract or in the belief that a contract existed.[14]

The objects of this chapter are threefold:

5. See, eg *Fibrosa Spolka Akcyjna v Fairbairn Lawson Combe Barbour Ltd* [1943] AC 32 at 47.
6. See further [2308].
7. See [105].
8. [1941] AC 1 at 29.
9. [1943] AC 32 at 63.
10. (1912) 14 CLR 17 at 25.
11. (1760) 2 Burr 1005 at 1012; 97 ER 676 at 681.
12. See, eg [520], [816] (claims where contract unenforceable for want of writing or capacity); [1707], [1717], [1720], [1727]–[1728], cf [1721]–[1724] (claims enforceable notwithstanding that contract void tainted with illegality); [2057]–[2098] (restitution following frustration); [2229], [2232], [2234], [2235], [2237], [2238], [2240] (claim in restitution as defence to recovery of liquidated sum following termination for breach or repudiation).
13. See Mason and Carter, *Restitution Law in Australia*, 1995, Chapter 4.
14. Cf [1209].

- to provide a statement of the theory which underlies restitution, including those claims already discussed;
- since that theory is of general application, to provide an introduction to restitutionary claims in general; and
- to investigate controversial aspects of the application of the law of restitution in the contract context.

[2302] Nature of the remedy. A defendant is subject to a liability in restitution whenever the circumstances indicate that the receipt or retention of a benefit obtained by the defendant from the plaintiff is unjust. There are therefore three elements of unjust enrichment:[15]

- 'benefit';
- 'at the plaintiff's expense'; and
- 'injustice'.

Satisfaction of all these elements is essential for a 'prima facie claim' in restitution. Assuming that they are satisfied, attention may turn to a fourth element, namely, no 'defence' is applicable or available. However, for the purposes of this work[16] restitutionary defences can be largely ignored.[17]

Our concern is with *pecuniary* restitution. Unlike the obligation to pay damages, which assumes the breach of a primary obligation, and provides an additional or substitutionary form of relief in the form of enforcement of a secondary obligation,[18] the obligation to make restitution is a species of primary obligation. The award is not given in substitution for an obligation assumed by the defendant, for example, under a contract. Nor is the award given in substitution for an obligation imposed by law, for example, under tort law. This means that, generally,[19] a claim for restitution is independent of wrongdoing, and does not assume that the defendant breached a contract or committed a tort. Instead, it assumes that the defendant has been unjustly enriched at the expense of the plaintiff.

Claims for pecuniary restitution are 'personal claims', that is, they are available against a particular person, and do not attach to a person's property. Accordingly, although we often refer, for example, to a claim to recover money which was paid to the defendant, the claim is really for a sum of money equal to that received. The principal significance of this is that the plaintiff is entitled to restitution even though the defendant has disposed of the benefit received. Equally, however, since the plaintiff cannot claim an interest in property, usually the claim will rank with those of other unsecured creditors in bankruptcy proceedings.[20]

---

15. See further [2309].
16. For analysis see Mason and Carter, *Restitution Law in Australia*, 1995, Part VII.
17. See further [2336] (restitutio in integrum). Reference may also be made to [520] (statutory policy); [1727]–[1728] (illegality); [1042]–[1062] (restrictions on rescission); [1967]–[1978], [1981]–[1984] (restrictions on termination).
18. See [1989], [2101].
19. But see [2326].
20. See *Re Goldcorp Exchange Ltd* [1995] 1 AC 74. But sometimes the claim is proprietary in character. See generally Mason and Carter, *Restitution Law in Australia*, 1995, paras 325–8, 1727–33.

[2303] **Relevance of contract and contract law.**[21] An action for restitution is not contractual. It differs from an action for damages because it is not based on a wrong. Moreover, whereas claims for contract damages rely on the fact that the plaintiff has suffered loss or damage, those for restitution rely on the fact that the defendant has been unjustly benefited. A claim in restitution differs from an action for a contract debt because the sum is fixed by reference to a benefit received, not the prior agreement of the parties to the claim. It follows that contract rules, such as privity of contract, do not govern claims for restitution. Nevertheless, the fact that a third party is benefited by performance under a contract does not in itself imply that the third party must make restitution for the benefit.[22]

That is not to say that contract law, or the contract itself, is irrelevant to restitution. There are six points to be made. First, since a loss to the plaintiff is sometimes a benefit to the defendant, some claims may be based in either contract or restitution.[23]

Second, although it is perfectly acceptable to have alternative bases for a defendant's liability, it would be intolerable to countenance two conflicting regimes of liability. Most of the relevant claims in restitution arise because a contract is ineffective: where it never became a source of enforceable obligations or has ceased to bind the parties. Indeed, while an enforceable contract exists between the parties no action can be brought for restitution for a benefit conferred in discharge of an obligation to confer it.[24]

Third, although most claims in restitution which arise in the contract context do so because the contract is ineffective, the mere fact that a contract is ineffective is not sufficient to give rise to a claim for restitution: there must also be an unjust enrichment.

Fourth, restitution is not the only source of relief outside contract law. Thus, as we have already seen,[25] principles of estoppel may operate. The danger, or at least difficulty, here is that estoppel or restitution may be used to cure perceived defects in contract law, and so detract attention from the fundamental issue, namely, the need to develop contract law to meet new problems and changed economic and social conditions.[26]

Fifth, just as it is open to parties to exclude claims in contract, so also is it open to them to exclude restitutionary relief. The most common example of this is a forfeiture clause.[27]

---

21. Cf Andrew Kull, 'Restitution and the Noncontractual Transfer' (1997) 11 *JCL* 93 (and see Keith Mason, 'Commentary on "Restitution and the Noncontractual Transfer"' (1997) 11 *JCL* 111).
22. See, eg *J Gadsden Pty Ltd v Strider 1 Ltd (The AES Express)* (1990) 20 NSWLR 57 (see David Fung, (1991) 4 *JCL* 273).
23. Cf [2112].
24. See, eg *Pavey & Matthews Pty Ltd v Paul* (1987) 162 CLR 221 at 256; 69 ALR 577; *Foran v Wight* (1989) 168 CLR 385 at 413, 432; 88 ALR 413; *Baltic Shipping Co v Dillon (The Mikhail Lermontov)* (1993) 176 CLR 344 at 356, 385; 111 ALR 289.
25. See [374]–[377].
26. See J M Perillo, 'Restitution in a Contractual Context' (1973) 73 *Col L Rev* 1208.
27. However, such a clause is not conclusive. See [2332], [2333].

Sixth, where it is necessary to *value* a restitutionary claim, the terms of the contract are relevant, because ignoring the contract might result in an allocation of risk different from that agreed by the parties.[28]

[2304] Recovery based on statute. In considering restitution under statute it is important to distinguish cases in which a statutory right to restitution is recognised or conferred from cases in which a court is given a discretion in relation to a contract or claim in terms which include a *power* to award restitution. For example, we saw earlier[29] that the frustrated contracts legislation operates to confer rights of restitution where a contract is discharged by frustration. One significant feature of legislative intervention is that it may, as in that legislation, go further than merely recognising common law rights. Another feature is that the statutory claim may go beyond what can be justified under the broadest concept of unjust enrichment. For example, the *Frustrated Contracts Act* 1978 (NSW)[30] goes beyond the reversal of unjust enrichment by apportioning losses and gains following frustration.

A discretionary power to award restitution need not rely on unjust enrichment. Thus, where a contract is reopened by the court in reliance on a statutory power to review a harsh or unconscionable contract or provision,[31] although it may be necessary for the court to address restitutionary issues,[32] the statute may do no more than confer a discretion. This is the case, for example, under certain provisions of the trade practices and fair trading legislation.[33]

Quasi-contract[34]

[2305] Common counts. The 'common counts' were pleading devices employed to assist in the recovery of debts.[35] For example, a debt might arise from the defendant's receipt of money paid by a plaintiff as a result of a mistake, or from a sale of goods or the execution of work at the defendant's request. In the third edition of *Bullen and Leake*[36] it was emphasised that the pleading was in general terms, specific details of the debt being left to the evidence. An action in assumpsit would lie, quasi ex contractu, on an implied obligation or debt without there being any genuine agreement to pay the debt.

Although the common counts are the historical antecedents of many modern restitutionary claims, because they were used to recover debts they were not restricted to restitutionary claims. For example, the count for work done applied equally to a restitutionary claim — where there was an

---

28. See further [2337]–[2339].
29. See generally [2057]–[2098].
30. See generally [2069]–[2078].
31. See generally [1515]–[1528].
32. See, eg *Contracts Review Act* 1980 (NSW), s 8 and Sch 1.
33. See [1526]. See also [2334] (statutory power operates to order the return of a deposit).
34. See Mason and Carter, *Restitution Law in Australia*, 1995, Chapter 1.
35. See Fifoot, *History and Sources of the Common Law*, 1949, pp 368ff.
36. Bullen and Leake, *Precedents of Pleadings*, 3rd ed, 1868, p 35.

ineffective contract — and to a claim in contract for a reasonable sum due under an express contract to pay a reasonable sum.[37]

It is sufficient for our purposes to deal with two areas: claims for the recovery of money on the basis of a total failure of consideration and claims for the reasonable value of work done, as on a quantum meruit.

[2306] Total failure of consideration. One group of common counts applied to money had and received by the defendant to the use of the plaintiff. Most important was the count to recover money on a total failure of consideration. Where money is paid pursuant to an obligation created by a contract, in the expectation of receiving contractual performance from the defendant, the failure of the defendant to perform the contract is a failure of consideration since it deprives the plaintiff of the performance for which he or she bargained. The terminology is a little confusing. The word 'consideration' here refers to performance of the contract rather than the criterion for enforceability of promises which was discussed earlier.[38] The fact that the consideration has 'failed' does not mean that the contract becomes void. Rather, it refers to a total failure by the defendant to render the agreed return for the plaintiff's payment.

The common law applied if two requirements were met. These continue to govern modern restitutionary claims, in which the failure of consideration signifies an unjust enrichment of the defendant. First, the failure must be *total*. The issue is whether the plaintiff received any of the performance which was stipulated by the contract as the agreed return for the payment which the plaintiff seeks to recover.[39] For example, in *Rowland v Divall*[40] the plaintiff recovered the price of a motor car, which had been paid to the defendant, when the defendant was found to have no title to the vehicle. Since he had not bargained for the use of the vehicle, it was immaterial that the plaintiff had the use of the car for a time. The consideration for the payment was the transfer of ownership in the vehicle and the right to possession, but the plaintiff received neither. Since the consideration for the payment therefore failed the plaintiff was entitled to restitution.

At one time the view was taken that a transfer of title by a seller of goods prevented the recovery of money paid by the buyer on the basis of a total failure of consideration.[41] However, the rationale was that for a total failure of consideration to occur the contract had to be rescinded ab initio, and restitutio in integrum achieved by the buyer's termination. Now that it is established that termination for breach is a sufficient basis for restitution,[42] the buyer's election revests title in the seller.[43]

---

37. See further [2307].
38. See Chapter 3.
39. See [2229]. See also [1215].
40. [1923] 2 KB 500.
41. See, eg *Hunt v Silk* (1804) 5 East 449; 102 ER 114; *Street v Blay* (1831) 2 B & Ad 456; 109 ER 1212.
42. The sale of goods legislation preserves this right of recovery. See *Sale of Goods Act* 1923 (NSW), s 55 (for corresponding provisions see [2144]). Cf *Goods Act* 1958 (Vic), s 101(1)(f). See also [1991], [2067].

When applied to a severable contract, under which payments are made for distinct portions of contract performance,[44] the requirement of a total failure of consideration applies to each severable part. Under the law of quasi-contract, a court cannot apportion a payment if the parties have not done so. Thus, in *Whincup v Hughes*[45] the plaintiff apprenticed his son to Hughes and paid a premium of £25. Hughes agreed to instruct the apprentice and to pay him wages. After giving one year's instruction Hughes died and the plaintiff sued to recover the money paid. The court held that as the contract had been partly performed the plaintiff could not recover. At best there had been a partial failure and this did not justify the recovery of the whole sum. Moreover, because there had been no apportionment of the money paid to the years of instruction contemplated, the plaintiff was unable to recover part of the money paid. However, the approach has been questioned in recent cases applying unjust enrichment. Thus, in *David Securities Pty Ltd v Commonwealth Bank of Australia*[46] Mason CJ, Deane, Toohey, Gaudron and McHugh JJ said that in 'cases where consideration can be apportioned or where counter-restitution is relatively simple, insistence on total failure of consideration can be misleading or confusing'.

The second requirement is the absence of a provision (express or implied) in the contract stating that the money in question is to be retained by the defendant. For example, the contract may contain a provision for the forfeiture of money paid to the defendant in the event of breach on the plaintiff's part.[47]

It is not a requirement of the claim that the defendant breached the contract. Thus, the claim is available where the contract is ineffective for reasons other than breach, such as frustration. It therefore also follows that, so long as the two requirements are met, a party who breached the contract is entitled to recover money paid under the contract if it is subsequently terminated.[48]

[2307] Quantum meruit. Another common count was to recover a reasonable sum (quantum meruit) for work done and materials supplied to the defendant by the plaintiff at the defendant's request.[49] This form of claim arose in response to the shortcomings of the action in debt, namely, the necessity of a liquidated sum,[50] and the inability to maintain assumpsit where there was no express promise to pay. By the middle of the 17th

---

43. See *McDougall v Aeromarine of Emsworth Ltd* [1958] 1 WLR 1126; *Berger & Co Inc v Gill & Duffus SA* [1984] 1 AC 382 at 395. For express provisions to this effect in the consumer context see **Cth:** *Trade Practices Act* 1974, s 75A(3)(a); **NT:** *Consumer Affairs and Fair Trading Act* 1990, s 67(3)(a); **SA:** *Consumer Transactions Act* 1972, s 12(3); **Vic:** *Goods Act* 1958, s 101(1)(e); **WA:** *Fair Trading Act* 1987, s 41(3)(a).
44. See [1825].
45. (1871) LR 6 CP 78.
46. (1992) 175 CLR 353 at 383; 109 ALR 57. See also *Goss v Chilcott* [1996] AC 788 where this dictum was applied (see J W Carter and Gregory Tolhurst, (1997) 11 JCL 162).
47. See [2332].
48. See further [2324].
49. See Bullen and Leake, *Precedents of Pleadings*, 3rd ed, 1868, p 40.
50. Simpson, *A History of the Common Law of Contract*, 1975, p 65.

century quantum meruit was established as a means of recovering the reasonable value of services rendered under an ineffective contract, or a valid contract which failed to state a price for work or services.

The modern perspective was stated in *Pavey & Matthews Pty Ltd v Paul*.[51] It will be recalled[52] that a builder sued to recover the value of the work done under an oral building contract where the customer agreed to pay a reasonable sum. The claim could not be framed in contract due to non-compliance with s 45 of the *Builders Licensing Act* 1971 (NSW), which required the contract to be in writing. Deane J said[53] that quantum meruit had been developed in the law of quasi-contract to accommodate two distinct categories of claim. First, to recover a debt arising under a genuine contract, whether express or implied. The action was on the contract, and this was so whether it took the form of a 'special' or a 'common' count. The claim was not for restitution. Today we would see it as a claim for a contract debt based on an implied term of the contract.

Second, Deane J referred to a claim to recover a debt owing in circumstances where *the law* imposed (or imputed) an obligation or promise to make payment for a benefit accepted. This action was not based on a genuine agreement at all. Although lawyers continued to speak in terms of an implied contract, a valid and enforceable agreement would in fact preclude such a claim. So, the claim is today available only where there is no genuine agreement, or where the agreement is frustrated, avoided or unenforceable. Indeed, as Deane J pointed out,[54] it is the absence of a genuine agreement, or the fact that it is not applicable, frustrated, avoided or unenforceable 'that provides the occasion for (and part of the circumstances giving rise to) the imposition by law of the obligation to make restitution'.

Treating the claim in *Pavey* as analogous to one made in the context of the *Statute of Frauds* 1677 (Imp),[55] it belonged in the second category, and was maintainable as a claim in restitution not contract. A majority of the High Court held that the builder could succeed despite the inability to sue on the contract. For Deane J there was no need to resort to a fictional promise to explain why the statute did not preclude the action to recover a quantum meruit. The obligation to pay, as Jordan CJ had explained in *Horton v Jones (No 2)*,[56] is 'imposed by law, and does not depend on an inference of an implied promise'.

Since the indebitatus form of action is no longer pleaded, and notwithstanding the continued use of the expression 'quantum meruit',[57] it is better to see the restitutionary claim as one for 'reasonable remuneration'. It applies in a variety of situations, analysed below from the perspective of unjust enrichment.[58]

---

51. (1987) 162 CLR 221.
52. See [520].
53. Mason CJ and Wilson J substantially agreed.
54. (1987) 162 CLR 221 at 256.
55. See generally [519]–[520].
56. (1939) 39 SR (NSW) 305 at 320.
57. Where a plaintiff sought to recover a reasonable price for goods sold the claim was formerly referred to as a quantum valebat. However, as a consequence of the sale of goods legislation (see [2318]), very little is heard of this terminology today.

Unjust Enrichment[59]

[2308] Recognition. In *Pavey & Matthews Pty Ltd v Paul*[60] the rationale for the *imposition* of a liability was expressed in terms of unjust enrichment, rather than the consensual assumption of responsibility which typifies contract.[61] Deane J described[62] unjust enrichment as a 'unifying legal concept' which

> explains why the law recognises, in a variety of distinct categories of case, an obligation on the part of the defendant to make fair and just restitution for a benefit derived at the expense of a plaintiff and which assists in the determination, by the ordinary processes of legal reasoning, of the question whether the law should, in justice, recognise such an obligation in a new or developing category of case.

It was a bold step for the High Court to adopt unjust enrichment as the basis for restitution, and a very strong indication that the High Court is prepared to take seriously arguments that the diverse situations in which restitution is ordered have the same underlying elements.[63] At the practical level, there is no need for a plaintiff to recite the terminology of the forms of action.[64] Two things must, however, be appreciated. First, the fact that unjust enrichment is the proper basis does not imply that the court can order restitution simply because that appears to be a 'fair' result: there must be a recognised basis for the claim.

Second, the displacement of implied contract by unjust enrichment does not mean that all the old cases were wrongly decided. The impact is that we now have a different explanation, with the potential for reconsideration of established principles and application of the law to new areas.

[2309] Elements. It is worth restating[65] (in more detail) the elements which make up the concept of unjust enrichment:

(1) an element of benefit received, retained, realised or realisable by the defendant;

---

58. See further [2320]–[2325].
59. See Mason and Carter, *Restitution Law in Australia*, 1995, Chapter 2.
60. (1987) 162 CLR 221.
61. In England, see *Lipkin Gorman v Karpnale Ltd* [1991] 2 AC 548 (see Peter Birks, 'The English Recognition of Unjust Enrichment' [1991] *LMCLQ* 473); *Woolwich Equitable Building Society v IRC* [1993] AC 70.
62. (1987) 162 CLR 221 at 256–7. See also at 227; *Australia and New Zealand Banking Group Ltd v Westpac Banking Corp* (1988) 164 CLR 662 at 673; 78 ALR 157.
63. A coherent theory is presented by Birks, *An Introduction to the Law of Restitution*, 1985, but not everyone has welcomed the concept. See, eg Steve Hedley, 'Unjust Enrichment as the Basis of Restitution — An Overworked Concept' (1985) 5 *Legal Studies* 56; S J Stoljar, 'Unjust Enrichment and Unjust Sacrifice' (1987) 50 *MLR* 603. And restitution is still seen by some as purely 'improvisational' (T J Sullivan, 'The Concept of Benefit in the Law of Quasi-Contract' (1975) 64 *Geo LJ* 1).
64. It ought also to follow that a plaintiff is able to plead the concept and particularise its elements in order to lay the foundation for proof of the claim in court. But the cases deny that this is the effect of *Pavey*. See, eg *Winterton Constructions Pty Ltd v Hambros Australia Ltd* (1992) 111 ALR 649; *Christiani & Nielsen Pty Ltd v Goliath Portland Cement Co Ltd* (1993) 2 Tas R 122 at 131, 169; but cf *Baltic Shipping Co v Dillon (The Mikhail Lermontov)* (1993) 176 CLR 344 at 375, 379 and see generally Mason and Carter, *Restitution Law in Australia*, 1995, paras 305–9.
65. See [2302].

(2) an element which provides the plaintiff with 'title' to make the claim, namely, that the benefit was at the plaintiff's expense and not at the expense of some other person; and

(3) an element of injustice, that is, some *recognised* circumstance showing that it was unjust, unfair, unconscionable or inequitable for the defendant to obtain (or retain) the benefit.

Because there are few cases which contain analysis from the perspective of unjust enrichment, the analysis below is to some extent an *evaluation* of old cases from a new perspective.

Benefit

Types of Benefits

[2310] Money and other benefits. It might be thought that the concept of benefit is a simple one. In fact, it attracts complex ideas, and virtually the only straightforward proposition is that money is always a benefit for the purpose of unjust enrichment. Where a defendant receives a benefit in the form of money, the benefit to the defendant is obvious or 'incontrovertible'. Restitution in the repayment of the money does not involve the return of the benefit *in specie*, but the plaintiff receives an equivalent sum.

Similarly, where restitution is sought in respect of other forms of benefit, such as services, the order will be for a money sum.[66] Unlike the receipt of money, the receipt of services is not necessarily a benefit: services are not necessarily realisable, even where there is, in an objective sense, an increase in the defendant's wealth. One reason the law is complex is that the layperson's idea that any contractual performance, or increase in the assets of the defendant, is a benefit does not correspond to the restitutionary concept of enrichment. In other words, a simple *objective* concept does not match the restitutionary concept which incorporates an important subjective element in most cases.

[2311] Services. A distinctive feature of many categories of services is that they are either consumed by the defendant or form an unrealisable part of the defendant's wealth. Frequently, a person who receives such services is entitled to say that there is no benefit.[67] There are two perspectives. First, to what extent must the benefit alleged to be received match a benefit requested? The inquiry here is whether request is essential, and whether the plaintiff has fully or partially performed the task requested. The focus of discussion of the cases has, principally, been directed to the extent to which the benefit alleged to be received matches the benefit requested. *Pavey & Matthews Pty Ltd v Paul*[68] illustrates the strength of a claim of a plaintiff who has fully performed the task requested in a way which corresponds to the performance requested. But once the alleged

---

66. Specific restitution may be ignored for our purposes.
67. 'Subjective devaluation' is a description of the right of a person who receives such services to say that there was no enrichment. See Birks, *An Introduction to the Law of Restitution*, 1985, pp 109ff.
68. (1987) 162 CLR 221 (see [2308]).

benefit is not that which the defendant requested the stocks of the plaintiff drop dramatically. In order to explain the authorities which illustrate successful claims in respect of partial satisfaction of a request the concept of benefit must be refined. This helps to provide a theoretical framework for unjust enrichment.

Second, do all services count as benefits under the unjust enrichment concept? The plaintiff may have performed services which involved the combination of labour and materials. If so there will usually be an end product. Alternatively, the plaintiff may have performed services which involved no more than the supply of information or the application of skill, learning, expertise or talent, a typical example being the work of a professional person such as a solicitor.

We address these issues below.[69]

[2312] Unrequested benefits. Assume that A builds a house on B's land. Is B obliged to pay for the house even though B did not request it? The answer is no, and the simplest explanation is that for the purposes of restitution there is no enrichment. Even if we also assume that B's land has increased in value there is still no benefit for which B can be required to make restitution.

More elaborate explanations could be given to explain why, because B is not benefited, that is, to explain why B may keep what is, objectively, a benefit without paying for it. Thus, it could be pointed out that most restitutionary claims in respect of non-monetary benefits rely on the existence of a request that the benefit be conferred, or we could analyse the concept of risk in relation to benefits and say that in doing the work A took the risk that B would refuse to pay for it. Again, it could be pointed out that there is no benefit because B did not have the opportunity to say 'I do not want a house on my land'. It makes no difference to say that B now owns, and perhaps lives in, a valuable house, that is merely the consequence of B being the owner of the land.

In the final analysis the approach of the unjust enrichment concept, in denying benefit, is simply a reflection of the policy of the law against rewarding unrequested benefits. The policy is strongest where the benefit was conferred officiously,[70] but it also applies, generally, to unrequested benefits. This helps to explain aspects of the law which, at first sight, seem to be inexplicable. Thus, even where a request is made, but the work does not correspond to the request, it may be appropriate to say that the person who did the work is in the same position as if no request was made.[71]

[2313] Incontrovertible benefit. Where a court orders restitution in respect of a non-monetary benefit, the award is for a sum of money.[72] Another explanation of why B, in the example above,[73] need not pay for the house is that B should not be compelled to pay a substantial sum of money, and be treated as if the benefit which A conferred has been realised, when

---

69. See [2312]–[2315].
70. Cf [229].
71. Certainly many of the old cases can be explained on this basis. See, eg [2325].
72. See [2310].
73. See [2312].

the benefit has not been converted into cash. Indeed, an order in A's favour might force B to sell the land in order to meet the judgment.

Nevertheless, a concept of incontrovertible benefit has been suggested as a way around the narrow — subjective — concept found in the cases. The anticipation of a necessary expenditure, or a benefit realised in money will constitute an 'incontrovertible benefit' which must be paid for. The test to be satisfied is that no reasonable person would deny that a benefit was received,[74] whether or not it was requested. However, except where the principle of restitutio in integrum operates,[75] there are relatively few illustrations in the cases.[76] *Craven-Ellis v Canons Ltd*[77] may be an example. The articles of association of the defendants required their directors to acquire qualification shares in the company within two months of their appointment. The plaintiff was appointed managing director, but the directors who made the appointment had not obtained their qualification shares in accordance with the articles with the result that the agreement was void. Greer LJ said[78] that the defendants had been saved a necessary expenditure: if the plaintiff had not performed the services, the defendants 'would have had to get some other agent' to carry them out.

[2314] Acceptance of benefit. A feature which distinguishes services from money is the absence, in many cases, of a free choice to keep or reject the benefit conferred. The inability to restore the benefit in cases where services are rendered arises from the fact that there is no question of supply of equivalent services by the defendant. If we add to this the plain fact that in many cases services are consumed, or performed on a defendant's property, so that the defendant immediately enjoys or becomes the owner of the benefit, there is a very real problem in saying that services have been *accepted* by the defendant. The absence of an intention on the part of a plaintiff who has rendered unrequested services to make a gift of those services is not enough to found a restitutionary claim. The same is true where a contractual request was only partially satisfied. The benefit must have been accepted.[79]

The Australian cases treat 'acceptance of benefit' as a key factor in establishing a claim for restitution in relation to non-monetary benefits.[80] 'Free acceptance' shows a defendant's choice to accept a benefit which could have been rejected. It introduces two notions: *opportunity* (to reject); and *knowledge* (sufficient to make a choice).[81] 'Constructive acceptance', the concept applied in *Pavey & Matthews Pty Ltd v Paul*,[82] operates where,

---

74. Cf *Craven-Ellis v Canons Ltd* [1936] 2 KB 403 (see [2318]).
75. See [2336].
76. See generally Birks, *An Introduction to the Law of Restitution*, 1985, pp 117ff; Mason and Carter, *Restitution Law in Australia*, 1995, paras 213–15, 932.
77. [1936] 2 KB 403. See further [2318] (acceptance).
78. [1936] 2 KB 403 at 412.
79. See further [2322], [2325].
80. The main cases are *Steele v Tardiani* (1946) 72 CLR 386 at 402; *Pavey & Matthews Pty Ltd v Paul* (1987) 162 CLR 221 at 227–8, 229, 255–6, 257, 259, 260, 262–3, 264; *Baltic Shipping Co v Dillon (The Mikhail Lermontov)* (1993) 176 CLR 344 at 374.
81. The important feature of free acceptance is that it may satisfy both the 'benefit' and 'injustice' elements of unjust enrichment. See Birks, *An Introduction to the Law of Restitution*, 1985, pp 114, 266, 283.

although the contract was ineffective, the defendant received the benefit which was requested. It applies, principally, where an unenforceable contract is fully performed or a distinct ('severable') part of a discharged unenforceable contract is performed. Although not defined as such in the cases, a third form of acceptance, which might be termed 'deemed acceptance', operates where the defendant is precluded from denying that a benefit was received. This applies, mainly, to a claim against a defendant in breach of contract.

[2315] **Reliance and restitution.** A payment of money or the rendering of services following a request involves reliance by the plaintiff on the words or conduct of the defendant. Does the law of restitution provide a way of responding to a benefit received by the defendant, or a way of responding to the benefit to the defendant of the plaintiff's reliance? If the former is correct, the only possible cases for restitution are where there is an accretion to the wealth of the defendant. This is obviously satisfied by a payment of money, but what is the position where the request was to do work?

Where a builder is asked to perform work, in a situation where it is clear that the work is to be remunerated, the work (if accepted) is an asset in the hands of the customer which must be paid for even though the contract is unenforceable, or indeed never existed.[83] It has been argued that 'pure services',[84] that is, work which does not result in an increase in the tangible assets of the defendant do not come within the concept of unjust enrichment. If restitution may be based on the benefit of reliance, restitution is available in cases where there is no increase in the assets of the defendant, but merely a benefit in the satisfaction of the request. However, this would be unsatisfactory. Either the performance of such services constitutes a benefit for the purposes of unjust enrichment or there is no possibility of restitution at all. Restitution is a response to benefit, not to reliance per se. Accordingly, in the recent cases it has become clear that restitution may be available even though all that the plaintiff has done is to provide services which produce no tangible end product.[85]

Inherently Ineffective Contracts[86]

[2316] **General.** The description 'inherently ineffective contracts' is not a precise one. It encompasses a range of defects, such as failure to agree, uncertainty, failure to comply with a statutory requirement of writing, lack of capacity, mistake, illegality, and so on which show that the contract failed to materialise, was 'void' or 'unenforceable'.

---

82. (1987) 162 CLR 221 (see [2308]).
83. See H O Hunter and J W Carter, 'Quantum Meruit and Building Contracts — Part I' (1989) 2 *JCL* 95.
84. See J Beatson, 'Benefit, Reliance and the Structure of Unjust Enrichment' [1987] *CLP* 71.
85. See *Brenner v First Artists' Management Pty Ltd* [1993] 2 VR 221; *Independent Grocers Co-operative Ltd v Noble Lowndes Superannuation Consultants Ltd* (1993) 60 SASR 525. See generally Fung, *Pre-contractual Liability Rights and Remedies: Restitution and Promissory Estoppel*, 1999.
86. See generally Mason and Carter, *Restitution Law in Australia*, 1995, Chapter 10.

We are therefore dealing with cases in which no contract exists,[87] or where the contract which came into existence is not enforceable,[88] rather than cases where the contract, although initially valid, has been discharged or rescinded.

[2317] **Contracts which fail to materialise.** *Sabemo Pty Ltd v North Sydney Municipal Council*[89] concerned a claim by Sabemo in respect of services rendered to the council in the following circumstances. In 1969 the council advertised that it planned to build a civic centre, and to award a building lease for development of the land in question. Tenders were called for, for the purpose of bringing the council into a negotiating relationship with the successful tenderer. Sabemo was the successful tenderer and it prepared various schemes, at least one of which was satisfactory to all interested parties, but no contract was entered into even though development approval was received. The decision not to proceed had nothing to do with the conduct of Sabemo or the quality of its work. The position was simply that the council decided to reject the idea of a commercial project in favour of a more modest development. Although he was unable to characterise the claim as based on unjust enrichment, Sheppard J held that Sabemo could not be deprived of payment for its labours. He said[90] that Sabemo was entitled to 'compensation or restitution'.

The justifiable complaint of Sabemo was that it had relied on the council's conduct, and provided services from which the council benefited, in determining the building scheme which would meet its needs. However, since the work was not used by the council it is impossible to say that the benefit was realised. Moreover, given that the commercial development was finally dropped, the benefit was not realisable. *Sabemo* is a case involving 'pure' services. It does not seem arguable, on the findings in *Sabemo*, that Sheppard J's decision was wrong. Equally, however, the basis of the decision is far from clear. The council got what it asked for, and the argument that it therefore obtained a benefit is quite sensible. Accordingly, the best explanation is that the concept of benefit does extend to pure services, that the council accepted the benefit of the services which Sabemo rendered, and that it would have been unjustly enriched if it did not have to pay for the work.[91] The fact that Sheppard J rejected unjust enrichment is easily explained since the concept had not been recognised in Australia at the time of the decision.

---

87. See, eg Alistair Wyvill, 'Enrichment, Restitution and the Collapsed Negotiations Cases' (1993) 11 *Aust Bar Rev* 93; Sharon Christensen, 'Recovery for Work Performed in Anticipation of Contract: Is Reliance an Element of Benefit?' (1993) 11 *Aust Bar Rev* 144.
88. See J W Carter, 'Ineffective Transactions' in Finn, ed, *Essays on Restitution*, 1990, p 206; Peter Birks, 'Restitution after Ineffective Contracts: Issues for the 1990s' (1990) 2 *JCL* 227.
89. [1977] 2 NSWLR 880 (see J D Davies, [1981] *OJLS* 300).
90. [1977] 2 NSWLR 880 at 903. It is not clear whether Sheppard J was treating restitution as a form of compensation. Cf *Austotel Pty Ltd v Franklins Selfserve Pty Ltd* (1989) 16 NSWLR 582 at 621.
91. Cf *Earhart v William Low Co* 600 P 2d 1344 (1979). See also J P Dawson, 'Restitution Without Enrichment' (1981) 61 *Boston ULR* 563.

Alternatively, Sheppard J may have been correct in saying that there was an obligation on the council to pay compensation. The difficulty is in finding a basis for damages, bearing in mind that rights to compensation arise from acts or omissions constituting wrongs. There was no breach of contract by the council, but Sheppard J may have had in mind the breach of a duty of good faith in negotiating.[92] Another argument, again not available at the time of Sheppard J's decision, relies on the principle of promissory estoppel as discussed in *Waltons Stores (Interstate) Ltd v Maher*.[93] As was explained earlier,[94] satisfaction of the requirements of that concept may result in a damages claim being available. Assuming there was an implied promise to enter into the building lease once the project received the necessary approval, Sabemo had done its work in reliance on that promise. An equity may then have arisen for the enforcement of the promise when the necessary approvals were given. The conduct of the council in seeking to withdraw its promise was unconscionable conduct and a remedy was available to Sabemo, to obtain damages equal to the market rate for the work done.[95]

A less controversial case is *British Steel Corp v Cleveland Bridge and Engineering Co Ltd*.[96] Work was done under a letter of intent which Robert Goff J held had no contractual effect. The anticipated contract never materialised or was void for incompleteness. However, the work which the parties contemplated as being done under contract was substantially completed. This involved the manufacture and delivery of steel nodes by BSC to CBE. The work was not done gratuitously, and Robert Goff J held that a quantum meruit was available. Given that CBE actually received the nodes — they were accepted by CBE — restitution could be based on unjust enrichment. But he emphasised execution of the request that the work be done and the understanding of BSC that it be paid for.

One difficulty[97] with allowing restitution in cases such as *British Steel* is that it looks to make the defendant liable without an opportunity to claim in respect of defects in the work done or late performance. In fact, CBE made a claim against BSC for breach of contract. This claim could not succeed because there was no contract. BSC argued that there was no contract for the very purpose of shutting out the claim for compensation. But there are two general answers to this criticism. First, if work is defective a plaintiff may fail in the claim, for example, because acceptance assumes that the work will correspond to the request. Second, and more importantly, the valuation process[98] may take account of at least some of

---

92. Cf Sir Anthony Mason and S J Gageler, 'The Contract' in Finn, ed, *Essays on Contract*, 1987, pp 15–16. See also [113].
93. (1988) 164 CLR 387; 76 ALR 513 (see [376]).
94. See [383]–[387].
95. See J W Carter, 'Contract, Restitution and Promissory Estoppel' (1989) 12 *UNSWLJ* 30. Cf Gareth Jones, 'Claims Arising Out of Anticipated Contracts Which Do Not Materialize' (1980) 18 *U W Ontario LR* 447 at 457 (analogy of proprietary estoppel). But cf Peter Birks, 'Restitution for Services' [1974] *CLP* 13 at 16. Other concepts may operate. See generally Mason and Carter, *Restitution Law in Australia*, 1995, paras 1042–7.
96. (1981) [1984] 1 All ER 504.
97. See S N Ball, 'Work Carried Out in Pursuance of Letters of Intent — Contract or Restitution?' (1983) 99 *LQR* 572.

the circumstances which cause a defendant to complain, and would, if there was a contract, constitute a breach giving rise to a claim for damages. This is because valuation relates to the work done rather than the work requested.

Where the benefit which is at issue takes the form of preparatory work it will be more difficult to establish an entitlement to restitution.[99] There may be no intention that the work is to be paid for, or there may be no benefit.[100] Indeed, where contract is the only rational basis for the liability of the defendant, a court should not allow a claim for restitution, the plaintiff having taken the risk that no contract would materialise.[101]

[2318] **Void contracts.**[102] Where a contract is void, for example, on the ground of uncertainty, but one of the parties made payments for performance under the contract, the money so paid is recoverable if there is a total failure of consideration. Thus, if a contract for the sale of land is held to be void because both parties believed that the vendor owned the land when in fact it was owned by the purchaser, the money paid by the purchaser can be recovered on the ground of total failure of consideration.[103] Alternatively, according to the recent English cases,[104] the money is recoverable on the basis of mistake.

The right of a plaintiff to recover the reasonable value of services rendered depends on proof of acceptance by the defendant. For example, in *Stinchcombe v Thomas*[105] the plaintiff sued the defendant, as executor and trustee of the deceased for whom the plaintiff had served as housekeeper until his death. There was a request that these services be performed, and the deceased had in fact promised to 'well reward' the plaintiff and to leave her a reasonable sum in his will. The deceased left her property to the value of £1000, but the plaintiff alleged that this sum was not sufficient. The court held the alleged contract was void for uncertainty, but allowed recovery of restitution in respect of the benefits conferred by the plaintiff at the deceased's request. Acceptance of benefit is an alternative explanation for *Craven-Ellis v Canons Ltd*.[106] The court held the contract to be void but found the defendants liable. Their liability was based on 'an implied

---

98. See [2335]–[2339].
99. Compare and contrast *Marston Construction Co Ltd v Kigass Ltd* (1989) 46 BLR 109; *Regalian Properties Plc v London Docklands Development Corp* [1995] 1 WLR 212 (see Paul Key, (1995) 111 *LQR* 576).
100. But it may be possible, in cases where the understanding is that the work is to be paid for, to find a collateral contract dealing with the preparatory work. See *Turriff Construction Ltd v Regalia Knitting Mills Ltd* [1972] EG (Dig) 257.
101. But see Ewan McKendrick, 'The Battle of the Forms and the Law of Restitution' (1988) 8 *OJLS* 197.
102. See Ben Kremer, 'Recovering Money Under Void Contracts: "Absence of Consideration" and Failure of Consideration' (2001) 17 *JCL* 37.
103. See *Svanosio v McNamara* (1956) 96 CLR 186 at 207. See also *George v Roach* (1942) 67 CLR 253 (failure of condition precedent to the existence of a contract).
104. See *Kleinwort Benson Ltd v Lincoln City Council* [1999] 2 AC 349 (contract fully performed); *Guinness Mahon & Co Ltd v Kensington and Chelsea Royal London Borough Council* [1999] QB 215. Cf *David Securities Pty Ltd v Commonwealth Bank of Australia* (1992) 175 CLR 353 (mistake of law is now the same as a mistake of fact for the purposes of restitution).
105. [1957] VR 509.
106. [1936] 2 KB 403. See [2318].

promise to pay on a quantum meruit basis' which arose, as Greer LJ went on to say,[107] 'from the performance of the services and the implied acceptance of the same by the company'. More recently, in *Brenner v First Artists' Management Pty Ltd*[108] Byrne J held that performance of a management agreement and a record agreement entered into as part of a project for the 'comeback' of a famous singer of the 1970s, namely, one Daryl Braithwaite, gave rise to a claim for reasonable remuneration where the agreements were too uncertain to count as contracts.

Where a contract is void (but not illegal) by virtue of statute, although no claim can be made in contract, a claim in restitution may be available, because it is based on unjust enrichment and therefore independent of contract. However, it is essential for the plaintiff to show that there is a basis for restitution, such as total failure of consideration or mistake, and also necessary to take into account the policy behind the statute. In some cases the legislation will be found to apply to restitution as well as contract. But this is rare. Moreover, a statute which merely recognises a common law basis for voidness will not generally preclude a claim for restitution.

However, the claim may not in fact be restitutionary. Thus, where a contract for the sale of goods is void for incompleteness due to the parties' failure to agree on a price, in circumstances where the parties intended the contract to be binding only in the event of a price being fixed by the parties,[109] the 'buyer' will, under the sale of goods legislation,[110] be liable to pay a reasonable price for goods actually supplied and accepted. This liability is statutory or contractual rather than restitutionary.[111]

[2319] Unenforceable contracts. Most of the unenforceable contract cases concern claims in respect of contracts affected by the *Statute of Frauds* 1677 (Imp) or derivative legislation. These claims were dealt with earlier.[112]

Contracts Discharged after Partial Performance[113]

Introduction

[2320] General. If a contract has been partially performed, the first question to be asked is whether the plaintiff has performed a part of the contract to be separately paid for by the defendant. For example, if a seller under an instalment goods contract has made deliveries which have been

---

107. [1936] 2 KB 403 at 409. Cf A T Denning, 'Quantum Meruit: The Case of *Craven-Ellis v Canons Ltd*' (1939) 55 *LQR* 54.
108. [1993] 2 VR 221.
109. See *May and Butcher Ltd v R* (1929) [1934] 2 KB 17n, and generally [267]–[269].
110. See **ACT:** *Sale of Goods Act* 1954, s 13(2); **NSW:** *Sale of Goods Act* 1923, s 13(2); **NT:** *Sale of Goods Act* 1972, s 13(2); **Qld:** *Sale of Goods Act* 1896, s 11(2); **SA:** *Sale of Goods Act* 1895, s 8(2); **Tas:** *Sale of Goods Act* 1896, s 13(2); **Vic:** *Goods Act* 1958, s 13(2); **WA:** *Sale of Goods Act* 1895, s 8(2).
111. The provision refers to other situations where the seller would otherwise be required to bring a claim for restitution based on the buyer's acceptance of the goods.
112. See [520]. See also [2308] and J W Carter, 'Services Rendered Under Ineffective Contracts' [1990] *LMCLQ* 495.
113. See generally Mason and Carter, *Restitution Law in Australia*, 1995, Chapter 11; J W Carter, 'Discharged Contracts: Claims for Restitution' (1997) 11 *JCL* 130.

accepted by the buyer, restitution is not relevant: an action for the agreed price is available. This is true even if the contract has been validly terminated by the buyer for breach by the seller.[114]

On the other hand, if the plaintiff has performed part of an 'entire'[115] contract, no action can be brought on the contract and the issue of restitution is raised. In evaluating such a claim, it is necessary to consider:

- the nature of the benefit;
- whether the performance of the contract was not completed because of a breach by the plaintiff or defendant; and
- whether the defendant is unjustly enriched.

Recovery by the terminating party

[2321] Recovery of money. Where a payment is made under a contract, and the agreed return is a non-monetary benefit, a total failure of consideration[116] will occur if the contract is discharged at a time when no part of the agreed return has been received. There is then an unjust enrichment of the defendant.

As the law currently stands,[117] unless the contract was severable and the payment was made for the receipt of a severable part of the defendant's performance obligations,[118] there is no unjust enrichment if the failure is less than total. A recent example is *Baltic Shipping Co v Dillon (The Mikhail Lermontov)*.[119] The passenger was not entitled to restitution, although she had paid the whole fare for a cruise in advance, because she enjoyed eight of the promised 14 days when the vessel sank. However, she was not without remedy since she was able to claim compensation for the loss which she suffered.[120]

[2322] Recovery as on a quantum meruit. If the defendant's breach prevented performance by the plaintiff, the plaintiff will be entitled to recover as on a quantum meruit following termination of the performance of the contract. For example, in *Stevenson v Hook*,[121] a surveyor recovered the value of work done when the contract was discharged for repudiation on the part of the defendant after the work which the plaintiff had been requested to do was partially completed. More recently, in *Renard Constructions (ME) Pty Ltd v Minister for Public Works*[122] a builder's claim for reasonable remuneration succeeded following discharge of a schedule of

---

114. See [2234]. The buyer retains the right to claim damages for breach.
115. See [1822].
116. See [2306].
117. But see [2306].
118. See *Fibrosa Spolka Akcyjna v Fairbairn Lawson Combe Barbour Ltd* [1943] AC 32 at 64–5; *Baltic Shipping Co v Dillon (The Mikhail Lermontov)* (1993) 176 CLR 344 at 375.
119. (1993) 176 CLR 344 (see [2153]). See Jane Swanton, (1993) 67 *ALJ* 379; Hugh Stowe, [1993] *CLJ* 384; Kit Barker, [1993] *LMCLQ* 291; J W Carter and Gregory Tolhurst, (1994) 7 *JCL* 273.
120. Contrast the position of a party in breach: [2324].
121. (1956) 73 WN (NSW) 307.
122. (1992) 26 NSWLR 234. See also *Iezzi Constructions Pty Ltd v Watkins Pacific (Qld) Pty Ltd* [1995] 2 Qd R 350 (see M R Lawson, (1998) 13 *JCL* 274).

rates building contract on the principal's repudiation, in wrongfully taking over the work and excluding the contractor from the site after the builder had carried out part of the work.

The importance of asking whether the defendant was in breach is also illustrated by a lump sum employment contract which has been partially performed by the employee. An employee who is wrongfully dismissed is entitled to terminate the performance of the contract. Having done so the employee has the choice between claiming damages and claiming restitution in respect of the benefits conferred on the employer in partially performing the contract.[123]

[2323] Unjust enrichment without benefit. In *Planché v Colburn*[124] the plaintiff agreed to write a volume on costume and ancient armour for publication by the defendants in *The Juvenile Library*. After the plaintiff had spent money viewing a collection of ancient armour, and completed (but not delivered) a portion of the manuscript, the defendants abandoned the project and repudiated their obligations. The jury brought in a verdict in favour of the plaintiff and £50 was awarded. A motion to set aside the verdict failed, but there was no clear decision on whether the judgment in the plaintiff's favour was to be supported on the ground of damages — for breach by the defendants — or for restitution. It is, however, clear that the court regarded restitution as available, and there are many later cases in which this has been treated as the actual decision. Thus, it has often been said that the mere fact of discharge for breach provides the plaintiff with a right to elect between suing for compensation and suing in restitution to recover the value of reliance expenditure or work done.[125]

The approach based on *Planché* creates a number of problems.[126] First, the idea that the plaintiff is entitled to choose between restitution and damages is misconceived if it is suggested that the choice of one precludes the other. In fact, so long as the plaintiff does not recover the same sum twice,[127] there is no objection to a plaintiff recovering both damages and restitution.

Second, the cases run counter to the cases on unjust enrichment which explain that the benefit in respect of which the claim is made must have been accepted by the defendant. Apparently, in cases where the defendant breached the contract, the defendant is deemed to have accepted the benefit, by virtue of its actual or notional prevention of performance by the plaintiff.

Third, there is no analysis of whether the defendant was in fact benefited. In *Planché* itself, the benefit bargained for must have been the completed manuscript. Since this was not received — and was in fact retained by the

---

123. See, eg *Goodman v Pocock* (1850) 15 QB 576 at 580, 582, 583; 117 ER 577 at 579, 580; *Automatic Fire Sprinklers Pty Ltd v Watson* (1946) 72 CLR 435 at 450, 462.
124. (1831) 8 Bing 14; 131 ER 305.
125. See, eg *Ettridge v Vermin Board of the District of Murat Bay* [1928] SASR 124 at 131; *Brooks Robinson Pty Ltd v Rothfield* [1951] VLR 405 (see [2339]); *Bolwell Fibreglass Pty Ltd v Foley* [1984] VR 97 at 114.
126. Cf [2315]. See further [2339].
127. See Mason and Carter, *Restitution Law in Australia*, 1995, paras 1405, 1410, 1411, 1737–38.

plaintiff — it is difficult to see how the defendant was enriched.[128] Accordingly, the cases also appear to say that the defendant is deemed to have been benefited. This is unsatisfactory. Logically, the plaintiff should be restricted to a claim for damages.[129]

Position of party in breach

[2324] Recovery of money. The concept of total failure of consideration does not depend on the plaintiff not being in breach of contract. For example, if a contract for the sale of land provides for instalment payments to be made by the purchaser, and the purchaser breaches the contract in such a way that the vendor is justified in electing to terminate, termination by the vendor results in a total failure of consideration. The purchaser is then entitled to recover payments made on the basis that the agreed return for the payments — conveyance of title — has totally failed.[130] Since the total failure shows that the vendor was unjustly enriched, neither the fact that the purchaser has been let into possession nor the fact that the purchaser was in breach of contract prevents recovery.[131]

On the other hand, where the failure is less than total, the party in breach will be denied recovery. This is not because of the breach, but rather because[132] a *total* failure is required for there to be an unjust enrichment. A court will not inquire into the value of the benefit. For example, in *Shaw v Ball*[133] termination of a contract for the sale of a business did not cause a total failure of consideration because the purchaser had taken possession of the business and enjoyed its goodwill for a time. The goodwill was part of the performance for which the purchaser bargained, and having enjoyed it for a time he could not show that there had been a total failure of consideration. This approach means that a plaintiff will be denied restitution even if the sum paid to the defendant is out of all proportion to the benefit obtained by performance.[134]

In *Dies v British and International Mining and Finance Corp Ltd*[135] Stable J suggested a wider principle in the context of a sale of goods contract. Although the decision is in fact explicable on the basis that there was on the facts a total failure of consideration, he said that a total failure of consideration is not required. However, this was doubted by the House of Lords in *Hyundai Heavy Industries Co Ltd v Papadopoulos*.[136] On the other

---

128. This looks to allow restitution for reliance loss. See Mason and Carter, *Restitution Law in Australia*, 1995, paras 1168, 1408. Cf [2339].
129. Cf *Commonwealth of Australia v Amann Aviation Pty Ltd* (1991) 174 CLR 64; 104 ALR 1 (see [2111]).
130. *McDonald v Dennys Lascelles Ltd* (1933) 48 CLR 457 at 470, 478. See also *Mayson v Clouet* [1924] AC 980; *Frankcombe v Foster Investments Pty Ltd* [1978] 2 NSWLR 41 at 55.
131. For a sale of goods illustration see *Rowland v Divall* [1923] 2 KB 500 (see [2306]).
132. Subject to statute. See Mason and Carter, *Restitution Law in Australia*, 1995, paras 1146–9.
133. (1962) 63 SR (NSW) 910. Cf *Hodder v Watters* [1946] VLR 222. Contrast *Rover International Ltd v Cannon Film Sales Ltd* [1989] 1 WLR 912.
134. But see [2336] (requirement of restitutio in integrum).
135. [1939] 1 KB 724 at 743.
136. [1980] 1 WLR 1129 at 1134, 1142, 1148. Cf *Baltic Shipping Co v Dillon (The Mikhail Lermontov)* (1993) 176 CLR 344 at 352, 390.

hand, a plaintiff who has been benefited will not be denied recovery unless the benefit was part of the agreed return for the payment, that is, the benefit must have been bargained for under the contract.

The total failure principle may be excluded by the parties' agreement. Accordingly, if there is an express or implied term of the contract providing that any payment received may be forfeited, the plaintiff will be unable to rely on total failure of consideration as a basis for recovering the payment. In such cases the plaintiff must invoke principles governing relief against forfeiture.[137]

[2325] Recovery as on a quantum meruit. Where the plaintiff is the party in breach, a restitutionary claim for the value of a non-monetary benefit conferred will not generally be available. Thus, where an employee is lawfully dismissed under a lump sum employment contract, the employer is not obliged to pay the value of the employee's service prior to dismissal.[138]

The classic decision is *Sumpter v Hedges*,[139] where the plaintiff abandoned a building contract after doing work on the defendant's land. It was taken for granted that, as the contract was entire, the plaintiff was unable to recover on the contract.[140] The plaintiff's claim to a quantum meruit was rejected because it was impossible to imply a right of recovery while the contract between the parties governed their rights and obligations. In addition, the defendant had no choice but to accept the work as it had been done on his land.[141] Therefore, no obligation to pay could be implied from the receipt of partial performance. However, when completing the work himself, the defendant had used certain building materials which the plaintiff had left on the ground. As the defendant had clearly accepted the benefit of these materials, which could have been returned, the plaintiff was entitled to be paid the value of these materials.

In *Sumpter v Hedges* the court said that the express contractual provision for payment prevented reliance on a claim in the nature of quantum meruit, based on an implied promise to pay for the benefit conferred. This reasoning cannot now be accepted: reliance on the implied promise reasoning will not do because the High Court has rejected the implied contract theory of restitution.[142] The relevant question is whether the defendant was unjustly enriched at the plaintiff's expense. Since the case has been approved by the High Court[143] it would be difficult to say that adoption of the unjust enrichment concept is a sufficient basis for treating the decision as inapplicable today.

The other basis for the decision was that the defendant did not freely accept the benefit of the plaintiff's performance.[144] Thus, unlike the

---

137. See [2331]–[2333].
138. *Boston Deep Sea Fishing & Ice Co v Ansell* (1888) 39 Ch D 339 at 364–5. But see [1827].
139. [1898] 1 QB 673.
140. See [1824].
141. See also *Forman & Co Pty Ltd v The Ship 'Liddesdale'* [1900] AC 190; *Cooper v Australian Electric Co (1922) Ltd* (1922) 25 WALR 66.
142. See *Pavey & Matthews Pty Ltd v Paul* (1987) 162 CLR 221 (see [2308]).
143. See *Steele v Tardiani* (1946) 72 CLR 386.

position where the defendant is in breach of contract,[145] the plaintiff must establish that the defendant had a free choice of whether to accept or reject the alleged benefit. Although this remains as an acceptable basis for the decision, unjust enrichment suggests two possible views. One is that in the absence of free acceptance the defendant is not, on facts conforming to that decision, benefited. The other view is that, although the defendant is benefited, the benefit is not an unjust one. It would seem that, because of the emphasis on acceptance in the Australian cases,[146] the first view is correct, so that the absence of evidence of acceptance means that no issue of injustice arises.

There will, however, be cases in which acceptance is established. The leading case is *Steele v Tardiani*.[147] Steele employed the plaintiffs, who were released Italian internees during the second world war, to cut timber. Their performance was not in accordance with the contract, since it did not comply with a term specifying the dimensions of the timber. The High Court said that the contract was not an 'entire' contract. Rather it was 'infinitely divisible',[148] with the contract price indicating the *rate* at which the cut timber was to be paid for. That did not help the plaintiffs in their contract claim. As Dixon J said,[149] 'each divisible application of the contract is entire and is only satisfied by performance, not partial, but substantially complete'. Although the plaintiffs cut 1500 tons of timber, their performance was not substantial under the doctrine discussed earlier,[150] and recovery on the contract was not possible.

To recover in respect of such timber the plaintiffs had to show 'circumstances removing their right to remuneration from the exact conditions of the special contract'.[151] This was Dixon J's expression of the way of distinguishing *Sumpter v Hedges*. However, it was 'not enough that the work has been beneficial',[152] in this case by turning standing timber into valuable firewood. The evidence had to be examined to see the circumstances under which Steele obtained that benefit. The evidence showed that the defendant had allowed the plaintiffs to leave their employment under the impression that he was not insisting on the contract, and that he had stood by while the timber was cut and made no complaint, and subsequently sold the cut timber. Indeed, the point as to dimensions was only taken late in the day, during cross-examination. Therefore, the deviation from contract being acquiesced in, the conduct of the defendant could be regarded as 'a taking of the benefit of the work and so, as involving

---

144. But see A S Burrows, 'Free Acceptance in the Law of Restitution' (1988) 104 *LQR* 576.
145. See [2322].
146. See [2314].
147. (1946) 72 CLR 386.
148. (1946) 72 CLR 386 at 401 per Dixon J.
149. (1946) 72 CLR 386 at 401.
150. See [1830]–[1832].
151. (1946) 72 CLR 386 at 402.
152. (1946) 72 CLR 386 at 402 per Dixon J. Suggestions in *Miles v Wakefield MDC* [1987] AC 539 at 553, 561, that an employer may be liable as on a quantum meruit for work accepted when the employee intentionally breaches the contract but is not dismissed are not consistent with Australian law. See Mason and Carter, *Restitution Law in Australia*, 1995, para 909.

either a dispensation from precise performance or an implication at law of a new obligation to pay the value of the work done'.[153] The proper (modern) rationalisation of this decision is that, because the defendant had accepted the benefit of the plaintiffs' work, he was unjustly enriched.

A plaintiff in breach may sometimes recover under statute. Indeed, some law reform bodies have recommended a general reform, by treating benefit as a purely factual matter, not dependent on whether the contract is entire.[154] However, this may go too far. On a rising market it takes away the incentive of the plaintiff to perform the contract. It also deprives the defendant of the main defence to a claim for incomplete work. At present, statutory bases are more limited.[155]

At the Expense of the Plaintiff[156]

[2326] Primary and secondary senses of unjust enrichment. So far we have been dealing exclusively with cases where the benefit to the defendant is an increase in the defendant's assets acquired at the expense of the plaintiff in the sense that the plaintiff's assets have been correspondingly decreased. This is the 'substantive' or autonomous part of restitution law, where there is an imposed *primary* liability to make restitution. Where the only principles at work are those of the law of restitution, the 'primary' sense of unjust enrichment is at issue. This is an appropriate description not just because the benefit to the defendant is a 'subtraction' from the plaintiff's assets but also, and more importantly, because the law does not rely on the identification of conduct as wrongful under the law of contract or tort. Thus, restitution is available — the defendant is unjustly enriched — whether or not the defendant has committed a wrong to the plaintiff.

However, another — secondary — sense of unjust enrichment has been recognised,[157] which relies on the fact that the defendant has committed a wrong. Although in some cases the benefit to the defendant is also at the plaintiff's expense in the sense that it was a subtraction from the plaintiff's assets, when asserting the secondary sense of 'at the plaintiff's expense' the plaintiff relies on the fact that the defendant committed a wrong, such as a tort or a crime. In this secondary sense the benefit is at the plaintiff's expense because the defendant has benefited by reason of a wrong done to

---

153. (1946) 72 CLR 386 at 405 per Dixon J. See also *Horton v Jones (No 2)* (1939) 39 SR (NSW) 305 at 319–20.
154. See Law Commission, *Pecuniary Restitution on Breach of Contract*, Law Commission No 121, 1983; Law Reform Committee of South Australia, *Nineteenth Report*, 1986. However, both suggestions have been criticised. See Mason and Carter, *Restitution Law in Australia*, 1995, para 1177. But cf C J F Kidd, 'Partial Performance of Lump Sum Contracts: Proposals for Reform' (1985) 59 *ALJ* 96.
155. See Mason and Carter, *Restitution Law in Australia*, 1995, para 1172–6.
156. See Peter Birks, 'Restitutionary Damages for Breach of Contract: Snepp and the Fusion of Law and Equity' [1987] *LMCLQ* 421; I M Jackman, 'Restitution for Wrongs' [1989] *CLJ* 302; P B H Birks, 'Civil Wrongs: A New World' in *Butterworth Lectures 1990–91*, 1992.
157. See *Winterton Constructions Pty Ltd v Hambros Australia Ltd* (1991) 101 ALR 363 at 374; *Bryson v Bryant* (1992) 29 NSWLR 188 at 222; *Commissioner of State Revenue (Vic) v Royal Insurance Australia Ltd* (1994) 182 CLR 51 at 73; 126 ALR 1.

the plaintiff.[158] Therefore, as Professor Birks explains,[159] there is a distinction between asserting a remedy on the ground of unjust enrichment — ignoring the wrong — and reliance on the wrong itself. Only if there is no independent unjust enrichment will it be essential for the plaintiff to rely on the wrong.

There are two main types of case. In the first, the plaintiff relies on the wrong for the purpose of showing that a benefit obtained by the defendant was unjustly obtained, as where the benefit accrued as a result of the tort of deceit. The second relies on the contrast drawn earlier[160] between primary and secondary obligations. If the defendant breached a primary duty arising in tort or contract the plaintiff is entitled to enforce a secondary obligation, namely, to pay damages. Although, as we also saw earlier,[161] in contract the secondary duty is treated as one requiring the payment of compensation, in this branch of the law of restitution[162] the idea is that the defendant may come under an obligation to pay restitutionary (rather than compensatory) damages. In other words, damages may be available, even though the plaintiff did not suffer a loss, if a benefit accrued to the defendant as a result of the wrong.

Potentially, this analysis has very important implications for the assessment of damages in contract. However, although the ultimate rationalisation is the need to prevent unjust enrichment, that is, to ensure that persons do not benefit from their own wrongs,[163] it would be incorrect to say that there is a legal principle to the effect that a defendant who has obtained a benefit as a result of his or her own wrong must always pay restitutionary damages. So far, the cases in which restitutionary damages are available are fairly limited in scope. It is clear that the analysis is often applicable where a tort has been committed.[164] It is also clear — although the cases do not rely heavily on unjust enrichment — that the obligation of a fiduciary to account for profits made in breach of the fiduciary relation produces the same result as restitutionary damages.[165] On the other hand, the courts have usually denied that restitutionary damages can be recovered for a mere breach of contract.[166]

[2327] **Waiver of tort.** In *United Australia Ltd v Barclays Bank Ltd*[167] United Australia was the payee of a cheque payable to their order. It was received and endorsed by one Emons (their secretary) in favour of MFG Trust Ltd. Subsequently, the cheque was received by Barclays who credited the account of MFG at one of their branches. In fact, Emons had no authority to endorse the cheque in MFG's favour. On these facts the House of Lords said that United Australia had a choice. They could sue MFG for

---

158. Mason and Carter, *Restitution Law in Australia*, 1995, paras 221–5, Chapter 15.
159. Birks, *An Introduction to the Law of Restitution*, 1985, p 322.
160. See [2302].
161. See [2101].
162. Sometimes termed the 'remedial' side of the law. See Birks, *Restitution — The Future*, 1992, p 1.
163. See Mason and Carter, *Restitution Law in Australia*, 1995, para 1502.
164. See [2327].
165. See [2328].
166. See [2329].
167. [1941] AC 1.

the amount of the cheque, alleging that it had been endorsed without authority to recover the amount which it represented as restitution. Alternatively, they could sue Barclays for damages for conversion or negligence. Originally, United Australia had sued MFG in restitution, but this action had not been brought to judgment, and there was no obstacle to the claim in tort for conversion, and the recovery of damages.[168]

Under this analysis, the idea of 'waiver of tort' is misleading[169] and we should distinguish three situations. First, where the basis for a claim in restitution is that the defendant both committed a wrong and received a benefit directly at the expense of the plaintiff (as would have been the position in a claim against MFG for restitution), the tort is asserted as the basis for a primary (but perhaps 'dependent') claim in restitution.

Second, where the plaintiff seeks damages (which were available against MFG, and were recovered from Barclays) the tort is relied upon for the purpose of enforcing the secondary obligation to pay (restitutionary) damages.

Third, the defendant may have held itself out as the agent of the plaintiff when committing the tort. If, by virtue of the wrong, the defendant has obtained a benefit, the plaintiff may adopt the conduct of the defendant by ratifying the agency.

In neither of the first two cases is the tort actually 'waived'. Instead, it is in both cases relied on, but for different remedies. However, the plaintiff cannot have both remedies, because that would lead to double recovery. Accordingly, the plaintiff must choose (elect) in favour of one or the other. The decision of the House of Lords was that United Australia had not made any election because it had not brought the claim against MFG to judgment. But had it done so the tort would have been 'waived' only in the limited sense of an election not to sue Barclays for its wrong. On the other hand, in the third situation — not applicable in the *United Australia* case — the tort is waived in the sense that it is extinguished. It is not a wrong at all, and the claim in restitution is justifiable simply on the basis that the money in the defendant's hands was received as agent for the plaintiff.

A breach of contract is not usually also a tort, and the waiver of tort analysis will rarely be applicable in the breach of contract context.[170] However, if, for example, a seller sells a specific motor car to a buyer, and although ownership in the vehicle has been transferred to the buyer, the seller purports to sell it to a third party, the seller's conduct will amount both to a tort and a breach of contract. Moreover, since the tort is conversion the buyer is entitled to restitutionary damages. Nevertheless, this is on the basis of the wrong to the buyer's property interest rather than the seller's breach of contract. Therefore, if the subject matter of the contract is unascertained goods, so that property cannot pass merely by virtue of the contract of sale, it is not meaningful to speak of the seller

---

168. In fact it was never brought to trial and MFG went into liquidation. The appellants put in a proof in the liquidation but at the time of the present action the proof had not been admitted.
169. Cf Stephen Hedley, 'The Myth of Waiver of Tort' (1984) 100 *LQR* 653.
170. For the torts which have been subjected to this analysis see Mason and Carter, *Restitution Law in Australia*, 1995, Chapter 16.

committing the tort of conversion. Even if it sells all of its stock to a third party, the buyer cannot claim restitutionary damages.

[2328] **Breach of fiduciary obligation.** The distinctive features of a fiduciary obligation are that the fiduciary must not abuse its position or, unless the beneficiary consents, allow interest and duty to conflict. The mischief which equity seeks to avoid is the 'sacrifice'[171] of the beneficiary's interests. The high standard guards against actual and possible abuses of position: there is a breach of duty even if there is in fact no sacrifice.[172] A person who, whether honestly or dishonestly, obtains a benefit as a result of the breach of a fiduciary relationship must therefore account to the other party (the beneficiary of the duty) for the amount of the benefit.[173] Although usually justified by reference to the nature of the relationship rather than principles of restitution, there is no doubt that the liability of the fiduciary has a restitutionary character. Indeed, in the case of fiduciaries, equity requires restitution of a benefit which the beneficiary of the duty could not have made itself.[174] It is because of the high standards which a fiduciary obligation attracts that the law imposes the greater incentive.

Although an obligation to compensate for breaches of a duty no doubt serves to discourage breach, the imposition of a duty going beyond compensation is a much greater disincentive. A contract may create a relationship which is also fiduciary, because it belongs to a class which is generally so regarded or because the particular circumstances justify the conclusion that the contractual relation is also of a fiduciary nature.[175] It follows that the imposition of a duty to account for the amount of the benefit obtained in breach of a fiduciary obligation may occur in the contract context.[176] Therefore, where contracting parties are in a fiduciary relationship, and the defendant receives a bribe or secret commission, this may be recovered by the plaintiff.[177]

Generally, in contract the parties are concerned with their individual objectives (usually assumed to be profit based) and are not concerned to look after each other's interests. By contrast, a fiduciary must give precedence to the beneficiary's interests. It follows that, generally, contracting parties do not stand in a fiduciary relationship to one another.[178] Although the courts have been reluctant to impose a fiduciary

---

171. Birks, *An Introduction to the Law of Restitution*, 1985, p 333.
172. See Birks, *An Introduction to the Law of Restitution*, 1985, pp 339–40 (where the plaintiff could not have made the profit or benefit, it is the 'non-subtractive receipt' which is the measure of restitution).
173. See, eg *United Dominions Corp Ltd v Brian* (1985) 157 CLR 1; 60 ALR 741 (sale of property at a substantial profit).
174. See, eg *Boardman v Phipps* [1967] 2 AC 46. Cf *Snepp v United States* 444 US 507 (1980).
175. See generally *Hospital Products Ltd v United States Surgical Corp* (1984) 156 CLR 41; 55 ALR 417.
176. See, eg *Thornley v Tilley* (1925) 36 CLR 1.
177. See, eg *Islamic Republic of Iran Shipping Lines v Denby* [1987] 1 Lloyd's Rep 367.
178. See, eg [2112].

relationship in ordinary commercial contracts,[179] there is no doubt that this may occur.

[2329] Breach of contract as a wrong.[180] In *Hospital Products Ltd v United States Surgical Corp*[181] Deane J, in his dissenting judgment, countenanced an award of restitution for breach of contract (on equitable principles) even though there was no breach of a fiduciary duty. There is, however, no general support for the treatment of a breach of contract as a wrong which justifies an award of restitutionary damages or an account of profits. For example, in *Surrey County Council v Bredero Homes Ltd*[182] a local council (the plaintiff) sold land to a developer (the defendant). The contract contained a covenant requiring the defendant to limit the development to 72 houses, and planning permission was granted to build that number of houses. However, the defendant later applied for (and was granted) permission to build five additional houses. Although the plaintiff was required by statute to grant the permission, the conduct of the defendant was nevertheless a breach of contract. The plaintiff's claim for damages was not based on any loss suffered, because there was no loss. Instead, the claim was for the sum which would have been a fair price for the relaxation of the covenant.[183] In other words, the claim was for some of the profit which the defendant had made by breaching the contract. The claim was refused, on the basis that where a plaintiff has suffered no quantifiable loss or damage, only nominal damages can be awarded.

This approach is also supported by a theory of 'efficient breach'.[184] This is an economic analysis which says that the law should assist the movement of resources to their highest value user. Therefore, a defendant should not be required to pay over money obtained in breaching a contract if this would discourage conduct which is economically beneficial. Of course, the 'efficient breach' analysis pays little regard for a basic idea of contract, that is, that promises should be performed. Accordingly, the real support for the current approach of the courts is based more on the primacy of the compensation principle than a concern to promote economic analysis.[185] Accordingly, unless the breach is also an infringement of a property right, or the breach of a fiduciary duty, the compensation principle is applied.

---

179. See, eg Jonathan Gill, 'A Man Cannot Serve Two Masters' (1989) 2 *JCL* 115 at 139–40.
180. See generally Catherine Mitchell, 'Remedial Inadequacy in Contract and the Role of Restitutionary Damages' (1999) 15 *JCL* 133.
181. (1984) 156 CLR 41 at 124–5. Cf *Trident General Insurance Co Ltd v McNiece Bros Pty Ltd* (1988) 165 CLR 107 at 146; 80 ALR 574.
182. [1993] 1 WLR 1361. See Peter Birks, (1993) 109 *LQR* 518; Andrew Burrows, [1993] *LMCLQ* 453; Richard O'Dair, [1993] *RLR* 31; S A Smith, 'Of Remedies and Restrictive Covenants' (1994) 7 *JCL* 164. Cf *Jaggard v Sawyer* [1995] 1 WLR 269 (see [2170]).
183. See generally R J Sharpe and S M Waddams, 'Damages for Lost Opportunity to Bargain' (1982) 2 *OJLS* 290; S M Waddams, 'Restitution as Part of Contract Law' in Burrows, ed, *Essays on the Law of Restitution*, 1991, p 211; S M Waddams, 'Profits Derived from Breach of Contract: Damages or Restitution?' (1997) 11 *JCL* 115 (and see H O Hunter 'Commentary on "Profits Derived from Breach of Contract: Damages or Restitution?"' (1997) 11 *JCL* 127).
184. See, eg C J Goetz and R E Scott, 'Enforcing Promises: An Examination of the Basis of Contract' (1980) 89 *Yale LJ* 1261.

Recently, however, the House of Lords has distanced itself from the decision in *Bredero*. Lord Nicholls in *Attorney-General v Blake*[186] said that it would be a 'sorry reflection on the law' if a defendant who had covenanted not to erect further houses was permitted to breach the obligation with impunity. In that case the majority held that an account of profits may in some cases be awarded for breach of contract. Although Blake did at one time owe a fiduciary duty to the Crown, and a duty to keep confidential the information which he obtained in connection with his employment by the Secret Intelligence Service, by the time the breach of contract occurred it was accepted that these duties had expired. All that remained was his life-long undertaking not to divulge official information. That duty was breached when he published his autobiography. The reasoning of the majority to justify the conclusion that Blake was liable to account to the Crown is not easy to follow. Of course, the object was to ensure that Blake did not profit from his wrongdoing. Although the majority was not prepared to recognise account of profits as a general remedy for breach of contract, Lord Nicholls concluded that there was 'in principle' no reason to rule out the remedy in all cases.[187] The precise basis for the actual decision was that Blake's life-long undertaking was analogous to a fiduciary obligation.[188] In the context of the intelligence services this was thought to be sufficient to justify the conclusion that even though the information disclosed was not confidential the award of an account of profits was available to the Crown.[189]

It remains to be seen whether the Australian courts will apply *Blake*. That could in our view only occur at the level of the High Court.[190] At present, the position remains that there is no obligation on a contracting party to account for profits made in breach of contract unless:

- the profit represents the plaintiff's loss, in which case the damages award is compensatory in nature;
- the defendant breached a term of the contract to the effect that the plaintiff would receive the benefits obtained by the defendant — again, the damages are compensatory;
- the profit resulted from a wrongful dealing with the plaintiff's property, bringing the principle of waiver of tort into play; or
- the profit was made in breach of a fiduciary obligation or a duty of confidence arising from the contract.

---

185. See J W Carter and Andrew Stewart, 'Commerce and Conscience: The High Court's Developing View of Contract' (1993) 23 *UWALR* 49 at 68–9. Cf S M Waddams, 'The Choice of Remedy for Breach of Contract' in Beatson and Friedmann, eds, *Good Faith and Fault in Contract Law*, 1995, p 481.
186. [2001] 1 AC 268 at 283. Lords Goff and Browne-Wilkinson agreed.
187. See [2001] 1 AC 268 at 284.
188. See [2001] 1 AC 268 at 287, 291.
189. For discussion see David Fox, [2001] *CLJ* 33; Furmston, *How Modern is English Contract Law?*, 2000.
190. See *Hospitality Group Pty Ltd v Australian Rugby Union Ltd* [2001] FCA 1040 (3 August 2001).

Injustice

[2330] Generally. Assuming that the other requirements of unjust enrichment have been satisfied, the final element is whether it was unjust for the defendant to receive (or retain) the benefit. The suspicion which has surrounded the unjust enrichment concept is almost certainly due to the fear that its adoption would result in great uncertainty, by an unprincipled approach to restitutionary claims. The discussion of the ideas of 'benefit' and 'at the expense of' clearly shows that the law is anything but unprincipled. So also with the requirement of injustice.

One significant feature of *Pavey & Matthews Pty Ltd v Paul*[191] is Deane J's statement[192] that adopting unjust enrichment does not amount to the assertion of a 'judicial discretion to do whatever idiosyncratic notions of what is fair and just might dictate'. Injustice is not determined simply by asking where the merits of the case lie. Injustice is thus determined by the interaction of principle, precedent and policy. The rule is that a *recognised basis* for the conclusion must be found. In the contract context, careful attention must be paid to the bargain: if the parties have expressed their intention on how the benefit is to be dealt with this must be respected.

Some cases will be very easy indeed. Assume that A makes a gift of $100 to B. B has obtained a benefit at A's expense, but there is no question of A obtaining restitution. The circumstances of the payment — the fact of gift — indicate that the receipt is not an unjust enrichment of B. The same is true where A pays money to B in discharge of a contractual obligation: if A has received the agreed return for the payment, no question of unjust enrichment can arise. On the other hand, where A pays money to B as a result of mistake, there is no doubt that, prima facie, the receipt is an unjust enrichment of B.

We have already seen the operation of two important bases for the conclusion that the defendant's enrichment was unjust:

- total failure of consideration;[193] and
- acceptance of benefit.[194]

The discussion below deals with the impact of contractual provisions and statute in relation to those bases.

[2331] Effect of provision for forfeiture. Where there is an express or implied provision in a contract that a benefit conferred by the plaintiff's performance is to be retained or forfeited by the defendant if the plaintiff breaches the contract, restitution on the basis of a total failure of consideration is excluded. If restitution is to be ordered it must be based on rules governing relief against forfeiture.

Typically, the benefit will be monetary, for example, part payments under a sale of land contract. But the benefit may be of some other form, that is, personal or real property.[195]

---

191. (1987) 162 CLR 221.
192. (1987) 162 CLR 221 at 256.
193. See [2306].
194. See [2314].

[2332] **Relief against forfeiture.** If the defendant terminated the performance of the contract for breach or repudiation by the plaintiff, and has forfeited any payments made, the plaintiff may apply for relief against forfeiture if there is an element of unconscionability in the defendant's conduct.[196]

Assume that a contract for the sale of land provides for instalment payments to be made by the purchaser, and that there is a provision for the forfeiture of payments made by the purchaser. There is support for the application of an equitable principle permitting restitution in respect of the payments made. Thus, in *McDonald v Dennys Lascelles Ltd*[197] Dixon J said that 'in equity such a contract is considered to involve a forfeiture from which the purchaser is entitled to be relieved'. For example, in *Pitt v Curotta*[198] Long Innes J granted the plaintiff relief (on terms) against the forfeiture of moneys (other than the deposit) paid under a contract for the sale of land on the basis that an express provision for forfeiture was in the nature of a penalty. In *Tropical Traders Ltd v Goonan*,[199] the High Court granted a purchaser of land liberty to apply for relief against the forfeiture of instalments paid under a contract for the sale of land where the vendor had terminated performance because the purchaser had failed to comply with an essential time stipulation.[200]

There seems no reason why these cases should not be applied to contracts dealing with goods or services. In *Stockloser v Johnson*[201] a majority of the English Court of Appeal rejected the view that termination is conclusive against a plaintiff unless there is fraud or sharp practice. Denning LJ recognised the possibility that a buyer of goods might be granted relief against an express provision for forfeiture. He said[202] that if the sum in question is in the nature of a penalty and the buyer possesses an 'equity of restitution' because it would be 'unconscionable' for the seller to retain the money, relief will be granted.[203]

[2333] **Deposit payments.** A deposit paid under a void or ineffective contract will usually be recoverable by the plaintiff, on the basis of the intention of the parties or as restitution to reverse an unjust enrichment. For example, if the existence of a binding contract is subject to the

---

195. Cf *P C Developments Pty Ltd v Revell* (1991) 22 NSWLR 615. See also the discussion in [1979], which was more concerned with the prevention of unjust enrichment than its reversal.
196. For the recovery of *unpaid* part payments see [2239].
197. (1933) 48 CLR 457 at 478. Rich and McTiernan JJ agreed. See also (1933) 48 CLR 457 at 470.
198. (1931) 31 SR (NSW) 477, approved *McDonald v Dennys Lascelles Ltd* (1933) 48 CLR 457 at 478 (see also at 470). See also *Steedman v Drinkle* [1916] 1 AC 275; *Berry v Mahony* [1933] VLR 314. But cf *Mussen v Van Dieman's Land Co* [1938] 1 Ch 253 at 265.
199. (1964) 111 CLR 41.
200. For the subsequent proceedings see *Tropical Traders Ltd v Goonan (No 2)* [1965] WAR 174.
201. [1954] 1 QB 476.
202. [1954] 1 QB 476 at 490. Somervell LJ said (at 487–8) that the cases do not support the proposition that in no circumstances can a plaintiff be granted relief unless in a position to show, 'financially', a readiness and willingness and ability to perform. Contrast the narrow view of Romer LJ.

occurrence of an unfulfilled contingency, a deposit paid is recoverable.[204] But the contingency need not relate to formation. For example, in *Clifton v Coffey*[205] the plaintiff agreed to purchase the lease, goodwill and so on, of a hotel partly out of money to be advanced by a brewery company. The company failed to advance any money and the contract was held to be discharged and to that extent was ineffective. There was no default by the plaintiff and the High Court held that he was entitled to recover a deposit which he had paid to the defendant. Similar principles apply where the contract, although valid, is abandoned by the parties.[206] Where the plaintiff has terminated the performance of a contract for breach or repudiation on the part of the defendant, any deposit paid by the plaintiff is recoverable.[207]

There are, however, two situations in which the deposit may not be recoverable. One is where illegality is present, or the ineffectiveness of the contract arises from a statutory provision which forbids restitution of the deposit.[208] The other is where the plaintiff's wrongful conduct caused the contract to be ineffective.[209] Thus, the general approach, where a breach or repudiation on the part of the plaintiff has led to termination by the defendant, is to refuse recovery. The express or implied provision for forfeiture of a conventional deposit, usually 10 per cent, will be respected and the retention of such a sum will not be considered unjust. However, the simple proposition that breach is generally conclusive should not detract attention from some very significant issues created by advance payments made under a contract. Three points are important.[210]

First, as Hale J recognised in *Coates v Sarich*,[211] there is a distinction between payments described as 'deposits' but not subject to any express provision for forfeiture and payments similarly described but subject to an express forfeiture provision. In respect of the former, the question is whether the court should imply a right of forfeiture. The amount of the payment is important in deciding whether the payment was accurately

---

203. See also *O'Dea v Allstates Leasing System (WA) Pty Ltd* (1983) 152 CLR 359 at 392; 45 ALR 632. Cf *Esanda Finance Corp Ltd v Plessnig* (1989) 166 CLR 131 at 151; 84 ALR 99. However, in *Legione v Hateley* (1983) 152 CLR 406 at 443–4; 46 ALR 1, Mason and Deane JJ left open for future decision whether the majority view in *Stockloser* should be accepted by the High Court. See also *Scandinavian Trading Tanker Co AB v Flota Petrolera Ecuatoriana* [1983] 2 AC 694 at 702–3. See further [2333] (deposit payments).
204. See, eg *Masters v Cameron* (1954) 91 CLR 353 (a 'subject to contract' case (see [273])).
205. (1924) 34 CLR 434. See also *Christie v Robinson* (1907) 4 CLR 1338 (contract cancelled).
206. *Summers v The Commonwealth* (1918) 25 CLR 144 (affirmed (1919) 26 CLR 180); *DTR Nominees Pty Ltd v Mona Homes Pty Ltd* (1978) 138 CLR 423; 19 ALR 223.
207. See *Ward v Ellerton* [1927] VLR 494; *Torr v Harpur* (1940) 40 SR (NSW) 585; *Lombok Pty Ltd v Supetina Pty Ltd* (1987) 71 ALR 333. The contrary decision in *Landers v Schmidt* [1983] 1 Qd R 188 relies on the discredited decision in *Hunt v Silk* (1804) 5 East 449; 102 ER 114 (see [2306]) and is incorrect (see *Sibbles v Highfern Pty Ltd* (1987) 164 CLR 214 at 232; 76 ALR 13). Cf *Marsh v Mackay* [1948] St R Qd 113.
208. See [1727].
209. Cf *Duncan v Mell* (1914) 14 SR (NSW) 333. This includes cases where a *Statute of Frauds* provision applies: see [520].
210. For the recovery of *unpaid* deposits see [2239].
211. [1964] WAR 2 at 15.

described. In the latter case, since there is an express forfeiture, the question is whether the court has jurisdiction to grant relief against the forfeiture provision, and the amount of the deposit may be important.

Second, there is support for granting a plaintiff relief against the forfeiture of an 'extravagant' deposit, representing a large part payment for the subject matter of the contract, where the defendant has acted unconscionably in purporting to forfeit what is, in effect, a penalty.[212] The fact that the payment is described as a 'deposit' does not, therefore, preclude the possibility of recovery,[213] although the usual approach has been for the court to permit the defendant to retain out of the deposit an amount which would not be extravagant.[214]

Third, where relief against forfeiture is relevant, it will be necessary to have regard to the particular circumstances of the case. For example, in *Smyth v Jessep*[215] Monahan AJ granted relief against the forfeiture of a deposit which, on one interpretation of the agreement, represented 40 per cent of the purchase money payable under two contracts for the sale of land. Applying Denning LJ's statement in *Stockloser v Johnson*,[216] he said that, tested at the time of the agreement, the sum sought to be forfeited was penal in nature. When the forfeiture provision was invoked there was an 'equity of restitution' operating in the purchaser's favour, by reason of an element of unconscionable conduct. Monahan AJ gave effect to the purchaser's equity of restitution by relieving him from the forfeiture provision. The vendors were protected by an order for damages including, but not confined to, the difference between the net value of the land and the contract price. On the other hand, a sum which looks to be penal may be found, on examination, to be legitimately forfeited. Thus, in *Re Hoobin*[217] O'Bryan J refused relief against forfeiture of a 25 per cent deposit paid under a contract for sale of a hotel freehold. He did not regard the sum as a penalty, since the balance of the price was payable eight years after possession was given, and the contract permitted re-sale by the purchaser. Although sceptical of Denning LJ's statements in *Stockloser*, he added that there was no evidence of unfair conduct.

[2334] **Statute.** The decision whether to make an order for restitution may, as was indicated earlier,[218] be affected by statutory provisions. For example, in *Pavey & Matthews Pty Ltd v Paul*[219] the High Court had to consider whether the statutory prohibition on enforcement of the contract

---

212. *Stockloser v Johnson* [1954] 1 QB 476 at 491. Cf *NLS Pty Ltd v Hughes* (1966) 120 CLR 583 at 588–9. See also *Yardley v Saunders* [1982] WAR 231 at 237.
213. *Coates v Sarich* [1964] WAR 2 at 6, 15. Cf *Palmer v Temple* (1839) 9 Ad & E 508; 112 ER 1304. See also *Union Eagle Ltd v Golden Achievement Ltd* [1997] AC 514 at 518 (if a deposit is described as 'liquidated damages' this does not deprive it of its character as a deposit).
214. Contrast see *Workers Trust & Merchant Bank Ltd v Dojap Investments Ltd* [1993] AC 573 (see Hugh Beale, (1993) 109 *LQR* 524; Charles Harpum, [1993] *CLJ* 389; J W Carter, 'Two Privy Council Cases' (1993) 6 *JCL* 266).
215. [1956] VLR 230.
216. [1954] 1 QB 476 at 490 (see [2332]).
217. [1957] VR 341. See also the more questionable decision in *Coates v Sarich* [1964] WAR 2.
218. See [2304].
219. (1987) 162 CLR 221 (see [2308]).

extended to a claim in the nature of restitution. Although this was treated as purely a matter of statutory interpretation, once a prima facie right to restitution was established, an argument may be made that the scope of the statutory provision was part and parcel of the unjust enrichment analysis, in particular the element of injustice.

Another example, directly relevant to the recovery of deposit payments, is s 55(2A) of the *Conveyancing Act* 1919 (NSW)[220] which provides that in every case where the court 'refuses to grant specific performance' of a contract for the sale of land, or in any proceedings for the return of a deposit, the court may, if it thinks fit, 'order the repayment of any deposit with or without interest thereon'. An order may be made, in the discretion of the court, even if the defendant (vendor under the contract) has exercised a contractual right to forfeit the deposit.[221] The basic issue under the provision is whether it would be 'unjust and inequitable'[222] to permit the defendant to retain the deposit. If, for example, the defendant has been guilty of unconscionable conduct, there is a basis on which the court can exercise its discretion in the plaintiff's favour,[223] because forfeiture of the deposit would unjustly enrich the defendant.[224]

Adjustment and Valuation Issues[225]

General

[2335] Time and basis for valuation. Of the restitutionary claims discussed above, an issue of valuation will arise where the plaintiff is successful in a restitutionary claim based on the defendant's receipt (and retention) of a non-monetary benefit.[226] Unless based on a subsequent realisation of benefit, the appropriate date for valuation of such claims is generally the date of receipt.[227]

The usual description of the basis for valuation is the market or current price of the work done or services rendered in conferring the benefit.[228] This will contain an element of profit. It applies in all cases where the basis for restitution is the defendant's acceptance of benefit.[229] However, in cases of 'incontrovertible benefit', the amount by which the defendant's assets

---

220. See also *Property Law Act* 1958 (Vic), s 49(2).
221. *A A Jones & Son Pty Ltd v Weeden* (1964) 82 WN (Pt 1) (NSW) 326; *Zsadony v Pizer* [1955] VLR 496.
222. *Lucas & Tait (Investments) Pty Ltd v Victoria Securities Ltd* [1973] 2 NSWLR 268 at 272; *Thors v Weekes* (1989) 92 ALR 131 at 145. Cf *Frankcombe v Foster Investments Pty Ltd* [1978] 2 NSWLR 41 at 54. A narrower view may have been taken in *Poort v Development Underwriting (Victoria) Pty Ltd* [1976] VR 779 (affirmed [1977] VR 454).
223. See *A A Jones & Son Pty Ltd v Weeden* (1964) 82 WN (Pt 1) (NSW) 326.
224. But exercise of the court's discretion in the plaintiff's favour does not absolve the plaintiff from liability in damages for breach of contract and the deposit may be set-off against that liability. See *Lucas & Tait (Investments) Pty Ltd v Victoria Securities Ltd* [1973] 2 NSWLR 268.
225. See H O Hunter, 'Measuring the Unjust Enrichment in a Restitution Case' (1989) 12 *Syd LR* 76.
226. See also [2318] (goods).
227. See, eg *Flett v Deniliquin Publishing Co Ltd* [1964–65] NSWR 383 at 386.

are increased is the appropriate measure, unless this exceeds the value of the work done. An example would be the increase in the value of the defendant's land resulting from services rendered.[230]

We deal separately with the most controversial issue in relation to valuation, namely, the relevance of the contract price.[231]

[2336] **Adjustment.** Adjustments required where a restitutionary claim succeeds in relation to a benefit obtained under an ineffective contract are of various kinds.[232] However, they fall into two main categories. First, on the success of either party, it may be necessary to consider the impact on damages claims. For example, in *Baltic Shipping Co v Dillon (The Mikhail Lermontov)*[233] the High Court pointed out that since the plaintiff's damages award included a component representing the loss incurred in paying for a cruise which was cut short due to the defendant's breach of contract, an adjustment would have been necessary had the plaintiff been entitled to restitution of the fare.

Second, adjustment is necessary where the 'price' of rescission of a contract is restitutio in integrum. Whenever a contract is rescinded (or set aside) for a vitiating factor, and the parties are restored to their pre-contractual positions, the *plaintiff* must make restitution.[234] As Isaacs and Rich JJ pointed out in *Brown v Smitt*,[235] '[o]ne condition is always inseparable from rescission — restitution by the plaintiff to the defendant of the property transferred'. Expressed in terms of the unjust enrichment concept, the requirement is one of counter-restitution to ensure that the plaintiff is not unjustly enriched at the defendant's expense.[236] A total failure of consideration need not be established in relation to money paid under the contract, and a merely partial failure may lead to a successful claim in restitution. Under the modern law, the requirement is one of *substantial restitution*. For example, where an order is made for restitution of the price paid under a sale of land contract, substantial restitution will be achieved by orders, for example, that the purchaser pay for benefits obtained by use of the land. More generally, as we saw earlier,[237] rescission of a contract will be ordered (or confirmed) so long as orders for

---

228. See, eg *Flett v Deniliquin Publishing Co Ltd* [1964–65] NSWR 383 at 386; *BP Exploration Co (Libya) Ltd v Hunt (No 2)* [1979] 1 WLR 783 at 805 (affirmed [1983] 2 AC 352). An award on a commission basis may be appropriate where this is customary within the industry. See *Brenner v First Artists' Management Pty Ltd* [1993] 2 VR 221.
229. Gareth Jones, 'Restitutionary Claims for Services Rendered' (1977) 93 *LQR* 273 at 275.
230. See *Van den Berg v Giles* [1979] 2 NZLR 111.
231. See [2337]–[2339].
232. See generally Mason and Carter, *Restitution Law in Australia*, 1995, Chapter 14.
233. (1993) 176 CLR 344 (see [2153], [2321]). See also [2239], [2333] (damages claim against plaintiff granted relief against forfeiture).
234. See, eg *Alati v Kruger* (1955) 94 CLR 216 (see [1045]); *Vadasz v Pioneer Concrete (SA) Pty Ltd* (1995) 184 CLR 102; 130 ALR 570 (see [1045]) and generally [1043]–[1046].
235. (1924) 34 CLR 160 at 168.
236. See *Spence v Crawford* [1939] 3 All ER 271 at 288; *Akron Securities Ltd v Iliffe* (1997) 41 NSWLR 353 at 370; 143 ALR 457. Cf *Maguire v Makaronis* (1997) 188 CLR 449 at 496–7; 144 ALR 729 at 763–4.
237. See [1044], [1045]. See also [1228], [1255]; [1402]; cf [1526].

adjustment do what is practically just between the parties.[238] This means that, where the intervention of the court is necessary to achieve substantial restitution, the *plaintiff* must submit to orders which ensure that the plaintiff is not unjustly enriched.[239]

On the other hand, restitutio in integrum is not a general requirement for valid discharge, because parties are not restored to former positions on discharge,[240] and counter-restitution is not insisted on in this context. There are, however, exceptional cases where substantial restitution does apply. For example, if a contract for the sale of land is discharged, restitution may be claimed in respect of permanent improvements made to the land while the purchaser was in possession[241] even though the improvements were not requested. Again, as Dixon J said in *McDonald v Dennys Lascelles Ltd*,[242] where a plaintiff is granted relief against forfeiture, the plaintiff must submit to equity as a condition of obtaining relief. Terms will therefore be imposed, and although the plaintiff is entitled to restitution, the plaintiff must make restitution to the defendant, so as to achieve substantial restitution.[243] Finally, counter-restitution may be required under statute. An unusual example of this is s 101(1)(g) of the *Goods Act* 1958 (Vic). If a buyer used goods prior to termination by the buyer for breach by the seller in not transferring title, and the seller acted 'honestly and reasonably' in selling the goods, the court may allow the seller to recover from the buyer something for the use of the goods. The justice of this solution is not, however, self-evident. Why should a seller, who is not the owner of the goods, receive payment for use which, so far as the true owner is concerned, was wrongful?[244]

Relevance of Contract Price

[2337] Evidence of value. As a general principle, the contract, or so much of it as was the subject of negotiation, may be referred to when valuing the plaintiff's claim even if the contract was inherently ineffective. It may be relevant as evidence of:

- what was requested;
- the extent to which the performance corresponds to what was in fact requested;[245] and
- the value of the work done or services rendered.[246]

---

238. See *Vadasz v Pioneer Concrete (SA) Pty Ltd* (1995) 184 CLR 102 (see [1045]).
239. See, eg *O'Sullivan v Management Agency and Music Ltd* [1985] QB 428 (see [1402]).
240. See [1982]. For criticism of this perspective see Mason and Carter, *Restitution Law in Australia*, 1995, paras 1305, 2329.
241. See, eg *Rawson v Hobbs* (1961) 107 CLR 466 (see [1982]); *Stern v McArthur* (1988) 165 CLR 489 at 509. Cf *T M Burke Estates Pty Ltd v P J Constructions (Vic) Pty Ltd* [1991] 1 VR 610.
242. (1933) 48 CLR 457 at 478.
243. See also *Lexane Pty Ltd v Highfern Pty Ltd* [1985] 1 Qd R 446 and [2332].
244. The benefit is obtained at the expense of the true owner rather than at the seller's expense. See Peter Birks, 'Restitution after Ineffective Contracts: Issues for the 1990s' (1990) 2 *JCL* 227 at 238.
245. *BP Exploration Co (Libya) Ltd v Hunt (No 2)* [1979] 1 WLR 783 at 805 (affirmed [1983] 2 AC 352).

However, evidence is not restricted to the contract price, and in cases such as *Pavey & Matthews Pty Ltd v Paul*,[247] where the contract price is in terms of 'prevailing' rates of payment, there is no course open, unless the parties have agreed on a value, other than to obtain evidence of the market price.

More controversial is whether the contract price should constitute a ceiling on the plaintiff's recovery. Account must be taken of the basis upon which the contract is found to be ineffective.

[2338] **Unenforceable and void contracts.** Where the restitutionary claim arises from the acceptance of work or services amounting to the full execution of an unenforceable contract, the claim will not be permitted to exceed the contract price. The same is true where the contract is partially performed, although in such cases the plaintiff may be limited to the proportion of the contract price which represents the extent of work done or services rendered. The obvious justification for this is that, usually, unenforceability results from statute, and it would be absurd to suggest that the plaintiff is in a better position where the contract does not comply with the statute than if the statute had been complied with. Thus, in *Pavey & Matthews Pty Ltd v Paul*[248] Deane J said that the contract price is a limit in cases involving executed contracts unenforceable by reason of statute.

Where the contract is void there is less justification for treating the contract price as a limitation, because the negotiations may not have been complete. Indeed, if the reason for voidness may be the failure to agree on price, it would be wrong to say that the plaintiff is limited to whatever sum was discussed during negotiations. But where voidness is due to a factor which does not affect the parties' agreement on price, it may represent the maximum sum recoverable.[249] And, where the contract (although fully negotiated) is void under statute, the price will generally — on policy grounds — constitute a ceiling on recovery.

[2339] **Discharged contracts.** The problem is more acute where the contract is discharged for breach or repudiation. We saw earlier[250] that in cases where the claim is brought against a defendant in breach, the claim in restitution is based on the plaintiff's ability to choose between restitution and damages.

As originally conceived, this was a choice between rescission of the contract (ab initio) and enforcement of the contract in a claim for damages.

---

246. See, eg *Scarisbrick v Parkinson* (1869) 20 LT 175; *Ward v Griffiths Bros Ltd* (1928) 28 SR (NSW) 425; *Way v Latilla* [1937] 3 All ER 759; *Phillips v Ellinson Bros Pty Ltd* (1941) 65 CLR 221 at 246; *Stinchcombe v Thomas* [1957] VR 509 at 513; *Flett v Deniliquin Publishing Co Ltd* [1964–65] NSWR 383 at 386, 388.
247. (1987) 162 CLR 221.
248. (1987) 162 CLR 221 at 257. He excluded rescinded contracts from this statement, presumably on the basis that where a contract is rescinded (for example, for misrepresentation) the contract is treated as never having existed. See also *Scarisbrick v Parkinson* (1869) 20 LT 175; Gareth Jones, 'Restitution: Unjust Enrichment as a Unifying Element in Australia?' (1988) 1 *JCL* 8 at 13.
249. But cf *Rover International Ltd v Cannon Film Sales Ltd* [1989] 1 WLR 912 (see J Beatson, (1989) 105 *LQR* 179; N H Andrews, [1990] *CLJ* 15).
250. See [2323].

Thus, in *De Bernardy v Harding*[251] the plaintiff agreed to sell tickets to view the funeral of the Duke of Wellington. After the plaintiff had spent money in employing clerks and so on, but before any tickets had been sold, the defendant repudiated his obligations. The plaintiff returned the tickets and sued to recover a reasonable sum for the work done and expenses incurred. The court considered that the plaintiff was entitled to recover in restitution for the work actually done, on the basis of rescission ab initio. The same reasoning is found in some Australian cases. For example, in *Brooks Robinson Pty Ltd v Rothfield*[252] the plaintiffs contracted to build a cocktail cabinet and to install it in the defendant's house. After the work had been partially completed the defendant repudiated the contract. The plaintiffs sued to recover the reasonable value of the work completed and the court held that they were entitled to recover on a quantum meruit basis.

The impact is that the contract price is not a limitation, and the plaintiff may therefore recover a substantial sum even if a claim for damages would have resulted in the recovery of a nominal sum. Thus, in *Brooks Robinson*, because the contract was treated as rescinded, it was no answer to such a claim that the contract would have been unprofitable. In coming to this conclusion the court followed *Slowey v Lodder*,[253] where a contractor was there allowed to elect between damages and restitution (on a quantum meruit), after the defendants breached the contract and excluded the contractor from the site, thereby preventing him from completing the work. Although the trial judge refused to award more than a nominal sum as damages, because there was no evidence that the contract would have been profitable, and also rejected the claim for restitution, the Court of Appeal of New Zealand disagreed. The Privy Council affirmed the decision.[254] That the contract must be rescinded (rather than merely discharged) to achieve this result is confirmed by a line of United States cases of which *Boomer v Muir*[255] is the best known. Although the plaintiff's damages claim would have amounted to about $20,000, his suit on a quantum meruit brought him $250,000. This was justified by the view[256] that, as a 'rescinded contract ceases to exist for all purposes', the amount fixed as the contract price was not a restriction on the restitution claim.

It is, however, now absolutely clear that (under Australian law) a plaintiff is not entitled to rescind (rather than terminate) a contract for breach or repudiation.[257] On this basis alone one would have thought that the reasoning in the above cases should now be regarded as erroneous. However, in *Renard Constructions (ME) Pty Ltd v Minister for Public Works*,[258] the New South Wales Court of Appeal held that although a schedule of rates building contract was merely discharged by the

---

251. (1853) 8 Ex 822; 155 ER 1586.
252. [1951] VLR 405 at 409.
253. (1901) 20 NZLR 321.
254. Sub nom *Lodder v Slowey* [1904] AC 442.
255. 24 P 2d 570 (1933). See H O Hunter and J W Carter, 'Quantum Meruit and Building Contracts — Part II' (1990) 2 *JCL* 189; Andrew Kull, 'Restitution as a Remedy for Breach of Contract' (1994) 67 *Southern California Law Review* 1465.
256. 24 P 2d 570 at 577 (1933).
257. See [1904].
258. (1992) 26 NSWLR 234. Special leave to appeal to the High Court was refused: see (1992) 20 Legal Rep SL 1.

contractor, the contract price was not a ceiling on recovery. Accordingly, and notwithstanding that the work was only partially completed, the contractor's award of reasonable remuneration was, when combined with the payments made under the contract, substantially in excess of the contract price. *Slowey* was approved on the basis that it is not open to a defendant in breach of contract to set up the contract price as a term operating in its favour.

For a number of reasons it is suggested that this approach is not satisfactory.[259] To begin with, since the reason why the contract was ineffective — discharge for breach — does not impugn the parties' initial risk allocation, it is impossible to see how the contract price can be ignored. There is, in other words, no justification for allowing the contractor to deny the agreed price as the maximum sum available for the work required under the contract.[260]

Second, the suggestion that a party in breach of contract cannot put forward the terms of the bargain as a defence to the claim is inconsistent with the exclusion clause cases. As we have seen,[261] where a contract is terminated a clause may restrict the plaintiff's non-contractual rights in the same way as it restricts contractual rights.

Third, from the restitutionary perspective, in claims for restitution brought against defendants in breach, there is no real analysis of 'acceptance of benefit'. The receipt of the contractual performance is regarded as a benefit even if 'acceptance' is merely referable to the defendant's obligation to accept a performance complying with the contract. Since this is acceptance under the contract, it is proper to regard the contract as setting a limit on recovery. The position is otherwise, however, if the facts indicate an acceptance which is truly independent of the contract, since in such cases there is a genuine restitutionary liability.

---

259. For a more detailed analysis see Mason and Carter, *Restitution Law in Australia*, 1995, paras 1428–30.
260. See J W Carter, 'Restitution and Contract Risk' in McInnes, ed, *Restitution: Developments in Unjust Enrichment*, 1996, p 137.
261. See, eg [763].

Chapter 24

Specific Performance and Injunction

Specific Performance	**2401**
General	2401
Specific Contracts	2404
Discretionary Factors	2407
Injunction	**2413**
General	2413
Injunction to Restrain a Breach of Contract	2415

Specific Performance[1]

General

[2401] The remedy. In *J C Williamson Ltd v Lukey*[2] Dixon J explained that specific performance, 'in the proper sense, is a remedy to compel the execution in specie of a contract which requires some definite thing to be done before the transaction is complete and the parties' rights are settled and defined in the manner intended'. He had earlier given an illustration by referring to a contract to assure land, where the parties must execute a formal instrument in order to achieve the transfer of legal title to the land. The fact that the defendant is required to execute the contract 'in specie' clearly distinguishes the remedy from damages which are, in most cases, awarded in *substitution for actual performance*.

The expression 'specific performance' is used in a second sense, as can be implied from Dixon J's statement. This describes an order applied to an executed contract, that is, one which is the final expression of the parties for the regulation of their relations,[3] which requires specific performance of obligations under the contract. Although in *Australian Hardwoods Pty Ltd v Commissioner for Railways*[4] the Privy Council did not see any reason why

---

1. See Meagher, Gummow and Lehane, *Equity: Doctrines and Remedies*, 3rd ed, 1992, Chapter 20.
2. (1931) 45 CLR 282 at 297. Cf *McMahon v Ambrose* [1987] VR 817 at 826.
3. *J C Williamson Ltd v Lukey* (1931) 45 CLR 282 at 297.

specific performance in the second sense should be governed by 'principles which are in any way different from those applicable to executory agreements "proper"', the distinction is important.[5]

[2402] Inadequacy of damages. Generally, specific performance is not ordered until a breach of contract has occurred.[6] Since there is a remedy in damages,[7] it is only if that remedy is inadequate to protect the plaintiff that a court will order specific performance. The basis for ordering specific performance of the contract is therefore the inadequacy of a damages award as a remedy.[8] This is the sense in which the expression 'jurisdiction to order specific performance' is used.

For example, if damages are very difficult to assess, or would not do justice between the parties, the court will say that there is a 'jurisdiction' to make the order. Similarly, if there is no contract remedy, for example, because a requirement of writing has not been complied with, part performance of the contract may provide a basis for ordering specific performance.[9]

Given the general need for an enforceable contract with executory obligations, specific performance is not usually available to a plaintiff if the defendant validly terminated the performance of the contract for breach by the plaintiff. However, relief against forfeiture by an order for specific performance is sometimes (but rarely) made notwithstanding the defendant's election to terminate.[10]

[2403] Contracts to which the remedy is applicable. It should not be thought that specific performance, in either of the two senses referred to above,[11] is the usual remedy where a defendant is in breach of contract. There has, however, been a general tendency to enlarge the situations in which the remedy is available.[12] For example, although in *J C Williamson Ltd v Lukey*,[13] Dixon J explained that specific performance is 'inapplicable when the continued supervision of the court is necessary in order to ensure the fulfilment of the contract', the better view is that the concept of continued supervision by the court is no longer an effective or useful criterion for the refusal of specific performance.[14]

---

4. [1961] 1 WLR 425 at 434.
5. See Meagher, Gummow and Lehane, *Equity: Doctrines and Remedies*, 3rd ed, 1992, para 2003.
6. But the order for specific performance will, if necessary, be postponed in its operation to the time of performance under the contract: see *Hasham v Zenab* [1960] AC 316.
7. See generally Chapter 21.
8. *Hewett v Court* (1983) 149 CLR 639 at 665; 46 ALR 87; *Co-operative Insurance Society Ltd v Argyll Stores (Holdings) Ltd* [1998] AC 1 at 11–12, 14; [1997] 2 WLR 898 at 902–3, 905 (see Andrew Phang, (1998) 61 *MLR* 421).
9. See [521]–[524]. But there is no general principle that specific performance can be obtained in respect of unenforceable contracts.
10. See [1979]–[1980].
11. See [2401].
12. See further [2406].
13. (1931) 45 CLR 282 at 297–8.
14. See *Patrick Stevedores Operations No 2 Pty Ltd v Maritime Union of Australia* (1998) 195 CLR 1; 153 ALR 643 (approving *Co-operative Insurance Society Ltd v Argyll Stores (Holdings) Ltd* [1998] AC 1).

Nevertheless, the courts continue to insist, for a variety of reasons, that specific performance is not appropriate in some situations. For example, specific performance of the contract may be impossible, or it may be a futile order because of the defendant's ability, under the contract, to terminate the contractual relationship without notice.[15] Again, because of the element of personal service, specific performance is rarely ordered in respect of a contract of employment.[16] The courts have generally said that for specific performance to be ordered the whole contract must be the subject of the order.[17] Specific performance of part of a severable contract may, however, be ordered if the order relates to a severable part.[18]

There are also discretionary factors to be considered, such as hardship. The ability to refuse relief on the basis of discretion distinguishes equitable relief from damages recovered at common law, where the remedy is not subject to the exercise of a judicial discretion in the plaintiff's favour. One reason specific performance is now more generally available than in the past is a refusal to draw a sharp distinction between discretionary defences, such as hardship, and factors such as an element of personal service in the contract, which have in the past been treated as going to the 'jurisdiction' of the court.

Although, as Windeyer J said in *Coulls v Bagot's Executor and Trustee Co Ltd*,[19] there is no reason today for 'limiting by particular categories, rather than by general principle, the cases in which orders for specific performance will be made', it is appropriate in a book of this nature to consider the remedy in the context of specific types of contracts.

Specific Contracts

[2404] Sale of land. Specific performance has its main application to contracts for the sale of land or an interest in land. Thus, if the defendant has agreed to convey title to a particular parcel of land, but refuses to complete the transaction, the plaintiff will usually be entitled to specific performance. This will include an order that the defendant execute the formal document conveying title or in a form registrable at the land titles office.

The reason that the remedy has its main application to land contracts is historical. Specific performance has been granted on the basis that land is unique, that is, that the purchaser cannot go into the market and buy an equivalent parcel. Damages sufficient to purchase a replacement are therefore not an adequate remedy. In addition, the fact that a binding contract exists between the parties means that the purchaser possesses an

---

15. See, eg *Heppingstone v Stewart* (1910) 12 CLR 126 at 129, 138.
16. See *Byrne v Australian Airlines Ltd* (1995) 185 CLR 410 at 428; 131 ALR 422 at 432 per Brennan CJ, Dawson and Toohey JJ ('save in exceptional circumstances') and further [2420].
17. See, eg *J C Williamson Ltd v Lukey* (1931) 45 CLR 282 at 314.
18. *Wilkinson v Clements* (1872) LR 8 Ch App 96. See also *J C Williamson Ltd v Lukey* (1931) 45 CLR 282 at 294.
19. (1967) 119 CLR 460 at 503. See also *McMahon v Ambrose* [1987] VR 817 at 837 and S M Waddams, 'The Choice of Remedy for Breach of Contract' in Beatson and Friedmann, eds, *Good Faith and Fault in Contract Law*, 1995, p 471.

equitable interest in the land.[20] This is an illustration of what the Privy Council described in *Palmer v Carey*[21] as the 'familiar doctrine of equity that a contract for valuable consideration to transfer or charge a specific subject matter passes a beneficial interest by way of property in that subject matter'. The proprietary interest is coextensive with the purchaser's ability to claim specific performance.[22] Specific performance may therefore be ordered even though the purchaser is a developer, purchasing with a view to profit.[23] Although in such a case it may be difficult to justify saying that the land is unique, damages are still regarded as inadequate.

[2405] Sale of goods. Specific performance of a contract for the sale of goods is the exception rather than the rule, because damages will almost invariably be an adequate remedy for the plaintiff. The position is perhaps clearest where the contract relates to a commodity available on the market. For example, if A agrees to sell 100 tonnes of a particular grade of wheat to B, breach by A can be adequately compensated by an award of damages because B can buy the same quantity from a different seller.

However, the sale of goods legislation does not rule out the possibility of specific performance. Section 56 of the *Sale of Goods Act* 1923 (NSW) states that nothing in the Act affects 'any remedy in equity of the buyer or seller in respect of any breach of a contract of sale'. This includes the (equitable) remedy of specific performance. Section 58 of the *Goods Act* 1958 (Vic)[24] is more explicit. It provides:

> In any action for breach of contract to deliver specific or ascertained goods the court may if it thinks fit on the application of the plaintiff by its judgment direct that the contract shall be performed specifically without giving the defendant the option of retaining the goods on payment of damages. The judgment may be unconditional or upon such terms and conditions as to damages payment of the price and otherwise as to the court may seem just, and the application by the plaintiff may be made at any time before judgment.

The words which restrict the operation of this provision to 'specific or ascertained' goods exclude the commodity contract example referred to above unless the seller has appropriated a particular parcel of wheat to the contract and the buyer has consented to the appropriation.

Specific performance is frequently refused because the goods in question, even though specific or ascertained, have no special value or interest,[25] sometimes on the ground that there is no jurisdiction in respect of ordinary articles of commerce.[26] However, the better view is that expressed by

---

20. See, eg *Legione v Hateley* (1983) 152 CLR 406; 46 ALR 1.
21. (1926) 37 CLR 545 at 548.
22. See *Stern v McArthur* (1988) 165 CLR 489; 81 ALR 463. This includes enforcement by injunction: *Chan v Cresdon Pty Ltd* (1989) 168 CLR 242 at 253; 89 ALR 522.
23. See, eg *Pianta v National Finance & Trustees Ltd* (1964) 180 CLR 146. And note the difference of opinion in *Loan Investment Corp of Australasia v Bonner* [1970] NZLR 724.
24. See also **ACT:** *Sale of Goods Act* 1954, s 55; **NT:** *Sale of Goods Act* 1972, s 56; **Qld:** *Sale of Goods Act* 1896, s 53; **SA:** *Sale of Goods Act* 1895, s 51; **Tas:** *Sale of Goods Act* 1896, s 56; **WA:** *Sale of Goods Act* 1895, s 51.
25. See, eg *Cohen v Roche* [1927] 1 KB 169 at 181.
26. See *Cook v Rodgers* (1946) 46 SR (NSW) 229.

Jacobs J in *Aristoc Industries Pty Ltd v R A Wenham (Builders) Pty Ltd*,[27] namely, that the rarity of the chattel in question is one aspect of the general question of inadequacy of damages. Accordingly, if 'damages at law are an inadequate remedy then there is no principle which will prevent the interference of the court of equity simply because the subject matter is a chattel'.[28]

Dougan v Ley[29] is an illustration. The defendant agreed to sell a licensed taxi-cab registered under the *Transport Act* 1930 (NSW) to the plaintiffs for the sum of £1850. The evidence established not only that the number of licensed taxi-cabs was limited, but also that the number of such vehicles which could be sold was even less because of a statutory restriction on transfer of registration. Roper J's order for specific performance[30] was affirmed by the High Court. Dixon J said that the contract was not, in substance, a simple sale of goods. In fact, the contract was 'for the transfer of a valuable privilege annexed to a chattel'.[31] He pointed out that the greater part of the price which the plaintiffs had agreed to pay was represented by the registration and licence.

[2406] Contracts to pay money. The fact that a contract obliges the plaintiff (or defendant) to pay money does not necessarily preclude the court making an order for specific performance. For example, the remedy is available to a vendor under a contract for the sale of land even if all that remains for performance is the purchaser's obligation to pay money.[32] Outside the sale of land context there has been a certain reluctance to order specific performance in such cases. This can be justified on the basis that there is an adequate remedy under the common law, namely, to recover the sum which the defendant agreed to pay, as a debt due or as damages.[33]

If the remedy at common law is not adequate, there is at least a basis for arguing that specific performance should be available to the plaintiff. For example, the House of Lords found no difficulty in ordering specific performance in *Beswick v Beswick*.[34] Peter Beswick (A) assigned his coal merchant's business to John Beswick (B) in return, among other things, for a promise by B to pay a weekly sum of £5 to A's wife (C), who was not a party to the contract of sale. After A's death B repudiated his obligations and A's wife successfully claimed specific performance in her capacity as A's legal personal representative. It was assumed that on the facts A would have been entitled to nominal damages, but no more, because C was the person who would suffer by B's breach. Accordingly, damages would not have been an adequate remedy for B's breach. Moreover, multiple actions in debt or damages would have been necessary, but were avoided by the order for specific performance. Lord Pearce, who rejected the assumption

---

27. [1965] NSWR 581. Cf *Eximenco Handels AG v Partrederiet Oro Chief (The Oro Chief)* [1983] 2 Lloyd's Rep 509.
28. [1965] NSWR 581 at 588.
29. (1946) 71 CLR 142. See also *ANZ Executors & Trustees Ltd v Humes Ltd* [1990] VR 615 (shares not available on the market).
30. Sub nom *Ley v Dougan* (1945) 63 WN (NSW) 224.
31. See (1946) 71 CLR 142 at 149.
32. *Turner v Bladin* (1951) 82 CLR 463.
33. See *Wight v Haberdan Pty Ltd* [1984] 2 NSWLR 280 at 289. But see [2151].
34. [1968] AC 58 (see [912]).

that damages would have been nominal, considered that specific performance could be justified on the ground that it was the more appropriate remedy. Similarly, in *Coulls v Bagot's Executor and Trustee Co Ltd*[35] Barwick CJ and Windeyer J, in separate judgments, expressed the view that if B promises A, for consideration supplied by A, to pay money to C, then A may obtain specific performance if B defaults.

Beswick v Beswick illustrates that where the plaintiff has fully performed his or her contractual obligations the court will be more willing to order specific performance, to ensure that the plaintiff receives the defendant's performance rather than an inadequate damages award. From a wider perspective the decision suggests that specific performance should be ordered unless there are good reasons for not doing so.[36]

Discretionary Factors

[2407] Readiness and willingness of plaintiff. There is no doubt that the readiness and willingness of the plaintiff to perform the contract, or the existence of a breach on the plaintiff's part, is relevant to the court's decision whether to exercise its discretion in the plaintiff's favour.[37] However, the Privy Council adopted too rigid a stance[38] in *Australian Hardwoods Pty Ltd v Commissioner for Railways*[39] when it stated that the plaintiff must fail if in breach of a term in a contract containing dependent obligations, or not ready and willing to perform where the contract states continuing or future acts to be performed by the plaintiff. As was explained earlier,[40] a plaintiff in breach of a time stipulation is not necessarily precluded from obtaining specific performance by reason of the breach, because of the statutory rule applicable to such terms. Some inquiry must be made into the seriousness of the breach[41] and the extent of any absence of readiness or willingness. The same is true of other types of terms.[42] Thus, generally, if the plaintiff's breach formed the basis for a valid termination by the defendant equitable relief will not be given.[43] The *Australian Hardwoods* case illustrates this as the defendants had there exercised a right to terminate. But to say that a prior breach is necessarily

35. (1967) 119 CLR 460 at 478, 503.
36. Cf *Wight v Haberdan Pty Ltd* [1984] 2 NSWLR 280.
37. For the meaning of readiness and willingness see [1929]. In *King v Poggioli* (1923) 32 CLR 222 the High Court treated an absence of readiness or willingness as conclusive against the plaintiff; but that may, perhaps, be explained on the ground that the plaintiff was not ready and willing at the time of the lower court's order for specific performance.
38. See *Bahr v Nicolay (No 2)* (1988) 164 CLR 604 at 620; 78 ALR 1.
39. [1961] 1 WLR 425 at 432–3. For the distinction between dependent and independent obligations see [1805]–[1808].
40. See [1852].
41. See, eg *Ray v Davies* (1909) 9 CLR 160; *Bahr v Nicolay (No 2)* (1988) 164 CLR 604 at 619.
42. The words or conduct of the defendant may be relevant to the readiness and willingness of the plaintiff; see generally [1947] and, in the context of specific performance, eg *Carpentaria Investments Pty Ltd v Airs* [1972] Qd R 436. On pleading readiness and willingness see *Tsangaris v Gaymark Investments Pty Ltd* (1986) 82 FLR 269 at 285 and [1811]).
43. Subject to the possibility of relief against forfeiture; see [1979].

fatal would deny that the court has any discretion to exercise, and that is inconsistent with the authorities.

Of course, the plaintiff must be ready, willing and able to comply with the order for specific performance. For example, in *Mehmet v Benson*[44] the plaintiff brought an action for the specific performance of a sale of land contract which required the plaintiff to make instalment payments of the price on specified dates. Default on the plaintiff's part took place but the defendant did not immediately exercise his contractual right to terminate for breach. In fact, before the defendant purported to terminate he accepted money on account of the price of the land and this was held to make the election of the defendant ineffective. Because there was no right to terminate, the court held that the plaintiff's breach did not disentitle him to an order for specific performance. So far as the readiness and willingness of the plaintiff to perform was concerned, Barwick CJ said:[45]

> The question as to whether or not the plaintiff has been and is ready and willing to perform the contract is one of substance not to be resolved in any technical or narrow sense. It is important to bear in mind what is the substantial thing for which the parties contract and what on the part of the plaintiff in a suit for specific performance are his essential obligations.

On the facts the defendant would receive the price by virtue of the order for specific performance and the ancillary orders compensated him for loss or damage occasioned by the plaintiff's delay. Accordingly, the court exercised its discretion in the plaintiff's favour.

[2408] **Mutuality.** The question of mutuality of remedy has been the subject of disagreement among text writers.[46] Two questions may arise: first, whether the defendant could have obtained specific performance against the plaintiff; and, second, whether the defendant has a remedy on the contract which can be enforced against the plaintiff if specific performance is ordered. It would be wrong to refuse a plaintiff specific performance just because, had the defendant petitioned for that relief, it would have been refused as a matter of discretion. On the other hand, it would be unfair to order specific performance in favour of a plaintiff if the order would not secure performance by the plaintiff, because that would leave the defendant without adequate compensation in respect of any breach on the plaintiff's part.[47]

Assuming that mutuality becomes relevant to the proceedings a further question may arise, namely, whether mutuality must be present both at the time of the proceedings and at the time the contract was entered into. The better view is that mutuality at the time of suit is sufficient. Thus, in *Dougan v Ley*[48] Williams J said that mutuality was not lacking at the time

---

44. (1965) 113 CLR 295. See also *Bahr v Nicolay (No 2)* (1988) 164 CLR 604 at 621, 640–1, 658–9; *Darter Pty Ltd v Malloy* [1993] 2 Qd R 615 at 621. Cf *Thors v Weekes* (1989) 92 ALR 131 at 144.
45. (1965) 113 CLR 295 at 307. See also *Fullers' Theatres Ltd v Musgrove* (1923) 31 CLR 524 at 550.
46. See Meagher, Gummow and Lehane, *Equity: Doctrines and Remedies*, 3rd ed, 1992, para 2030.
47. See *J C Williamson Ltd v Lukey* (1931) 45 CLR 282 at 298.
48. (1946) 71 CLR 142 at 154. See also *Macaulay v Greater Paramount Theatres Ltd* (1921) 22 SR (NSW) 66; *McMahon v Ambrose* [1987] VR 817 at 849.

the contract was entered into; but 'even if it had been, the better opinion would appear to be that a contract is capable of being specifically performed if, notwithstanding that it was not mutually enforceable at that time, it has become mutually enforceable at the date the suit is instituted'. When the law was considered by the English Court of Appeal in *Price v Strange*,[49] the same conclusion reached. The plaintiff there sought specific performance of an oral agreement for an underlease which the plaintiff conceded would not originally have been amenable to the remedy of specific performance.[50] The plaintiff's obligation was to carry out repair work on the building the subject of the head lease. However, by the time the proceedings were commenced the work had been done (by the defendant) and mutuality was not lacking. The terms of the court's order protected the defendant by requiring the plaintiff to make proper compensation for the work done, on the basis of the actual cost to the defendant. The court also emphasised that lack of mutuality goes to the court's discretion, and is not necessarily fatal to the plaintiff's claim.

It therefore appears that the crucial time for considering whether mutuality is present is the time of the court's order. If mutuality is lacking at that time, the court may refuse relief, even if mutuality was present at the time of the contract or the institution of proceedings.[51] However, the defendant may 'waive' the want of mutuality. For example, where specific performance would not be ordered against a purchaser under a contract for the sale of land because of a defect in the vendor's title, the purchaser may claim specific performance by electing not to rely on the want of mutuality.[52]

[2409] **Delay.** Delay on the plaintiff's part in pursuing a right or remedy is always relevant, and that is true whether the right or remedy is legal or equitable in nature. Principles of election between inconsistent rights or remedies clearly illustrate that point.[53] But the principles governing delay in equity have an independent existence. For example, where an equitable right of rescission arises out of lack of mutuality of remedy under a contract for the sale of land, the purchaser must act promptly in order to avoid a suit for specific performance by the vendor.[54]

More generally, in considering a plaintiff's delay in the context of specific performance, the discretion of the court is exercised according to whether it amounts to 'laches'.[55] In *Fitzgerald v Masters*[56] an action for specific performance of a contract for the sale of land was commenced more than 26 years after the execution of the contract document. That delay was held

---

49. [1978] Ch 337.
50. Cf *Greetings Oxford Koala Hotel Pty Ltd v Oxford Square Investments Pty Ltd* (1989) 18 NSWLR 33.
51. See *E Johnson & Co (Barbados) Ltd v NSR Ltd* [1997] AC 400. See Meagher, Gummow and Lehane, *Equity: Doctrines and Remedies*, 3rd ed, 1992, para 2032.
52. *Halkett v Earl of Dudley* [1907] 1 Ch 590.
53. See [1050], [1971]–[1973].
54. *Halkett v Earl of Dudley* [1907] 1 Ch 590. The right of rescission is conferred by **NSW:** *Conveyancing Act* 1919, s 55; **Qld:** *Property Law Act* 1974, s 69.
55. For the relationship between laches, estoppel and acquiescence see *Orr v Ford* (1989) 167 CLR 316 at 339ff; 84 ALR 146.
56. (1956) 95 CLR 420.

by a majority of the court to disentitle the plaintiff.[57] However, the discussion by the court, and particularly the joint judgment of Dixon CJ and Fullagar J (who dissented) indicates that it is not length of time per se which disentitles a plaintiff. Rather, the court must consider whether, having regard to the delay, it is in the circumstances fair and just to order specific performance.[58] This involves a consideration of whether the defendant can be adequately compensated, as part of the order for specific performance, in respect of any disadvantage caused by the plaintiff's delay. Therefore, apart from considering the length of time, it will be necessary to ask what has actually been done in the period relied upon as constituting laches in order to see whether an element of injustice is present which would not have been present had the proceedings been brought punctually.[59]

[2410] Hardship or unfairness. The presence of hardship to the defendant, and the existence of conduct on the part of the plaintiff which renders it unfair for specific performance to be granted in his or her favour, are factors relevant to the exercise of the court's discretion.[60] It would seem that the matter 'falls to be answered as at the time when the decree would otherwise be made',[61] rather than the time of entry into the contract.

Of course, the mere fact that the contract has turned sour for the defendant is not a basis for refusing specific performance: there must be genuine hardship not just an unprofitable or hard bargain.[62]

[2411] Mistake. The ability of a party to rescind a contract on the ground of mistake was discussed earlier.[63] Clearly, if the contract has been validly rescinded for mistake (or was void) no claim for specific performance will lie. Equally, even if there is no rescission, a court may refuse to order specific performance if there is an element of mistake in relation to the contract.

In *Tamplin v James*[64] Baggallay LJ said:[65]

> It is doubtless well established that a court of equity will refuse specific performance of an agreement when the defendant has entered into it under a mistake, and where injustice would be done to him were performance to be enforced. The most common instances of such refusal on the ground of mistake are cases in which there has been some unintentional misrepresentation on the part of the plaintiff ... or where from the ambiguity of the agreement different meanings have been given to it by the different parties.

---

57. But when regard was had to moratorium legislation, there was no delay of which the defendant could take advantage and so specific performance was ordered.
58. See, eg *Baxton v Kara* [1982] 1 NSWLR 604.
59. See *Carter v Hyde* (1923) 33 CLR 115 at 127.
60. For an illustration of hardship see *Norton v Angus* (1926) 38 CLR 523 (see [2170]). Cf *Demagogue Pty Ltd v Ramensky* (1992) 110 ALR 608 at 622 (impact of misleading or deceptive conduct).
61. *Hewett v Court* (1983) 149 CLR 639 at 664. And see *Patel v Ali* [1984] Ch 283.
62. Cf *ANZ Executors & Trustees Ltd v Humes Ltd* [1990] VR 615.
63. See Chapter 12.
64. (1880) 15 Ch D 215.
65. (1880) 15 Ch D 215 at 217.

A court may exercise its discretion in the defendant's favour irrespective of whether the mistake was common,[66] mutual[67] or unilateral.[68] Therefore, classification of the mistake is not crucial. However, provided specific performance would not cause undue hardship to the defendant, the court will generally order specific performance if the plaintiff did not contribute to the defendant's mistake.[69] Thus, Baggallay LJ said in *Tamplin v James*:[70]

> But where there has been no misrepresentation, and where there is no ambiguity in the terms of the contract, the defendant cannot be allowed to evade the performance of it by the simple statement that he has made a mistake. Were such to be the law the performance of a contract could rarely be enforced upon an unwilling party who was also unscrupulous.

Tamplin v James involved a vendor's action for specific performance. The purchaser resisted on the ground of his mistake as to the identity of the subject matter of the contract. The description and plans of the property being auctioned were unambiguous, and although the purchaser, when bidding, had mistakenly believed that 'The Ship Inn' being auctioned included two pieces of garden ground at the rear of the premises, he was ordered to perform. The case shows that subjective mistake must be accompanied by something else, such as disentitling conduct by the unmistaken party, or the objective circumstances of the case.[71]

Cases where specific performance has been refused even though the defendant's mistake was not known to the plaintiff are commonly cases where specific performance would, in view of the mistake, involve hardship amounting to injustice.[72] Where the defendant's mistake relates to the meaning of the contract the position is, as O'Connor J explained in *Goldsbrough Mort & Co Ltd v Quinn*,[73] that the court 'must be clearly convinced that the party resisting specific performance was in fact mistaken as to the meaning of the contract by which he bound himself'. For example, a clear case of ambiguity in relation to a material term of the contract might be sufficient. The mistake alleged in the *Goldsbrough Mort* case was that the defendant was bound by a contract which required him to sell his land for less than half of that for which he intended to part with it. The court said that this mistake would have been a sufficient ground for the exercise of its discretion in the defendant's favour. But on the facts the defendant could not make out his allegation.

---

66. See, eg *Dell v Beasley* [1959] NZLR 89. And cf *Jones v Clifford* (1876) 3 Ch D 779. Contrast *Jeffries v Fairs* (1876) 4 Ch D 448.
67. See [1237].
68. See, eg *Cochrane v Willis* (1865) 1 Ch App 58; *Jericho v Guglielmin* [1938] SASR 292.
69. *Slee v Warke* (1949) 86 CLR 271. See also *Fragomeni v Fogliani* (1968) 42 ALJR 263.
70. (1880) 15 Ch D 215 at 217–18.
71. Contrast *Denny v Hancock* (1870) LR 6 Ch App 1, where the purchaser succeeded because the plan supplied by the vendors coupled with the physical characteristics of the land had been misleading and had in fact misled the purchaser.
72. See *Goldsbrough Mort & Co Ltd v Quinn* (1910) 10 CLR 674; *Gall v Mitchell* (1924) 35 CLR 222; *Jericho v Guglielmin* [1938] SASR 292; *Slee v Warke* (1949) 86 CLR 271; *Fragomeni v Fogliani* (1968) 42 ALJR 263.
73. (1910) 10 CLR 674 at 687.

[2412] Misrepresentation.[74] As in the case of mistake, rescission for misrepresentation[75] will prevent specific performance being ordered. But, in the context of the court's discretion to refuse specific performance to a plaintiff who has otherwise made out a case for relief, it would seem to be clear that a defendant with no right of rescission may nevertheless be in a position to convince the court that specific performance should not be ordered. It is a question, for the court, of doing justice between the parties, and the existence of the misrepresentation is a material factor against the plaintiff.

Injunction[76]

General

[2413] The remedy. Like the remedy of specific performance, the injunction is a remedy which is equitable in origin and, in the context of contractual disputes, is concerned with securing contractual performance in specie. It is, as Dixon J explained in *J C Williamson Ltd v Lukey*,[77] 'a remedy appropriate to restrain the violation of a provision or term of a contract which is the final expression of the parties' legal relations'.

[2414] Types of injunctions. Injunctions may be classified in various ways.[78] For example, if the injunction is designed to prevent the breach of a negative term of a contract it is 'prohibitory' in character, whereas if it is designed to compel performance of a term it is 'mandatory' in character. Another classification is by reference to time. If granted prior to a breach of contract it is 'quia timet' and distinguishable from an injunction designed to prevent repetition of a breach. If the injunction is intended to last for a limited time it is 'interlocutory', otherwise the injunction is 'final'. A third classification is based on whether the defendant in the action has been served with the plaintiff's initiating process. If the defendant has been served the injunction is granted 'inter partes', if not it is 'ex parte'. Recent developments have given rise to further refinements, for example, in the appearance of the so-called '*Mareva* injunction'.[79]

Injunction to Restrain a Breach of Contract

[2415] Introduction. The context most relevant to this work is where an injunction is granted (issued) to restrain a breach of contract which the defendant has threatened to commit, or the continuance or repetition of a

---

74. See generally Spry, *Equitable Remedies*, 5th ed, 1997, pp 161–73.
75. See generally Chapter 10.
76. See Meagher, Gummow and Lehane, *Equity: Doctrines and Remedies*, 3rd ed, 1992, Chapter 21.
77. (1931) 45 CLR 282 at 298.
78. See Meagher, Gummow and Lehane, *Equity: Doctrines and Remedies*, 3rd ed, 1992, para 2102.
79. See Meagher, Gummow and Lehane, *Equity: Doctrines and Remedies*, 3rd ed, 1992, paras 2185ff.

breach already committed. A convenient starting point is the famous statement of Lord Cairns LC in *Doherty v Allman*:[80]

> [I]f there had been a negative covenant, I apprehend, according to well-settled practice, a court of equity would have had no discretion to exercise. If parties, for valuable consideration, with their eyes open, contract that a particular thing shall not be done, all that a court of equity has to do is to say, by way of injunction, that which the parties have already said by way of covenant, that the thing shall not be done; and in such case the injunction does nothing more than give the sanction of the process of the court to that which already is the contract between the parties. It is not then a question of the balance of convenience or inconvenience, or of the amount of damage or of injury — it is the specific performance, by the court, of that negative bargain which the parties have made, with their eyes open, between themselves. But ... if there be not a negative covenant but only an affirmative covenant, it appears to me that the case admits of a very different construction. I entirely admit that an affirmative covenant may be of such a character that a court of equity, although it cannot enforce affirmatively the performance of the covenant, may, in special cases, interpose to prevent that being done which would be a departure from, and a violation of, the covenant. That is a well-settled and well-known jurisdiction of the court of equity. But in that case ... there appear to me to come in considerations which do not occur in the case of a negative covenant. It may be that a court of equity will see that, by interposing in a case of that kind, in place of leaving the parties to their remedy in damages, it would be doing more harm than it could possibly do good, and there are, as we well know, different matters which the court of equity will, under those circumstances, take into its view.

The present relevance of Lord Cairns' statement lies not so much in its accuracy, for in fact in some respects it is now regarded as inaccurate,[81] as in the way it highlights the pertinent issues, and provides a framework for discussion of those issues.

[2416] Discretion. Lord Cairns' statement in *Doherty v Allman*[82] draws a distinction between negative and positive covenants or terms.[83] It suggests that in the former there is no discretion for the court to exercise. However, as Mason J said in *Dalgety Wine Estates Pty Ltd v Rizzon*,[84] there is 'general agreement' that the statement is 'not accurate'. It may be that discretionary factors do not figure quite so prominently where an injunction is sought to restrain the breach of a negative term, but there is no reason for saying that discretion is never relevant to a negative term but always relevant to other types of terms.[85] The true position is that the court will not grant an injunction where it would, in the circumstances of the case, be 'inequitable'[86] to do so.

---

80. (1878) 3 App Cas 709 at 719–20.
81. See *Curro v Beyond Productions Pty Ltd* (1993) 30 NSWLR 337 at 346–8.
82. (1878) 3 App Cas 709 at 719–20 (see [2415]).
83. See further [2419].
84. (1979) 141 CLR 552 at 573; 26 ALR 355.
85. See, eg *Shaw v Applegate* [1978] 1 All ER 123; *Broken Hill Pty Co Ltd v Hapag-Lloyd Aktiengesellschaft* [1980] 2 NSWLR 572 at 581; *Sanderson Motors (Sales) Pty Ltd v Yorkstar Motors Pty Ltd* [1983] 1 NSWLR 513 at 516. Cf *Hawthorn Football Club Ltd v Harding* [1988] VR 49 at 60 ('residual discretion').
86. See, eg *Measures Bros Ltd v Measures* [1910] 2 Ch 248.

[2417] Position where specific performance not available. Although Lord Cairns in *Doherty v Allman*[87] describes the grant of an injunction as the specific performance of a 'negative bargain', it is clear that an injunction may be obtained even though specific performance of the whole contract is not asked for, or available to the plaintiff. Therefore the rule[88] against specific performance of part of a contract is not infringed. In truth, an injunction to enforce a negative stipulation is at most specific performance in the second of the two senses described earlier.[89]

In many cases where specific performance has been refused injunctive relief has also been refused, on the basis that the unavailability of specific performance implies that no injunction should issue to restrain the defendant's breach. But these are cases in which the injunction would have the same effect as specific performance. Thus, in *J C Williamson Ltd v Lukey*[90] the defendants, lessees of a theatre, granted the plaintiffs the exclusive right to sell sweets and confectionery in the theatre but later repudiated their obligations and granted the right to a third party. The plaintiffs' claim for specific performance was rejected because the contract was not of a type which the court would enforce by that remedy. There would, for example, have been a need for constant supervision by the court. The plaintiffs' claim, to enforce their right to sell sweets and confectionery by means of an injunction restraining the defendants from granting the right to the third party, was refused because it was equivalent to specific performance of the whole contract. Dixon J said[91] it was not possible to order specific performance where the plaintiffs' breach would sound only in damages, and also that the reason for not ordering specific performance 'ought not to be forgotten' when the injunction was considered. The defendants would have been compelled to perform their side of the bargain in specie even though their obligation to perform depended on future performance by the plaintiffs. At best the defendants would have had a remedy in damages.

[2418] Adequacy of damages. Is it true to say, as Lord Cairns did in *Doherty v Allman*,[92] that the adequacy of the plaintiff's remedy in damages is not relevant to the decision to grant an injunction to restrain a breach of contract?

In *Sanderson Motors (Sales) Pty Ltd v Yorkstar Motors Pty Ltd*[93] the plaintiffs sought an injunction to restrain the defendants from terminating a distributorship agreement without cause except in accordance with a contractual provision dealing with termination. In granting the injunction, Yeldham J gave a negative answer to the question formulated by Sachs LJ in *Evans Marshall & Co Ltd v Bertola SA*[94] and which he regarded as expressing the relevance of damages, 'is it just, in all the circumstances, that

---

87. (1878) 3 App Cas 709 at 719–20 (see [2415]).
88. See [2403].
89. See [2401].
90. (1931) 45 CLR 282.
91. (1931) 45 CLR 282 at 298.
92. (1878) 3 App Cas 709 at 719–20 (see [2415]).
93. [1983] 1 NSWLR 513. Contrast *Kurt Keller Pty Ltd v BMW Australia Ltd* [1984] 1 NSWLR 353.
94. [1973] 1 All ER 992 at 1005.

a plaintiff should be confined to his remedy in damages?' Accordingly, in the context of injunction, inadequacy of damages is not so much a basis for jurisdiction as a factor relevant to the justice of the case.

[2419] **Negative and positive duties.** Lord Cairns in *Doherty v Allman*[95] treated the form of the term sought to be enforced by injunction, that is whether it is positive or negative, as crucial. An 'affirmative' term, Lord Cairns said, is enforceable only in 'special cases' and even then subject to a discretion which does not otherwise apply. It is now accepted that it is the substance of the term which matters, not its form.[96] Nevertheless, as Mason J said in *Dalgety Wine Estates Pty Ltd v Rizzon*[97] it is not entirely clear how Lord Cairns' statement should be reformed, the reason being that it is 'quite impossible to formulate an illuminating statement of principle which is capable of universal application'. Mason J went on to explain that the

> attitudes of the courts to the enforcement of negative stipulations has varied according to the nature of the stipulation, the nature of the contract in which it is found, the effect which enforcement will have on the relationship of the parties under the contract and the character of the order required to enforce the stipulation.

In order to decide whether the substance of the term in question is negative in character the court will ask whether mere inactivity on the part of the defendant constitutes performance of the term. For example, in *Administrative and Clerical Officers Association v The Commonwealth*[98] the plaintiffs sought an injunction to restrain the Commonwealth from ceasing its practice of deducting union dues of the plaintiffs' members from the salary, paid by the Commonwealth, except on giving notice. Assuming that the practice was part of a legally binding contract between the plaintiffs and the Commonwealth, Mason J found the substance of the terms relied on to be positive, not negative. This was because inactivity on the part of the Commonwealth would involve a failure to deduct dues from salary and therefore not constitute performance of the term, which required the deduction to be made and to be paid to the plaintiffs. On the other hand, a promise to grant an exclusive licence to the plaintiff naturally implies a negative, that is, not to grant a licence to someone else, which is performed by mere inactivity on the defendant's part.

A positive term may, however, sometimes be enforced by a mandatory injunction, that is, one which requires the performance of a contractual obligation. For example, in *Burns Philp Trust Co Pty Ltd v Kwikasair Freightlines Ltd*[99] the plaintiffs sought an injunction to restrain the defendants from preventing their inspection of a register pursuant to a deed of trust between the parties, one term of which conferred a right to inspect. The Full Court of the Supreme Court of New South Wales held that the plaintiffs were entitled to the injunction sought. The court admitted that the term was primarily affirmative, rather than negative in its nature, but

---

95. (1878) 3 App Cas 709 at 719–20 (see [2415]).
96. See, eg *J C Williamson Ltd v Lukey* (1931) 45 CLR 282 at 299.
97. (1979) 141 CLR 552 at 573.
98. (1979) 26 ALR 497.
99. (1963) 80 WN (NSW) 801.

found that an insufficient reason for refusing the relief claimed. In effect, the court was ordering specific performance of part of the deed, but the term was not of a type to which equity would deny enforcement, by reason of the need for continuous supervision or otherwise. Moreover, damages were not an adequate remedy for the plaintiffs, and the court was not enforcing the principal or substantial part of the deed which would not, as a whole, have been properly the subject of the remedy of specific performance.

[2420] Employment contracts. In *Lumley v Wagner*[100] the plaintiff sought an injunction to restrain the defendant from singing at Covent Garden in breach of a contract which bound her to sing at Her Majesty's Theatre, London, for a period of three months. The contract contained a term which stated that the defendant would not 'use her talents at any other theatre, nor in any concert or reunion, public or private, without the written authorisation' of the plaintiff. Lord St Leonards' decision to grant the injunction has given rise to considerable controversy[101] and led to many subsequent decisions which it is difficult, if not impossible, to reconcile. To a large extent the problem arises because *Lumley v Wagner* itself sits uneasily with equitable principles governing the issue of injunctions.

It might be argued that the court was seized of jurisdiction in *Lumley v Wagner* because of the existence of the negative term and therefore had no option but to issue the injunction. Although that would be in accordance with Lord Cairns' statement of the law in *Doherty v Allman*,[102] it ignores the point that the court will not grant an injunction which is, in effect, specific performance of the contract because an employment contract is not specifically enforceable. In other words, the court should not grant an injunction which requires the defendant to choose between working for the plaintiff and not working at all. In *Lumley v Wagner* the order was not equivalent to specific performance, but it arguably placed the defendant in the position where she could either work for the plaintiff or not sing at all in England. Lord St Leonards denied that he had the power to compel the defendant to sing for the plaintiff, and although the injunction looks to have been strongly coercive in that regard (because she was hardly likely to remain idle or obtain some other form of employment in England) there was nothing to prevent her singing in Europe.[103]

The decision can be contrasted with *Heine Bros (Aust) Pty Ltd v Forrest*[104] where the plaintiffs sought to restrain the defendant, an employee subject to a three-year contract of employment, from breaching the contract. Clause 4 required the defendant to serve the plaintiffs and to 'devote his whole time and attention during usual business hours' to his duties under

---

100. (1852) 1 De G M & G 604; 42 ER 687. See S M Waddams, 'Johanna Wagner and the Rival Opera Houses' (2001) 117 *LQR* 431. See also *Buckenara v Hawthorn Football Club Ltd* [1988] VR 39; *Hawthorn Football Club Ltd v Harding* [1988] VR 49.
101. See Spry, *Equitable Remedies*, 5th ed, 1997, pp 574–606.
102. (1878) 3 App Cas 709 at 719–20 (see [2415]).
103. It is perhaps significant that the contract had less than two months to run when the injunction was granted. See the discussion in *Warren v Mendy* [1989] 1 WLR 853 esp at 865ff (doubting *Warner Bros Pictures Inc v Nelson* [1937] 1 KB 209).
104. [1963] VR 383.

the contract. It went on to state that the defendant should 'not be concerned in any other business' than that of the plaintiffs 'either directly or indirectly, for or on behalf of any other person, firm or company or on his own account or as shareholder, director or officer of any other company, save as a shareholder in a public company listed on a recognised stock exchange, unless the company shall expressly consent or request in writing'. There was no question of enforcing the positive part, but could the court enforce the negative aspect of the term? Dean J concluded[105] that if he prohibited the defendant in the terms of the negative part of the term he would be 'virtually putting him out of work altogether', and held that the injunction should be refused on that ground.

A similar approach is taken where an injunction is sought against a *third party* attempting to induce the employee to breach the contract with the employer. If to restrain the third party would, having regard to the realities of the situation, compel the employee either to work for the employer or to be unemployed, the injunction will not be granted.[106]

The main reason for not granting an injunction to an employer, namely, that the court will not make an order equivalent to specific performance, applies equally where it is the employee who seeks the injunction. Thus, the court will not grant an injunction (or give equivalent relief)[107] to restrain a wrongful dismissal because that would compel the employer to retain the employee's services and be equivalent to specific performance. But in *Hill v C A Parsons & Co Ltd*[108] a majority of the English Court of Appeal did just that. The justification for the decision perhaps lies in the special circumstance that on the facts of the case there was no loss of confidence between the employee and his employers. The defendants had reached an agreement with a trade union to employ only union labour and their dismissal of the plaintiff took place because he refused to join the union. On the other hand, the case may be illustrative of a new approach to wrongful dismissal cases.[109]

---

105. [1963] VR 383 at 386.
106. *Warren v Mendy* [1989] 1 WLR 853.
107. See *Lucy v The Commonwealth* (1923) 33 CLR 229.
108. [1972] 1 Ch 305 (approved *Turner v Australasian Coal and Shale Employees Federation* (1984) 55 ALR 635; see G J McCarry, (1985) 59 *ALJ* 284).
109. See Andrew Stewart, 'New Directions in the Law of Employment Termination' (1989) 1 *Bond LR* 233, which also examines the impact of reinstatement under industrial awards. See also K D Ewing, 'Remedies for Breach of the Contract of Employment' [1993] *CLJ* 405 at 415ff.

Bibliography

Books

Adams, J N and Brownsword, R, *Understanding Contract Law*, Fontana Press, London, 1987.

Amos and Walton's Introduction to French Law, 3rd ed, 1967.

Association of American Law Schools, *Selected Readings on the Law of Contracts*, Macmillan, New York, 1931.

Atiyah, P S, *Consideration in Contracts: a Fundamental Restatement*, ANU Press, Canberra, 1971.

Atiyah, P S, *Essays on Contract*, Clarendon Press, Oxford, 1986.

Atiyah, P S, *An Introduction to the Law of Contract*, 5th ed, Clarendon Press, Oxford, 1995.

Atiyah, P S, *The Rise and Fall of Freedom of Contract*, Clarendon Press, Oxford, 1979.

Balate, E, ed, *Unfair Advertising and Comparative Advertising*, Story-Scientia, Brussels, 1988.

Beale, H, *Remedies for Breach of Contract*, Sweet & Maxwell, London, 1980.

Beatson, J, *Anson's Law of Contract*, 27th ed, Clarendon Press, Oxford, 1998.

Beatson, Jack and Friedmann, Daniel, eds, *Good Faith and Fault in Contract Law*, Clarendon Press, Oxford, 1995.

Benjamin's Sale of Goods, 5th ed, Sweet & Maxwell, London, 1997.

Birks, Peter, *An Introduction to the Law of Restitution*, Clarendon Press, Oxford, 1985.

Birks, Peter, *Restitution — The Future*, Federation Press, Sydney, 1992.

Birks, P B H, *The Frontiers of Liability*, Vol 2, OUP, Oxford, 1994.

Bradbrook, A J and Neave, M A, *Easements and Restrictive Covenants in Australia*, Butterworths, Sydney, 1981.

Brownsword, Roger, Hird, Norma J and Howells, Geraint, eds, *Good Faith in Contract*, Aldershot, Ashgate, 1999.

Bullen, H and Leake, S M, *Precedents of Pleadings*, 3rd ed, Stevens & Sons, London, 1868.

Burrows, Andrew, ed, *Essays on the Law of Restitution*, Clarendon Press, Oxford, 1991.

Butterworth Lectures 1989-90, Butterworths, London, 1990.

Butterworth Lectures 1990–91, Butterworths, London, 1992.

Cane, Peter and Stapleton, Jane, eds, *Essays for Patrick Atiyah*, Clarendon Press, Oxford, 1991.

Carter, J W, *Breach of Contract*, 2nd ed, Law Book Co Ltd, Sydney, 1991.

Carter, J W, *Outline of Contract Law in Australia*, 2nd ed, Butterworths, Sydney, 1994.

Carter, J W, ed, *Rights and Remedies for Breach of Contract*, University of Sydney Law School, Sydney, 1986.

Carter, J W, and D J Harland, *Cases and Materials on Contract Law in Australia*, 3rd ed, Butterworths, Sydney, 1998.

Chen-Wishart, M, *Unconscionable Bargains*, Butterworths, Wellington, 1989.

Cheshire, G C and Fifoot, C H S, *The Law of Contract*, 3rd ed, Butterworths, London, 1952.

Chissick, M, and Kelman, A, *Electronic Commerce: Law and Practice*, Sweet & Maxwell, London, 1999.

Chitty on Contracts, 28th ed, Sweet & Maxwell, London, 2 vols, 1999.

Cohn, E J, *Manual of German Law*, Vol 1, 2nd ed, Oceana Publications, New York, 1968.

Coote, Brian, *Contract — An Underview*, Legal Research Foundation, Auckland, 1995.

Coote, Brian, *Exception Clauses*, Sweet & Maxwell, London, 1964.

Corbin, A L, *Corbin on Contracts*, West Publishing Co, St Paul, 12 vols, 1951–64.

Current Developments in International Transfers of Goods and Services, Butterworths, Singapore, 1994.

Davies, P L, *Gower's Principles of Modern Company Law*, 6th ed, Stevens & Sons, London, 1997.

Deutch, Sinai, *Unfair Contracts — the Doctrine of Unconscionability*, Lexington Books, Lexington, Massachusetts, 1977.

Dorter, J B and Sharkey, J J A, *Building and Construction Contracts in Australia*, 2nd ed, Law Book Co Ltd, Sydney, 1990.

Ewart, J S, *Waiver Distributed*, Harvard University Press, Cambridge Massachusetts, 1917.

Farrands, D J, *The Law of Options*, Law Book Co Ltd, Sydney, 1992.

Fifoot, C H S, *History and Sources of the Common Law*, Stevens & Sons, London, 1949.

Finn, P D, ed, *Essays in Equity*, Law Book Co Ltd, Sydney, 1985.

Finn, P D, ed, *Essays on Contract*, Law Book Co Ltd, Sydney, 1987.

Finn, P D, ed, *Essays on Restitution*, Law Book Co Ltd, Sydney, 1990.

Finn, P D, ed, *Essays on Torts*, Law Book Co Ltd, Sydney, 1989.

Ford, H A J, Austin, R P, and Ramsay, I M, *Ford's Principles of Corporations Law*, 10th ed, Butterworths, Sydney, 2001.

Francis, E A, *Law and Practice Relating to Torrens Title in Australasia*, Butterworths, Sydney, 1973.

Fried, Charles, *Contract as Promise*, Harvard University Press, Cambridge Massachusetts, 1981.

Fuller, L F and Eisenberg, M A, *Basic Contract Law*, 5th ed, West Publishing Co, St Paul, 1990.

Fung, D Y K, *Pre-contractual Liability Rights and Remedies: Restitution and Promissory Estoppel*, Sweet & Maxwell Asia, Selangor, 1999.

Furmston, M P, *Cheshire, Fifoot and Furmston's Law of Contract*, 12th ed, Butterworth & Co, London, 1991.

Furmston, M P, *How Modern is English Contract Law?* Centro di studi e richerche di diritto comparato e straniero, Rome, 2000.

Gilmore, G, *The Death of Contract*, Ohio State University Press, Ohio, 1974.

Halsbury's Laws of Australia, Vol 6, 'Contract', Butterworths, Sydney, 1992.

Halsbury's Laws of England, 4th ed, Vol 9 'Contract', Butterworths, London, 1974.

Harland, D J, *Law of Minors in Relation to Contracts and Property*, Butterworths, Sydney, 1974.

Healey, D and Terry, A, *Misleading and Deceptive Conduct*, CCH, Sydney, 1991.

Hogg, P W, *Liability of the Crown in Australia, New Zealand and the United Kingdom*, 2nd ed, Law Book Co Ltd, Sydney, 1989.

Holmes, O W, *The Common Law*, ed Howe, M De W, Little Brown & Co, Boston, 1963.

Hondius, Ewoud, *Unfair Terms in Consumer Contracts*, Molengraaff Institute for Private Law, Utrecht, 1987.

Honnold, J O, *Uniform Law for International Sales Under the 1980 United Nations Convention*, 2nd ed, Kluwer, Deventer, 1991.

Jones, Gareth, *Anglo-American Trends in Restitution*, Kluwer, Deventer, 1978.

Kercher, B, and Noone, M, *Remedies*, 2nd ed, Law Book Co Ltd, Sydney, 1990.

Laws of Australia, Vol 35, 'Unconscionable Dealing', Law Book Co Ltd, Sydney, 1993.

Lindgren, K E, *Time in the Performance of Contracts*, 2nd ed, Butterworths, Sydney, 1982.

Lockhart, C, *The Law of Misleading or Deceptive Conduct*, Butterworths, Sydney, 1998.

McElroy, R G, and Williams, G L, *Impossibility of Performance*, Cambridge University Press, Cambridge, 1941.

McInnes, Mitchell, ed, *Restitution: Developments in Unjust Enrichment*, LBC Ltd, Sydney, 1996.

McKendrick, Ewan, ed, *Force Majeure and Frustration of Contract*, 2nd ed, Lloyd's of London Press Ltd, London, 1995.

MacNeil, I R, *The New Social Contract; an Inquiry into Modern Contractual Relations*, Yale University, New Haven, Connecticut, 1980.

Maitland, F W, *The Forms of Action at Common Law*, ed Chaytor, A H and Whittaker, W J, Cambridge University Press, Cambridge, 1936.

Mason, Keith and Carter, J W, *Restitution Law in Australia*, Butterworths, Sydney, 1995.

Meagher, R P and Gummow, W M C, *Jacobs' Law of Trusts in Australia*, 6th ed, Butterworths, Sydney, 1997.

Meagher, R P, Gummow, W M C and Lehane, J R F, *Equity: Doctrines and Remedies*, 3rd ed, Butterworths, Sydney, 1992.

Merkin, R, *Privity of Contract*, Lloyd's of London Press, London, 2000.

Murray, J E, *Cases and Materials on Contracts*, Bobbs Merrill Co Inc, New York, 1969.

Norton on Deeds, 2nd ed, 1928.

Nygh P E, *Conflict of Laws in Australia*, 6th ed, Butterworths, Sydney, 1995.

Palmer, N E, *Bailment*, 2nd ed, Law Book Co Ltd, Sydney, 1991.

Parkinson, Patrick, ed, *The Principles of Equity*, LBC Information Services, Sydney, 1996.

Peden, J R, *The Law of Unjust Contracts*, Butterworths, Sydney, 1982.

Pettit, P H, *Equity and the Law of Trusts*, 5th ed, Butterworths, London, 1984.

Phillips, J, Horrigan, B, and Collier, B, *Guarantees and Solicitors' Certificates — Guidelines for Lawyers, Financiers and Guarantors*, QUT, Centre for Commercial and Property Law, Brisbane, 1999.

Pollock, F E and Maitland, F W, *History of English Law Before the Time of Edward I*, 2nd ed, Cambridge University Press, Cambridge, 1968.

Rachagan, S, ed, *Developing Consumer Law in Asia*, University of Malaya, Kuala Lumpur, 1994.

Rawls, J, *A Theory of Justice*, Clarendon Press, Oxford, 1973.

Reich, N and Micklitz, H-W, *Consumer Legislation in the Federal Republic of Germany*, Van Nostrand Reinhold, London, 1981.

Reiter, B J and Swan, John, eds, *Studies in Contract Law*, Butterworth & Co (Canada) Ltd, Toronto, 1980.

Reynolds, F M B, and Davenport, B J, eds, *Bowstead and Reynolds on Agency*, 16th ed, Sweet & Maxwell, London, 1996.

Rose, F D, ed, *Lex Mercatoria: Essays on International Commercial Law in Honour of Francis Reynolds*, LLP, London, 2000.

Rossiter, C J, *Penalties and Forfeiture*, Law Book Co Ltd, Sydney, 1992.

Salmond, J W and Williams, J, *Principles of the Law of Contracts*, 2nd ed, Sweet & Maxwell, London, 1945.

Salmond, J W and Winfield, P H, *Principles of the Law of Contracts*, Sweet & Maxwell, London, 1927.

Schlesinger, R B, ed, *Formation of Contracts*, Oceana, Dobbs Ferry, New York, 1968.

Seddon, N C, *Government Contracts: Federal, State and Local*, 2nd ed, Federation Press, Leichardt, 1999.

Seddon, N C, and Ellinghaus, M P, *Cheshire & Fifoot's Law of Contract*, 7th Aust ed, Butterworths, Sydney, 1997.

Simpson, A W B, *A History of the Common Law of Contract: the Rise of the Action of Assumpsit*, Clarendon Press, Oxford, 1975.

Spry, I C F, *Equitable Remedies*, 5th ed, LBC Information Services, Sydney, 1997.

Starke, J G, *Assignments of Choses in Action in Australia*, Butterworths, Sydney, 1972.

Stonham, R M, *Law of Vendor and Purchaser*, Law Book Co Ltd, Sydney, 1964.

Street, H A, *Ultra Vires*, Sweet & Maxwell, London, 1930.

Street, T A, *Foundations of Legal Liability*, New York, 3 Vols, 1906.

Sutton, K C T, *Consideration Reconsidered*, University of Queensland Press, St Lucia, Qld, 1974.

Sutton, K C T, *Sales and Consumer Law in Australia and New Zealand*, 4th ed, Law Book Co Ltd, Sydney, 1995.

Taperell, G Q, Vermeesch, R B and Harland, D J, *Trade Practices and Consumer Protection*, 3rd ed, Butterworths, Sydney, 1983.

Tilbury, M J, *Civil Remedies*, Butterworths, Sydney, 2 vols, 1990, 1993.

Treitel, G H, *Doctrine and Discretion in the Law of Contract*, Clarendon Press, Oxford, 1981.

Treitel, G H, *The Law of Contract*, 6th ed, Sweet & Maxwell, London, 1983.

Treitel, G H, *The Law of Contract*, 10th ed, Sweet & Maxwell, London, 1999.

Treitel, G H, *Remedies for Breach of Contract*, Clarendon Press, Oxford, 1988.

Turner, Sir A K, *Spencer Bower and Turner on Estoppel by Representation*, 3rd ed, Butterworths, London, 1977.

White, Michael, ed, *Australian Maritime Law*, 2nd ed, Federation Press, Leichardt, 2000.

Williams, G L, *Joint Obligations*, Butterworths, London, 1949.

Williams, G L, *The Law Reform (Frustrated Contracts) Act 1943*, Stevens & Sons Ltd, London, 1944.

Williston, S, *Williston on Contracts*, 3rd ed, ed Jaeger, W H E, Baker Voorhis & Co Inc, New York, 22 vols, 1957–79.

Winfield, Sir P H, ed, *Pollock's Principles of Contract*, 13th ed, Stevens & Sons, London, 1950.

Yates, D, *Exclusion Clauses in Contracts*, 2nd ed, Sweet & Maxwell, London, 1982.

Law Reform Reports

English Law Revision Committee, *Sixth Interim Report*, Cmd 5449, 1937.

Final Report of the Special Committee to Review the Companies Act, New Zealand, 1973.

Forty-first Report of the Law Reform Committee of South Australia Relating to the Contractual Capacity of Infants, 1977.

Ghana Report.

Law Commission, *Law of Contract — Minors' Contracts*, Law Com No 131, 1984.

Law Commission, *The Parol Evidence Rule*, Law Com No 154, 1986.

Law Commission, *Privity of Contract: Contracts for the Benefit of Third Parties*, Law Com No 242, 1996.

Law Commission, *Transfer of Land, The Rule in Bain v Fothergill*, Law Com No 166, 1987.

Law Commission, *Working Paper No 70*, 1976.

Law Reform Committee, *Tenth Report*, Cmd 1782, 1962.

NSW Law Reform Commission, *Barratry, Maintenance and Champerty*, Discussion Paper No 36, 1994.

NSW Law Reform Commission, *Damages for Vendor's Inability to Convey Good Title*, LRC 64, 1990.

NSW Law Reform Commission, *Issues Paper on Sale of Goods*, IP 5, 1988.

NSW Law Reform Commission, *Report on Frustrated Contracts*, LRC 25, 1976.

NSW Law Reform Commission, *Report on Infancy in Relation to Contracts & Property*, LRC 6, 1969.

NSW Law Reform Commission, *Report on Sale of Goods Law*, LRC 51, 1987.

NSW Law Reform Commission, *Representations as to Credit*, LRC 57, 1988.

New Zealand Contracts and Commercial Law Reform Committee, *Report on Misrepresentation and Breach of Contract*, 1967.

Reid Report, *Finding a Balance Towards Fair Trading in Australia*, 1998.

Report of the Cohen Committee, 1945, Cmnd 6659.

Report of the Committee on the Age of Majority ('The Latey Committee Report') 1967, Cmnd 3342.

Report of the Jenkins Committee, 1962, Cmnd 1749.

Tas Law Reform Commission, *Report on Contracts and the Disposition of Property by Minors*, Report No 48, 1987.

Trade Practices Act Review Committee, *Report to the Minister for Business and Consumer Affairs*, 1976.

Trade Practices Commission, *Advertising and Selling*, 2nd ed, TPC, Canberra, 1991.

Bibliography

Trade Practices Commission, *Unconscionable Conduct in Commercial Dealings*, TPC, Canberra, 1993.

Victorian Chief Justice's Law Reform Committee, *Infancy* (No 3) 1970.

Victorian Law Reform Commission, *Sale of Land*, Report No 20, 1989.

WA Law Reform Commission, *Report on Innocent Misrepresentation*, Project No 22, 1973.

WA Law Reform Commission, *Report on Minors' Contracts* (Project No 25, Part 11), 1988.

WA Law Reform Commission, *Report on the Sale of Goods Act 1895*, Project No 89, 1998.

Index

References are to paragraphs

Acceptance see **Offer and Acceptance**
Accord and Satisfaction, 332, 354
Agent
  commission, right to
    implied term and, 628
    wagering and, 1616
  contracts by, 866–873 see also **Corporations**
  privity of contract and, 906
  self-styled, 1242
Agreed Damages see **Liquidated Damages**
Agreed Sum see also **Debt; Price**
  acceleration of, 2202, 2206, 2217, 2231, 2240
  accrued right to, 2225
  characteristics of, 2202
  damages as, 2207–2217 see also **Liquidated Damages**
  deposit as, 2236
  instalments, payable in, 2206, 2232
  nature of, 2204
  price as, 2204, 2205, 2218–2224, 2231 see also **Price**
  recovery of
    election to continue performance, after, 2218–2224
    frustration, after, 2065
    frustration and, 2227
    generally, 2201–2207
    mitigation and, 2137
    restrictions on, 2207, 2221–2224, 2238–2241
      equitable relief as, 2239–2240
      failure of consideration as, 2238
      statute as, 2241
    termination, after, 2210, 2225–2241 see also **Termination**
    time and, 2202, 2226
  White and Carter case, and, 2220, 2221, 2223, 2224
Agreement
  conduct, inferred from, 205
  importance of, 201
  incompleteness, 267
    agreement to negotiate, 271
    discretion as to performance and, 270
    executed contracts in, 269
    generally, 258

    implication of terms and, 268
    negotiate, to, 271
    offer and acceptance test, 202–206 see also **Offer and Acceptance**
  uncertainty
    absence of meaning as, 260
    conditional contracts in, 275
    effect in future, 263
    external standard, 261
    generally, 258
    intention to contract, and, 266
    interpretation, difficulty of, 260
    operation, area of, 265
    reasonableness, and, 262
    'rise and fall' clauses, 264
    severance, 272, 1730
    'subject to contract', 273
    'subject to finance', 274
    upholding of, 259
    Vienna Convention, impact of, 276
Aleatory Contract
  nature of, 1838
  performance of, 1838
Anticipatory Breach see **Breach; Termination**
Arbitration Clause
  nature of, 1936
  public policy and, 1626
  repudiation of, 1936
  Scott v Avery, 1626, 1993
  stay of proceedings, 1626
  termination of contract and, 1993, 1994
Assignment
  'bare' right of action, of, 1629
  choses in action, of, 909
  maintenance and, 1629
  privity of contract and, 909 see also **Privity**
  public policy and, 1629
  vicarious performance and, 1818
Auction, 211, see also **Offer and Acceptance**

Bankruptcy
  composition with creditors, 360
  consideration and, 360, 389
  effect of, 874–876
    post-bankruptcy contracts, on, 876
    pre-bankruptcy contracts, on, 875

Bankruptcy — *continued*
generally, 874
preference void, 1618
Bill of Exchange
anticipatory breach of, 1966
consideration and, 333, 358
deposit, as, 2236
payment by, 1816, 1936
repudiation of, 1936
Breach, 1841–1859
anticipatory
contractual right and, 1935
damages and, 2146–2149, *see also*
Damages
defined, 1841
duty, standard of, and, 1853
meaning of, 1906
apportionment legislation and, 1827
arbitration clause, of, 1626
bad faith performance, by, 1842
consequences of, 1858–1859, *see also*
Termination
co-operation, absence of, by, 2221
deviation, by, 761
duty, standard of, and, 1853–1857
absolute, 1856
'actual' breach, and, 1853
anticipatory breach, and, 1853
care, reasonable, 1854, 1857
determination of, 1855
meaning, 1853
relevance, 1853
strict, 1854, 1856
types of, 1854
failure to perform, by, 1844–1857
anticipatory breach and, 1841, 1929
concept of, 1844
consequences of
damages, right to, 1858
defective performance, 1846
definition, 1841
duty, standard of, and, 1853
commercial contract, in, 1856
construction, based on, 1855
exclusion clause and, 1855
express term, 1855
frustration, doctrine of, and, 1856
implied term, 1855
informal contracts, in, 1855
skill, special, and, 1857
excuse for, 1811
late performance, 1847–1852
termination for, 1948–1964
non-performance, 1845
readiness and willingness and, 1929
repudiation and, 1929, 1947
forms of, 1841
frustration and, 2015, 2045, 2046

fundamental *see also* **Fundamental Breach**; **Terms**
breach of fundamental term as, 755
confusion over, 754
definition, 754
total breach, compared with, 757
generally, 1841–1843
illegality and, 2021
inevitable, concept of, 1933
late performance, by
equitable remedies and, 1849, 1850, 1852
statutory rule, 1851–1852
commercial contract
application to, 1852
common law rule, 1848
statutory rule and, 1851
conflict, law and equity, between, 1850
English approach to, 1852
equitable rule, 1849
statutory rule and, 1851
generally, 1847
option contract and, 1852
traditional approach to, 1852
negligence, by, 2131
onus of proof, 1843
partial, distinguished from total, 757
prospective, problems of, 1935
remedy of, 1927, 1968
termination and, 1968
repetition of, repudiation and, 1938
repudiation, by, 1906
repudiatory, 1908
substantial performance doctrine and, 1832
termination for *see* **Termination**
total, 757
termination for, 1907

Capacity *see* **Bankrupts**; **Corporations**; **Crown**; **Married Women**; **Mental Disability**; **Minors**; **Unincorporated Associations**
Champerty *see* **Maintenance**
Chose in Action
assignment of, 909
debt as, 2226
Collateral Contract
consideration for, 611, 614, 1726
consistency requirement, 613, 614
elements of, 612
evidence of, 711
exclusion clause and, 766
guarantee of trust in, 612
illegality and, 1726
intention and, 612
nature of, 611

References are to paragraphs

Index

pre-contractual statement, based on, 611–614
privity rule and, 614
reliance and, 612
third party, with, 614
types, 611
Compromise *see also* **Consideration**
public policy and, 1626
Condition *see also* **Condition Precedent; Condition Subsequent**
breach of
  damages and, 2159
contingency, where, 730
definition, 727
distinguished from warranty, 726–732
  weaknesses of, 729
goods, sale of, in, 727, 742
important term, as, 726
intermediate term and, 727
'proper' meaning, 730
synonym for 'term', where, 730
term of art, as, 730
termination and *see* **Termination**
types of, 1911
Condition Precedent
distinguished from, condition subsequent, 741
failure, 1824
meaning, 741
pleading of, 741
sale of goods law, 743
term of contract, as, 742
Condition Subsequent
distinguished from condition precedent, 741
meaning, 741
pleading of, 741
term of contract, as, 742
Consideration
accord and satisfaction, 332, 354
act as, 303
adequacy of, 325–327
  nominal, 327
  restraint of trade, where, 1644
  severance and, 1736
  undue influence and, 1414
assumpsit, 305
benefit/detriment, as, 308, 317
bilateral contracts, and, 313
collateral contract, in, 611, 614, 1726
compositions with creditors, 360
compromise, 350–355
  bad claim, 351
  forbearance to sue, 355
  frivolous claim, 353
  honesty and, 352
  identification of consideration, 354
  vexatious claim, 353

condition, and, 303
conditional gift promises, 316
debt, part payment of, 356–360
  deed and, 358
  nominal consideration and, 358
  rule, 356, 357
  third party, by, 359
definition, 307–311
  bargain theory, 309
  benefit as, 308
  conclusion on, 311
  detriment as, 308
  generally, 307
  reason for enforcement as, 312
discharge of contract, and, 388
evidence as, 306
executed, 314, 318, 323, 329–332
  concept, 329
  implied promise and, 331
  request for, 330
executory contracts, in, 311
failure of, 333, 2053, 2054, 2065, 2238, 2306, *see also* **Restitution**
'for' promise, 302, 303, 304
forbearance as, 307–309
form and, 306
illusory, 336–340
  concept of, 336
  discretionary promise, 338
  executory consideration, 337
  promise not to complain, 339
  requirements contract, 340
  uncertain, 339
  vague, 339
intention to create legal relations, 306, 401, 402
legal duty, existing, 332, 341–364
  classes of duty, 341
  contractual, 344–364
    exceptions, 346–348
      content different, 346
      exclusion clause, and, 349
      factual benefit, 348
      termination of contract, 347
      third party, owed to, 349
    generally, 344–345
    promise to exceed, 345
  criticism, 361–364
    business practice, 364
    economic duress, and, 363
  public duties, 342–343
    policy and, 342
    promise to exceed, 343
  rule, 341, 342, 344
legality of, 324
  severance and, 1731
Lord Mansfield and, 306
moral obligation, 306

References are to paragraphs

Consideration — *continued*
motive, and, 315, 329
movement from promisee, 319–322
  joint promisees, 322
  privity, and, 320
  promisor, not to, 321
  rule, 319
necessity of, 301, 302
past, 328–335
  exceptions to, 333–335
    acknowledgment of debt, 334
    bill of exchange, 333
    ratification, 355
  executed consideration and, 329–332
  rule, 328
performance as, 1736
price of promise, as, 307, 309
promissory estoppel, 365–387, *see also* **Estoppel**
reasons for doctrine, 301
referability of, 315–318
  gift promises and, 316
  Woollen Mills case and, 318
sufficiency, 325
tortious liability, 303
unilateral contract, and, 308, 314, 315
variation of contract, and, 389
waiver and, 390–393
  election as, 391
  estoppel as, 392
writing, and, 306
Consumer Protection *see also* **Misleading or Deceptive Conduct** and **Unconscionability**
credit contract, 1617
exclusion clause, 770–772, 1617
Contra Proferentem *see* **Exclusion Clause**
Contract
bilateral, 308
'contract' or 'contracts', 103
'death of', 105
definition, 113
formal, 312
history, 104–107
importance, decline of, 113
intent, 110
role of, 114–116
  business, in, 116
  certainty and, 114
  cost and, 115
  dispute resolution, 115
simple, 312
unilateral, 249, 314
Contract Law
assumptions of, 108–109, 113
'Australian', 117–119
  'flavour' of, 117

innovation, 118
internationalisation, 119
modernisation, 119
content, 104
obligations, law of, and, 107
role of, 114–116
theory of, 110–113
  objective, 110, 206, 1213
  perspectives on, 112
  subjective, 110, 206
  unitary, 106
  will, 110, 111, 206
tort law, and, 107
Contracts Requiring Written Evidence
absence of writing, effect of, 519–524
  common law, at, 519–520
    contract unenforceable, 519
    debt, recovery of, 520
    quantum meruit, 520
    restitutionary claim, 520
    severable promises, 519
  equity, in, 521–524
    part performance doctrine, 521–524
      basis for, 521
      damages claim and, 524
      land, mainly applied to, 524
      payment of money and, 521
      performance of contract, 522
      possession of land and, 521
      referability of acts to contract, 522
      scope of, 524
      specific performance and, 524
      uncertainty of law, 521
bill of exchange, 512
compliance with requirements, 513–518
credit contract, 512
estoppel and, 521, 527
general rule, 501
goods, sale of, 516–518
  'acceptance', 511, 517
  note or memorandum, 516
    alternatives to, 516–518
  payment, earnest, in, 518
  payment, part, 518
hire-purchase, 512
marine insurance, 512
misrepresentation, and, 1005
note or memorandum, 513–515
  authenticated signature fiction, 514
  contents of, 513
  documents, joinder of, 515
  signature, 514
rescission of contract, 526
Statute of Frauds and, 502–512
  administrator, special promises of, 506
  Australian law and, 505
  executor, special promises of, 506
  goods, sale of, 511

Index

'goods', 511
'value', 511
work and materials and, 511
guarantee, contracts of, 507
land, contract involving, 509
legislation, other, and, 512
marriage, contracts in consideration of, 508
one year, contract not to be performed in, 510
purpose of, 502
section 4, 503
section 17, 504
variation of contract, 525
  distinguished from rescission, 526
  estoppel, distinguished from, 527
  forbearance, distinguished from, 527
  manner of performance, and, 527
  mode of performance, and, 527
  test of, 526

Contributory Negligence see **Damages**
Co-promisees see **Plurality of Parties**
Co-promisors see **Plurality of Parties**
Corporations
contracts by, 850
definition, 849
formation and expression of assent, 857–861
  agency principles, 857
  assent, appearance of, 861
  common seal, 858
  company agents, contracts by, 859
    Corporations Law, under, 859, 861
    other corporations, of, 860
  constructive notice, 861
  positive corporate seal rule, 858
pre-incorporation contracts, 862–863
  Corporations Law, under, 873
  general law, under, 862
ultra vires, 851–856
  Australian legislation, 855, 856
    Corporations Law, 856
  chartered companies, 852
  doctrine of, 851
  registered companies, 854
  statutory companies, 853

Crown
agency principles, 873
capacity to contract, 869–873
fettering of discretion, 872
litigant, as, 869
Parliamentary control, 871
procedure, 869
ultra vires, 870

Damages
acceleration of, 2217
accrued right, to, 1989
adequacy of
  condition, breach of, and, 1918
  specific performance and, 2402, 2404, 2406
anticipatory breach, for, 2146–2149, 2161
  date of, 2148
  goods, sale of, in, 2148, 2149
  market prices and, 2149
  mitigation and, 2149
  problems of, 2147
  termination of contract and, 2102
  termination, required for, 2146
assessment of, 2110–2118
  basis of, 2110–2113
    combined claim, 2113
    expectation interest, 2110
    general rule, 2110
    reliance interest, 2111
    restitution, 2112
  date for, 2114–2116
    anticipatory breach, 2148
    'appropriate', 2115
    general rule, 2114
      breach, date of, as, 2114
      exceptions to, 2115
    hearing, at, 2115
    justice and, 2115
    Lord Cairns' Act under, 2172, 2173
  difficulty of, 2117–2118
    bar, no, 2117
    basis for, and, 2118
    chance, loss of, and, 2163
    liquidated damages and, 2215
    speculative claim, where, 2117
award
  accrued rights and, 2161
  contingencies, effect of, on, 2161
  discount of, 2116, 2160, 2168
  method of limiting, 2119
  subsequent events and, 2161
Bain v Fothergill rule in, 2111, 2165–2166
  common law, at, 2165
  exceptions to, 2165
  statute, under, 2165, 2166
bargain, loss of, for, 2110, 2158
breach, confers right to, 1858
building, reinstatement of, by, 2155–2156
  diminished value and, 2155
  intention of plaintiff and, 2156
  mitigation and, 2156
causation and, 2103, 2119–2122
  'but for' test, 2120
  chain of, 2120, 2122
    breaks in, 2122
  concurrent causes, 2121
  connection required, 2120
  contributory negligence, 2129, 2132

References are to paragraphs

Damages — *continued*
  knowledge of parties, 2121
  multiple causes, 2121
  plaintiff and, 2122
  termination and, 2159
chance, loss of, for, 2163–2164
  concept of, 2163
  principles, 2164
compensation principle, 2103
contract and tort compared, 2126
contributory negligence and, 2129–2131
  application of
    negligence, where, 2131, 2132
    strict liability, cases of, 2132
  causation and, 2129, 2132
  concurrent duty and, 2131
  defence, as, 2129, 2131
    generally, 2129
    tort in, 2129, 2130
    statute, under, 2130–2132
      application of, 2129, 2130, 2131
        contract, to, 2129, 2131, 2132
        tort, to, 2129, 2130
      generally, 2129
      'wrong' and, 2129, 2131
debt and, 2201–2206
delay, for, 2150–2151
  generally, 2150
  goods, sale of, in, 2139, 2141, 2151
  Hadley v Baxendale rule in, and, 2151
  liquidated, 2215
  money, payment of, in, 2151
disappointment, for, 2152, 2153
  entertainment contract, 2153
discomfort, for, 2153
distress, mental, for, 2152
equity, in, 2169
exemplary, 2103
expectation, 2110
expenditure and, 2111, 2145
  generally, 2111
  pre-contract, 2145
failure of consideration and, 2238
frustration and, 2063, 2072
general, distinguished from special, 2109
generally, 2101–2118
goods, sale of, in, 2102, 2111, 2112, 2138–2144, 2161
  anticipatory breach, for, 2148, 2149
  buyer, recovery of, by, 2138, 2141–2142, 2143, 2144
  condition, breach of, 2138
  delay, for, 2139, 2141
    acceptance, in, 2139
    delivery, in, 2141
  non-acceptance, for, 1815, 2140, 2143, 2151
  market, availability of, and, 2143
  resale by seller and, 1815
  non-delivery, for, 1845, 2142, 2143
    anticipatory breach and, 2148
    market, availability of, and, 2143
    warranty, breach of, and, 2138
  physical loss and, 2138
  prima facie rules, 2138, 2140, 2141, 2142
  secondhand, 2140, 2143
  seller, recovery of, by, 2139–2140, 2143, 2144
  supply and demand in, 2140
  warranty, breach of, for, 2138
Hadley v Baxendale rule in, 2108–2109
  general damages and, 2109
  limbs of, 2108, 2124–2128
    first, 2108, 2124–2126, 2138, 2140, 2142
    second, 2108, 2127–2128, 2144, 2151
  special damages and, 2109
  stated, 2108
illegality and, 1706
inconvenience, for, 2153
inflation, relevance of, to 2168
injured feelings, for, 2152
Lord Cairns' Act under, 2169–2173
  assessment, date of, 2172
  common law and, 2169, 2171, 2173
  discretion and, 2169
  injunction and, 2169
  specific performance and, 2169, 2170, 2171, 2173
    addition to, in 2169, 2171
    substitution for, in, 2169, 2170
loss, proof of, and, 2105–2107
  identification of, 2107
  nominal, and, 2106
  onus of, 2105
  substantial, and, 2106
misrepresentation, for, *see* **Misrepresentation**
mitigation of, 2133–2137
  anticipatory breach, where, 2149
  benefit obtained and, 2134
  breach and, 2134, 2137
  debt and, 2137, 2201, 2220
  definition, 2133
  duty, 2135
  generally, 2133
  losses and, 2135–2136
    increasing, 2136
    minimising, 2135
  scope of, 2137
money, payment of, and, 2116, 2151
nominal, 2106, 2117, 2118
pain and suffering, for, 2152
performance, method of, and, 2162

Index

primary obligation, breach of, 2101
publicity, loss of, for, 2154
punitive, 2103, 2152
purpose of, 2103–2104
  compensation as, 2103
  contract and tort, in, 2104
reliance, 2111
remoteness of, 2119, 2123–2128
  concept, 2123
  contract and tort, 2104, 2126
  fact, question of, 2123
  Hadley v Baxendale under, 2124–2128
    certainty, degree of, 2124
    criterion for, 2124
    knowledge, special, and, 2127, 2128
    risk of loss, acceptance of, and, 2128
    'usual course of things', 2124–2125, 2126
      foresight and, 2124, 2126
      illustrations, 2125
  termination and, 2159
repudiation and, 2116
reputation, loss of, for, 2154
restitution and, 2112, 2113, 2303, 2323, 2326
right to, 2101–2102
  breach, existence of, and, 2101
  termination of contract and, 2102
secondary obligation, as, 2101, 2326
substantial, 2106
taxation, relevance of, to, 2167
termination, after, 2116, 2146, 2157–2161
  anticipatory breach, and, 2161
  bargain, loss of, and, 2158
  causation and, 2159
  condition, breach of, and, 2159
  contractual right and, 2159
  divested, not, 2157
  essential term, breach of, and, 2159
  frustration, by, 2157
  remoteness and, 2159
  right to, and, 2157
vexation, for, 2152
waiver and, 1972

Debt
damages and, 2201–2206
  distinguished from, 2201, 2220
  illustrations, 2204
  set-off against, 2202
discharge of, 1816
  third party, by, 1818
due, demand for, 1814
illegality and, 1706
liquidated sum, as, 2202
non-payment of, breach and, 2201, 2202
  damages and, 2201
recovery of
  indebitatus assumpsit, by, 2201
  mitigation of loss and, 2201, 2220
  onus of proof and, 2201
  performance, prevention of, and, 2202
  procedural advantages of, 2201
  tender and, 2201
  termination, after, 1989
tender of money and, 1815

Deceit *see* **Misrepresentation**

Deed, 312, 327
severance in, 1731

Dependency of Obligation
severance and, 1736

Deposit *see also* **Restitution**
earnest, payment in, as, 2236
extravagant, 2333
forfeiture of, 2239
forfeiture, relief against, and, 2241
  statute, under, 2334
liquidated sum, as, 2236
option in, 2237
payment of
  breach and, 2237
  existence of contract and, 2237
penalty, as, 2239
possession of, 2237
price, portion of, as, 2236
recovery of, 2236–2237, 2239, 2241, 2333
  basis for, 2236
  cases on, 2237
  forfeiture clause and, 2236
  law, uncertainty of, 2237
security for performance, as, 2236, 2237

Discharge
abandonment, by, 1978
agreement, by, *see* **Consideration**
frustration, by, *see* **Frustration**
termination, by, *see* **Termination**

Duress
economic, 1311–1313
  consideration and, 1313
  payments under compulsion, 1311
effects of, 1302–1306
  basis for, 1303
  causation and, 1305
  'overborne' will and, 1304
  voidable contract, 1302
elements of, 1314–1316
  analysis of, 1315
  consideration and, 1316
  generally, 1314
forms of, 1307–1313
  generally, 1307
  goods, to, 1309
  payment/agreement distinction and, 1310
  person, to, 1308

Duress — *continued*
  generally, 1301
  paradigm case, 1304
  pressure, illegitimacy of, 1317–1323
    bona fides and, 1320
    commercial pressure, as, 1318
    consequences of, 1322
    generally, 1317
    lawful, 1319
    protest and, 1323
    wrongful conduct as, 1321
  proof, burden of, 1306
  remedies for, 1326–1330
    damages as, 1329
    generally, 1326
    rescission as, 1327
    restitution for, 1312, 1328
    statute, under, 1330
  third parties, and, 1324–1325
    against, 1325
    by, 1324
  unconscionability, and, 1301, 1321, 1416, 1509
  undue influence, and, 1301, 1416

Election
  acceptance of repudiation, as, 1945
  breach, continuing, where, 1972
  breach, once and for all, where, 1972
  common law, at, 1970
  communication of, 1970
  consideration and, 390–393
  continue performance, to, 1971, 1972, 2218–2224
    co-operation and, 2221–2222
      active, 2221
      passive, 2222
    finality of, 1972
    legitimate interest to, 2223–2224
      basis of, 2224
      equitable jurisdiction and, 2223
      onus of proof in, 2224
      uncertainty about, 2224
    repudiation and, 1947
    right of, 2218
    specific performance and, 2219
    White and Carter case and, 2220, 2221, 2223, 2224
  contractual provision, under, 1979
  delay in, 1984
  finality of, 1972
  forfeiture and, 1970
  frustration and, 2059
  inconsistent conduct and, 1971, 1973
  knowledge and, 1971
  performance, methods of, between, 1817
  remedies, between, 1971, 1973
  repudiation, and, 1930

  requirement of, 1968
  rights, between, 1971
  specific performance and, 1973
  statute, under, 1970
  terminate, to, 1967–1973
    finality of, 1972
    requirements of, 1970
  termination and continuation, between, 1859, 1967, 1968
  time allowed, 1984
  unequivocal, must be, 1970
  waiver as, 1972

Entire Contracts, 1822–1835
  construction, issue of, 1823
  definition, 1822
  'doctrine' of, 1824
    breach and, 1824
    criticism, 1833–1835
      substantial performance and, 1834
      unjust enrichment and, 1835
    exceptions to, 1827–1835
      statutory, 1827–1829
        apportionment, 1827
        employment contracts, 1828
        frustrated contracts, 1829
      substantial performance, 1830–1835
        basis for, 1834
        condition precedent and, 1832
        effect of, 1831
        origin of law, 1830
        scope of, 1832
        severable contracts and, 1832
        uncertainty of, 1832, 1834
        what constitutes, 1832
  examples of, 1823
  severable contracts and
    defined, 1825
    distinguished from, 1825–1826, 1833
    enforcement of contract and, 1826
  terminology of, 1833

Essential Term *see also* **Terms**
  classification of term as, 743

Estoppel
  assurance, based on, 1976
  common law, at, 382
  detriment, requirement of, 1974, 1975, 1976
  effect of, 1974
  equity, in, 366
  forms, 366
  frustration and, 2059
  generally, 365–370
  illegality, in cases of, 1709
  impact, 365
  knowledge and, 1974
  object of, 367, 1974
  performance, co-operation in, and, 1809
  promise, based on, 1976

Index

promissory, 365–387, 1976
  elements of, 378–382
    detriment as, 380
    express, promise 379
    generally, 378
    implied, promise 379
    reliance as, 380
    representation and, 382, 1976
    unconscionability and, 381
  operation of, 383–387
    American law, under, 387
    assumption, giving effect to, 386
    equity, enforcement of, 385
    generally, 383
    suspension of rights, 384
    termination of rights, 384
  pre-existing legal relation, no, 374–377
    agreed terms, where, 376
    consideration and, 375
    generally, 373
    proprietary interest and, 377
  pre-existing legal relation, where, 371–373
    Australian law, 373
    generally, 371
    Hughes' case and, 372
  remedies for, 383–387
    damages, 385
    equity, enforcement of, 385
  sword, as, 375
proprietary, 366, 377
public policy and, 1733
relevance, 370
reliance and, 368
representation, by, 1974
  clear, must be, 1976
  fact, of, 1975
repudiation and, 1945, 1947
silence and, 1974
termination, right of, as restriction on, 1974, 1975, 1983
unconscionability and, 369, 381, 1983
waiver and, 390–393
Exception Clause *see* **Exclusion Clause**
Exclusion Clause, 748–772
  analogous terms, 748
  benefit of one party only, 748
  contractual intent, destruction of, by, 760
  damages and, 766
  defence to action for breach, as, 749
  definition of duty, as, 749
    standard of, and, 1855
  function of, 749
  generally, 748–749
  incorporation of, 615–619 *see also* **Terms**
  misleading or deceptive conduct, 1122–1124
  misrepresentation, 766, 1123
  operation of, 750–772
    bailment contract, 761, 762
    collateral contract, and, 766
    construction of, 750–768
      basic issue, as, 750
      contra proferentem, 751, 752, 764
      'deviation' cases, 761
      different article, supply of, 758, 759
      Flight v Booth rule in, 759
      'four corners' rule, 762
      fundamental breach, where, 754, 755
      fundamental term, where, 755
      limitation clause, 752
      'main purpose' rule, 760
      negligence, where, 763–764
        construction, issue of, 763
        contra proferentem rule and, 764
        express reference to negligence, 764
        head of damage, relevance to, 764
        liability for, exclusion of
          'all liability', 763
          'any loss', 763
      reasonableness of, 765
      seriousness of breach and, 753–759
      strict liability, where, 764
      termination and, 768
      'total' breach, where, 757, 758
      'wilful' breach, where, 756
    estoppel and, 766
    oral promise, where, 766
    oral representation, where, 766
    rule of law, no, 754, 755, 757
    statute, under, 769–772
      construction and, 770
      consumer contract, where, 772
      fairness and, 771
      forms of control, 769
      goods, sale of, where, 770, 771, 772
      permitted use of, 771
      prohibition of, 770
      scope of, 772
  privity and, 767, 923–926 *see also* **Privity of Contract**
  right to terminate for breach and, 748
  termination of contract and, 1977, 1993, 1995
  statute and, 1995
  traditional approach to, 749
  tripartite classification and, 745
  types, 748
  void, 770, 772, 1617
Exemption Clause *see* **Exclusion Clause**

Forfeiture
  deposit, of, 2236
  provision for, security, as, 1979

Forfeiture — *continued*
  relief against
    acceleration clause and, 2240
    agreed sum and, 2239
    appropriate, when, 1979
    commercial contract, in, 1979
    credit contract and, 2241
    deposit and, 2239, 2241, 2333
    discharge and, 1987
    interest required, 1979
    jurisdiction to grant, 1979, 1980
      inherent, 1979
      statutory, 1837, 1980
    land, in
      lease of, 1837, 1980
      sale of, 1979, 2332, 2333
    liquidated damages, where, 2210, 2217, 2239, 2240
    object of contract and, 1979
    option contract and, 1979
    part payment, 2240
    penalty, of, 2332
    restitution and *see* **Restitution**
    service contract, in, 1979
    'special heads', 1979
    specific performance and, 2240, 2332, 2334
    statute, under, 1978
    termination and, 1979–1980, 2239, 2240
    uncertainty and, 1979
    unconscionability and, 1979
Formalities *see* **Contracts Requiring Written Evidence**
Forms of Action *see also* **Restitution**
  assumpsit, 105
  covenant, 105
  debt, 105
  indebitatus assumpsit, 105
  trespass, 105
Fraud *see* **Misrepresentation**
Freedom of Contract
  conceptions of contract and, 113
  generally, 108, 113
  illegality and, 1619
  restraint of trade and, 1636
Frustration
  absolute contract and, 2003, 2051
  concept of, 2001
  consideration, failure of, and, 2054
    discharge and, 2065
    impossibility of performance, 2053
  construction and, 2006, 2008
  delay, by, 2013, 2025–2027
    assessment of, time for, 2026
    certainty and, 2026
    commercial contract in, 2025, 2026
    criterion of, 2025
    'frustrating' as, 2025
    inference of, 2026, 2027
    prospective, 2027
    repudiation and, 1944
    'unreasonable' as, 2025
  descriptions of, 2001, 2002
  doctrine of, 2001–2037
    basis for, 2049–2056
      consideration, failure of, as, 2053, 2054
      construction as, 2049, 2056
      foundation, disappearance of, as, 2052, 2056
      implied term as, 2050, 2052, 2056
      importance of, 2056
      impossibility as, 2053, 2054
      'just' solution as, 2051
      mistake as, 2055
    generally, 2001–2004
    scope of, 2011–2037
    type of contract and, 2004
  duty, standard of, and, 1856
  effect of, 2057–2098
    common law, at, 2057–2067, 2068
      defects in, 2068
      discharge as, 2058–2061
        automatic, 2058
        delay and, 2058
        election and, 2059
        estoppel and, 2059
        partial, 2060
        suspension of performance, and, 2061
      liabilities, on, 2065
      liquidated sum, on, 2225, 2227
      relevance of, 2057
      rescission, no, 2062
      restitution and, 2066–2067, *see also* **Restitution**
        partial performance, after, 2066
      rights, on, 2062–2065
        damages, to, 2063
        unconditional, 2065
        terms, 2064
    statute, under, 2068–2098
      New South Wales, in, 2069–2078
        apportionment under, 2069
        attributable value and, 2074
        benefits received and, 2073–2074
          'attributable cost' and, 2074
          full performance, 2073
          partial performance, 2074
          'value' of agreed return for, and, 2073
        court, adjustment by, 2078
        damages and, 2072
        discharge and, 2071
        expenditure, wasted, and, 2076

Index

function of, 2078
money paid and, 2075
recovery, basis of, 2077
scope of, 2070
severable contracts, in, 2070
South Australia, in, 2092–2098
  adjustment under, 2095
  application of, 2093
  discharge under, 2094
  discretion under, 2095
  generally, 2092
  recovery, basis of, 2098
  valuation under, 2096–2097
    benefit, 2096
    cost, 2097
Victoria, in, 2079–2091
  benefits obtained, 2083
  discharge and, 2080
  expenses and, 2082, 2084
  insurance and, 2085
  'just sum' and, 2083
  model for, 2079
  money paid and, 2081
  recovery, basis of, 2091
  scope of, 2079, 2088, 2089
  severable contracts, 2090
  terms dealing with, 2087
  third parties and, 2086
evidence of, 2007–2010
  cases, relevance of, 2010
  conduct of parties as, 2009
  construction and, 2008
  event, 2009
  factual matrix and, 2008
  generally, 2007
  purpose of, 2009
  time, relevant, 2009
factual elements, 2006
fault and, 2014, 2043
force majeure and, 2061
foresight of, 2038–2039
  extent of, and, 2039
  general rule of, 2038
  standard of, 2039
illegality as, 2021–2024, 2029, 2060
  enemy, contract with, 2023, 2041
  foundation of contract and, 2024
  generally, 2021
  impossibility and, 2022
  suspension of performance, 2061
  temporary, 2024
impossibility as, 2011–2017, 2029, 2053
  breach and, 2015
  death and, 2015
  illegality and, 2022
  illness as, 2015
  incapacity and, 2015
  performance and, 2016–2017

  burden of, 2017
  method of, 2016
  physical, 2011
  risk and, 2012, 2031, 2033, 2035, 2038
  scope of, 2011
  subject matter of contract and, 2012–2013
    availability of, 2013
    destruction of, 2012
  supply, source of, and, 2014
intermediate term, breach of, and, 1925
land contract, of, 2031–2037
  generally, 2031
  lease, of, 2034–2037
    agreement for, 2034
    Australian law, 2036
    duration of and, 2037
    English law, 2035
    illustrations, 2037
    licence and, 2035
  option contract, 2032
  sale of, 2033
law, conclusion of, as, 2005, 2006
Paradine v Jane rule in, 2003
price, recovery of, after, 1821
purpose, of, 2018–2020
  disappointment and, 2020
  expectations of parties and, 2020
  Krell v Henry and, 2018
  scope of, 2018
  uncontemplated event and, 2019
repudiation and, 1945
risk and, 2020
self-induced, 2014, 2043–2048
  act of party, 2043, 2044, 2045
  both parties, by, 2048
  breach and, 2045
  causation and, 2047
  deliberateness of, 2044, 2045
  discharge and, 2058
  general rule, 2043
  omission by party, 2043, 2044
  onus of proof in, 2046
terms dealing with, 2040–2042
  frustration under, 2042
  public policy and, 2041
  scope of, 2040
war as, 2028–2030
  contract, time of, and, 2030
  declaration of, 2028
  generally, 2028
  illegality and, 2029
  impossibility and, 2029

Fundamental Breach
anticipatory breach, and, 1935
intermediate term, and, 1925
termination for, 1907

References are to paragraphs

Fundamental Term *see also* **Terms**
 breach of, 755
 classification of term as, 743
 distinguished from condition, 743, 755

Gaming *see* **Illegal Contracts**

Good Faith
 breach and, 1842, 1983
 compromise and, 353
 contract to negotiate and, 271
 development of, 113, 1809, 1983, 2317
 performance and, 1809, 1842
 term requiring, 624, 1809, 1842
 termination and, 1983
 unconscionability and, 1503

Goods, sale of, *see* **Sale of Goods**

Illegal Contracts *see also* **Public Policy**
 analysis of, 1602
 betting, 1616
 distinguished from other contracts, 1601
 ex facie, 1621
 gaming, 1616
 generally, 1601–1606, 1607–1610
 inconsistencies in law, 1602
 law, uncertainty of, 1602
 nature of, 1601
 performance of, 1715–1717, 1723
 prohibited by statute, 1607–1615
  commission of offence and, 1609
  consequences, 1614, 1615
  express provisions, 1611–1612
   permission, 1612
   prohibition, 1611
  illegal as formed, where, 1610
  illegal performance, where, 1610
  implied, 1613–1615
   difficulties of, 1612
   object of statute, from, 1613
   penalty, from, 1614
   protection of public, 1613
   public policy and, 1619
   reasonableness of, 1615
   securing the revenue, 1613
  intention and
   legislature, of, 1607
   parties, of, 1607
  meaning of 'statute', 1608
 prosecution, to stifle, 1628, 1718
 rescission of, 1716–1718
 restitution and, 1727–1728
 severance in, 1737
 void by statute, 1616
  against third person, 1618
  credit legislation, 1617
  particular provisions only, 1617
 wagering, 1616
 wrongs, commission of, 1621–1623

Illegality *see also* **Illegal Contracts; Public Policy; Severance**
 breach and, 2021
 common law *see* **Public Policy**
 contract to commit, 1604
 effects of
  cause of action, independent, 1701, 1721–1728
   bailment, 1721, 1723, 1724
   basis of, and, 1704
   Bowmakers principle, 1721–1724
   conversion, 1721, 1723
   detinue, 1724
   goods, sale of, 1721, 1722, 1723, 1725
   hire-purchase contract, 1721, 1723
   property, recovery of, 1721
   restitution as, 1727–1728
   trespass, 1722
  contract, on, 1701
  damages claims, on, 1706
  debt claim for, on, 1706
  equitable relief, on, 1708, 1713, 1714, 1716, 1719
  ex turpi maxim and, 1705–1709
   application of, 1705
   damages, claim for, 1706
   equitable remedies, 1708
   estoppel and, 1709
   meaning of, 1705
   money, recovery of, 1707
   pleading and, 1705
   property, recovery of, 1707
   status of contract and, 1705
  execution of contract and, 1704
  fault and, 1710–1720
   generally, 1710
  generally, 1701–1704
  goods, sale of, on, 1721
  in pari delicto maxim, 1710
   exceptions to, 1711–1720
    knowledge, absence of, 1711
    oppression, 1712
     duress, 1712
     fiduciary relationship, 1714
     fraud, 1712
     mistake, 1713
    statutory, 1720
    protection of public and, 1719, 1720
    repentance from illegality and, 1718
     motive for, 1718
     statutory illegality and, 1718
  knowledge of parties and, 1704
  money, recovery of, on, 1707, 1715, 1720, 1727, 1728
  performance of contract and, 1701, 1715–1718
   frustration of purpose, 1715

Index

in pari delicto maxim and, 1715
   partial, 1716
   purpose not carried out, 1715
policy considerations and, 1703, 1704
prohibition of contract and, 1703
property, recovery of, on, 1707, 1715, 1719, 1721
   goods, in relation to, 1721–1724
   land, in relation to, 1721
property, transfer of, on, 1721, 1722, 1724, 1725
   Bowmakers principle
      Australia, application, in, 1723
   collateral contract, 1726
   restitution, 1727–1728
      money paid, of, 1727, 1728
      quantum meruit claim, 1728
   statute, based on, 1725
remedies, on, 1701, 1702
rights, on, 1701
source of illegality, and, 1704, 1716, 1718
stakeholder, payment to, 1717
status of contract and, 1704
wagering contract, 1616
enforcement of contract, where, 1702
evidence of, 1603
frustration and, 2029, 2060
intention and, 1604
law, uncertainty of, 1702, 1704
penalties for, 1703
pleading of, 1603, 1705
rules governing, 1603–1606
scope of, 2022
statutory, 1605, 1607–1618
   severance and, 1732, 1737
supervening *see* **Frustration**
terminology of, 1702
Impossibility *see* **Frustration**
Infants *see* **Minors**
Inflation *see* **Damages**
Injunction, 2413–2420
breach, to restrain, 2415–2420
   damages, inadequacy of, and, 2418
   discretion and, 2416
   employment contract, in, 2420
   generally, 2415
   negative duty, 2419
   positive duty, 2419
   specific performance and, 2417, 2420
co-operation in performance and, 2222
damages and, 2169–2172
final, 2414
forfeiture, relief against, and, 1979
generally, 2413–2420
illegality of contract and, 1708
interlocutory, 2414
Mareva, 2414

performance, late, and, 1849
prohibitory, 2414
quia timet, 2414
remedy of, 2413
termination of contract and, 1989
third party, against, 2420
types of, 2414
Innominate Term *see* **Intermediate Term**
Intention to Create Legal Relations
advertising puff and, 407
agreement and, 412
commercial agreements, in, 405–408
consideration and, 306, 406, 412
discretion as to performance, 411
domestic agreements, in, 403–404
essential to contract, 401
exclusion of, 406
express, 402
family agreements, in, 403–404
governmental schemes, 409
'honour' clauses and, 406
implied, 402
onus of proof, 405
social agreements, and, 403–404
voluntary associations, rules of, and, 410
Intermediate Term
breach of, termination for, *see* **Termination**
condition/warranty distinction and, 731
criticism, 738
definition, 732
goods, sale of, in, 736
innominate term as, 732
origin of, 731
right to terminate and, 731
seaworthiness term as, 731
Intoxication *see* **Mental Disability**

Liquidated Damages
clause for, purpose of, 2207
extravagant, 2212
forfeiture, relief against, and, 2210, 2217
hire, contract of, in, 2217
hire-purchase, in, 2216
money, failure to pay, for, 2213
penalty, as, 2211
penalty, distinguished from, 2207–2209, 2212–2217
   acceleration clause and, 2217
   basis for, 2208
   breach, payable on, 2216, 2217, 2224
   construction and, 2208
   contractual rights and, 2216
   description by parties, 2209
   factors relevant to, 2212–2215
   defendant's obligation, 2213
   estimating loss, difficulty of, 2215

Liquidated Damages — *continued*
   payment, size of, 2212
   scope of clause, 2213
  forfeiture and, 2217
  onus of proof, 2208
  'present debt' and, 2217
  presumption of, 2214
  scope of, 2216–2217
  time for, 2208
  pre-estimates, as, 2207
  purpose of, 747
  recovery of, 2207–2217
  statute and, 2208
  termination and, 1993, 2210, 2217
   acceleration clause, where, 2217
   effect of, 2210
Lump Sum Contract *see* **Entire Contracts**

Maintenance
  bare right to action, assignment of, as, 1629
  champerty, 1630
  definition, 1629
  modern approach to, 1629
  proprietary interest and, 1629
  public policy, and, 1629–1630
  solicitors, position of, 1630
Married Women
  anti-discrimination legislation, 882
  capacity to contract, 877–882
  common law, at, 877
  equity, in, 878
  legislation, 879, 881, 882
  restraints on anticipation, 880
Mental Disability, 838–848
  awareness of other party, 841
  contracts void or voidable, 842
  equitable approach, 845
  executed and executory contracts, 843
  extent of effect on mind, 840
  mental health legislation, 838
  necessaries, 847
  non est factum, 838
  onus of proof, 848
  ratification, 846
  terminology, 838
  'unfair' contracts, 844
Minors
  classification of contracts, 805
  contracts not for necessaries
   effect of repudiation, 821–822
    adult, on, 822
    minor, on, 821
   repudiation of, 820
   voidable, 817–819
    binding unless repudiated, 818
    not binding unless affirmed, 819

  contractual capacity of, 804
  'degrees' of minority, 807
  fraud of minor, 823
  guarantees of obligations, 826
  incapacity, duration of, 806
  majority, age of, 802–803
  necessaries, contracts for
   beneficial contracts, 813
   benefit overall, 814
   concept of, 809
   employment, 812
   executory, contracts for, 816
   loans for, 815
   services as, 811
   trading contracts, 813
  New South Wales statute
   adjustment where presumptively binding, 834
   affirmation, 831
   background, 827
   beneficial contracts, 829
   'civil acts', 828
   grant of capacity, 830
   'presumptively binding', 828
   repudiation, 832
    adjustment on, 833–836
   tort, liability in, 837
  privilege, personal, 808
  statutory modification, 824
  tort, liability in, 825
Misleading or Deceptive Conduct
  general law, compared with, 1117–1121
   damages and, 1118
   misrepresentation, absence of, 1119
   rescission and, 1120
  generally, 1101
   application of, 1103–1104
    consumers and, 1106
   impact of, 1117
  misrepresentation and, 1101, 1104, 1107, 1108, 1110, 1115, 1117–1120, 1123
  prohibition of, 1101–1110
   breach of contract and, 1109
   conduct prohibited, 1101
   exclusion clauses, 1122–1124
   fair trading legislation, 1102
   financial services, 1103
   generally, 1101
   literal truth and, 1107
   'misleading or deceptive', 1105
   opinions and, 1108
   overall impression and, 1107
   predictions and, 1108
   promises and, 1108
   provisions, relevant, 1101, 1102, 1103
   puffery and, 1107
   silence and, 1110
   trade or commerce, in, required, 1104

References are to paragraphs

Index

Trade Practices Act, 1101
  remedies for, 1111–1116, 1121
    damages, right to, 1112, 1114
      measure of, 1113
    discretionary orders, 1115
      limitation on, 1116
    generally, 1111
    limitation periods, 1113
    persons involved, 1114, 1121
    reliance and, 1112
Misrepresentation
  acknowledgment clause and, 1124
  collateral contract, and, 1001
  common law and equity contrasted, 1003, 1037
  damages for, 1063–1078
    common law, at, 1066–1072
      affirmation, assessment after, 1071
      causation and, 1068
      cause of action, accrual of, 1067
      damage, proof of, 1066
      market value, relevance of, 1070
      measure of, 1069
      remoteness and, 1068
      rescission, assessment after, 1072
      warranty and, 1069
    generally, 1063–1065
      deceit, remedy for, 1063
      equity, and, 1037, 1065
      rescission and, 1064
    statute, under, 1073–1078
      generally, 1073
  definition, 1002
  disclaimer clause and, 1122
  elements of, 1006–1024
    false and factual, 1006–1018
      advertising puff, 1006
      circumstances, change in, 1017
      concealment, fraudulent, 1018
      fact, question of, 1013
      generally, 1006–1007
      intention, statement of and, 1009
      law, not, 1010–1012
      non-disclosure, not, 1014
        duty to disclose, 1015
      opinion, statement of and, 1009
      partially true statement, 1016
      promise, not, 1008
      silence and, 1013–1018
      representor's mind, state of, 1026
    materiality, 1023–1024
      relevance of, 1023
      requirement of, 1023
    reliance by representee, 1019–1022
      fact, question of, 1020
      intention of representor and, 1019
      knowledge and, 1022
      proof, burden of, 1021
      verify, opportunity to, and, 1022
  exclusion of liability for, 766, 1123, *see also* **Exclusion Clause**
  fraudulent, 1023, 1025–1028
    concept of, 1025
    damages for, 1066–1072
    deceit, tort of, 1077
    intention and, 1027
    motive and, 1027
    pleading of, 1028
    proof of, 1028
    representor's mind, state of, 1026
  generally, 1001–1005
  innocent, 1023, 1037–1038
    approach to, 1038
    generally, 1037
  law, of, 1010–1012
    fraud, as, 1012
    private rights, 1011
    rule applicable to, 1010
    status of person, 1011
  legislation and, 1074–1078, 1117–1120
    Australian Capital Territory and South Australia, in, 1074–1078, 1123
      application of, 1074
      damages under, 1075–1078
      defences to, 1078
      measure of, 1077
      nature of, 1077
      rescission, in lieu of, 1075
      right to, 1076
    damages and, 1074–1078, 1118
    exclusion clauses and, 1123
    generally, 1074, 1117
    goods, sale of, 1060–1062 *see also* **Sale of Goods**
  merger clause and, 1124
  misleading or deceptive conduct and, *see* **Misleading or Deceptive Conduct**
  negligent, 1029–1036
    damages, measure of, 1065
    duty of care, 1029
    elements of, 1029
    fiduciary relationship, where, 1032
    foreseeability and, 1031
    Hedley Byrne principle, 1030
    pre-contract misrepresentation as, 1033
    reliance, and, 1034, 1035
    representation as term, 1036
    special relationship, where, 1032
  rescission for, 1039–1062, 1120 and *see* **Rescission**
  specific performance and, 2412
  types of, 1004
  writing, when required, 1005
Mistake
  approaches to, 1205–1209
    common law, at, 1206

Mistake — *continued*
  equity, in, 1207
  generally, 1205
  common, 1214–1232
    generally, 1214
    nature of, 1202
    rescission for, 1226–1232
      equitable fraud and, 1231
      fault and, 1232
      fundamental, 1230
      innocent misrepresentation and, 1206
      justification of, 1228
      modern formulation, 1229
      origins of, 1227
      rectification for, 1207 and *see* **Rectification**
      specific performance, refusal of, 2411
      unconscionability and, 1231
    voidness by, 1215–1225
      failure of consideration and, 1215
      negligence, and, 1217
      reliance on, 1220
      subject matter, absence of, 1215–1220
        goods, 1216, 1217
        land, 1218
        partial, 1219
      subject matter, quality of, 1221–1225
        Bell v Lever Bros and, 1222, 1224
        'chance', where, 1219
        failure of consideration and, 1215
        generally, 1221
        identification of, 1223
        motive and, 1225
      void/voidable distinction, 1226
  factual, 1209
  frustration, and, 1210, 2055
  generally, 1201
  law, of, 1209
  misrepresentation, and, 1211
  mutual, 1233–1237
    nature of, 1203
    rescission for, 1236–1237
      equitable relief for, 1237
      generally, 1236
    specific performance, refusal of, 1235
    voidness by, 1233–1235
      illustrations, 1234
      legal effect as to, 1235
      offer and acceptance and, 1233
  non est factum, 1267–1275 and *see* **Non Est Factum**
  objective theory of contract, 1213
  rectification for, 1256–1266 *see also* **Rectification**
  remedies for, 1208
  specific performance and, 1207, 1237, 2411

  types of, 1202–1204
  unilateral mistake, 1238–1254
    generally, 1238–1239
    mutual mistake and, 1239
    nature of, 1203
    rescission for, 1252–1254
      generally, 1252
      knowledge and, 1253
      unconscionable conduct and, 1254
    voidness, for, 1240–1251
      identity of party, as to, 1240–1248
        Australian cases, 1247
        aversion to dealing with, 1242
        characteristics and, 1244
        distance, at, 1240–1243
        face to face where, 1244–1248
        generally, 1240, 1244
        illustrations, 1245, 1246
        non-existent party, 1243
        offer, acceptance of, and, 1241
        principle, search for, 1248
        self-styled agent, 1242
      terms, as to, 1249–1251
        generally, 1249
        Smith v Hughes and, 1250
        'snapping' at offer, 1251
    warranty, and, 1212
Money
  legal tender, 1815
  payment of, 1816
  tender of, 1815

Negligence
  exclusion clause, and, 763–764, *see also* **Exclusion Clause**
Negotiable Instruments *see also* **Bill of Exchange**
  bet, as payment for, 1616
Non Est Factum, 1267–1275
  blanks, filling in, 1275
  carelessness and, 1273
  character/contents distinction and, 1272
  generally, 1267
  history, 1269
  mental incapacity and, 838, 1268
  proof of, 1271
  Saunders v Anglia Building Society and, 1270
  third party absent, 1274
  undue influence, and, 1415

Offer and Acceptance
  acceptance, 218–241
    additional terms, 222
    alternative offers and, 221
    communication of, 226, 227
    correspondence with offer, 219
    counter-offer, 219, 220, 221

Index

different terms, 222
inertia selling, 228
instantaneous communication, 238
knowledge of offer and
   necessity of, 239
   sufficiency of, 240
method of, 228
necessity of, 218
offeree, must be by, 225
postal rule, 230–237
   application of, 231
   displacement of, 232
   intermediate situations, 234
   justifications for, 235
   'lost in post', 233
   'ordinary course of post', 234
   place of contracting, 236, 238
   time of contracting, 237
   withdrawal by post, 237
qualified, 222
reward cases, in, 241
silence as, 229
tenders, of, 223
unequivocal, 220
withdrawal by post, 237
agreement, traditional test of, 202
'battle of forms', 224
email, 238
limitations on, 203
negotiations, lengthy, 204
offer, 207–217, 242–257
   advertisement as, 208
   alternatives, of, 221
   auction sale, 211
   bait advertising, 215
   communication of, 217
   debenture or shares for, 210
   definition, 207
   duration of, 242–257
      conditional offer, 256
      death of offeror/offeree, 257
   intent, statements of, and, 207
   invitation to treat, 208–215
   land, sale of, 209
   lapse of, 254–255
      period of offer indefinite, 255
      period of offer stated, 254
   multiple, revocation of, 245
   price, statement of, 209
   price lists, and, 208
   prospectus, 210
   public, to, 216
      revocation of, 246
   'puff', 208
   rejection of, 251–253
   revocable, 223
   revocation of, 243
      communication of, 244
      multiple offer, 245
      option contracts, 247
      postal rule inapplicable, 244
      public offer, 246
      unilateral contract, in, 249, 250
   self-service stores, 213
   shares or debentures, 210
   standing, 223
   statutory offences and, 214
   tenders as, 213
   traditional test, as, 202–206

Option Contracts
deposit required by, 2237
enforcement of, 1837
   exercise, time of, 1852
forfeiture of, 1979
   statute and, 1980
frustration of, 2032
juristic nature, 248
leases, in, 1837
performance of, 1837
privilege, species of, as, 1852
revocation of offer, 247

Penalty see **Liquidated Damages**
Performance, 1801–1840 see also **Entire Contract**
aleatory contract, of, 1838
apportionment of
   statute, by, 1827
   terms of contract, by, 1822, 1825
bad faith, in, 1842
bill of exchange, acceptance of, as, 1816
consideration meaning, 1736
co-operation in, 1800, 2221–2222
defective see **Breach**
delay in
   damages for, 2150–2151
   generally, 1847–1852, see also **Breach**
demand for, 1814
discharge by, 1812–1818
   enforcement of contract and, 1819
   exact performance required, 1812
   generally, 1812–1813
   substantial performance, by, 1813
enforcement of contract after, 1819–1838
   aleatory contract, 1838
   entire contracts, 1822–1824
   nature of claim and, 1820
   option contract, 1837
   severable contracts, 1825–1826
   unilateral contract, 1836
frustration and, 2015, 2073
illegal contract, of, 1715, 1718, 1723, 1725
impossibility of see **Frustration**
interruption in, 2039
issues, 1801

References are to paragraphs

Performance — *continued*
late *see* **Breach**
method of, 1814–1818
  alternative, 1817
  damages and, 2162
  express provision, 1818
  frustration and, 2016
  skill, and, 1818
  third party, by, 1818
  vicarious, 1818
order of, 1805–1811
  concurrent, 1808
  construction, depends on, 1802
  co-operation and, 1809
  dependent obligations, 1805, 1807, 1808
  good faith and, 1809
  goods, sale of, in, 1807–1808
  history, 1806
  independent obligations, 1805, 1806
  plea of, implied, 1811
  presumption of, 1808
  prevention of performance and, 1810
partial, restitution and *see* **Restitution**
payment, by, 1816
prevention of, 1810, 2202
refusal of, 1806, 1839, 1937–1938
repudiation and, 1939
substantial *see also* **Entire Contracts**
  doctrine of, 1830–1832, 1834
  unilateral contract and, 1836
suspension of, 1806, 1839, 2061
tender of, 1815
termination of, 1840, 2228 *see also* **Termination**
time of, 1803–1804
  construction, depends on, 1802
  demand, when required, 1814
  express provision, 1803
  reasonable, 1804
  tender of performance and, 1815
withholding of, 1839
Plurality of Parties, 927–930
consideration by, 322, 927, 930
co-promisees, 929
  concept, 927
  consideration moving from one, 930
  joint, 322, 929, 930
  joint and several, 929
  several, 929, 930
co-promisors, 928
  concept, 927
  discharge of, 928
  joint, 928
  joint and several, 928
  several, 928
generally, 927
intention and, 928

release of, 927
Price
conditional payment, as, 2238
reasonable, 2307, 2318
recovery of, 1809, 1820–1834
  acceleration of, 2206
  damages and, 2100
  election, after, 2220–2224
    co-operation and, 2221–2222
  frustration, after, 2065
  goods, sale of, in, 2204, 2206, 2221
    instalments, 2206, 2234
    property, passing of, and, 2204, 2221, 2231
  land, sale of, in, 1808, 2235, *see also* **Termination**
  nature of contract and, 1820
  piecemeal, 2206
  termination and, 1821, 2206
Privity of Contract, 901–926
assignment of rights and, 909, *see also* **Assignment**
benefit third parties, attempts to, 910–912
  damages, 912
  generally, 910
  enforcement by, 912
  performance of contract and, 911
  remedies in favour of, 912
  specific performance and, 912
  variation of contract and, 911
burden third parties, attempts to, 913
  goods, and, 913
  Tulk v Moxhay, 913
collateral contract, and, 614
doctrine, 901–909
exceptions to, 905–909
  agency, 906
  assignment and, 909
  generally, 905
  privity of estate, 908
  trusteeship, 907
exclusion clauses, 767, 923–926
  carriage of goods, 923–926
  Elder Dempster, 923
  The Eurymedon, 925
  Midland Silicones, 924
  The New York Star, 925
  vicarious immunity and, 923
future of, 917–922
  conclusion on, 922
history of, 903
illustrations, 904
legislation, 914–916
  consumers, in favour of, 916
  insurance contracts, 916
  manufacturers' liability, 916
  motor vehicle insurance, 916
  property interest, 914

Index

reform of, 914–916
  recommendation, 915
rule, 901
Trident case, and
  conclusion on, 922
  contractual action, 918
  decision, 917
  dissenting judgments, 921
  impact of, 902, 922
  trust device, revival of, 919
  unjust enrichment and, 920

Promise
condition precedent and, 741
condition subsequent and, 741
contingency, distinguished from, 739–742
  basis for, 739
  confusion between, 742
  similarity between, 740

Promissory Estoppel *see* **Estoppel**

Public Policy
changing face of, 1620, 1632
concept of, 1619
effect of, 1619, *see also* **Illegality**
English decisions, application of, 1619
frustration and, 2041
generally, 1619–1620
heads of, 1620
illegality and, 1606
infringement of, 1621–1653
  administration of justice, prejudice to, 1628–1630
    champerty, 1630
    maintenance, 1629
    private rights and, 1628
    public interest and, 1628
    stifling prosecution, 1628
  corruption in public life, by, 1624
  foreign relations, injury to, by, 1625
  immoral contract, by, 1631, 1632
    current approach to, 1632
    illicit cohabitation, for, 1632
    sexual immorality, limited to, 1631
    sexual services, for, 1632
    statute and, 1632
  marriage, status of, contract prejudicial to, 1633
  ouster of courts' jurisdiction, by, 1626–1627
    arbitration clause, 1626
    certificate of third person, and, 1626
    common law jurisdiction, 1626
    compromise of dispute, and, 1626
    'honour' clause, 1626
    maintenance agreement, 1627
    private right, where, 1627
    public right, where, 1627
    statutory jurisdiction, 1627
    unincorporated association, 1626
  restraint of trade, by, *see* **Restraint of Trade**
  separation agreement, and, 1632, 1633
  trading with the enemy, by, 1625
  wrong, commission of, by, 1621–1623
    common law, 1621
    crime, contract to commit, 1623
    ex facie illegality and, 1622
    intent, requirement of, 1621
    intention of one party, 1622
    knowledge of law and, 1621
    statutory, 1621
      minor offence, where, 1623
    tort, contract to commit, 1623
maintenance agreement, and, 1627
relevant, 1619
restraint of trade, 1619 and *see* **Restraint of Trade**
termination of contract and, 1992, 1994, 1995
test of, 1619

Rectification, 1256–1266
agreement, nature of, and, 1259–1261
  content, must be as to, 1261
  continuing intention, 1259
  document as whole agreement, 1260
  enforceable, need not be, 1261
bars to, 1258
common mistake, where, 1256
evidence of, 722
generally, 1256–1258
  bars to, 1258
  dangers of, 1257
  effect of, 1256
  instruments, correction of, 1256
illegality and, 1708
intention and, 1262–1263
  common, 1259
  proof of, 1262–1263
    manifestation of, 1263
    standard of, 1262
scope of, 1256
unilateral mistake, where, 1264–1266
  equitable fraud, 1265
  knowledge and, 1264
  rescission and, 1266

Repudiation *see also* **Breach**; **Termination**
doctrine of
  'acceptance' and, 1945
  basis for, 1933
  scope of, 1936
frustration and, 1945
retraction of, 1933, 1946
termination for, 1928–1947

Rescission
breach, for, no, 1904

References are to paragraphs

Rescission — *continued*
discharge of duties and, 1985
duress for, 1303, 1325
equitable right of, 1904
frustration and, 2062, 2067
illegal contract, of, 1716–1718
liquidated sum recovery of, and, 2225
misrepresentation, for, 1039–1062, *see also* **Misrepresentation**
    damages and, 1002
    effect of, 1041
    elements of, 1039–1040
        generally, 1039
        unequivocal conduct as, 1040
    frustration and, 2062
    statute and, 1120
mistake, for, *see also* **Mistake**
    frustration and, 2062
    restrictions on, 1255
restitution and, 2322
restrictions on, 1042–1062
    affirmation as, 1047–1051
        conduct and, 1049
        delay and, 1050
        duress, where, 1327
        generally, 1047
        knowledge and, 1048
        scope of, 1051
    execution of contract, as, 1054–1056
        amendment, statute, by, 1056
        fraud, where, 1055
        Seddon's case, rule in, 1054, 1055
    generally, 1042
    goods, sale of, in, 1060–1062, *see also* **Sale of Goods**
    mistake, where, 1255
    representation, incorporation as term, 1057–1059
        amendment, statute, by, 1059
        fraud, where, 1058
        generally, 1057
    restitutio in integrum as, 1043–1046
        common law and equity contrasted, 1044
        illustrations, 1046
        process of, 1043
        rule for, 1045
    third parties' rights, 1052–1053
        generally, 1052
        illustration, 1053
    types of, 1042
termination and, 1981, 1982, 1988
terminology of, 1988

Restitution
action, forms of, and, 2301, 2308
adjustment issues, 2335–2339
    damages and, 2336, 2339
    generally, 2335
    restitutio in integrum, 2306, 2313, 2336
claims for, 2301–2309
consideration, failure of, as basis for, 1728, 2238, 2306
    discharged contract, 2321, 2324
    frustration where, 2067
    illegality and, 1728
    intention and, 2333
    mistake and, 1215
    total, must be, 2067, 2306
contract law, relevance of, 2303
damages and, 2112
debt and, 2301, 2305, 2307
deposit, of, 2333, 2334
discharge of contract, sufficient and, 1991, 2067, 2301, 2336
duress for, 1312, 1313, 1328
forfeiture, relief against, as, 2331–2333, 2334
    deposits and, 2333
    land, sale of, in, 2332
    relevance of, 2331
    statute, under, 2334
frustration after, 2066–2098 *see also* **Frustration**
generally, 2301–2304
illegality, where, 1707, 1715, 1716, 1727–1728
implied contract and, 2301, 2307
implied term and, 2307
ineffective contract, in, 520, 2303, 2305, 2306, 2307, 2314
inherently ineffective contract, in, 2316–2319
    failure to materialise, 2317
    generally, 2316
    goods and, 2318
    money, recovery of, 2318
    services rendered under, 2317, 2318
    unenforceable, 2319
    void, 2318
justice and, 2301
liquidated sum and, 2202, 2237
nature of, 2302
partially performed contract, under, 2320–2325
    benefit, absence of, and, 2323
    breach and, 2321–2325
        defendant, by, 2324–2325
        plaintiff, by, 2321–2323
    entire contracts and, 1824
    frustration and, 2066, 2067, 2304, 2306
    generally, 2320
    illegality and, 1728
    quantum meruit claim, 2305, 2322, 2323, 2325, 2339

quasi–contract and, 2305–2307
  common counts, 2305
  consideration, total failure of, and, 2306
  indebitatus assumpsit, based on, 2301, 2307
  quantum meruit, 2307
  quantum valebat, 2066, 2307
reliance and, 2315
rescission of contract and, 1991, 2067, 2306, 2336
statute, based on, 2304, 2334
  frustrated contracts legislation, 2069–2098, *see also* **Frustration**
substantial, 2336
unjust enrichment, based on, 2301, 2308–2309 *see also* **Unjust Enrichment**
valuation issues, 2335–2339
  adjustment and, 2336
  basis for, 2335
  contract price, relevance of, 2337–2339
    ceiling, as, 2339
    discharged contract, 2339
    evidence, as 2337
    unenforceable contract, 2338
    unprofitable contract and, 2339
    void contract, 2338
  damages and, 2336, 2339
  generally, 2335
  price, reasonable, and, 2307, 2318
  time for, 2335
wrong, for, 2327–2329
  breach of contract as, 2329
  fiduciary duty and, 2328
  tort, waiver of, 2327

Restraint of Trade
covenantee, meaning of, 1634
covenantor, meaning of, 1634
definition, 1634
doctrine
  personal restraints, not limited to, 1638
  scope of, 1637, 1638
enforceability of, 1636
examples, 1634
exclusive service contract, where, 1637
existence of, 1637
generally, 1634–1641
justification of, 1636
  accepted standards and, 1638
  business, sale of, in, 1636, 1642, 1644, 1647
  commercial contract, in, 1652
  employment contract, in, 1636, 1643, 1648
    illustrations, 1649
  exclusive dealing contract, in, 1652
  exclusive service contract, in, 1653
  fiduciary relationship, where, 1651

nature of contract and, 1636
onus of proof, 1639
partnership deed, in, 1650, 1651
  business, sale of, compared with, 1650, 1651
  generally, 1650
  solicitors, between, 1651
protectable interests, 1642
  confidential information, 1642
  economies of trade, 1642, 1653
  goodwill, 1642, 1647
  property, not limited to, 1642
  trade secrets, 1642
public interest and, 1636, 1640, 1651, 1655
reasonableness
  advantage to individual and, 1640, 1651
  construction of contract and, 1649
  economic theory and, 1644
  intention and, 1641
  particular contracts, in, 1647–1653
  relevant factors, 1642–1646
    bargaining position, 1646
    benefits to parties, 1644
    consideration, quantum of, 1644, 1651
    duration of restraint, 1643, 1647, 1651
      unlimited, 1643
    employment contract, in, 1648
    interest of covenantee, 1642
    scope of restraint, 1643, 1647, 1649, 1650, 1651
      world–wide, where, 1647
    termination of contract and, 1643
    unconscionability, 1645
  time of inquiry, 1641
  two questions, 1640
  unfair bargain, where, 1653
  'solus' agreement, in, 1652
land, sale of, where, 1638
lease of land, where, 1638
mortgage of land, where, 1638
non-contractual, 1634
popular sense of, 1634
practical working of contract and, 1637
pre-existing freedom, need for, 1637
prima facie rule, 1635
safety standards and, 1656
severance, 1731, 1733, 1734, 1735, 1737, 1738–1739
  statutory, 1738–1739
statutory control of, 1654
statutory penalty for, 1656
termination of contract and, 1994
Trade Practices Act and, 1654–1656
  common law, contrast with, 1655

Restraint of Trade — *continued*
   contravention of, 1656
   generally, 1654
   remedies under, 1656
   'unfair practices' and, 1654
  void or unenforceable, 1692

Sale of Goods *see also* **Damages**
  implied terms in, 637–641
  misrepresentation and, 1060–1062
   equitable rules and, 1061
   goods, acceptance of, and, 1062
   issues, 1060
  mistake and, 1216
  repudiation of, 1938

Severance
  associated transaction, of, 1732–1733
   illegal contract, 1732
   restraint of trade, contract in, 1731, 1733, 1734, 1735
  bailment contract, in, 1737
  common law, at, 1732–1737
   defects of, 1738
  court, powers of, 1734
   'blue pencil' test, 1735
  deed, 1731, 1739
  factors relevant to, 1731
  forms of, 1729
  generally, 1729–1731
  illegality and, 1729–1739
  intention and, 1730, 1735
  land, lease of, and, 1733
  public policy and, 1737
  restraint of trade contract, in, 1737, *see also* **Restraint of Trade**
  scope of contract and, 1735
  statute, under, 1738–1739
   approach to, 1739
  test of, 1730, 1735
  uncertainty, where, 1730
  within the contract, 1729, 1734–1739
   illegal contract, 1737
   term, part of, 1735
   term, whole of, 1736

Simple Contracts, 312
Specialties, 306, 312
Specific Performance, 2401–2412
  consideration and, 2406
  co-operation in performance and, 2221
  damages, inadequacy of, and, 2402, 2404, 2406
  damages and, 2169–2173
  discretion in, 2403, 2407–2414
   breach and, 2407
   delay and, 2409
   hardship and, 2410
   misrepresentation and, 2412
   mistake and, 1208, 1235, 2411
   mutuality and, 2408
   readiness and willingness, and, 2407
   unfairness and, 2410
  election and, 1973, 2219, 2409
  employment contract, of, 2403
  forfeiture, relief against and, 1979, 2240, 2402
  futility of, 2403
  generally, 2401–2403
  goods, sale of, 2405
  illegality of contract and, 1708
  impossibility of, 2403
  injunction and, 2417, 2420
  land, sale of, 2404
  money, contract for payment, of, 2219, 2406
  option contract, 248
  performance, late, and, 1849
  'proper', 2401
  proprietary, interest and, 2404
  readiness and willingness and, 2240
  remedy of, 2401
  scope of, 2403
  senses of, 2401
  severable contract, of, 2403
  supervision and, 2403
  termination of contract and, 1989, 2402

Statute of Frauds *see* **Contracts Requiring Written Evidence**

Taxation *see* **Damages**
Tenders, 212, 223 *see also* **Offer and Acceptance**
Termination *see also* **Election; Frustration**
  abandonment, by, 1978
  anticipatory breach, by, 1930
   election, requirement of, 1930
  automatic, 1859, 1967
   breach and, 1967
   contractual provision for, 1967
   force majeure, where, 1967
  breach, for, 1909–1927
   automatic, not, 1859
   condition, of, 1911–1921
    agreement for, 1912–1919
     cases, prior, and, 1914
     contractual right and, 1912
     express, 1912
     implied, 1913–1919
      agreement by parties, 1921
      conduct, subsequent, and, 1917
      consequences of breach, and, 1917
      contract, nature of, and, 1919
      contract, structure of, and, 1916
      damages, assessment of, and, 1918

Index

entry into contract, motivation for, and, 1915
    establishment of, 1913
    negotiations, and, 1915
    parol evidence rule, and, 1913
    result, reasonableness of, and, 1918
    standard form, where, 1914, 1919
    statutory classification, 1920
    subject matter, nature of, and, 1919
    term, structure of, and, 1916, 1919
    test of, 1915, 1917, 1919
  implied term, 1920–1921
contractual right to, 1909
generally, 1901–1910
intermediate term of, 1922–1927
  express, 1922
  implied, 1923
  seriousness required for, 1924–1927
    actual, 1926
    agreement on, 1924–1925
      express, 1924
      implied, 1925
    common law, at, 1925
    conduct of parties and, 1927
    foreseeable, 1927
    substantially different performance as, 1925
partially executed contract, 1966
statutory right to, 1910
substantial performance and, 1832
unilateral contracts, of, 1965
court, by, 1973
damages and, 2157–2161
delay, for, 1948–1964
  consequences of breach and, 1957–1958
    actual, 1958
    criterion for, 1957
    foreseeable, 1958
  forms of, 1948
  generally, 1948–1949
  notice procedure and
    anticipated, 1956
    breach required for, 1960, 1962
    effect of, 1964
    form of notice, 1961
    generally, 1959
    parties bound by, 1963
    readiness and willingness and, 1962
    scope of, 1962
    service, time of, 1960
    unreasonable delay and, 1955, 1956, 1969, 1961
  relevance of, 1948

time stipulation, breach of
  classification of, 1949
    agreement for, 1950–1951
      express, 1950
      implied, 1951
    essential, breach of, 1950–1953
      commercial contract, in, 1951, 1952
      condition as, 1949
      intermediate term, and, 1952
      standard form contract, in, 1951
      express, 1950–1952
      implied, 1953
    intermediate term and, 1949
    non-essential, breach of, 1954–1956
      detriment and, 1955
      disadvantage and, 1955
      frustrating delay, 1955
      generally, 1954
      loss and, 1955
      nature of contract and, 1955
      unreasonable delay, 1955
    treatment of, 1949
    warranty and, 1949
effect of
  anticipatory breach and, 1933
  breach, for, 1985–1995
  frustration and, 2058, 2059, 2062, 2065, 2067
  damages, on, 2063
  deposit, recovery of, on, 2236–2237, *see also* **Deposit**
  discharge as, 1985–1987
    duties, of, 1985, 1989
    finality of, 1987
    forfeiture, relief against, and, 1987
    parties, of, 1901, 1985
    primary duties, of, 1985, 1986, 1989
    'rescission' and, 1985
    retrospective, not, 1986
    scope of, 1986
    secondary duties, of, 1989
    time of, 1986
  instalment payments, recovery of, on, 2232–2235
    charterparty, 2232
    construction contract, 2233
    employment contract, 2233
    goods, sale of, 2234
    hire, contract of, 2232
    hire-purchase, 2232
    land, sale of, 2235
    lease, 2232
  liquidated sum, recovery of, on 2225–2241
    accrued right to, 2225
    breach, for, 2228–2237
    breach, party in, and, 2230

Termination — *continued*
- consideration, failure of, and, 2229, 2238
- contractual right and, 2229
- frustration, by, 2227
- generally, 2225–2227
- intention and, 2228
- performance and, 2228, 2229
- repudiation, for, 2228–2237
- time of, 2226
- price, recovery of, on, 1821, 2231
- restitution and, 1990–1991
- rights, on, 1989
- terms, on, 1992–1995, 2064
  - agreed damages clause, 1993
  - breach, party in, and, 1994
  - construction and, 1992
  - exclusion clause, 1993
  - primary obligations, 1993
  - procedural, 1993, 1994
  - public policy and, 1992, 1995
  - statute and, 1992, 1995
  - substantive, 1993, 1994
- employment contract, of, 1967
- exclusion clause, effect on, 768
- frustration and, 2058, 2059, 2062, 2065
- grounds for, alternative, 1969
- illegal contract, of, 1721
- justification of, 1969
- performance and, 1839, 1840
- repudiation, for, 1928–1947
  - acceptance as, 1945–1947
    - effect, 1946
    - election, as, 1946
    - meaning of, 1945
    - non-acceptance, 1947
    - readiness and willingness and, 1947
    - reasons for, 1945
    - required for, 1945
  - anticipatory breach on, 1930
  - basis of, 1933
  - bill of exchange, application to, 1936
  - concept of, 1928
  - condition, breach of, and, 1934, 1935
  - contractual right and, 1941
  - exclusion of, 1936
  - generally, 1901–1910, 1928–1936
  - inability, based on, 1942–1944
    - actual, 1943
    - declared, 1942
    - disabling conduct, by, 1942
    - inferred, 1944
  - inevitable breach, based on, 1933
  - instalment goods contract, of, 1938
  - intermediate term, breach of, and, 1934
  - lease, application to, 1936
  - partially executed contract, 1966
  - proof of, 1931
  - seriousness required for, 1932
  - prospective breach and, 1932, 1935
  - readiness and willingness and, 1929
  - retraction of, 1933
  - termination for breach, compared with, 1928
  - test of, 1932, 1935, 1938
    - intention and, 1941
    - objective, 1941
  - theories of, 1933
  - unilateral contract, of, 1965
  - warranty and, 1934
  - wilful, 1937
  - words or conduct, based on, 1937–1941
    - absoluteness of, and, 1941
    - bona fides and, 1941
    - construction of contract and, 1939
    - refusal to perform as, 1937–1938
      - contingent obligation, where, 1937
      - express, 1937
      - implied, 1938
    - termination, wrongful, as, 1940
- rescission, distinguished from 1904
- rescission and, 1981, 1982
  - confused with, 1981
- restitution, requirement for, as, 1991
- right of, 1901–1904
  - common law, conferred by, 1903
  - contractual, 1903
  - express, 1903
  - law, issue of, 1901
  - nature, 1901
  - onus of proof, 1902
  - rescission and, 1904
- restrictions on, 1967–1984
  - breach as, 1978
  - delay as, 1984
  - election, as, 1967–1973
  - equitable relief as, 1973
  - estoppel as, 1974–1976, 1983
    - factual representation, where, 1975
    - promise, where, 1976
  - exclusion clause, 1977
  - 'fair conduct' requirement, 1983
  - forfeiture, relief against, as, 1979–1980
    - jurisdiction, 1979, 1980
      - inherent, 1979
      - statutory, 1980
  - good faith, as, 1983
  - goods, acceptance of, as, 1981
  - goods, title to, and, 1981
  - permanent, 1972
  - reasonableness, as, 1983
  - restitutio in integrum as, 1982
  - statute as, 1981, 1984
  - unconscionability as, 1979, 1983
- statute, conferred by, 1903

terminology and, 1905–1907
  anticipatory breach, 1906
  fundamental breach, 1907
  repudiation, 1906
  terms of contract, 1905
  total breach, 1907
rights, effect on, 1988–1989
  rescission and, 1988
  types of, 1989
suspension of performance and, 1839, 1840
wrongful repudiation as, 1940

Terms
agreed damages clauses *see* **Liquidated Damages**
classification of, 724–747
  breach, gravity of, and, 729
  construction, by, 729
  consumer contracts, in, 737
  conventional descriptions and, 734
  exclusion clauses and, 737
  goods, sale of, in, 727, 728, 736, 737
    English and Australian law, 736
  intention and, 737
  purpose, 724
  statutory, 727, 728, 734, 736, 737, 1920
  time stipulation, 1949
  tripartite, 725–738
    agreed damages clauses and, 747
    basis of, 725
    definitional terms and, 744
    essential terms and, 743
    exclusion clauses and, 745
    fundamental terms and, 743
    procedural terms and, 746
    scope of, 733
composite, 729
conditions *see* **Condition**
conditions precedent, 741, 1807, *see also* **Condition Precedent**
conditions subsequent, 741, *see also* **Condition Subsequent**
construction of
  approach to, 704
  contractual right and, 1909
  definition, 701
  duty, standard of, and, 1855
  'entire' contract and, 1823
  factual matrix, evidence of, and, 713–715
    aim of contract, 713
    commercial purpose, 713
    concept, 713
    frustration and, 2008
    object of contract, 713
    surrounding circumstances, 714
  frustration and, 2049

  implied terms, 1920–1921
  intention and, 703
  intermediate, as, 1922–1923
  issues of, 704
  law, issue of, 702, 2005
  legal effect, determining, 701
  meaning, determining, 701
  merger clause, 708, 1124
  parol evidence rule, 705–712
    application of, 707–708
      integration and, 708
      terms of the bargain, 707
    conclusion on, 716
    condition, breach of, and, 1913, 1917
    evidence excluded, 709–712
      conduct of parties, 712
      documentary evidence, 709
      intention, 710
      negotiations, 711
    exceptions to, 716–723
      ambiguity, 718
      conduct of parties and, 712, 718, 719, 720
      consideration, 721
      contract, enforceability of, and, 716
      course of dealing, 720
      custom, 720
      estoppel and, 712, 718, 720
      generally, 716
      identity of parties, 722
      implied terms, 719
      pleadings and, 723
      rectification, 723
      relationship of parties, 722
      rights, enforceability of, and, 716
      subject matter of contract, 717
      usage, 720
    formulations of, 701
      suggested, 702
    generally, 705
  penalty, as, 2208
  performance and, 1802
  reasonableness of, 704
  restitution and, 2066–2067, 2301
contingencies stated by, 735
definitional, 744
essential, 743, *see also* **Essential Term**
exclusion clauses *see* **Exclusion Clause**
frustration and, 2040–2042
fundamental, 743, *see also* **Fundamental Term**
identification of, 602–644
  express, 602–619
    incorporation of, 615–619
      character of document, and, 615, 617

Terms — *continued*
- commercial contract, where, 618, 619
- course of dealing, by, 618
- effect of misrepresentation, 615
- knowledge of terms and, 615, 617, 618
- notice, by, 616
- onerous terms, 617
- reference, by, 619
- signature, by, 615
- 'ticket' cases, 617
- unusual terms, 617
- pre-contractual statements as, 602–614
  - classification of, 602–605
    - puffs, as, 603
    - purpose of, 602
    - representations, as, 604
    - term, as, 605
  - collateral contracts, as, *see* **Collateral Contract**
  - factors relevant to, 606–610
    - content of statement as, 608
    - expertise as, 610
    - intention as, 606
    - knowledge as, 610
    - time of statement as, 607
    - writing as, 609
  - fault and, 610
  - opinion, of, 610
  - reliance on, 610
- implied, 620–644
  - custom, 644
  - evidence admissible, 623, 719
  - express term, and, 630, 635, 644
  - factual, 625–630
    - requirements, for, 625, 626–630
      - business efficacy, 627
      - clarity, 629
      - consistency, 630
      - equitable, 626
      - necessity, 627
      - obviousness, 628
      - reasonableness, 626
  - frustration and, 2050
  - generally, 620–624
  - good faith, 633
  - implied legal duties and, 624
  - intention of parties and, 632
  - law, issue of, 622
  - legal, 631–643
    - concurrent duties and, 635
    - consistency and, 635
    - distinguished from factual, 632
    - illustrations, 633
    - nature of contract, 631
    - requirements for, 631
- unjust term, 634
- unreasonable term, 634
- onus of proof, 621
- reasons for, 620
- usage, 644
- statutory, 636–643
  - general, 636
  - goods
    - description, 638
    - exchange of, 642
    - fitness for purpose, 639
    - hire of, 642
    - lease of, 642
    - merchantable quality, 640
    - sale of, 637–641
    - sample, by, 641
    - title, 637
  - hire-purchase, 642
  - services, 643
- intermediate *see* **Intermediate Term**
- procedural, 746
- promises *see* **Promise**
- types, 601
- warranties *see* **Warranty**

Time
- election, for, 1900
- essence, of, 1848, 1849, 1851, 1949, 1950–1953
- notice procedure
  - origin of, 1849
  - statute and, 1851
- payment, late, 1951
- performance, for, 1803–1804
  - repudiation and, 1929
- reasonable
  - fact, question of, 1804
  - implied, 1803
- unreasonable, termination after, 1984

Unconscionability
- application of, 1513
- basis of relief, 1503
- catching bargains, 1504–1506
  - disadvantaged persons, 1506
  - expectants, with, 1504
  - statutory intervention and, 1505
- concept of, 1501, 1503, 1513
- duress and, 1301, 1321, 1509
- election and, 2224
- equitable principles, 1504–1514
- estoppel and, 369, 381
- forfeiture, relief against, and, 1501, 1979
- generally, 1501–1503
- limits on, 1502
- modern law, 1507–1514
  - circumstances, variety of, 1508
  - *Commercial Bank of Australia v Amadio*, 1512

Index

guiding principle, search for, 1509
illustrations, 1507
independent advice and, 1513
inequality of bargaining and, 1510, 1511
  rejection of, 1511
remedies under, 1513
relevance of, 1501
relief from, 1502, 1503, 1513
restraint of trade and, 1510, 1645
termination of contract and, 1983
undue influence, and, 1416, 1501, 1504
unfair contracts legislation, under, 1515–1530
  abstract control and, 1529–1530
    'access to justice' and, 1529
    Australia, in, 1530
    other jurisdictions, in, 1529
  class of contract and, 1516
  Contracts Review Act, 1517–1522
    considerations relevant to, 1520
    consumers and, 1518
    generally, 1517
    interpretation of, 1522
    relief under, 1521
    scope of, 1518
    section 7, 1519
  fair trading legislation, 1523–1528
    provisions of, 1525
    rights and remedies, 1526
  generally, 1515
  Trade Practices Act, 1523–1528
    commercial contracts and, 1523–1528
    consumers, 1523–1528
    federal legislation, 1523
    implications of, 1527
    provisions of, 1524
    rights and remedies, 1526
    small business, 1523–1528
    unconscionability
      different meanings of, 1527–1528

Undue Influence
actual, 1413–1414
  consideration, adequacy of, 1414
  presumed, distinguished from, 1413
categories of, 1404
  relationship between, 1407
concept, 1401
concerns of, 1403
damages for, no, 1402
duress, and, 1301
generally, 1401–1402
non est factum and, 1415
presumed, 1406–1412
  generally, 1406–1407
  rebuttal of, 1411–1412
    disadvantageous transaction and, 1412
    proof, burden of, 1411
  relationships generating, 1408–1410
    established classes, 1408
    scope of, 1409
    special, 1410
remedies for, 1402
third party situations, 1405
unconscionability, and, 1416, 1501, 1504
wife, where guarantor of husband's debt, 1405

Unfair Contracts *see* **Unconscionability**

Unilateral Contract, 208, 249, 250
aleatory contract, compared with, 1838
bilateral, distinguished from, 1836
consideration for, 308, 314, 315
offer for, 249–250
  revocation of, 250
option, compared with, 1837
performance of, 1836
termination of, 1965

Unincorporated Association
capacity to contract, 864–868
contracting party, identification of, 865
employer, as, 867
long-term contracts of, 866
nature of, 864
reform of law, 868
rules of, public policy and, 1626

Unjust Enrichment
action, forms of, and, 2301, 2308
benefit element, 2310–2325
  acceptance of, 2314, 2318, 2325, 2335
  discharge of contract and, 2320
  failure of contract to materialise and, 2317
  generally, 2310
  incontrovertible, 2313, 2335
  money as, 2310, 2321, 2324
  officious, not, 2312
  quantum meruit and, 2317, 2318, 2322, 2323, 2325
  reliance and, 2315
  requested, 2312
  services as, 2311
  types of, 2310–2315
  unenforceable contract and, 520, 2319
  unrequested, 2312
  valuation of, 2335
  void contract and, 2318
damages and, 2112, 2328
duress and, 1307, 1309, 1312, 1313, 1328
elements of, 2309
frustration and, 2066, 2067, 2079, 2082
illegality and, 1727, 1728
injustice element, 2330–2334
  benefit and, 2325

Unjust Enrichment — *continued*
    deposit payments and, 2333
    discretion and, 2304, 2330
    forfeiture, relief against, and, 2331, 2332
    generally, 2330
    recognised, must be, 2309
    statute and, 2334
    total failure of consideration and, 2306, 2318
  misrepresentation and, 1065
  mistake and, 1205, 1208
  Pavey & Matthews, recognition in, 520, 2308
  plaintiff's expense element, 2326–2329
    fiduciary obligation, breach of, and, 2328
    primary sense of, 2326
    secondary sense of, 2326
    tort, waiver of, and, 2378
    wrong, breach of contract as, 2329
  privity of contract and, 919, 920
  restitutio in integrum, 1065, 2306, 2313, 2336
  restitution, as basis for, 2301, 2308–2309, *see also* **Restitution**
  Statute of Frauds and, 520, 2308
  substantial performance and, 1835
  undue influence and, 1402

Waiver
  consideration and, 390–393
  damages and, 1972
  effect of, 393, 1972
  election as, 391, 1972
  estoppel and, 392
  termination and, 1972

Warranty
  breach of, failure of consideration by, 738
  collateral contract, in, 730
  collateral term, as, 728
  contractually binding promise, as, 730
  defined, 728
  distinguished from condition, 726–732
  essential promise, as, 730
  goods, sale of, in, 728